STREET ATLAS North Yorkshire

Contents

III **Key to map symbols**

IV **Key to map pages**

VI **Route planning**

X **Administrative and Postcode boundaries**

1 **Street maps** at 1¾ inches to 1 mile

208 **Street maps** at 3½ inches to 1 mile

233 **Street map of York city centre** at 7 inches to 1 mile

234 **Index** of towns and villages

238 **Index** of streets, hospitals, industrial estates, railway stations, schools, shopping centres, universities and places of interest

First published in 2002 by

Philip's, a division of
Octopus Publishing Group Ltd
2–4 Heron Quays, London E14 4JP

First colour edition 2002
Second impression 2002

ISBN 0-540-08143-4 (spiral)

© Philip's 2002

Ordnance Survey®

This product includes mapping data licensed from Ordnance Survey® with the permission of the Controller of Her Majesty's Stationery Office. © Crown copyright 2002. All rights reserved. Licence number 100011710

No part of this publication may be reproduced, stored in a retrieval system or transmitted in any form or by any means, electronic, mechanical, photocopying, recording or otherwise, without the permission of the Publishers and the copyright owner.

To the best of the Publishers' knowledge, the information in this atlas was correct at the time of going to press. No responsibility can be accepted for any errors or their consequences.

The representation in this atlas of a road, track or path is no evidence of the existence of a right of way.

Ordnance Survey and the OS Symbol are registered trademarks of Ordnance Survey, the national mapping agency of Great Britain

Printed and bound in Spain
by Cayfosa-Quebecor

Digital Data

The exceptionally high-quality mapping found in this atlas is available as digital data in TIFF format, which is easily convertible to other bit mapped (raster) image formats.

The index is also available in digital form as a standard database table. It contains all the details found in the printed index together with the National Grid reference for the map square in which each entry is named.

For further information and to discuss your requirements, please contact Philip's on 020 7531 8439 or george.philip@philips-maps.co.uk

Key to map symbols

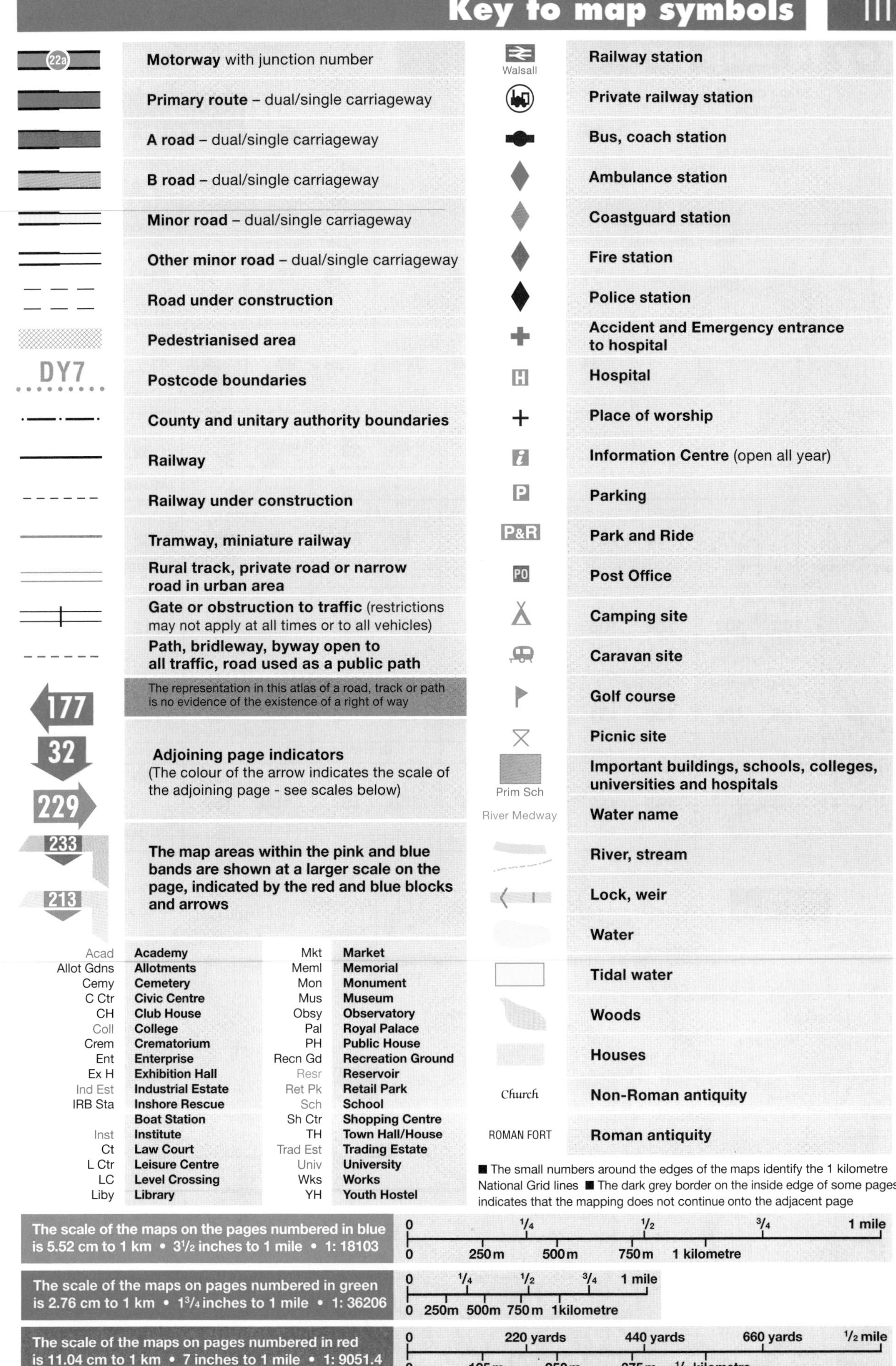

Motorway with junction number

Primary route – dual/single carriageway

A road – dual/single carriageway

B road – dual/single carriageway

Minor road – dual/single carriageway

Other minor road – dual/single carriageway

Road under construction

Pedestrianised area

Postcode boundaries

County and unitary authority boundaries

Railway

Railway under construction

Tramway, miniature railway

Rural track, private road or narrow road in urban area

Gate or obstruction to traffic (restrictions may not apply at all times or to all vehicles)

Path, bridleway, byway open to all traffic, road used as a public path

The representation in this atlas of a road, track or path is no evidence of the existence of a right of way

Adjoining page indicators
(The colour of the arrow indicates the scale of the adjoining page - see scales below)

The map areas within the pink and blue bands are shown at a larger scale on the page, indicated by the red and blue blocks and arrows

Railway station

Private railway station

Bus, coach station

Ambulance station

Coastguard station

Fire station

Police station

Accident and Emergency entrance to hospital

Hospital

Place of worship

Information Centre (open all year)

Parking

Park and Ride

Post Office

Camping site

Caravan site

Golf course

Picnic site

Important buildings, schools, colleges, universities and hospitals

Water name

River, stream

Lock, weir

Water

Tidal water

Woods

Houses

Non-Roman antiquity

Roman antiquity

Acad	**Academy**	Mkt	**Market**
Allot Gdns	**Allotments**	Meml	**Memorial**
Cemy	**Cemetery**	Mon	**Monument**
C Ctr	**Civic Centre**	Mus	**Museum**
CH	**Club House**	Obsy	**Observatory**
Coll	**College**	Pal	**Royal Palace**
Crem	**Crematorium**	PH	**Public House**
Ent	**Enterprise**	Recn Gd	**Recreation Ground**
Ex H	**Exhibition Hall**	Resr	**Reservoir**
Ind Est	**Industrial Estate**	Ret Pk	**Retail Park**
IRB Sta	**Inshore Rescue Boat Station**	Sch	**School**
		Sh Ctr	**Shopping Centre**
Inst	**Institute**	TH	**Town Hall/House**
Ct	**Law Court**	Trad Est	**Trading Estate**
L Ctr	**Leisure Centre**	Univ	**University**
LC	**Level Crossing**	Wks	**Works**
Liby	**Library**	YH	**Youth Hostel**

■ The small numbers around the edges of the maps identify the 1 kilometre National Grid lines ■ The dark grey border on the inside edge of some pages indicates that the mapping does not continue onto the adjacent page

The scale of the maps on the pages numbered in blue is 5.52 cm to 1 km • 3½ inches to 1 mile • 1: 18103

0 ¼ ½ ¾ 1 mile
0 250 m 500 m 750 m 1 kilometre

The scale of the maps on pages numbered in green is 2.76 cm to 1 km • 1¾ inches to 1 mile • 1: 36206

0 ¼ ½ ¾ 1 mile
0 250m 500m 750m 1kilometre

The scale of the maps on pages numbered in red is 11.04 cm to 1 km • 7 inches to 1 mile • 1: 9051.4

0 220 yards 440 yards 660 yards ½ mile
0 125 m 250 m 375 m ½ kilometre

Key to map pages

214 Map pages at 7 inches to 1 mile

122 Map pages at 3½ inches to 1 mile

186 Map pages at 1¾ inches to 1 mile

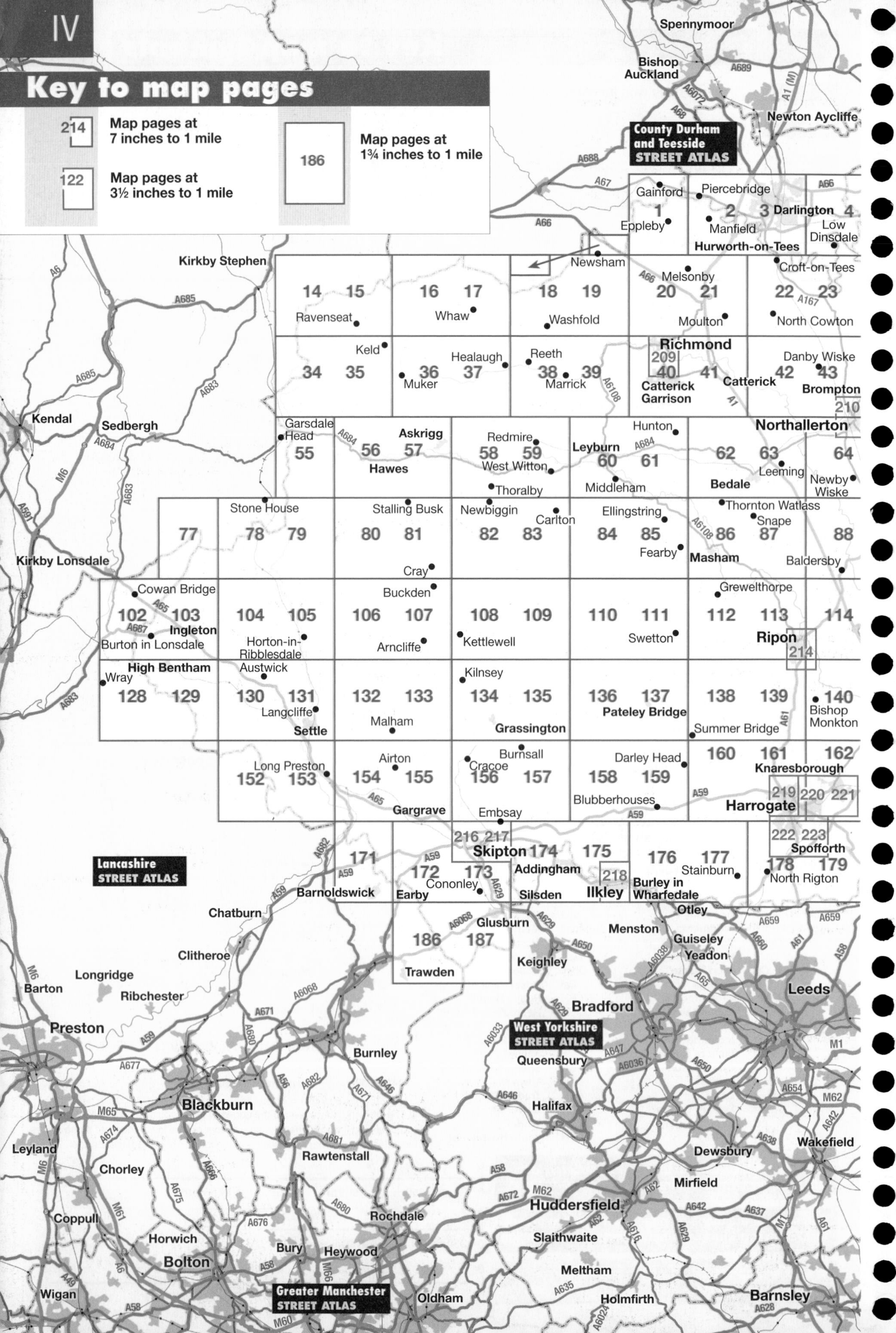

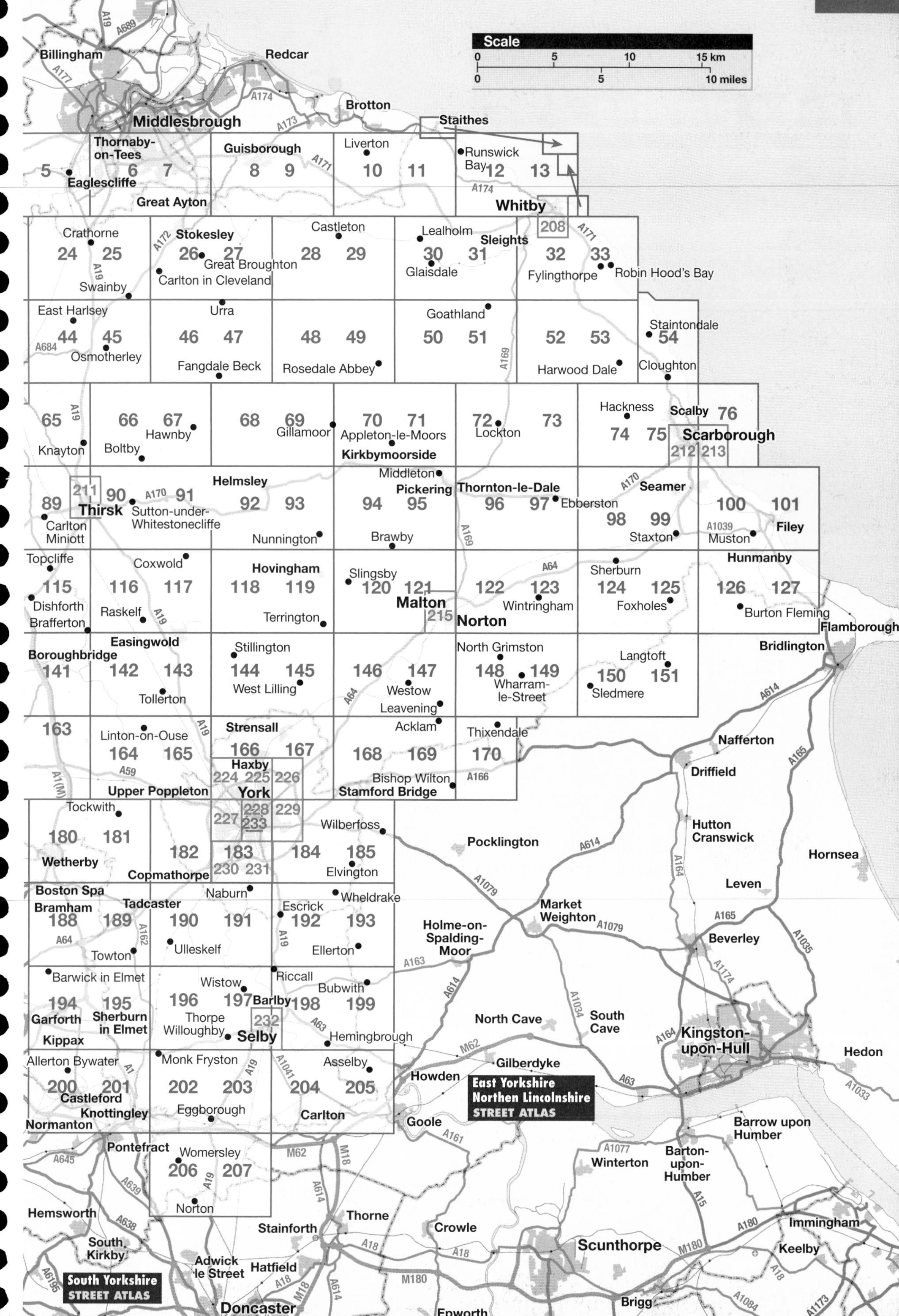
Scale
0 5 10 15 km
0 5 10 miles
Hartlepool
Billingham
Redcar
Middlesbrough
Brotton
Staithes
Thornaby-on-Tees
Guisborough
Liverton
Runswick Bay
Eaglescliffe
Great Ayton
Whitby
Crathorne
Stokesley
Castleton
Lealholm
Sleights
Great Broughton
Glaisdale
Fylingthorpe
Robin Hood's Bay
Swainby
Carlton in Cleveland
East Harlsey
Urra
Goathland
Staintondale
Osmotherley
Fangdale Beck
Rosedale Abbey
Harwood Dale
Cloughton
Knayton
Boltby
Hawnby
Gillamoor
Appleton-le-Moors
Kirkbymoorside
Lockton
Hackness
Scalby
Scarborough
Helmsley
Middleton
Pickering
Thornton-le-Dale
Ebberston
Seamer
Thirsk
Sutton-under-Whitestonecliffe
Carlton Miniott
Nunnington
Brawby
Staxton
Muston
Filey
Topcliffe
Coxwold
Hovingham
Slingsby
Sherburn
Hunmanby
Dishforth
Raskelf
Terrington
Malton
Norton
Wintringham
Foxholes
Burton Fleming
Flamborough
Brafferton
Easingwold
Boroughbridge
Stillington
North Grimston
Langtoft
Bridlington
West Lilling
Westow
Wharram-le-Street
Sledmere
Tollerton
Leavening
Acklam
Thixendale
Linton-on-Ouse
Strensall
Haxby
York
Upper Poppleton
Bishop Wilton
Stamford Bridge
Nafferton
Driffield
Tockwith
Wilberfoss
Pocklington
Hutton Cranswick
Wetherby
Copmathorpe
Elvington
Hornsea
Boston Spa
Bramham
Tadcaster
Naburn
Escrick
Wheldrake
Leven
Market Weighton
Holme-on-Spalding-Moor
Towton
Ulleskelf
Ellerton
Beverley
Barwick in Elmet
Riccall
Wistow
Bubwith
Barlby
Garforth
Sherburn in Elmet
Thorpe Willoughby
Selby
Kippax
Hemingbrough
North Cave
South Cave
Kingston-upon-Hull
Hedon
Allerton Bywater
Monk Fryston
Asselby
Gilberdyke
Howden
Castleford
Knottingley
Eggborough
Carlton
Normanton
East Yorkshire Northen Lincolnshire STREET ATLAS
Goole
Barrow upon Humber
Pontefract
Womersley
Winterton
Barton-upon-Humber
Norton
Hemsworth
Thorne
Crowle
Immingham
South Kirkby
Stainforth
Scunthorpe
Keelby
Adwick le Street
Hatfield
South Yorkshire STREET ATLAS
Doncaster
Epworth
Brigg
5 6 7 8 9 10 11 12 13
24 25 26 27 28 29 30 31 32 33 208
44 45 46 47 48 49 50 51 52 53 54
65 66 67 68 69 70 71 72 73 74 75 76 212 213
89 211 90 91 92 93 94 95 96 97 98 99 100 101
115 116 117 118 119 120 121 215 122 123 124 125 126 127
141 142 143 144 145 146 147 148 149 150 151
163 164 165 166 167 168 169 170 224 225 226
180 181 182 227 228 229 233 183 230 231 184 185
188 189 190 191 192 193
194 195 196 197 198 199 232
200 201 202 203 204 205
206 207
A19 A689 A177 A174 A173 A171 A172 A684 A169 A170 A1039 A64 A59 A1(M) A166 A614 A165 A1079 A1164 A162 A163 A1034 A1174 A1035 A164 A63 M62 A1041 A1 A1033 A645 A639 A638 A6195 M18 A161 A1077 A15 A180 M180 A18 A1084 A1173

Route planning

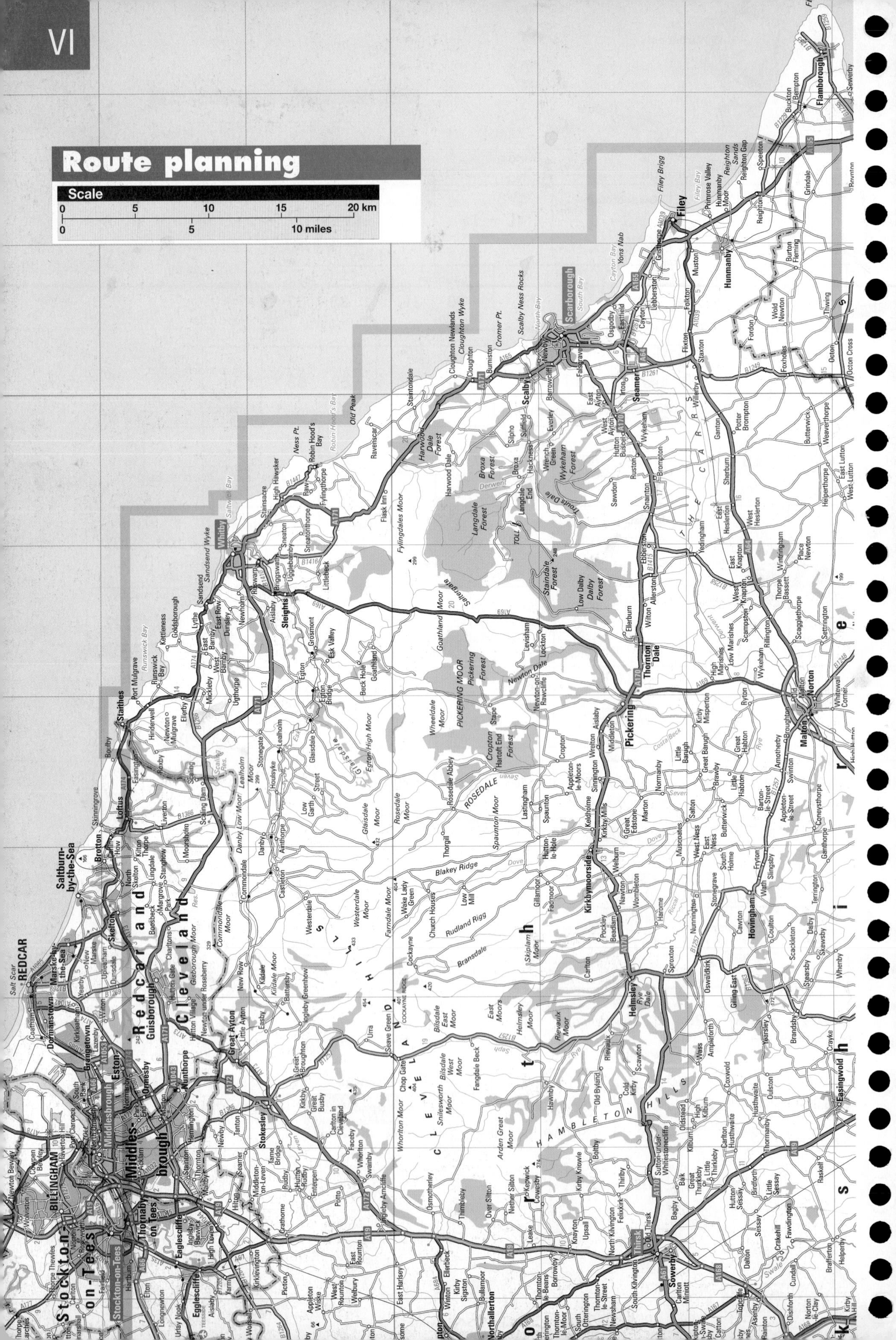

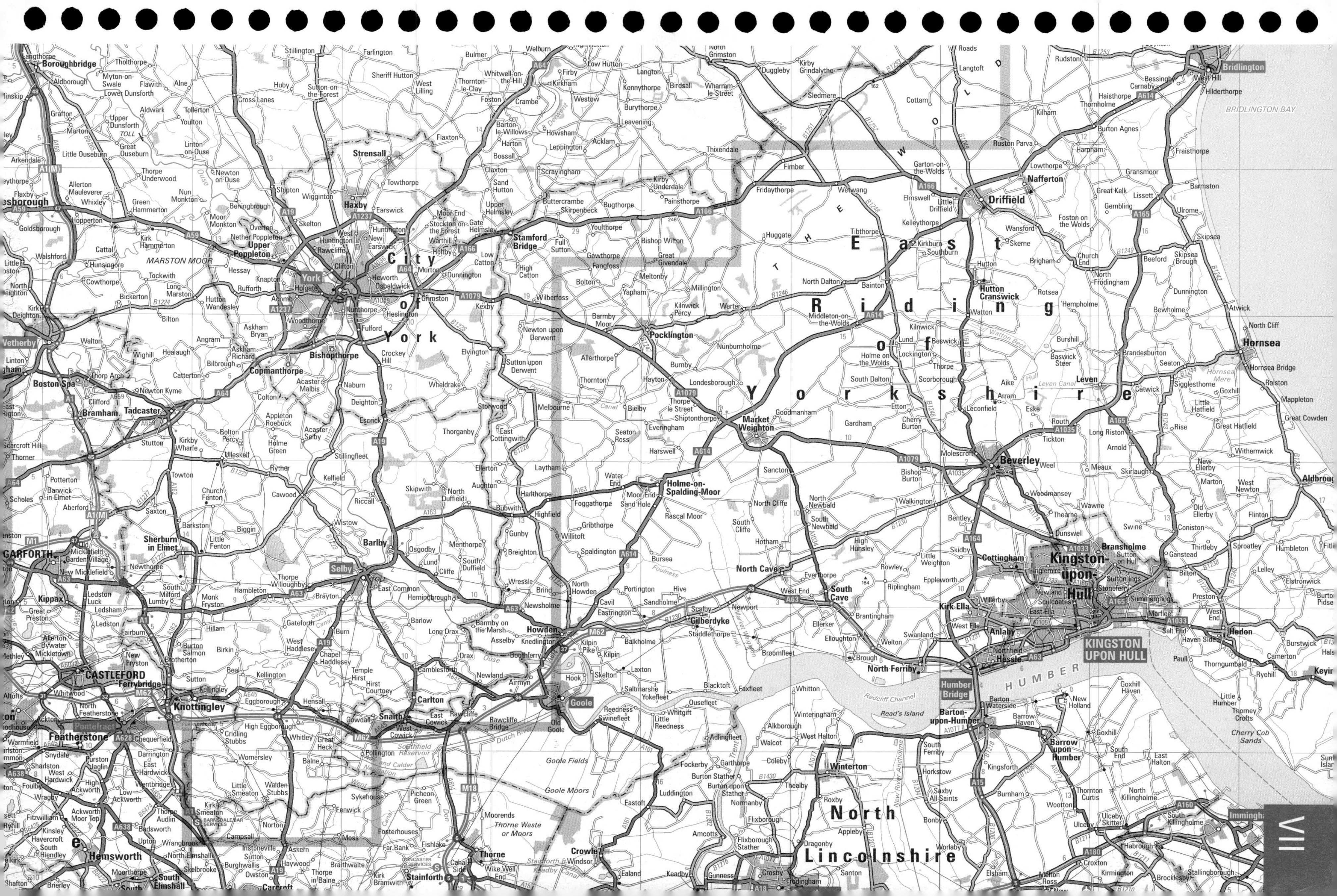
BRIDLINGTON BAY
Bridlington
Hornsea
Aldbrough
Hedon
KINGSTON UPON HULL
Kingston-upon-Hull
HUMBER
Humber Bridge
Barton-upon-Humber
Barrow upon Humber
Immingham
Beverley
Driffield
Nafferton
Hutton Cranswick
Leven
Cottingham
Hessle
Anlaby
Kirk Ella
North Ferriby
Brough
South Cave
North Cave
Market Weighton
Pocklington
Holme-on-Spalding-Moor
Gilberdyke
Howden
Goole
Stamford Bridge
York
City of York
Haxby
Strensall
Upper Poppleton
Bishopthorpe
Copmanthorpe
Selby
Barlby
Snaith
Carlton
Tadcaster
Boston Spa
Bramham
Sherburn in Elmet
Knottingley
CASTLEFORD
Ferrybridge
Pontefract
Featherstone
Hemsworth
Kippax
GARFORTH
Boroughbridge
Thorne
Stainforth
Crowle
Winterton
Thorne Waste or Moors
Goole Moors
Goole Fields
MARSTON MOOR
East Riding of Yorkshire
North Lincolnshire
THE WOLDS

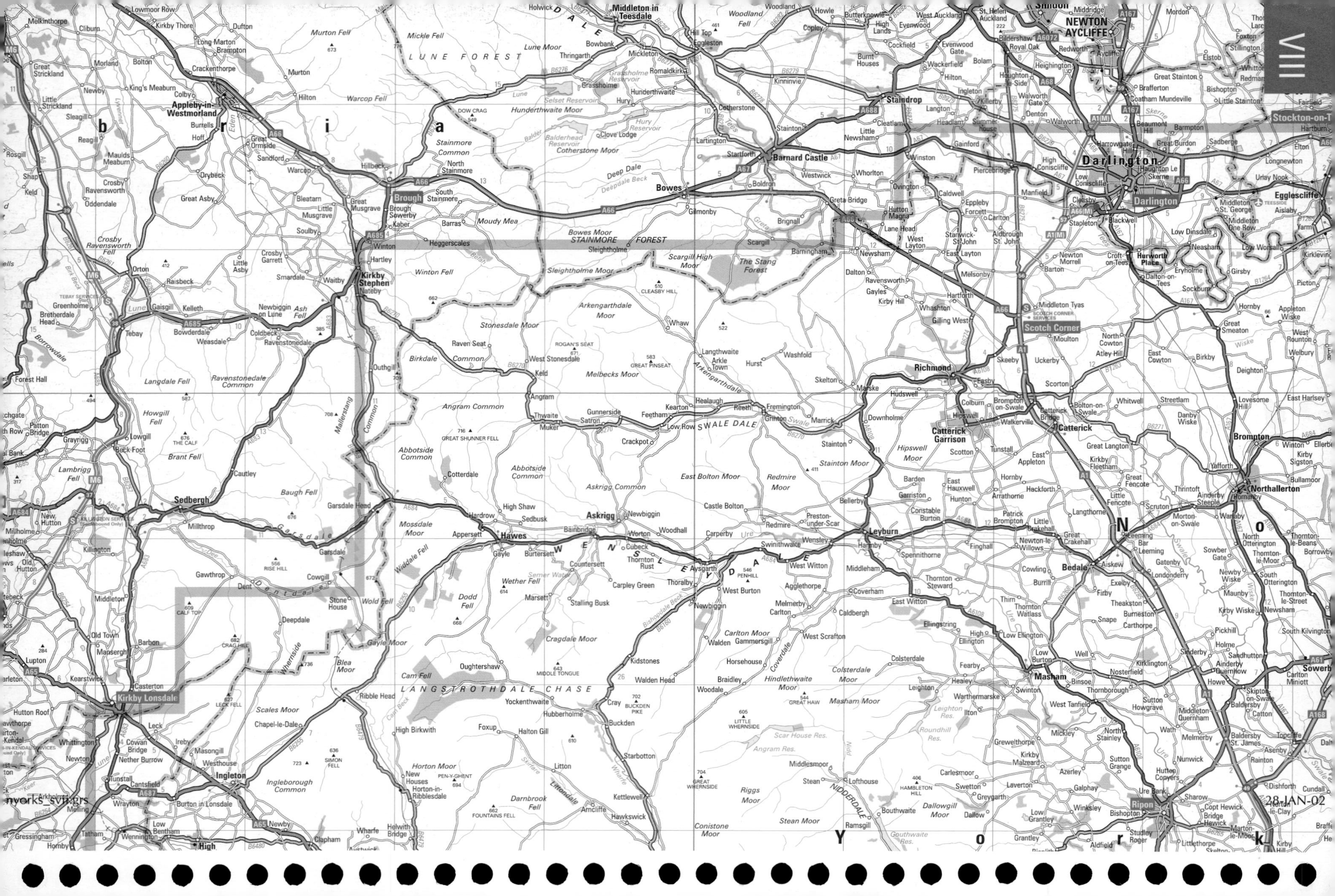

VIII
28-JAN-02
nyorks_svii.grs
Darlington
Newton Aycliffe
Northallerton
Richmond
Catterick
Catterick Garrison
Scotch Corner
Bedale
Masham
Ripon
Leyburn
Hawes
Askrigg
Barnard Castle
Staindrop
Bowes
Middleton in Teesdale
Brough
Kirkby Stephen
Appleby-in-Westmorland
Sedbergh
Kirkby Lonsdale
Ingleton
Stockton-on-T
Swale Dale
Wensleydale
Langstrothdale Chase
Stainmore Forest
Lune Forest

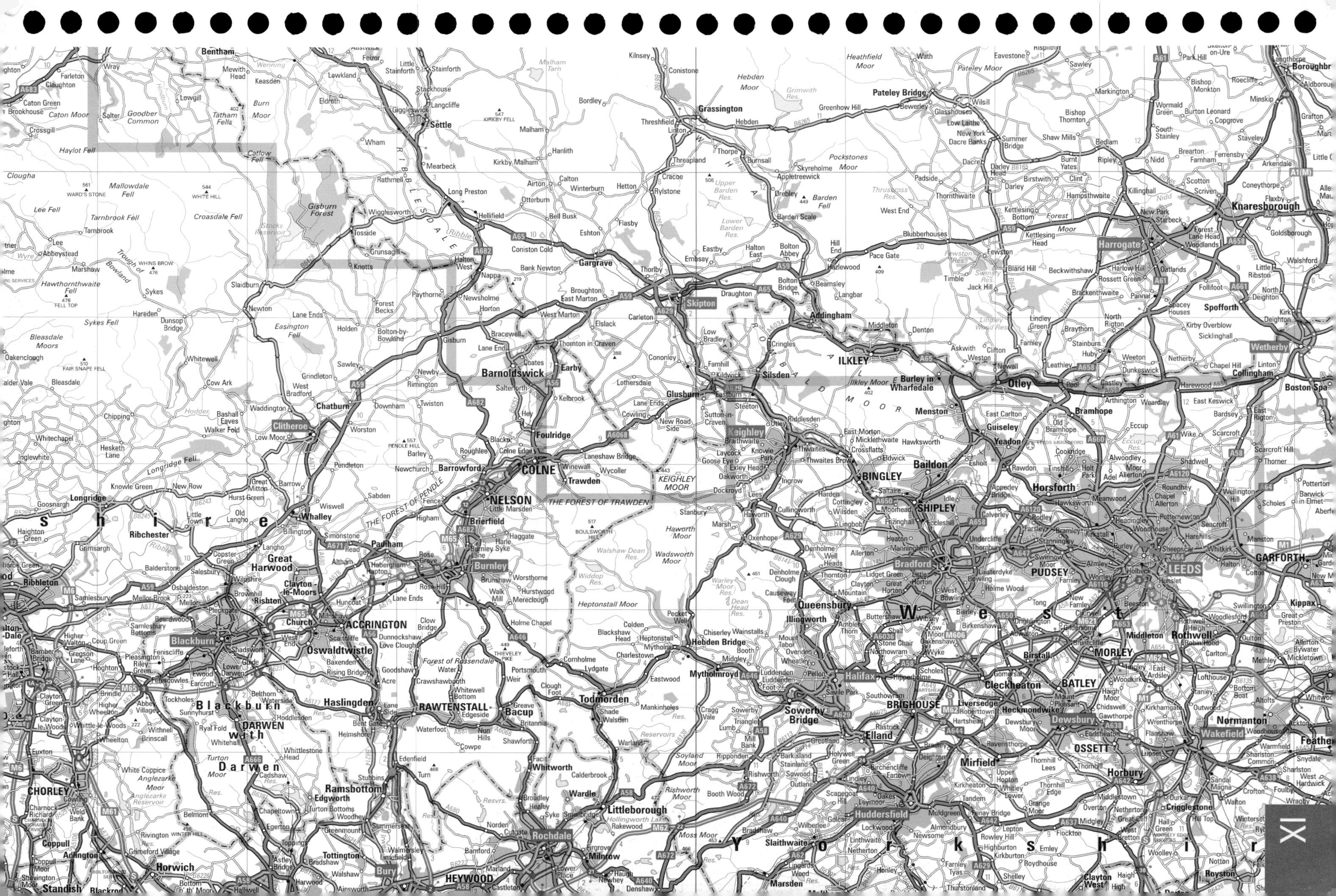
Knaresborough
Harrogate
Wetherby
Boston Spa
Spofforth
Collingham
Pateley Bridge
Grassington
Otley
Ilkley
Burley in Wharfedale
Guiseley
Yeadon
Horsforth
Pudsey
Leeds
Garforth
Kippax
Rothwell
Morley
Batley
Dewsbury
Ossett
Wakefield
Normanton
Horbury
Shipley
Bingley
Baildon
Bradford
Keighley
Silsden
Skipton
Addingham
Queensbury
Halifax
Brighouse
Elland
Huddersfield
Mirfield
Cleckheaton
Sowerby Bridge
Hebden Bridge
Mytholmroyd
Todmorden
Littleborough
Rochdale
Milnrow
Heywood
Bacup
Rawtenstall
Haslingden
Ramsbottom
Accrington
Oswaldtwistle
Clayton-le-Moors
Great Harwood
Blackburn
Darwen
Burnley
Padiham
Nelson
Colne
Trawden
Barnoldswick
Earby
Foulridge
Gargrave
Settle
Clitheroe
Whalley
Chatburn
Ribchester
Longridge
Bentham
Horwich
Chorley
Coppull
Standish
Harwood
Tottington
Edgworth
Forest of Bowland
Gisburn Forest
Ribblesdale
Ilkley Moor
Keighley Moor
The Forest of Trawden
West Yorkshire
Lancashire

Administrative and Postcode boundaries

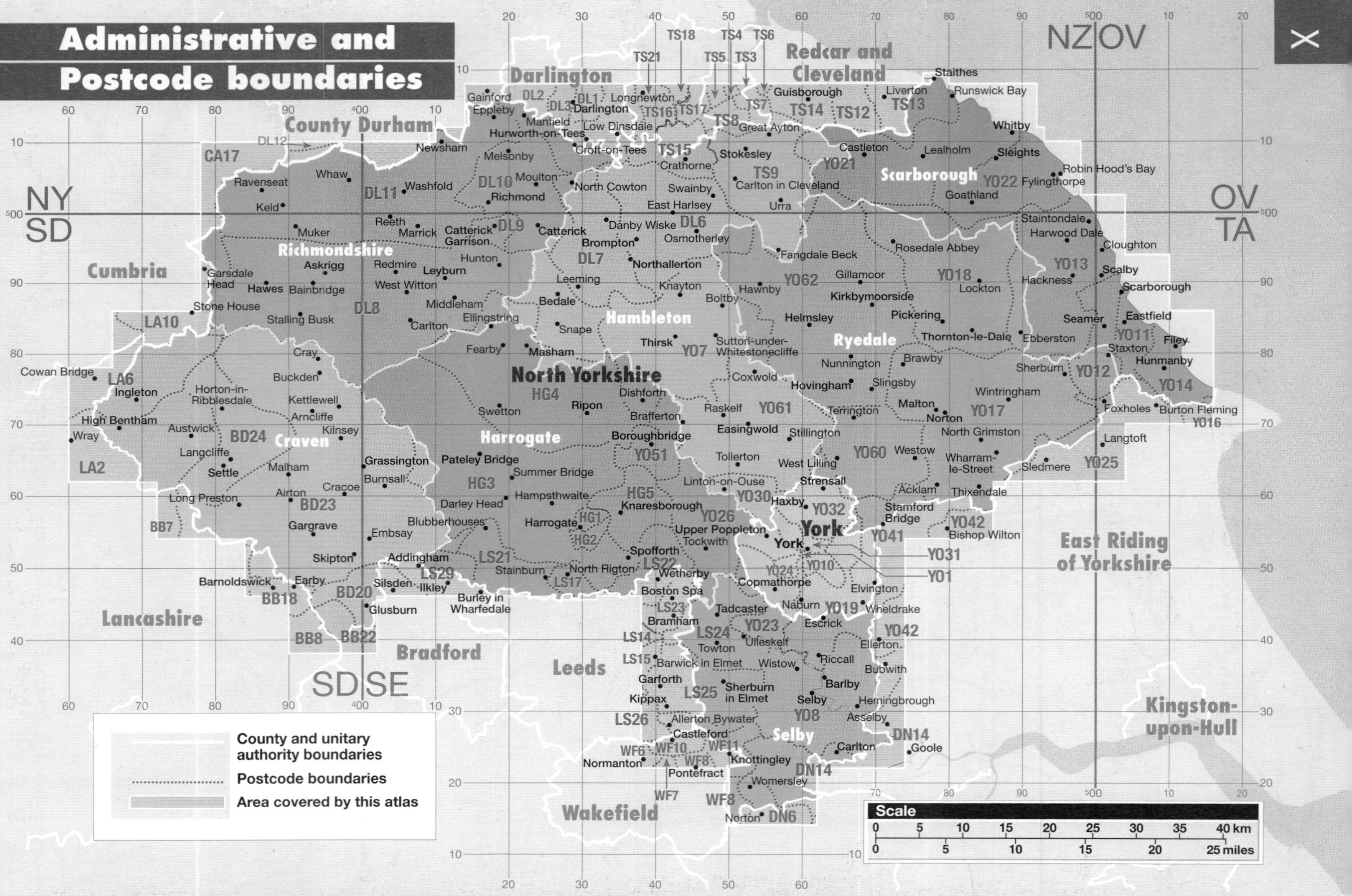

(white line)	County and unitary authority boundaries
(dotted line)	Postcode boundaries
(shaded)	Area covered by this atlas

Scale

0 5 10 15 20 25 30 35 40 km

0 5 10 15 20 25 miles

Durham & Teesside STREET ATLAS
A67 Barnard Castle
Gainford
Caldwell
Eppleby
Forcett
Carlton
Stanwick-St-John
DL2
DL11
Westholme Bridge
Station Farm
Primrose Hill Farm
Selaby Basses
Gainford Great Wood
West Tees Bridge
Grant Bank Wood
Burn House
Field House
Park Farm
Hill House
Dyance
Cock Lane
Hedgeholme Wood
Sewage Works
Barforth Hall
Gainford Hall
CE Prim Sch
Cemy
Hedgeholme
Hedgeholme Bank
Hill Top
St Lawrence's Chapel
Boat Scar
Black Scar
Sewage Works
Greystone Hall
East Greystone
White Cross
Snow Hall
Gallow Hill
Winston Bridge
Chapel Bridge
Chapel Gill
Barforth Whins
Low Fields
Low Close Farm
Chapel House
River Tees
Teesdale Way
West Scar
Hill Top East
Moor Row
Greener Hill
Moor House Farm
Barforth Grange
High Close
Low Field
Lowfield Farm
Berry Bank
Pudding Hl
Pudding Hill Road
Ovington Lane
Boat Lane
Lower Chapel House
Burnthouse Plantation
Little Allan's Plantation
Main Moor Hill
Long Riggs
West La
Curtain Lane
Carr Plantation
Cote Hill
Sough Hill
Sough Hill Farm
Greystone
Rennison
Greystone Plantation
Greystone Lane
Low Moor
Village Farm
High Row
Hall La
High House Farm
New Row
Little Hutton La
West Lane
Caldwell Farm
Church Farm
Eppleby Forcett CE Prim Sch
The Curtain
Village Farm
Carlton Grange
Mill Farm
Mill Bridge
School La
Foxberry
Mill Farm
Meadow Side
Aldbrough Beck
Keld Down Plantation
Caldwell Beck
Home Farm
Oak Wood
Foxberry Rush
Forcett Gd
Forcett Gill
Layton Fields
Foxclose Plantation
Forcett Valley
Garden Wood
Forcett Park
Earthworks
Kirk Bridge
Kirkbridge Farm
Henah Hill Plantation
The Tofts Fort
Greenless Lane
New House
Forcett Valley Farm
Fir Groves
Sandwath House
Mary Wild Bridge
White House
Hillhouse Plantation
Elm Grove
Brantcas
Forcett Quarry
Earthwork
Hergill Plantation
Fox Covert Wood
Carkin Fields
Primrose Gill
Park House
Appleby La
Collier Lane
Honey Pot Plantation
Hallmires Plantation
Sorrowful Hill
Long Plantation
Limekiln Lane
West Farm
Ashes Well
Moat
Oak Wood
Old Bye Plantation
Gill Wells Plantation
Suddels Wood
Forcett Barns
Gallop
West Lane
Wood Lane
North Lane
Balmer Hl
Station Rd
North Tr
Academy Gd
Eden Cres
Eden Lane
Eden Pk
Piggy La
Spa Rd
Main Rd
Low Rd
Old Rd
Waters End
PH
PO
P
A67
B6274
Way Wood
A B C D E F
8 17 7 16 6 15 5 14 4 13 3 12 2 11 1 10
14 15 16 17 18 19

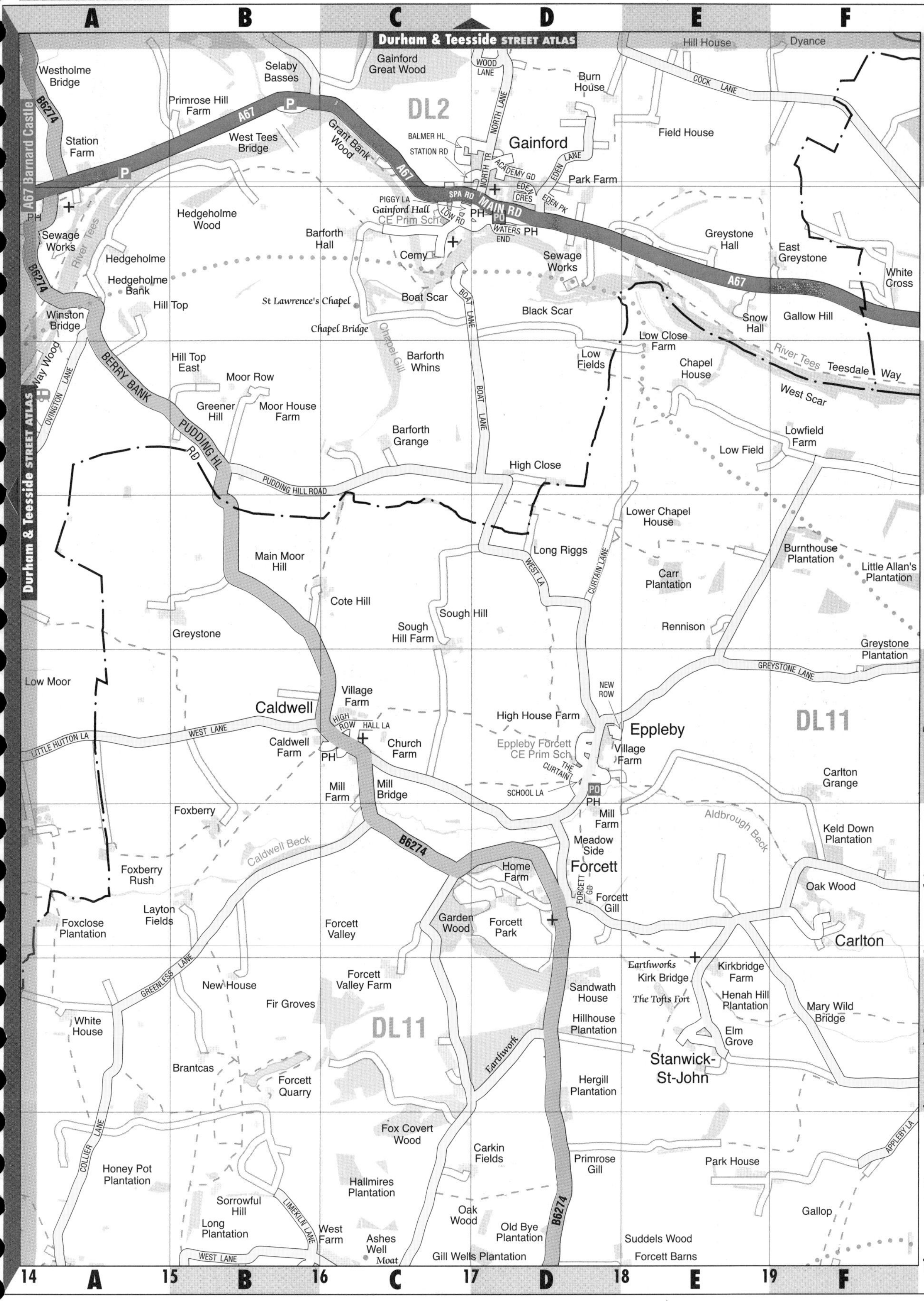

1

Scale: 1¾ inches to 1 mile

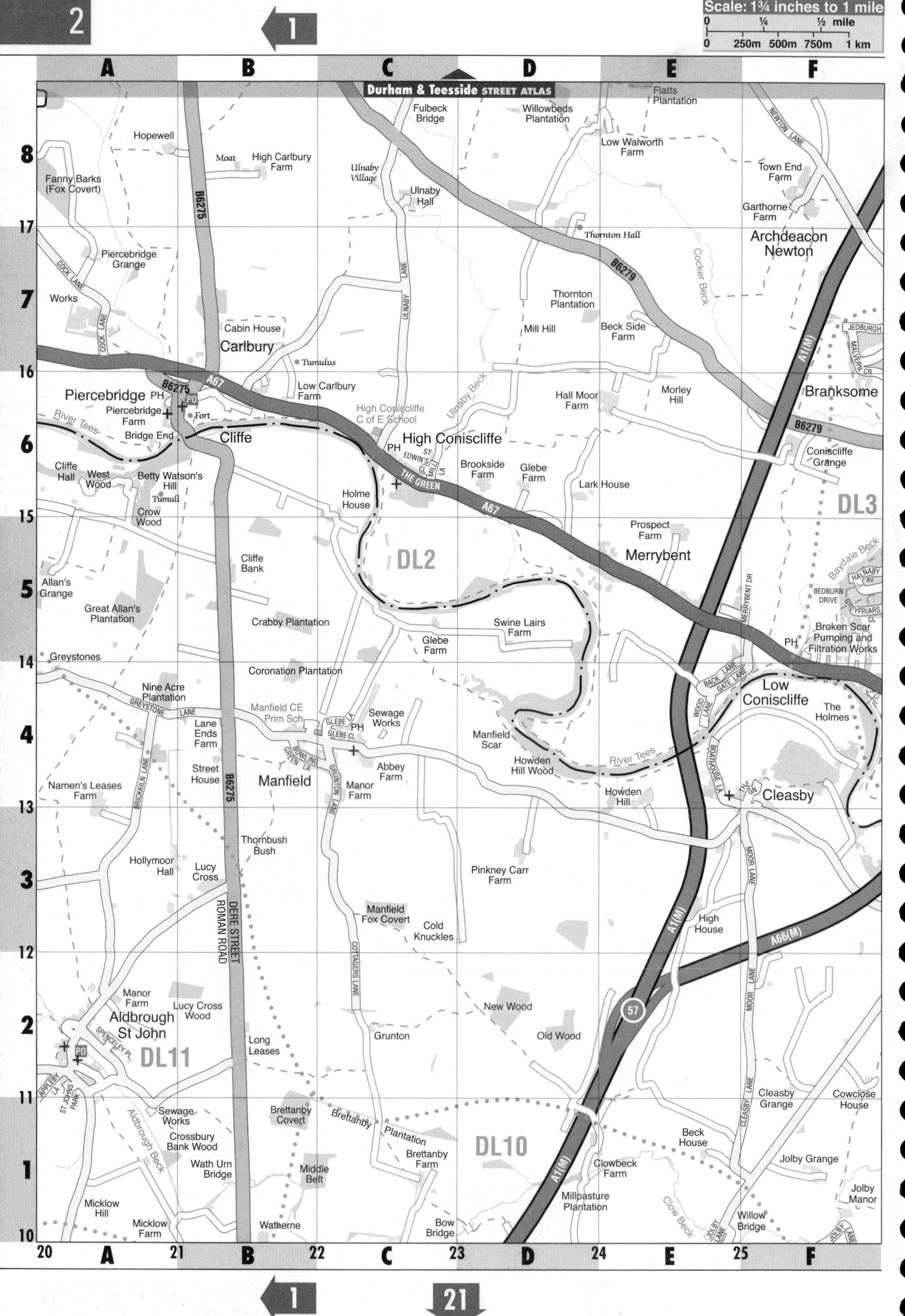

1

21

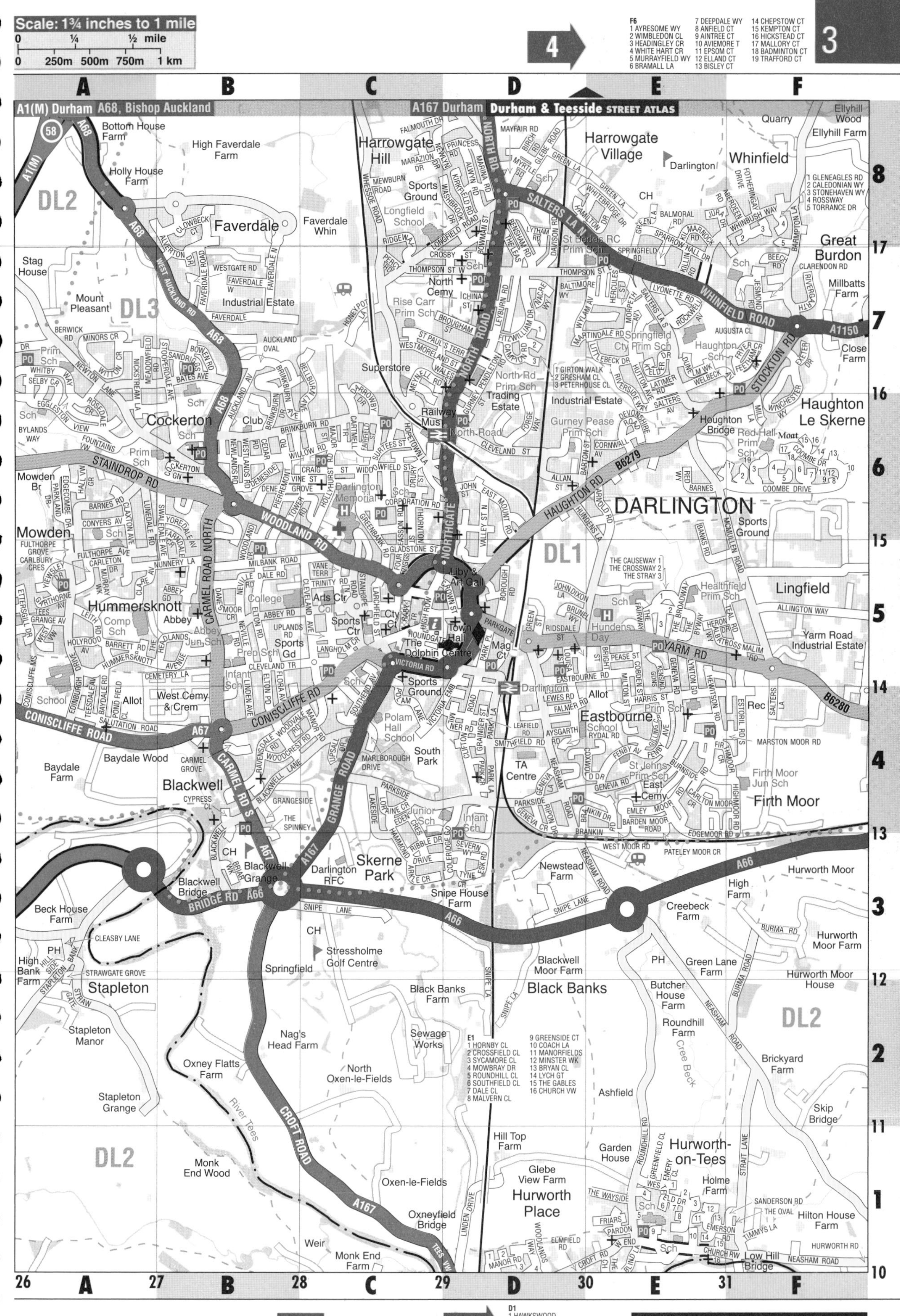

Scale: 1¾ inches to 1 mile
0 ¼ ½ mile
0 250m 500m 750m 1 km
4
F6
1 AYRESOME WY
2 WIMBLEDON CL
3 HEADINGLEY CR
4 WHITE HART CR
5 MURRAYFIELD WY
6 BRAMALL LA
7 DEEPDALE WY
8 ANFIELD CT
9 AINTREE CT
10 AVIEMORE T
11 EPSOM CT
12 ELLAND CT
13 BISLEY CT
14 CHEPSTOW CT
15 KEMPTON CT
16 HICKSTEAD CT
17 MALLORY CT
18 BADMINTON CT
19 TRAFFORD CT
3
A B C D E F
A1(M) Durham A68, Bishop Auckland
A167 Durham
Durham & Teesside STREET ATLAS
Bottom House Farm
High Faverdale Farm
Holly House Farm
DL2
Faverdale
Faverdale Whin
Industrial Estate
Stag House
Mount Pleasant
DL3
Harrowgate Hill
Sports Ground
Longfield School
Harrowgate Village
Darlington
Whinfield
Quarry
Ellyhill Wood
Ellyhill Farm
1 GLENEAGLES RD
2 CALEDONIAN WY
3 STONEHAVEN WY
4 ROSSWAY
5 TORRANCE DR
Great Burdon
Millbatts Farm
Close Farm
WHINFIELD ROAD
A1150
Rise Carr Prim Sch
North Cemy
Superstore
Springfield Cty Prim Sch
Haughton Sch
1 GIRTON WALK
2 GRESHAM CL
3 PETERHOUSE CL
Industrial Estate
North Rd Prim Sch
Trading Estate
Railway Mus
North Road
Cockerton
Club
Gurney Pease Prim Sch
Haughton Bridge
Red Hall Prim Sch
Moat
Haughton Le Skerne
STAINDROP RD
Mowden Br
Mowden
WOODLAND RD
HAUGHTON RD
B6279
DARLINGTON
Sports Ground
Darlington Memorial
NORTHGATE
DL1
THE CAUSEWAY 1
THE CROSSWAY 2
THE STRAY 3
Healthfield Prim Sch
Lingfield
Hummersknott
Comp Sch
Abbey
Abbey Jun Sch
College
Arts Ctr
Sports Ctr
Sports Gd
City Ct
Liby & Art Gall
Town Hall
The Dolphin Centre
Mag Ct
Hundens Day
YARM RD
Yarm Road Industrial Estate
Prep Sch
Infant Sch
School
Allot
West Cemy & Crem
CONISCLIFFE RD
CONISCLIFFE ROAD
A67
Sports Ground
Darlington
Allot
Eastbourne
Prim Sch
Rec
B6280
MARSTON MOOR RD
Baydale Wood
Baydale Farm
Blackwell
Polam Hall School
South Park
TA Centre
St Johns Prim Sch
East Cemy
Firth Moor Jun Sch
Firth Moor
GRANGE ROAD
CARMEL RD S
A167
CH
Blackwell Grange
Blackwell Bridge
BRIDGE RD A66
Darlington RFC
Skerne Park
Newstead Farm
Hurworth Moor
High Farm
Snipe House Farm
A66
Beck House Farm
Creebeck Farm
Hurworth Moor Farm
CH
Stressholme Golf Centre
PH
High Bank Farm
Stapleton
Springfield
Blackwell Moor Farm
Black Banks
Green Lane Farm
Hurworth Moor House
Butcher House Farm
Black Banks Farm
Roundhill Farm
DL2
Stapleton Manor
Nag's Head Farm
Sewage Works
E1
1 HORNBY CL
2 CROSSFIELD CL
3 SYCAMORE CL
4 MOWBRAY DR
5 ROUNDHILL CL
6 SOUTHFIELD CL
7 DALE CL
8 MALVERN CL
9 GREENSIDE CT
10 COACH LA
11 MANORFIELDS
12 MINSTER WK
13 BRYAN CL
14 LYCH GT
15 THE GABLES
16 CHURCH VW
Cree Beck
Brickyard Farm
Oxney Flatts Farm
North Oxen-le-Fields
Ashfield
Stapleton Grange
River Tees
Skip Bridge
CROFT ROAD
Hill Top Farm
Garden House
Hurworth-on-Tees
DL2
Monk End Wood
Glebe View Farm
Oxen-le-Fields
Hurworth Place
Holme Farm
Hilton House Farm
Oxneyfield Bridge
Weir
Monk End Farm
Low Hill Bridge
HURWORTH RD
NEASHAM ROAD
26 A 27 B 28 C 29 D 30 E 31 F
8 17 7 16 6 15 5 14 4 13 3 12 2 11 1 10
22
4
D1
1 HAWKSWOOD
2 EDEN CL
3 GRANGE AVE
4 HUNTERS CL
For full street detail of Darlington see Philip's STREET ATLAS of Co. Durham and Teesside

Burdon Hall
Burdon Grange Farm
Carcut Beck
HILL HOUSE LANE
NORTON BACK LANE
DARLINGTON BACK LA
Salter Carr Farm
Sewage Works
C of E Sch
Hill House Farm
Bewley Hill
BACK LANE
Sadberge
EAST CL
NORTON CR
NORTON RD
DALE RD
ABBEY RD
PH
PO
MIDDLETON RD
STOCKTON RD
Newton Grange Farm
Longnewton Reservoir
Farfields Farm
Carcut Bridge
BISHOPTON LA
Sadberge Reservoir
Rectory Farm
DL1
BEACON HILL
A66
Eddlethorpe Farm
Hang Thorn Farm
THE WILLOW CHASE 1
VANE COURT 2
THE CLOSE 3
WOODLAND WAY 4
THE YEW WALK 5
A1150
A66
1 WEST ROW
2 THE ORCHARD
3 BEACON GRANGE PK
4 CHURCH LANE
5 HILLHOUSE
Bumper Hall
Little Burdon
Toft Hill
West End Farm
FARFIELDS CL
PH
BUESS LANE
Middle Town Farm
Spring House Farm
Sadberge Hall Farm
Street House Farm
Hardstones Farm
MILL LANE
Sadberge Hall
A66
Mill Hill Farm
South Burdon
White House Farm
SADBERGE ROAD
LINGFIELD CL
Midway Farm
DL2
West Moor
LINGFIELD WAY
DUDLEY RD
ALLINGTON WAY
LINGFIELD WAY
Highfield
High Goosepool Farm
West Gate Fox Covert
Morton Palms Farm
Palm Bridge
Long Plantation
Westgate Farm
MORTON RD
SADBERGE RD
West Hartburn Village
MILL LANE
Maxgate Farm
A67
A67
HAMBY RD
HEATHFIELD PK
STATION ROAD
Low Goosepool Farm
HARPERS TR
PH
Sewage Works
WILD RD
PH
SHANNON LEA
STANSTED GR
Foster House
Morton Grange
OAKTREE JUNC
B6280
Resr
WOOLSINGTON DRIVE
A67
HIGH STELL
Teesside Airport
Middleton St George
PH
PO
YARM ROAD
ALEXANDRIA DR
FAIRFAX RD
WASHINGTON AVE
YARM ROAD
A66
Stodhoe Farm
Prim Sch
Dinsdale
THE SPINNEY 1
DENVER DR 2
ASHDALE CL
OAK TREE CL
PH
Maidendale Farm
Thorntree Farm
THORNTREE GD
CHAPEL ST
Oak Tree Farm
OAK THE CRES
PINE TREE GR
High Scrog Farm
Middleton Hall
Oak Tree
Teesside International Airport
Morton Farm
C4
1 GRENDON GDNS
2 THE GREENWAY
3 CEDARWOOD
4 POUNTEYS CL
5 WESTACRES
6 DINSDALE CT
7 DINSDALE CL
8 THE MEADOWS
9 MT PLEASANT CL
10 FARNBOROUGH CT
11 RINGWAY GR
12 YEADON WALK
13 HEATHROW CL
14 MANSTON CT
15 PRESTWICK CT
NEASHAM ROAD
MIDDLETON LANE
1 ST MARGARETS CL
2 ST ANNES GDNS
Sewage Works
Robinson's Plantation
COATHAM AV
DESMOND RD
THE PADDOCK
CASTLE CL
HUNTERS GN
Hunger Hill Farm
East Flat Plantation
1 THE OAKLANDS
2 EAST VIEW
CHURCH LA
PH
ARCHER RD
HILL RISE
Middleton One Row
CHURCH CL
Motte
THE FRONT
Featherstone House
Low Maidendale Farm
Woodhead Farm
Dinsdale Park
Sewage Works
Brass Castle Farm
River Tees
Over Dinsdale Grange
East Middleton Farm
CH
Dinsdale Wood
West Middleton Farm
Birch Carr Plantation
Over Dinsdale Hall
Church House Farm
Neasham Springs
Over Dinsdale Wood
Cold Comfort Farm
Manor House
Earthworks
Trafford Hill
DIBDALE ROAD
Low Dinsdale
Howe Hill Cottages
Low Middleton
Stonybank Plantation
Crosshill Wood
Low Neasham Springs
THE CLOSE
Dibdale Plantation
Neasham
NEASHAM HILL
Neasham Hill Farm
Rose Hill
Low Moor Farm
TS16
Hill Top House
Spa Wells (Sulphur)
Hill House
Fatten Hill
NEASHAM RD
NEW LA
TEESWAY
TEESWAY
HURWORTH RD
Paddock Wood
SOCKBURN LA
Scarhill Plantation
The Gill
Newsham Grange
Black Wood

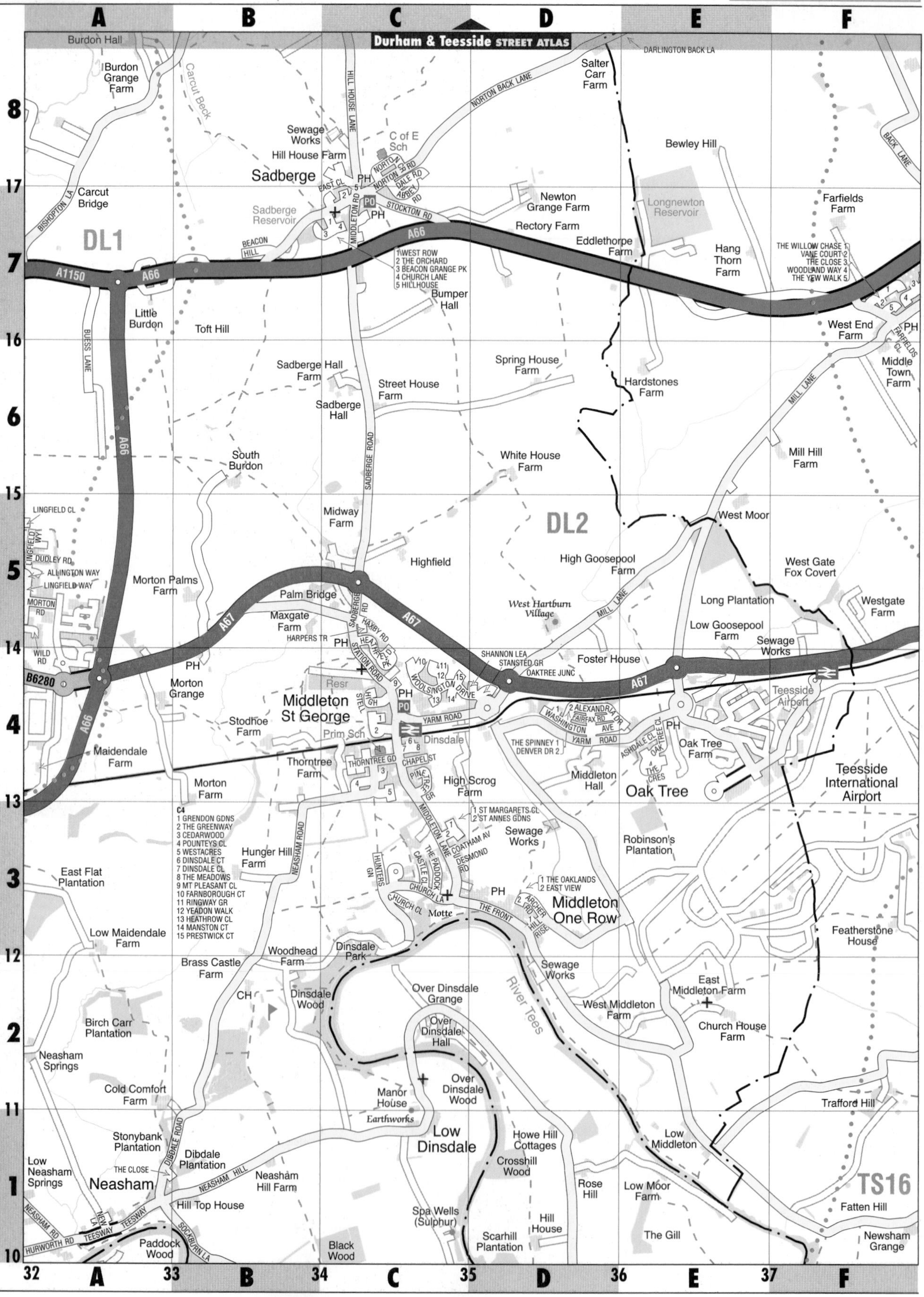

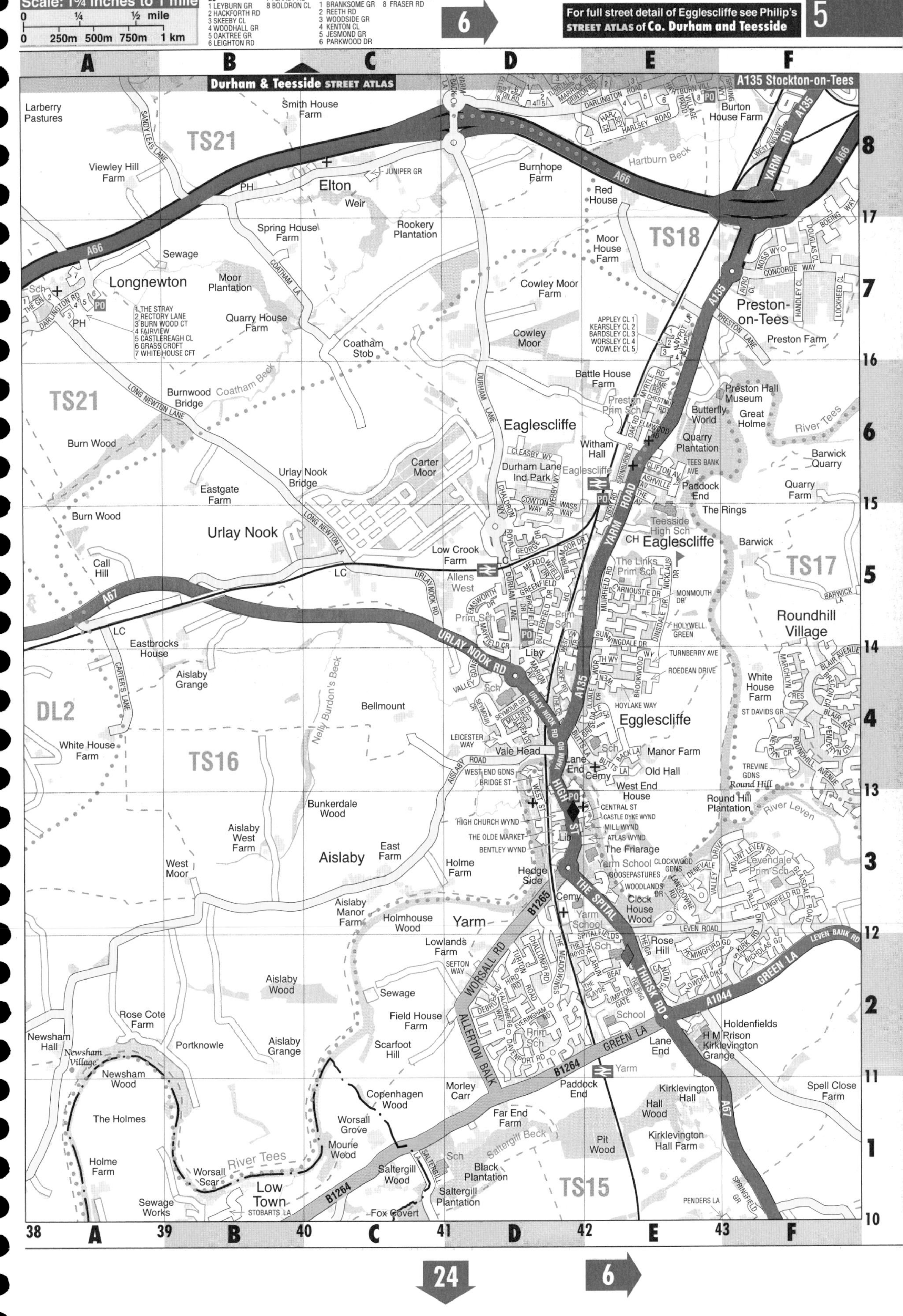
Scale: 1¾ inches to 1 mile
0 ¼ ½ mile
0 250m 500m 750m 1 km
D8
1 LEYBURN GR
2 HACKFORTH RD
3 SKEEBY CL
4 WOODHALL GR
5 OAKTREE GR
6 LEIGHTON RD
7 FEARBY RD
8 BOLDRON CL
E8
1 BRANKSOME GR
2 REETH RD
3 WOODSIDE GR
4 KENTON CL
5 JESMOND GR
6 PARKWOOD DR
7 HARPER TERR
8 FRASER RD
6
For full street detail of Egglescliffe see Philip's STREET ATLAS of Co. Durham and Teesside
Durham & Teesside STREET ATLAS
A135 Stockton-on-Tees
Larberry Pastures
Smith House Farm
TS21
Viewley Hill Farm
Elton
Weir
Burnhope Farm
Red House
Hartburn Beck
Burton House Farm
Spring House Farm
Rookery Plantation
Moor House Farm
TS18
Sewage
Longnewton
Moor Plantation
Quarry House Farm
Cowley Moor Farm
Preston-on-Tees
Preston Farm
1 THE STRAY
2 RECTORY LANE
3 BURN WOOD CT
4 FAIRVIEW
5 CASTLEREAGH CL
6 GRASS CROFT
7 WHITE HOUSE CFT
Coatham Stob
Cowley Moor
APPLEY CL 1
KEARSLEY CL 2
BARDSLEY CL 3
WORSLEY CL 4
COWLEY CL 5
TS21
Burnwood Bridge
Coatham Beck
Battle House Farm
Preston Hall Museum
Butterfly World
Great Holme
River Tees
Burn Wood
Eaglescliffe
Witham Hall
Quarry Plantation
Barwick Quarry
Carter Moor
Urlay Nook Bridge
Durham Lane Ind Park
Paddock End
Quarry Farm
Eastgate Farm
The Rings
Burn Wood
Urlay Nook
Teesside High Sch
Eaglescliffe
Barwick
TS17
Low Crook Farm
Call Hill
The Links Prim Sch
Allens West
Roundhill Village
Eastbrocks House
Aislaby Grange
URLAY NOOK RD
White House Farm
Bellmount
Nelly Burdon's Beck
DL2
Egglescliffe
Manor Farm
White House Farm
TS16
Vale Head
Old Hall
West End House
Round Hill Plantation
River Leven
Bunkerdale Wood
Aislaby West Farm
The Friarage
East Farm
Aislaby
Holme Farm
Hedge Side
West Moor
Yarm School
Levendale Prim Sch
Aislaby Manor Farm
Holmhouse Wood
Yarm
Clock House Wood
Lowlands Farm
Rose Hill
Aislaby Wood
Sewage
Field House Farm
Rose Cote Farm
Holdenfields
H M Prison Kirklevington Grange
Newsham Hall
Portknowle
Aislaby Grange
Scarfoot Hill
Lane End
Newsham Village
Newsham Wood
Copenhagen Wood
Morley Carr
Paddock End
Kirklevington Hall
Spell Close Farm
The Holmes
Worsall Grove
Far End Farm
Hall Wood
Holme Farm
Mourie Wood
Saltergill Beck
Pit Wood
Kirklevington Hall Farm
River Tees
Worsall Scar
Saltergill Wood
Black Plantation
TS15
Low Town
Sewage Works
Saltergill Plantation
Fox Covert
A66
A67
A135
A1044
B1264
B1265
A B C D E F
38 39 40 41 42 43
8 17 7 16 6 15 5 14 4 13 3 12 2 11 1 10
24
6

Scale: 1¾ inches to 1 mile
0 ¼ ½ mile
0 250m 500m 750m 1 km

A66 Middlesbrough | A1130 Stockton-on-Tees (A1305) | A19 Peterlee | A1032 Middlesbrough (A66) | Durham & Teesside STREET ATLAS

Stockton Football Club
Lanehouse Rd
Acklam Road A1130
Mandale Road
Rugby & Cricket Clubs
Acklam
North Wood Coll
East Wood
Sixth Form Coll
Swimming Baths
Bowesfield Industrial Estate
TS18
Thornaby-on-Tees
Jolly Farmer Inn
Low Wood
River Tees
The Holmes
Acklam Grange Secondary Sch
Stainsby Hill Farm
West Plantation
Hallgarth Comp Sch
St Davids Sec Sch
TS5
Acklam Cemy
Medieval Village of Stansby
Stainsby Beck
Bassleton Wood
TS17
Thorntree Farm
Thornaby Wood
Rec Ctr
Stainton Vale Farm
Brookfield
Ladgate La
Low La A1044
A174
Hollybush Farm
Stainsby Wood
Teesside Industrial Estate
Stainton Vale
Stainton Beck
Stainton
Hemlington Hall
Liby
Low Farm
Myton House Farm
Thornaby Plantation
Plum Tree Farm
Upper Farm
Quarry Plantation
Hemlington
Rec Ctr
Ingleby Barwick
Superstore
Maltby
Oxhill Farm
Thornton
TS8
Stainton Grange
Holme Farm
Larchfield Community
Little Maltby Farm
Thornton Grange
Maltby Farm
Sleepy Hollow Farm
Thornton Low Moor Farm
Fox Covert
Severs' Plantation
Thornton Moor
Maltby Grange
Mount Leven
High Leven
The Fox Covert
Ingleby Hill
Sober Hall
White House Farm
Maltby Beck
Seamer Road
Leven Bridge
Leven Bank Rd
High Farm
Low Fields
Barley Flatts Wood
Antelope Farm
Leven Bridge Plantation
East Gill
Crow Wood
Leven Close Farm
Red Hall Wood
Greenfields Farm
High Plantation
Low Fields Farm
Low House Farm
Hilton House Farm
Hilton
Oxhill Farm
TS9
Stockdale Wood
Red Hall Wood
TS15
Brewsdale
Red Hall Farm
Ravenscar Wood
Hilton Wood
Scriddles Wood
White Hall Farm
Middleton Lodge
Castle Hill
Blackwell Crook Wood
Seamer Grange Farm
Boy Hill Farm
West End
Greystone Farm
Village Farm
Seamer

For full street detail of Middlesbrough see Philip's STREET ATLAS of Co. Durham and Teesside

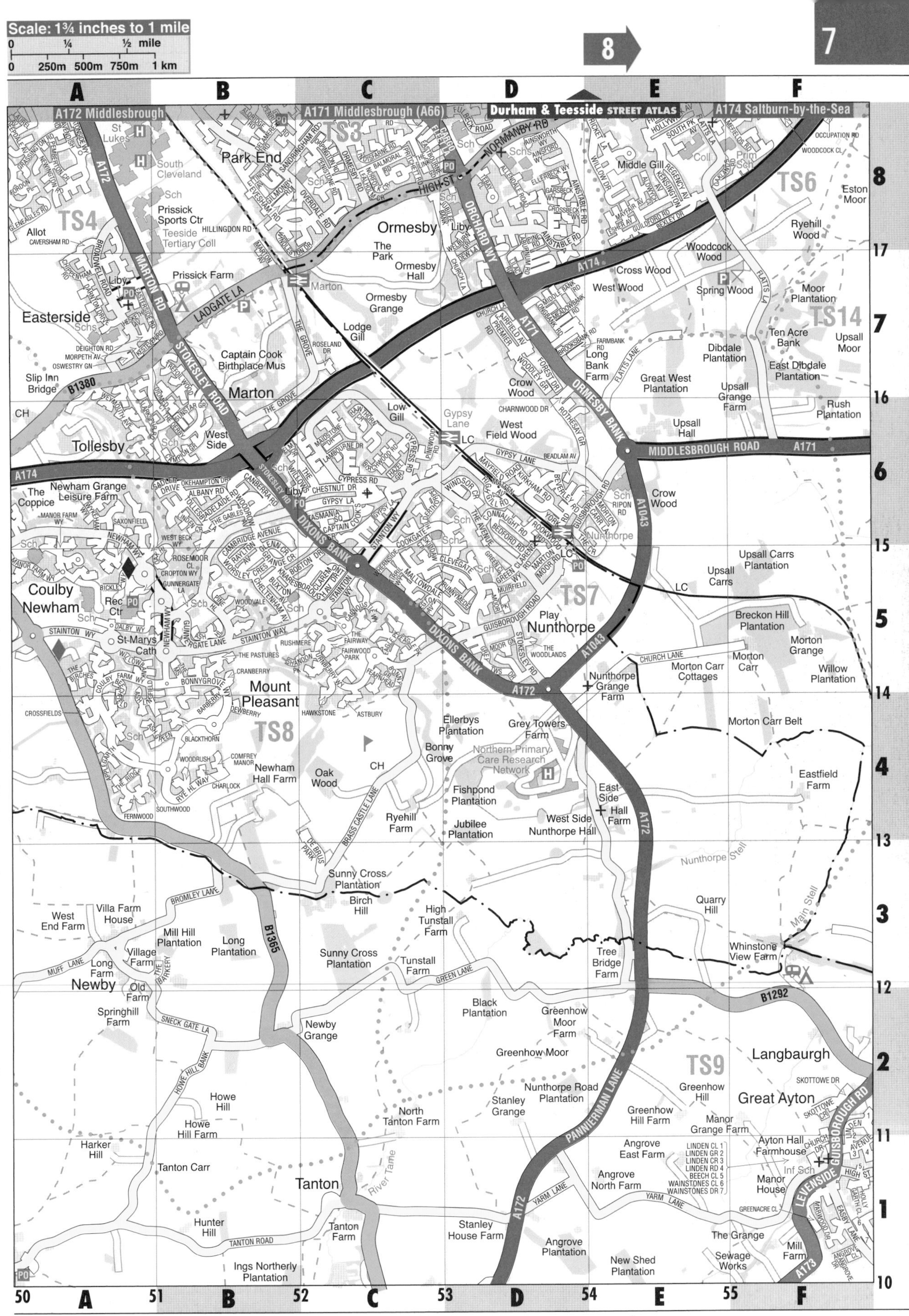

For full street detail of Middlesbrough see Philip's STREET ATLAS of Co. Durham and Teesside

26
8

Scale: 1¾ inches to 1 mile
0 ¼ ½ mile
0 250m 500m 750m 1 km

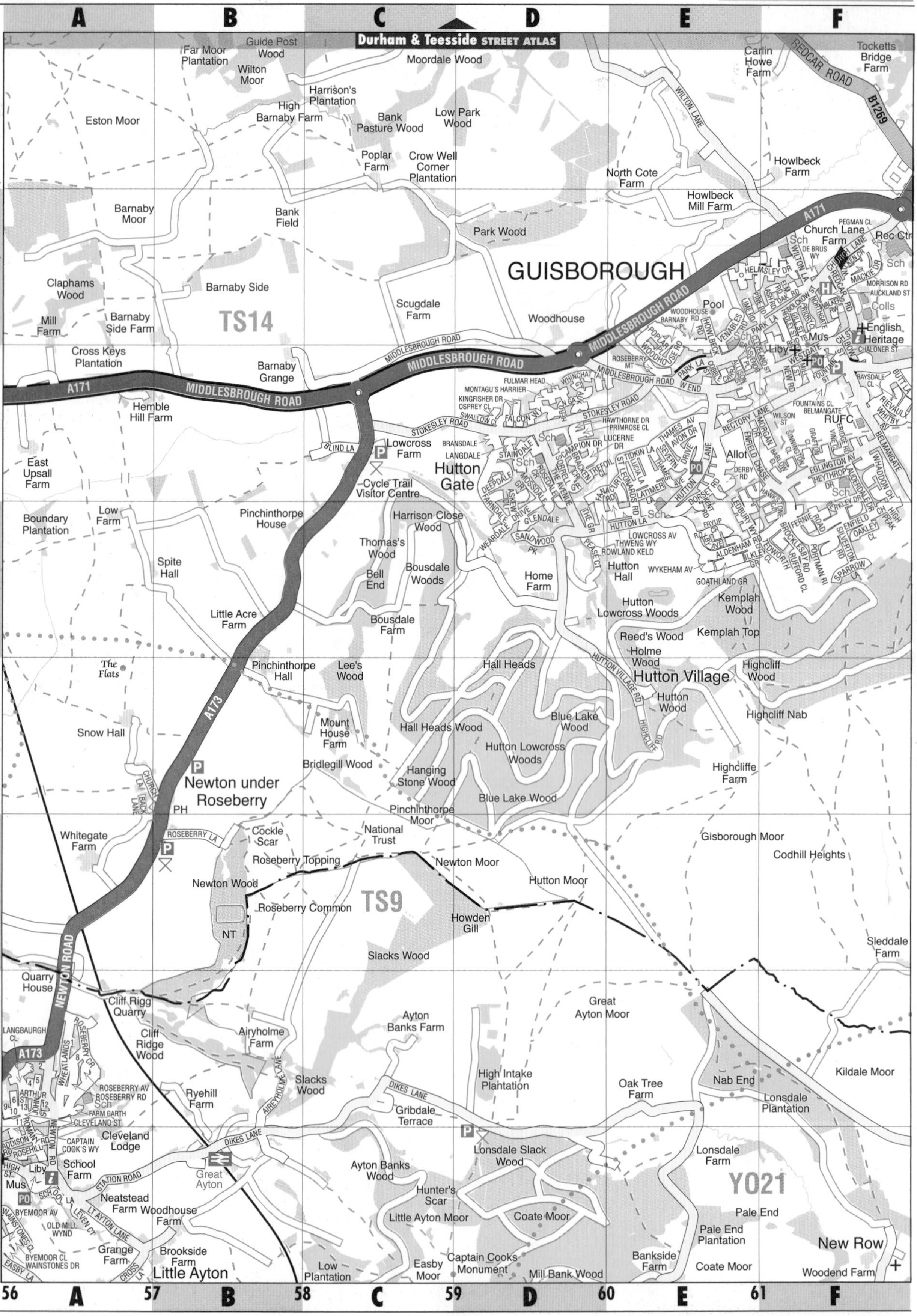
A B C D E F
Durham & Teesside STREET ATLAS
8
17
7
16
6
15
5
14
4
13
3
12
2
11
1
10
56 57 58 59 60 61
Guide Post Wood
Far Moor Plantation
Wilton Moor
Moordale Wood
Harrison's Plantation
High Barnaby Farm
Bank Pasture Wood
Low Park Wood
Eston Moor
Poplar Farm
Crow Well Corner Plantation
Carlin Howe Farm
REDCAR ROAD
B1269
Tocketts Bridge Farm
WILTON LANE
Howlbeck Farm
North Cote Farm
Howlbeck Mill Farm
Barnaby Moor
Bank Field
Park Wood
A171
Church Lane Farm
Rec Ctr
GUISBOROUGH
Claphams Wood
Barnaby Side
Scugdale Farm
Woodhouse
MIDDLESBROUGH ROAD
Pool
Colls
English Heritage
Mill Farm
Barnaby Side Farm
TS14
Cross Keys Plantation
Barnaby Grange
MIDDLESBROUGH ROAD
Liby
Mus
PO
A171
MIDDLESBROUGH ROAD
Hemble Hill Farm
STOKESLEY ROAD
RUFC
East Upsall Farm
BLIND LA
Lowcross Farm
Hutton Gate
Cycle Trail Visitor Centre
Allot
Boundary Plantation
Low Farm
Pinchinthorpe House
Harrison Close Wood
Thomas's Wood
Spite Hall
Bell End
Bousdale Woods
Home Farm
Hutton Hall
Little Acre Farm
Bousdale Farm
Hutton Lowcross Woods
Kemplah Wood
Reed's Wood
Kemplah Top
Holme Wood
The Flats
Pinchinthorpe Hall
Lee's Wood
Hall Heads
Hutton Village
Highcliff Wood
HUTTON VILLAGE RD
A173
Mount House Farm
Blue Lake Wood
Hutton Wood
Snow Hall
Hall Heads Wood
Highcliff Nab
Hutton Lowcross Woods
Bridlegill Wood
Hanging Stone Wood
Highcliffe Farm
Newton under Roseberry
PH
Blue Lake Wood
Pinchinthorpe Moor
ROSEBERRY LA
Whitegate Farm
Cockle Scar
National Trust
Gisborough Moor
Codhill Heights
Roseberry Topping
Newton Moor
Hutton Moor
Newton Wood
Roseberry Common
TS9
Howden Gill
NT
Slacks Wood
Sleddale Farm
Quarry House
NEWTON ROAD
Cliff Rigg Quarry
Great Ayton Moor
Cliff Ridge Wood
Ayton Banks Farm
Airyholme Farm
A173
Kildale Moor
Slacks Wood
High Intake Plantation
Oak Tree Farm
Nab End
Ryehill Farm
Lonsdale Plantation
DIKES LANE
Gribdale Terrace
Cleveland Lodge
Lonsdale Slack Wood
School Farm
Lonsdale Farm
Ayton Banks Wood
Great Ayton
Hunter's Scar
YO21
Neatstead Farm
Woodhouse Farm
Little Ayton Moor
Coate Moor
Pale End
Pale End Plantation
New Row
Grange Farm
Brookside Farm
Little Ayton
Low Plantation
Easby Moor
Captain Cooks Monument
Mill Bank Wood
Bankside Farm
Coate Moor
Woodend Farm

A2
1 ORCHARD CL
2 BRADLEYS TR
3 CHURCHILL CL
4 SPENCE CT
5 ROWAN DR
6 CENTRAL WY
7 CALIFORNIA GR
8 ROSEBERRY DR
9 OAKLANDS
10 THE HAWTHORNS
11 ROMANY RD
12 WOODBINE CL
13 WHINSTONE VW

For full street detail of Guisborough see Philip's STREET ATLAS of Co. Durham and Teesside

Scale: 1¾ inches to 1 mile

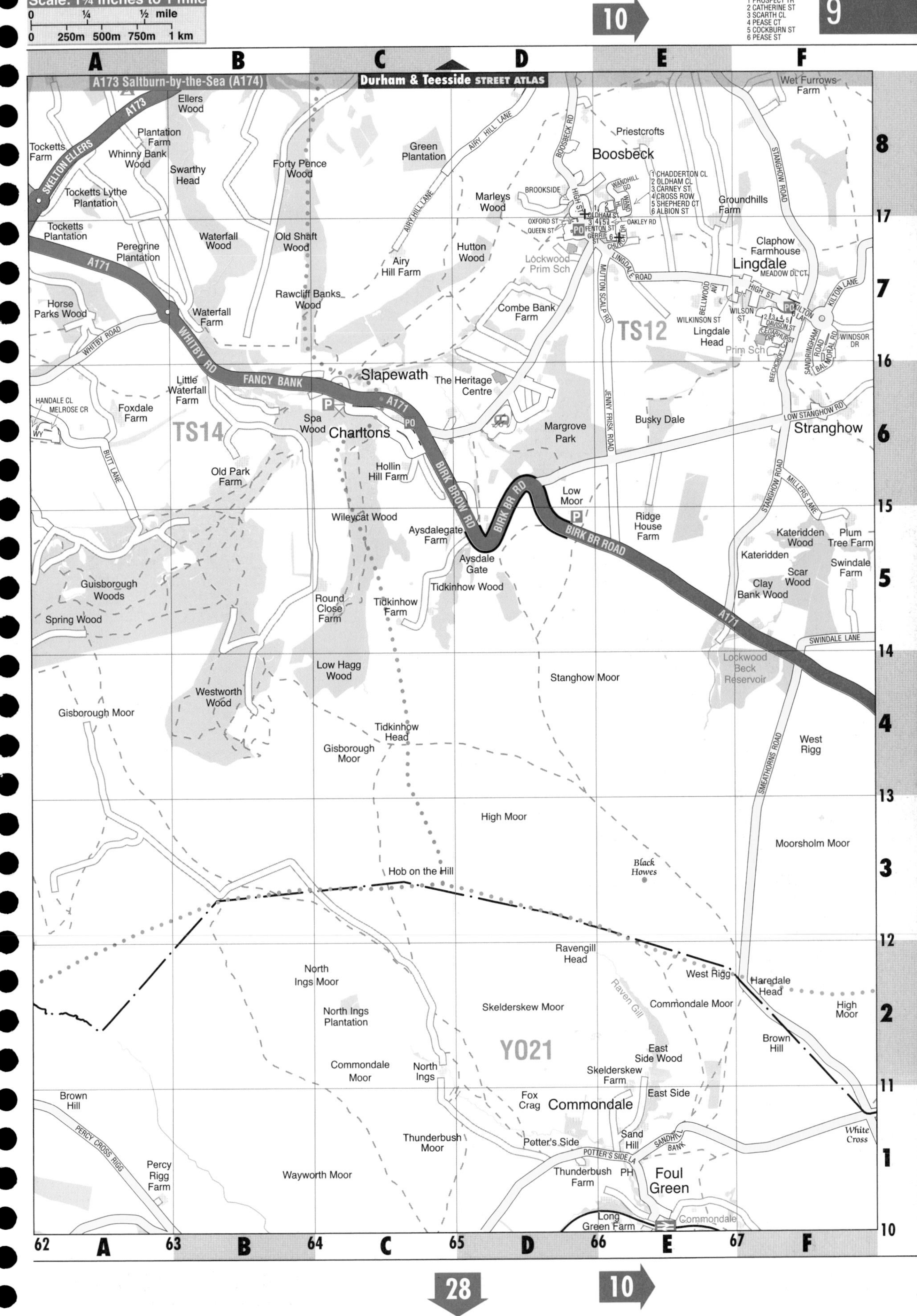

28
10

9

Scale: 1¾ inches to 1 mile
0 ¼ ½ mile
0 250m 500m 750m 1 km

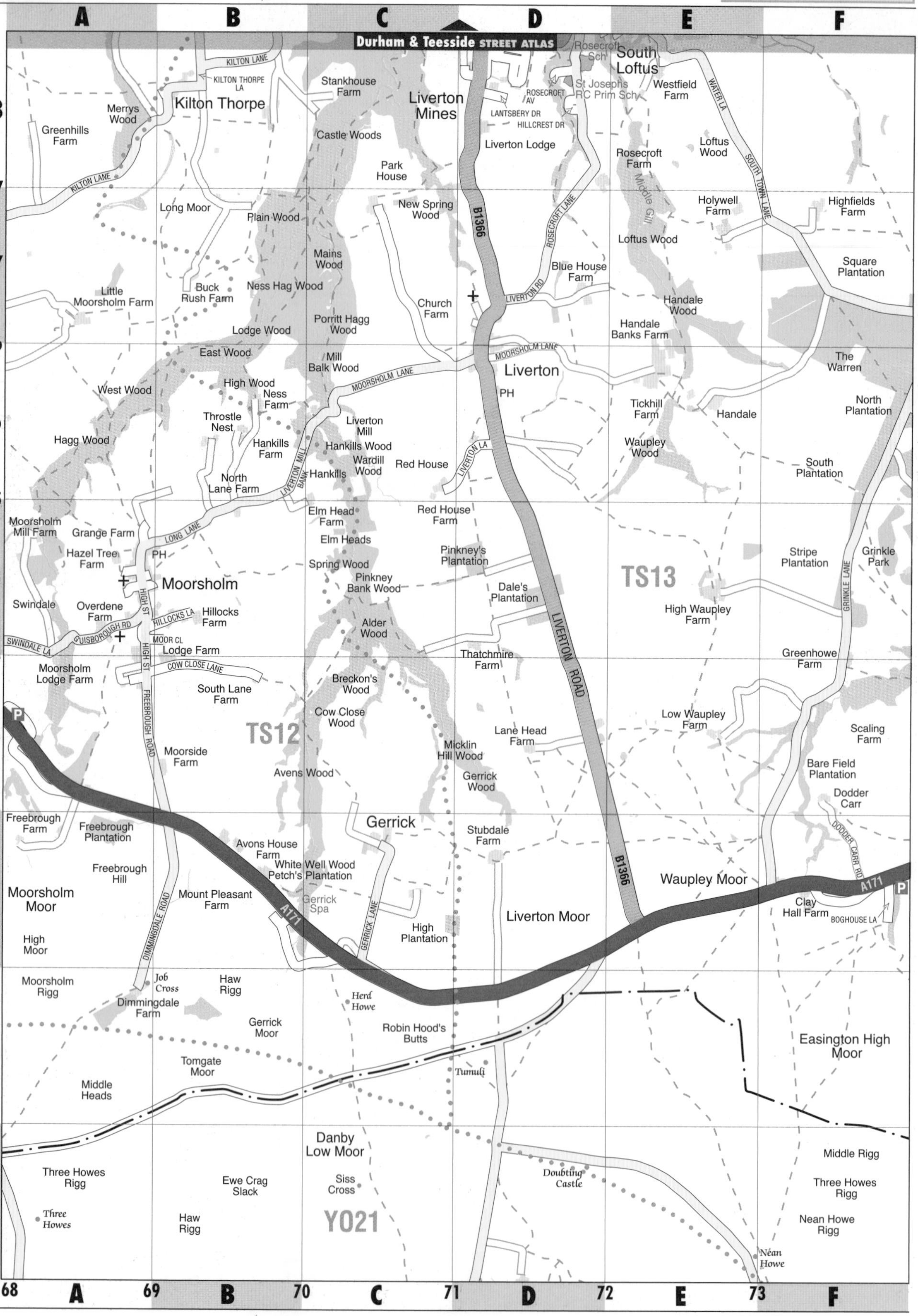

A B C D E F

8 17 7 16 6 15 5 14 4 13 3 12 2 11 1 10

Kilton Thorpe
Kilton Lane
Kilton Thorpe La
Merrys Wood
Greenhills Farm
Stankhouse Farm
Liverton Mines
Castle Woods
Park House
Rosecroft Sch
South Loftus
St Josephs RC Prim Sch
Rosecroft Av
Lantsbery Dr
Hillcrest Dr
Liverton Lodge
Westfield Farm
Water La
Loftus Wood
Rosecroft Farm
Middle Gill
South Town Lane
Holywell Farm
Highfields Farm
Long Moor
Plain Wood
New Spring Wood
B1366
Rosecroft Lane
Loftus Wood
Mains Wood
Blue House Farm
Square Plantation
Little Moorsholm Farm
Buck Rush Farm
Ness Hag Wood
Church Farm
Liverton Rd
Handale Wood
Porritt Hagg Wood
Handale Banks Farm
Lodge Wood
East Wood
Mill Balk Wood
Moorsholm Lane
Liverton
The Warren
West Wood
High Wood
Ness Farm
PH
Tickhill Farm
Handale
North Plantation
Hagg Wood
Throstle Nest
Liverton Mill
Hankills Farm
Hankills Wood
Red House
Liverton La
Waupley Wood
Wardill Wood
Hankills
Liverton Mill Bank
South Plantation
North Lane Farm
Moorsholm Mill Farm
Grange Farm
Long Lane
Elm Head Farm
Red House Farm
Elm Heads
Hazel Tree Farm
Pinkney's Plantation
Stripe Plantation
Grinkle Park
Spring Wood
TS13
Moorsholm
Pinkney Bank Wood
Dale's Plantation
Grinkle Lane
Swindale
Overdene Farm
High St
Hillocks La
Hillocks Farm
High Waupley Farm
Guisborough Rd
Alder Wood
Liverton Road
Swindale La
Moor Cl
Lodge Farm
Thatchmire Farm
Greenhowe Farm
Moorsholm Lodge Farm
Cow Close Lane
South Lane Farm
Breckon's Wood
Freebrough Road
Cow Close Wood
Low Waupley Farm
P
TS12
Lane Head Farm
Scaling Farm
Micklin Hill Wood
Moorside Farm
Bare Field Plantation
Avens Wood
Gerrick Wood
Dodder Carr
Freebrough Farm
Freebrough Plantation
Gerrick
Stubdale Farm
Dodder Carr Rd
Avons House Farm
White Well Wood
Petch's Plantation
Freebrough Hill
Waupley Moor
A171
Moorsholm Moor
Mount Pleasant Farm
Clay Hall Farm
Boghouse La
Gerrick Spa
Gerrick Lane
Liverton Moor
High Plantation
Dimmingdale Road
High Moor
Moorsholm Rigg
Job Cross
Haw Rigg
Herd Howe
Dimmingdale Farm
Gerrick Moor
Robin Hood's Butts
Easington High Moor
Tomgate Moor
Tumuli
Middle Heads
Danby Low Moor
Middle Rigg
Three Howes Rigg
Ewe Crag Slack
Siss Cross
Doubting Castle
Three Howes Rigg
Three Howes
Haw Rigg
YO21
Nean Howe Rigg
Nean Howe

68 A 69 B 70 C 71 D 72 E 73 F

9
29

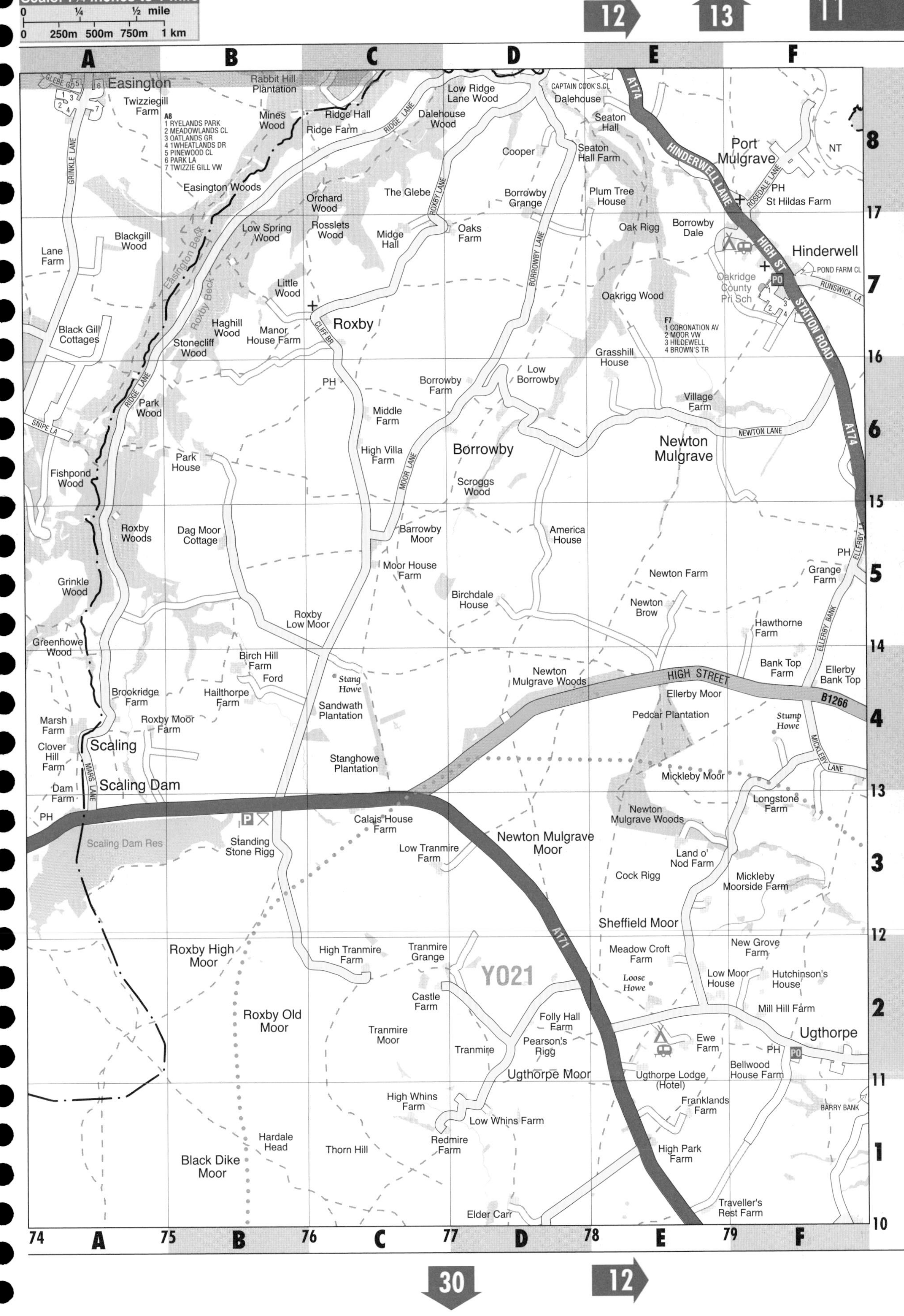
Scale: 1¾ inches to 1 mile
0 ¼ ½ mile
0 250m 500m 750m 1 km
12
13
Easington
Twizziegill Farm
Rabbit Hill Plantation
Mines Wood
Ridge Hall
Ridge Farm
Low Ridge Lane Wood
Dalehouse Wood
CAPTAIN COOK'S CL
Dalehouse
Seaton Hall
Seaton Hall Farm
Cooper
Port Mulgrave
NT
PH
St Hildas Farm
A8
1 RYELANDS PARK
2 MEADOWLANDS CL
3 OATLANDS GR
4 1WHEATLANDS DR
5 PINEWOOD CL
6 PARK LA
7 TWIZZIE GILL VW
GRINKLE LANE
Easington Woods
Orchard Wood
The Glebe
Borrowby Grange
Plum Tree House
HINDERWELL LANE
ROSEDALE LANE
Blackgill Wood
Low Spring Wood
Rosslets Wood
Midge Hall
Oaks Farm
Oak Rigg
Borrowby Dale
Hinderwell
HIGH ST
POND FARM CL
RUNSWICK LA
Lane Farm
Easington Beck
Roxby Beck
Little Wood
Roxby
Oakrigg Wood
Oakridge County Pri Sch
STATION ROAD
F7
1 CORONATION AV
2 MOOR VW
3 HILDEWELL
4 BROWN'S TR
Black Gill Cottages
Haghill Wood
Manor House Farm
Stonecliff Wood
CLIFF BR
BORROWBY LANE
ROXBY LANE
RIDGE LANE
Grasshill House
PH
Borrowby Farm
Low Borrowby
Village Farm
Park Wood
Middle Farm
NEWTON LANE
SNIPE LA
Newton Mulgrave
A174
Borrowby
High Villa Farm
Park House
Fishpond Wood
MOOR LANE
Scroggs Wood
Roxby Woods
Dag Moor Cottage
Barrowby Moor
America House
ELLERBY LA
PH
Grange Farm
Moor House Farm
Newton Farm
Grinkle Wood
Birchdale House
Newton Brow
Roxby Low Moor
Hawthorne Farm
ELLERBY BANK
Greenhowe Wood
Birch Hill Farm
Newton Mulgrave Woods
HIGH STREET
Bank Top Farm
Ellerby Bank Top
Stang Howe
Ford
Ellerby Moor
B1266
Brookridge Farm
Hailthorpe Farm
Sandwath Plantation
Pedcar Plantation
Marsh Farm
Roxby Moor Farm
Stump Howe
Clover Hill Farm
Scaling
MICKLEBY LANE
Stanghowe Plantation
Mickleby Moor
MARS LANE
Dam Farm
Scaling Dam
Longstone Farm
PH
Calais House Farm
Newton Mulgrave Woods
Standing Stone Rigg
Newton Mulgrave Moor
Scaling Dam Res
Low Tranmire Farm
Land o' Nod Farm
Cock Rigg
Mickleby Moorside Farm
Sheffield Moor
A171
Roxby High Moor
High Tranmire Farm
Tranmire Grange
Meadow Croft Farm
New Grove Farm
YO21
Loose Howe
Low Moor House
Hutchinson's House
Castle Farm
Roxby Old Moor
Mill Hill Farm
Folly Hall Farm
Tranmire Moor
Pearson's Rigg
Ewe Farm
Ugthorpe
Tranmire
PH
PO
Ugthorpe Moor
Ugthorpe Lodge (Hotel)
Bellwood House Farm
High Whins Farm
Franklands Farm
BARRY BANK
Low Whins Farm
Hardale Head
Redmire Farm
Thorn Hill
High Park Farm
Black Dike Moor
Traveller's Rest Farm
Elder Carr
A B C D E F
74 75 76 77 78 79
17 16 15 14 13 12 11 10
8 7 6 5 4 3 2 1
30
12

11

Scale: 1¾ inches to 1 mile

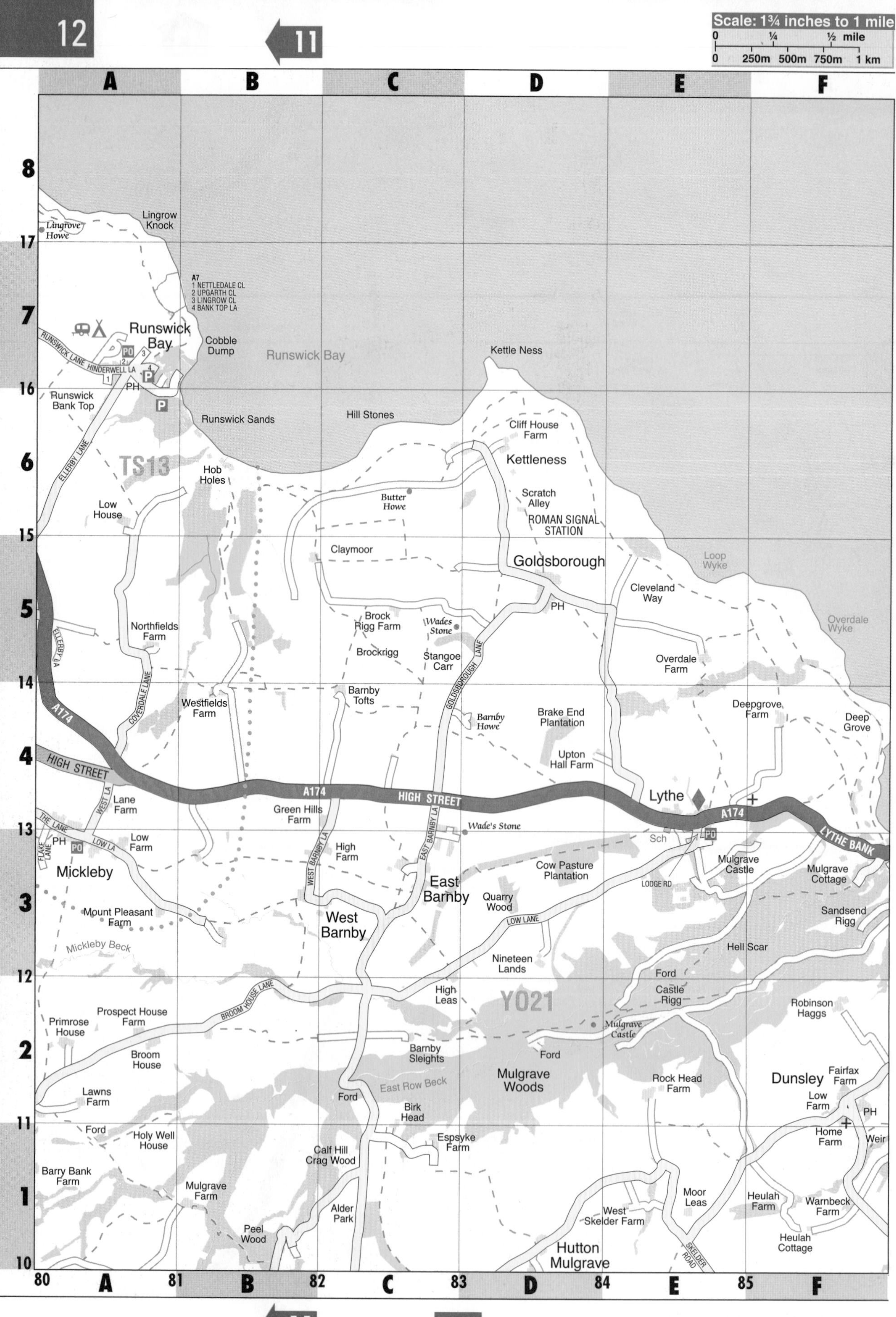

11

31

Scale: 1¾ inches to 1 mile

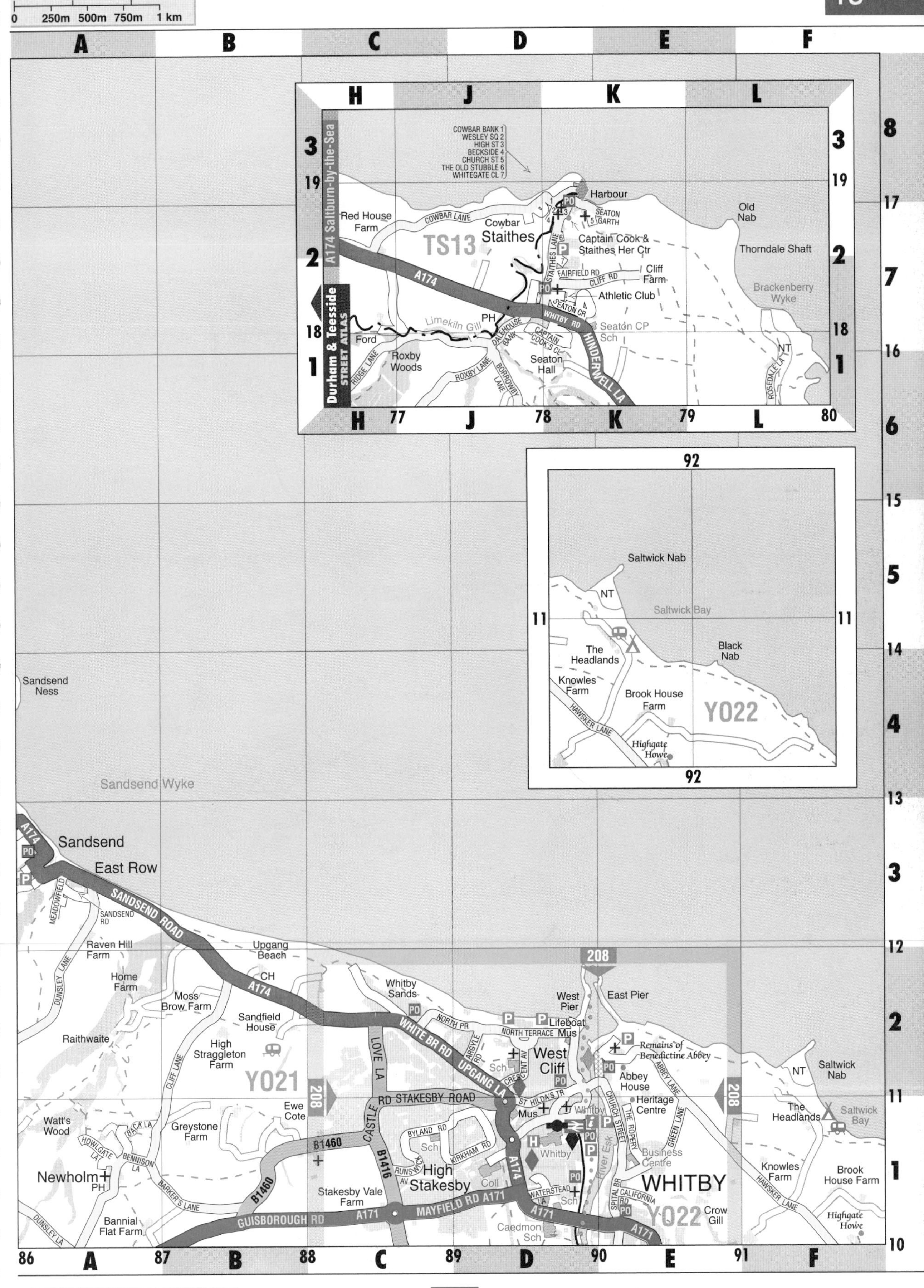

For full street detail of the highlighted area see page 208.

32

Scale: 1¾ inches to 1 mile
0 ¼ ½ mile
0 250m 500m 750m 1 km

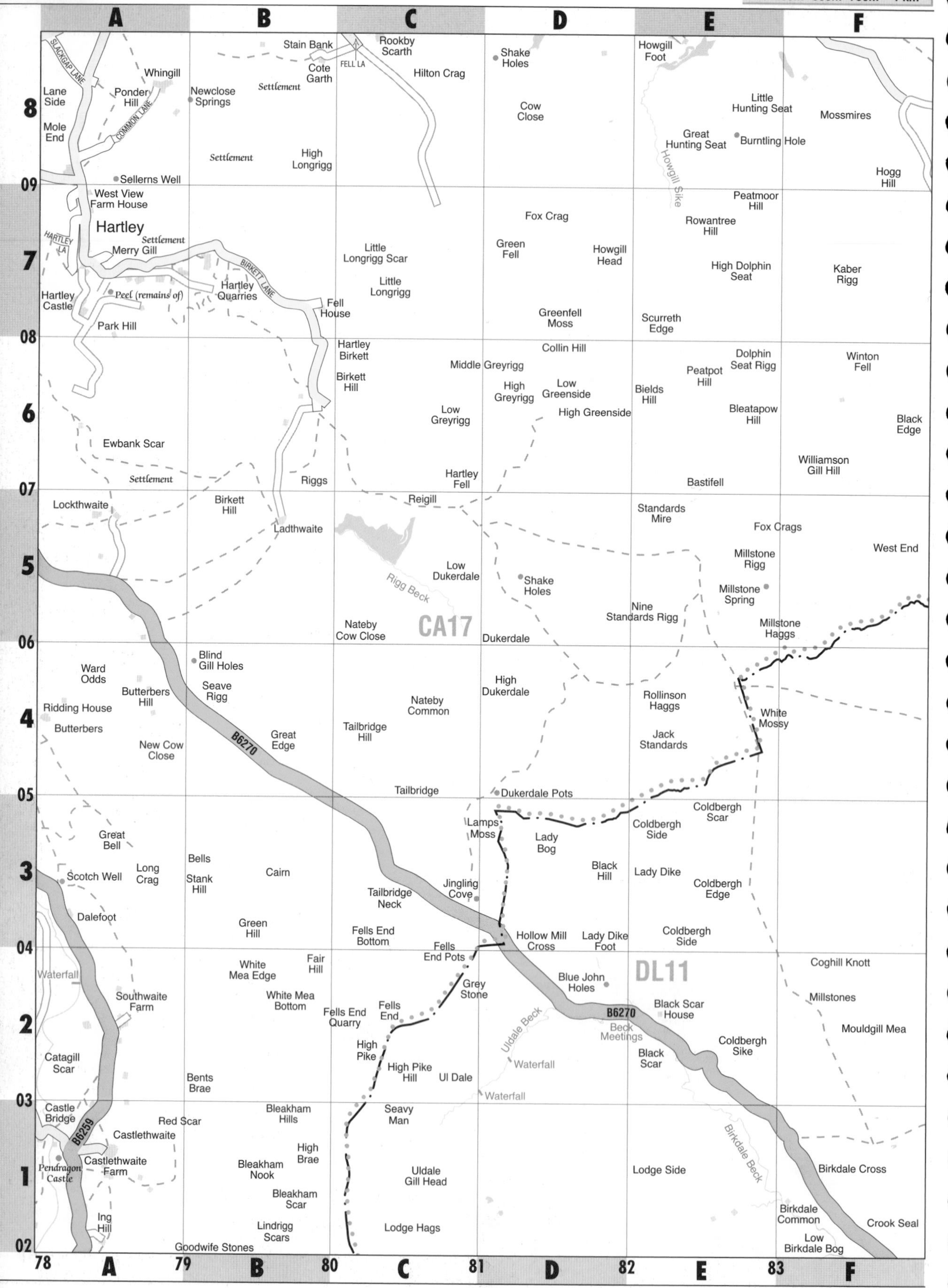

34

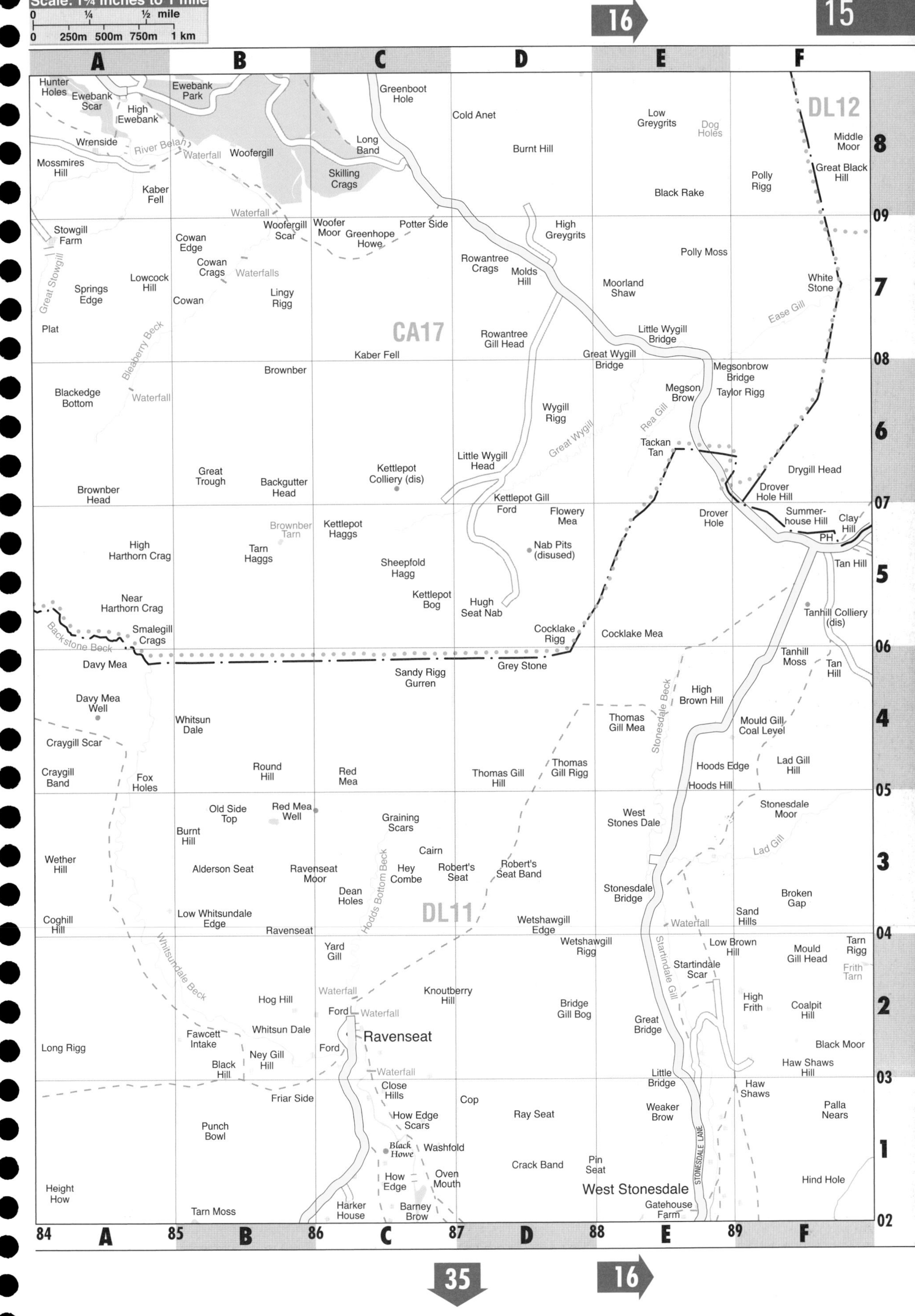
Scale: 1¾ inches to 1 mile
0 ¼ ½ mile
0 250m 500m 750m 1 km
16
A B C D E F
Hunter Holes
Ewebank Scar
Ewebank Park
High Ewebank
Greenboot Hole
Cold Anet
Low Greygrits
Dog Holes
DL12
Middle Moor
Wrenside
River Belah
Waterfall
Woofergill
Long Band
Burnt Hill
Mossmires Hill
Skilling Crags
Great Black Hill
Polly Rigg
Kaber Fell
Black Rake
Waterfall
Stowgill Farm
Woofergill Scar
Woofer Moor
Greenhope Howe
Potter Side
High Greygrits
Cowan Edge
Polly Moss
Cowan Crags
Waterfalls
Rowantree Crags
Molds Hill
White Stone
Great Stowgill
Lowcock Hill
Springs Edge
Lingy Rigg
Moorland Shaw
Cowan
Ease Gill
Plat
CA17
Rowantree Gill Head
Little Wygill Bridge
Bleaberry Beck
Kaber Fell
Great Wygill Bridge
Megsonbrow Bridge
Brownber
Megson Brow
Taylor Rigg
Blackedge Bottom
Waterfall
Wygill Rigg
Rea Gill
Great Wygill
Tackan Tan
Little Wygill Head
Kettlepot Colliery (dis)
Drygill Head
Great Trough
Backgutter Head
Drover Hole Hill
Brownber Head
Kettlepot Gill Ford
Summer-house Hill
Clay Hill
Flowery Mea
Drover Hole
Brownber Tarn
Kettlepot Haggs
PH
High Harthorn Crag
Tarn Haggs
Nab Pits (disused)
Tan Hill
Sheepfold Hagg
Kettlepot Bog
Hugh Seat Nab
Near Harthorn Crag
Tanhill Colliery (dis)
Smalegill Crags
Backstone Beck
Cocklake Rigg
Cocklake Mea
Davy Mea
Grey Stone
Tanhill Moss
Tan Hill
Sandy Rigg Gurren
Davy Mea Well
High Brown Hill
Whitsun Dale
Thomas Gill Mea
Stonesdale Beck
Mould Gill Coal Level
Craygill Scar
Round Hill
Hoods Edge
Lad Gill Hill
Craygill Band
Fox Holes
Red Mea
Thomas Gill Hill
Thomas Gill Rigg
Hoods Hill
Old Side Top
Red Mea Well
Stonesdale Moor
West Stones Dale
Burnt Hill
Graining Scars
Wether Hill
Cairn
Lad Gill
Alderson Seat
Ravenseat Moor
Hey Combe
Robert's Seat
Robert's Seat Band
Hodds Bottom Beck
Dean Holes
Stonesdale Bridge
Broken Gap
DL11
Coghill Hill
Low Whitsundale Edge
Ravenseat
Wetshawgill Edge
Waterfall
Sand Hills
Yard Gill
Wetshawgill Rigg
Low Brown Hill
Mould Gill Head
Tarn Rigg
Startindale Scar
Frith Tarn
Whitsundale Beck
Waterfall
Knoutberry Hill
Startindale Gill
High Frith
Hog Hill
Ford
Waterfall
Bridge Gill Bog
Coalpit Hill
Great Bridge
Fawcett Intake
Whitsun Dale
Ravenseat
Long Rigg
Ney Gill Hill
Ford
Black Moor
Black Hill
Waterfall
Haw Shaws Hill
Little Bridge
Close Hills
Haw Shaws
Friar Side
Cop
Weaker Brow
Palla Nears
How Edge Scars
Ray Seat
Punch Bowl
Black Howe
Washfold
Stonesdale Lane
Crack Band
Pin Seat
How Edge
Oven Mouth
Hind Hole
Height How
West Stonesdale
Harker House
Barney Brow
Gatehouse Farm
Tarn Moss
8 09 7 08 6 07 5 06 4 05 3 04 2 03 1 02
84 A 85 B 86 C 87 D 88 E 89 F
35
16

15

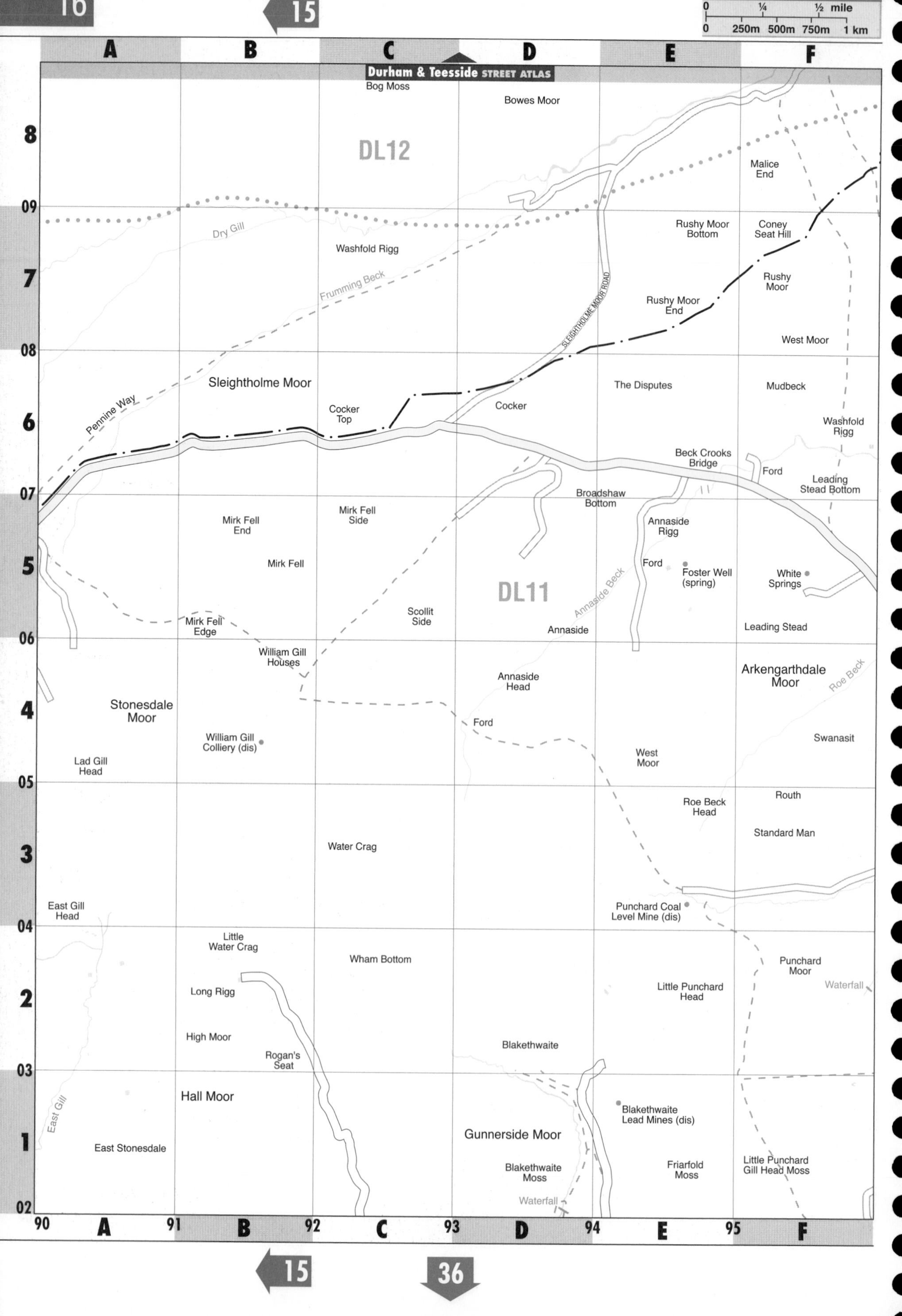
Scale: 1¾ inches to 1 mile
0 ¼ ½ mile
0 250m 500m 750m 1 km
A B C D E F
Durham & Teesside STREET ATLAS
Bog Moss
Bowes Moor
DL12
8
09
Malice End
Dry Gill
Rushy Moor Bottom
Coney Seat Hill
Washfold Rigg
7
Frumming Beck
Rushy Moor
Rushy Moor End
SLEIGHTHOLME MOOR ROAD
08
West Moor
Sleightholme Moor
The Disputes
Mudbeck
Pennine Way
Cocker Top
Cocker
6
Washfold Rigg
Beck Crooks Bridge
Ford
Leading Stead Bottom
07
Broadshaw Bottom
Mirk Fell End
Mirk Fell Side
Annaside Rigg
Mirk Fell
5
Ford
Foster Well (spring)
White Springs
DL11
Annaside Beck
Scollit Side
Mirk Fell Edge
Annaside
Leading Stead
06
William Gill Houses
Annaside Head
Arkengarthdale Moor
Roe Beck
Stonesdale Moor
4
Ford
Swanasit
William Gill Colliery (dis)
Lad Gill Head
West Moor
05
Roe Beck Head
Routh
Standard Man
Water Crag
3
East Gill Head
Punchard Coal Level Mine (dis)
04
Little Water Crag
Wham Bottom
Punchard Moor
Waterfall
2
Long Rigg
Little Punchard Head
High Moor
Blakethwaite
Rogan's Seat
03
Hall Moor
East Gill
Blakethwaite Lead Mines (dis)
1
Gunnerside Moor
East Stonesdale
Blakethwaite Moss
Friarfold Moss
Little Punchard Gill Head Moss
Waterfall
02
90 A 91 B 92 C 93 D 94 E 95 F

15

36

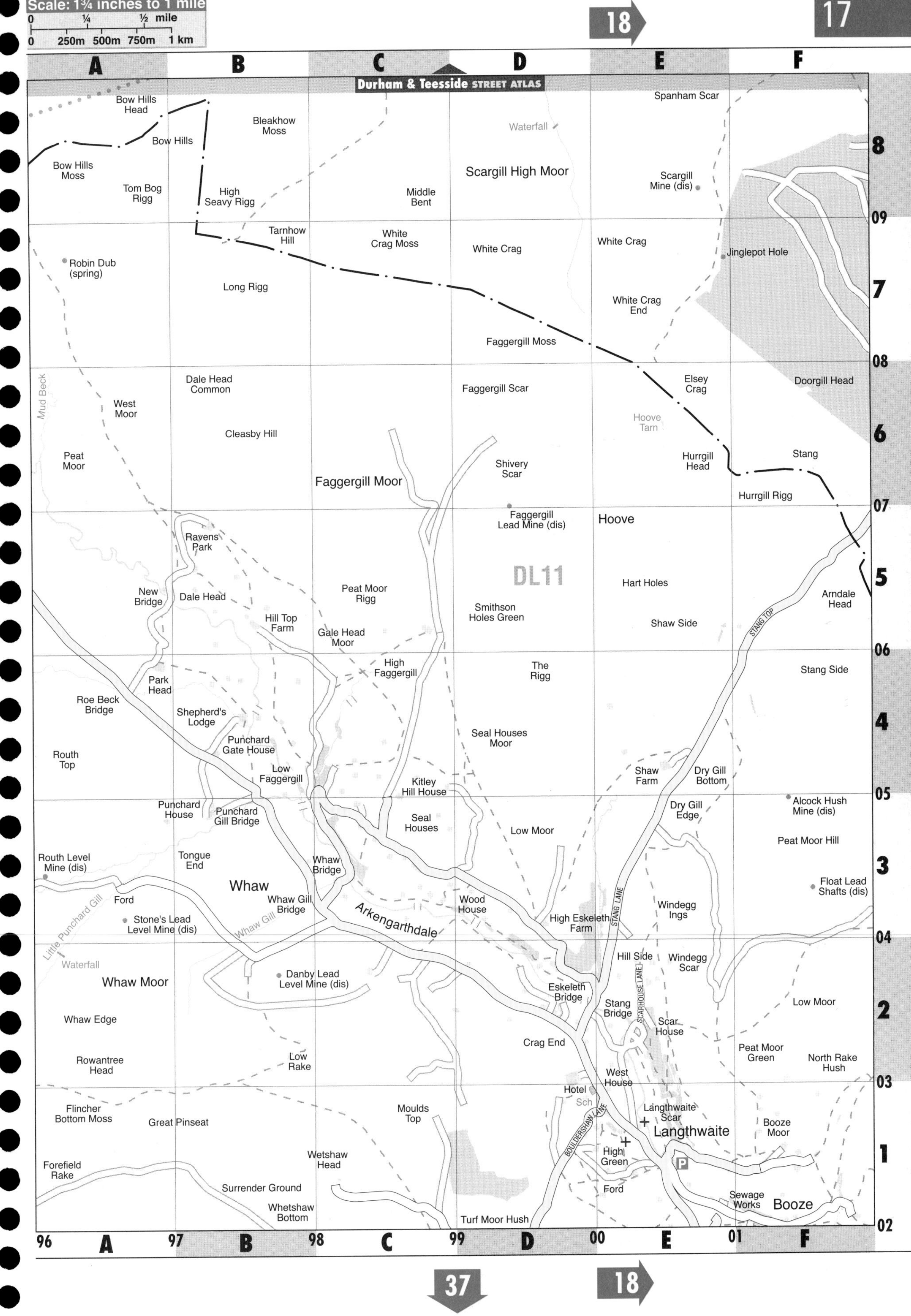
Scale: 1¾ inches to 1 mile
0 ¼ ½ mile
0 250m 500m 750m 1 km
18
Durham & Teesside STREET ATLAS
A B C D E F
8 09 7 08 6 07 5 06 4 05 3 04 2 03 1 02
96 97 98 99 00 01
Bow Hills Head
Bow Hills
Bow Hills Moss
Tom Bog Rigg
High Seavy Rigg
Bleakhow Moss
Middle Bent
Waterfall
Scargill High Moor
Spanham Scar
Scargill Mine (dis)
Tarnhow Hill
White Crag Moss
White Crag
White Crag
Jinglepot Hole
Robin Dub (spring)
Long Rigg
White Crag End
Faggergill Moss
Dale Head Common
Faggergill Scar
Elsey Crag
Doorgill Head
Mud Beck
West Moor
Cleasby Hill
Hoove Tarn
Peat Moor
Shivery Scar
Hurrgill Head
Stang
Faggergill Moor
Hurrgill Rigg
Faggergill Lead Mine (dis)
Hoove
Ravens Park
DL11
New Bridge
Dale Head
Peat Moor Rigg
Hart Holes
Arndale Head
Hill Top Farm
Gale Head Moor
Smithson Holes Green
Shaw Side
STANG TOP
High Faggergill
The Rigg
Stang Side
Park Head
Roe Beck Bridge
Shepherd's Lodge
Punchard Gate House
Seal Houses Moor
Routh Top
Low Faggergill
Kitley Hill House
Shaw Farm
Dry Gill Bottom
Punchard House
Punchard Gill Bridge
Seal Houses
Dry Gill Edge
Alcock Hush Mine (dis)
Low Moor
Peat Moor Hill
Routh Level Mine (dis)
Tongue End
Whaw Bridge
Whaw
Float Lead Shafts (dis)
Ford
Whaw Gill Bridge
Wood House
Windegg Ings
Stone's Lead Level Mine (dis)
Arkengarthdale
High Eskeleth Farm
STANG LANE
Little Punchard Gill
Whaw Gill
Waterfall
Hill Side
Windegg Scar
Whaw Moor
Danby Lead Level Mine (dis)
Esketeth Bridge
Stang Bridge
SCARHOUSE LANE
Low Moor
Whaw Edge
Scar House
Crag End
Rowantree Head
Low Rake
Peat Moor Green
North Rake Hush
West House
Hotel
Sch
Flincher Bottom Moss
Great Pinseat
Moulds Top
Langthwaite Scar
Langthwaite
Booze Moor
BOULDERSHAW LANE
High Green
Wetshaw Head
Forefield Rake
P
Surrender Ground
Ford
Whetshaw Bottom
Turf Moor Hush
Sewage Works
Booze
37
18

17

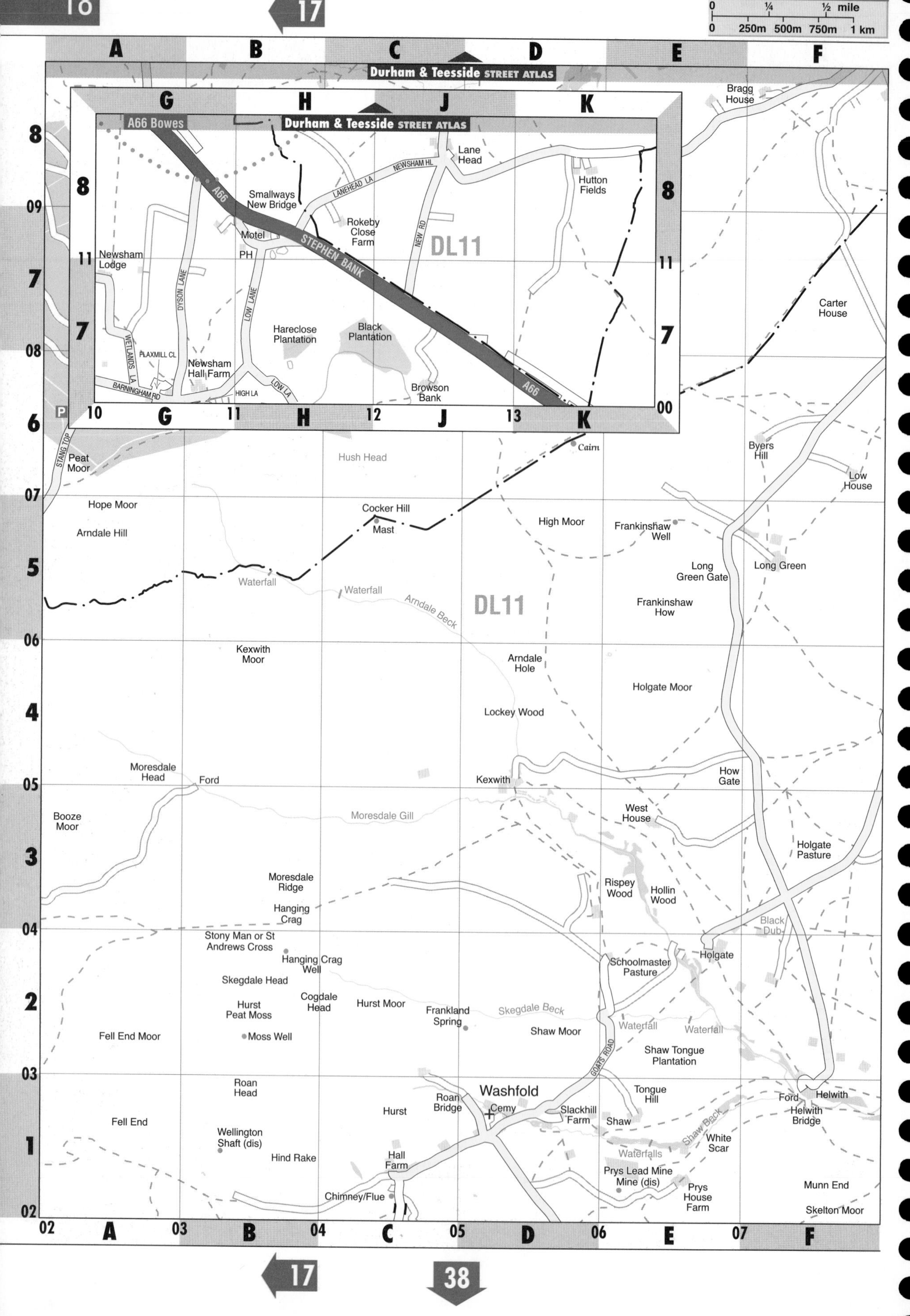
Scale: 1¾ inches to 1 mile
0 ¼ ½ mile
0 250m 500m 750m 1 km
Durham & Teesside STREET ATLAS
Durham & Teesside STREET ATLAS
A66 Bowes
Lane Head
NEWSHAM HL
LANEHEAD LA
Hutton Fields
Smallways New Bridge
Rokeby Close Farm
NEW RD
DL11
A66
Motel
PH
STEPHEN BANK
Newsham Lodge
DYSON LANE
LOW LANE
Hareclose Plantation
Black Plantation
WETLANDS LA
FLAXMILL CL
Newsham Hall Farm
LOW LA
Browson Bank
BARNINGHAM RD
HIGH LA
A66
Bragg House
Carter House
Byers Hill
Low House
STANG TOP
Peat Moor
Cairn
Hush Head
Hope Moor
Arndale Hill
Cocker Hill
Mast
High Moor
Frankinshaw Well
Long Green Gate
Long Green
Waterfall
Waterfall
Arndale Beck
DL11
Frankinshaw How
Kexwith Moor
Arndale Hole
Holgate Moor
Lockey Wood
Moresdale Head
Ford
Kexwith
How Gate
Booze Moor
Moresdale Gill
West House
Holgate Pasture
Moresdale Ridge
Rispey Wood
Hollin Wood
Hanging Crag
Stony Man or St Andrews Cross
Black Dub
Hanging Crag Well
Schoolmaster Pasture
Holgate
Skegdale Head
Cogdale Head
Hurst Moor
Frankland Spring
Skegdale Beck
Hurst Peat Moss
Waterfall
Waterfall
Fell End Moor
Moss Well
Shaw Moor
GOATS ROAD
Shaw Tongue Plantation
Roan Head
Washfold
Tongue Hill
Roan Bridge
Cemy
Slackhill Farm
Ford
Helwith
Hurst
Shaw
Helwith Bridge
Fell End
Shaw Beck
Wellington Shaft (dis)
White Scar
Hind Rake
Waterfalls
Hall Farm
Prys Lead Mine Mine (dis)
Prys House Farm
Munn End
Chimney/Flue
Skelton Moor

17

38

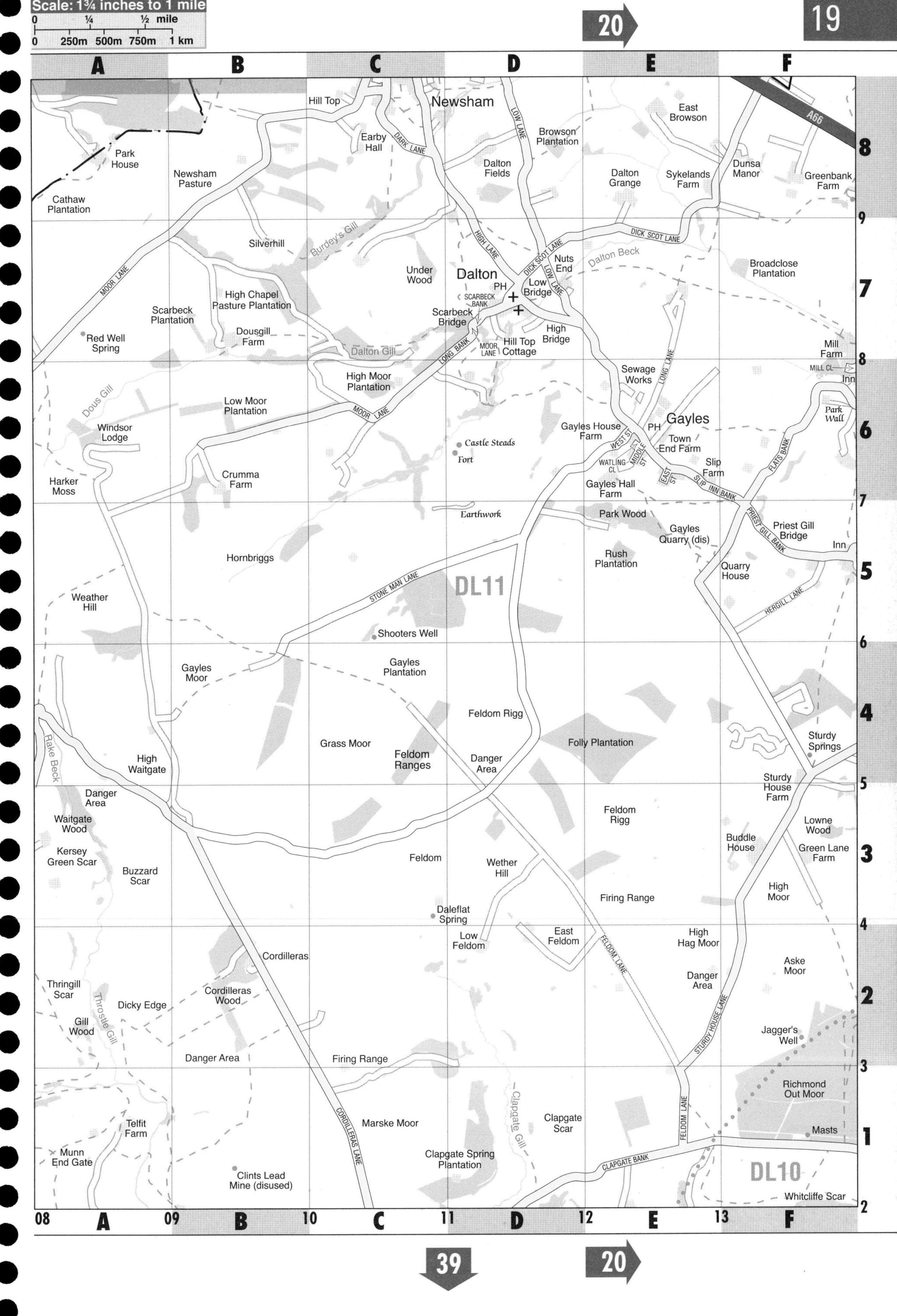

Scale: 1¾ inches to 1 mile
0 ¼ ½ mile
0 250m 500m 750m 1 km
20
Newsham
Hill Top
Earby Hall
Park House
Newsham Pasture
Cathaw Plantation
Browson Plantation
East Browson
Dalton Fields
Dalton Grange
Sykelands Farm
Dunsa Manor
Greenbank Farm
A66
Silverhill
Burdey's Gill
Under Wood
Dalton
Nuts End
Low Bridge
Dalton Beck
Broadclose Plantation
DICK SCOT LANE
High Chapel Pasture Plantation
Scarbeck Plantation
Scarbeck Bridge
SCARBECK BANK
High Bridge
Hill Top Cottage
Dougsgill Farm
Red Well Spring
Dalton Gill
Mill Farm
MILL CL
Inn
High Moor Plantation
Sewage Works
LONG LANE
Gayles
Low Moor Plantation
Windsor Lodge
Dous Gill
Gayles House Farm
Town End Farm
Park Wall
Castle Steads
Fort
Slip Farm
FLATS BANK
Harker Moss
Crumma Farm
Gayles Hall Farm
WATLING CL
SLIP INN BANK
Earthwork
Park Wood
Gayles Quarry (dis)
Priest Gill Bridge
PRIEST GILL BANK
Hornbriggs
Rush Plantation
Quarry House
DL11
STONE MAN LANE
Weather Hill
HERGILL LANE
Shooters Well
Gayles Moor
Gayles Plantation
Feldom Rigg
Folly Plantation
Grass Moor
Feldom Ranges
Danger Area
Sturdy Springs
High Waitgate
Rake Beck
Sturdy House Farm
Waitgate Wood
Kersey Green Scar
Buzzard Scar
Feldom
Wether Hill
Buddle House
Lowne Wood
Green Lane Farm
Firing Range
High Moor
Daleflat Spring
Low Feldom
East Feldom
High Hag Moor
Cordilleras
Aske Moor
Thringill Scar
Throstle Gill
Dicky Edge
Cordilleras Wood
Gill Wood
Danger Area
Jagger's Well
Firing Range
Richmond Out Moor
Telfit Farm
Marske Moor
Clapgate Gill
Clapgate Scar
Masts
Munn End Gate
Clapgate Spring Plantation
CLAPGATE BANK
FELDOM LANE
STURDY HOUSE LANE
CORDILLERAS LANE
Clints Lead Mine (disused)
DL10
Whitcliffe Scar
08 A 09 B 10 C 11 D 12 E 13 F
39
20

19
1

Scale: 1¾ inches to 1 mile
0 ¼ ½ mile
0 250m 500m 750m 1 km

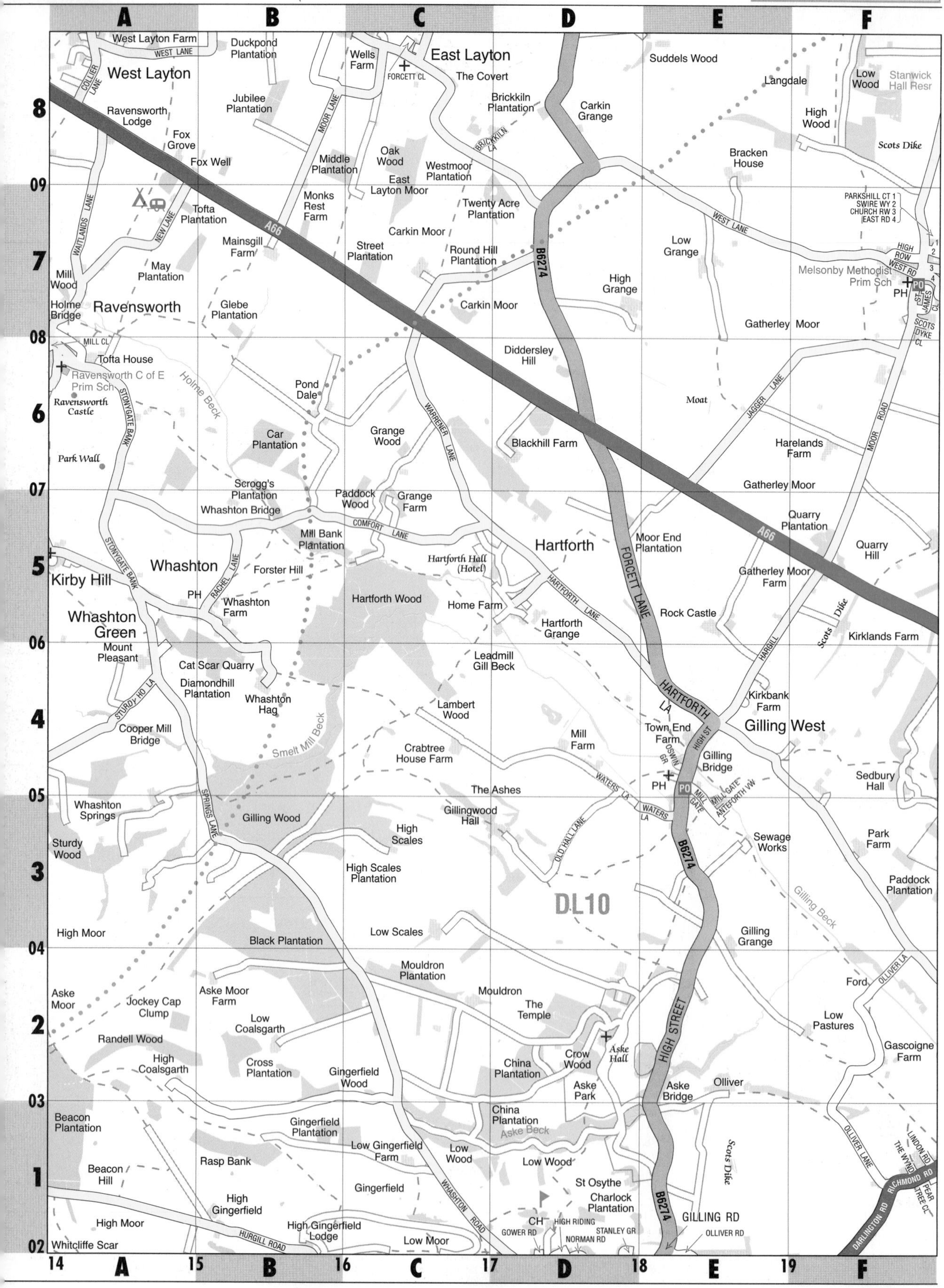

A B C D E F

8
09
7
6
07
5
06
4
05
3
04
2
03
1
02

West Layton Farm
WEST LANE
Duckpond Plantation
Wells Farm
East Layton
FORCETT CL
The Covert
Suddels Wood
Langdale
Low Wood
Stanwick Hall Resr
West Layton
COLLIER LANE
Jubilee Plantation
MOOR LANE
Brickkiln Plantation
Carkin Grange
High Wood
Ravensworth Lodge
Fox Grove
BRICKKILN LA
Scots Dike
Fox Well
Middle Plantation
Oak Wood
Westmoor Plantation
Bracken House
East Layton Moor
Monks Rest Farm
Twenty Acre Plantation
PARKSHILL CT 1
SWIRE WY 2
CHURCH RW 3
EAST RD 4
WAITLANDS LANE
Tofta Plantation
NEW LANE
A66
Carkin Moor
WEST LANE
Low Grange
HIGH ROW
WEST RD
Mainsgill Farm
Street Plantation
Round Hill Plantation
B6274
Melsonby Methodist Prim Sch
PO
PH
Mill Wood
May Plantation
High Grange
ST JAMES CL
Holme Bridge
Ravensworth
Glebe Plantation
Carkin Moor
Gatherley Moor
SCOTS DYKE CL
MILL CL
Tofta House
Diddersley Hill
Ravensworth C of E Prim Sch
Holme Beck
Pond Dale
JAGGER LANE
Ravensworth Castle
Moat
MOOR ROAD
STONYGATE BANK
Car Plantation
Grange Wood
WARRENER LANE
Blackhill Farm
Harelands Farm
Park Wall
Scrogg's Plantation
Gatherley Moor
Paddock Wood
Grange Farm
Whashton Bridge
Quarry Plantation
COMFORT LANE
Mill Bank Plantation
Hartforth
Moor End Plantation
A66
Quarry Hill
STONYGATE BANK
Whashton
Forster Hill
RACHEL LANE
Hartforth Hall (Hotel)
FORCETT LANE
Gatherley Moor Farm
Kirby Hill
PH
Whashton Farm
Hartforth Wood
Home Farm
HARTFORTH LANE
Rock Castle
Whashton Green
Hartforth Grange
Scots Dike
Kirklands Farm
Mount Pleasant
Leadmill Gill Beck
HARGILL
Cat Scar Quarry
Diamondhill Plantation
Whashton Hag
HARTFORTH LA
Kirkbank Farm
STURDY HO LA
Lambert Wood
Cooper Mill Bridge
Smelt Mill Beck
Mill Farm
Town End Farm
Gilling West
Crabtree House Farm
HIGH ST
OSWIN GR
Gilling Bridge
Sedbury Hall
WATERS LA
PH
PO
MILL GATE
ANTEFORTH VW
The Ashes
Whashton Springs
SPRINGS LANE
Gilling Wood
Gillingwood Hall
OLD HALL LANE
WATERS LA
Sewage Works
Park Farm
Sturdy Wood
High Scales
B6274
High Scales Plantation
Paddock Plantation
DL10
Gilling Beck
High Moor
Black Plantation
Low Scales
Gilling Grange
OLLIVER LA
Mouldron Plantation
Aske Moor
Jockey Cap Clump
Aske Moor Farm
Mouldron
The Temple
Ford
Low Coalsgarth
Low Pastures
HIGH STREET
Randell Wood
Aske Hall
Gascoigne Farm
High Coalsgarth
Cross Plantation
Gingerfield Wood
China Plantation
Crow Wood
Aske Park
Aske Bridge
Olliver
Beacon Plantation
Gingerfield Plantation
China Plantation
Aske Beck
Scots Dike
Low Gingerfield Farm
Low Wood
OLLIVER LANE
LINDON RD
THE WYND
Beacon Hill
Rasp Bank
Low Wood
RICHMOND RD
PEAR TREE CL
Gingerfield
WHASHTON ROAD
St Osythe
High Gingerfield
Charlock Plantation
B6274
High Moor
CH
HIGH RIDING
GILLING RD
DARLINGTON RD
High Gingerfield Lodge
STANLEY GR
GOWER RD
NORMAN RD
OLLIVER RD
Low Moor
HURGILL ROAD
Whitcliffe Scar

14 A 15 B 16 C 17 D 18 E 19 F

19
40
209

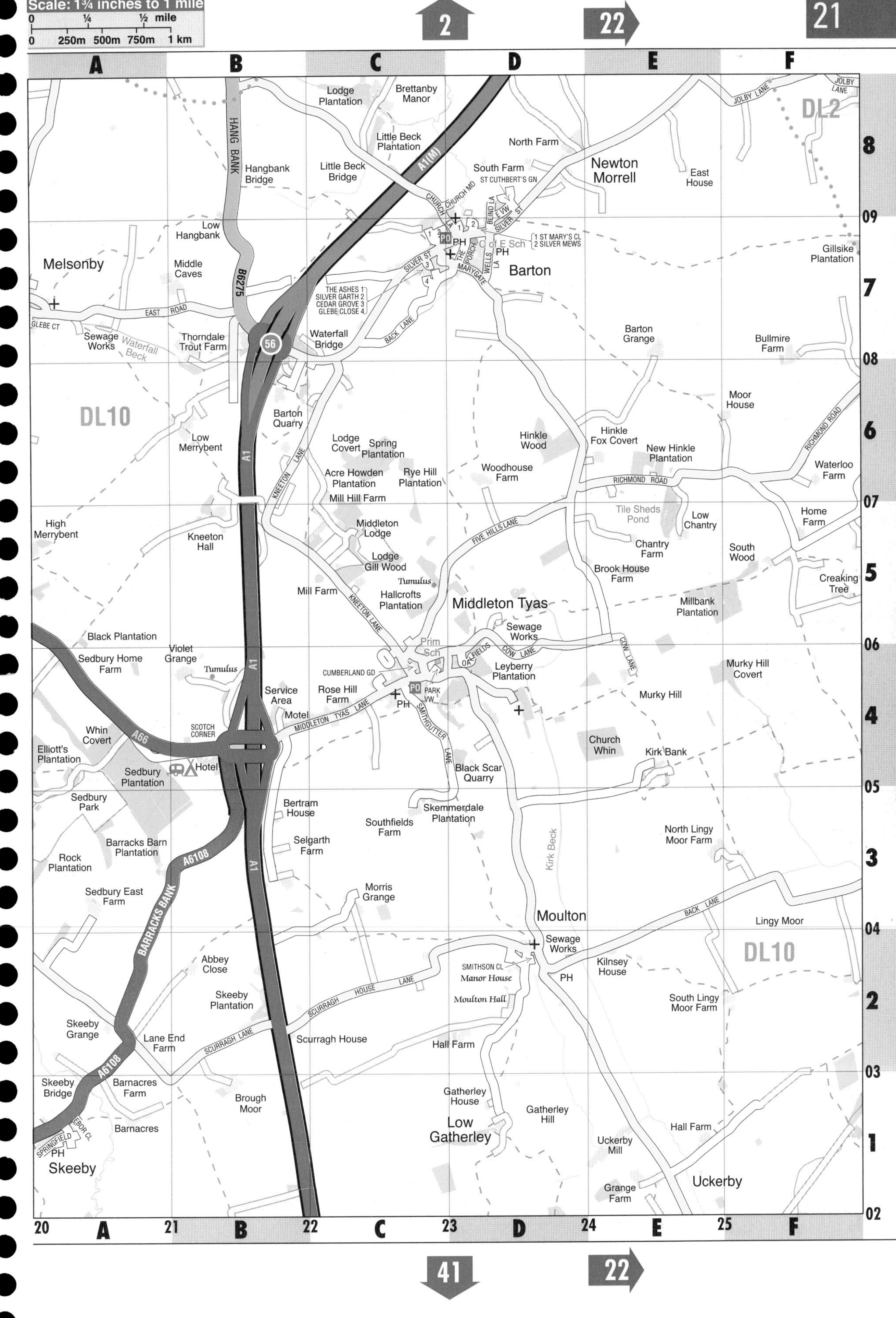
Scale: 1¾ inches to 1 mile
0 ¼ ½ mile
0 250m 500m 750m 1 km
2
22
Lodge Plantation
Brettanby Manor
Little Beck Plantation
North Farm
Newton Morrell
East House
Hangbank Bridge
Little Beck Bridge
South Farm
HANG BANK
A1(M)
Low Hangbank
Melsonby
Middle Caves
B6275
Barton
Gillsike Plantation
EAST ROAD
GLEBE CT
Sewage Works
Waterfall Beck
Thorndale Trout Farm
56
Waterfall Bridge
BACK LANE
Barton Grange
Bullmire Farm
DL10
DL2
Barton Quarry
Low Merrybent
Lodge Covert
Spring Plantation
Acre Howden Plantation
Rye Hill Plantation
Mill Hill Farm
Hinkle Wood
Hinkle Fox Covert
New Hinkle Plantation
Moor House
Woodhouse Farm
RICHMOND ROAD
Waterloo Farm
Home Farm
High Merrybent
Kneeton Hall
KNEETON LANE
Middleton Lodge
Lodge Gill Wood
Tumulus
FIVE HILLS LANE
Tile Sheds Pond
Low Chantry
Chantry Farm
Brook House Farm
South Wood
Creaking Tree
Mill Farm
Hallcrofts Plantation
Middleton Tyas
Millbank Plantation
Black Plantation
Violet Grange
Sedbury Home Farm
Tumulus
Prim Sch
Sewage Works
COW LANE
Leyberry Plantation
Murky Hill Covert
Murky Hill
CUMBERLAND GD
Service Area
Rose Hill Farm
PO
PH
PARK VW
Motel
MIDDLETON TYAS LANE
SMITHGUTTER LANE
Whin Covert
SCOTCH CORNER
A66
Elliott's Plantation
Hotel
Sedbury Plantation
Church Whin
Kirk Bank
Black Scar Quarry
Sedbury Park
Bertram House
Skemmerdale Plantation
Southfields Farm
North Lingy Moor Farm
Barracks Barn Plantation
Selgarth Farm
Kirk Beck
Rock Plantation
A6108
A1
Sedbury East Farm
BARRACKS BANK
Morris Grange
Moulton
BACK LANE
Lingy Moor
Sewage Works
Abbey Close
SMITHSON CL
Manor House
PH
Kilnsey House
Skeeby Plantation
SCURRAGH HOUSE LANE
Moulton Hall
South Lingy Moor Farm
Skeeby Grange
Lane End Farm
SCURRAGH LANE
Scurragh House
Hall Farm
Skeeby Bridge
Barnacres Farm
Brough Moor
Gatherley House
Gatherley Hill
Barnacres
Low Gatherley
Uckerby Mill
Hall Farm
SPRINGFIELD
EBOR CL
Skeeby
Grange Farm
Uckerby
41
22

C8
1 LEWIS CL
2 CARROLL PL
3 RECTORY LA
4 THE MILL RACE

D8
1 LINDEN DRIVE
2 BAXBY TERRACE
3 BELGRAVE TERR
4 CEDAR MEWS
5 GRANGE AVE
6 FOX CL
7 WOODLANDS WAY
8 AVON ROAD
9 ASHVILLE DRIVE

Scale: 1¾ inches to 1 mile

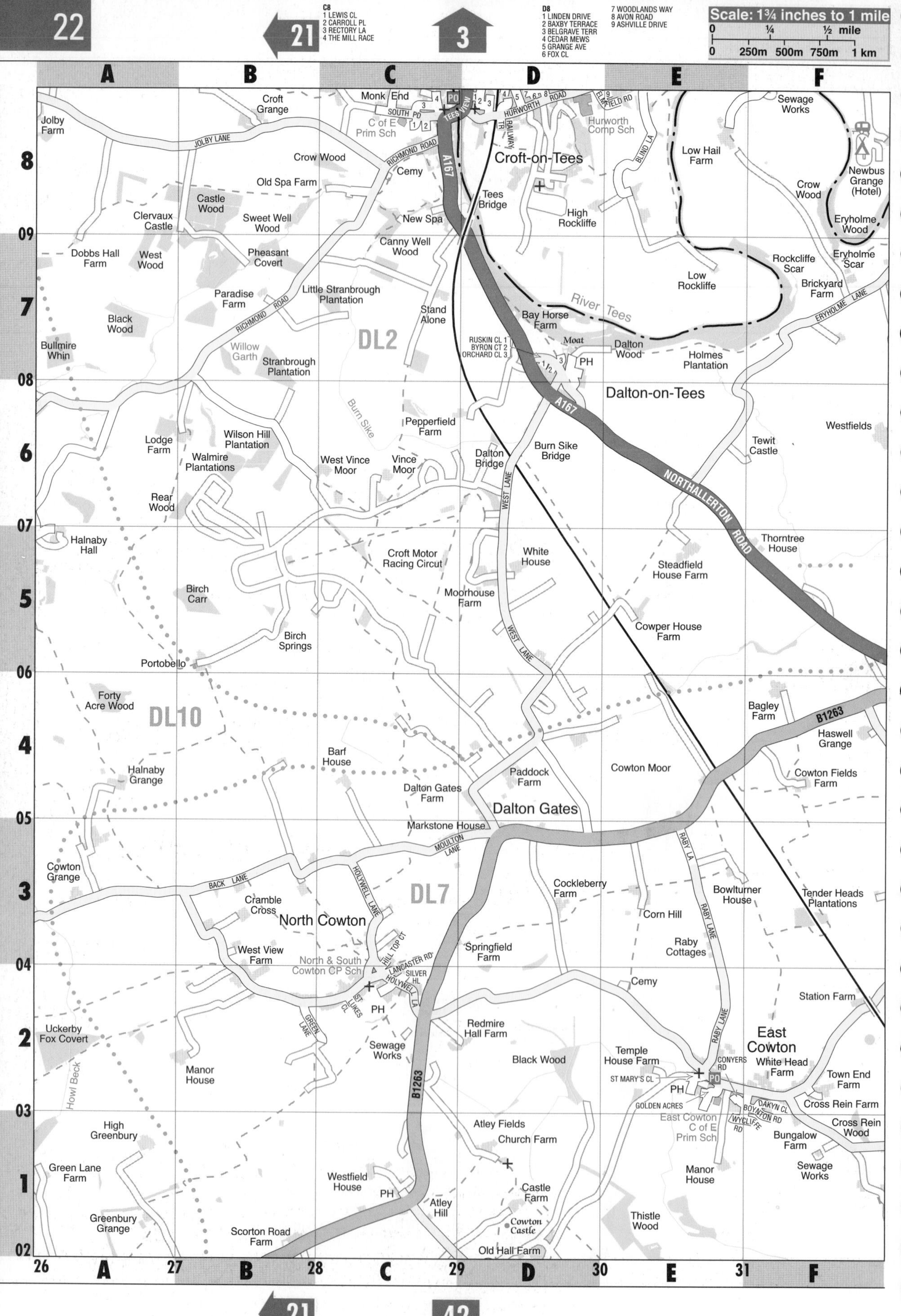

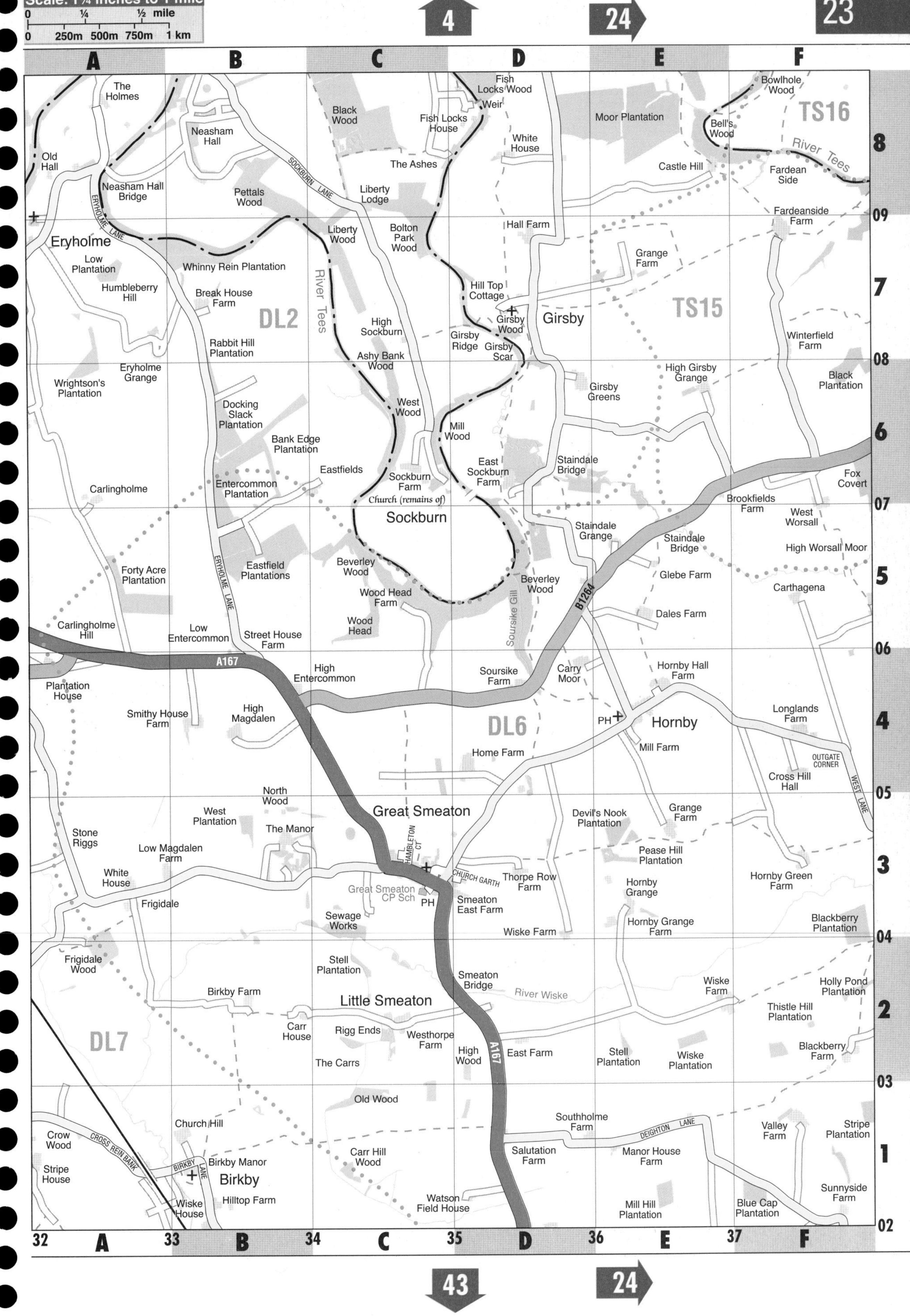
Scale: 1¾ inches to 1 mile
0 ¼ ½ mile
0 250m 500m 750m 1 km
4
24
A B C D E F
The Holmes
Old Hall
Neasham Hall
Neasham Hall Bridge
Pettals Wood
Eryholme
Low Plantation
Humbleberry Hill
Whinny Rein Plantation
Break House Farm
DL2
Rabbit Hill Plantation
Eryholme Grange
Wrightson's Plantation
Docking Slack Plantation
Bank Edge Plantation
Carlingholme
Entercommon Plantation
Forty Acre Plantation
Eastfield Plantations
Carlingholme Hill
Low Entercommon
Street House Farm
A167
Plantation House
Smithy House Farm
High Magdalen
High Entercommon
Black Wood
Fish Locks House
The Ashes
Liberty Lodge
Liberty Wood
Bolton Park Wood
River Tees
High Sockburn
Ashy Bank Wood
West Wood
Eastfields
Sockburn Farm
Church (remains of)
Sockburn
Beverley Wood
Wood Head Farm
Wood Head
Fish Locks Wood
Weir
White House
Hall Farm
Hill Top Cottage
Girsby Wood
Girsby
Girsby Ridge
Girsby Scar
Mill Wood
East Sockburn Farm
Beverley Wood
Soursike Gill
Soursike Farm
Carry Moor
DL6
Moor Plantation
Castle Hill
Grange Farm
TS15
Girsby Greens
High Girsby Grange
Staindale Bridge
Staindale Grange
Staindale Bridge
Glebe Farm
B1264
Dales Farm
Hornby Hall Farm
PH
Hornby
Mill Farm
Bowlhole Wood
Bell's Wood
TS16
River Tees
Fardean Side
Fardeanside Farm
Winterfield Farm
Black Plantation
Fox Covert
Brookfields Farm
West Worsall
High Worsall Moor
Carthagena
Longlands Farm
OUTGATE CORNER
Cross Hill Hall
WEST LANE
SOCKBURN LANE
ERYHOLME LANE
Home Farm
North Wood
West Plantation
Great Smeaton
The Manor
Stone Riggs
Low Magdalen Farm
White House
Frigidale
HAMBLETON CT
CHURCH GARTH
Great Smeaton CP Sch
PH
Thorpe Row Farm
Smeaton East Farm
Sewage Works
Wiske Farm
Devil's Nook Plantation
Grange Farm
Pease Hill Plantation
Hornby Grange
Hornby Grange Farm
Hornby Green Farm
Blackberry Plantation
Frigidale Wood
Stell Plantation
Smeaton Bridge
River Wiske
Birkby Farm
Little Smeaton
Carr House
Rigg Ends
Westhorpe Farm
High Wood
East Farm
Stell Plantation
Wiske Plantation
Wiske Farm
Holly Pond Plantation
Thistle Hill Plantation
Blackberry Farm
DL7
The Carrs
Old Wood
Church Hill
Crow Wood
CROSS REIN BANK
Stripe House
BIRKBY LANE
Birkby Manor
Birkby
Wiske House
Hilltop Farm
Carr Hill Wood
Watson Field House
Southholme Farm
Salutation Farm
DEIGHTON LANE
Manor House Farm
Mill Hill Plantation
Valley Farm
Stripe Plantation
Sunnyside Farm
Blue Cap Plantation
8 09 7 08 6 07 5 06 4 05 3 04 2 03 1 02
32 33 34 35 36 37
43
24

23
5

E8
1 ASH GR
2 BIRCH CL
3 BRAESIDE
4 GR BANK
5 KNOWLES CL
6 WESTLANDS
7 HALL MOOR CL
8 THE GN
9 STRATHMORE DR
10 MOOR CL
11 ST MARTINS WY
12 MANOR GARTH

Scale: 1¾ inches to 1 mile
0 ¼ ½ mile
0 250m 500m 750m 1 km

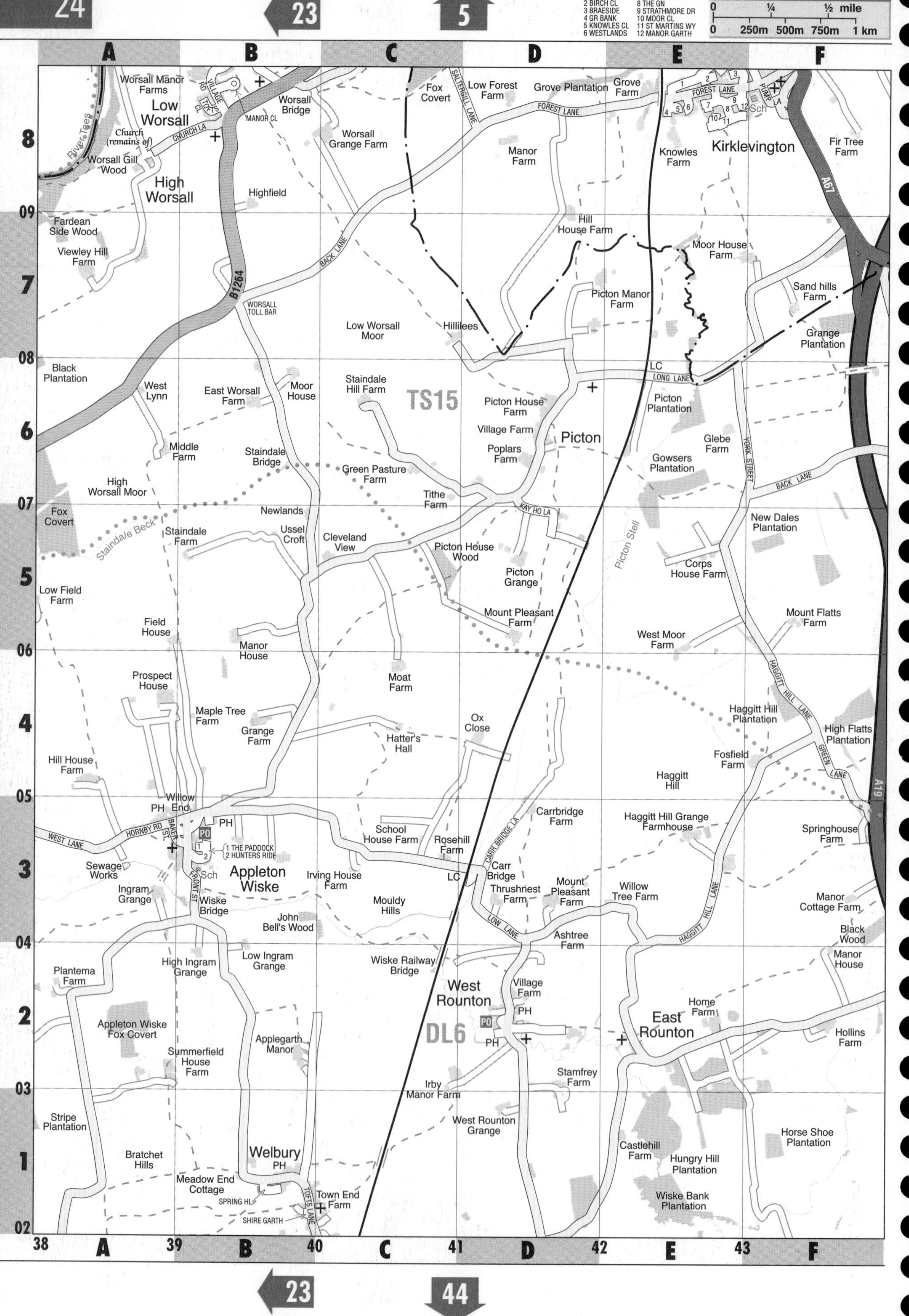

23
44

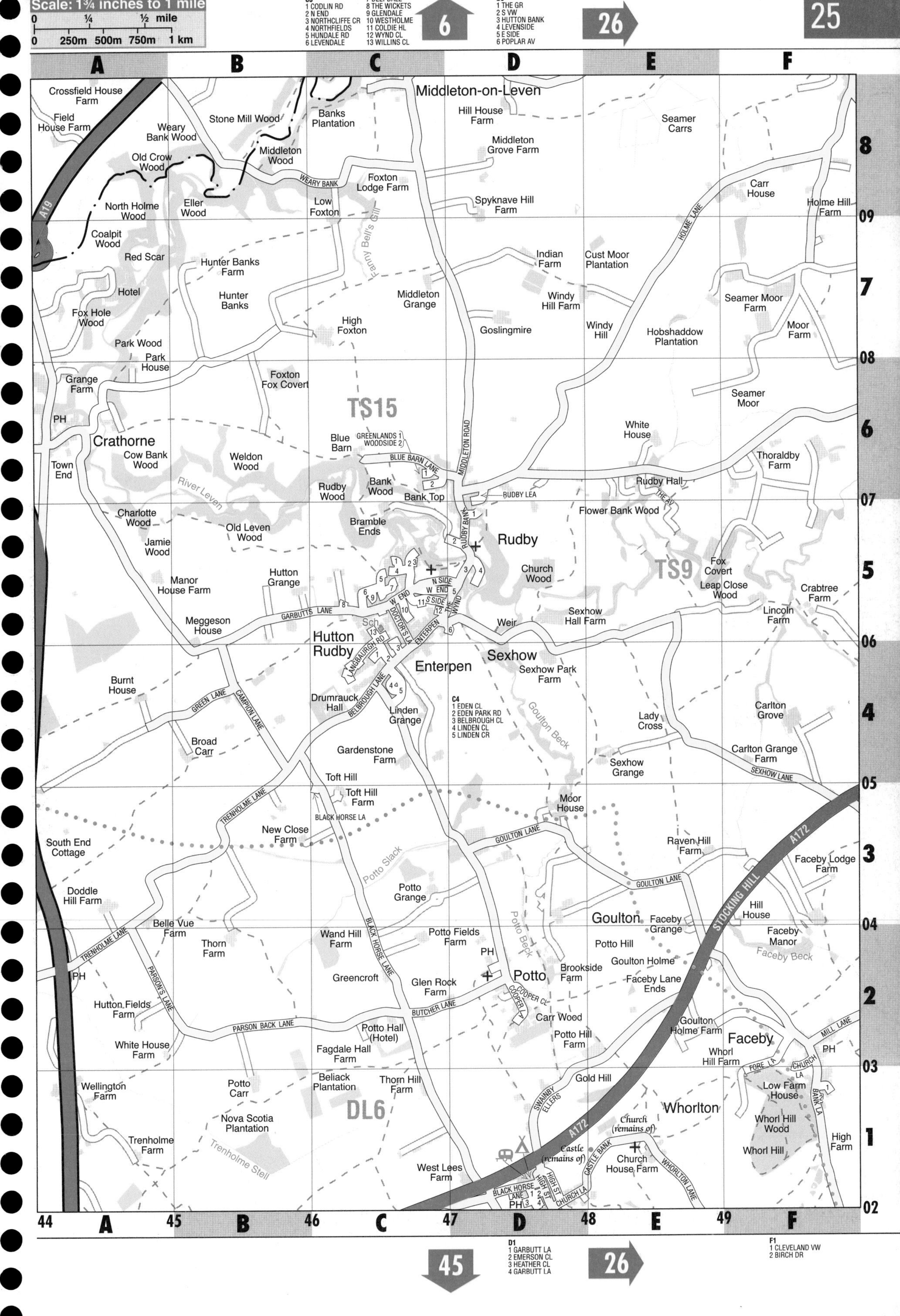

Scale: 1¾ inches to 1 mile
0 ¼ ½ mile
0 250m 500m 750m 1 km
C5
1 CODLIN RD
2 N END
3 NORTHCLIFFE CR
4 NORTHFIELDS
5 HUNDALE RD
6 LEVENDALE
7 DEEPDALE
8 THE WICKETS
9 GLENDALE
10 WESTHOLME
11 COLDIE HL
12 WYND CL
13 WILLINS CL
6
D5
1 THE GR
2 S VW
3 HUTTON BANK
4 LEVENSIDE
5 E SIDE
6 POPLAR AV
26
25
A B C D E F
Crossfield House Farm
Field House Farm
Weary Bank Wood
Stone Mill Wood
Banks Plantation
Middleton-on-Leven
Hill House Farm
Seamer Carrs
Old Crow Wood
Middleton Wood
Middleton Grove Farm
WEARY BANK
Foxton Lodge Farm
Carr House
North Holme Wood
Eller Wood
Low Foxton
Spyknave Hill Farm
Holme Hill Farm
A19
HOLME LANE
Coalpit Wood
Fanny Bell's Gill
Red Scar
Hunter Banks Farm
Indian Farm
Cust Moor Plantation
Hotel
Hunter Banks
Middleton Grange
Windy Hill Farm
Seamer Moor Farm
Fox Hole Wood
High Foxton
Goslingmire
Windy Hill
Hobshaddow Plantation
Moor Farm
Park Wood
Park House
Grange Farm
Foxton Fox Covert
Seamer Moor
TS15
PH
White House
Crathorne
Blue Barn
GREENLANDS 1
WOODSIDE 2
Cow Bank Wood
Weldon Wood
BLUE BARN LANE
MIDDLETON ROAD
Thoraldby Farm
Town End
River Leven
Rudby Wood
Bank Wood
Bank Top
RUDBY LEA
Rudby Hall
THE AV
Charlotte Wood
Flower Bank Wood
Old Leven Wood
Bramble Ends
RUDBY BANK
Rudby
Jamie Wood
TS9
Fox Covert
Manor House Farm
Hutton Grange
Church Wood
Leap Close Wood
Crabtree Farm
N SIDE
W END
E SIDE
S SIDE
GARBUTTS LANE
Sexhow Hall Farm
Lincoln Farm
Meggeson House
Sch
DOCTOR'S LA
ENTERPEN
THE WYND
Weir
Hutton Rudby
LANGBAURGH RD
Sexhow
Enterpen
Sexhow Park Farm
Burnt House
Drumrauck Hall
BELBROUGH LANE
Linden Grange
C4
1 EDEN CL
2 EDEN PARK RD
3 BELBROUGH CL
4 LINDEN CL
5 LINDEN CR
Goulton Beck
Lady Cross
Carlton Grove
GREEN LANE
CAMPION LANE
Broad Carr
Gardenstone Farm
Sexhow Grange
Carlton Grange Farm
SEXHOW LANE
Toft Hill
Toft Hill Farm
TRENHOLME LANE
Moor House
BLACK HORSE LA
New Close Farm
GOULTON LANE
South End Cottage
Raven Hill Farm
A172
Potto Slack
Faceby Lodge Farm
Doddle Hill Farm
Potto Grange
STOCKING HILL
Hill House
Belle Vue Farm
Potto Beck
Goulton
Faceby Grange
Faceby Manor
Thorn Farm
Wand Hill Farm
Potto Fields Farm
Potto Hill
Faceby Beck
BLACK HORSE LANE
Brookside Farm
Goulton Holme
Greencroft
Potto
Faceby Lane Ends
Hutton Fields Farm
PARSON'S LANE
Glen Rock Farm
COOPER CL
Carr Wood
BUTCHER LANE
Goulton Holme Farm
Faceby
MILL LANE
White House Farm
PARSON BACK LANE
Potto Hall (Hotel)
Potto Hill Farm
Whorl Hill Farm
Fagdale Hall Farm
FORE LA
CHURCH LA
Wellington Farm
Potto Carr
Beliack Plantation
Thorn Hill Farm
Gold Hill
Low Farm House
ELLERS
SWAINBY
BANK LA
Nova Scotia Plantation
DL6
Whorlton
Whorl Hill Wood
Church (remains of)
Trenholme Farm
Trenholme Stell
Castle (remains of)
Church House Farm
Whorl Hill
High Farm
West Lees Farm
CASTLE BANK
WHORLTON LANE
BLACK HORSE LANE
HIGH ST
CHURCH LA
8 09 7 08 6 07 5 06 4 05 3 04 2 03 1 02
44 45 46 47 48 49
45
D1
1 GARBUTT LA
2 EMERSON CL
3 HEATHER CL
4 GARBUTT LA
26
F1
1 CLEVELAND VW
2 BIRCH DR

25

C8
1 CEDARWOOD AV
2 BEECHWOOD AV
3 DALEWOOD WK
4 CHERRYWOOD AV
5 COPSEWOOD WK
6 ELMWOOD CL
7 PINEWOOD WK
8 MEADOWFIELD
9 QUEENS DR

7

Scale: 1¾ inches to 1 mile
0 ¼ ½ mile
0 250m 500m 750m 1 km

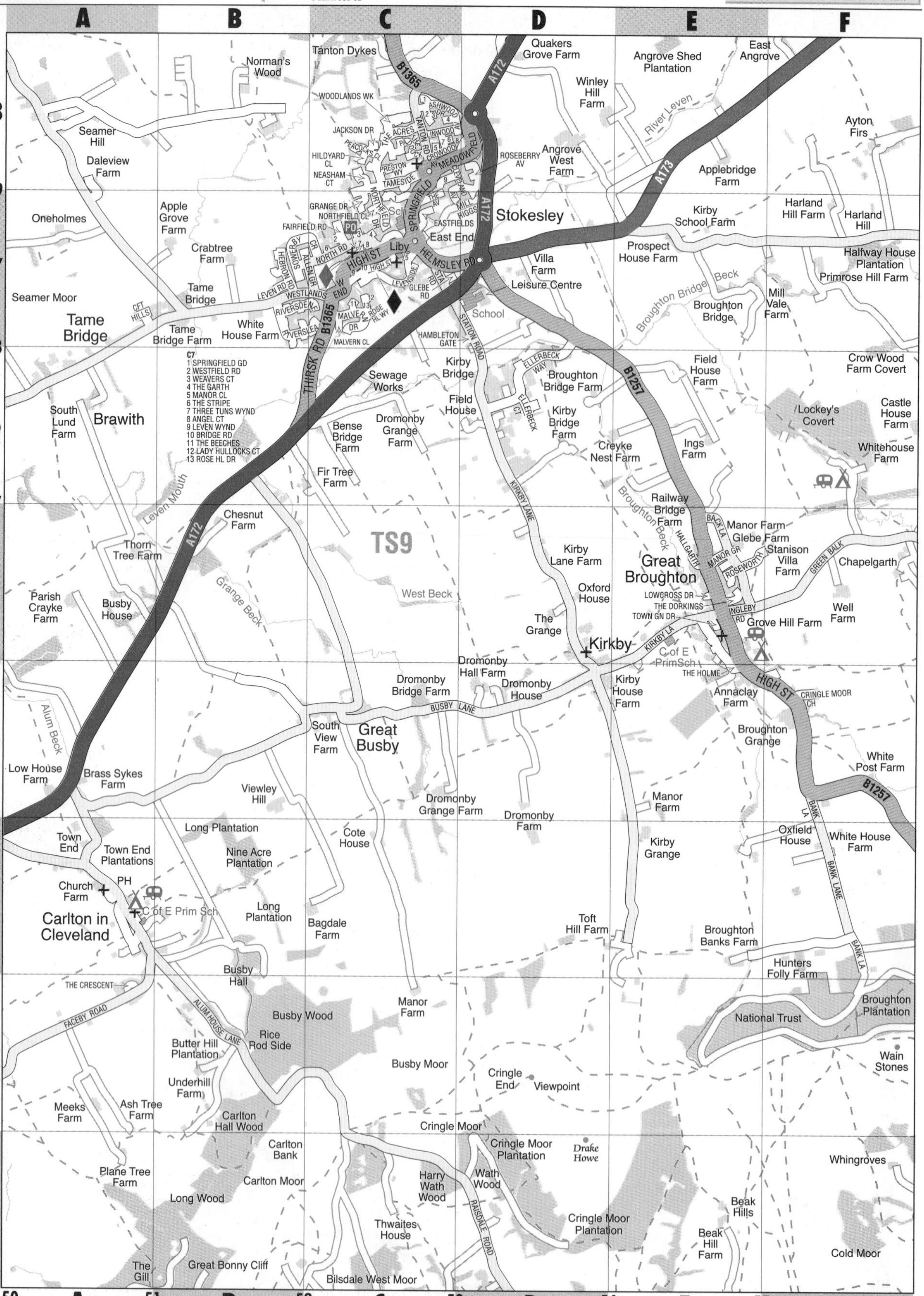

A B C D E F

8 09 7 08 6 07 5 06 4 05 3 04 2 03 1 02

Tanton Dykes
Norman's Wood
Quakers Grove Farm
Angrove Shed Plantation
East Angrove
Winley Hill Farm
River Leven
Ayton Firs
Seamer Hill
Daleview Farm
WOODLANDS WK
ASHWOOD
THE ACRES
JACKSON DR
TANTON RD
INWOOD
PEACOCKS CL
HILDYARD CL
PRESTON WY
CROWOOD AV
MEADOWFIELD
NEASHAM CT
TAMESIDE
ROSEBERRY AV
Angrove West Farm
Applebridge Farm
GRANGE DR
NORTHFIELD CL
NORTHFIELD DR
SPRINGFIELD
MILL RIGGS
A172
A173
Oneholmes
Apple Grove Farm
FAIRFIELD RD
PO
Sch
EASTFIELDS
Stokesley
East End
Kirby School Farm
Harland Hill Farm
Harland Hill
Crabtree Farm
HEBRON RD
SOWERBY CR
ALLEN GR
NORTH RD
HIGH ST
Liby
HELMSLEY RD
Prospect House Farm
Villa Farm
Halfway House Plantation
Primrose Hill Farm
Seamer Moor
Tame Bridge
CFT HILLS
LEVEN RD
WESTLANDS
W END
LEVENSIDE
GLEBE RD
STA RD
Leisure Centre
Broughton Bridge Beck
Mill Vale Farm
Broughton Bridge
RIVERSDEN
MALVE DR
ROSE HL WY
School
Tame Bridge
Tame Bridge Farm
White House Farm
LEVERSLEA
B1365
THIRSK RD
MALVERN CL
HAMBLETON GATE
STATION ROAD
Crow Wood Farm Covert
C7
1 SPRINGFIELD GD
2 WESTFIELD RD
3 WEAVERS CT
4 THE GARTH
5 MANOR CL
6 THE STRIPE
7 THREE TUNS WYND
8 ANGEL CT
9 LEVEN WYND
10 BRIDGE RD
11 THE BEECHES
12 LADY HULLOCKS CT
13 ROSE HL DR
Sewage Works
Kirby Bridge
ELLERBECK WAY
Broughton Bridge Farm
B1257
Field House Farm
Castle House Farm
South Lund Farm
Brawith
Bense Bridge Farm
Dromonby Grange Farm
Field House
ELLERBECK CT
Kirby Bridge Farm
Lockey's Covert
Creyke Nest Farm
Ings Farm
Whitehouse Farm
Fir Tree Farm
Leven Mouth
Broughton Beck
Railway Bridge Farm
Chesnut Farm
KIRKBY LANE
BACK LA
Manor Farm
Glebe Farm
TS9
HALLGARTH
MANOR GR
Stanison Villa Farm
GREEN BALK
Chapelgarth
Thorn Tree Farm
Kirby Lane Farm
Great Broughton
ROSEWORTH
Grange Beck
West Beck
Oxford House
LOWCROSS DR
THE DORKINGS
TOWN GN DR
INGLEBY RD
Parish Crayke Farm
Busby House
The Grange
Grove Hill Farm
Well Farm
KIRKBY LA
Kirkby
C of E PrimSch
Dromonby Hall Farm
THE HOLME
Alum Beck
Dromonby Bridge Farm
Dromonby House
Kirby House Farm
HIGH ST
CRINGLE MOOR CH
Annaclay Farm
BUSBY LANE
South View Farm
Great Busby
Broughton Grange
Low House Farm
Brass Sykes Farm
Viewley Hill
White Post Farm
Dromonby Grange Farm
Manor Farm
BANK LA
Long Plantation
Dromonby Farm
Town End
Town End Plantations
Nine Acre Plantation
Cote House
Oxfield House
White House Farm
Kirby Grange
BANK LANE
PH
Church Farm
Carlton in Cleveland
C of E Prim Sch
Long Plantation
Bagdale Farm
Toft Hill Farm
Broughton Banks Farm
BANK LA
Busby Hall
Hunters Folly Farm
THE CRESCENT
FACEBY ROAD
ALUM HOUSE LANE
Busby Wood
Manor Farm
National Trust
Broughton Plantation
Rice Rod Side
Butter Hill Plantation
Busby Moor
Wain Stones
Underhill Farm
Cringle End
Viewpoint
Meeks Farm
Ash Tree Farm
Carlton Hall Wood
Cringle Moor
Carlton Bank
Cringle Moor Plantation
Drake Howe
Whingroves
Plane Tree Farm
Carlton Moor
Harry Wath Wood
Wath Wood
Long Wood
Beak Hills
RAISDALE ROAD
Thwaites House
Cringle Moor Plantation
Beak Hill Farm
Cold Moor
The Gill
Great Bonny Cliff
Bilsdale West Moor

50 A 51 B 52 C 53 D 54 E 55 F

25

46

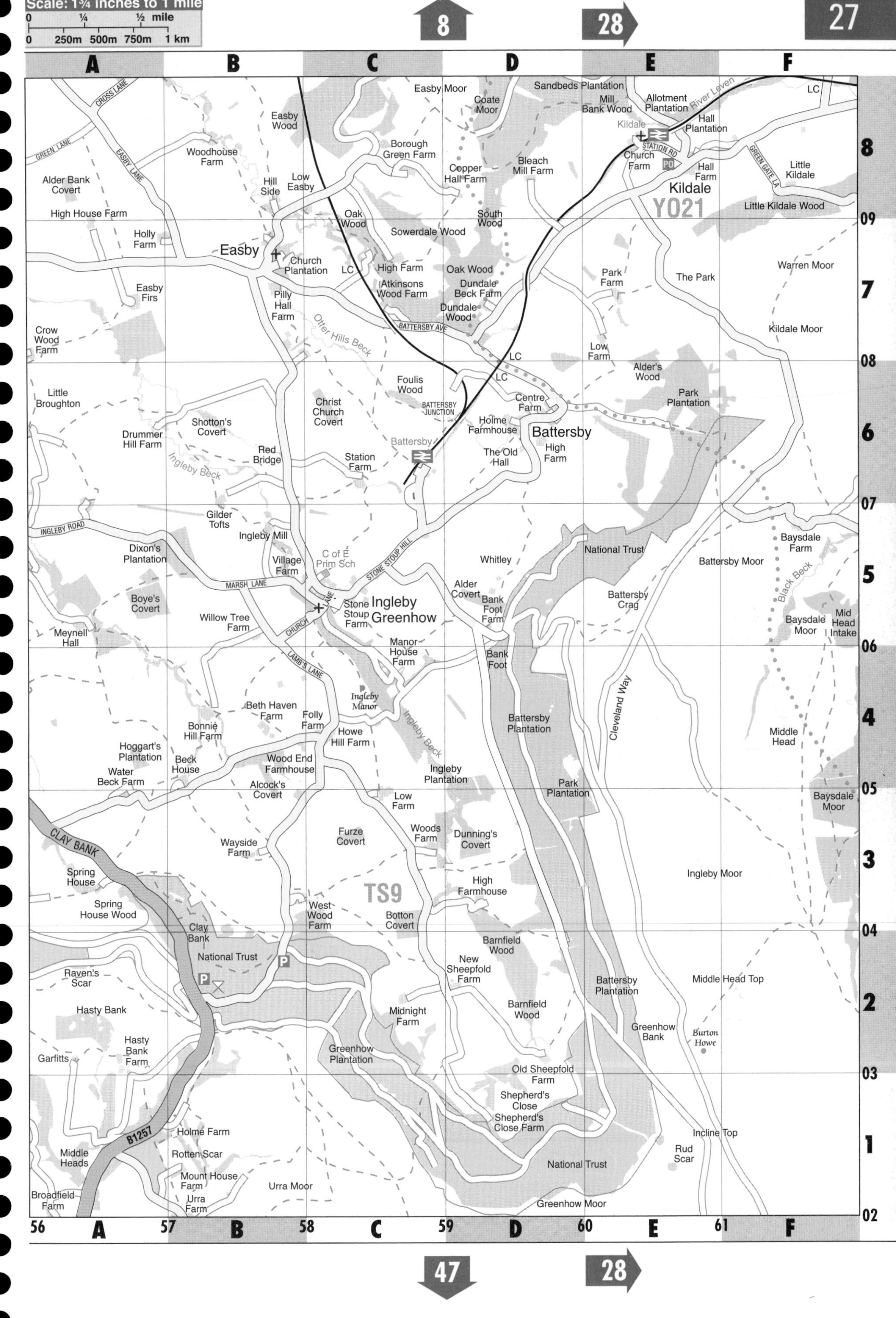
Scale: 1¾ inches to 1 mile
0 ¼ ½ mile
0 250m 500m 750m 1 km
8
28
A B C D E F
Easby Moor
Coate Moor
Sandbeds Plantation
Mill Bank Wood
Allotment Plantation
River Leven
Kildale
Hall Plantation
Church Farm
Station Rd
Hall Farm
Kildale
YO21
Little Kildale
Little Kildale Wood
Green Gate La
LC
Easby Wood
Woodhouse Farm
Borough Green Farm
Copper Hall Farm
Bleach Mill Farm
Cross Lane
Green Lane
Easby Lane
Alder Bank Covert
Hill Side
Low Easby
High House Farm
Oak Wood
Sowerdale Wood
South Wood
Holly Farm
Easby
Church Plantation
LC
High Farm
Oak Wood
Dundale Beck Farm
Atkinsons Wood Farm
Dundale Wood
Park Farm
The Park
Warren Moor
Easby Firs
Pilly Hall Farm
Battersby Ave
Kildale Moor
Crow Wood Farm
Otter Hills Beck
LC
LC
Low Farm
Alder's Wood
Foulis Wood
Battersby Junction
Centre Farm
Park Plantation
Little Broughton
Christ Church Covert
Holme Farmhouse
Battersby
Drummer Hill Farm
Shotton's Covert
Battersby
High Farm
Red Bridge
Station Farm
The Old Hall
Ingleby Beck
Gilder Tofts
Ingleby Road
Ingleby Mill
Dixon's Plantation
C of E Prim Sch
Village Farm
Stone Stoup Hill
Whitley
National Trust
Baysdale Farm
Battersby Moor
Black Beck
Marsh Lane
Alder Covert
Bank Foot Farm
Battersby Crag
Boye's Covert
Lane
Stone Stoup Farm
Ingleby Greenhow
Willow Tree Farm
Church
Meynell Hall
Baysdale Moor
Mid Head Intake
Manor House Farm
Bank Foot
Lamb's Lane
Ingleby Manor
Cleveland Way
Beth Haven Farm
Folly Farm
Battersby Plantation
Ingleby Beck
Bonnie Hill Farm
Howe Hill Farm
Middle Head
Hoggart's Plantation
Beck House
Wood End Farmhouse
Ingleby Plantation
Water Beck Farm
Alcock's Covert
Park Plantation
Low Farm
Baysdale Moor
Clay Bank
Wayside Farm
Furze Covert
Woods Farm
Dunning's Covert
Spring House
Ingleby Moor
High Farmhouse
TS9
Spring House Wood
West Wood Farm
Botton Covert
Clay Bank
Barnfield Wood
National Trust
Raven's Scar
New Sheepfold Farm
Battersby Plantation
Middle Head Top
Hasty Bank
Barnfield Wood
Midnight Farm
Greenhow Bank
Burton Howe
Hasty Bank Farm
Garfitts
Greenhow Plantation
Old Sheepfold Farm
Shepherd's Close
Shepherd's Close Farm
Holme Farm
Incline Top
B1257
Middle Heads
Rotten Scar
Rud Scar
National Trust
Mount House Farm
Urra Moor
Broadfield Farm
Urra Farm
Greenhow Moor
8 09 7 08 6 07 5 06 4 05 3 04 2 03 1 02
56 A 57 B 58 C 59 D 60 E 61 F
47
28

27
9

Scale: 1¾ inches to 1 mile

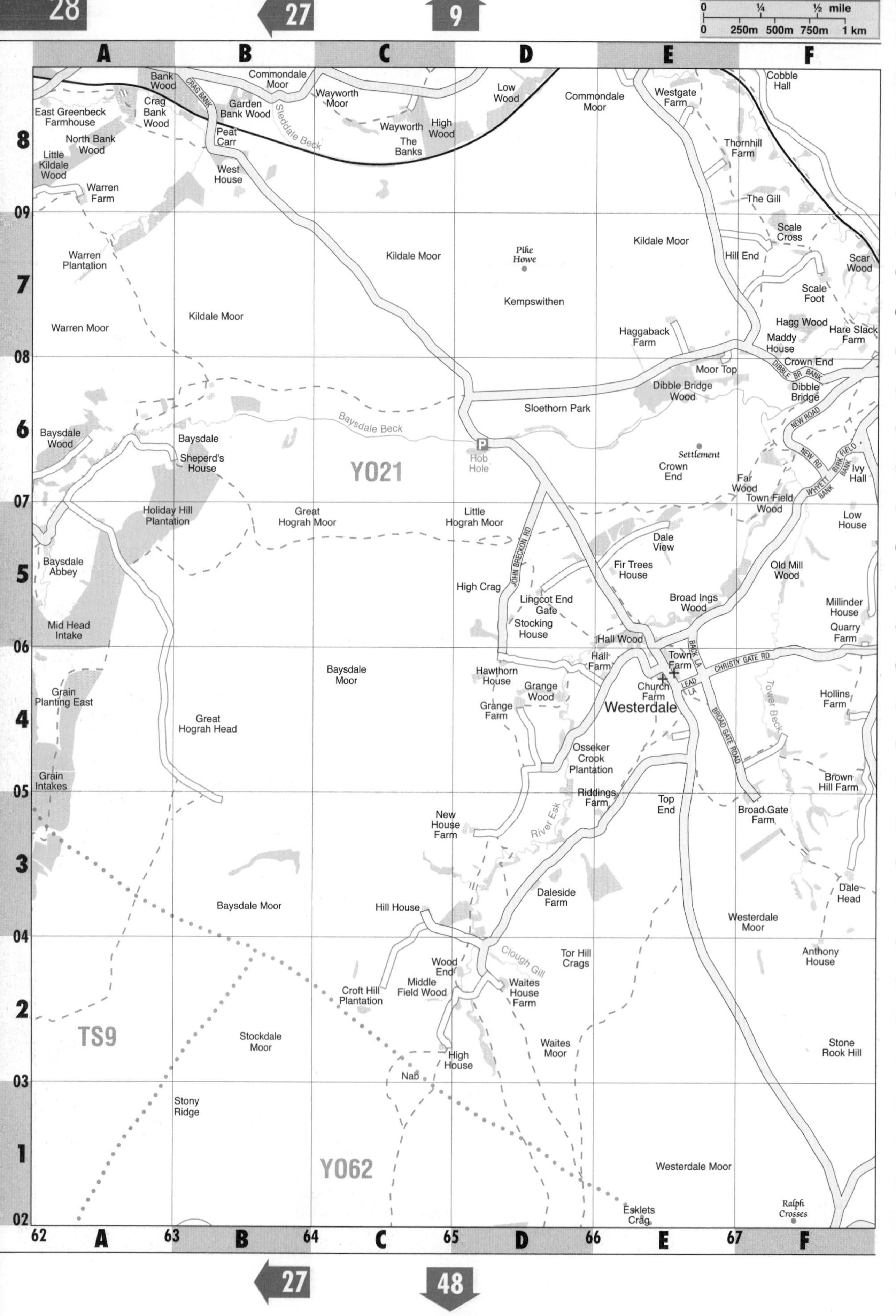

27
48

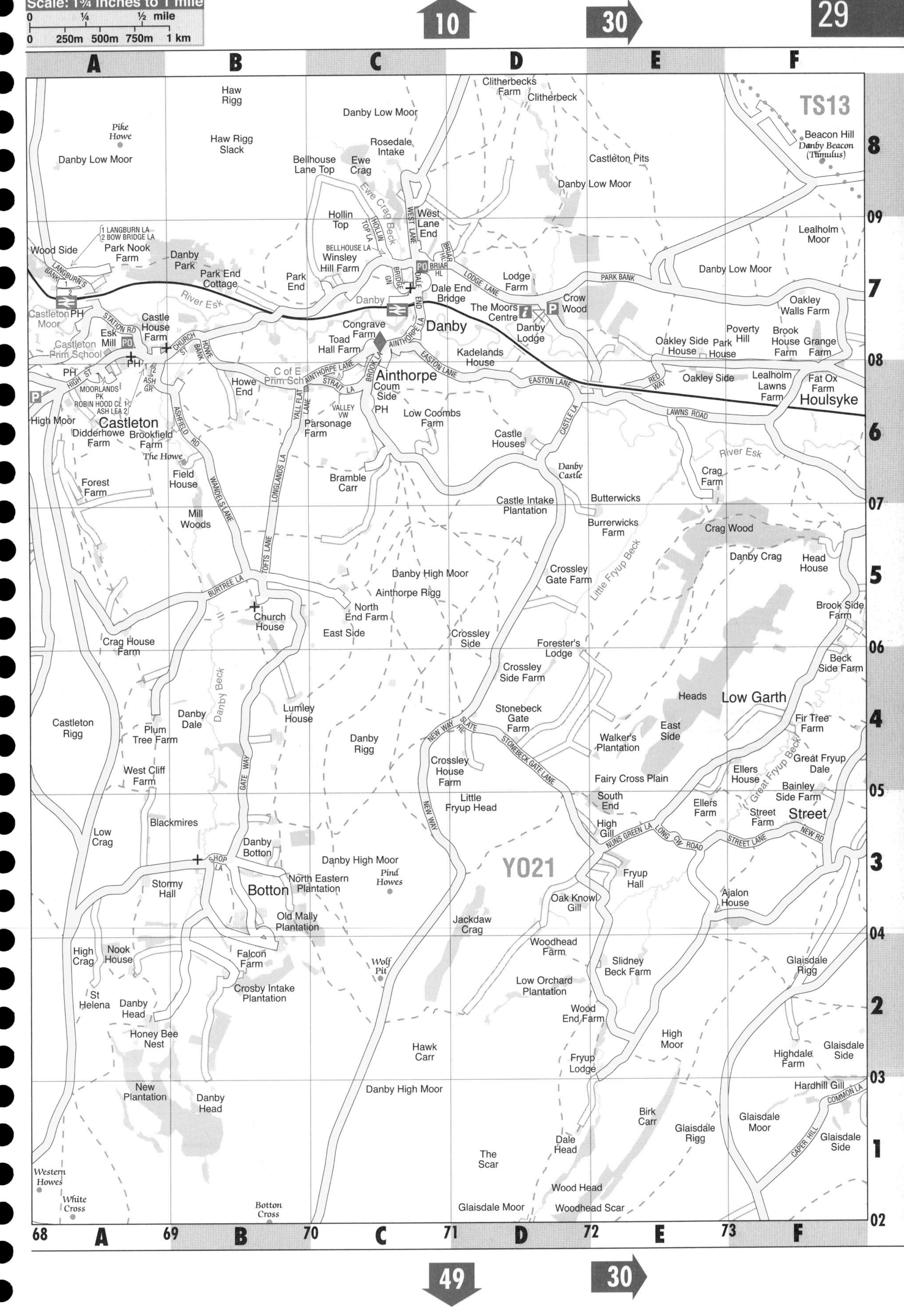

Scale: 1¾ inches to 1 mile
0 ¼ ½ mile
0 250m 500m 750m 1 km
10
30
TS13
Clitherbecks Farm
Clitherbeck
Haw Rigg
Danby Low Moor
Pike Howe
Haw Rigg Slack
Rosedale Intake
Beacon Hill
Danby Beacon (Tumulus)
Danby Low Moor
Bellhouse Lane Top
Ewe Crag
Castleton Pits
Danby Low Moor
Hollin Top
Ewe Crag Beck
West Lane End
Lealholm Moor
Wood Side
Park Nook Farm
Danby Park
Park End Cottage
Park End
Winsley Hill Farm
Danby Low Moor
Lodge Farm
Dale End Bridge
Oakley Walls Farm
Castleton Moor
River Esk
Danby
The Moors Centre
Crow Wood
Castle House Farm
Congrave Farm
Danby
Danby Lodge
Poverty Hill
Brook House Farm
Grange Farm
Esk Mill
Castleton Prim School
Toad Hall Farm
Kadelands House
Oakley Side House
Park House
C of E Prim Sch
Ainthorpe
Coum Side
Oakley Side
Lealholm Lawns Farm
Fat Ox Farm
Houlsyke
Howe End
High Moor
Castleton
Didderhowe Farm
Brookfield Farm
The Howe
Parsonage Farm
Low Coombs Farm
Castle Houses
River Esk
Field House
Danby Castle
Crag Farm
Forest Farm
Bramble Carr
Castle Intake Plantation
Butterwicks
Mill Woods
Burrerwicks Farm
Crag Wood
Little Fryup Beck
Danby Crag
Head House
Danby High Moor
Crossley Gate Farm
Ainthorpe Rigg
North End Farm
Brook Side Farm
Church House
East Side
Crossley Side
Crag House Farm
Forester's Lodge
Beck Side Farm
Crossley Side Farm
Heads
Low Garth
Danby Beck
Lumley House
Stonebeck Gate Farm
Castleton Rigg
Danby Dale
Plum Tree Farm
Danby Rigg
East Side
Walker's Plantation
Fir Tree Farm
Crossley House Farm
Great Fryup Beck
Great Fryup Dale
West Cliff Farm
Fairy Cross Plain
Ellers House
Bainley Side Farm
Little Fryup Head
South End
Ellers Farm
Street Farm
Street
Blackmires
Low Crag
High Gill
Danby Botton
Danby High Moor
YO21
Pind Howes
Fryup Hall
Stormy Hall
Botton
North Eastern Plantation
Ajalon House
Oak Knowl Gill
Old Mally Plantation
Jackdaw Crag
High Crag
Nook House
Falcon Farm
Woodhead Farm
Wolf Pit
Slidney Beck Farm
Glaisdale Rigg
Crosby Intake Plantation
Low Orchard Plantation
St Helena
Danby Head
Wood End Farm
Honey Bee Nest
Hawk Carr
High Moor
Glaisdale Side
Highdale Farm
Fryup Lodge
Hardhill Gill
New Plantation
Danby Head
Danby High Moor
Birk Carr
Glaisdale Moor
Glaisdale Rigg
Glaisdale Side
Dale Head
The Scar
Western Howes
White Cross
Botton Cross
Wood Head
Glaisdale Moor
Woodhead Scar
1 LANGBURN LA
2 BOW BRIDGE LA
LANGBURN'S BANK
STATION RD
CHURCH ST
HOWE BANK
HIGH ST
MOORLANDS PK
ROBIN HOOD CL
ASH LEA
ASH GR
ASHFIELD RD
WANDELS LANE
LONGLANDS LA
TOFTS LANE
BURTREE LA
YALL FLAT LANE
AINTHORPE LANE
STRAIT LA
VALLEY VW
BROOK LA
AINTHORPE LA
EASTON LANE
EASTON LANE
CASTLE LA
LAWNS ROAD
RED WAY
PARK BANK
LODGE LANE
BRIAR HL
WEST LANE
HOLLIN TOP LA
BELLHOUSE LA
BRIDGE GN
DALE END
GATE WAY
SHOP LA
NEW WAY
SLATE HL
NEW WAY
STONEBECK GATE LANE
NUNS GREEN LA
LONG CW ROAD
STREET LANE
NEW RD
COMMON LA
CAPER HILL
PH
PO
A B C D E F
8 7 6 5 4 3 2 1
09 08 07 06 05 04 03 02
68 69 70 71 72 73
49
30

29
11

Scale: 1¾ inches to 1 mile
0 ¼ ½ mile
0 250m 500m 750m 1 km

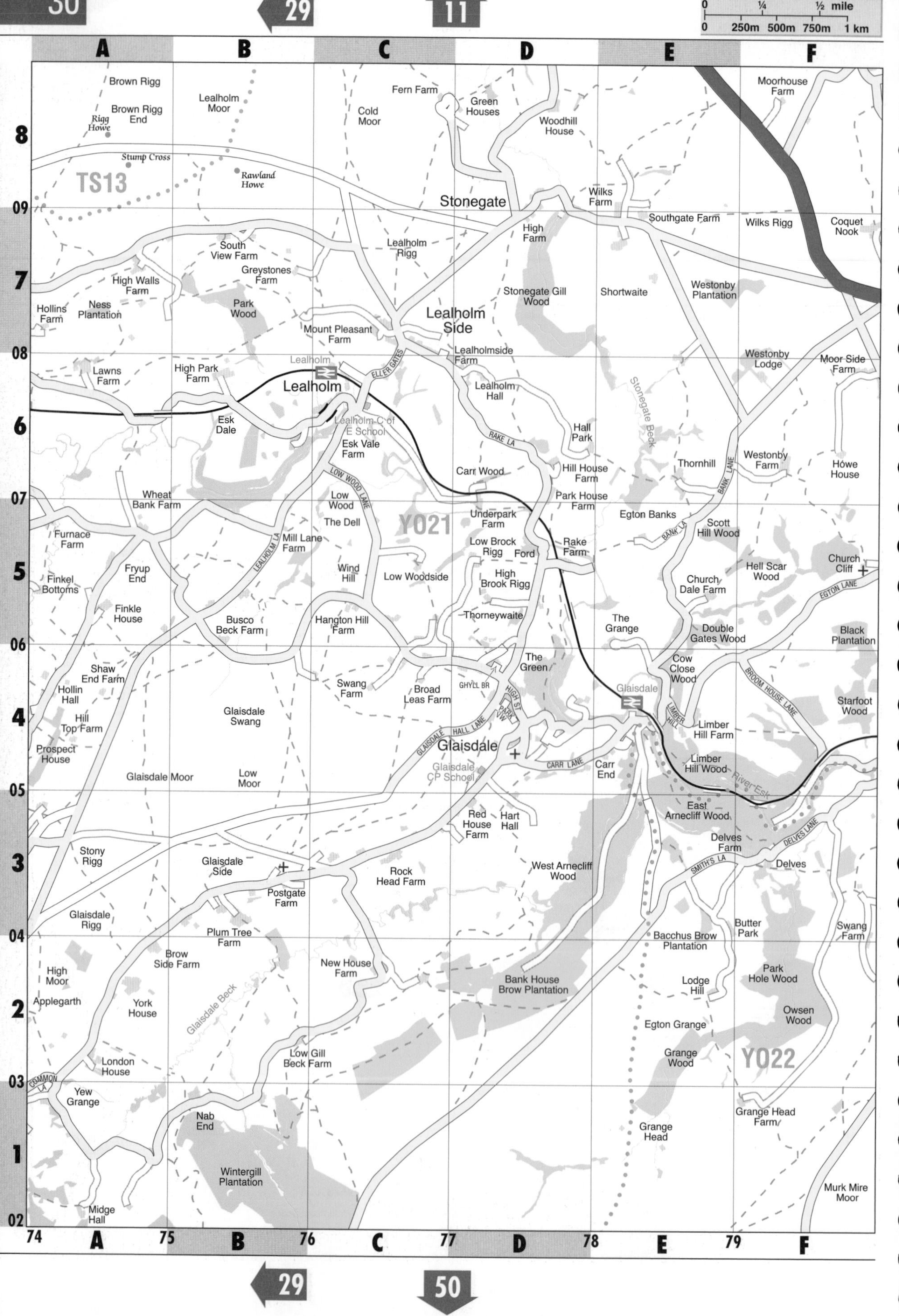

29
50

12
32

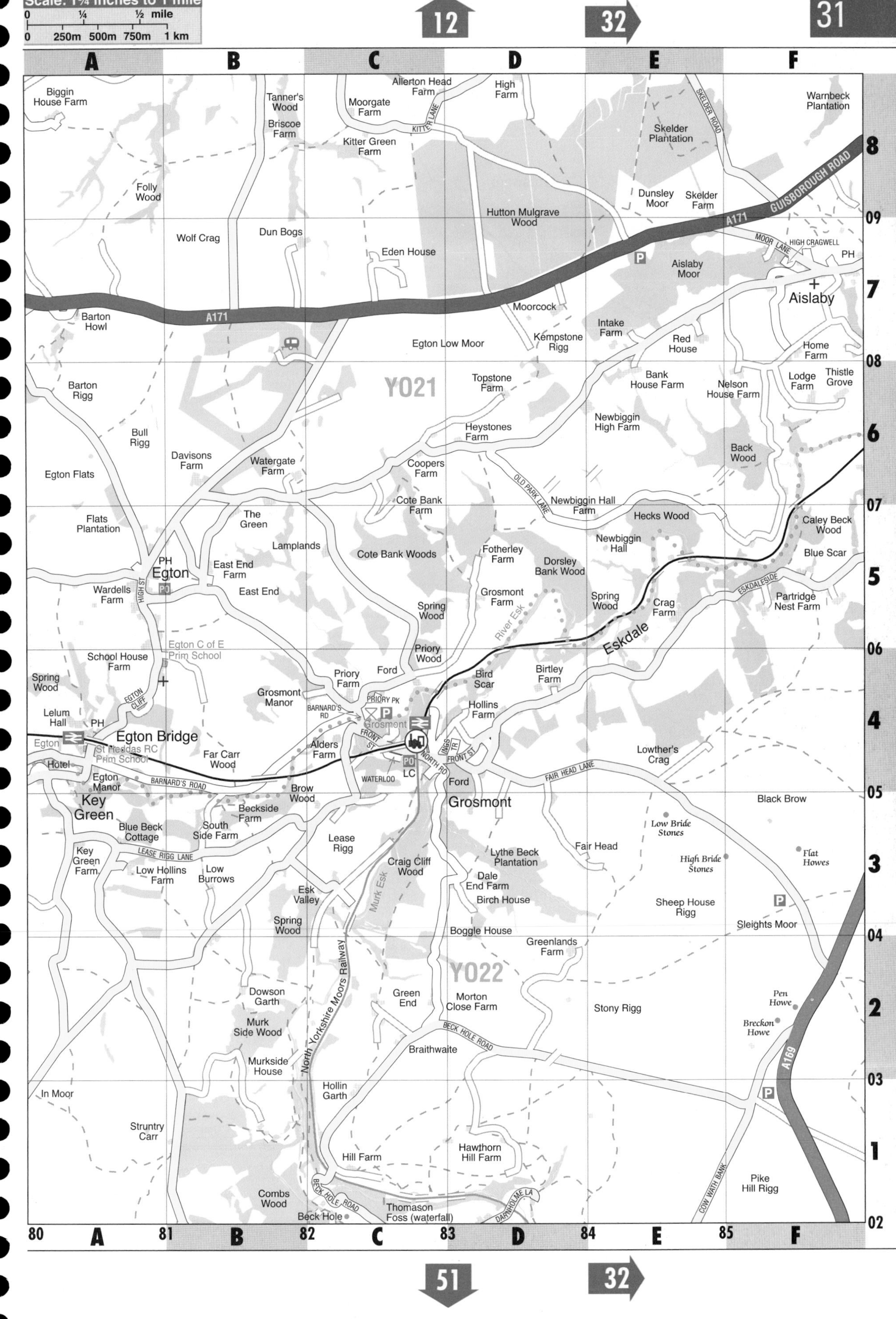
Scale: 1¾ inches to 1 mile
0 ¼ ½ mile
0 250m 500m 750m 1 km
A
B
C
D
E
F
Biggin House Farm
Tanner's Wood
Briscoe Farm
Moorgate Farm
Allerton Head Farm
KITTER LANE
Kitter Green Farm
High Farm
SKELDER ROAD
Skelder Plantation
Warnbeck Plantation
Folly Wood
Hutton Mulgrave Wood
Dunsley Moor
Skelder Farm
GUISBOROUGH ROAD
A171
Wolf Crag
Dun Bogs
Eden House
MOOR LANE
HIGH CRAGWELL
PH
Aislaby Moor
Aislaby
Barton Howl
Moorcock
Intake Farm
Kempstone Rigg
Egton Low Moor
Red House
Home Farm
Barton Rigg
YO21
Topstone Farm
Bank House Farm
Nelson House Farm
Lodge Farm
Thistle Grove
Bull Rigg
Heystones Farm
Newbiggin High Farm
Davisons Farm
Watergate Farm
Coopers Farm
Back Wood
Egton Flats
OLD PARK LANE
Cote Bank Farm
Newbiggin Hall Farm
Hecks Wood
Caley Beck Wood
Flats Plantation
The Green
Newbiggin Hall
Lamplands
Cote Bank Woods
Fotherley Farm
Blue Scar
PH
Egton
East End Farm
Dorsley Bank Wood
Wardells Farm
HIGH ST
PO
East End
Grosmont Farm
ESKDALESIDE
Spring Wood
Spring Wood
Crag Farm
Partridge Nest Farm
River Esk
Eskdale
Egton C of E Prim School
Priory Wood
School House Farm
Priory Farm
Ford
Bird Scar
Birtley Farm
Spring Wood
EGTON CLIFF
Grosmont Manor
PRIORY PK
Hollins Farm
Lelum Hall
PH
BARNARD'S RD
Grosmont
Egton
Egton Bridge
FRONT ST
Alders Farm
INGS TR
FRONT ST
Lowther's Crag
St Heddas RC Prim School
Far Carr Wood
NORTH RD
PO
LC
Hotel
WATERLOO
Ford
FAIR HEAD LANE
Egton Manor
BARNARD'S ROAD
Brow Wood
Grosmont
Black Brow
Key Green
Beckside Farm
Low Bride Stones
Blue Beck Cottage
South Side Farm
Lease Rigg
Lythe Beck Plantation
Fair Head
High Bride Stones
Flat Howes
Key Green Farm
LEASE RIGG LANE
Craig Cliff Wood
Low Hollins Farm
Low Burrows
Dale End Farm
Esk Valley
Murk Esk
Birch House
Sheep House Rigg
Sleights Moor
Spring Wood
Boggle House
Greenlands Farm
YO22
Dowson Garth
Green End
Morton Close Farm
Stony Rigg
Pen Howe
North Yorkshire Moors Railway
Murk Side Wood
Brecken Howe
BECK HOLE ROAD
Murkside House
Braithwaite
A169
In Moor
Hollin Garth
Struntry Carr
Hill Farm
Hawthorn Hill Farm
Pike Hill Rigg
COW WATH BANK
Combs Wood
BECK HOLE ROAD
DARNHOLME LA
Thomason Foss (waterfall)
Beck Hole
8
09
7
08
6
07
5
06
4
05
3
04
2
03
1
02
80
81
82
83
84
85

51
32

A6
1 THE AV
2 BANK CL
3 ORCHARD RD
4 LOWDALE CT
5 SMIDDYFIELDS
6 NETHERBY CL
7 SELSTONE CR
8 NARROWFIELD
9 HALL PASTURE
10 BIRCH CR
11 FOURACRE DR
12 SPRING CL
13 YEWTREE CL

31

13

E8
1 LARPOOL CR
2 HELREDALE GD
3 ST PETER'S RD
4 ST PETER'S CT
5 FAIRMEAD WY
6 ELLERBECK WY
7 QUEENS DR
8 BRACKEN CL
9 STAINSACRE LA
10 PLEASANT MOUNT
11 KINGFISHER DR
12 HEATHER DR
13 CHOLMLEY WY

Scale: 1¾ inches to 1 mile
0 ¼ ½ mile
0 250m 500m 750m 1 km

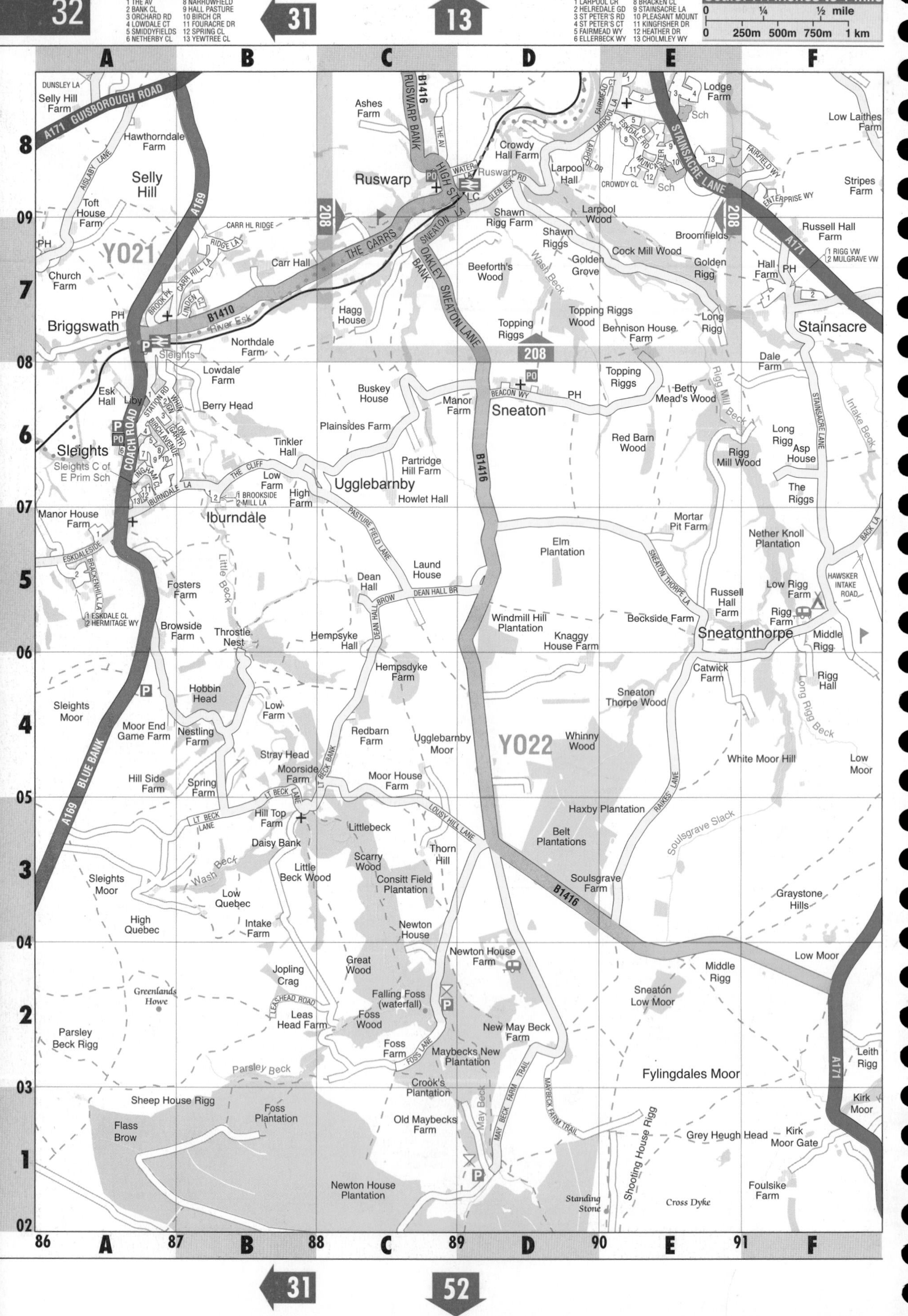

31

52

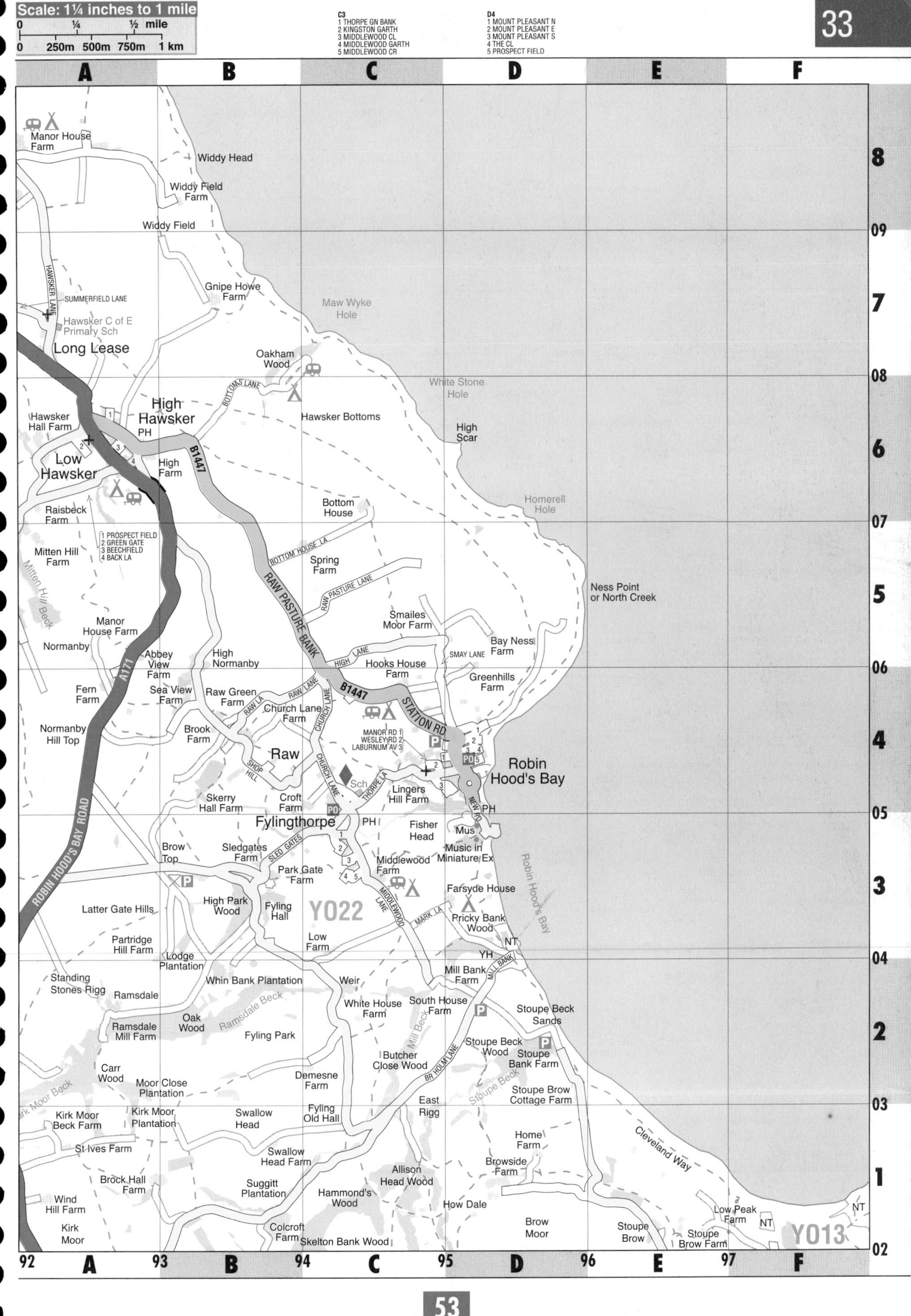

Scale: 1¼ inches to 1 mile
0 ¼ ½ mile
0 250m 500m 750m 1 km
C3
1 THORPE GN BANK
2 KINGSTON GARTH
3 MIDDLEWOOD CL
4 MIDDLEWOOD GARTH
5 MIDDLEWOOD CR
D4
1 MOUNT PLEASANT N
2 MOUNT PLEASANT E
3 MOUNT PLEASANT S
4 THE CL
5 PROSPECT FIELD
33
A B C D E F
8 09 7 08 6 07 5 06 4 05 3 04 2 03 1 02
92 93 94 95 96 97
Manor House Farm
Widdy Head
Widdy Field Farm
Widdy Field
HAWSKER LANE
SUMMERFIELD LANE
Hawsker C of E Primary Sch
Gnipe Howe Farm
Maw Wyke Hole
Long Lease
Oakham Wood
BOTTOMS LANE
White Stone Hole
High Hawsker
Hawsker Hall Farm
PH
Hawsker Bottoms
High Scar
Low Hawsker
High Farm
B1447
Raisbeck Farm
Bottom House
Homerell Hole
1 PROSPECT FIELD
2 GREEN GATE
3 BEECHFIELD
4 BACK LA
Mitten Hill Farm
BOTTOM HOUSE LA
Spring Farm
Mitten Hill Beck
RAW PASTURE BANK
RAW PASTURE LANE
Ness Point or North Creek
Smailes Moor Farm
Manor House Farm
Normanby
Bay Ness Farm
SMAY LANE
Abbey View Farm
High Normanby
HIGH LANE
Hooks House Farm
A171
Greenhills Farm
Fern Farm
Sea View Farm
Raw Green Farm
RAW LA
RAW LANE
B1447
Church Lane Farm
CHURCH LANE
STATION RD
Normanby Hill Top
Brook Farm
MANOR RD 1
WESLEY RD 2
LABURNUM AV 3
Raw
Robin Hood's Bay
SHOP HILL
P
PO
Sch
THORPE LA
Lingers Hill Farm
Skerry Hall Farm
Croft Farm
CHURCH LANE
NEW RD
PH
ROBIN HOOD'S BAY ROAD
Fylingthorpe
PH
Fisher Head
Mus
Brow Top
Sledgates Farm
SLED GATES
Music in Miniature Ex
Middlewood Farm
Robin Hood's Bay
Park Gate Farm
Farsyde House
Latter Gate Hills
High Park Wood
Fylling Hall
YO22
MIDDLEWOOD LANE
MARK LA
Pricky Bank Wood
Partridge Hill Farm
Low Farm
NT
Lodge Plantation
YH
MILL BANK
Standing Stones Rigg
Whin Bank Plantation
Weir
Mill Bank Farm
Ramsdale
Ramsdale Beck
White House Farm
South House Farm
Stoupe Beck Sands
Ramsdale Mill Farm
Oak Wood
Fyling Park
Mill Beck
Stoupe Beck Wood
Stoupe Bank Farm
Carr Wood
Butcher Close Wood
BR HOLM LANE
Moor Close Plantation
Demesne Farm
Stoupe Beck
Stoupe Brow Cottage Farm
Kirk Moor Beck
Kirk Moor Beck Farm
Kirk Moor Plantation
Swallow Head
Fyling Old Hall
East Rigg
Cleveland Way
St Ives Farm
Swallow Head Farm
Home Farm
Browside Farm
Brock Hall Farm
Allison Head Wood
Suggitt Plantation
Hammond's Wood
Wind Hill Farm
How Dale
Low Peak Farm
NT
Kirk Moor
Colcroft Farm
Skelton Bank Wood
Brow Moor
Stoupe Brow
Stoupe Brow Farm
YO13

53

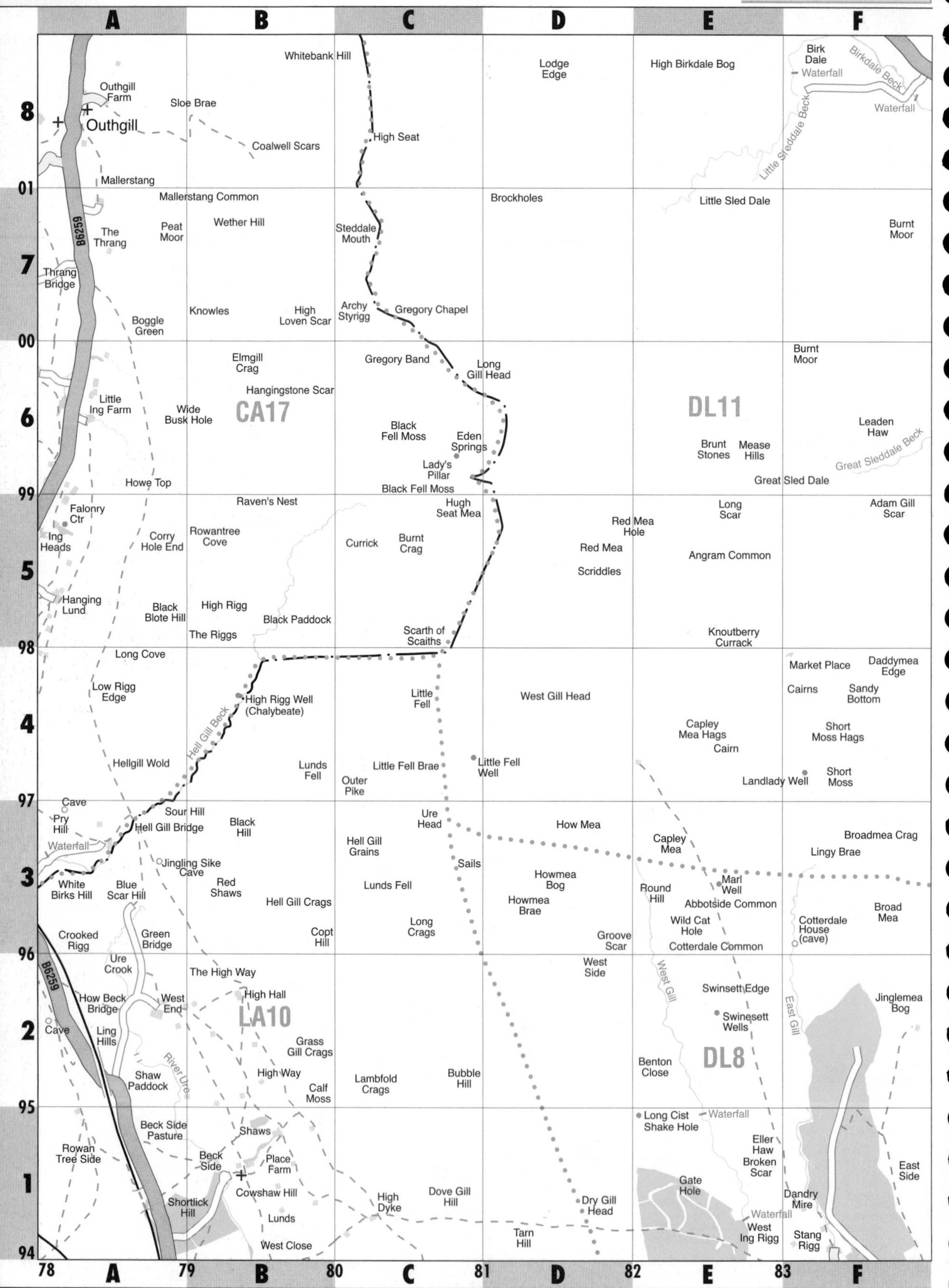
14
Scale: 1¾ inches to 1 mile
0 ¼ ½ mile
0 250m 500m 750m 1 km
A B C D E F
Whitebank Hill
Lodge Edge
High Birkdale Bog
Birk Dale
Waterfall
Birkdale Beck
Outhgill Farm
Sloe Brae
Outhgill
Coalwell Scars
High Seat
Little Sleddale Beck
Mallerstang
Mallerstang Common
Brockholes
Little Sled Dale
B6259
The Thrang
Peat Moor
Wether Hill
Steddale Mouth
Burnt Moor
Thrang Bridge
Knowles
High Loven Scar
Archy Styrigg
Gregory Chapel
Boggle Green
Elmgill Crag
Gregory Band
Long Gill Head
Hangingstone Scar
Little Ing Farm
Wide Busk Hole
CA17
DL11
Leaden Haw
Black Fell Moss
Eden Springs
Brunt Stones
Mease Hills
Great Sleddale Beck
Lady's Pillar
Howe Top
Black Fell Moss
Great Sled Dale
Raven's Nest
Hugh Seat Mea
Long Scar
Adam Gill Scar
Falonry Ctr
Red Mea Hole
Ing Heads
Corry Hole End
Rowantree Cove
Curick
Burnt Crag
Red Mea
Angram Common
Scriddles
Hanging Lund
Black Blote Hill
High Rigg
Black Paddock
The Riggs
Scarth of Scaiths
Knoutberry Currack
Long Cove
Market Place
Daddymea Edge
Low Rigg Edge
Little Fell
High Rigg Well (Chalybeate)
West Gill Head
Cairns
Sandy Bottom
Hell Gill Beck
Capley Mea Hags
Short Moss Hags
Cairn
Hellgill Wold
Lunds Fell
Little Fell Brae
Little Fell Well
Outer Pike
Landlady Well
Short Moss
Cave
Pry Hill
Sour Hill
Black Hill
Ure Head
How Mea
Hell Gill Bridge
Waterfall
Hell Gill Grains
Capley Mea
Broadmea Crag
Lingy Brae
Jingling Sike Cave
Sails
Howmea Bog
Marl Well
White Birks Hill
Blue Scar Hill
Red Shaws
Lunds Fell
Round Hill
Hell Gill Crags
Howmea Brae
Abbotside Common
Broad Mea
Crooked Rigg
Green Bridge
Copt Hill
Long Crags
Wild Cat Hole
Cotterdale House (cave)
Groove Scar
Cotterdale Common
Ure Crook
The High Way
West Side
West Gill
Swinsett Edge
B6259
How Beck Bridge
West End
High Hall
LA10
East Gill
Jinglemea Bog
Cave
Ling Hills
Swinesett Wells
Grass Gill Crags
River Ure
Benton Close
DL8
Shaw Paddock
High Way
Lambfold Crags
Bubble Hill
Calf Moss
Long Cist Shake Hole
Waterfall
Beck Side Pasture
Shaws
Eller Haw Broken Scar
Rowan Tree Side
Beck Side
Place Farm
Gate Hole
East Side
Cowshaw Hill
High Dyke
Dove Gill Hill
Dry Gill Head
Dandry Mire
Shortlick Hill
Lunds
Waterfall
Tarn Hill
West Ing Rigg
Stang Rigg
West Close
78 79 80 81 82 83
55

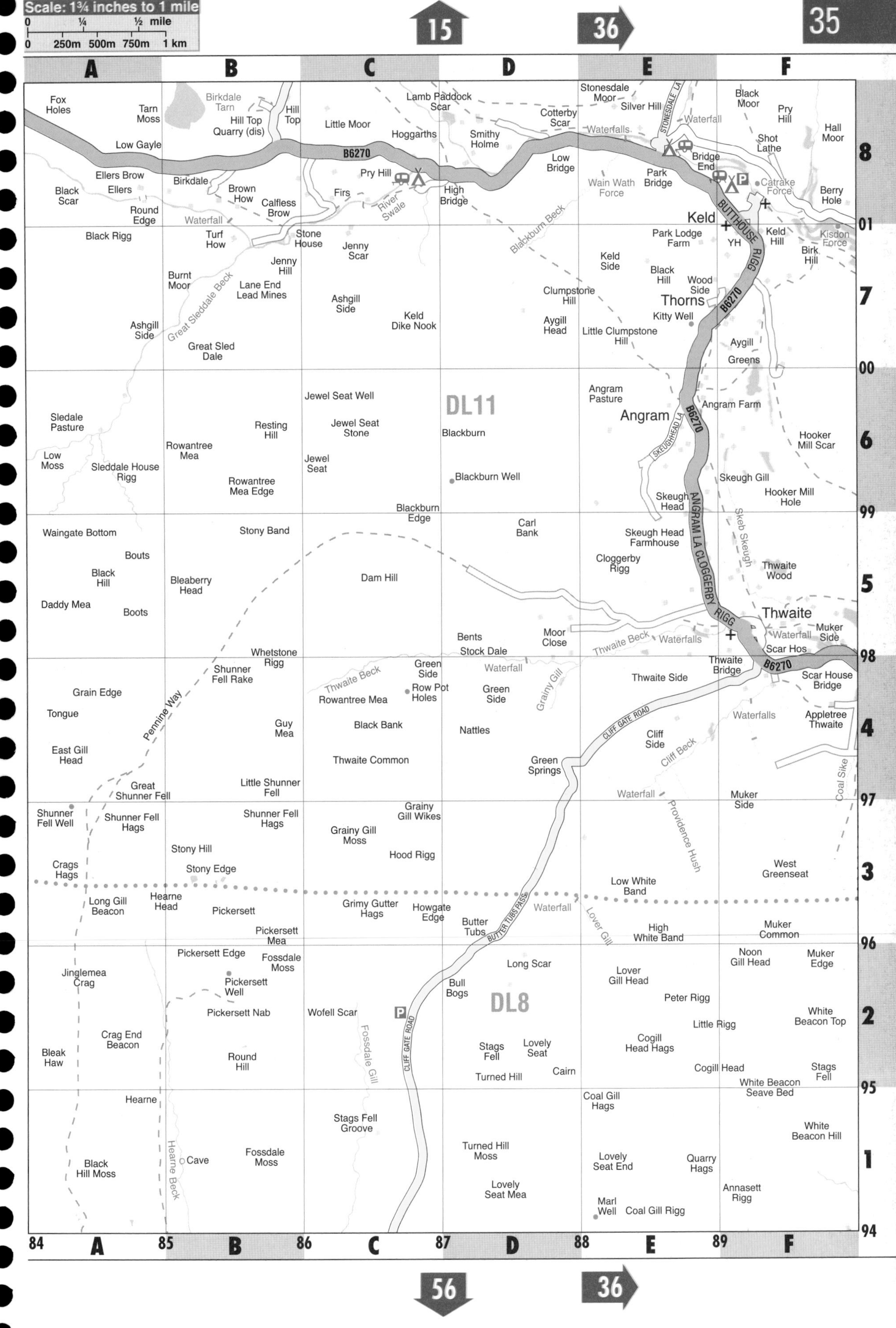
Scale: 1¾ inches to 1 mile
0 ¼ ½ mile
0 250m 500m 750m 1 km
15
36
A B C D E F
Fox Holes
Tarn Moss
Birkdale Tarn
Hill Top Quarry (dis)
Hill Top
Little Moor
Lamb Paddock Scar
Hoggarths
Smithy Holme
Cotterby Scar
Stonesdale Moor
Silver Hill
STONESDALE LA
Waterfalls
Waterfall
Black Moor
Pry Hill
Hall Moor
Shot Lathe
Low Gayle
B6270
Ellers Brow
Ellers
Black Scar
Round Edge
Birkdale
Brown How
Calfless Brow
Pry Hill
Firs
River Swale
High Bridge
Low Bridge
Wain Wath Force
Park Bridge
Bridge End
Catrake Force
Berry Hole
Waterfall
Keld
BUTTHOUSE RIGG
Black Rigg
Turf How
Stone House
Jenny Scar
Blackburn Beck
Park Lodge Farm
YH
Keld Hill
Kisdon Force
Birk Hill
Jenny Hill
Burnt Moor
Great Sleddale Beck
Lane End Lead Mines
Ashgill Side
Keld Side
Black Hill
Wood Side
Clumpstone Hill
Thorns
Kitty Well
Ashgill Side
Keld Dike Nook
Aygill Head
Little Clumpstone Hill
Great Sled Dale
Aygill
Greens
8
01
7
00
6
99
5
98
4
97
3
96
2
95
1
94
Jewel Seat Well
DL11
Angram Pasture
Angram
Angram Farm
Sledale Pasture
Resting Hill
Jewel Seat Stone
Blackburn
B6270
SKEUGHEAD LA
Hooker Mill Scar
Rowantree Mea
Low Moss
Sleddale House Rigg
Jewel Seat
Rowantree Mea Edge
Blackburn Well
Skeugh Gill
Hooker Mill Hole
Skeugh Head
ANGRAM LA CLOGGERBY RIGG
Blackburn Edge
Carl Bank
Waingate Bottom
Stony Band
Skeugh Head Farmhouse
Skeb Skeugh
Bouts
Cloggerby Rigg
Thwaite Wood
Black Hill
Bleaberry Head
Dam Hill
Daddy Mea
Boots
Thwaite
Moor Close
Bents
Muker Side
Waterfall
Whetstone Rigg
Stock Dale
Thwaite Beck
Waterfalls
Scar Hos
Shunner Fell Rake
Green Side
Waterfall
Thwaite Bridge
Thwaite Side
B6270
Scar House Bridge
Grain Edge
Thwaite Beck
Row Pot Holes
Green Side
Grainy Gill
Rowantree Mea
Tongue
Pennine Way
Guy Mea
Black Bank
Nattles
CLIFF GATE ROAD
Waterfalls
Appletree Thwaite
Cliff Side
Cliff Beck
East Gill Head
Thwaite Common
Green Springs
Great Shunner Fell
Little Shunner Fell
Waterfall
Coal Sike
Muker Side
Shunner Fell Well
Shunner Fell Hags
Shunner Fell Hags
Grainy Gill Wikes
Grainy Gill Moss
Providence Hush
Stony Hill
Hood Rigg
Crags Hags
Stony Edge
West Greenseat
Low White Band
Long Gill Beacon
Hearne Head
Pickersett
Grimy Gutter Hags
Howgate Edge
Waterfall
BUTTER TUBS PASS
Lover Gill
Butter Tubs
Pickersett Mea
High White Band
Muker Common
Pickersett Edge
Fossdale Moss
Long Scar
Lover Gill Head
Noon Gill Head
Muker Edge
Jinglemea Crag
Pickersett Well
Bull Bogs
DL8
Peter Rigg
Pickersett Nab
Wofell Scar
Fossdale Gill
CLIFF GATE ROAD
White Beacon Top
Little Rigg
Crag End Beacon
Cogill Head Hags
Bleak Haw
Round Hill
Stags Fell
Lovely Seat
Cairn
Turned Hill
Cogill Head
Stags Fell
White Beacon Seave Bed
Hearne
Coal Gill Hags
Stags Fell Groove
White Beacon Hill
Turned Hill Moss
Hearne Beck
Cave
Black Hill Moss
Fossdale Moss
Lovely Seat End
Quarry Hags
Lovely Seat Mea
Annasett Rigg
Marl Well
Coal Gill Rigg
84 A 85 B 86 C 87 D 88 E 89 F
56
36

35

16

Scale: 1¾ inches to 1 mile

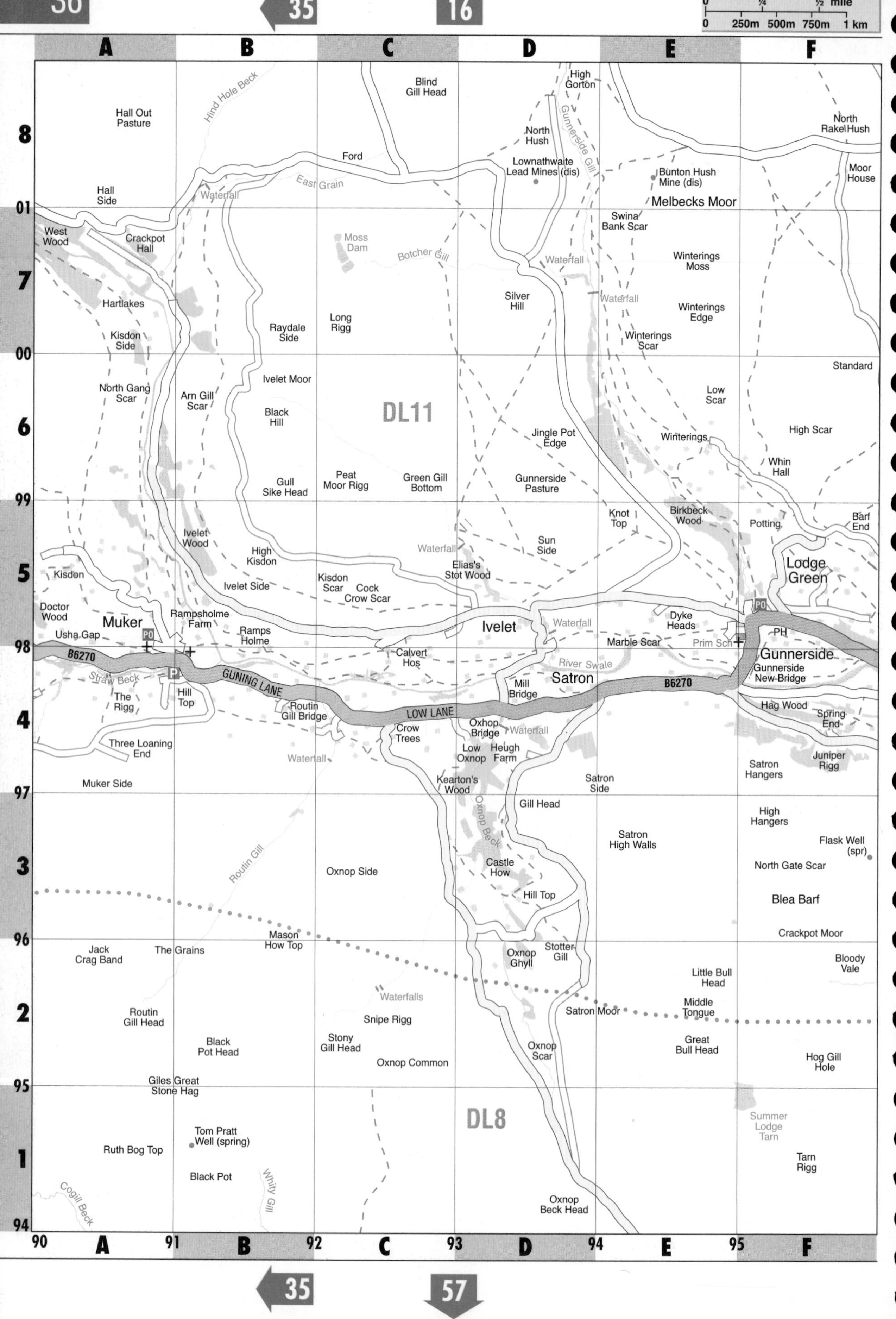

35

57

17
38

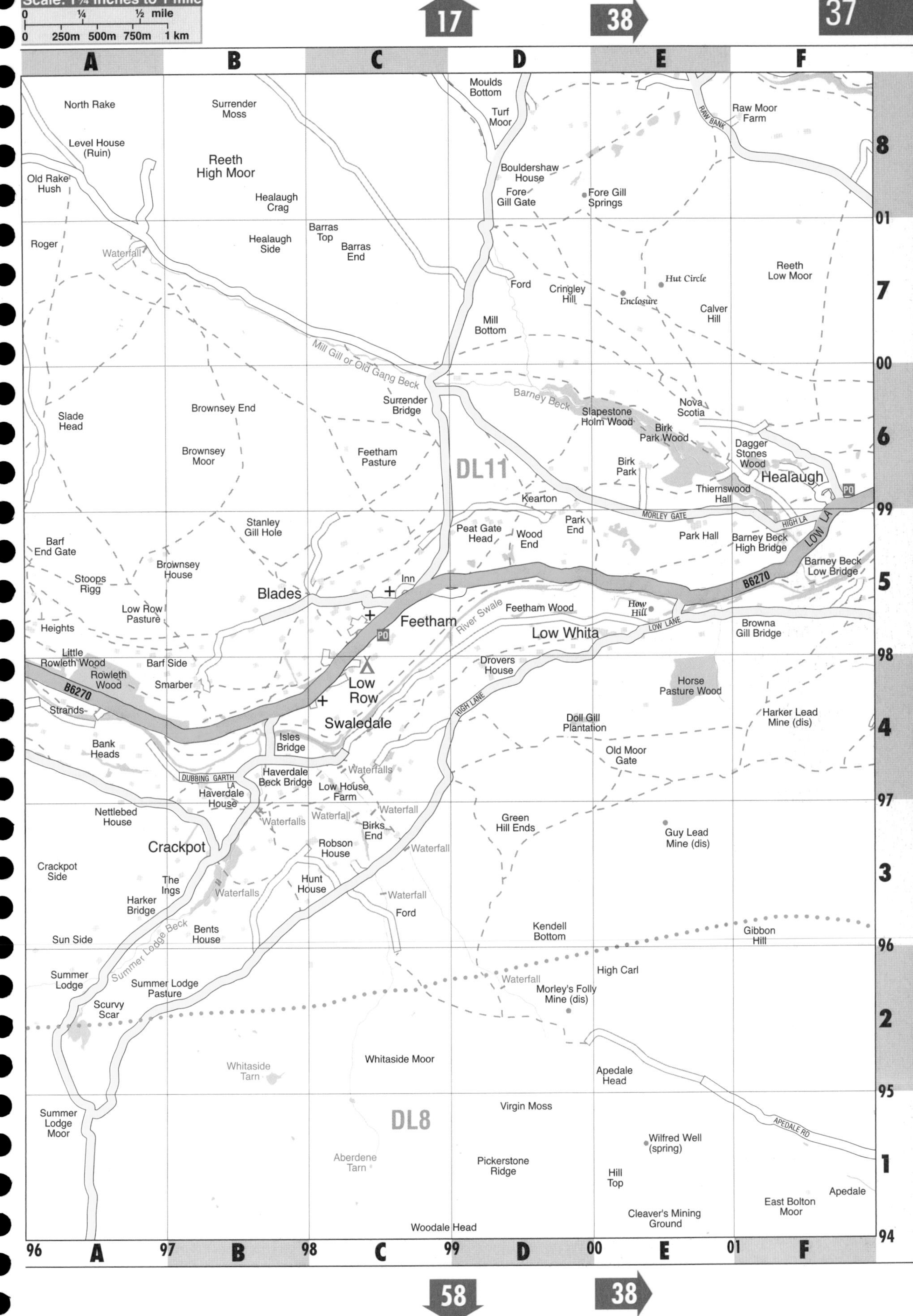
Scale: 1¾ inches to 1 mile
0 ¼ ½ mile
0 250m 500m 750m 1 km
A B C D E F
North Rake
Surrender Moss
Moulds Bottom
Turf Moor
Raw Moor Farm
RAW BANK
Level House (Ruin)
Reeth High Moor
Old Rake Hush
Healaugh Crag
Bouldershaw House
Fore Gill Gate
Fore Gill Springs
8
01
Roger
Waterfall
Healaugh Side
Barras Top
Barras End
Ford
Cringley Hill
Enclosure
Hut Circle
Reeth Low Moor
Calver Hill
7
Mill Bottom
Mill Gill or Old Gang Beck
00
Barney Beck
Surrender Bridge
Slapestone Holm Wood
Nova Scotia
Slade Head
Brownsey End
Birk Park Wood
Dagger Stones Wood
6
Brownsey Moor
Feetham Pasture
DL11
Birk Park
Healaugh
Thiernswood Hall
Kearton
PO
99
MORLEY GATE
HIGH LA
LOW LA
Barf End Gate
Stanley Gill Hole
Peat Gate Head
Wood End
Park End
Park Hall
Barney Beck High Bridge
Barney Beck Low Bridge
Stoops Rigg
Brownsey House
Inn
B6270
5
Low Row Pasture
Blades
Feetham
River Swale
Feetham Wood
How Hill
Low Whita
LOW LANE
Browna Gill Bridge
Heights
PO
Little Rowleth Wood
Rowleth Wood
Barf Side
Drovers House
98
Smarber
Low Row
Horse Pasture Wood
B6270
Strands
HIGH LANE
Swaledale
Harker Lead Mine (dis)
Doll Gill Plantation
4
Bank Heads
Isles Bridge
Old Moor Gate
Waterfalls
DUBBING GARTH LA
Haverdale Beck Bridge
Low House Farm
Haverdale House
97
Nettlebed House
Waterfalls
Waterfall
Waterfall
Birks End
Green Hill Ends
Guy Lead Mine (dis)
Crackpot
Robson House
Waterfall
Crackpot Side
3
The Ings
Hunt House
Harker Bridge
Waterfalls
Waterfall
Ford
Kendell Bottom
Gibbon Hill
Sun Side
Bents House
Summer Lodge Beck
96
Summer Lodge
Summer Lodge Pasture
Waterfall
High Carl
Morley's Folly Mine (dis)
Scurvy Scar
2
Whitaside Tarn
Whitaside Moor
Apedale Head
95
Summer Lodge Moor
DL8
Virgin Moss
APEDALE RD
Wilfred Well (spring)
Aberdene Tarn
Pickerstone Ridge
1
Hill Top
Apedale
East Bolton Moor
Cleaver's Mining Ground
Woodale Head
94
96 A 97 B 98 C 99 D 00 E 01 F

58
38

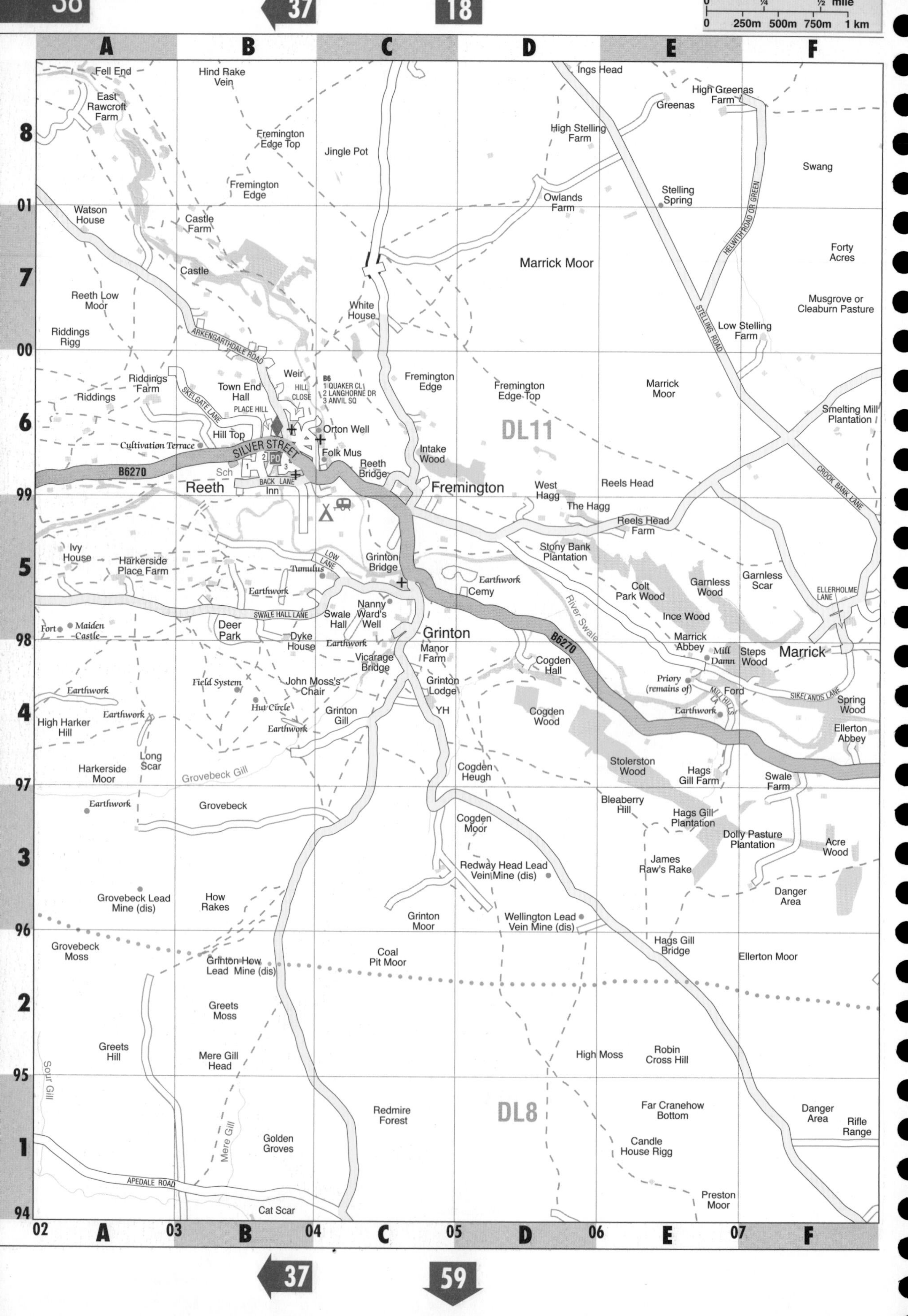
37
18
Scale: 1¾ inches to 1 mile
A B C D E F
Fell End
Hind Rake Vein
Ings Head
High Greenas Farm
Greenas
East Rawcroft Farm
High Stelling Farm
Fremington Edge Top
Jingle Pot
Swang
Fremington Edge
Stelling Spring
Owlands Farm
Watson House
Castle Farm
Forty Acres
Castle
Marrick Moor
Reeth Low Moor
White House
Musgrove or Cleaburn Pasture
Riddings Rigg
Low Stelling Farm
ARKENGARTHDALE ROAD
STELLING ROAD
HEWITH ROAD OR GREEN
Weir
Riddings Farm
Town End Hall
Fremington Edge
Fremington Edge Top
Marrick Moor
Riddings
1 QUAKER CL
2 LANGHORNE DR
3 ANVIL SQ
SKELGATE LANE
PLACE HILL
Smelting Mill Plantation
Orton Well
DL11
Hill Top
Cultivation Terrace
SILVER STREET
Folk Mus
Intake Wood
CROOK BANK LANE
B6270
Sch
Reeth Bridge
Reeth
BACK LANE
Inn
Fremington
West Hagg
Reels Head
The Hagg
Reels Head Farm
Ivy House
Harkerside Place Farm
LOW LANE
Grinton Bridge
Stony Bank Plantation
Garnless Wood
Garnless Scar
Tumulus
Earthwork
Colt Park Wood
Earthwork
Cemy
River Swale
ELLERHOLME LANE
Nanny Ward's Well
SWALE HALL LANE
Swale Hall
Ince Wood
Fort
Maiden Castle
Deer Park
Dyke House
Grinton
Marrick Abbey
Mill Dam
Steps Wood
Marrick
Earthwork
Manor Farm
Vicarage Bridge
Cogden Hall
Earthwork
Field System
John Moss's Chair
Grinton Lodge
Priory (remains of)
Ford
MILL HILLS LA
SIKELANDS LANE
Hut Circle
YH
Grinton Gill
Cogden Wood
Spring Wood
High Harker Hill
Earthwork
Earthwork
Ellerton Abbey
Long Scar
Cogden Heugh
Stolerston Wood
Hags Gill Farm
Swale Farm
Harkerside Moor
Grovebeck Gill
Earthwork
Grovebeck
Bleaberry Hill
Hags Gill Plantation
Cogden Moor
Dolly Pasture Plantation
Acre Wood
James Raw's Rake
Redway Head Lead Vein Mine (dis)
Grovebeck Lead Mine (dis)
How Rakes
Danger Area
Grinton Moor
Wellington Lead Vein Mine (dis)
Grovebeck Moss
Hags Gill Bridge
Coal Pit Moor
Ellerton Moor
Grinton How Lead Mine (dis)
Greets Moss
Greets Hill
Mere Gill Head
High Moss
Robin Cross Hill
Sour Gill
Far Cranehow Bottom
Redmire Forest
DL8
Danger Area
Rifle Range
Mere Gill
Golden Groves
Candle House Rigg
APEDALE ROAD
Preston Moor
Cat Scar
8
01
7
00
6
99
5
98
4
97
3
96
2
95
1
94
02 03 04 05 06 07
37
59

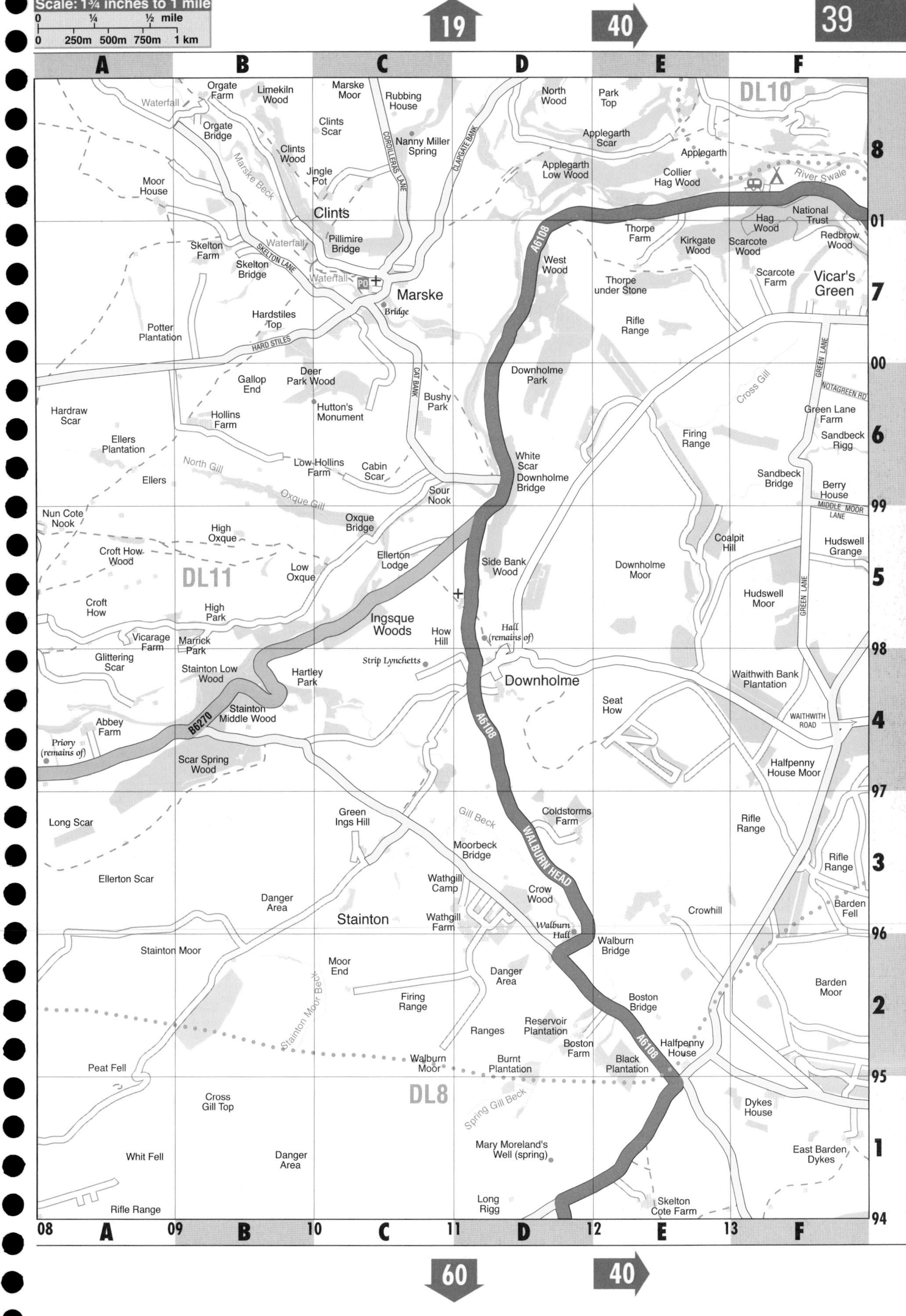
Scale: 1¾ inches to 1 mile
0 ¼ ½ mile
0 250m 500m 750m 1 km
19
40
A B C D E F
Orgate Farm
Limekiln Wood
Marske Moor
Rubbing House
North Wood
Park Top
DL10
Waterfall
Orgate Bridge
Clints Scar
Nanny Miller Spring
Applegarth Scar
Clints Wood
Applegarth
Marske Beck
Jingle Pot
Applegarth Low Wood
Collier Hag Wood
River Swale
Moor House
Clints
CORDILLERAS LANE
CLAPGATE BANK
Hag Wood
National Trust
Thorpe Farm
Redbrow Wood
Skelton Farm
Pillimire Bridge
Kirkgate Wood
Scarcote Wood
SKELTON LANE
West Wood
Skelton Bridge
Waterfall
PO
Marske
Thorpe under Stone
Scarcote Farm
Vicar's Green
Bridge
Hardstiles Top
Rifle Range
Potter Plantation
HARD STILES
GREEN LANE
Downholme Park
Deer Park Wood
Gallop End
CAT BANK
NOTAGREEN RD
Cross Gill
Hardraw Scar
Hutton's Monument
Bushy Park
Green Lane Farm
Hollins Farm
Firing Range
Sandbeck Rigg
Ellers Plantation
White Scar
Low Hollins Farm
Cabin Scar
Downholme Bridge
North Gill
Sandbeck Bridge
Berry House
Ellers
Sour Nook
Oxque Gill
Nun Cote Nook
Oxque Bridge
MIDDLE MOOR LANE
High Oxque
Coalpit Hill
Hudswell Grange
Croft How Wood
Ellerton Lodge
Side Bank Wood
Downholme Moor
DL11
Low Oxque
Hudswell Moor
Croft How
High Park
Ingsque Woods
How Hill
Hall (remains of)
Vicarage Farm
Marrick Park
Glittering Scar
Strip Lynchetts
Waithwith Bank Plantation
Stainton Low Wood
Hartley Park
Downholme
Seat How
Stainton Middle Wood
WAITHWITH ROAD
Abbey Farm
B6270
A6108
Priory (remains of)
Scar Spring Wood
Halfpenny House Moor
Coldstorms Farm
Long Scar
Green Ings Hill
Gill Beck
Rifle Range
Moorbeck Bridge
WALBURN HEAD
Rifle Range
Ellerton Scar
Wathgill Camp
Crow Wood
Danger Area
Barden Fell
Stainton
Wathgill Farm
Walburn Hall
Crowhill
Walburn Bridge
Stainton Moor
Moor End
Danger Area
Barden Moor
Firing Range
Boston Bridge
Stainton Moor Beck
Reservoir Plantation
Ranges
Boston Farm
Halfpenny House
Walburn Moor
Burnt Plantation
Black Plantation
Peat Fell
DL8
Spring Gill Beck
Dykes House
Cross Gill Top
Mary Moreland's Well (spring)
East Barden Dykes
Whit Fell
Danger Area
Long Rigg
Skelton Cote Farm
Rifle Range
8 01 7 00 6 99 5 98 4 97 3 96 2 95 1 94
08 09 10 11 12 13
60
40

39

F5
1 WESTRIDGE CR
2 FALKLAND RD
3 ALBERMARLE DR
4 CRAVENDALE RD
5 MAPLE CL
6 CHESTNUT CL
7 GRANGE RD
8 MANOR GR

20

For full street detail of the highlighted area see page 209.

Scale: 1¾ inches to 1 mile
0 ¼ ½ mile
0 250m 500m 750m 1 km

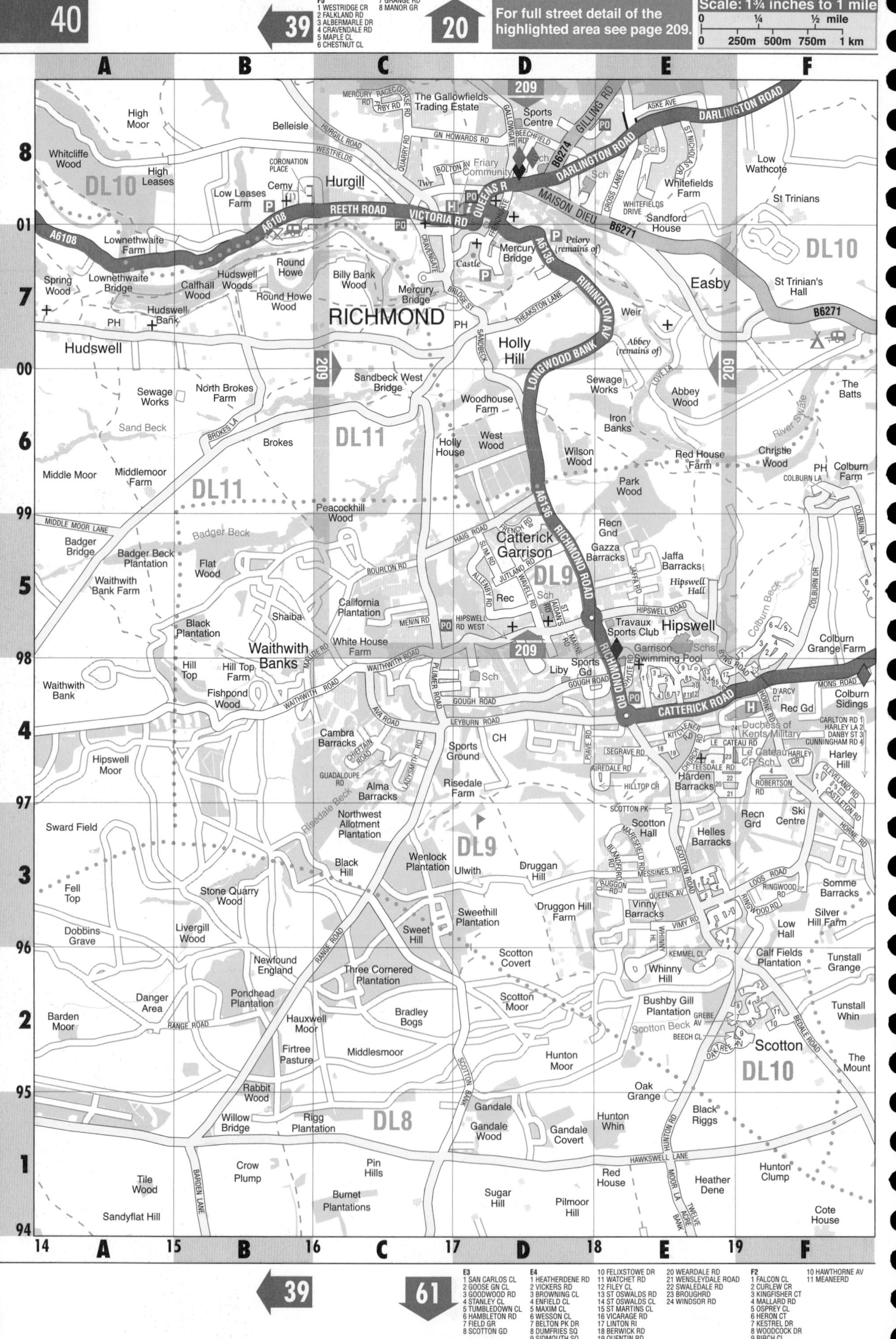

39

61

E3
1 SAN CARLOS CL
2 GOOSE GN CL
3 GOODWOOD RD
4 STANLEY CL
5 TUMBLEDOWN CL
6 HAMBLETON RD
7 FIELD GR
8 SCOTTON GD

E4
1 HEATHERDENE RD
2 VICKERS RD
3 BROWNING CL
4 ENFIELD CL
5 MAXIM CL
6 WESSON CL
7 BELTON PK DR
8 DUMFRIES SQ
9 SIDMOUTH SQ
10 FELIXSTOWE DR
11 WATCHET RD
12 FILEY CL
13 ST OSWALDS RD
14 ST OSWALDS CL
15 ST MARTINS CL
16 VICARAGE RD
17 LINTON RI
18 BERWICK RD
19 QUENTIN RD
20 WEARDALE RD
21 WENSLEYDALE ROAD
22 SWALEDALE RD
23 BROUGHRD
24 WINDSOR RD

F2
1 FALCON CL
2 CURLEW CR
3 KINGFISHER CT
4 MALLARD RD
5 OSPREY CL
6 HERON CT
7 KESTREL DR
8 WOODCOCK DR
9 BIRCH CL
10 HAWTHORNE AV
11 MEANEERD

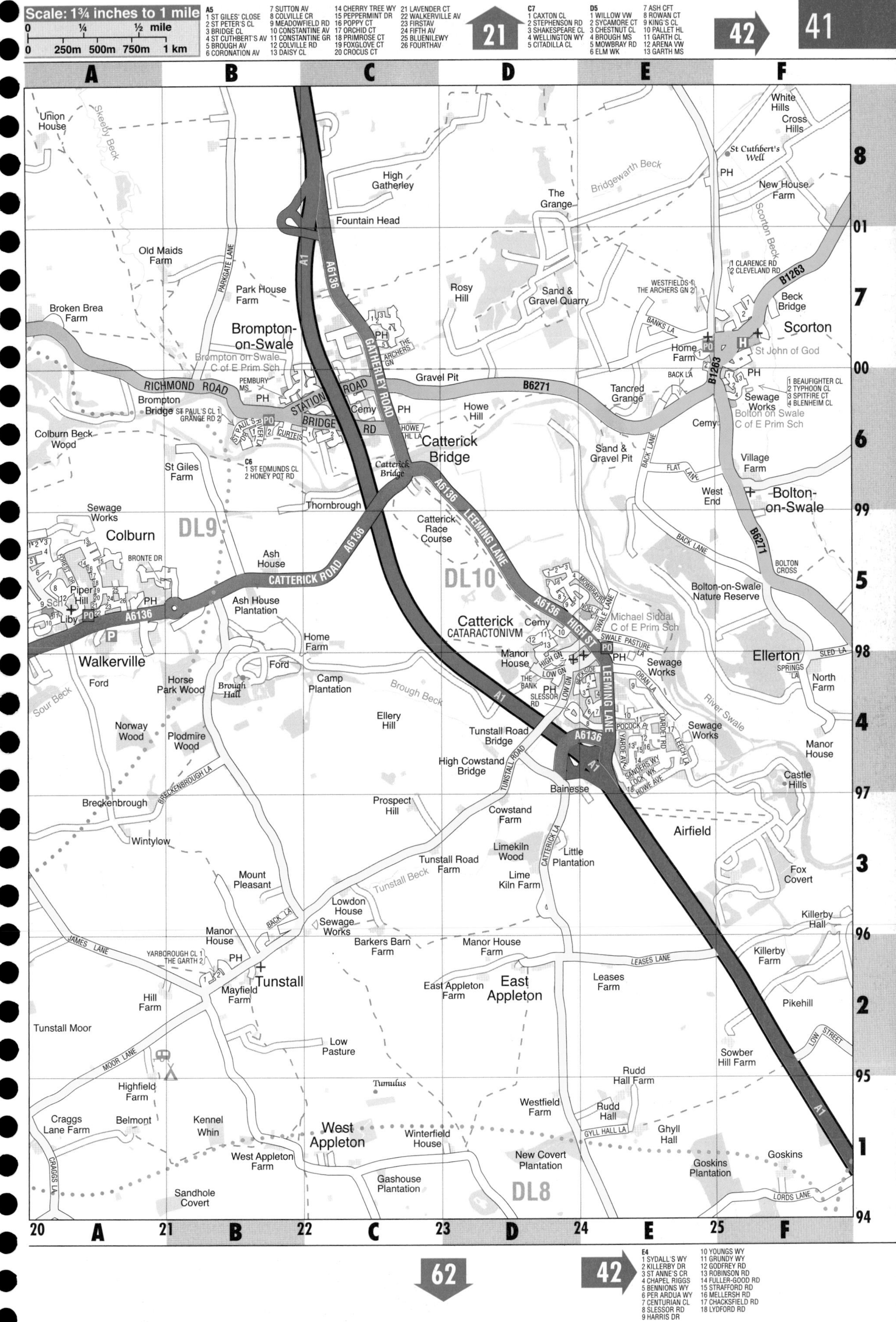
Scale: 1¾ inches to 1 mile
0 ¼ ½ mile
0 250m 500m 750m 1 km
A5
1 ST GILES' CLOSE
2 ST PETER'S CL
3 BRIDGE CL
4 ST CUTHBERT'S AV
5 BROUGH AV
6 CORONATION AV
7 SUTTON AV
8 COLVILLE CR
9 MEADOWFIELD RD
10 CONSTANTINE AV
11 CONSTANTINE GR
12 COLVILLE RD
13 DAISY CL
14 CHERRY TREE WY
15 PEPPERMINT DR
16 POPPY CT
17 ORCHID CT
18 PRIMROSE CT
19 FOXGLOVE CT
20 CROCUS CT
21 LAVENDER CT
22 WALKERVILLE AV
23 FIRSTAV
24 FIFTH AV
25 BLUENILEWY
26 FOURTHAV
21
C7
1 CAXTON CL
2 STEPHENSON RD
3 SHAKESPEARE CL
4 WELLINGTON WY
5 CITADILLA CL
D5
1 WILLOW VW
2 SYCAMORE CT
3 CHESTNUT CL
4 BROUGH MS
5 MOWBRAY RD
6 ELM WK
7 ASH CFT
8 ROWAN CT
9 KING'S CL
10 PALLET HL
11 GARTH CL
12 ARENA VW
13 GARTH MS
42
A B C D E F
Union House
Skeeby Beck
White Hills
Cross Hills
St Cuthbert's Well
PH
Bridgewarth Beck
High Gatherley
The Grange
New House Farm
Scorton Beck
Fountain Head
Old Maids Farm
PARKGATE LANE
A1
A6136
1 CLARENCE RD
2 CLEVELAND RD
B1263
Park House Farm
Rosy Hill
Sand & Gravel Quarry
WESTFIELDS 1
THE ARCHERS GN 2
Beck Bridge
Broken Brea Farm
Brompton-on-Swale
BANKS LA
Scorton
Brompton on Swale C of E Prim Sch
GATHERLEY ROAD
THE ARCHERS GN
Home Farm
PO
H
St John of God
B1263
PEMBURY MS
RICHMOND ROAD
STATION ROAD
Gravel Pit
B6271
Tancred Grange
BACK LA
1 BEAUFIGHTER CL
2 TYPHOON CL
3 SPITFIRE CT
4 BLENHEIM CL
Brompton Bridge
ST PAUL'S CL 1
GRANGE RD 2
ST PAUL'S DR
RIVER LA
CURTEIS
BRIDGE RD
Cemy
Howe Hill
HOWE HILL LA
Sewage Works
Bolton on Swale C of E Prim Sch
Colburn Beck Wood
Catterick Bridge
BACK LANE
Sand & Gravel Pit
Village Farm
St Giles Farm
C6
1 ST EDMUNDS CL
2 HONEY POT RD
FLAT LANE
West End
Bolton-on-Swale
Thornbrough
Sewage Works
Colburn
DL9
Catterick Race Course
LEEMING LANE
BACK LANE
B6271
BRONTE DR
FOREST DR
Ash House
CATTERICK ROAD
DL10
BOLTON CROSS
Piper Hill
Sch
Liby
Ash House Plantation
MOWBRAY RD
SWALE LANE
Bolton-on-Swale Nature Reserve
Catterick
CATARACTONIVM
Michael Siddal C of E Prim Sch
Walkerville
Home Farm
HIGH ST
SWALE PASTURE LA
Ellerton
SLED LA
SPRINGS LA
Ford
Manor House
HIGH GN
LOW GN
North Farm
Sour Beck
Horse Park Wood
Brough Hall
Camp Plantation
Brough Beck
THE BANK
SLESSOR RD
BACKSIDE
ORAN LA
River Swale
Norway Wood
Plodmire Wood
Ellery Hill
Tunstall Road Bridge
POCOCK PL
HARDEY RD
LEECH LA
Sewage Works
Manor House
High Cowstand Bridge
TUNSTALL ROAD
YARDE AV
SANDERS WY
LOCK WK
HOWE AVE
Castle Hills
BRECKENBROUGH LA
Breckenbrough
Prospect Hill
Bainesse
Cowstand Farm
Airfield
Wintylow
Limekiln Wood
CATTERICK LA
Little Plantation
Mount Pleasant
Tunstall Road Farm
Tunstall Beck
Lime Kiln Farm
Fox Covert
Lowdon House
BACK LA
Sewage Works
Killerby Hall
Manor House
JAMES LANE
YARBOROUGH CL 1
THE GARTH 2
PH
Barkers Barn Farm
Manor House Farm
LEASES LANE
Killerby Farm
Tunstall
Mayfield Farm
East Appleton Farm
East Appleton
Leases Farm
Hill Farm
Pikehill
Tunstall Moor
MOOR LANE
Low Pasture
LOW STREET
Sowber Hill Farm
Tumulus
Rudd Hall Farm
Highfield Farm
Westfield Farm
Rudd Hall
Craggs Lane Farm
Belmont
Kennel Whin
West Appleton
Winterfield House
GYLL HALL LA
Ghyll Hall
West Appleton Farm
New Covert Plantation
Goskins Plantation
Goskins
CRAGGS LA
Sandhole Covert
Gashouse Plantation
DL8
LORDS LANE
8 01 7 00 6 99 5 98 4 97 3 96 2 95 1 94
20 21 22 23 24 25
62
42
E4
1 SYDALL'S WY
2 KILLERBY DR
3 ST ANNE'S CR
4 CHAPEL RIGGS
5 BENNIONS WY
6 PER ARDUA WY
7 CENTURIAN CL
8 SLESSOR RD
9 HARRIS DR
10 YOUNGS WY
11 GRUNDY WY
12 GODFREY RD
13 ROBINSON RD
14 FULLER-GOOD RD
15 STRAFFORD RD
16 MELLERSH RD
17 CHACKSFIELD RD
18 LYDFORD RD

41
22

Scale: 1¾ inches to 1 mile

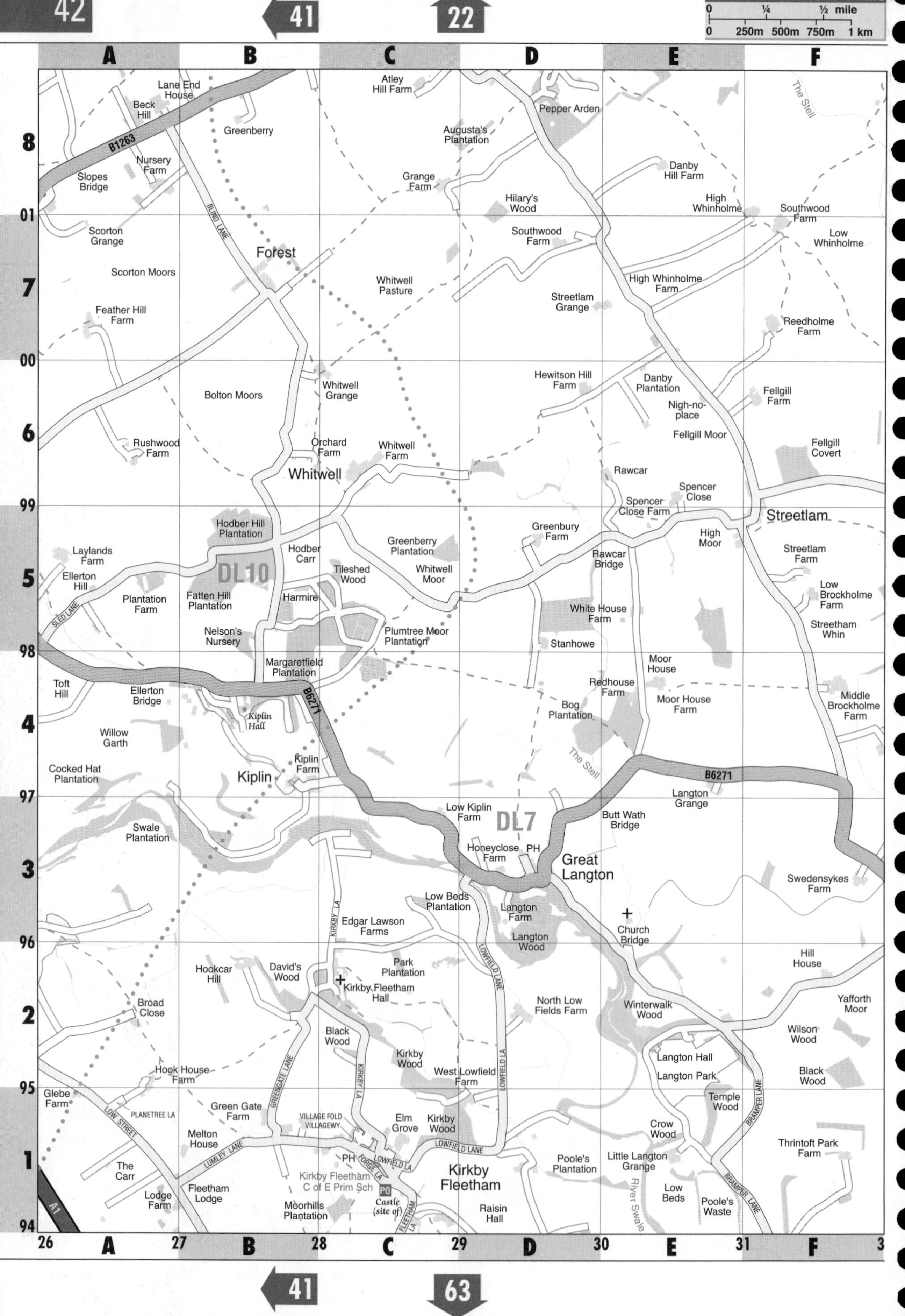

41
63

23
44

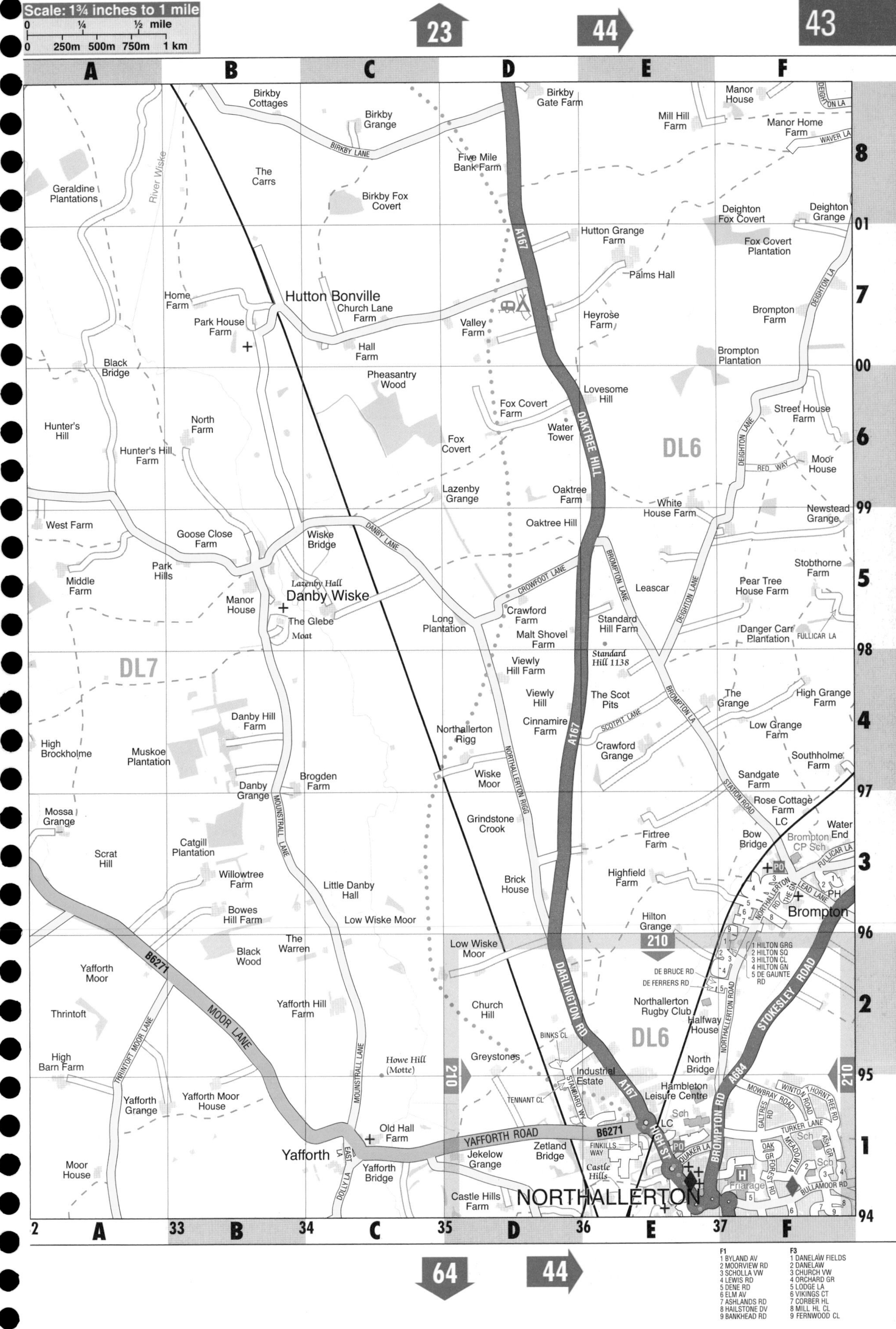

64
44

F1
1 BYLAND AV
2 MOORVIEW RD
3 SCHOLLA VW
4 LEWIS RD
5 DENE RD
6 ELM AV
7 ASHLANDS RD
8 HAILSTONE DV
9 BANKHEAD RD

F3
1 DANELAW FIELDS
2 DANELAW
3 CHURCH VW
4 ORCHARD GR
5 LODGE LA
6 VIKINGS CT
7 CORBER HL
8 MILL HL CL
9 FERNWOOD CL

43 24

Scale: 1¾ inches to 1 mile
0 ¼ ½ mile
0 250m 500m 750m 1 km

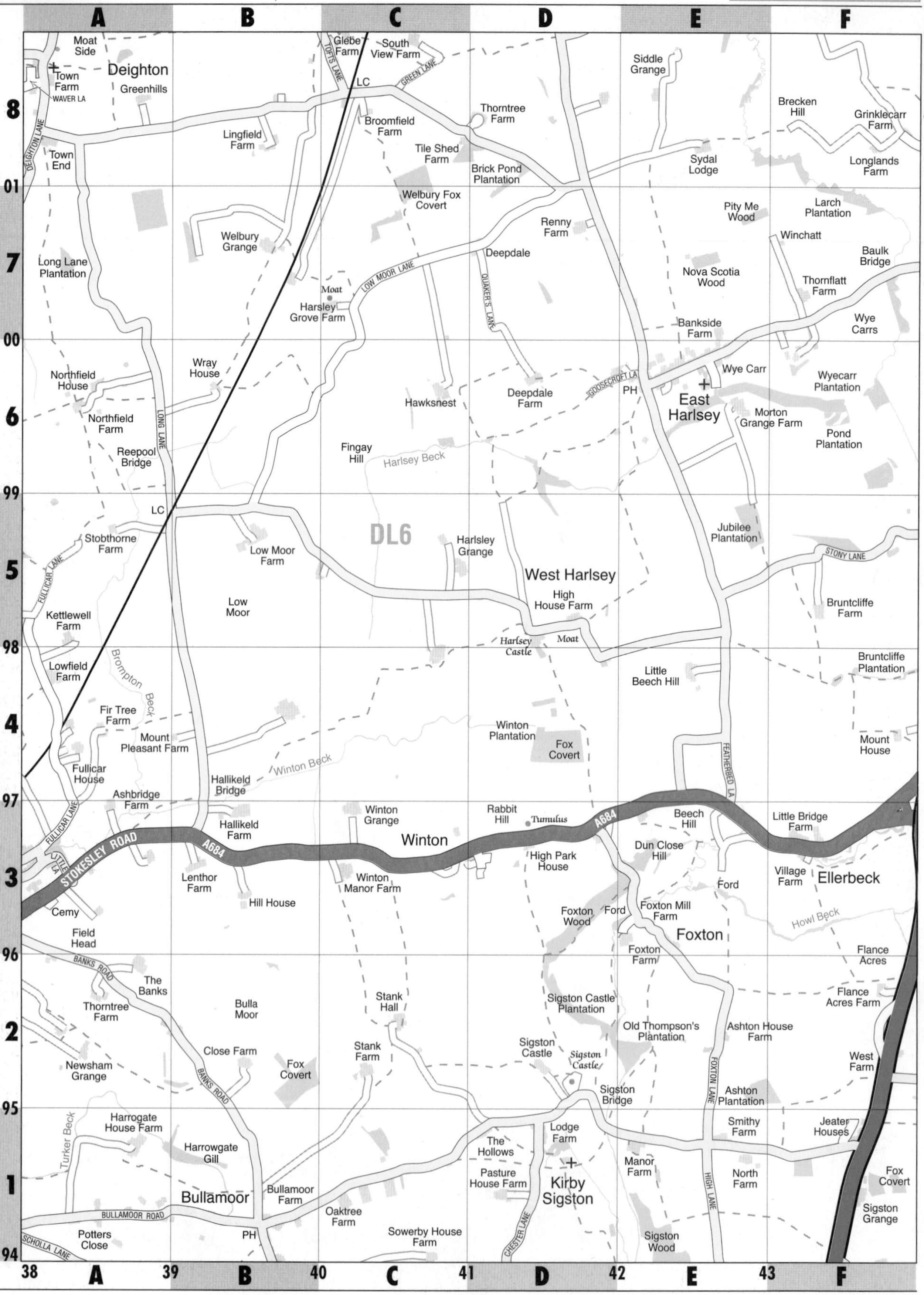

A B C D E F

Moat Side
Town Farm
Deighton
Greenhills
WAVER LA
Glebe Farm
TOFTS LANE
South View Farm
GREEN LANE
LC
Siddle Grange
8
DEIGHTON LANE
Lingfield Farm
Broomfield Farm
Thorntree Farm
Brecken Hill
Grinklecarr Farm
Town End
Tile Shed Farm
Brick Pond Plantation
Sydal Lodge
Longlands Farm
01
Welbury Fox Covert
Pity Me Wood
Larch Plantation
Renny Farm
Welbury Grange
Winchatt
Baulk Bridge
7
Long Lane Plantation
Deepdale
LOW MOOR LANE
QUAKER'S LANE
Moat
Nova Scotia Wood
Thornflatt Farm
Harsley Grove Farm
Bankside Farm
Wye Carrs
00
Northfield House
Wray House
GOOSECROFT LA
PH
Wye Carr
Wyecarr Plantation
Hawksnest
Deepdale Farm
East Harlsey
6
Northfield Farm
LONG LANE
Morton Grange Farm
Pond Plantation
Reepool Bridge
Fingay Hill
Harlsey Beck
99
LC
Jubilee Plantation
Stobthorne Farm
DL6
Harlsey Grange
STONY LANE
Low Moor Farm
5
FULLICAR LANE
West Harlsey
Low Moor
High House Farm
Bruntcliffe Farm
Kettlewell Farm
98
Harlsey Castle
Moat
Bruntcliffe Plantation
Lowfield Farm
Brompton Beck
Little Beech Hill
Fir Tree Farm
4
Winton Plantation
Mount Pleasant Farm
Fox Covert
Mount House
Fullicar House
Winton Beck
FEATHERBED LA
Hallikeld Bridge
97
Ashbridge Farm
Winton Grange
Rabbit Hill
Tumulus
Beech Hill
Little Bridge Farm
FULLICAR LANE
Hallikeld Farm
A684
Winton
Dun Close Hill
STOKESLEY ROAD
A684
LITTLE LA
High Park House
3
Lenthor Farm
Winton Manor Farm
Village Farm
Ellerbeck
Ford
Hill House
Cemy
Foxton Wood
Ford
Foxton Mill Farm
Howl Beck
Field Head
Foxton
96
Foxton Farm
Flance Acres
BANKS ROAD
The Banks
Stank Hall
Sigston Castle Plantation
Flance Acres Farm
Thorntree Farm
Bulla Moor
2
Old Thompson's Plantation
Ashton House Farm
Close Farm
Stank Farm
Sigston Castle
Sigston Castle
Newsham Grange
Fox Covert
West Farm
BANKS ROAD
FOXTON LANE
95
Sigston Bridge
Ashton Plantation
Turker Beck
Harrogate House Farm
Lodge Farm
Smithy Farm
Jeater Houses
Harrowgate Gill
The Hollows
1
Manor Farm
Fox Covert
Pasture House Farm
Kirby Sigston
North Farm
Bullamoor
Bullamoor Farm
HIGH LANE
Sigston Grange
BULLAMOOR ROAD
Oaktree Farm
CHESTER LANE
Potters Close
PH
Sowerby House Farm
Sigston Wood
SCHOLLA LANE
94

38 A 39 B 40 C 41 D 42 E 43 F

43 65

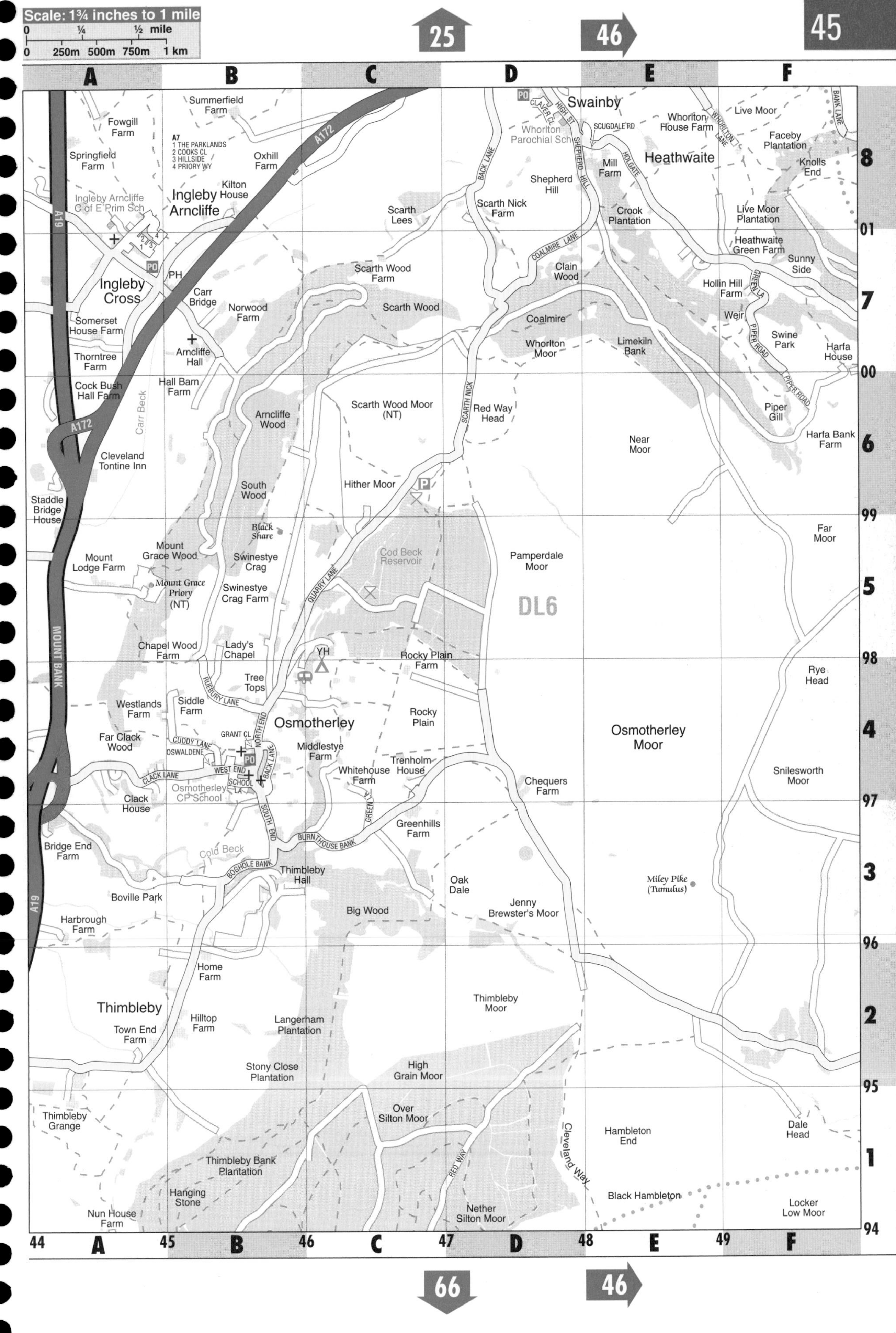

Scale: 1¾ inches to 1 mile
0 ¼ ½ mile
0 250m 500m 750m 1 km
25
46
A B C D E F
Summerfield Farm
Fowgill Farm
Springfield Farm
A7
1 THE PARKLANDS
2 COOKS CL
3 HILLSIDE
4 PRIORY WY
Oxhill Farm
Kilton House
Ingleby Arncliffe
Ingleby Arncliffe C of E Prim Sch
A172
A19
Ingleby Cross
PH
Carr Bridge
Norwood Farm
Somerset House Farm
Thorntree Farm
Arncliffe Hall
Cock Bush Hall Farm
Hall Barn Farm
Carr Beck
Cleveland Tontine Inn
Staddle Bridge House
Arncliffe Wood
South Wood
Black Share
Mount Lodge Farm
Mount Grace Wood
Mount Grace Priory (NT)
Swinestye Crag
Swinestye Crag Farm
Chapel Wood Farm
Lady's Chapel
Tree Tops
RUEBURY LANE
Westlands Farm
Siddle Farm
Far Clack Wood
CUDDY LANE
GRANT CL
OSWALDENE
NORTH END
BACK LANE
WEST END
CLACK LANE
SCHOOL LA
Osmotherley CP School
Clack House
SOUTH END
Osmotherley
MOUNT BANK
Bridge End Farm
Cold Beck
BOGHOLE BANK
Thimbleby Hall
Boville Park
Harbrough Farm
Home Farm
Thimbleby
Town End Farm
Hilltop Farm
Langerham Plantation
Stony Close Plantation
Thimbleby Grange
Thimbleby Bank Plantation
Hanging Stone
Nun House Farm
Scarth Lees
Scarth Wood Farm
Scarth Wood
Scarth Wood Moor (NT)
Hither Moor
QUARRY LANE
Cod Beck Reservoir
YH
Middlestye Farm
Whitehouse Farm
GREEN LA
Trenholm House
BURN HOUSE BANK
Greenhills Farm
Big Wood
Oak Dale
Rocky Plain Farm
Rocky Plain
High Grain Moor
Over Silton Moor
RED WAY
Nether Silton Moor
PO
Swainby
CLAVER CL
HIGH ST
Whorlton Parochial Sch
SCUGDALE RD
SHEPHERD HILL
BACK LANE
Shepherd Hill
Mill Farm
HOLGATE
Scarth Nick Farm
COALMIRE LANE
Clain Wood
Coalmire
Whorlton Moor
SCARTH NICK
Red Way Head
Pamperdale Moor
DL6
Chequers Farm
Jenny Brewster's Moor
Thimbleby Moor
Cleveland Way
Whorlton House Farm
WHORLTON LANE
Heathwaite
Crook Plantation
Limekiln Bank
Live Moor
Faceby Plantation
BANK LANE
Knolls End
Live Moor Plantation
Heathwaite Green Farm
Sunny Side
Hollin Hill Farm
GREEN LA
Weir
PIPER ROAD
Swine Park
Harfa House
Piper Gill
Harfa Bank Farm
Near Moor
Far Moor
Rye Head
Osmotherley Moor
Snilesworth Moor
Miley Pike (Tumulus)
Hambleton End
Dale Head
Black Hambleton
Locker Low Moor
8 01 7 00 6 99 5 98 4 97 3 96 2 95 1 94
44 45 46 47 48 49
66
46

45
26

Scale: 1¾ inches to 1 mile

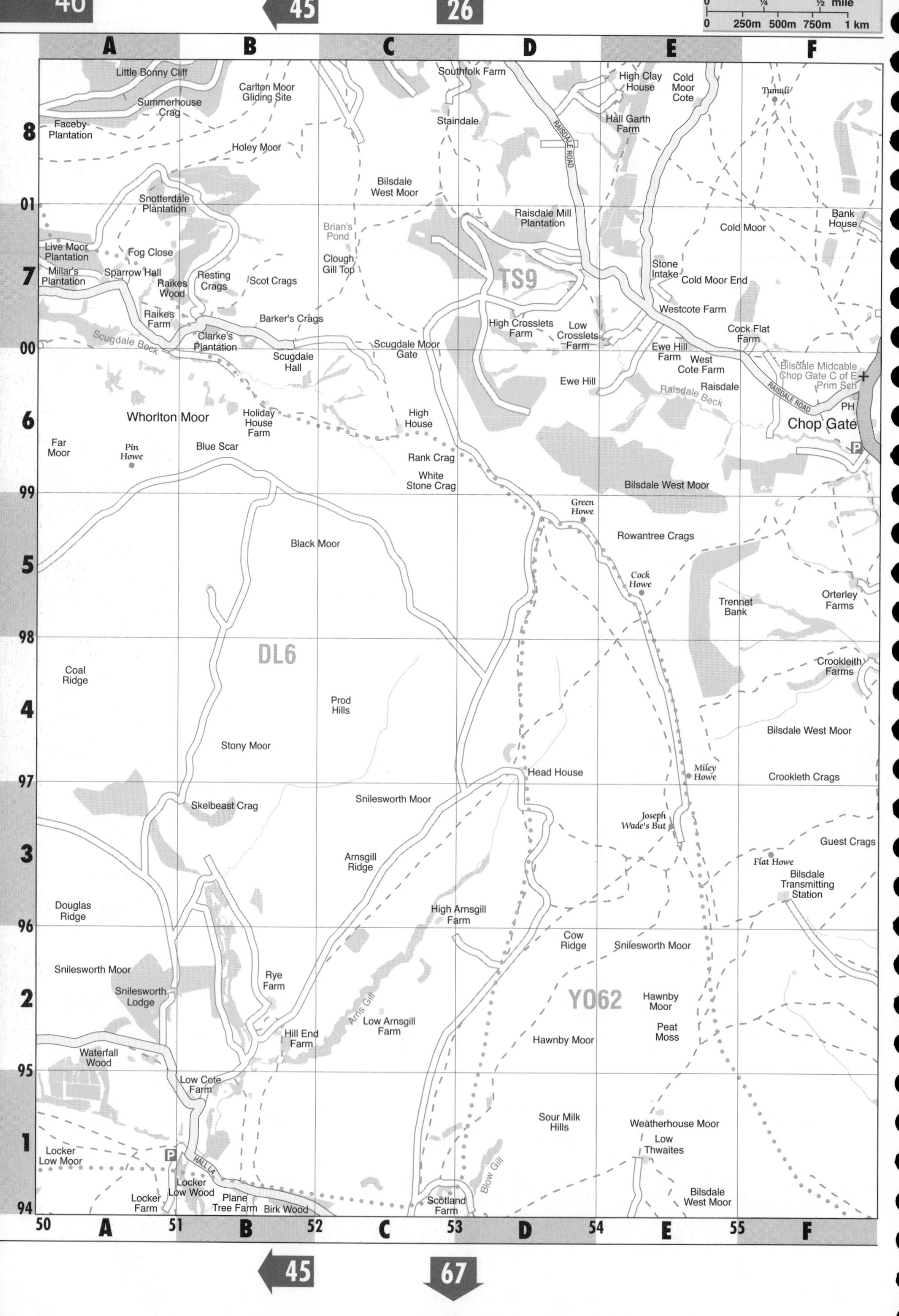

45
67

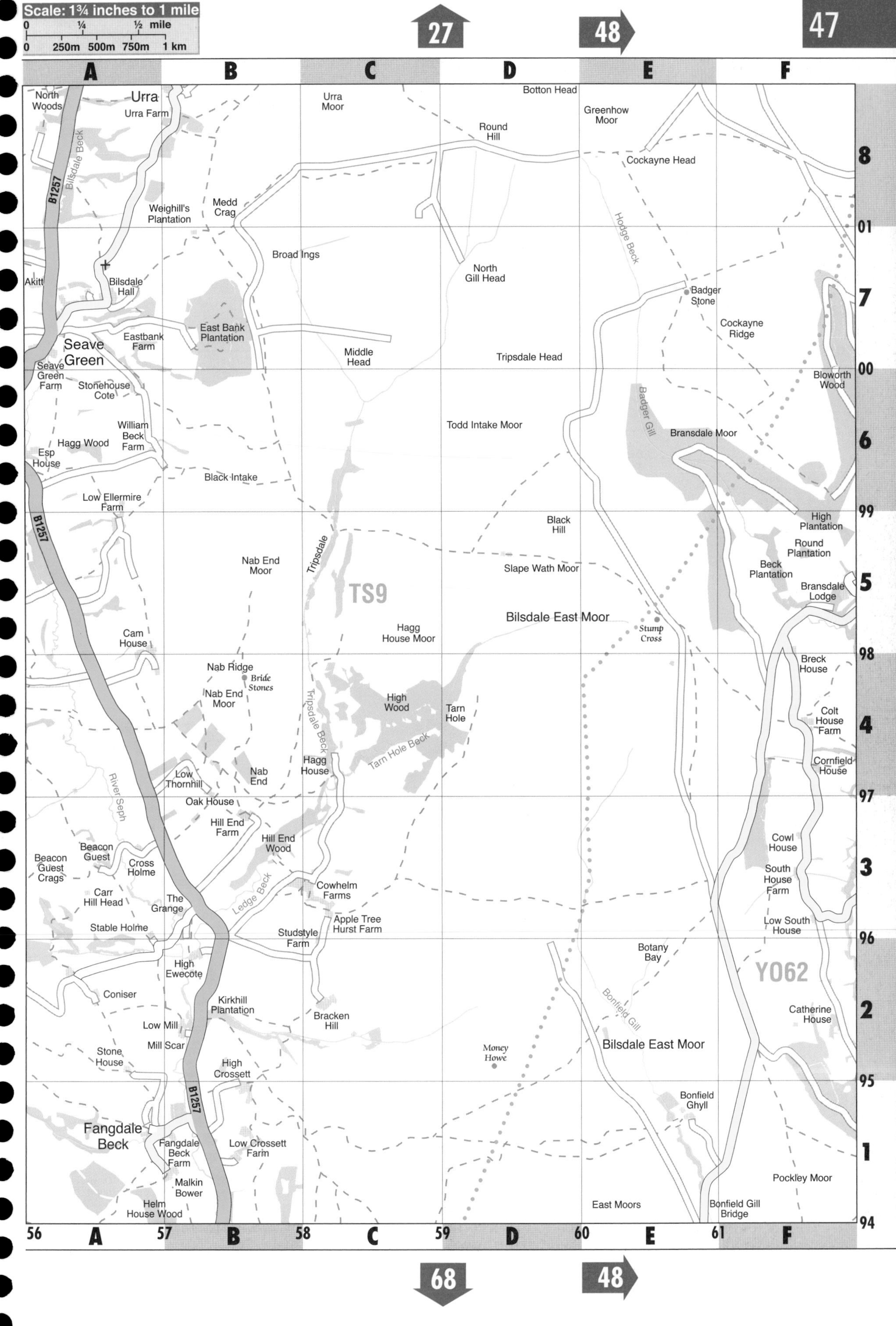
Scale: 1¾ inches to 1 mile
0 ¼ ½ mile
0 250m 500m 750m 1 km
27
48
A B C D E F
North Woods
Urra
Urra Farm
Urra Moor
Botton Head
Greenhow Moor
Round Hill
Cockayne Head
Bilsdale Beck
B1257
Weighill's Plantation
Medd Crag
Hodge Beck
Broad Ings
North Gill Head
Akitt
Bilsdale Hall
Badger Stone
Cockayne Ridge
Eastbank Farm
East Bank Plantation
Seave Green
Middle Head
Tripsdale Head
Seave Green Farm
Stonehouse Cote
Bloworth Wood
Badger Gill
William Beck Farm
Todd Intake Moor
Bransdale Moor
Hagg Wood
Esp House
Black Intake
Low Ellermire Farm
High Plantation
Black Hill
Round Plantation
Tripsdale
Nab End Moor
Slape Wath Moor
Beck Plantation
TS9
Bransdale Lodge
Bilsdale East Moor
Cam House
Hagg House Moor
Stump Cross
Breck House
Nab Ridge
Bride Stones
Nab End Moor
Tripsdale Beck
High Wood
Tarn Hole
Colt House Farm
Tarn Hole Beck
Hagg House
Nab End
Low Thornhill
Cornfield House
River Seph
Oak House
Hill End Farm
Hill End Wood
Cowl House
Beacon Guest
Beacon Guest Crags
Cross Holme
South House Farm
Ledge Beck
Cowhelm Farms
Carr Hill Head
The Grange
Apple Tree Hurst Farm
Low South House
Stable Holme
Studstyle Farm
Botany Bay
High Ewecote
YO62
Coniser
Kirkhill Plantation
Bonfield Gill
Catherine House
Bracken Hill
Low Mill
Mill Scar
Money Howe
Bilsdale East Moor
Stone House
High Crossett
Bonfield Ghyll
Fangdale Beck
Fangdale Beck Farm
Low Crossett Farm
Malkin Bower
Pockley Moor
Helm House Wood
East Moors
Bonfield Gill Bridge
8 01 7 00 6 99 5 98 4 97 3 96 2 95 1 94
56 57 58 59 60 61
68
48

47
28

Scale: 1¾ inches to 1 mile

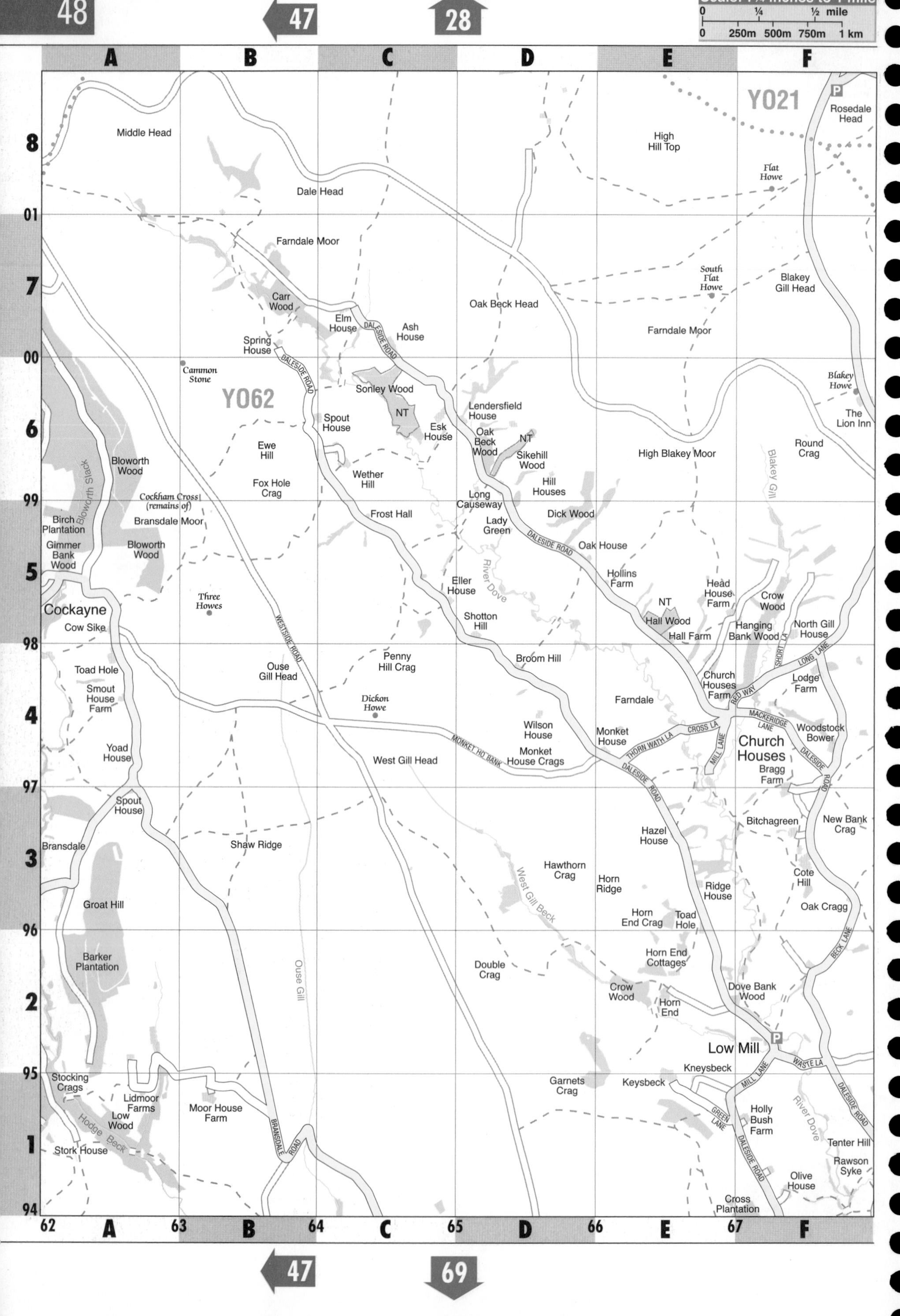

47
69

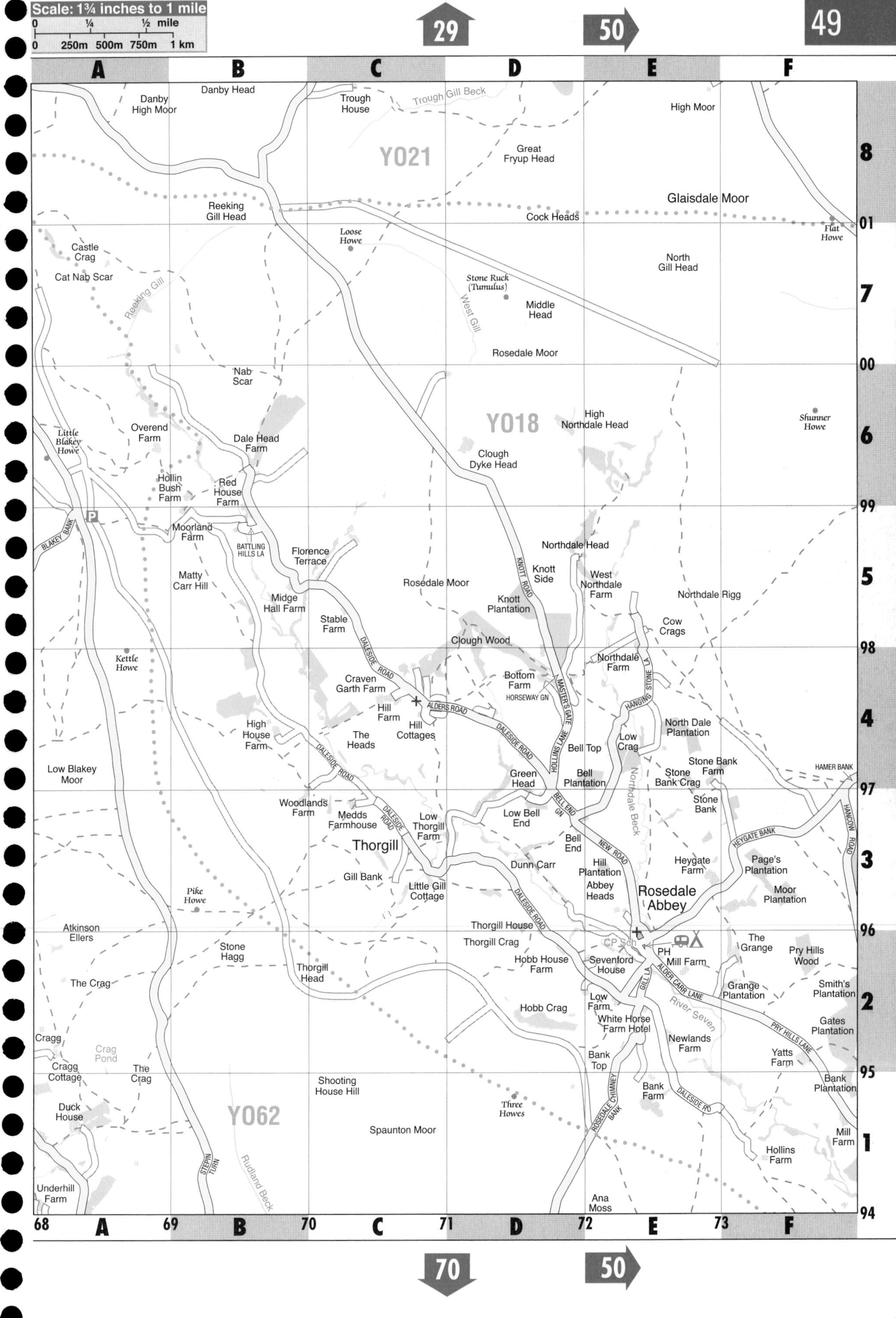
Scale: 1¾ inches to 1 mile
0 ¼ ½ mile
0 250m 500m 750m 1 km
29
50
A B C D E F
Danby High Moor
Danby Head
Trough House
Trough Gill Beck
High Moor
YO21
Great Fryup Head
Glaisdale Moor
Reeking Gill Head
Cock Heads
Flat Howe
Castle Crag
Loose Howe
North Gill Head
Cat Nab Scar
Reeking Gill
Stone Ruck (Tumulus)
West Gill
Middle Head
Rosedale Moor
Nab Scar
YO18
High Northdale Head
Shunner Howe
Little Blakey Howe
Overend Farm
Dale Head Farm
Clough Dyke Head
Hollin Bush Farm
Red House Farm
P
Blakey Bank
Moorland Farm
Battling Hills La
Northdale Head
Florence Terrace
Knott Road
Knott Side
West Northdale Farm
Matty Carr Hill
Rosedale Moor
Northdale Rigg
Midge Hall Farm
Knott Plantation
Stable Farm
Cow Crags
Clough Wood
Kettle Howe
Daleside Road
Northdale Farm
Bottom Farm
Craven Garth Farm
Horseway Gn
Master's Gate
Stone La
Hill Farm
Alders Road
Hanging
High House Farm
Hill Cottages
North Dale Plantation
Low Crag
The Heads
Daleside Road
Hollins Lane
Bell Top
Low Blakey Moor
Stone Bank Farm
Daleside Road
Green Head
Bell Plantation
Stone Bank Crag
Hamer Bank
Northdale Beck
Woodlands Farm
Bell End Gn
Stone Bank
Medds Farmhouse
Daleside Road
Low Thorgill Farm
Low Bell End
Hancow Road
Heygate Bank
Thorgill
Bell End
New Road
Dunn Carr
Hill Plantation
Heygate Farm
Page's Plantation
Gill Bank
Pike Howe
Little Gill Cottage
Abbey Heads
Rosedale Abbey
Moor Plantation
Daleside Road
Atkinson Ellers
Thorgill House
Thorgill Crag
CP Sch
The Grange
Stone Hagg
PH
Pry Hills Wood
Hobb House Farm
Sevenford House
Mill Farm
Thorgill Head
The Crag
Gill La
Alder Carr Lane
Grange Plantation
Smith's Plantation
Low Farm
Hobb Crag
River Seven
White Horse Farm Hotel
Gates Plantation
Pry Hills Lane
Cragg
Crag Pond
Newlands Farm
Bank Top
Yatts Farm
Cragg Cottage
The Crag
Shooting House Hill
Bank Plantation
Rosedale Chimney Bank
Bank Farm
Daleside Rd
Duck House
YO62
Three Howes
Spaunton Moor
Mill Farm
Stepin Turn
Rudland Beck
Hollins Farm
Underhill Farm
Ana Moss
8
01
7
00
6
99
5
98
4
97
3
96
2
95
1
94
68 69 70 71 72 73
70
50

49
30

Scale: 1¾ inches to 1 mile

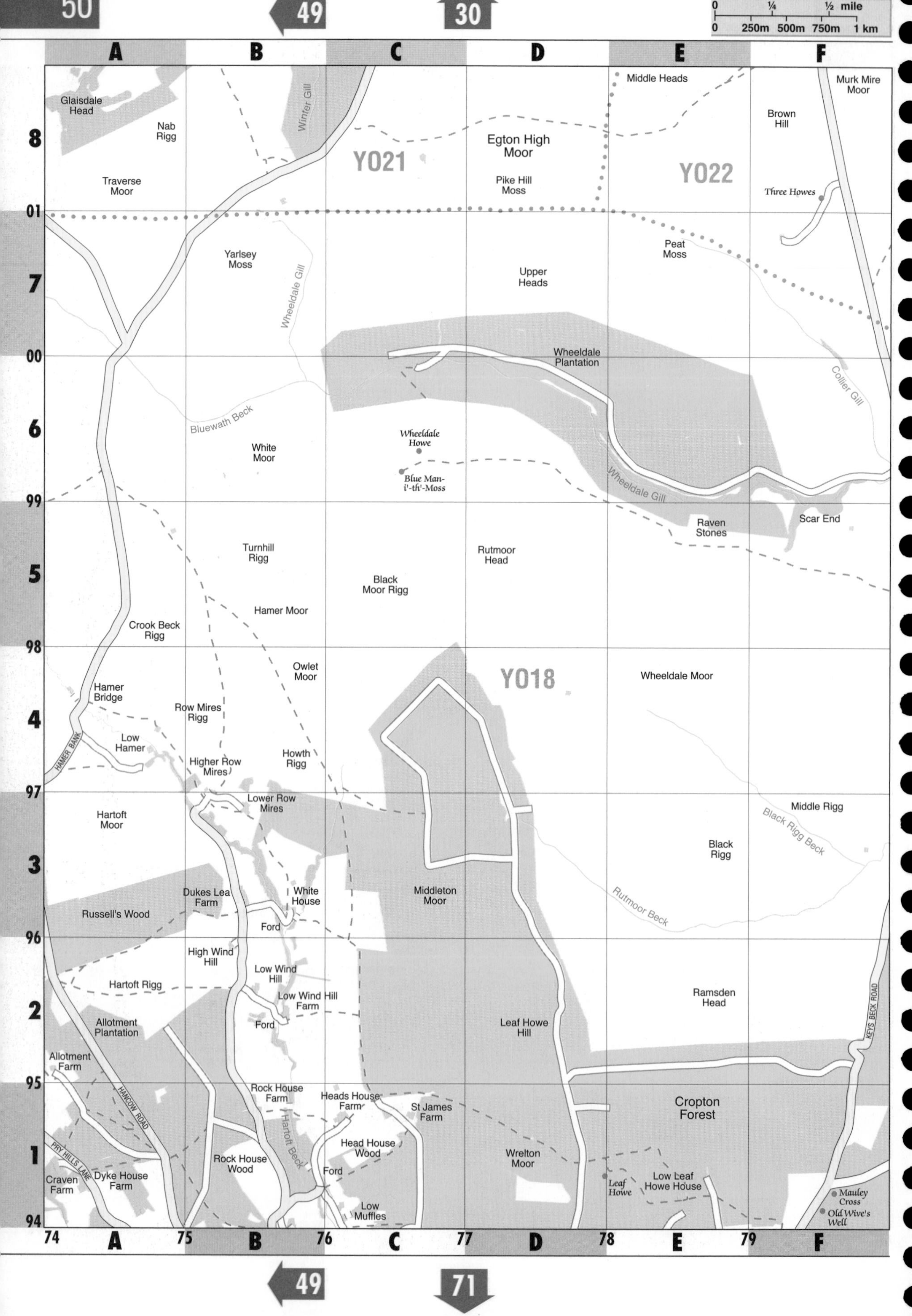

49
71

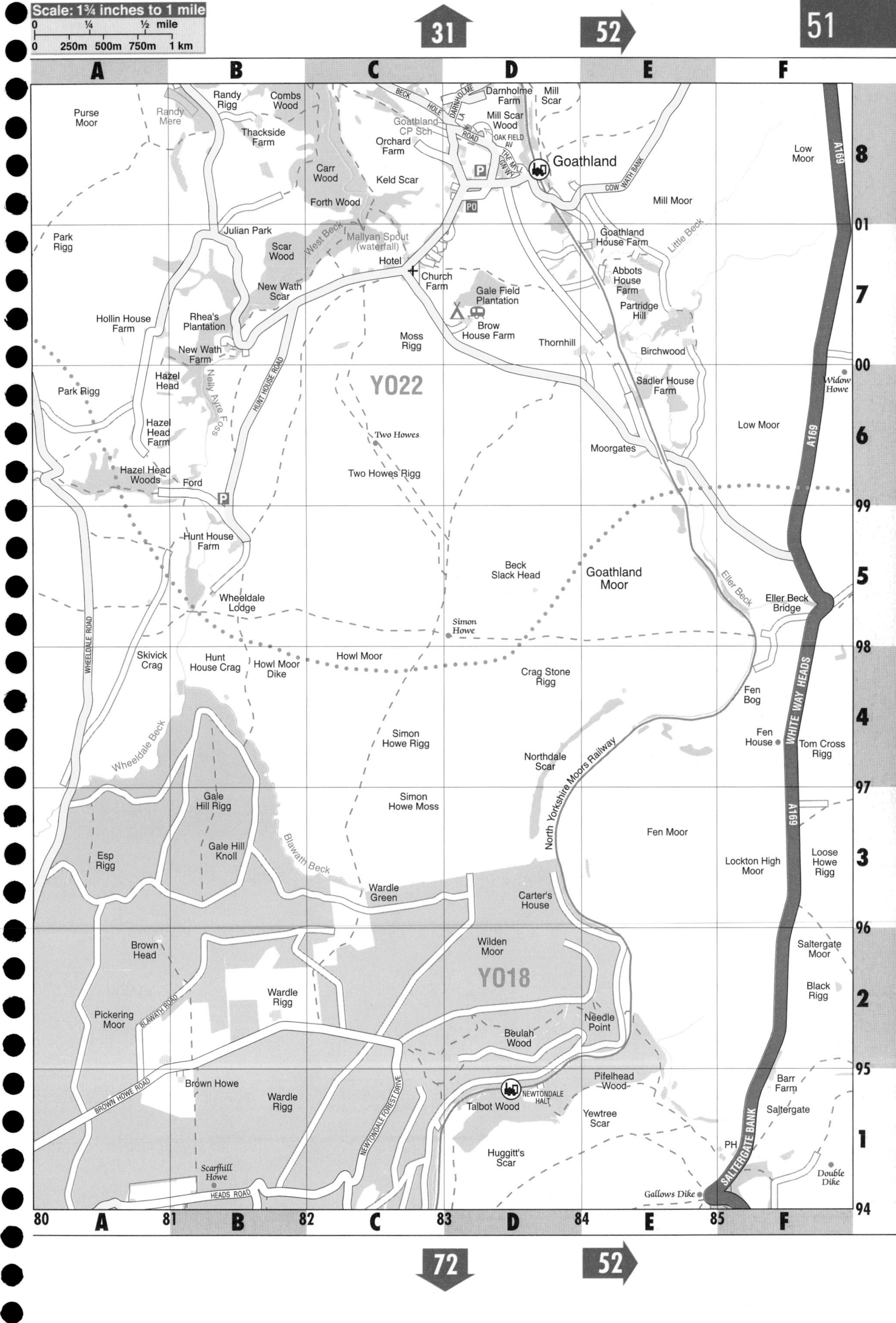

Scale: 1¾ inches to 1 mile
0 ¼ ½ mile
0 250m 500m 750m 1 km
31
52
A B C D E F
Purse Moor
Randy Mere
Randy Rigg
Combs Wood
Thackside Farm
Goathland CP Sch
Darnholme Farm
Mill Scar
Mill Scar Wood
Orchard Farm
Goathland
Low Moor
Carr Wood
Keld Scar
Forth Wood
Mill Moor
Park Rigg
Julian Park
Scar Wood
West Beck
Mallyan Spout (waterfall)
Goathland House Farm
Little Beck
Hotel
Church Farm
Abbots House Farm
New Wath Scar
Gale Field Plantation
Partridge Hill
Hollin House Farm
Rhea's Plantation
Brow House Farm
Moss Rigg
Thornhill
New Wath Farm
Birchwood
Hazel Head
Park Rigg
YO22
Sadler House Farm
Widow Howe
Nelly Ayre Foss
Hazel Head Farm
HUNT HOUSE ROAD
Two Howes
Low Moor
Moorgates
Hazel Head Woods
Ford
Two Howes Rigg
A169
Hunt House Farm
Beck Slack Head
Goathland Moor
Eller Beck
Eller Beck Bridge
Wheeldale Lodge
Simon Howe
WHEELDALE ROAD
Skivick Crag
Hunt House Crag
Howl Moor Dike
Howl Moor
Crag Stone Rigg
Fen Bog
Wheeldale Beck
Simon Howe Rigg
Northdale Scar
North Yorkshire Moors Railway
Fen House
Tom Cross Rigg
WHITE WAY HEADS
Gale Hill Rigg
Simon Howe Moss
Fen Moor
Gale Hill Knoll
Blawath Beck
Esp Rigg
Lockton High Moor
Loose Howe Rigg
Wardle Green
Carter's House
Brown Head
Wilden Moor
Saltergate Moor
YO18
Black Rigg
Wardle Rigg
Pickering Moor
BLAWATH ROAD
Needle Point
Beulah Wood
Brown Howe
Pifelhead Wood
Barr Farm
Wardle Rigg
BROWN HOWE ROAD
NEWTONDALE FOREST DRIVE
Talbot Wood
NEWTONDALE HALT
Yewtree Scar
Saltergate
SALTERGATE BANK
PH
Huggitt's Scar
Scarfhill Howe
HEADS ROAD
Gallows Dike
Double Dike
80 81 82 83 84 85
8 01 7 00 6 99 5 98 4 97 3 96 2 95 1 94
72
52

51
32

Scale: 1¾ inches to 1 mile

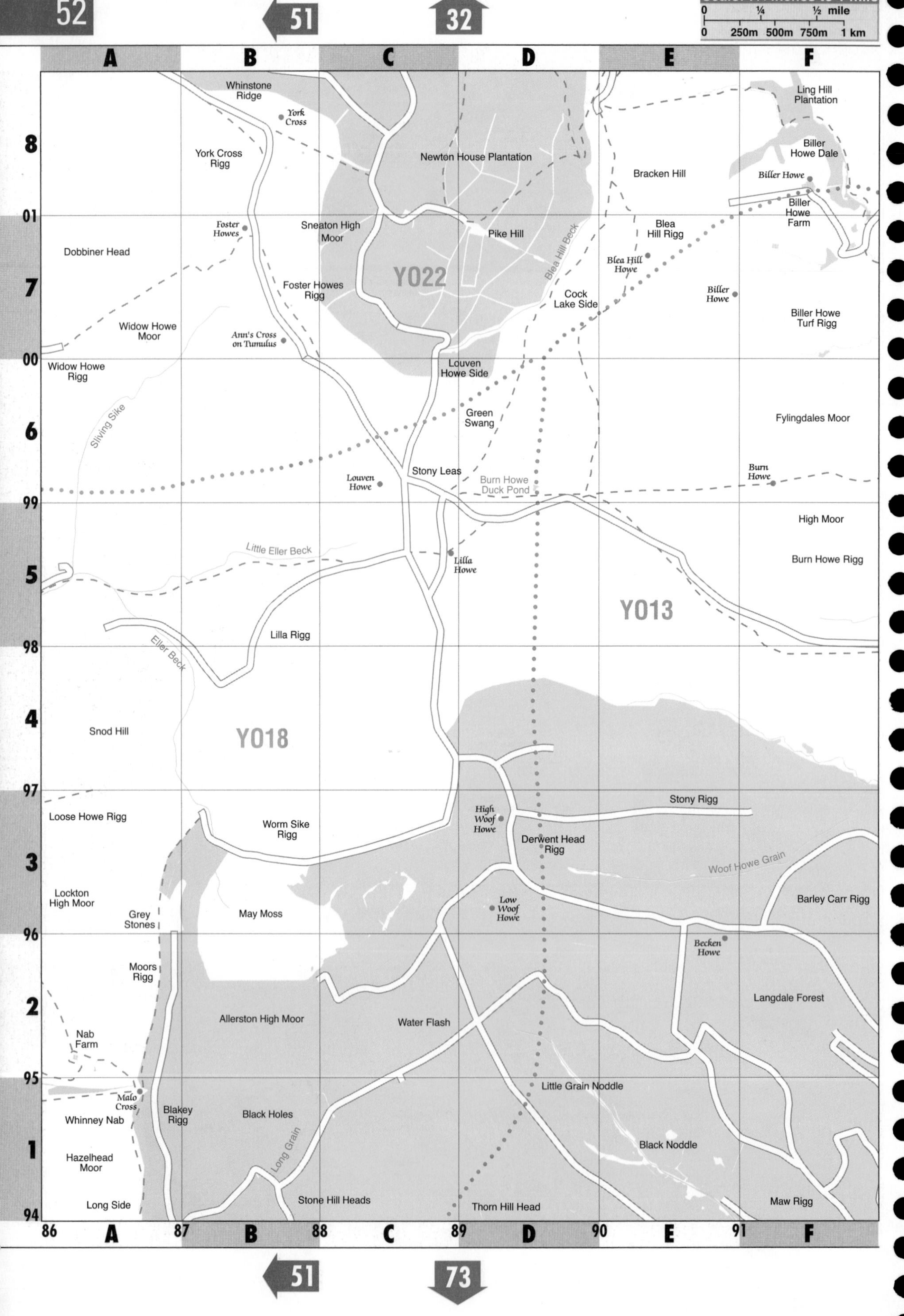

51
73

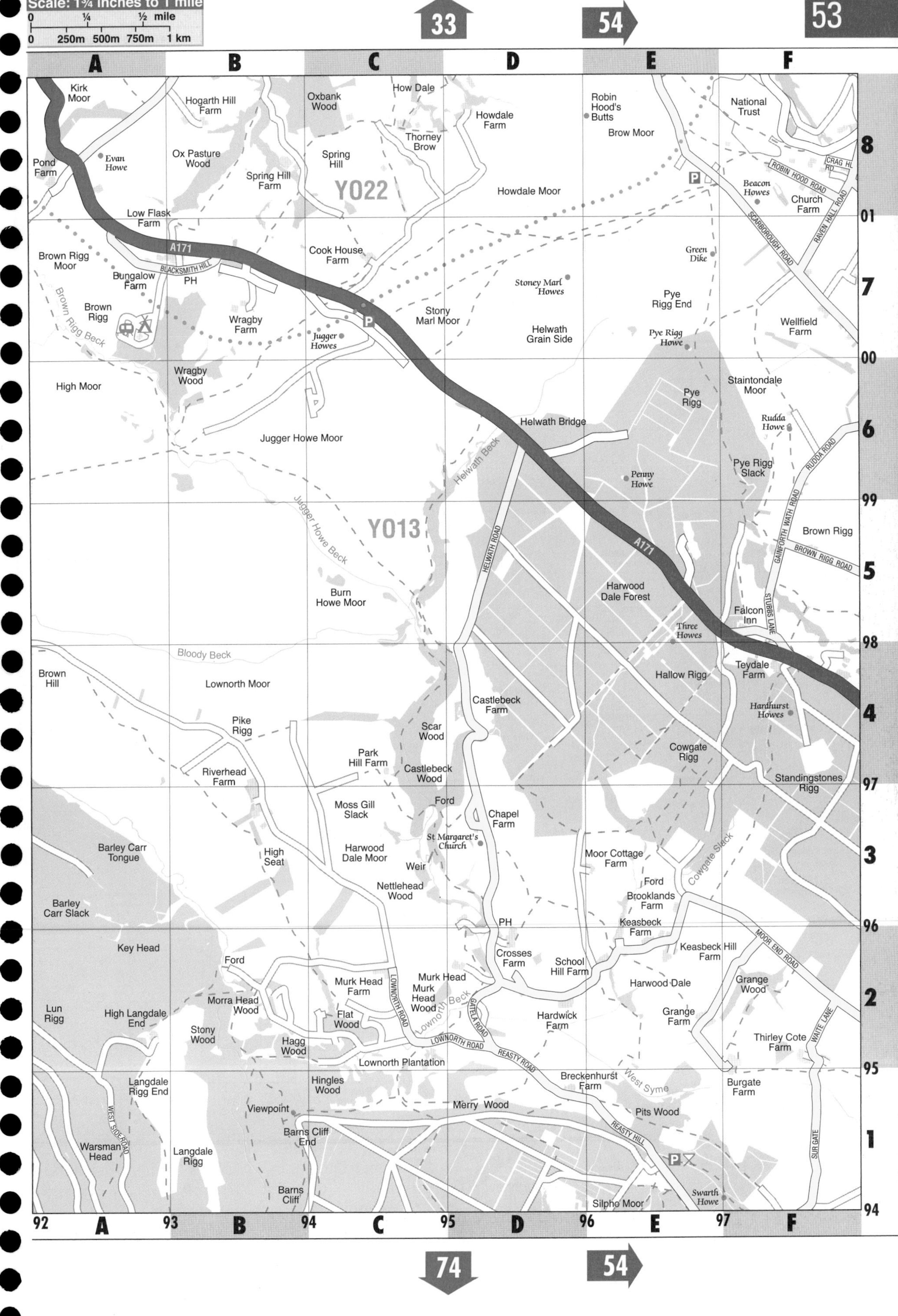

Scale: 1¾ inches to 1 mile
0 ¼ ½ mile
0 250m 500m 750m 1 km
33
54
A B C D E F
Kirk Moor
Hogarth Hill Farm
Oxbank Wood
How Dale
Robin Hood's Butts
National Trust
Howdale Farm
Thorney Brow
Brow Moor
Pond Farm
Evan Howe
Ox Pasture Wood
Spring Hill
Spring Hill Farm
YO22
Howdale Moor
Crag Hl Rd
Robin Hood Road
Beacon Howes
Church Farm
Raven Hall Road
Scarborough Road
Low Flask Farm
A171
Brown Rigg Moor
Blacksmith Hill
Cook House Farm
Green Dike
Bungalow Farm
PH
Stoney Marl Howes
Pye Rigg End
Brown Rigg
Wragby Farm
Stony Marl Moor
Wellfield Farm
Brown Rigg Beck
Jugger Howes
Helwath Grain Side
Pye Rigg Howe
Wragby Wood
Staintondale Moor
High Moor
Pye Rigg
Rudda Howe
Helwath Bridge
Jugger Howe Moor
Helwath Beck
Rudda Road
Pye Rigg Slack
Penny Howe
Gainforth Wath Road
Brown Rigg
Jugger Howe Beck
YO13
Helwath Road
Brown Rigg Road
Harwood Dale Forest
Burn Howe Moor
Falcon Inn
Stubbs Lane
Three Howes
Bloody Beck
Brown Hill
Lownorth Moor
Teydale Farm
Hallow Rigg
Castlebeck Farm
Hardhurst Howes
Pike Rigg
Scar Wood
Cowgate Rigg
Park Hill Farm
Castlebeck Wood
Riverhead Farm
Standingstones Rigg
Moss Gill Slack
Ford
Chapel Farm
Barley Carr Tongue
St Margaret's Church
High Seat
Harwood Dale Moor
Moor Cottage Farm
Cowgate Slack
Weir
Ford
Nettlehead Wood
Brooklands Farm
Barley Carr Slack
PH
Keasbeck Farm
Key Head
Ford
Crosses Farm
School Hill Farm
Keasbeck Hill Farm
Moor End Road
Murk Head
Murk Head Farm
Murk Head Wood
Harwood Dale
Grange Wood
Lownorth Road
Morra Head Wood
Lownorth Beck
Lun Rigg
High Langdale End
Flat Wood
Gatela Road
Hardwick Farm
Grange Farm
Waite Lane
Stony Wood
Hagg Wood
Lownorth Road
Reasty Road
Thirley Cote Farm
Lownorth Plantation
Langdale Rigg End
Hingles Wood
Breckenhurst Farm
West Syme
Burgate Farm
Viewpoint
Merry Wood
Pits Wood
West Side Road
Barns Cliff End
Reasty Hill
Warsman Head
Langdale Rigg
Sur Gate
Barns Cliff
Swarth Howe
Silpho Moor
8 01 7 00 6 99 5 98 4 97 3 96 2 95 1 94
92 93 94 95 96 97
74
54

Scale: 1¾ inches to 1 mile
0 ¼ ½ mile
0 250m 500m 750m 1 km

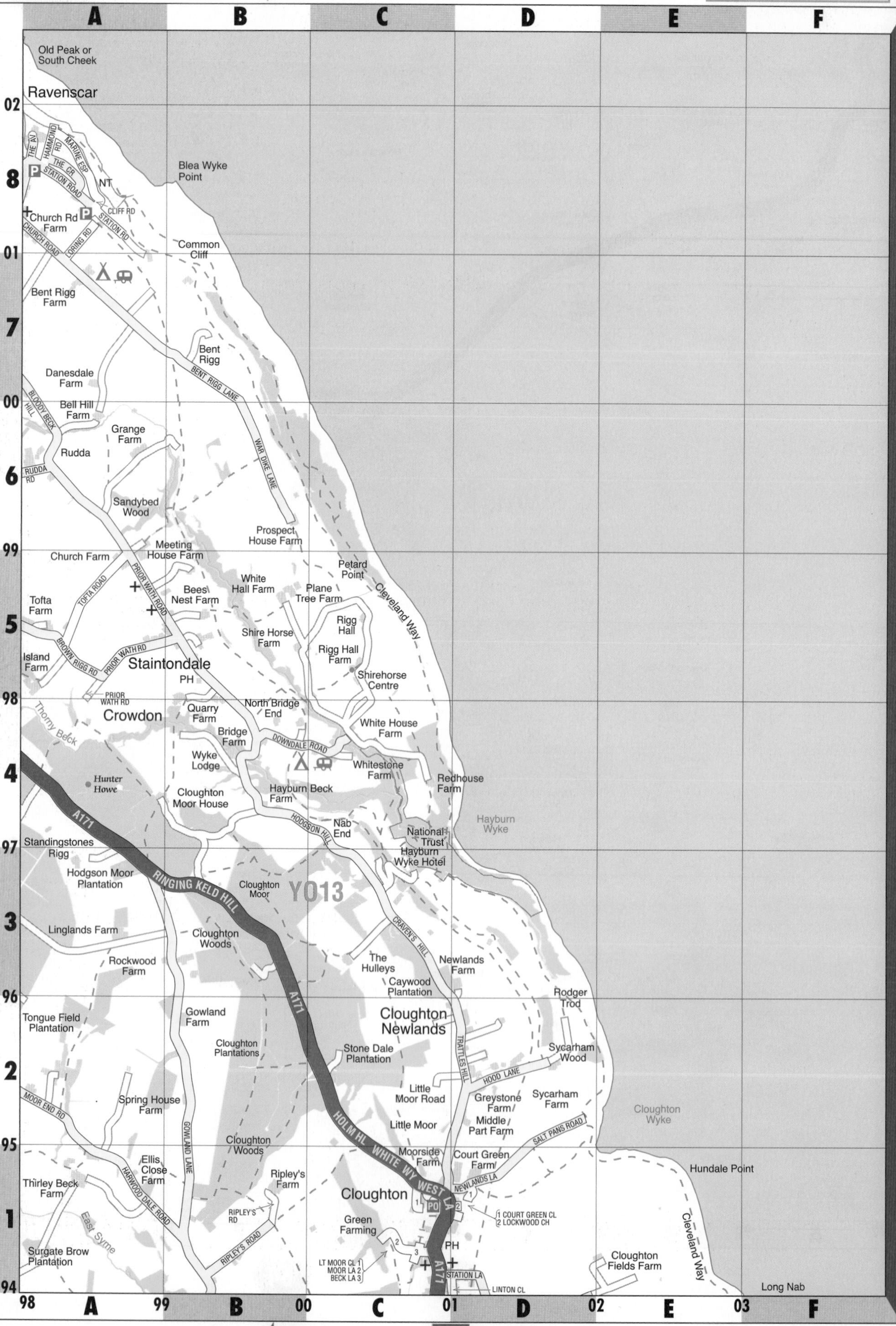

A B C D E F

Old Peak or South Cheek
Ravenscar
02
THE AV
HAMMOND RD
MARINE ESP
THE CR
STATION ROAD
8
NT
Blea Wyke Point
CLIFF RD
Church Rd Farm
STATION RD
CHURCH ROAD
LORING RD
01
Common Cliff
Bent Rigg Farm
7
Bent Rigg
BENT RIGG LANE
Danesdale Farm
BLOODY BECK HILL
00
Bell Hill Farm
Grange Farm
Rudda
WAR DIKE LANE
RUDDA RD
6
Sandybed Wood
Prospect House Farm
99
Church Farm
Meeting House Farm
Petard Point
TOFTA ROAD
PRIOR WATH ROAD
White Hall Farm
Plane Tree Farm
Cleveland Way
Tofta Farm
Bees Nest Farm
Rigg Hall
5
Shire Horse Farm
Rigg Hall Farm
BROWN RIGG RD
PRIOR WATH RD
Island Farm
Staintondale
Shirehorse Centre
PH
PRIOR WATH RD
98
Crowdon
Quarry Farm
North Bridge End
Thorny Beck
Bridge Farm
White House Farm
DOWNDALE ROAD
Wyke Lodge
Whitestone Farm
4
Hunter Howe
Redhouse Farm
Cloughton Moor House
Hayburn Beck Farm
Hayburn Wyke
A171
HODGSON HILL
Nab End
National Trust
97
Standingstones Rigg
Hayburn Wyke Hotel
Hodgson Moor Plantation
RINGING KELD HILL
Cloughton Moor
YO13
3
Linglands Farm
Cloughton Woods
CRAVEN'S HILL
The Hulleys
Newlands Farm
Rockwood Farm
Caywood Plantation
96
Rodger Trod
A171
Tongue Field Plantation
Gowland Farm
Cloughton Newlands
Cloughton Plantations
TRAITLES HILL
Sycarham Wood
Stone Dale Plantation
2
HOOD LANE
Little Moor Road
Greystone Farm
Sycarham Farm
MOOR END RD
Spring House Farm
Middle Part Farm
Cloughton Wyke
Little Moor
GOWLAND LANE
SALT PANS ROAD
HOLM HL
WHITE WY
WEST LA
95
Cloughton Woods
Moorside Farm
Court Green Farm
Ellis Close Farm
Hundale Point
Ripley's Farm
NEWLANDS LA
Thirley Beck Farm
Cloughton
HARWOOD DALE ROAD
PO
1
RIPLEY'S RD
1 COURT GREEN CL
2 LOCKWOOD CH
Green Farming
East Syme
PH
Cleveland Way
RIPLEY'S ROAD
LT MOOR CL 1
MOOR LA 2
BECK LA 3
Surgate Brow Plantation
Cloughton Fields Farm
A171
STATION LA
94
LINTON CL
Long Nab

98 A 99 B 00 C 01 D 02 E 03 F

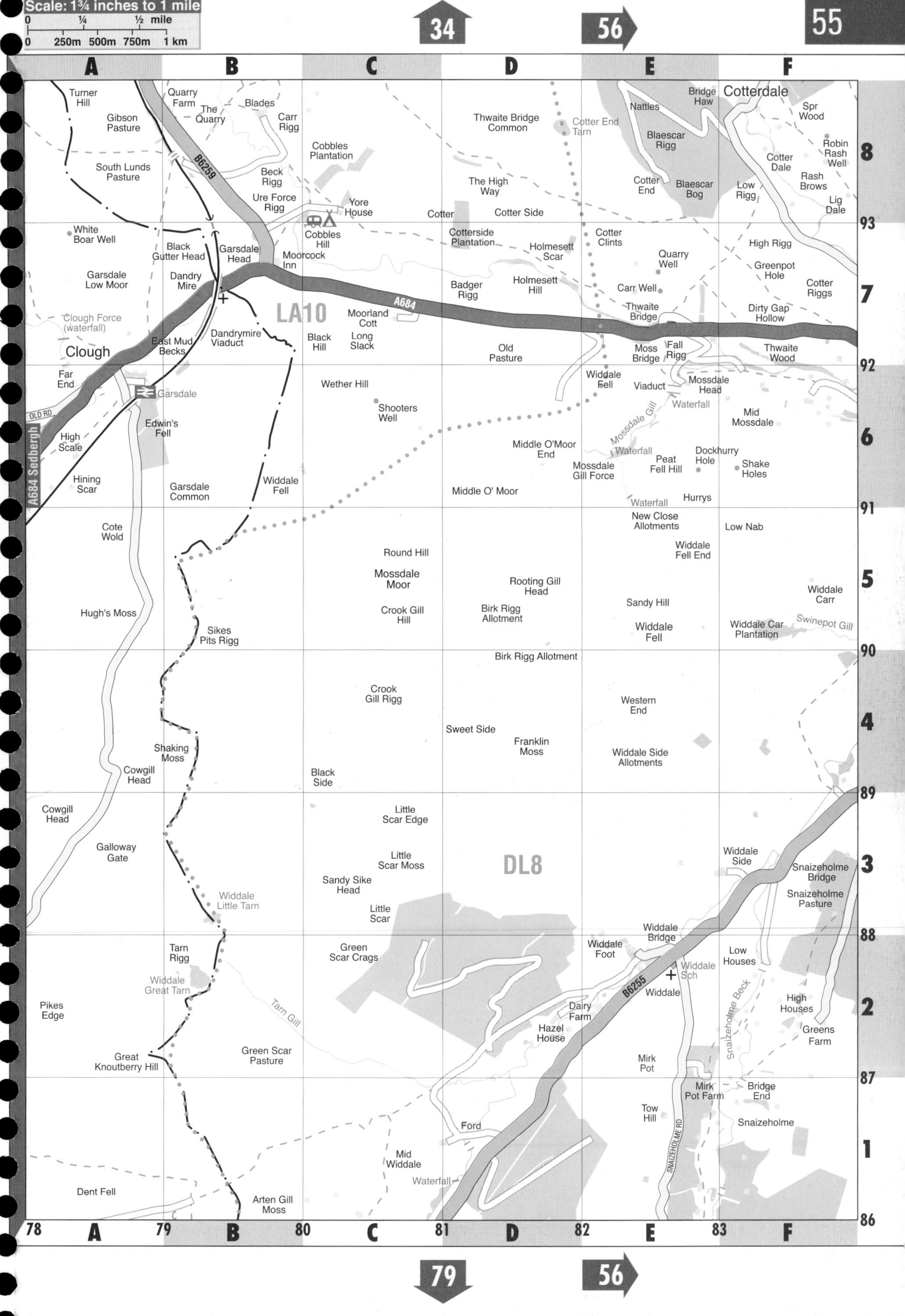
Scale: 1¾ inches to 1 mile
34
56
A
B
C
D
E
F
Turner Hill
Gibson Pasture
Quarry Farm
The Quarry
Blades
Carr Rigg
Cobbles Plantation
Thwaite Bridge Common
Cotter End Tarn
Nattles
Bridge Haw
Cotterdale
Spr Wood
Blaescar Rigg
Robin Rash Well
South Lunds Pasture
B6259
Beck Rigg
The High Way
Cotter End
Blaescar Bog
Cotter Dale
Low Rigg
Rash Brows
Ure Force Rigg
Yore House
Cotter
Cotter Side
Lig Dale
White Boar Well
Black Gutter Head
Garsdale Head
Cobbles Hill
Cotterside Plantation
Holmesett Scar
Cotter Clints
Quarry Well
High Rigg
Moorcock Inn
Greenpot Hole
Garsdale Low Moor
Dandry Mire
Badger Rigg
Holmesett Hill
Carr Well
Cotter Riggs
LA10
A684
Thwaite Bridge
Dirty Gap Hollow
Clough Force (waterfall)
Moorland Cott
Clough
East Mud Becks
Dandrymire Viaduct
Black Hill
Long Slack
Old Pasture
Moss Bridge
Fall Rigg
Thwaite Wood
Far End
Garsdale
Wether Hill
Widdale Fell
Viaduct
Mossdale Head
OLD RD
Shooters Well
Waterfall
Mid Mossdale
Edwin's Fell
Mossdale Gill
A684 Sedbergh
High Scale
Middle O'Moor End
Peat Fell Hill
Dockhurry Hole
Shake Holes
Mossdale Gill Force
Hining Scar
Garsdale Common
Widdale Fell
Middle O' Moor
Hurrys
Cote Wold
New Close Allotments
Low Nab
Widdale Fell End
Round Hill
Mossdale Moor
Rooting Gill Head
Widdale Carr
Sandy Hill
Hugh's Moss
Crook Gill Hill
Birk Rigg Allotment
Widdale Fell
Widdale Car Plantation
Swinepot Gill
Sikes Pits Rigg
Birk Rigg Allotment
Crook Gill Rigg
Western End
Sweet Side
Franklin Moss
Shaking Moss
Widdale Side Allotments
Cowgill Head
Black Side
Cowgill Head
Little Scar Edge
Galloway Gate
Little Scar Moss
DL8
Widdale Side
Snaizeholme Bridge
Sandy Sike Head
Widdale Little Tarn
Snaizeholme Pasture
Little Scar
Widdale Bridge
Tarn Rigg
Green Scar Crags
Widdale Foot
Low Houses
Widdale Sch
Widdale Great Tarn
B6255
Widdale
Snaizeholme Beck
High Houses
Pikes Edge
Tarn Gill
Dairy Farm
Greens Farm
Hazel House
Great Knoutberry Hill
Green Scar Pasture
Mirk Pot
Mirk Pot Farm
Bridge End
Tow Hill
Ford
Snaizeholme
Mid Widdale
SNAIZEHOLME RD
Dent Fell
Waterfall
Arten Gill Moss
78
79
80
81
82
83
86
87
1
2
88
3
89
4
90
5
91
6
92
7
93
8
79
56

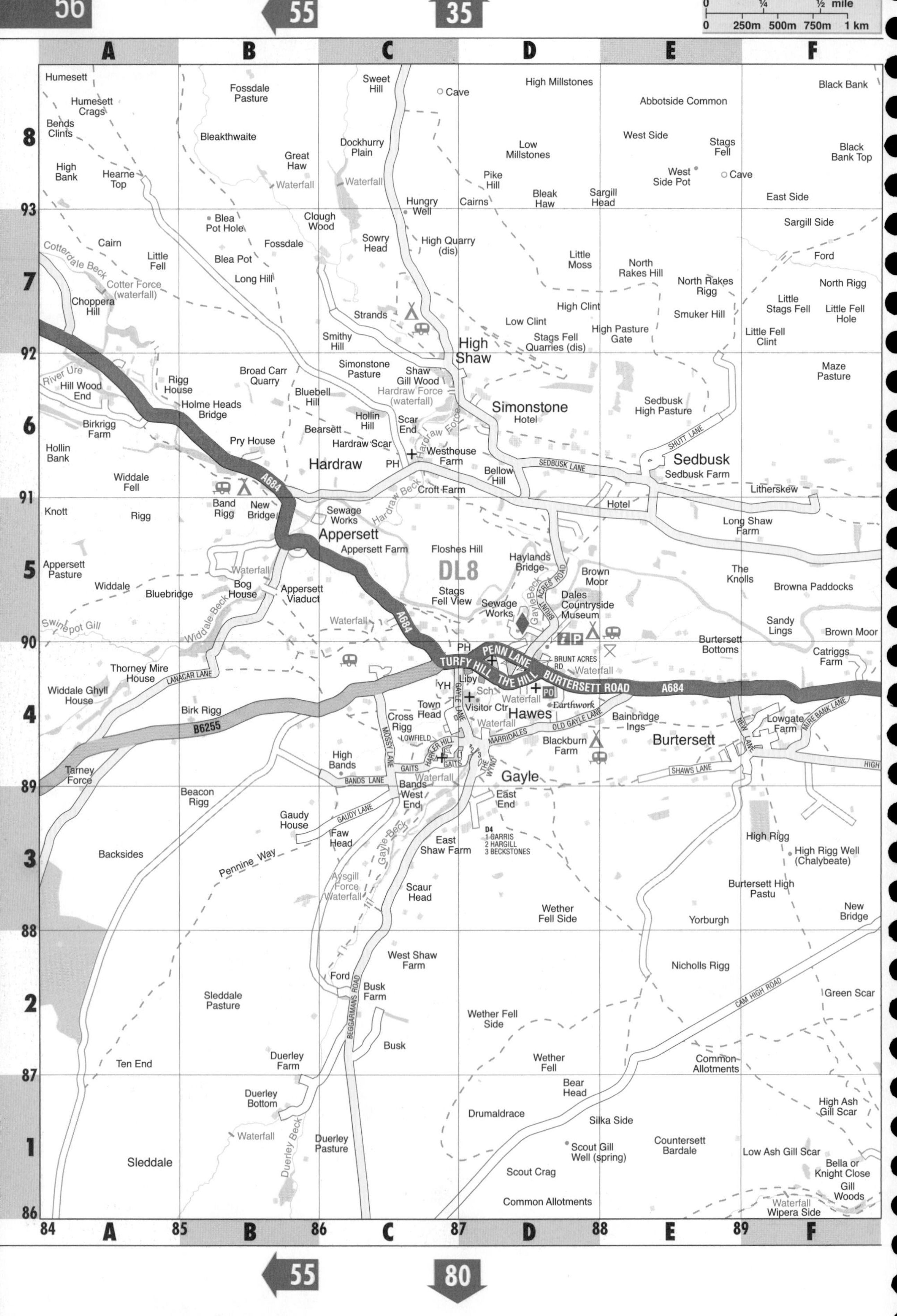
55
35
Scale: 1¾ inches to 1 mile
0 ¼ ½ mile
0 250m 500m 750m 1 km
A B C D E F
8 93 7 92 6 91 5 90 4 89 3 88 2 87 1 86
84 85 86 87 88 89
Humesett
Humesett Crags
Bends Clints
High Bank
Hearne Top
Fossdale Pasture
Bleakthwaite
Great Haw
Waterfall
Sweet Hill
Dockhurry Plain
Cave
High Millstones
Low Millstones
Pike Hill
Abbotside Common
West Side
Stags Fell
West Side Pot
Cave
Black Bank
Black Bank Top
East Side
Sargill Side
Hungry Well
Cairns
Bleak Haw
Sargill Head
Blea Pot Hole
Clough Wood
Fossdale
Sowry Head
High Quarry (dis)
Cairn
Little Fell
Blea Pot
Long Hill
Cotterdale Beck
Cotter Force (waterfall)
Choppera Hill
Little Moss
North Rakes Hill
North Rakes Rigg
Ford
North Rigg
Strands
Smithy Hill
High Clint
Low Clint
Stags Fell Quarries (dis)
High Pasture Gate
Smuker Hill
Little Stags Fell
Little Fell Hole
Little Fell Clint
High Shaw
River Ure
Hill Wood End
Rigg House
Broad Carr Quarry
Holme Heads Bridge
Bluebell Hill
Simonstone Pasture
Shaw Gill Wood
Hardraw Force (waterfall)
Simonstone
Hotel
Sedbusk High Pasture
Maze Pasture
Birkrigg Farm
Hollin Bank
Pry House
Bearsett
Hollin Hill
Scar End
Hardraw Force
Hardraw Scar
Westhouse Farm
SHUTT LANE
Sedbusk
Sedbusk Farm
Widdale Fell
A684
Hardraw
PH
Bellow Hill
SEDBUSK LANE
Croft Farm
Hardraw Beck
Litherskew
Knott
Rigg
Band Rigg
New Bridge
Sewage Works
Appersett
Hotel
Long Shaw Farm
Appersett Pasture
Appersett Farm
Floshes Hill
Haylands Bridge
DL8
BRUNT ACRES ROAD
Brown Moor
The Knolls
Browna Paddocks
Widdale
Bluebridge
Waterfall
Bog House
Appersett Viaduct
Stags Fell View
Sewage Works
Gayle Beck
Dales Countryside Museum
Sandy Lings
Brown Moor
Swinepot Gill
Widdale Beck
Waterfall
Burtersett Bottoms
Catriggs Farm
PH
PENN LANE
BRUNT ACRES RD
TURFY HILL
THE HILL
Waterfall
BURTERSETT ROAD
Thorney Mire House
LANACAR LANE
Widdale Ghyll House
YH
Liby
Sch
Waterfall
PO
Earthwork
Town Head
Visitor Ctr
Hawes
GAYLE LANE
OLD GAYLE LANE
Bainbridge Ings
Lowgate Farm
MIRE BANK LANE
Birk Rigg
B6255
Cross Rigg
Waterfall
LOWFIELD
MARRIDALES
Blackburn Farm
Burtersett
NEW LANE
HARKER HILL
MOSSY LANE
SHAWS LANE
HIGH
Tarney Force
High Bands
GAITS
THE WYND
Gayle
BANDS LANE
Waterfall
Bands West End
East End
Beacon Rigg
Gaudy House
GAUDY LANE
D4
1 GARRIS
2 HARGILL
3 BECKSTONES
High Rigg
High Rigg Well (Chalybeate)
Backsides
Faw Head
Gayle Beck
East Shaw Farm
Pennine Way
Aysgill Force Waterfall
Scar Head
Burtersett High Pastu
Wether Fell Side
Yorburgh
New Bridge
West Shaw Farm
Nicholls Rigg
Ford
Busk Farm
BEGGARMANS ROAD
Sleddale Pasture
CAM HIGH ROAD
Green Scar
Wether Fell Side
Busk
Ten End
Duerley Farm
Wether Fell
Common Allotments
Bear Head
Duerley Bottom
Drumaldrace
High Ash Gill Scar
Silka Side
Waterfall
Duerley Beck
Duerley Pasture
Scout Gill Well (spring)
Countersett Bardale
Low Ash Gill Scar
Sleddale
Scout Crag
Bella or Knight Close
Gill Woods
Common Allotments
Waterfall
Wipera Side
55
80

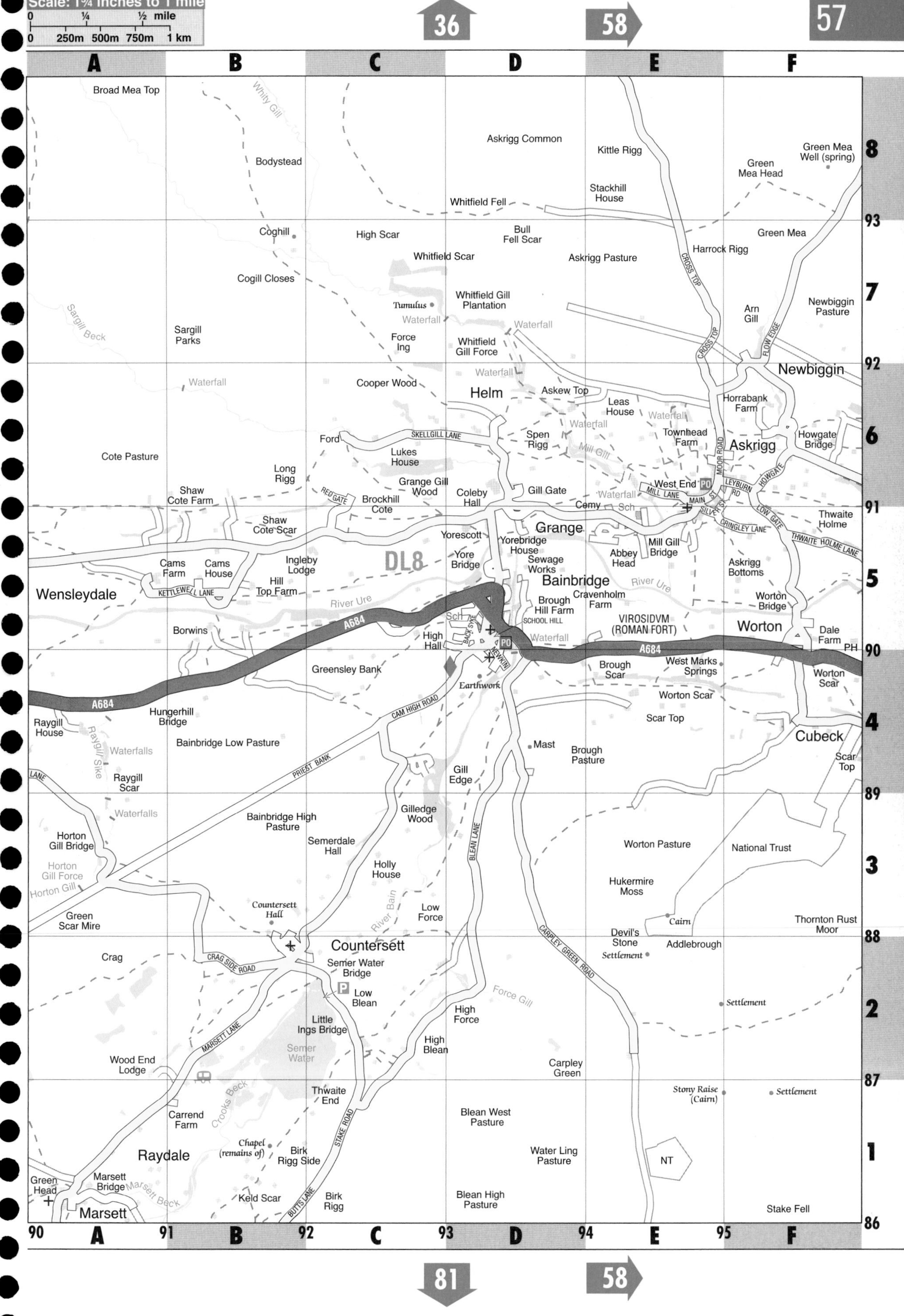
Scale: 1¾ inches to 1 mile
0 ¼ ½ mile
0 250m 500m 750m 1 km
36
58
A B C D E F
Broad Mea Top
Whity Gill
Bodystead
Askrigg Common
Kittle Rigg
Green Mea Well (spring)
Green Mea Head
Stackhill House
Whitfield Fell
Coghill
High Scar
Bull Fell Scar
Green Mea
Harrock Rigg
Whitfield Scar
Askrigg Pasture
Cross Top
Cogill Closes
Whitfield Gill Plantation
Tumulus
Newbiggin Pasture
Sargill Beck
Waterfall
Arn Gill
Sargill Parks
Force Ing
Whitfield Gill Force
Flow Edge
Newbiggin
Cooper Wood
Helm
Askew Top
Leas House
Horrabank Farm
Ford
Skellgill Lane
Spen Rigg
Mill Gill
Townhead Farm
Askrigg
Moor Road
Howgate Bridge
Cote Pasture
Lukes House
Long Rigg
Grange Gill Wood
West End
PO
Leybourn Rd
Howgate
Shaw Cote Farm
Red Gate
Brockhill Cote
Coleby Hall
Gill Gate
Mill Lane
Main St
Silver St
Low Gate
Cemy
Sch
Thwaite Holme
Shaw Cote Scar
Yorescott
Grange
Gringley Lane
Thwaite Holme Lane
Yorebridge House
Mill Gill Bridge
Cams Farm
Cams House
Ingleby Lodge
DL8
Yore Bridge
Sewage Works
Abbey Head
Askrigg Bottoms
Hill Top Farm
Bainbridge
River Ure
Wensleydale
Kettlewell Lane
Brough Hill Farm
Cravenholm Farm
Worton Bridge
Borwins
A684
Back Syke
School Hill
VIROSIDVM (ROMAN FORT)
Worton
Dale Farm
High Hall
Newkin
PH
Greensley Bank
Brough Scar
West Marks Springs
Worton Scar
Earthwork
Worton Scar
Cam High Road
Scar Top
Raygill House
Hungerhill Bridge
Cubeck
Raygill Sike
Waterfalls
Bainbridge Low Pasture
Mast
Brough Pasture
Scar Top
Lane
Raygill Scar
Priest Bank
Gill Edge
Gilledge Wood
Bainbridge High Pasture
Blean Lane
Worton Pasture
National Trust
Horton Gill Bridge
Semerdale Hall
Horton Gill Force
Holly House
Hukermire Moss
Horton Gill
River Bain
Green Scar Mire
Countersett Hall
Low Force
Cairn
Thornton Rust Moor
Devil's Stone
Countersett
Carpley Green Road
Settlement
Addlebrough
Crag
Crag Side Road
Semer Water Bridge
Low Blean
Force Gill
P
High Force
Settlement
Little Ings Bridge
Marsett Lane
Semer Water
High Blean
Wood End Lodge
Carpley Green
Crooks Beck
Thwaite End
Stony Raise (Cairn)
Settlement
Carrend Farm
Blean West Pasture
Stake Road
Chapel (remains of)
Raydale
Birk Rigg Side
Water Ling Pasture
NT
Green Head
Marsett Bridge
Marsett Beck
Keld Scar
Butts Lane
Birk Rigg
Blean High Pasture
Stake Fell
Marsett
90 91 92 93 94 95
8 93 7 92 6 91 5 90 4 89 3 88 2 87 1 86
81
58

57
37

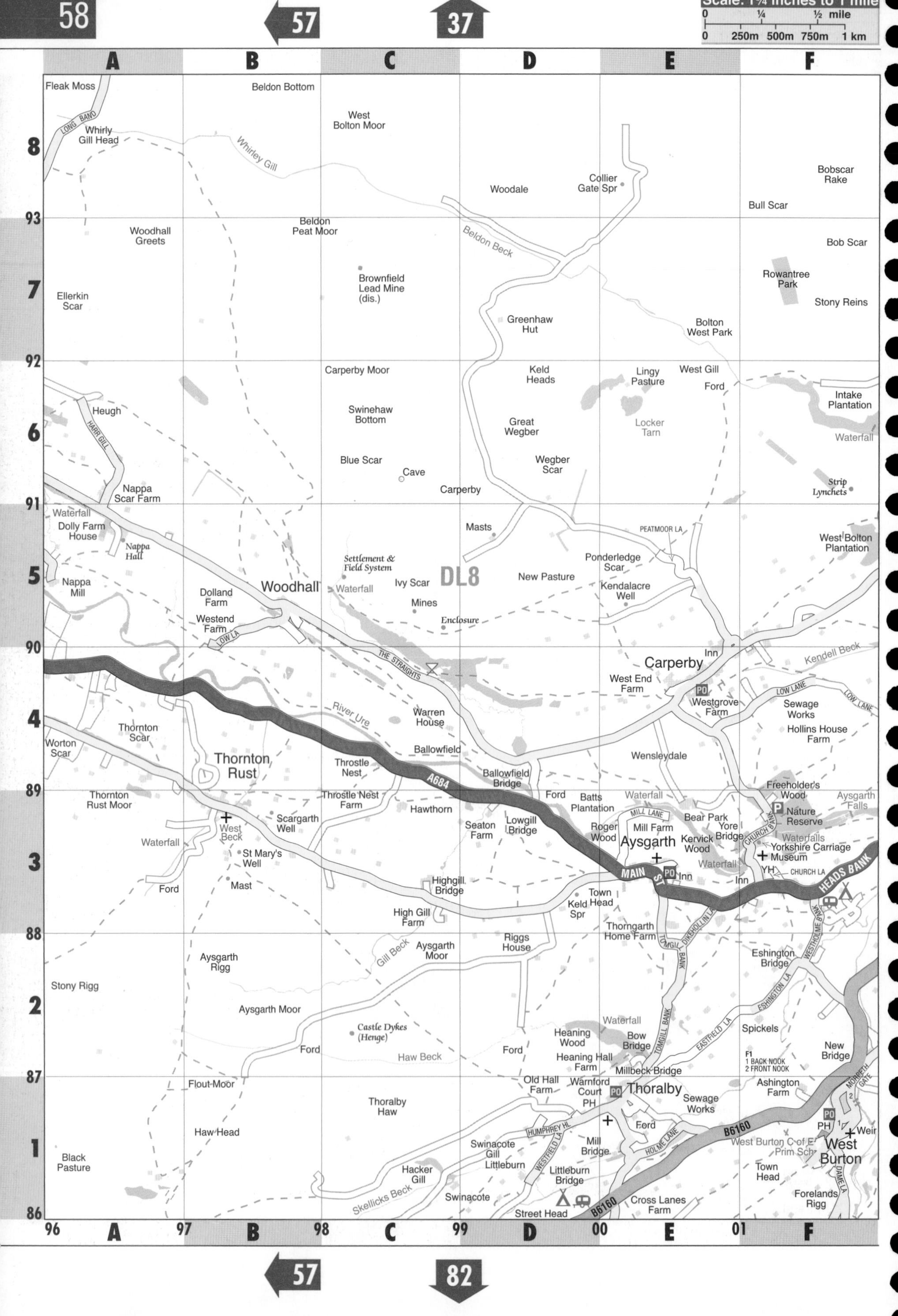
Scale: 1¾ inches to 1 mile
0 ¼ ½ mile
0 250m 500m 750m 1 km
A
B
C
D
E
F
8
93
7
92
6
91
5
90
4
89
3
88
2
87
1
86
96
97
98
99
00
01
Fleak Moss
Beldon Bottom
West Bolton Moor
LONG BAND
Whirly Gill Head
Whirley Gill
Collier Gate Spr
Woodale
Bobscar Rake
Bull Scar
Woodhall Greets
Beldon Peat Moor
Beldon Beck
Bob Scar
Brownfield Lead Mine (dis.)
Rowantree Park
Ellerkin Scar
Stony Reins
Greenhaw Hut
Bolton West Park
Carperby Moor
Keld Heads
Lingy Pasture
West Gill
Ford
Intake Plantation
Heugh
Swinehaw Bottom
Great Wegber
Locker Tarn
HARR GILL
Waterfall
Blue Scar
Cave
Wegber Scar
Carperby
Strip Lynchets
Nappa Scar Farm
Waterfall
Dolly Farm House
Masts
PEATMOOR LA
West Bolton Plantation
Nappa Hall
Settlement & Field System
Ponderledge Scar
Nappa Mill
DL8
New Pasture
Dolland Farm
Woodhall
Waterfall
Ivy Scar
Kendalacre Well
Mines
Westend Farm
Enclosure
LOW LA
Inn
Kendell Beck
THE STRAIGHTS
Carperby
West End Farm
PO
LOW LANE
LOW LANE
Westgrove Farm
Sewage Works
River Ure
Warren House
Thornton Scar
Hollins House Farm
Worton Scar
Ballowfield
Thornton Rust
Throstle Nest
Wensleydale
Ballowfield Bridge
A684
Freeholder's Wood
Thornton Rust Moor
Throstle Nest Farm
Ford
Batts Plantation
Waterfall
Aysgarth Falls
Hawthorn
P
Nature Reserve
MILL LANE
Bear Park
Scargarth Well
Seaton Farm
Lowgill Bridge
Roger Wood
Mill Farm
Yore Bridge
West Beck
Aysgarth
Kervick Wood
Waterfalls
Waterfall
CHURCH BANK
Yorkshire Carriage Museum
St Mary's Well
Waterfall
MAIN ST
PO
Inn
YH
CHURCH LA
HEADS BANK
Ford
Mast
Highgill Bridge
Town Head
Inn
Keld Spr
High Gill Farm
Thorngarth Home Farm
Riggs House
TOMGILL BANK
DIKEHOLLIN LA
WESTHOLME BANK
Gill Beck
Aysgarth Moor
Eshington Bridge
Aysgarth Rigg
Stony Rigg
ESHINGTON LA
Aysgarth Moor
Waterfall
Spickels
Castle Dykes (Henge)
Heaning Wood
Bow Bridge
EASTFIELD LA
TOMGILL BANK
Ford
Ford
New Bridge
Haw Beck
Heaning Hall Farm
F1
1 BACK NOOK
2 FRONT NOOK
Millbeck Bridge
Flout Moor
Old Hall Farm
Warnford Court
PO
Thoralby
Ashington Farm
MORPETH GATE
Thoralby Haw
PH
Sewage Works
HUMPHREY HL
Ford
PO
Haw Head
B6160
PH
Weir
Swinacote Gill
Mill Bridge
HOLME LANE
West Burton C of E Prim Sch
West Burton
Black Pasture
Littleburn
WESTFIELD LA
Hacker Gill
Littleburn Bridge
Town Head
Skellicks Beck
Swinacote
Cross Lanes Farm
Forelands Rigg
DAME LA
Street Head
B6160

57
82

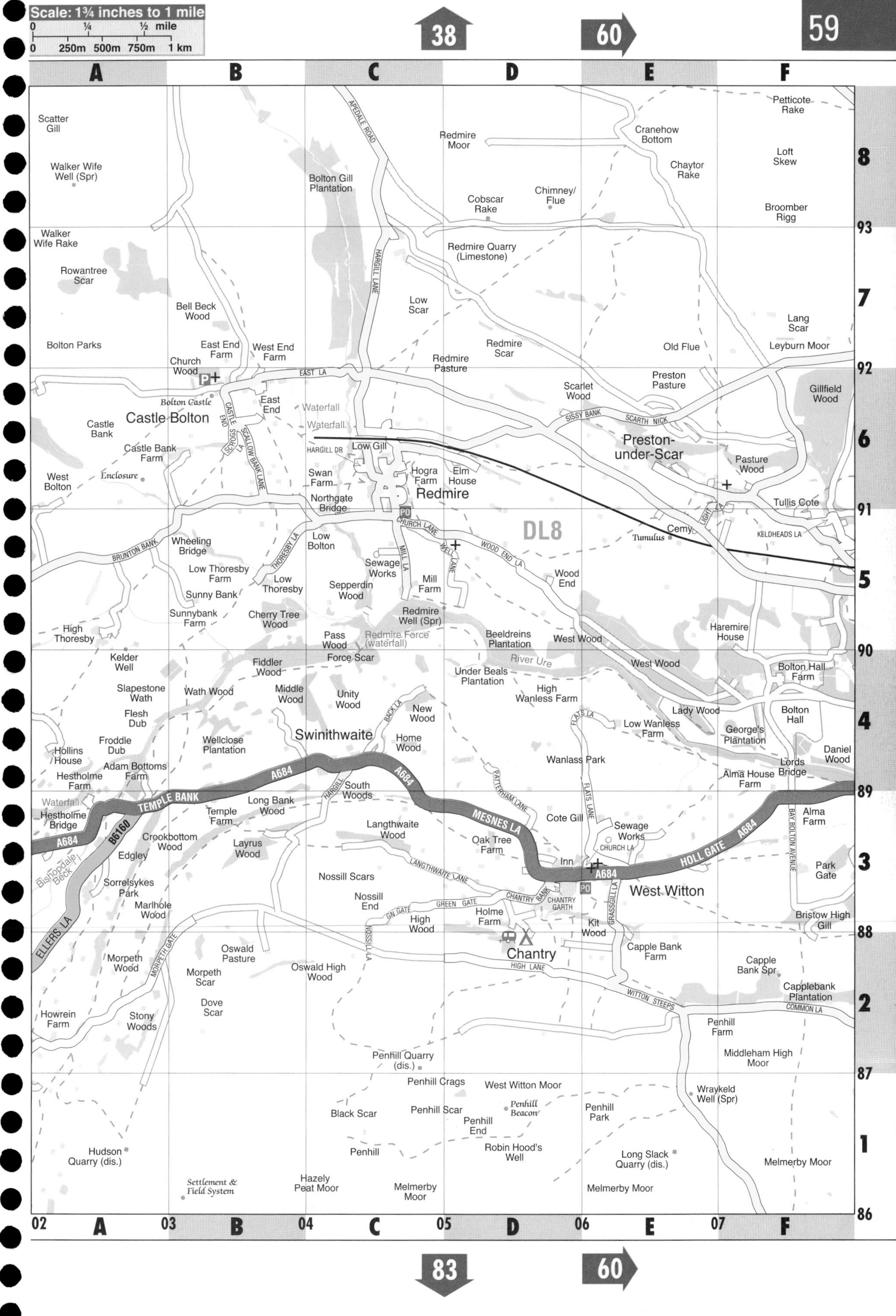
Scale: 1¾ inches to 1 mile
0 ¼ ½ mile
0 250m 500m 750m 1 km
38
60
A B C D E F
Scatter Gill
Walker Wife Well (Spr)
Walker Wife Rake
Rowantree Scar
Bell Beck Wood
Bolton Parks
Church Wood
East End Farm
West End Farm
Bolton Gill Plantation
APEDALE ROAD
HARGILL LANE
Redmire Moor
Cobscar Rake
Chimney/ Flue
Redmire Quarry (Limestone)
Low Scar
Redmire Pasture
Redmire Scar
Cranehow Bottom
Chaytor Rake
Petticote Rake
Loft Skew
Broomber Rigg
Lang Scar
Leyburn Moor
Old Flue
Preston Pasture
Gillfield Wood
EAST LA
Bolton Castle
Castle Bolton
Castle Bank
Castle Bank Farm
CASTLE END
SCROGS LA
SCALLOW BANK LANE
East End
Waterfall
Waterfall
HARGILL DR
Low Gill
Swan Farm
Hogra Farm
Elm House
Redmire
Northgate Bridge
Scarlet Wood
SISSY BANK
SCARTH NICK
Preston-under-Scar
Pasture Wood
Tullis Cote
West Bolton
Enclosure
BRUNTON BANK
Wheeling Bridge
Low Thoresby Farm
THORESBY LA
Low Bolton
Low Thoresby
PO
CHURCH LANE
MILL LA
WELL LANE
WOOD END LA
DL8
Cemy
Tumulus
LIGHT LA
KELDHEADS LA
Sunny Bank
Sunnybank Farm
Sewage Works
Sepperdin Wood
Mill Farm
Wood End
High Thoresby
Cherry Tree Wood
Redmire Well (Spr)
Pass Wood
Redmire Force (waterfall)
Force Scar
Beeldreins Plantation
West Wood
Haremire House
Kelder Well
Fiddler Wood
River Ure
Under Beals Plantation
West Wood
Bolton Hall Farm
Slapestone Wath
Wath Wood
Middle Wood
Unity Wood
High Wanless Farm
Lady Wood
Bolton Hall
Flesh Dub
New Wood
BACK LA
FLATS LA
Low Wanless Farm
George's Plantation
Froddle Dub
Hollins House
Wellclose Plantation
Swinithwaite
Home Wood
Daniel Wood
Adam Bottoms Farm
Hestholme Farm
Wanlass Park
Lords Bridge
Alma House Farm
A684
A684
PATTERHAM LANE
FLATS LANE
Waterfall
Hestholme Bridge
TEMPLE BANK
Temple Farm
Long Bank Wood
HARGILL
South Woods
MESNES LA
Cote Gill
Sewage Works
Alma Farm
A684
B6160
Crookbottom Wood
Langthwaite Wood
Oak Tree Farm
CHURCH LA
HOLL GATE
BAY BOLTON AVENUE
Edgley
Layrus Wood
Inn
A684
Park Gate
Bishopdale Beck
LANGTHWAITE LANE
Nossill Scars
CHANTRY BANK
PO
West Witton
Sorrelsykes Park
Nossill End
GREEN GATE
CHANTRY GARTH
Marlhole Wood
GN GATE
High Wood
Holme Farm
GRASSGILL LA
Bristow High Gill
ELLERS LA
Kit Wood
NOSSILL LA
Chantry
Morpeth Wood
MORPETH GATE
Oswald Pasture
Capple Bank Farm
Capple Bank Spr
HIGH LANE
Morpeth Scar
Oswald High Wood
Capplebank Plantation
WITTON STEEPS
COMMON LA
Dove Scar
Howrein Farm
Stony Woods
Penhill Farm
Middleham High Moor
Penhill Quarry (dis.)
Penhill Crags
West Witton Moor
Wraykeld Well (Spr)
Black Scar
Penhill Scar
Penhill Beacon
Penhill Park
Penhill End
Hudson Quarry (dis.)
Penhill
Robin Hood's Well
Long Slack Quarry (dis.)
Melmerby Moor
Settlement & Field System
Hazely Peat Moor
Melmerby Moor
Melmerby Moor
8
93
7
92
6
91
5
90
4
89
3
88
2
87
1
86
02 A 03 B 04 C 05 D 06 E 07 F
83
60

59
39

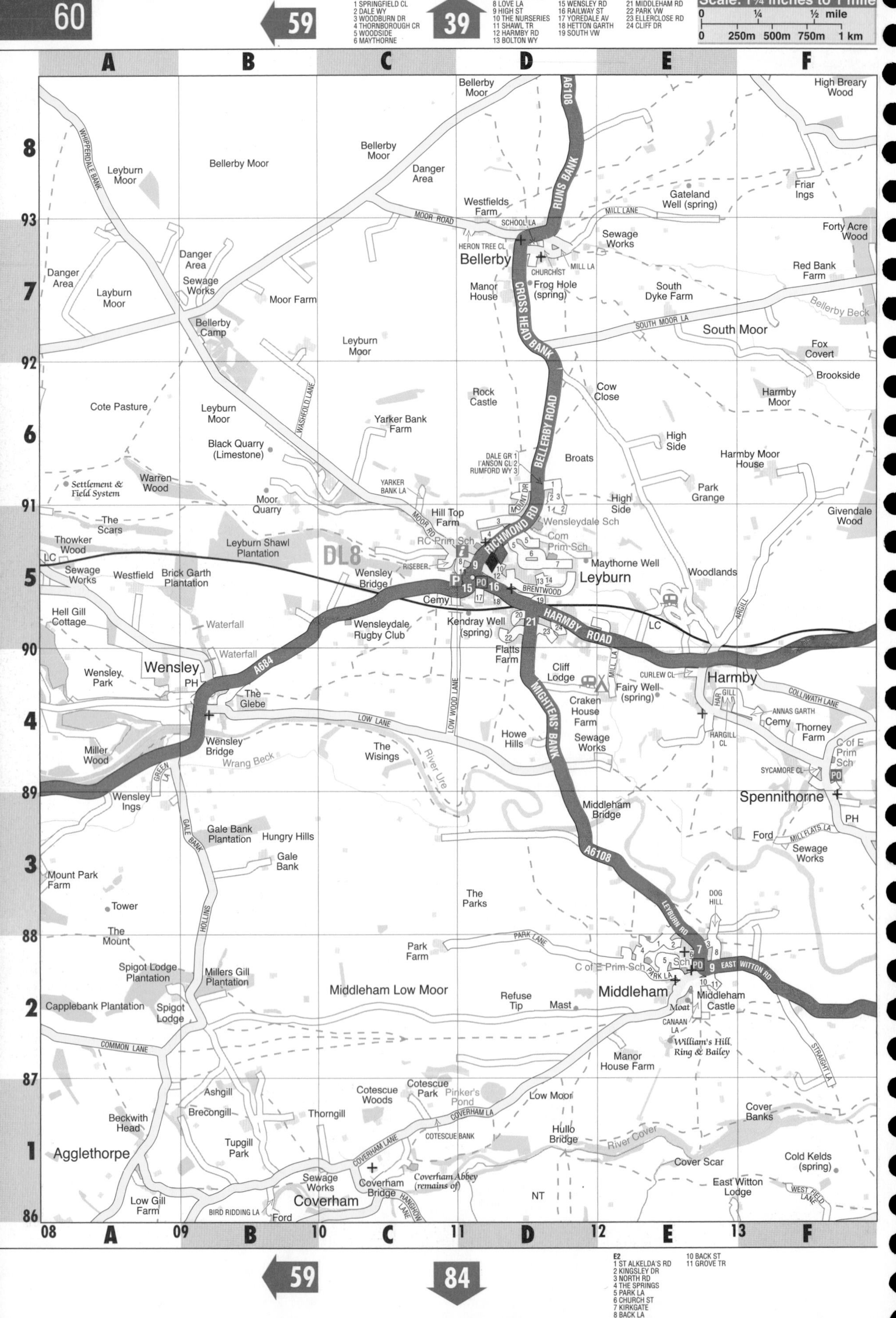
D5
1 SPRINGFIELD CL
2 DALE WY
3 WOODBURN DR
4 THORNBOROUGH CR
5 WOODSIDE
6 MAYTHORNE
7 WENSLEYDALE AV
8 LOVE LA
9 HIGH ST
10 THE NURSERIES
11 SHAWL TR
12 HARMBY RD
13 BOLTON WY
14 BOLTON CT
15 WENSLEY RD
16 RAILWAY ST
17 YOREDALE AV
18 HETTON GARTH
19 SOUTH VW
20 ST MATTHEW'S CL
21 MIDDLEHAM RD
22 PARK VW
23 ELLERCLOSE RD
24 CLIFF DR
Scale: 1¾ inches to 1 mile
0 ¼ ½ mile
0 250m 500m 750m 1 km
A B C D E F
8
93
7
92
6
91
5
90
4
89
3
88
2
87
1
86
08 09 10 11 12 13
Bellerby Moor
High Breary Wood
A6108
WHIPPERDALE BANK
Leyburn Moor
Bellerby Moor
Danger Area
RUNS BANK
Gateland Well (spring)
Friar Ings
Westfields Farm
MOOR ROAD
SCHOOL LA
MILL LANE
Forty Acre Wood
HERON TREE CL
Sewage Works
Danger Area
Bellerby
MILL LA
Red Bank Farm
Danger Area
Sewage Works
CHURCH ST
Frog Hole (spring)
Manor House
South Dyke Farm
Layburn Moor
Moor Farm
CROSS HEAD BANK
Bellerby Beck
Bellerby Camp
SOUTH MOOR LA
South Moor
Leyburn Moor
Fox Covert
Brookside
Rock Castle
Cow Close
Harmby Moor
Cote Pasture
Leyburn Moor
WASHFOLD LANE
Yarker Bank Farm
BELLERBY ROAD
High Side
Black Quarry (Limestone)
DALE GR 1
I'ANSON CL 2
RUMFORD WY 3
Broats
Harmby Moor House
Settlement & Field System
Warren Wood
YARKER BANK LA
Park Grange
Moor Quarry
MOUNT DR
High Side
Givendale Wood
The Scars
MOOR RD
Hill Top Farm
RICHMOND RD
Wensleydale Sch
Thowker Wood
Leyburn Shawl Plantation
RC Prim Sch
Com Prim Sch
DL8
LC
RISEBER
Maythorne Well
Sewage Works
Westfield
Brick Garth Plantation
Wensley Bridge
Leyburn
Woodlands
BRENTWOOD
Cemy
P
PO
Hell Gill Cottage
Waterfall
Wensleydale Rugby Club
Kendray Well (spring)
HARMBY ROAD
LC
ARGILL
Waterfall
Flatts Farm
Wensley
Wensley Park
A684
Cliff Lodge
MILL LA
CURLEW CL
Harmby
Fairy Well (spring)
PH
The Glebe
Craken House Farm
HAR GILL
COLLIWATH LANE
ANNAS GARTH
Cemy
Thorney Farm
LOW LANE
LOW WOOD LANE
MIGHTENS' BANK
Miller Wood
Wensley Bridge
Howe Hills
Sewage Works
HARGILL CL
C of E Prim Sch
Wrang Beck
The Wisings
River Ure
SYCAMORE CL
PO
GREEN LA
Wensley Ings
Middleham Bridge
Spennithorne
PH
Gale Bank Plantation
Hungry Hills
Ford
MILL FLATS LA
GALE BANK
Sewage Works
Gale Bank
A6108
Mount Park Farm
The Parks
DOG HILL
LEYBURN RD
Tower
HOLLINS
The Mount
PARK LANE
Park Farm
EAST WITTON RD
Spigot Lodge Plantation
Millers Gill Plantation
C of E Prim Sch
Sch
PO
PARK LA
Middleham Low Moor
Refuse Tip
Middleham
Middleham Castle
Capplebank Plantation
Spigot Lodge
Mast
Moat
CANAAN LA
William's Hill Ring & Bailey
COMMON LANE
STRAIGHT LA
Manor House Farm
Ashgill
Cotescue Woods
Cotescue Park
Pinker's Pond
Low Moor
Beckwith Head
Brecongill
Thorngill
COVERHAM LA
Cover Banks
Hullo Bridge
River Cover
COTESCUE BANK
Agglethorpe
Tupgill Park
COVERHAM LANE
Cover Scar
Cold Kelds (spring)
Sewage Works
Coverham Bridge
Coverham Abbey (remains of)
East Witton Lodge
WEST FIELD LANE
Low Gill Farm
HANGHOW LANE
NT
BIRD RIDDING LA
Ford
Coverham
E2
1 ST ALKELDA'S RD
2 KINGSLEY DR
3 NORTH RD
4 THE SPRINGS
5 PARK LA
6 CHURCH ST
7 KIRKGATE
8 BACK LA
9 MARKET PL
10 BACK ST
11 GROVE TR

59
84

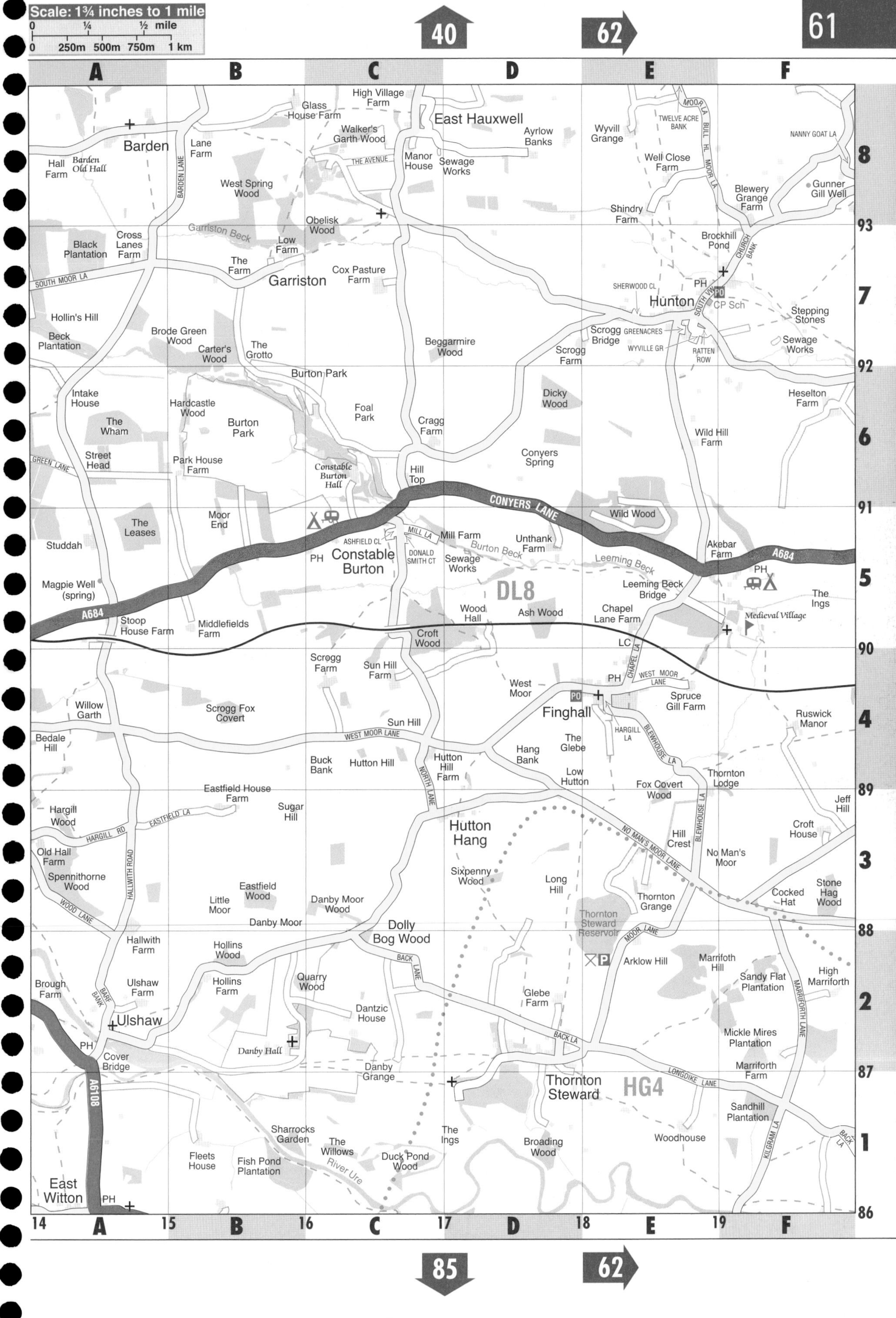
Scale: 1¾ inches to 1 mile
0 ¼ ½ mile
0 250m 500m 750m 1 km
40
62
A B C D E F
8
93
7
92
6
91
5
90
4
89
3
88
2
87
1
86
14 15 16 17 18 19
Barden
Hall Farm
Barden Old Hall
Lane Farm
BARDEN LANE
Glass House Farm
High Village Farm
Walker's Garth Wood
East Hauxwell
Aylrow Banks
Manor House
Sewage Works
THE AVENUE
Wyvill Grange
TWELVE ACRE BANK
MOOR LA
BULL HL
MOOR LA
Well Close Farm
NANNY GOAT LA
Gunner Gill Well
Blewery Grange Farm
West Spring Wood
Obelisk Wood
Shindry Farm
Garriston Beck
Black Plantation
Cross Lanes Farm
Low Farm
The Farm
Garriston
Cox Pasture Farm
Brockhill Pond
CHURCH BANK
SOUTH MOOR LA
SHERWOOD CL
PH
PO
Hunton
SOUTH VW
CP Sch
Stepping Stones
Hollin's Hill
Beck Plantation
Brode Green Wood
Carter's Wood
The Grotto
Beggarmire Wood
Scrogg Bridge
GREENACRES
WYVILLE GR
Scrogg Farm
RATTEN ROW
Sewage Works
Burton Park
Intake House
Hardcastle Wood
Dicky Wood
Heselton Farm
The Wham
Burton Park
Foal Park
Cragg Farm
Wild Hill Farm
Street Head
GREEN LANE
Park House Farm
Constable Burton Hall
Hill Top
Conyers Spring
CONYERS LANE
Wild Wood
The Leases
Moor End
MILL LA
Mill Farm
Unthank Farm
Burton Beck
ASHFIELD CL
Studdah
PH
Constable Burton
DONALD SMITH CT
Sewage Works
Leeming Beck
Akebar Farm
A684
Magpie Well (spring)
DL8
Leeming Beck Bridge
The Ings
A684
Stoop House Farm
Middlefields Farm
Wood Hall
Ash Wood
Chapel Lane Farm
Medieval Village
Croft Wood
LC
Scrogg Farm
Sun Hill Farm
West Moor
PH
CHAPEL LA
WEST MOOR LANE
Willow Garth
Scrogg Fox Covert
PO
Finghall
Spruce Gill Farm
Ruswick Manor
Bedale Hill
Sun Hill
WEST MOOR LANE
HARGILL LA
The Glebe
BLEWHOUSE LA
Buck Bank
Hutton Hill
Hutton Hill Farm
Hang Bank
Low Hutton
Thornton Lodge
NORTH LANE
Eastfield House Farm
Fox Covert Wood
Hargill Wood
Sugar Hill
Jeff Hill
EASTFIELD LA
HARGILL RD
Hutton Hang
Hill Crest
BLEWHOUSE LA
Croft House
NO MAN'S MOOR LANE
Old Hall Farm
No Man's Moor
Spennithorne Wood
HALLWITH ROAD
Sixpenny Wood
Long Hill
Stone Hag Wood
WOOD LANE
Eastfield Wood
Little Moor
Danby Moor Wood
Thornton Grange
Cocked Hat
Danby Moor
Thornton Steward Reservoir
Dolly Bog Wood
MOOR LANE
Hallwith Farm
Hollins Wood
P
Arklow Hill
Marrifoth Hill
BACK LANE
High Marriforth
Brough Farm
Ulshaw Farm
Hollins Farm
Quarry Wood
Sandy Flat Plantation
BARF BANK
MARRIFORTH LANE
Glebe Farm
Ulshaw
Dantzic House
Mickle Mires Plantation
PH
BACK LA
Cover Bridge
Danby Hall
Marriforth Farm
Danby Grange
LONGDIKE LANE
A6108
Thornton Steward
HG4
Sandhill Plantation
Sharrocks Garden
The Ings
The Willows
Broading Wood
Woodhouse
BACK LA
Fleets House
Fish Pond Plantation
Duck Pond Wood
KILGRAM LA
River Ure
East Witton
PH
85
62

61 41

Scale: 1¾ inches to 1 mile

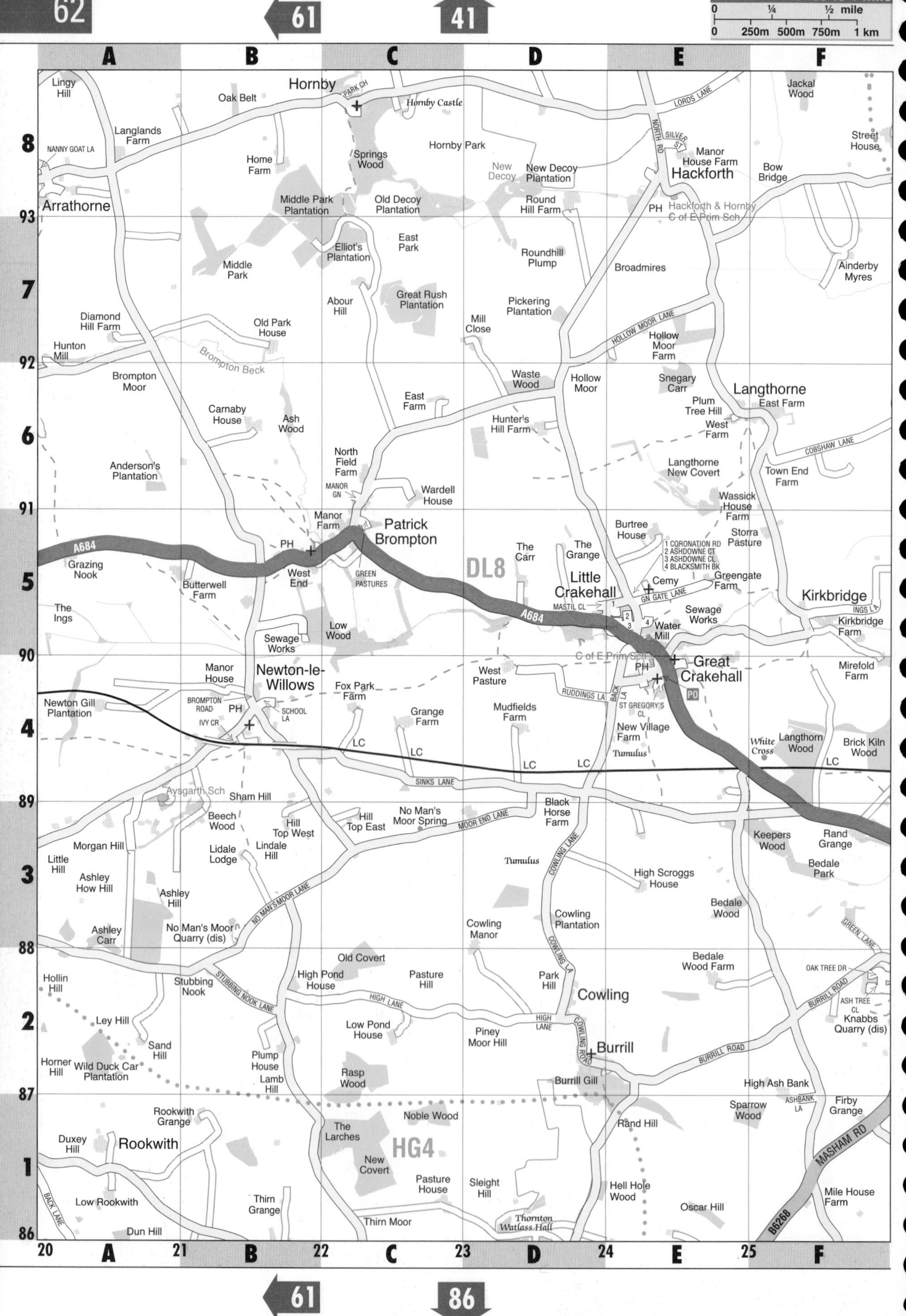

61 86

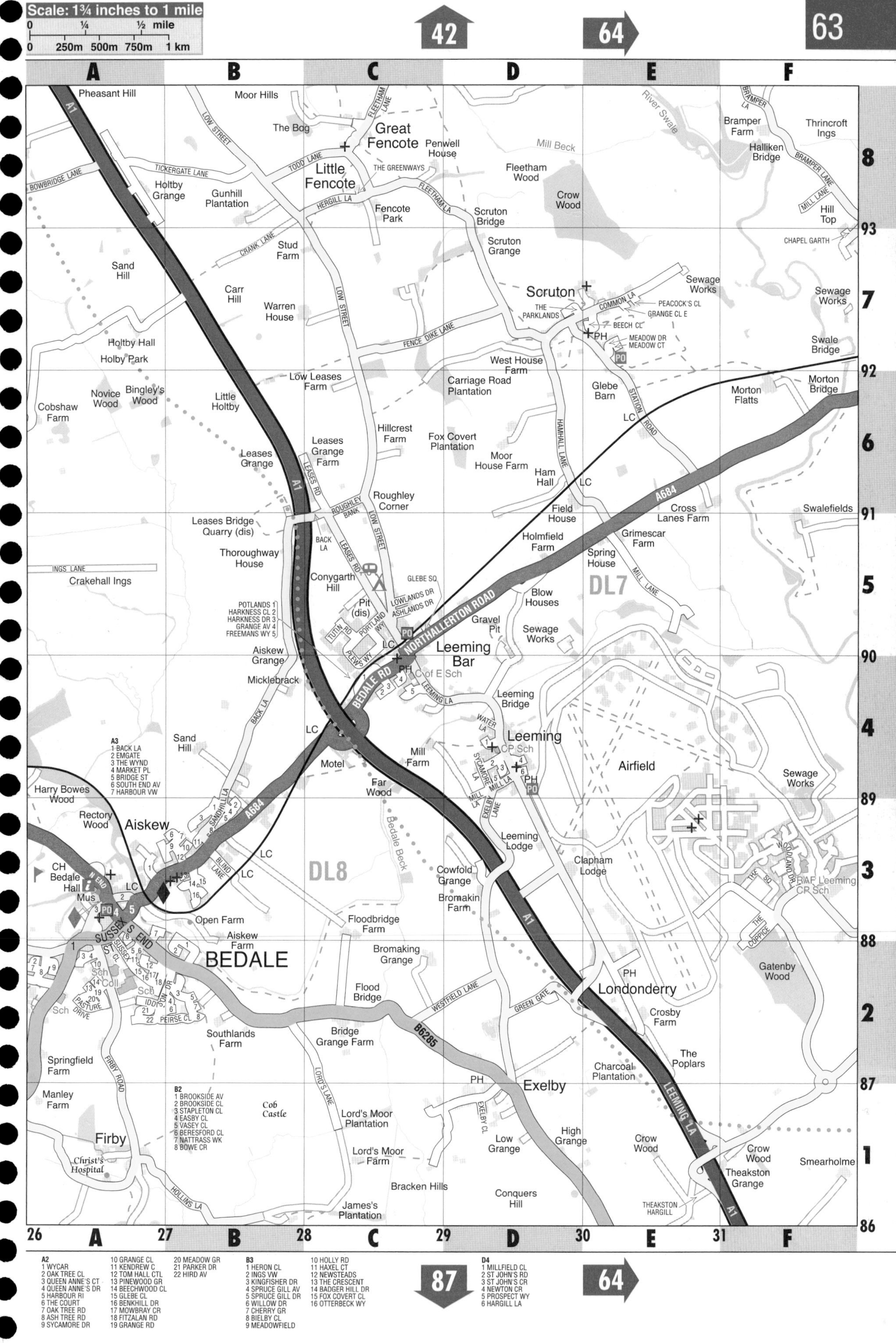

A2
1 WYCAR
2 OAK TREE CL
3 QUEEN ANNE'S CT
4 QUEEN ANNE'S DR
5 HARBOUR RI
6 THE COURT
7 OAK TREE RD
8 ASH TREE RD
9 SYCAMORE DR
10 GRANGE CL
11 KENDREW C
12 TOM HALL CTL
13 PINEWOOD GR
14 BEECHWOOD CL
15 GLEBE CL
16 BENKHILL DR
17 MOWBRAY CR
18 FITZALAN RD
19 GRANGE RD
20 MEADOW GR
21 PARKER DR
22 HIRD AV

B3
1 HERON CL
2 INGS VW
3 KINGFISHER DR
4 SPRUCE GILL AV
5 SPRUCE GILL DR
6 WILLOW DR
7 CHERRY GR
8 BIELBY CL
9 MEADOWFIELD
10 HOLLY RD
11 HAXEL CT
12 NEWSTEADS
13 THE CRESCENT
14 BADGER HILL DR
15 FOX COVERT CL
16 OTTERBECK WY

D4
1 MILLFIELD CL
2 ST JOHN'S RD
3 ST JOHN'S CR
4 NEWTON CR
5 PROSPECT WY
6 HARGILL LA

87
64

43 63 210

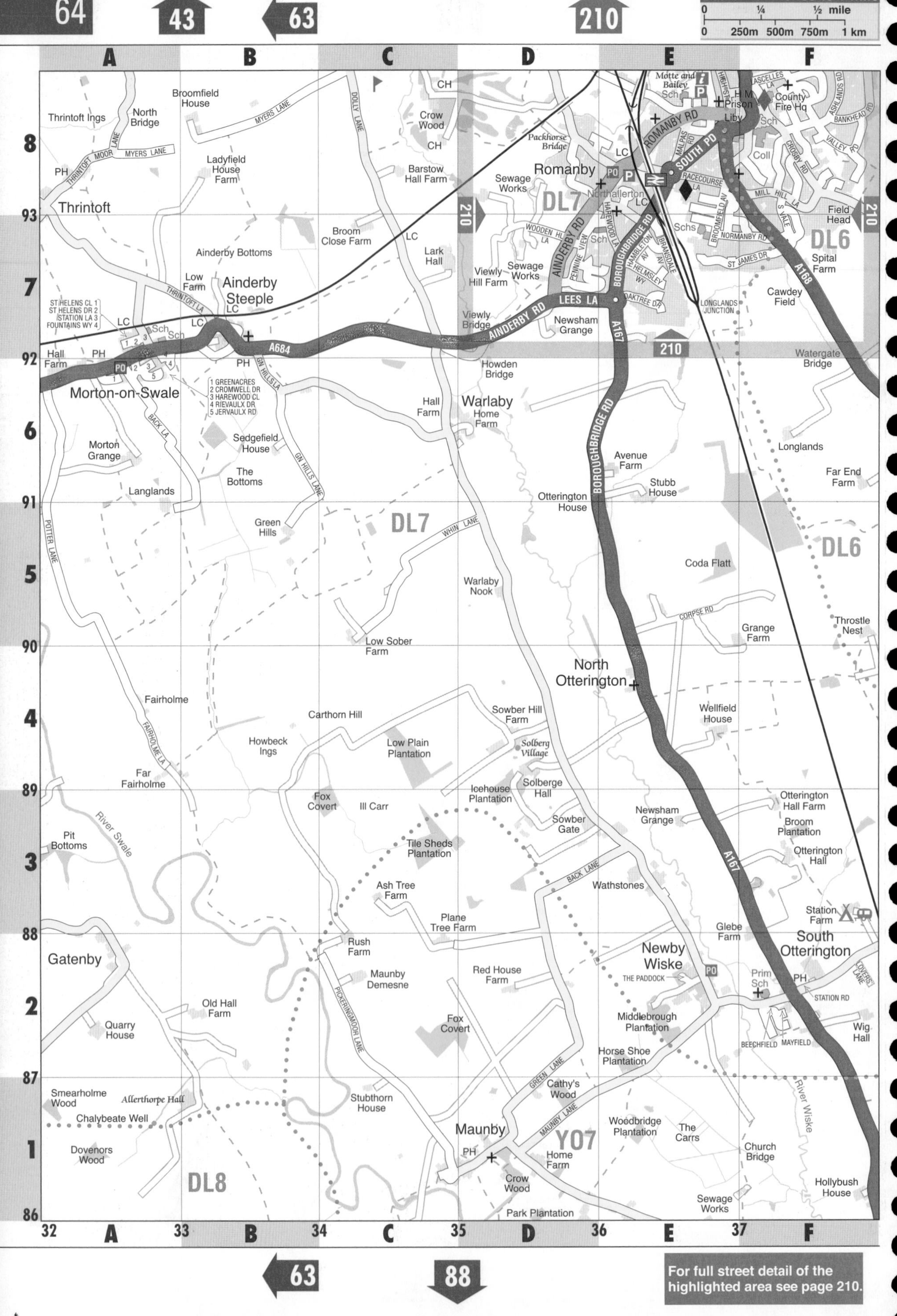

63 88

For full street detail of the highlighted area see page 210.

44
66

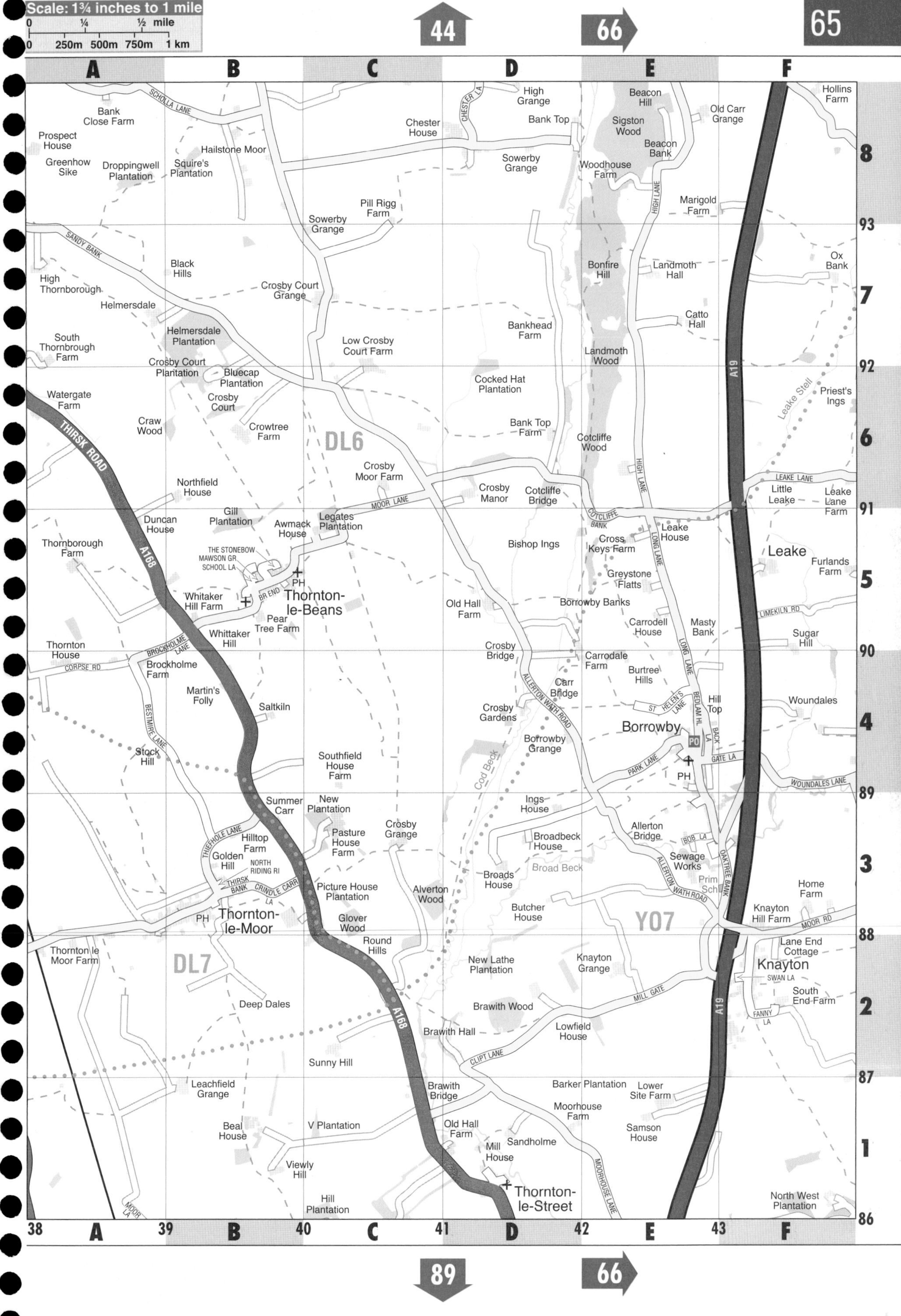
Scale: 1¾ inches to 1 mile
0 ¼ ½ mile
0 250m 500m 750m 1 km
A B C D E F
8 93 7 92 6 91 5 90 4 89 3 88 2 87 1 86
38 39 40 41 42 43
Bank Close Farm
Prospect House
Greenhow Sike
Droppingwell Plantation
Squire's Plantation
Hailstone Moor
SCHOLLA LANE
Chester House
CHESTER LA
High Grange
Bank Top
Sowerby Grange
Beacon Hill
Sigston Wood
Beacon Bank
Old Carr Grange
Hollins Farm
Woodhouse Farm
HIGH LANE
Marigold Farm
Pill Rigg Farm
Sowerby Grange
SANDY BANK
High Thornborough
Black Hills
Crosby Court Grange
Helmersdale
Bonfire Hill
Landmoth Hall
Ox Bank
Catto Hall
South Thornbrough Farm
Helmersdale Plantation
Low Crosby Court Farm
Bankhead Farm
Landmoth Wood
Crosby Court Plantation
Bluecap Plantation
Cocked Hat Plantation
A19
Watergate Farm
Crosby Court
Priest's Ings
Leake Stell
THIRSK ROAD
Craw Wood
Crowtree Farm
DL6
Bank Top Farm
Cotcliffe Wood
Crosby Moor Farm
Northfield House
MOOR LANE
Crosby Manor
Cotcliffe Bridge
LEAKE LANE
Little Leake
Leake Lane Farm
Duncan House
Gill Plantation
Awmack House
Legates Plantation
COTCLIFFE BANK
Leake House
Thornborough Farm
A168
THE STONEBOW
MAWSON GR
SCHOOL LA
PH
Bishop Ings
Cross Keys Farm
LONG LANE
Leake
Furlands Farm
Greystone Flatts
BR END
Thornton-le-Beans
Whitaker Hill Farm
Old Hall Farm
Borrowby Banks
LIMEKILN RD
Pear Tree Farm
Whittaker Hill
Carrodell House
Masty Bank
Sugar Hill
Thornton House
BROCKHOLME LANE
Crosby Bridge
Carrodale Farm
CORPSE RD
Brockholme Farm
Burtree Hills
Martin's Folly
ALLERTON WATH ROAD
Carr Bridge
Hill Top
BESTMIRE LANE
Saltkiln
Crosby Gardens
ST HELEN'S LANE
BEDLAM HL
Woundales
Borrowby
Stock Hill
Borrowby Grange
PO
BACK LA
Cod Beck
GATE LA
Southfield House Farm
PARK LANE
PH
WOUNDALES LANE
Summer Carr
New Plantation
Ings House
Crosby Grange
THIEFHOLE LANE
Hilltop Farm
Pasture House Farm
Allerton Bridge
Broadbeck House
BOB LA
Golden Hill
NORTH RIDING RI
Sewage Works
Broads House
Broad Beck
OAKTREE BANK
THIRSK BANK
CRINDLE CARR LA
Picture House Plantation
Alverton Wood
Prim Sch
Home Farm
ALLERTON WATH ROAD
Butcher House
PH
Thornton-le-Moor
Glover Wood
YO7
Knayton Hill Farm
MOOR RD
Round Hills
Lane End Cottage
Thornton le Moor Farm
DL7
New Lathe Plantation
Knayton Grange
Knayton
SWAN LA
Deep Dales
MILL GATE
South End Farm
Brawith Wood
FANNY LA
Brawith Hall
Lowfield House
Sunny Hill
CLIPT LANE
Leachfield Grange
Brawith Bridge
Barker Plantation
Lower Site Farm
Moorhouse Farm
Beal House
V Plantation
Old Hall Farm
Samson House
Mill House
Sandholme
Viewly Hill
MOORHOUSE LANE
Thornton-le-Street
Hill Plantation
MOOR LA
North West Plantation

89
66

65
45

Scale: 1¾ inches to 1 mile

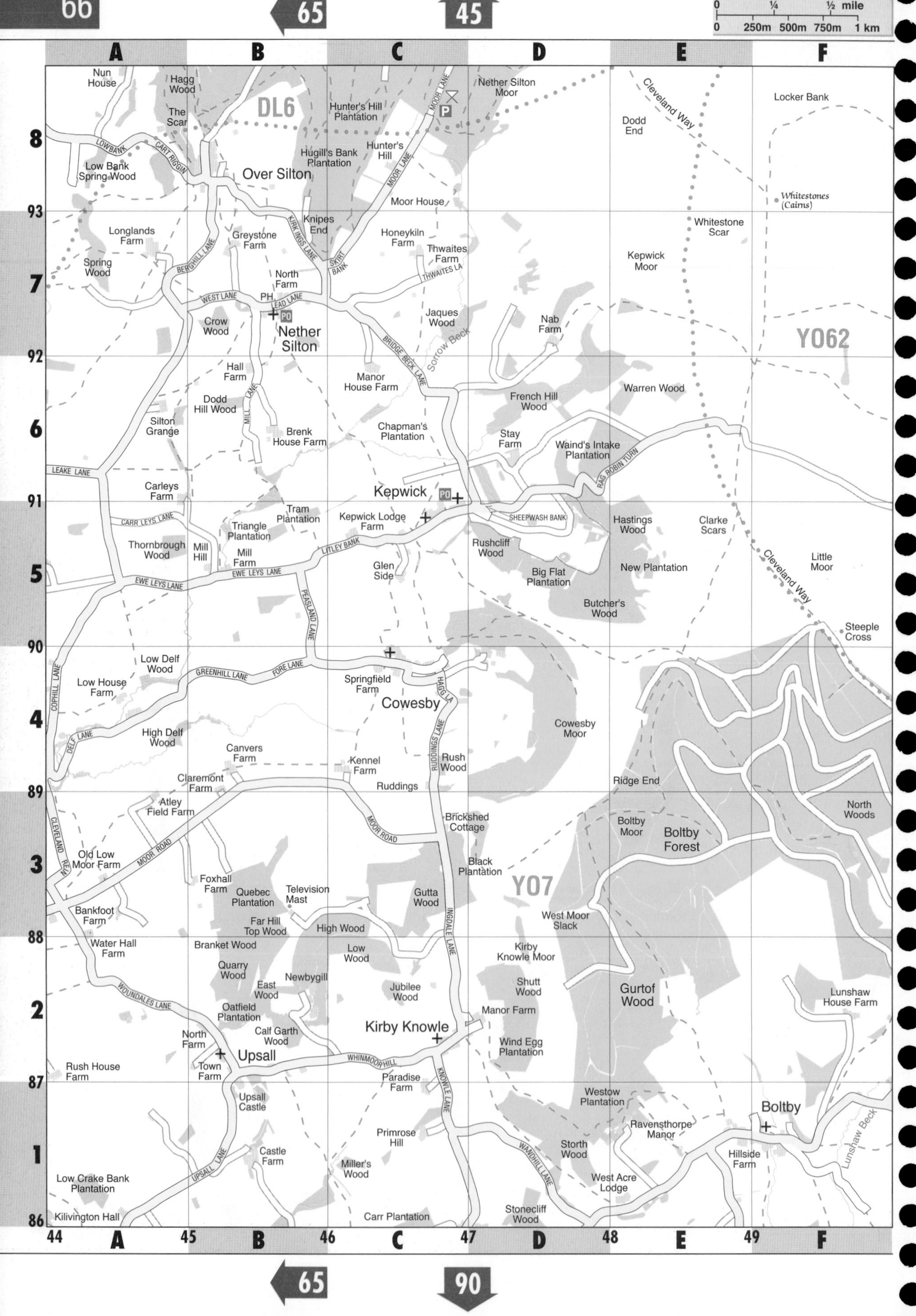

65
90

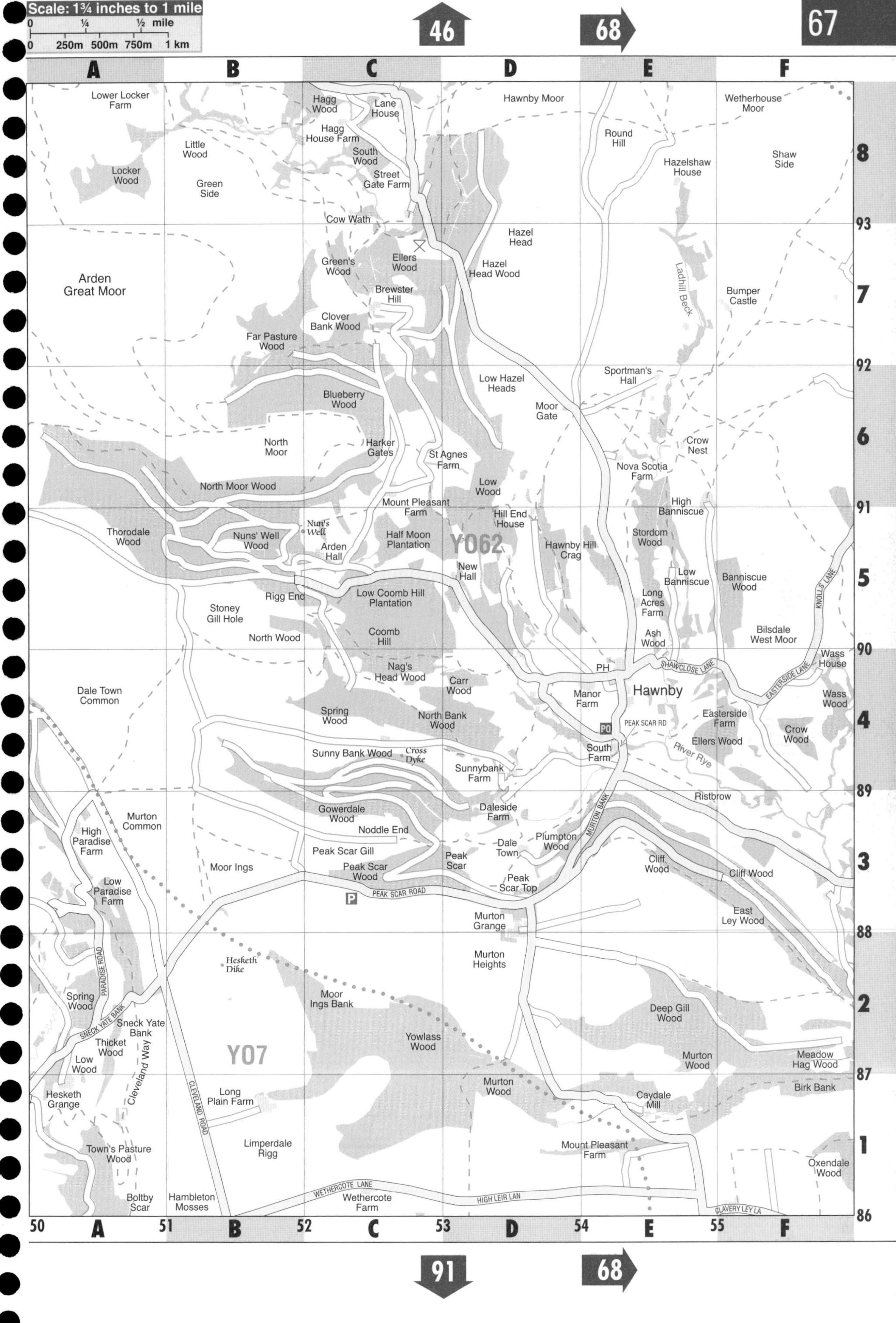
Scale: 1¾ inches to 1 mile
0 ¼ ½ mile
0 250m 500m 750m 1 km
46
68
A B C D E F
Lower Locker Farm
Hagg Wood
Lane House
Hawnby Moor
Round Hill
Wetherhouse Moor
Hagg House Farm
Little Wood
South Wood
Hazelshaw House
Shaw Side
Locker Wood
Green Side
Street Gate Farm
Cow Wath
Hazel Head
Ellers Wood
Green's Wood
Hazel Head Wood
Arden Great Moor
Brewster Hill
Ladhill Beck
Bumper Castle
Clover Bank Wood
Far Pasture Wood
Sportman's Hall
Low Hazel Heads
Blueberry Wood
Moor Gate
North Moor
Harker Gates
St Agnes Farm
Crow Nest
Nova Scotia Farm
Low Wood
North Moor Wood
Mount Pleasant Farm
High Banniscue
Hill End House
Thorodale Wood
Nun's Well
Nuns' Well Wood
Arden Hall
Half Moon Plantation
YO62
Hawnby Hill Crag
Stordom Wood
Low Banniscue
Banniscue Wood
New Hall
KNOLLS LANE
Low Coomb Hill Plantation
Long Acres Farm
Rigg End
Stoney Gill Hole
Coomb Hill
Ash Wood
Bilsdale West Moor
North Wood
Nag's Head Wood
PH
SHAWCLOSE LANE
Wass House
Carr Wood
Hawnby
EASTERSIDE LANE
Dale Town Common
Manor Farm
Wass Wood
Spring Wood
North Bank Wood
PO
PEAK SCAR RD
Easterside Farm
Crow Wood
Ellers Wood
Sunny Bank Wood
Cross Dyke
South Farm
River Rye
Sunnybank Farm
Ristbrow
MURTON BANK
Murton Common
Gowerdale Wood
Daleside Farm
High Paradise Farm
Noddle End
Dale Town
Plumpton Wood
Cliff Wood
Peak Scar Gill
Peak Scar
Cliff Wood
Moor Ings
Peak Scar Wood
Low Paradise Farm
Peak Scar Top
PEAK SCAR ROAD
P
East Ley Wood
Murton Grange
Hesketh Dike
Murton Heights
PARADISE ROAD
Moor Ings Bank
Spring Wood
Deep Gill Wood
SNECK YATE BANK
Sneck Yate Bank
Yowlass Wood
Thicket Wood
Cleveland Way
YO7
Murton Wood
Meadow Hag Wood
Low Wood
Murton Wood
Birk Bank
Hesketh Grange
CLEVELAND ROAD
Long Plain Farm
Caydale Mill
Town's Pasture Wood
Limperdale Rigg
Mount Pleasant Farm
Oxendale Wood
WETHERCOTE LANE
Boltby Scar
Hambleton Mosses
Wethercote Farm
HIGH LEIR LAN
CLAVERY LEY LA
8
93
7
92
6
91
5
90
4
89
3
88
2
87
1
86
50 51 52 53 54 55
91
68

67 47

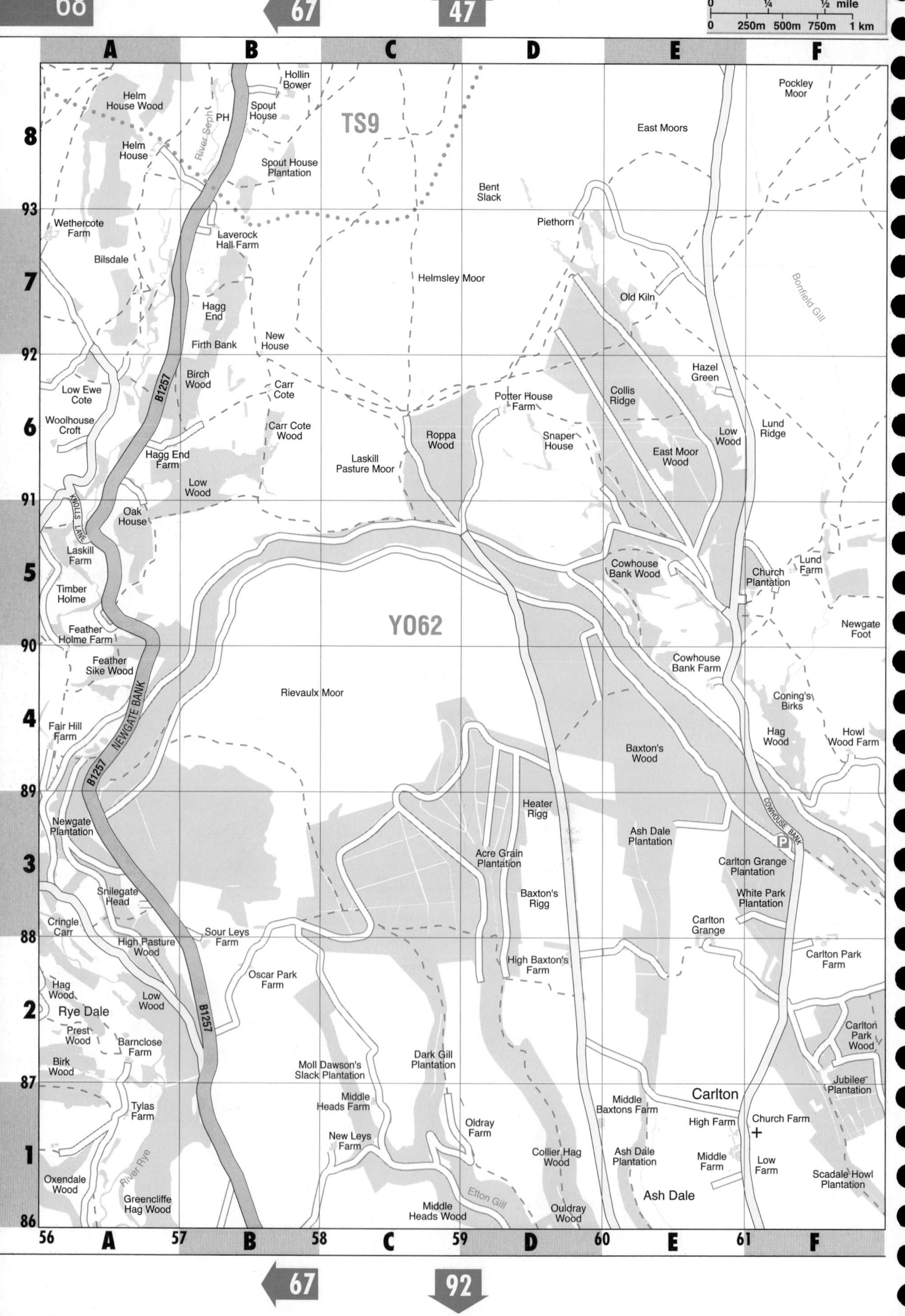
Scale: 1¾ inches to 1 mile
0 ¼ ½ mile
0 250m 500m 750m 1 km
A B C D E F
TS9
YO62
Hollin Bower
Helm House Wood
PH
Spout House
River Seph
Helm House
Spout House Plantation
Pockley Moor
East Moors
Bent Slack
Piethorn
Wethercote Farm
Laverock Hall Farm
Bilsdale
Helmsley Moor
Old Kiln
Bonfield Gill
Hagg End
Firth Bank
New House
Hazel Green
Birch Wood
Carr Cote
Potter House Farm
Collis Ridge
Low Ewe Cote
B1257
Woolhouse Croft
Carr Cote Wood
Roppa Wood
Snaper House
Low Wood
Lund Ridge
Hagg End Farm
Laskill Pasture Moor
East Moor Wood
Low Wood
KNOLLS LANE
Oak House
Laskill Farm
Cowhouse Bank Wood
Church Plantation
Lund Farm
Timber Holme
Feather Holme Farm
Newgate Foot
Feather Sike Wood
Cowhouse Bank Farm
NEWGATE BANK
Rievaulx Moor
Coning's Birks
Fair Hill Farm
Baxton's Wood
Hag Wood
Howl Wood Farm
Newgate Plantation
Heater Rigg
COWHOUSE BANK
Ash Dale Plantation
Acre Grain Plantation
Carlton Grange Plantation
White Park Plantation
Baxton's Rigg
Snilegate Head
Cringle Carr
Sour Leys Farm
Carlton Grange
High Pasture Wood
High Baxton's Farm
Carlton Park Farm
Oscar Park Farm
Hag Wood
Rye Dale
Low Wood
Prest Wood
Barnclose Farm
Carlton Park Wood
Birk Wood
Moll Dawson's Slack Plantation
Dark Gill Plantation
Jubilee Plantation
Carlton
Middle Heads Farm
Middle Baxtons Farm
Tylas Farm
Oldray Farm
High Farm
Church Farm
New Leys Farm
Collier Hag Wood
Ash Dale Plantation
Middle Farm
Low Farm
Oxendale Wood
River Rye
Scadale Howl Plantation
Etton Gill
Greencliffe Hag Wood
Middle Heads Wood
Ouldray Wood
Ash Dale
8 93 7 92 6 91 5 90 4 89 3 88 2 87 1 86
56 57 58 59 60 61

67 92

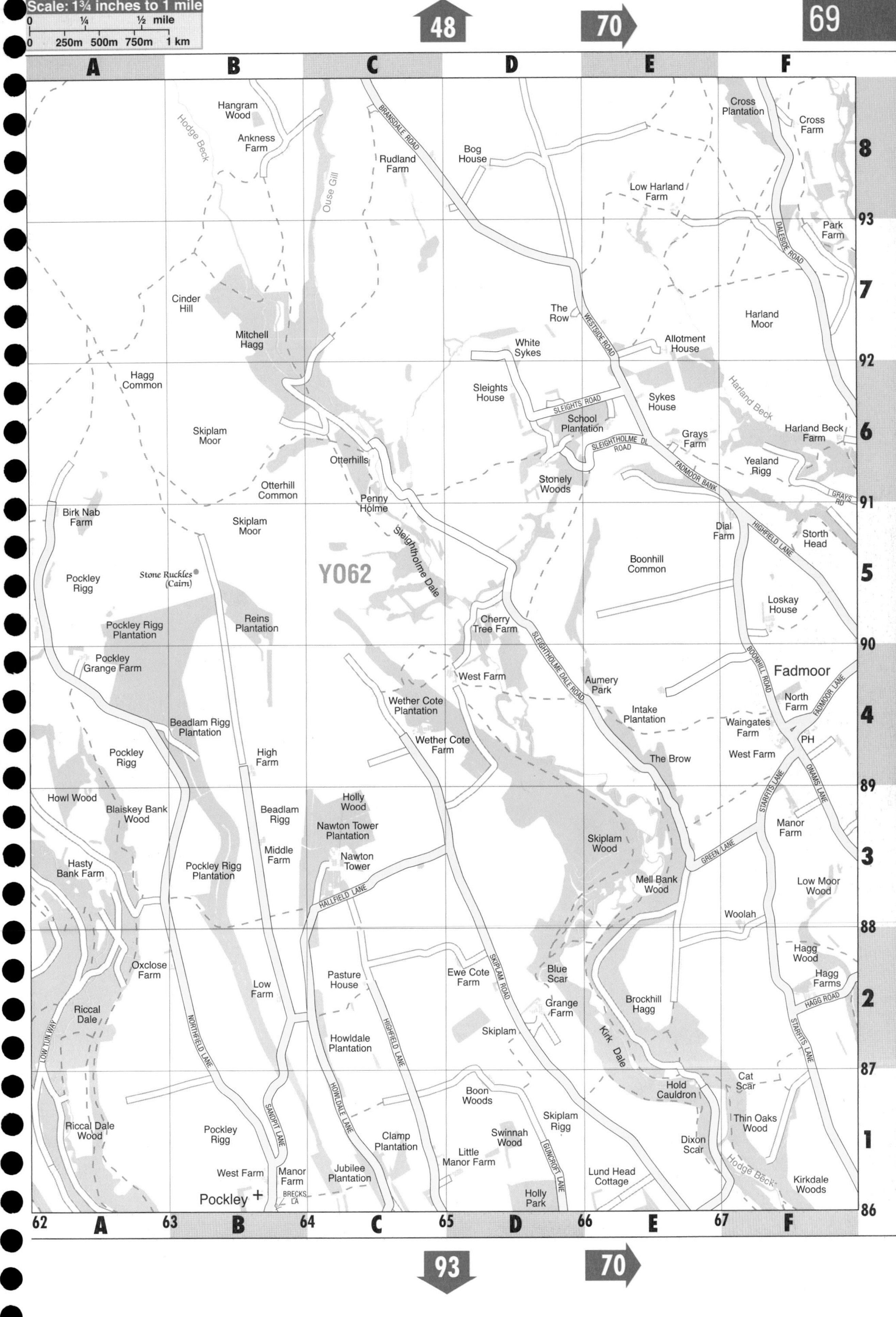
Scale: 1¾ inches to 1 mile
0 ¼ ½ mile
0 250m 500m 750m 1 km
48
70
A B C D E F
Hangram Wood
Ankness Farm
Hodge Beck
Rudland Farm
Bog House
Cross Plantation
Cross Farm
Low Harland Farm
Park Farm
Ouse Gill
BRANSDALE ROAD
DALESIDE ROAD
Cinder Hill
Mitchell Hagg
The Row
WESTSIDE ROAD
Allotment House
Harland Moor
White Sykes
Hagg Common
Sleights House
SLEIGHTS ROAD
School Plantation
Sykes House
Harland Beck
Skiplam Moor
Grays Farm
Harland Beck Farm
SLEIGHTHOLME DL ROAD
Otterhills
Otterhill Common
Stonely Woods
FADMOOR BANK
Yealand Rigg
GRAYS RD
Penny Holme
Birk Nab Farm
Skiplam Moor
Dial Farm
HIGHFIELD LANE
Storth Head
Sleightholme Dale
Pockley Rigg
Stone Ruckles (Cairn)
YO62
Boonhill Common
Loskay House
Pockley Rigg Plantation
Reins Plantation
Cherry Tree Farm
SLEIGHTHOLME DALE ROAD
Pockley Grange Farm
West Farm
Aumery Park
BOONHILL ROAD
Fadmoor
FADMOOR LANE
North Farm
Wether Cote Plantation
Intake Plantation
Waingates Farm
Beadlam Rigg Plantation
Wether Cote Farm
PH
Pockley Rigg
High Farm
The Brow
West Farm
STARFITS LANE
ONAMS LANE
Howl Wood
Blaiskey Bank Wood
Holly Wood
Beadlam Rigg
Nawton Tower Plantation
Manor Farm
Skiplam Wood
Hasty Bank Farm
Middle Farm
Nawton Tower
GREEN LANE
Pockley Rigg Plantation
Mell Bank Wood
Low Moor Wood
HALLFIELD LANE
Woolah
Hagg Wood
Oxclose Farm
Pasture House
Ewe Cote Farm
Blue Scar
Hagg Farms
Low Farm
SKIPLAM ROAD
HAGG ROAD
Riccal Dale
Grange Farm
Brockhill Hagg
LOW TUN WAY
NORTHFIELD LANE
Howldale Plantation
HIGHFIELD LANE
Skiplam
Kirk Dale
STARFITS LANE
Boon Woods
Hold Cauldron
Cat Scar
SANDPIT LANE
HOWLDALE LANE
Skiplam Rigg
Thin Oaks Wood
Riccal Dale Wood
Pockley Rigg
Clamp Plantation
Swinnah Wood
Dixon Scar
Little Manor Farm
GUNCROFT LANE
Hodge Beck
Jubilee Plantation
Lund Head Cottage
Kirkdale Woods
West Farm
Manor Farm
Pockley
BRECKS LA
Holly Park
8 93 7 92 6 91 5 90 4 89 3 88 2 87 1 86
62 63 64 65 66 67
93
70

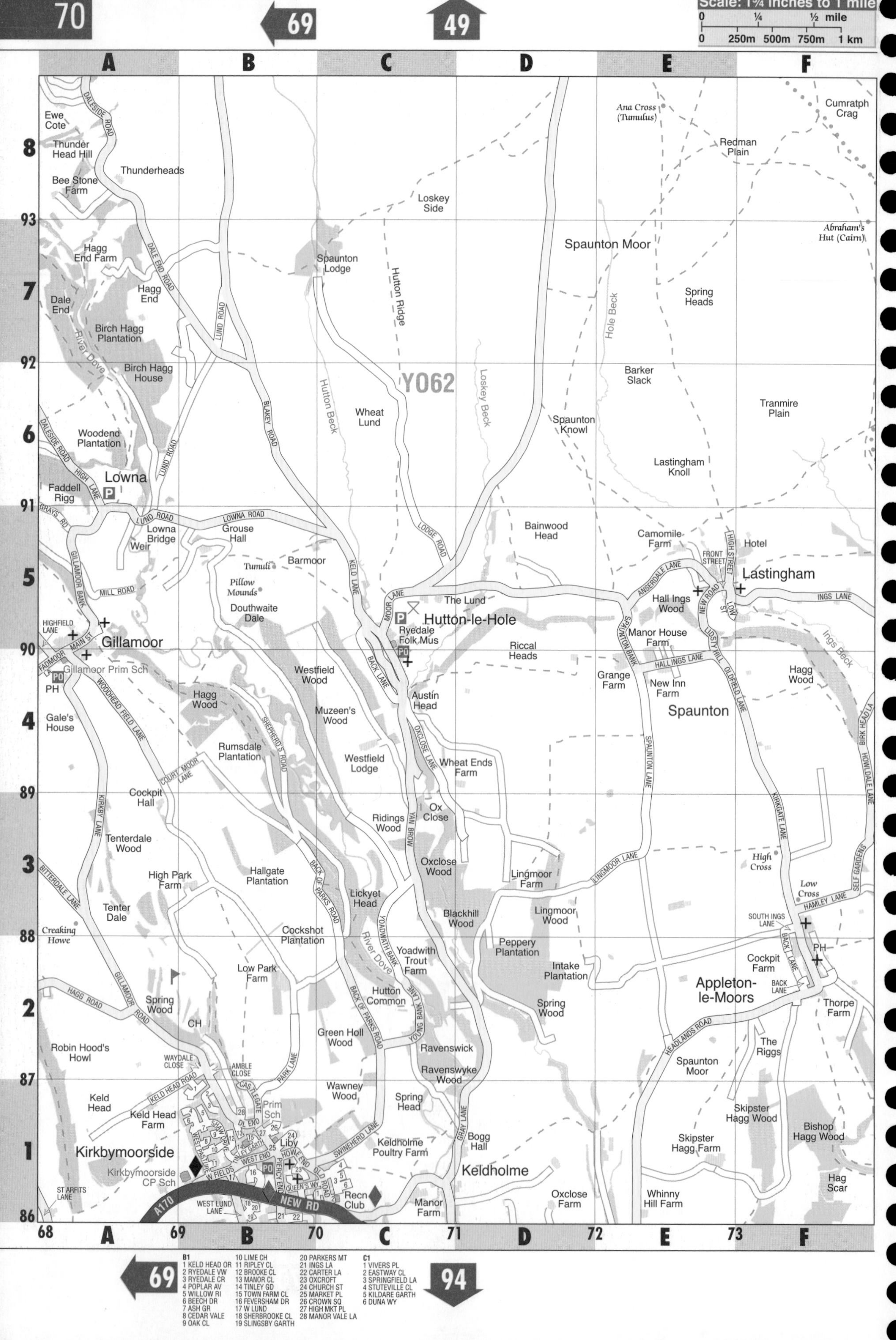

B1
1 KELD HEAD OR
2 RYEDALE VW
3 RYEDALE CR
4 POPLAR AV
5 WILLOW RI
6 BEECH DR
7 ASH GR
8 CEDAR VALE
9 OAK CL
10 LIME CH
11 RIPLEY CL
12 BROOKE CL
13 MANOR CL
14 TINLEY GD
15 TOWN FARM CL
16 FEVERSHAM DR
17 W LUND
18 SHERBROOKE CL
19 SLINGSBY GARTH
20 PARKERS MT
21 INGS LA
22 CARTER LA
23 OXCROFT
24 CHURCH ST
25 MARKET PL
26 CROWN SQ
27 HIGH MKT PL
28 MANOR VALE LA

C1
1 VIVERS PL
2 EASTWAY CL
3 SPRINGFIELD LA
4 STUTEVILLE CL
5 KILDARE GARTH
6 DUNA WY

69
94

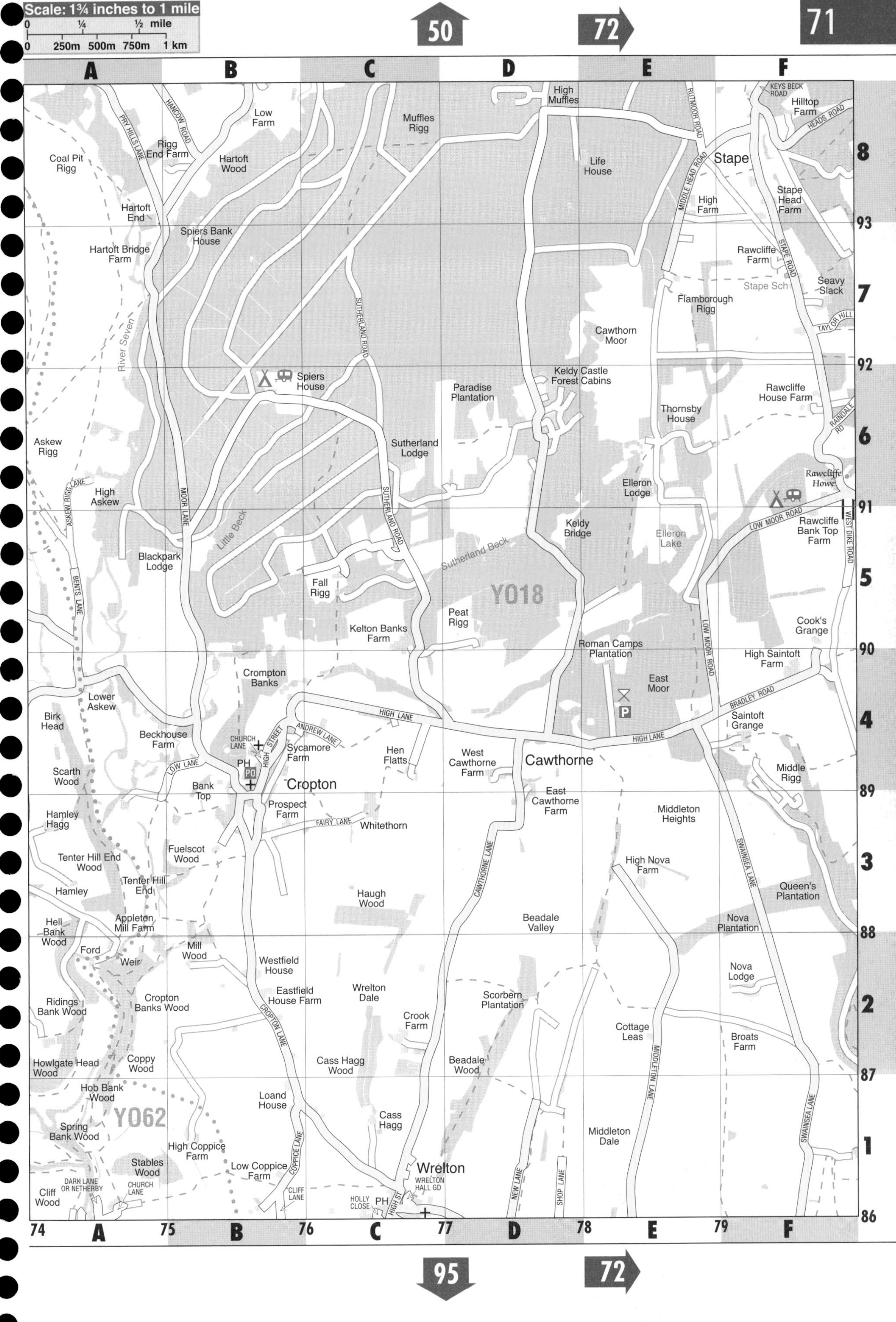
Scale: 1¾ inches to 1 mile
0 ¼ ½ mile
0 250m 500m 750m 1 km
50
72
A B C D E F
Low Farm
Muffles Rigg
High Muffles
Hilltop Farm
Coal Pit Rigg
Rigg End Farm
Hartoft Wood
Life House
Stape
Hartoft End
High Farm
Stape Head Farm
Spiers Bank House
Hartoft Bridge Farm
Rawcliffe Farm
Stape Sch
Seavy Slack
Flamborough Rigg
Cawthorn Moor
River Seven
Spiers House
Keldy Castle Forest Cabins
Paradise Plantation
Rawcliffe House Farm
Thornsby House
Askew Rigg
Sutherland Lodge
Rawcliffe Howe
High Askew
Elleron Lodge
Rawcliffe Bank Top Farm
Keldy Bridge
Elleron Lake
Little Beck
Blackpark Lodge
Sutherland Beck
Fall Rigg
YO18
Peat Rigg
Cook's Grange
Kelton Banks Farm
Roman Camps Plantation
High Saintoft Farm
Crompton Banks
East Moor
Lower Askew
Birk Head
Beckhouse Farm
Saintoft Grange
Sycamore Farm
Hen Flatts
West Cawthorne Farm
Cawthorne
Middle Rigg
Scarth Wood
PH
PO
Cropton
Bank Top
East Cawthorne Farm
Hamley Hagg
Prospect Farm
Middleton Heights
Whitethorn
Fuelscot Wood
Tenter Hill End Wood
High Nova Farm
Tenter Hill End
Hamley
Haugh Wood
Queen's Plantation
Appleton Mill Farm
Beadale Valley
Nova Plantation
Hell Bank Wood
Mill Wood
Ford
Weir
Westfield House
Nova Lodge
Ridings Bank Wood
Crompton Banks Wood
Eastfield House Farm
Wrelton Dale
Scorbern Plantation
Crook Farm
Cottage Leas
Broats Farm
Howlgate Head Wood
Coppy Wood
Cass Hagg Wood
Beadale Wood
Hob Bank Wood
YO62
Loand House
Cass Hagg
Spring Bank Wood
Middleton Dale
High Coppice Farm
Stables Wood
Low Coppice Farm
Wrelton
Cliff Wood
WRELTON HALL GD
PRY HILLS LANE
HANCOW ROAD
RUTMOOR ROAD
KEYS BECK ROAD
HEADS ROAD
MIDDLE HEAD ROAD
STAPE ROAD
TAYLOR HILL
SUTHERLAND ROAD
RAINDALE RD
ASKEW RIGG LANE
MOOR LANE
LOW MOOR ROAD
WEST DIKE ROAD
BENTS LANE
HIGH LANE
BRADLEY ROAD
CHURCH LANE
HIGH STREET
ANDREW LANE
LOW LANE
FAIRY LANE
CAWTHORNE LANE
SWAINSEA LANE
CROPTON LANE
MIDDLETON LANE
COPPICE LANE
NEW LANE
SHOP LANE
DARK LANE OR NETHERBY
CHURCH LANE
CLIFF LANE
HOLLY CLOSE
HIGH ST
8 93 7 92 6 91 5 90 4 89 3 88 2 87 1 86
74 75 76 77 78 79
95
72

71
51

Scale: 1¾ inches to 1 mile

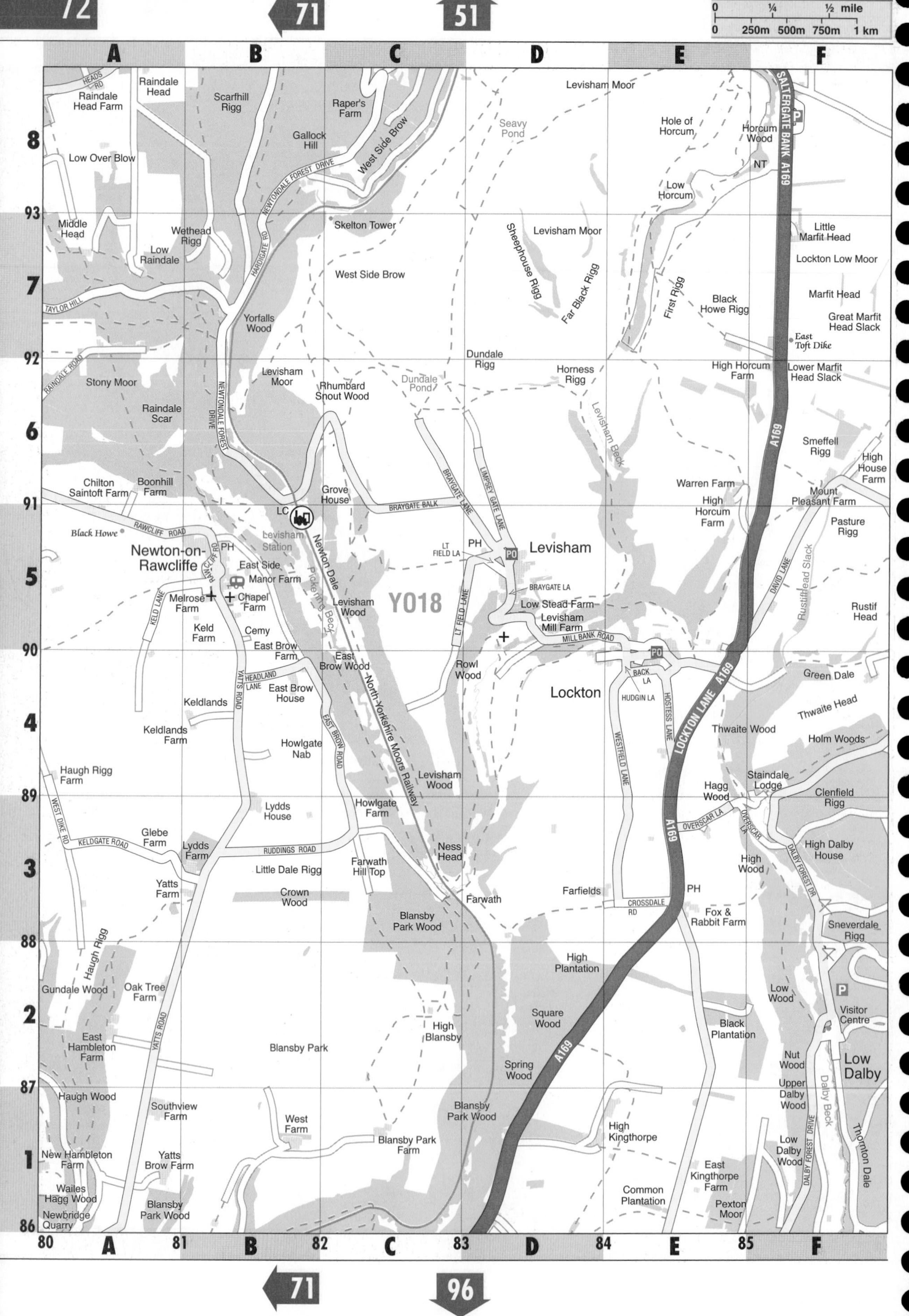

71
96

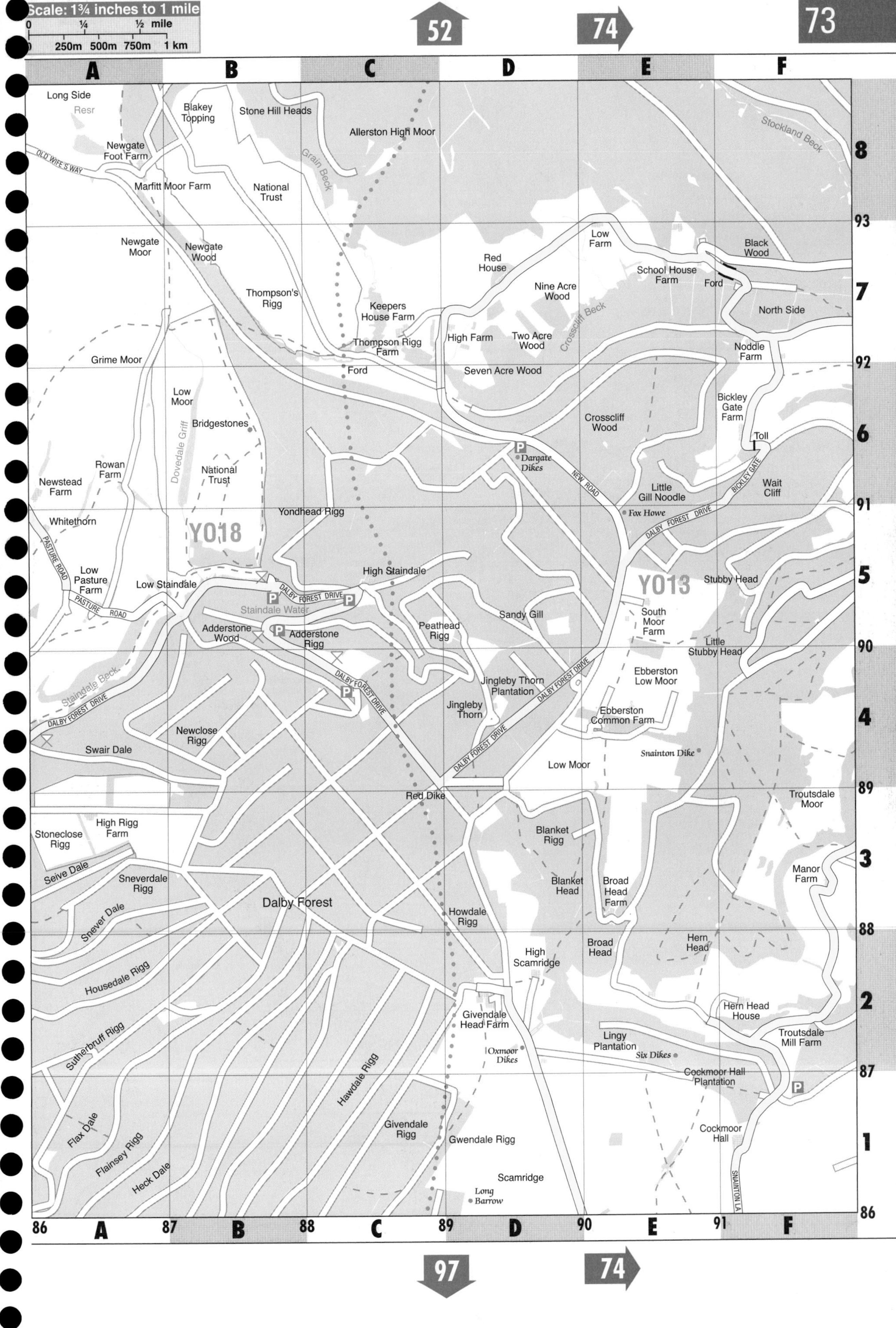
Scale: 1¾ inches to 1 mile
0
¼
½ mile
250m 500m 750m 1 km
52
74
A B C D E F
Long Side
Resr
Blakey Topping
Stone Hill Heads
Allerston High Moor
Stockland Beck
Newgate Foot Farm
OLD WIFE'S WAY
Grain Beck
Marfitt Moor Farm
National Trust
Low Farm
Black Wood
Newgate Moor
Newgate Wood
Red House
School House Farm
Ford
Nine Acre Wood
Thompson's Rigg
North Side
Keepers House Farm
Crosscliff Beck
High Farm
Two Acre Wood
Thompson Rigg Farm
Noddle Farm
Grime Moor
Ford
Seven Acre Wood
Low Moor
Bickley Gate Farm
Crosscliff Wood
Bridgestones
Dovedale Griff
Toll
Rowan Farm
Dargate Dikes
National Trust
NEW ROAD
Newstead Farm
Little Gill Noodle
BICKLEY GATE
Wait Cliff
Whitethorn
Yondhead Rigg
Fox Howe
DALBY FOREST DRIVE
YO18
PASTURE ROAD
Low Pasture Farm
High Staindale
YO13
Stubby Head
Low Staindale
DALBY FOREST DRIVE
Sandy Gill
South Moor Farm
PASTURE ROAD
Staindale Water
Adderstone Wood
Adderstone Rigg
Peathead Rigg
Little Stubby Head
Staindale Beck
DALBY FOREST DRIVE
Ebberston Low Moor
Jingleby Thorn Plantation
DALBY FOREST DRIVE
DALBY FOREST DRIVE
Jingleby Thorn
Ebberston Common Farm
Newclose Rigg
DALBY FOREST DRIVE
Swair Dale
Snainton Dike
Low Moor
Red Dike
Troutsdale Moor
High Rigg Farm
Blanket Rigg
Stoneclose Rigg
Seive Dale
Manor Farm
Sneverdale Rigg
Blanket Head
Broad Head Farm
Dalby Forest
Snever Dale
Howdale Rigg
Hern Head
Broad Head
High Scamridge
Housedale Rigg
Hern Head House
Givendale Head Farm
Troutsdale Mill Farm
Sutherbruff Rigg
Lingy Plantation
Oxmoor Dikes
Six Dikes
Hawdale Rigg
Cockmoor Hall Plantation
Flax Dale
Givendale Rigg
Cockmoor Hall
Gwendale Rigg
Flainsey Rigg
Heck Dale
Scamridge
Long Barrow
SNAINTON LA
8
93
7
92
6
91
5
90
4
89
3
88
2
87
1
86
86 A 87 B 88 C 89 D 90 E 91 F
97
74

73
53

Scale: 1¾ inches to 1 mile
0 ¼ ½ mile
0 250m 500m 750m 1 km

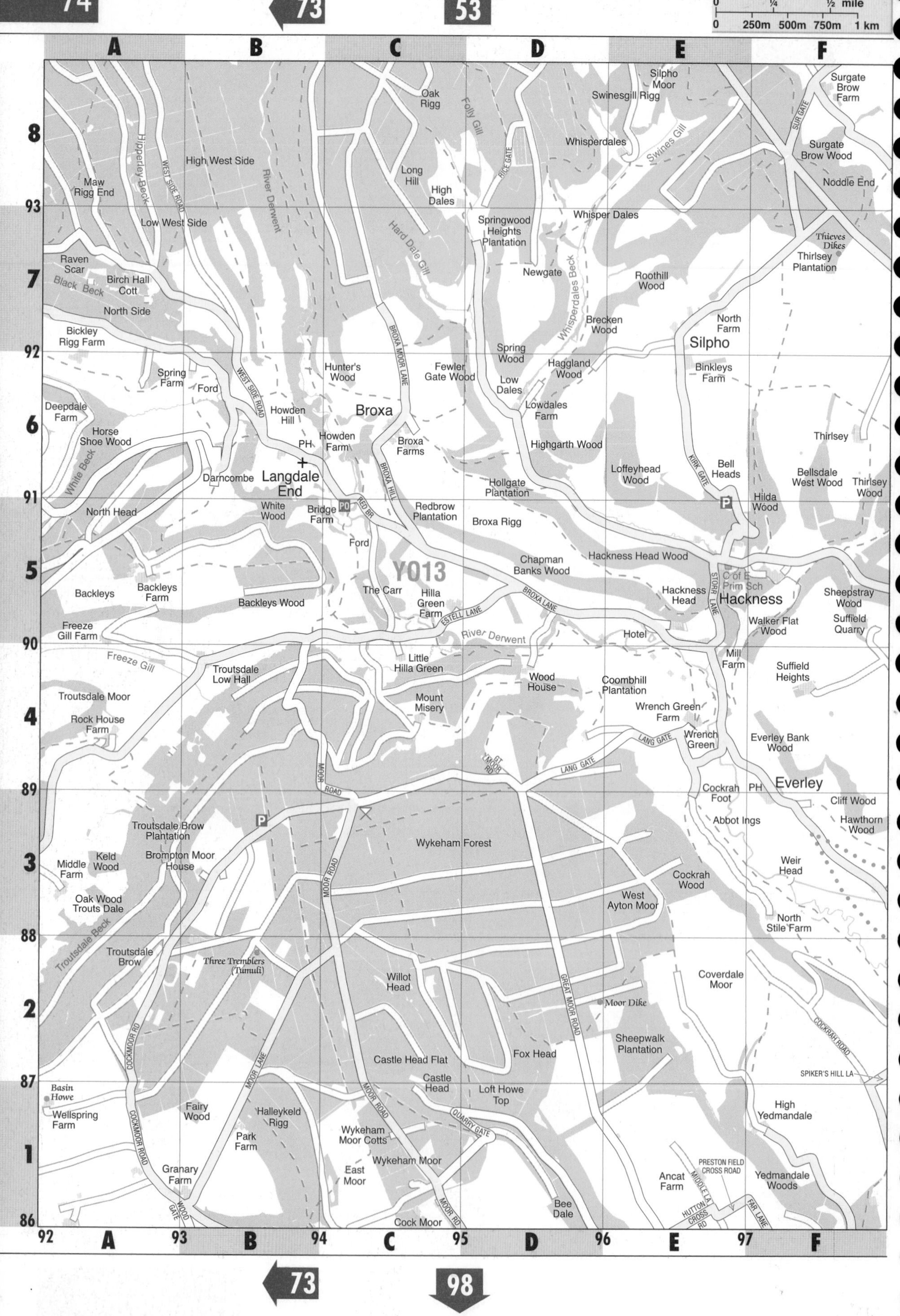

73
98

54
76

Scale: 1¾ inches to 1 mile
0 ¼ ½ mile
0 250m 500m 750m 1 km

D5
1 ANNADALE GR
2 WREA HEAD CL
3 COOKS GD
4 IVY BANK CT
5 STONY CT
6 ELLIS GD
7 CASTLE VW
8 STONY LA
9 LANCASTER CL
10 QUEEN ELIZABETH DR
11 DUCHY AV
12 BEECH DR
13 WEST PARK RD
14 THE PARK
15 EAST PARK RD
16 FIELD CL RD
17 LANCASTER WY
18 CHICHESTER CL
19 WEST AV
20 SOUTH AV
21 EAST AV
22 LOW ST
23 HALL PK CL
24 FLOCK LEYS
25 HALL PK GR
26 TIBBY BUTTS
27 SCALBY BECK RD
28 RIVERSIDE
29 THOMPSON CL
30 COW WATH CL
31 HAGUE AV
32 ELLISON AV
33 BIELBY CL
34 DANES DYKE
35 NEWBY FARM CL
36 NEWBY FARM CR

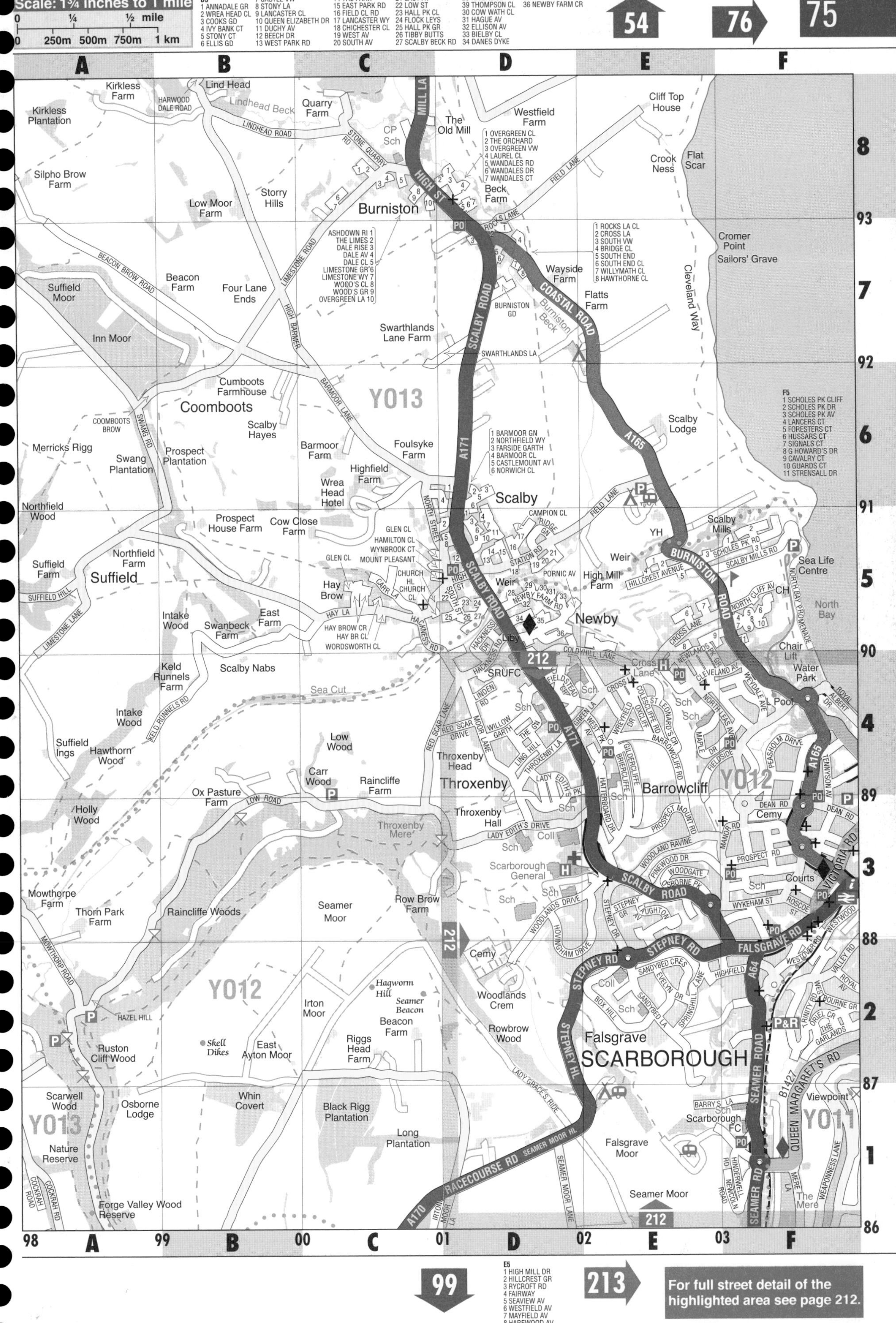

99

E5
1 HIGH MILL DR
2 HILLCREST GR
3 RYCROFT RD
4 FAIRWAY
5 SEAVIEW AV
6 WESTFIELD AV
7 MAYFIELD AV
8 HAREWOOD AV
9 BRIARDENE AV

213

For full street detail of the highlighted area see page 212.

75

Scale: 1¾ inches to 1 mile

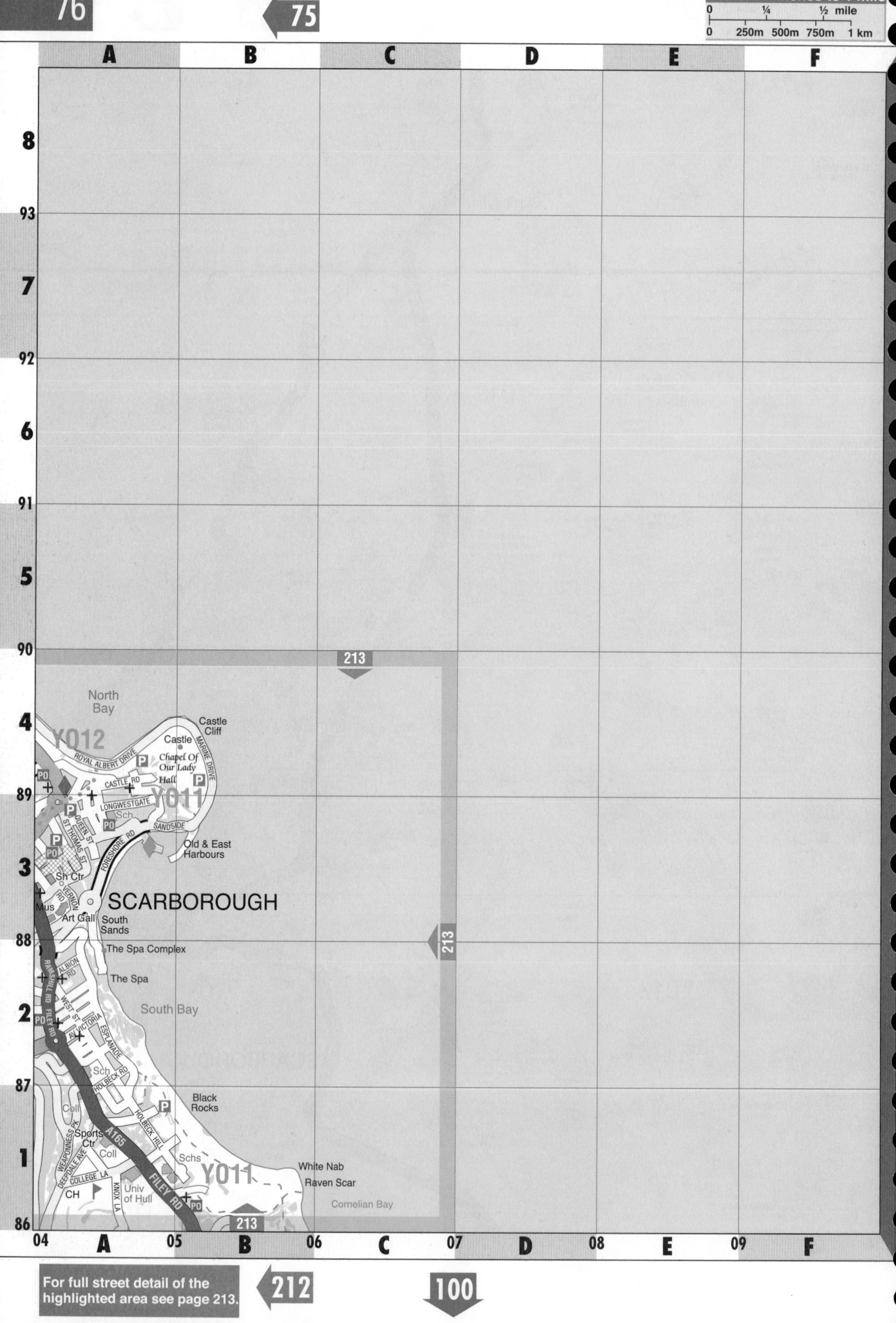

For full street detail of the highlighted area see page 213.

212

100

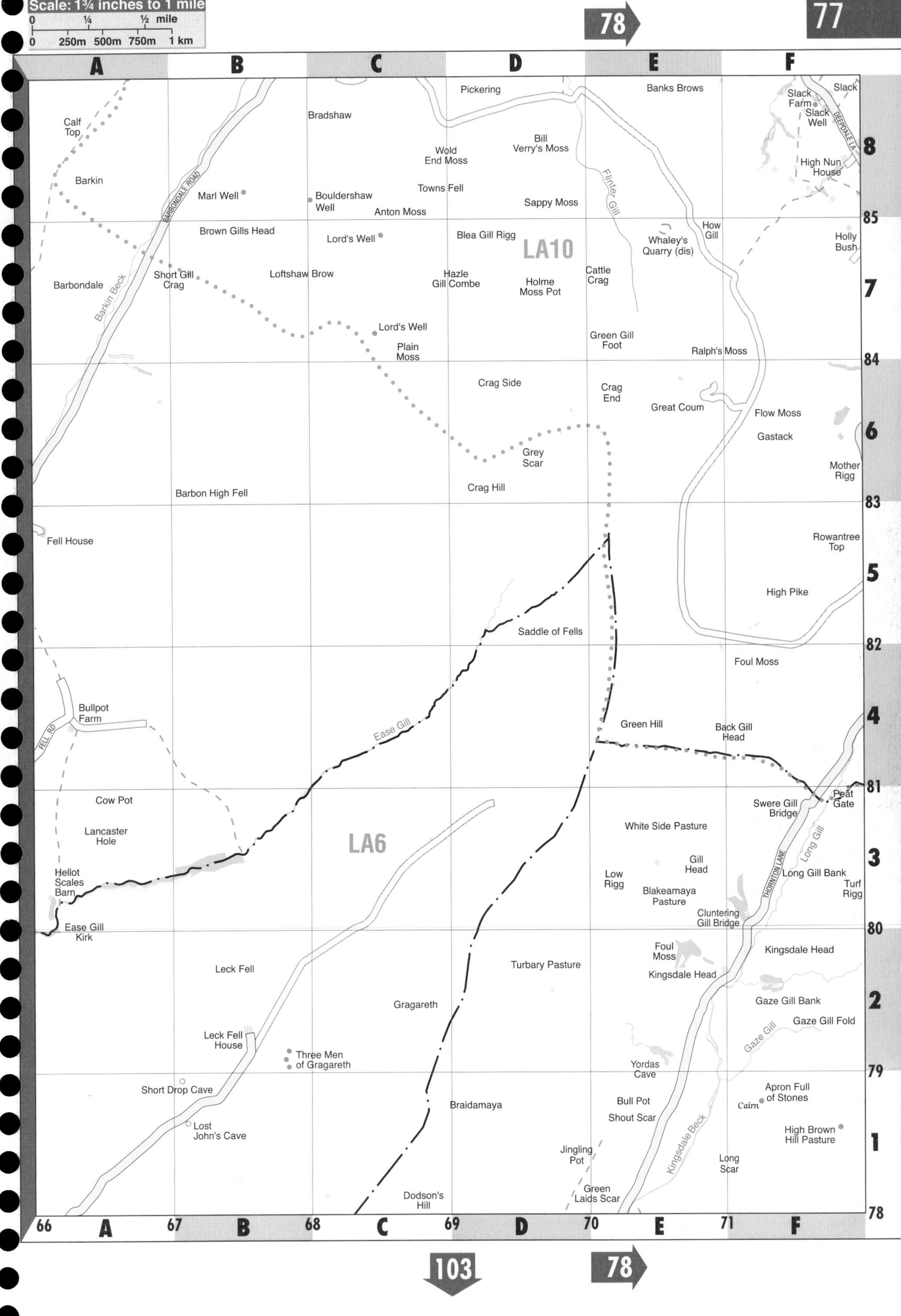
Scale: 1¾ inches to 1 mile
0 ¼ ½ mile
0 250m 500m 750m 1 km
78
A B C D E F
Calf Top
Barkin
Bradshaw
Pickering
Banks Brows
Slack Farm
Slack Well
Slack
DEEPDALE LA
High Nun House
Wold End Moss
Bill Verry's Moss
Marl Well
Boldershaw Well
Towns Fell
Anton Moss
Sappy Moss
Flinter Gill
BARBONDALE ROAD
Brown Gills Head
Lord's Well
Blea Gill Rigg
LA10
Whaley's Quarry (dis)
How Gill
Holly Bush
Barbondale
Barkin Beck
Short Gill Crag
Loftshaw Brow
Hazle Gill Combe
Holme Moss Pot
Cattle Crag
Lord's Well
Plain Moss
Green Gill Foot
Ralph's Moss
Crag Side
Crag End
Great Coum
Flow Moss
Gastack
Grey Scar
Mother Rigg
Crag Hill
Barbon High Fell
Fell House
Rowantree Top
High Pike
Saddle of Fells
Foul Moss
Bullpot Farm
FELL RD
Ease Gill
Green Hill
Back Gill Head
Peat Gate
Swere Gill Bridge
Cow Pot
Lancaster Hole
LA6
White Side Pasture
Gill Head
Long Gill
THORNTON LANE
Long Gill Bank
Hellot Scales Barn
Low Rigg
Blakeamaya Pasture
Turf Rigg
Cluntering Gill Bridge
Ease Gill Kirk
Foul Moss
Kingsdale Head
Leck Fell
Turbary Pasture
Kingsdale Head
Gragareth
Gaze Gill Bank
Gaze Gill Fold
Gaze Gill
Leck Fell House
Three Men of Gragareth
Yordas Cave
Short Drop Cave
Apron Full of Stones
Cairn
Braidamaya
Bull Pot
Shout Scar
Lost John's Cave
High Brown Hill Pasture
Kingsdale Beck
Jingling Pot
Long Scar
Green Laids Scar
Dodson's Hill
8 85 7 84 6 83 5 82 4 81 3 80 2 79 1 78
66 67 68 69 70 71

103
78

77

Scale: 1¾ inches to 1 mile

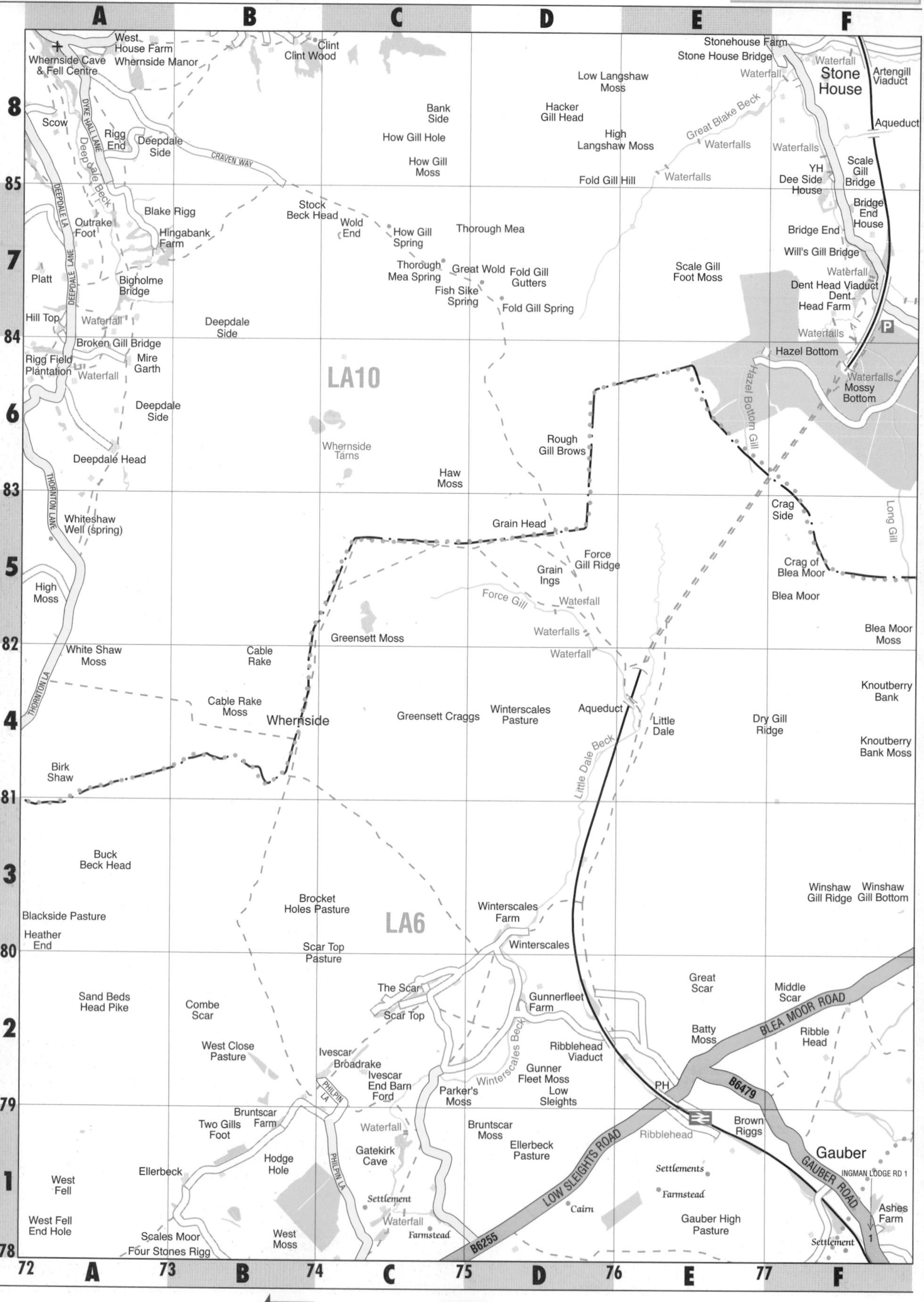

77

104

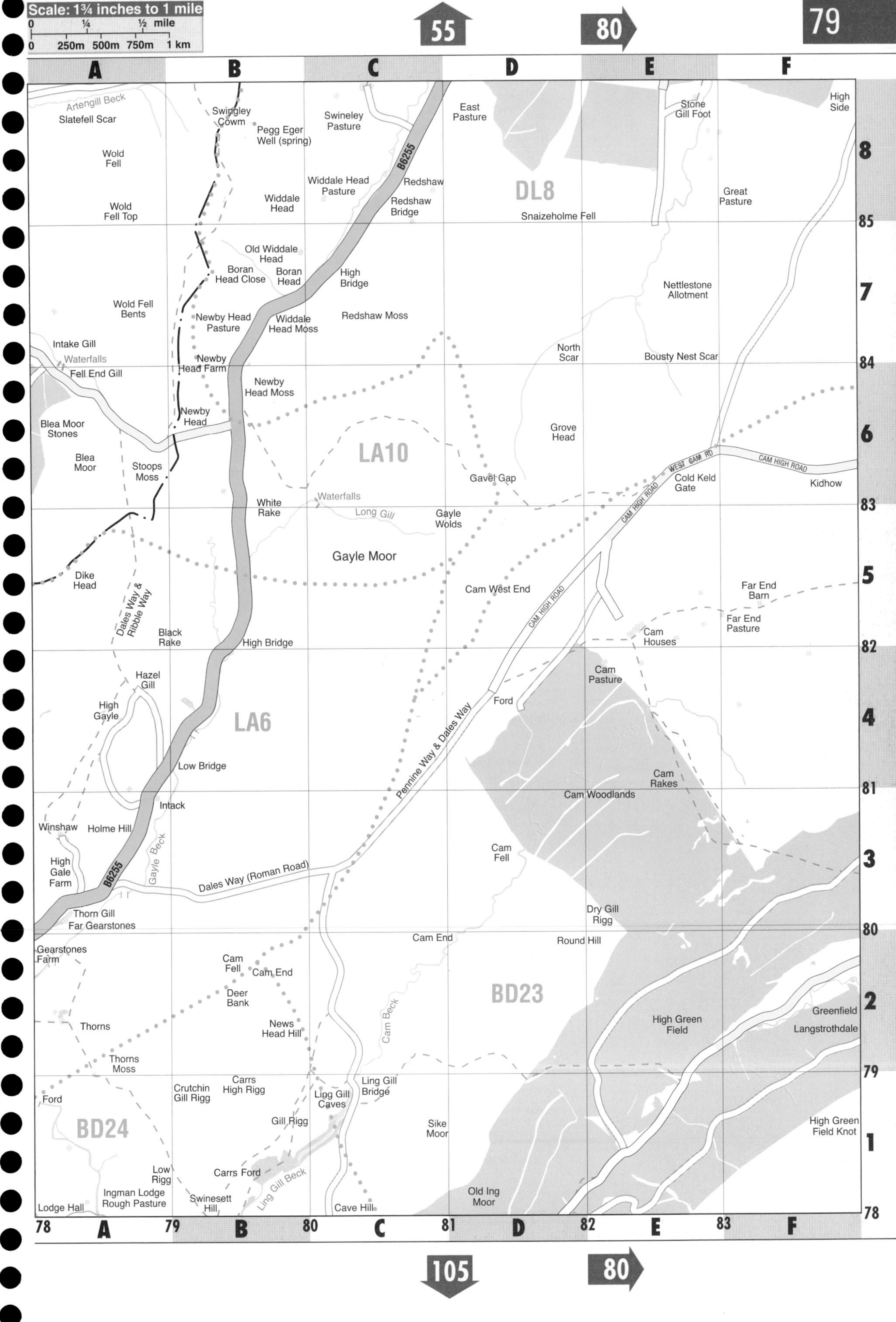
Scale: 1¾ inches to 1 mile
0 ¼ ½ mile
0 250m 500m 750m 1 km
55
80
A B C D E F
Artengill Beck
Slatefell Scar
Swingley Cowm
Pegg Eger Well (spring)
Swineley Pasture
East Pasture
Stone Gill Foot
High Side
Wold Fell
Wold Fell Top
Widdale Head
Widdale Head Pasture
B6255
Redshaw
Redshaw Bridge
DL8
Great Pasture
Snaizeholme Fell
Old Widdale Head
Boran Head Close
Boran Head
High Bridge
Nettlestone Allotment
Wold Fell Bents
Newby Head Pasture
Widdale Head Moss
Redshaw Moss
Intake Gill
Waterfalls
Fell End Gill
Newby Head Farm
North Scar
Bousty Nest Scar
Newby Head Moss
Blea Moor Stones
Newby Head
Grove Head
Blea Moor
Stoops Moss
LA10
WEST CAM RD
CAM HIGH ROAD
Gavel Gap
Cold Keld Gate
Kidhow
Waterfalls
White Rake
Long Gill
Gayle Wolds
Gayle Moor
Dike Head
Dales Way & Ribble Way
Cam West End
Far End Barn
Far End Pasture
Black Rake
High Bridge
Cam Houses
Hazel Gill
Cam Pasture
High Gayle
Ford
LA6
Pennine Way & Dales Way
Low Bridge
Cam Rakes
Cam Woodlands
Intack
Winshaw
Holme Hill
Gayle Beck
Cam Fell
High Gale Farm
Dales Way (Roman Road)
Thorn Gill
Far Gearstones
Dry Gill Rigg
Gearstones Farm
Cam End
Round Hill
Cam Fell
Cam End
Deer Bank
BD23
Thorns
News Head Hill
Cam Beck
High Green Field
Greenfield
Langstrothdale
Thorns Moss
Crutchin Gill Rigg
Carrs High Rigg
Ling Gill Caves
Ling Gill Bridge
Ford
BD24
Gill Rigg
Sike Moor
High Green Field Knot
Low Rigg
Carrs Ford
Ling Gill Beck
Ingman Lodge Rough Pasture
Swinesett Hill
Old Ing Moor
Lodge Hall
Cave Hill
8 85 7 84 6 83 5 82 4 81 3 80 2 79 1 78
78 79 80 81 82 83
105
80

79
56

Scale: 1¾ inches to 1 mile

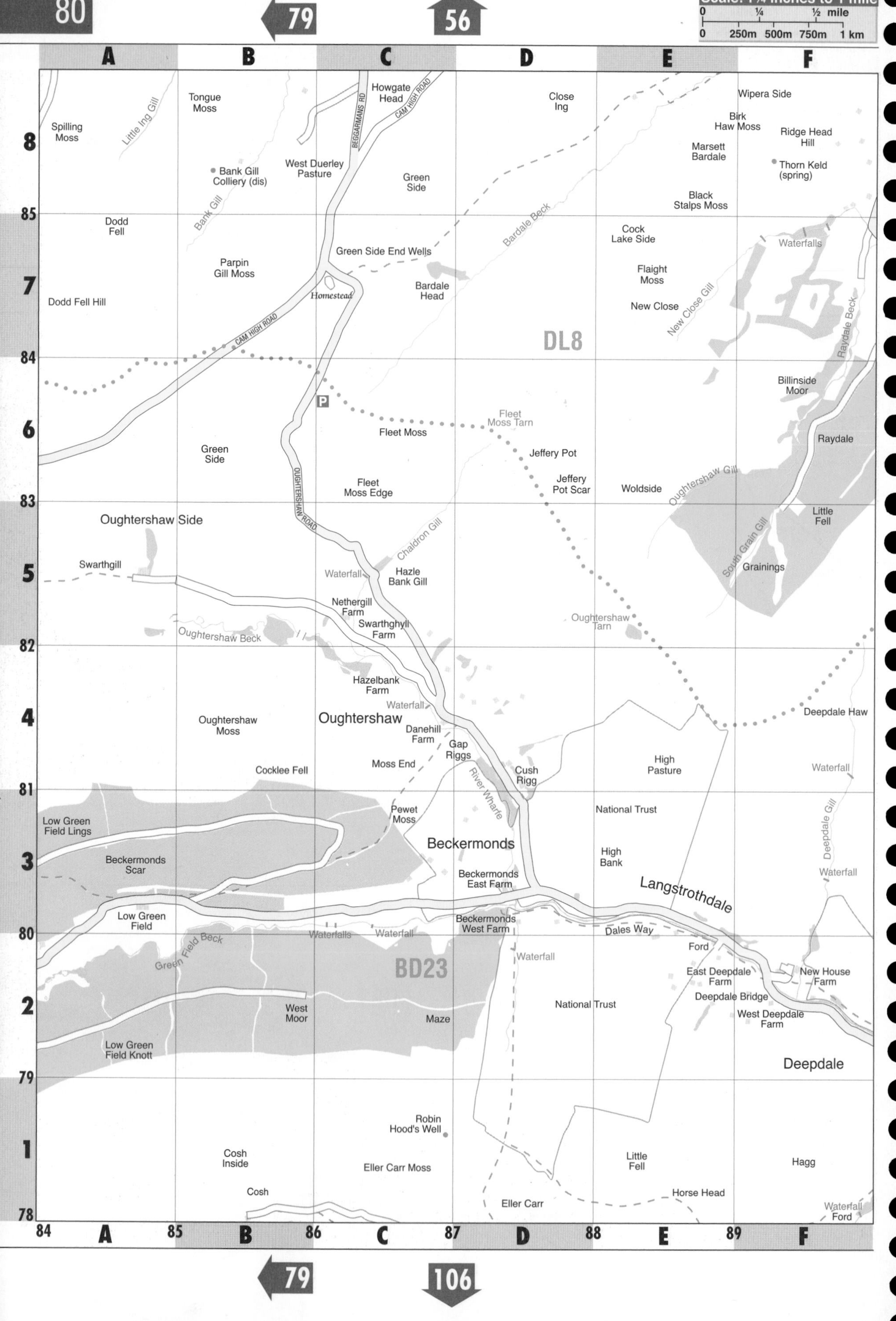

79
106

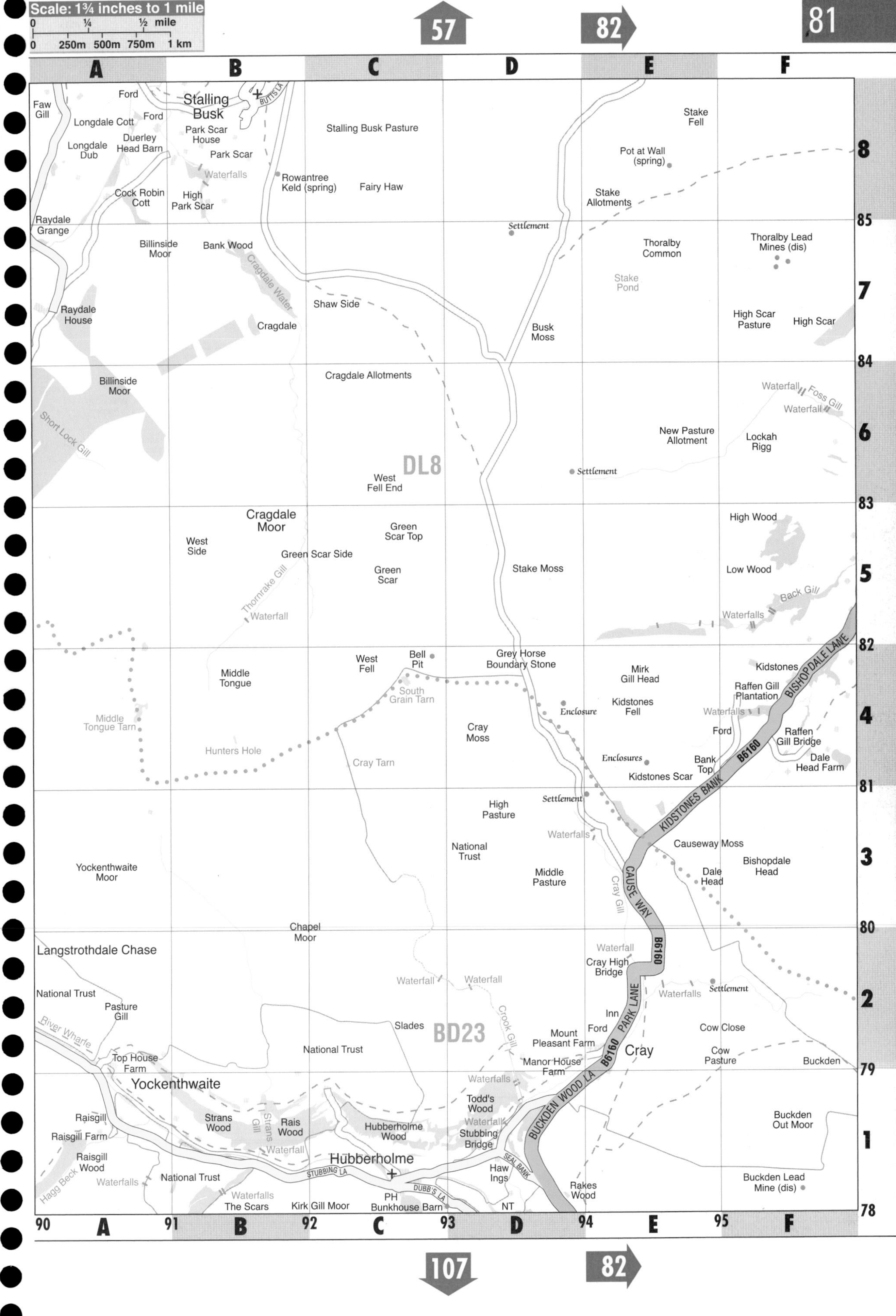
Scale: 1¾ inches to 1 mile
57
82
Stalling Busk
Stalling Busk Pasture
Stake Fell
Pot at Wall (spring)
Rowantree Keld (spring)
Fairy Haw
Stake Allotments
Raydale Grange
Thoralby Common
Thoralby Lead Mines (dis)
Cragdale
Shaw Side
Busk Moss
High Scar Pasture
High Scar
Cragdale Allotments
New Pasture Allotment
Lockah Rigg
DL8
West Fell End
Cragdale Moor
Stake Moss
Grey Horse Boundary Stone
Kidstones
Hunters Hole
Cray Tarn
Cray Moss
Kidstones Scar
Yockenthwaite Moor
Causeway Moss
Bishopdale Head
Chapel Moor
Langstrothdale Chase
BD23
Cray
Buckden
Yockenthwaite
Hubberholme
Buckden Out Moor
Buckden Lead Mine (dis)
107
82

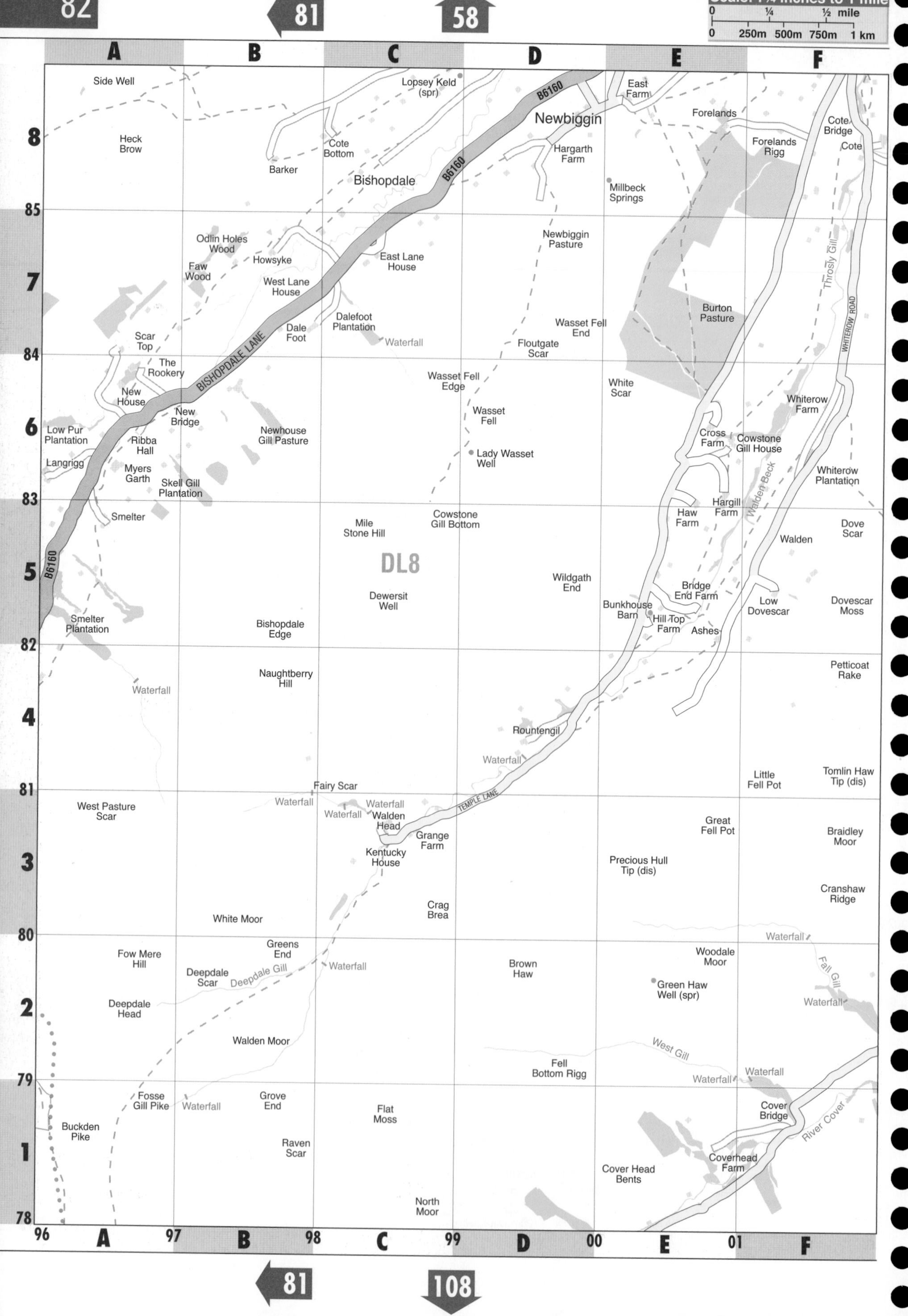
81
58
Scale: 1¾ inches to 1 mile
A
B
C
D
E
F
Side Well
Lopsey Keld (spr)
East Farm
B6160
Newbiggin
Forelands
Cote Bridge
Cote
Heck Brow
Cote Bottom
Barker
Bishopdale
Hargarth Farm
Forelands Rigg
Millbeck Springs
Odlin Holes Wood
Faw Wood
Howsyke
East Lane House
West Lane House
Newbiggin Pasture
Throsly Gill
Scar Top
Dale Foot
Dalefoot Plantation
Waterfall
Wasset Fell End
Floutgate Scar
Burton Pasture
WHITEROW ROAD
The Rookery
BISHOPDALE LANE
New House
New Bridge
Wasset Fell Edge
White Scar
Whiterow Farm
Low Pur Plantation
Ribba Hall
Newhouse Gill Pasture
Wasset Fell
Cross Farm
Cowstone Gill House
Langrigg
Myers Garth
Skell Gill Plantation
Lady Wasset Well
Whiterow Plantation
Smelter
Mile Stone Hill
Cowstone Gill Bottom
Haw Farm
Hargill Farm
Walden Beck
Walden
Dove Scar
DL8
Dewersit Well
Wildgath End
Bridge End Farm
Bunkhouse Barn
Hill Top Farm
Ashes
Low Dovescar
Dovescar Moss
Smelter Plantation
Bishopdale Edge
Naughtberry Hill
Petticoat Rake
Rountengil
Fairy Scar
TEMPLE LANE
Little Fell Pot
Tomlin Haw Tip (dis)
West Pasture Scar
Walden Head
Grange Farm
Great Fell Pot
Braidley Moor
Kentucky House
Precious Hull Tip (dis)
Cranshaw Ridge
White Moor
Crag Brea
Fow Mere Hill
Greens End
Deepdale Scar
Deepdale Gill
Brown Haw
Woodale Moor
Fall Gill
Green Haw Well (spr)
Deepdale Head
Walden Moor
West Gill
Fell Bottom Rigg
Fosse Gill Pike
Grove End
Flat Moss
Cover Bridge
River Cover
Buckden Pike
Raven Scar
Coverhead Farm
Cover Head Bents
North Moor
81
108

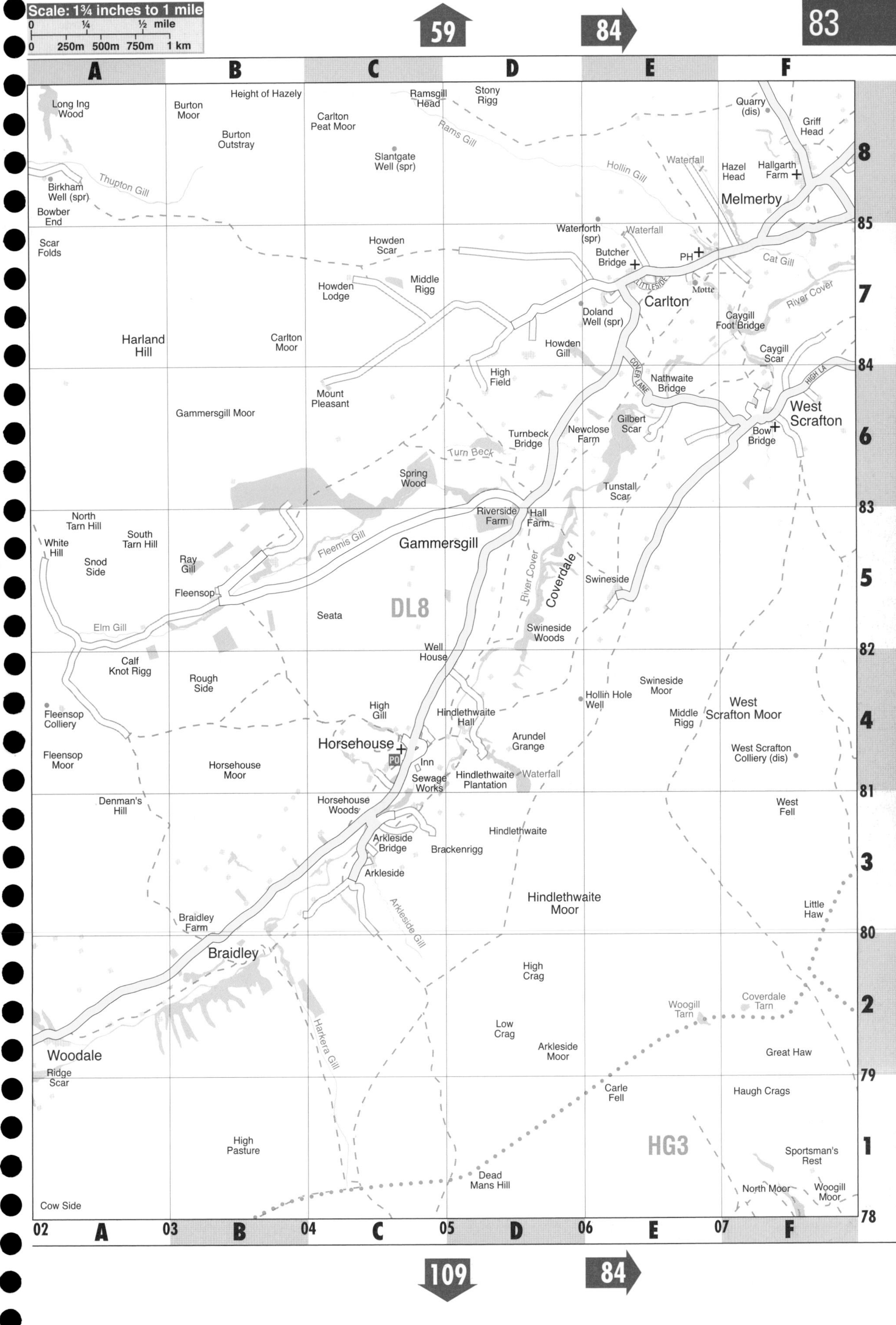
Scale: 1¾ inches to 1 mile
0 ¼ ½ mile
0 250m 500m 750m 1 km
59
84
A B C D E F
Long Ing Wood
Burton Moor
Height of Hazely
Burton Outstray
Carlton Peat Moor
Ramsgill Head
Stony Rigg
Rams Gill
Slantgate Well (spr)
Quarry (dis)
Griff Head
Hazel Head
Hallgarth Farm
Melmerby
Waterfall
Hollin Gill
Birkham Well (spr)
Thupton Gill
Bowber End
Scar Folds
Howden Scar
Waterforth (spr)
Butcher Bridge
PH
Cat Gill
Howden Lodge
Middle Rigg
Littleside
Motte
Carlton
River Cover
Doland Well (spr)
Caygill Foot Bridge
Caygill Scar
Harland Hill
Carlton Moor
Howden Gill
High Field
Cover Lane
Nathwaite Bridge
High La
Mount Pleasant
West Scrafton
Gammersgill Moor
Gilbert Scar
Turnbeck Bridge
Newclose Farm
Bow Bridge
Turn Beck
Spring Wood
Tunstall Scar
North Tarn Hill
South Tarn Hill
White Hill
Riverside Farm
Hall Farm
Fleemis Gill
Gammersgill
Snod Side
Ray Gill
Coverdale
River Cover
Swineside
Fleensop
Seata
DL8
Elm Gill
Swineside Woods
Well House
Calf Knot Rigg
Rough Side
Swineside Moor
Hollin Hole Well
High Gill
Hindlethwaite Hall
Middle Rigg
West Scrafton Moor
Fleensop Colliery
Horsehouse
PO
Inn
Arundel Grange
West Scrafton Colliery (dis)
Fleensop Moor
Horsehouse Moor
Sewage Works
Hindlethwaite Plantation
Waterfall
Denman's Hill
Horsehouse Woods
West Fell
Arkleside Bridge
Hindlethwaite
Brackenrigg
Arkleside
Hindlethwaite Moor
Little Haw
Arkleside Gill
Braidley Farm
Braidley
High Crag
Coverdale Tarn
Woogill Tarn
Harkera Gill
Low Crag
Arkleside Moor
Great Haw
Woodale
Ridge Scar
Carle Fell
Haugh Crags
High Pasture
HG3
Sportsman's Rest
Dead Mans Hill
North Moor
Woogill Moor
Cow Side
8 85 7 84 6 83 5 82 4 81 3 80 2 79 1 78
02 03 04 05 06 07
109
84

83
60

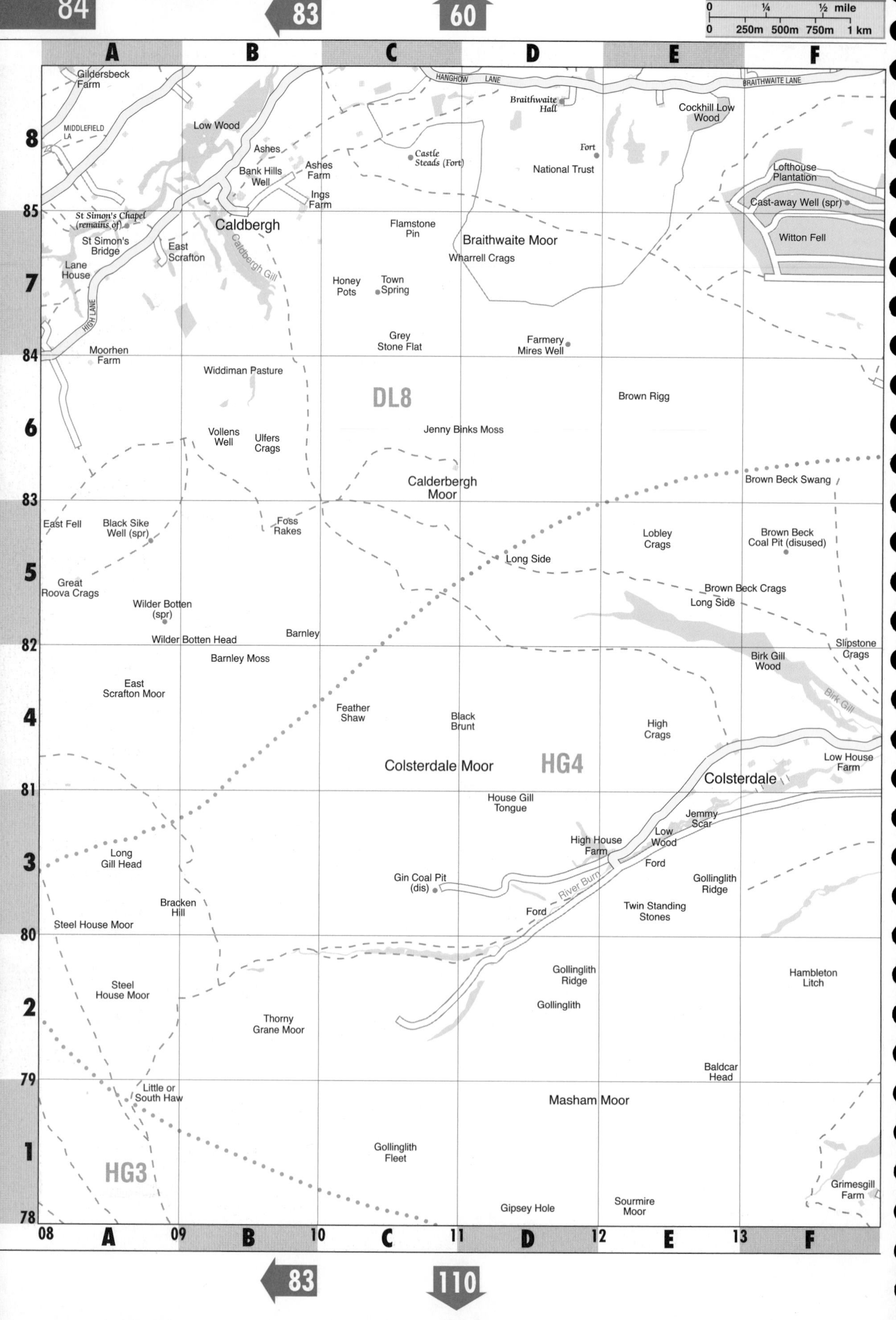
Scale: 1¾ inches to 1 mile
0 ¼ ½ mile
0 250m 500m 750m 1 km
A B C D E F
Gildersbeck Farm
MIDDLEFIELD LA
Low Wood
Ashes
Bank Hills Well
Ashes Farm
Ings Farm
HANGHOW LANE
Braithwaite Hall
Castle Steads (Fort)
Fort
National Trust
BRAITHWAITE LANE
Cockhill Low Wood
Lofthouse Plantation
Cast-away Well (spr)
Witton Fell
St Simon's Chapel (remains of)
St Simon's Bridge
Caldbergh
Caldbergh Gill
East Scrafton
Lane House
HIGH LANE
Flamstone Pin
Braithwaite Moor
Wharrell Crags
Honey Pots
Town Spring
Grey Stone Flat
Farmery Mires Well
Moorhen Farm
Widdiman Pasture
DL8
Brown Rigg
Vollens Well
Ulfers Crags
Jenny Binks Moss
Calderbergh Moor
Brown Beck Swang
East Fell
Black Sike Well (spr)
Foss Rakes
Lobley Crags
Brown Beck Coal Pit (disused)
Long Side
Great Roova Crags
Wilder Botten (spr)
Brown Beck Crags
Long Side
Wilder Botten Head
Barnley
Barnley Moss
Slipstone Crags
Birk Gill Wood
Birk Gill
East Scrafton Moor
Feather Shaw
Black Brunt
High Crags
Colsterdale Moor
HG4
Low House Farm
Colsterdale
House Gill Tongue
Jemmy Scar
Low Wood
High House Farm
Long Gill Head
Ford
Gin Coal Pit (dis)
Gollinglith Ridge
River Burn
Bracken Hill
Ford
Twin Standing Stones
Steel House Moor
Gollinglith Ridge
Hambleton Litch
Steel House Moor
Gollinglith
Thorny Grane Moor
Baldcar Head
Little or South Haw
Masham Moor
Gollinglith Fleet
HG3
Grimesgill Farm
Gipsey Hole
Sourmire Moor
8 85 7 84 6 83 5 82 4 81 3 80 2 79 1 78
08 A 09 B 10 C 11 D 12 E 13 F

83
110

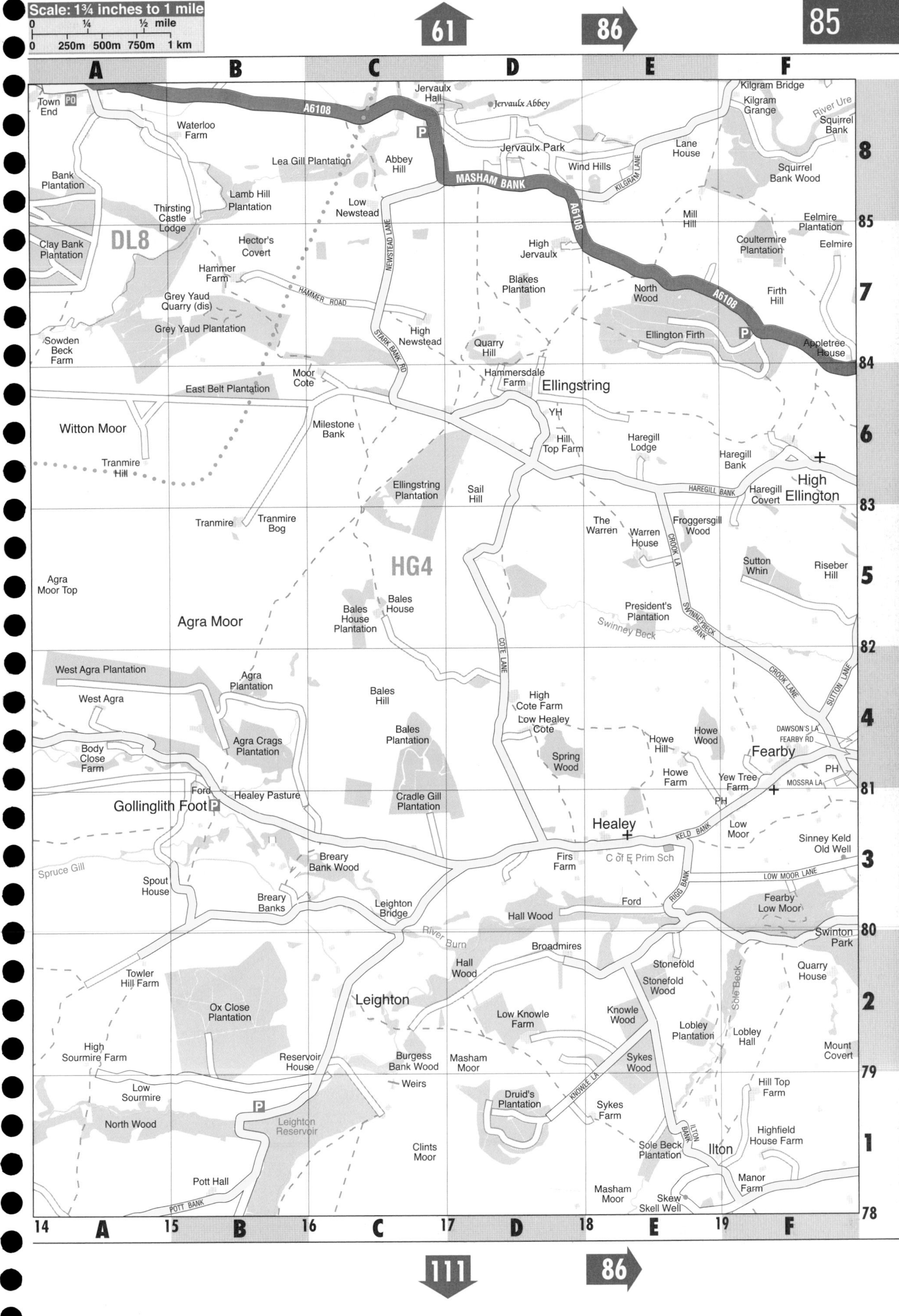
Scale: 1¾ inches to 1 mile
61
86
Jervaulx Hall
Jervaulx Abbey
Kilgram Bridge
Kilgram Grange
River Ure
Squirrel Bank
Town End
Waterloo Farm
A6108
Lea Gill Plantation
Abbey Hill
Jervaulx Park
Wind Hills
Lane House
Squirrel Bank Wood
Bank Plantation
Lamb Hill Plantation
MASHAM BANK
KILGRAM LANE
Thirsting Castle Lodge
Low Newstead
Mill Hill
Eelmire Plantation
DL8
Clay Bank Plantation
Hector's Covert
High Jervaulx
Coultermire Plantation
Eelmire
Hammer Farm
HAMMER ROAD
NEWSTEAD LANE
Blakes Plantation
North Wood
Firth Hill
Grey Yaud Quarry (dis)
Grey Yaud Plantation
High Newstead
Ellington Firth
Sowden Beck Farm
STARK BANK RD
Quarry Hill
Appletree House
Moor Cote
Hammersdale Farm
Ellingstring
East Belt Plantation
YH
Witton Moor
Milestone Bank
Hill Top Farm
Haregill Lodge
Haregill Bank
Tranmire Hill
Ellingstring Plantation
Sail Hill
HAREGILL BANK
Haregill Covert
High Ellington
Tranmire
Tranmire Bog
The Warren
Warren House
Froggersgill Wood
CROOK LA
HG4
Sutton Whin
Riseber Hill
Agra Moor Top
Bales House
Bales House Plantation
President's Plantation
Agra Moor
Swinney Beck
SWINNEY BECK BANK
COTE LANE
West Agra Plantation
Agra Plantation
CROOK LANE
SUTTON LANE
West Agra
Bales Hill
High Cote Farm
Low Healey Cote
Bales Plantation
Howe Hill
Howe Wood
DAWSON'S LA
FEARBY RD
Body Close Farm
Agra Crags Plantation
Spring Wood
Fearby
Howe Farm
PH
Yew Tree Farm
MOSSRA LA
Ford
Healey Pasture
Cradle Gill Plantation
Gollinglith Foot
Healey
KELD BANK
Low Moor
Sinney Keld Old Well
Spruce Gill
Breary Bank Wood
Firs Farm
C of E Prim Sch
LOW MOOR LANE
Spout House
RIGG BANK
Breary Banks
Leighton Bridge
Ford
Fearby Low Moor
Hall Wood
River Burn
Swinton Park
Broadmires
Towler Hill Farm
Hall Wood
Stonefold
Quarry House
Stonefold Wood
Ox Close Plantation
Leighton
Sole Beck
Low Knowle Farm
Knowle Wood
Lobley Plantation
Lobley Hall
High Sourmire Farm
Reservoir House
Burgess Bank Wood
Masham Moor
Sykes Wood
Mount Covert
Low Sourmire
Weirs
Hill Top Farm
Druid's Plantation
KNOWLE LA
Sykes Farm
North Wood
Leighton Reservoir
Highfield House Farm
ILTON BANK
Clints Moor
Sole Beck Plantation
Ilton
Pott Hall
Manor Farm
POTT BANK
Masham Moor
Skew Skell Well
111
86

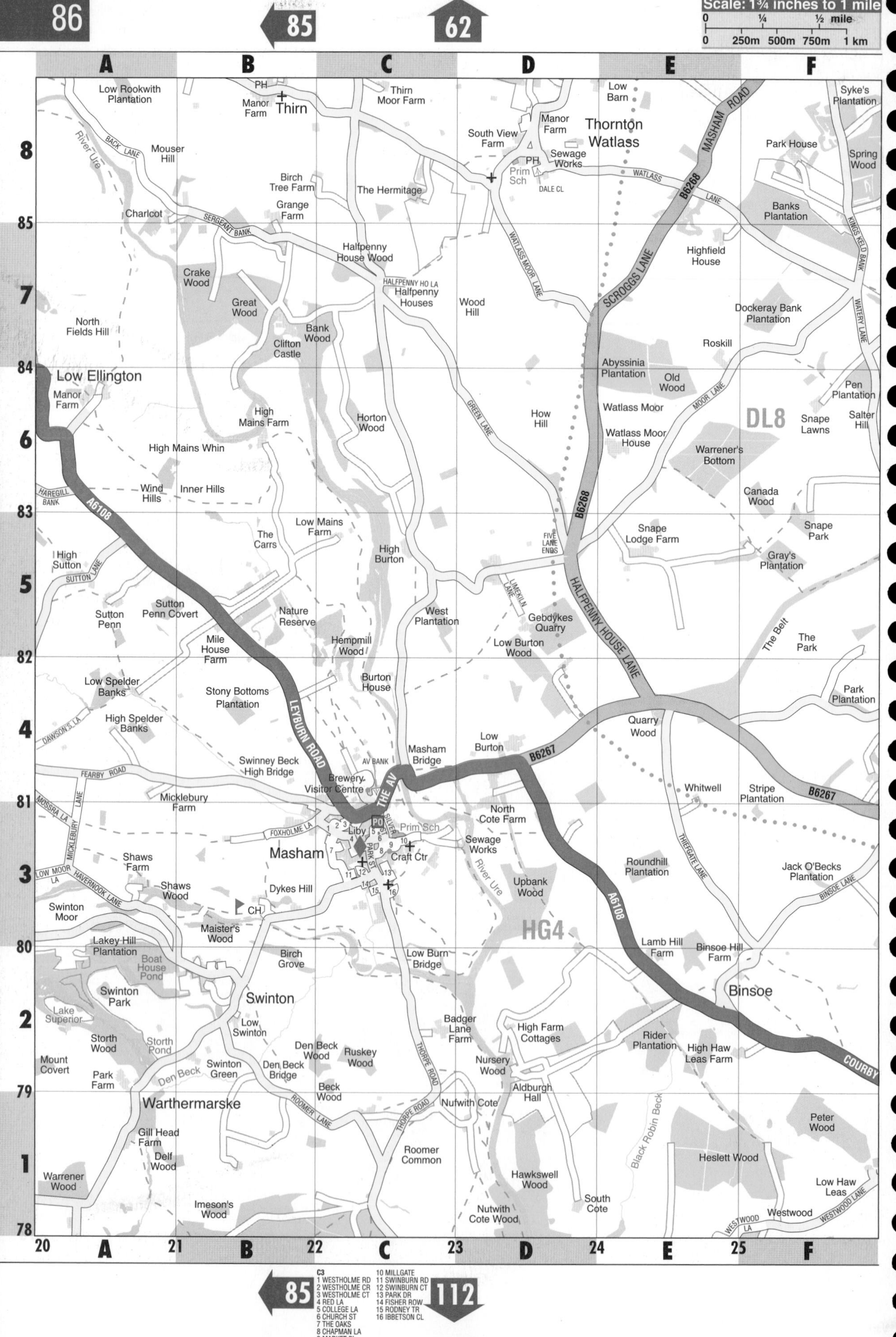

C3
1 WESTHOLME RD
2 WESTHOLME CR
3 WESTHOLME CT
4 RED LA
5 COLLEGE LA
6 CHURCH ST
7 THE OAKS
8 CHAPMAN LA
9 MARKET PL
10 MILLGATE
11 SWINBURN RD
12 SWINBURN CT
13 PARK DR
14 FISHER ROW
15 RODNEY TR
16 IBBETSON CL

Scale: 1¾ inches to 1 mile

63
88

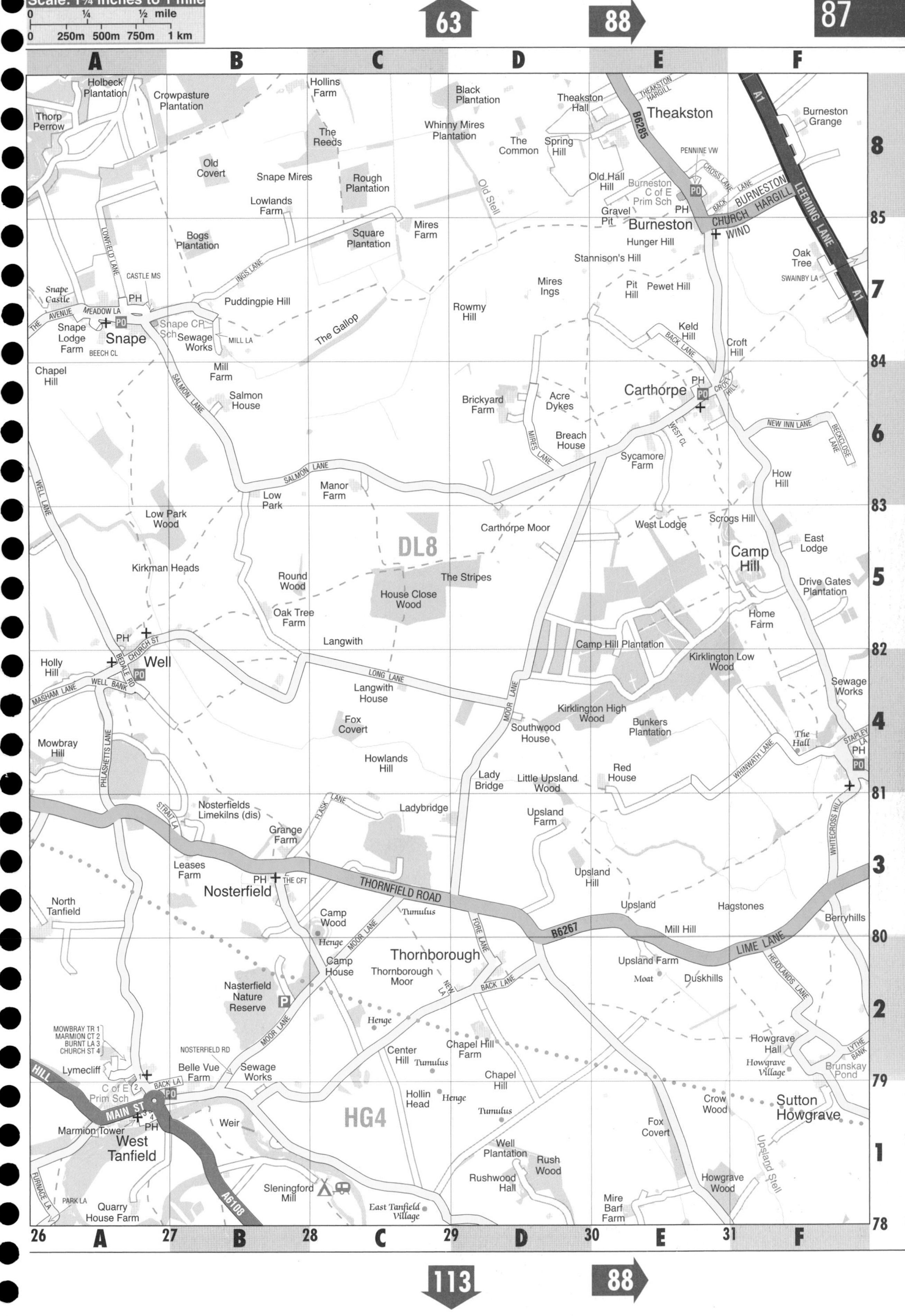

A B C D E F
8 85 7 84 6 83 5 82 4 81 3 80 2 79 1 78
26 27 28 29 30 31

113
88

87
64

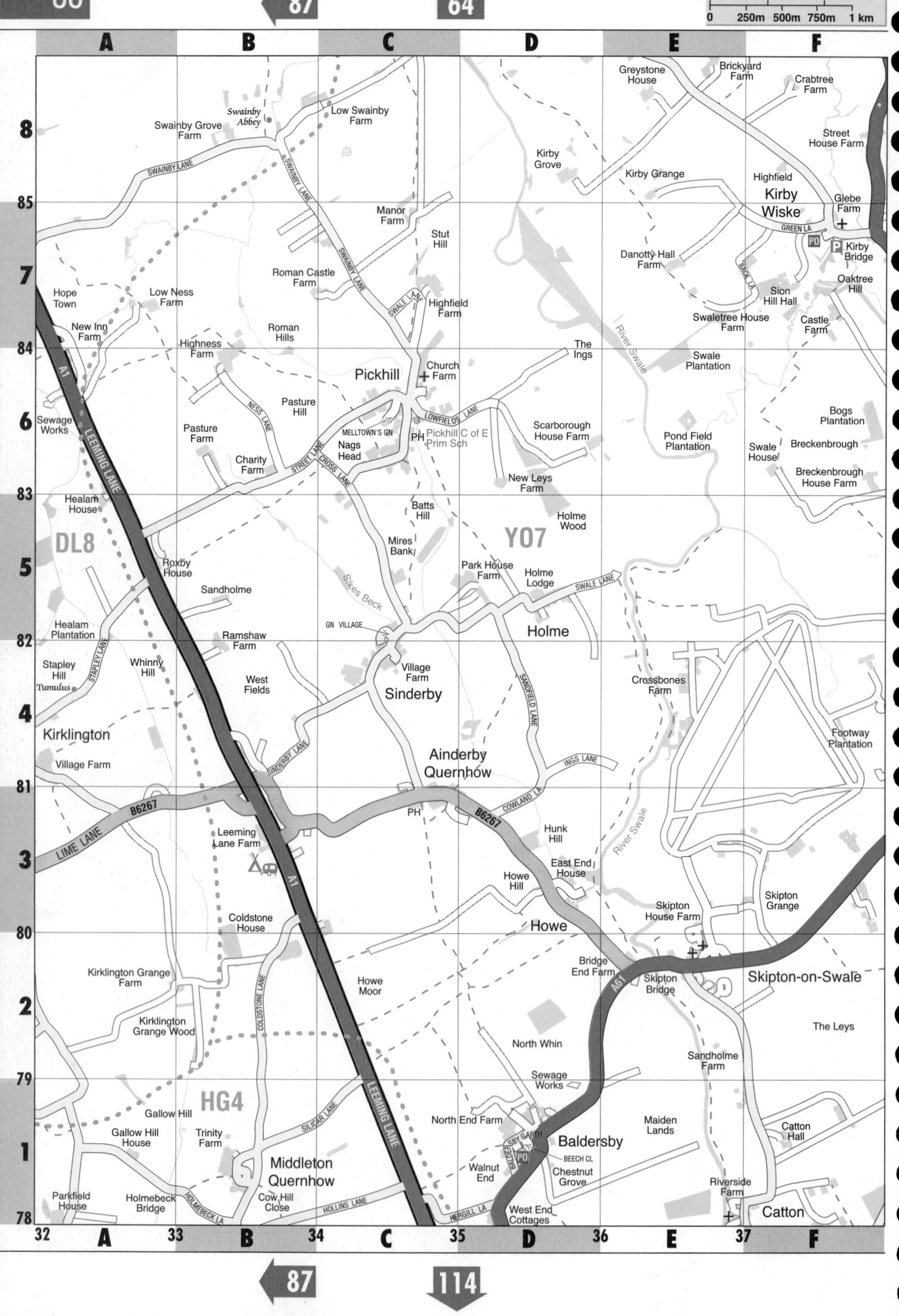
Scale: 1¾ inches to 1 mile
Swainby Abbey
Swainby Grove Farm
Low Swainby Farm
Greystone House
Brickyard Farm
Crabtree Farm
Street House Farm
Kirby Grove
Kirby Grange
Highfield
Kirby Wiske
Glebe Farm
Manor Farm
Stut Hill
Danotty Hall Farm
Kirby Bridge
Oaktree Hill
Roman Castle Farm
Hope Town
Low Ness Farm
Highfield Farm
Sion Hill Hall
Swaletree House Farm
Castle Farm
New Inn Farm
Roman Hills
Highness Farm
The Ings
River Swale
Swale Plantation
Pickhill
Church Farm
Pasture Hill
Sewage Works
Pasture Farm
Pickhill C of E Prim Sch
Scarborough House Farm
Pond Field Plantation
Bogs Plantation
Swale House
Breckenbrough
Breckenbrough House Farm
Nags Head
Charity Farm
New Leys Farm
Healam House
Batts Hill
Holme Wood
DL8
YO7
Mires Bank
Roxby House
Park House Farm
Holme Lodge
Sandholme
Sikes Beck
Healam Plantation
Ramshaw Farm
Holme
Stapley Hill
Tumulus
Whinny Hill
West Fields
Village Farm
Sinderby
Crossbones Farm
Kirklington
Village Farm
Ainderby Quernhow
Footway Plantation
Leeming Lane Farm
Hunk Hill
East End House
Howe Hill
Skipton House Farm
Skipton Grange
Coldstone House
Howe
Bridge End Farm
Kirklington Grange Farm
Howe Moor
Skipton Bridge
Skipton-on-Swale
Kirklington Grange Wood
North Whin
The Leys
Sandholme Farm
Sewage Works
HG4
Gallow Hill
Gallow Hill House
Trinity Farm
North End Farm
Baldersby
Maiden Lands
Catton Hall
Middleton Quernhow
Walnut End
Chestnut Grove
Riverside Farm
Parkfield House
Holmebeck Bridge
Cow Hill Close
West End Cottages
Catton

87
114

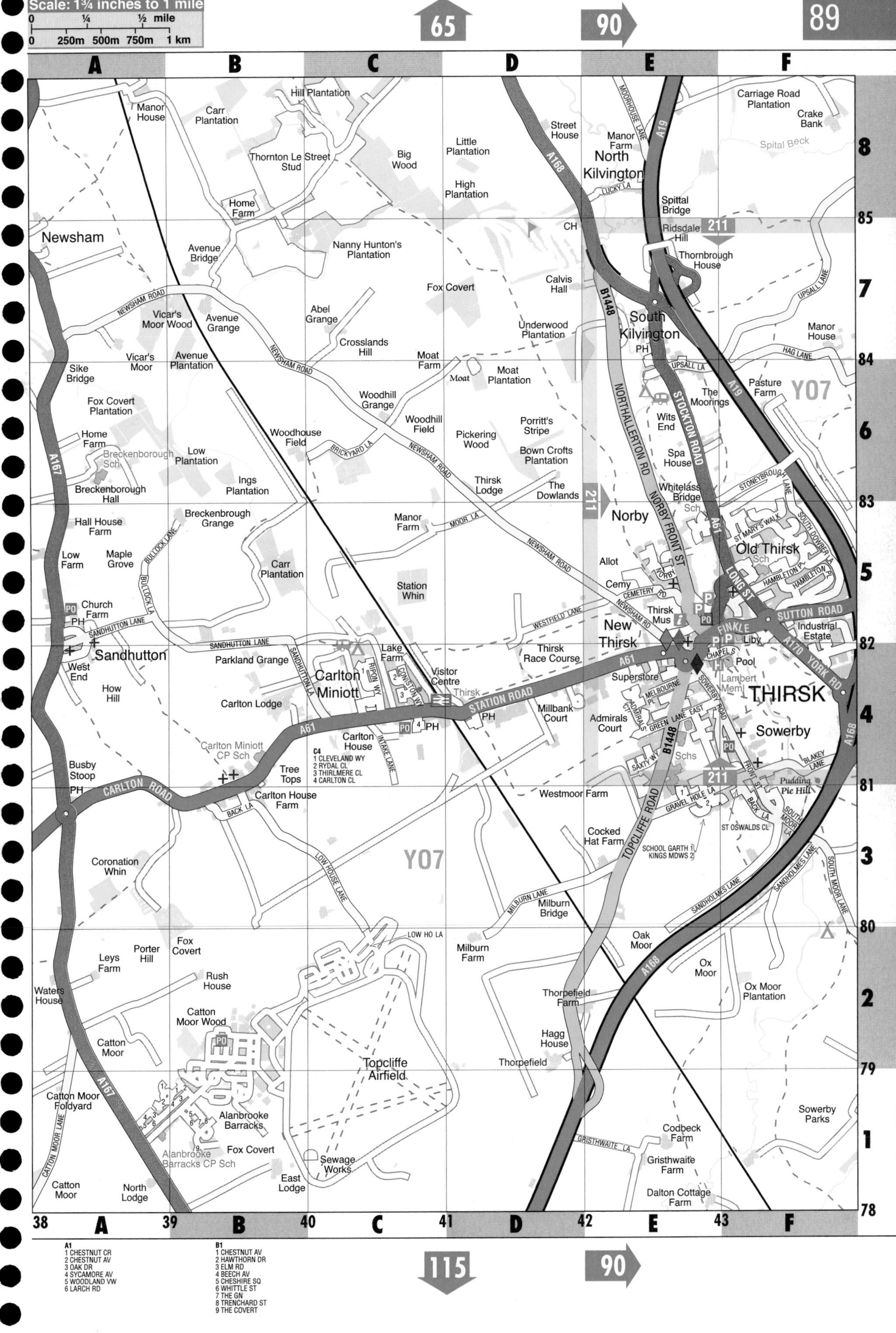

Scale: 1¾ inches to 1 mile
0 ¼ ½ mile
0 250m 500m 750m 1 km
65
90
A B C D E F
Manor House
Carr Plantation
Hill Plantation
Thornton Le Street Stud
Big Wood
Little Plantation
High Plantation
Street House
Manor Farm
North Kilvington
MOORHOUSE LANE
A19
A168
LUCKY LA
Carriage Road Plantation
Crake Bank
Spital Beck
Spittal Bridge
Home Farm
Newsham
Avenue Bridge
Nanny Hunton's Plantation
CH
Ridsdale Hill
211
Thornbrough House
Calvis Hall
Fox Covert
NEWSHAM ROAD
Vicar's Moor Wood
Avenue Grange
Abel Grange
Crosslands Hill
Underwood Plantation
B1448
South Kilvington
PH
UPSALL LANE
Manor House
HAG LANE
Sike Bridge
Vicar's Moor
Avenue Plantation
Moat Farm
Moat
Moat Plantation
UPSALL LA
Pasture Farm
YO7
Fox Covert Plantation
Woodhill Grange
The Moorings
Home Farm
Breckenborough Sch
Low Plantation
Woodhouse Field
Woodhill Field
Pickering Wood
Porritt's Stripe
Bown Crofts Plantation
Wits End
Spa House
NORTHALLERTON RD
STOCKTON ROAD
A167
BRICKYARD LA
Breckenborough Hall
Ings Plantation
Thirsk Lodge
The Dowlands
Whitelass Bridge
Sch
STONEYBROUGH LANE
Hall House Farm
Breckenbrough Grange
Manor Farm
MOOR LA
Norby
NORBY FRONT ST
A61
ST MARY'S WALK
SOUTH DOWBER LA
Old Thirsk
Low Farm
Maple Grove
BULLOCK LANE
Carr Plantation
Allot
Station Whin
Cemy
CEMETERY RD
LONG ST
HAMBLETON PL
Church Farm
BULLOCK LA
WESTFIELD LANE
Thirsk Mus
SUTTON ROAD
Industrial Estate
FINKLE ST
SANDHUTTON LANE
New Thirsk
Liby
Sandhutton
Parkland Grange
Lake Farm
Thirsk Race Course
A170
YORK RD
West End
RIPON WY
CONISTON WY
Visitor Centre
Thirsk
CHAPEL ST
Pool
How Hill
Carlton Minott
Carlton Lodge
STATION ROAD
Superstore
Lambert Meml
THIRSK
Millbank Court
MELBOURNE PL
ADMIRALS CT
Admirals Court
GREEN LANE EAST
SOWERBY ROAD
Sowerby
Carlton House
INTAKE LANE
Carlton Minott CP Sch
C4
1 CLEVELAND WY
2 RYDAL CL
3 THIRLMERE CL
4 CARLTON CL
Schs
SAXTY WY
BLAKEY LANE
Busby Stoop
Tree Tops
Carlton House Farm
Westmoor Farm
Pudding Pie Hill
CARLTON ROAD
BACK LA
TOPCLIFFE ROAD
GRAVEL HOLE LA
FRONT ST
SOUTH MOOR RD
ST OSWALDS CL
Cocked Hat Farm
SCHOOL GARTH 1
KINGS MDWS 2
Coronation Whin
LOW HOUSE LANE
SANDHOLMES LANE
SOUTH MOOR LANE
MILBURN LANE
Milburn Bridge
LOW HO LA
Fox Covert
Porter Hill
Leys Farm
Milburn Farm
Oak Moor
Ox Moor
Rush House
Waters House
Thorpefield Farm
Ox Moor Plantation
Catton Moor Wood
Catton Moor
Topcliffe Airfield
Hagg House
Thorpefield
Catton Moor Foldyard
Alanbrooke Barracks
Sowerby Parks
Codbeck Farm
CATTON MOOR LANE
Alanbrooke Barracks CP Sch
Fox Covert
Sewage Works
GRISTHWAITE LA
Gristhwaite Farm
Catton Moor
North Lodge
East Lodge
Dalton Cottage Farm
8 85 7 84 6 83 5 82 4 81 3 80 2 79 1 78
38 39 40 41 42 43
115
90
A1
1 CHESTNUT CR
2 CHESTNUT AV
3 OAK DR
4 SYCAMORE AV
5 WOODLAND VW
6 LARCH RD
B1
1 CHESTNUT AV
2 HAWTHORN DR
3 ELM RD
4 BEECH AV
5 CHESHIRE SQ
6 WHITTLE ST
7 THE GN
8 TRENCHARD ST
9 THE COVERT

89

66

For full street detail of the highlighted area see page 211.

Scale: 1¾ inches to 1 mile
0 ¼ ½ mile
0 250m 500m 750m 1 km

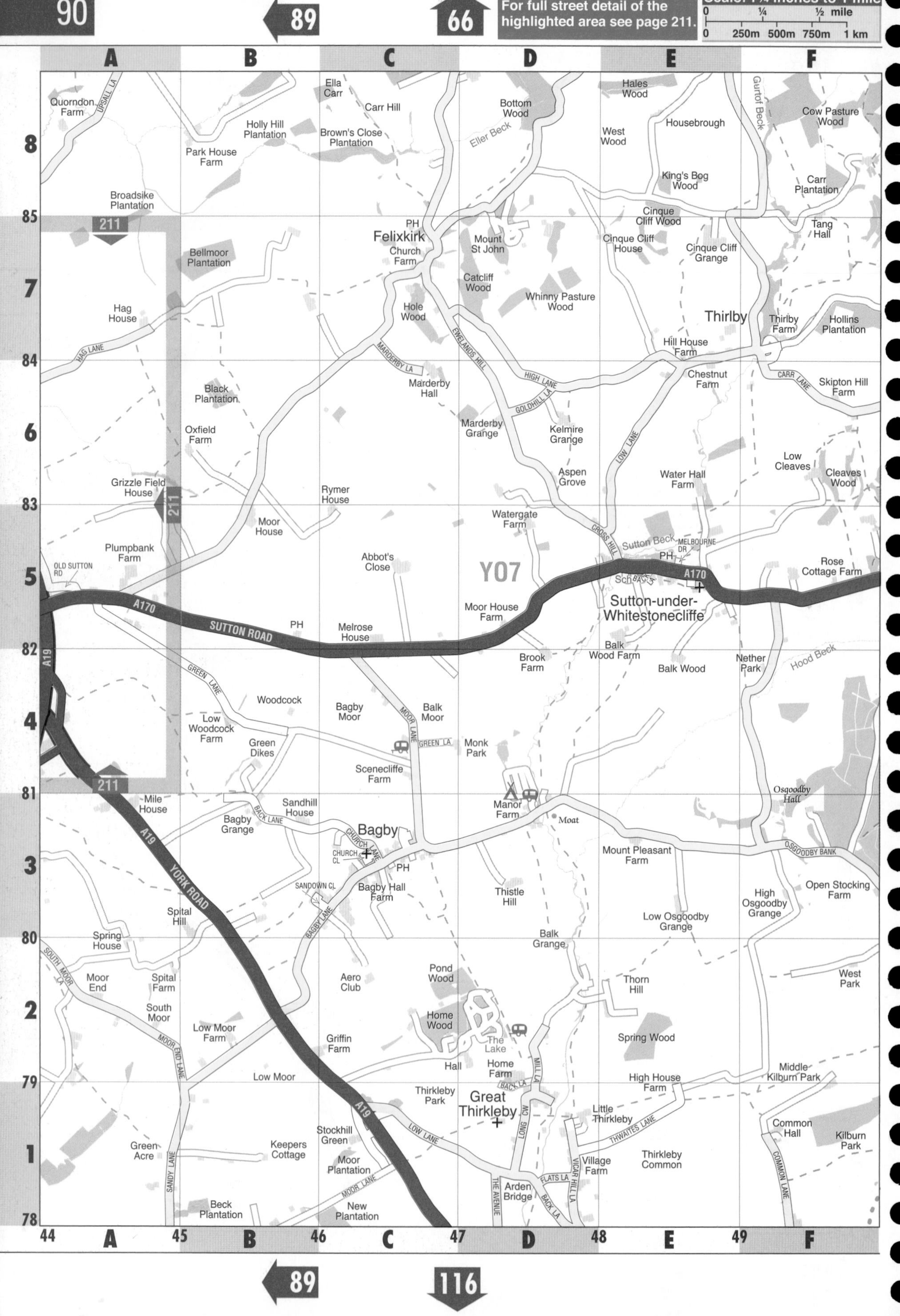

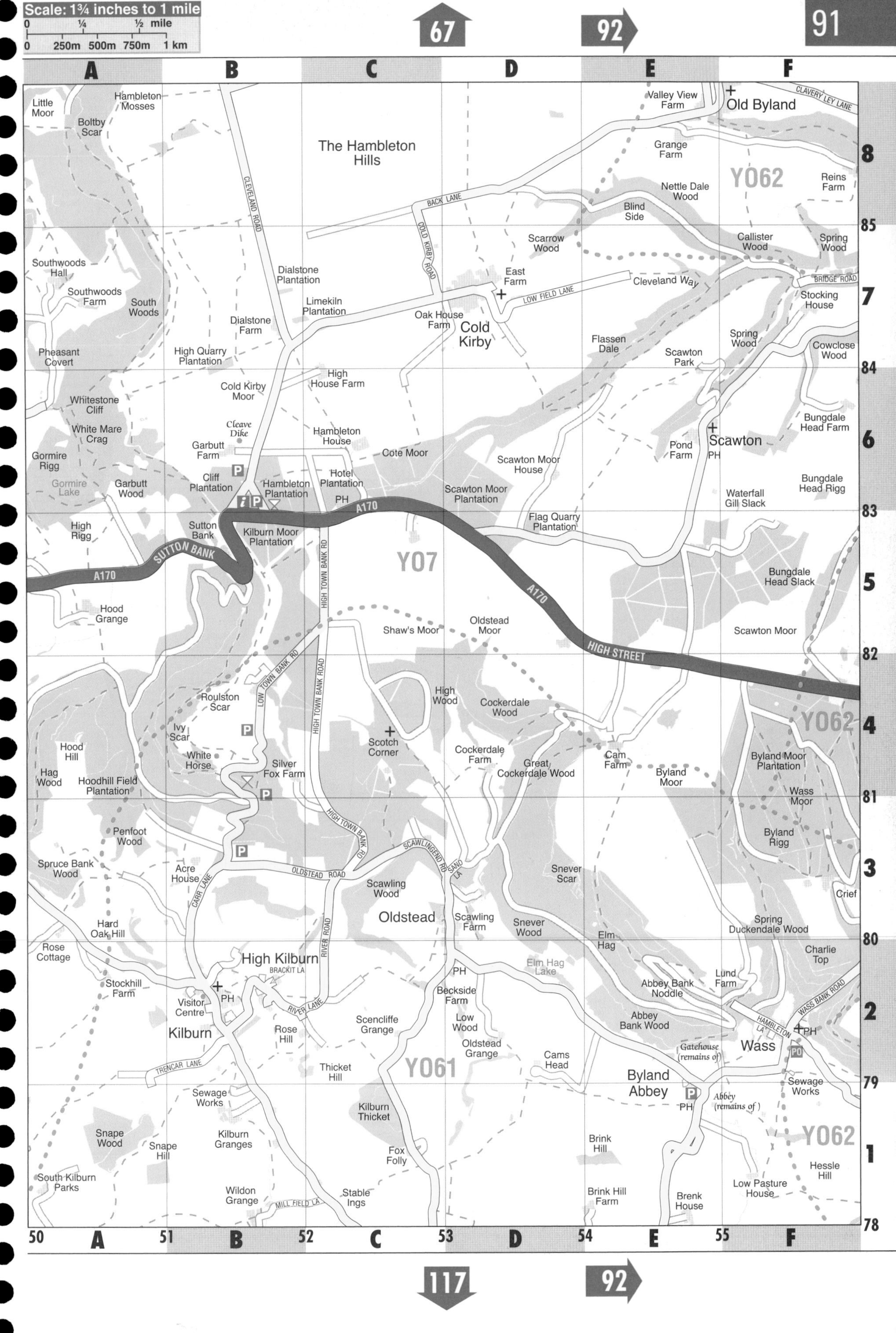
Scale: 1¾ inches to 1 mile
0 ¼ ½ mile
0 250m 500m 750m 1 km
67
92
A B C D E F
Little Moor
Hambleton Mosses
Boltby Scar
The Hambleton Hills
Valley View Farm
Old Byland
CLAVERY LEY LANE
Grange Farm
YO62
Reins Farm
Nettle Dale Wood
Blind Side
BACK LANE
CLEVELAND ROAD
COLD KIRBY ROAD
Scarrow Wood
Callister Wood
Spring Wood
Southwoods Hall
Dialstone Plantation
East Farm
Cleveland Way
BRIDGE ROAD
Southwoods Farm
South Woods
Limekiln Plantation
LOW FIELD LANE
Stocking House
Dialstone Farm
Oak House Farm
Cold Kirby
Flassen Dale
Spring Wood
Cowclose Wood
Pheasant Covert
High Quarry Plantation
Scawton Park
High House Farm
Cold Kirby Moor
Whitestone Cliff
Cleave Dike
Hambleton House
Bungdale Head Farm
White Mare Crag
Garbutt Farm
Cote Moor
Pond Farm
Scawton
PH
Gormire Rigg
Scawton Moor House
Gormire Lake
Garbutt Wood
Cliff Plantation
Hambleton Plantation
Hotel Plantation
PH
Scawton Moor Plantation
Waterfall Gill Slack
Bungdale Head Rigg
A170
High Rigg
Sutton Bank
Kilburn Moor Plantation
Flag Quarry Plantation
SUTTON BANK
A170
HIGH TOWN BANK RD
YO7
Bungdale Head Slack
Hood Grange
A170
Shaw's Moor
Oldstead Moor
Scawton Moor
HIGH STREET
LOW TOWN BANK RD
HIGH TOWN BANK ROAD
Roulston Scar
High Wood
Cockerdale Wood
YO62
Ivy Scar
Scotch Corner
Hood Hill
White Horse
Silver Fox Farm
Cockerdale Farm
Great Cockerdale Wood
Cam Farm
Byland Moor
Byland Moor Plantation
Hag Wood
Hoodhill Field Plantation
Wass Moor
Penfoot Wood
HIGH TOWN BANK RD
Byland Rigg
Spruce Bank Wood
Acre House
SCAWLINGEND RD
SAND LA
Snever Scar
CARR LANE
OLDSTEAD ROAD
Scawling Wood
Crief
Hard Oak Hill
Oldstead
Scawling Farm
Snever Wood
Spring Duckendale Wood
RIVER ROAD
Elm Hag
Rose Cottage
High Kilburn
BRACKIT LA
Elm Hag Lake
Charlie Top
PH
Stockhill Farm
Beckside Farm
Abbey Bank Noddle
Lund Farm
WASS BANK ROAD
Visitor Centre
PH
RIVER LANE
Scencliffe Grange
Low Wood
Abbey Bank Wood
HAMBLETON LA
PH
Kilburn
Rose Hill
Oldstead Grange
Gatehouse (remains of)
Wass
PO
TRENCAR LANE
Thicket Hill
YO61
Cams Head
Byland Abbey
Sewage Works
Sewage Works
PH
Abbey (remains of)
Kilburn Thicket
YO62
Snape Wood
Snape Hill
Kilburn Granges
Brink Hill
Hessle Hill
Fox Folly
South Kilburn Parks
Wildon Grange
Stable Ings
MILL FIELD LA
Brink Hill Farm
Brenk House
Low Pasture House
8 85 7 84 6 83 5 82 4 81 3 80 2 79 1 78
50 A 51 B 52 C 53 D 54 E 55 F
117
92

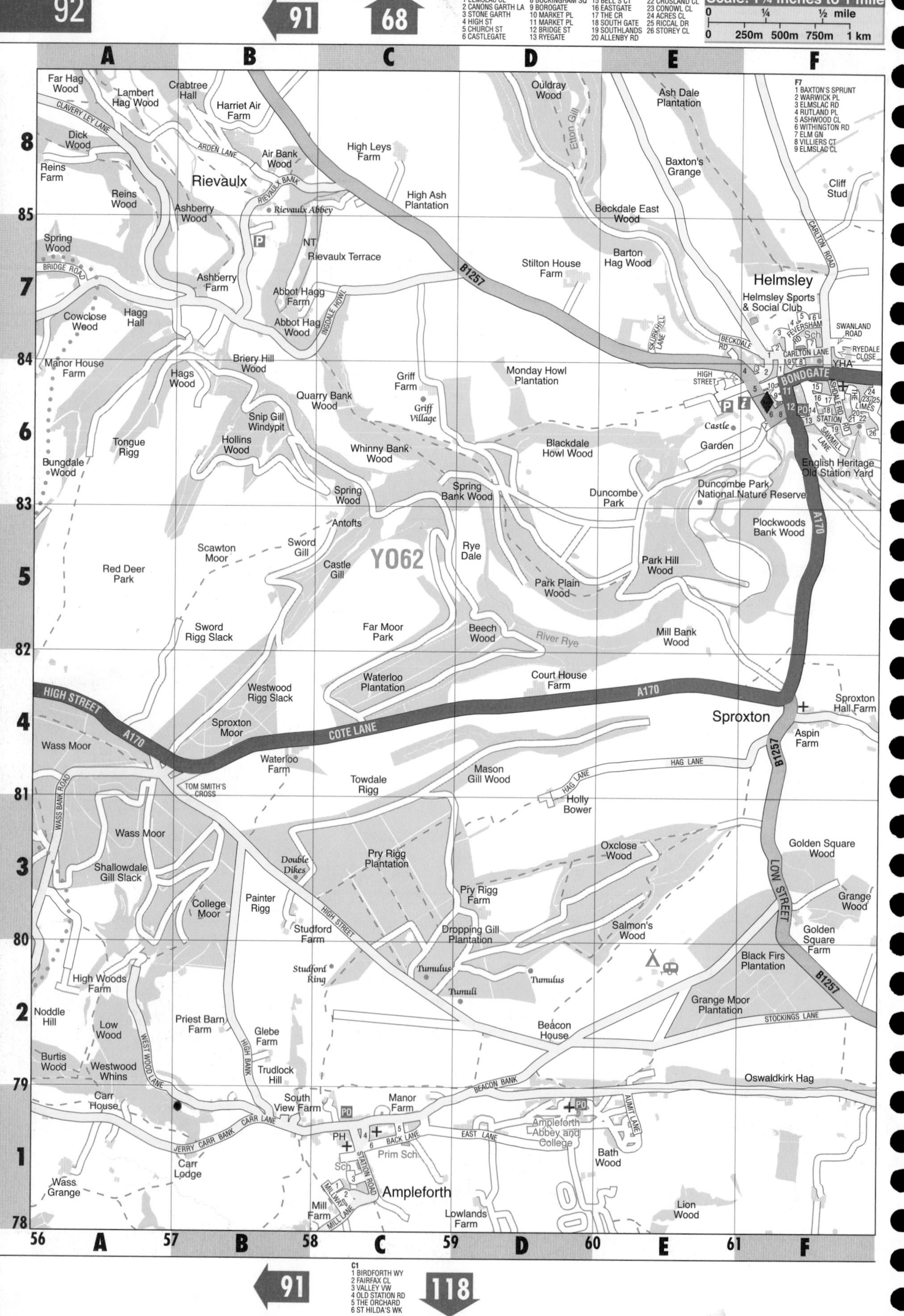
91
68
F6
1 ELMSLAC CL
2 CANONS GARTH LA
3 STONE GARTH
4 HIGH ST
5 CHURCH ST
6 CASTLEGATE
7 BUCKINGHAM SQ
8 BUCKINGHAM SQ
9 BOROGATE
10 MARKET PL
11 MARKET PL
12 BRIDGE ST
13 RYEGATE
14 POTTERGATE
15 BELL'S CT
16 EASTGATE
17 THE CR
18 SOUTH GATE
19 SOUTHLANDS
20 ALLENBY RD
21 CHAPEL CL
22 CROSLAND CL
23 CONOWL CL
24 ACRES CL
25 RICCAL DR
26 STOREY CL
Scale: 1¾ inches to 1 mile
0 ¼ ½ mile
0 250m 500m 750m 1 km
A B C D E F
F7
1 BAXTON'S SPRUNT
2 WARWICK PL
3 ELMSLAC RD
4 RUTLAND PL
5 ASHWOOD CL
6 WITHINGTON RD
7 ELM GN
8 VILLIERS CT
9 ELMSLAC CL
8 85 7 84 6 83 5 82 4 81 3 80 2 79 1 78
Far Hag Wood
Lambert Hag Wood
Crabtree Hall
Harriet Air Farm
CLAVERY LEY LANE
Dick Wood
ARDEN LANE
Air Bank Wood
High Leys Farm
Ouldray Wood
Etton Gill
Ash Dale Plantation
Reins Farm
Rievaulx
RIEVAULX BANK
Reins Wood
Ashberry Wood
Rievaulx Abbey
High Ash Plantation
Baxton's Grange
Cliff Stud
Beckdale East Wood
Spring Wood
BRIDGE ROAD
NT
Rievaulx Terrace
B1257
Stilton House Farm
Barton Hag Wood
CARLTON ROAD
Ashberry Farm
Abbot Hagg Farm
INGDALE HOWL
Helmsley
Helmsley Sports & Social Club
Cowclose Wood
Hagg Hall
Abbot Hag Wood
SKIPKROLL LANE
BECKDALE RD
FEVERSHAM RD
Sch
SWANLAND ROAD
RYEDALE CLOSE
CARLTON LANE
YHA
Manor House Farm
Briery Hill Wood
Hags Wood
Griff Farm
Monday Howl Plantation
HIGH STREET
BONDGATE
Quarry Bank Wood
Griff Village
BUCKINGHAM SQ
STATION RD
THE LIMES
Snip Gill Windypit
Tongue Rigg
Hollins Wood
Whinny Bank Wood
Blackdale Howl Wood
Castle
Garden
SAWMILL LANE
Bungdale Wood
English Heritage Old Station Yard
Spring Wood
Spring Bank Wood
Duncombe Park
Duncombe Park National Nature Reserve
Antofts
Plockwoods Bank Wood
A170
Scawton Moor
Sword Gill
Castle Gill
YO62
Rye Dale
Red Deer Park
Park Hill Wood
Park Plain Wood
Sword Rigg Slack
Far Moor Park
Beech Wood
River Rye
Mill Bank Wood
Westwood Rigg Slack
Waterloo Plantation
Court House Farm
HIGH STREET
A170
Sproxton
Sproxton Hall Farm
Sproxton Moor
COTE LANE
Aspin Farm
Wass Moor
Waterloo Farm
B1257
Towdale Rigg
Mason Gill Wood
HAG LANE
TOM SMITH'S CROSS
WASS BANK ROAD
Holly Bower
Wass Moor
Shallowdale Gill Slack
Double Dikes
Pry Rigg Plantation
Oxclose Wood
Golden Square Wood
Painter Rigg
College Moor
HIGH STREET
Pry Rigg Farm
LOW STREET
Grange Wood
Studford Farm
Dropping Gill Plantation
Salmon's Wood
Golden Square Farm
Studford Ring
Tumulus
Tumuli
Black Firs Plantation
High Woods Farm
Grange Moor Plantation
STOCKINGS LANE
Noddle Hill
Low Wood
WEST WOOD LANE
Priest Barn Farm
Glebe Farm
HIGH BANK
Beacon House
Burtis Wood
Westwood Whins
Trudlock Hill
BEACON BANK
Oswaldkirk Hag
Carr House
South View Farm
Manor Farm
PO
AUMIT LANE
CARR LANE
JERRY CARR BANK
PH
BACK LANE
EAST LANE
Ampleforth Abbey and College
Carr Lodge
Prim Sch
Sch
STATION ROAD
Bath Wood
Wass Grange
MILLWAY
Ampleforth
Mill Farm
MILL LANE
Lowlands Farm
Lion Wood
56 A 57 B 58 C 59 D 60 E 61 F
C1
1 BIRDFORTH WY
2 FAIRFAX CL
3 VALLEY VW
4 OLD STATION RD
5 THE ORCHARD
6 ST HILDA'S WK
91
118

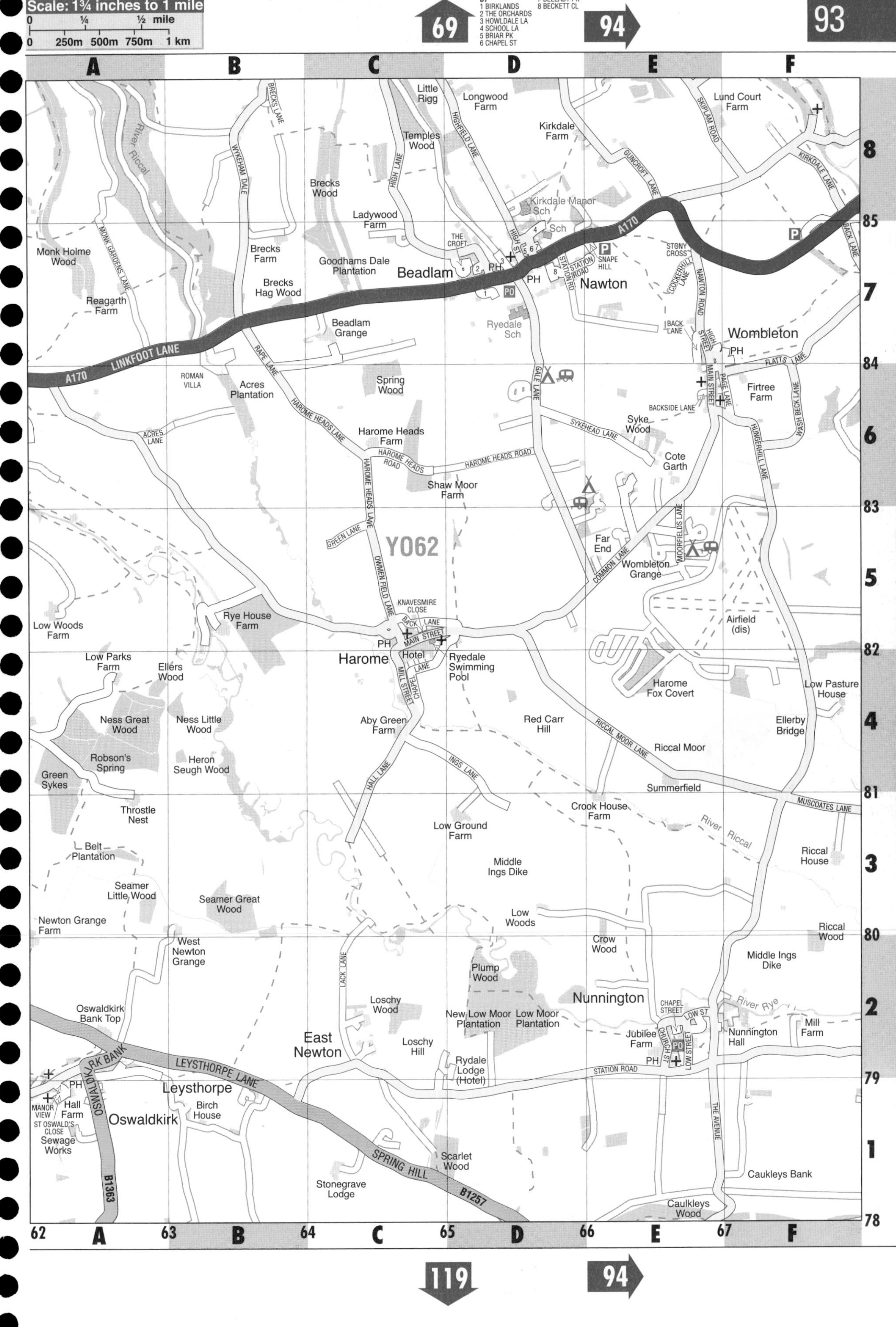
Scale: 1¾ inches to 1 mile
0 ¼ ½ mile
0 250m 500m 750m 1 km
69
94
D7
1 BIRKLANDS
2 THE ORCHARDS
3 HOWLDALE LA
4 SCHOOL LA
5 BRIAR PK
6 CHAPEL ST
7 BELLABY PK
8 BECKETT CL
A B C D E F
8 85 7 84 6 83 5 82 4 81 3 80 2 79 1 78
62 63 64 65 66 67
Beadlam
Nawton
Wombleton
Harome
Nunnington
East Newton
Leysthorpe
Oswaldkirk
YO62
A170
LINKFOOT LANE
Little Rigg
Longwood Farm
Kirkdale Farm
Lund Court Farm
Temples Wood
Brecks Wood
Ladywood Farm
Kirkdale Manor Sch
Monk Holme Wood
Brecks Farm
Goodhams Dale Plantation
Brecks Hag Wood
Reagarth Farm
Beadlam Grange
Ryedale Sch
Acres Plantation
ROMAN VILLA
Spring Wood
Harome Heads Farm
Shaw Moor Farm
Syke Wood
Cote Garth
Firtree Farm
Far End
Wombleton Grange
Airfield (dis)
Rye House Farm
Low Woods Farm
Low Parks Farm
Ellers Wood
Hotel
Ryedale Swimming Pool
Harome Fox Covert
Low Pasture House
Ellerby Bridge
Ness Great Wood
Ness Little Wood
Aby Green Farm
Red Carr Hill
Riccal Moor
Robson's Spring
Heron Seugh Wood
Green Sykes
Summerfield
Throstle Nest
Crook House Farm
Low Ground Farm
River Riccal
Riccal House
Belt Plantation
Middle Ings Dike
Seamer Little Wood
Seamer Great Wood
Low Woods
Riccal Wood
Newton Grange Farm
Crow Wood
West Newton Grange
Plump Wood
Loschy Wood
New Low Moor Plantation
Low Moor Plantation
River Rye
Oswaldkirk Bank Top
Loschy Hill
Rydale Lodge (Hotel)
Jubilee Farm
Nunnington Hall
Mill Farm
Hall Farm
Birch House
Sewage Works
Scarlet Wood
Stonegrave Lodge
Caukleys Bank
Caulkleys Wood
BRECKS LANE
WYKEHAM DALE
HIGHFIELD LANE
HIGH LANE
MONK GARDENS LANE
GUNCROFT LANE
SKIPLAM ROAD
KIRKDALE LANE
BACK LANE
THE CROFT
HIGH ST
STATION ROAD
SNAPE HILL
STONY CROSS
COCKERHILL LANE
NAWTON ROAD
BACK LANE
HIGH STREET
FLATTS LANE
RAPE LANE
GALE LANE
MAIN STREET
PAGE LANE
BACKSIDE LANE
WASH BECK LANE
HAROME HEADS LANE
ACRES LANE
SYKEHEAD LANE
HUNGERHILL LANE
HAROME HEADS ROAD
HAROME HEADS LANE
GREEN LANE
MOORFIELDS LANE
COMMON LANE
OWMEN FIELD LANE
KNAVESMIRE CLOSE
BACK LANE
MILL STREET
CHAPEL LANE
RICCAL MOOR LANE
INGS LANE
HALL LANE
MUSCOATES LANE
LACK LANE
CHAPEL STREET
LOW ST
CHURCH ST
LOW STREET
STATION ROAD
THE AVENUE
OSWALDKIRK BANK
LEYSTHORPE LANE
MANOR VIEW
ST OSWALD'S CLOSE
SPRING HILL
B1257
B1363
PH
PO
Sch
119
94

93
70

Scale: 1¾ inches to 1 mile

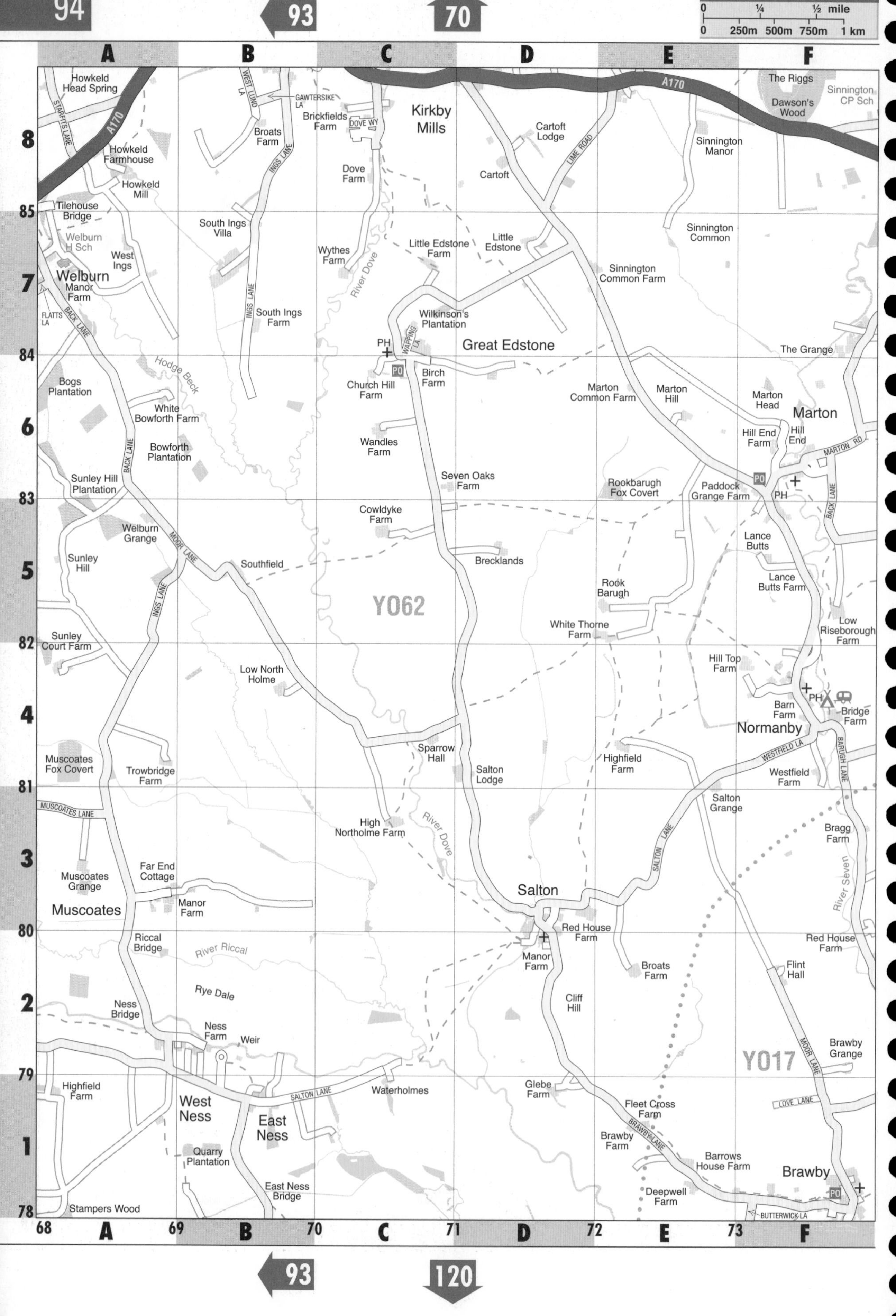

93
120

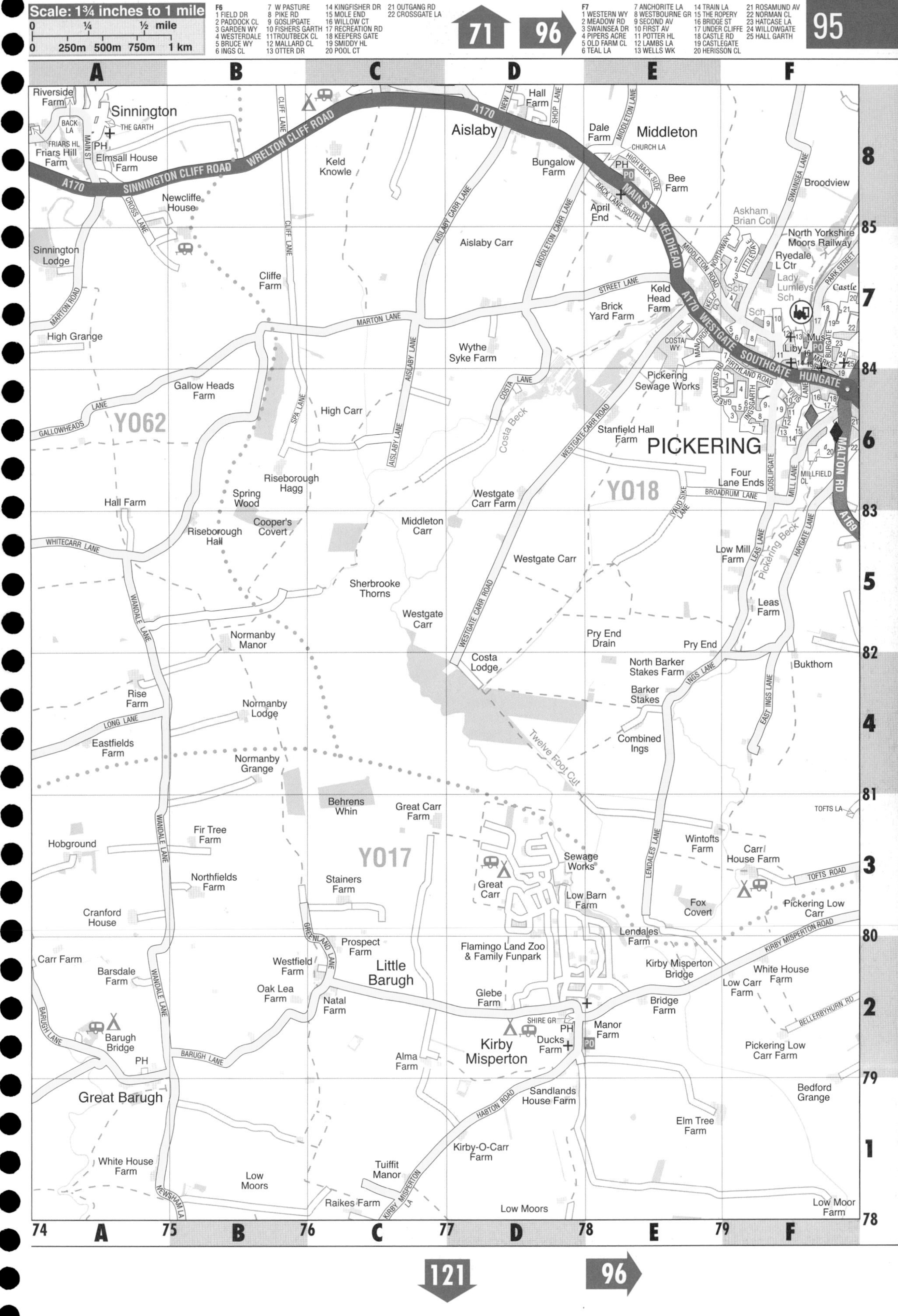

Scale: 1¾ inches to 1 mile
0 ¼ ½ mile
0 250m 500m 750m 1 km
F6
1 FIELD DR
2 PADDOCK CL
3 GARDEN WY
4 WESTERDALE
5 BRUCE WY
6 INGS CL
7 W PASTURE
8 PIKE RD
9 GOSLIPGATE
10 FISHERS GARTH
11 TROUTBECK CL
12 MALLARD CL
13 OTTER DR
14 KINGFISHER DR
15 MOLE END
16 WILLOW CT
17 RECREATION RD
18 KEEPERS GATE
19 SMIDDY HL
20 POOL CT
21 OUTGANG RD
22 CROSSGATE LA
71
96
F7
1 WESTERN WY
2 MEADOW RD
3 SWAINSEA DR
4 PIPERS ACRE
5 OLD FARM CL
6 TEAL LA
7 ANCHORITE LA
8 WESTBOURNE GR
9 SECOND AV
10 FIRST AV
11 POTTER HL
12 LAMBS LA
13 WELLS WK
14 TRAIN LA
15 THE ROPERY
16 BRIDGE ST
17 UNDER CLIFFE
18 CASTLE RD
19 CASTLEGATE
20 HERISSON CL
21 ROSAMUND AV
22 NORMAN CL
23 HATCASE LA
24 WILLOWGATE
25 HALL GARTH
95
A B C D E F
Riverside Farm
Sinnington
THE GARTH
Friars Hill Farm
Elmsall House Farm
SINNINGTON CLIFF ROAD
WRELTON CLIFF ROAD
A170
Keld Knowle
Hall Farm
Aislaby
Dale Farm
Middleton
CHURCH LA
Bungalow Farm
Bee Farm
MAIN ST
BACK LANE SOUTH
April End
Newcliffe House
Sinnington Lodge
Aislaby Carr
Askham Brian Coll
North Yorkshire Moors Railway
Ryedale L Ctr
Lady Lumleys Sch
Castle
KELDHEAD
Cliffe Farm
MARTON ROAD
MARTON LANE
STREET LANE
Brick Yard Farm
Keld Head Farm
High Grange
Wythe Syke Farm
WESTGATE
SOUTHGATE
HUNGATE
Mus
Liby
Pickering Sewage Works
Gallow Heads Farm
GALLOWHEADS LANE
YO62
High Carr
COSTA LANE
Costa Beck
Stanfield Hall Farm
PICKERING
MALTON RD
Four Lane Ends
BROADRUM LANE
YO18
MILLFIELD CL
Riseborough Hagg
Spring Wood
Hall Farm
Cooper's Covert
Westgate Carr Farm
Middleton Carr
Riseborough Hall
WHITECARR LANE
Westgate Carr
Low Mill Farm
Pickering Beck
HAYGATE LANE
A169
Sherbrooke Thorns
Westgate Carr
Leas Farm
WANDALE LANE
Normanby Manor
Pry End Drain
Pry End
Costa Lodge
WESTGATE CARR ROAD
North Barker Stakes Farm
Bukthorn
Barker Stakes
INGS LANE
EAST INGS LANE
Rise Farm
Normanby Lodge
LONG LANE
Eastfields Farm
Combined Ings
Twelve Foot Cut
Normanby Grange
TOFTS LA
Behrens Whin
Great Carr Farm
Fir Tree Farm
Hobground
YO17
Sewage Works
Wintofts Farm
Carr House Farm
TOFTS ROAD
Northfields Farm
Stainers Farm
Great Carr
Low Barn Farm
LENDALES LANE
Fox Covert
Pickering Low Carr
Cranford House
Lendales Farm
KIRBY MISPERTON ROAD
Carr Farm
Prospect Farm
Flamingo Land Zoo & Family Funpark
GREENLAND LANE
Westfield Farm
Little Barugh
Kirby Misperton Bridge
White House Farm
Barsdale Farm
Oak Lea Farm
Natal Farm
Glebe Farm
Bridge Farm
Low Carr Farm
BELLERBYHURN RD
BARUGH LANE
Barugh Bridge
SHIRE GR
Manor Farm
PH
Kirby Misperton
Ducks Farm
Pickering Low Carr Farm
Alma Farm
Great Barugh
Sandlands House Farm
HABTON ROAD
Bedford Grange
Elm Tree Farm
Kirby-O-Carr Farm
White House Farm
Tuiffit Manor
Low Moors
NEWSHAM LA
KIRBY MISPERTON LA
Raikes Farm
Low Moors
Low Moor Farm
74 75 76 77 78 79
8 85 7 84 6 83 5 82 4 81 3 80 2 79 1 78
121
96

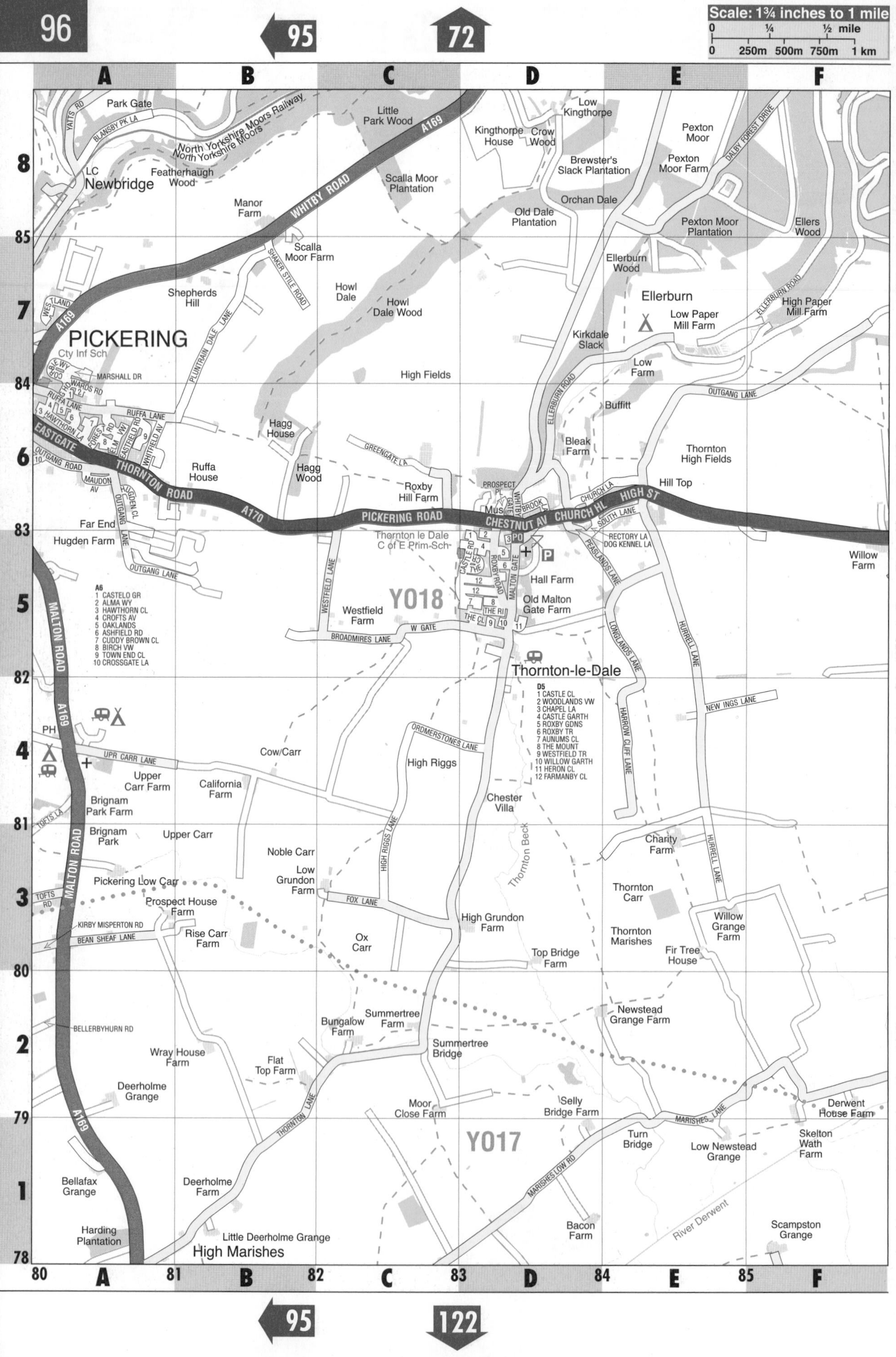
A
B
C
D
E
F
Park Gate
YATTS RD
BLANSBY PK LA
North Yorkshire Moors Railway
North Yorkshire Moors
Little Park Wood
A169
Low Kingthorpe
Kingthorpe House
Crow Wood
Pexton Moor
DALBY FOREST DRIVE
Brewster's Slack Plantation
Pexton Moor Farm
LC
Newbridge
Featherhaugh Wood
Scalla Moor Plantation
Orchan Dale
Manor Farm
WHITBY ROAD
Old Dale Plantation
Pexton Moor Plantation
Ellers Wood
Scalla Moor Farm
SHAKER STILE ROAD
Ellerburn Wood
Shepherds Hill
Howl Dale
Howl Dale Wood
Ellerburn
ELLERBURN ROAD
High Paper Mill Farm
Low Paper Mill Farm
WESTLAND
PICKERING
PLUNTRAIN DALE LANE
Kirkdale Slack
Cty Inf Sch
MARSHALL DR
High Fields
Low Farm
WARDS RD
RUFFA LANE
OUTGANG LANE
Buffitt
ELLERBURN ROAD
HAWTHORN LA
FOREST RD
ELM
EASTFIELD RD
WHITFIELD AV
Hagg House
Bleak Farm
Thornton High Fields
EASTGATE
OUTGANG ROAD
GREENGATE LA
Ruffa House
Hagg Wood
Roxby Hill Farm
Hill Top
MAUDON AV
THORNTON ROAD
HUGDEN CL
PROSPECT PL
WHITBY GATE
BROOK
CHURCH LA
HIGH ST
A170
Mus
CHESTNUT AV
CHURCH HL
SOUTH LANE
Far End
PICKERING ROAD
Hugden Farm
Thornton le Dale C of E Prim Sch
PO
RECTORY LA
DOG KENNEL LA
CASTLE RD
ROXBY ROAD
MALTON GATE
PEASLANDS LANE
Willow Farm
OUTGANG LANE
Hall Farm
A6
1 CASTELO GR
2 ALMA WY
3 HAWTHORN CL
4 CROFTS AV
5 OAKLANDS
6 ASHFIELD RD
7 CUDDY BROWN CL
8 BIRCH VW
9 TOWN END CL
10 CROSSGATE LA
MALTON ROAD
WESTFIELD LANE
Westfield Farm
Y018
THE RI
Old Malton Gate Farm
THE CL
W GATE
BROADMIRES LANE
HURRELL LANE
LONGLANDS LANE
Thornton-le-Dale
D5
1 CASTLE CL
2 WOODLANDS VW
3 CHAPEL LA
4 CASTLE GARTH
5 ROXBY GDNS
6 ROXBY TR
7 AUNUMS CL
8 THE MOUNT
9 WESTFIELD TR
10 WILLOW GARTH
11 HERON CL
12 FARMANBY CL
NEW INGS LANE
HARROW CLIFF LANE
PH
ORDMERSTONES LANE
UPR CARR LANE
Cow Carr
High Riggs
Upper Carr Farm
California Farm
Chester Villa
Brignam Park Farm
TOFTS LA
Brignam Park
Upper Carr
HIGH RIGGS LANE
Charity Farm
Noble Carr
Thornton Beck
Low Grundon Farm
Pickering Low Carr
Thornton Carr
TOFTS RD
Prospect House Farm
FOX LANE
High Grundon Farm
Willow Grange Farm
KIRBY MISPERTON RD
Rise Carr Farm
BEAN SHEAF LANE
Ox Carr
Thornton Marishes
Fir Tree House
Top Bridge Farm
Summertree Farm
Newstead Grange Farm
Bungalow Farm
BELLERBYHURN RD
Wray House Farm
Summertree Bridge
Flat Top Farm
Deerholme Grange
Moor Close Farm
Selly Bridge Farm
Derwent House Farm
MARISHES LANE
THORNTON LANE
Turn Bridge
Skelton Wath Farm
Y017
Low Newstead Grange
MARISHES LOW RD
Bellafax Grange
Deerholme Farm
River Derwent
Scampston Grange
Bacon Farm
Harding Plantation
Little Deerholme Grange
High Marishes
8
85
7
84
6
83
5
82
4
81
3
80
2
79
1
78
80
81
82
83
84
85

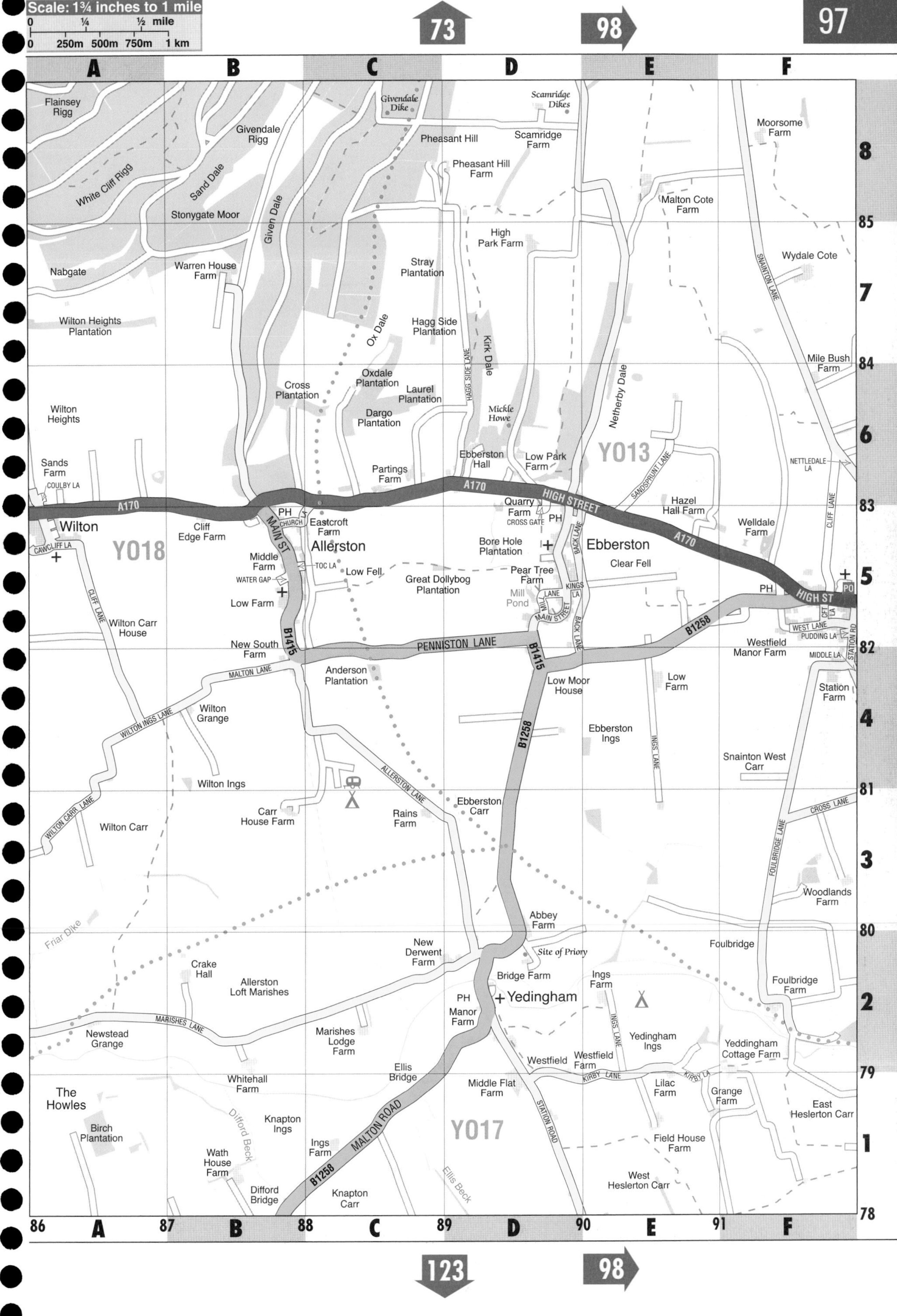
Scale: 1¾ inches to 1 mile
0 ¼ ½ mile
0 250m 500m 750m 1 km
73
98
A B C D E F
Flainsey Rigg
Givendale Dike
Scamridge Dikes
Givendale Rigg
Pheasant Hill
Scamridge Farm
Moorsome Farm
White Cliff Rigg
Sand Dale
Pheasant Hill Farm
Stonygate Moor
Given Dale
Malton Cote Farm
High Park Farm
Nabgate
Warren House Farm
Stray Plantation
Wydale Cote
SNAINTON LANE
Wilton Heights Plantation
Hagg Side Plantation
Ox Dale
Kirk Dale
Mile Bush Farm
Cross Plantation
Oxdale Plantation
Laurel Plantation
HAGG SIDE LANE
Netherby Dale
Wilton Heights
Dargo Plantation
Mickle Howe
YO13
Sands Farm
COULBY LA
Partings Farm
Ebberston Hall
Low Park Farm
SANDSPRUNT LANE
NETTLEDALE LA
A170
HIGH STREET
Quarry Farm
CROSS GATE
Hazel Hall Farm
CLIFF LANE
Wilton
Cliff Edge Farm
PH
CHURCH
MAIN ST
Eastcroft Farm
Welldale Farm
YO18
CAWCLIFF LA
Allerston
Bore Hole Plantation
BACK LANE
Ebberston
Middle Farm
TOC LA
Low Fell
Clear Fell
WATER GAP
Pear Tree Farm
Great Dollybog Plantation
Mill Pond
MILL LANE
KINGS LA
PO
HIGH ST
CLIFF LANE
Low Farm
MAIN STREET
Wilton Carr House
B1258
WEST LANE
CFT LA
PUDDING LA
STATION RD
New South Farm
B1415
PENNISTON LANE
Westfield Manor Farm
MIDDLE LA
MALTON LANE
Anderson Plantation
Low Moor House
Low Farm
Station Farm
Wilton Grange
WILTON INGS LANE
Ebberston Ings
INGS LANE
Snainton West Carr
Wilton Ings
ALLERSTON LANE
Ebberston Carr
CROSS LANE
Carr House Farm
Rains Farm
WILTON CARR LANE
Wilton Carr
FOULBRIDGE LANE
Woodlands Farm
Abbey Farm
Friar Dike
New Derwent Farm
Site of Priory
Foulbridge
Crake Hall
Allerston Loft Marishes
Bridge Farm
Ings Farm
Foulbridge Farm
PH
Yedingham
Manor Farm
MARISHES LANE
Newstead Grange
Marishes Lodge Farm
Yedingham Ings
Yeddingham Cottage Farm
Ellis Bridge
Westfield
Westfield Farm
KIRBY LANE
KIRBY LA
Whitehall Farm
Middle Flat Farm
Lilac Farm
Grange Farm
The Howles
East Heslerton Carr
Knapton Ings
MALTON ROAD
YO17
STATION ROAD
Birch Plantation
Difford Beck
Ings Farm
Field House Farm
Wath House Farm
Ellis Beck
West Heslerton Carr
B1258
Difford Bridge
Knapton Carr
8 85 7 84 6 83 5 82 4 81 3 80 2 79 1 78
86 87 88 89 90 91

97
74

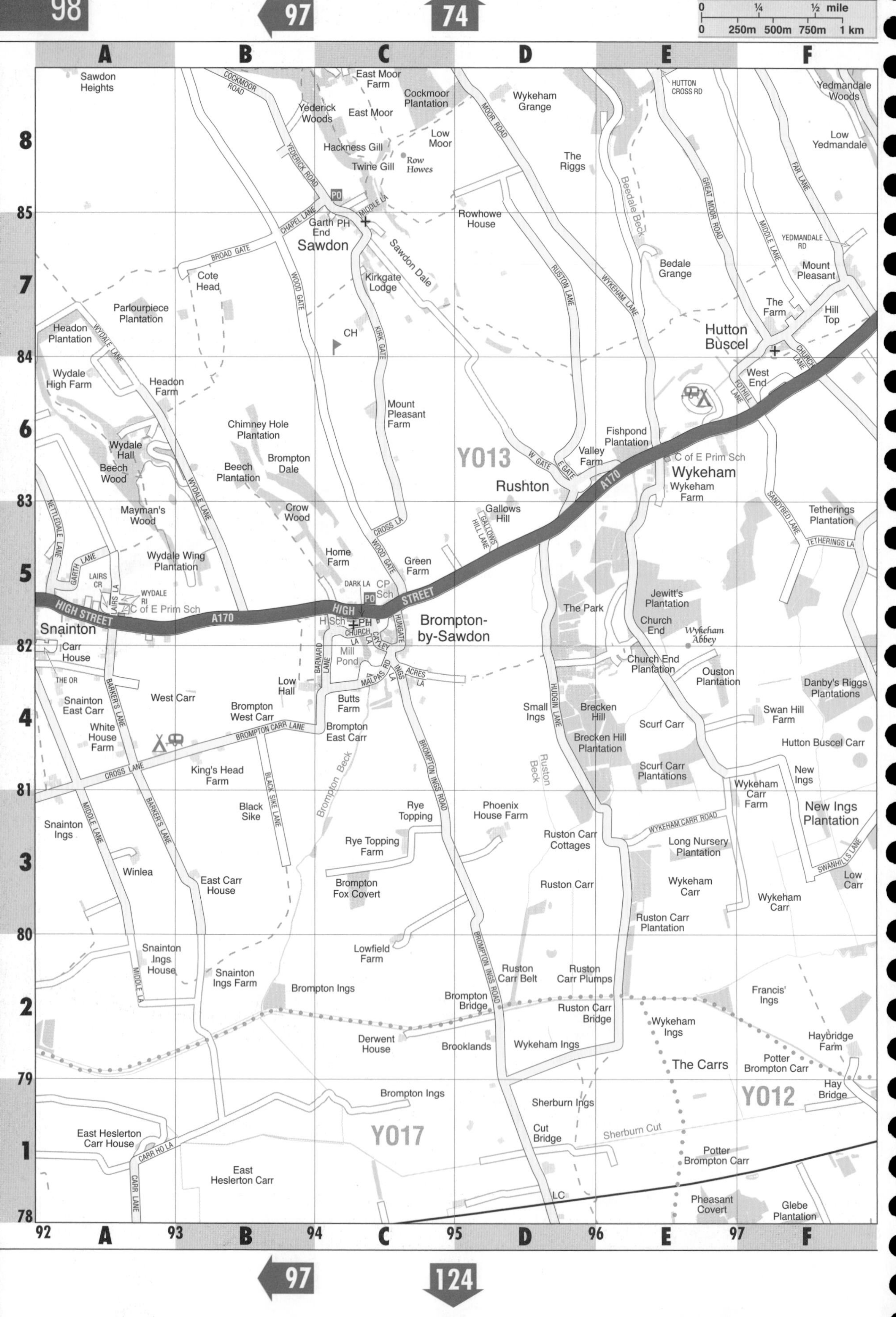
Scale: 1¾ inches to 1 mile
Sawdon Heights
Yederick Woods
East Moor Farm
East Moor
Cockmoor Plantation
Low Moor
Hackness Gill
Twine Gill
Row Howes
Wykeham Grange
The Riggs
Yedmandale Woods
Low Yedmandale
Sawdon
Garth End
Sawdon Dale
Rowhowe House
Beedale Beck
Bedale Grange
Mount Pleasant
Cote Head
Kirkgate Lodge
Parlourpiece Plantation
Headon Plantation
The Farm
Hill Top
Hutton Buscel
West End
Wydale High Farm
Headon Farm
Mount Pleasant Farm
Chimney Hole Plantation
Fishpond Plantation
Valley Farm
Wydale Hall
Beech Wood
Beech Plantation
Brompton Dale
YO13
Rushton
Wykeham
Wykeham Farm
C of E Prim Sch
Mayman's Wood
Crow Wood
Gallows Hill
Tetherings Plantation
Wydale Wing Plantation
Home Farm
Green Farm
Jewitt's Plantation
The Park
Snainton
Brompton-by-Sawdon
Church End
Wykeham Abbey
Carr House
Mill Pond
Church End Plantation
Ouston Plantation
Danby's Riggs Plantations
Low Hall
Snainton East Carr
West Carr
Brompton West Carr
Butts Farm
Small Ings
Brecken Hill
Swan Hill Farm
White House Farm
Brompton East Carr
Scurf Carr
Brecken Hill Plantation
Hutton Buscel Carr
King's Head Farm
Brompton Beck
Ruston Beck
Scurf Carr Plantations
New Ings
Wykeham Carr Farm
Snainton Ings
Black Sike
Rye Topping
Phoenix House Farm
New Ings Plantation
Rye Topping Farm
Ruston Carr Cottages
Long Nursery Plantation
Winlea
East Carr House
Brompton Fox Covert
Ruston Carr
Wykeham Carr
Low Carr
Ruston Carr Plantation
Snainton Ings House
Lowfield Farm
Snainton Ings Farm
Brompton Ings
Ruston Carr Belt
Ruston Carr Plumps
Brompton Bridge
Ruston Carr Bridge
Francis' Ings
Wykeham Ings
Derwent House
Brooklands
Haybridge Farm
The Carrs
Potter Brompton Carr
Hay Bridge
YO12
Brompton Ings
Sherburn Ings
East Heslerton Carr House
YO17
Cut Bridge
Sherburn Cut
East Heslerton Carr
Pheasant Covert
Glebe Plantation

97
124

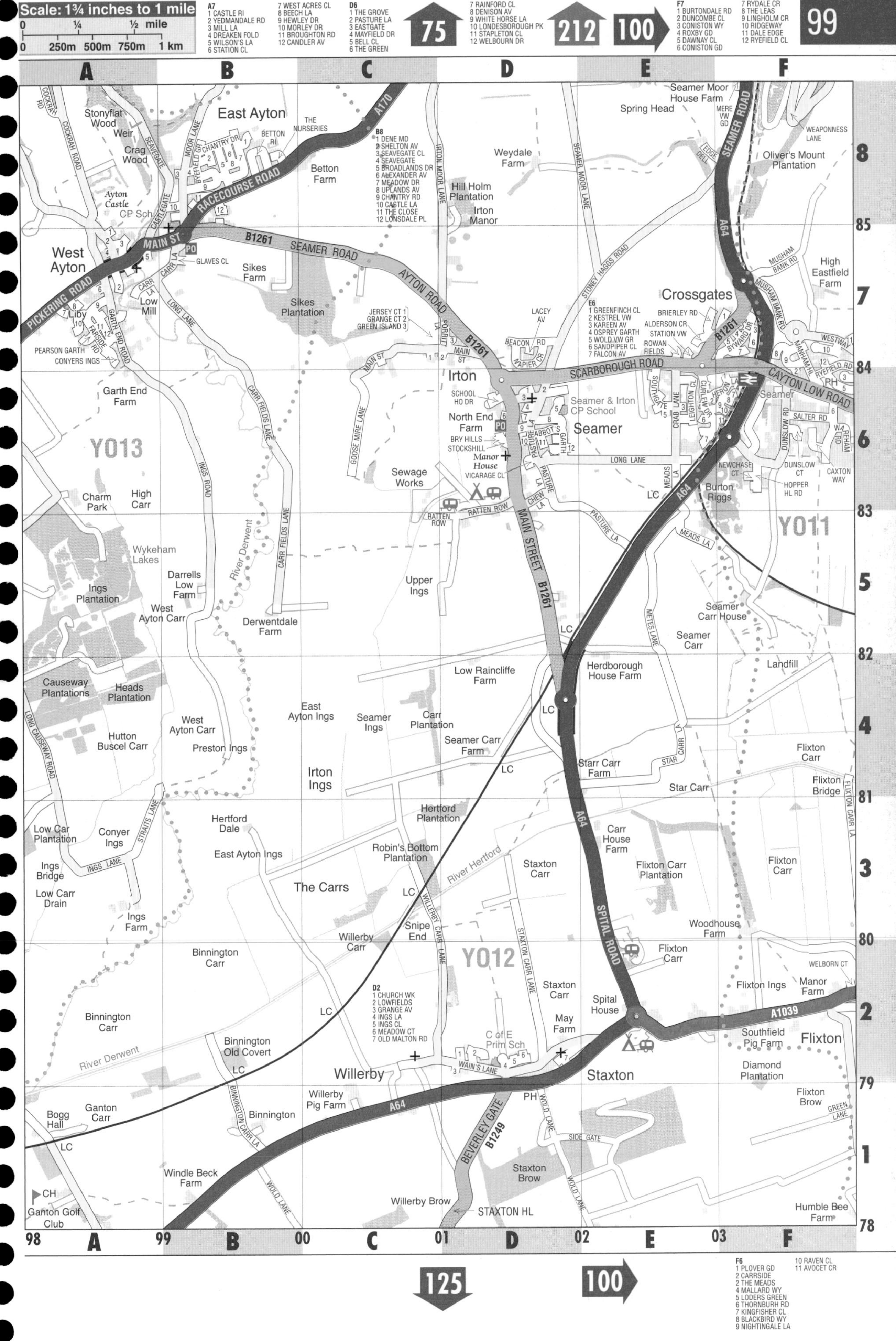

Scale: 1¾ inches to 1 mile
0
¼
½ mile
0
250m
500m
750m
1 km
A7
1 CASTLE RI
2 YEDMANDALE RD
3 MILL LA
4 DREAKEN FOLD
5 WILSON'S LA
6 STATION CL
7 WEST ACRES CL
8 BEECH LA
9 HEWLEY DR
10 MORLEY DR
11 BROUGHTON RD
12 CANDLER AV
D6
1 THE GROVE
2 PASTURE LA
3 EASTGATE
4 MAYFIELD DR
5 BELL CL
6 THE GREEN
75
7 RAINFORD CL
8 DENISON AV
9 WHITE HORSE LA
10 LONDESBOROUGH PK
11 STAPLETON CL
12 WELBOURN DR
212
100
F7
1 BURTONDALE RD
2 DUNCOMBE CL
3 CONISTON WY
4 ROXBY GD
5 DAWNAY CL
6 CONISTON GD
7 RYDALE CR
8 THE LEAS
9 LINGHOLM CR
10 RIDGEWAY
11 DALE EDGE
12 RYEFIELD CL
99
A
B
C
D
E
F
East Ayton
Stonyflat Wood
Weir
Crag Wood
Ayton Castle
CP Sch
West Ayton
PICKERING ROAD
MAIN ST
RACECOURSE ROAD
A170
THE NURSERIES
BETTON RI
Betton Farm
B8
1 DENE MD
2 SHELTON AV
3 SEAVEGATE CL
4 SEAVEGATE
5 BROADLANDS DR
6 ALEXANDER AV
7 MEADOW DR
8 UPLANDS AV
9 CHANTRY RD
10 CASTLE LA
11 THE CLOSE
12 LONSDALE PL
Weydale Farm
Hill Holm Plantation
Irton Manor
Seamer Moor House Farm
Spring Head
SEAMER ROAD
WEAPONNESS LANE
Oliver's Mount Plantation
B1261
SEAMER ROAD
GLAVES CL
Sikes Farm
Sikes Plantation
AYTON ROAD
Low Mill
LONG LANE
Liby
PEARSON GARTH
CONYERS INGS
GARTH END ROAD
Garth End Farm
JERSEY CT 1
GRANGE CT 2
GREEN ISLAND 3
STONEY HAGGS ROAD
Crossgates
MUSHAM BANK RD
High Eastfield Farm
E6
1 GREENFINCH CL
2 KESTREL VW
3 KAREEN AV
4 OSPREY GARTH
5 WOLD VW GR
6 SANDPIPER CL
7 FALCON AV
LACEY AV
BEACON RD
NAPIER CR
BRIERLEY RD
ALDERSON CR
STATION VW
ROWAN FIELDS
WESTWAY
Irton
SCARBOROUGH ROAD
CAYTON LOW ROAD
SCHOOL HO DR
North End Farm
BRY HILLS
STOCKSHILL
Manor House
VICARAGE CL
Seamer & Irton CP School
Seamer
ABBOT'S GARTH
LONG LANE
SALTER RD
DUNSLOW RD
Y013
GOOSE MIRE LANE
Sewage Works
Charm Park
High Carr
RATTEN ROW
MAIN STREET
PASTURE LA
MEADS LA
Burton Riggs
NEWCHASE CT
DUNSLOW CT
HOPPER HL RD
CAXTON WAY
Y011
Wykeham Lakes
River Derwent
CARR FIELDS LANE
Darrells Low Farm
Ings Plantation
West Ayton Carr
Upper Ings
Derwentdale Farm
METES LANE
Seamer Carr House
Seamer Carr
Low Raincliffe Farm
Herdborough House Farm
Landfill
Causeway Plantations
Heads Plantation
Hutton Buscel Carr
East Ayton Ings
Seamer Ings
Carr Plantation
Seamer Carr Farm
West Ayton Carr
Preston Ings
Irton Ings
Starr Carr Farm
STAR CARR LA
Star Carr
Flixton Carr
Flixton Bridge
LONG CAUSEWAY ROAD
STRAITS LANE
Low Car Plantation
Conyer Ings
Hertford Dale
East Ayton Ings
Hertford Plantation
Robin's Bottom Plantation
River Hertford
Carr House Farm
Staxton Carr
Flixton Carr Plantation
Flixton Carr
Ings Bridge
INGS LANE
Low Carr Drain
The Carrs
Ings Farm
Snipe End
Willerby Carr
WILLERBY CARR LANE
Y012
STAXTON CARR LANE
SPITAL ROAD
Woodhouse Farm
Flixton Carr
Binnington Carr
WELBORN CT
Flixton Ings
Manor Farm
D2
1 CHURCH WK
2 LOWFIELDS
3 GRANGE AV
4 INGS LA
5 INGS CL
6 MEADOW CT
7 OLD MALTON RD
Staxton Carr
Spital House
A1039
May Farm
Binnington Carr
Southfield Pig Farm
Flixton
Binnington Old Covert
C of E Prim Sch
River Derwent
Willerby
WAIN'S LANE
Staxton
Diamond Plantation
A64
Willerby Pig Farm
BEVERLEY GATE
B1249
WOLD LANE
Bogg Hall
Ganton Carr
Binnington
BINNINGTON CARR LA
SIDE GATE
Flixton Brow
GREEN LANE
Windle Beck Farm
Staxton Brow
WOLD LANE
CH
Ganton Golf Club
Willerby Brow
STAXTON HL
Humble Bee Farm
98
99
00
01
02
03
78
79
80
81
82
83
84
85
8
7
6
5
4
3
2
1
125
100
F6
1 PLOVER GD
2 CARRSIDE
3 THE MEADS
4 MALLARD WY
5 LODERS GREEN
6 THORNBURH RD
7 KINGFISHER CL
8 BLACKBIRD WY
9 NIGHTINGALE LA
10 RAVEN CL
11 AVOCET CR

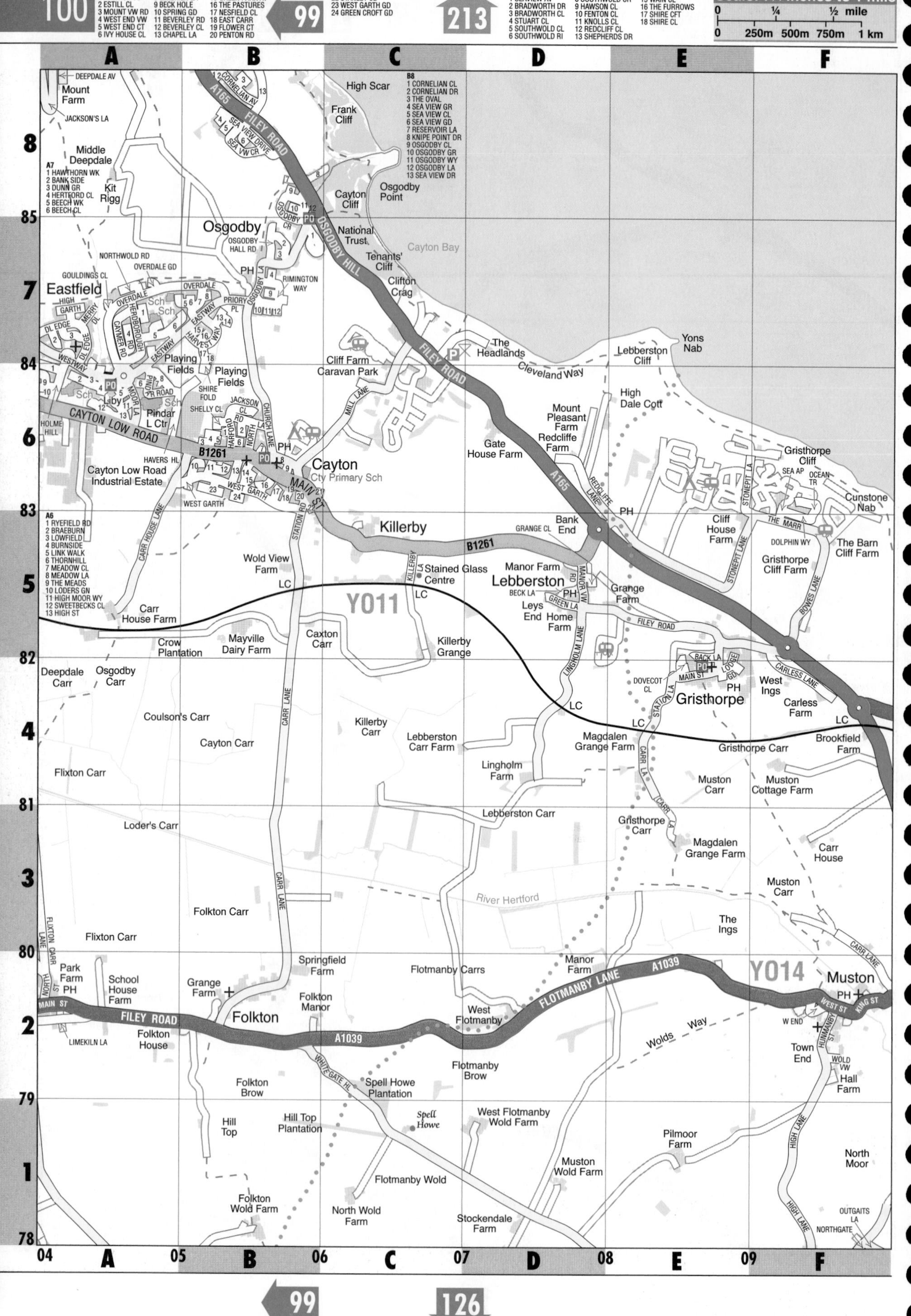

100
B6
1 FENWICK CL
2 ESTILL CL
3 MOUNT VW RD
4 WEST END VW
5 WEST END CT
6 IVY HOUSE CL
7 LODGE CL
8 LIMEKILN LA
9 BECK HOLE
10 SPRING GD
11 BEVERLEY RD
12 BEVERLEY CL
13 CHAPEL LA
14 GREEN PARK RD
15 GREEN PARK AV
16 THE PASTURES
17 NESFIELD CL
18 EAST CARR
19 FLOWER CT
20 PENTON RD
99
21 EAST LEA VW
22 STANLEY CL
23 WEST GARTH GD
24 GREEN CROFT GD
213
B7
1 SEAVIEW AV
2 BRADWORTH DR
3 BRADWORTH CL
4 STUART CL
5 SOUTHWOLD CL
6 SOUTHWOLD RI
7 SOUTHWOLD
8 SOUTHWOLD CR
9 HAWSON CL
10 FENTON CL
11 KNOLLS CL
12 REDCLIFF CL
13 SHEPHERDS DR
14 PLOUGHMANS CT
15 WAIN CL
16 THE FURROWS
17 SHIRE CFT
18 SHIRE CL
Scale: 1¾ inches to 1 mile
0 ¼ ½ mile
0 250m 500m 750m 1 km
A B C D E F
B8
1 CORNELIAN CL
2 CORNELIAN DR
3 THE OVAL
4 SEA VIEW GR
5 SEA VIEW CL
6 SEA VIEW GD
7 RESERVOIR LA
8 KNIPE POINT DR
9 OSGODBY CL
10 OSGODBY GR
11 OSGODBY WY
12 OSGODBY LA
13 SEA VIEW DR
A7
1 HAWTHORN WK
2 BANK SIDE
3 DUNN GR
4 HERTFORD CL
5 BEECH WK
6 BEECH CL
A6
1 RYEFIELD RD
2 BRAEBURN
3 LOWFIELD
4 BURNSIDE
5 LINK WALK
6 THORNHILL
7 MEADOW CL
8 MEADOW LA
9 THE MEADS
10 LODERS GN
11 HIGH MOOR WY
12 SWEETBECKS CL
13 HIGH ST
Mount Farm
Middle Deepdale
Kit Rigg
Osgodby
High Scar
Frank Cliff
Osgodby Point
Cayton Cliff
National Trust
Cayton Bay
Tenants' Cliff
Clifton Crag
Eastfield
FILEY ROAD
OSGODBY HILL
Cliff Farm Caravan Park
The Headlands
Cleveland Way
Lebberston Cliff
Yons Nab
High Dale Cott
Mount Pleasant Farm
Redcliffe Farm
Gate House Farm
Playing Fields
Pindar L Ctr
CAYTON LOW ROAD
B1261
Cayton
Cty Primary Sch
Cayton Low Road Industrial Estate
MAIN ST
Killerby
Bank End
Gristhorpe Cliff
Cunstone Nab
Cliff House Farm
The Barn Cliff Farm
Gristhorpe Cliff Farm
Wold View Farm
Stained Glass Centre
Manor Farm
Lebberston
Leys End
Home Farm
Grange Farm
YO11
Carr House Farm
Crow Plantation
Mayville Dairy Farm
Caxton Carr
Killerby Grange
Deepdale Carr
Osgodby Carr
Gristhorpe
West Ings
Carless Farm
Coulson's Carr
Cayton Carr
Killerby Carr
Lebberston Carr Farm
Magdalen Grange Farm
Gristhorpe Carr
Brookfield Farm
Flixton Carr
Lingholm Farm
Muston Carr
Muston Cottage Farm
Loder's Carr
Lebberston Carr
Gristhorpe Carr
Carr House
River Hertford
Folkton Carr
The Ings
Flixton Carr
Park Farm
School House Farm
Grange Farm
Springfield Farm
Flotmanby Carrs
Manor Farm
FLOTMANBY LANE
A1039
YO14
Muston
Folkton
Folkton Manor
West Flotmanby
Folkton House
Wolds Way
Town End
Hall Farm
Folkton Brow
Spell Howe Plantation
Flotmanby Brow
Hill Top
Hill Top Plantation
Spell Howe
West Flotmanby Wold Farm
Pilmoor Farm
North Moor
Flotmanby Wold
Muston Wold Farm
Folkton Wold Farm
North Wold Farm
Stockendale Farm
04 05 06 07 08 09
99
126

Scale: 1¾ inches to 1 mile
0 ¼ ½ mile
0 250m 500m 750m 1 km

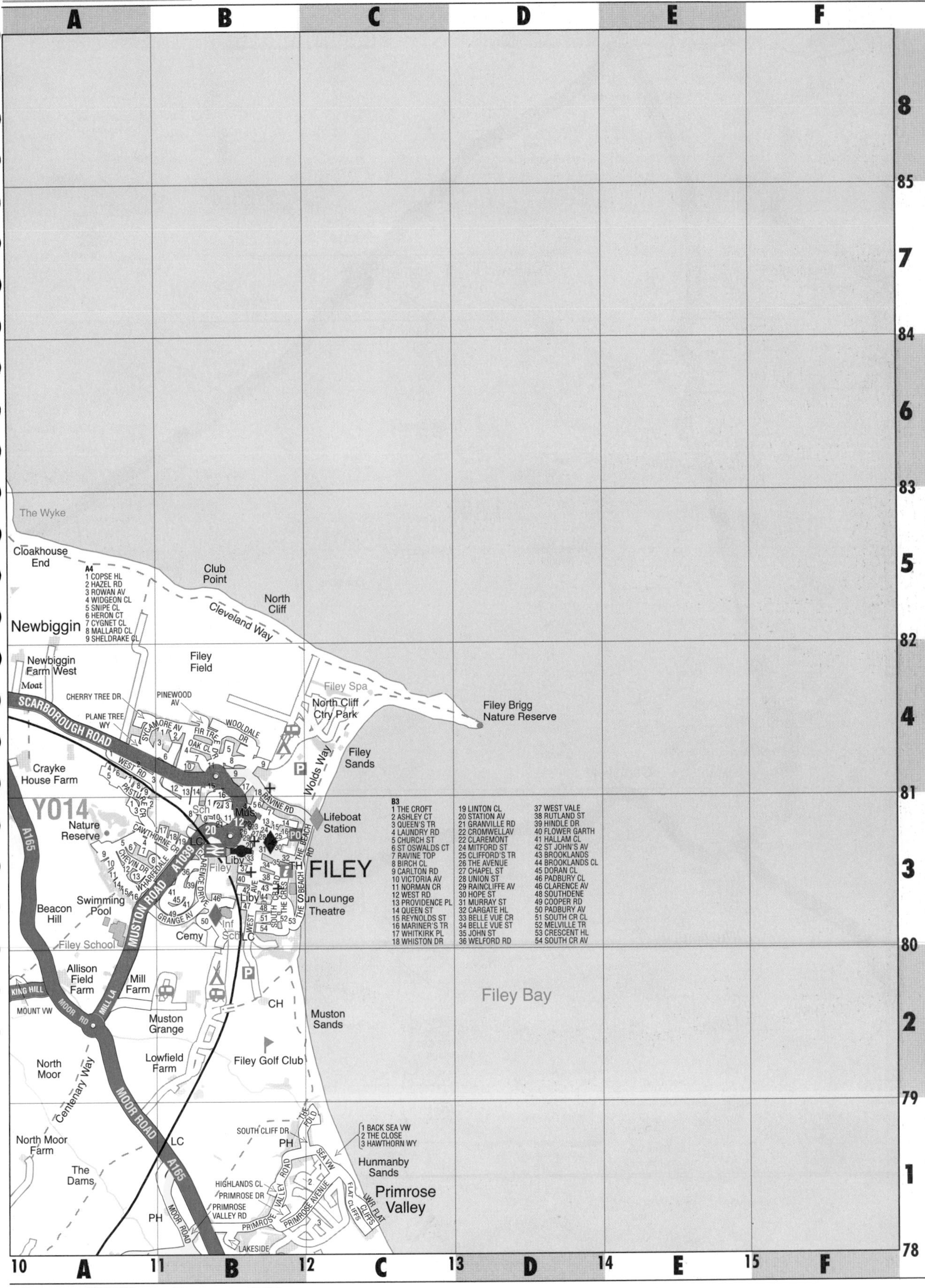

The Wyke
Cloakhouse End
Club Point
North Cliff
Cleveland Way
Newbiggin
Newbiggin Farm West
Moat
Filey Field
Filey Spa
North Cliff Ctry Park
Filey Brigg Nature Reserve
Filey Sands
Wolds Way
SCARBOROUGH ROAD
Crayke House Farm
YO14
Nature Reserve
Lifeboat Station
FILEY
Sun Lounge Theatre
Beacon Hill
Swimming Pool
MUSTON ROAD
A1039
Filey School
Cemy
Allison Field Farm
Mill Farm
KING HILL
MOOR RD
MILL LA
MOUNT VW
Muston Grange
CH
Muston Sands
Filey Bay
North Moor
Lowfield Farm
Filey Golf Club
Centenary Way
MOOR ROAD
A165
North Moor Farm
The Dams
SOUTH CLIFF DR
THE FOLD
PH
Hunmanby Sands
Primrose Valley
HIGHLANDS CL
PRIMROSE DR
PRIMROSE VALLEY RD
LAKESIDE

A4
1 COPSE HL
2 HAZEL RD
3 ROWAN AV
4 WIDGEON CL
5 SNIPE CL
6 HERON CT
7 CYGNET CL
8 MALLARD CL
9 SHELDRAKE CL

B3
1 THE CROFT
2 ASHLEY CT
3 QUEEN'S TR
4 LAUNDRY RD
5 CHURCH ST
6 ST OSWALDS CT
7 RAVINE TOP
8 BIRCH CL
9 CARLTON RD
10 VICTORIA AV
11 NORMAN CR
12 WEST RD
13 PROVIDENCE PL
14 QUEEN ST
15 REYNOLDS ST
16 MARINER'S TR
17 WHITKIRK PL
18 WHISTON DR
19 LINTON CL
20 STATION AV
21 GRANVILLE RD
22 CROMWELLAV
22 CLAREMONT
24 MITFORD ST
25 CLIFFORD'S TR
26 THE AVENUE
27 CHAPEL ST
28 UNION ST
29 RAINCLIFFE AV
30 HOPE ST
31 MURRAY ST
32 CARGATE HL
33 BELLE VUE CR
34 BELLE VUE ST
35 JOHN ST
36 WELFORD RD
37 WEST VALE
38 RUTLAND ST
39 HINDLE DR
40 FLOWER GARTH
41 HALLAM CL
42 ST JOHN'S AV
43 BROOKLANDS
44 BROOKLANDS CL
45 DORAN CL
46 PADBURY CL
46 CLARENCE AV
48 SOUTHDENE
49 COOPER RD
50 PADBURY AV
51 SOUTH CR CL
52 MELVILLE TR
53 CRESCENT HL
54 SOUTH CR AV

1 BACK SEA VW
2 THE CLOSE
3 HAWTHORN WY

A3
1 SANDPIPER CL
2 TEAL CL
3 CURLEW DR
4 HAREWOOD DR
5 SILVERWOOD AV
6 BURNSALL CL
7 LANGSETT AV
8 LEYBURN PL
9 BARDEN PL
10 RIVELIN WY
11 FEWSTON CL
12 COLLINGHAM WY
13 WASHBURN CL
14 WHARNCLIFFE PL
15 MIDHOPE WY
16 EWDEN CL

B4
1 LARCH GR
2 WILLOW CL
3 CEDAR GR
4 GROVE HILL RD
5 HORNDALE RD
6 THORN TREE AV
7 ALMOND CL
8 ARNDALE WY
9 CHURCH CLIFF DR
10 ELM CL
11 ALMOND GR
12 ASH GR
13 ASH RD
14 GROVE RD
15 THE GARDENS
16 THE CROFT
17 RAVINE HL
18 CHURCH CL

127

Scale: 1¾ inches to 1 mile

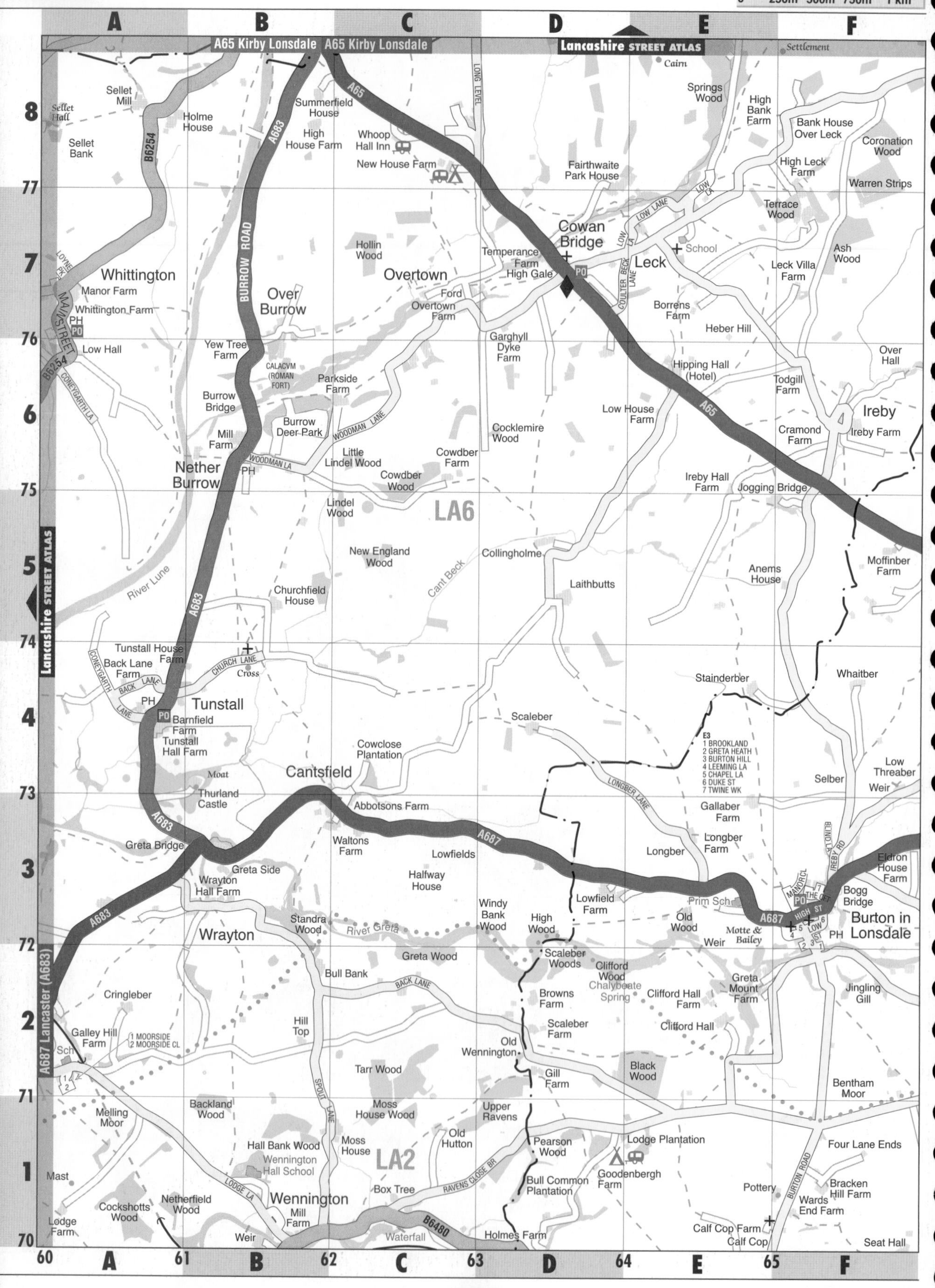

77
104

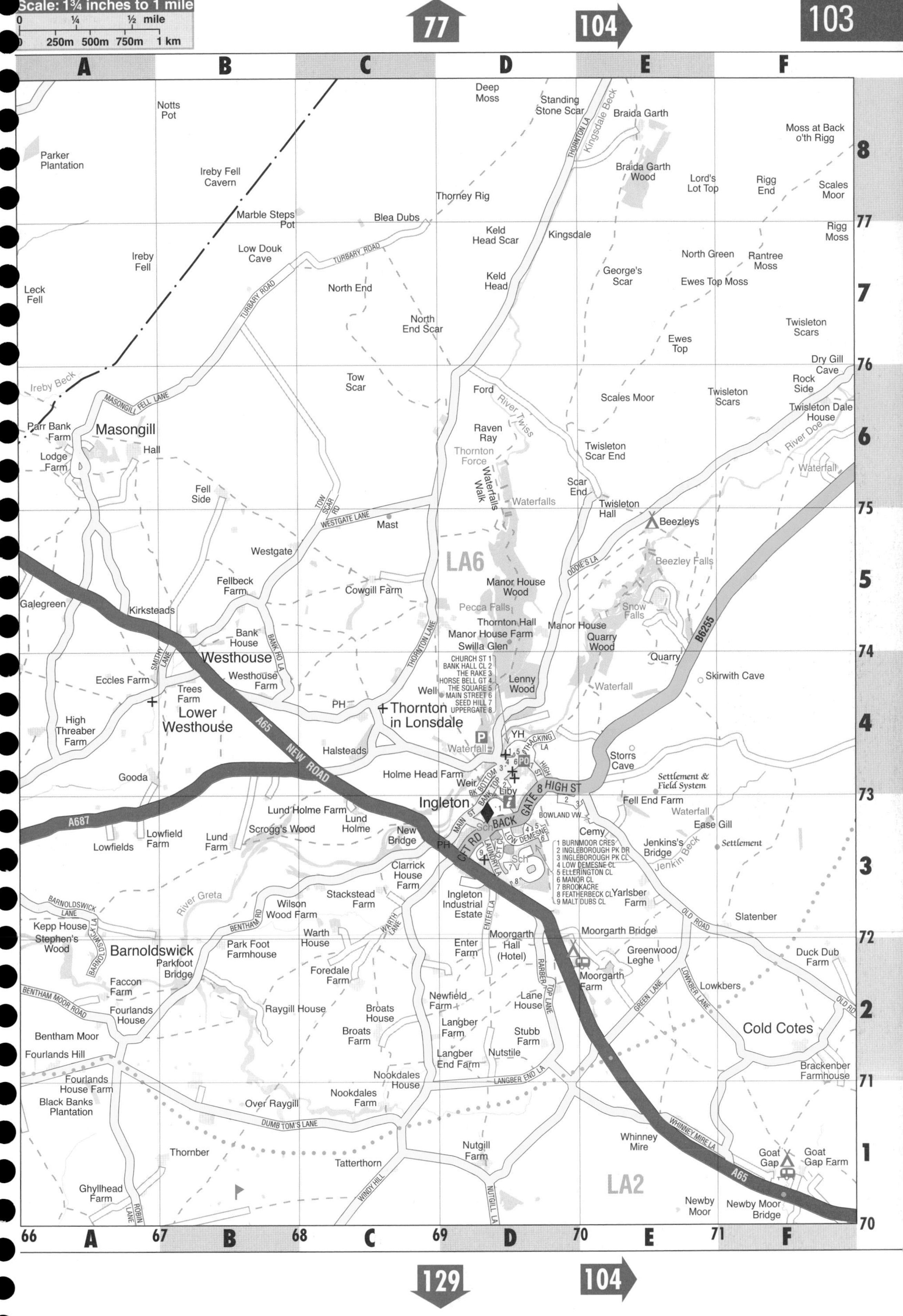

129
104

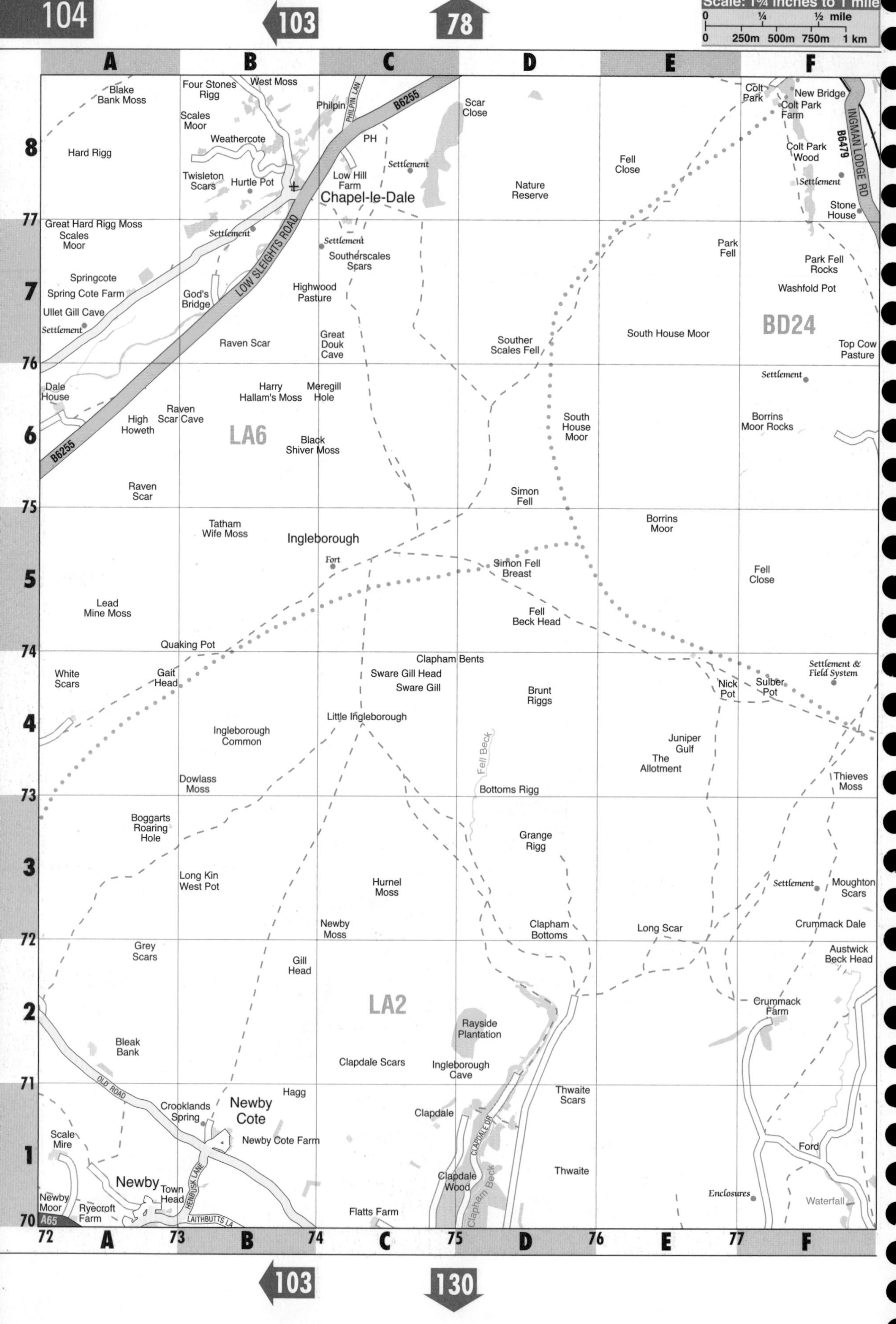
103
78
Scale: 1¾ inches to 1 mile
0 ¼ ½ mile
0 250m 500m 750m 1 km
A B C D E F
8 77 7 76 6 75 5 74 4 73 3 72 2 71 1 70
72 73 74 75 76 77
Blake Bank Moss
Four Stones Rigg
West Moss
Philpin
PHILPIN LAN
B6255
Scar Close
Colt Park
New Bridge
Colt Park Farm
INGMAN LODGE RD
B6479
Scales Moor
Weathercote
PH
Hard Rigg
Settlement
Fell Close
Colt Park Wood
Twisleton Scars
Hurtle Pot
Low Hill Farm
Nature Reserve
Chapel-le-Dale
Stone House
Great Hard Rigg Moss
Scales Moor
Southerscales Scars
Park Fell
Park Fell Rocks
Springcote
LOW SLEIGHTS ROAD
Spring Cote Farm
God's Bridge
Highwood Pasture
Washfold Pot
Ullet Gill Cave
BD24
Raven Scar
Great Douk Cave
Souther Scales Fell
South House Moor
Top Cow Pasture
Dale House
Harry Hallam's Moss
Meregill Hole
Raven Scar Cave
High Howeth
LA6
South House Moor
Borrins Moor Rocks
Black Shiver Moss
B6255
Raven Scar
Simon Fell
Tatham Wife Moss
Borrins Moor
Ingleborough
Fort
Simon Fell Breast
Fell Close
Lead Mine Moss
Fell Beck Head
Quaking Pot
Clapham Bents
Settlement & Field System
White Scars
Gait Head
Sware Gill Head
Sware Gill
Brunt Riggs
Nick Pot
Sulber Pot
Little Ingleborough
Ingleborough Common
Juniper Gulf
The Allotment
Fell Beck
Dowlass Moss
Bottoms Rigg
Thieves Moss
Boggarts Roaring Hole
Grange Rigg
Long Kin West Pot
Hurnel Moss
Moughton Scars
Newby Moss
Clapham Bottoms
Long Scar
Crummack Dale
Grey Scars
Gill Head
Austwick Beck Head
LA2
Crummack Farm
Rayside Plantation
Bleak Bank
Clapdale Scars
Ingleborough Cave
OLD ROAD
Hagg
Thwaite Scars
Crooklands Spring
Newby Cote
Clapdale
Scale Mire
Newby Cote Farm
CLAPDALE DR
Ford
HENBUSK LANE
Newby
Town Head
Clapdale Wood
Thwaite
Clapham Beck
Enclosures
Newby Moor
Ryecroft Farm
Waterfall
A65
LAITHBUTTS LA
Flatts Farm

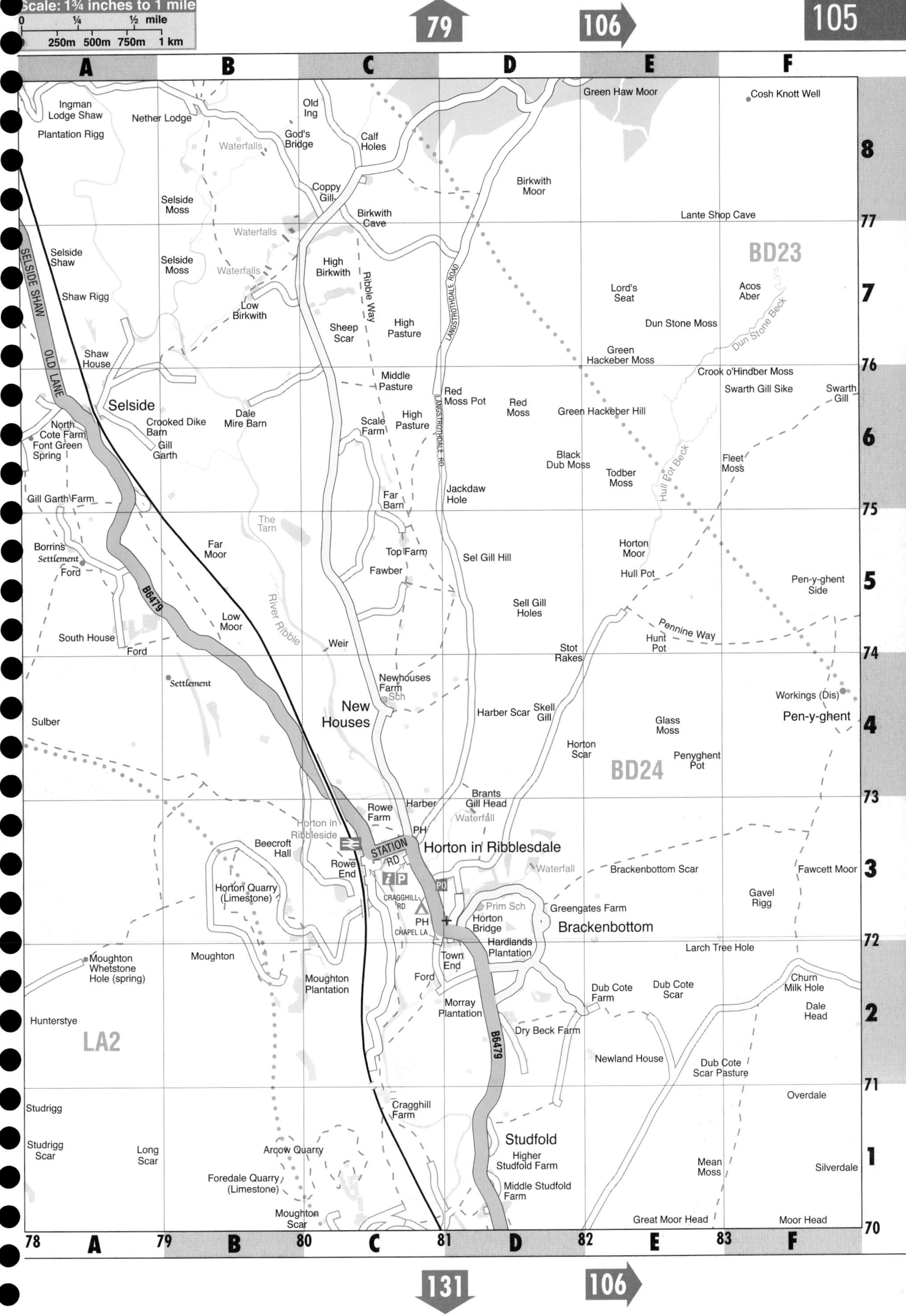
Scale: 1¾ inches to 1 mile
0 ¼ ½ mile
250m 500m 750m 1 km
79
106
A B C D E F
8 7 6 5 4 3 2 1
77 76 75 74 73 72 71 70
78 79 80 81 82 83
Ingman Lodge Shaw
Plantation Rigg
Nether Lodge
Old Ing
God's Bridge
Waterfalls
Calf Holes
Green Haw Moor
Cosh Knott Well
Coppy Gill
Birkwith Moor
Selside Moss
Birkwith Cave
Lante Shop Cave
Selside Shaw
High Birkwith
BD23
Shaw Rigg
Low Birkwith
Ribble Way
Langstrothdale Road
Lord's Seat
Acos Aber
Dun Stone Moss
Dun Stone Beck
High Pasture
Sheep Scar
Shaw House
Green Hackeber Moss
Crook o'Hindber Moss
Selside Shaw
Old Lane
Middle Pasture
Swarth Gill Sike
Swarth Gill
Selside
Dale Mire Barn
Red Moss Pot
Red Moss
Green Hackeber Hill
North Cote Farm
Font Green Spring
Crooked Dike Barn
Gill Garth
Scale Farm
High Pasture
Black Dub Moss
Todber Moss
Fleet Moss
Hull Pot Beck
Gill Garth Farm
Far Barn
Jackdaw Hole
The Tarn
Borrins
Settlement
Ford
Far Moor
Top Farm
Sel Gill Hill
Horton Moor
Hull Pot
Pen-y-ghent Side
Fawber
B6479
Low Moor
River Ribble
Sell Gill Holes
South House
Ford
Weir
Pennine Way
Hunt Pot
Stot Rakes
Settlement
Newhouses Farm
Sch
Workings (Dis)
Pen-y-ghent
Sulber
New Houses
Harber Scar
Skell Gill
Glass Moss
Horton Scar
Penyghent Pot
BD24
Brants Gill Head
Rowe Farm
Harber
Waterfall
Horton in Ribbleside
Beecroft Hall
PH
Station Rd
Horton in Ribblesdale
Rowe End
Waterfall
Brackenbottom Scar
Fawcett Moor
Horton Quarry (Limestone)
Cragghill Rd
PO
Prim Sch
Greengates Farm
Gavel Rigg
PH
Horton Bridge
Brackenbottom
Chapel La
Hardlands Plantation
Larch Tree Hole
Moughton Whetstone Hole (spring)
Moughton
Town End
Ford
Moughton Plantation
Dub Cote Farm
Dub Cote Scar
Churn Milk Hole
Morray Plantation
Dale Head
Dry Beck Farm
Hunterstye
LA2
Newland House
Dub Cote Scar Pasture
Overdale
Studrigg
Cragghill Farm
Studrigg Scar
Long Scar
Arcow Quarry
Studfold
Higher Studfold Farm
Mean Moss
Silverdale
Foredale Quarry (Limestone)
Middle Studfold Farm
Moughton Scar
Great Moor Head
Moor Head
131
106

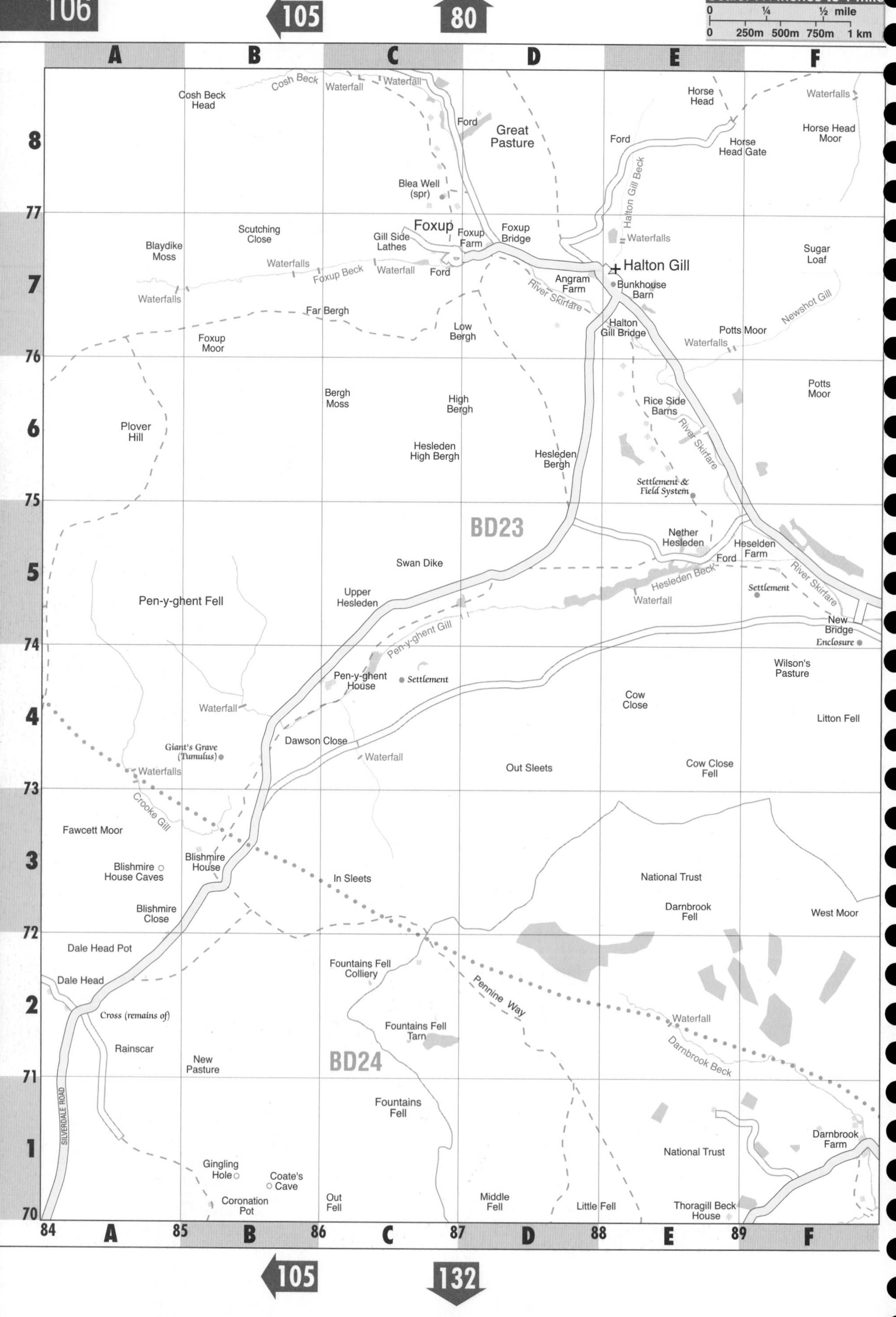
Scale: 1¾ inches to 1 mile
0 ¼ ½ mile
0 250m 500m 750m 1 km
Cosh Beck Head
Cosh Beck
Waterfall
Ford
Great Pasture
Horse Head
Horse Head Gate
Horse Head Moor
Waterfalls
Blea Well (spr)
Halton Gill Beck
Foxup
Scutching Close
Blaydike Moss
Gill Side Lathes
Foxup Farm
Foxup Bridge
Waterfalls
Halton Gill
Sugar Loaf
Foxup Beck
Angram Farm
Bunkhouse Barn
River Skirfare
Far Bergh
Newshot Gill
Low Bergh
Halton Gill Bridge
Potts Moor
Foxup Moor
Bergh Moss
High Bergh
Rice Side Barns
Plover Hill
Hesleden High Bergh
Hesleden Bergh
Settlement & Field System
BD23
Nether Hesleden
Heselden Farm
Swan Dike
Hesleden Beck
Settlement
Pen-y-ghent Fell
Upper Hesleden
New Bridge
Enclosure
Pen-y-ghent Gill
Pen-y-ghent House
Settlement
Wilson's Pasture
Cow Close
Litton Fell
Dawson Close
Giant's Grave (Tumulus)
Out Sleets
Cow Close Fell
Crooke Gill
Fawcett Moor
Blishmire House
Blishmire House Caves
In Sleets
National Trust
Darnbrook Fell
West Moor
Blishmire Close
Dale Head Pot
Fountains Fell Colliery
Dale Head
Pennine Way
Cross (remains of)
Fountains Fell Tarn
Rainscar
New Pasture
BD24
Darnbrook Beck
Fountains Fell
SILVERDALE ROAD
Darnbrook Farm
National Trust
Gingling Hole
Coate's Cave
Coronation Pot
Out Fell
Middle Fell
Little Fell
Thoragill Beck House
A B C D E F
8 77 7 76 6 75 5 74 4 73 3 72 2 71 1 70
84 85 86 87 88 89

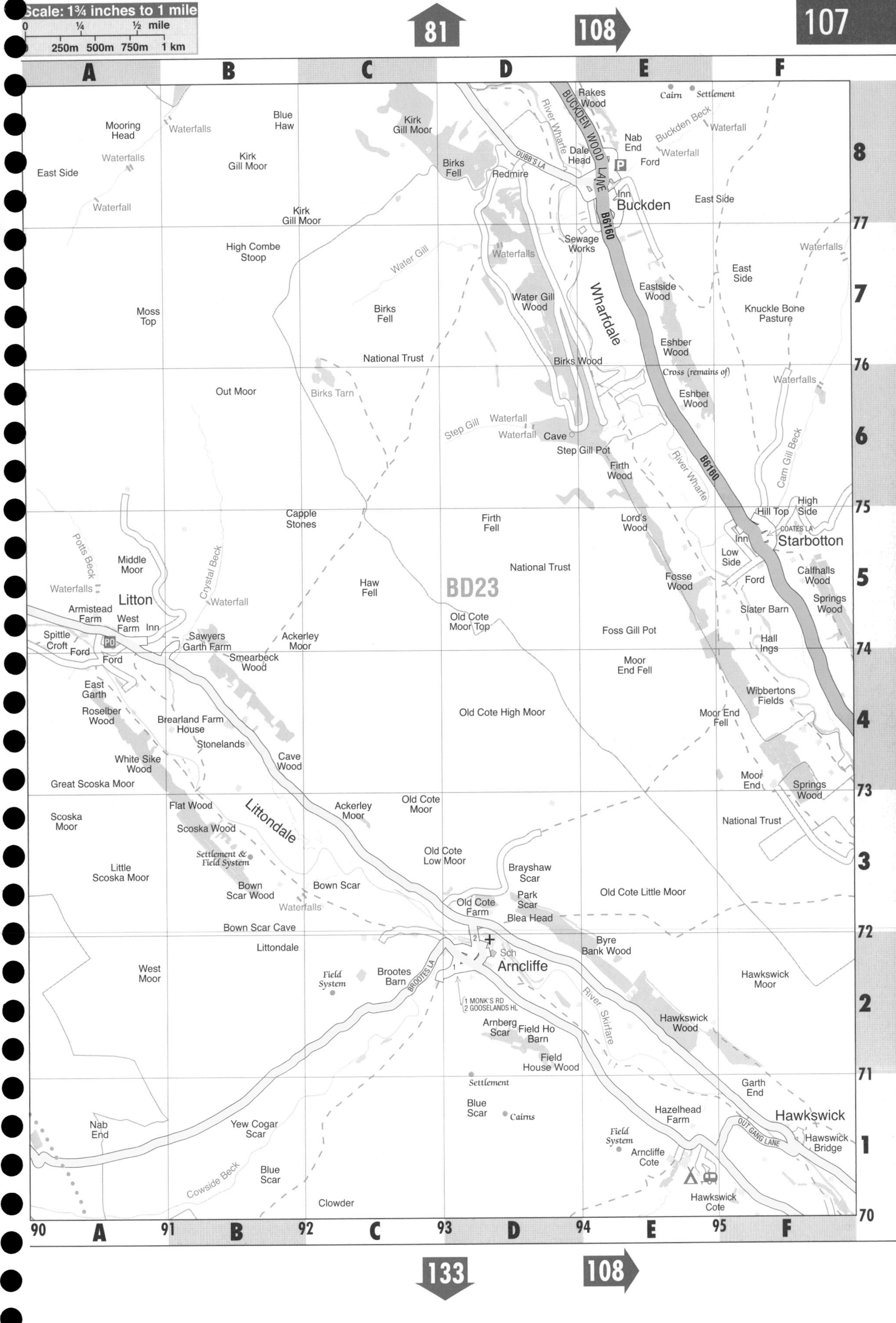
Scale: 1¾ inches to 1 mile
0 ¼ ½ mile
0 250m 500m 750m 1 km
81
108
133
108
Mooring Head
Waterfalls
Blue Haw
Kirk Gill Moor
East Side
Waterfall
Kirk Gill Moor
Birks Fell
Redmire
Rakes Wood
River Wharfe
BUCKDEN WOOD LANE
Dale Head
Nab End
Buckden Beck
Waterfall
Ford
Inn
Buckden
East Side
Cairn
Settlement
High Combe Stoop
Water Gill
Sewage Works
B6160
Waterfalls
Eastside Wood
East Side
Knuckle Bone Pasture
Moss Top
Birks Fell
Water Gill Wood
Wharfdale
Eshber Wood
National Trust
Birks Wood
Cross (remains of)
Out Moor
Birks Tarn
Eshber Wood
Step Gill
Waterfall
Cave
Step Gill Pot
Firth Wood
River Wharfe
Cam Gill Beck
Capple Stones
Firth Fell
Lord's Wood
Hill Top
High Side
COATES LA
Starbotton
Low Side
Potts Beck
Middle Moor
Crystal Beck
Waterfall
Litton
Haw Fell
BD23
National Trust
Fosse Wood
Ford
Calfhalls Wood
Springs Wood
Slater Barn
Armistead Farm
West Farm
Inn
Spittle Croft
Ford
PO
Sawyers Garth Farm
Ackerley Moor
Old Cote Moor Top
Foss Gill Pot
Hall Ings
Smearbeck Wood
Moor End Fell
East Garth
Roselber Wood
Brearland Farm House
Stonelands
Old Cote High Moor
Wibbertons Fields
Moor End Fell
White Sike Wood
Cave Wood
Great Scoska Moor
Moor End
Springs Wood
Scoska Moor
Flat Wood
Littondale
Ackerley Moor
Old Cote Moor
National Trust
Scoska Wood
Settlement & Field System
Little Scoska Moor
Old Cote Low Moor
Brayshaw Scar
Bown Scar Wood
Bown Scar
Waterfalls
Old Cote Farm
Park Scar
Blea Head
Old Cote Little Moor
Bown Scar Cave
Littondale
Sch
Arncliffe
Byre Bank Wood
West Moor
Field System
Brootes Barn
BROOTES LA
1 MONK'S RD
2 GOOSELANDS HL
River Skirfare
Hawkswick Moor
Arnberg Scar
Field Ho Barn
Hawkswick Wood
Field House Wood
Settlement
Garth End
Blue Scar
Cairns
Hazelhead Farm
Hawkswick
Nab End
Yew Cogar Scar
Field System
Arncliffe Cote
OUT GANG LANE
Hawswick Bridge
Cowside Beck
Blue Scar
Clowder
Hawkswick Cote
A B C D E F
8 77 7 76 6 75 5 74 4 73 3 72 2 71 1 70
90 91 92 93 94 95

107
82

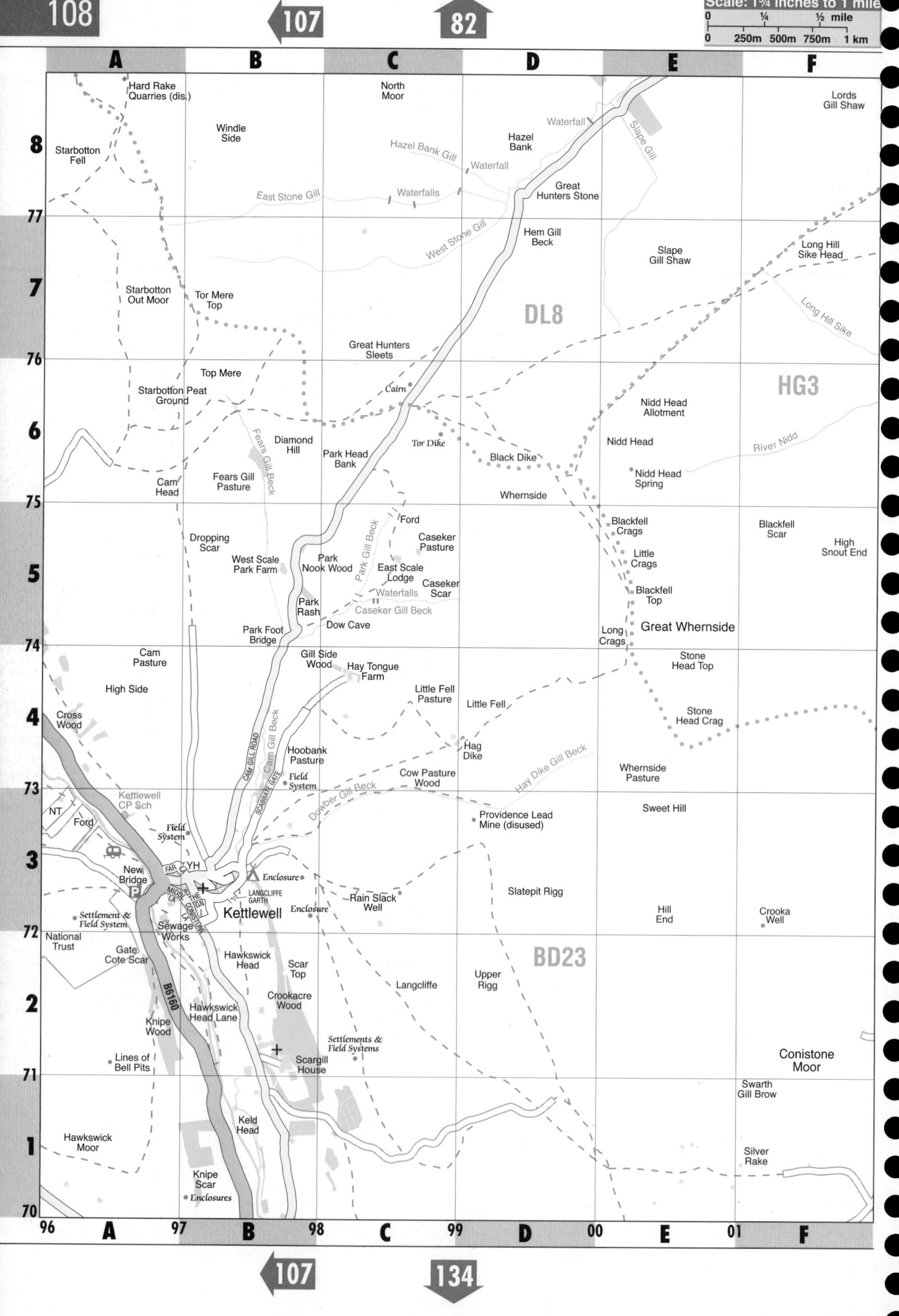

107
134

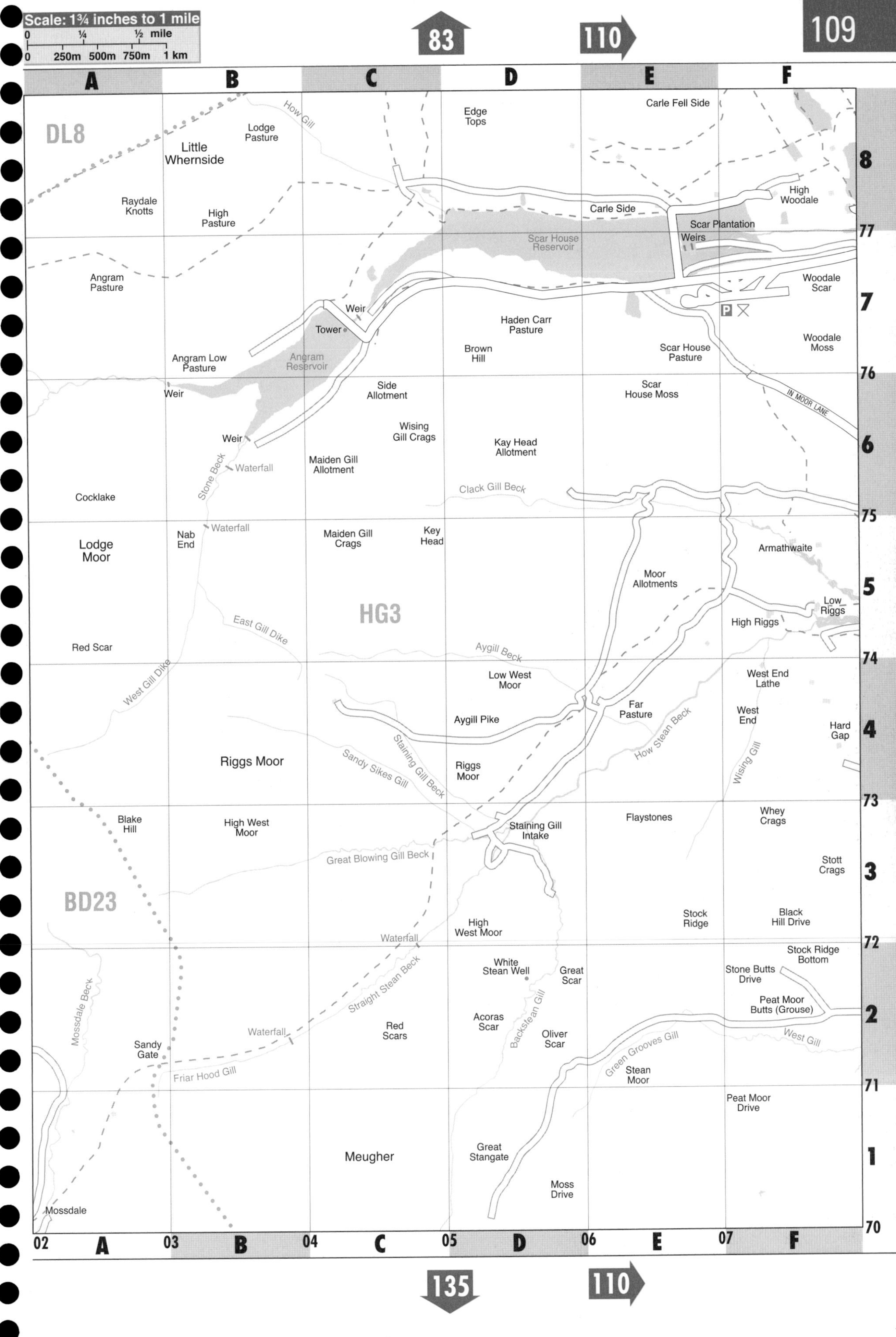
Scale: 1¾ inches to 1 mile
0 ¼ ½ mile
0 250m 500m 750m 1 km
83
110
A B C D E F
DL8
How Gill
Lodge Pasture
Little Whernside
Edge Tops
Carle Fell Side
Raydale Knotts
High Pasture
Carle Side
High Woodale
Scar Plantation
Scar House Reservoir
Weirs
Angram Pasture
Woodale Scar
Weir
Tower
Haden Carr Pasture
Brown Hill
Scar House Pasture
Woodale Moss
Angram Low Pasture
Angram Reservoir
Side Allotment
Scar House Moss
IN MOOR LANE
Weir
Wising Gill Crags
Kay Head Allotment
Weir
Stone Beck
Waterfall
Maiden Gill Allotment
Clack Gill Beck
Cocklake
Waterfall
Nab End
Maiden Gill Crags
Key Head
Armathwaite
Lodge Moor
Moor Allotments
HG3
East Gill Dike
Low Riggs
High Riggs
Red Scar
Aygill Beck
West End Lathe
West Gill Dike
Low West Moor
Far Pasture
Aygill Pike
West End
How Stean Beck
Hard Gap
Staining Gill Beck
Riggs Moor
Sandy Sikes Gill
Riggs Moor
Wising Gill
Blake Hill
High West Moor
Staining Gill Intake
Flaystones
Whey Crags
Great Blowing Gill Beck
Stott Crags
BD23
High West Moor
Stock Ridge
Black Hill Drive
Waterfall
Stock Ridge Bottom
White Stean Well
Great Scar
Stone Butts Drive
Straight Stean Beck
Mossdale Beck
Peat Moor Butts (Grouse)
Acoras Scar
Red Scars
Backstean Gill
Oliver Scar
Waterfall
West Gill
Sandy Gate
Green Grooves Gill
Friar Hood Gill
Stean Moor
Peat Moor Drive
Meugher
Great Stangate
Moss Drive
Mossdale
8 77 7 76 6 75 5 74 4 73 3 72 2 71 1 70
02 03 04 05 06 07
135
110

109
84

Scale: 1¾ inches to 1 mile

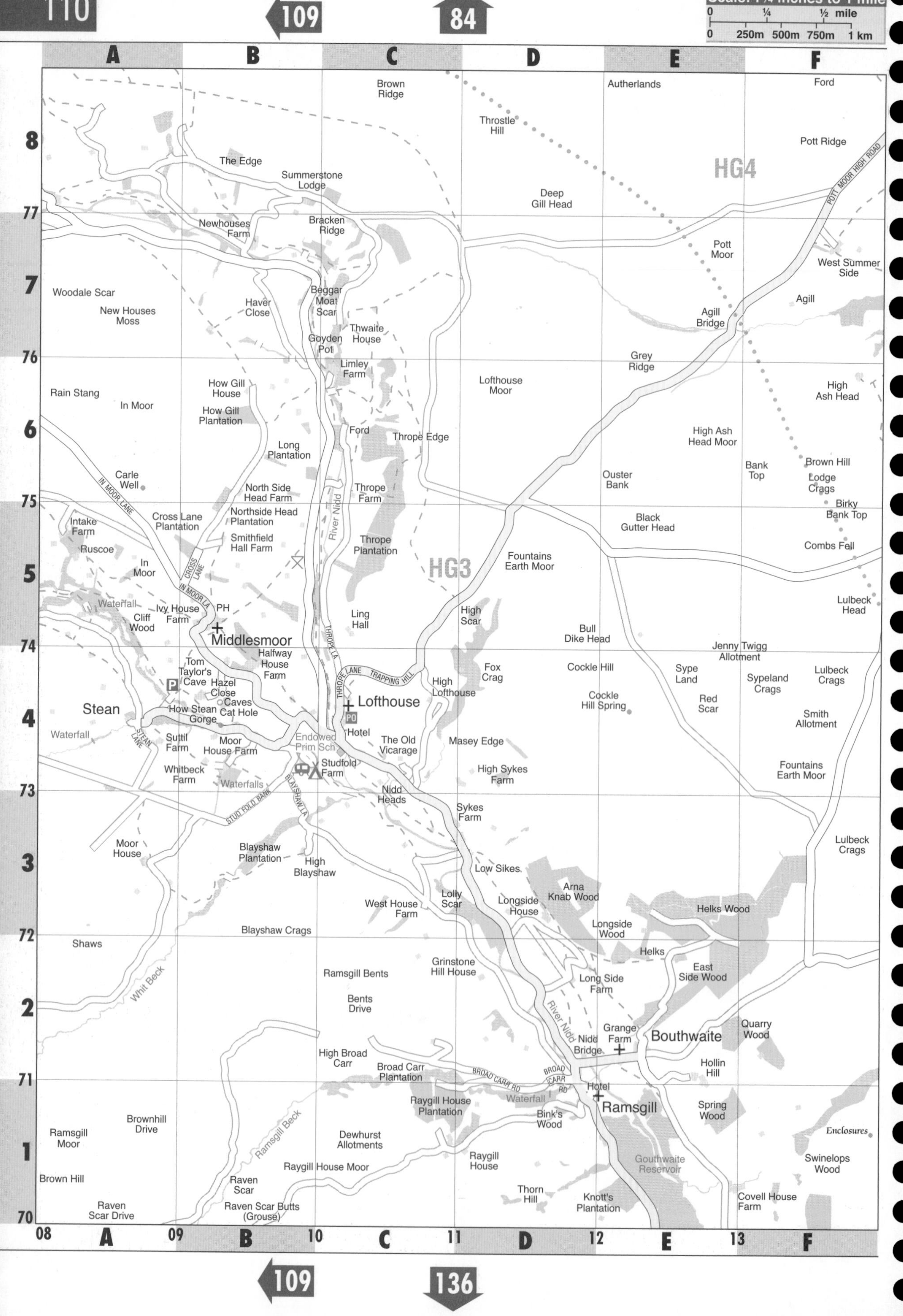

109
136

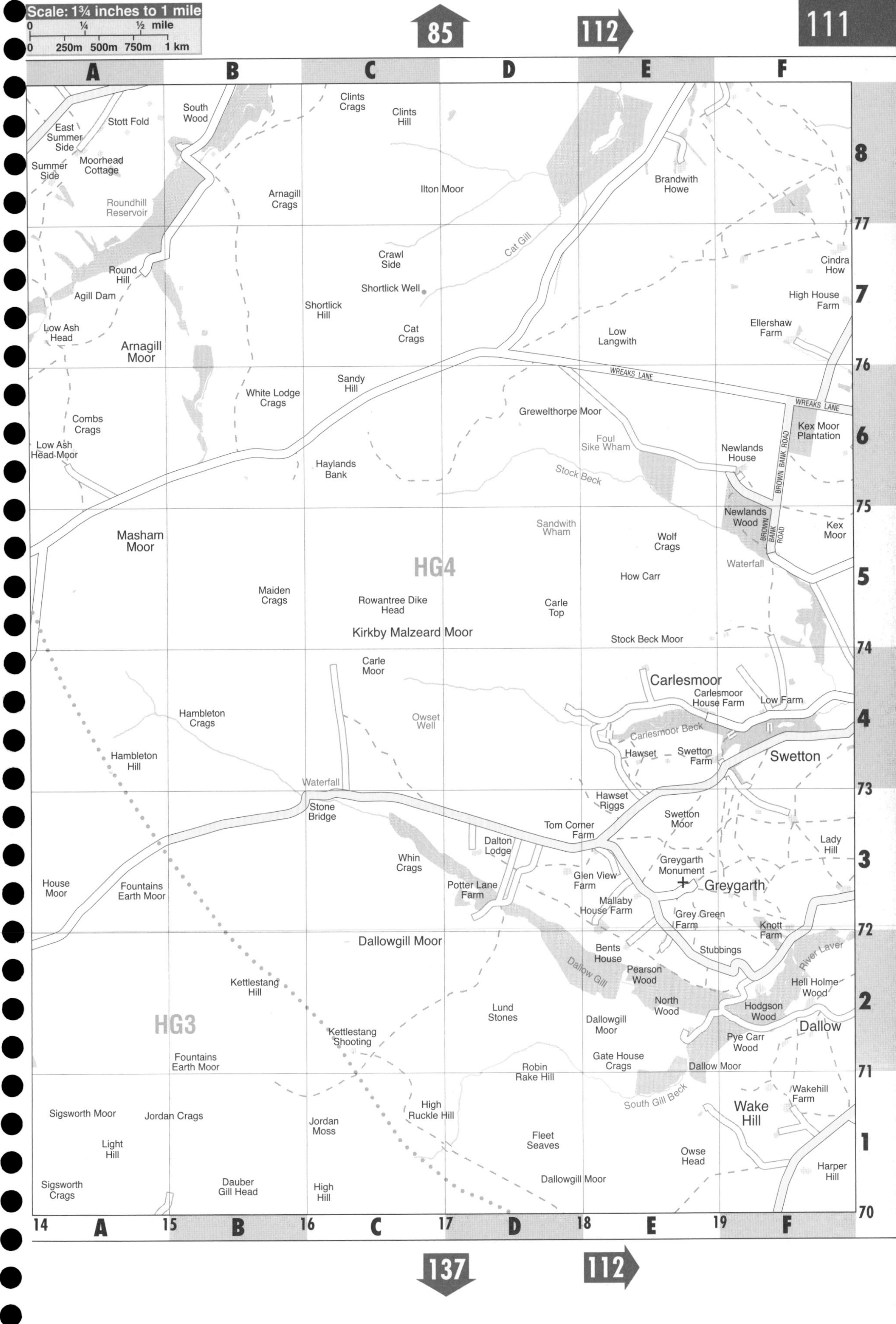
Scale: 1¾ inches to 1 mile
0 ¼ ½ mile
0 250m 500m 750m 1 km
85
112
A B C D E F
Clints Crags
Clints Hill
South Wood
Stott Fold
East Summer Side
Summer Side
Moorhead Cottage
Roundhill Reservoir
Arnagill Crags
Ilton Moor
Brandwith Howe
Cat Gill
Crawl Side
Round Hill
Agill Dam
Shortlick Well
Shortlick Hill
Cindra How
High House Farm
Ellershaw Farm
Low Ash Head
Arnagill Moor
Cat Crags
Low Langwith
Sandy Hill
White Lodge Crags
WREAKS LANE
Grewelthorpe Moor
Kex Moor Plantation
Combs Crags
Low Ash Head Moor
Foul Sike Wham
Newlands House
BROWN BANK ROAD
Haylands Bank
Stock Beck
Newlands Wood
Kex Moor
Sandwith Wham
Wolf Crags
Masham Moor
HG4
Waterfall
Maiden Crags
Rowantree Dike Head
How Carr
Carle Top
Kirkby Malzeard Moor
Stock Beck Moor
Carle Moor
Carlesmoor
Carlesmoor House Farm
Low Farm
Hambleton Crags
Owset Well
Carlesmoor Beck
Hawset
Swetton Farm
Swetton
Hambleton Hill
Waterfall
Hawset Riggs
Stone Bridge
Swetton Moor
Tom Corner Farm
Dalton Lodge
Lady Hill
Whin Crags
Greygarth Monument
House Moor
Fountains Earth Moor
Potter Lane Farm
Glen View Farm
Greygarth
Mallaby House Farm
Grey Green Farm
Knott Farm
Dallowgill Moor
Bents House
Stubbings
River Laver
Dallow Gill
Pearson Wood
Hell Holme Wood
Kettlestang Hill
North Wood
Hodgson Wood
Lund Stones
Dallowgill Moor
HG3
Kettlestang Shooting
Pye Carr Wood
Dallow
Fountains Earth Moor
Robin Rake Hill
Gate House Crags
Dallow Moor
Wakehill Farm
South Gill Beck
High Ruckle Hill
Wake Hill
Sigsworth Moor
Jordan Crags
Jordan Moss
Light Hill
Fleet Seaves
Owse Head
Harper Hill
Dallowgill Moor
Sigsworth Crags
Dauber Gill Head
High Hill
77 76 75 74 73 72 71 70
8 7 6 5 4 3 2 1
14 15 16 17 18 19
137
112

111
86

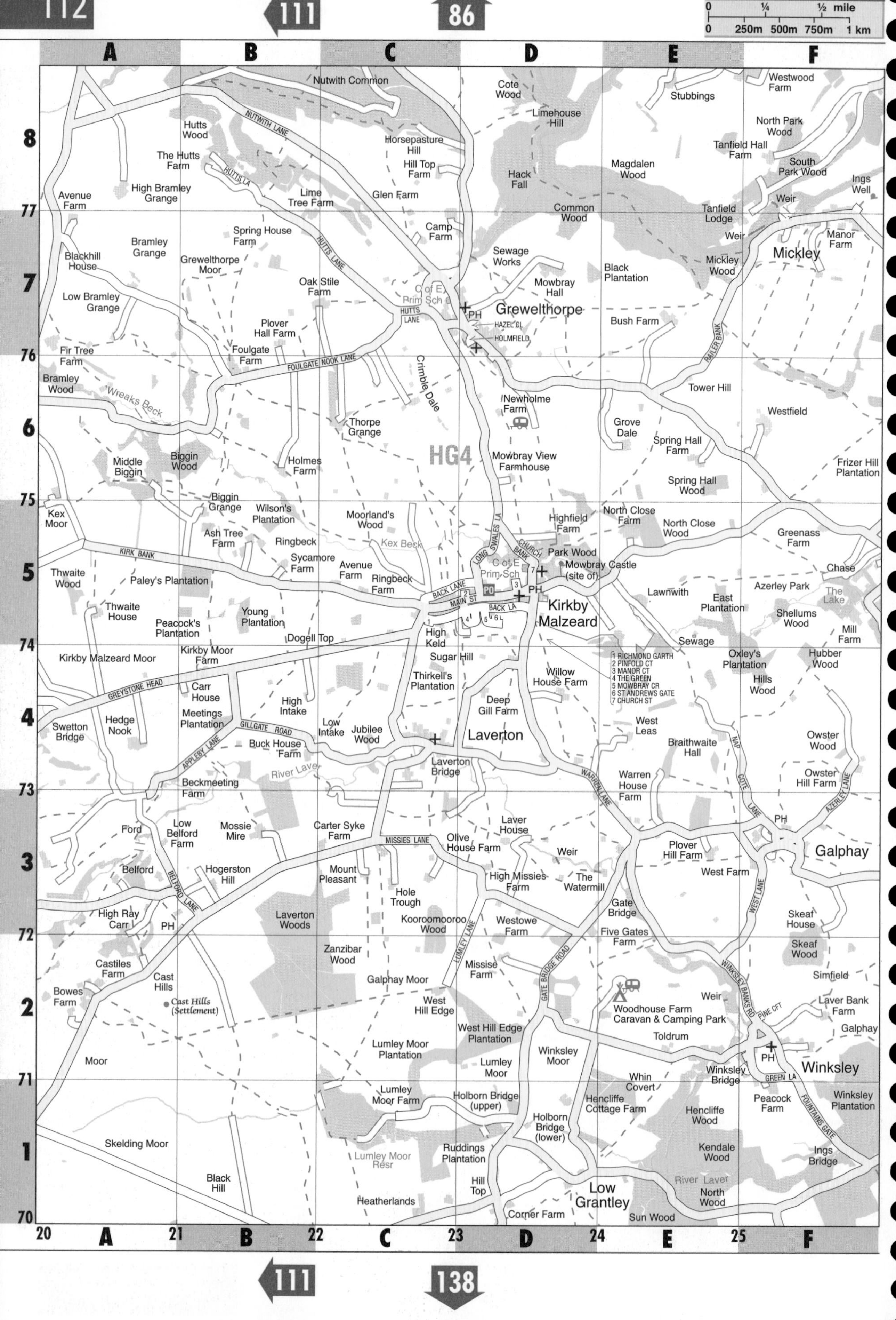

111
138

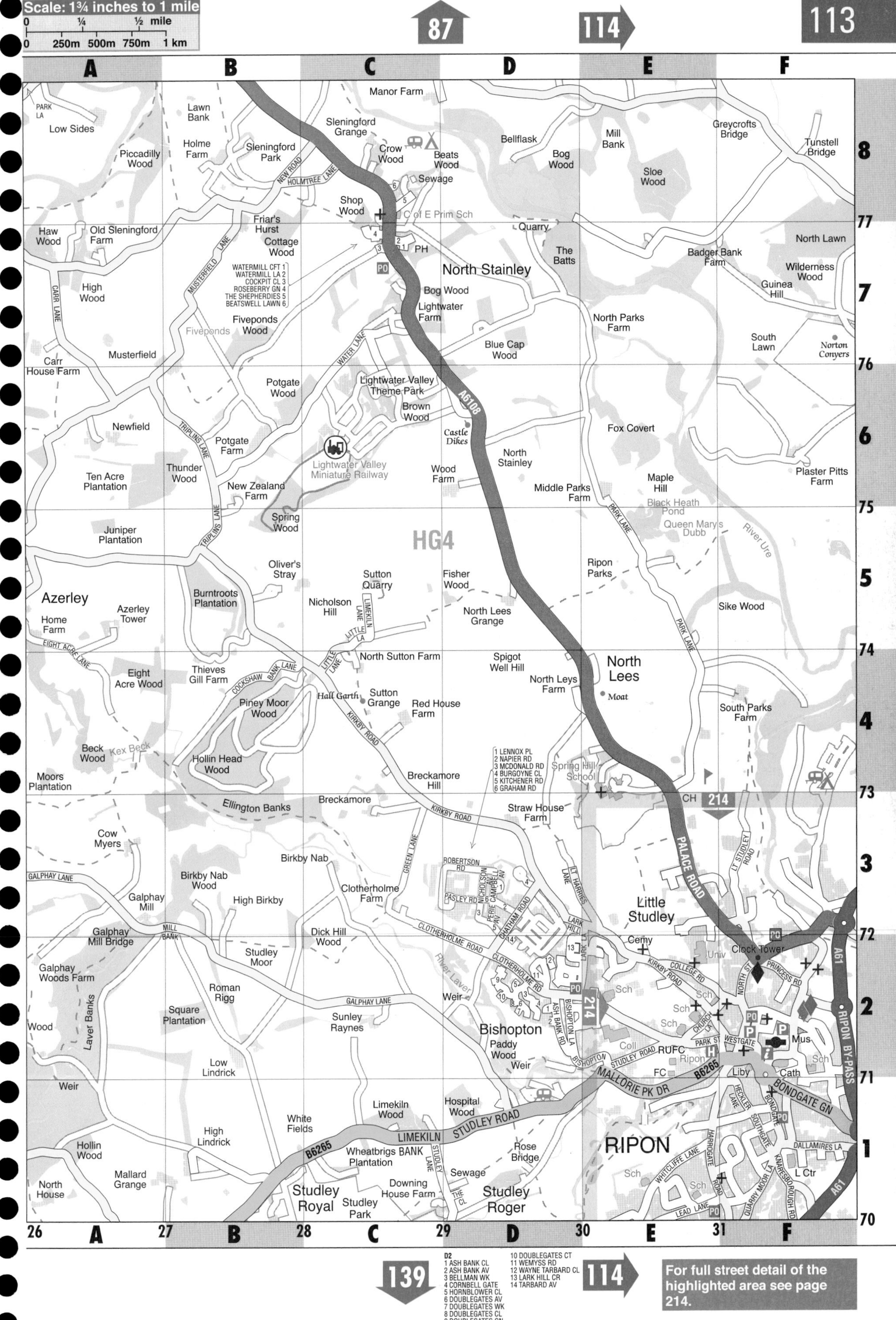

139

D2
1 ASH BANK CL
2 ASH BANK AV
3 BELLMAN WK
4 CORNBELL GATE
5 HORNBLOWER CL
6 DOUBLEGATES AV
7 DOUBLEGATES WK
8 DOUBLEGATES CL
9 DOUBLEGATES GN
10 DOUBLEGATES CT
11 WEMYSS RD
12 WAYNE TARBARD CL
13 LARK HILL CR
14 TARBARD AV

114

For full street detail of the highlighted area see page 214.

Scale: 1¾ inches to 1 mile
0 ¼ ½ mile
0 250m 500m 750m 1 km

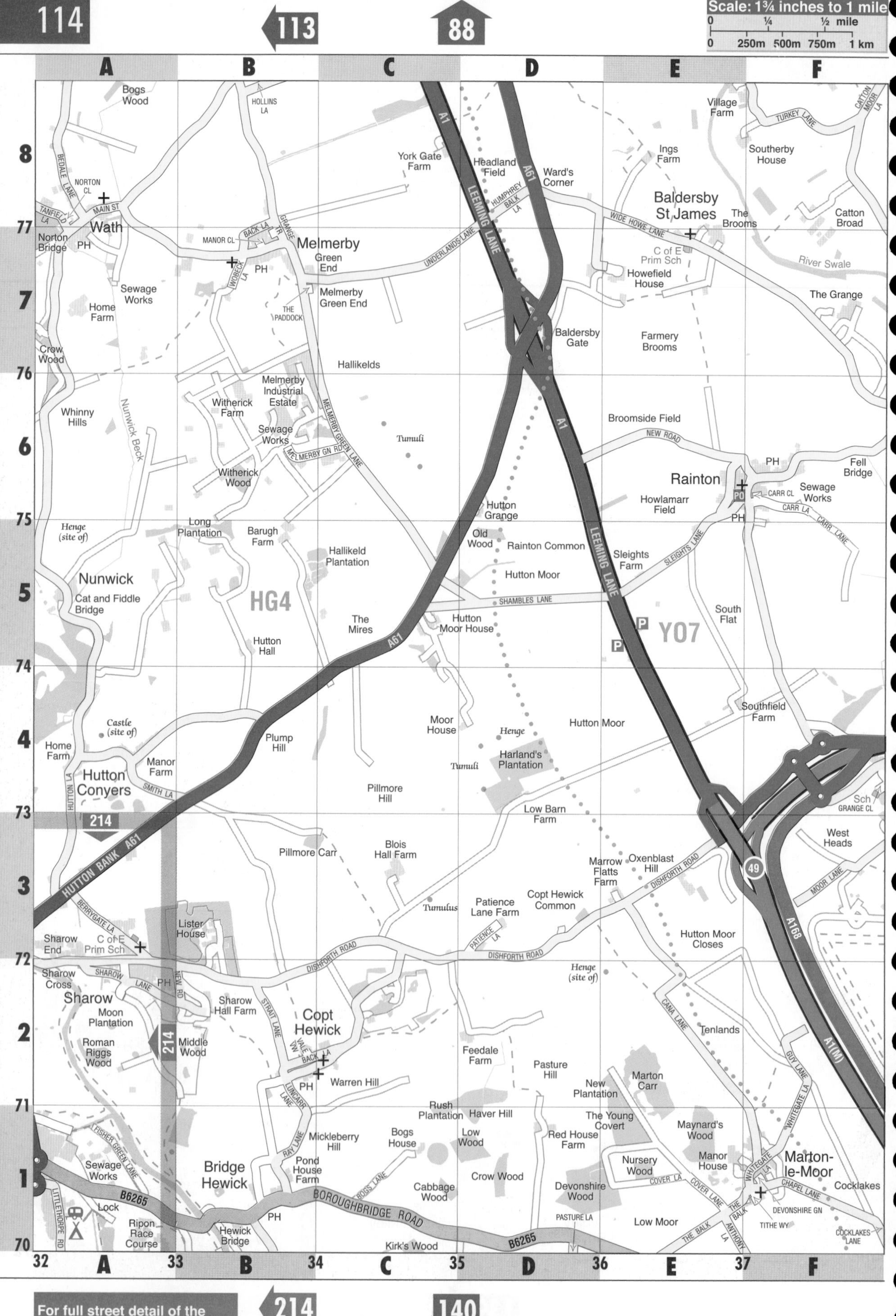

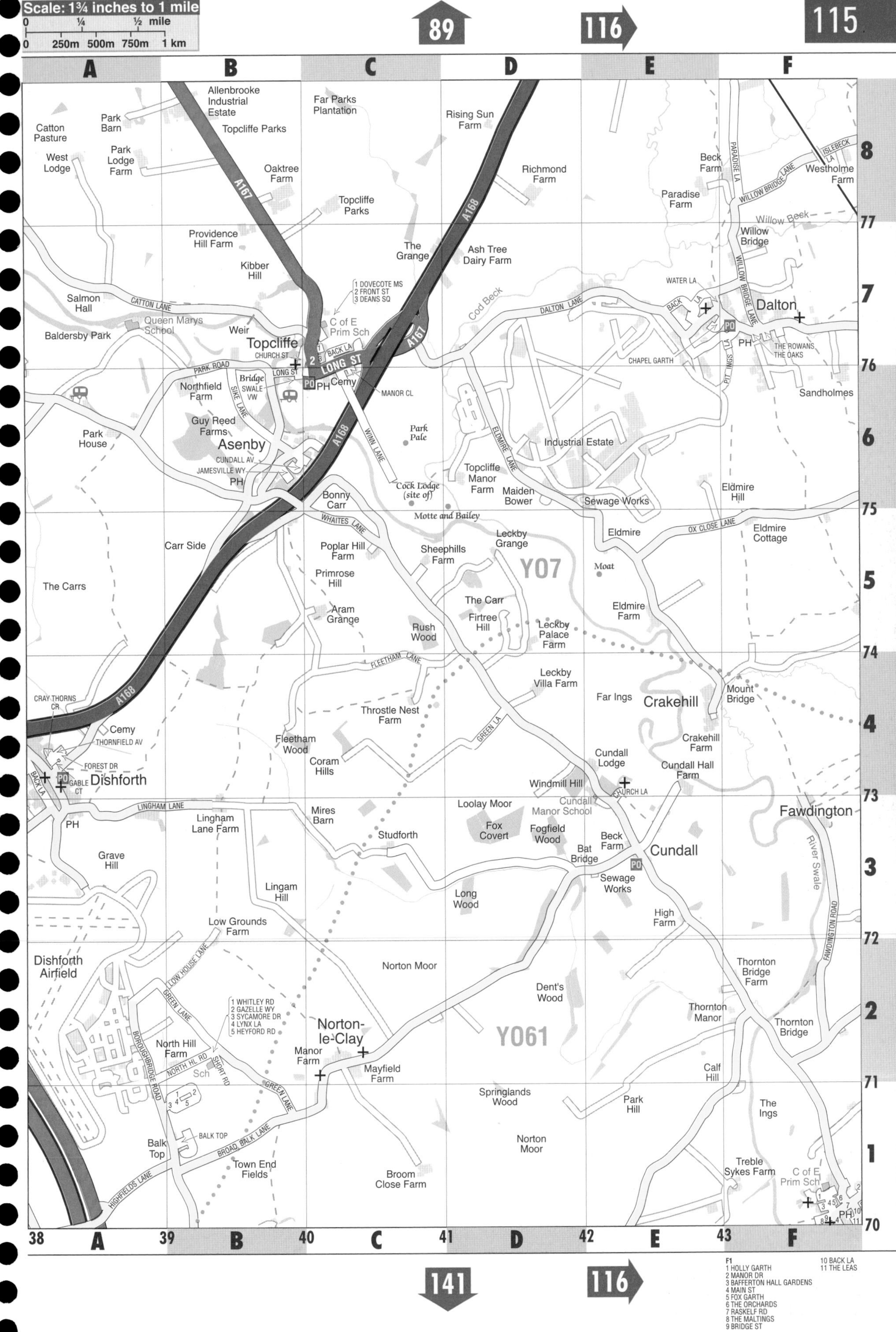

Scale: 1¾ inches to 1 mile
0 ¼ ½ mile
0 250m 500m 750m 1 km
89
116
115
A B C D E F
Allenbrooke Industrial Estate
Far Parks Plantation
Rising Sun Farm
Catton Pasture
Park Barn
Topcliffe Parks
West Lodge
Park Lodge Farm
Oaktree Farm
Richmond Farm
Beck Farm
PARADISE LA
ISLEBECK LA
Westholme Farm
WILLOW BRIDGE LANE
Paradise Farm
A167
Topcliffe Parks
A168
Willow Beck
Willow Bridge
Providence Hill Farm
The Grange
Ash Tree Dairy Farm
Kibber Hill
1 DOVECOTE MS
2 FRONT ST
3 DEANS SQ
WATER LA
WILLOW BRIDGE LANE
Salmon Hall
CATTON LANE
Cod Beck
DALTON LANE
BACK LA
Dalton
Queen Marys School
C of E Prim Sch
Baldersby Park
Weir
Topcliffe
CHURCH ST
BACK LA
LONG ST
A167
PO
PH
CHAPEL GARTH
PIT INS
THE ROWANS
THE OAKS
PARK ROAD
LONG ST
Northfield Farm
Bridge
SWALE VW
SIKE LANE
PO PH
Cemy
MANOR CL
Sandholmes
Park House
Guy Reed Farms
Asenby
Park Pale
WINN LANE
ELDMIRE LANE
Industrial Estate
CUNDALL AV
JAMESVILLE WY
PH
Topcliffe Manor Farm
Maiden Bower
Cock Lodge (site of)
Eldmire Hill
Bonny Carr
Motte and Bailey
Sewage Works
WHAITES LANE
Leckby Grange
Eldmire
OX CLOSE LANE
Eldmire Cottage
Carr Side
Poplar Hill Farm
Sheephills Farm
YO7
Moat
Primrose Hill
The Carrs
The Carr
Eldmire Farm
Aram Grange
Firtree Hill
Leckby Palace Farm
Rush Wood
FLEETHAM LANE
Leckby Villa Farm
Mount Bridge
Far Ings
Crakehill
CRAY THORNS CR
Throstle Nest Farm
Cemy
THORNFIELD AV
Fleetham Wood
GREEN LA
Crakehill Farm
FOREST DR
Coram Hills
Cundall Lodge
Cundall Hall Farm
BACK LA
PO
GABLE CT
Dishforth
Windmill Hill
CHURCH LA
LINGHAM LANE
Lingham Lane Farm
Mires Barn
Loolay Moor
Cundall Manor School
Fawdington
PH
Fox Covert
Fogfield Wood
Beck Farm
Studforth
River Swale
Grave Hill
Bat Bridge
Cundall
PO
Sewage Works
Lingam Hill
Long Wood
High Farm
Low Grounds Farm
FAWDINGTON ROAD
Dishforth Airfield
LOW HOUSE LANE
Norton Moor
Thornton Bridge Farm
GREEN LANE
Dent's Wood
1 WHITLEY RD
2 GAZELLE WY
3 SYCAMORE DR
4 LYNX LA
5 HEYFORD RD
Norton-le-Clay
Thornton Manor
Thornton Bridge
YO61
BOROUGHBRIDGE ROAD
North Hill Farm
Manor Farm
NORTH HL RD
SHORT RD
Sch
Mayfield Farm
Calf Hill
GREEN LANE
Springlands Wood
Park Hill
The Ings
BALK TOP
Balk Top
BROAD BALK LANE
Norton Moor
Treble Sykes Farm
C of E Prim Sch
HIGHFIELDS LANE
Town End Fields
Broom Close Farm
PH
8 77 7 76 6 75 5 74 4 73 3 72 2 71 1 70
38 39 40 41 42 43
141
116
F1
1 HOLLY GARTH
2 MANOR DR
3 BAFFERTON HALL GARDENS
4 MAIN ST
5 FOX GARTH
6 THE ORCHARDS
7 RASKELF RD
8 THE MALTINGS
9 BRIDGE ST
10 BACK LA
11 THE LEAS

115
90

Scale: 1¾ inches to 1 mile
0 ¼ ½ mile
0 250m 500m 750m 1 km

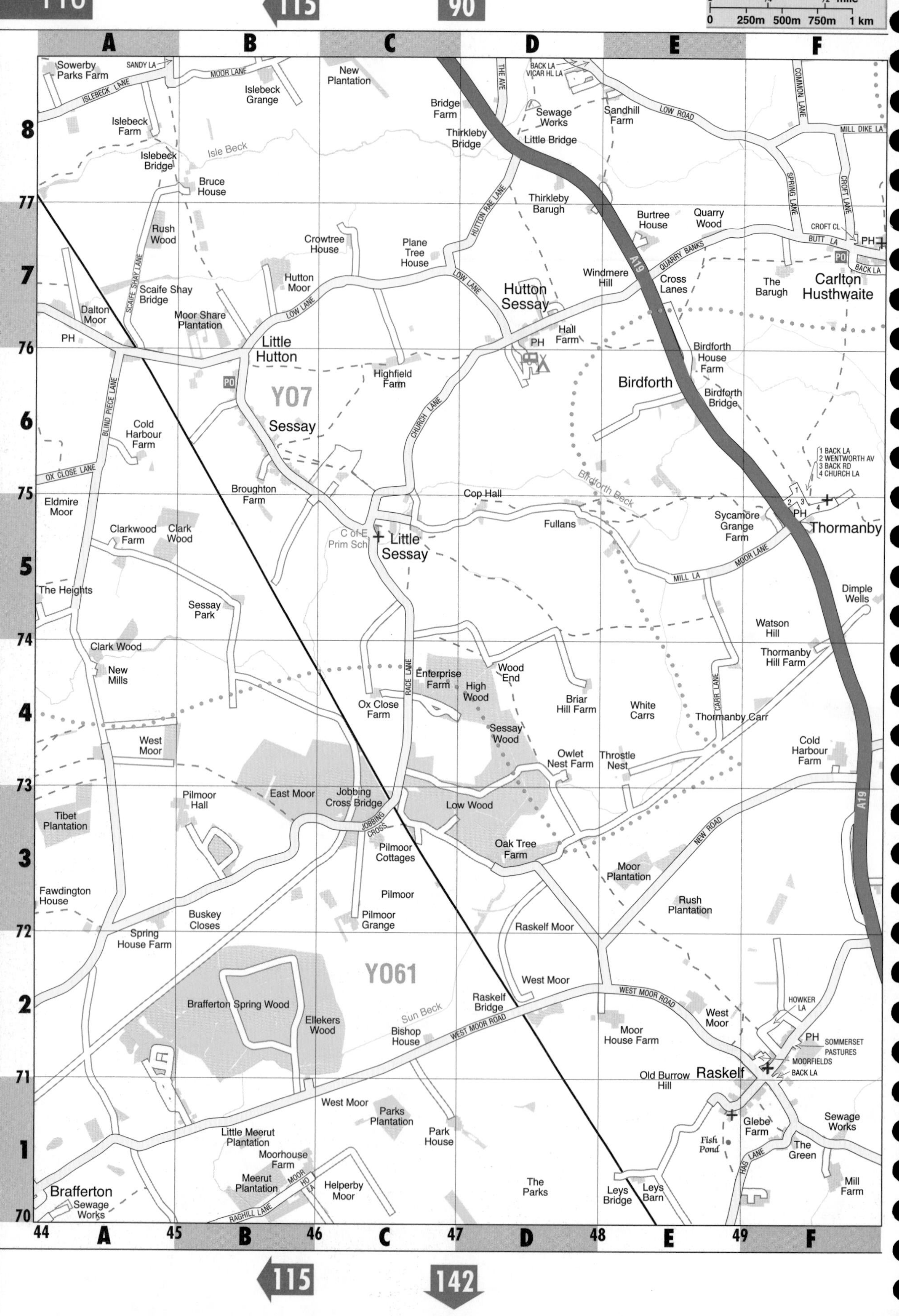

115
142

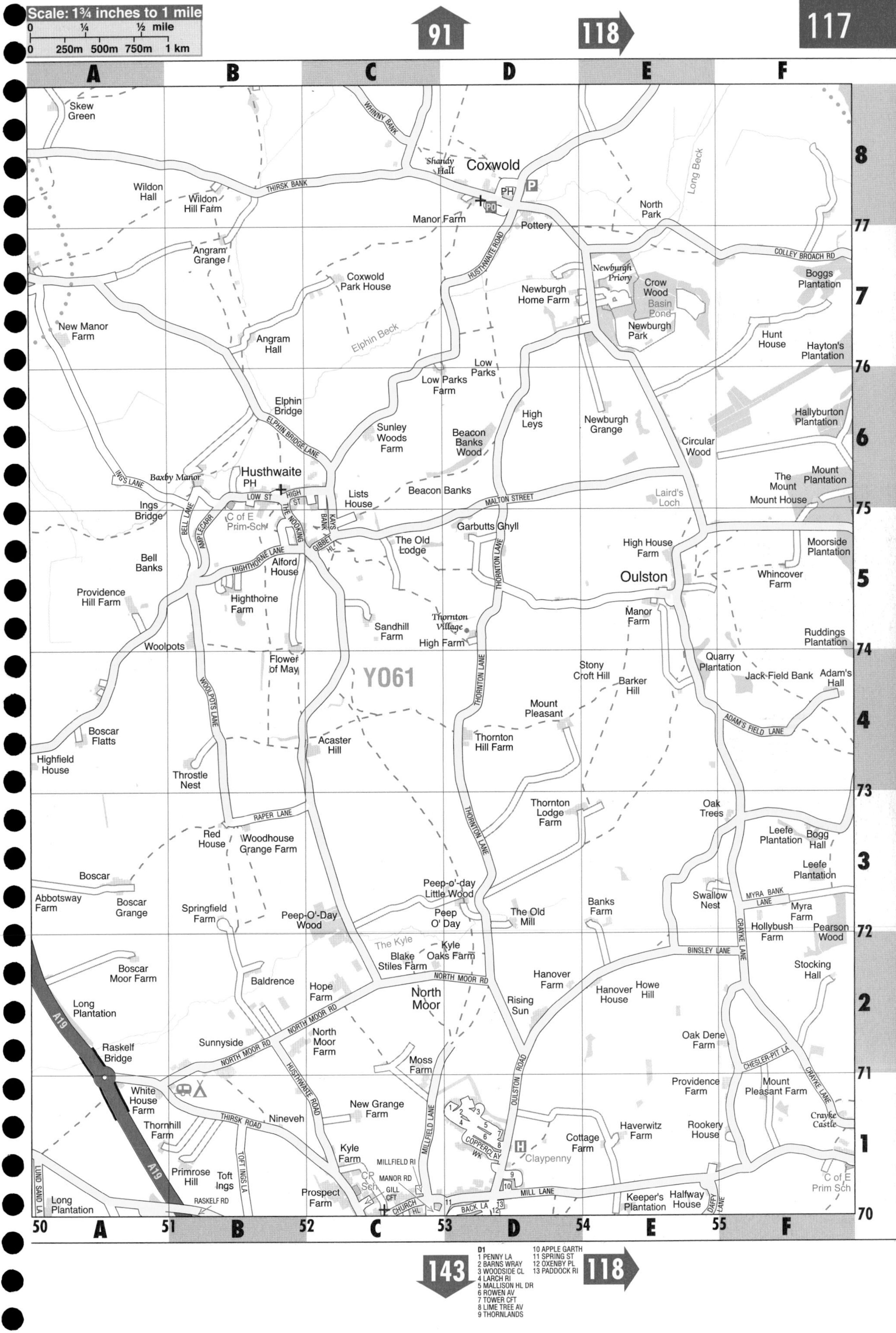
Scale: 1¾ inches to 1 mile
0 ¼ ½ mile
0 250m 500m 750m 1 km
91
118
A B C D E F
Skew Green
Wildon Hall
Wildon Hill Farm
THIRSK BANK
WHINNY BANK
Shandy Hall
Coxwold
PH
P
PO
Manor Farm
Pottery
North Park
Long Beck
COLLEY BROACH RD
Angram Grange
Coxwold Park House
HUSTHWAITE ROAD
Newburgh Priory
Crow Wood
Basin Pond
Newburgh Home Farm
Boggs Plantation
New Manor Farm
Angram Hall
Elphin Beck
Newburgh Park
Hunt House
Hayton's Plantation
Low Parks
Low Parks Farm
Elphin Bridge
ELPHIN BRIDGE LANE
Sunley Woods Farm
Beacon Banks Wood
High Leys
Newburgh Grange
Circular Wood
Hallyburton Plantation
Husthwaite
PH
Baxby Manor
INGS LANE
Ings Bridge
LOW ST
HIGH ST
Lists House
Beacon Banks
MALTON STREET
Laird's Loch
The Mount
Mount Plantation
Mount House
BELL LANE
AMPLECARR
C of E Prim Sch
THE NOOKING
BANK
KAYS
GIBBET HL
The Old Lodge
Garbutts Ghyll
High House Farm
Moorside Plantation
Bell Banks
HIGHTHORNE LANE
Alford House
THORNTON LANE
Oulston
Whincover Farm
Providence Hill Farm
Highthorne Farm
Thornton Village
Manor Farm
Sandhill Farm
High Farm
Ruddings Plantation
Woolpots
Flower of May
YO61
Stony Croft Hill
Quarry Plantation
Barker Hill
Jack Field Bank
Adam's Hall
WOOLPOTS LANE
Mount Pleasant
ADAM'S FIELD LANE
Boscar Flatts
Acaster Hill
Thornton Hill Farm
Highfield House
Throstle Nest
Thornton Lodge Farm
Oak Trees
RAPER LANE
Red House
Woodhouse Grange Farm
Leefe Plantation
Bogg Hall
Leefe Plantation
Boscar
Peep-o'-day Little Wood
Swallow Nest
MYRA BANK LANE
Abbotsway Farm
Boscar Grange
Springfield Farm
Peep-O'-Day Wood
Peep O' Day
The Old Mill
Banks Farm
Myra Farm
Hollybush Farm
Pearson Wood
The Kyle
Kyle Oaks Farm
Blake Stiles Farm
BINSLEY LANE
CRAYKE LANE
Stocking Hall
Boscar Moor Farm
Baldrence
NORTH MOOR RD
Hanover Farm
Hope Farm
North Moor
Hanover House
Howe Hill
Long Plantation
Rising Sun
A19
NORTH MOOR RD
North Moor Farm
Oak Dene Farm
Raskelf Bridge
Sunnyside
NORTH MOOR RD
Moss Farm
CHESLER-PIT LA
HUSTHWAITE ROAD
OULSTON ROAD
Providence Farm
Mount Pleasant Farm
CRAYKE LANE
White House Farm
New Grange Farm
Crayke Castle
Thornhill Farm
THIRSK ROAD
Nineveh
MILLFIELD LANE
COPPERCLAY WK
H
Claypenny
Cottage Farm
Haverwitz Farm
Rookery House
Primrose Hill
Toft Ings
TOFT INGS LA
Kyle Farm
MILLFIELD RI
CP Sch
MANOR RD
GILL CFT
Prospect Farm
CHURCH HL
BACK LA
MILL LANE
Keeper's Plantation
Halfway House
DAFFY LANE
C of E Prim Sch
LUND SAND LA
Long Plantation
RASKELF RD
77 76 75 74 73 72 71 70
8 7 6 5 4 3 2 1
50 A 51 B 52 C 53 D 54 E 55 F
143
118
D1
1 PENNY LA
2 BARNS WRAY
3 WOODSIDE CL
4 LARCH RI
5 MALLISON HL DR
6 ROWEN AV
7 TOWER CFT
8 LIME TREE AV
9 THORNLANDS
10 APPLE GARTH
11 SPRING ST
12 OXENBY PL
13 PADDOCK RI

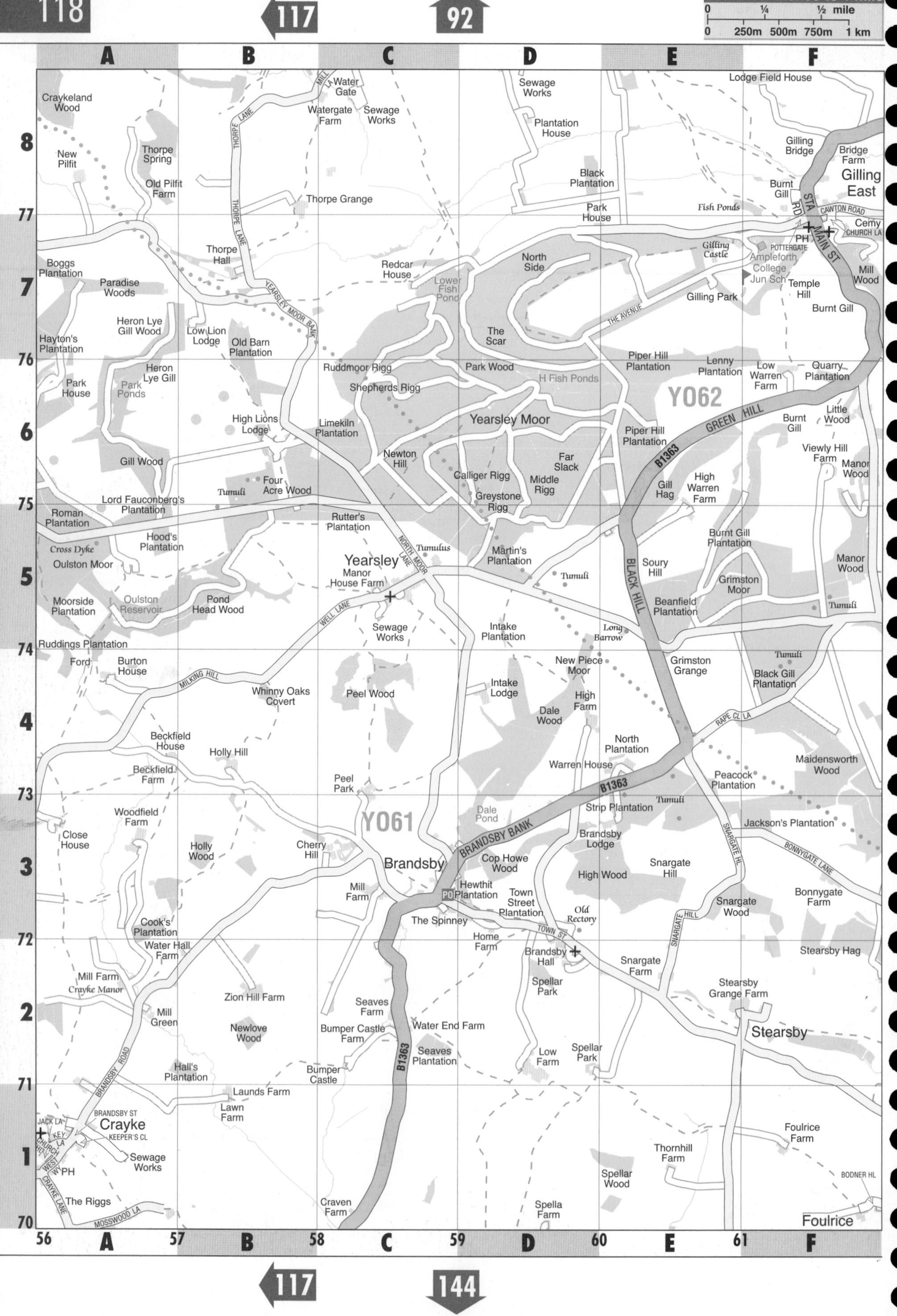
Scale: 1¾ inches to 1 mile
0 ¼ ½ mile
0 250m 500m 750m 1 km
Craykeland Wood
New Pilfit
Thorpe Spring
Old Pilfit Farm
Water Gate
Watergate Farm
Sewage Works
Thorpe Grange
Plantation House
Black Plantation
Park House
Lodge Field House
Gilling Bridge
Bridge Farm
Gilling East
Burnt Gill
Fish Ponds
Cawton Road
Cemy
Church La
PH
Pottergate
Main St
Sta Rd
Gilling Castle
Ampleforth College Jun Sch
Temple Hill
Mill Wood
Burnt Gill
Gilling Park
The Avenue
Boggs Plantation
Paradise Woods
Thorpe Hall
Redcar House
Lower Fish Pond
North Side
The Scar
Heron Lye Gill Wood
Low Lion Lodge
Old Barn Plantation
Hayton's Plantation
Yearsley Moor Bank
Thorpe Lane
Ruddmoor Rigg
Shepherds Rigg
Park Wood
H Fish Ponds
Piper Hill Plantation
Lenny Plantation
Low Warren Farm
Quarry Plantation
YO62
Park House
Park Ponds
Heron Lye Gill
High Lions Lodge
Limekiln Plantation
Yearsley Moor
Piper Hill Plantation
Green Hill
B1363
Burnt Gill
Little Wood
Viewly Hill Farm
Manor Wood
Gill Wood
Newton Hill
Calliger Rigg
Far Slack
Middle Rigg
Greystone Rigg
Gill Hag
High Warren Farm
Tumuli
Four Acre Wood
Lord Fauconberg's Plantation
Roman Plantation
Rutter's Plantation
Cross Dyke
Hood's Plantation
Oulston Moor
Tumulus
North Moor Lane
Martin's Plantation
Burnt Gill Plantation
Yearsley
Manor House Farm
Soury Hill
Grimston Moor
Manor Wood
Moorside Plantation
Oulston Reservoir
Pond Head Wood
Well Lane
Black Hill
Beanfield Plantation
Sewage Works
Intake Plantation
Long Barrow
Ruddings Plantation
Ford
Burton House
Milking Hill
Whinny Oaks Covert
Peel Wood
Intake Lodge
New Piece Moor
High Farm
Grimston Grange
Black Gill Plantation
Dale Wood
Rape Cl La
Beckfield House
Holly Hill
North Plantation
Warren House
Maidensworth Wood
Beckfield Farm
Peel Park
Peacock Plantation
Strip Plantation
Woodfield Farm
Close House
Dale Pond
YO61
Jackson's Plantation
Brandsby Bank
Holly Wood
Cherry Hill
Brandsby
Brandsby Lodge
Snargate Hill
Snargate Hl
Bonnygate Lane
Cop Howe Wood
High Wood
Mill Farm
PO
Hewthit Plantation
Town Street Plantation
Bonnygate Farm
Snargate Wood
Snargate Hill
Old Rectory
The Spinney
Cook's Plantation
Home Farm
Town St
Brandsby Hall
Water Hall Farm
Snargate Farm
Stearsby Hag
Mill Farm
Crayke Manor
Spellar Park
Stearsby Grange Farm
Zion Hill Farm
Mill Green
Seaves Farm
Newlove Wood
Bumper Castle Farm
Water End Farm
Stearsby
Brandsby Road
Seaves Plantation
Spellar Park
Low Farm
Hall's Plantation
Bumper Castle
Launds Farm
Lawn Farm
Brandsby St
Jack La
Crayke
Key La
Keeper's Cl
Church Hill
West Way
Foulrice Farm
Sewage Works
PH
Thornhill Farm
Crayke Lane
Spellar Wood
Bodner Hl
The Riggs
Craven Farm
Mosswood La
Spella Farm
Foulrice
A B C D E F
56 57 58 59 60 61
70 71 1 2 72 3 73 4 74 5 75 6 76 7 77 8

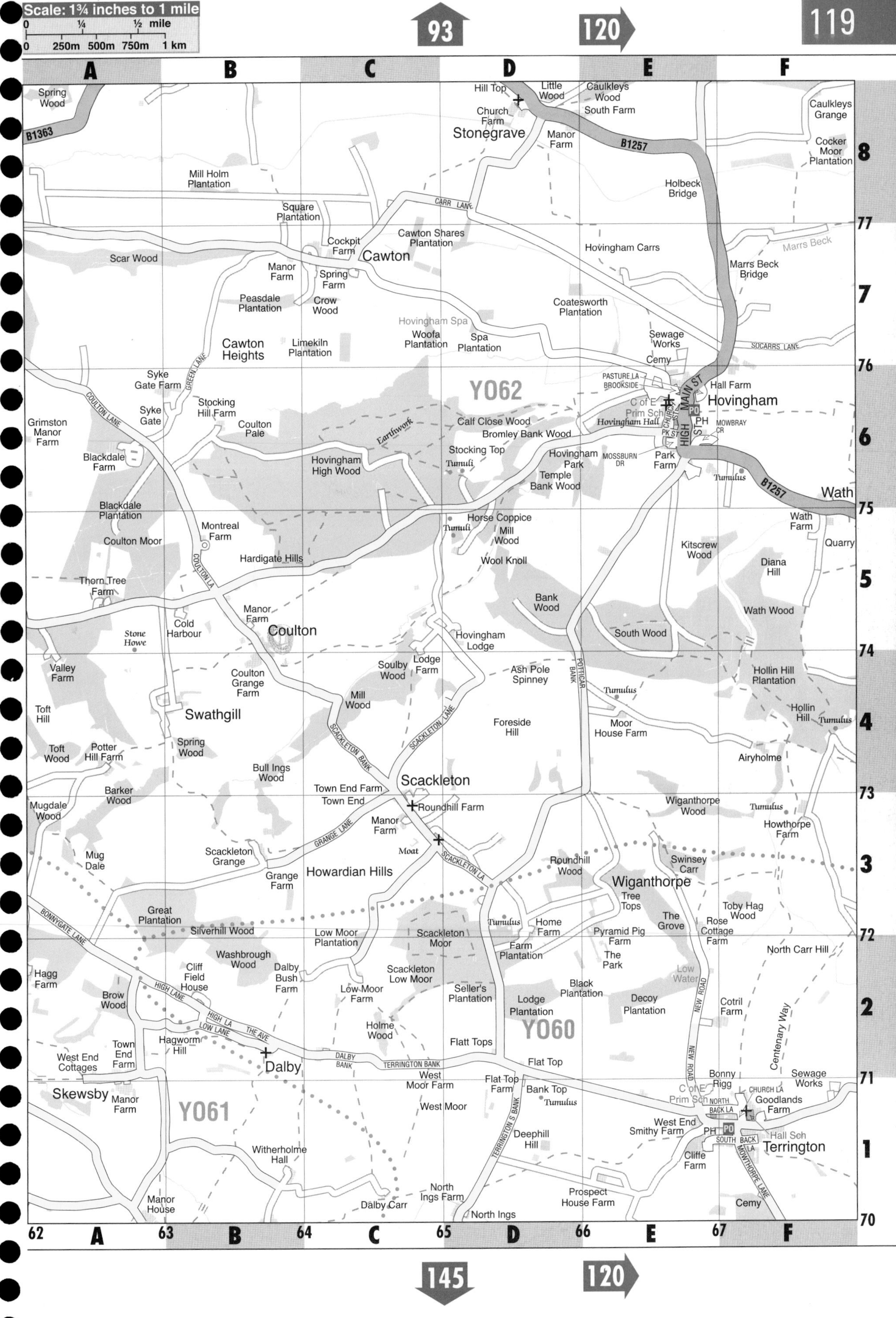
Scale: 1¾ inches to 1 mile
0 ¼ ½ mile
0 250m 500m 750m 1 km
93
120
A B C D E F
Spring Wood
B1363
Hill Top
Little Wood
Caulkleys Wood
South Farm
Caulkleys Grange
Church Farm
Stonegrave
Manor Farm
B1257
Cocker Moor Plantation
Mill Holm Plantation
Holbeck Bridge
Square Plantation
CARR LANE
Cockpit Farm
Cawton Shares Plantation
Cawton
Hovingham Carrs
Marrs Beck
Marrs Beck Bridge
Scar Wood
Manor Farm
Spring Farm
Peasdale Plantation
Crow Wood
Coatesworth Plantation
Hovingham Spa
Woofa Plantation
Spa Plantation
Sewage Works
Cawton Heights
Limekiln Plantation
SOCARRS LANE
Cemy
Syke Gate Farm
GREEN LANE
YO62
PASTURE LA
BROOKSIDE
Hall Farm
Hovingham
C of E Prim Sch
PO
COULTON LANE
Syke Gate
Stocking Hill Farm
Calf Close Wood
Hovingham Hall
HIGH
MAIN ST
ST
PH
MOWBRAY CR
Grimston Manor Farm
Coulton Pale
Earthwork
Bromley Bank Wood
PK ST
Blackdale Farm
Hovingham High Wood
Stocking Top
Tumuli
Hovingham Park
MOSSBURN DR
Park Farm
Temple Bank Wood
Tumulus
Wath
Blackdale Plantation
Horse Coppice
Wath Farm
Montreal Farm
Tumuli
Mill Wood
Quarry
Coulton Moor
Kitscrew Wood
Hardigate Hills
Wool Knoll
Diana Hill
COULTON LA
Thorn Tree Farm
Bank Wood
Wath Wood
Manor Farm
Cold Harbour
Coulton
Stone Howe
Hovingham Lodge
South Wood
Lodge Farm
Valley Farm
Soulby Wood
Ash Pole Spinney
POTTICAR BANK
Hollin Hill Plantation
Coulton Grange Farm
Tumulus
Mill Wood
Toft Hill
Swathgill
Foreside Hill
Hollin Hill
Tumulus
SCACKLETON BANK
SCACKLETON LANE
Moor House Farm
Spring Wood
Toft Wood
Potter Hill Farm
Airyholme
Bull Ings Wood
Scackleton
Barker Wood
Town End Farm
Town End
Wiganthorpe Wood
Mugdale Wood
Roundhill Farm
Tumulus
Manor Farm
GRANGE LANE
Howthorpe Farm
Moat
Mug Dale
Scackleton Grange
Roundhill Wood
Swinsey Carr
SCACKLETON LA
Grange Farm
Howardian Hills
Wiganthorpe
Tree Tops
Toby Hag Wood
Great Plantation
The Grove
BONNYGATE LANE
Silverhill Wood
Tumulus
Home Farm
Rose Cottage Farm
Low Moor Plantation
Scackleton Moor
Pyramid Pig Farm
Farm Plantation
North Carr Hill
Washbrough Wood
The Park
Cliff Field House
Dalby Bush Farm
Scackleton Low Moor
Low Water
Hagg Farm
HIGH LANE
Low Moor Farm
Seller's Plantation
Black Plantation
NEW ROAD
Brow Wood
Lodge Plantation
Decoy Plantation
Cotril Farm
Centenary Way
HIGH LA
LOW LANE
THE AVE
Holme Wood
YO60
Town End Farm
Hagworm Hill
Flatt Tops
West End Cottages
DALBY BANK
TERRINGTON BANK
Flat Top
NEW ROAD
Dalby
Bonny Rigg
Sewage Works
West Moor Farm
Flat Top Farm
Bank Top
C of E Prim Sch
CHURCH LA
Skewsby
Manor Farm
YO61
Tumulus
NORTH BACK LA
Goodlands Farm
West Moor
West End Smithy Farm
TERRINGTON BANK
Deephill Hill
PH
PO
Hall Sch
SOUTH BACK LA
Terrington
Witherholme Hall
Cliffe Farm
MOWTHORPE LANE
Prospect House Farm
North Ings Farm
Manor House
Dalby Carr
Cemy
North Ings
62 A 63 B 64 C 65 D 66 E 67 F
8 77 7 76 6 75 5 74 4 73 3 72 2 71 1 70
145
120

119
94

Scale: 1¾ inches to 1 mile
0 ¼ ½ mile
0 250m 500m 750m 1 km

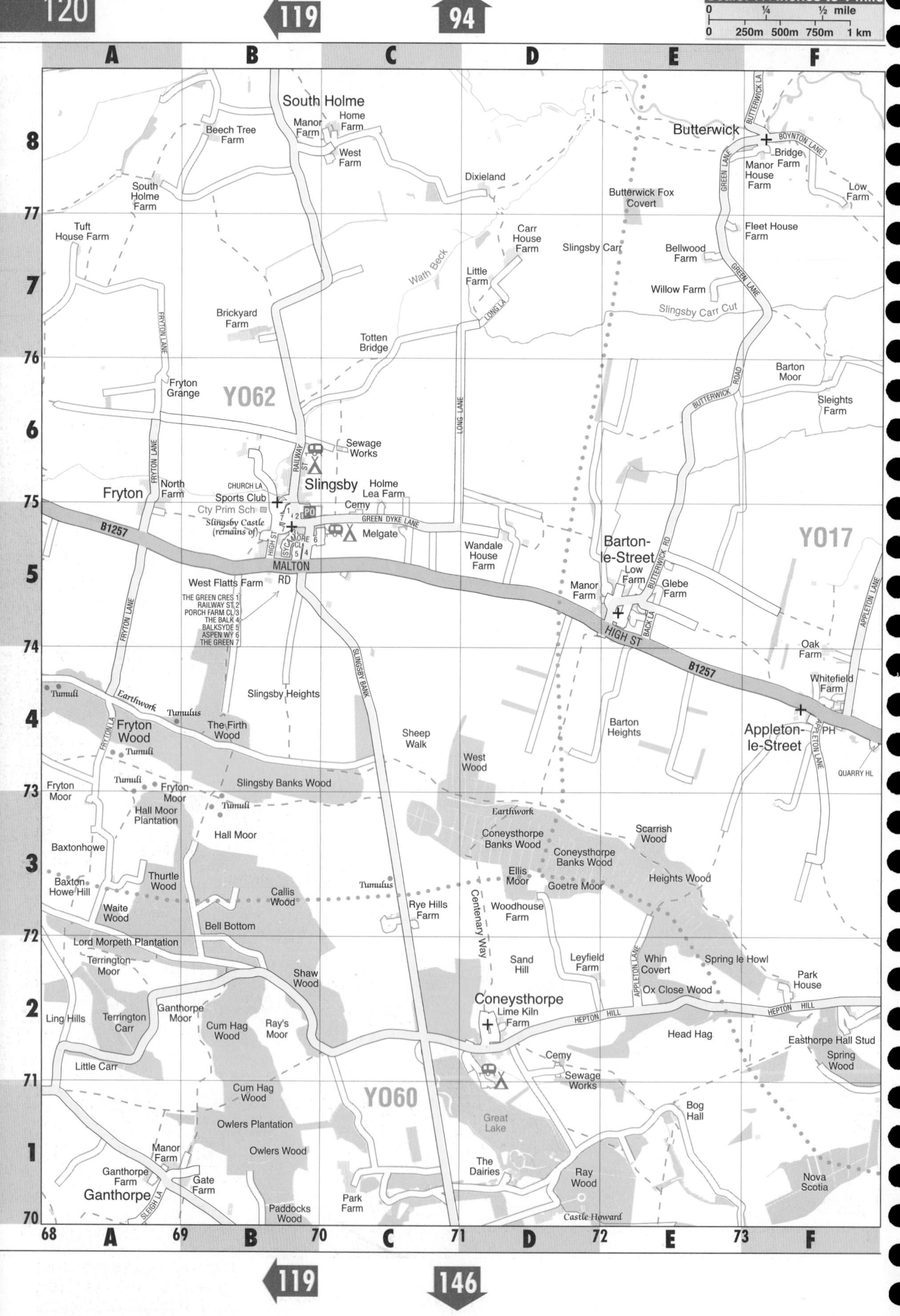

119
146

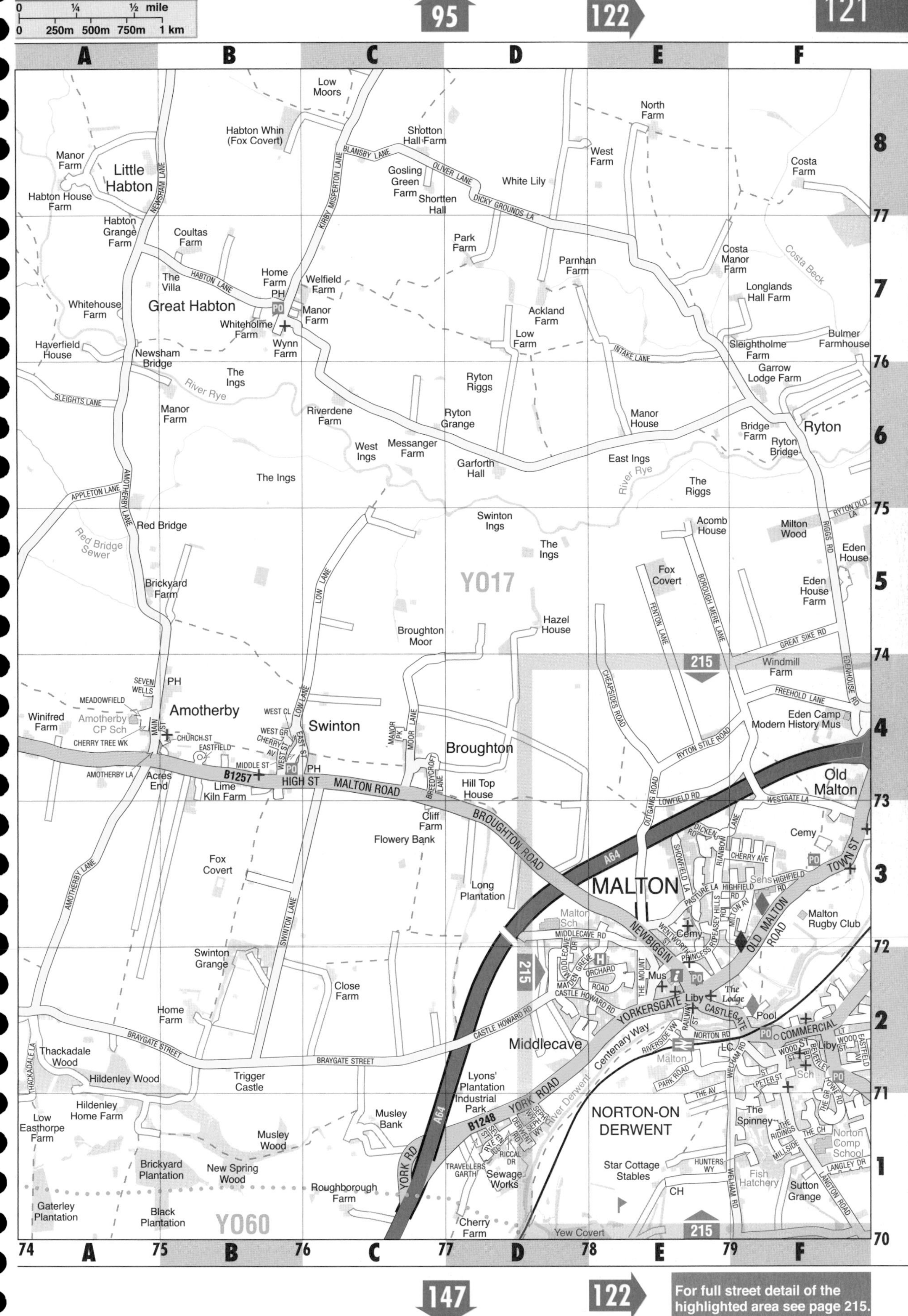

For full street detail of the highlighted area see page 215.

121
96

Scale: 1¾ inches to 1 mile
0 ¼ ½ mile
0 250m 500m 750m 1 km

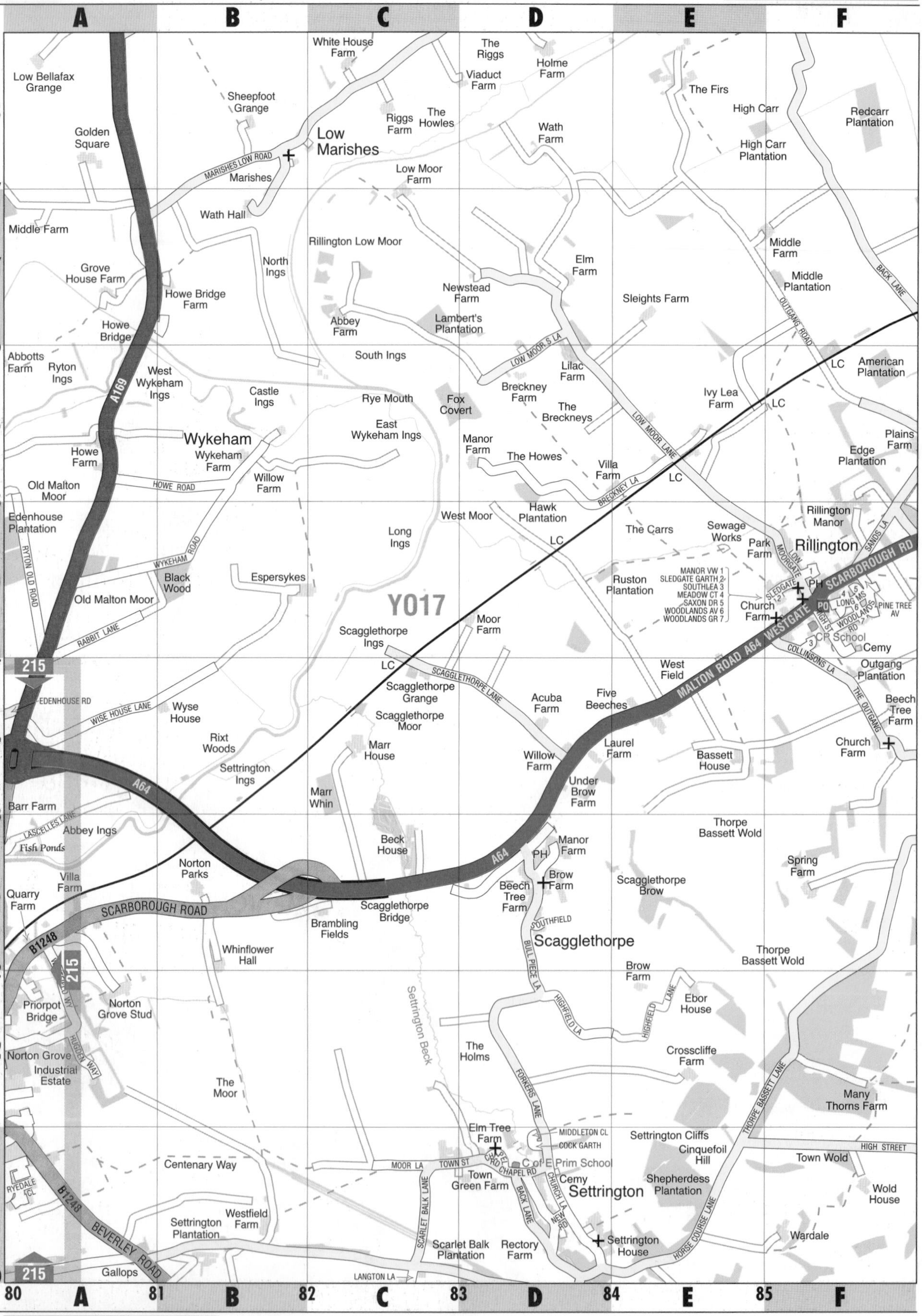

Low Bellafax Grange
Golden Square
Sheepfoot Grange
White House Farm
Riggs Farm
The Howles
The Riggs
Viaduct Farm
Holme Farm
Wath Farm
The Firs
High Carr
High Carr Plantation
Redcarr Plantation
Low Marishes
Marishes
MARISHES LOW ROAD
Low Moor Farm
Wath Hall
Middle Farm
Rillington Low Moor
North Ings
Grove House Farm
Howe Bridge Farm
Howe Bridge
Newstead Farm
Lambert's Plantation
Abbey Farm
Elm Farm
Sleights Farm
Middle Farm
Middle Plantation
BACK LANE
OUTGANG ROAD
South Ings
LOW MOOR S LA
Lilac Farm
Abbotts Farm
Ryton Ings
West Wykeham Ings
Castle Ings
A169
Rye Mouth
Fox Covert
Breckney Farm
The Breckneys
Ivy Lea Farm
LC
American Plantation
Wykeham
Wykeham Farm
East Wykeham Ings
Manor Farm
The Howes
LOW MOOR LANE
Plains Farm
Edge Plantation
Howe Farm
Willow Farm
Villa Farm
BRECKNEY LA
LC
Old Malton Moor
HOWE ROAD
Edenhouse Plantation
West Moor
Hawk Plantation
Rillington Manor
Long Ings
The Carrs
Sewage Works
Park Farm
Rillington
LC
SANDS LA
RYTON OLD ROAD
WYKEHAM ROAD
Black Wood
Espersykes
Ruston Plantation
LOW MOORGATE
SCARBOROUGH RD
MANOR VW 1
SLEDGATE GARTH 2
SOUTHLEA 3
MEADOW CT 4
SAXON DR 5
WOODLANDS AV 6
WOODLANDS GR 7
SLEDGATE
PH
Old Malton Moor
YO17
Church Farm
PO
LONG MS
PINE TREE AV
WOODLANDS RD
HIGH ST
RABBIT LANE
Moor Farm
Scagglethorpe Ings
CP School
Cemy
WESTGATE
MALTON ROAD A64
COLLINSONS LA
Outgang Plantation
LC
SCAGGLETHORPE LANE
West Field
EDENHOUSE RD
Scagglethorpe Grange
Acuba Farm
Five Beeches
THE OUTGANG
Beech Tree Farm
WISE HOUSE LANE
Wyse House
Scagglethorpe Moor
Rixt Woods
Marr House
Laurel Farm
Willow Farm
Bassett House
Church Farm
Settrington Ings
A64
Under Brow Farm
Barr Farm
Marr Whin
LASCELLES LANE
Abbey Ings
Fish Ponds
Beck House
Manor Farm
Thorpe Bassett Wold
PH
A64
Spring Farm
Norton Parks
Villa Farm
Brow Farm
Quarry Farm
Beech Tree Farm
Scagglethorpe Brow
SCARBOROUGH ROAD
Scagglethorpe Bridge
Brambling Fields
SOUTHFIELD
Scagglethorpe
B1248
Whinflower Hall
Thorpe Bassett Wold
215
Brow Farm
BULL PIECE LA
HIGHFIELD LA
HIGHFIELD LANE
Ebor House
Priorpot Bridge
Norton Grove Stud
Settrington Beck
The Holms
Crosscliffe Farm
Norton Grove Industrial Estate
HUGDEN WAY
The Moor
FORKERS LANE
THORPE BASSETT LANE
Many Thorns Farm
Elm Tree Farm
MIDDLETON CL
COCK GARTH
Settrington Cliffs
Cinquefoil Hill
HIGH STREET
Town Wold
Centenary Way
MOOR LA
TOWN ST
CHAPEL RD
C of E Prim School
RYEDALE CL
Town Green Farm
Cemy
CHURCH LA
Settrington
Shepherdess Plantation
Wold House
B1248
SCARLET BALK LANE
BACK LANE
NEW RD
Settrington Plantation
Westfield Farm
BEVERLEY ROAD
Scarlet Balk Plantation
Rectory Farm
Settrington House
HORSE COURSE LANE
Wardale
Gallops
LANGTON LA

Grid columns: A B C D E F; grid rows: 8 7 6 5 4 3 2 1; grid references 77 76 75 74 73 72 71 70; 80 81 82 83 84 85

215
215
215
For full street detail of the highlighted area see page 215.
215
148

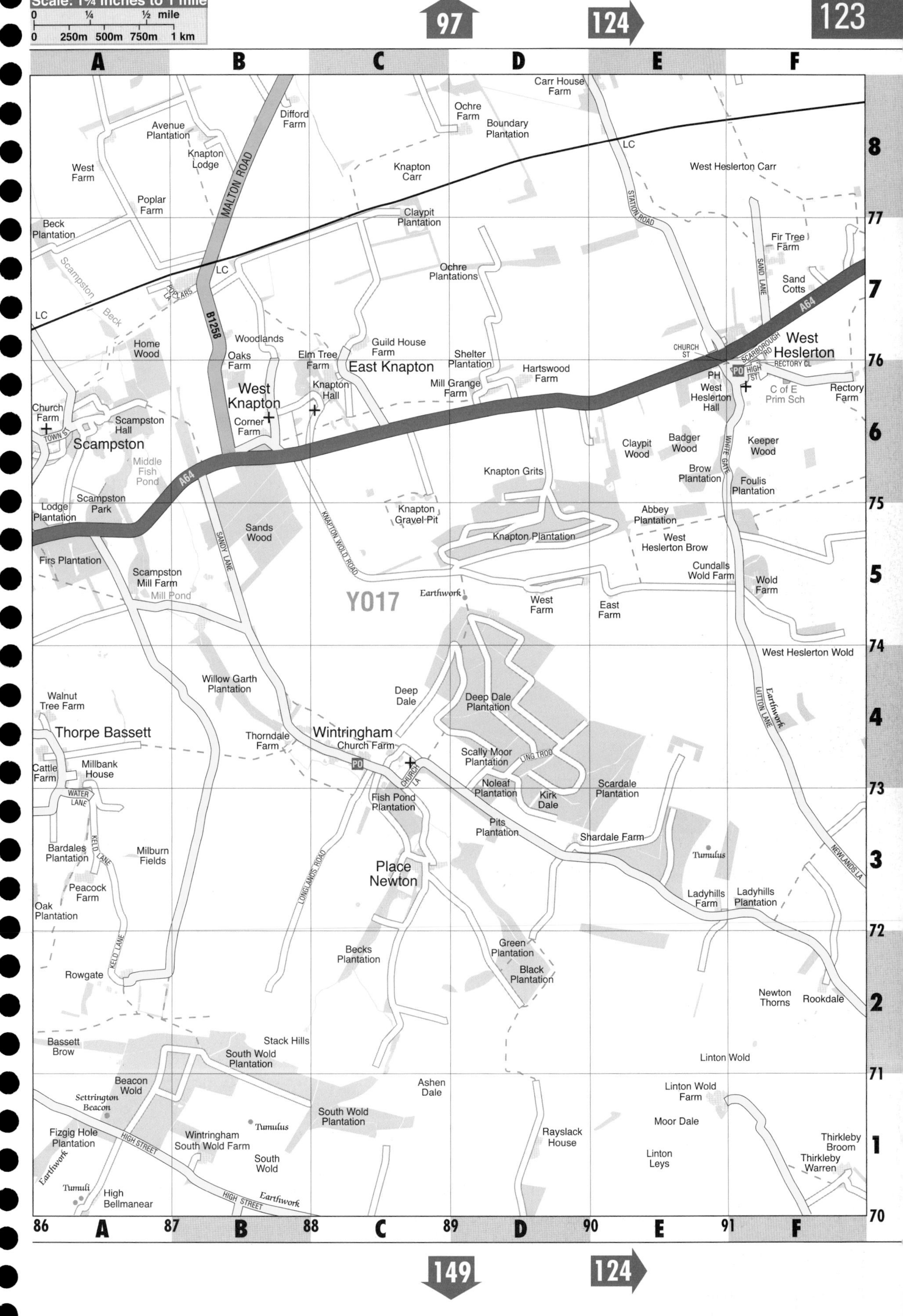
Scale: 1¾ inches to 1 mile
0 ¼ ½ mile
0 250m 500m 750m 1 km
97
124
A B C D E F
Carr House Farm
Ochre Farm
Boundary Plantation
Difford Farm
Avenue Plantation
Knapton Lodge
MALTON ROAD
West Farm
Poplar Farm
Knapton Carr
LC
West Heslerton Carr
STATION ROAD
Beck Plantation
Claypit Plantation
Fir Tree Farm
Scampston Beck
LC
POPLARS LA
Ochre Plantations
SAND LANE
Sand Cotts
LC
B1258
A64
Woodlands
Home Wood
Guild House Farm
Oaks Farm
Elm Tree Farm
East Knapton
Shelter Plantation
CHURCH ST
SCARBOROUGH RD
West Heslerton
Hartswood Farm
PO
HIGH ST
RECTORY CL
West Knapton
Knapton Hall
Mill Grange Farm
PH
West Heslerton Hall
C of E Prim Sch
Rectory Farm
Church Farm
Scampston Hall
Corner Farm
TOWN ST
Scampston
Claypit Wood
Badger Wood
Keeper Wood
Middle Fish Pond
WHITE GATE
Knapton Grits
Brow Plantation
Foulis Plantation
Scampston Park
Lodge Plantation
Knapton Gravel Pit
Abbey Plantation
Sands Wood
KNAPTON WOLD ROAD
Knapton Plantation
West Heslerton Brow
SANDY LANE
Firs Plantation
Cundalls Wold Farm
Wold Farm
Scampston Mill Farm
Mill Pond
YO17
Earthwork
West Farm
East Farm
West Heslerton Wold
Willow Garth Plantation
Deep Dale
Deep Dale Plantation
Walnut Tree Farm
LUTTON LANE
Earthwork
Thorpe Bassett
Thorndale Farm
Wintringham
Church Farm
Scally Moor Plantation
LING TROD
Cattle Farm
Millbank House
PO
CHURCH LA
WATER LANE
Noleaf Plantation
Scardale Plantation
Fish Pond Plantation
Kirk Dale
Pits Plantation
Shardale Farm
KELD LANE
Bardales Plantation
Milburn Fields
Tumulus
NEWLANDS LA
LONGLANDS ROAD
Place Newton
Peacock Farm
Ladyhills Farm
Ladyhills Plantation
Oak Plantation
KELD LANE
Green Plantation
Becks Plantation
Black Plantation
Rowgate
Newton Thorns
Rookdale
Stack Hills
Bassett Brow
South Wold Plantation
Linton Wold
Beacon Wold
Ashen Dale
Linton Wold Farm
Settrington Beacon
South Wold Plantation
Moor Dale
Tumulus
Wintringham South Wold Farm
Rayslack House
Fizgig Hole Plantation
HIGH STREET
South Wold
Linton Leys
Thirkleby Broom
Thirkleby Warren
Earthwork
Tumuli
High Bellmanear
HIGH STREET
Earthwork
8
77
7
76
6
75
5
74
4
73
3
72
2
71
1
70
86 A 87 B 88 C 89 D 90 E 91 F
149
124

123
98

Scale: 1¾ inches to 1 mile

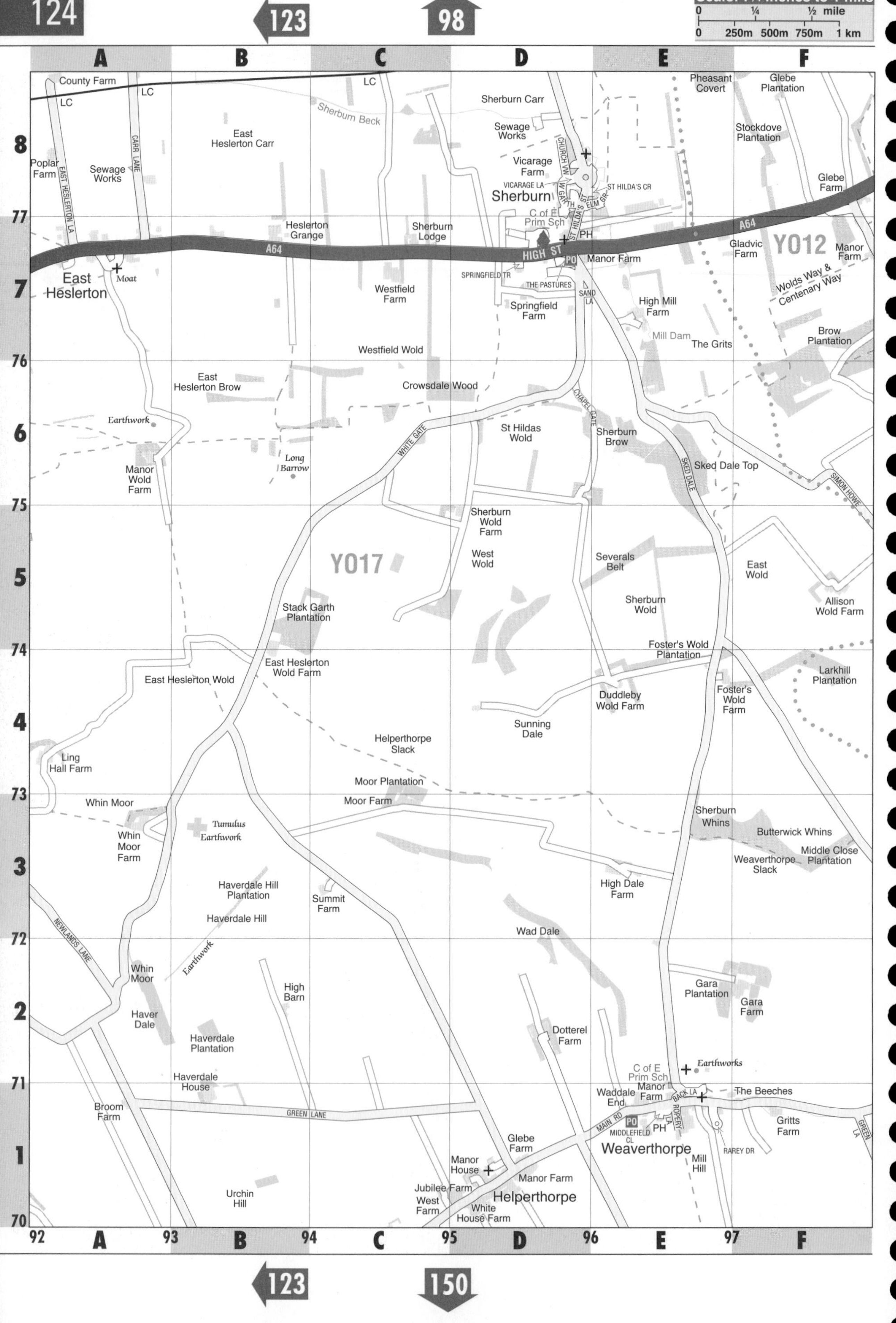

123
150

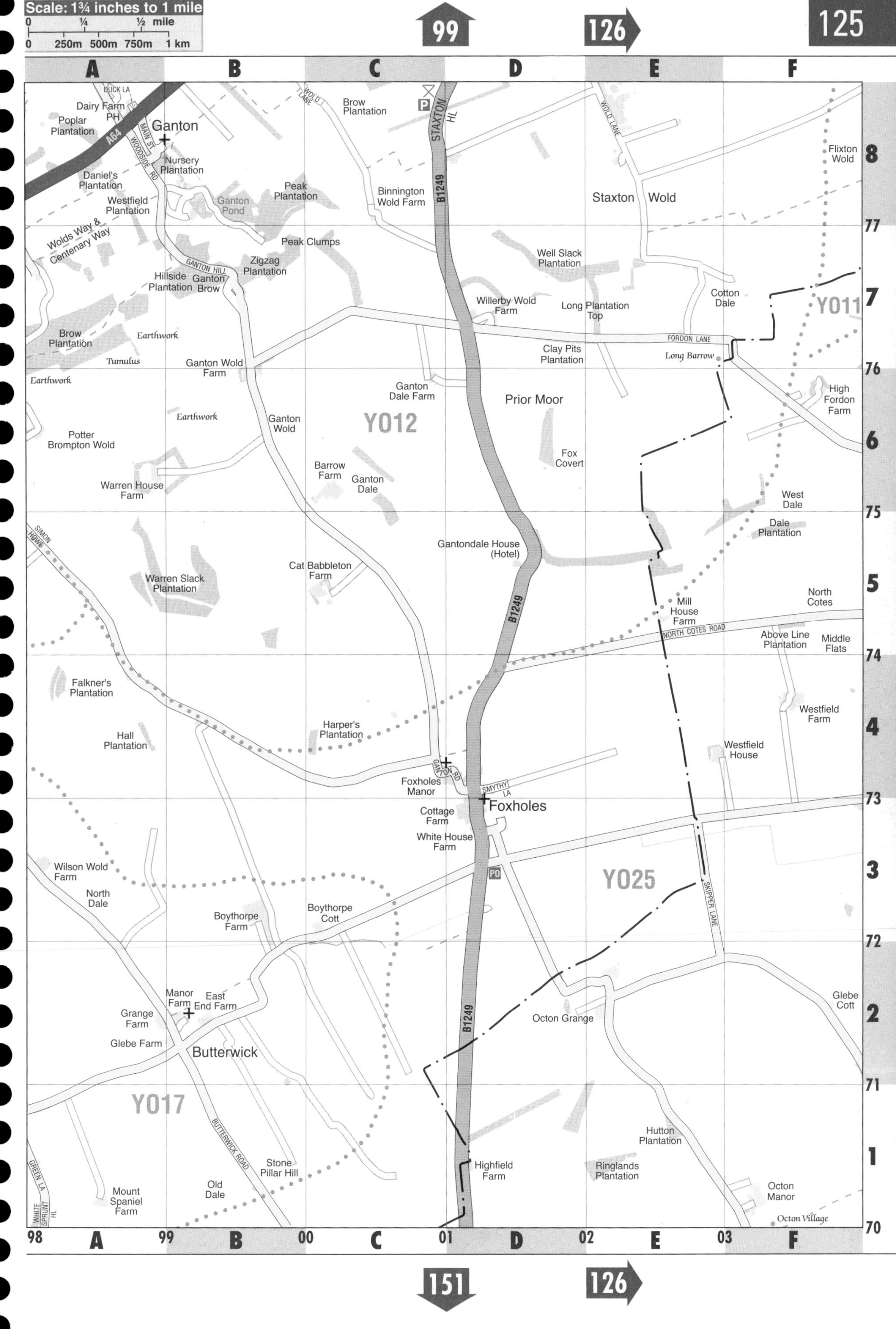
Scale: 1¾ inches to 1 mile
0
¼
½ mile
0
250m
500m
750m
1 km
99
126
A
B
C
D
E
F
Ganton
Dairy Farm
PH
Poplar Plantation
Nursery Plantation
Daniel's Plantation
Westfield Plantation
Ganton Pond
Peak Plantation
Brow Plantation
Binnington Wold Farm
STAXTON HL
B1249
Staxton Wold
WOLD LANE
Flixton Wold
Wolds Way & Centenary Way
Peak Clumps
Zigzag Plantation
GANTON HILL
Hillside Plantation
Ganton Brow
Well Slack Plantation
Willerby Wold Farm
Long Plantation Top
Cotton Dale
YO11
Brow Plantation
Earthwork
Tumulus
Ganton Wold Farm
FORDON LANE
Clay Pits Plantation
Long Barrow
Earthwork
Ganton Dale Farm
Prior Moor
High Fordon Farm
Ganton Wold
YO12
Potter Brompton Wold
Earthwork
Barrow Farm
Ganton Dale
Fox Covert
Warren House Farm
West Dale
Dale Plantation
SIMON HOWE
Gantondale House (Hotel)
Cat Babbleton Farm
Warren Slack Plantation
Mill House Farm
North Cotes
NORTH COTES ROAD
Above Line Plantation
Middle Flats
Falkner's Plantation
Westfield Farm
Harper's Plantation
Hall Plantation
Westfield House
GANTON RD
Foxholes Manor
SMYTHY LA
Foxholes
Cottage Farm
White House Farm
Wilson Wold Farm
PO
YO25
North Dale
SKIPPER LANE
Boythorpe Farm
Boythorpe Cott
Manor Farm
East End Farm
Grange Farm
Octon Grange
Glebe Cott
Glebe Farm
Butterwick
YO17
BUTTERWICK ROAD
Hutton Plantation
Stone Pillar Hill
Highfield Farm
Ringlands Plantation
GREEN LA
Mount Spaniel Farm
Old Dale
Octon Manor
WHITE SPRUNT HL
Octon Village
8
77
7
76
6
75
5
74
4
73
3
72
2
71
1
70
98
99
00
01
02
03
151
126

125
100

F8
1 OWSTON RD
2 MITFORD RD
3 MITFORD CL
4 OUTGAITS CL
5 WENTWORTH WY
6 SIMPSON AV
7 HIGH CFT
8 CASTLE HL
9 BOWLING GN LA
10 CHURCH HL
11 HUNGATE CT
12 VICARAGE CL
13 FONTAYNE RD
14 BARDNEY RD
15 ROWEDALE CL
16 AMBREY CL
17 PARK RISE
18 OLIVER'S CL
19 ROSEMOOR CL
20 HARBOROUGH CL

Scale: 1¾ inches to 1 mile
0 ¼ ½ mile
0 250m 500m 750m 1 km

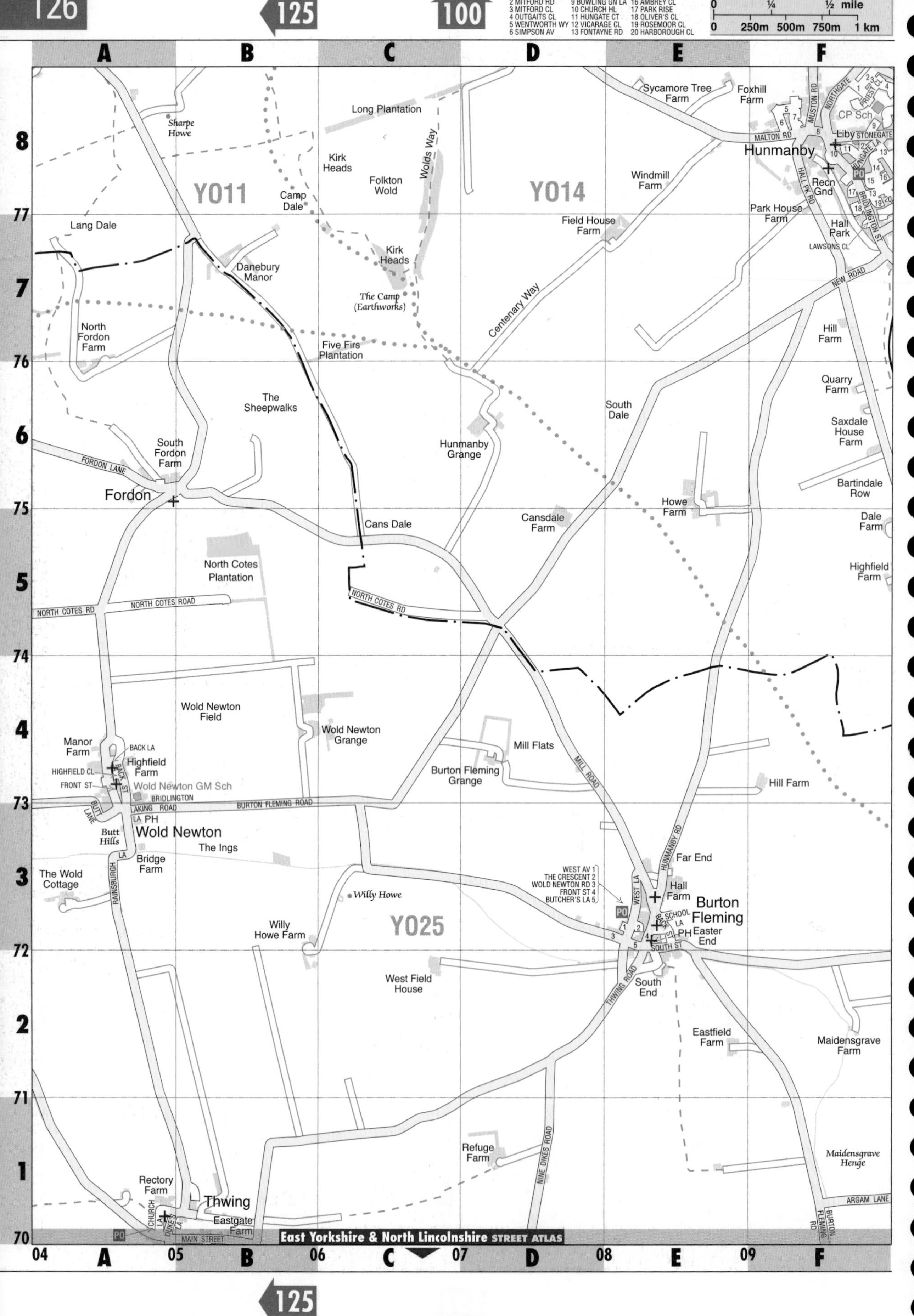

125

Scale: 1¾ inches to 1 mile

A8
1 WRANGHAM DR
2 LENNOX CL
3 BURLYN RD
4 CHERRY RD
5 HAWKE GARTH
6 MANOR GD
7 CECIL RD
8 HOWES RD
9 WATSON CL
10 HAMERTON RD
11 HAMERTON CL
12 GRIMSTON RD
13 STRICKLAND RD
14 PERCY RD
15 HAVERCROFT RD
16 COWLINGS CL

101

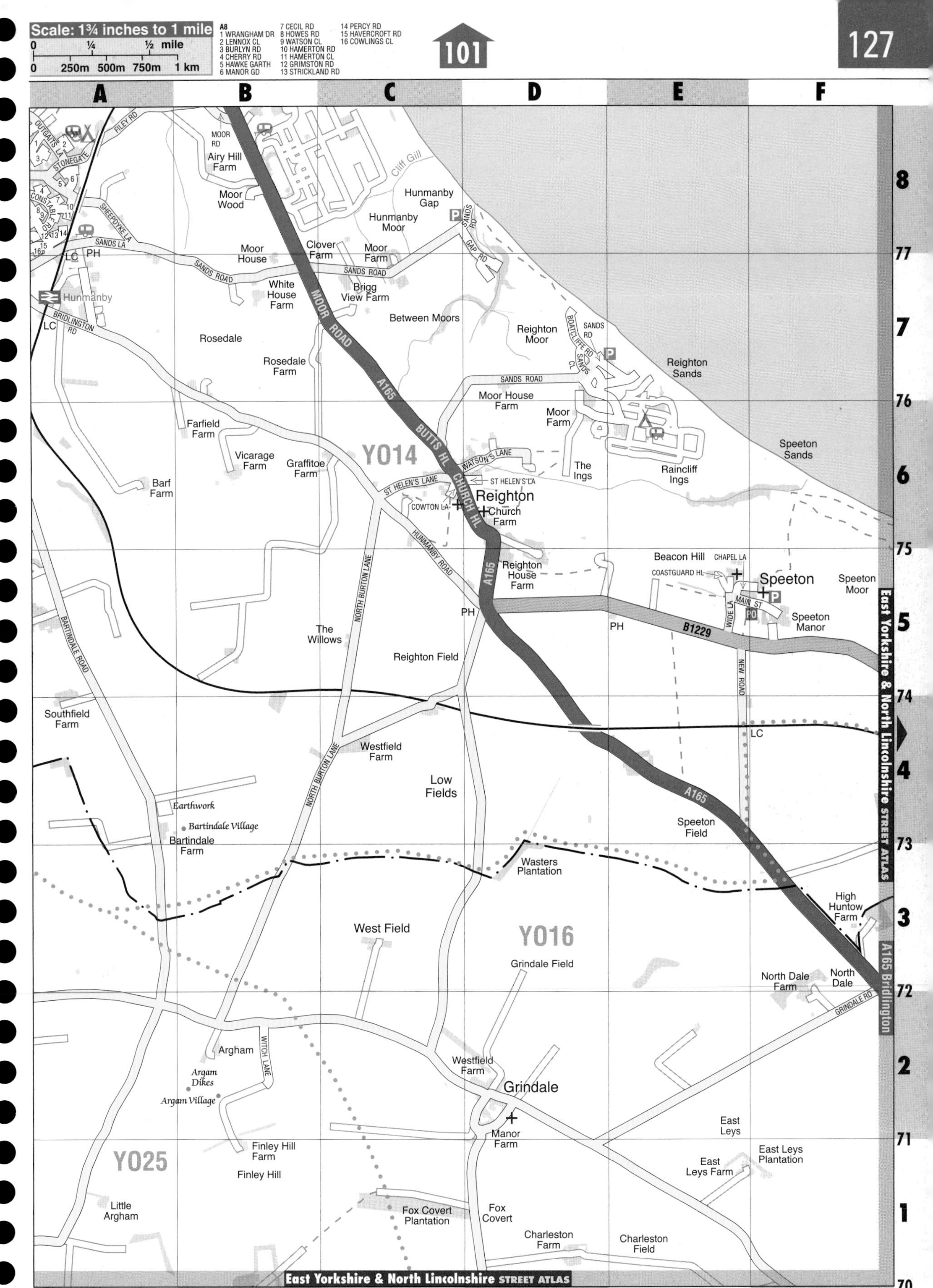

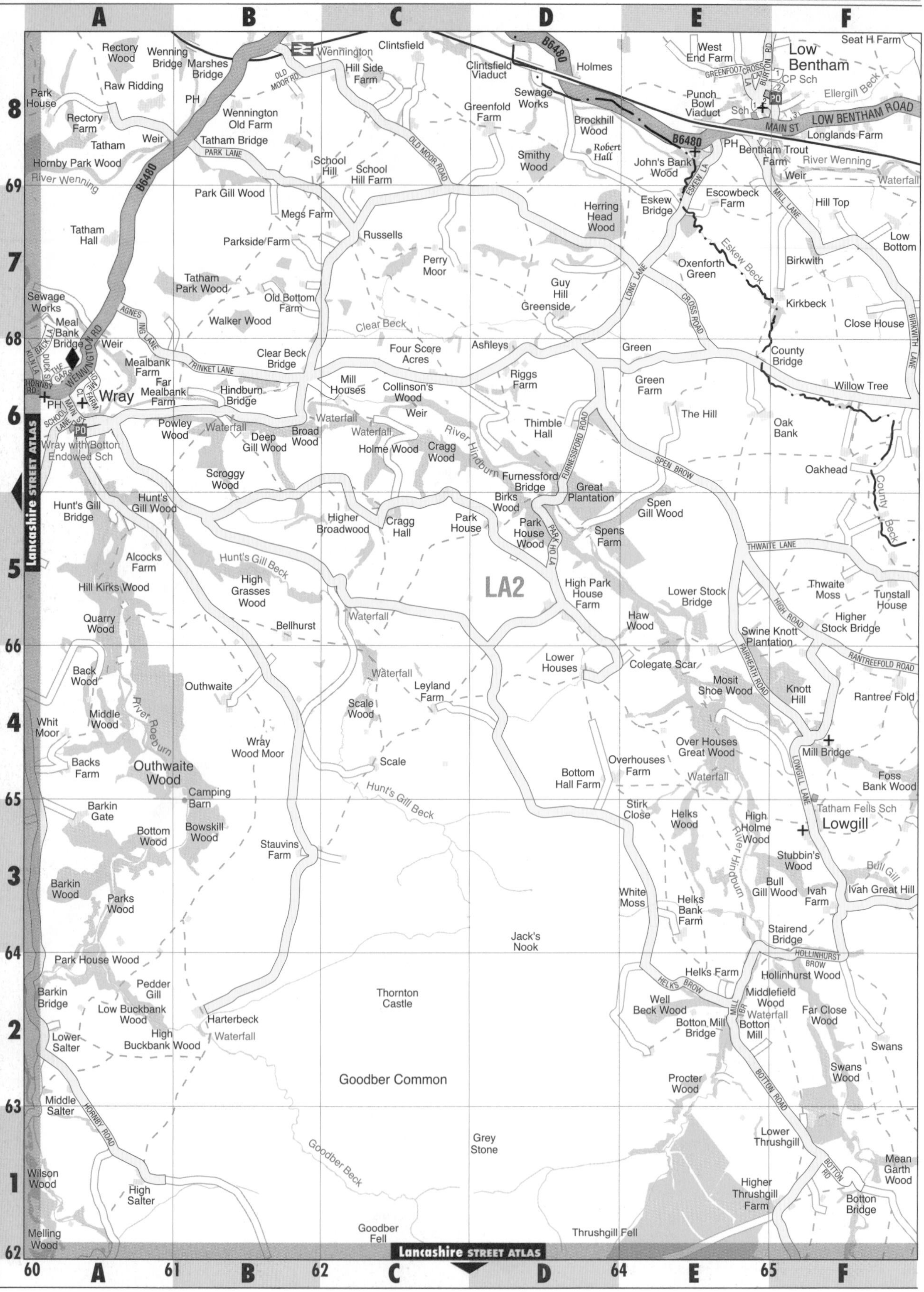

102

E8
1 CROWTREES
2 DOCTOR'S HL

F8
1 YEWTREE DR
2 HILLSIDE RD
3 HARLEY CL

Scale: 1¾ inches to 1 mile
0 ¼ ½ mile
0 250m 500m 750m 1 km

A B C D E F

8 69 7 68 6 5 66 4 65 3 64 2 63 1 62

Rectory Wood, Wenning Bridge, Marshes Bridge, Wennington, Clintsfield, Hill Side Farm, Clintsfield Viaduct, Holmes, West End Farm, Low Bentham, Seat H Farm, Park House, Raw Ridding, PH, Wennington Old Farm, Sewage Works, Greenfold Farm, Brockhill Wood, Punch Bowl Viaduct, Sch, CP Sch, Ellergill Beck, LOW BENTHAM ROAD, MAIN ST, Rectory Farm, Tatham, Weir, Tatham Bridge, PARK LANE, Longlands Farm, Hornby Park Wood, School Hill, School Hill Farm, Smithy Wood, Robert Hall, John's Bank Wood, Bentham Trout Farm, River Wenning, Waterfall, River Wenning, B6480, OLD MOOR RD, OLD MOOR ROAD, GREENFOOT, CROSSLEY, LA, BURTON RD, PO, Park Gill Wood, Megs Farm, Eskew Bridge, Escowbeck Farm, ESKEW LA, MILL LANE, Hill Top, Herring Head Wood, Tatham Hall, Russells, Parkside Farm, Low Bottom, Perry Moor, Oxenforth Green, Eskew Beck, Birkwith, Tatham Park Wood, Guy Hill, Greenside, LONG LANE, CROSS ROAD, Sewage Works, Old Bottom Farm, Kirkbeck, Meal Bank, Walker Wood, Clear Beck, Close House, BIRKWITH LANE, Bridge, Weir, AGNES, ING LANE, WENNINGTON RD, BACK LA, KILN LA, DUCK ST, THE GARS, Clear Beck Bridge, Four Score Acres, Ashleys, Green, County Bridge, Mealbank Farm, TRINKET LANE, Far Mealbank Farm, Mill Houses, Collinson's Wood, Riggs Farm, Green Farm, Willow Tree, HORNBY RD, Wray, Hindburn Bridge, MAIN ST, FARM, PH, SCHOOL LANE, Weir, The Hill, Waterfall, Powley Wood, Waterfall, Deep Gill Wood, Broad Wood, Waterfall, Holme Wood, Cragg Wood, River Hindburn, Thimble Hall, FURNESSFORD ROAD, Oak Bank, Wray with Botton Endowed Sch, Furnessford Bridge, SPEN BROW, Oakhead, Scroggy Wood, Great Plantation, Hunt's Gill Bridge, Hunt's Gill Wood, Birks Wood, Spen Gill Wood, County Beck, Higher Broadwood, Cragg Hall, Park House, Park House Wood, PARK HO LA, Spens Farm, THWAITE LANE, Alcocks Farm, Hunt's Gill Beck, LA2, Thwaite Moss, Tunstall House, High Grasses Wood, High Park House Farm, Lower Stock Bridge, Hill Kirks Wood, Haw Wood, HIGH ROAD, Higher Stock Bridge, Quarry Wood, Waterfall, Bellhurst, Swine Knott Plantation, RANTREEFOLD ROAD, Back Wood, Waterfall, Lower Houses, Colegate Scar, Outhwaite, Leyland Farm, Mosit Shoe Wood, FAIRHEATH ROAD, Knott Hill, Rantree Fold, River Roeburn, Scale Wood, Middle Wood, Whit Moor, Wray Wood Moor, Over Houses Great Wood, Mill Bridge, Backs Farm, Scale, Overhouses Farm, LOWGILL LANE, Outhwaite Wood, Bottom Hall Farm, Waterfall, Foss Bank Wood, Camping Barn, Hunt's Gill Beck, Barkin Gate, Stirk Close, Tatham Fells Sch, Helks Wood, High Holme Wood, Lowgill, Bottom Wood, Bowskill Wood, Stauvins Farm, River Hindburn, Stubbin's Wood, Bull Gill, Barkin Wood, Bull Gill Wood, Ivah Farm, Ivah Great Hill, Parks Wood, White Moss, Helks Bank Farm, Jack's Nook, Stairend Bridge, HOLLINHURST BROW, Park House Wood, Helks Farm, Hollinhurst Wood, HELKS BROW, Pedder Gill, Thornton Castle, Middlefield Wood, Barkin Bridge, Well Beck Wood, Far Close Wood, Low Buckbank Wood, Harterbeck, MILL BR, Waterfall, Bottom Mill, Botton Mill Bridge, Lower Salter, High Buckbank Wood, Waterfall, Swans, Goodber Common, Procter Wood, BOTTON ROAD, Swans Wood, Middle Salter, HORNBY ROAD, Grey Stone, Lower Thrushgill, Goodber Beck, Mean Garth Wood, Wilson Wood, BOTTON RD, High Salter, Higher Thrushgill Farm, Botton Bridge, Melling Wood, Goodber Fell, Thrushgill Fell

Lancashire STREET ATLAS

60 A 61 B 62 C D 64 E 65 F

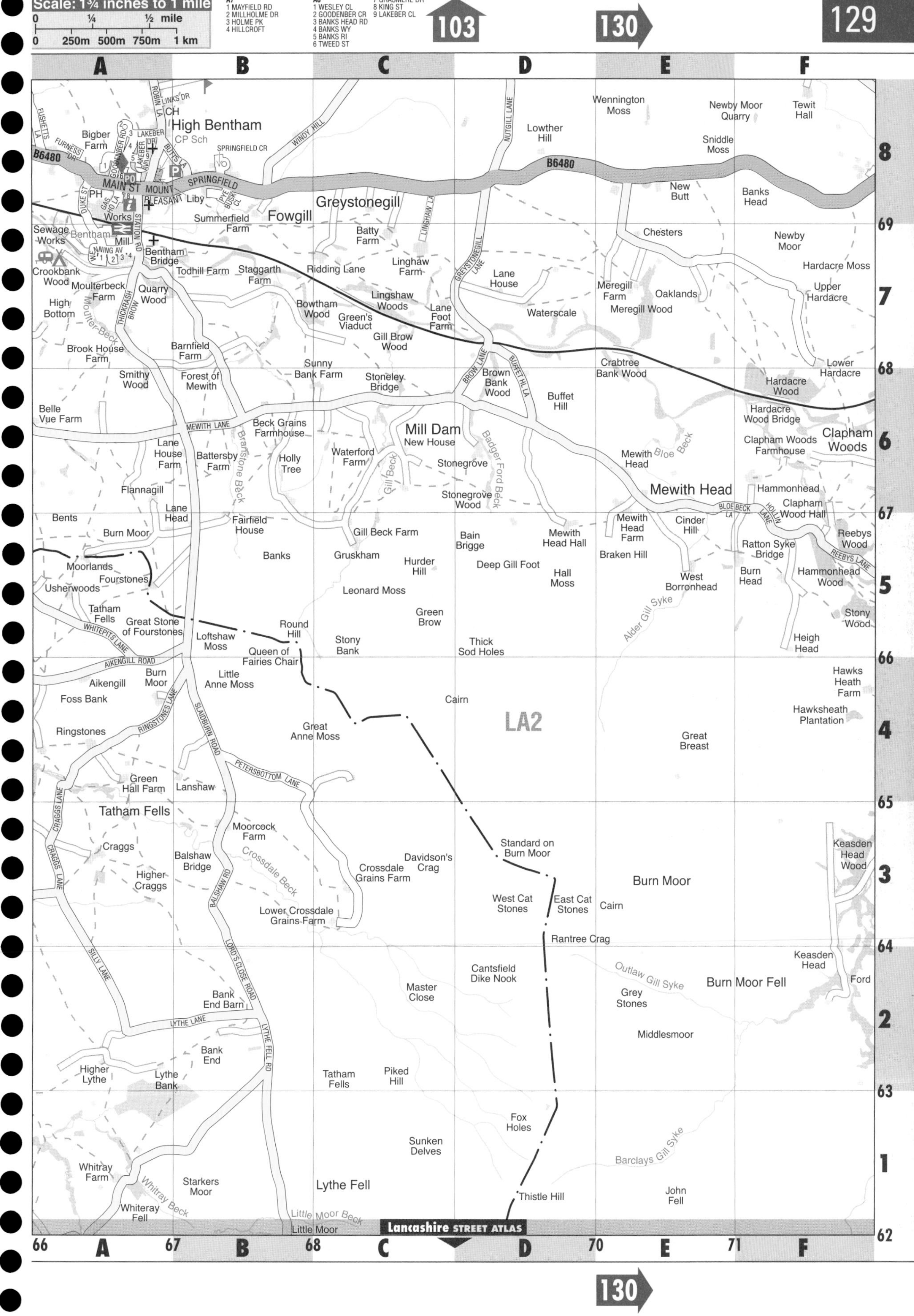
Scale: 1¾ inches to 1 mile
0 ¼ ½ mile
0 250m 500m 750m 1 km
A7
1 MAYFIELD RD
2 MILLHOLME DR
3 HOLME PK
4 HILLCROFT
A8
1 WESLEY CL
2 GOODENBER CR
3 BANKS HEAD RD
4 BANKS WY
5 BANKS RI
6 TWEED ST
7 GRASMERE DR
8 KING ST
9 LAKEBER CL
103
130
A B C D E F
8
69
7
68
6
67
5
66
4
65
3
64
2
63
1
62
66 67 68 70 71
High Bentham
CP Sch
Bigber Farm
B6480
MAIN ST
SPRINGFIELD CR
SPRINGFIELD
MOUNT PLEASANT
Liby
Greystonegill
Fowgill
Summerfield Farm
Sewage Works
Bentham
Mill
Works
STATION RD
Bentham Bridge
Crookbank Wood
Todhill Farm
Staggarth Farm
Ridding Lane
Batty Farm
Linghaw Farm
Lingshaw Woods
Bowtham Wood
Green's Viaduct
Lane Foot Farm
Gill Brow Wood
Moulterbeck Farm
Quarry Wood
High Bottom
Moulter Beck
Brook House Farm
Barnfield Farm
Sunny Bank Farm
Stoneley Bridge
Smithy Wood
Forest of Mewith
Belle Vue Farm
MEWITH LANE
Beck Grains Farmhouse
Mill Dam
New House
Lane House Farm
Battersby Farm
Holly Tree
Waterford Farm
Gill Beck
Stonegrove
Badger Ford Beck
Stonegrove Wood
Flannagill
Branstone Beck
Lane Head
Fairfield House
Bents
Burn Moor
Gill Beck Farm
Bain Brigge
Moorlands
Fourstones
Usherwoods
Banks
Gruskham
Hurder Hill
Deep Gill Foot
Leonard Moss
Tatham Fells
Great Stone of Fourstones
WHITEPITS LANE
Loftshaw Moss
Round Hill
Queen of Fairies Chair
Green Brow
Stony Bank
Thick Sod Holes
AIKENGILL ROAD
Aikengill
Burn Moor
Little Anne Moss
Foss Bank
Cairn
LA2
RINGSTONES LANE
SLAIDBURN ROAD
Ringstones
Great Anne Moss
PETERSBOTTOM LANE
Green Hall Farm
Lanshaw
Tatham Fells
CRAGGS LANE
Moorcock Farm
Craggs
Balshaw Bridge
Crossdale Beck
Crossdale Grains Farm
Davidson's Crag
Standard on Burn Moor
Higher Craggs
BALSHAW RD
Lower Crossdale Grains Farm
West Cat Stones
East Cat Stones
Cairn
Rantree Crag
SILLY LANE
LORD'S CLOSE ROAD
Bank End Barn
Cantsfield Dike Nook
Master Close
LYTHE LANE
LYTHE FELL RD
Bank End
Higher Lythe
Lythe Bank
Tatham Fells
Piked Hill
Fox Holes
Sunken Delves
Whitray Farm
Whitray Beck
Starkers Moor
Lythe Fell
Thistle Hill
Whiteray Fell
Little Moor Beck
Little Moor
NUTGILL LANE
WINDY HILL
Lowther Hill
Wennington Moss
Newby Moor Quarry
Tewit Hall
Sniddle Moss
New Butt
Banks Head
Chesters
Newby Moor
Hardacre Moss
LINGHAW LA
GREYSTONEGILL LANE
Lane House
Meregill Farm
Oaklands
Upper Hardacre
Meregill Wood
Waterscale
BROW LANE
BUFFET HILL LA
Brown Bank Wood
Crabtree Bank Wood
Lower Hardacre
Hardacre Wood
Buffet Hill
Hardacre Wood Bridge
Clapham Woods Farmhouse
Clapham Woods
Mewith Head
Bloe Beck
Hammonhead
Mewith Head
Clapham Wood Hall
BLOE BECK LA
HOLLIN LANE
Mewith Head Farm
Cinder Hill
Mewith Head Hall
Reebys Wood
Ratton Syke Bridge
REEBYS LANE
Braken Hill
Hall Moss
West Borronhead
Burn Head
Hammonhead Wood
Alder Gill Syke
Stony Wood
Heigh Head
Hawks Heath Farm
Hawksheath Plantation
Great Breast
Keasden Head Wood
Burn Moor
Keasden Head
Outlaw Gill Syke
Burn Moor Fell
Ford
Grey Stones
Middlesmoor
Barclays Gill Syke
John Fell
Lancashire STREET ATLAS

129 104

C8
1 THE GN
2 CLAPDALE WY
3 CROSS HAW LA

Scale: 1¾ inches to 1 mile
0 ¼ ½ mile
0 250m 500m 750m 1 km

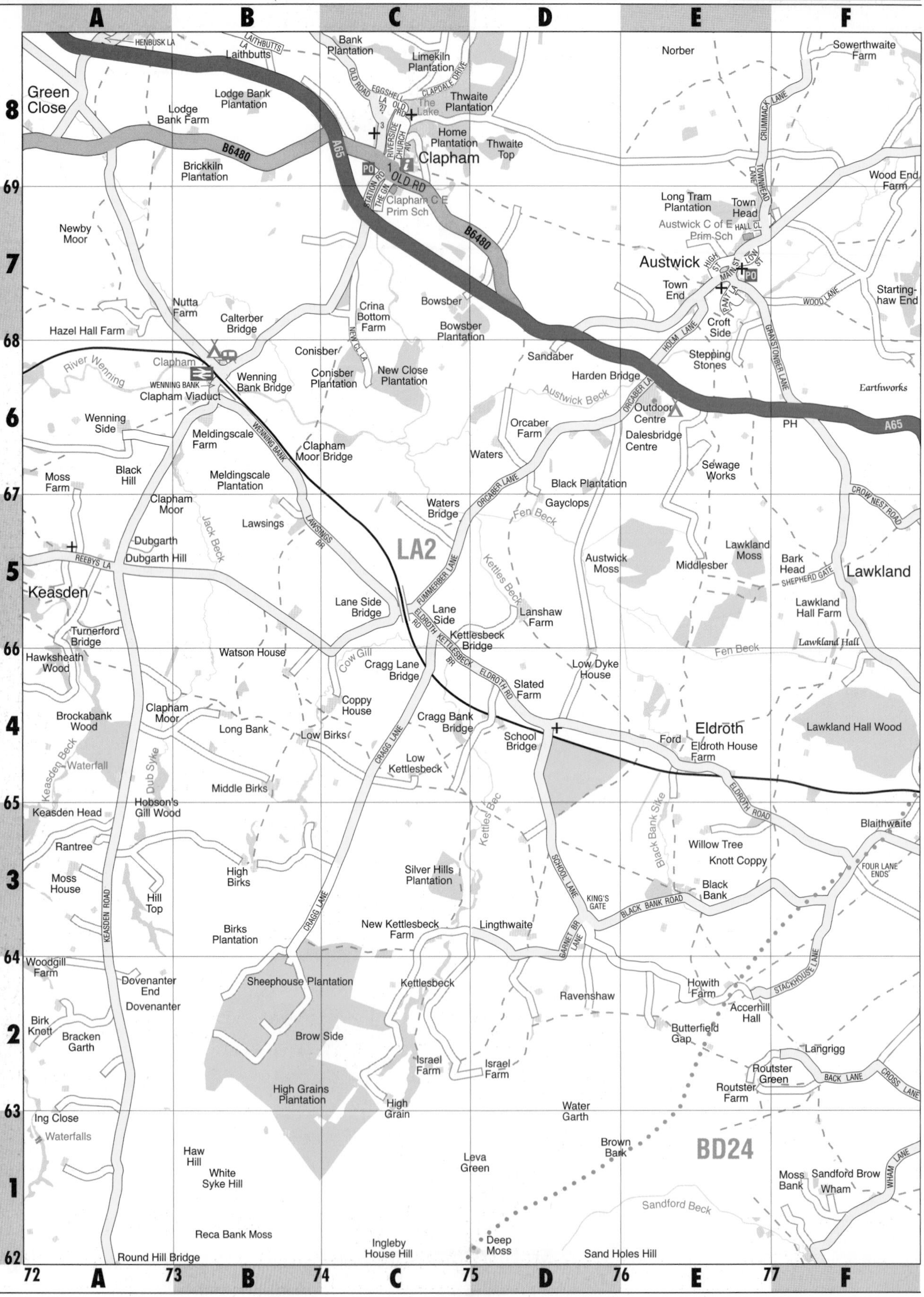

129 152

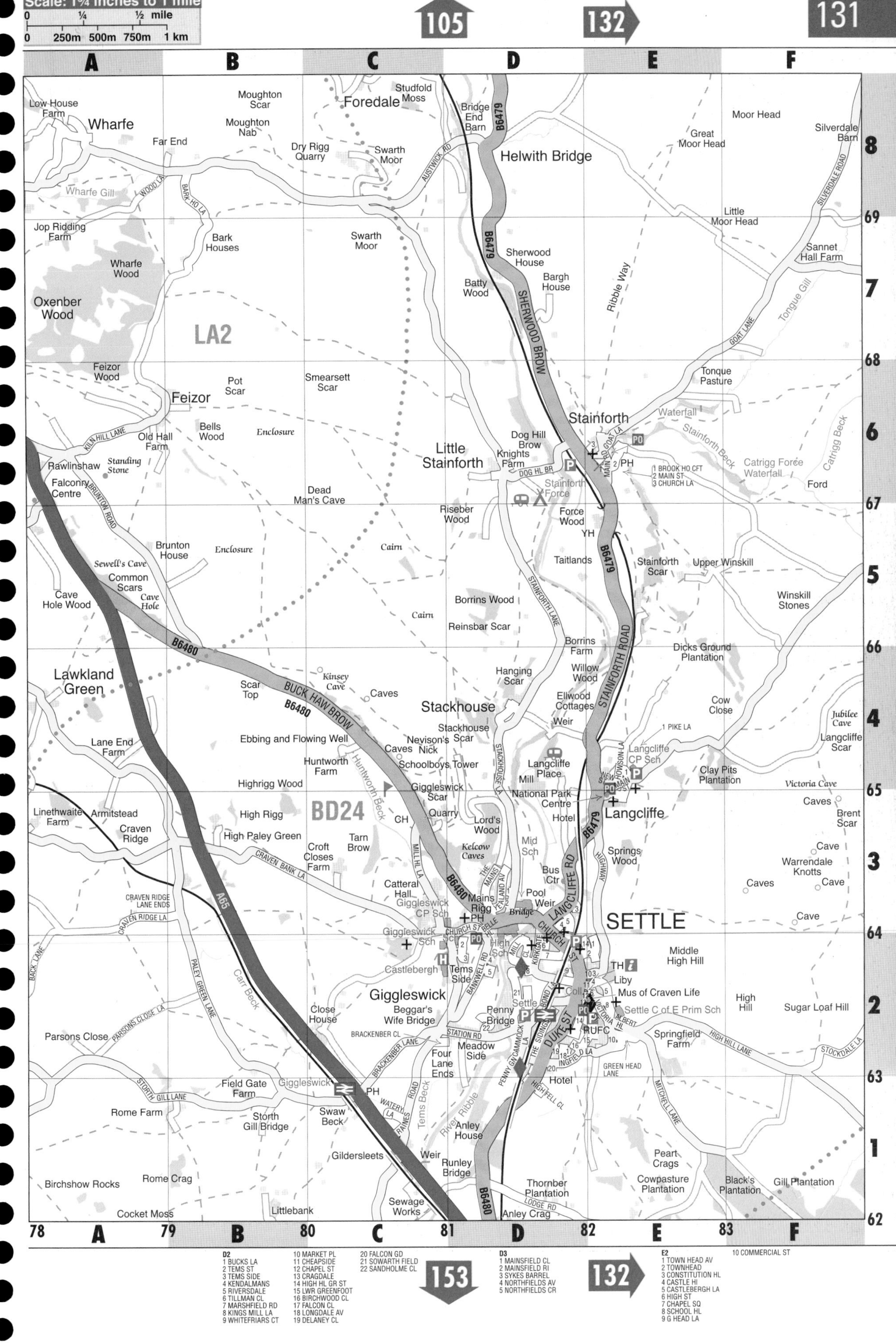

D2
1 BUCKS LA
2 TEMS ST
3 TEMS SIDE
4 KENDALMANS
5 RIVERSDALE
6 TILLMAN CL
7 MARSHFIELD RD
8 KINGS MILL LA
9 WHITEFRIARS CT
10 MARKET PL
11 CHEAPSIDE
12 CHAPEL ST
13 CRAGDALE
14 HIGH HL GR ST
15 LWR GREENFOOT
16 BIRCHWOOD CL
17 FALCON CL
18 LONGDALE AV
19 DELANEY CL
20 FALCON GD
21 SOWARTH FIELD
22 SANDHOLME CL

D3
1 MAINSFIELD CL
2 MAINSFIELD RI
3 SYKES BARREL
4 NORTHFIELDS AV
5 NORTHFIELDS CR

E2
1 TOWN HEAD AV
2 TOWNHEAD
3 CONSTITUTION HL
4 CASTLE HI
5 CASTLEBERGH LA
6 HIGH ST
7 CHAPEL SQ
8 SCHOOL HL
9 G HEAD LA
10 COMMERCIAL ST

Scale: 1¾ inches to 1 mile

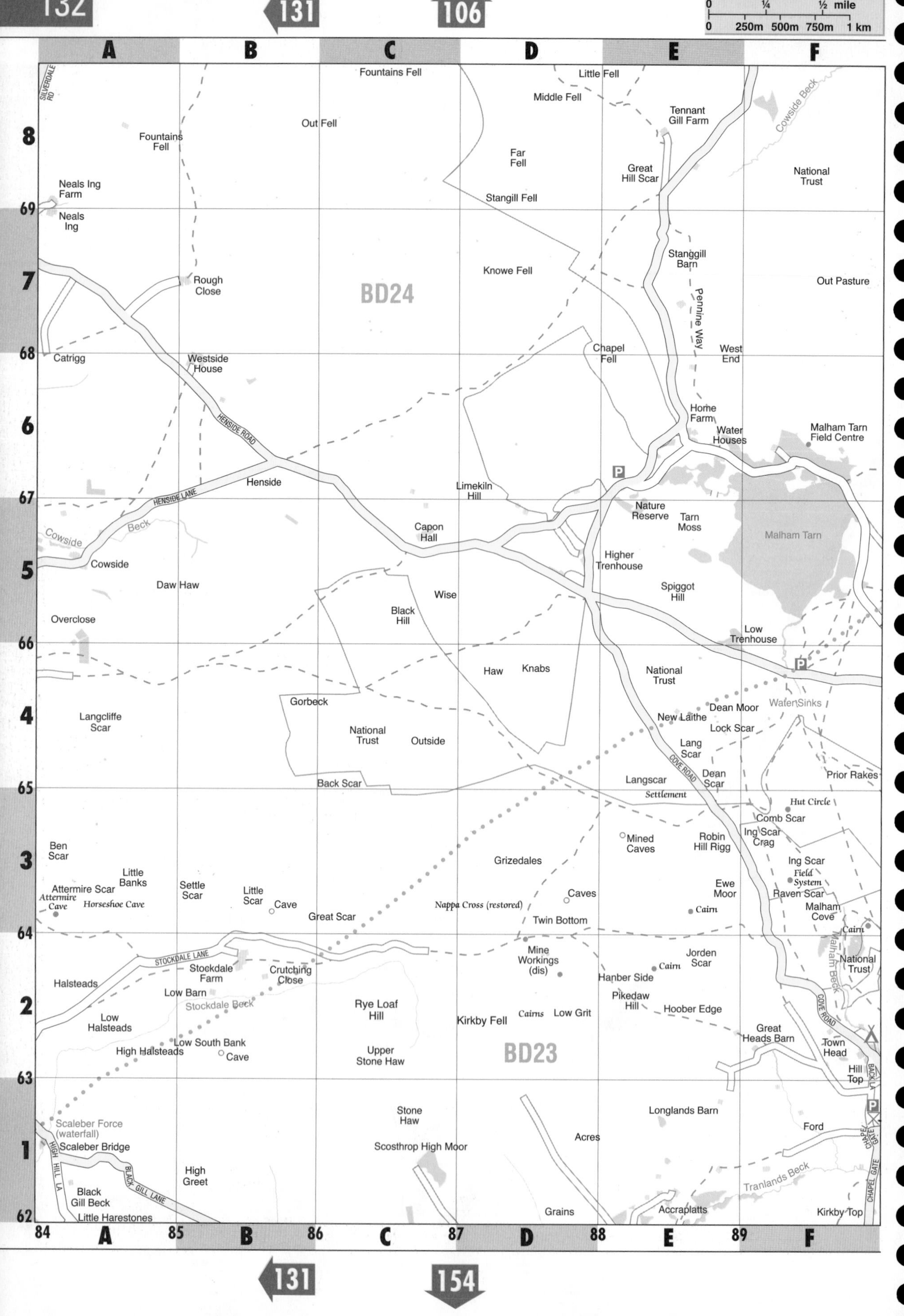

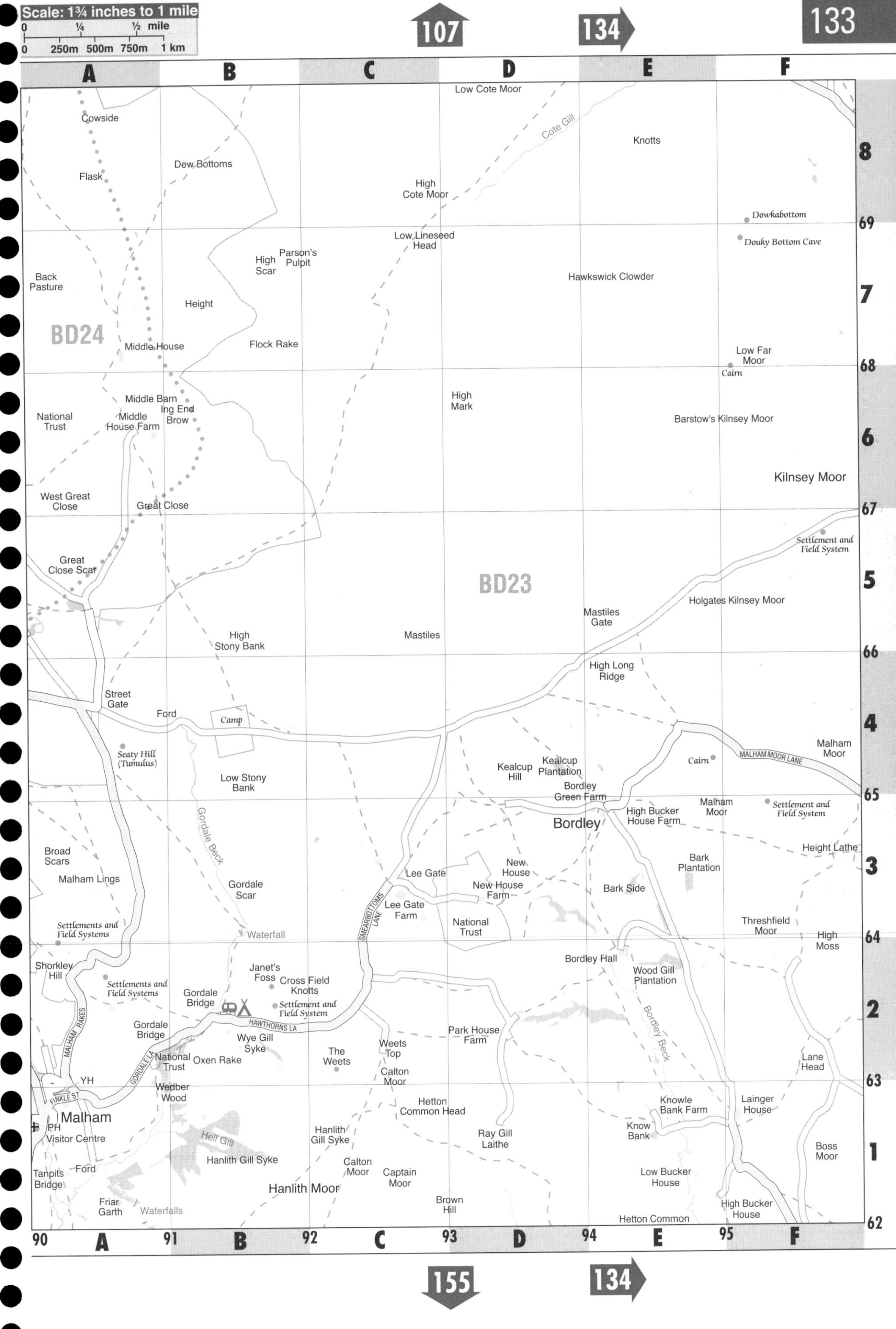
Scale: 1¾ inches to 1 mile
0 ¼ ½ mile
0 250m 500m 750m 1 km
107
134
155
134
Low Cote Moor
Cowside
Cote Gill
Knotts
Dew Bottoms
Flask
High
Cote Moor
Dowkabottom
Douky Bottom Cave
Low Lineseed
Head
Parson's
Pulpit
High
Scar
Back
Pasture
Hawkswick Clowder
Height
BD24
Middle House
Flock Rake
Low Far
Moor
Cairn
Middle Barn
Ing End
Brow
High
Mark
National
Trust
Middle
House Farm
Barstow's Kilnsey Moor
Kilnsey Moor
West Great
Close
Great Close
Settlement and
Field System
Great
Close Scar
BD23
Holgates Kilnsey Moor
Mastiles
Gate
High
Stony Bank
Mastiles
High Long
Ridge
Street
Gate
Ford
Camp
Seaty Hill
(Tumulus)
Malham
Moor
Cairn
MALHAM MOOR LANE
Kealcup
Hill
Kealcup
Plantation
Low Stony
Bank
Bordley
Green Farm
Malham
Moor
Settlement and
Field System
High Bucker
House Farm
Bordley
Gordale Beck
Broad
Scars
Height Lathe
New
House
Bark
Plantation
Lee Gate
Malham Lings
New House
Farm
Gordale
Scar
Bark Side
SMEARBOTTOMS LANE
Lee Gate
Farm
Threshfield
Moor
Settlements and
Field Systems
National
Trust
Waterfall
High
Moss
Shorkley
Hill
Bordley Hall
Janet's
Foss
Wood Gill
Plantation
Cross Field
Knotts
Settlements and
Field Systems
Gordale
Bridge
Settlement and
Field System
MALHAM RAKES
Bordley Beck
HAWTHORNS LA
Gordale
Bridge
Park House
Farm
Wye Gill
Syke
Weets
Top
The
Weets
National
Trust
Oxen Rake
Lane
Head
GORDALE LA
Calton
Moor
YH
Wedber
Wood
FINKLE ST
Hetton
Common Head
Knowle
Bank Farm
Lainger
House
Malham
PH
Know
Bank
Visitor Centre
Hell Gill
Hanlith
Gill Syke
Ray Gill
Laithe
Hanlith Gill Syke
Boss
Moor
Calton
Moor
Tanpits
Bridge
Ford
Captain
Moor
Low Bucker
House
Hanlith Moor
Friar
Garth
Waterfalls
Brown
Hill
High Bucker
House
Hetton Common
A
B
C
D
E
F
8
69
7
68
6
67
5
66
4
65
3
64
2
63
1
62
90
91
92
93
94
95

133
108

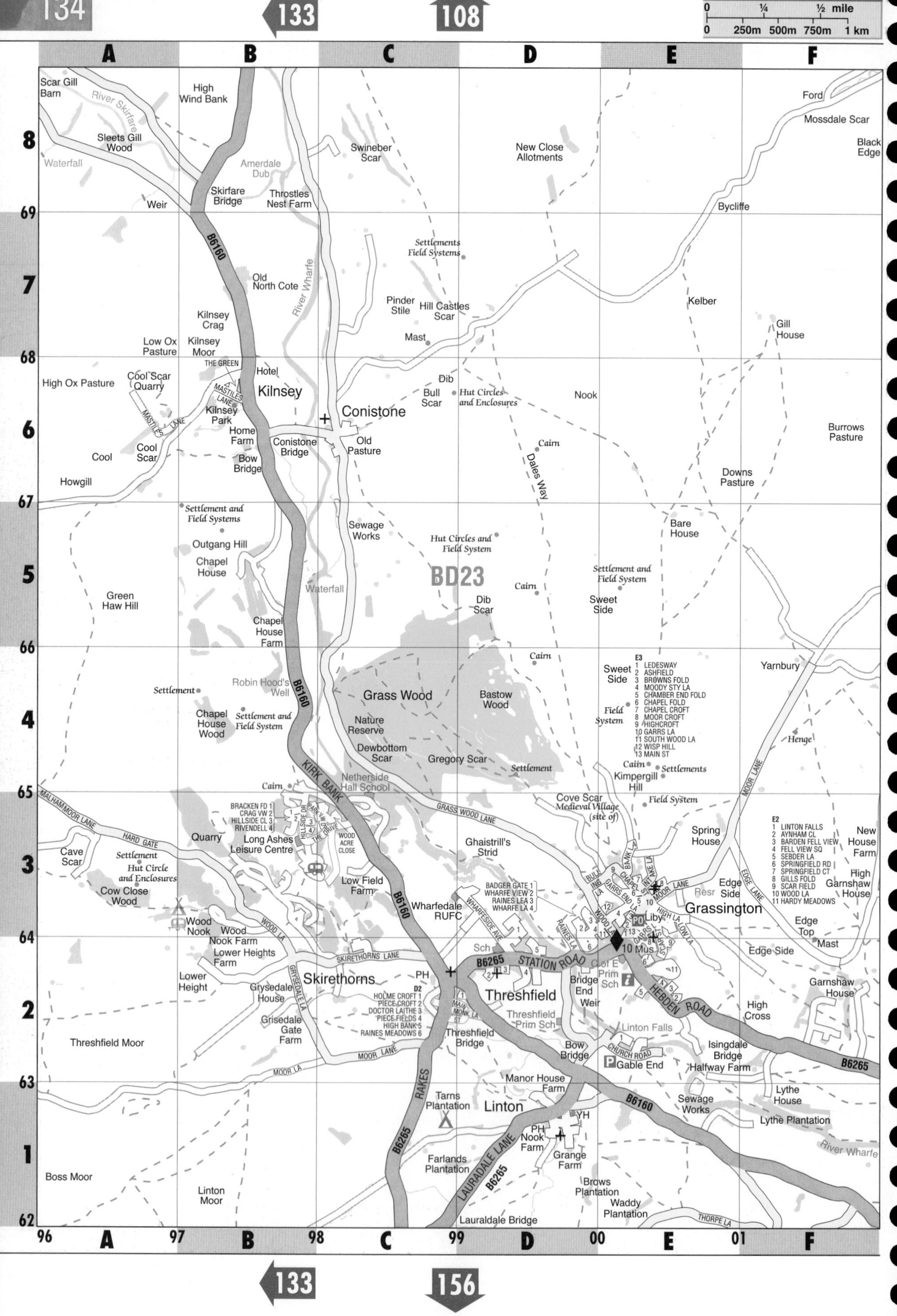

133
156

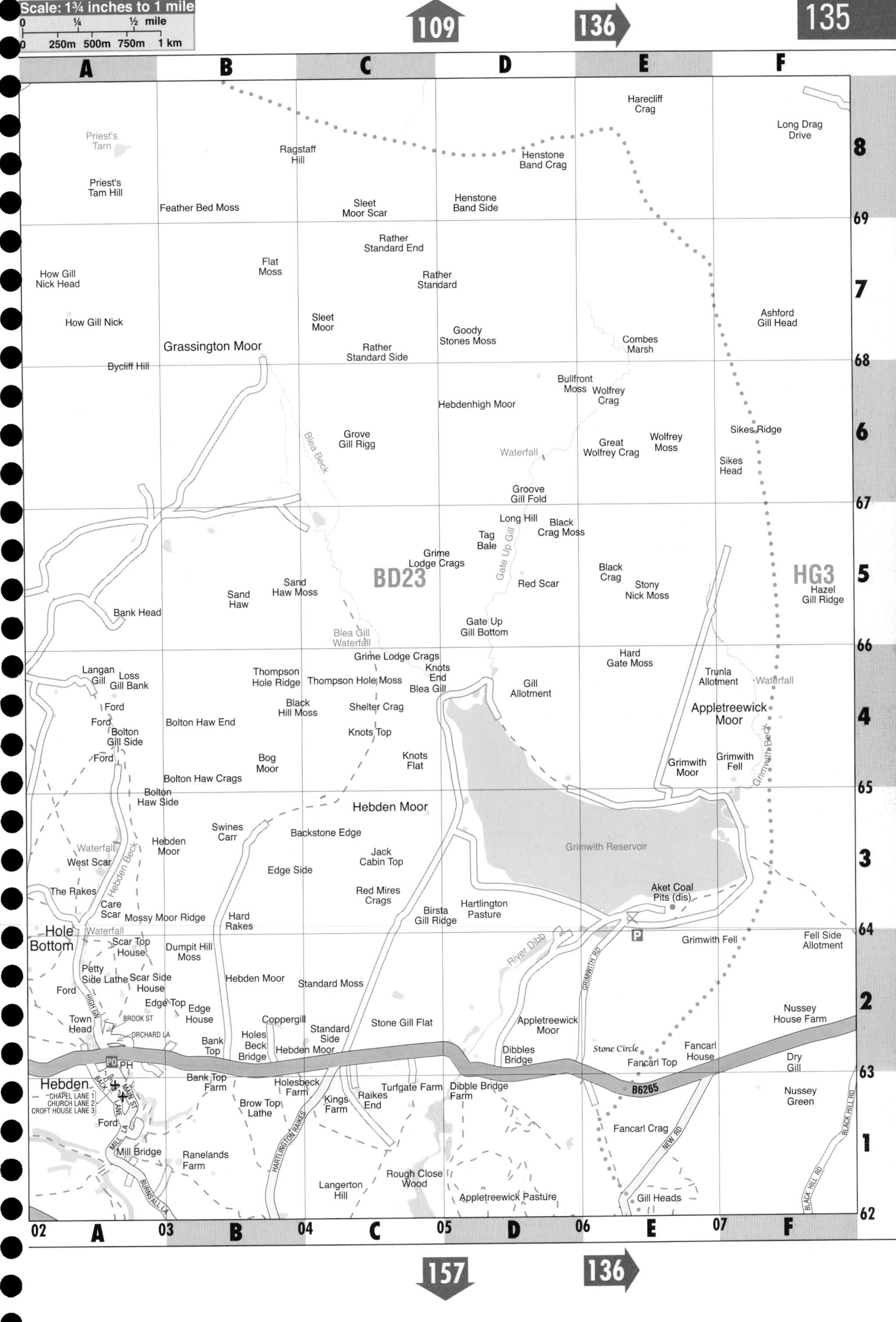

Scale: 1¾ inches to 1 mile
0 ¼ ½ mile
0 250m 500m 750m 1 km
109
136
A B C D E F
Priest's Tarn
Ragstaff Hill
Harecliff Crag
Long Drag Drive
Henstone Band Crag
Priest's Tarn Hill
Feather Bed Moss
Sleet Moor Scar
Henstone Band Side
Rather Standard End
How Gill Nick Head
Flat Moss
Rather Standard
How Gill Nick
Sleet Moor
Goody Stones Moss
Ashford Gill Head
Grassington Moor
Rather Standard Side
Combes Marsh
Bycliff Hill
Bullfront Moss
Wolfrey Crag
Hebdenhigh Moor
Grove Gill Rigg
Blea Beck
Waterfall
Great Wolfrey Crag
Wolfrey Moss
Sikes Ridge
Sikes Head
Groove Gill Fold
Long Hill
Black Crag Moss
Tag Bale
Gate Up Gill
Grime Lodge Crags
BD23
Sand Haw Moss
Sand Haw
Red Scar
Black Crag
Stony Nick Moss
HG3
Hazel Gill Ridge
Bank Head
Gate Up Gill Bottom
Blea Gill Waterfall
Grime Lodge Crags
Hard Gate Moss
Langan Gill
Loss Gill Bank
Thompson Hole Ridge
Thompson Hole Moss
Knots End
Blea Gill
Gill Allotment
Trunla Allotment
Waterfall
Ford
Black Hill Moss
Shelter Crag
Appletreewick Moor
Ford
Bolton Gill Side
Bolton Haw End
Knots Top
Ford
Bog Moor
Knots Flat
Grimwith Moor
Grimwith Fell
Grimwith Beck
Bolton Haw Crags
Bolton Haw Side
Hebden Moor
Swines Carr
Backstone Edge
Waterfall
Hebden Moor
Hebden Beck
West Scar
Jack Cabin Top
Grimwith Reservoir
Edge Side
The Rakes
Red Mires Crags
Aket Coal Pits (dis)
Care Scar
Mossy Moor Ridge
Hard Rakes
Birsta Gill Ridge
Hartlington Pasture
Hole Bottom
Waterfall
Scar Top House
Dumpit Hill Moss
River Dibb
P
Grimwith Fell
Fell Side Allotment
Petty Side Lathe
Scar Side House
Hebden Moor
Standard Moss
Grimwith Rd
Ford
High Gn
Edge Top
Edge House
Nussey House Farm
Town Head
Brook St
Orchard La
Coppergill
Standard Side
Stone Gill Flat
Appletreewick Moor
Bank Top
Holes Beck Bridge
Hebden Moor
Dibbles Bridge
Stone Circle
Fancarl House
PO PH
Fancarl Top
Dry Gill
Hebden
Back La
Main St
Chapel Lane 1
Church Lane 2
Croft House Lane 3
Bank Top Farm
Holesbeck Farm
Turfgate Farm
Dibble Bridge Farm
B6265
Nussey Green
Brow Top Lathe
Kings Farm
Raikes End
Lane
Ford
Mill La
Hartlington Raikes
Fancarl Crag
New Rd
Black Hill Rd
Mill Bridge
Ranelands Farm
Rough Close Wood
Langerton Hill
Burnsall La
Appletreewick Pasture
Gill Heads
Black Hill Rd
8 69 7 68 6 67 5 66 4 65 3 64 2 63 1 62
02 03 04 05 06 07
A B C D E F
157
136

135
110

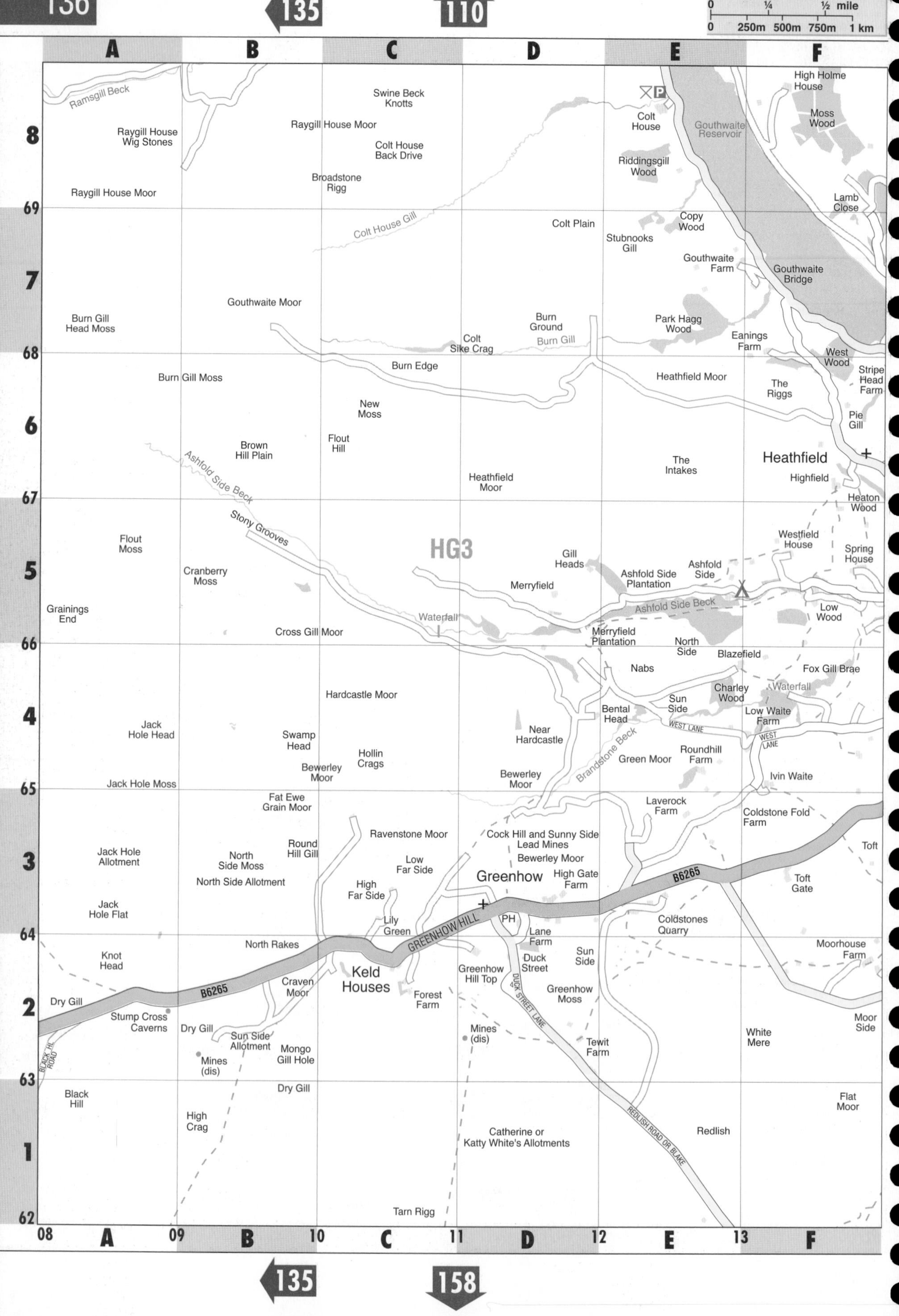

135
158

111
138

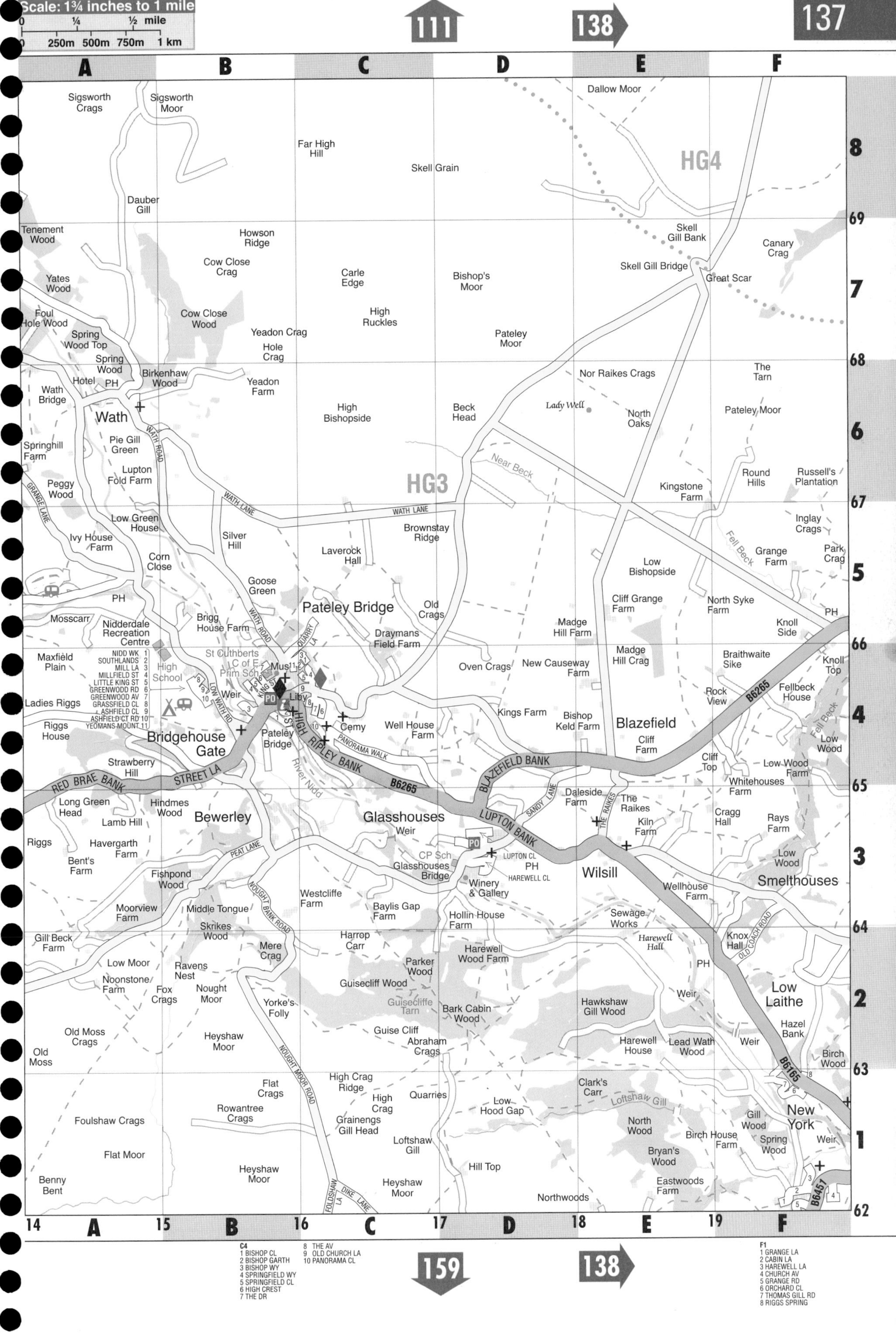

C4
1 BISHOP CL
2 BISHOP GARTH
3 BISHOP WY
4 SPRINGFIELD WY
5 SPRINGFIELD CL
6 HIGH CREST
7 THE DR
8 THE AV
9 OLD CHURCH LA
10 PANORAMA CL

F1
1 GRANGE LA
2 CABIN LA
3 HAREWELL LA
4 CHURCH AV
5 GRANGE RD
6 ORCHARD CL
7 THOMAS GILL RD
8 RIGGS SPRING

159
138

137
112

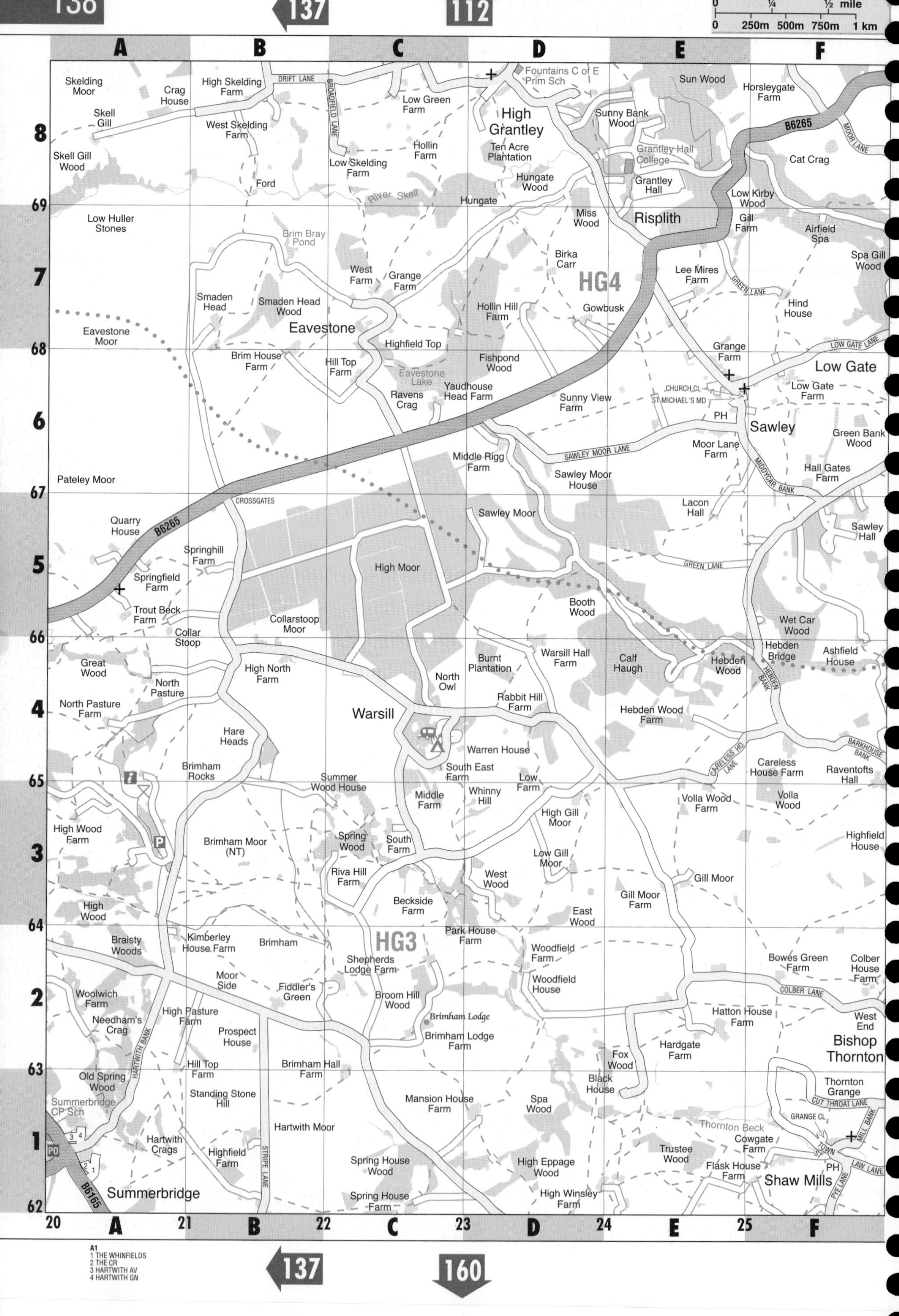

A1
1 THE WHINFIELDS
2 THE CR
3 HARTWITH AV
4 HARTWITH GN

137
160

For full street detail of the highlighted area see page 214.
113
140

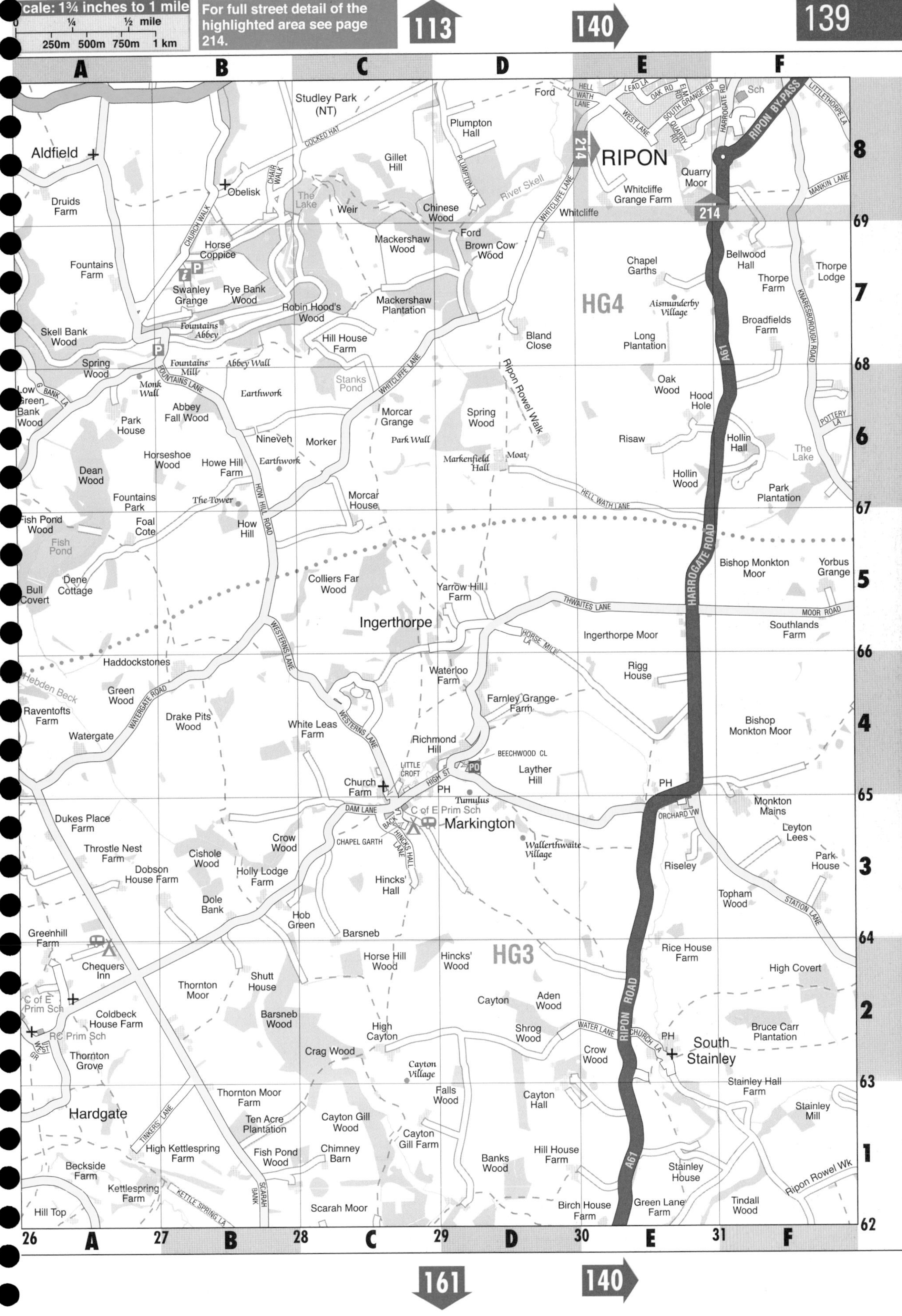

161
140

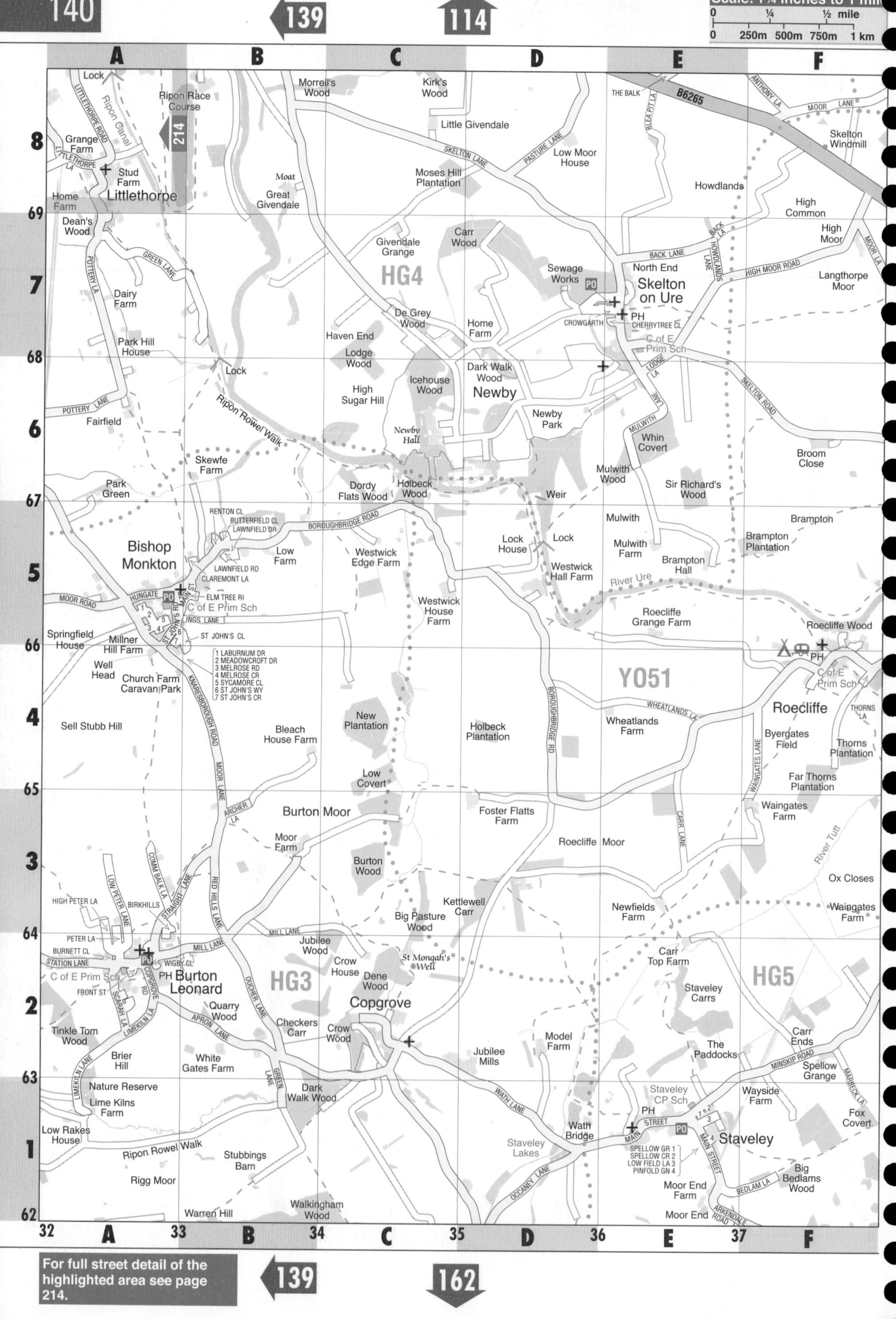

For full street detail of the highlighted area see page 214.

139

162

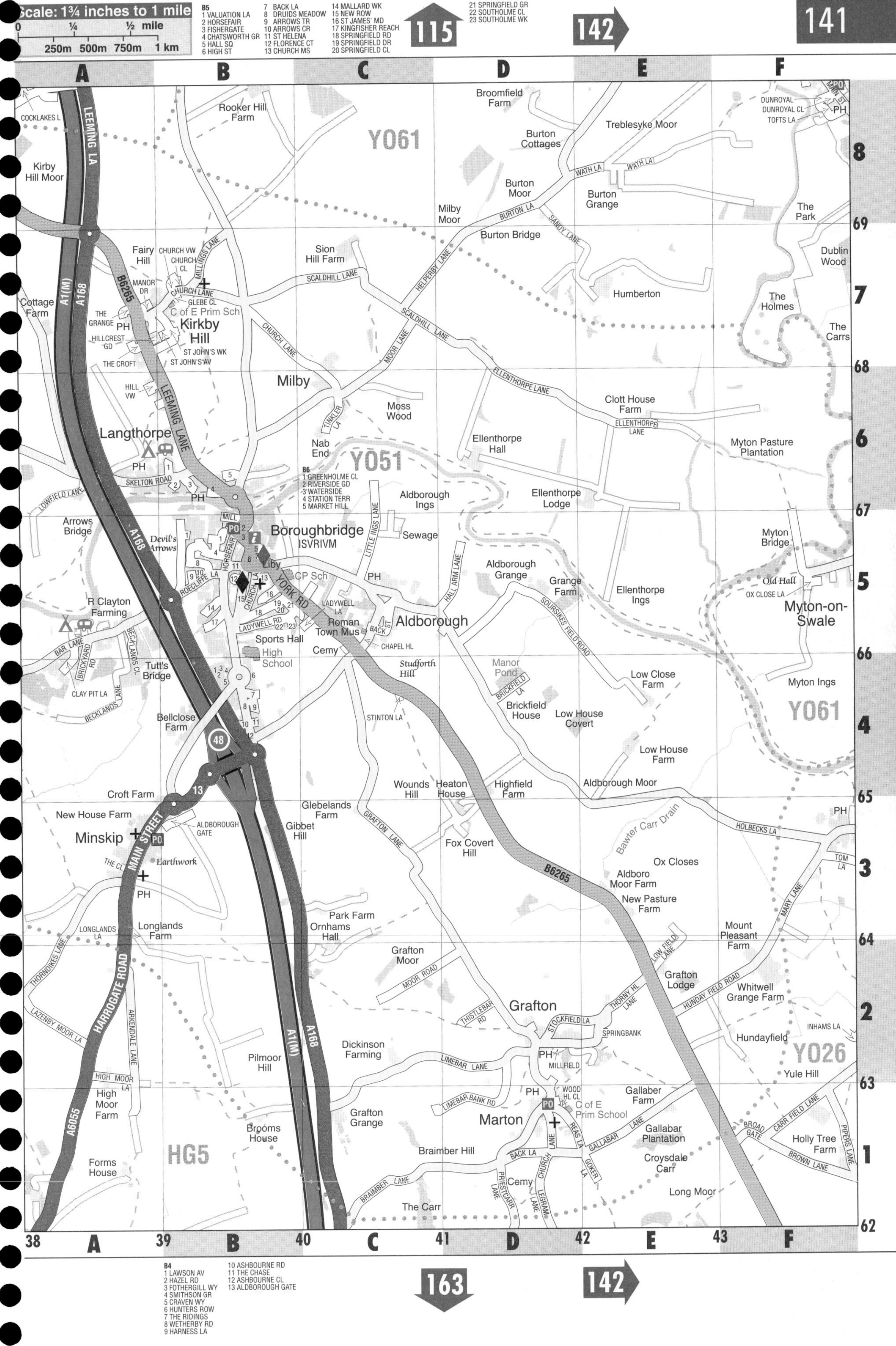

Scale: 1¾ inches to 1 mile
0 ¼ ½ mile
250m 500m 750m 1 km
B5
1 VALUATION LA
2 HORSEFAIR
3 FISHERGATE
4 CHATSWORTH GR
5 HALL SQ
6 HIGH ST
7 BACK LA
8 DRUIDS MEADOW
9 ARROWS TR
10 ARROWS CR
11 ST HELENA
12 FLORENCE CT
13 CHURCH MS
14 MALLARD WK
15 NEW ROW
16 ST JAMES' MD
17 KINGFISHER REACH
18 SPRINGFIELD RD
19 SPRINGFIELD DR
20 SPRINGFIELD CL
21 SPRINGFIELD GR
22 SOUTHOLME CL
23 SOUTHOLME WK
115
142
A B C D E F
Broomfield Farm
Rooker Hill Farm
COCKLAKES L
LEEMING LA
Kirby Hill Moor
YO61
Burton Cottages
Treblesyke Moor
DUNROYAL
DUNROYAL CL
TOFTS LA
PO
MAIN ST
PH
8
WATH LA
Burton Moor
Burton Grange
Milby Moor
BURTON LA
Burton Bridge
SANDY LANE
The Park
69
Dublin Wood
Fairy Hill
CHURCH VW
CHURCH CL
MILLINGS LANE
Sion Hill Farm
SCALDHILL LANE
HELPERBY LANE
Humberton
The Holmes
7
MANOR DR
CHURCH LANE
GLEBE CL
Cottage Farm
THE GRANGE
PH
C of E Prim Sch
Kirkby Hill
HILLCREST GD
THE CROFT
ST JOHN'S WK
ST JOHN'S AV
CHURCH LANE
SCALDHILL LANE
MOOR LANE
The Carrs
68
A1(M)
A168
B6265
Milby
HILL VW
ELLENTHORPE LANE
Clott House Farm
Moss Wood
TINKLER LA
Langthorpe
LEEMING LANE
ELLENTHORPE LANE
Ellenthorpe Hall
Myton Pasture Plantation
6
PH
Nab End
YO51
SKELTON ROAD
LOWFIELD LANE
B6
1 GREENHOLME CL
2 RIVERSIDE GD
3 WATERSIDE
4 STATION TERR
5 MARKET HILL
Aldborough Ings
Ellenthorpe Lodge
67
Arrows Bridge
MILL
PO
Boroughbridge
ISVRIVM
LITTLE INGS LANE
Sewage
Myton Bridge
Devil's Arrows
A168
Liby
HALL ARM LANE
Aldborough Grange
HORSEFAIR
ROECLIFFE LA
CP Sch
PH
Grange Farm
Ellenthorpe Ings
Old Hall
OX CLOSE LA
5
R Clayton Farming
CHURCH LA
YORK RD
LADYWELL LA
Aldborough
Myton-on-Swale
LADYWELL RD
Roman Town Mus
BACK ST
SOURSIKES FIELD ROAD
BAR LANE
BRICKYARD RD
BECKLANDS CL
Sports Hall
High School
Cemy
CHAPEL HL
66
Tutt's Bridge
Studforth Hill
Manor Pond
Low Close Farm
Myton Ings
CLAY PIT LA
BECKLANDS LANE
BRICKFIELD LA
Brickfield House
Low House Covert
YO61
Bellclose Farm
STINTON LA
48
Low House Farm
4
13
Wounds Hill
Heaton House
Highfield Farm
Aldborough Moor
Croft Farm
65
New House Farm
Glebelands Farm
Bawter Carr Drain
PH
HOLBECKS LA
Minskip
MAIN STREET
PO
ALDBOROUGH GATE
Gibbet Hill
GRAFTON LANE
Fox Covert Hill
TOM LA
THE CL
Earthwork
B6265
Ox Closes
Aldboro Moor Farm
3
PH
MARY LANE
New Pasture Farm
Park Farm
LONGLANDS LA
Longlands Farm
Ornhams Hall
Mount Pleasant Farm
64
THORNDIKES LANE
HARROGATE ROAD
Grafton Moor
LOW FIELD LANE
Grafton Lodge
MOOR ROAD
HUNDAY FIELD ROAD
Whitwell Grange Farm
LAZENBY MOOR LA
ARKENDALE LANE
A1(M)
A168
THISTLEBAR RD
Grafton
THORNY HL LANE
STOCKFIELD LA
SPRINGBANK
2
INHAMS LA
Dickinson Farming
Hundayfield
Pilmoor Hill
LIMEBAR LANE
PH
MILLFIELD
YO26
HIGH MOOR LA
PH
WOOD HL CL
Gallaber Farm
Yule Hill
63
High Moor Farm
LIMEBAR BANK RD
PO
C of E Prim School
Grafton Grange
Marton
REAS LA
GALLABAR LANE
Gallabar Plantation
BROAD GATE
CARR FIELD LANE
A6055
Brooms House
HG5
Braimber Hill
BACK LA
CHURCH LANE
Holly Tree Farm
PIPERS LANE
Croysdale Carr
BROWN LANE
1
Forms House
GOKER LA
PRIESTCARR LANE
Cemy
LEGRAM LANE
BRAIMBER LANE
Long Moor
The Carr
62
38 A 39 B 40 C 41 D 42 E 43 F
B4
1 LAWSON AV
2 HAZEL RD
3 FOTHERGILL WY
4 SMITHSON GR
5 CRAVEN WY
6 HUNTERS ROW
7 THE RIDINGS
8 WETHERBY RD
9 HARNESS LA
10 ASHBOURNE RD
11 THE CHASE
12 ASHBOURNE CL
13 ALDBOROUGH GATE
163
142

Scale: 1¾ inches to 1 mile

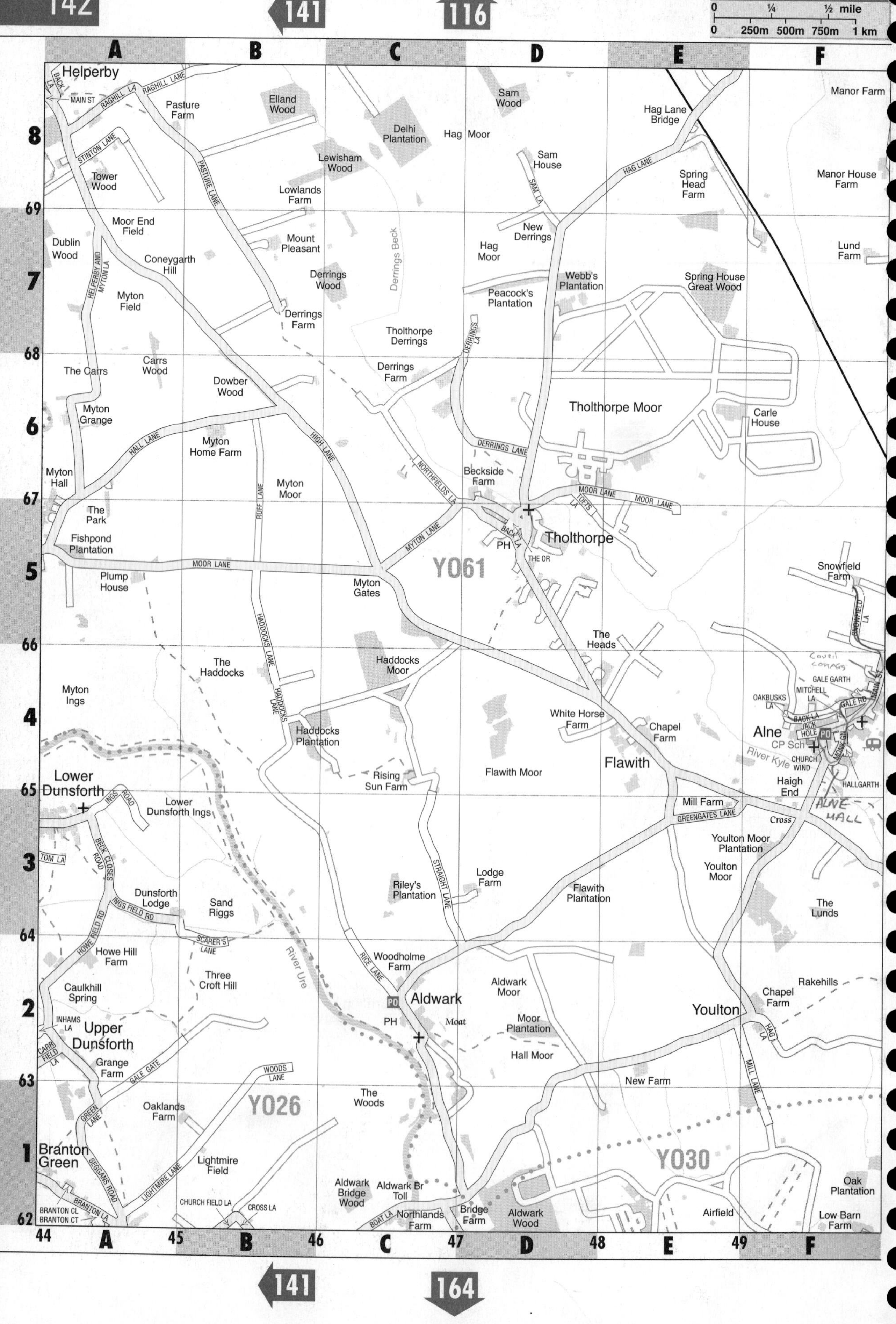

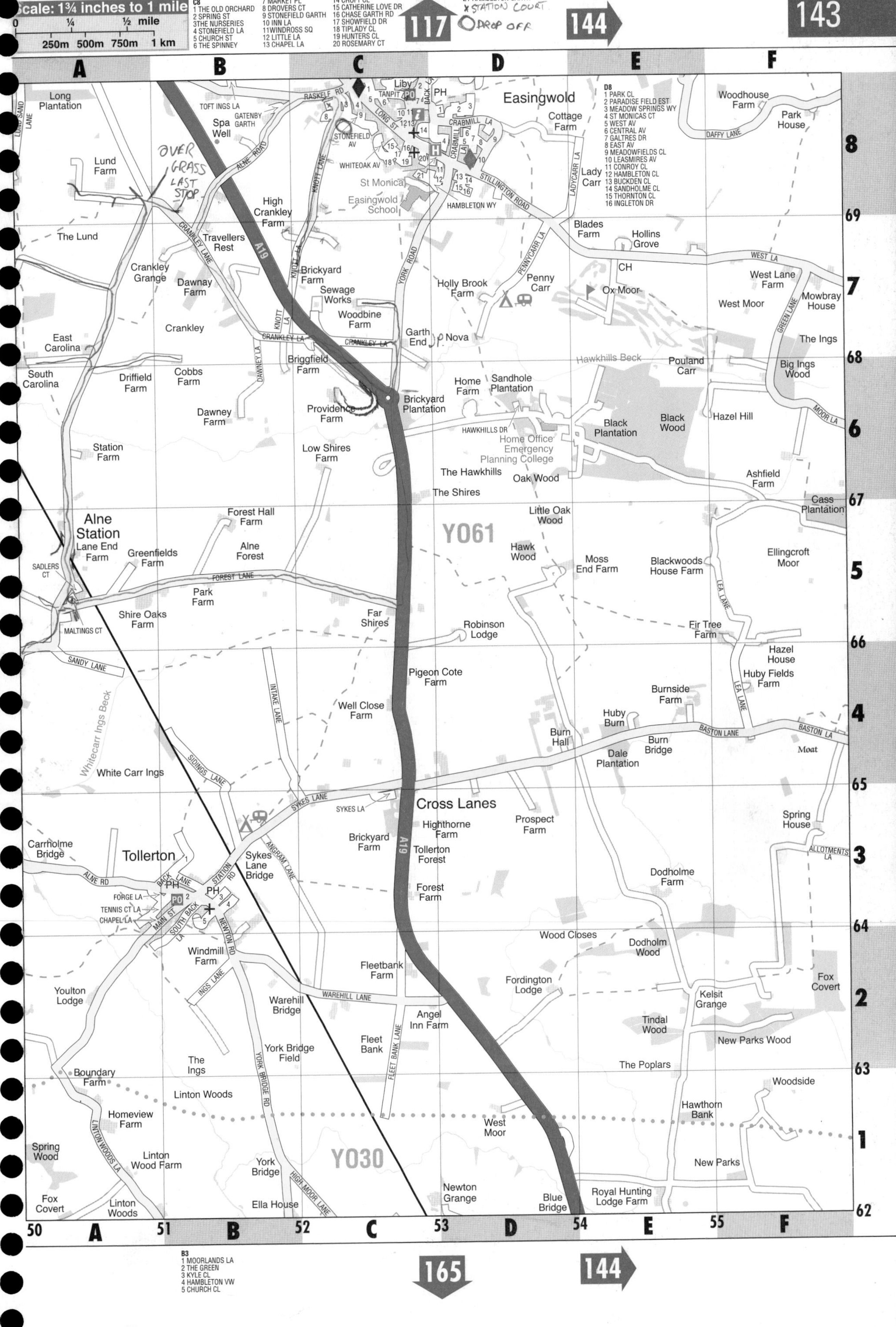

Scale: 1¾ inches to 1 mile
0 ¼ ½ mile
250m 500m 750m 1 km
C8
1 THE OLD ORCHARD
2 SPRING ST
3 THE NURSERIES
4 STONEFIELD LA
5 CHURCH ST
6 THE SPINNEY
7 MARKET PL
8 DROVERS CT
9 STONEFIELD GARTH
10 INN LA
11 WINDROSS SQ
12 LITTLE LA
13 CHAPEL LA
14 CROFT CL
15 CATHERINE LOVE DR
16 CHASE GARTH RD
17 SHOWFIELD DR
18 TIPLADY CL
19 HUNTERS CL
20 ROSEMARY CT
21 HAMBLETON GARTH
117
144
143
A B C D E F
D8
1 PARK CL
2 PARADISE FIELD EST
3 MEADOW SPRINGS WY
4 ST MONICAS CT
5 WEST AV
6 CENTRAL AV
7 GALTRES DR
8 EAST AV
9 MEADOWFIELDS CL
10 LEASMIRES AV
11 CONROY CL
12 HAMBLETON CL
13 BUCKDEN CL
14 SANDHOLME CL
15 THORNTON CL
16 INGLETON DR
Easingwold
Long Plantation
Lund Farm
Spa Well
TOFT INGS LA
GATENBY GARTH
ALNE ROAD
RASKELF RD
Liby
PO
PH
TANPIT
LONG ST
BACK LA
CRABMILL LA
STONEFIELD AV
WHITEOAK AV
St Monica
Easingwold School
STILLINGTON ROAD
HAMBLETON WY
Cottage Farm
Lady Carr
LADYCARR LA
Woodhouse Farm
Park House
DAFFY LANE
The Lund
High Crankley Farm
Travellers Rest
CRANKLEY LANE
A19
KNOTT LANE
YORK ROAD
Blades Farm
Hollins Grove
WEST LA
PENNYCARR LA
Penny Carr
CH
Ox Moor
West Lane Farm
Mowbray House
West Moor
GREEN LANE
Crankley Grange
Dawnay Farm
Brickyard Farm
Sewage Works
Woodbine Farm
Holly Brook Farm
Crankley
East Carolina
KNOTT LA
CRANKLEY LA
Garth End
Nova
The Ings
Hawkhills Beck
South Carolina
Driffield Farm
Cobbs Farm
DAWNEY LA
Briggfield Farm
Home Farm
Sandhole Plantation
Pouland Carr
Big Ings Wood
Dawney Farm
Providence Farm
Brickyard Plantation
Black Plantation
Black Wood
Hazel Hill
MOOR LA
HAWKHILLS DR
Home Office Emergency Planning College
Station Farm
Low Shires Farm
The Hawkhills
Oak Wood
Ashfield Farm
The Shires
Cass Plantation
Alne Station
Forest Hall Farm
Little Oak Wood
Y061
Ellingcroft Moor
Lane End Farm
Greenfields Farm
Alne Forest
Hawk Wood
Moss End Farm
Blackwoods House Farm
SADLERS CT
FOREST LANE
Park Farm
LEA LANE
Shire Oaks Farm
Far Shires
Robinson Lodge
Fir Tree Farm
MALTINGS CT
Hazel House
SANDY LANE
Huby Fields Farm
Pigeon Cote Farm
Burnside Farm
INTAKE LANE
Well Close Farm
Huby Burn
Whitecar Ings Beck
Burn Hall
BASTON LANE
BASTON LA
Burn Bridge
Moat
White Carr Ings
Dale Plantation
SIDINGS LANE
SYKES LANE
SYKES LA
Cross Lanes
Prospect Farm
Spring House
Highthorne Farm
Carrholme Bridge
Tollerton
Brickyard Farm
Tollerton Forest
ALLOTMENTS LA
Sykes Lane Bridge
ANGRAM LANE
Dodholme Farm
ALNE RD
BACK LANE
STATION RD
FORGE LA
TENNIS CT LA
CHAPEL LA
MAIN ST
SOUTH BACK LA
NEWTON RD
Forest Farm
Wood Closes
Dodholm Wood
Windmill Farm
Fleetbank Farm
Fordington Lodge
Fox Covert
Youlton Lodge
INGS LANE
Warehill Bridge
WAREHILL LANE
Kelsit Grange
Angel Inn Farm
Tindal Wood
New Parks Wood
York Bridge Field
FLEET BANK LANE
Fleet Bank
The Ings
The Poplars
Boundary Farm
YORK BRIDGE RD
Woodside
Linton Woods
Hawthorn Bank
Homeview Farm
West Moor
LINTON WOODS LA
Spring Wood
Linton Wood Farm
York Bridge
Y030
New Parks
Newton Grange
Royal Hunting Lodge Farm
Fox Covert
Linton Woods
Ella House
HIGH MOOR LANE
Blue Bridge
8 69 7 68 6 67 5 66 4 65 3 64 2 63 1 62
50 51 52 53 54 55
B3
1 MOORLANDS LA
2 THE GREEN
3 KYLE CL
4 HAMBLETON VW
5 CHURCH CL
165
144

143
118

Scale: 1¾ inches to 1 mile
0 ¼ ½ mile
0 250m 500m 750m 1 km

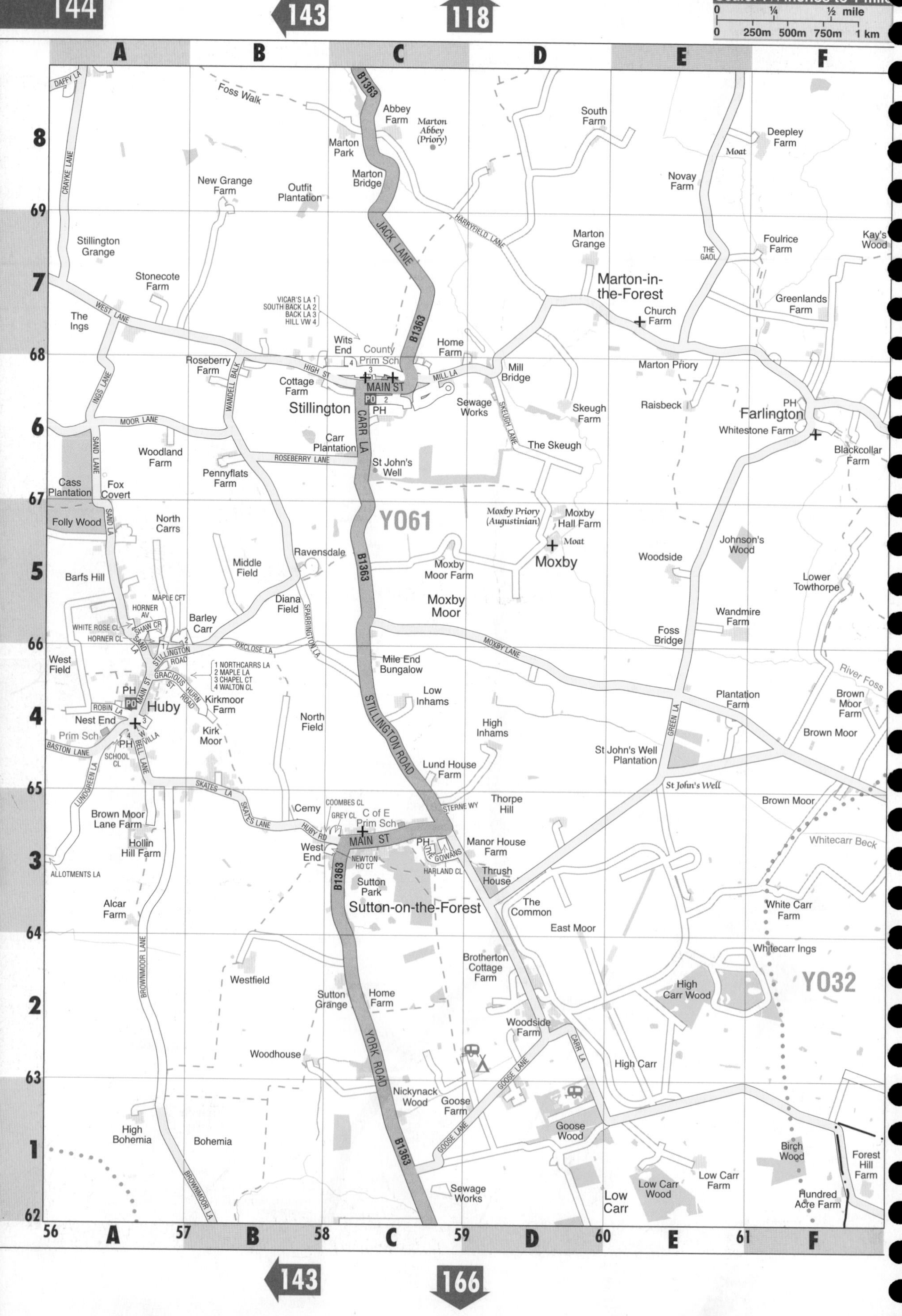

Scale: 1¾ inches to 1 mile

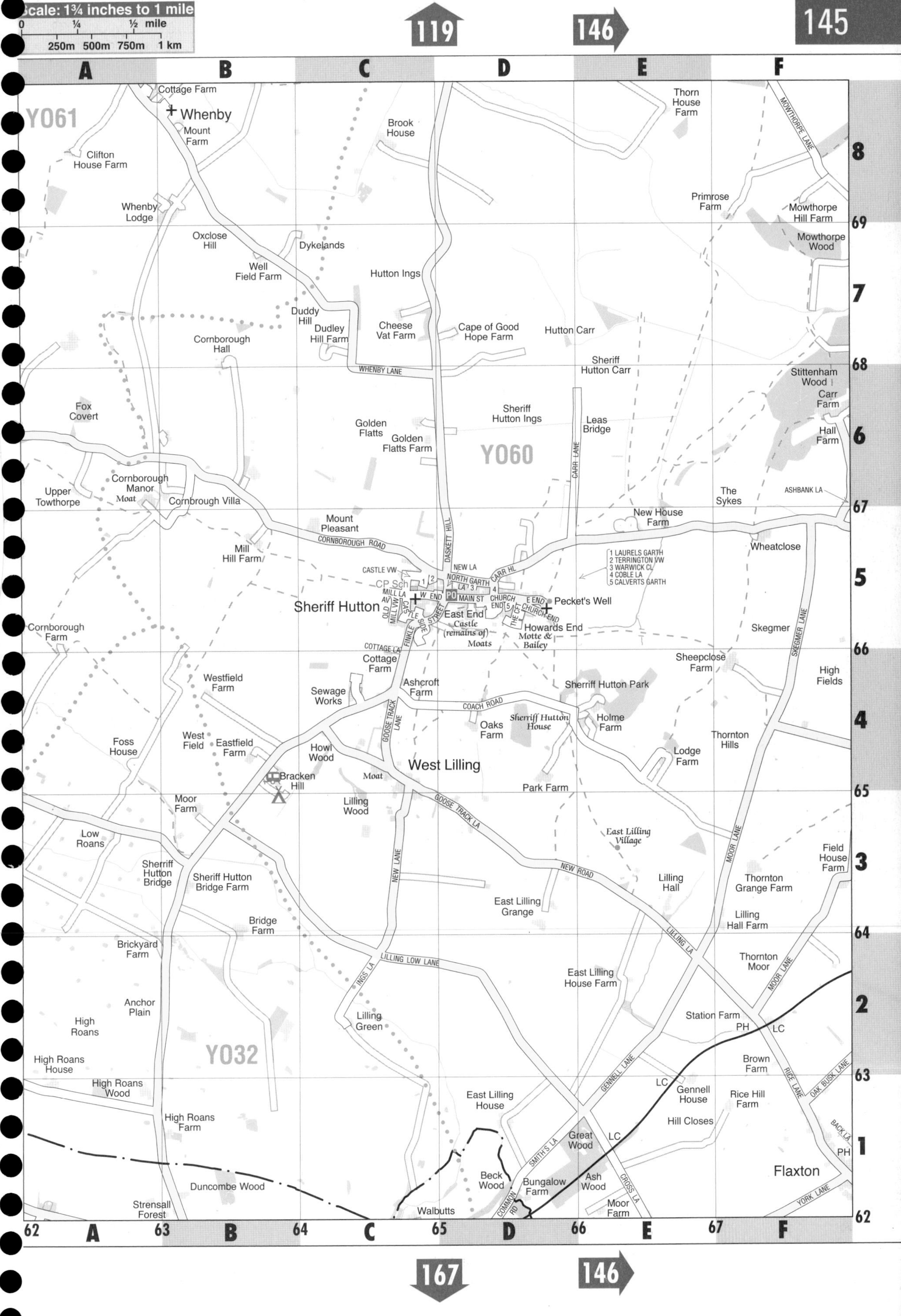

145
120

Scale: 1¾ inches to 1 mile
0 ¼ ½ mile
0 250m 500m 750m 1 km

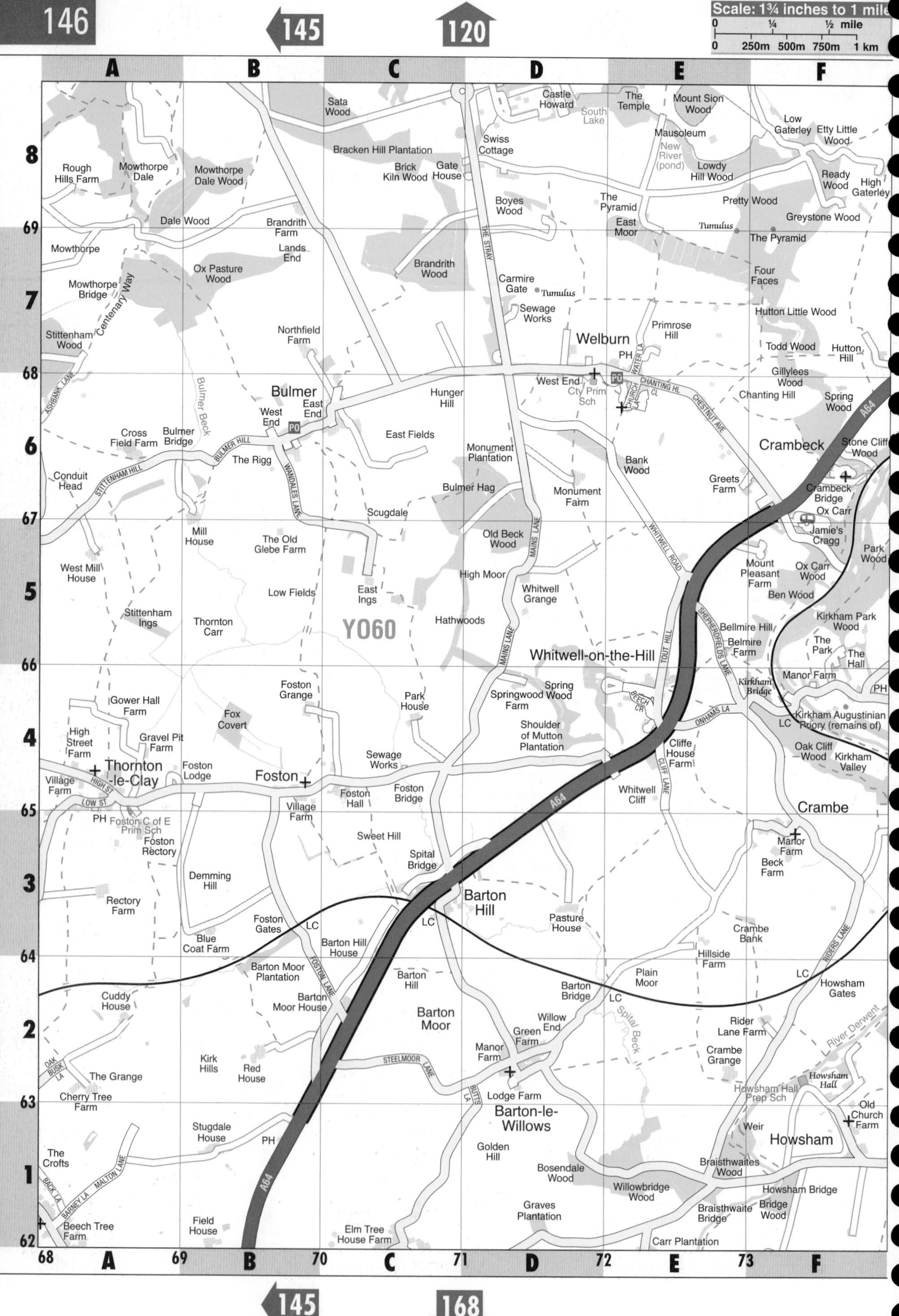

145
168

121
148
215

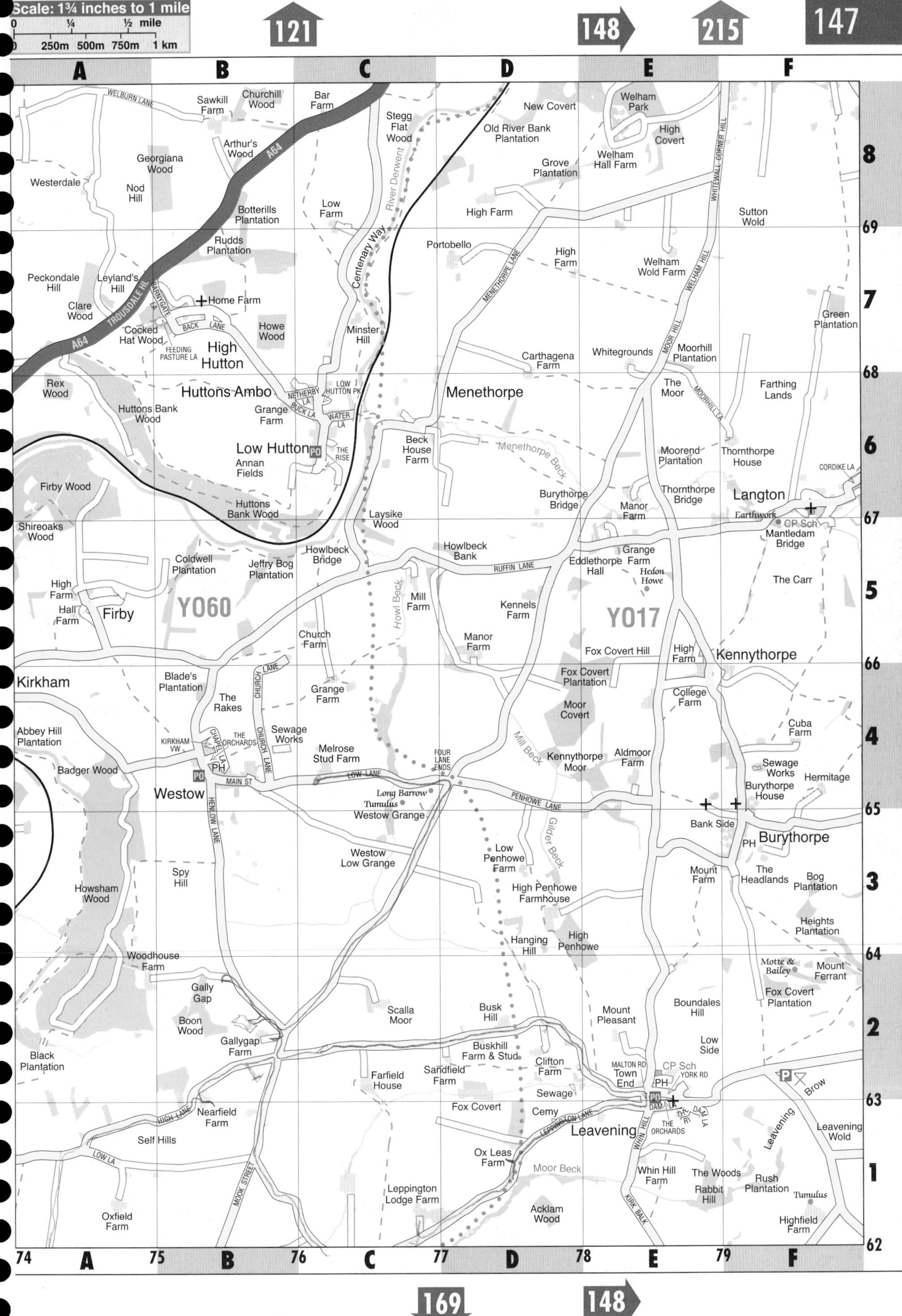

169
148

147
122

Scale: 1¾ inches to 1 mile
0 ¼ ½ mile
0 250m 500m 750m 1 km

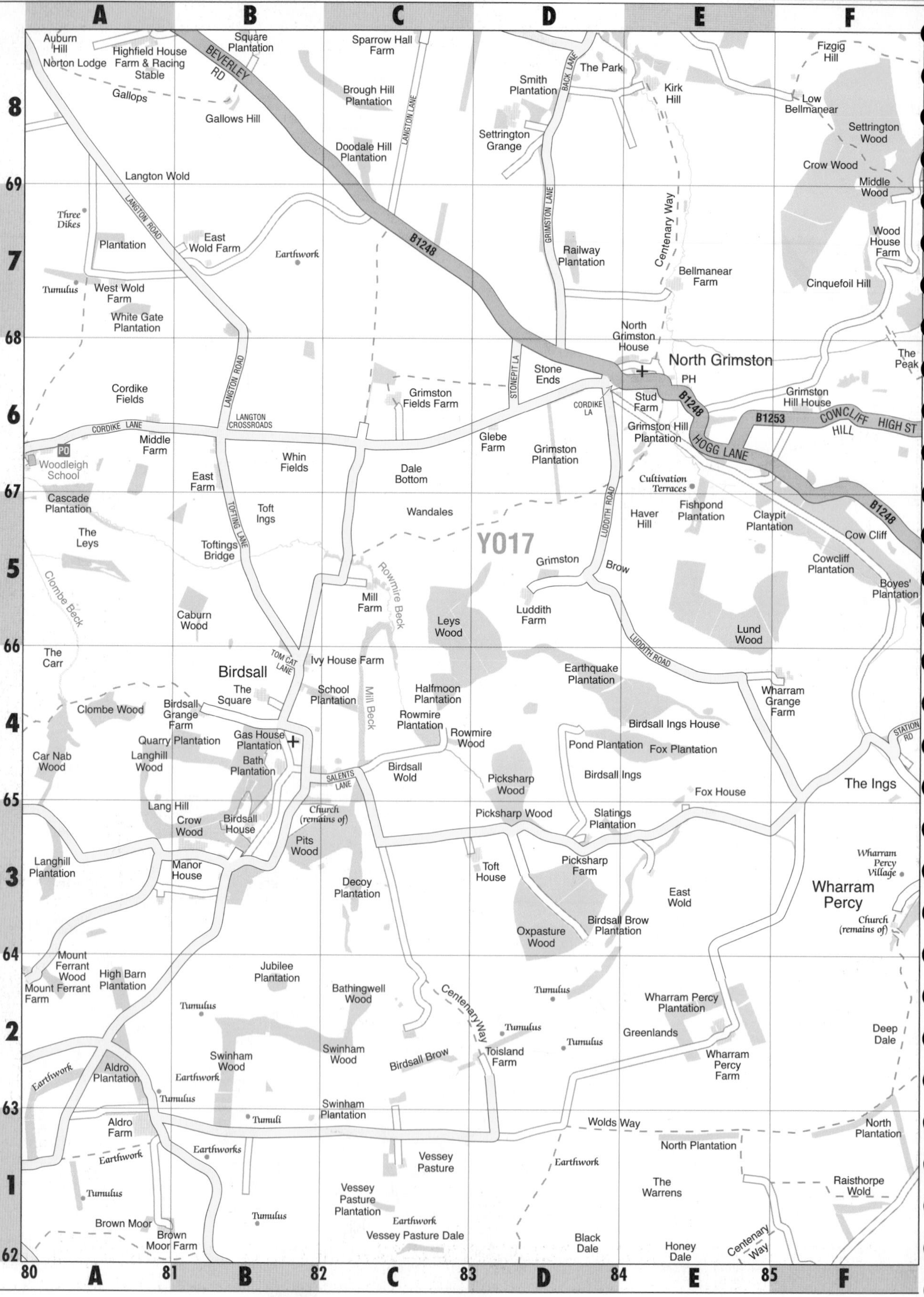

A B C D E F

8
69
7
68
6
67
5
66
4
65
3
64
2
63
1
62

Auburn Hill
Norton Lodge
Highfield House Farm & Racing Stable
Square Plantation
BEVERLEY RD
Sparrow Hall Farm
Back Lane
The Park
Fizgig Hill
Gallops
Gallows Hill
Brough Hill Plantation
Langton Lane
Smith Plantation
Kirk Hill
Low Bellmanear
Settrington Wood
Doodale Hill Plantation
Settrington Grange
Crow Wood
Middle Wood
Langton Wold
Three Dikes
Langton Road
Grimston Lane
Centenary Way
Wood House Farm
Plantation
East Wold Farm
Earthwork
B1248
Railway Plantation
Bellmanear Farm
Tumulus
West Wold Farm
Cinquefoil Hill
White Gate Plantation
North Grimston House
North Grimston
The Peak
Stonepit La
Stone Ends
PH
Cordike Fields
Langton Road
Grimston Fields Farm
Stud Farm
Grimston Hill House
Langton Crossroads
Cordike La
Cordike Lane
Middle Farm
Glebe Farm
Grimston Plantation
Grimston Hill Plantation
B1253
Cowcliff Hill
High St
Hogg Lane
PO
Woodleigh School
Whin Fields
Dale Bottom
East Farm
Cultivation Terraces
Cascade Plantation
Toft Ings
Tofting Lane
Wandales
Luddith Road
Haver Hill
Fishpond Plantation
Claypit Plantation
B1248
The Leys
Toftings Bridge
YO17
Grimston
Brow
Cow Cliff
Cowcliff Plantation
Clombe Beck
Rowmire Beck
Mill Farm
Boyes' Plantation
Caburn Wood
Leys Wood
Luddith Farm
Lund Wood
The Carr
Birdsall
Tom Cat Lane
Ivy House Farm
Luddith Road
Earthquake Plantation
The Square
School Plantation
Mill Beck
Halfmoon Plantation
Wharram Grange Farm
Clombe Wood
Birdsall Grange Farm
Rowmire Plantation
Birdsall Ings House
Station Rd
Quarry Plantation
Gas House Plantation
Rowmire Wood
Pond Plantation
Fox Plantation
Car Nab Wood
Langhill Wood
Bath Plantation
Birdsall Wold
Salents Lane
Picksharp Wood
Birdsall Ings
The Ings
Fox House
Lang Hill
Crow Wood
Birdsall House
Church (remains of)
Picksharp Wood
Slatings Plantation
Pits Wood
Langhill Plantation
Manor House
Toft House
Picksharp Farm
Wharram Percy Village
Decoy Plantation
East Wold
Wharram Percy
Church (remains of)
Birdsall Brow Plantation
Oxpasture Wood
Mount Ferrant Wood
Jubilee Plantation
High Barn Plantation
Mount Ferrant Farm
Bathingwell Wood
Centenary Way
Tumulus
Wharram Percy Plantation
Tumulus
Tumulus
Deep Dale
Tumulus
Greenlands
Swinham Wood
Swinham Wood
Birdsall Brow
Toisland Farm
Wharram Percy Farm
Earthwork
Aldro Plantation
Earthwork
Tumulus
Swinham Plantation
Aldro Farm
Tumuli
Wolds Way
North Plantation
North Plantation
Earthwork
Earthworks
Vessey Pasture
Earthwork
The Warrens
Raisthorpe Wold
Tumulus
Vessey Pasture Plantation
Earthwork
Tumulus
Brown Moor
Brown Moor Farm
Vessey Pasture Dale
Black Dale
Honey Dale
Centenary Way

80 A 81 B 82 C 83 D 84 E 85 F

147
170

Scale: 1¾ inches to 1 mile

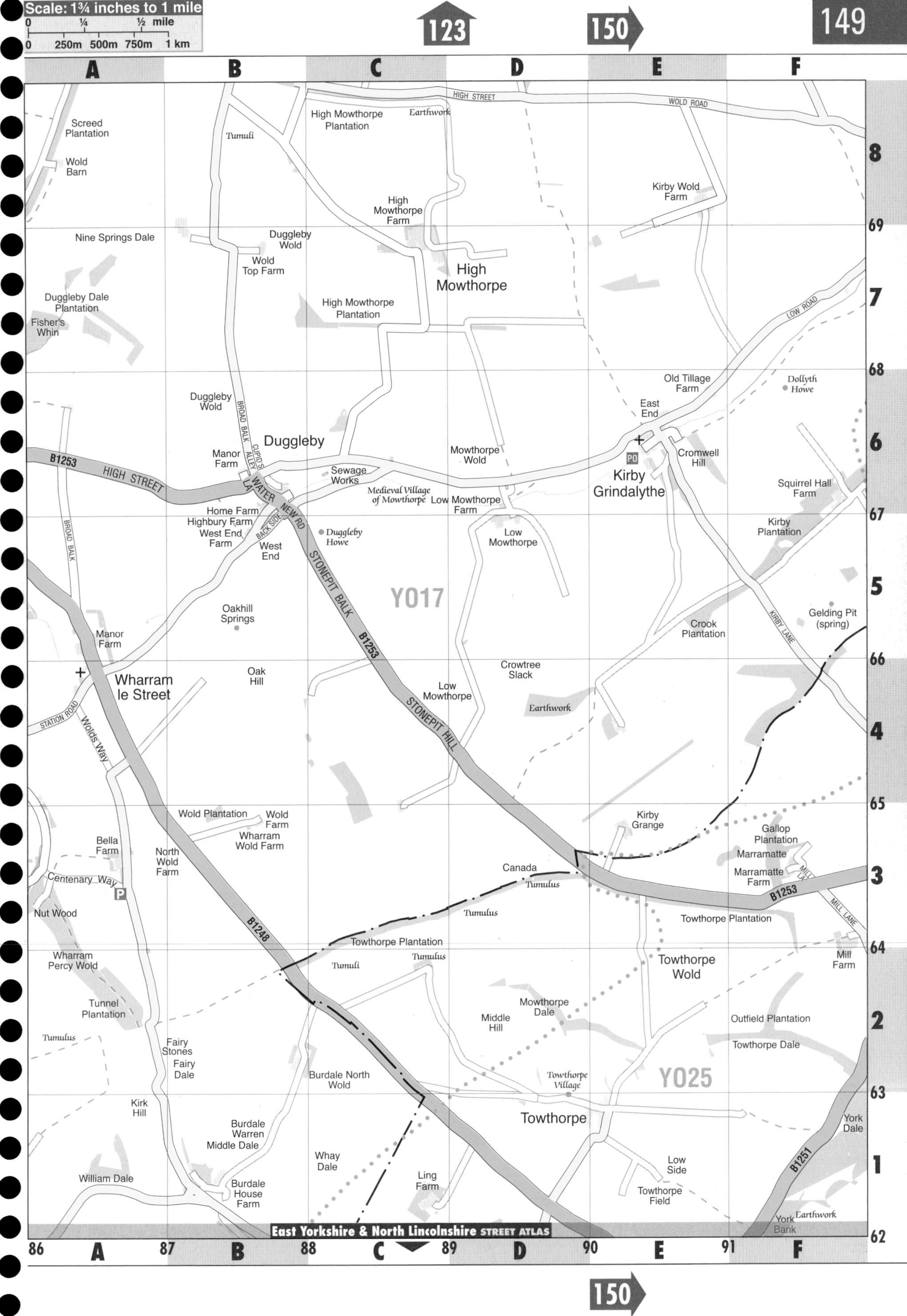

150

149
124

Scale: 1¾ inches to 1 mile

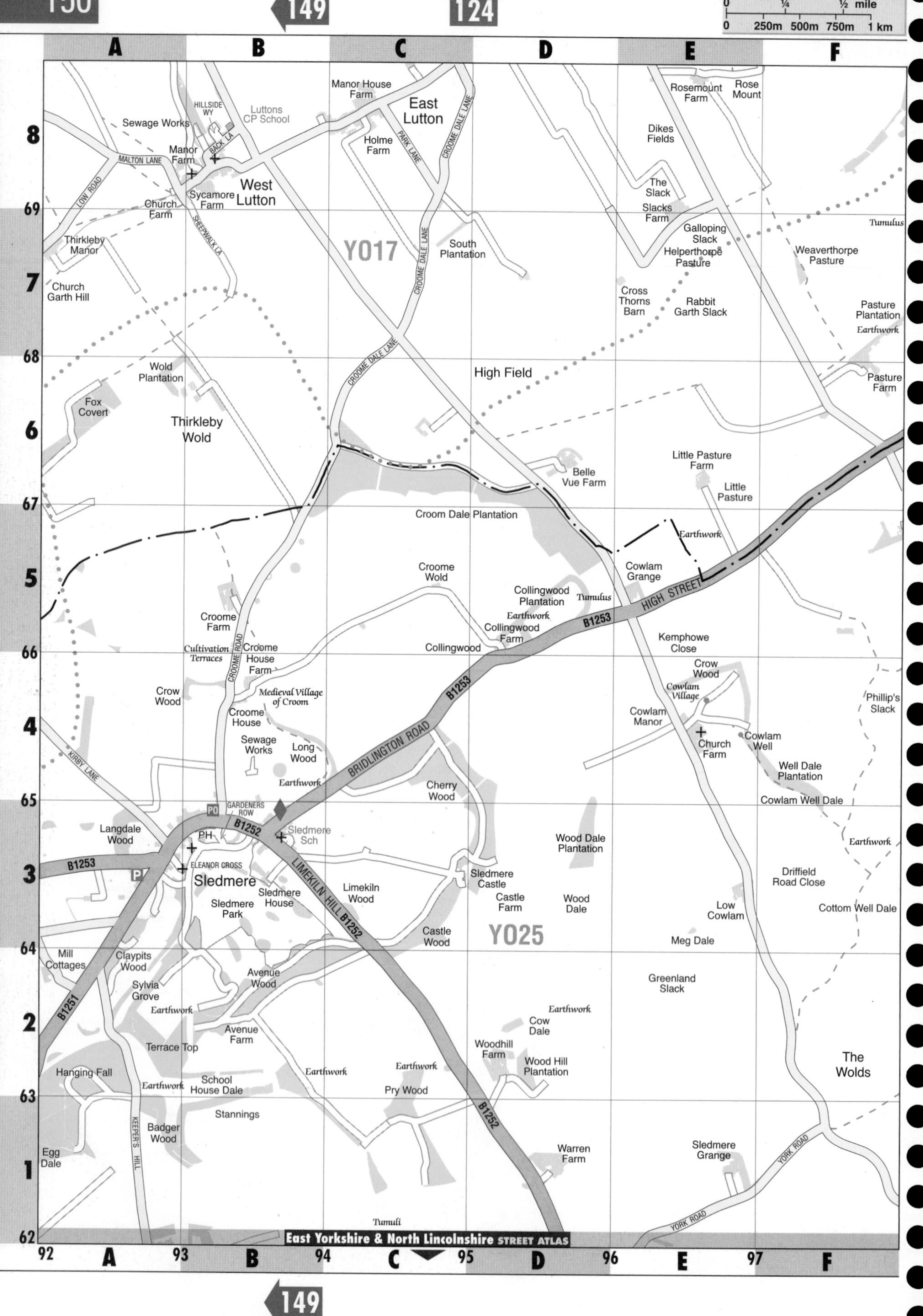

149

Scale: 1¾ inches to 1 mile

125

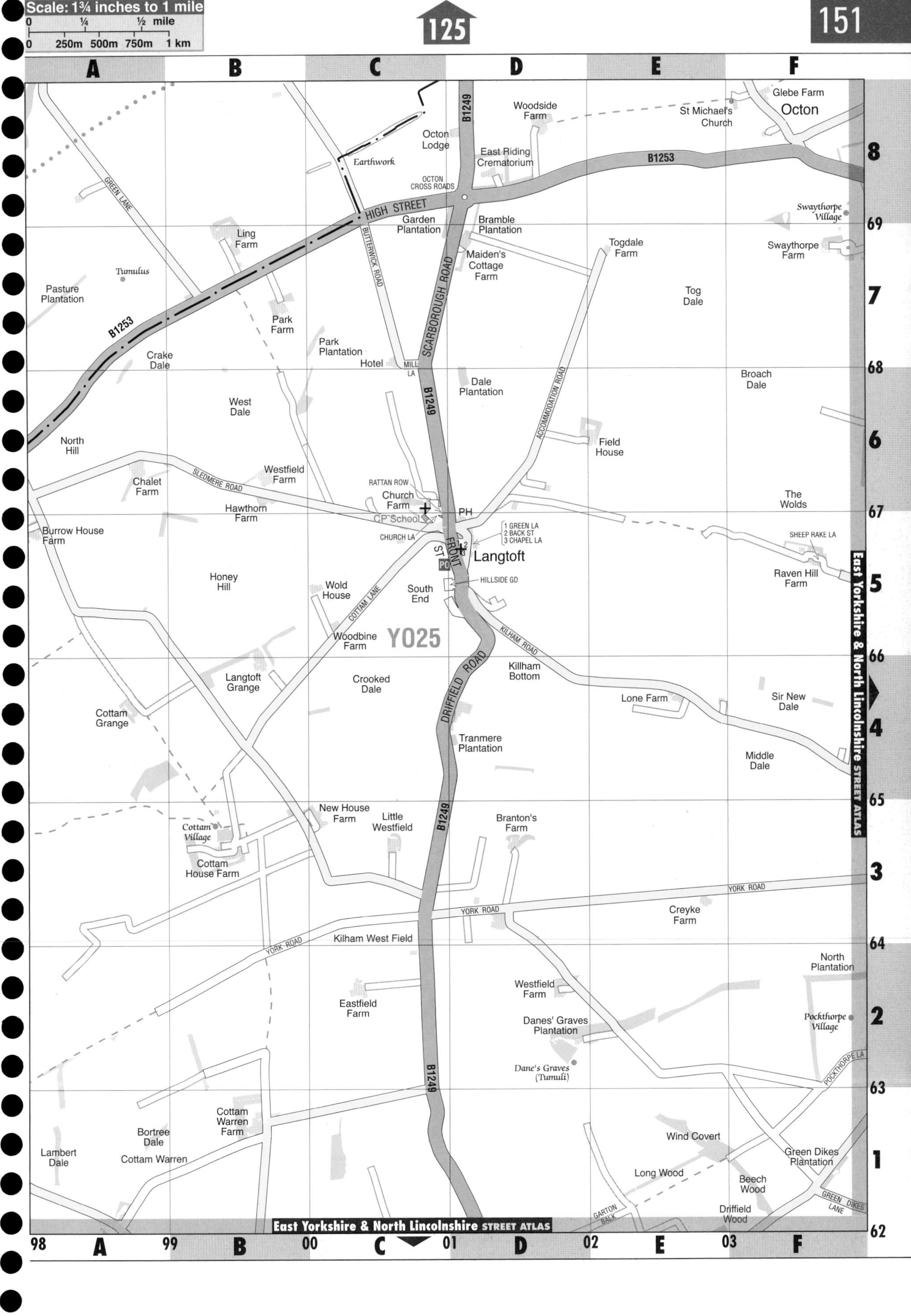

130

Scale: 1¾ inches to 1 mile
0 ¼ ½ mile
0 250m 500m 750m 1 km

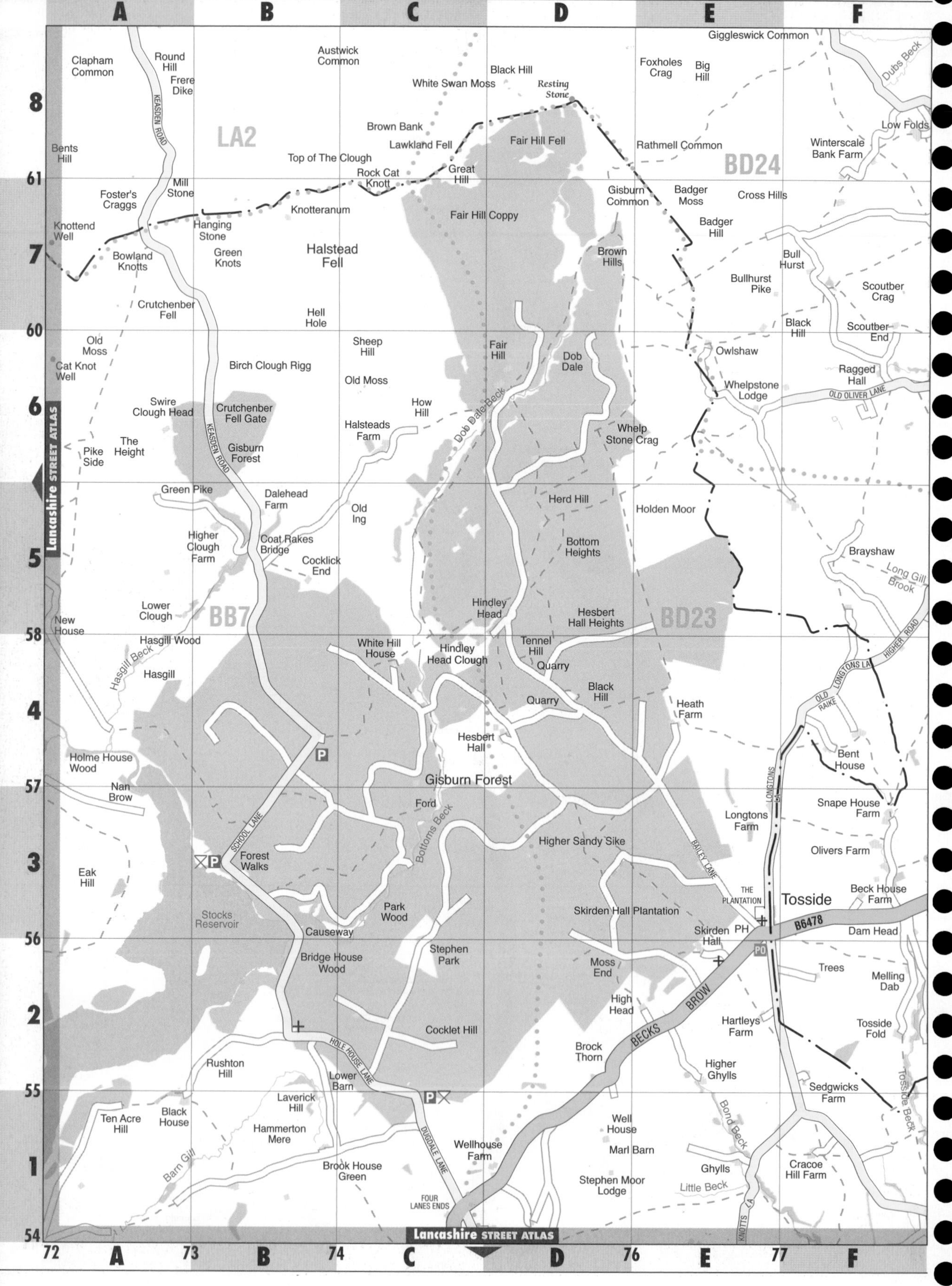

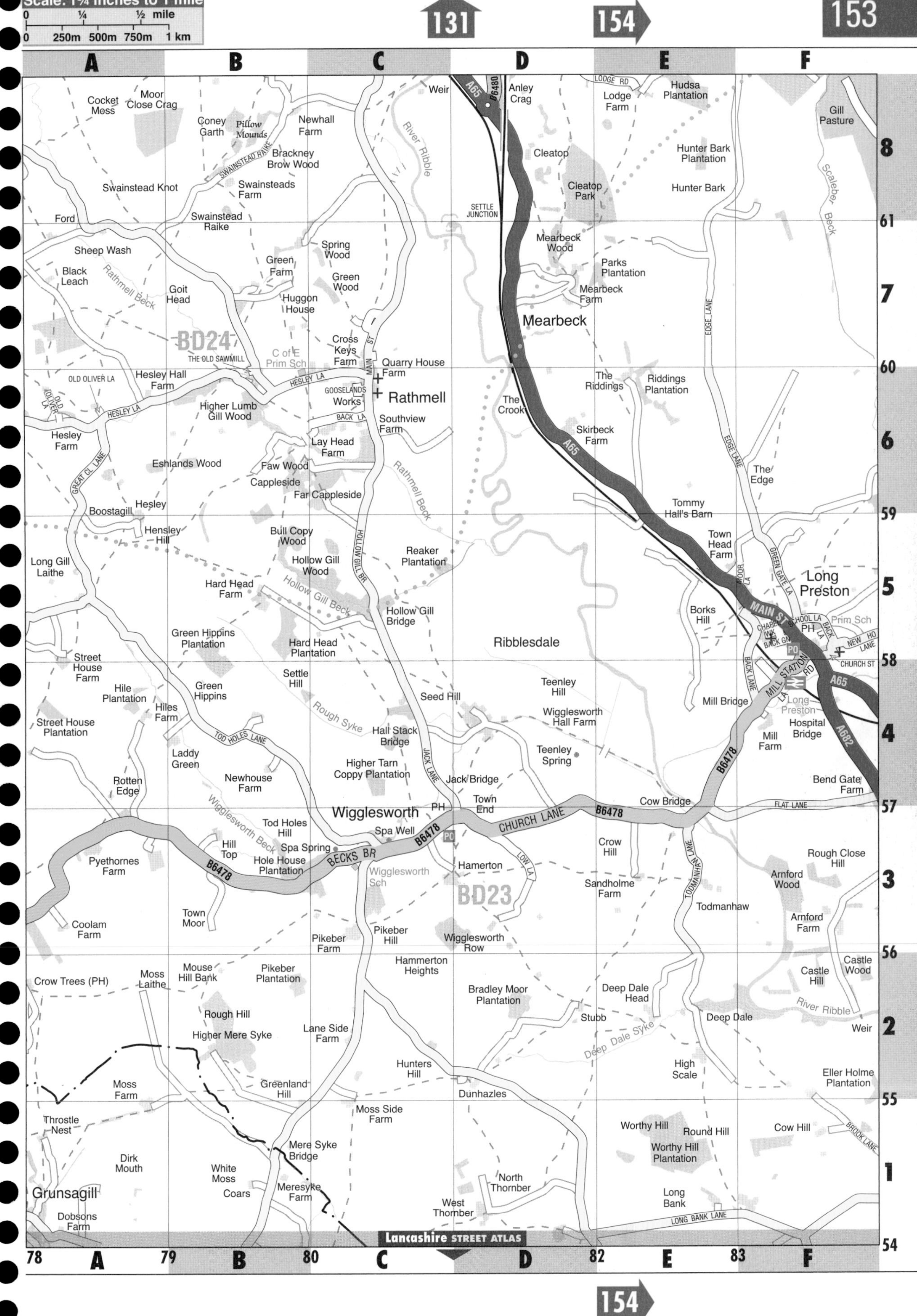
Scale: 1¾ inches to 1 mile
131
154
Cocket Moss
Moor Close Crag
Coney Garth
Pillow Mounds
Newhall Farm
Bracknev Brow Wood
Swainstead Knot
Swainsteads Farm
Swainstead Raike
Ford
Sheep Wash
Black Leach
Rathmell Beck
Goit Head
Green Farm
Spring Wood
Green Wood
Huggon House
BD24
THE OLD SAWMILL
C of E Prim Sch
Cross Keys Farm
Quarry House Farm
Rathmell
OLD OLIVER LA
Hesley Hall Farm
HESLEY LA
Higher Lumb Gill Wood
GOOSELANDS Works
BACK LA
Southview Farm
Hesley Farm
Lay Head Farm
Eshlands Wood
Faw Wood
Cappleside
Far Cappleside
Boostagill
Hesley
Hensley Hill
Bull Copy Wood
Hollow Gill Wood
Reaker Plantation
Long Gill Laithe
Hard Head Farm
Hollow Gill Beck
Hollow Gill Bridge
Green Hippins Plantation
Hard Head Plantation
Ribblesdale
Street House Farm
Hile Plantation
Green Hippins
Settle Hill
Seed Hill
Teenley Hill
Hiles Farm
Street House Plantation
Rough Syke
Hall Stack Bridge
Wigglesworth Hall Farm
TOD HOLES LANE
Laddy Green
Teenley Spring
Rotten Edge
Newhouse Farm
Higher Tarn Coppy Plantation
Jack Bridge
JACK LANE
Town End
Wigglesworth
PH
Tod Holes Hill
Spa Well
Hill Top
Spa Spring
B6478
CHURCH LANE
Cow Bridge
Pyethornes Farm
Hole House Plantation
BECKS BR
Hamerton
LOW LA
Crow Hill
Wigglesworth Sch
BD23
Sandholme Farm
Town Moor
Coolam Farm
Pikeber Farm
Pikeber Hill
Wigglesworth Row
Todmanhaw
TODMANHAW LANE
Hammerton Heights
Crow Trees (PH)
Moss Laithe
Mouse Hill Bank
Pikeber Plantation
Bradley Moor Plantation
Deep Dale Head
Rough Hill
Stubb
Deep Dale
Higher Mere Syke
Lane Side Farm
Deep Dale Syke
Hunters Hill
High Scale
Moss Farm
Greenland Hill
Dunhazles
Throstle Nest
Moss Side Farm
Worthy Hill
Round Hill
Mere Syke Bridge
Worthy Hill Plantation
Dirk Mouth
White Moss
Coars
Meresyke Farm
North Thornber
Grunsagill
Long Bank
West Thornber
Dobsons Farm
LONG BANK LANE
Weir
River Ribble
A65
B6480
Anley Crag
LODGE RD
Lodge Farm
Hudsa Plantation
Gill Pasture
Cleatop
Hunter Bark Plantation
Cleatop Park
Hunter Bark
Scaleber Beck
SETTLE JUNCTION
Mearbeck Wood
Parks Plantation
Mearbeck Farm
Mearbeck
EDGE LANE
The Riddings
Riddings Plantation
The Crook
Skirbeck Farm
The Edge
Tommy Hall's Barn
Town Head Farm
GREEN GATE LA
MOOR LA
Long Preston
Borks Hill
MAIN ST
SCHOOL LA
Prim Sch
CHAPEL
BACK GN
PO
BACK LA
NEW HO LANE
CHURCH ST
BACK LANE
MILL STATION RD
A65
Mill Bridge
Long Preston
Hospital Bridge
Mill Farm
A682
B6478
Bend Gate Farm
FLAT LANE
Rough Close Hill
Arnford Wood
Arnford Farm
Castle Hill
Castle Wood
River Ribble
Weir
Eller Holme Plantation
Cow Hill
BROOK LANE
Lancashire STREET ATLAS
78
79
80
82
83
54
55
56
57
58
59
60
61
1
2
3
4
5
6
7
8
A
B
C
D
E
F

154

153
132

Scale: 1¾ inches to 1 mile

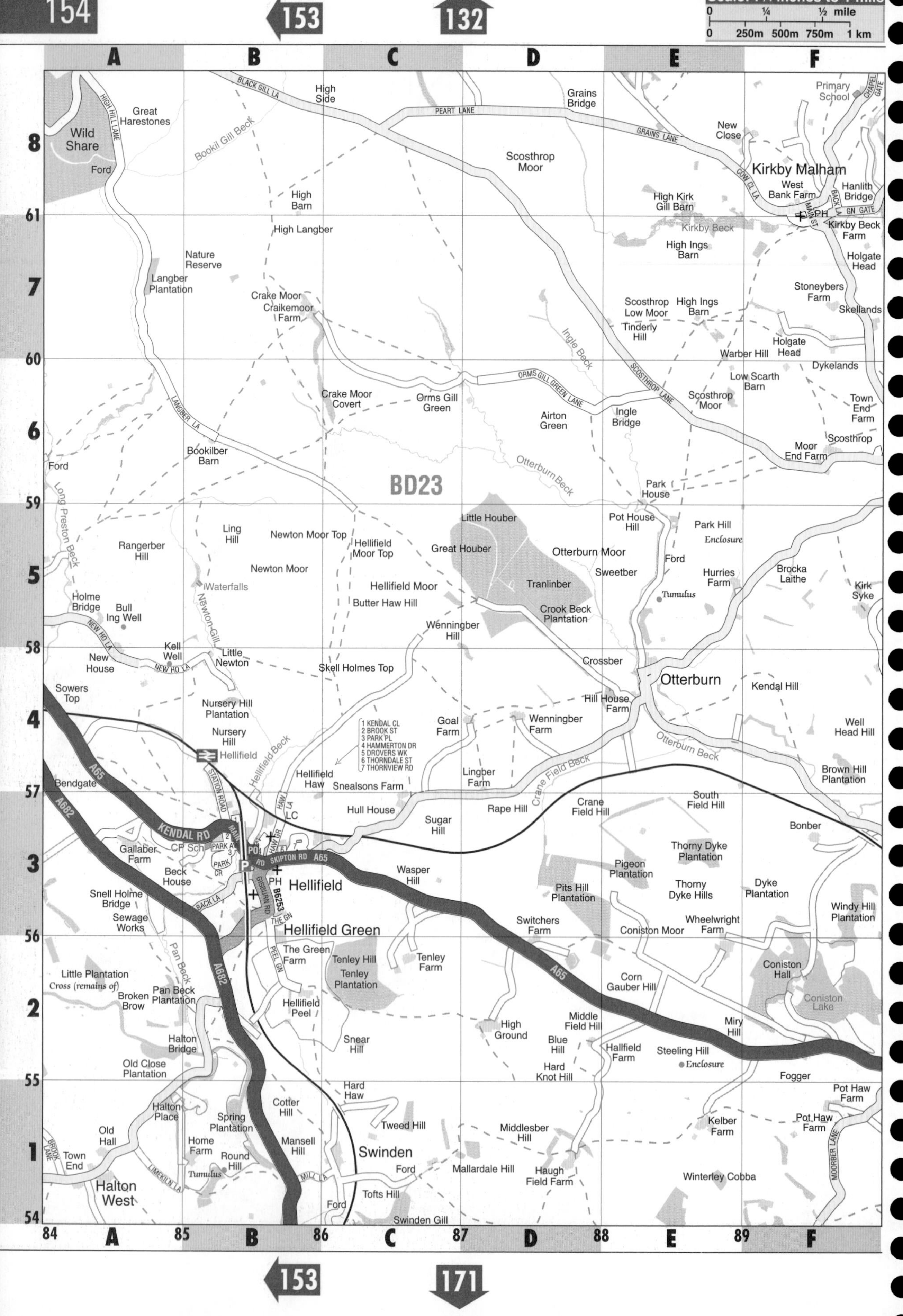

153
171

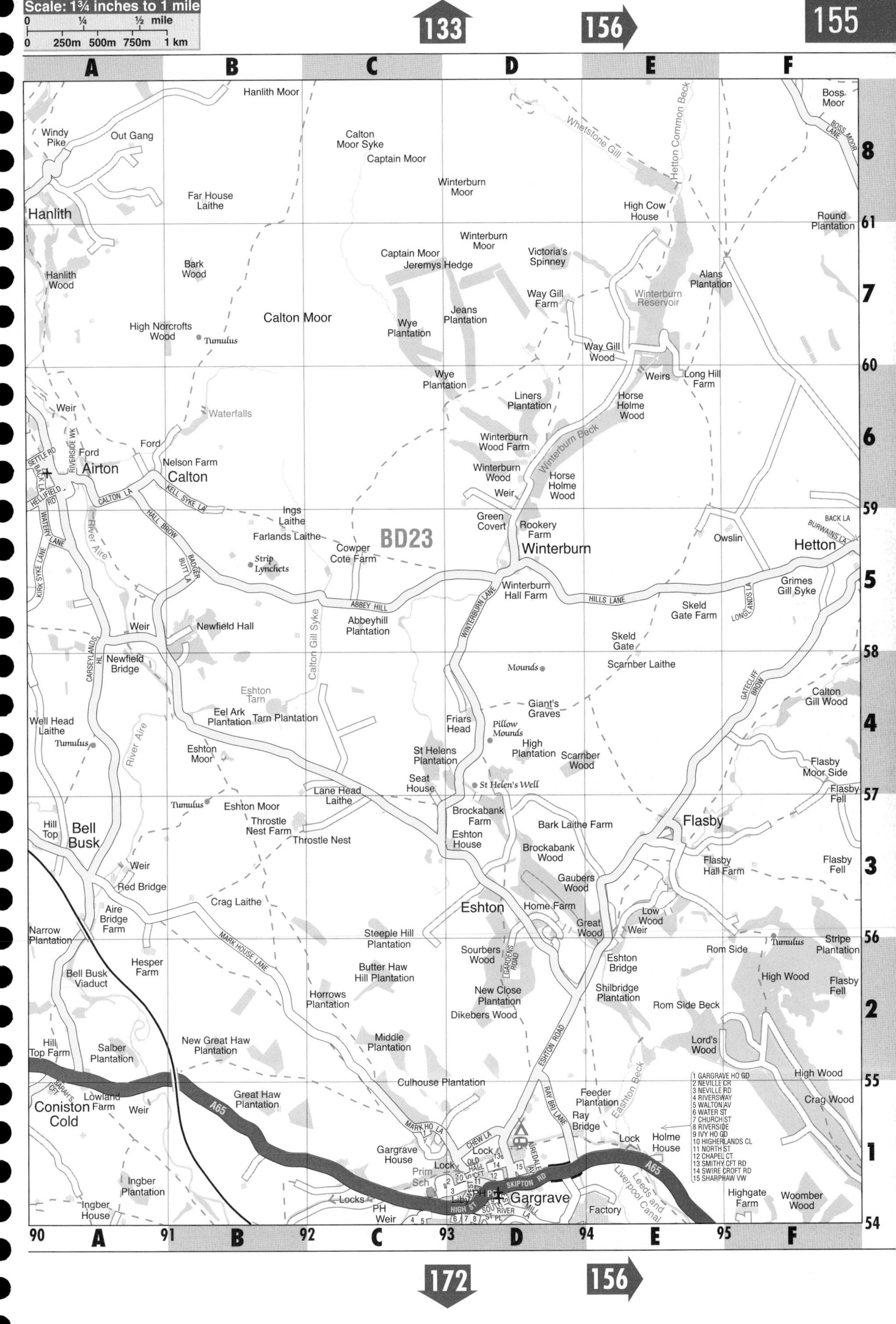
Scale: 1¾ inches to 1 mile
133
156
Hanlith Moor
Windy Pike
Out Gang
Hanlith
Far House Laithe
Calton Moor Syke
Captain Moor
Winterburn Moor
High Cow House
Hetton Common Beck
Whetstone Gill
Boss Moor
Round Plantation
Hanlith Wood
Bark Wood
Captain Moor
Jeremys Hedge
Victoria's Spinney
Alans Plantation
Winterburn Reservoir
Way Gill Farm
Jeans Plantation
Calton Moor
High Norcrofts Wood
Tumulus
Wye Plantation
Way Gill Wood
Weirs
Long Hill Farm
Wye Plantation
Liners Plantation
Horse Holme Wood
Weir
Waterfalls
Winterburn Beck
Winterburn Wood Farm
Ford
Ford
Airton
Nelson Farm
Calton
Winterburn Wood
Horse Holme Wood
Weir
Ings Laithe
Green Covert
Rookery Farm
Winterburn
Owslin
Hetton
Farlands Laithe
BD23
Cowper Cote Farm
Strip Lynchets
River Aire
Winterburn Hall Farm
Grimes Gill Syke
Skeld Gate Farm
Abbeyhill Plantation
Newfield Hall
Weir
Skeld Gate
Scarnber Laithe
Newfield Bridge
Calton Gill Syke
Mounds
Eshton Tarn
Calton Gill Wood
Giant's Graves
Eel Ark Plantation
Tarn Plantation
Friars Head
Pillow Mounds
Well Head Laithe
Tumulus
River Aire
Eshton Moor
St Helens Plantation
High Plantation
Scarnber Wood
Flasby Moor Side
Seat House
St Helen's Well
Flasby Fell
Lane Head Laithe
Tumulus
Eshton Moor
Brockabank Farm
Bark Laithe Farm
Flasby
Hill Top
Bell Busk
Throstle Nest Farm
Throstle Nest
Eshton House
Brockabank Wood
Flasby Hall Farm
Flasby Fell
Weir
Red Bridge
Gaubers Wood
Crag Laithe
Eshton
Home Farm
Aire Bridge Farm
Low Wood
Great Wood
Weir
Narrow Plantation
Steeple Hill Plantation
Tumulus
Stripe Plantation
Hesper Farm
Sourbers Wood
Eshton Bridge
Rom Side
Butter Haw Hill Plantation
High Wood
Bell Busk Viaduct
Shilbridge Plantation
Flasby Fell
New Close Plantation
Horrows Plantation
Dikebers Wood
Rom Side Beck
Hill Top Farm
Salber Plantation
New Great Haw Plantation
Middle Plantation
Lord's Wood
High Wood
Lowland Farm
Great Haw Plantation
Culhouse Plantation
Feeder Plantation
Eshton Beck
Coniston Cold
Weir
Ray Bridge
Crag Wood
Lock
Holme House
Gargrave House
Lock
Lock
Prim Sch
Leeds and Liverpool Canal
Locks
PH
Liby
Gargrave
Factory
Highgate Farm
Woomber Wood
Ingber Plantation
Ingber House
PH Weir
1 GARGRAVE HO GD
2 NEVILLE CR
3 NEVILLE RD
4 RIVERSWAY
5 WALTON AV
6 WATER ST
7 CHURCH ST
8 RIVERSIDE
9 IVY HO GD
10 HIGHERLANDS CL
11 NORTH ST
12 CHAPEL CT
13 SMITHY CFT RD
14 SWIRE CROFT RD
15 SHARPHAW VW
172
156

155
134

Scale: 1¾ inches to 1 mile

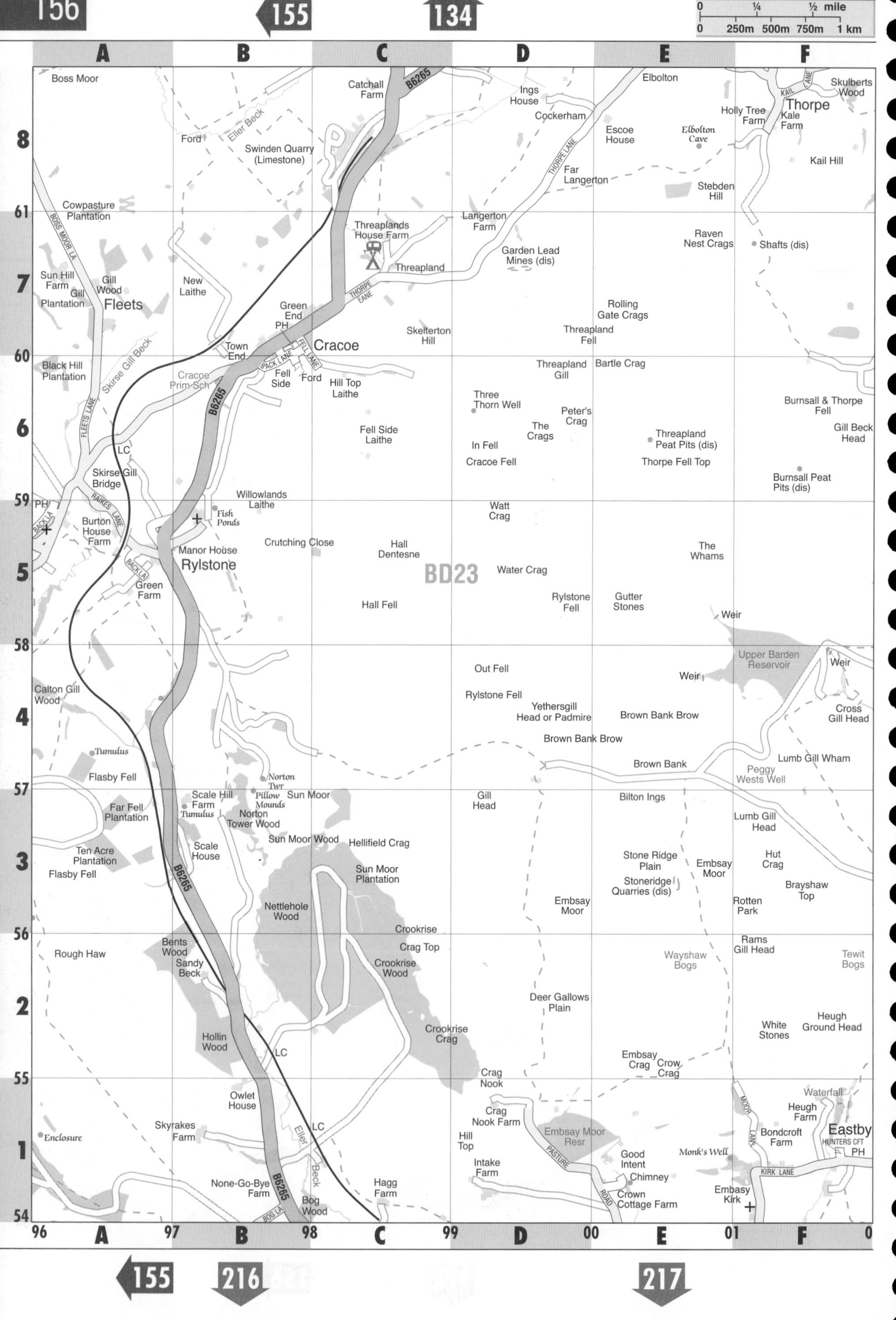

155
216
217

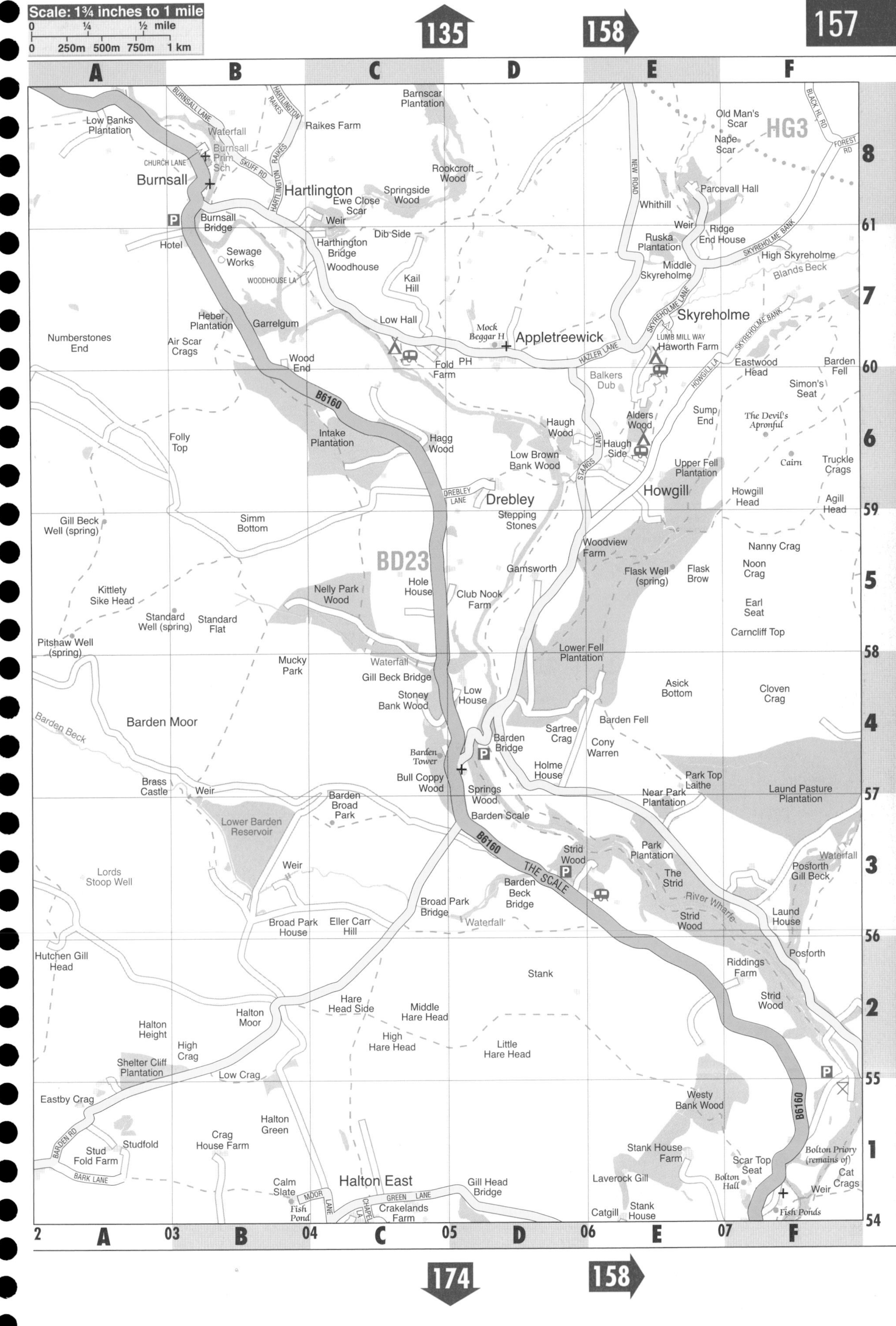
Scale: 1¾ inches to 1 mile
135
158
A B C D E F
Low Banks Plantation
Burnsall
Hartlington
Raikes Farm
Barnscar Plantation
Rookcroft Wood
Springside Wood
Ewe Close Scar
Weir
Dib Side
Burnsall Bridge
Hotel
Sewage Works
Harthington Bridge
Woodhouse
Kail Hill
Low Hall
Heber Plantation
Garrelgum
Numberstones End
Air Scar Crags
Wood End
Mock Beggar H
Appletreewick
Fold Farm
PH
Old Man's Scar
Nape Scar
HG3
Parcevall Hall
Whithill
Ruska Plantation
Ridge End House
Middle Skyreholme
High Skyreholme
Blands Beck
Skyreholme
Haworth Farm
Eastwood Head
Barden Fell
Balkers Dub
Simon's Seat
Intake Plantation
Hagg Wood
Folly Top
Haugh Wood
Alders Wood
Haugh Side
Low Brown Bank Wood
Sump End
The Devil's Apronful
Cairn
Truckle Crags
Upper Fell Plantation
Drebley
Howgill
Howgill Head
Agill Head
Stepping Stones
Gill Beck Well (spring)
Simm Bottom
BD23
Woodview Farm
Nanny Crag
Gamsworth
Flask Well (spring)
Flask Brow
Noon Crag
Hole House
Nelly Park Wood
Club Nook Farm
Kittlety Sike Head
Standard Well (spring)
Standard Flat
Earl Seat
Carncliff Top
Pitshaw Well (spring)
Mucky Park
Waterfall
Lower Fell Plantation
Gill Beck Bridge
Stoney Bank Wood
Low House
Asick Bottom
Cloven Crag
Barden Moor
Barden Beck
Barden Fell
Sartree Crag
Barden Bridge
Cony Warren
Barden Tower
Holme House
Bull Coppy Wood
Park Top Laithe
Brass Castle
Weir
Barden Broad Park
Springs Wood
Near Park Plantation
Laund Pasture Plantation
Lower Barden Reservoir
Barden Scale
Lords Stoop Well
Strid Wood
Park Plantation
Posforth Gill Beck
The Strid
Barden Beck Bridge
Broad Park Bridge
THE SCALE
River Wharfe
Laund House
Broad Park House
Eller Carr Hill
Strid Wood
Hutchen Gill Head
Posforth
Riddings Farm
Stank
Hare Head Side
Middle Hare Head
Halton Moor
Halton Height
High Crag
High Hare Head
Little Hare Head
Shelter Cliff Plantation
Low Crag
Eastby Crag
Westy Bank Wood
Halton Green
Studfold
Stud Fold Farm
Crag House Farm
Stank House Farm
Scar Top Seat
Bolton Priory (remains of)
Cat Crags
Calm Slate
Halton East
Gill Head Bridge
Laverock Gill
Bolton Hall
Weir
Fish Pond
Crakelands Farm
Catgill
Stank House
Fish Ponds
B6160
2 03 04 05 06 07
8 61 7 60 6 59 5 58 4 57 3 56 2 55 1 54
174
158

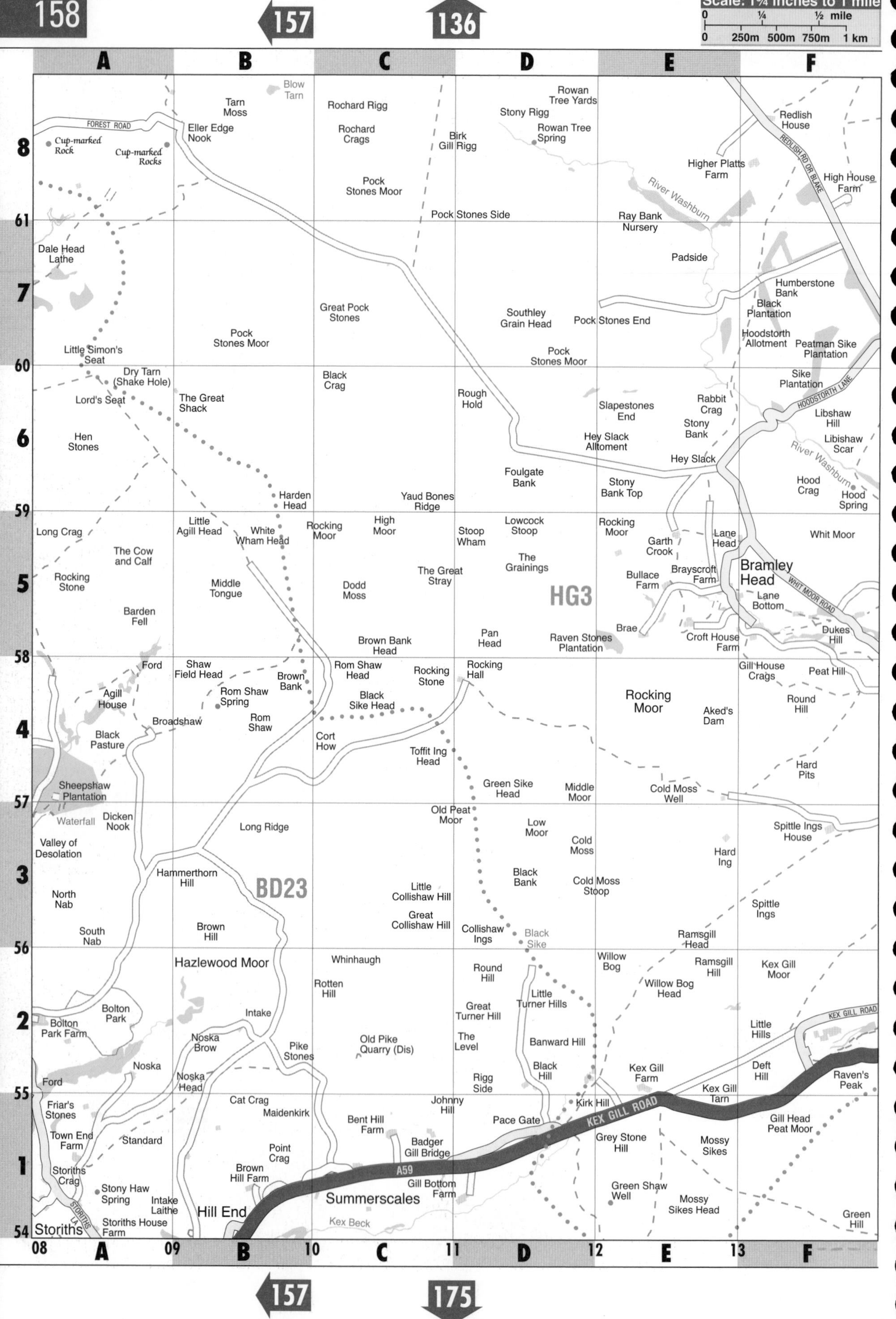
157
136
Scale: 1¾ inches to 1 mile
0 ¼ ½ mile
0 250m 500m 750m 1 km
A
B
C
D
E
F
Blow Tarn
Tarn Moss
Rochard Rigg
Rowan Tree Yards
Stony Rigg
Redlish House
FOREST ROAD
Eller Edge Nook
Rochard Crags
Birk Gill Rigg
Rowan Tree Spring
Cup-marked Rock
Cup-marked Rocks
REDLISH RD OR BLAKE
8
Higher Platts Farm
High House Farm
Pock Stones Moor
River Washburn
61
Pock Stones Side
Ray Bank Nursery
Dale Head Lathe
Padside
7
Humberstone Bank
Great Pock Stones
Black Plantation
Southley Grain Head
Pock Stones End
Pock Stones Moor
Hoodstorth Allotment
Peatman Sike Plantation
Little Simon's Seat
Pock Stones Moor
60
Dry Tarn (Shake Hole)
Black Crag
Sike Plantation
Lord's Seat
The Great Shack
Rough Hold
Slapestones End
Rabbit Crag
HOODSTORTH LANE
Libshaw Hill
Hen Stones
Stony Bank
6
Hey Slack Allotment
Libishaw Scar
River Washburn
Hey Slack
Foulgate Bank
Hood Crag
Harden Head
Yaud Bones Ridge
Stony Bank Top
Hood Spring
59
Long Crag
Little Agill Head
White Wham Head
Rocking Moor
High Moor
Stoop Wham
Lowcock Stoop
Rocking Moor
Lane Head
Whit Moor
The Cow and Calf
Garth Crook
The Grainings
Bramley Head
Rocking Stone
Middle Tongue
Dodd Moss
The Great Stray
Bullace Farm
Brayscroft Farm
5
HG3
Lane Bottom
WHIT MOOR ROAD
Barden Fell
Brae
Pan Head
Dukes Hill
Brown Bank Head
Raven Stones Plantation
Croft House Farm
58
Ford
Shaw Field Head
Rom Shaw Head
Rocking Stone
Rocking Hall
Gill House Crags
Peat Hill
Brown Bank
Rom Shaw Spring
Black Sike Head
Agill House
Rocking Moor
Round Hill
Aked's Dam
Broadshaw
Rom Shaw
4
Black Pasture
Cort How
Toffit Ing Head
Hard Pits
Sheepshaw Plantation
Green Sike Head
Middle Moor
Cold Moss Well
57
Old Peat Moor
Waterfall
Dicken Nook
Long Ridge
Low Moor
Spittle Ings House
Valley of Desolation
Cold Moss
Hard Ing
Hammerthorn Hill
3
BD23
Black Bank
Little Collishaw Hill
Cold Moss Stoop
North Nab
Spittle Ings
Great Collishaw Hill
Brown Hill
Collishaw Ings
South Nab
Black Sike
Ramsgill Head
56
Hazlewood Moor
Whinhaugh
Willow Bog
Ramsgill Hill
Kex Gill Moor
Round Hill
Rotten Hill
Willow Bog Head
Little Turner Hills
Great Turner Hill
Bolton Park
Intake
2
KEX GILL ROAD
Bolton Park Farm
Little Hills
Noska Brow
Old Pike Quarry (Dis)
The Level
Banward Hill
Pike Stones
Noska
Deft Hill
Black Hill
Kex Gill Farm
Noska Head
Raven's Peak
Ford
Rigg Side
55
Kex Gill Tarn
Cat Crag
Johnny Hill
Kirk Hill
Friar's Stones
Maidenkirk
KEX GILL ROAD
Bent Hill Farm
Pace Gate
Gill Head Peat Moor
Town End Farm
Standard
Badger Gill Bridge
Grey Stone Hill
Mossy Sikes
Point Crag
1
A59
Storiths Crag
Brown Hill Farm
Gill Bottom Farm
Green Shaw Well
Stony Haw Spring
Intake Laithe
Summerscales
Mossy Sikes Head
Green Hill
STORITHS LA
Hill End
Kex Beck
Storiths House Farm
54
Storiths
08
09
10
11
12
13
157
175

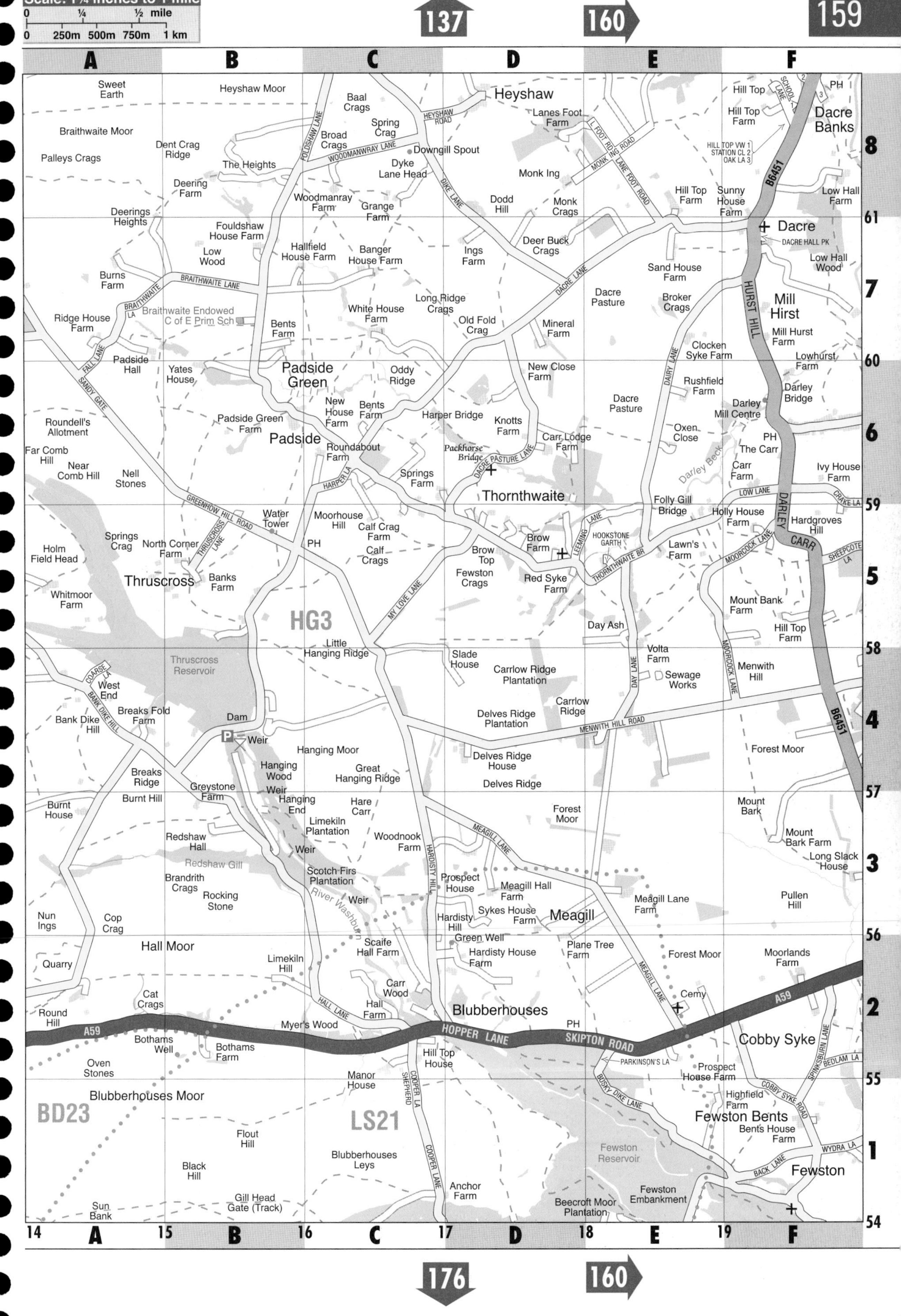
Scale: 1¾ inches to 1 mile
0 ¼ ½ mile
0 250m 500m 750m 1 km
137
160
176
160
A B C D E F
8 61 7 60 6 59 5 58 4 57 3 56 2 55 1 54
14 15 16 17 18 19
Sweet Earth
Heyshaw Moor
Baal Crags
Spring Crag
Heyshaw
Lanes Foot Farm
Hill Top
Hill Top Farm
Dacre Banks
PH
Braithwaite Moor
Palleys Crags
Dent Crag Ridge
Broad Crags
The Heights
Downgill Spout
Dyke Lane Head
Monk Ing
HILL TOP VW 1
STATION CL 2
OAK LA 3
Deering Farm
Woodmanray Farm
Grange Farm
Dodd Hill
Monk Crags
Hill Top Farm
Sunny House Farm
Low Hall Farm
Deerings Heights
Fouldshaw House Farm
Low Wood
Hallfield House Farm
Banger House Farm
Ings Farm
Deer Buck Crags
Dacre
DACRE HALL PK
Low Hall Wood
Burns Farm
Sand House Farm
Dacre Pasture
Broker Crags
Mill Hirst
Mill Hurst Farm
Ridge House Farm
Braithwaite Endowed C of E Prim Sch
Bents Farm
White House Farm
Long Ridge Crags
Old Fold Crag
Mineral Farm
Clocken Syke Farm
Lowhurst Farm
Padside Hall
Yates House
Padside Green
Oddy Ridge
New Close Farm
Rushfield Farm
Darley Bridge
New House Farm
Bents Farm
Dacre Pasture
Darley Mill Centre
Roundell's Allotment
Padside Green Farm
Harper Bridge
Knotts Farm
Oxen Close
PH
Padside
Roundabout Farm
Carr Lodge Farm
The Carr
Far Comb Hill
Near Comb Hill
Packhorse Bridge
Carr Farm
Ivy House Farm
Nell Stones
Springs Farm
Thornthwaite
Darley Beck
Folly Gill Bridge
Holly House Farm
Hardgroves Hill
Water Tower
Moorhouse Hill
Calf Crag Farm
Holm Field Head
Springs Crag
North Corner Farm
PH
Calf Crags
Brow Top
Brow Farm
HOOKSTONE GARTH
Lawn's Farm
Thruscross
Banks Farm
Fewston Crags
Red Syke Farm
Mount Bank Farm
Whitmoor Farm
HG3
Day Ash
Hill Top Farm
Little Hanging Ridge
Slade House
Volta Farm
Thruscross Reservoir
Carrolow Ridge Plantation
Sewage Works
Menwith Hill
West End
Carrlow Ridge
Bank Dike Hill
Breaks Fold Farm
Dam
Delves Ridge Plantation
Weir
Hanging Moor
Forest Moor
Delves Ridge House
Breaks Ridge
Hanging Wood
Great Hanging Ridge
Greystone Farm
Weir
Delves Ridge
Burnt House
Burnt Hill
Hanging End
Hare Carr
Forest Moor
Mount Bark
Limekiln Plantation
Redshaw Hall
Woodnook Farm
Mount Bark Farm
Weir
Long Slack House
Redshaw Gill
Brandrith Crags
Scotch Firs Plantation
Prospect House
Meagill Hall Farm
Rocking Stone
River Washburn
Weir
Meagill Lane Farm
Pullen Hill
Nun Ings
Cop Crag
Hardisty Hill
Sykes House Farm
Meagill
Green Well
Hall Moor
Scaife Hall Farm
Hardisty House Farm
Plane Tree Farm
Forest Moor
Moorlands Farm
Quarry
Limekiln Hill
Carr Wood
Cemy
Cat Crags
Hall Farm
Blubberhouses
Round Hill
A59
Myer's Wood
PH
A59
Bothams Well
Bothams Farm
HOPPER LANE
SKIPTON ROAD
Cobby Syke
Hill Top House
PARKINSON'S LA
Oven Stones
Manor House
Prospect House Farm
Highfield Farm
Blubberhouses Moor
Fewston Bents
BD23
LS21
Bents House Farm
Flout Hill
Fewston Reservoir
Blubberhouses Leys
Fewston
Black Hill
Anchor Farm
Fewston Embankment
Sun Bank
Gill Head Gate (Track)
Beecroft Moor Plantation
FOLDSHAW LANE
WOODMANWRAY LANE
HEYSHAW ROAD
DIKE LANE
L FOOT RD
MONK ING ROAD
LANE FOOT ROAD
SCHOOL LANE
B6451
BRAITHWAITE LANE
BRAITHWAITE LA
DACRE LANE
HURST HILL
DAIRY LANE
FALL LANE
SANDY GATE
HARPER LA
DACRE PASTURE LANE
LOW LANE
CRAKE LA
DARLEY
CARR
GREENHOW HILL ROAD
THRUSCROSS LANE
LEEMING LANE
THORNTHWAITE BR
MOORCOCK LANE
SHEEPCOTE LA
MY LOVE LANE
COARSE LA
BANK DIKE HILL
DAY LANE
MOORCOCK LANE
MENWITH HILL ROAD
B6451
MEAGILL LANE
HARDISTY HILL
MEAGILL LANE
HALL LANE
SPINKSBURN LANE
BEDLAM LA
COBBY SYKE ROAD
BUSKY DIKE LANE
COOPER LA
SHEPHERD
COOPER LANE
WYDRA LA
BACK LANE

Scale: 1¾ inches to 1 mile
0 ¼ ½ mile
0 250m 500m 750m 1 km

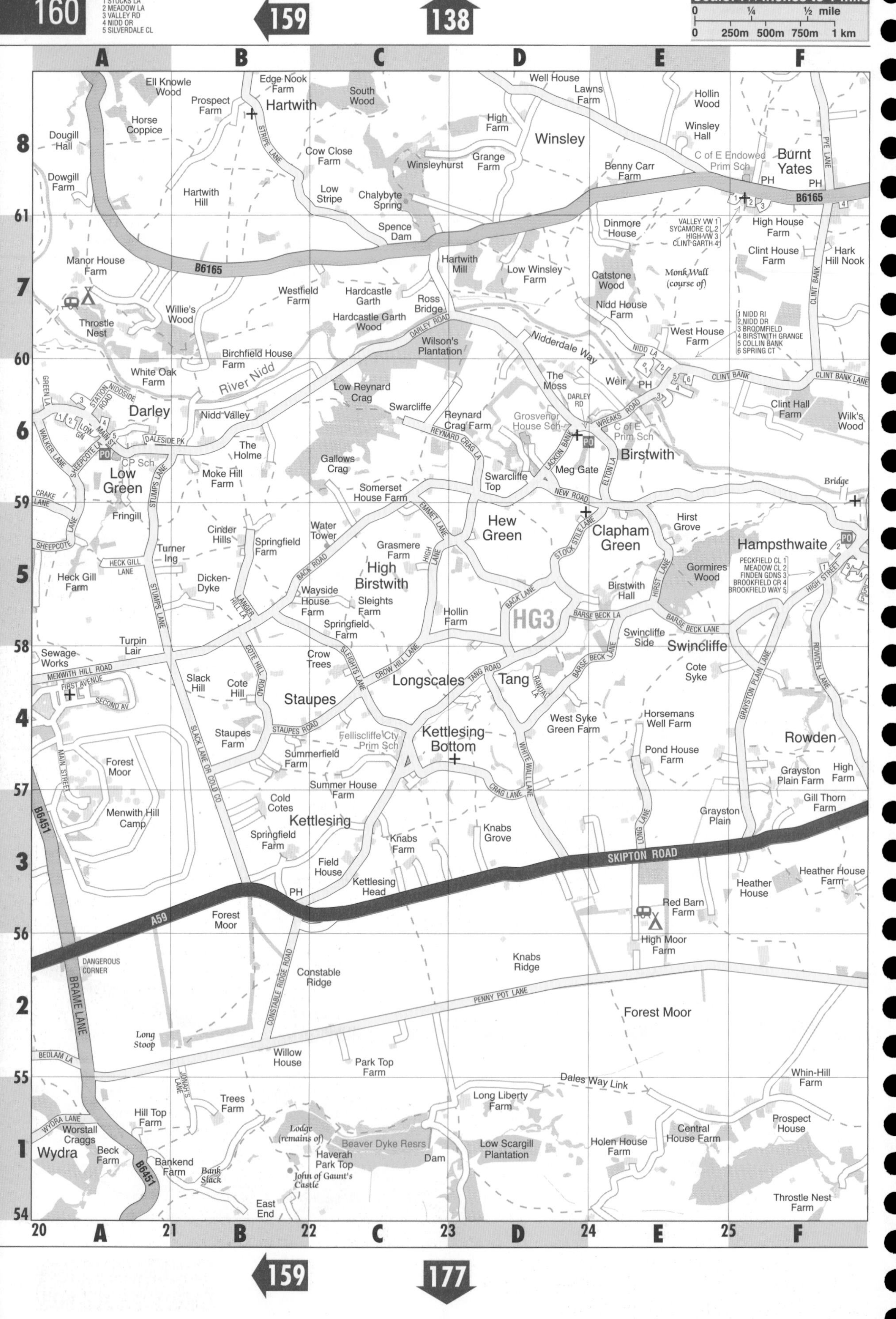

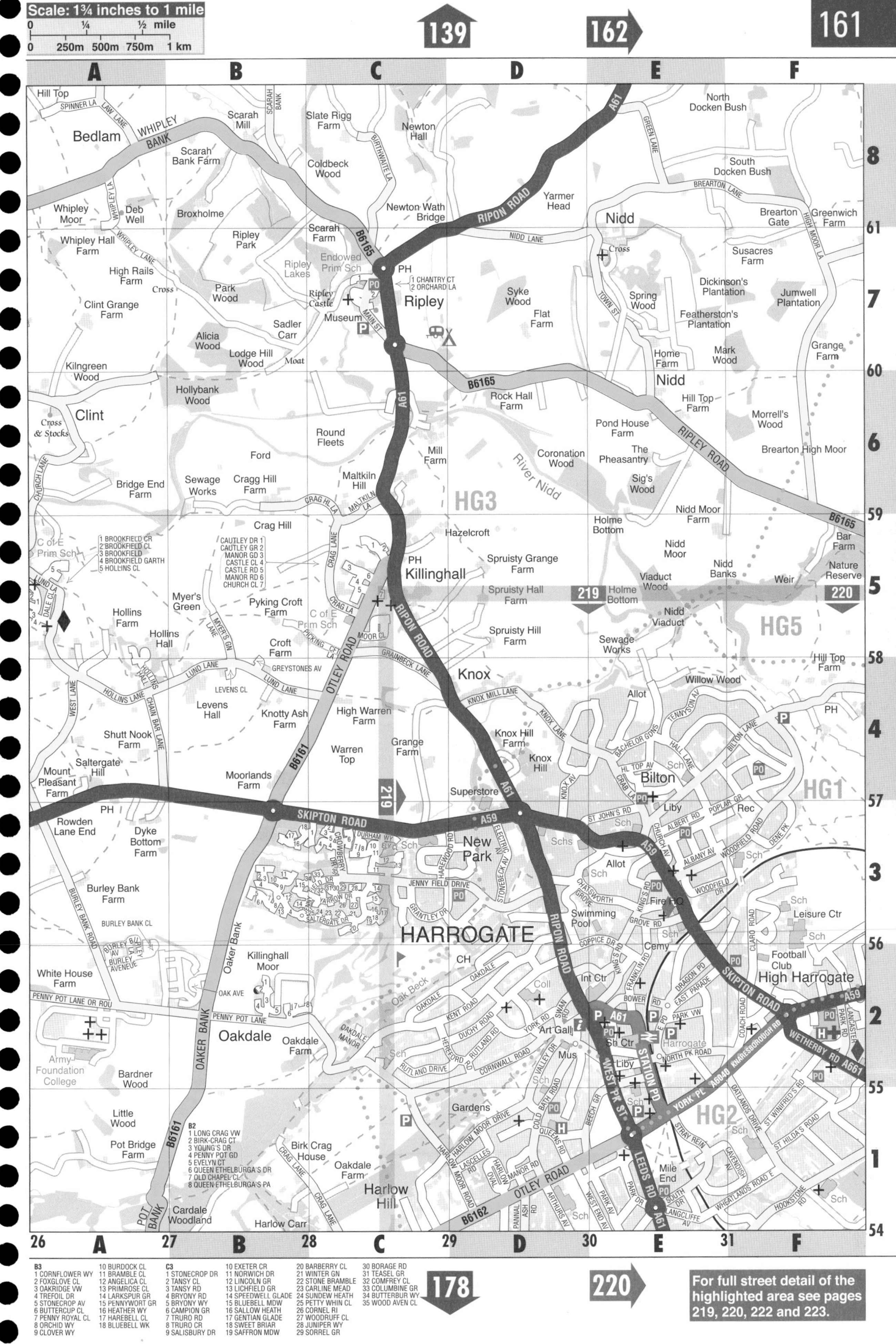
Scale: 1¾ inches to 1 mile
0 ¼ ½ mile
0 250m 500m 750m 1 km
139
162
A B C D E F
Hill Top
Bedlam
Whipley Bank
Scarah Mill
Scarah Bank Farm
Slate Rigg Farm
Newton Hall
North Docken Bush
South Docken Bush
Coldbeck Wood
Ripon Road
Yarmer Head
Whipley Moor
Deb Well
Broxholme
Newton Wath Bridge
Nidd
Brearton Gate
Greenwich Farm
Whipley Hall Farm
Ripley Park
Scarah Farm
Nidd Lane
Susacres Farm
High Rails Farm
Ripley Lakes
Endowed Prim Sch
Ripley Castle
Ripley
Syke Wood
Dickinson's Plantation
Jumwell Plantation
Clint Grange Farm
Park Wood
Museum
Sadler Carr
Flat Farm
Spring Wood
Featherston's Plantation
Alicia Wood
Lodge Hill Wood
Moat
Home Farm
Mark Wood
Grange Farm
Kilngreen Wood
Hollybank Wood
B6165
Rock Hall Farm
Hill Top Farm
Clint
Cross & Stocks
Round Fleets
Pond House Farm
Morrell's Wood
Ford
Mill Farm
Coronation Wood
The Pheasantry
Ripley Road
Brearton High Moor
River Nidd
Bridge End Farm
Sewage Works
Cragg Hill Farm
Maltkiln Hill
HG3
Sig's Wood
Nidd Moor Farm
Holme Bottom
Crag Hill
Hazelcroft
Bar Farm
C of E Prim Sch
Killinghall
Spruisty Grange Farm
Nidd Moor
Nidd Banks
Nature Reserve
Myer's Green
Pyking Croft Farm
Spruisty Hall Farm
Viaduct Wood
Weir
219
220
Holme Bottom
Hollins Farm
Hollins Hall
Nidd Viaduct
HG5
Croft Farm
Spruisty Hill Farm
Sewage Works
Hill Top Farm
Otley Road
Knox
Willow Wood
Levens Hall
Knotty Ash Farm
High Warren Farm
Allot
Shutt Nook Farm
Warren Top
Grange Farm
Knox Hill Farm
Knox Hill
Bilton
HG1
Mount Pleasant Farm
Saltergate Hill
Moorlands Farm
Superstore
Rec
Rowden Lane End
Skipton Road
Dyke Bottom Farm
New Park
Allot
Burley Bank Farm
Fire HQ
Swimming Pool
Leisure Ctr
HARROGATE
Football Club
High Harrogate
White House Farm
Killinghall Moor
CH
Int Ctr
Oakdale
Oakdale Farm
Art Gall
Sh Ctr
Harrogate
Army Foundation College
Bardner Wood
Mus
HG2
Little Wood
Gardens
Pot Bridge Farm
Birk Crag House
Oakdale Farm
Mile End
Harlow Hill
Cardale Woodland
Harlow Carr
B6162
26 27 28 29 30 31
54 55 56 57 58 59 60 61
1 2 3 4 5 6 7 8
B3
1 CORNFLOWER WY
2 FOXGLOVE CL
3 OAKRIDGE VW
4 TREFOIL DR
5 STONECROP AV
6 BUTTERCUP CL
7 PENNY ROYAL CL
8 ORCHID WY
9 CLOVER WY
10 BURDOCK CL
11 BRAMBLE CL
12 ANGELICA CL
13 PRIMROSE CL
14 LARKSPUR GR
15 PENNYWORT GR
16 HEATHER WY
17 HAREBELL CL
18 BLUEBELL WK
C3
1 STONECROP DR
2 TANSY CL
3 TANSY RD
4 BRYONY RD
5 BRYONY WY
6 CAMPION GR
7 TRURO RD
8 TRURO CR
9 SALISBURY DR
10 EXETER CR
11 NORWICH DR
12 LINCOLN GR
13 LICHFIELD GR
14 SPEEDWELL GLADE
15 BLUEBELL MDW
16 SALLOW HEATH
17 GENTIAN GLADE
18 SWEET BRIAR
19 SAFFRON MDW
20 BARBERRY CL
21 WINTER GN
22 STONE BRAMBLE
23 CARLINE MEAD
24 SUNDEW HEATH
25 PETTY WHIN CL
26 CORNEL RI
27 WOODRUFF CL
28 JUNIPER WY
29 SORREL GR
30 BORAGE RD
31 TEASEL GR
32 COMFREY CL
33 COLUMBINE GR
34 BUTTERBUR WY
35 WOOD AVEN CL
178
220
For full street detail of the highlighted area see pages 219, 220, 222 and 223.

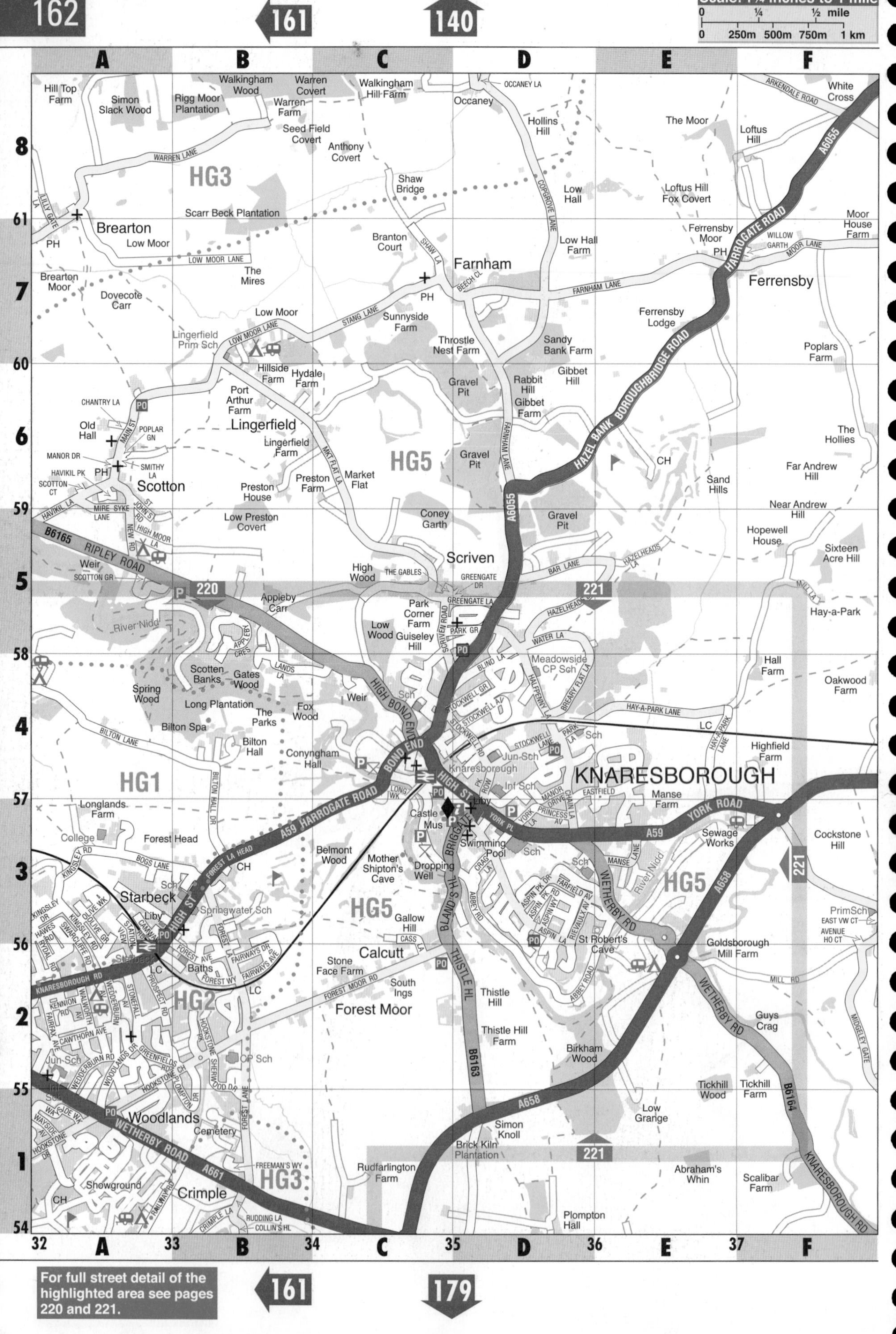

For full street detail of the highlighted area see pages 220 and 221.

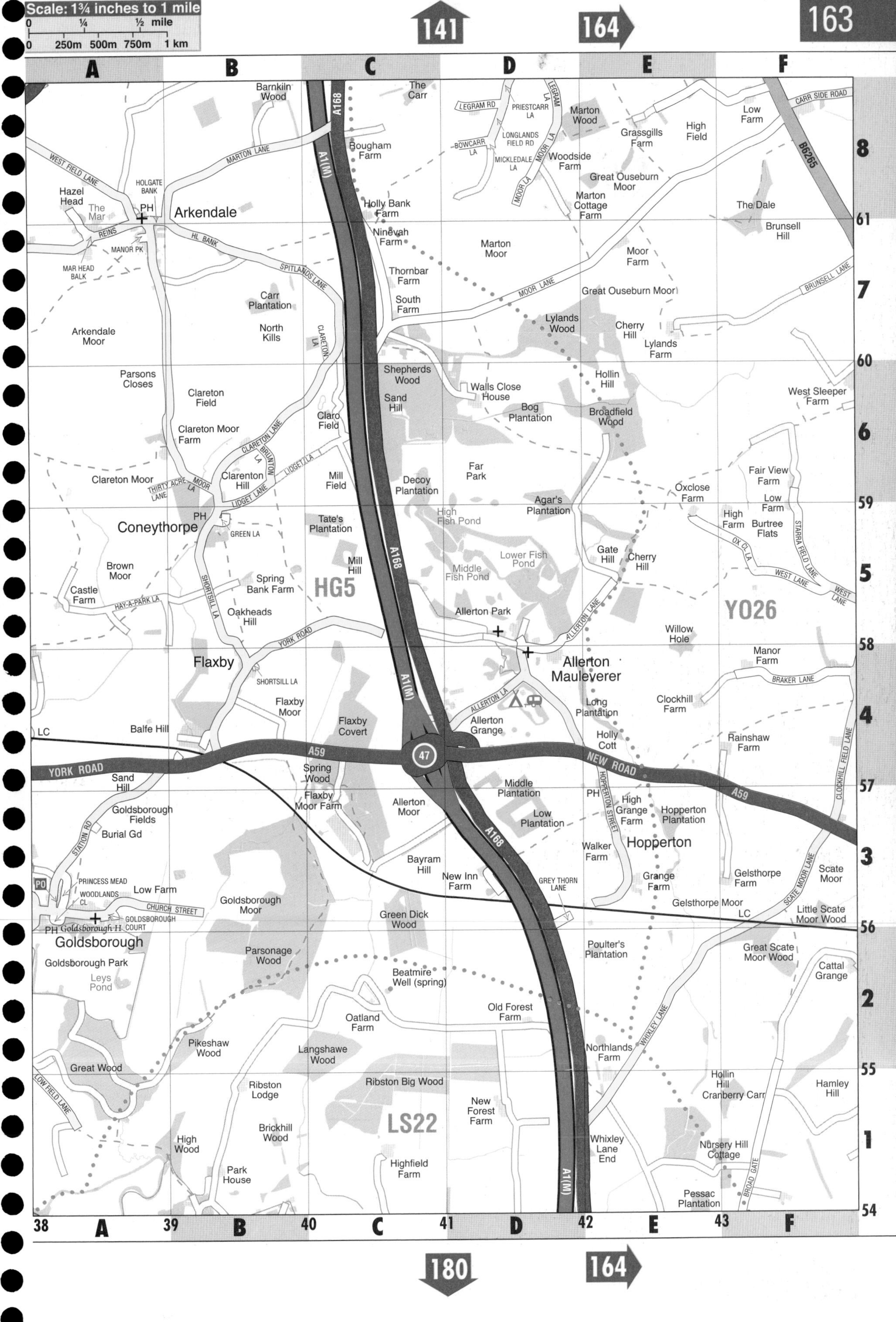
Scale: 1¾ inches to 1 mile
0 ¼ ½ mile
0 250m 500m 750m 1 km
141
164
Barnkiln Wood
The Carr
Bougham Farm
Marton Wood
Grassgills Farm
High Field
Low Farm
CARR SIDE ROAD
B6265
LEGRAM RD
PRIESTCARR LA
LONGLANDS FIELD RD
BOWCARR LA
MICKLEDALE LA
Woodside Farm
Great Ouseburn Moor
WEST FIELD LANE
MARTON LANE
HOLGATE BANK
Hazel Head
The Mar
PH
Arkendale
REINS
MANOR PK
MAR HEAD BALK
HL BANK
SPITLANDS LANE
Holly Bank Farm
Nineveh Farm
Marton Cottage Farm
The Dale
Brunsell Hill
Marton Moor
Moor Farm
Thornbar Farm
Carr Plantation
South Farm
MOOR LANE
Great Ouseburn Moor
BRUNSELL LANE
Arkendale Moor
North Kills
CLARETON LA
Lylands Wood
Cherry Hill
Lylands Farm
Shepherds Wood
Parsons Closes
Clareton Field
Sand Hill
Walls Close House
Hollin Hill
West Sleeper Farm
Bog Plantation
Broadfield Wood
Claro Field
Clareton Moor Farm
CLARETON LANE
BRUNTON LA
LIDGET LA
Clareton Moor
THIRTY ACRE LANE
MOOR LA
Clarenton Hill
LIDGET LANE
Mill Field
Decoy Plantation
Far Park
Fair View Farm
Oxclose Farm
Low Farm
Agar's Plantation
High Fish Pond
High Farm
Burtree Flats
PH
Coneythorpe
GREEN LA
Tate's Plantation
Mill Hill
A168
Lower Fish Pond
Gate Hill
Cherry Hill
OX CL LA
STARRA FIELD LANE
Brown Moor
Castle Farm
Spring Bank Farm
HG5
Middle Fish Pond
WEST LANE
WEST LANE
HAY-A-PARK LA
SHORTSILL LA
Oakheads Hill
YORK ROAD
Allerton Park
ALLERTON LANE
YO26
Willow Hole
Flaxby
SHORTSILL LA
Allerton Mauleverer
Manor Farm
BRAKER LANE
Flaxby Moor
A1(M)
ALLERTON LA
Long Plantation
Clockhill Farm
LC
Balfe Hill
Flaxby Covert
Allerton Grange
Holly Cott
Rainshaw Farm
CLOCKHILL FIELD LANE
A59
47
NEW ROAD
YORK ROAD
Sand Hill
Spring Wood
Middle Plantation
A59
Goldsborough Fields
Flaxby Moor Farm
Allerton Moor
PH
HOPPERTON STREET
High Grange Farm
Hopperton Plantation
STATION RD
Burial Gd
Low Plantation
Hopperton
Walker Farm
Bayram Hill
PO
PRINCESS MEAD
New Inn Farm
GREY THORN LANE
Grange Farm
Gelsthorpe Farm
Scate Moor
SCATE MOOR LANE
WOODLANDS CL
Low Farm
CHURCH STREET
Goldsborough Moor
Gelsthorpe Moor
LC
Little Scate Moor Wood
GOLDSBOROUGH COURT
PH Goldsborough H.
Green Dick Wood
Goldsborough
Poulter's Plantation
Great Scate Moor Wood
Parsonage Wood
Goldsborough Park
Cattal Grange
Leys Pond
Beatmire Well (spring)
Oatland Farm
Old Forest Farm
Pikeshaw Wood
Langshawe Wood
Northlands Farm
WHIXLEY LANE
Great Wood
LOW FIELD LANE
Ribston Lodge
Ribston Big Wood
Hollin Hill
Cranberry Carr
Hamley Hill
New Forest Farm
LS22
Brickhill Wood
High Wood
Whixley Lane End
Nursery Hill Cottage
Park House
Highfield Farm
BROAD GATE
Pessac Plantation
A B C D E F
8 61 7 60 6 59 5 58 4 57 3 56 2 55 1 54
38 39 40 41 42 43
180
164

A8
1 SPRINGFIELD RI
2 CHURCH FIELD LA
3 TOWNEND CT

163

142

F7
1 HALF MOON ST
2 BEECH TREE CT
3 GARTH GRANGE
4 LINTON PL
5 LINTON MDW
6 MILL LA
7 MAPLE GR
8 WHITE ROSE CL

F8
1 THE PADDOCK
2 GREEN CL
3 GROSVENOR SQ

Scale: 1¾ inches to 1 mile
0 ¼ ½ mile
0 250m 500m 750m 1 km

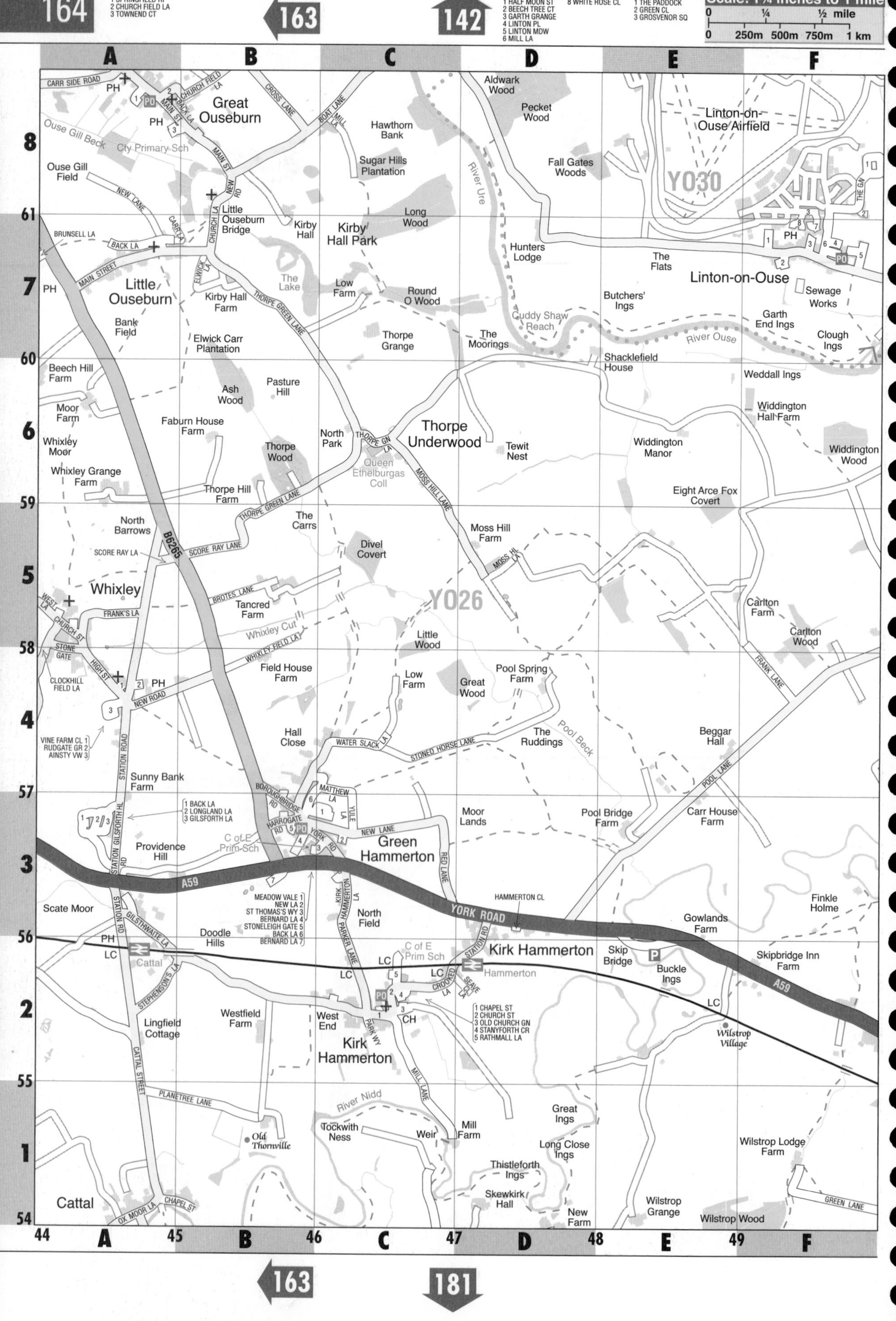

163

181

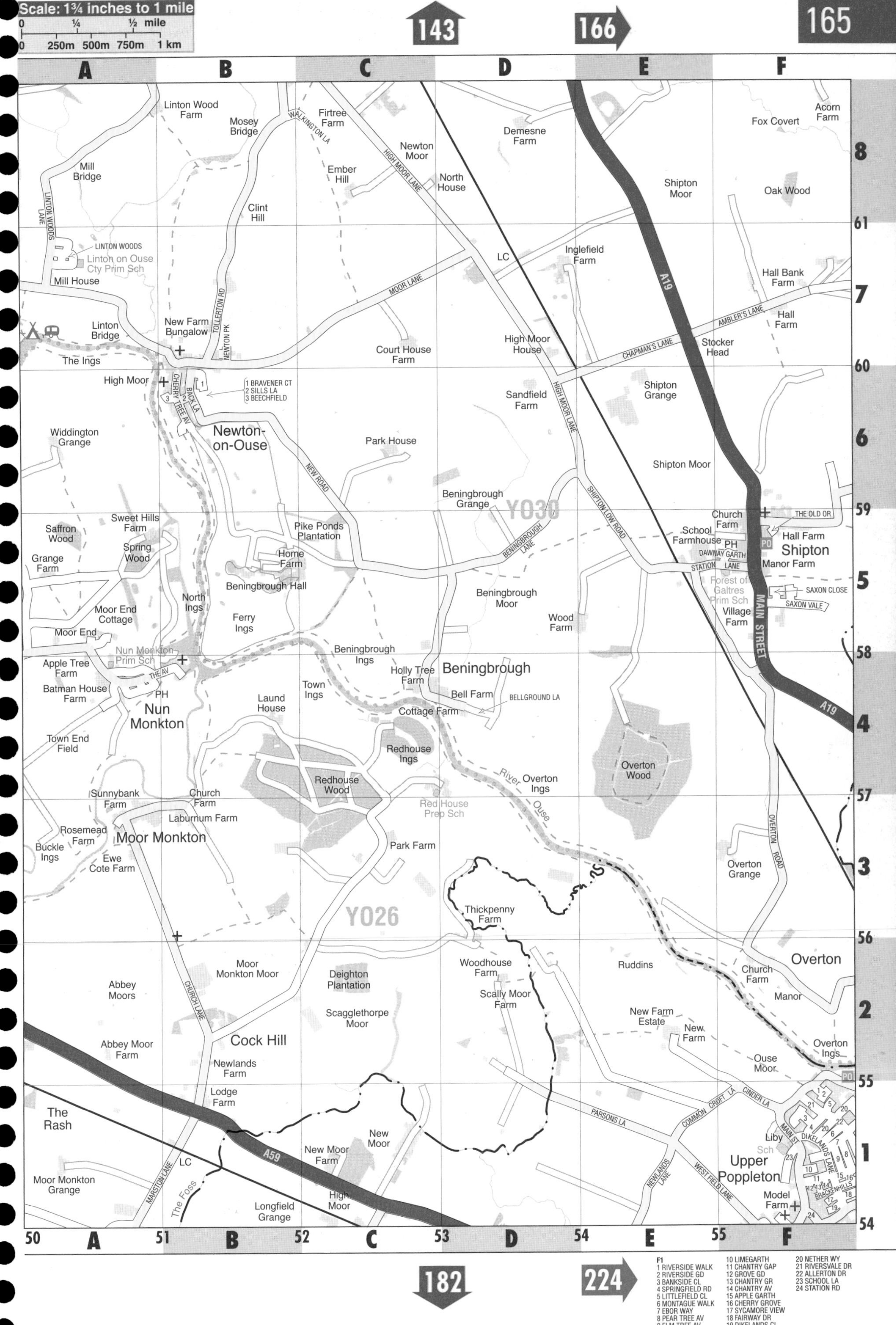
Scale: 1¾ inches to 1 mile
143
166
Linton Wood Farm
Mosey Bridge
Firtree Farm
Newton Moor
Demesne Farm
Fox Covert
Acorn Farm
Mill Bridge
Ember Hill
North House
Shipton Moor
Oak Wood
Clint Hill
Linton on Ouse Cty Prim Sch
Mill House
Inglefield Farm
Hall Bank Farm
Hall Farm
Linton Bridge
New Farm Bungalow
Court House Farm
High Moor House
Stocker Head
The Ings
High Moor
1 BRAVENER CT
2 SILLS LA
3 BEECHFIELD
Sandfield Farm
Shipton Grange
Widdington Grange
Newton-on-Ouse
Park House
Shipton Moor
Beningbrough Grange
YO30
Church Farm
School Farmhouse
Hall Farm
Shipton
Manor Farm
Saffron Wood
Sweet Hills Farm
Spring Wood
Pike Ponds Plantation
Home Farm
Grange Farm
Beningbrough Hall
Beningbrough Moor
Forest of Galtres Prim Sch
Village Farm
North Ings
Moor End Cottage
Ferry Ings
Wood Farm
Moor End
Nun Monkton Prim Sch
Beningbrough Ings
Apple Tree Farm
Holly Tree Farm
Beningbrough
Batman House Farm
Town Ings
Laund House
Bell Farm
Nun Monkton
Cottage Farm
Town End Field
Redhouse Ings
Overton Wood
Redhouse Wood
River Ouse
Overton Ings
Sunnybank Farm
Church Farm
Laburnum Farm
Red House Prep Sch
Rosemead Farm
Moor Monkton
Buckle Ings
Ewe Cote Farm
Park Farm
Overton Grange
Thickpenny Farm
YO26
Moor Monkton Moor
Woodhouse Farm
Ruddins
Church Farm
Overton
Abbey Moors
Deighton Plantation
Scally Moor Farm
Manor
Scagglethorpe Moor
New Farm Estate
New Farm
Abbey Moor Farm
Cock Hill
Overton Ings
Ouse Moor
Newlands Farm
Lodge Farm
The Rash
New Moor
New Moor Farm
Liby
Sch
Upper Poppleton
Moor Monkton Grange
High Moor
Longfield Grange
Model Farm
The Foss
A19
A59
50 51 52 53 54 55
A B C D E F
54 55 1 2 3 56 57 4 58 5 59 6 60 7 61 8
182
224
F1
1 RIVERSIDE WALK
2 RIVERSIDE GD
3 BANKSIDE CL
4 SPRINGFIELD RD
5 LITTLEFIELD CL
6 MONTAGUE WALK
7 EBOR WAY
8 PEAR TREE AV
9 ELM TREE AV
10 LIMEGARTH
11 CHANTRY GAP
12 GROVE GD
13 CHANTRY GR
14 CHANTRY AV
15 APPLE GARTH
16 CHERRY GROVE
17 SYCAMORE VIEW
18 FAIRWAY DR
19 DIKELANDS CL
20 NETHER WY
21 RIVERSVALE DR
22 ALLERTON DR
23 SCHOOL LA
24 STATION RD

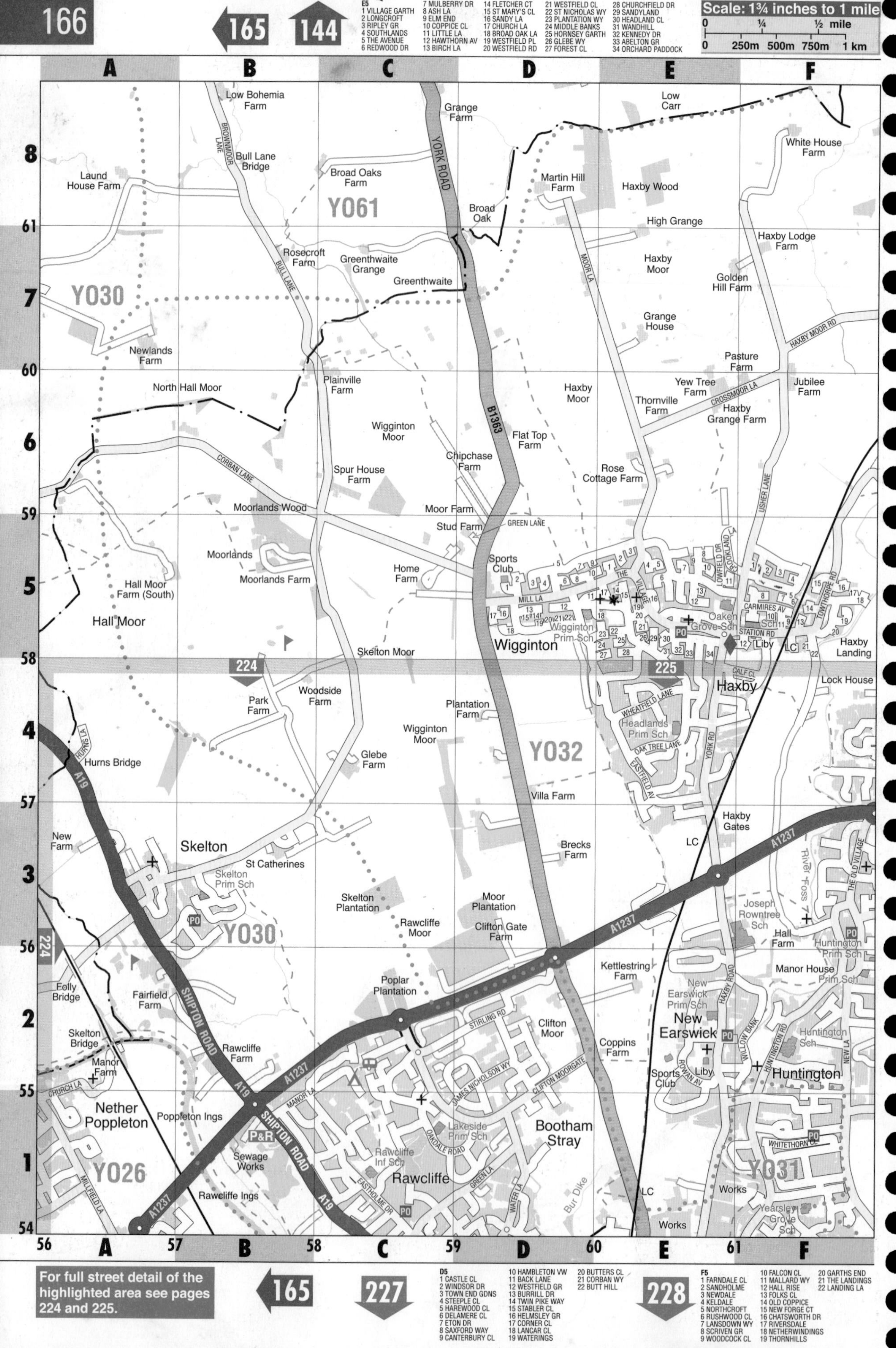

166
165
144
* St. MARYS MEWS
E5
1 VILLAGE GARTH
2 LONGCROFT
3 RIPLEY GR
4 SOUTHLANDS
5 THE AVENUE
6 REDWOOD DR
7 MULBERRY DR
8 ASH LA
9 ELM END
10 COPPICE CL
11 LITTLE LA
12 HAWTHORN AV
13 BIRCH LA
14 FLETCHER CT
15 ST MARY'S CL
16 SANDY LA
17 CHURCH LA
18 BROAD OAK LA
19 WESTFIELD PL
20 WESTFIELD RD
21 WESTFIELD CL
22 ST NICHOLAS WY
23 PLANTATION WY
24 MIDDLE BANKS
25 HORNSEY GARTH
26 GLEBE WY
27 FOREST CL
28 CHURCHFIELD DR
29 SANDYLAND
30 HEADLAND CL
31 WANDHILL
32 KENNEDY DR
33 ABELTON GR
34 ORCHARD PADDOCK
Scale: 1¾ inches to 1 mile
0 ¼ ½ mile
0 250m 500m 750m 1 km
A B C D E F
8
61
7
60
6
59
5
58
4
57
3
56
2
55
1
54
Low Bohemia Farm
Grange Farm
Low Carr
White House Farm
BROWNMOOR LANE
YORK ROAD
Bull Lane Bridge
Laund House Farm
Broad Oaks Farm
YO61
Martin Hill Farm
Haxby Wood
Broad Oak
High Grange
Rosecroft Farm
Greenthwaite Grange
Greenthwaite
BULL LANE
MOOR LA
Haxby Moor
Haxby Lodge Farm
Golden Hill Farm
YO30
Grange House
HAXBY MOOR RD
Newlands Farm
Pasture Farm
North Hall Moor
Plainville Farm
Haxby Moor
Yew Tree Farm
Thornville Farm
CROSSMOOR LA
Jubilee Farm
Haxby Grange Farm
B1363
Wigginton Moor
Flat Top Farm
CORBAN LANE
Chipchase Farm
Spur House Farm
Rose Cottage Farm
USHER LANE
Moorlands Wood
Moor Farm
Stud Farm
GREEN LANE
Moorlands
Sports Club
Home Farm
THE VILLAGE
LOWFIELD DR
BROOKLAND LA
Moorlands Farm
Hall Moor Farm (South)
TOWTHORPE RD
MILL LA
CARMIRES AV
Hall Moor
Wigginton Prim Sch
Oaken Grove Sch
PO
STATION RD
Liby
LC
Haxby Landing
Wigginton
Skelton Moor
224
225
CALF CL
Haxby
Lock House
Woodside Farm
Park Farm
Plantation Farm
WHEATFIELD LANE
Headlands Prim Sch
Wigginton Moor
YO32
HURNS LA
OAK TREE LANE
YORK RD
Hurns Bridge
Glebe Farm
EASTFIELD AV
A19
Villa Farm
New Farm
Haxby Gates
Skelton
Brecks Farm
LC
A1237
St Catherines
Skelton Prim Sch
THE OLD VILLAGE
River Foss
Skelton Plantation
Moor Plantation
Joseph Rowntree Sch
Rawcliffe Moor
Clifton Gate Farm
Hall Farm
YO30
Huntington Prim Sch
Kettlestring Farm
Manor House Prim Sch
Folly Bridge
Poplar Plantation
New Earswick Prim Sch
Fairfield Farm
HAXBY ROAD
SHIPTON ROAD
STIRLING RD
Clifton Moor
New Earswick
Skelton Bridge
Rawcliffe Farm
Coppins Farm
WILLOW BANK
HUNTINGTON RD
Huntington Sch
Manor Farm
JAMES NICHOLSON WY
CLIFTON MOORGATE
ROWAN AV
NEW LA
CHURCH LA
MANOR LA
Sports Club
Huntington
Nether Poppleton
Poppleton Ings
Bootham Stray
P&R
Lakeside Prim Sch
OAKDALE ROAD
WHITETHORN CL
Sewage Works
Rawcliffe Inf Sch
YO26
Rawcliffe
YO31
MILLFIELD LA
EASTHOLME DR
GREEN LA
WATER LA
Bur Dike
Works
Rawcliffe Ings
LC
Yearsley Grove Sch
Works
56 A 57 B 58 C 59 D 60 E 61 F
For full street detail of the highlighted area see pages 224 and 225.
165
227
D5
1 CASTLE CL
2 WINDSOR DR
3 TOWN END GDNS
4 STEEPLE CL
5 HAREWOOD CL
6 DELAMERE CL
7 ETON DR
8 SAXFORD WAY
9 CANTERBURY CL
10 HAMBLETON VW
11 BACK LANE
12 WESTFIELD GR
13 BURRILL DR
14 TWIN PIKE WAY
15 STABLER CL
16 HELMSLEY GR
17 CORNER CL
18 LANCAR CL
19 WATERINGS
20 BUTTERS CL
21 CORBAN WY
22 BUTT HILL
228
F5
1 FARNDALE CL
2 SANDHOLME
3 NEWDALE
4 KELDALE
5 NORTHCROFT
6 RUSHWOOD CL
7 LANSDOWN WY
8 SCRIVEN GR
9 WOODCOCK CL
10 FALCON CL
11 MALLARD WY
12 HALL RISE
13 FOLKS CL
14 OLD COPPICE
15 NEW FORGE CT
16 CHATSWORTH DR
17 RIVERSDALE
18 NETHERWINDINGS
19 THORNHILLS
20 GARTHS END
21 THE LANDINGS
22 LANDING LA
SWARTHDALE

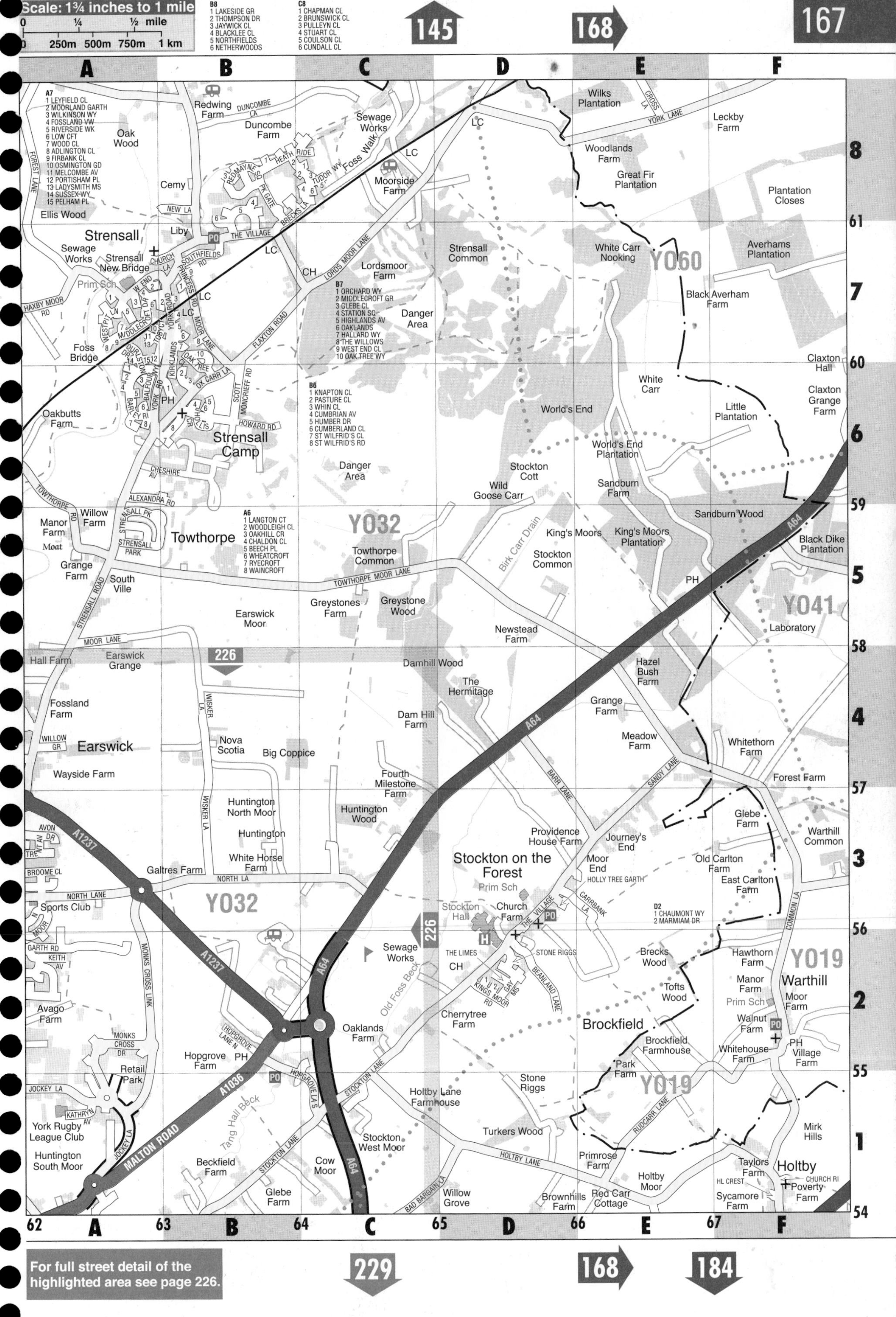

For full street detail of the highlighted area see page 226.

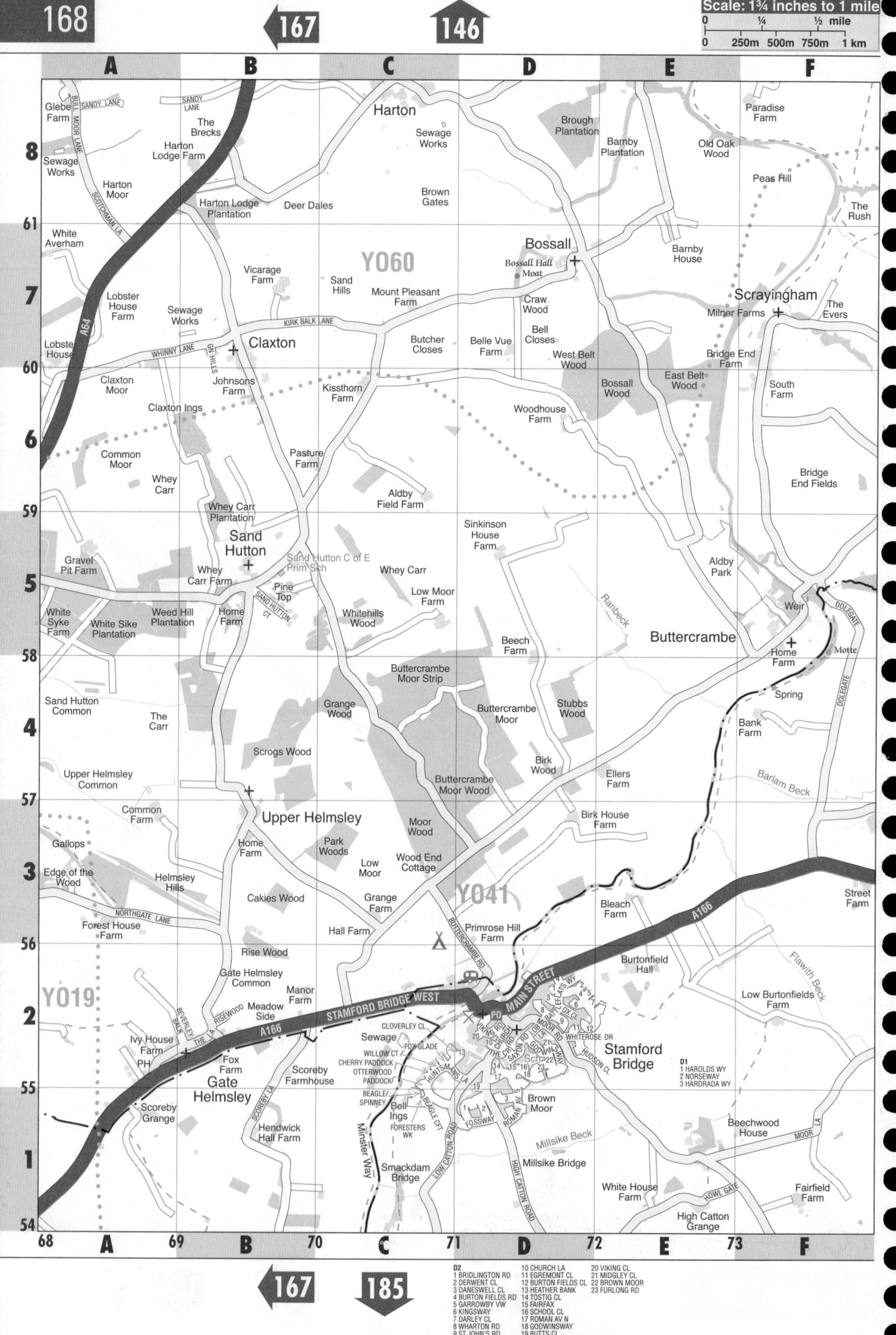
167
146
Scale: 1¾ inches to 1 mile
0 ¼ ½ mile
0 250m 500m 750m 1 km
A
B
C
D
E
F
Glebe Farm
SANDY LANE
BULL MOOR LANE
SANDY LANE
The Brecks
Harton
Sewage Works
Brough Plantation
Barnby Plantation
Paradise Farm
Old Oak Wood
8
Sewage Works
Harton Lodge Farm
Harton Moor
SCOTCHMAN LA
Harton Lodge Plantation
Deer Dales
Brown Gates
Peas Hill
The Rush
61
White Averham
Bossall
Barnby House
Vicarage Farm
YO60
Bossall Hall Moat
Sand Hills
Mount Pleasant Farm
Lobster House Farm
Sewage Works
A64
Craw Wood
Scrayingham
Milner Farms
The Evers
7
KIRK BALK LANE
Lobster House
WHINNY LANE
GN HILLS
Claxton
Butcher Closes
Belle Vue Farm
Bell Closes
West Belt Wood
Bridge End Farm
60
Claxton Moor
Johnsons Farm
Kissthorn Farm
Bossall Wood
East Belt Wood
South Farm
Claxton Ings
Woodhouse Farm
6
Common Moor
Pasture Farm
Whey Carr
Aldby Field Farm
Bridge End Fields
59
Whey Carr Plantation
Sinkinson House Farm
Sand Hutton
Gravel Pit Farm
Sand Hutton C of E Prim Sch
Whey Carr
Aldby Park
5
Whey Carr Farm
Pine Top
Low Moor Farm
Ranbeck
Weir
White Syke Farm
White Sike Plantation
Weed Hill Plantation
Home Farm
SAND HUTTON CT
Whitehills Wood
DOLEGATE
Buttercrambe
Beech Farm
Home Farm
Motte
58
Buttercrambe Moor Strip
Spring
Sand Hutton Common
The Carr
Grange Wood
Buttercrambe Moor
Stubbs Wood
DOLEGATE
4
Bank Farm
Scrogs Wood
Birk Wood
Upper Helmsley Common
Buttercrambe Moor Wood
Ellers Farm
Barlam Beck
57
Common Farm
Upper Helmsley
Birk House Farm
Gallops
Moor Wood
Home Farm
Park Woods
3
Edge of the Wood
Helmsley Hills
Low Moor
Wood End Cottage
YO41
Street Farm
Cakies Wood
Grange Farm
Bleach Farm
NORTHGATE LANE
Forest House Farm
Hall Farm
BUTTERCRAMBE RD
Primrose Hill Farm
A166
56
Rise Wood
Burtonfield Hall
Flawith Beck
Gate Helmsley Common
MAIN STREET
YO19
Manor Farm
STAMFORD BRIDGE WEST
Low Burtonfields Farm
2
Meadow Side
BEVERLEY BALK
RISEWOOD
THE LA
A166
PO
CLOVERLEY CL
VIKING RD
CHURCH RD
WHITEROSE DR
Ivy House Farm
Sewage
FOX GLADE
THE CROFT
SAXON RD
Stamford Bridge
Fox Farm
WILLOW CT
CHERRY PADDOCK
OTTERWOOD PADDOCK
HUNTSMANS LA
GODWINSWAY
HUDSON CL
PH
Scoreby Farmhouse
D1
1 HAROLDS WY
2 NORSEWAY
3 HARDRADA WY
Gate Helmsley
55
BEAGLE SPINNEY
Brown Moor
Scoreby Grange
SCOREBY LA
Bell Ings
BEAGLE CFT
ROMAN AV S
FOSSWAY
Beechwood House
Hendwick Hall Farm
FORESTERS WK
MOOR LA
Minster Way
LOW CATTON ROAD
Millsike Beck
1
Smackdam Bridge
HIGH CATTON ROAD
Millsike Bridge
White House Farm
HOWL GATE
Fairfield Farm
High Catton Grange
54
68
69
70
71
72
73
167
185
D2
1 BRIDLINGTON RD
2 DERWENT CL
3 DANESWELL CL
4 BURTON FIELDS RD
5 GARROWBY VW
6 KINGSWAY
7 DARLEY CL
8 WHARTON RD
9 ST JOHN'S RD
10 CHURCH LA
11 EGREMONT CL
12 BURTON FIELDS CL
13 HEATHER BANK
14 TOSTIG CL
15 FAIRFAX
16 SCHOOL CL
17 ROMAN AV N
18 GODWINSWAY
19 BUTTS CL
20 VIKING CL
21 MIDGLEY CL
22 BROWN MOOR
23 FURLONG RD

147
170

Scale: 1¾ inches to 1 mile

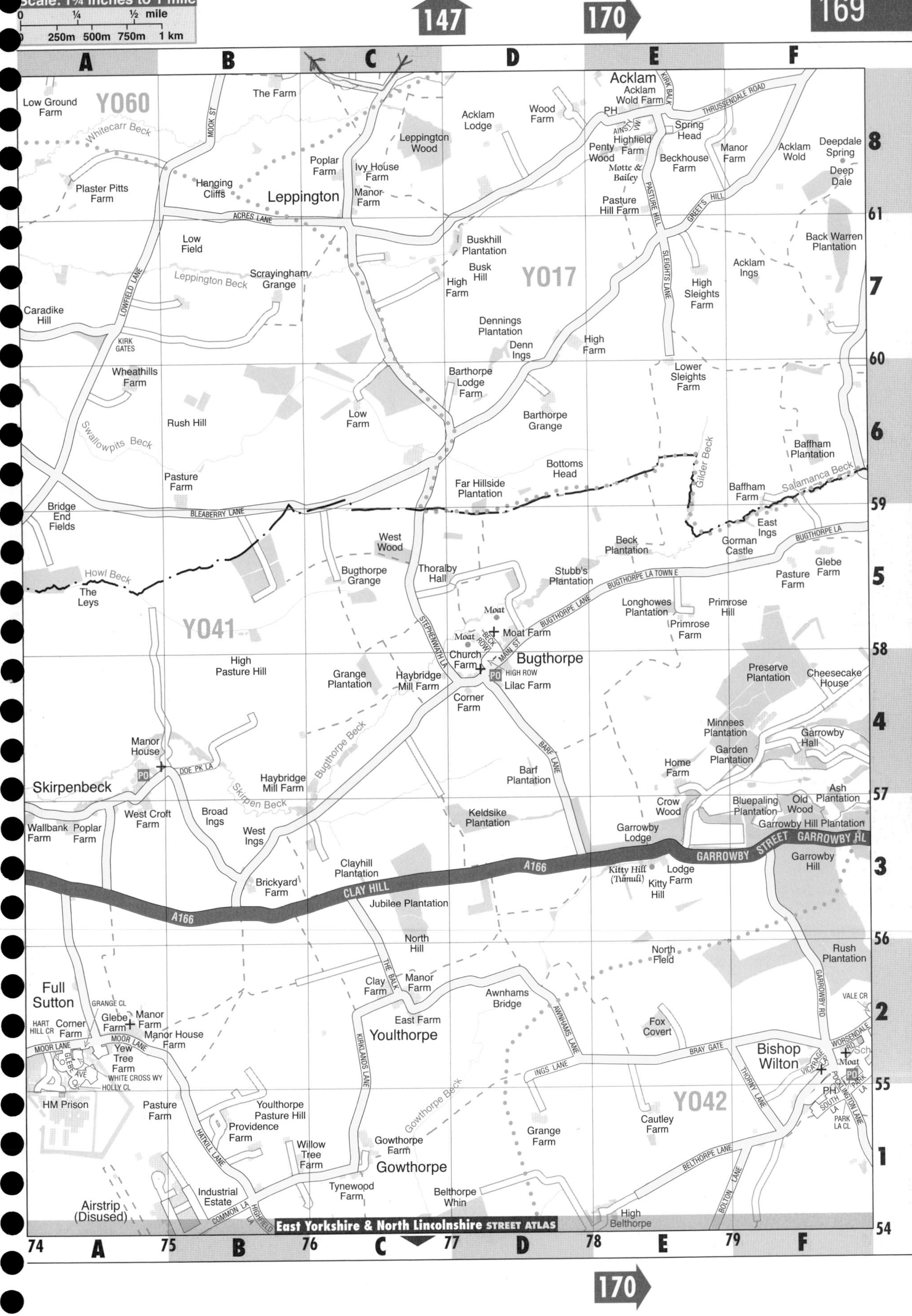

170

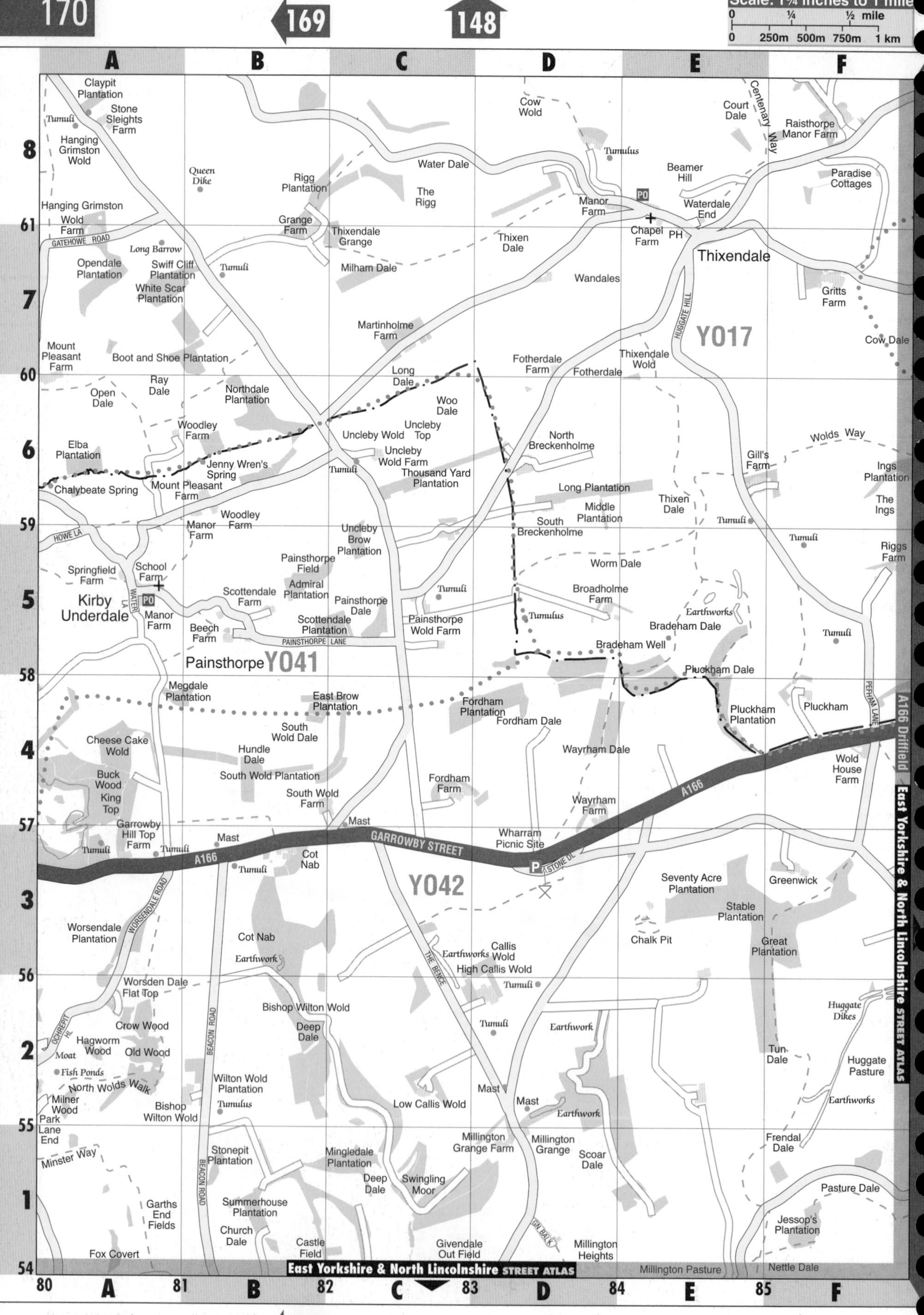
Claypit Plantation
Stone Sleights Farm
Hanging Grimston Wold
Queen Dike
Rigg Plantation
Water Dale
The Rigg
Cow Wold
Tumulus
Court Dale
Centenary Way
Raisthorpe Manor Farm
Beamer Hill
Paradise Cottages
Hanging Grimston Wold Farm
Gatehowe Road
Grange Farm
Thixendale Grange
Manor Farm
Chapel Farm
Waterdale End
Thixen Dale
Thixendale
Long Barrow
Opendale Plantation
Swiff Cliff Plantation
White Scar Plantation
Milham Dale
Wandales
Gritts Farm
Huggate Hill
YO17
Martinholme Farm
Mount Pleasant Farm
Boot and Shoe Plantation
Fotherdale Farm
Fotherdale
Thixendale Wold
Cow Dale
Ray Dale
Open Dale
Northdale Plantation
Long Dale
Woo Dale
Uncleby Top
Uncleby Wold
Woodley Farm
Elba Plantation
Jenny Wren's Spring
Uncleby Wold Farm
North Breckenholme
Wolds Way
Gill's Farm
Ings Plantation
Thousand Yard Plantation
Chalybeate Spring
Mount Pleasant Farm
Long Plantation
Thixen Dale
The Ings
Middle Plantation
Woodley Farm
Howe La
Manor Farm
Uncleby Brow Plantation
South Breckenholme
Riggs Farm
Painsthorpe Field
Worm Dale
Springfield Farm
School Farm
Admiral Plantation
Broadholme Farm
Kirby Underdale
Scottendale Farm
Painsthorpe Dale
Earthworks
Water La
Manor Farm
Scottendale Plantation
Painsthorpe Wold Farm
Bradeham Dale
Beech Farm
Painsthorpe Lane
Bradeham Well
Painsthorpe
YO41
Pluckham Dale
Megdale Plantation
East Brow Plantation
Fordham Plantation
Fordham Dale
Pluckham
Pluckham Plantation
Peryham Lane
A166 Driffield
South Wold Dale
Cheese Cake Wold
Hundle Dale
Wayrham Dale
Wold House Farm
Buck Wood
South Wold Plantation
King Top
South Wold Farm
Fordham Farm
Wayrham Farm
A166
Mast
Garrowby Hill Top Farm
Mast
Wharram Picnic Site
Garrowby Street
Cot Nab
Stone Dl
YO42
Seventy Acre Plantation
Greenwick
Worsendale Road
Worsendale Plantation
Stable Plantation
Cot Nab
Callis Wold
Chalk Pit
Great Plantation
Earthwork
The Bence
High Callis Wold
Worsden Dale
Flat Top
Bishop Wilton Wold
Huggate Dikes
Crow Wood
Deep Dale
Earthwork
Ochrepit Hl
Hagworm Wood
Old Wood
Beacon Road
Tun Dale
Moat
Huggate Pasture
Fish Ponds
North Wolds Walk
Wilton Wold Plantation
Mast
Earthworks
Milner Wood
Bishop Wilton Wold
Low Callis Wold
Mast
Earthwork
Park Lane End
Millington Grange Farm
Millington Grange
Frendal Dale
Minster Way
Stonepit Plantation
Mingledale Plantation
Scoar Dale
Deep Dale
Swingling Moor
Garths End Fields
Summerhouse Plantation
Pasture Dale
Jessop's Plantation
Church Dale
Castle Field
Givendale Out Field
Gn Balk
Millington Heights
Fox Covert
Millington Pasture
Nettle Dale
East Yorkshire & North Lincolnshire STREET ATLAS

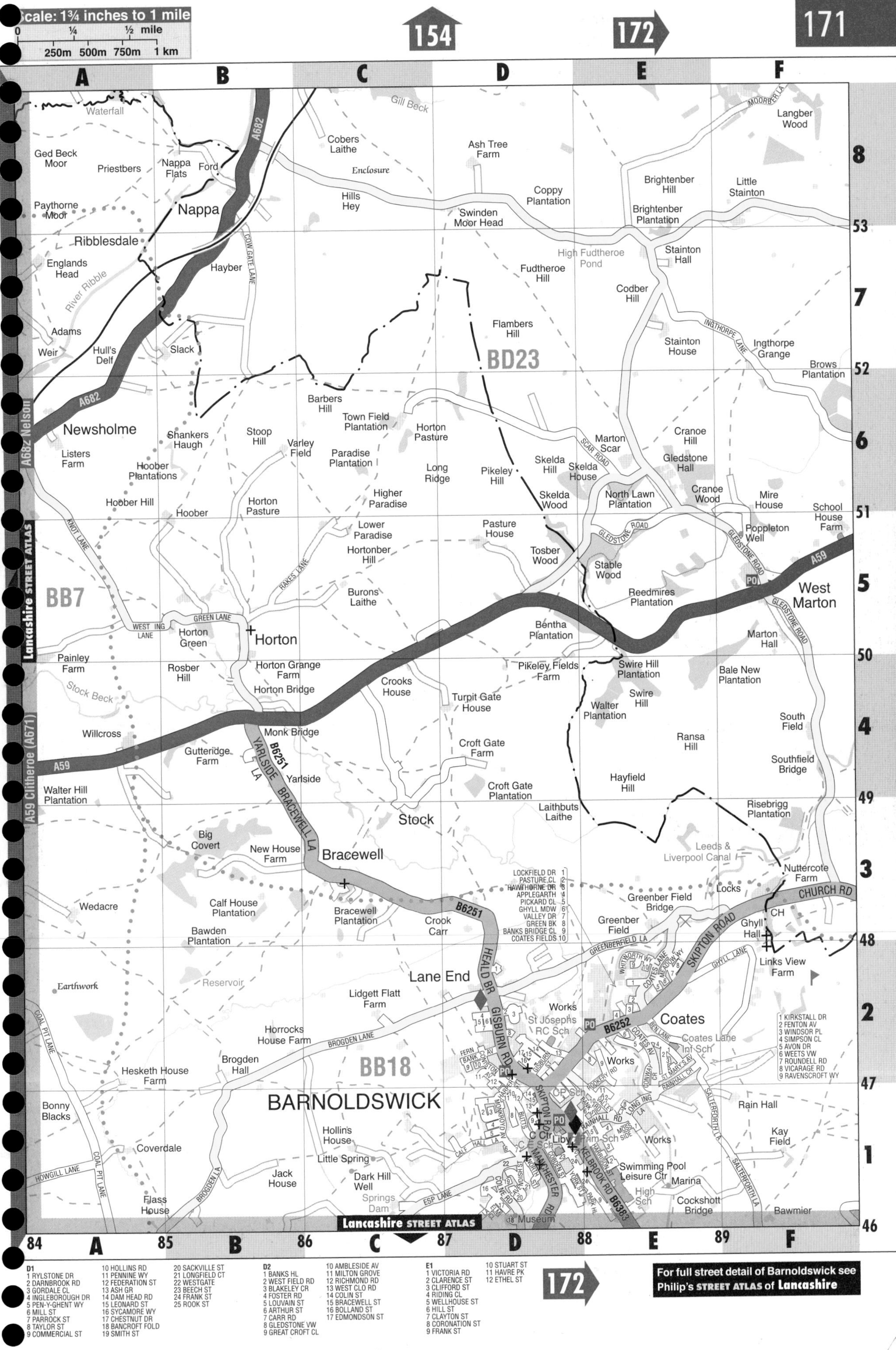
Scale: 1¾ inches to 1 mile
0 ¼ ½ mile
250m 500m 750m 1 km
154
172
Waterfall
Gill Beck
Ged Beck Moor
Priestbers
Nappa Flats
Ford
Nappa
Cobers Laithe
Enclosure
Ash Tree Farm
Hills Hey
Swinden Moor Head
Coppy Plantation
Brightenber Hill
Brightenber Plantation
Little Stainton
Langber Wood
Paythorne Moor
Ribblesdale
Englands Head
River Ribble
Hayber
High Fudtheroe Pond
Fudtheroe Hill
Stainton Hall
Codber Hill
Adams
Weir
Hull's Delf
Slack
Flambers Hill
BD23
Stainton House
Ingthorpe Grange
Brows Plantation
Newsholme
Listers Farm
Shankers Haugh
Barbers Hill
Town Field Plantation
Horton Pasture
Stoop Hill
Varley Field
Paradise Plantation
Long Ridge
Pikeley Hill
Skelda Hill
Skelda House
Marton Scar
Cranoe Hill
Gledstone Hall
Hoober Plantations
Hoober Hill
Hoober
Horton Pasture
Higher Paradise
Skelda Wood
North Lawn Plantation
Cranoe Wood
Mire House
School House Farm
Lower Paradise
Hortonber Hill
Pasture House
Tosber Wood
Stable Wood
Poppleton Well
BB7
Burons Laithe
Reedmires Plantation
West Marton
Horton Green
Horton
Bentha Plantation
Marton Hall
Painley Farm
Rosber Hill
Horton Grange Farm
Horton Bridge
Crooks House
Pikeley Fields Farm
Swire Hill Plantation
Bale New Plantation
Stock Beck
Turpit Gate House
Swire Hill
Walter Plantation
South Field
Willcross
Monk Bridge
Gutteridge Farm
Croft Gate Farm
Ransa Hill
Southfield Bridge
Yarlside
Walter Hill Plantation
Croft Gate Plantation
Hayfield Hill
Risebrigg Plantation
Stock
Laithbuts Laithe
Big Covert
New House Farm
Bracewell
Leeds & Liverpool Canal
Nuttercote Farm
Calf House Plantation
Bracewell Plantation
Greenber Field Bridge
Locks
Wedacre
Crook Carr
Greenber Field
Ghyll Hall
Bawden Plantation
Links View Farm
Earthwork
Reservoir
Lane End
Lidgett Flatt Farm
Works
St Josephs RC Sch
Coates
Coates Lane Inf Sch
Horrocks House Farm
Brogden Hall
BB18
Hesketh House Farm
Works
Rain Hall
Bonny Blacks
BARNOLDSWICK
Hollins House
Works
Kay Field
Coverdale
Little Spring
Swimming Pool Leisure Ctr
Marina
Jack House
Dark Hill Well
Springs Dam
High Sch
Flass House
Cockshott Bridge
Bawmier
Museum
LOCKFIELD DR 1
PASTURE CL 2
HAWTHORNE DR 3
APPLEGARTH 4
PICKARD CL 5
GHYLL MDW 6
VALLEY DR 7
GREEN BK 8
BANKS BRIDGE CL 9
COATES FIELDS 10
1 KIRKSTALL DR
2 FENTON AV
3 WINDSOR PL
4 SIMPSON CL
5 AVON DR
6 WEETS VW
7 ROUNDELL RD
8 VICARAGE RD
9 RAVENSCROFT WY
A682
A682 Nelson
A59
A59 Clitheroe (A671)
B6251
B6252
B6383
CHURCH RD
SKIPTON ROAD
Lancashire STREET ATLAS
A B C D E F
84 85 86 87 88 89
8 53 7 52 6 51 5 50 4 49 3 48 2 47 1 46
D1
1 RYLSTONE DR
2 DARNBROOK RD
3 GORDALE CL
4 INGLEBOROUGH DR
5 PEN-Y-GHENT WY
6 MILL ST
7 PARROCK ST
8 TAYLOR ST
9 COMMERCIAL ST
10 HOLLINS RD
11 PENNINE WY
12 FEDERATION ST
13 ASH GR
14 DAM HEAD RD
15 LEONARD ST
16 SYCAMORE WY
17 CHESTNUT DR
18 BANCROFT FOLD
19 SMITH ST
20 SACKVILLE ST
21 LONGFIELD CT
22 WESTGATE
23 BEECH ST
24 FRANK ST
25 ROOK ST
D2
1 BANKS HL
2 WEST FIELD RD
3 BLAKELEY CR
4 FOSTER RD
5 LOUVAIN ST
6 ARTHUR ST
7 CARR RD
8 GLEDSTONE VW
9 GREAT CROFT CL
10 AMBLESIDE AV
11 MILTON GROVE
12 RICHMOND RD
13 WEST CLO RD
14 COLIN ST
15 BRACEWELL ST
16 BOLLAND ST
17 EDMONDSON ST
E1
1 VICTORIA RD
2 CLARENCE ST
3 CLIFFORD ST
4 RIDING CL
5 WELLHOUSE ST
6 HILL ST
7 CLAYTON ST
8 CORONATION ST
9 FRANK ST
10 STUART ST
11 HAVRE PK
12 ETHEL ST
172
For full street detail of Barnoldswick see Philip's STREET ATLAS of Lancashire

171
155

Scale: 1¾ inches to 1 mile
0 ¼ ½ mile
0 250m 500m 750m 1 km

A B C D E F

Viaduct
Weir
Lock
Weir
Weir
MARTON ROAD
WALTON CL
MOSBER LA
CHURCH CFT
PH
CHURCH LA
Gargrave
Weir
River Aire
Sewage Works
Woomber Wood
Aqueduct
Priest Holme Bridge
Gargrave
Moat
Lobby Bridge
Leeds and Liverpool Canal
Mosber La Bridge
Highgate Bridge (swing)
Sulber Laithe
8
Ivy End
Lock
Kelber Hill Farm
Kirk Sink Farm
Newton Hall
Lock
Parkers Farm
Scaleber
Bank Newton
53
Lock
Robin Wood
A65
Butter Haw Farm
Pennine Way
Moorber Hill
Broughton Quarry
Thorlby Bridge (swing)
Newton Bridge
Newton Grange Farm
CHURCH STREET
Smellows Quarry
Copy Hill Plantation
River Aire
7
Small House
Copy Hill
Pasture House
52
Oxen Close
Turnbers Hill Plantation
Acliffe Hill Plantation
Oxenclose Farm
Greenbank Farm
Trenet Laithe
Clints Delf (dis)
Hall Close Wood
Brows Plantation
Broughton Copy Farm
6
Green Bank
Langber Plantation
Skinnerground Wood
INGTHORPE LANE
Corringer Hill
GARGRAVE ROAD
Broughton
A59
BD23
OLD LA
Skinner Ground Farm
Deer Haw Plantation
Heslaker Bridge
Tempest Farm
Williamson Bridge
51
HEBER DR
PH
East Marton
PH
Weir
Dancliff Plantation
OLD LA
The Grove Hall
Church Farm Barn
CHURCH LA
Micklethorne Farm
Mill Wood
A59
Broughton Fields Farm
Primrose Hill
Home Farm
Denbers Plantation
5
Sewage Works
Crickle Farm
EDMONDSON'S LANE
COLNE AND BROUGHTON RD
Pennine Way
50
Pasture House Farm
Low Ground Farm
PH
Gubbs Hill Farm
Elslack Bridge
ELLER GILL LANE
Langber
CHURCH LANE
ELSLACK LA
BURWEN CASTLE RD
Far Fence End Farm
Yellison House
Croft Wood
4
Johnsons Gate Farm
White House Farm
Yellison Wood
Smearber Farm
Lower Scarcliffe Farm
Fence End
Elslack Hall Farm
Higher Scarcliff
Scarcliffe Farm
BURWEN CASTLE (ROMAN FORT)
Merlinwood
Mitton House
Lane Head Quarry
49
Old Cote Farm
Thompson House Farm
A56
Thornton in Craven CP Sch
CAM LA
BREARLANDS
MOOR LANE
Redfirth Gill Cote
Thornton-in-Craven
Earby Beck
Stories House Farm
Baxter House
OLD RD
OLD RD
Rectory Farm
Cowgill Farm
Brown House Bridge
Park House Farm
Mill Fold
Standrise Plantation
3
PO
1 THE FOLD
2 QUEENS GARTH
Brown House
Wood House
Baxter House Farm
B6252 CHURCH RD
Hotel
BOOTH BR LANE
Elslack Resr
Thornton Hall Farm
Frozen Well
Gawthorpe House
48
CLOGGER LANE
Pennine Way
Ransable Well
Booth Bridge Farm
Clarke Moss Hill
Carleton Moor
SKIPTON RD
Little Moor
Elslack Moor
2
Pendle Way
PH
Batty House
Broughton Hill
Pinhaw Moor
SCHOOL FIELDS
Sewage Works
Oak Slack Farm
P
Kirk Sykes Farm
Grange Farm
Mine Mus
Cowgarth Farm
Thornton Moor
Pinhaw
Pennine Way
OLD LA
Marl Field Farm
47
YH
GAYLANDS LANE
Wentcliff Brook
Hill Top
SCHOOL
HEWITTS LA
RED LION ST
MILL BR RD
BIRCH HALL LA
DARK LA
Hewitts Farm
Mill Bridge
B81
Sunny Side
Pennine Way
HILL TOP LA
STONEY BANK RD
MILL LANE
P
PO
DODGSON LA
Windle Field Farm
A56
NEW
Out Laithe Farm
1
Raike Bank Farm
Calf Edge Farm
Knott Farm
Hill Top
Prim School
STANDRIDGE CLOUGH LA
MITTON LA
WHITE HL LA
Highbank Farm
Lower Verjuice Farm
Dodgsons Farm
Harrow Ings Farm
SALTERFORTH RD
BARNWOOD RD
BARNWOOD CR
COOLHAM LANE
WINTER GAP LANE
CALF WOOD LANE
The Fold
COLNE RD
Green End
EARBY
Bleara Moor
Mitton House
COW LA
46

90 A 91 B 92 C 93 D 94 E 95 F

A1
1 BEECH AVE
2 WARWICK DR
3 KENILWORTH DR
4 TYSELEY GR
5 GREEN WLK
6 DALE VW
7 BROOKFIELD WY
8 JAGOE RD
9 LINDEN RD
10 ROSTLE TOP RD
11 JOHN ST
12 HARTLEY ST
13 BARRET ST
14 CROSS ST
15 APPLEGARTH ST
16 WILLIAM ST
17 COWGILL ST
18 BROOK ST
19 GEORGE ST
20 JAMES ST
21 RUSHTON AVE
22 CHAPEL ST
23 BAWHEAD RD
24 VICTORIA ST
25 ALBION RD
26 BOOT ST
27 EDWARD ST
28 ALBION ST
29 HIGHFIELD RD
30 LINCOLN RD
31 GOODALL CL
32 VALLEY RD
33 ALBERT ST
34 GREEN END RD
35 GREEN END AVE
36 SHUTTLEWORTH ST
37 WADDINGTON ST
38 GROVE ST
39 LOWER CROFT ST
40 CEMETERY RD
41 RILEY ST

171
186

B1
1 ALDER HILL ST
2 WELBURY CL
3 SPRINGMOUNT
4 SPRINGFIELD AVE
5 PLEASANT VW
6 MOORLAND AVE
7 LONG GREEN
8 STOOPES HL
9 SELBOURNE
10 EARLHAM ST
11 DUXBURY ST
12 CROFT ST
13 REEVAL CL
14 BROWNROYD
15 COWGARTH LA
16 HEATHER BROW

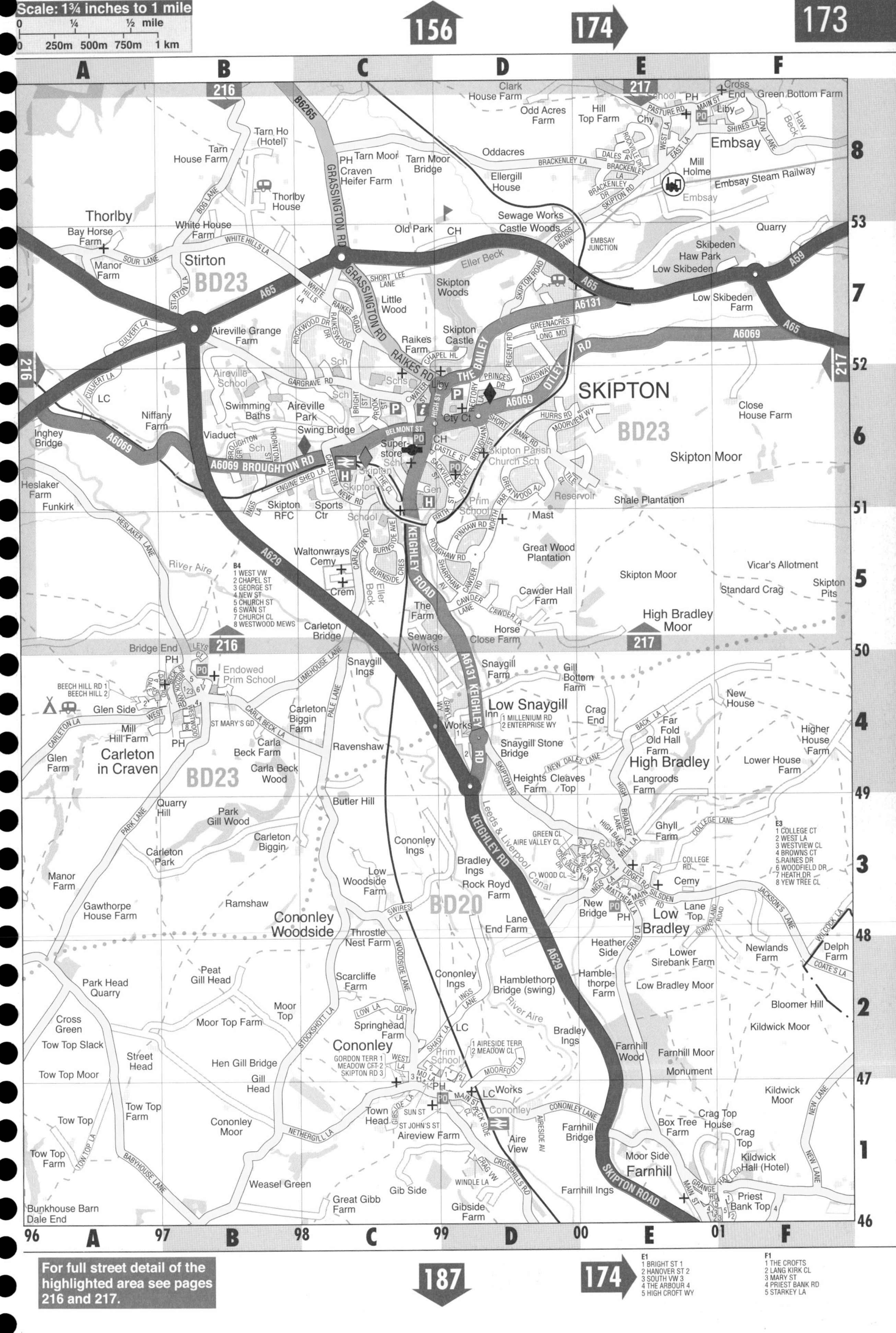

Scale: 1¾ inches to 1 mile
0 ¼ ½ mile
0 250m 500m 750m 1 km
156
174
173
A B C D E F
216
217
Clark House Farm
Odd Acres Farm
Hill Top Farm
Chy
PH
Cross End
Green Bottom Farm
Embsay
Haw Beck
Tarn Ho (Hotel)
Tarn House Farm
PH Tarn Moor
Craven Heifer Farm
Tarn Moor Bridge
Oddacres
BRACKENLEY LA
Ellergill House
Mill Holme
Embsay Steam Railway
Embsay
Thorlby House
Thorlby
GRASSINGTON RD
B6265
Bay Horse Farm
Manor Farm
White House Farm
WHITE HILLS LA
SOUR LANE
Stirton
BD23
Old Park
CH
Sewage Works
Castle Woods
EMBSAY JUNCTION
Quarry
Skibeden
Haw Park
Low Skibeden
Eller Beck
A65
Skipton Woods
Little Wood
SHORT LEE LANE
A6131
Low Skibeden Farm
A59
Aireville Grange Farm
Raikes Farm
Skipton Castle
GREENACRES
LONG MD
A6069
RD
52
RAIKES RD
CHAPEL HL
THE BAILEY
PRINCES DR
KINGSWAY
OTLEY
SKIPTON
Aireville School
GARGRAVE RD
Sch
Schs
LC
Niffany Farm
Swimming Baths
Aireville Park
Swing Bridge
Libr
Cty Ct
HIGH ST
A6069
HURRS RD
MOORVIEW WY
Close House Farm
BD23
Inghey Bridge
Viaduct
BELMONT ST
Super store
CH
Skipton Parish Church Sch
Skipton Moor
A6069 BROUGHTON RD
ENGINE SHED LA
Skipton
Gen
Prim School
Reservoir
Shale Plantation
Heslaker Farm
Funkirk
Skipton RFC
Sports Ctr
School
Mast
HESLAKER LANE
Waltonwrays Cemy
Crem
Eller Beck
KEIGHLEY ROAD
Great Wood Plantation
Vicar's Allotment
River Aire
B4
1 WEST VW
2 CHAPEL ST
3 GEORGE ST
4 NEW ST
5 CHURCH ST
6 SWAN ST
7 CHURCH CL
8 WESTWOOD MEWS
A629
The Farm
Cawder Hall Farm
Skipton Moor
Standard Crag
Skipton Pits
High Bradley Moor
Carleton Bridge
Sewage Works
Horse Close Farm
Bridge End
PH
Endowed Prim School
Snaygill Ings
Snaygill Farm
Gill Bottom Farm
BEECH HILL RD 1
BEECH HILL 2
Glen Side
Carleton Biggin Farm
Low Snaygill
Inn
1 MILLENNIUM RD
2 ENTERPRISE WY
Works
Craig End
Far Fold
Old Hall Farm
New House
Higher House Farm
Mill Hill Farm
PH
Carla Beck Farm
Ravenshaw
Snaygill Stone Bridge
Glen Farm
Carleton in Craven
BD23
Carla Beck Wood
High Bradley
Lower House Farm
Heights Farm
Cleaves Top
Langroods Farm
Quarry Hill
Butler Hill
Park Gill Wood
Carleton Biggin
Ghyll Farm
Carleton Park
Cononley Ings
Bradley Ings
Leeds & Liverpool Canal
E3
1 COLLEGE CT
2 WEST LA
3 WESTVIEW CL
4 BROWNS CT
5 RAINES DR
6 WOODFIELD DR
7 HEATH DR
8 YEW TREE CL
Manor Farm
Low Woodside Farm
Rock Royd Farm
Cemy
Gawthorpe House Farm
Ramshaw
BD20
New Bridge
PH
Low Bradley
Lane Top
Cononley Woodside
Throstle Nest Farm
Lane End Farm
Heather Side
Lower Sirebank Farm
Newlands Farm
Delph Farm
Park Head Quarry
Peat Gill Head
Scarcliffe Farm
Cononley Ings
Hamblethorpe Bridge (swing)
Hamble-thorpe Farm
Low Bradley Moor
Cross Green
Moor Top
Bloomer Hill
Tow Top Slack
Moor Top Farm
Springhead Farm
River Aire
Bradley Ings
Kildwick Moor
Street Head
Hen Gill Bridge
Cononley
Prim School
1 AIRESIDE TERR
2 MEADOW CL
Farnhill Wood
Farnhill Moor
Tow Top Moor
Gill Head
GORDON TERR 1
MEADOW CFT 2
SKIPTON RD 3
Monument
Tow Top Farm
Works
Kildwick Moor
Tow Top
Cononley Moor
Town Head
Aireview Farm
Cononley
Air View
Farnhill Bridge
Box Tree Farm
Crag Top House
Crag Top
Tow Top Farm
Moor Side
Farnhill
Kildwick Hall (Hotel)
Weasel Green
Great Gibb Farm
Gib Side
Gibside Farm
Farnhill Ings
SKIPTON ROAD
Priest Bank Top
Bunkhouse Barn
Dale End
96 97 98 99 00 01
8 53 7 52 6 51 5 50 4 49 3 48 2 47 1 46
For full street detail of the highlighted area see pages 216 and 217.
187
174
E1
1 BRIGHT ST 1
2 HANOVER ST 2
3 SOUTH VW 3
4 THE ARBOUR 4
5 HIGH CROFT WY
F1
1 THE CROFTS
2 LANG KIRK CL
3 MARY ST
4 PRIEST BANK RD
5 STARKEY LA

173
157

E4
1 PARSON'S LA
2 MOOR PK CL
3 MOOR PK CR
4 TURNER LA
5 BIG MD DR
6 GILL CL
7 STAMP HL CL
8 THE STREET
9 BROADFIELD WY
10 LIME CL
11 HAWTHORN CL

Scale: 1¾ inches to 1 mile
0 ¼ ½ mile
0 250m 500m 750m 1 km

A B C D E F

8
53
7
52
6
51
5
50
4
49
3
48
2
47
1
46

Fish Pond
Halton East
CHAPEL LA
GAW LA
Waterfall
Halton Gill Wood
Hesketh House
Bolton Abbey
Bank Wood
Struff Wood
LOW LANE
HOLME LANE
NEWBRIDGE LANE
Embsay Steam Railway
Holywell Holt
LONG CAUSEWAY
A59
Hambleton
Bolton Abbey
B6160
Dales Way
Holywell Bridge
PRIOR'S LA
Harry Wall Gill
Waterfall
Huffa Bridge
Hotel
Bolton Bridge
Boyle & Petyts Sch
High Skibeden Farm
Hayneholme
MEADOWCROFT
LOW LA
Banks Wood
BD23
Field House Farm
Draughton
THE CROFT
SPRING RI
Hawpike Farm
Lob Wood
Beamsley
BEAMSLEY LANE
River Wharfe
Home Farm
LOWFIELD LANE
Wheelam Rock
THE SPINNEY
WEST VW
Lane End Farm
Berwick
Haw Pike
Eller Carr Wood
BOLTON ROAD
Ellenber Farm
A65
Banks Gill
Wind Pumps
Draughton Heights Farm
Mines
Hag Head Laithe
Chelker Reservoir
Farfield Hall
Draughton Height
Berwick Intake Farm
Back Plantation
Chelker House Farm
Highfield Farm
Syke House Farm
HEIGHT LANE
Nor Hill Well
Upper White Well
Highfield House
Farfield Farm
Draughton Moor
Skipton Moor
High Sanfitt Farm
The Bogs
Riddings Farm
Snow Hill Farm
Snow Hill Plantation
Haygill Farm
MOOR LANE
High Cross Bank Farm
Cross Bank
CH
LONG RIDDINGS
SPRINGFIELD MOUNT
HAYGILL NOOK
High Edge
Bank End Farm
Addingham Low Moor
HEATHNESS RD
SKIPTON RD
Addingham
HARCOURT DR
High Bradley Moor
High Edge Farm
Middlesbrough Farm
HODGSON FOLD
Sch
SCHOOL GREEN LA
BACK BECK LA
Sch
Counter Hill
Round Dikes
Tumulus
MOOR LA
Low Edge Farm
Carr Bog Farm
JOWETT'S LA
BANK LANE
Earthwork
MOOR PK DR
MAIN ST
Old Sch
Hall
SILSDEN RD
ADDINGHAM WHARFEDALE
Cowburn Beck Farm
Woofa Bank Farm
PO
Liby
Moor Gate
Moorgate Farm
Jenkin
Great Gill
Lower Turner Lane Farm
STOCKINGER LA
Tumulus
Lower Marchup Farm
SILSDEN RD
ADDINGHAM WHARFEDALE
RIDGE LANE
WALKER'S LANE
Silsden Moor
CRINGLES LANE
Marchup Plantation
LS29
TURNER LA
Coppy Hill
Walton Hole
Middle Marchup Farm
Marchup Height
Nudge Hill Farm
Little Round Wood
Street Farm
Marlpit Plantation
High Bracken Hill Farm
BOLTON RD
Gildersber
GREEN LA
Foster Cliffe Farm North
Far Cringles Farm
Addingham Middle Moor
Deif Hill
KIT LANE
LOW LANE
Old Tower
COCKING LA
COCKING LA
Lane House Farm
KILN HILL LA
Silsden Moor
Foster Cliffe Farm South
Great Gill
Cringles
Brook's Hill
Sea Moor Hill
High Brockabank
Brocka Bank Moor
Small Banks
Silsden Moor
Brook's Crag
TURNER LA
School Wood
Horne House
Dales Bank Farm
A6034
Nudge Hill
Smoulden Farm
Heights Farm
HORN LANE
STRAIGHT LA
Sea Moor Farm
Hodson's Farm
Silsden Reservoir
Horn Crag
COATE'S LANE
HEIGHTS LANE
Stakehill Plantation
Lower Heights Farm
Hay Hills Farms
BD20
Asker Hill
Hang Goose Farm
Slade Farm
Addingham Moorside
HAYHILLS LA
FISHBECK LA
Crag House
LIGHT BANK LANE
Bloomer Hill Farm
Bridge House
HOLE LANE
Raikes Head Farm
Beck Wood
BROWN BANK LANE
NEW DENNIS LANE
Hole Farm
Well House Farm
Brown Bank
Addingham High Moor
Low Bracken Hill Farm
NAB VW
BREAKMOOR AV
SWARTHA LA
Windgate Nick
BURNSALL MEWS
BROWCLIFF
Light Bank
BRADLEY ROAD
SILSDEN
Nab End
KILNSEY FOLD
THORNER GV
Tar Topping
Town Head
White Crag
White Crag Plantation
High Cross Moor Farm
HIGH GREEN DR
BANKLANDS AV
HAWBER COTE DR
North End Farm
SKIPTON RD
Swartha
SKIPTON ROAD
KIRKGATE
Liby
Theatre
PICKARD LA
BACKLANDS
White Crag Moor
Cup and Ring Marked Rocks
Sch
CRAVEN CT
MIDDLEWAY
HAWBER LANE
Kildwick Grange
Sch
S VW TR
ELLIOTT STREET
PO
Brunthwaite
Brunthwaite Crag
JERRY LA
WOODSIDE ROAD
GLOUCESTER AVE
Goll
JACQUES GR
BRUNTHWAITE LANE
Airedale House Farm
Black Pots Farm

A6034 Keighley (A629) West Yorkshire STREET ATLAS

02 A 03 B 04 C D 06 E 07 F

F4
1 MOOR PK WY
2 MOOR PK GR
3 CRAVEN CR
4 BURNS HILL
5 COCKSHOTT PL
6 WHARFEDALE VW
7 HIGH BANK CL
8 CHAPEL ST
9 SUGAR HILL
10 AYNHOLME CL
11 KILNERS CFT
12 TOWNHEAD FOLD
13 BECKSIDE CL
14 RIDLEYS FOLD
15 GEORGE ST
16 DRUGGIST LA
17 JONATHAN GARTH
18 HILLSIDE CL
19 WEST CFT
20 OLD STATION WY
21 ACRE FOLD
22 SOUTHFIELD TR
23 SOUTHFIELD LA
24 BROWNSFIELD RD
25 ST JOHNS AV
26 MOUNT PLEASANT
27 ST CHRISTOPHERS DR
28 SOUTHFIELD RD
29 ST MICHAELS WY
30 ST LEONARDS CL
31 ST PETERS CT
32 ST IANS CFT

173

For full street detail of Silsden see Philip's STREET ATLAS of West Yorkshire

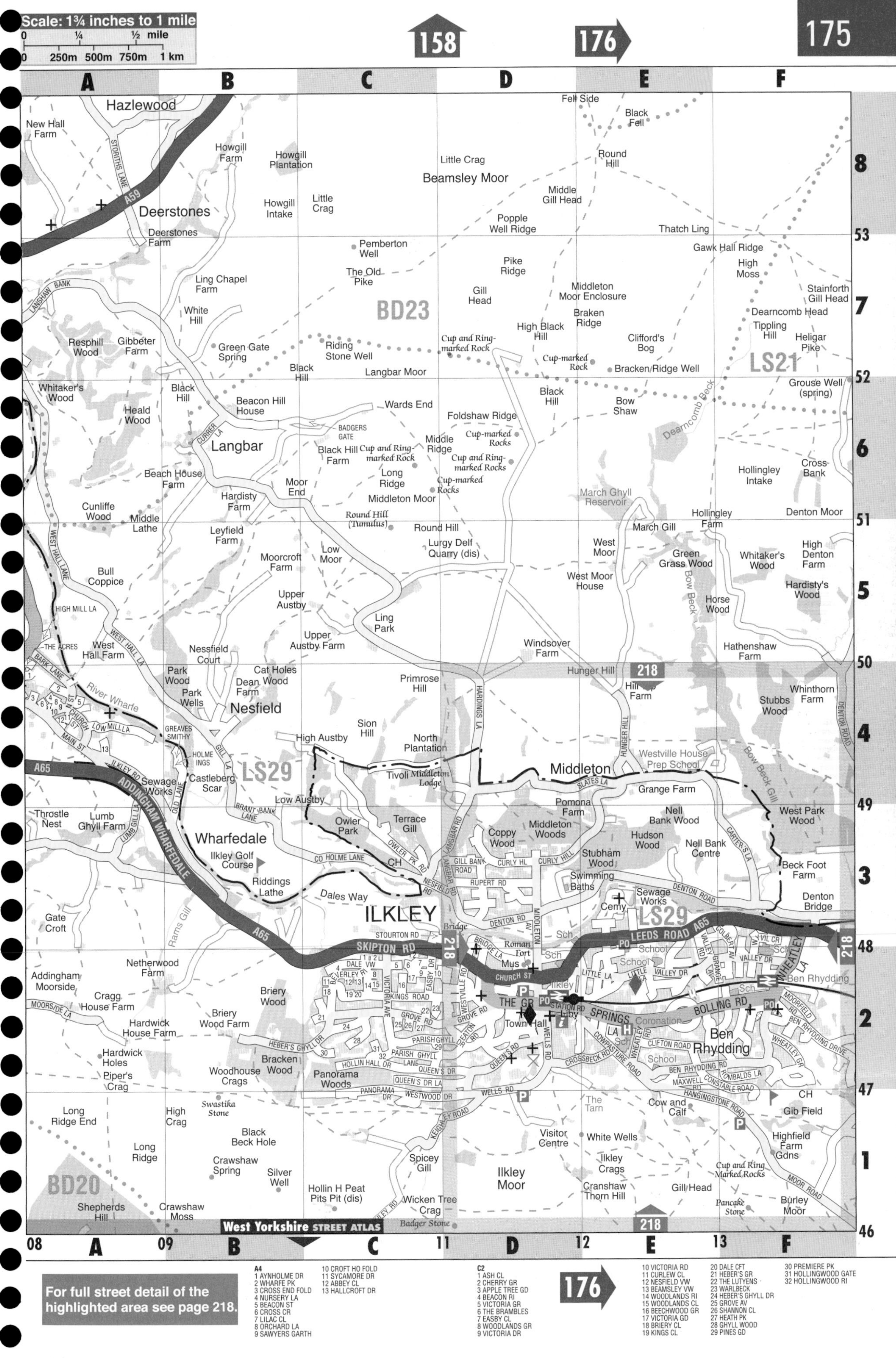
175
Scale: 1¾ inches to 1 mile
0 ¼ ½ mile
0 250m 500m 750m 1 km
158
176
Hazlewood
New Hall Farm
Howgill Farm
Howgill Plantation
Little Crag
Beamsley Moor
Fell Side
Black Fell
Round Hill
Middle Gill Head
Deerstones
Deerstones Farm
Howgill Intake
Popple Well Ridge
Thatch Ling
Pemberton Well
The Old Pike
Pike Ridge
Gawk Hall Ridge
High Moss
Ling Chapel Farm
Gill Head
Middleton Moor Enclosure
Stainforth Gill Head
BD23
White Hill
Braken Ridge
Dearncomb Head
Resphill Wood
Gibbeter Farm
Green Gate Spring
Riding Stone Well
Cup and Ring-marked Rock
High Black Hill
Clifford's Bog
Tippling Hill
Heligar Pike
Black Hill
Langbar Moor
Cup-marked Rock
Bracken Ridge Well
LS21
Whitaker's Wood
Beacon Hill House
Grouse Well (spring)
Heald Wood
Wards End
Bow Shaw
Foldshaw Ridge
Langbar
Badgers Gate
Black Hill Farm
Cup and Ring-marked Rock
Middle Ridge
Cup-marked Rocks
Cup and Ring-marked Rocks
Dearncomb Beck
Beach House Farm
Long Ridge
Hollingley Intake
Cross Bank
Moor End
Cup-marked Rocks
Hardisty Farm
Middleton Moor
March Ghyll Reservoir
Cunliffe Wood
Middle Lathe
Round Hill (Tumulus)
Round Hill
Hollingley Farm
Denton Moor
March Gill
Leyfield Farm
Lurgy Delf Quarry (dis)
West Moor
Green Grass Wood
Whitaker's Wood
High Denton Farm
Low Moor
Moorcroft Farm
West Moor House
Bull Coppice
Upper Austby
Hardisty's Wood
Horse Wood
High Mill La
Ling Park
Upper Austby Farm
Windsover Farm
Hathenshaw Farm
The Acres
West Hall Farm
Nessfield Court
Hunger Hill
Hill Top Farm
Park Wood
Cat Holes
Dean Wood
Primrose Hill
Whinthorn Farm
Stubbs Wood
Park Wells
Nesfield
River Wharfe
Sion Hill
High Austby
North Plantation
Greaves Smithy
Holme Ings
Westville House Prep School
Middleton
Tivoli
Middleton Lodge
Sewage Works
Castleberg Scar
LS29
Grange Farm
Low Austby
Pomona Farm
A65
Throstle Nest
Lumb Ghyll Farm
Owler Park
Terrace Gill
Nell Bank Wood
West Park Wood
Copy Wood
Middleton Woods
Hudson Wood
Nell Bank Centre
Wharfedale
Ilkley Golf Course
Stubham Wood
Beck Foot Farm
Swimming Baths
Riddings Lathe
Dales Way
Sewage Works
Cemy
Denton Bridge
Gate Croft
ILKLEY
LS29
Netherwood Farm
Roman Fort
Mus
Addingham Moorside
Cragg House Farm
Briery Wood
Town Hall
Ben Rhydding
Hardwick House Farm
Briery Wood Farm
Coronation
Hardwick Holes
Woodhouse Crags
Bracken Wood
Panorama Woods
Piper's Crag
The Tarn
Cow and Calf
Gib Field
Swastika Stone
Long Ridge End
High Crag
Black Beck Hole
Visitor Centre
White Wells
Highfield Farm Gdns
Long Ridge
Crawshaw Spring
Silver Well
Spicey Gill
Ilkley Moor
Ilkley Crags
Cup and Ring Marked Rocks
BD20
Hollin H Peat Pits Pit (dis)
Wicken Tree Crag
Cranshaw Thorn Hill
Gill Head
Pancake Stone
Burley Moor
Shepherds Hill
Crawshaw Moss
Badger Stone
218
West Yorkshire STREET ATLAS
For full street detail of the highlighted area see page 218.
A4
1 AYNHOLME DR
2 WHARFE PK
3 CROSS END FOLD
4 NURSERY LA
5 BEACON ST
6 CROSS CR
7 LILAC CL
8 ORCHARD LA
9 SAWYERS GARTH
10 CROFT HO FOLD
11 SYCAMORE DR
12 ABBEY CL
13 HALLCROFT DR
C2
1 ASH CL
2 CHERRY GR
3 APPLE TREE GD
4 BEACON RI
5 VICTORIA GR
6 THE BRAMBLES
7 EASBY CL
8 WOODLANDS GR
9 VICTORIA DR
10 VICTORIA RD
11 CURLEW CL
12 NESFIELD VW
13 BEAMSLEY VW
14 WOODLANDS RI
15 WOODLANDS CL
16 BEECHWOOD GR
17 VICTORIA GD
18 BRIERY CL
19 KINGS CL
20 DALE CFT
21 HEBER'S GR
22 THE LUTYENS
23 WARLBECK
24 HEBER'S GHYLL DR
25 GROVE AV
26 SHANNON CL
27 HEATH PK
28 GHYLL WOOD
29 PINES GD
30 PREMIERE PK
31 HOLLINGWOOD GATE
32 HOLLINGWOOD RI

175
159

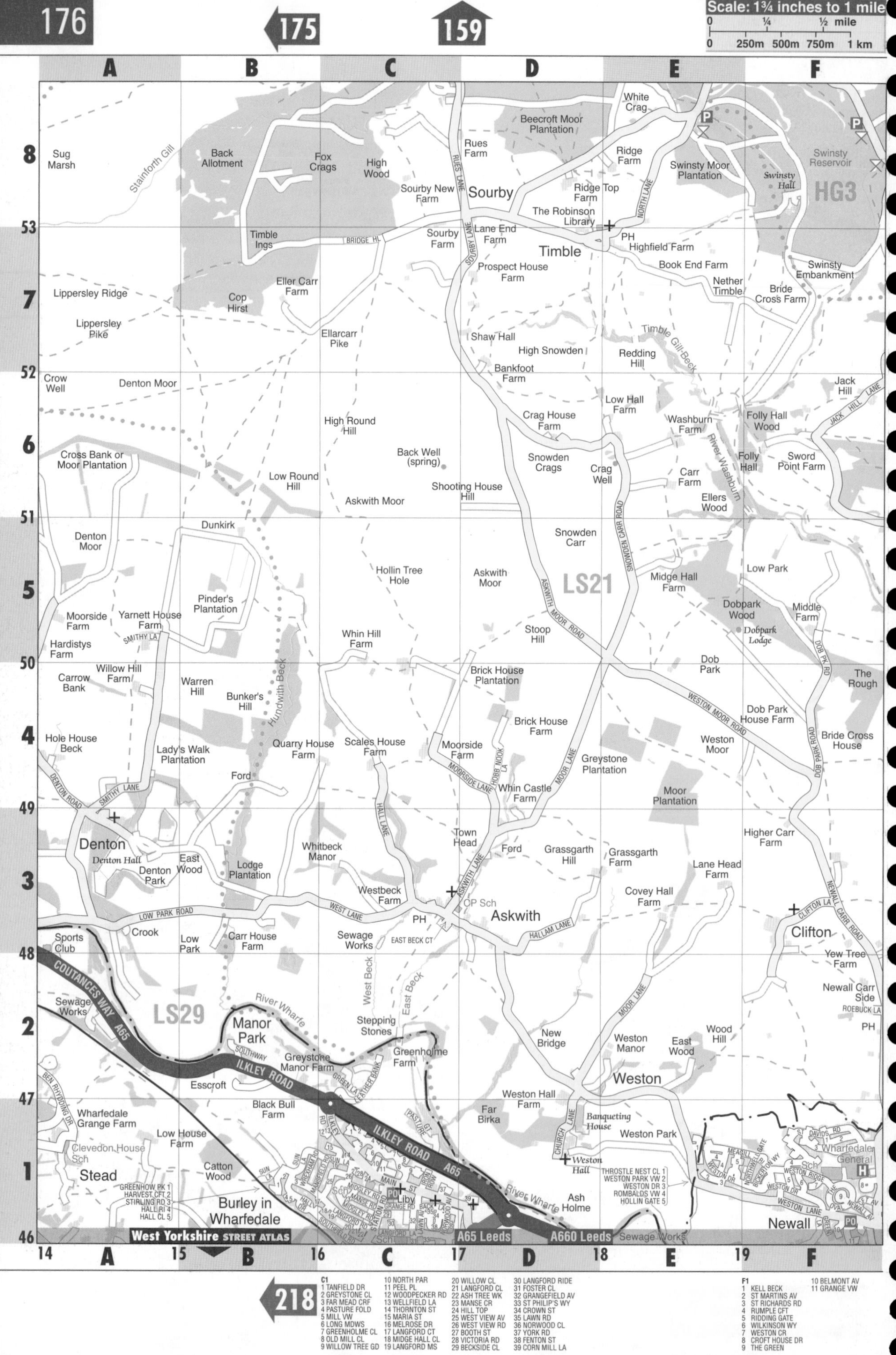

218

C1
1 TANFIELD DR
2 GREYSTONE CL
3 FAR MEAD CRF
4 PASTURE FOLD
5 MILL VW
6 LONG MDWS
7 GREENHOLME CL
8 OLD MILL CL
9 WILLOW TREE GD
10 NORTH PAR
11 PEEL PL
12 WOODPECKER RD
13 WELLFIELD LA
14 THORNTON ST
15 MARIA ST
16 MELROSE DR
17 LANGFORD CT
18 MIDGE HALL CL
19 LANGFORD MS
20 WILLOW CL
21 LANGFORD CL
22 ASH TREE WK
23 MANSE CR
24 HILL TOP
25 WEST VIEW AV
26 WEST VIEW RD
27 BOOTH ST
28 VICTORIA RD
29 BECKSIDE CL
30 LANGFORD RIDE
31 FOSTER CL
32 GRANGEFIELD AV
33 ST PHILIP'S WY
34 CROWN ST
35 LAWN RD
36 NORWOOD CL
37 YORK RD
38 FENTON ST
39 CORN MILL LA

F1
1 KELL BECK
2 ST MARTINS AV
3 ST RICHARDS RD
4 RUMPLE CFT
5 RIDDING GATE
6 WILKINSON WY
7 WESTON CR
8 CROFT HOUSE DR
9 THE GREEN
10 BELMONT AV
11 GRANGE VW

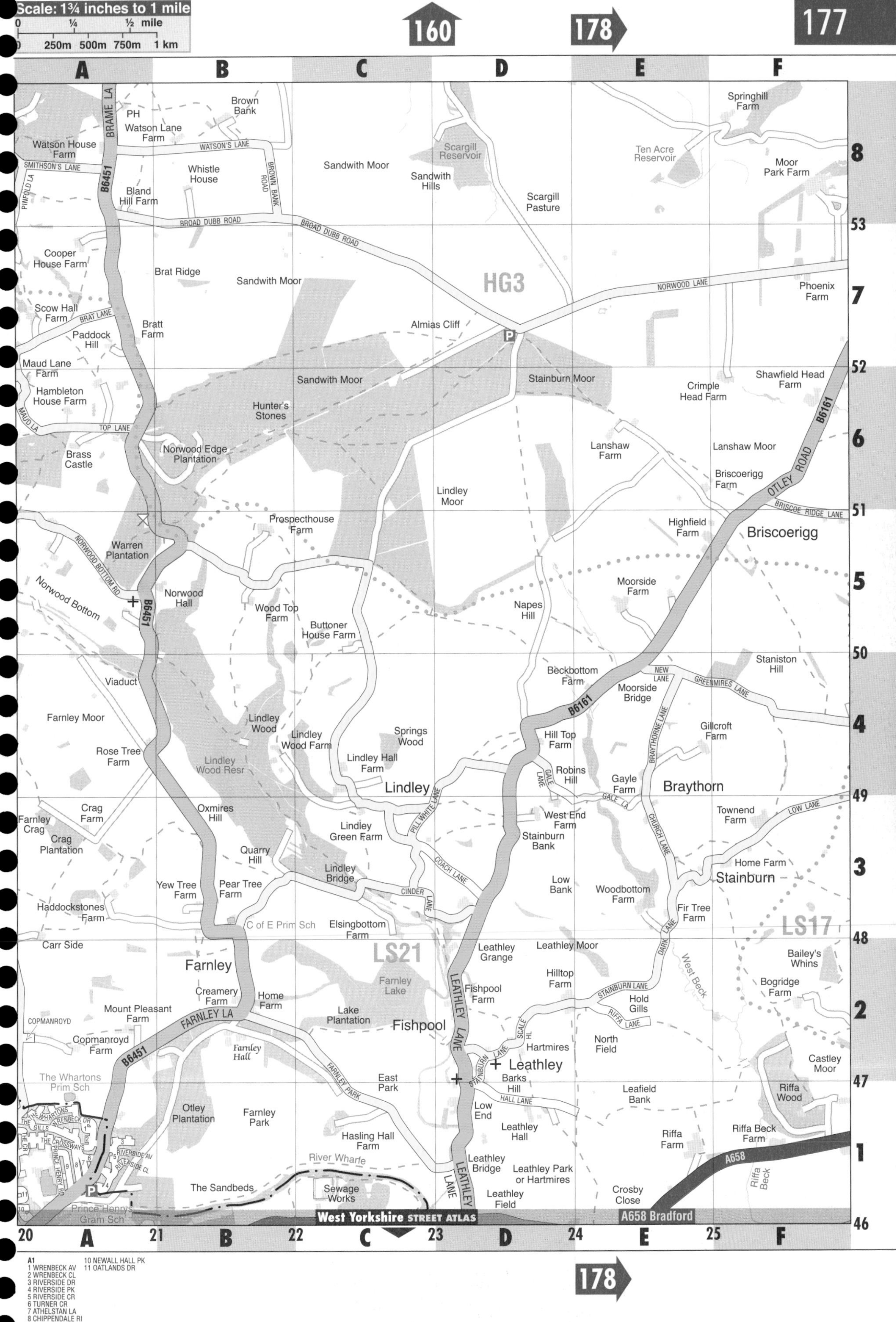

178

A1
1 WRENBECK AV
2 WRENBECK CL
3 RIVERSIDE DR
4 RIVERSIDE PK
5 RIVERSIDE CR
6 TURNER CR
7 ATHELSTAN LA
8 CHIPPENDALE RI
9 HARECROFT RD
10 NEWALL HALL PK
11 OATLANDS DR

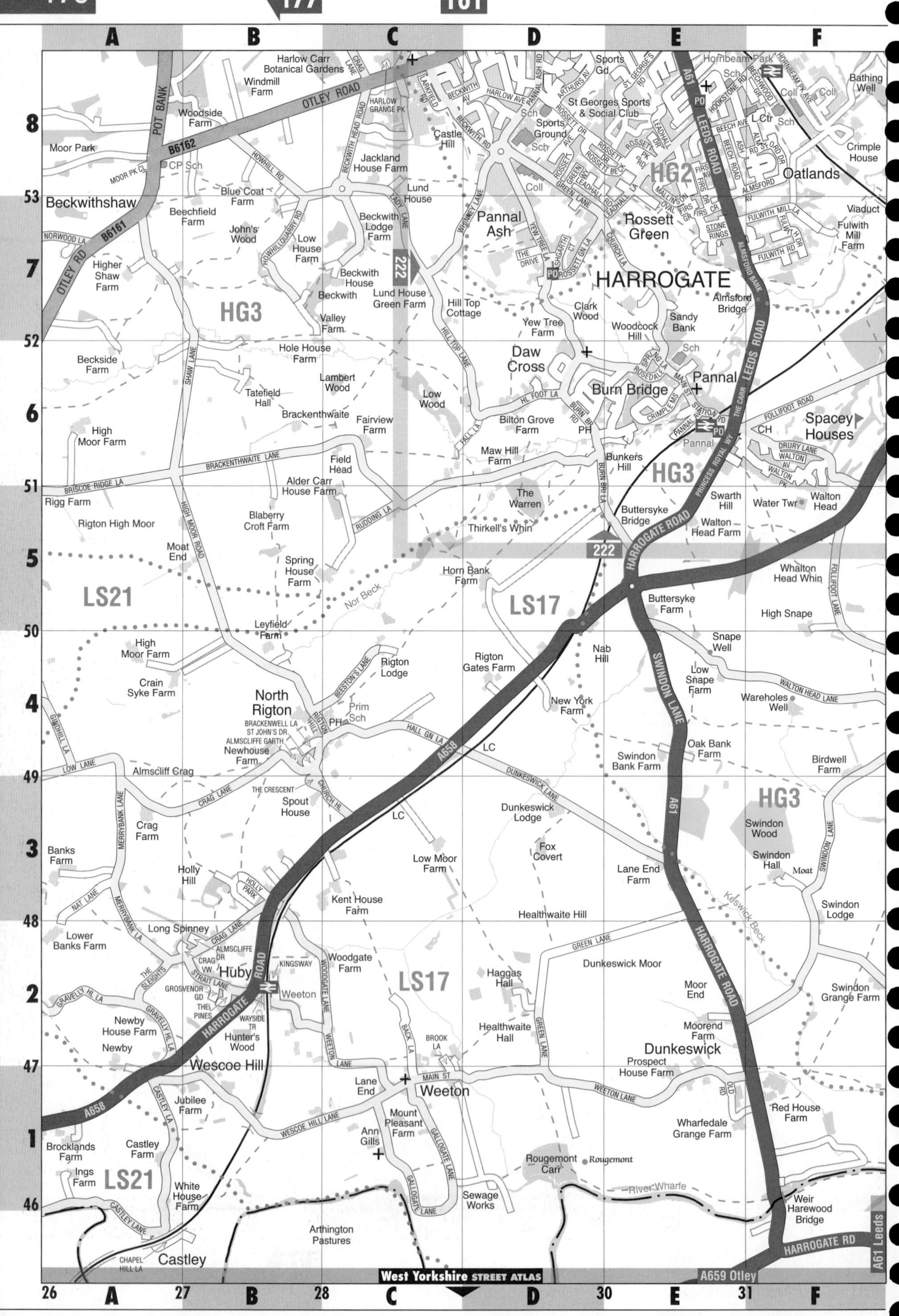
HARROGATE
Harlow Carr Botanical Gardens
Windmill Farm
Woodside Farm
Moor Park
Beckwithshaw
Blue Coat Farm
Beechfield Farm
John's Wood
Low House Farm
Higher Shaw Farm
Jackland House Farm
Lund House
Beckwith Lodge Farm
Beckwith House
Beckwith
Lund House Green Farm
Castle Hill
Pannal Ash
Rossett Green
Sports Gd
St Georges Sports & Social Club
Sports Ground
HG2
HG3
Oatlands
Crimple House
Bathing Well
Viaduct
Fulwith Mill Farm
Almsford Bridge
Sandy Bank
Clark Wood
Woodcock Hill
Yew Tree Farm
Hill Top Cottage
Valley Farm
Hole House Farm
Beckside Farm
Daw Cross
Burn Bridge
Pannal
Lambert Wood
Tatefield Hall
Brackenthwaite
Low Wood
Fairview Farm
Bilton Grove Farm
High Moor Farm
Field Head
Maw Hill Farm
Bunkers Hill
Spacey Houses
Swarth Hill
Water Twr
Walton Head
Walton Head Farm
Buttersyke Bridge
Rigg Farm
Rigton High Moor
Alder Carr House Farm
Blaberry Croft Farm
The Warren
Thirkell's Whin
Moat End
Spring House Farm
Horn Bank Farm
Whalton Head Whin
LS21
LS17
Nor Beck
Buttersyke Farm
High Snape
Leyfield Farm
High Moor Farm
Nab Hill
Snape Well
Rigton Lodge
Rigton Gates Farm
Low Snape Farm
Crain Syke Farm
North Rigton
Prim Sch
New York Farm
Wareholes Well
Newhouse Farm
Oak Bank Farm
Almscliff Crag
Swindon Bank Farm
Birdwell Farm
Spout House
Dunkeswick Lodge
Crag Farm
Swindon Wood
Banks Farm
Fox Covert
Low Moor Farm
Lane End Farm
Swindon Hall
Moat
Holly Hill
Kent House Farm
Swindon Lodge
Healthwaite Hill
Keswick Beck
Lower Banks Farm
Long Spinney
Woodgate Farm
Dunkeswick Moor
Huby
Weeton
Haggas Hall
Moor End
Swindon Grange Farm
Newby House Farm
Newby
Hunter's Wood
Healthwaite Hall
Moorend Farm
Dunkeswick
Prospect House Farm
Wescoe Hill
Lane End
Weeton
Jubilee Farm
Mount Pleasant Farm
Red House Farm
Wharfedale Grange Farm
Brocklands Farm
Castley Farm
Ann Gills
Rougemont Carr
Rougemont
Ings Farm
White House Farm
Sewage Works
River Wharfe
Weir
Harewood Bridge
Arthington Pastures
Castley
A658
A61
B6161
B6162
OTLEY ROAD
LEEDS ROAD
HARROGATE ROAD
SWINDON LANE
HARROGATE RD
222
A61 Leeds
A659 Otley

E6
1 CLIVE RD
2 CASTLE CL
3 BEECH LA
4 CANBY LA
5 CHURCH HL
6 MILL CL
7 MANOR GARTH
8 SCHOOL LA
9 CHURCH LA

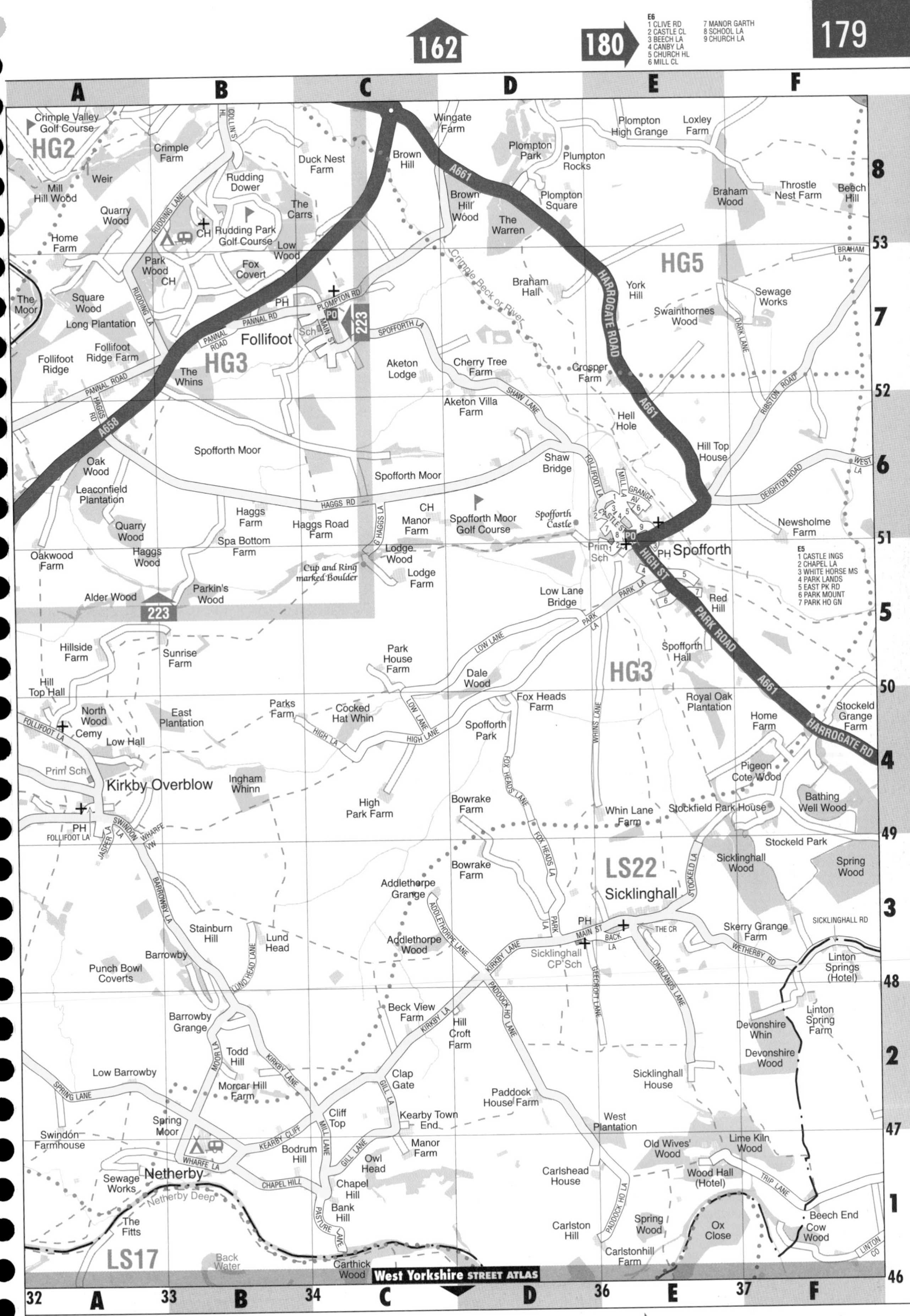

For full street detail of the highlighted area see pages 222 and 223.

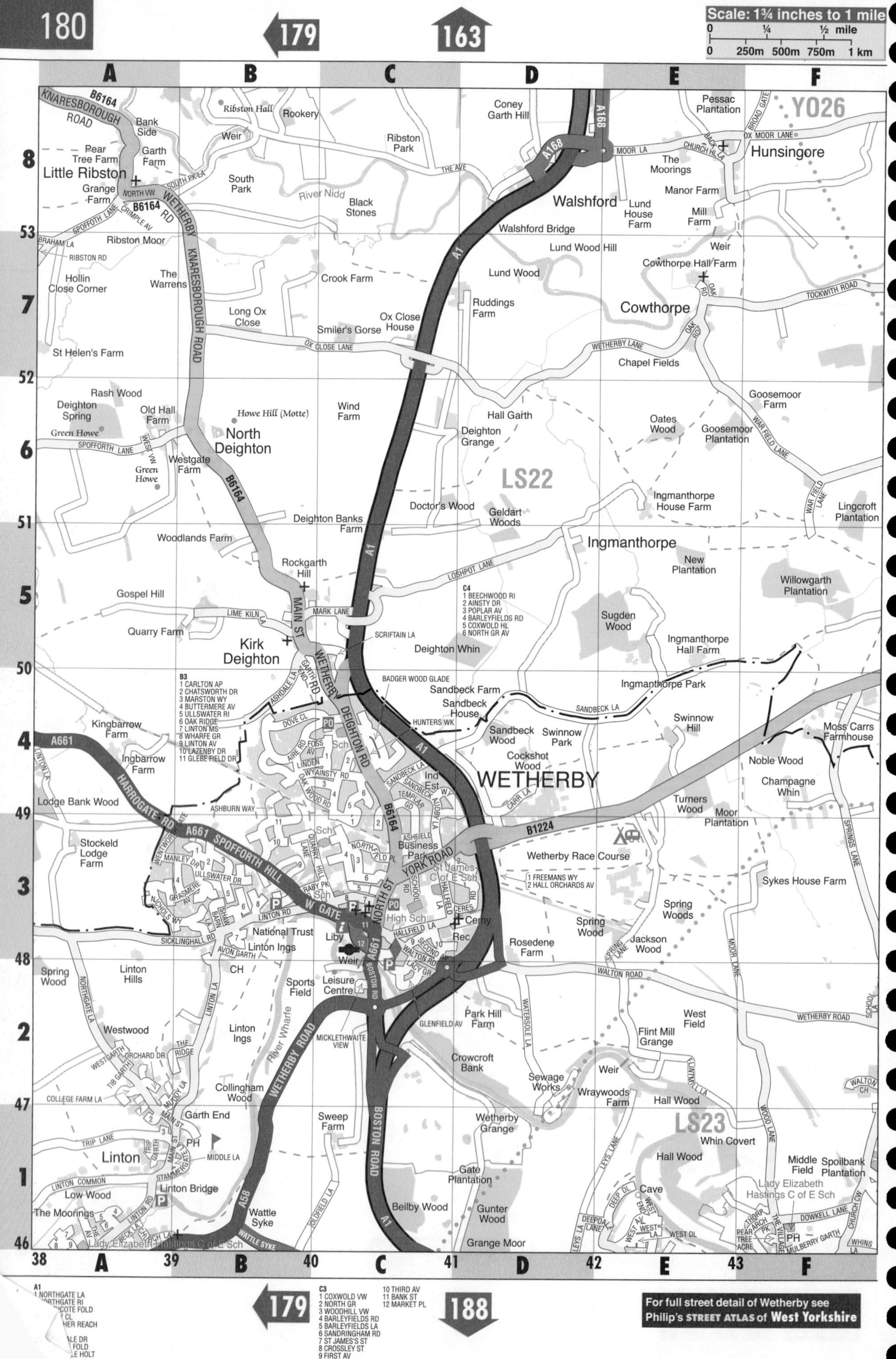
179
163
Scale: 1¾ inches to 1 mile
0 ¼ ½ mile
0 250m 500m 750m 1 km
Little Ribston
Hunsingore
Walshford
Cowthorpe
North Deighton
Kirk Deighton
Ingmanthorpe
WETHERBY
Linton
LS22
LS23
YO26
KNARESBOROUGH ROAD
WETHERBY KNARESBOROUGH ROAD
B6164
A168
A1
A661
A58
B1224
HARROGATE RD
SPOFFORTH HILL
WETHERBY ROAD
BOSTON ROAD
YORK ROAD
DEIGHTON RD
OX CLOSE LANE
LOSHPOT LANE
SANDBECK LA
WALTON ROAD
WETHERBY ROAD
TOCKWITH ROAD
WETHERBY LANE
Ribston Hall
Rookery
Ribston Park
South Park
River Nidd
Black Stones
Coney Garth Hill
Pessac Plantation
The Moorings
Manor Farm
Lund House Farm
Mill Farm
Walshford Bridge
Lund Wood Hill
Lund Wood
Cowthorpe Hall Farm
Ribston Moor
Hollin Close Corner
The Warrens
Crook Farm
Ruddings Farm
Long Ox Close
Smiler's Gorse
Ox Close House
St Helen's Farm
Chapel Fields
Goosemoor Farm
Rash Wood
Deighton Spring
Old Hall Farm
Howe Hill (Motte)
Wind Farm
Hall Garth
Deighton Grange
Oates Wood
Goosemoor Plantation
Green Howe
Westgate Farm
Doctor's Wood
Geldart Woods
Ingmanthorpe House Farm
Lingcroft Plantation
Deighton Banks Farm
Woodlands Farm
Rockgarth Hill
New Plantation
Willowgarth Plantation
Gospel Hill
Quarry Farm
Sugden Wood
Ingmanthorpe Hall Farm
Deighton Whin
Ingmanthorpe Park
Sandbeck Farm
Sandbeck House
Swinnow Hill
Kingbarrow Farm
Ingbarrow Farm
Sandbeck Wood
Swinnow Park
Cockshot Wood
Moss Carrs Farmhouse
Noble Wood
Champagne Whin
Lodge Bank Wood
Turners Wood
Moor Plantation
Stockeld Lodge Farm
Business Park
Wetherby Race Course
St James' C of E Sch
Sykes House Farm
High Sch
National Trust
Linton Ings
Spring Woods
Spring Wood
Jackson Wood
Rosedene Farm
Spring Wood
Linton Hills
Sports Field
Leisure Centre
West Field
Flint Mill Grange
Park Hill Farm
Westwood
River Wharfe
Crowcroft Bank
Sewage Works
Wraywoods Farm
Hall Wood
Collingham Wood
Garth End
Sweep Farm
Wetherby Grange
Whin Covert
Hall Wood
Middle Field
Spoilbank Plantation
Gate Plantation
Linton Bridge
Low Wood
Cave
Lady Elizabeth Hastings C of E Sch
The Moorings
Wattle Syke
Beilby Wood
Gunter Wood
Grange Moor
Lady Elizabeth Hastings C of E Sch
C4
1 BEECHWOOD RI
2 AINSTY DR
3 POPLAR AV
4 BARLEYFIELDS RD
5 COXWOLD HL
6 NORTH GR AV
B3
1 CARLTON AP
2 CHATSWORTH DR
3 MARSTON WY
4 BUTTERMERE AV
5 ULLSWATER RI
6 OAK RIDGE
7 LINTON MS
8 WHARFE GR
9 LINTON AV
10 LAZENBY DR
11 GLEBE FIELD DR
1 FREEMANS WY
2 HALL ORCHARDS AV
A1
1 NORTHGATE LA
ORTHGATE RI
COTE FOLD
CL
HER REACH
LE DR
FOLD
LE HOLT
179
C3
1 COXWOLD VW
2 NORTH GR
3 WOODHILL VW
4 BARLEYFIELDS RD
5 BARLEYFIELDS LA
6 SANDRINGHAM RD
7 ST JAMES'S ST
8 CROSSLEY ST
9 FIRST AV
10 THIRD AV
11 BANK ST
12 MARKET PL
188
For full street detail of Wetherby see Philip's STREET ATLAS of West Yorkshire

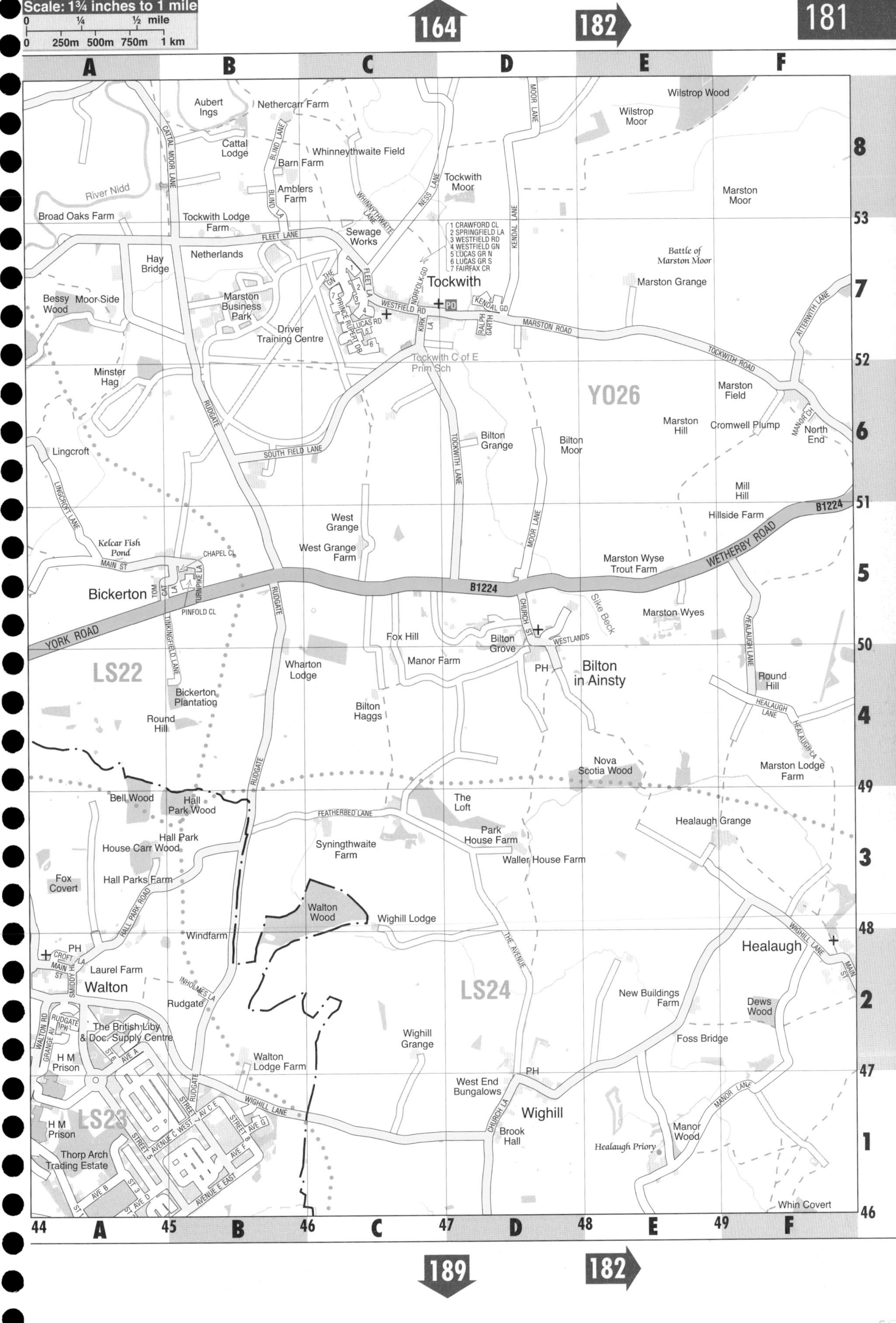
Scale: 1¾ inches to 1 mile
164
182
Tockwith
Bickerton
Bilton in Ainsty
Healaugh
Walton
Wighill
Marston Moor
Battle of Marston Moor
Marston Grange
Marston Business Park
Driver Training Centre
Tockwith C of E Prim Sch
The British Libry & Doc. Supply Centre
H M Prison
Thorp Arch Trading Estate
Healaugh Priory
YO26
LS22
LS23
LS24
B1224
YORK ROAD
WETHERBY ROAD
MARSTON ROAD
TOCKWITH ROAD
1 CRAWFORD CL
2 SPRINGFIELD LA
3 WESTFIELD RD
4 WESTFIELD GN
5 LUCAS GR N
6 LUCAS GR S
7 FAIRFAX CR
189
182

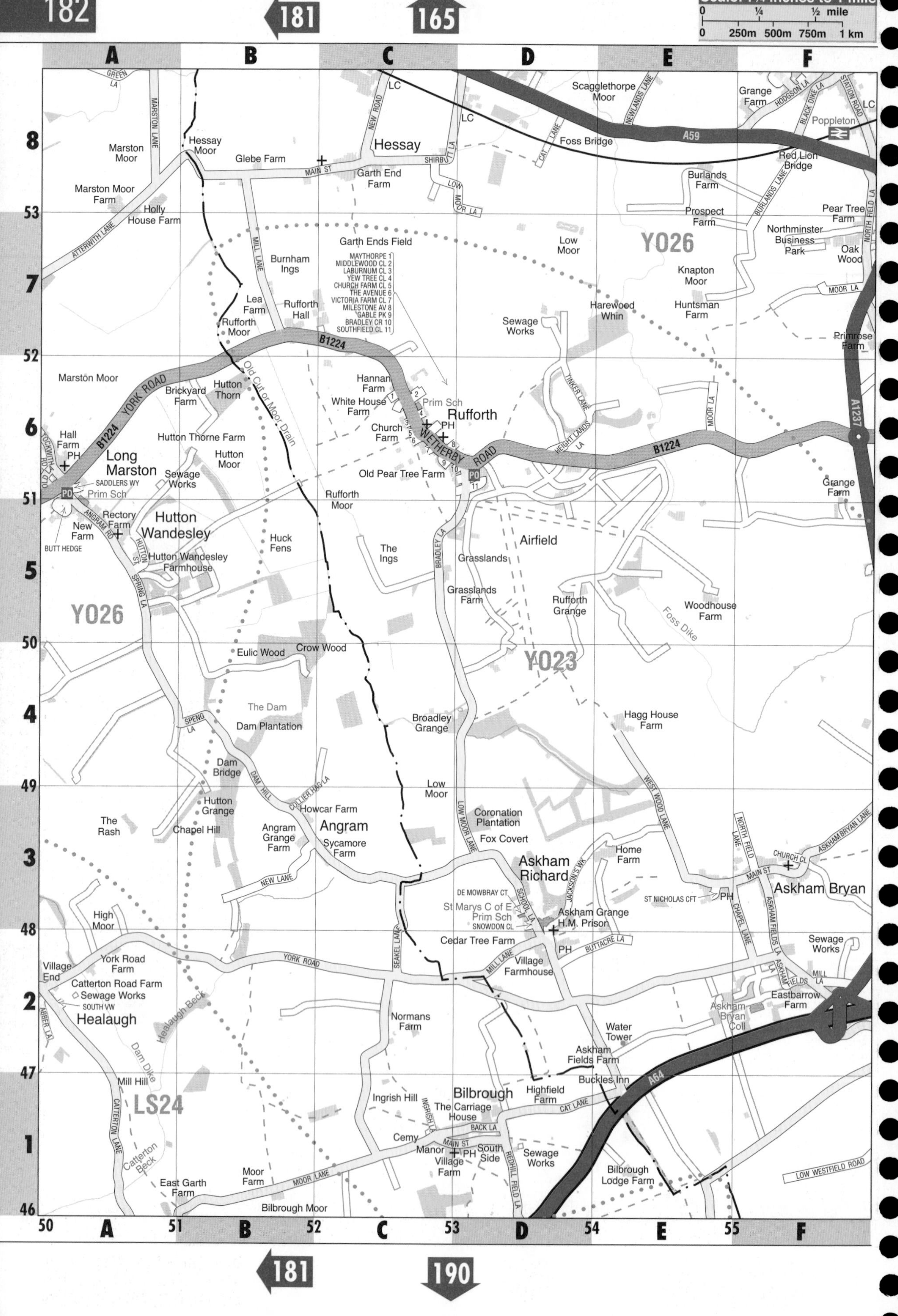
181
165
Scale: 1¾ inches to 1 mile
0 ¼ ½ mile
0 250m 500m 750m 1 km
A B C D E F
8
53
7
52
6
51
5
50
4
49
3
48
2
47
1
46
GREEN LA
MARSTON LANE
Marston Moor
Marston Moor Farm
Holly House Farm
ATTERWITH LANE
Hessay Moor
Glebe Farm
NEW ROAD
LC
Hessay
MAIN ST
SHIRBUTT LA
LOW MOOR LA
Garth End Farm
Scagglethorpe Moor
NEWLANDS LANE
CAT LANE
Foss Bridge
A59
Grange Farm
HODGSON LA
BLACK DIKE LA
STATION ROAD
Poppleton
Red Lion Bridge
Burlands Farm
BURLANDS LANE
Prospect Farm
Pear Tree Farm
NORTH FIELD LA
Northminster Business Park
Oak Wood
YO26
Garth Ends Field
MILL LANE
Burnham Ings
MAYTHORPE 1
MIDDLEWOOD CL 2
LABURNUM CL 3
YEW TREE CL 4
CHURCH FARM CL 5
THE AVENUE 6
VICTORIA FARM CL 7
MILESTONE AV 8
GABLE PK 9
BRADLEY CR 10
SOUTHFIELD CL 11
Low Moor
Knapton Moor
MOOR LA
Lea Farm
Rufforth Hall
Rufforth Moor
Harewood Whin
Huntsman Farm
Sewage Works
Primrose Farm
B1224
Marston Moor
YORK ROAD
Brickyard Farm
Hutton Thorn
Old Cut or Moor Drain
Hannah Farm
White House Farm
Prim Sch
Rufforth
PH
Church Farm
WETHERBY ROAD
TINKER LANE
MOOR LA
HEIGHT LANDS LA
A1237
Hall Farm
Long Marston
Hutton Thorne Farm
Hutton Moor
Sewage Works
SADDLERS WY
Prim Sch
PO
Old Pear Tree Farm
Grange Farm
Rufforth Moor
Rectory Farm
New Farm
ANGRAM RD
BUTT HEDGE
Hutton Wandesley
HUTTON ST
Huck Fens
The Ings
BRADLEY LA
Airfield
Grasslands
Hutton Wandesley Farmhouse
SPRING LA
YO26
Grasslands Farm
Rufforth Grange
Woodhouse Farm
Foss Dike
Eulic Wood
Crow Wood
YO23
The Dam
SPENG LA
Dam Plantation
Broadley Grange
Hagg House Farm
Dam Bridge
DAM HILL
COLLIER HAG LA
Low Moor
WEST WOOD LANE
Hutton Grange
Howcar Farm
LOW MOOR LANE
Coronation Plantation
NORTH FIELD LANE
ASKHAM BRYAN LANE
The Rash
Chapel Hill
Angram Grange Farm
Angram
Sycamore Farm
Fox Covert
Askham Richard
JACKSON'S WK
Home Farm
CHURCH CL
MAIN ST
NEW LANE
DE MOWBRAY CT
SCHOOL LA
ST NICHOLAS CFT
Askham Bryan
St Marys C of E Prim Sch
SNOWDON CL
Askham Grange H.M. Prison
CHAPEL LANE
ASKHAM FIELDS LA
High Moor
SEAKEL LANE
Cedar Tree Farm
BUTTACRE LA
Sewage Works
Village End
York Road Farm
YORK ROAD
MILL LANE
Village Farmhouse
MILL LA
Catterton Road Farm
Sewage Works
SOUTH VW
Healaugh
ABBER LA
Healaugh Beck
Normans Farm
Askham Bryan Coll
Eastbarrow Farm
Water Tower
Dam Dike
Askham Fields Farm
Mill Hill
LS24
Ingrish Hill
Bilbrough
Highfield Farm
Buckles Inn
A64
CATTERTON LANE
The Carriage House
CAT LANE
BACK LA
INGRISH LA
Cemy
MAIN ST
Manor
Village Farm
South Side
REDHILL FIELD LA
Sewage Works
Catterton Beck
Bilbrough Lodge Farm
LOW WESTFIELD ROAD
East Garth Farm
Moor Farm
MOOR LANE
Bilbrough Moor
50 51 52 53 54 55
181
190

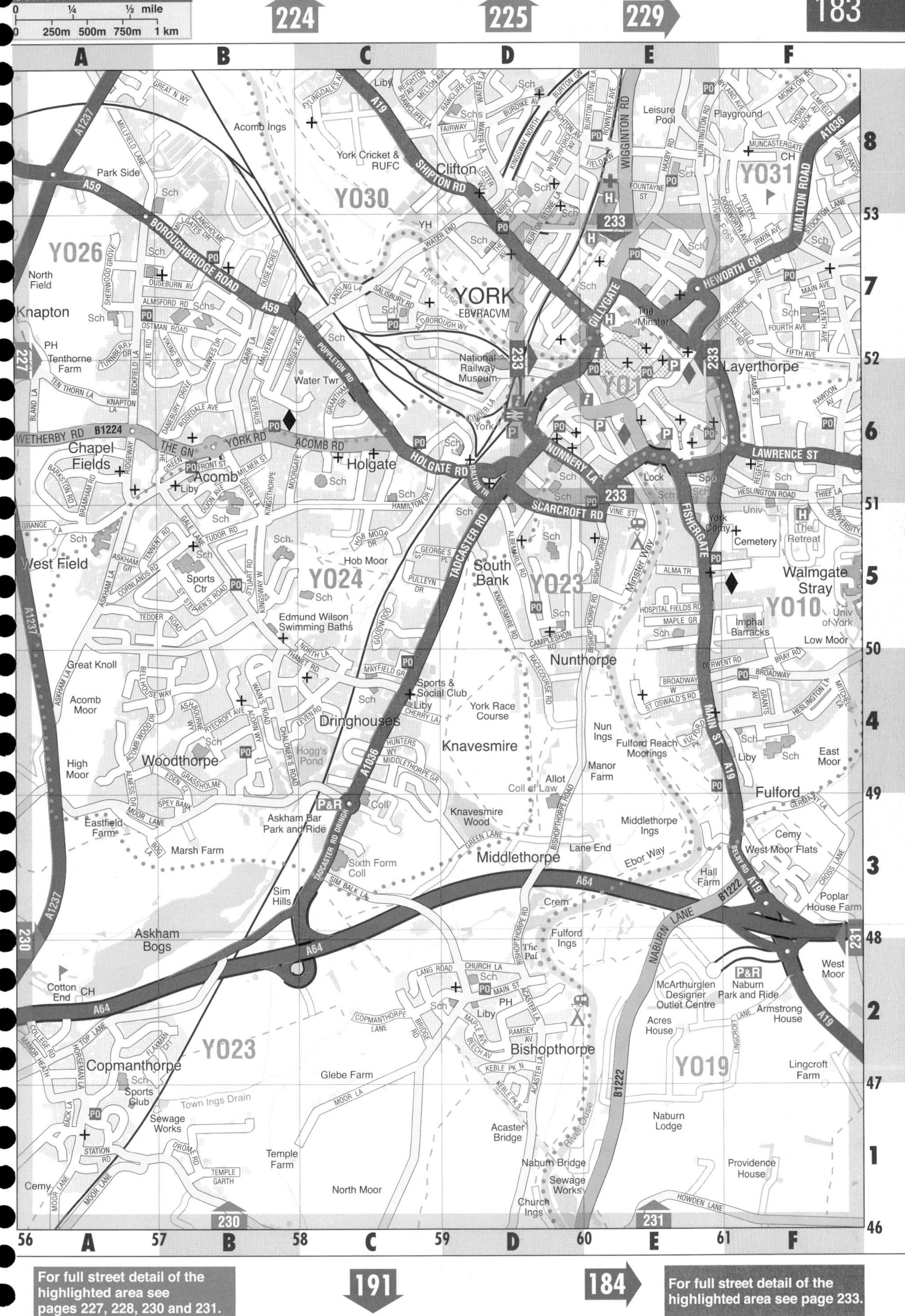

For full street detail of the highlighted area see pages 227, 228, 230 and 231.

For full street detail of the highlighted area see page 233.

228 226 167

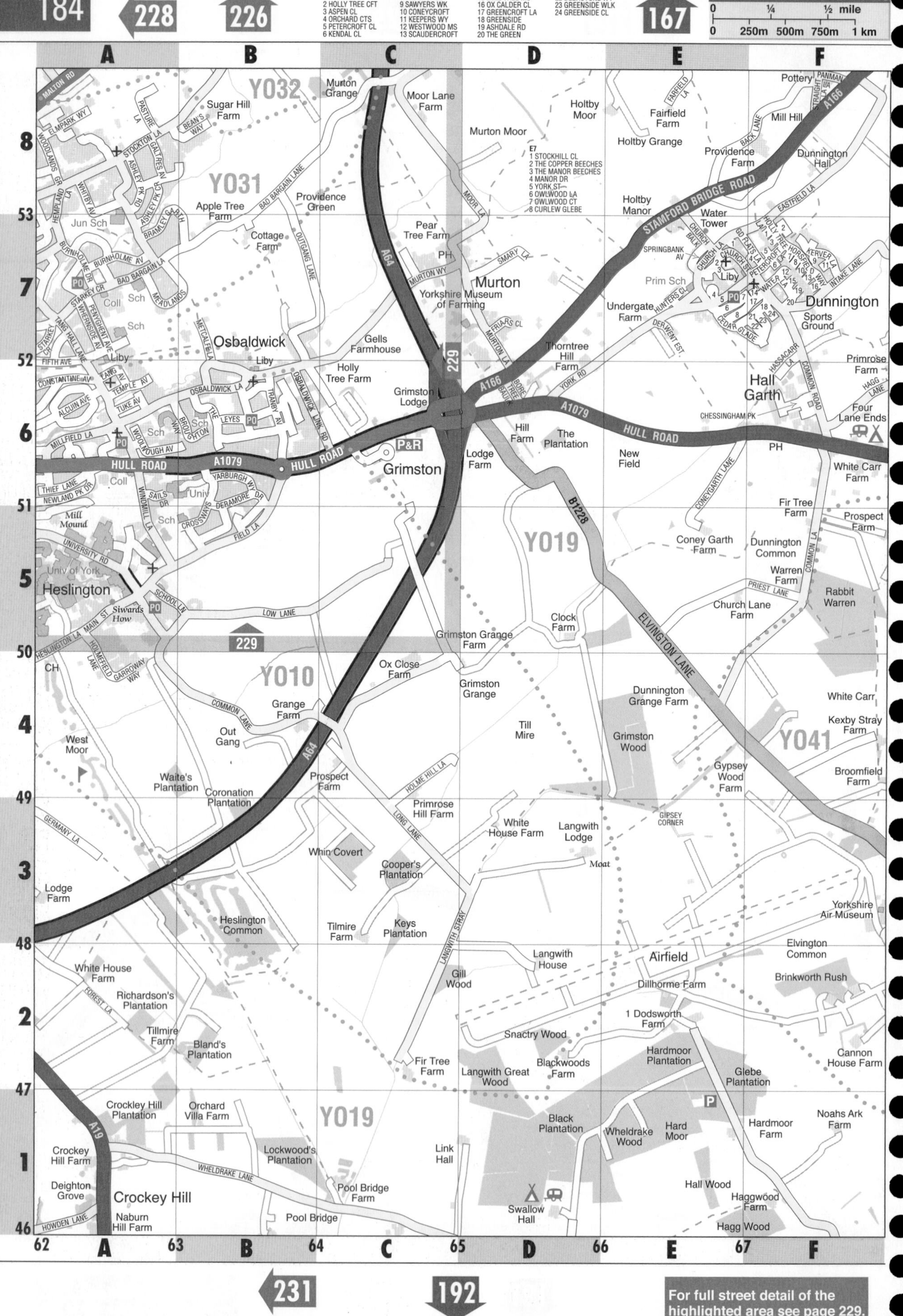

231 192

For full street detail of the highlighted area see page 229.

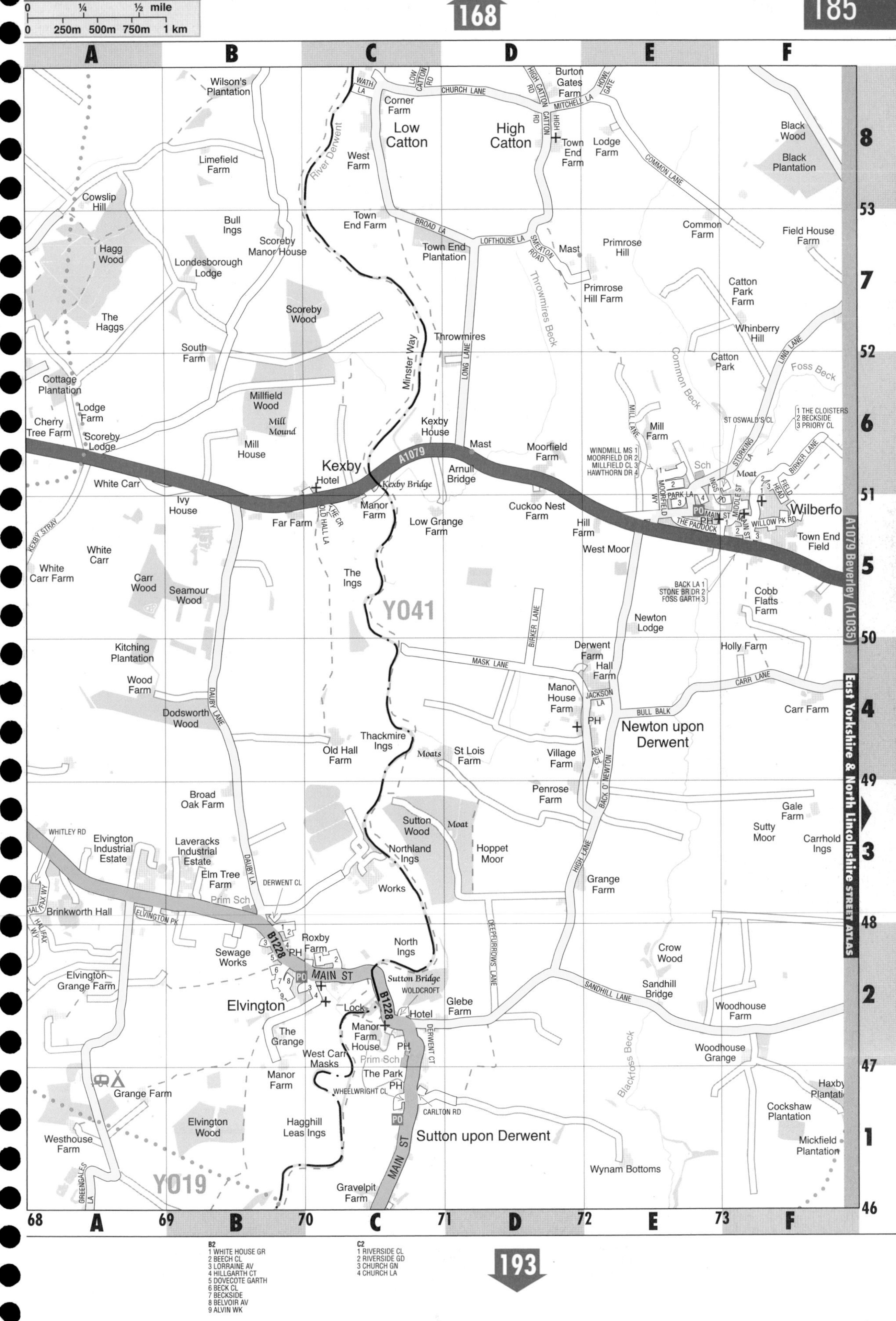
Scale: 1¾ inches to 1 mile
0 ¼ ½ mile
0 250m 500m 750m 1 km
168
A B C D E F
Low Catton
High Catton
Burton Gates Farm
Corner Farm
West Farm
Town End Farm
Lodge Farm
Black Wood
Black Plantation
Wilson's Plantation
Limefield Farm
Cowslip Hill
Bull Ings
Hagg Wood
Scoreby Manor House
Londesborough Lodge
Town End Plantation
Mast
Primrose Hill
Common Farm
Field House Farm
Primrose Hill Farm
Catton Park Farm
Scoreby Wood
The Haggs
Throwmires
Whinberry Hill
South Farm
Catton Park
Cottage Plantation
Millfield Wood
Lodge Farm
Cherry Tree Farm
Scoreby Lodge
Mill House
Kexby House
Mill Farm
Moorfield Farm
Kexby
Hotel
Arnull Bridge
Kexby Bridge
White Carr
Ivy House
Manor Farm
Far Farm
Low Grange Farm
Cuckoo Nest Farm
Hill Farm
West Moor
Wilberfoss
Town End Field
White Carr
White Carr Farm
Carr Wood
Seamour Wood
The Ings
YO41
Cobb Flatts Farm
Newton Lodge
Kitching Plantation
Derwent Farm
Hall Farm
Holly Farm
Wood Farm
Manor House Farm
Carr Farm
Dodsworth Wood
Newton upon Derwent
Thackmire Ings
Old Hall Farm
St Lois Farm
Village Farm
Broad Oak Farm
Penrose Farm
Elvington Industrial Estate
Laveracks Industrial Estate
Sutton Wood
Gale Farm
Sutty Moor
Carrhold Ings
Hoppet Moor
Elm Tree Farm
Northland Ings
Grange Farm
Works
Brinkworth Hall
Prim Sch
Roxby Farm
Sewage Works
North Ings
Crow Wood
Elvington Grange Farm
Sutton Bridge
Sandhill Bridge
Elvington
Lock
Hotel
Glebe Farm
Woodhouse Farm
The Grange
Manor Farm House
West Carr Masks
Prim Sch
Woodhouse Grange
Manor Farm
The Park
Grange Farm
Haxby Plantation
Cockshaw Plantation
Elvington Wood
Hagghill Leas Ings
Sutton upon Derwent
Westhouse Farm
Mickfield Plantation
Wynam Bottoms
YO19
Gravelpit Farm
A1079
B1228
MAIN ST
CHURCH LANE
MITCHELL LA
COMMON LANE
BROAD LA
LOFTHOUSE LA
SMEATON ROAD
LONG LANE
MASK LANE
BIRKER LANE
CARR LANE
BULL BALK
DAUBY LANE
HIGH LANE
SANDHILL LANE
DEEPFURROWS LANE
DERWENT CL
WHITLEY RD
ELVINGTON PK
WOLDCROFT
WHEELWRIGHT CL
CARLTON RD
GREENGALES LA
KEXBY STRAY
River Derwent
Minster Way
Throwmires Beck
Common Beck
Foss Beck
Blackfoss Beck
1 THE CLOISTERS
2 BECKSIDE
3 PRIORY CL
WINDMILL MS 1
MOORFIELD DR 2
MILLFIELD CL 3
HAWTHORN DR 4
BACK LA 1
STONE BR DR 2
FOSS GARTH 3
A1079 Beverley (A1035)
East Yorkshire & North Lincolnshire STREET ATLAS
8 53 7 52 6 51 5 50 4 49 3 48 2 47 1 46
68 69 70 71 72 73
B2
1 WHITE HOUSE GR
2 BEECH CL
3 LORRAINE AV
4 HILLGARTH CT
5 DOVECOTE GARTH
6 BECK CL
7 BECKSIDE
8 BELVOIR AV
9 ALVIN WK
C2
1 RIVERSIDE CL
2 RIVERSIDE GD
3 CHURCH GN
4 CHURCH LA
193

A7
1 UNITY ST
2 SCHOOL ST
3 VICARAGE RD

172

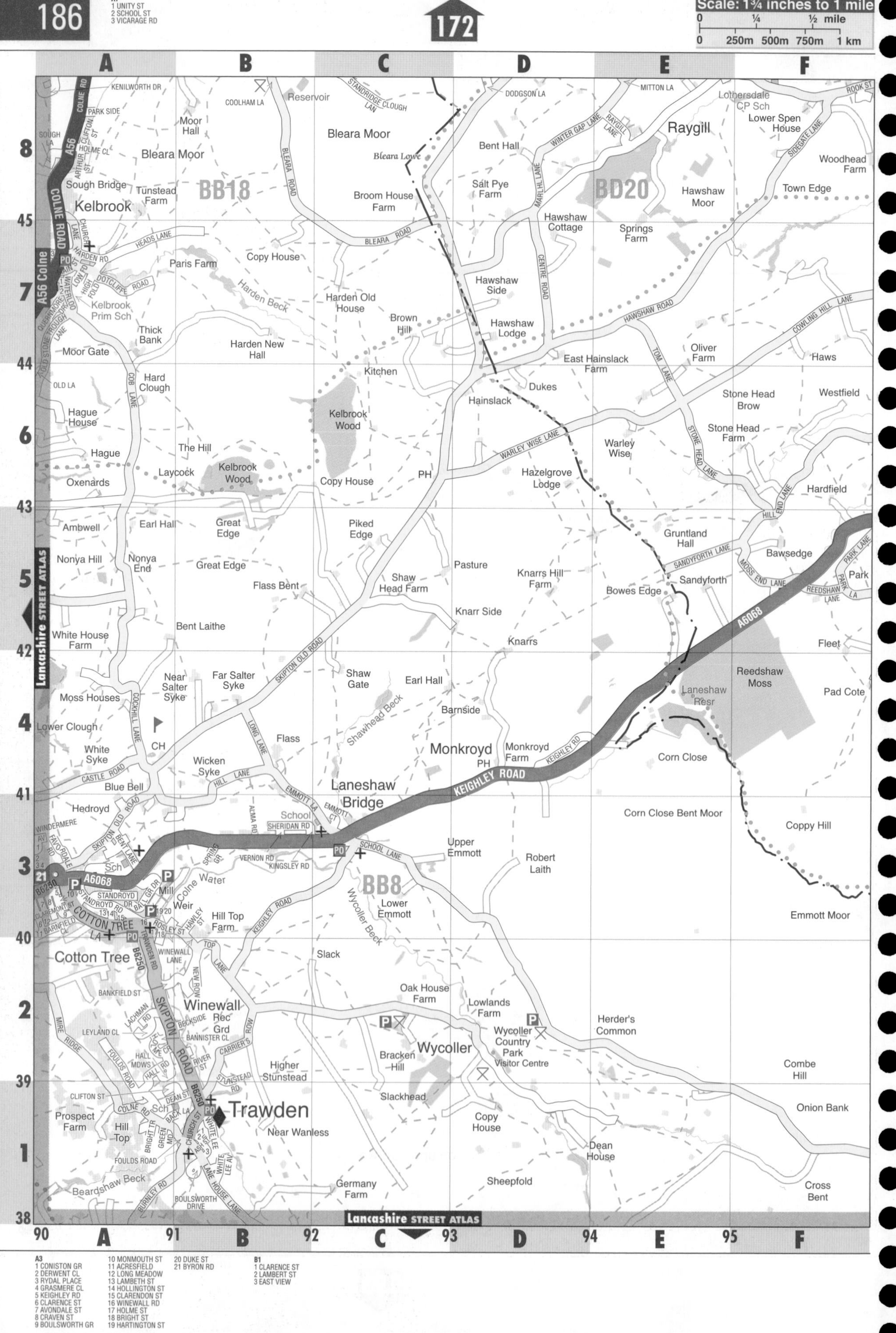

A3
1 CONISTON GR
2 DERWENT CL
3 RYDAL PLACE
4 GRASMERE CL
5 KEIGHLEY RD
6 CLARENCE ST
7 AVONDALE ST
8 CRAVEN ST
9 BOULSWORTH GR
10 MONMOUTH ST
11 ACRESFIELD
12 LONG MEADOW
13 LAMBETH ST
14 HOLLINGTON ST
15 CLARENDON ST
16 WINEWALL RD
17 HOLME ST
18 BRIGHT ST
19 HARTINGTON ST
20 DUKE ST
21 BYRON RD

B1
1 CLARENCE ST
2 LAMBERT ST
3 EAST VIEW

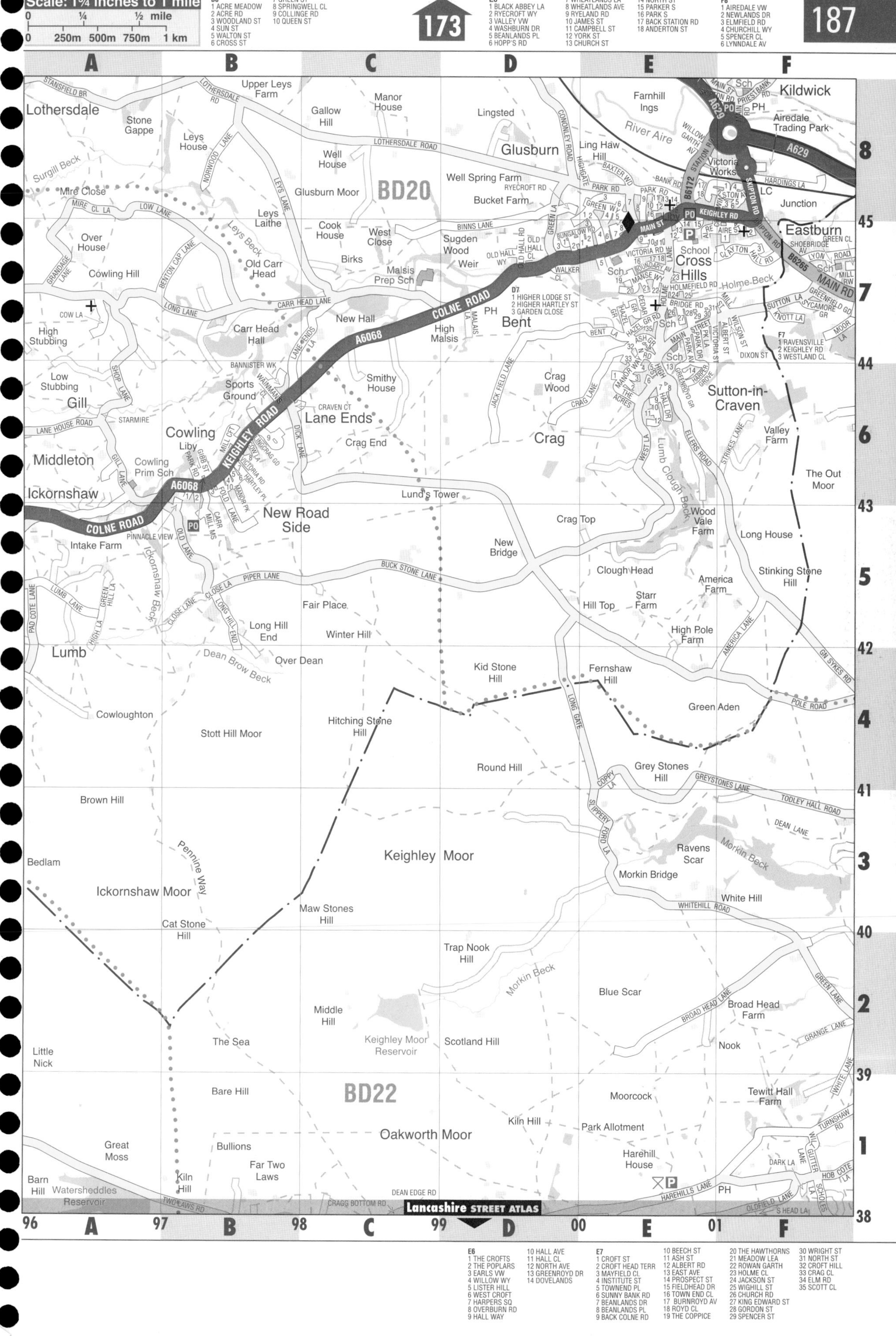

187
173
Scale: 1¾ inches to 1 mile
0 ¼ ½ mile
0 250m 500m 750m 1 km
B6
1 ACRE MEADOW
2 ACRE RD
3 WOODLAND ST
4 SUN ST
5 WALTON ST
6 CROSS ST
7 GREEN ST
8 SPRINGWELL CL
9 COLLINGE RD
10 QUEEN ST
E8
1 BLACK ABBEY LA
2 RYECROFT WY
3 VALLEY VW
4 WASHBURN DR
5 BEANLANDS PL
6 HOPP'S RD
7 WHEATLANDS LA
8 WHEATLANDS AVE
9 RYELAND RD
10 JAMES ST
11 CAMPBELL ST
12 YORK ST
13 CHURCH ST
14 NORTH ST
15 PARKER S
16 PARK S
17 BACK STATION RD
18 ANDERTON ST
F8
1 AIREDALE VW
2 NEWLANDS DR
3 ELMFIELD RD
4 CHURCHILL WY
5 SPENCER CL
6 LYNNDALE AV
A B C D E F
Lothersdale
Stone Gappe
Upper Leys Farm
Leys House
Gallow Hill
Manor House
Lingsted
Farnhill Ings
Kildwick
Airedale Trading Park
River Aire
Glusburn
Ling Haw Hill
Well House
BD20
Well Spring Farm
Bucket Farm
Glusburn Moor
Mire Close
Over House
Leys Laithe
Cook House
West Close
Sugden Wood
Weir
Cowling Hill
Old Carr Head
Birks
Malsis Prep Sch
Victoria Works
Junction
Eastburn
School
Cross Hills
High Stubbing
Carr Head Hall
New Hall
COLNE ROAD
A6068
High Malsis
Bent
Low Stubbing
Gill
Sports Ground
Smithy House
Crag Wood
Sutton-in-Craven
Lane Ends
Crag End
Crag
Valley Farm
Cowling
Middleton
Cowling Prim Sch
Ickornshaw
KEIGHLEY ROAD
Lund's Tower
The Out Moor
New Road Side
Crag Top
Wood Vale Farm
Long House
Intake Farm
New Bridge
Clough Head
America Farm
Stinking Stone Hill
Fair Place
Hill Top
Starr Farm
Long Hill End
Winter Hill
High Pole Farm
Lumb
Dean Brow Beck
Over Dean
Kid Stone Hill
Fernshaw Hill
Cowloughton
Stott Hill Moor
Hitching Stone Hill
Green Aden
Round Hill
Grey Stones Hill
Brown Hill
Pennine Way
Keighley Moor
Ravens Scar
Morkin Beck
Bedlam
Ickornshaw Moor
Morkin Bridge
White Hill
Maw Stones Hill
Cat Stone Hill
Trap Nook Hill
Blue Scar
Middle Hill
Broad Head Farm
Little Nick
The Sea
Keighley Moor Reservoir
Scotland Hill
Nook
BD22
Bare Hill
Moorcock
Tewitt Hall Farm
Kiln Hill
Park Allotment
Great Moss
Bullions
Oakworth Moor
Far Two Laws
Harehill House
Barn Hill
Watersheddles Reservoir
Kiln Hill
Lancashire STREET ATLAS
96 97 98 99 00 01
38 39 40 41 42 43 44 45
1 2 3 4 5 6 7 8
E6
1 THE CROFTS
2 THE POPLARS
3 EARLS VW
4 WILLOW WY
5 LISTER HILL
6 WEST CROFT
7 HARPERS SQ
8 OVERBURN RD
9 HALL WAY
10 HALL AVE
11 HALL CL
12 NORTH AVE
13 GREENROYD DR
14 DOVELANDS
E7
1 CROFT ST
2 CROFT HEAD TERR
3 MAYFIELD CL
4 INSTITUTE ST
5 TOWNEND PL
6 SUNNY BANK RD
7 BEANLANDS DR
8 BEANLANDS PL
9 BACK COLNE RD
10 BEECH ST
11 ASH ST
12 ALBERT RD
13 EAST AVE
14 PROSPECT ST
15 FIELDHEAD DR
16 TOWN END CL
17 BURNROYD AV
18 ROYD CL
19 THE COPPICE
20 THE HAWTHORNS
21 MEADOW LEA
22 ROWAN GARTH
23 HOLME CL
24 JACKSON ST
25 WIGHILL ST
26 CHURCH RD
27 KING EDWARD ST
28 GORDON ST
29 SPENCER ST
30 WRIGHT ST
31 NORTH ST
32 CROFT HILL
33 CRAG CL
34 ELM RD
35 SCOTT CL

A8
1 BISHOPDALE DR
2 COVERDALE GARTH
3 LANGWITH AV
4 GREEN LA
5 THE CROFT
6 THE CLOSE
7 MILLGARTH CT
8 THE GARTH
9 LOWCROFT
10 THE VALE

180

E7
1 MOOR AV
2 BRIDGE GARTH
3 WILLOW GR
4 ASHMEAD
5 WILLOW GLADE
6 ST LUKE'S CL
7 CHURCH VW MS
8 NURSERY WY
9 ALBION TR

Scale: 1¾ inches to 1 mile
0 ¼ ½ mile
0 250m 500m 750m 1 km

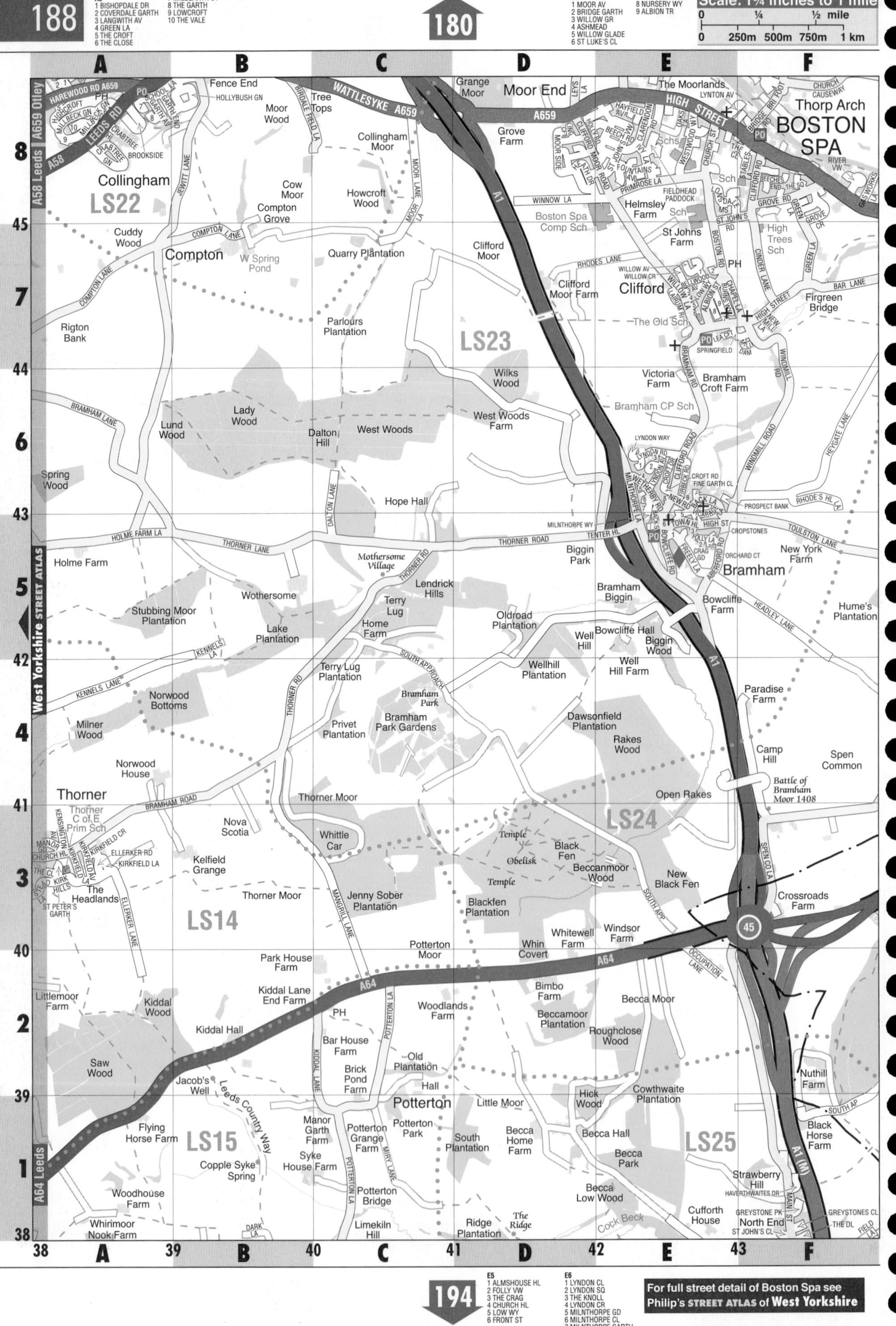

194

E5
1 ALMSHOUSE HL
2 FOLLY VW
3 THE CRAG
4 CHURCH HL
5 LOW WY
6 FRONT ST

E6
1 LYNDON CL
2 LYNDON SQ
3 THE KNOLL
4 LYNDON CR
5 MILNTHORPE GD
6 MILNTHORPE CL
7 MILNTHORPE GARTH
8 BRADFORDS CL
9 CHURCH MS

For full street detail of Boston Spa see Philip's STREET ATLAS of West Yorkshire

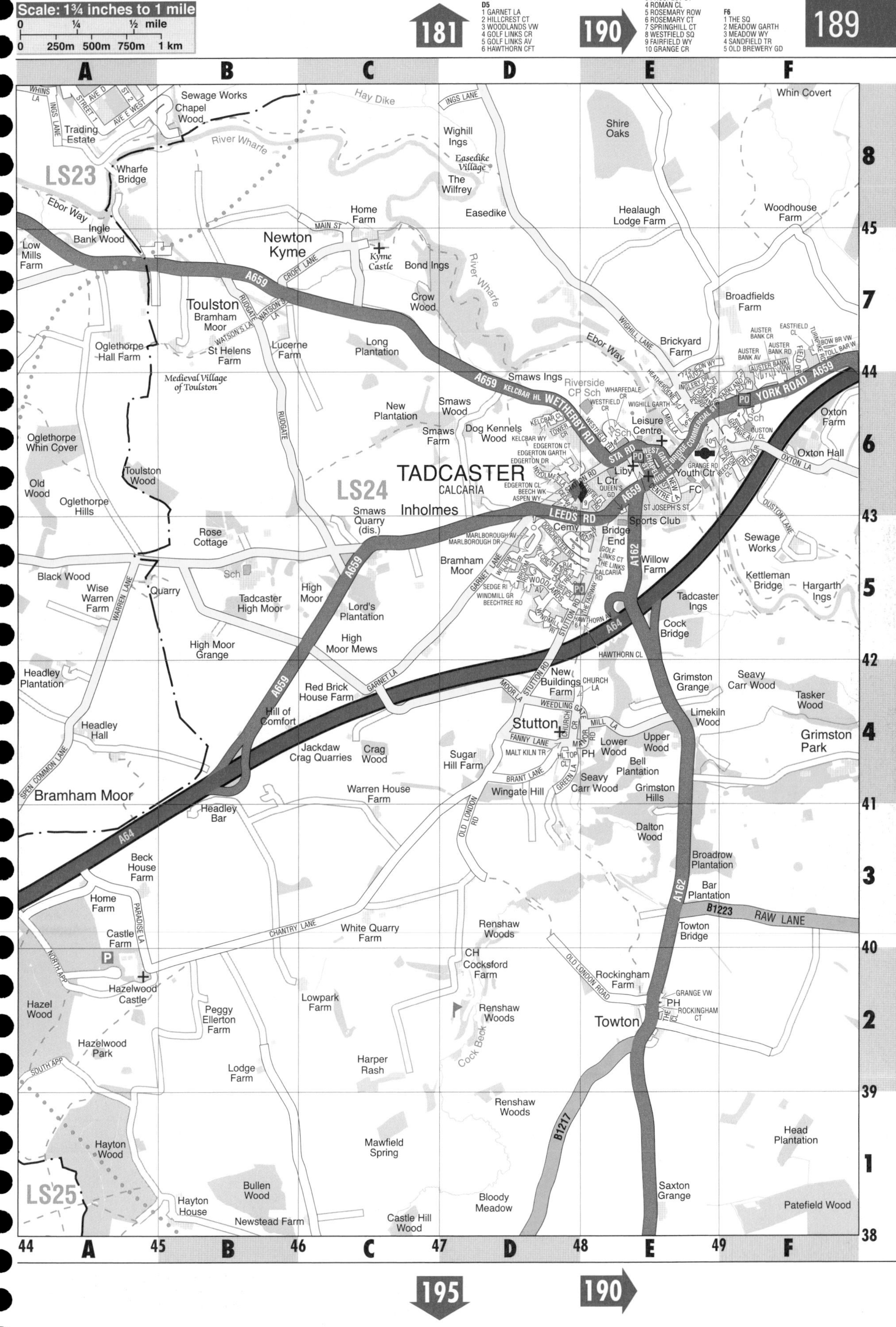
Scale: 1¾ inches to 1 mile
0 ¼ ½ mile
0 250m 500m 750m 1 km
181
190
D5
1 GARNET LA
2 HILLCREST CT
3 WOODLANDS VW
4 GOLF LINKS CR
5 GOLF LINKS AV
6 HAWTHORN CFT
1 HUDSON VW
2 HUDSON CL
3 PROSPECT CT
4 ROMAN CL
5 ROSEMARY ROW
6 ROSEMARY CT
7 SPRINGHILL CT
8 WESTFIELD SQ
9 FAIRFIELD WY
10 GRANGE CR
F6
1 THE SQ
2 MEADOW GARTH
3 MEADOW WY
4 SANDFIELD TR
5 OLD BREWERY GD
A B C D E F
Sewage Works
Chapel Wood
Trading Estate
Hay Dike
River Wharfe
LS23
Wharfe Bridge
Ebor Way
Ingle Bank Wood
Low Mills Farm
Wighill Ings
Easedike Village
The Wilfrey
Easedike
Shire Oaks
Whin Covert
Healaugh Lodge Farm
Woodhouse Farm
Home Farm
Newton Kyme
Kyme Castle
Bond Ings
Crow Wood
A659
Toulston
Bramham Moor
St Helens Farm
Lucerne Farm
Long Plantation
Oglethorpe Hall Farm
Medieval Village of Toulston
Broadfields Farm
Brickyard Farm
Smaws Ings
Riverside CP Sch
New Plantation
Smaws Wood
Smaws Farm
Dog Kennels Wood
WETHERBY RD
Leisure Centre
YORK ROAD
Oxton Farm
Oxton Hall
Oglethorpe Whin Cover
Toulston Wood
Old Wood
Oglethorpe Hills
TADCASTER
CALCARIA
LS24
Smaws Quarry (dis.)
Inholmes
LEEDS RD
Liby
L Ctr
Youth Ctr
FC
Sports Club
Cemy
Bridge End
Rose Cottage
Sewage Works
Black Wood
Wise Warren Farm
Quarry
Sch
Tadcaster High Moor
High Moor
Lord's Plantation
Bramham Moor
Willow Farm
Kettleman Bridge
Hargarth Ings
Tadcaster Ings
Cock Bridge
High Moor Grange
High Moor Mews
A64
A162
Headley Plantation
Red Brick House Farm
Hill of Comfort
New Buildings Farm
Grimston Grange
Seavy Carr Wood
Tasker Wood
Limekiln Wood
Headley Hall
Stutton
Jackdaw Crag Quarries
Crag Wood
Sugar Hill Farm
Lower Wood
Upper Wood
Grimston Park
Bell Plantation
Bramham Moor
Headley Bar
Warren House Farm
Wingate Hill
Seavy Carr Wood
Grimston Hills
Dalton Wood
Beck House Farm
Broadrow Plantation
Bar Plantation
Home Farm
B1223
RAW LANE
Castle Farm
White Quarry Farm
Renshaw Woods
Towton Bridge
CHANTRY LANE
Hazelwood Castle
CH Cocksford Farm
Rockingham Farm
Hazel Wood
Peggy Ellerton Farm
Lowpark Farm
Renshaw Woods
Towton
Hazelwood Park
Lodge Farm
Harper Rash
Cock Beck
Renshaw Woods
B1217
Hayton Wood
Mawfield Spring
Head Plantation
LS25
Bullen Wood
Hayton House
Newstead Farm
Castle Hill Wood
Bloody Meadow
Saxton Grange
Patefield Wood
8 45 7 44 6 43 5 42 4 41 3 40 2 39 1 38
44 45 46 47 48 49
195
190

189
182

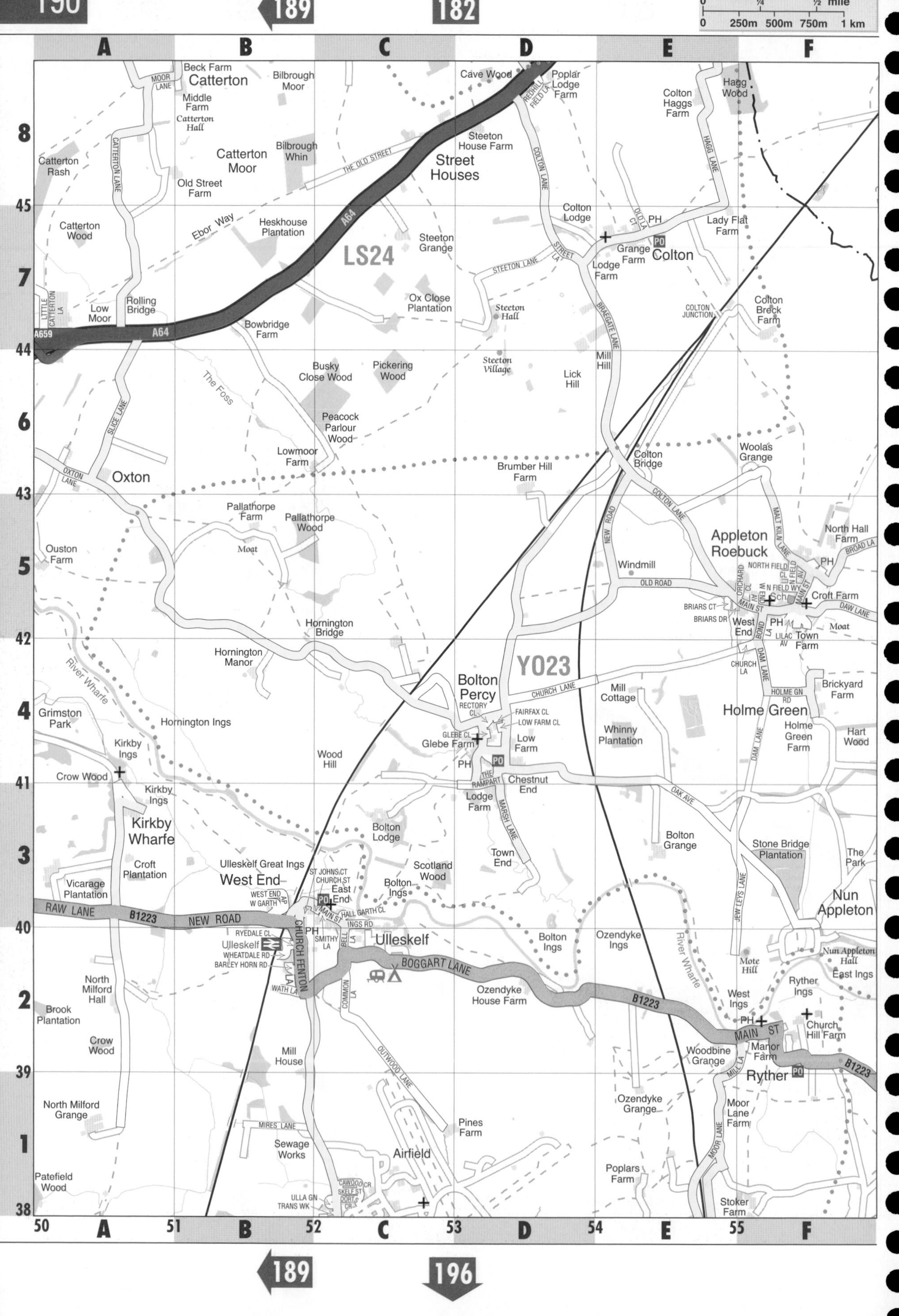

189
196

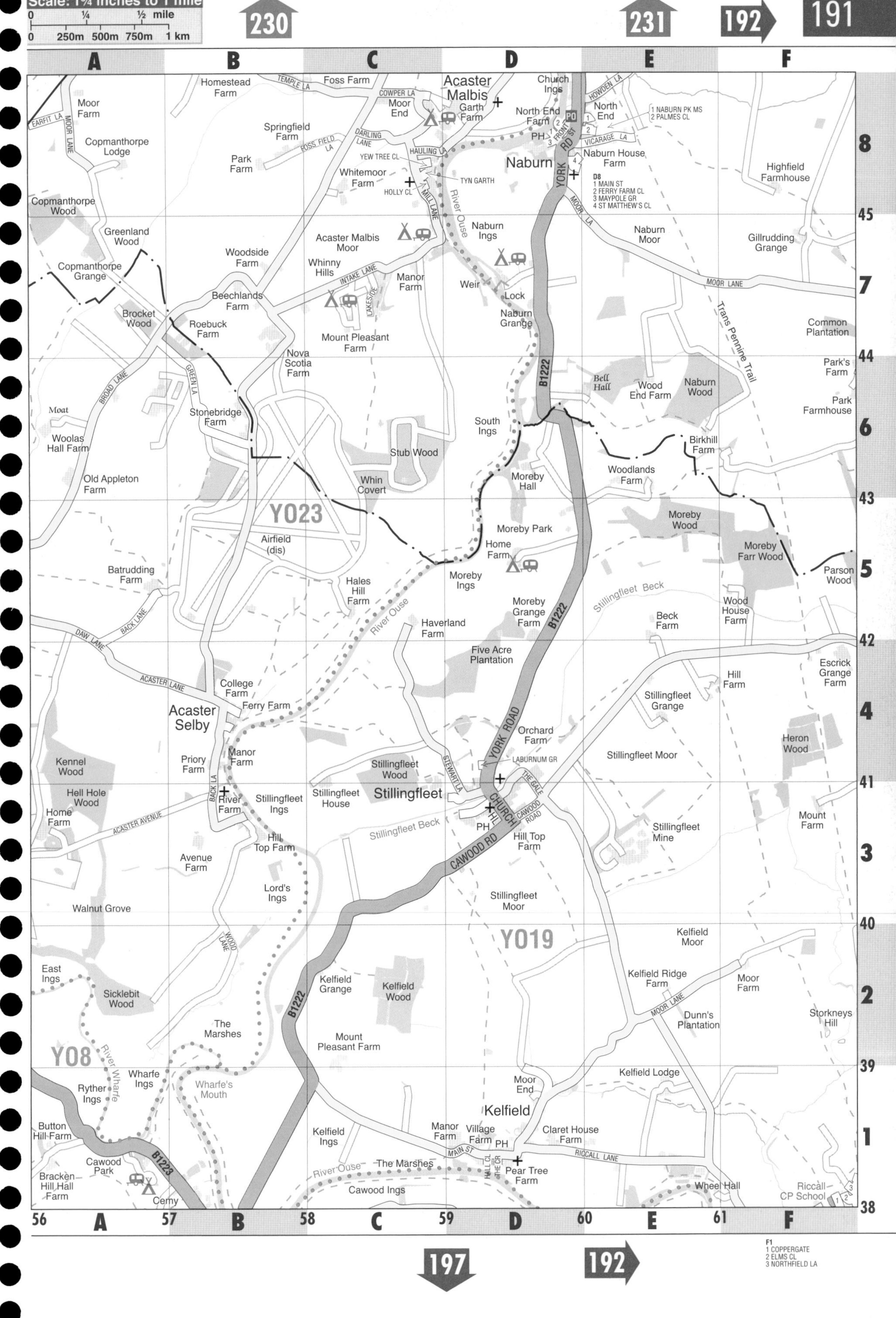

Scale: 1¾ inches to 1 mile
0 ¼ ½ mile
0 250m 500m 750m 1 km
230
231
192
191
A B C D E F
Homestead Farm
Temple La
Foss Farm
Acaster Malbis
Church Ings
Howden La
Moor Farm
Earfit La
Moor Lane
Cowper La
Moor End
Garth Farm
North End Farm
North End
1 Naburn Pk Ms
2 Palmes Cl
Springfield Farm
Foss Field La
Darling Lane
Copmanthorpe Lodge
Hauling La
Front St
Vicarage La
Park Farm
Yew Tree Cl
PH
York Rd
Naburn House Farm
Naburn
Whitemoor Farm
Holly Cl
Tyn Garth
D8
1 Main St
2 Ferry Farm Cl
3 Maypole Gr
4 St Matthew's Cl
Highfield Farmhouse
8
Copmanthorpe Wood
Mill Lane
River Ouse
Moor La
45
Greenland Wood
Acaster Malbis Moor
Naburn Ings
Naburn Moor
Gillrudding Grange
Woodside Farm
Whinny Hills
Intake Lane
Copmanthorpe Grange
Manor Farm
Weir
Lock
Moor Lane
7
Beechlands Farm
Lakeside
Brocket Wood
Naburn Grange
Trans Pennine Trail
Common Plantation
Roebuck Farm
Mount Pleasant Farm
44
Nova Scotia Farm
Park's Farm
Green La
Broad Lane
B1222
Bell Hall
Wood End Farm
Naburn Wood
Park Farmhouse
Moat
Stonebridge Farm
South Ings
Woolas Hall Farm
Birkhill Farm
6
Stub Wood
Moreby Hall
Woodlands Farm
Old Appleton Farm
Whin Covert
43
YO23
Moreby Wood
Moreby Park
Airfield (dis)
Home Farm
Moreby Farr Wood
Batrudding Farm
Moreby Ings
Parson Wood
5
Hales Hill Farm
Stillingfleet Beck
Back Lane
Moreby Grange Farm
Wood House Farm
Haverland Farm
Beck Farm
Daw Lane
42
Five Acre Plantation
Escrick Grange Farm
Acaster Lane
College Farm
Hill Farm
Stillingfleet Grange
Ferry Farm
4
Acaster Selby
York Road
Orchard Farm
Heron Wood
Manor Farm
Priory Farm
Stillingfleet Moor
Kennel Wood
Stillingfleet Wood
Laburnum Gr
Stewart La
41
Hell Hole Wood
Back La
River Farm
Stillingfleet Ings
Stillingfleet House
Stillingfleet
The Gale
Church Hl
Cawood Road
Home Farm
Acaster Avenue
PH
Mount Farm
Stillingfleet Mine
Hill Top Farm
Cawood Rd
3
Avenue Farm
Lord's Ings
Stillingfleet Moor
Walnut Grove
40
Wood Lane
YO19
Kelfield Moor
East Ings
Kelfield Ridge Farm
Moor Farm
Kelfield Grange
Kelfield Wood
2
Sicklebit Wood
B1222
Moor Lane
Dunn's Plantation
Storkneys Hill
The Marshes
Mount Pleasant Farm
YO8
River Wharfe
39
Wharfe Ings
Kelfield Lodge
Ryther Ings
Wharfe's Mouth
Moor End
Kelfield
Button Hill Farm
Manor Farm
Village Farm
PH
Claret House Farm
1
Kelfield Ings
Main St
Riccall Lane
Cawood Park
B1223
River Ouse
The Marshes
Hall Cl
The Cr
Pear Tree Farm
Bracken Hill Hall Farm
Cawood Ings
Wheel Hall
Riccall CP School
Cemy
38
56 A 57 B 58 C 59 D 60 E 61 F
197
192
F1
1 Coppergate
2 Elms Cl
3 Northfield La

191
184

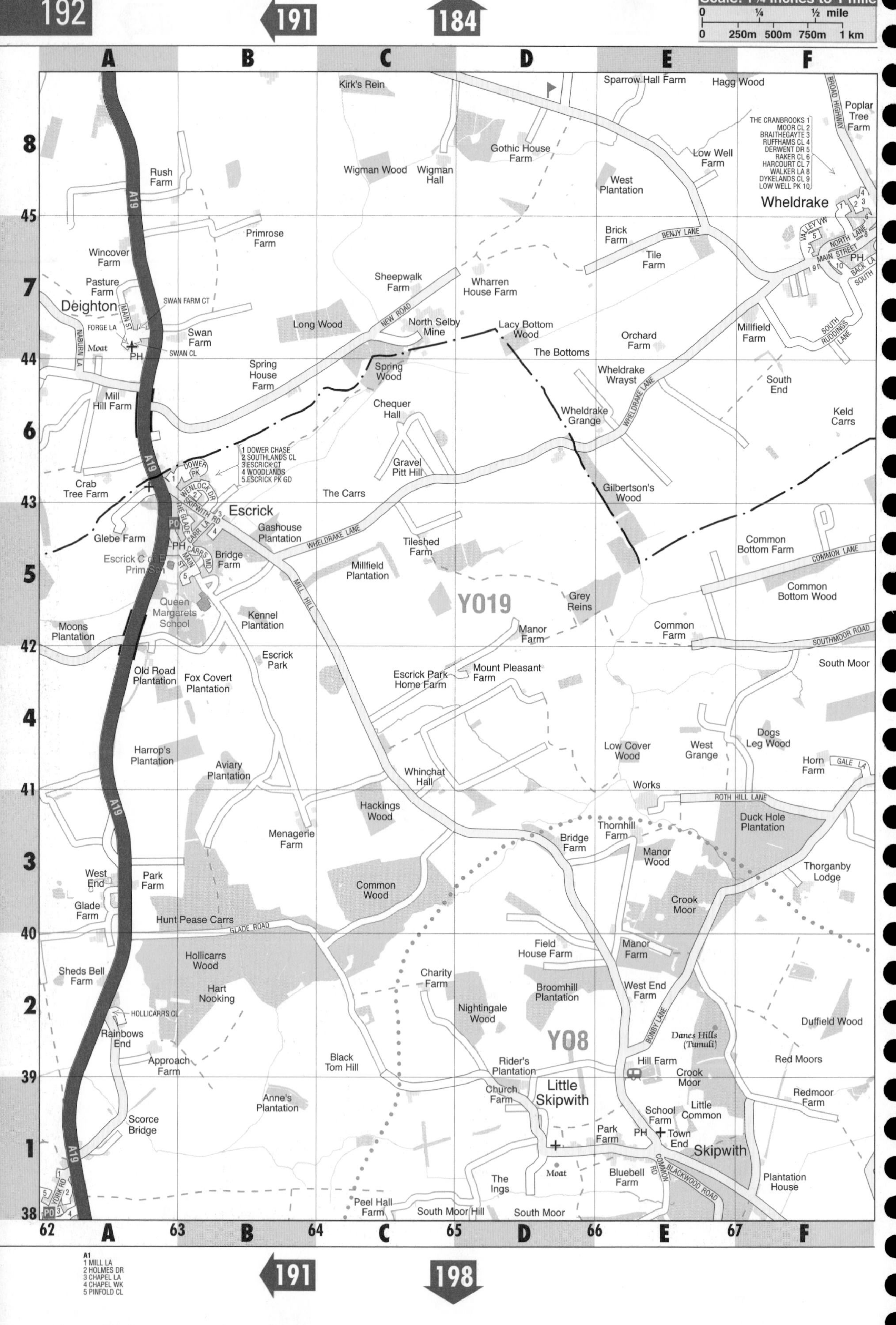

191
198

Scale: 1¾ inches to 1 mile

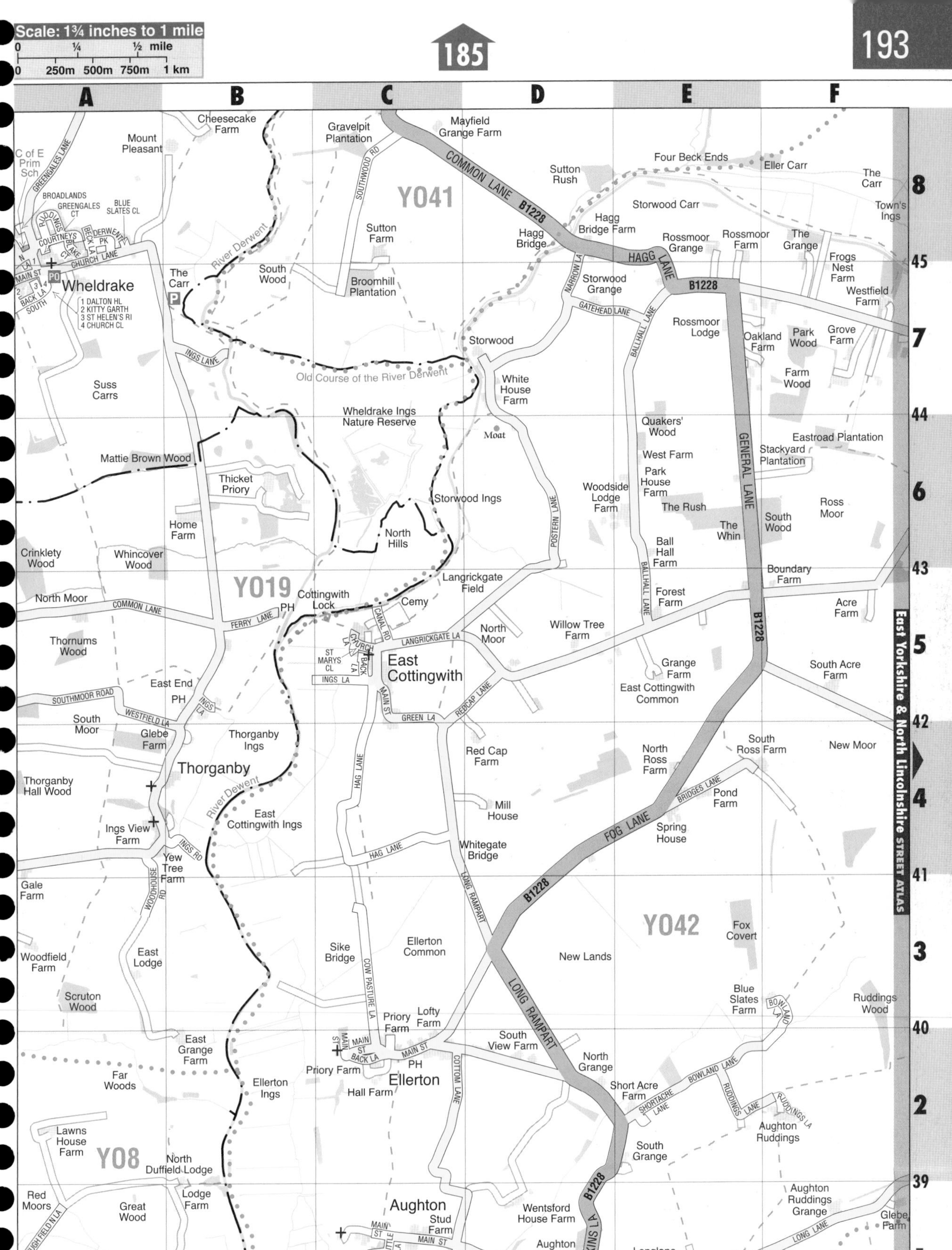

188

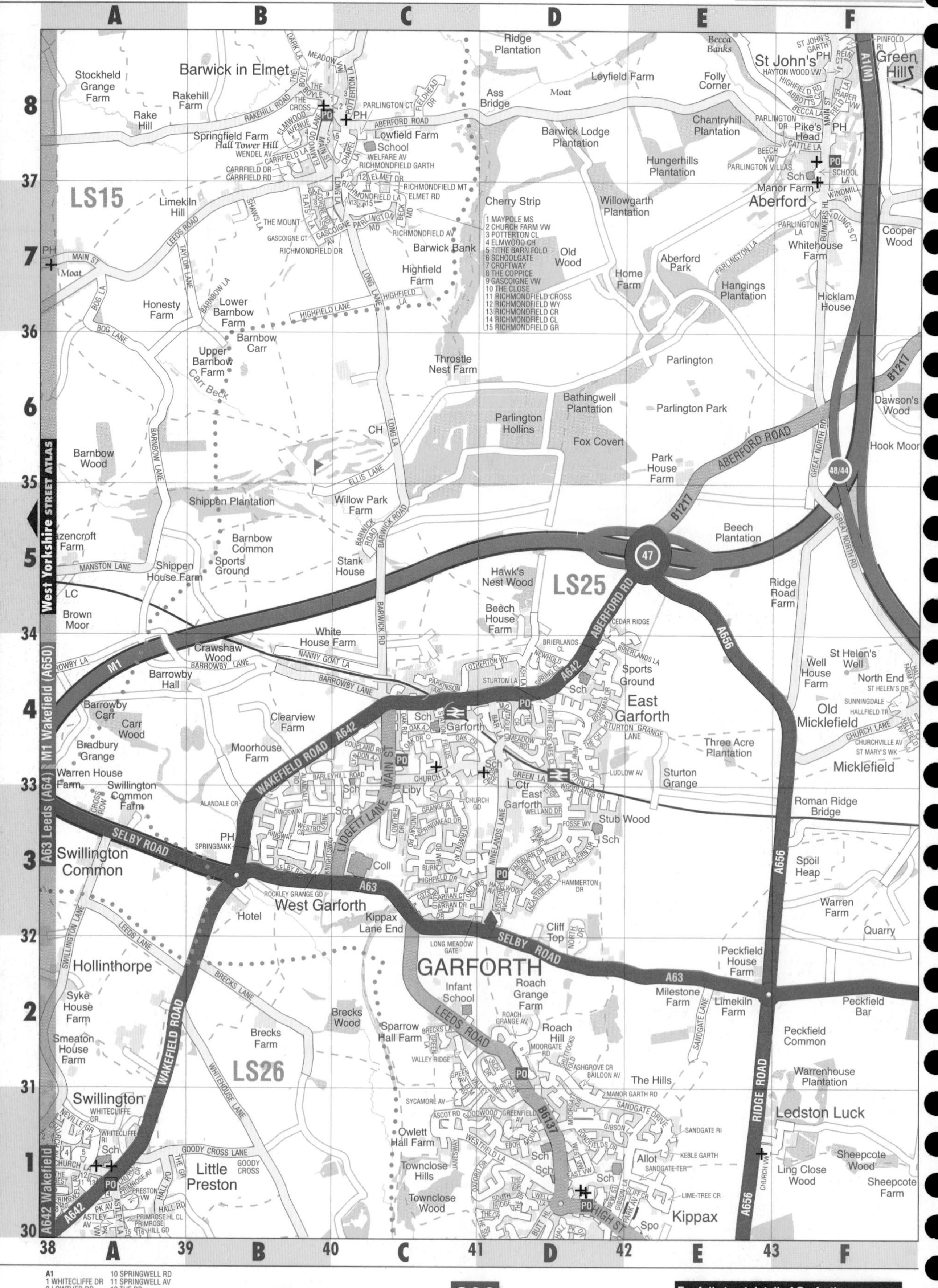

A1
1 WHITECLIFFE DR
2 LOWTHER DR
3 LOWTHER CR
4 CHURCH CL
5 SMEATON GR
6 THE PLEASANCE
7 WOODLAND GR
8 WOODLAND CR
9 WOODLAND AV
10 SPRINGWELL RD
11 SPRINGWELL AV
12 THE DR
13 SCOTT CL
14 ST MARY'S AV
15 PRIMROSE HL DR
16 PRIMROSE HL GR

200

For full street detail of Garforth see Philip's STREET ATLAS of West Yorkshire

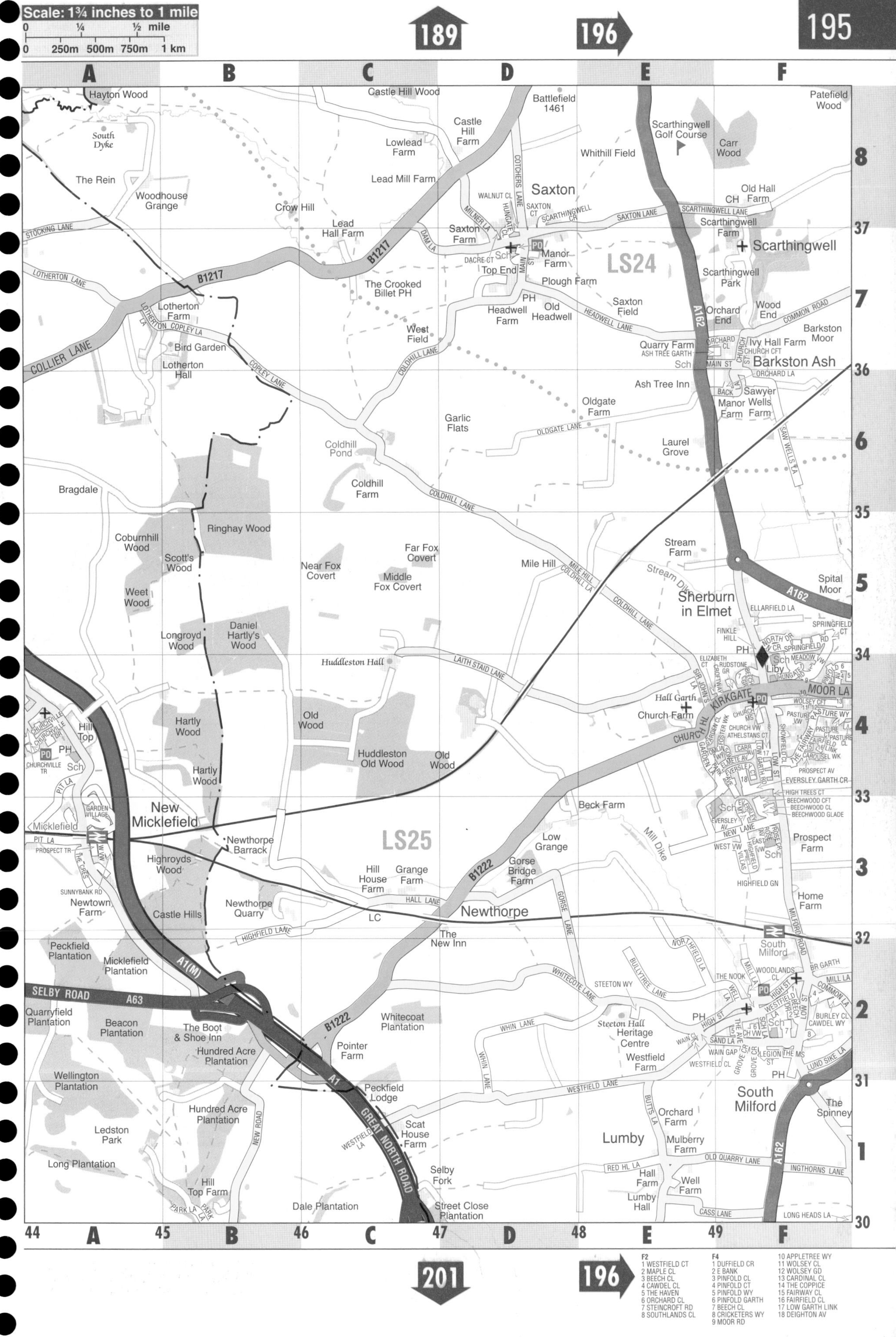

Scale: 1¾ inches to 1 mile
0 ¼ ½ mile
0 250m 500m 750m 1 km
189
196
195
A B C D E F
Hayton Wood
South Dyke
The Rein
Woodhouse Grange
Castle Hill Wood
Lowlead Farm
Castle Hill Farm
Battlefield 1461
Scarthingwell Golf Course
Carr Wood
Patefield Wood
Whithill Field
Lead Mill Farm
Crow Hill
Saxton
Old Hall Farm
Scarthingwell Farm
Scarthingwell
STOCKING LANE
Lead Hall Farm
Saxton Farm
Manor Farm
Top End
LS24
LOTHERTON LANE
B1217
The Crooked Billet PH
Plough Farm
Scarthingwell Park
Lotherton Farm
Headwell Farm
Old Headwell
Saxton Field
Orchard End
Wood End
COMMON ROAD
Barkston Moor
COLLIER LANE
Bird Garden
West Field
Quarry Farm
Ivy Hall Farm
Lotherton Hall
COPLEY LANE
COLDHILL LANE
Barkston Ash
Ash Tree Inn
Sawyer Wells Farm
Manor Farm
Oldgate Farm
Garlic Flats
OLDGATE LANE
Laurel Grove
Coldhill Pond
Coldhill Farm
Bragdale
Ringhay Wood
Coburnhill Wood
Scott's Wood
Weet Wood
Near Fox Covert
Far Fox Covert
Middle Fox Covert
Mile Hill
Stream Farm
Stream Dike
Sherburn in Elmet
Spital Moor
A162
Longroyd Wood
Daniel Hartly's Wood
Huddleston Hall
LAITH STAID LANE
MOOR LA
KIRKGATE
Hall Garth
Church Farm
Hill Top
Hartly Wood
Old Wood
Huddleston Old Wood
CHURCH HL
New Micklefield
Micklefield
Newthorpe Barrack
Beck Farm
Highroyds Wood
LS25
Low Grange
Mill Dike
Prospect Farm
Hill House Farm
Grange Farm
Gorse Bridge Farm
B1222
Newtown Farm
Castle Hills
Newthorpe Quarry
HALL LANE
Newthorpe
LC
Home Farm
HIGHFIELD LANE
The New Inn
South Milford
Peckfield Plantation
Micklefield Plantation
A1(M)
SELBY ROAD
A63
Quarryfield Plantation
Beacon Plantation
The Boot & Shoe Inn
Whitecoat Plantation
Steeton Hall Heritage Centre
Hundred Acre Plantation
Pointer Farm
Westfield Farm
Wellington Plantation
Peckfield Lodge
South Milford
The Spinney
Hundred Acre Plantation
A1
GREAT NORTH ROAD
Scat House Farm
Orchard Farm
Ledston Park
Lumby
Mulberry Farm
OLD QUARRY LANE
INGTHORNS LANE
Long Plantation
Selby Fork
Hall Farm
Well Farm
Hill Top Farm
Lumby Hall
Dale Plantation
Street Close Plantation
CASS LANE
LONG HEADS LA
8
37
7
36
6
35
5
34
4
33
3
32
2
31
1
30
44 A 45 B 46 C 47 D 48 E 49 F
201
196
F2
1 WESTFIELD CT
2 MAPLE CL
3 BEECH CL
4 CAWDEL CL
5 THE HAVEN
6 ORCHARD CL
7 STEINCROFT RD
8 SOUTHLANDS CL
F4
1 DUFFIELD CR
2 E BANK
3 PINFOLD CL
4 PINFOLD CT
5 PINFOLD WY
6 PINFOLD GARTH
7 BEECH CL
8 CRICKETERS WY
9 MOOR RD
10 APPLETREE WY
11 WOLSEY CL
12 WOLSEY GD
13 CARDINAL CL
14 THE COPPICE
15 FAIRWAY CL
16 FAIRFIELD CL
17 LOW GARTH LINK
18 DEIGHTON AV

195
190

Scale: 1¾ inches to 1 mile

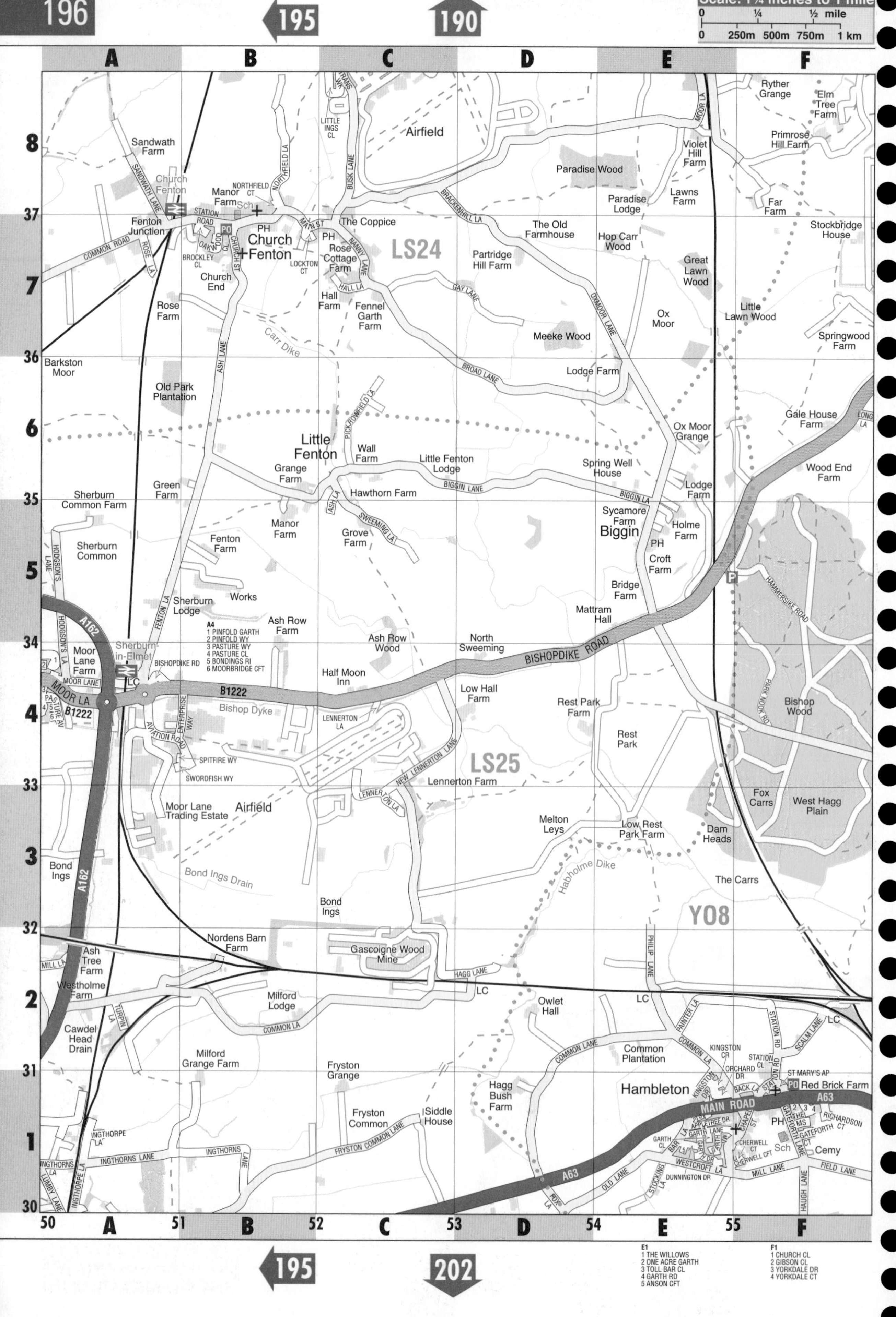

E1
1 THE WILLOWS
2 ONE ACRE GARTH
3 TOLL BAR CL
4 GARTH RD
5 ANSON CFT

F1
1 CHURCH CL
2 GIBSON CL
3 YORKDALE DR
4 YORKDALE CT

195
202

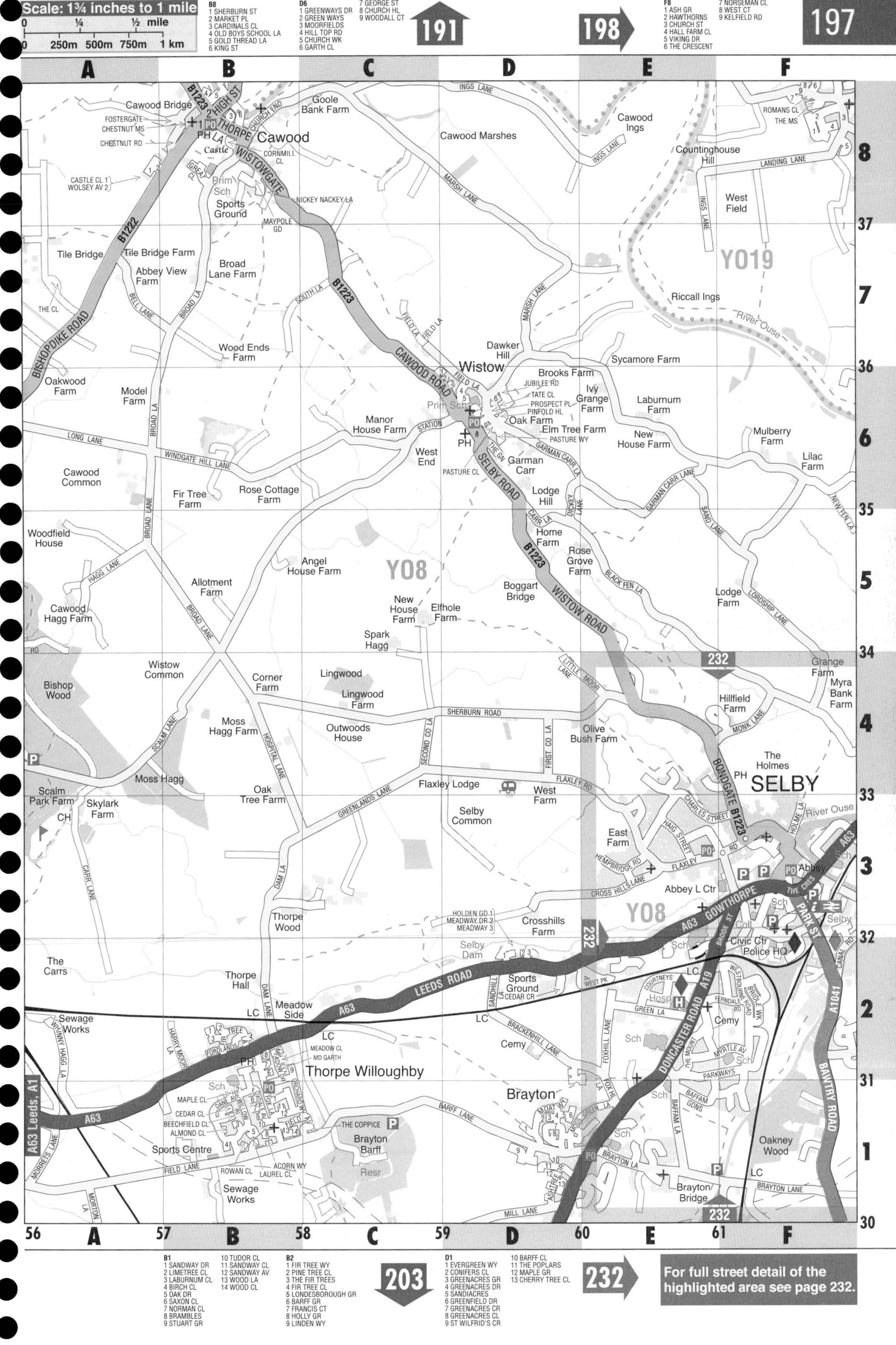

Scale: 1¾ inches to 1 mile
0 ¼ ½ mile
0 250m 500m 750m 1 km
B8
1 SHERBURN ST
2 MARKET PL
3 CARDINALS CL
4 OLD BOYS SCHOOL LA
5 GOLD THREAD LA
6 KING ST
D6
1 GREENWAYS DR
2 GREEN WAYS
3 MOORFIELDS
4 HILL TOP RD
5 CHURCH WK
6 GARTH CL
7 GEORGE ST
8 CHURCH HL
9 WOODALL CT
191
198
F8
1 ASH GR
2 HAWTHORNS
3 CHURCH ST
4 HALL FARM CL
5 VIKING DR
6 THE CRESCENT
7 NORSEMAN CL
8 WEST CT
9 KELFIELD RD
197
A B C D E F
Cawood Bridge
FOSTERGATE
CHESTNUT MS
CHESTNUT RD
B1223
HIGH ST
THORPE LA
CHURCH END
Goole Bank Farm
INGS LANE
Cawood Ings
Cawood
Castle
CORNMILL CL
WISTOWGATE
Cawood Marshes
INGS LANE
Countinghouse Hill
ROMANS CL
THE MS
LANDING LANE
CASTLE CL 1
WOLSEY AV 2
GREAT CL
Prim Sch
Sports Ground
NICKEY NACKEY LA
MAYPOLE GD
MARSH LANE
INGS LANE
West Field
B1222
Tile Bridge
Tile Bridge Farm
Abbey View Farm
Broad Lane Farm
B1223
YO19
SOUTH LA
MARSH LANE
Riccall Ings
River Ouse
BELL LANE
BROAD LA
THE CL
BISHOPDIKE ROAD
FIELD LA
FIELD LA
Wood Ends Farm
Dawker Hill
Sycamore Farm
CAWOOD ROAD
Wistow
Brooks Farm
JUBILEE RD
Oakwood Farm
Model Farm
FIELD LA
TATE CL
PROSPECT PL
PINFOLD HL
Ivy Grange Farm
Laburnum Farm
Prim Sch
Oak Farm
Manor House Farm
STATION
Elm Tree Farm
PASTURE WY
BROAD LA
LONG LANE
PH
New House Farm
Mulberry Farm
West End
THE GN
GARMAN CARR LA
WINDGATE HILL LANE
Cawood Common
PASTURE CL
Garman Carr
SELBY ROAD
Lilac Farm
GARMAN CARR LANE
Rose Cottage Farm
Fir Tree Farm
Lodge Hill
DICKEY LANE
NEW FEN LA
BROAD LANE
CARR LA
SAND LANE
Woodfield House
Home Farm
Rose Grove Farm
Angel House Farm
YO8
B1223
HAGG LANE
Allotment Farm
BLACK FEN LA
Boggart Bridge
Lodge Farm
Cawood Hagg Farm
New House Farm
Elfhole Farm
WISTOW ROAD
LORDSHIP LANE
BROAD LANE
Spark Hagg
RD
232
Grange Farm
Wistow Common
LITTLE MOOR LANE
Bishop Wood
Corner Farm
Lingwood
Myra Bank Farm
Lingwood Farm
Hillfield Farm
SHERBURN ROAD
MONK LANE
Moss Hagg Farm
Outwoods House
Olive Bush Farm
SCALM LANE
HOSPITAL LANE
SECOND CO LA
FIRST CO LA
The Holmes
BONDGATE B1223
P
PH
SELBY
Moss Hagg
Flaxley Lodge
FLAXLEY RD
Oak Tree Farm
West Farm
Scalm Park Farm
Skylark Farm
GREENLANDS LANE
Selby Common
CHARLES STREET
River Ouse
CH
HOLME LA
HAIG STREET
East Farm
RD
A63
HEMPBRIDGE RD
PO
FLAXLEY
P P
Abbey
CARR LANE
DAM LA
CROSS HILLS LANE
Abbey L Ctr
THE CRES
GOWTHORPE
Sch
HOLDEN GD 1
MEADWAY DR 2
MEADWAY 3
Crosshills Farm
YO8
PARK ST
Thorpe Wood
A63
BROOK ST
Selby
Coll
232
Civic Ctr
Selby Dam
Sch
Police HQ
CANAL RD
The Carrs
Thorpe Hall
Sports Ground
LC
CEDAR CR
WEST PK
COURTNEYS'
LEEDS ROAD
SANDHILL LA
Hosp
WESTBOURNE ROAD
BRIDLE WK
A1041
DAM LANE
Meadow Side
GREEN LA
FERNDALE RD
Sewage Works
A19
Cemy
LC
A63
LC
BRACKENHILL LANE
FOXHILL LANE
DONCASTER ROAD
Sch
WHINNY HAGG LA
HARRY MOOR LA
FIR TREE
FORDLANDS
MEADOW CL
MD GARTH
Cemy
THE MOUNT
MYRTLE AV
Sch
PH
Thorpe Willoughby
BAWTRY ROAD
PARKWAYS
Sch
PO
ORCHARD WY
Brayton
FOX HL LA
BAFFAM GDNS
Sch
BARFF LANE
MAPLE CL
DANE AV
WILLOW
LONDESBOROUGH GR
CEDAR CL
MOAT WY
A63 Leeds, A1
A63
BEECHFIELD CL
FIELD
THE COPPICE
P
Brayton Barff
BAFFAM LA
ALMOND CL
Sch
Oakney Wood
GREEN LA
MORRETS LANE
Sports Centre
PO
BRAYTON LA
P
ROWAN CL
ACORN WY
Resr
LC
FIELD LANE
LAUREL CL
Sewage Works
Brayton Bridge
BRAYTON LANE
MORTON LA
ASHTREE DR
MILL LANE
232
8 37 7 36 6 35 5 34 4 33 3 32 2 31 1 30
56 A 57 B 58 C 59 D 60 E 61 F
B1
1 SANDWAY DR
2 LIMETREE CL
3 LABURNUM CL
4 BIRCH CL
5 OAK DR
6 SAXON CL
7 NORMAN CL
8 BRAMBLES
9 STUART GR
10 TUDOR CL
11 SANDWAY CL
12 SANDWAY AV
13 WOOD LA
14 WOOD CL
B2
1 FIR TREE WY
2 PINE TREE CL
3 THE FIR TREES
4 FIR TREE CL
5 LONDESBOROUGH GR
6 BARFF GR
7 FRANCIS CT
8 HOLLY GR
9 LINDEN WY
203
D1
1 EVERGREEN WY
2 CONIFERS CL
3 GREENACRES GR
4 GREENACRES DR
5 SANDIACRES
6 GREENFIELD DR
7 GREENACRES CR
8 GREENACRES CL
9 ST WILFRID'S CR
10 BARFF CL
11 THE POPLARS
12 MAPLE GR
13 CHERRY TREE CL
232
For full street detail of the highlighted area see page 232.

A8
1 MANOR GARTH
2 BACK LA
3 SILVER ST
4 NOVA SCOTIA WY
5 DANES CT
6 KING RUDDING CL

197
192

Scale: 1¾ inches to 1 mile

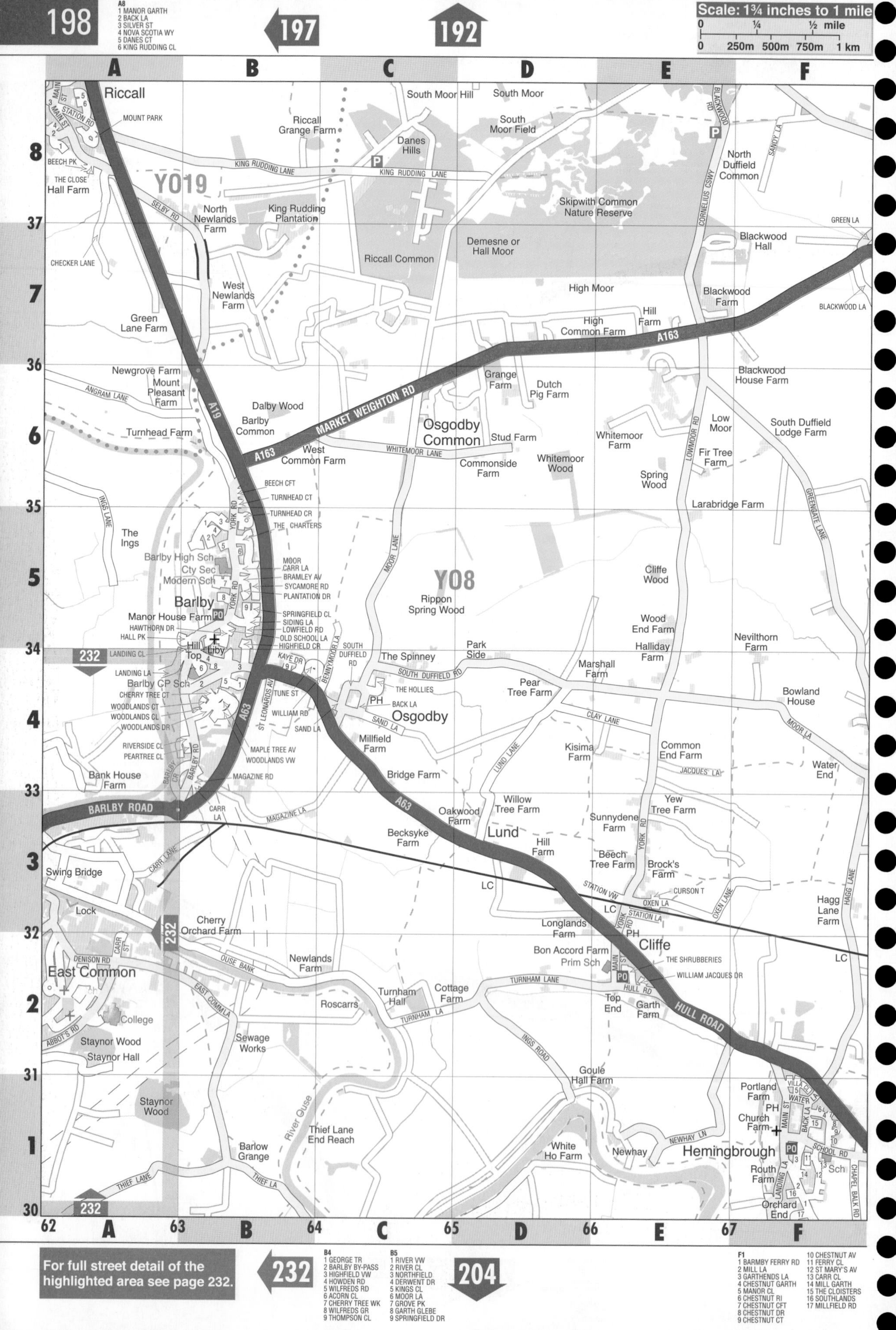

For full street detail of the highlighted area see page 232.
232
204

B4
1 GEORGE TR
2 BARLBY BY-PASS
3 HIGHFIELD VW
4 HOWDEN RD
5 WILFREDS RD
6 ACORN CL
7 CHERRY TREE WK
8 WILFREDS GR
9 THOMPSON CL

B5
1 RIVER VW
2 RIVER CL
3 NORTHFIELD
4 DERWENT DR
5 KINGS CL
6 MOOR LA
7 GROVE PK
8 GARTH GLEBE
9 SPRINGFIELD DR

F1
1 BARMBY FERRY RD
2 MILL LA
3 GARTHENDS LA
4 CHESTNUT GARTH
5 MANOR CL
6 CHESTNUT RI
7 CHESTNUT CFT
8 CHESTNUT DR
9 CHESTNUT CT
10 CHESTNUT AV
11 FERRY CL
12 ST MARY'S AV
13 CARR CL
14 MILL GARTH
15 THE CLOISTERS
16 SOUTHLANDS
17 MILLFIELD RD

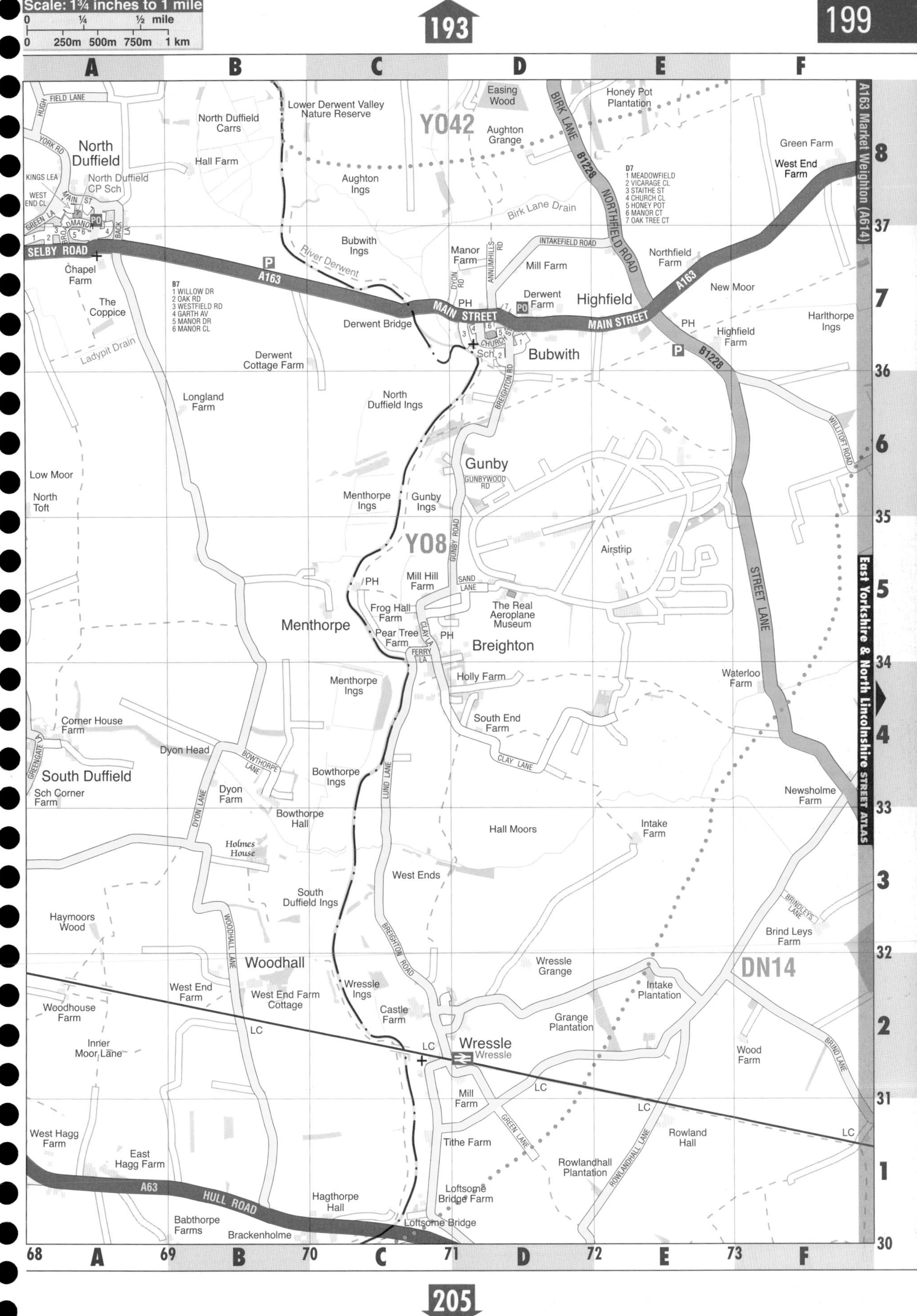
Scale: 1¾ inches to 1 mile
193
205
North Duffield
South Duffield
Bubwith
Highfield
Gunby
Breighton
Menthorpe
Woodhall
Wressle
YO42
YO8
DN14
A163 Market Weighton (A614)
East Yorkshire & North Lincolnshire STREET ATLAS
Lower Derwent Valley Nature Reserve
River Derwent
Derwent Bridge
Airstrip
The Real Aeroplane Museum
SELBY ROAD
MAIN STREET
HULL ROAD
STREET LANE
NORTHFIELD ROAD
BIRK LANE
B7
1 WILLOW DR
2 OAK RD
3 WESTFIELD RD
4 GARTH AV
5 MANOR DR
6 MANOR CL
D7
1 MEADOWFIELD
2 VICARAGE CL
3 STAITHE ST
4 CHURCH CL
5 HONEY POT
6 MANOR CT
7 OAK TREE CT

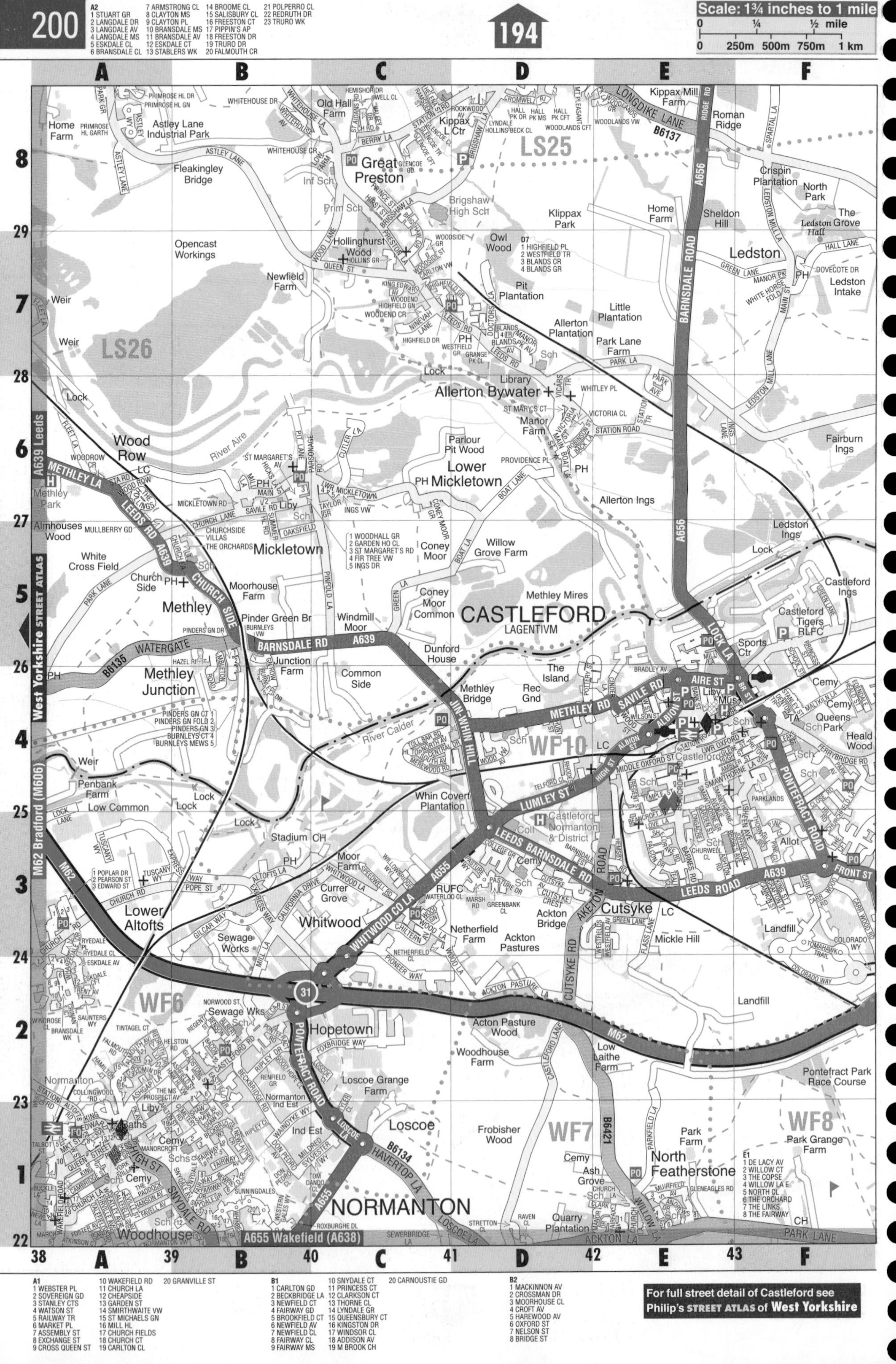

200
A2
1 STUART GR
2 LANGDALE DR
3 LANGDALE AV
4 LANGDALE MS
5 ESKDALE CL
6 BRANSDALE CL
7 ARMSTRONG CL
8 CLAYTON MS
9 CLAYTON PL
10 BRANSDALE MS
11 BRANSDALE AV
12 ESKDALE CT
13 STABLERS WK
14 BROOME CL
15 SALISBURY CL
16 FREESTON CT
17 PIPPIN'S AP
18 FREESTON DR
19 TRURO DR
20 FALMOUTH CR
21 POLPERRO CL
22 REDRUTH DR
23 TRURO WK
194
Scale: 1¾ inches to 1 mile
0 ¼ ½ mile
0 250m 500m 750m 1 km
A B C D E F
Home Farm
Astley Lane Industrial Park
Old Hall Farm
Kippax L Ctr
Kippax Mill Farm
Roman Ridge
LONGDIKE LANE
B6137
LS25
Great Preston
Fleakingley Bridge
Brigshaw High Sch
Crispin Plantation
North Park
Klippax Park
Home Farm
Sheldon Hill
The Grove
Ledston Hall
Opencast Workings
Hollinghurst Wood
Owl Wood
D7
1 HIGHFIELD PL
2 WESTFIELD TR
3 BLANDS CR
4 BLANDS GR
Ledston
Ledston Intake
Newfield Farm
Pit Plantation
Little Plantation
Allerton Plantation
BARNSDALE ROAD
Weir
LS26
Park Lane Farm
Lock
Library
Allerton Bywater
Wood Row
River Aire
Parlour Pit Wood
Lower Mickletown
Fairburn Ings
Methley Park
Allerton Ings
Almhouses Wood
Mickletown
1 WOODHALL GR
2 GARDEN HO CL
3 ST MARGARET'S RD
4 FIR TREE VW
5 INGS DR
Coney Moor
Willow Grove Farm
Ledston Ings
White Cross Field
Church Side
Methley
Moorhouse Farm
Coney Moor Common
Methley Mires
Castleford Ings
CASTLEFORD
LAGENTIVM
Castleford Tigers RLFC
Pinder Green Br
Windmill Moor
BARNSDALE RD
A639
Dunford House
Sports Ctr
WATERGATE
B6135
Methley Junction
Junction Farm
Common Side
The Island
Rec Gnd
Methley Bridge
Cemy
Queens Park
Heald Wood
WHIN HILL
METHLEY RD
SAVILE RD
AIRE ST
LOCK LA
1 PINDERS GN CT
2 PINDERS GN FOLD
3 PINDERS GN
4 BURNLEYS CT
5 BURNLEYS MEWS
River Calder
WF10
Weir
Penbank Farm
Low Common
Whin Covert Plantation
LUMLEY ST
PONTEFRACT ROAD
Castleford Normanton & District
Stadium
Allot
LEEDS BARNSDALE RD
Moor Farm
LEEDS ROAD
FRONT ST
1 POPLAR DR
2 PEARSON ST
3 EDWARD ST
Currer Grove
RUFC
Ackton Bridge
Cutsyke
Mickle Hill
Lower Altofts
Whitwood
WHITWOOD CO LA
Netherfield Farm
Ackton Pastures
Landfill
Sewage Works
CUTSYKE RD
WF6
Sewage Wks
Acton Pasture Wood
Landfill
Hopetown
M62
Woodhouse Farm
Low Laithe Farm
Pontefract Park Race Course
Normanton
Loscoe Grange Farm
Normanton Ind Est
WF8
Ind Est
Loscoe
Frobisher Wood
WF7
Park Farm
Park Grange Farm
B6134
North Featherstone
E1
1 DE LACY AV
2 WILLOW CT
3 THE COPSE
4 WILLOW LA E
5 NORTH CL
6 THE ORCHARD
7 THE LINKS
8 THE FAIRWAY
NORMANTON
Quarry Plantation
Woodhouse
A655 Wakefield (A638)
PARK LANE
A639 Leeds
West Yorkshire STREET ATLAS
M62 Bradford (M606)
38 39 40 41 42 43
A1
1 WEBSTER PL
2 SOVEREIGN GD
3 STANLEY CTS
4 WATSON ST
5 RAILWAY TR
6 MARKET PL
7 ASSEMBLY ST
8 EXCHANGE ST
9 CROSS QUEEN ST
10 WAKEFIELD RD
11 CHURCH LA
12 CHEAPSIDE
13 GARDEN ST
14 SMITHWAITE VW
15 ST MICHAELS GN
16 MILL HL
17 CHURCH FIELDS
18 CHURCH CT
19 CARLTON CL
20 GRANVILLE ST
B1
1 CARLTON GD
2 BECKBRIDGE LA
3 NEWFIELD CT
4 FAIRWAY GD
5 BROOKFIELD CT
6 NEWFIELD AV
7 NEWFIELD CL
8 FAIRWAY CL
9 FAIRWAY MS
10 SNYDALE CT
11 PRINCESS CT
12 CLARKSON CT
13 THORNE CL
14 LYNDALE GR
15 QUEENSBURY CT
16 KINGSTON DR
17 WINDSOR CL
18 ADDISON AV
19 M BROOK CH
20 CARNOUSTIE GD
B2
1 MACKINNON AV
2 CROSSMAN DR
3 MOORHOUSE CL
4 CROFT AV
5 HAREWOOD AV
6 OXFORD ST
7 NELSON ST
8 BRIDGE ST
For full street detail of Castleford see Philip's STREET ATLAS of West Yorkshire

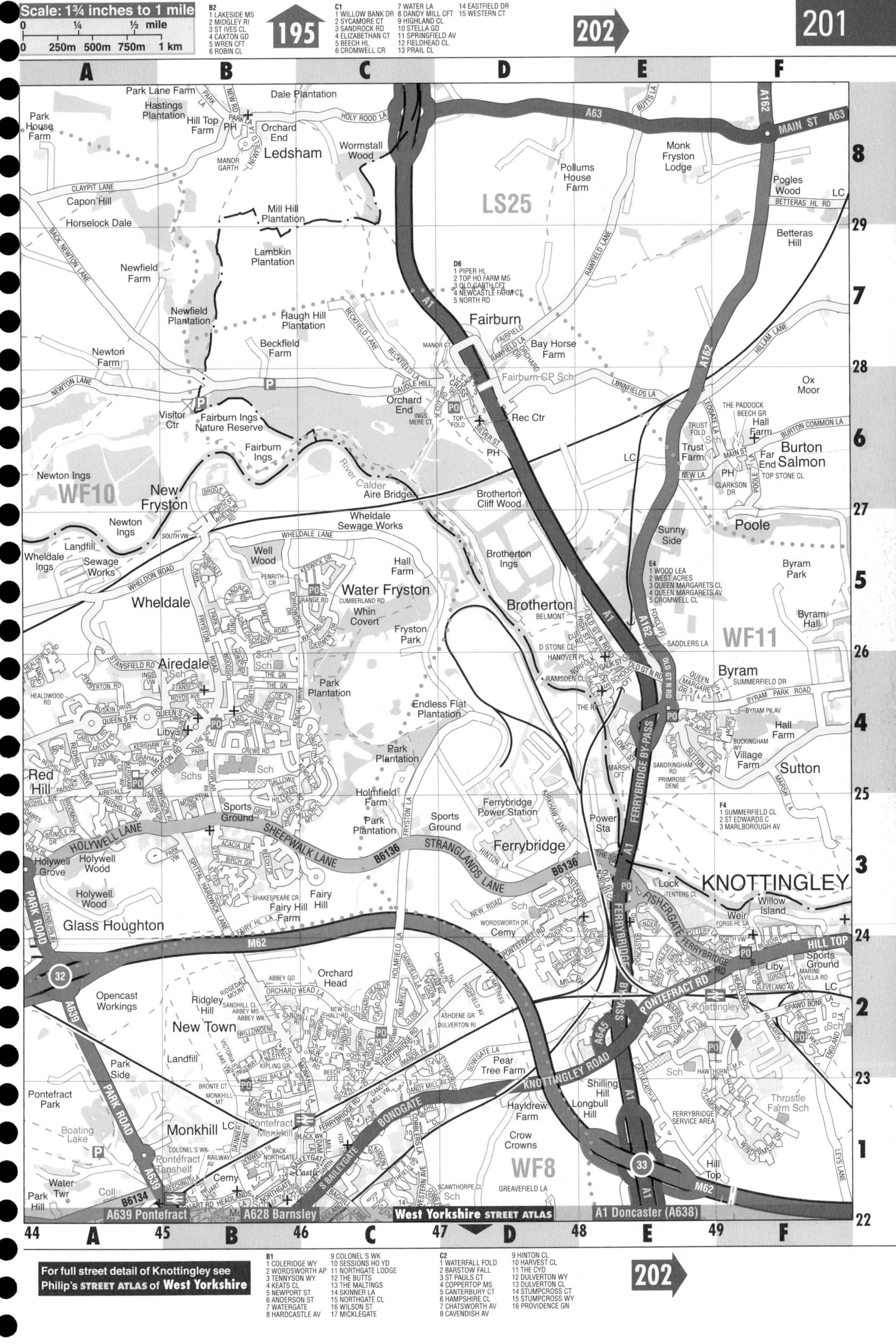
Scale: 1¾ inches to 1 mile
0 ¼ ½ mile
0 250m 500m 750m 1 km
B2
1 LAKESIDE MS
2 MIDGLEY RI
3 ST IVES CL
4 CAXTON GD
5 WREN CFT
6 ROBIN CL
195
C1
1 WILLOW BANK DR
2 SYCAMORE CT
3 SANDROCK RD
4 ELIZABETHAN CT
5 BEECH HL
6 CROMWELL CR
7 WATER LA
8 DANDY MILL CFT
9 HIGHLAND CL
10 STELLA GD
11 SPRINGFIELD AV
12 FIELDHEAD CL
13 PRAIL CL
14 EASTFIELD DR
15 WESTERN CT
202
A B C D E F
Park Lane Farm
Hastings Plantation
Hill Top Farm
Dale Plantation
Park House Farm
Orchard End
Ledsham
Wormstall Wood
HOLY ROOD LA
A63
MAIN ST
A162
Monk Fryston Lodge
Pollums House Farm
LS25
Pogles Wood
BETTERAS HL RD
Betteras Hill
CLAYPIT LANE
Capon Hill
Horselock Dale
Mill Hill Plantation
Lambkin Plantation
Newfield Farm
BACK NEWTON LANE
RAWFIELD LANE
D6
1 PIPER HL
2 TOP HO FARM MS
3 OLD GARTH CFT
4 NEWCASTLE FARM CT
5 NORTH RD
Newfield Plantation
Haugh Hill Plantation
Beckfield Farm
Fairburn
Bay Horse Farm
Newton Farm
NEWTON LANE
Fairburn CP Sch
LUNNFIELDS LA
HILLAM LANE
Ox Moor
Visitor Ctr
Fairburn Ings Nature Reserve
Orchard End
Rec Ctr
Fairburn Ings
THE PADDOCK
BEECH GR
Hall Farm
BURTON COMMON LA
Trust Farm
Burton Salmon
Newton Ings
WF10
New Fryston
River Calder
Aire Bridge
Brotherton Cliff Wood
TOP STONE CL
Newton Ings
Wheldale Sewage Works
WHELDALE LANE
Sunny Side
Poole
Wheldale Ings
Landfill
Sewage Works
Well Wood
Hall Farm
Brotherton Ings
E4
1 WOOD LEA
2 WEST ACRES
3 QUEEN MARGARETS CL
4 QUEEN MARGARETS AV
5 CROMWELL CL
Byram Park
WHELDON ROAD
Wheldale
Water Fryston
Whin Covert
Brotherton
Byram Hall
Fryston Park
WF11
SADDLERS LA
STANSFIELD RD
Airedale
Byram
SUMMERFIELD DR
Park Plantation
BYRAM PARK RD
Endless Flat Plantation
Hall Farm
Village Farm
Sutton
Red Hill
Park Plantation
Holmfield Farm
F4
1 SUMMERFIELD CL
2 ST EDWARDS C
3 MARLBOROUGH AV
Ferrybridge Power Station
Sports Ground
Park Plantation
Power Sta
FERRYBRIDGE BY-PASS
HOLYWELL LANE
SHEEPWALK LANE
B6136
STRANGLANDS LANE
Ferrybridge
Holywell Grove
Holywell Wood
Lock
KNOTTINGLEY
Willow Island
Holywell Wood
Fairy Hill
Fairy Hill Farm
Weir
Glass Houghton
Cemy
M62
PARK ROAD
32
Orchard Head
Opencast Workings
Ridgley Hill
New Town
A639
Knottingley
Landfill
Park Side
Pear Tree Farm
KNOTTINGLEY ROAD
Shilling Hill
Pontefract Park
Hayldrew Farm
Longbull Hill
Throstle Farm Sch
FERRYBRIDGE SERVICE AREA
Boating Lake
Monkhill
Pontefract Monkhill
Crow Crowns
BONDGATE
Pontefract Tanshelf
33
Hill Top
WF8
Water Twr
Park Hill
Coll
Castle
A639 Pontefract
A628 Barnsley
West Yorkshire STREET ATLAS
A1 Doncaster (A638)
44 45 46 47 48 49
8 29 7 28 6 27 5 26 4 25 3 24 2 23 1 22
For full street detail of Knottingley see Philip's STREET ATLAS of West Yorkshire
B1
1 COLERIDGE WY
2 WORDSWORTH AP
3 TENNYSON WY
4 KEATS CL
5 NEWPORT ST
6 ANDERSON ST
7 WATERGATE
8 HARDCASTLE AV
9 COLONEL'S WK
10 SESSIONS HO YD
11 NORTHGATE LODGE
12 THE BUTTS
13 THE MALTINGS
14 SKINNER LA
15 NORTHGATE CL
16 WILSON ST
17 MICKLEGATE
C2
1 WATERFALL FOLD
2 BARSTOW FALL
3 ST PAULS CT
4 COPPERTOP MS
5 CANTERBURY CT
6 HAMPSHIRE CL
7 CHATSWORTH AV
8 CAVENDISH AV
9 HINTON CL
10 HARVEST CL
11 THE CYD
12 DULVERTON WY
13 DULVERTON CL
14 STUMPCROSS CT
15 STUMPCROSS WY
16 PROVIDENCE GN
202

A8
1 DEER PK CT
2 PRIORY PARK GR
3 PRIORY PARK CL
4 CHURCH LA
5 OLD VICARAGE LA
6 ORCHARD CL
7 THE MEADOWS
8 HILLCREST
9 HILLSIDE CL

201

A7
1 PINE TREE LA
2 ROSE LEA CL
3 HILLAM HALL VW
4 HILLAM HALL LA
5 HILLIAM HALL CL
6 BEDFORDS FOLD

196

Scale: 1¾ inches to 1 mile

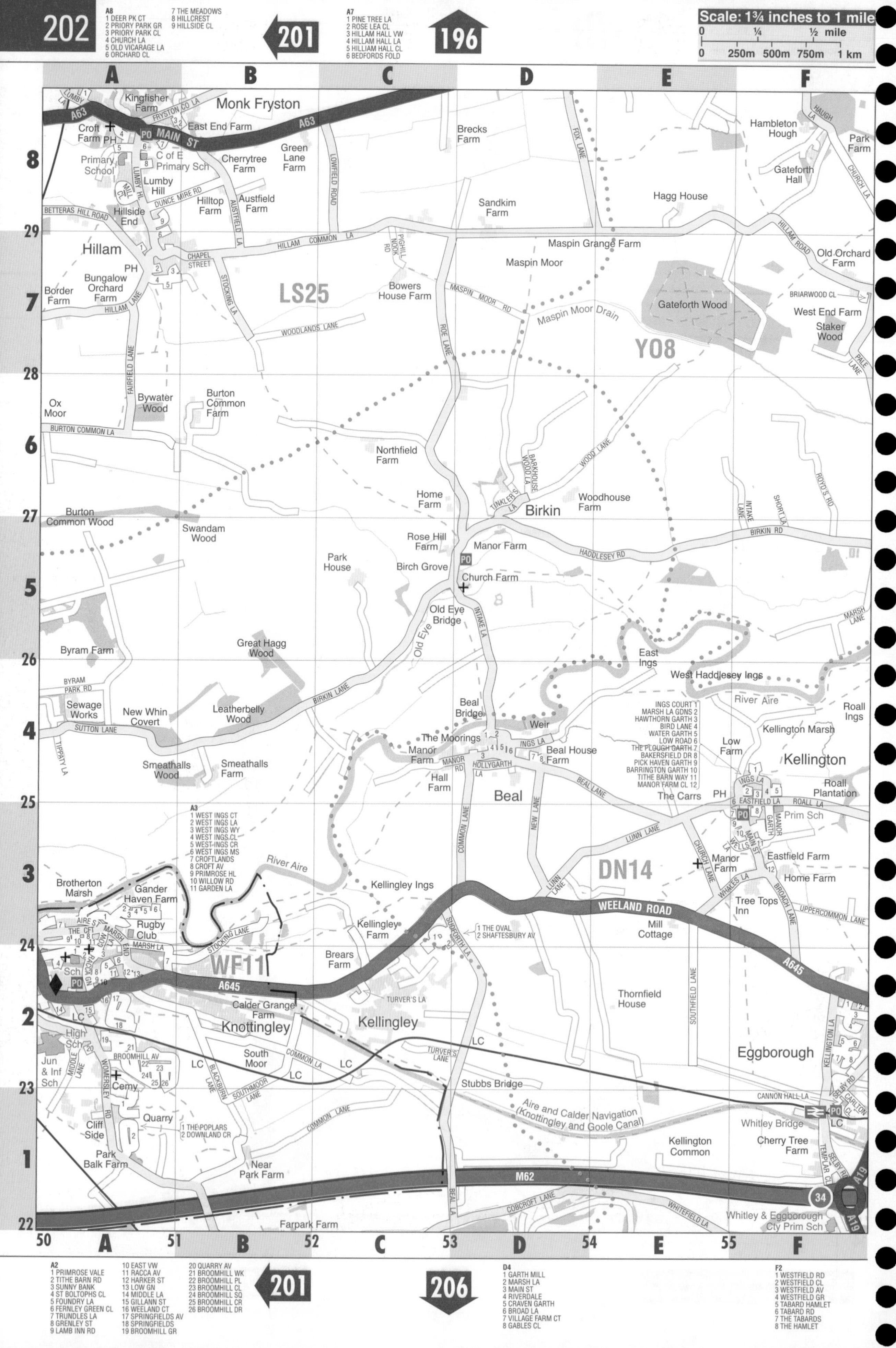

D4
1 GARTH MILL
2 MARSH LA
3 MAIN ST
4 RIVERDALE
5 CRAVEN GARTH
6 BROAD LA
7 VILLAGE FARM CT
8 GABLES CL

A2
1 PRIMROSE VALE
2 TITHE BARN RD
3 SUNNY BANK
4 ST BOLTOPHS CL
5 FOUNDRY LA
6 FERNLEY GREEN CL
7 TRUNDLES LA
8 GRENLEY ST
9 LAMB INN RD
10 EAST VW
11 RACCA AV
12 HARKER ST
13 LOW GN
14 MIDDLE LA
15 GILLANN ST
16 WEELAND CT
17 SPRINGFIELDS AV
18 SPRINGFIELDS
19 BROOMHILL GR
20 QUARRY AV
21 BROOMHILL WK
22 BROOMHILL PL
23 BROOMHILL CL
24 BROOMHILL SQ
25 BROOMHILL CR
26 BROOMHILL DR

201

206

D4
1 GARTH MILL
2 MARSH LA
3 MAIN ST
4 RIVERDALE
5 CRAVEN GARTH
6 BROAD LA
7 VILLAGE FARM CT
8 GABLES CL

F2
1 WESTFIELD RD
2 WESTFIELD CL
3 WESTFIELD AV
4 WESTFIELD GR
5 TABARD HAMLET
6 TABARD RD
7 THE TABARDS
8 THE HAMLET

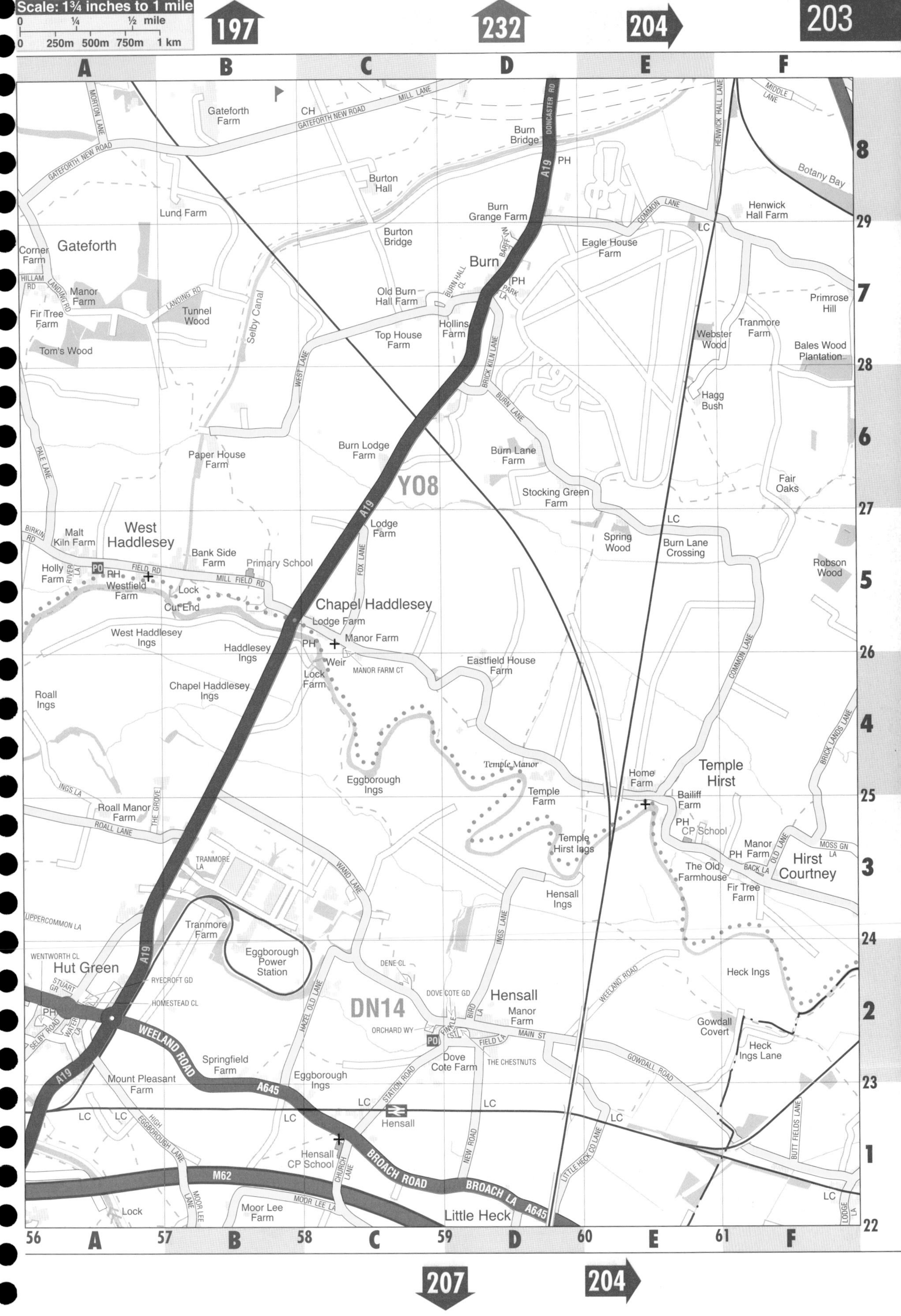
Scale: 1¾ inches to 1 mile
197
232
204
Gateforth Farm
Burton Hall
Lund Farm
Gateforth
Burton Bridge
Burn Grange Farm
Burn
Eagle House Farm
Henwick Hall Farm
Botany Bay
Old Burn Hall Farm
Top House Farm
Hollins Farm
Tunnel Wood
Manor Farm
Fir Tree Farm
Tom's Wood
Corner Farm
Selby Canal
Webster Wood
Tranmore Farm
Primrose Hill
Bales Wood Plantation
Hagg Bush
Paper House Farm
Burn Lodge Farm
Burn Lane Farm
YO8
Stocking Green Farm
Fair Oaks
West Haddlesey
Malt Kiln Farm
Bank Side Farm
Primary School
Lodge Farm
Spring Wood
Burn Lane Crossing
Robson Wood
Holly Farm
Westfield Farm
Lock
Cut End
Chapel Haddlesey
Lodge Farm
Manor Farm
West Haddlesey Ings
Haddlesey Ings
Weir
Lock Farm
Eastfield House Farm
Chapel Haddlesey Ings
Roall Ings
Temple Manor
Eggborough Ings
Home Farm
Temple Hirst
Temple Farm
Bailiff Farm
CP School
Roall Manor Farm
Temple Hirst Ings
Manor Farm
Hirst Courtney
The Old Farmhouse
Fir Tree Farm
Hensall Ings
Tranmore Farm
Eggborough Power Station
Hut Green
Heck Ings
DN14
Hensall
Manor Farm
Gowdall Covert
Heck Ings Lane
Springfield Farm
Dove Cote Farm
Mount Pleasant Farm
Eggborough Ings
Hensall
Hensall CP School
Moor Lee Farm
Little Heck
Lock
M62
A19
A645
WEELAND ROAD
BROACH ROAD
BROACH LA
56 A 57 B 58 C 59 D 60 E 61 F
8 29 7 28 6 27 5 26 4 25 3 24 2 23 1 22
207
204

232
203
198

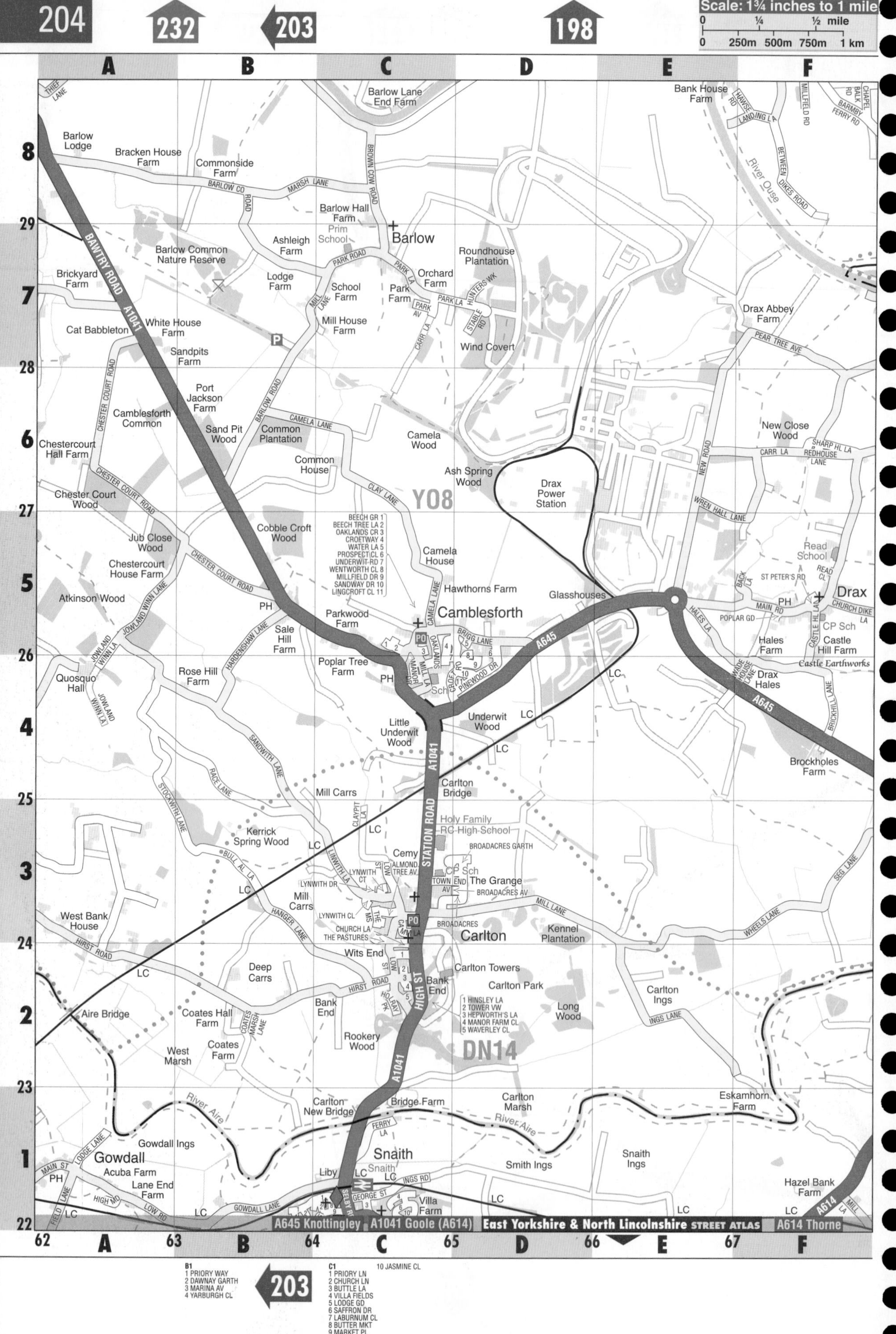

B1
1 PRIORY WAY
2 DAWNAY GARTH
3 MARINA AV
4 YARBURGH CL

203

C1
1 PRIORY LN
2 CHURCH LN
3 BUTTLE LA
4 VILLA FIELDS
5 LODGE GD
6 SAFFRON DR
7 LABURNUM CL
8 BUTTER MKT
9 MARKET PL
10 JASMINE CL

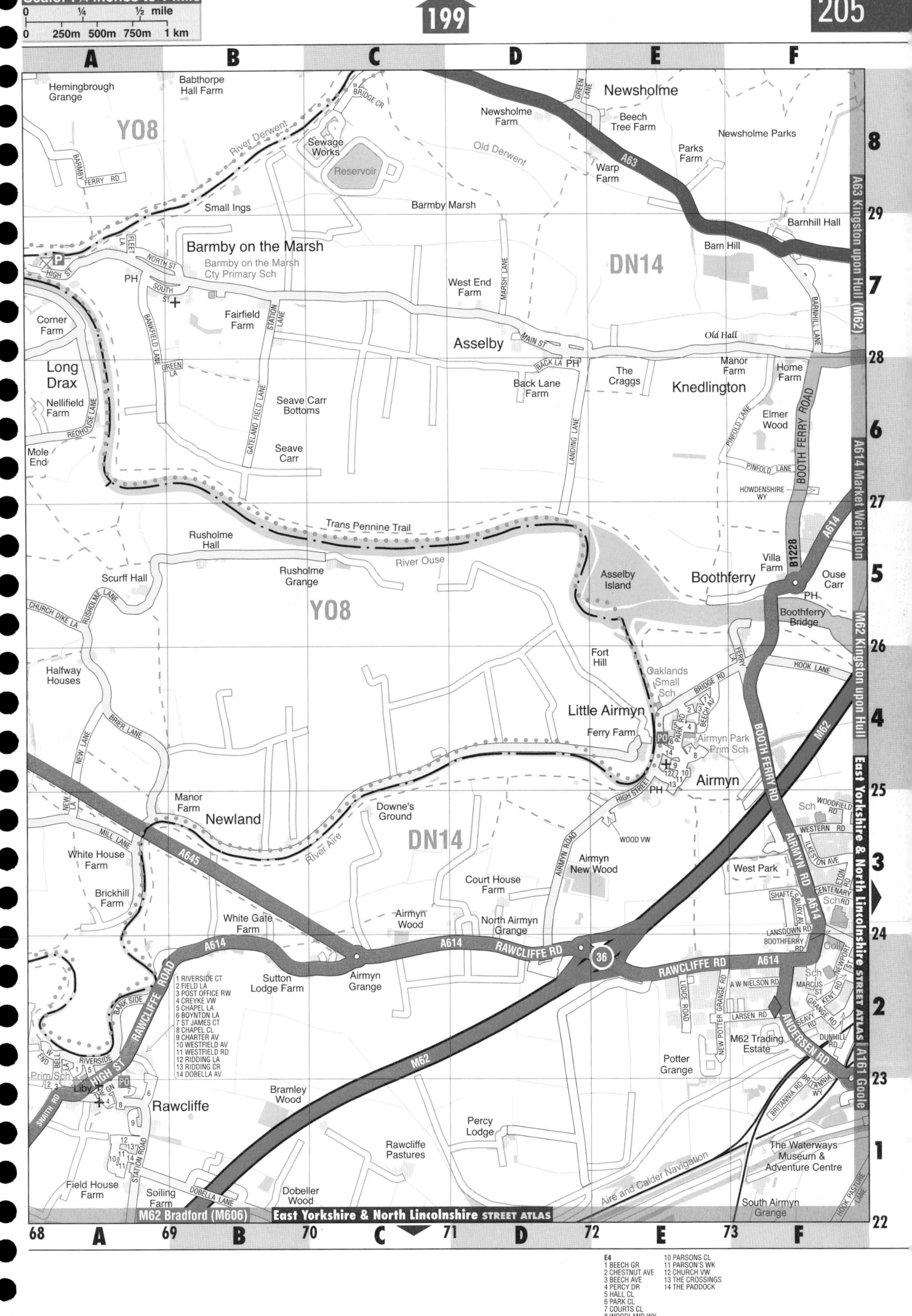
Scale: 1¾ inches to 1 mile
0 ¼ ½ mile
0 250m 500m 750m 1 km
199
A B C D E F
Hemingbrough Grange
Babthorpe Hall Farm
YO8
BARMBY FERRY RD
River Derwent
BRIDGE CR
Sewage Works
Reservoir
Newsholme
GREEN LANE
Newsholme Farm
Beech Tree Farm
Newsholme Parks
Old Derwent
Parks Farm
Warp Farm
A63
Small Ings
Barmby Marsh
Barnhill Hall
Barn Hill
Barmby on the Marsh
Barmby on the Marsh Cty Primary Sch
FLEET LA
NORTH ST
HIGH ST
SOUTH ST
PH
DN14
West End Farm
MARSH LANE
Corner Farm
Fairfield Farm
STATION LANE
BANKFIELD LANE
MAIN ST
Asselby
Old Hall
BARNHILL LANE
Long Drax
GREEN LA
BACK LA
Back Lane Farm
The Craggs
Manor Farm
Home Farm
Knedlington
Nellifield Farm
REDHOUSE LANE
Seave Carr Bottoms
GATELAND FIELD LANE
LANDING LANE
PINFOLD LANE
Elmer Wood
BOOTH FERRY ROAD
Mole End
Seave Carr
HOWDENSHIRE WY
Trans Pennine Trail
Rusholme Hall
River Ouse
Asselby Island
Villa Farm
B1228
A614
Boothferry
Ouse Carr
Scurff Hall
Rusholme Grange
YO8
CHURCH DIKE LA
RUSHOLME LANE
Boothferry Bridge
Fort Hill
FERRY LA
HOOK LANE
Halfway Houses
Oaklands Small Sch
BRIDGE RD
BRIER LANE
Little Airmyn
BEECH AV
PARK RD
Ferry Farm
Airmyn Park Prim Sch
NEW LANE
M62
BOOTH FERRY RD
Airmyn
HIGH STREET
Manor Farm
Newland
Downe's Ground
Sch
WOODFIELD RD
NEW LA
MILL LANE
DN14
WOOD VW
WESTERN RD
River Aire
A645
AIRMYN ROAD
Airmyn New Wood
AIRMYN RD
ILKESTON AVE
White House Farm
West Park
Court House Farm
ETON RD
CENTENARY RD
Brickhill Farm
SHAFTESBURY AV
Sch
A614
White Gate Farm
Airmyn Wood
North Airmyn Grange
LANSDOWN RD
BOOTHFERRY RD
Coll
A614
A614
RAWCLIFFE RD
36
RAWCLIFFE RD
A614
NEWPORT ST
Sch
RAWCLIFFE ROAD
Sutton Lodge Farm
Airmyn Grange
LIDICE ROAD
GRANGE RD
A W NIELSON RD
MARCUS ST
KENT RD
GRANGE RD
BANK SIDE
1 RIVERSIDE CT
2 FIELD LA
3 POST OFFICE RW
4 CREYKE VW
5 CHAPEL LA
6 BOYNTON LA
7 ST JAMES CT
8 CHAPEL CL
9 CHARTER AV
10 WESTFIELD AV
11 WESTFIELD RD
12 RIDDING LA
13 RIDDING CR
14 DOBELLA AV
NEW POTTER GRANGE RD
LARSEN RD
SEAVY RD
ANDERSEN RD
M62 Trading Estate
DUNHILL RD
W END
BELL LA
RIVERSIDE
Prim Sch
HIGH ST
M62
Potter Grange
Liby
THE GN
PO
BRITANNIA RD
BRITANNIA WY
SNAITH RD
Bramley Wood
Rawcliffe
Percy Lodge
STATION ROAD
Rawcliffe Pastures
The Waterways Museum & Adventure Centre
Aire and Calder Navigation
Field House Farm
Soiling Farm
DOBELLA LANE
Dobeller Wood
South Airmyn Grange
HOOK PASTURE LANE
M62 Bradford (M606)
East Yorkshire & North Lincolnshire STREET ATLAS
A63 Kingston upon Hull (M62)
A614 Market Weighton
M62 Kingston upon Hull
East Yorkshire & North Lincolnshire STREET ATLAS
A161 Goole
8 29 7 28 6 27 5 26 4 25 3 24 2 23 1 22
68 69 70 71 72 73
E4
1 BEECH GR
2 CHESTNUT AVE
3 BEECH AVE
4 PERCY DR
5 HALL CL
6 PARK CL
7 COURTS CL
8 WOODLAND WY
9 ST DAVID'S VW
10 PARSONS CL
11 PARSON'S WK
12 CHURCH VW
13 THE CROSSINGS
14 THE PADDOCK

202

Scale: 1¾ inches to 1 mile
0 ¼ ½ mile
0 250m 500m 750m 1 km

A B C D E F

WF11
Stubbs Lane
LC
Cobcroft Lane
Cobcroft La
Cridling Stubbs
PH
Wrights La
Works
South Moor
DN14
Whitefield Bungalows
Whitefield Lane
Leys La
Spring Lodge
Wormersley Quarry
Wake Wood
LC
Northfield Lane
Grange Farm
Kelseycroft Wood
Bell Lands Wood
Gravelhill Lane
Cathcart Cl
Whitley Thorpe La
Booty Lane
Whitley Thorpe
Fulham Lane
Fulham House
Beech House Farm
Scrombeck Farm
Rows Wood
Quarry (dis)
Womersley Common
Woodhall Lane
Bank Wood Road
Bank Wood
Well
Northfield Cl
Ricketcroft Wood
Hodgsoncroft Wood
Stapleton Park Farm
Kingsland Wood
Manor Farm
Prim Sch
LC
Cow La
Main St
Low Farm
Sewage Works
Womersley
Park La
Station Rd
Highfield La
LC
Grove Wood
Clipsall Wood
Saulcroft Wood
Fishpond Wood
Stapleton Park
Belt Plantation
The Rookery
Wormesley Park
Highfield Lane
Stocking Green Farm
Womersley Beck
Castle Farm
Castle Hill Wood
DN6
Brown Ings Wood
Ox Stocking Wood
Quarry (dis)
Nutwood End
Sod Wall Plantation
New Road
Dawland House Farm
Churchfield Lane
Birdspring Wood
Little Grove Farm
Smeaton Leys
Smeatley's La
Churchfield La
Smeaton Bridge
Grove Bridge
Brockadale Plantation
Leys Lane
Willowbridge Road
Little La
Smeaton Crags Quarry
River Went
Long Crag
Stubbs Common Farm
Common La
Wells Farm
Little Smeaton
Kirk Smeaton
West Edge Road
Chapel La
Hodge La
The Grove
Stubbs Bridge
Home Farm
LC
Walden Stubbs
PH
Main St
Water La
Manor Farm
WF8
Kirk Smeaton C of E Prim School
Manor Cl
Stubbs Road
Tanpit La
LC
Pinfold Cross
Pinfold La
Little Bottom Plantation
Willow Bridge
Sewage Works
Tanpit Bridge
Stubbs La
LC
Norton and Kirk Smeat
Middlefield Lane
Norton Priory
Walden Stubbs Road
Norton Mill La
Sewage Works
Long Lane
Barnsdale Vw
Stubbs Lane
Norton
LC
Middle Field
Linkway
Bradley's Spring
Coal Pit La
Back Lane
Back Lane
Priory Rd
Hall Rd
Spittlerush Lane
Highfield Farm
West End Road
High St
Station Rd
Quarry Rd
Westfield Lane
Cliff Hl Rd
PO
Pinfold La
LC
Norton Co La
Greengate Road
Cliff Hill
West End
Cridling Gd
New Road
Crab Tree Lane
PH
The Close
Common La
Sewage Works
Norton County Jun & Inf Sch
Fox Covert
East End Villas
Hotel
Windmill
Ryecroft Rd
Stygate La
Campsall Balk
Windhill Plantation
Windmill La
Norton Ings
Fox Covert Rd
Campsmount Sch
Shaft
Quarry
Long Lane
Whitley Rd
Cemy
Glebe Farm
Church Field Road
Glebe Rd
Park Dr
Shaft
Barnsdale
Campsmount Home Farm
Barnsdale Wood
The Ave
Woodlands Rise
Beech Rd
Church Vw
Askern & Campsall Sports Ctr
A1 Knottingley
A1
A639 Pontefract
A639 Doncaster Rd
A1 Doncaster (A638)
West Yorkshire STREET ATLAS

21 20 19 18 17 16 15 14
8 7 6 5 4 3 2 1
50 51 52 53 54 55

E1
1 TENNYSON AV
2 SHAKESPEARE AV
3 BYRON AV
4 WORDSWORTH AV
5 WELLINGTONIA DR
6 LANGLEYS RD
7 EAST VW
8 GRANGE RD
9 WILLOW RD
10 VAUGHAN RD
11 CAMPSALL PK RD
12 CAMPSALL HALL RD
13 SHERWOOD CL

C3
1 WENTDALE
2 STAN VALLEY
3 SPRINGFIELD CR

E2
1 BROC-O-BANK
2 NEWTHORPE RD
3 FORRESTER'S CL
4 TRAFFORD RD
5 ARUNDEL RD
6 ADELAIDE RD
7 HEADINGLEY RD
8 ORCHARD DR
9 ORCHARD CL
10 RYECROFT AV
11 FIR TREE DR
12 MANOR CL

F2
1 LYNDHURST DR
2 LYNDHURST CL
3 LYNDHURST RI
4 ASHBURNHAM CL
5 ASHBURNHAM WK
6 DENVER RD
7 MANOR GARTH
8 SWAN SYKE DR
9 DRYHURST CL

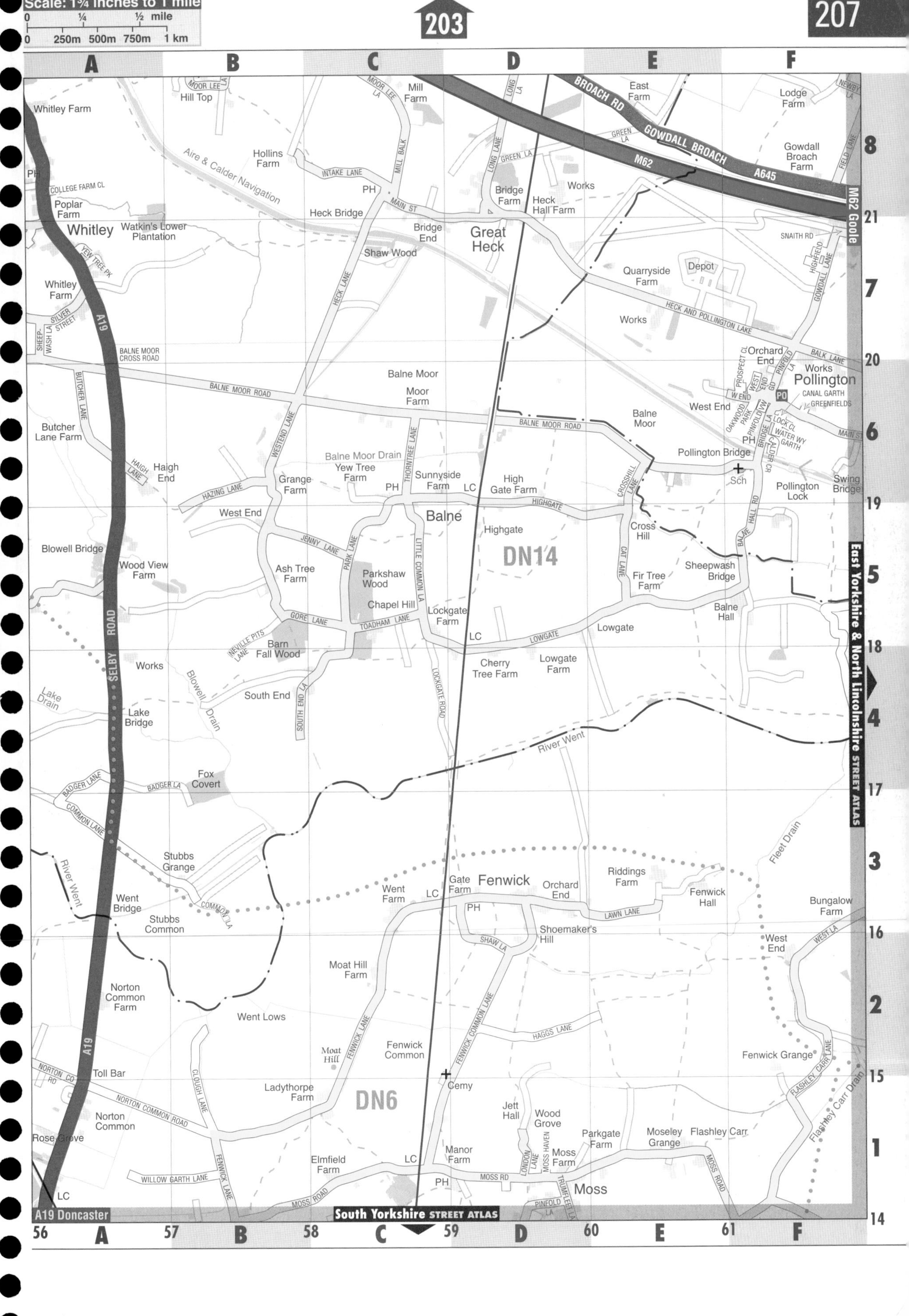
Scale: 1¾ inches to 1 mile
203
Whitley
Great Heck
Balne
Pollington
Fenwick
Moss
DN14
DN6
M62
A19
SELBY ROAD
River Went
Aire & Calder Navigation
East Yorkshire & North Lincolnshire STREET ATLAS
South Yorkshire STREET ATLAS
A19 Doncaster
M62 Goole

B6
1 ABBEVILLE AV
2 HOLLY TREE CT
3 THE NURSERIES
4 ELM GR
5 BYLAND CT
6 SUTCLIFFE CT

13

C6
1 FOUNTAINS CL
2 HARROWING DR
3 ROSEDALE CL
4 LIME GR
5 PINEWOOD CL
6 KIRKHAM CL
7 AUCKLAND WY
8 SOUTHEND GD
9 ARUNDEL PL

13

D5
1 WATERSTEAD CR
2 SCORESBY TR
3 RAGLAN TR
4 FISHBURN RD
5 OSWY ST

D6
1 ANGEL YD
2 WELINGTON RD
3 VICTORIA PL
4 STATION SQ
5 PRINCESS PL
6 ENDEAVOUR WHARF
7 WINDSOR CR
8 PANNETT WY
9 LYNDHURST CL
10 SPRING HL TR
11 FALCON TR
12 GEORGE ST
13 GRAY ST
14 ALBION PL
15 GROVE ST
16 ELGIN ST
17 MEADOWFIELDS CT

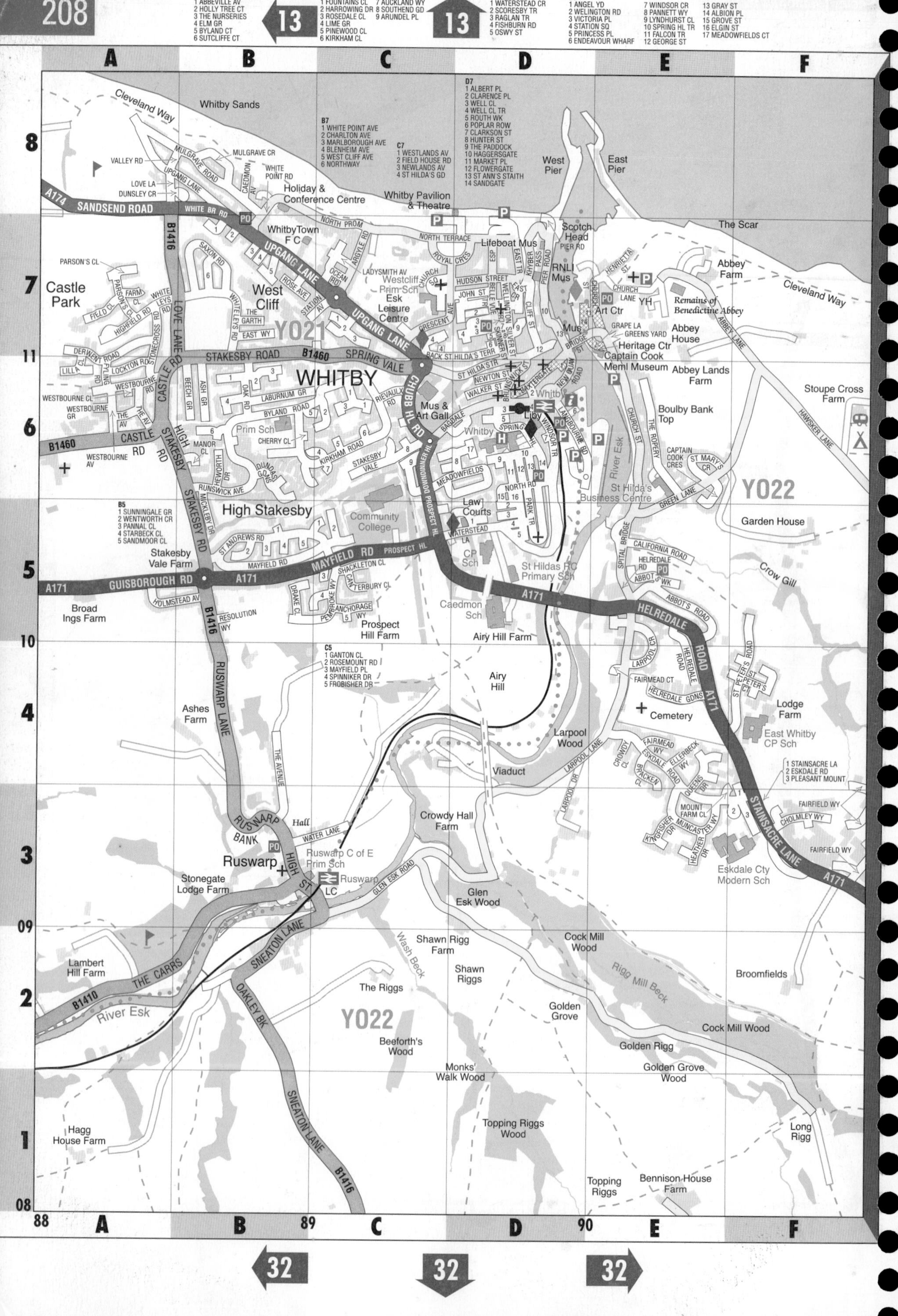

32
32
32

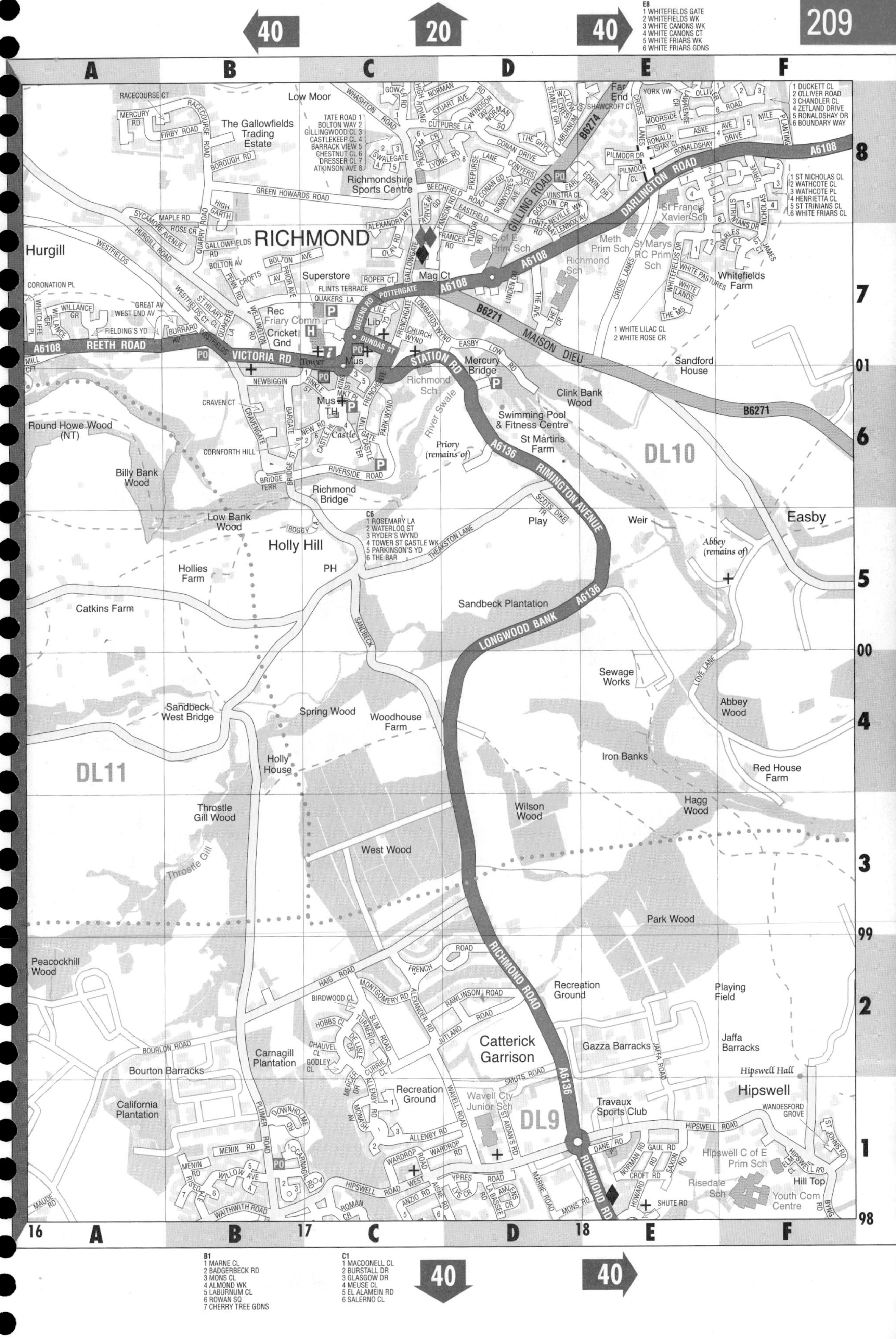
40
20
40
E8
1 WHITEFIELDS GATE
2 WHITEFIELDS WK
3 WHITE CANONS WK
4 WHITE CANONS CT
5 WHITE FRIARS WK
6 WHITE FRIARS GDNS
1 DUCKETT CL
2 OLLIVER ROAD
3 CHANDLER CL
4 ZETLAND DRIVE
5 RONALDSHAY DR
6 BOUNDARY WAY
1 ST NICHOLAS CL
2 WATHCOTE CL
3 WATHCOTE PL
4 HENRIETTA CL
5 ST TRINIANS CL
6 WHITE FRIARS CL
TATE ROAD 1
BOLTON WAY 2
GILLINGWOOD CL 3
CASTLEKEEP CL 4
BARRACK VIEW 5
CHESTNUT CL 6
DRESSER CL 7
ATKINSON AVE 8
1 WHITE LILAC CL
2 WHITE ROSE CR
C6
1 ROSEMARY LA
2 WATERLOO ST
3 RYDER'S WYND
4 TOWER ST CASTLE WK
5 PARKINSON'S YD
6 THE BAR
RICHMOND
Hurgill
Low Moor
The Gallowfields Trading Estate
Richmondshire Sports Centre
Far End
Superstore
Mag Ct
Rec
Friary Comm
Cricket Gnd
Lib
Mus
Tower
Mercury Bridge
Richmond Sch
Meth Prim Sch
St Marys RC Prim Sch
St Francis Xavier Sch
C of E Prim Sch
Whitefields Farm
Sandford House
Clink Bank Wood
Swimming Pool & Fitness Centre
St Martins Farm
Priory (remains of)
Castle
River Swale
Round Howe Wood (NT)
Billy Bank Wood
Richmond Bridge
Low Bank Wood
Holly Hill
Hollies Farm
PH
Play
Weir
Easby
Abbey (remains of)
DL10
Catkins Farm
Sandbeck Plantation
Sewage Works
Abbey Wood
Sandbeck West Bridge
Spring Wood
Woodhouse Farm
Iron Banks
Red House Farm
DL11
Holly House
Throstle Gill Wood
Throstle Gill
Wilson Wood
Hagg Wood
West Wood
Park Wood
Peacockhill Wood
Recreation Ground
Playing Field
Catterick Garrison
Gazza Barracks
Jaffa Barracks
Carnagill Plantation
Bourton Barracks
California Plantation
Recreation Ground
Wavell Cty Junior Sch
DL9
Travaux Sports Club
Hipswell Hall
Hipswell
Hipswell C of E Prim Sch
Risedale Sch
Hill Top
Youth Com Centre
A6108
B6274
B6271
A6136
REETH ROAD
VICTORIA RD
STATION RD
DARLINGTON ROAD
GILLING ROAD
MAISON DIEU
RIMINGTON AVENUE
LONGWOOD BANK
RICHMOND ROAD
HIPSWELL ROAD
A B C D E F
8 01 7 6 5 00 4 3 99 2 1 98
16 17 18
B1
1 MARNE CL
2 BADGERBECK RD
3 MONS CL
4 ALMOND WK
5 LABURNUM CL
6 ROWAN SQ
7 CHERRY TREE GDNS
C1
1 MACDONELL CL
2 BURSTALL DR
3 GLASGOW DR
4 MEUSE CL
5 EL ALAMEIN RD
6 SALERNO CL
40
40

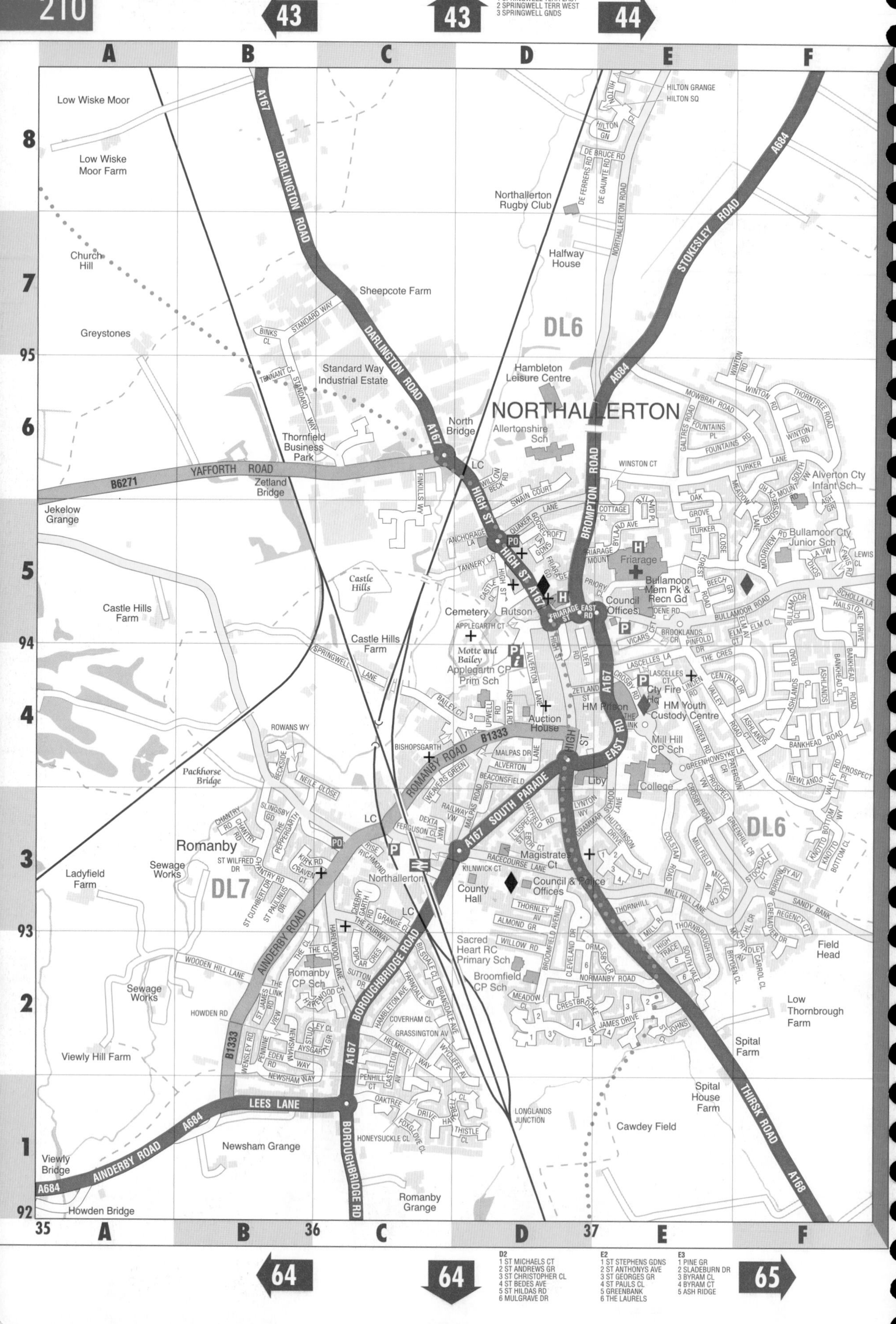
D4
1 SPRINGWELL TERR EAST
2 SPRINGWELL TERR WEST
3 SPRINGWELL GNDS
A
B
C
D
E
F
8
7
95
6
5
94
4
3
93
2
1
92
35
36
37
Low Wiske Moor
Low Wiske Moor Farm
Church Hill
Greystones
Jekelow Grange
Castle Hills Farm
Ladyfield Farm
Sewage Works
Viewly Hill Farm
Viewly Bridge
Howden Bridge
Newsham Grange
Romanby Grange
A167
DARLINGTON ROAD
Sheepcote Farm
BINKS CL
STANDARD WAY
TENNANT CL
Standard Way Industrial Estate
Thornfield Business Park
North Bridge
B6271
YAFFORTH ROAD
Zetland Bridge
FINKILLS WAY
Castle Hills
Castle Hills Farm
SPRINGWELL LANE
Packhorse Bridge
Romanby
DL7
ROWANS WY
BECKSIDE
NEILE CLOSE
CHANTRY RD
CHANTRY
SLINGSBY GD
PEPPERGARTH
THE RISE
ST WILFRED DR
CHANTRY DR
ST CUTHBERT DR
ST PAULINUS DR
KIRK RD
CRAVEN CT
AINDERBY ROAD
WOODEN HILL LANE
HOWDEN RD
B1333
WENSLEY RD
PENNINE
EDEN
NEWSHAM RD
AYSGARTH
NEWSHAM WAY
LEES LANE
A684
AINDERBY ROAD
BOROUGHBRIDGE RD
BOROUGHBRIDGE ROAD
Romanby CP Sch
HAREWOOD RD
HAREWOOD CH
THE CL
SUTTON DR
POPLAR CRES
THE FAIRWAY
CHERRY GARTH
GRANGE CL
RICHMOND
HAMBLETON AVE
FARNDALE AV
BILSDALE CL
BRANSDALE AVE
COVERHAM CL
GRASSINGTON AV
HELMSLEY WAY
WYCLIFFE AV
PENHILL CT
CASTLETON AV
OAKTREE DRIVE
HAREBELL CL
THISTLE CL
HONEYSUCKLE CL
FOXGLOVE CL
LONGLANDS JUNCTION
Northallerton Rugby Club
Halfway House
DL6
Hambleton Leisure Centre
NORTHALLERTON
Allertonshire Sch
WILLOW BECK RD
SWAIN COURT
HIGH ST
QUAKER LANE
GOOSECROFT
ANCHORAGE LA
TANNERY LA
FRIARAGE MOUNT
FRIARAGE ST
EAST RD
Cemetery
Rutson
APPLEGARTH CT
Motte and Bailey
Applegarth CP Prim Sch
ALVERTON LANE
ASHLEA RD
UPWELL RD
BAILEY CT
Auction House
ZETLAND ST
HM Prison
ELDER RD
BISHOPSGARTH
ROMANBY ROAD
B1333
MALPAS DR
ALVERTON
BEACONSFIELD
WEAVERS GREEN
RAILWAY VW
MALPAS ROAD
DEXTA WAY
FERGUSON CL
SOUTH PARADE
Liby
LYNTON WY
GRAMMAR SCHOOL LANE
HUTCHINSON DRIVE
RACECOURSE LANE
KILNWICK CT
Magistrates Ct
Council & Police Offices
County Hall
Northallerton
THORNLEY AV
ALMOND GR
WILLOW RD
BROOMFIELD AVENUE
CLEVELAND DR
Sacred Heart RC Primary Sch
Broomfield CP Sch
NORMANBY ROAD
MEADOW CL
CRESTBROOKE
ST JAMES DRIVE
ST JOHNS CL
HILTON GRANGE
HILTON SQ
HILTON GN
DE BRUCE RD
DE FERRERS RD
DE GAUNTE RD
NORTHALLERTON ROAD
BROMPTON ROAD
A684
STOKESLEY ROAD
WINSTON CT
COTTAGE CL
BYLAND AVE
BYLAND PL
Friarage
Bullamoor Mem Pk & Recn Gd
Council Offices
IDENE RD
VICARS CR
BROOKLANDS CR
PINFOLD DR
LASCELLES LA
LASCELLES CT
Cty Fire Hq
HM Youth Custody Centre
Mill Hill CP Sch
College
CROSBY RD
LINDEN RD
CENTRAL DR
VALLEY ROAD
GREENHOWSYKE LA
PATERSON CR
PROSPECT
COLSTAN ROAD
MILLFIELD AV
GREENHILL CR
STOCKDALE CT
MILL HILL LANE
THORNHILL
MILL RI
HIGH TRACE
SOUTH VALE
THORNBOROUGH RD
MAYFAIR
BRYDEN CL
CARROL CL
MOWBRAY ROAD
GALTRES ROAD
FOUNTAINS PL
FOUNTAINS RD
WINTON RD
THORNTREE ROAD
WINTON CT
TURKER LANE
MEADOW LANE
OAK GROVE
TURKER CLOSE
FOREST ROAD
BEECH GR
MOORVIEW RD
Alverton Cty Infant Sch
Bullamoor Cty Junior Sch
LA VW
LEWIS RD
LEWIS CL
SCHOLLA LA
HAILSTONE DRIVE
BULLAMOOR ROAD
ELM AV
ELM CL
THE CRES
ASHLANDS
BANKHEAD ROAD
NEWLANDS
PROSPECT PL
KNOTTO BOTTOM
DL6
BORROWBY AV
SANDY BANK
REGENCY CT
GRENADIER DR
Field Head
Low Thornbrough Farm
Spital Farm
Spital House Farm
Cawdey Field
THIRSK ROAD
A168
A
B
36
C
D
37
E
F
D2
1 ST MICHAELS CT
2 ST ANDREWS GR
3 ST CHRISTOPHER CL
4 ST BEDES AVE
5 ST HILDAS RD
6 MULGRAVE DR
E2
1 ST STEPHENS GDNS
2 ST ANTHONYS AVE
3 ST GEORGES GR
4 ST PAULS CL
5 GREENBANK
6 THE LAURELS
E3
1 PINE GR
2 SLADEBURN DR
3 BYRAM CL
4 BYRAM CT
5 ASH RIDGE

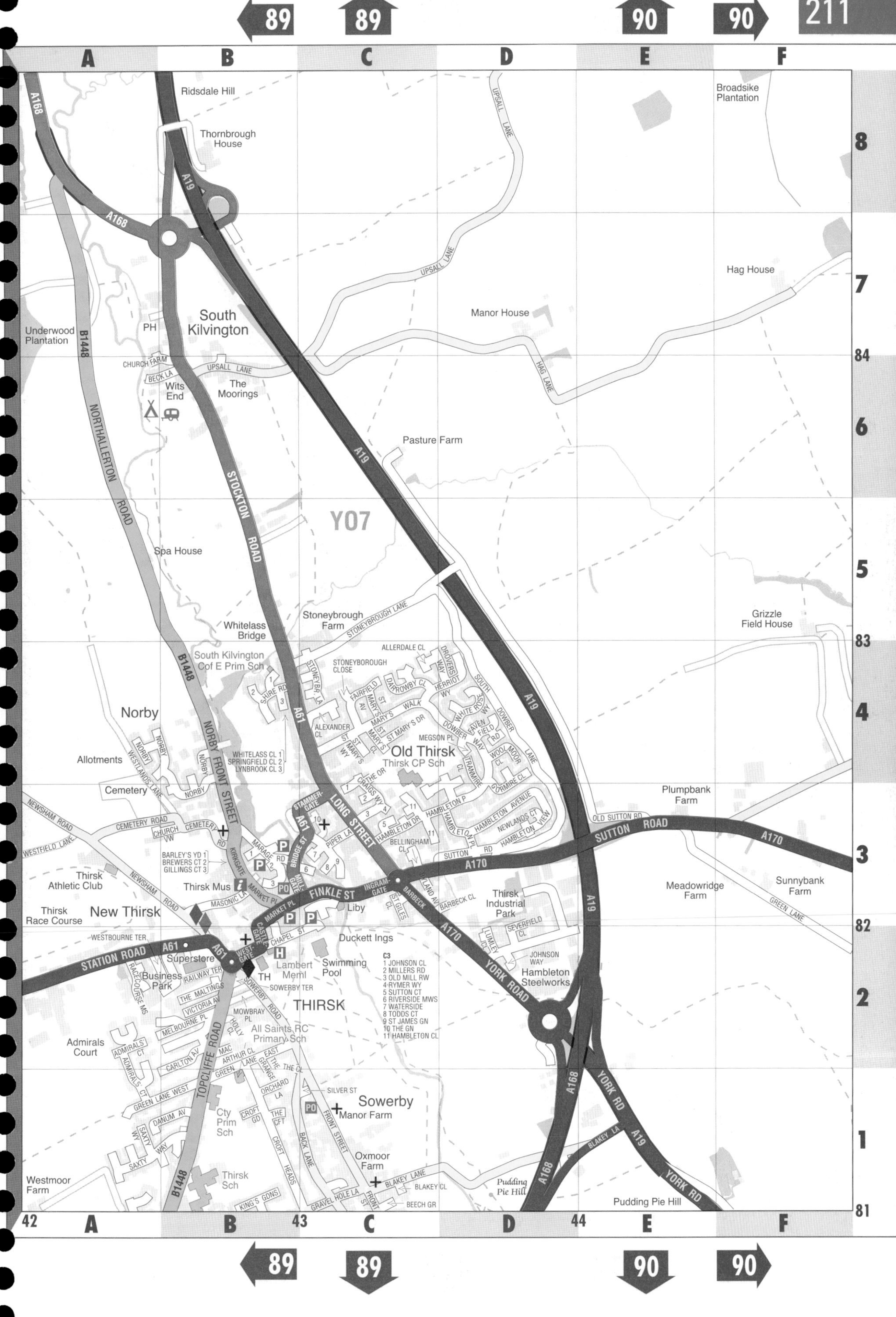
89
89
90
90
A
B
C
D
E
F
8
7
84
6
5
83
4
3
82
2
1
81
42
43
44
Ridsdale Hill
Thornbrough House
Broadsike Plantation
A168
A19
Hag House
Manor House
UPSALL LANE
UPSALL LANE
HAG LANE
South Kilvington
Underwood Plantation
PH
B1448
CHURCH FARM
BECK LA
Wits End
The Moorings
Pasture Farm
NORTHALLERTON ROAD
STOCKTON ROAD
YO7
Spa House
Stoneybrough Farm
STONEYBROUGH LANE
Whitelass Bridge
Grizzle Field House
South Kilvington Cof E Prim Sch
ALLERDALE CL
STONEYBOROUGH CLOSE
DROVERS WAY
HERRIOT WY
SOUTH DOWBER LANE
Norby
Allotments
Cemetery
Old Thirsk
Thirsk CP Sch
WHITELASS CL 1
SPRINGFIELD CL 2
LYNBROOK CL 3
NORBY FRONT STREET
LONG STREET
Plumpbank Farm
OLD SUTTON RD
SUTTON ROAD
A170
NEWSHAM ROAD
WESTFIELD LANE
CEMETERY ROAD
BARLEY'S YD 1
BREWERS CT 2
GILLINGS CT 3
Thirsk Athletic Club
Thirsk Mus
FINKLE ST
INGRAMGATE
Meadowridge Farm
Sunnybank Farm
GREEN LANE
Thirsk Race Course
New Thirsk
Liby
Thirsk Industrial Park
SEVERFIELD CL
WESTBOURNE TER
STATION ROAD
A61
Superstore
Duckett Ings
JOHNSON WAY
Hambleton Steelworks
Business Park
Lambert Meml
Swimming Pool
TH
C3
1 JOHNSON CL
2 MILLERS RD
3 OLD MILL RW
4 RYMER WY
5 SUTTON CT
6 RIVERSIDE MWS
7 WATERSIDE
8 TODDS CT
9 ST JAMES GN
10 THE GN
11 HAMBLETON CL
YORK ROAD
THIRSK
SOWERBY TER
All Saints RC Primary Sch
Admirals Court
TOPCLIFFE ROAD
YORK RD
SILVER ST
Sowerby
Manor Farm
City Prim Sch
Oxmoor Farm
BLAKEY LA
Westmoor Farm
Thirsk Sch
BLAKEY LANE
BLAKEY CL
BEECH GR
Pudding Pie Hill
Pudding Pie Hill

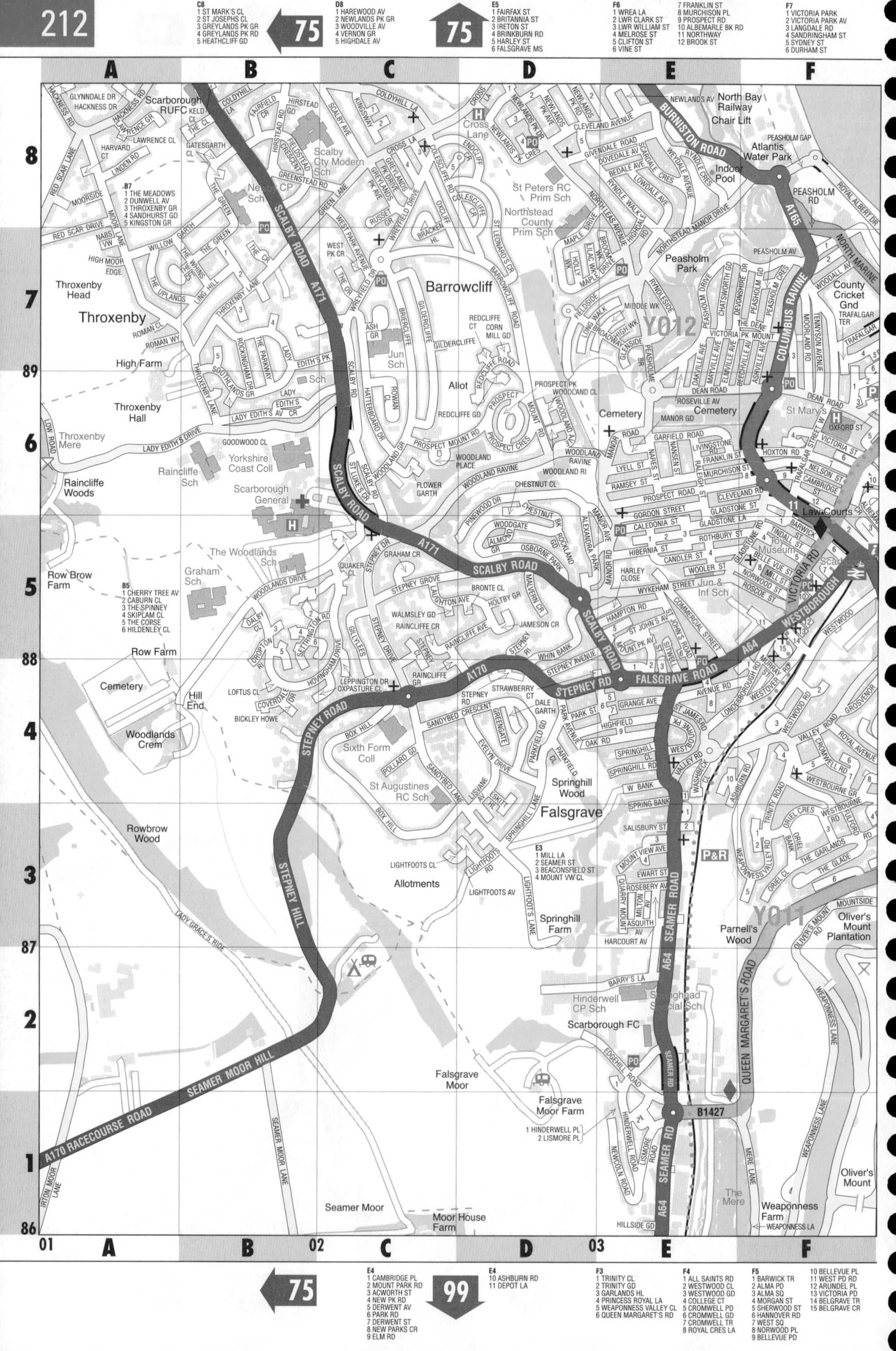
C8
1 ST MARK'S CL
2 ST JOSEPHS CL
3 GREYLANDS PK GR
4 GREYLANDS PK RD
5 HEATHCLIFF GD
75
D8
1 HAREWOOD AV
2 NEWLANDS PK GR
3 WOODVILLE AV
4 VERNON GR
5 HIGHDALE AV
75
E5
1 FAIRFAX ST
2 BRITANNIA ST
3 IRETON ST
4 BRINKBURN RD
5 HARLEY ST
6 FALSGRAVE MS
F6
1 WREA LA
2 LWR CLARK ST
3 LWR WILLIAM ST
4 MELROSE ST
5 CLIFTON ST
6 VINE ST
7 FRANKLIN ST
8 MURCHISON PL
9 PROSPECT RD
10 ALBEMARLE BK RD
11 NORTHWAY
12 BROOK ST
F7
1 VICTORIA PARK
2 VICTORIA PARK AV
3 LANGDALE RD
4 SANDRINGHAM ST
5 SYDNEY ST
6 DURHAM ST
B7
1 THE MEADOWS
2 DUNWELL AV
3 THROXENBY GR
4 SANDHURST GD
5 KINGSTON GR
B5
1 CHERRY TREE AV
2 CABURN CL
3 THE SPINNEY
4 SKIPLAM CL
5 THE CORSE
6 HILDENLEY CL
E3
1 MILL LA
2 SEAMER ST
3 BEACONSFIELD ST
4 MOUNT VW CL
1 HINDERWELL PL
2 LISMORE PL
Scarborough
Throxenby
Barrowcliff
Falsgrave
Y012
Y011
Scalby Road
Stepney Road
Stepney Hill
Seamer Moor Hill
A170 Racecourse Road
Seamer Road
Falsgrave Road
Westborough
Victoria Rd
Columbus Ravine
Burniston Road
Queen Margaret's Road
Peasholm Park
North Bay Railway
Scarborough FC
75
E4
1 CAMBRIDGE PL
2 MOUNT PARK RD
3 ACWORTH ST
4 NEW PK RD
5 DERWENT AV
6 PARK RD
7 DERWENT ST
8 NEW PARKS CR
9 ELM RD
99
E4
10 ASHBURN RD
11 DEPOT LA
F3
1 TRINITY CL
2 TRINITY GD
3 GARLANDS HL
4 PRINCESS ROYAL LA
5 WEAPONNESS VALLEY CL
6 QUEEN MARGARET'S RD
F4
1 ALL SAINTS RD
2 WESTWOOD CL
3 WESTWOOD GD
4 COLLEGE CT
5 CROMWELL PD
6 CROMWELL GD
7 CROMWELL TR
8 ROYAL CRES LA
F5
1 BARWICK TR
2 ALMA PD
3 ALMA SQ
4 MORGAN ST
5 SHERWOOD ST
6 HANNOVER RD
7 WEST SQ
8 NORWOOD PL
9 BELLEVUE PD
10 BELLEVUE PL
11 WEST PD RD
12 ARUNDEL PL
13 VICTORIA PD
14 BELGRAVE TR
15 BELGRAVE CR

76 76

A6
1 REGENT ST
2 JAMES PL
3 GEORGE ST
4 NORTH TR
5 AUBOROUGH ST
6 LANCASTER ST
7 CLARENCE PL
8 SILVER ST
9 MARIAS CT
10 FRIAR'S GD
11 FRIARS WY
12 UNION ST
13 BEDFORD ST
14 SUSSEX ST
15 PROVIDENCE PL
16 ABERDEEN WK
17 ABERDEEN ST
18 ALBERMARLE CR
19 ABERDEEN LA
20 ABERDEEN PL
21 ABERDEEN TR
22 NORTH ST LA
23 CHAPEL RD
24 MARKET ST
25 MARKET WY
26 ST HELEN'S SQ
27 BLAND'S CLIFF
28 PROSPECT PL
29 WATERHOUSE LA

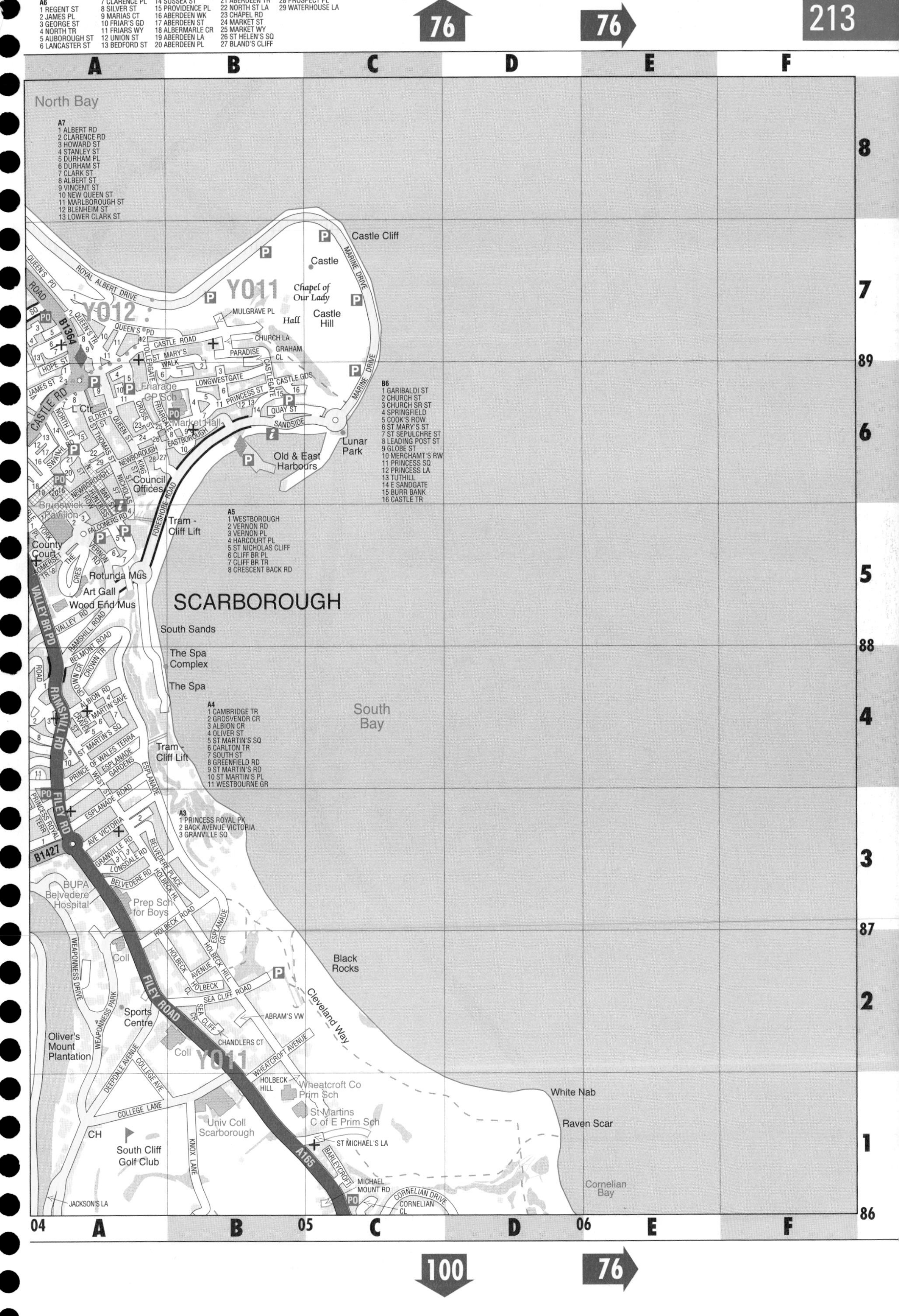

100 76

113 113 114

C5
1 ST WILFRID'S RD
2 ST WILFRID'S PL
3 WESTBOURNE GR
4 FINKLE CL
5 FINKLE ST
6 OLD MARKET PL
7 HIGH SKELLGATE
8 WILLIAMSON DR
9 WELLINGTON MS
10 WELLINGTON ST
11 KIRKGATE
12 BEDERN BANK
13 MINSTER CL
14 WILLIAMSON CL
15 LOWSKELLGATE
16 BEDERN CT
17 FISHERGATE
18 QUEEN ST
19 MARKET PLACE NORTH
20 MARKET PLACE EAST
21 MARKET PLACE SOUTH
22 MARKET PLACE WEST
23 MINSTER CLOSE

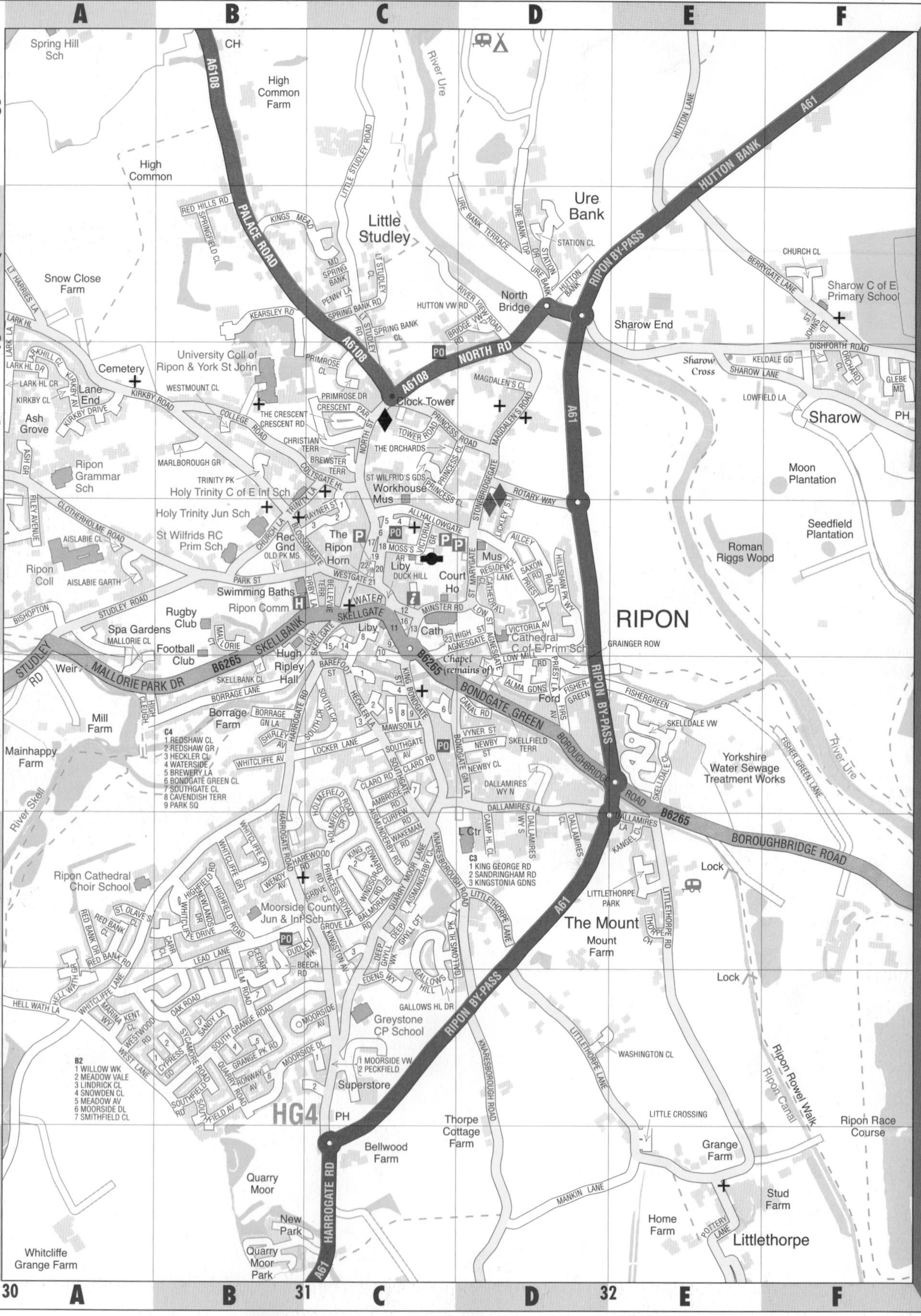

A B C D E F

RIPON

Little Studley

Ure Bank

Sharow

Littlethorpe

The Mount

C4
1 REDSHAW CL
2 REDSHAW GR
3 HECKLER CL
4 WATERSIDE
5 BREWERY LA
6 BONDGATE GREEN CL
7 SOUTHGATE CT
8 CAVENDISH TERR
9 PARK SQ

C3
1 KING GEORGE RD
2 SANDRINGHAM RD
3 KINGSTONIA GDNS

B2
1 WILLOW WK
2 MEADOW VALE
3 LINDRICK CL
4 SNOWDEN CL
5 MEADOW AV
6 MOORSIDE DL
7 SMITHFIELD CL

1 MOORSIDE VW
2 PECKFIELD

HG4

30 A B 31 C D 32 E F

139 139 140

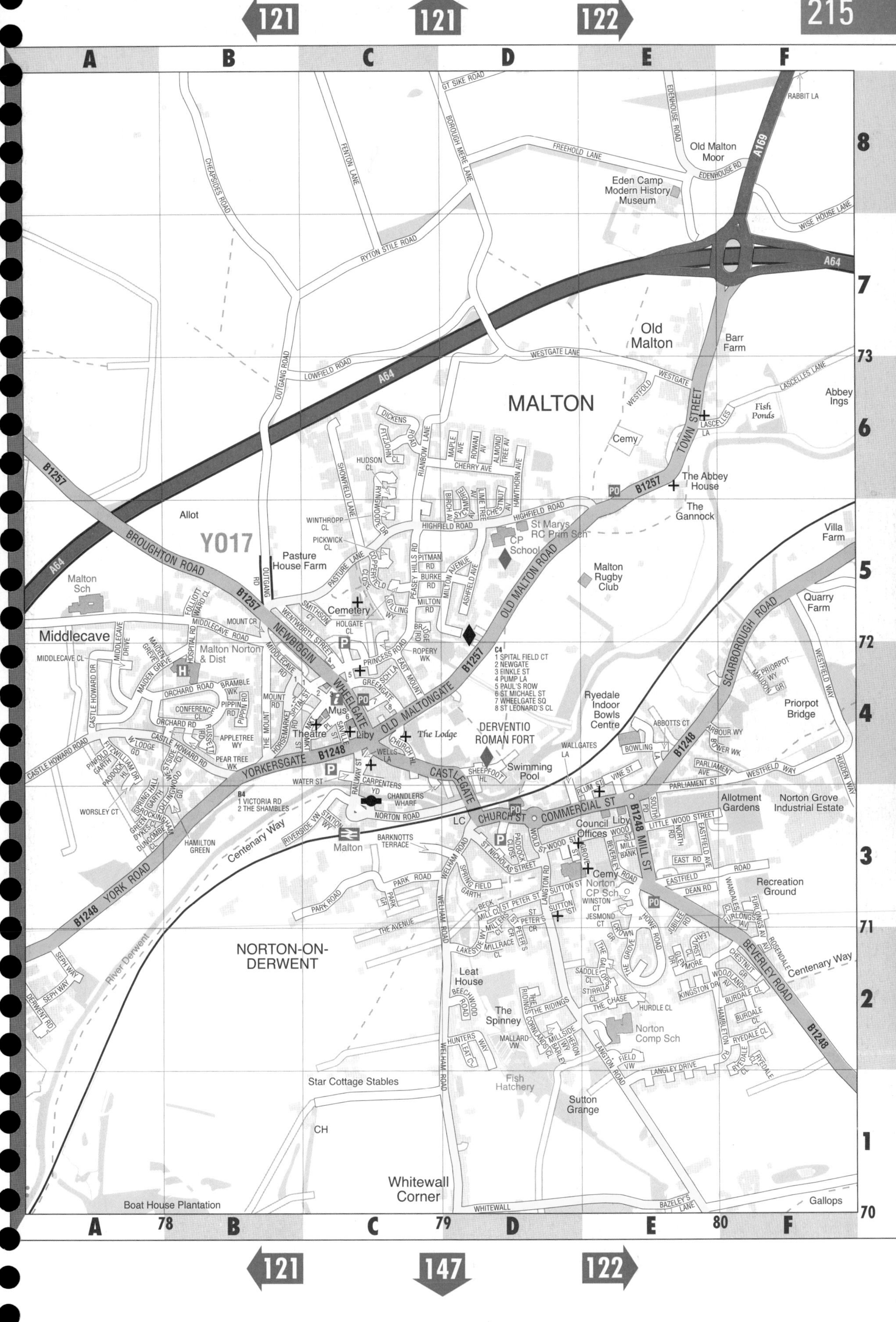
121
121
122
A
B
C
D
E
F
8
7
73
6
5
72
4
3
71
2
1
70
78
79
80
147
GT SIKE ROAD
RABBIT LA
EDENHOUSE ROAD
Old Malton Moor
FREEHOLD LANE
BOROUGH MERE LANE
FENTON LANE
CHEAPSIDES ROAD
EDENHOUSE RD
A169
Eden Camp Modern History Museum
WISE HOUSE LANE
RYTON STILE ROAD
A64
Old Malton
Barr Farm
WESTGATE LANE
WESTGATE
LASCELLES LANE
OUTGANG ROAD
LOWFIELD ROAD
Abbey Ings
MALTON
WESTFOLD
TOWN STREET
Fish Ponds
LASCELLES LA
Cemy
DICKENS ROAD
FITZJOHN CL
HUDSON CL
MAPLE AVE
ROWAN AV
ALMOND TREE AV
CHERRY AVE
HAWTHORN AVE
RIANBOW LANE
SHOWFIELD LANE
RYNGWOOD DR
B1257
The Abbey House
The Gannock
PO
BIRCH AV
SYCAMORE AV
LIME TREE AV
CHESTNUT AV
HIGHFIELD ROAD
WINTHROPP CL
HIGHFIELD ROAD
St Marys RC Prim Sch
Villa Farm
Allot
YO17
PICKWICK CL
CP School
BROUGHTON ROAD
Pasture House Farm
PASTURE LANE
COPPERFIELD CLOSE
PITMAN RD
PEASEY HILLS RD
BURKE RD
MILTON AVENUE
ASHFIELD AVE
OLD MALTON ROAD
Malton Rugby Club
Malton Sch
OUTGANG RD
SMITHSON CT
Cemetery
MILTON RD
Quarry Farm
SCARBOROUGH ROAD
Middlecave
MIDDLECAVE ROAD
MOUNT CR
FOLLIOTT WARD CL
NEWBIGGIN
WENTWORTH STREET
HOLGATE CL
GILLING WY
BR LODGE RD
ROPERY WK
PRINCESS ROAD
MIDDLECAVE CL
MIDDLECAVE DRIVE
MAIDEN GREVE
HOSPITAL RD
Malton Norton & Dist
H
GREEN SCH LA
EAST MOUNT
C4
1 SPITAL FIELD CT
2 NEWGATE
3 FINKLE ST
4 PUMP LA
5 PAUL'S ROW
6 ST MICHAEL ST
7 WHEELGATE SQ
8 ST LEONARD'S CL
WESTFIELD WAY
PRIORPOT WY
MAUDON GR
Priorpot Bridge
CASTLE HOWARD DR
ORCHARD ROAD
BRAMBLE WK
PIPPIN RD
CONFERENCE CL
ORCHARD RD
MOUNT RD
WHEELGATE
OLD MALTONGATE
Ryedale Indoor Bowls Centre
ABBOTTS CT
Mus
Theatre
Liby
The Lodge
DERVENTIO ROMAN FORT
APPLETREE WY
RUSSETT GD
THE MOUNT
HORSEMARKET RD
CASTLE HOWARD ROAD
PINFOLD GARTH
FITZWILLIAM DR
W LODGE GD
CASTLE HOWARD RD
PEAR TREE WK
WESTSIDE RD
YORKERSGATE
B1248
WELLS LA
CHURCH HILL
CASTLEGATE
WALLGATES LA
BOWLING LA
ARBOUR WY
BOWER WK
PARLIAMENT AVE
WESTFIELD WAY
HUGDEN WAY
SHEEPFOOT HL
Swimming Pool
VINE ST
PARLIAMENT ST
WATER ST
RAILWAY ST
CARPENTERS YD
CHANDLERS WHARF
B4
1 VICTORIA RD
2 THE SHAMBLES
PLUM ST
COMMERCIAL ST
SOUTH ST
Allotment Gardens
Norton Grove Industrial Estate
WORSLEY CT
SPRING HALL GARTH
COLLINGWOOD
GREEN DYKES CL
ROCKINGHAM
DUNCOMBE CL
HAMILTON GREEN
Centenary Way
RIVERSIDE VW
STATION WY
NORTON ROAD
LC
CHURCH ST
B1248 MILL ST
Council Offices
Liby
LITTLE WOOD STREET
NORTH RD
EASTFIELD AVE
Malton
BARKNOTTS TERRACE
WELHAM ROAD
PADDOCK CLOSE
WOLD ST
WOOD ST
GROVE ST
BEVERLEY ROAD
MILL BANK
EAST RD
ROAD
ST NICHOLAS STREET
Cemy
Norton CP Sch
EASTFIELD
DEAN RD
Recreation Ground
YORK ROAD
PARK ROAD
PARK GR
SPRING FIELD GARTH
LANGTON RD
SUTTON ST
WINSTON CT
JESMOND CT
PO
PARK ROAD
ST PETER ST
BECK MILL CL
ST PETER'S CR
SUTTON ST
WANDALES LA
FURLONGS AV
JUBILEE RD
THE AVENUE
WELHAM ROAD
MILLERS CR
MILLRACE CL
LAKESIDE WY
CROWN GR
HOWE ROAD
LEAT FIRST LA
BEVERLEY ROAD
ROSEDALE AV
Centenary Way
NORTON-ON-DERWENT
River Derwent
SEPH WAY
SEPH WAY
DERWENT RD
Leat House
BEECHWOOD ROAD
THE GALLOPS
THE GROVE
SADDLE CL
STIRRUP CL
THE CHASE
HURDLE CL
GLEN MORE DR
KINGSTON DR
CHESTNUT GR
WOODLANDS AV
BURDALE CL
BURDALE CL
The Spinney
THE RIDINGS
CORNLANDS CL
MILLSIDE WY
HERON WY
BARLEY
Norton Comp Sch
HAMBLETON CL
RYEDALE CL
B1248
HUNTERS WAY
LEAT CL
MALLARD VW
Fish Hatchery
LANGTON ROAD
FIELD VW
LANGLEY DRIVE
RYEDALE CL
Star Cottage Stables
Sutton Grange
CH
Whitewall Corner
Boat House Plantation
WHITEWALL
BAZELEY'S LANE
Gallops
121
147
122

172
156

F4
1 PARK ST
2 PRIMROSE HL
3 VICTORIA TR
4 HALLAM'S YD
5 THE PINFOLD
6 BACK O THE BECK
7 WATSON'S HO
8 CANAL YD
9 BAY HORSE YD
10 VICTORIA ST
11 SHEEP ST
12 DEVONSHIRE PL
13 COACH ST YD
14 GLADSTONE ST

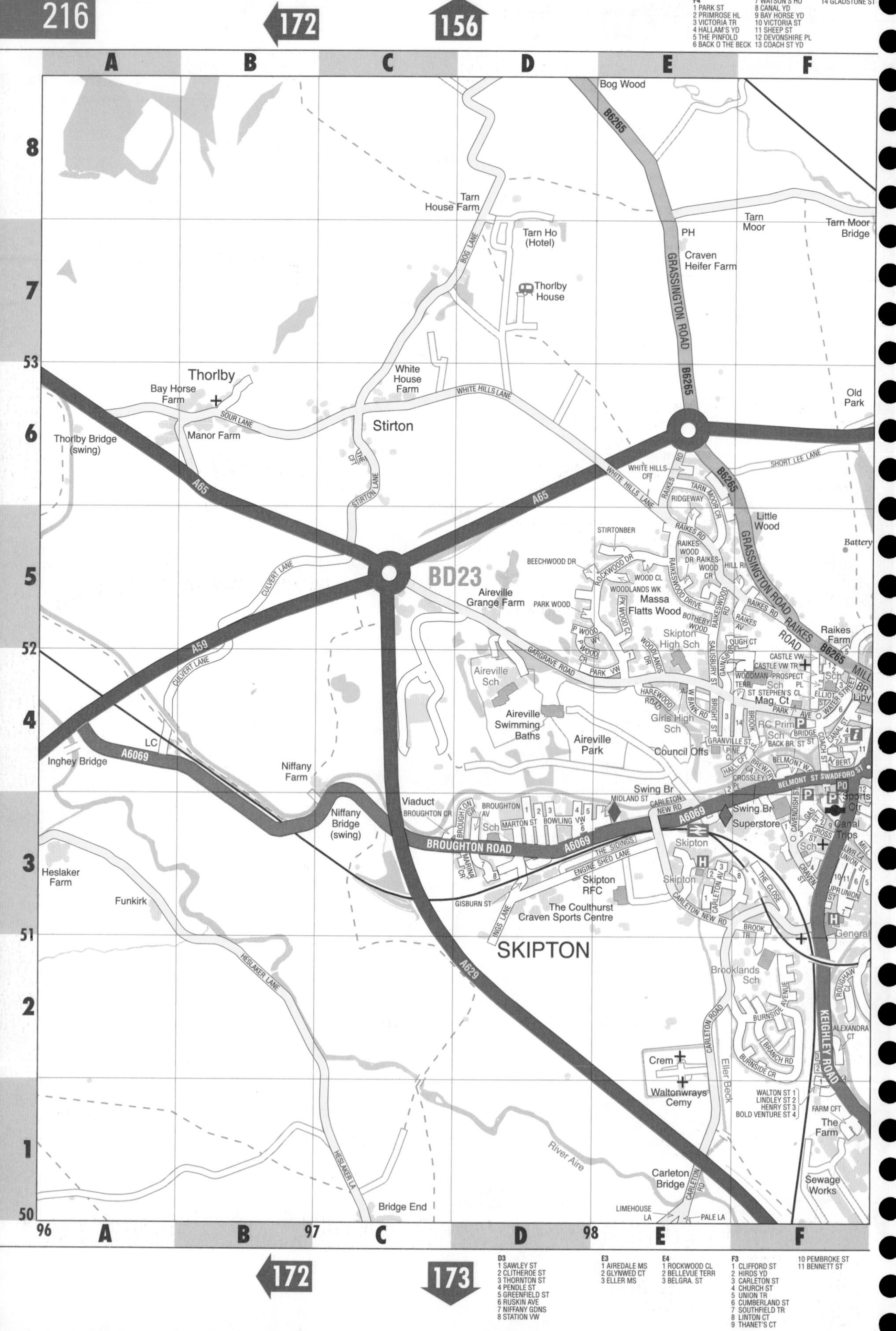

172
173

D3
1 SAWLEY ST
2 CLITHEROE ST
3 THORNTON ST
4 PENDLE ST
5 GREENFIELD ST
6 RUSKIN AVE
7 NIFFANY GDNS
8 STATION VW

E3
1 AIREDALE MS
2 GLYNWED CT
3 ELLER MS

E4
1 ROCKWOOD CL
2 BELLEVUE TERR
3 BELGRA. ST

F3
1 CLIFFORD ST
2 HIRDS YD
3 CARLETON ST
4 CHURCH ST
5 UNION TR
6 CUMBERLAND ST
7 SOUTHFIELD TR
8 LINTON CT
9 THANET'S CT
10 PEMBROKE ST
11 BENNETT ST

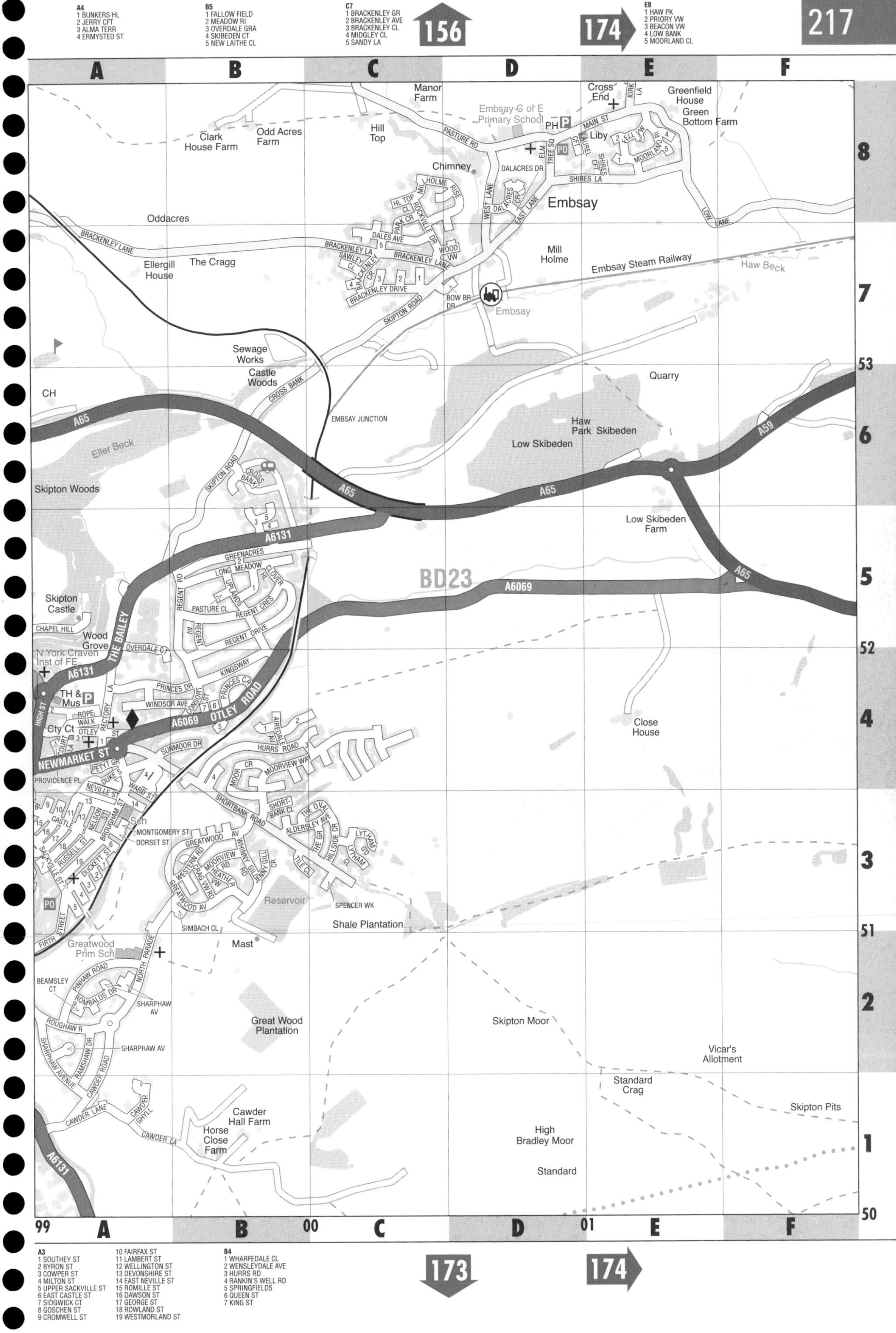
A4
1 BUNKERS HL
2 JERRY CFT
3 ALMA TERR
4 ERMYSTED ST
B5
1 FALLOW FIELD
2 MEADOW RI
3 OVERDALE GRA
4 SKIBEDEN CT
5 NEW LAITHE CL
C7
1 BRACKENLEY GR
2 BRACKENLEY AVE
3 BRACKENLEY CL
4 MIDGLEY CL
5 SANDY LA
156
174
E8
1 HAW PK
2 PRIORY VW
3 BEACON VW
4 LOW BANK
5 MOORLAND CL
Manor Farm
Cross End
Greenfield House
Green Bottom Farm
Embsay C of E Primary School
Clark House Farm
Odd Acres Farm
Hill Top
Liby
Chimney
DALACRES DR
SHIRES LA
Embsay
Oddacres
BRACKENLEY LANE
Ellergill House
The Cragg
Mill Holme
Embsay Steam Railway
Haw Beck
SKIPTON ROAD
Embsay
Sewage Works
Castle Woods
CROSS BANK
Quarry
CH
A65
Eller Beck
EMBSAY JUNCTION
Haw Park Skibeden
Low Skibeden
A59
Skipton Woods
Low Skibeden Farm
A6131
BD23
A6069
Skipton Castle
Wood Grove
THE BAILEY
N York Craven Inst of FE
CHAPEL HILL
OVERDALE CT
REGENT DRIVE
KINGSWAY
PRINCES DR
WINDSOR AVE
OTLEY ROAD
TH & Mus
Cty Ct
NEWMARKET ST
HIGH ST
Close House
HURRS ROAD
MOORVIEW WAY
SHORTBANK ROAD
PROVIDENCE PL
NEVILLE ST
MONTGOMERY ST
DORSET ST
GREATWOOD AV
Reservoir
SPENCER WK
Shale Plantation
SIMBACH CL
FIRTH STREET
Greatwood Prim Sch
Mast
NORTH PARADE
BEAMSLEY CT
PINHAW ROAD
SHARPHAW AV
ROUGHAW R
Great Wood Plantation
Skipton Moor
Vicar's Allotment
Standard Crag
Skipton Pits
CAWDER LANE
CAWDER ROAD
Cawder Hall Farm
Horse Close Farm
CAWDER LA
High Bradley Moor
Standard
99
00
01
173
174
A3
1 SOUTHEY ST
2 BYRON ST
3 COWPER ST
4 MILTON ST
5 UPPER SACKVILLE ST
6 EAST CASTLE ST
7 SIDGWICK CT
8 GOSCHEN ST
9 CROMWELL ST
10 FAIRFAX ST
11 LAMBERT ST
12 WELLINGTON ST
13 DEVONSHIRE ST
14 EAST NEVILLE ST
15 ROMILLE ST
16 DAWSON ST
17 GEORGE ST
18 ROWLAND ST
19 WESTMORLAND ST
B4
1 WHARFEDALE CL
2 WENSLEYDALE AVE
3 HURRS RD
4 RANKIN'S WELL RD
5 SPRINGFIELDS
6 QUEEN ST
7 KING ST

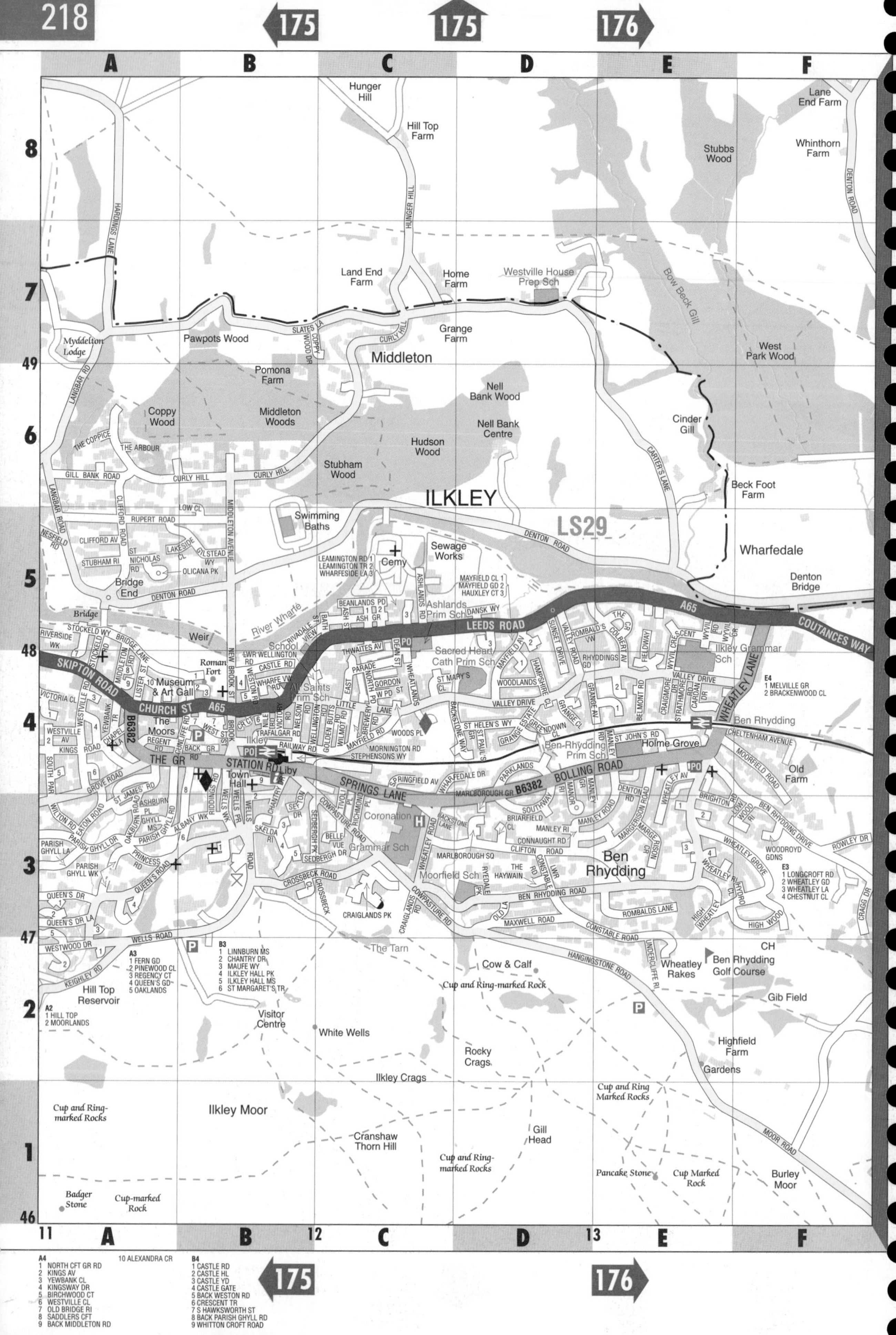
175
175
176
ILKLEY
LS29
Middleton
Ben Rhydding
Wharfedale
Ilkley Moor
Hunger Hill
Hill Top Farm
Lane End Farm
Whinthorn Farm
Stubbs Wood
Land End Farm
Home Farm
Westville House Prep Sch
Grange Farm
Myddelton Lodge
Pawpots Wood
Pomona Farm
West Park Wood
Nell Bank Wood
Nell Bank Centre
Coppy Wood
Middleton Woods
Hudson Wood
Stubham Wood
Cinder Gill
Beck Foot Farm
Swimming Baths
Sewage Works
Cemy
Denton Bridge
Bridge End
Bridge
Weir
River Wharfe
Roman Fort
Museum & Art Gall
The Moors
Town Hall
Liby
Ashlands Prim Sch
Sacred Heart Cath Prim Sch
All Saints Prim Sch
Ilkley Grammar Sch
Ben-Rhydding Prim Sch
Holme Grove
Old Farm
Coronation
Grammar Sch
Moorfield Sch
The Tarn
Cow & Calf
Cup and Ring-marked Rock
Wheatley Rakes
Ben Rhydding Golf Course
Gib Field
Hill Top Reservoir
Visitor Centre
White Wells
Rocky Crags
Ilkley Crags
Highfield Farm
Gardens
Cup and Ring-marked Rocks
Cup and Ring Marked Rocks
Cranshaw Thorn Hill
Gill Head
Cup and Ring-marked Rocks
Pancake Stone
Cup Marked Rock
Burley Moor
Badger Stone
Cup-marked Rock
SKIPTON ROAD
CHURCH ST
A65
LEEDS ROAD
COUTANCES WAY
B6382
THE GR
STATION RD
SPRINGS LANE
BOLLING ROAD
DENTON ROAD
CURLY HILL
GILL BANK ROAD
HARDINGS LANE
LANGBAR RD
HUNGER HILL
CARTER'S LANE
DENTON ROAD
WHEATLEY LANE
CHELTENHAM AVENUE
BEN RHYDDING ROAD
CONSTABLE ROAD
HANGINGSTONE ROAD
MOOR ROAD
WELLS ROAD
CROSSBECK ROAD
COWPASTURE RD
MIDDLETON AVENUE
E4
1 MELVILLE GR
2 BRACKENWOOD CL
E3
1 LONGCROFT RD
2 WHEATLEY GD
3 WHEATLEY LA
4 CHESTNUT CL
A3
1 FERN GD
2 PINEWOOD CL
3 REGENCY CT
4 QUEEN'S GD
5 OAKLANDS
B3
1 LINNBURN MS
2 CHANTRY DR
3 MAUFE WY
4 ILKLEY HALL PK
5 ILKLEY HALL MS
6 ST MARGARET'S TR
A2
1 HILL TOP
2 MOORLANDS
A4
1 NORTH CFT GR RD
2 KINGS AV
3 YEWBANK CL
4 KINGSWAY DR
5 BIRCHWOOD CT
6 WESTVILLE CL
7 OLD BRIDGE RI
8 SADDLERS CFT
9 BACK MIDDLETON RD
10 ALEXANDRA CR
B4
1 CASTLE RD
2 CASTLE HL
3 CASTLE YD
4 CASTLE GATE
5 BACK WESTON RD
6 CRESCENT TR
7 S HAWKSWORTH ST
8 BACK PARISH GHYLL RD
9 WHITTON CROFT ROAD

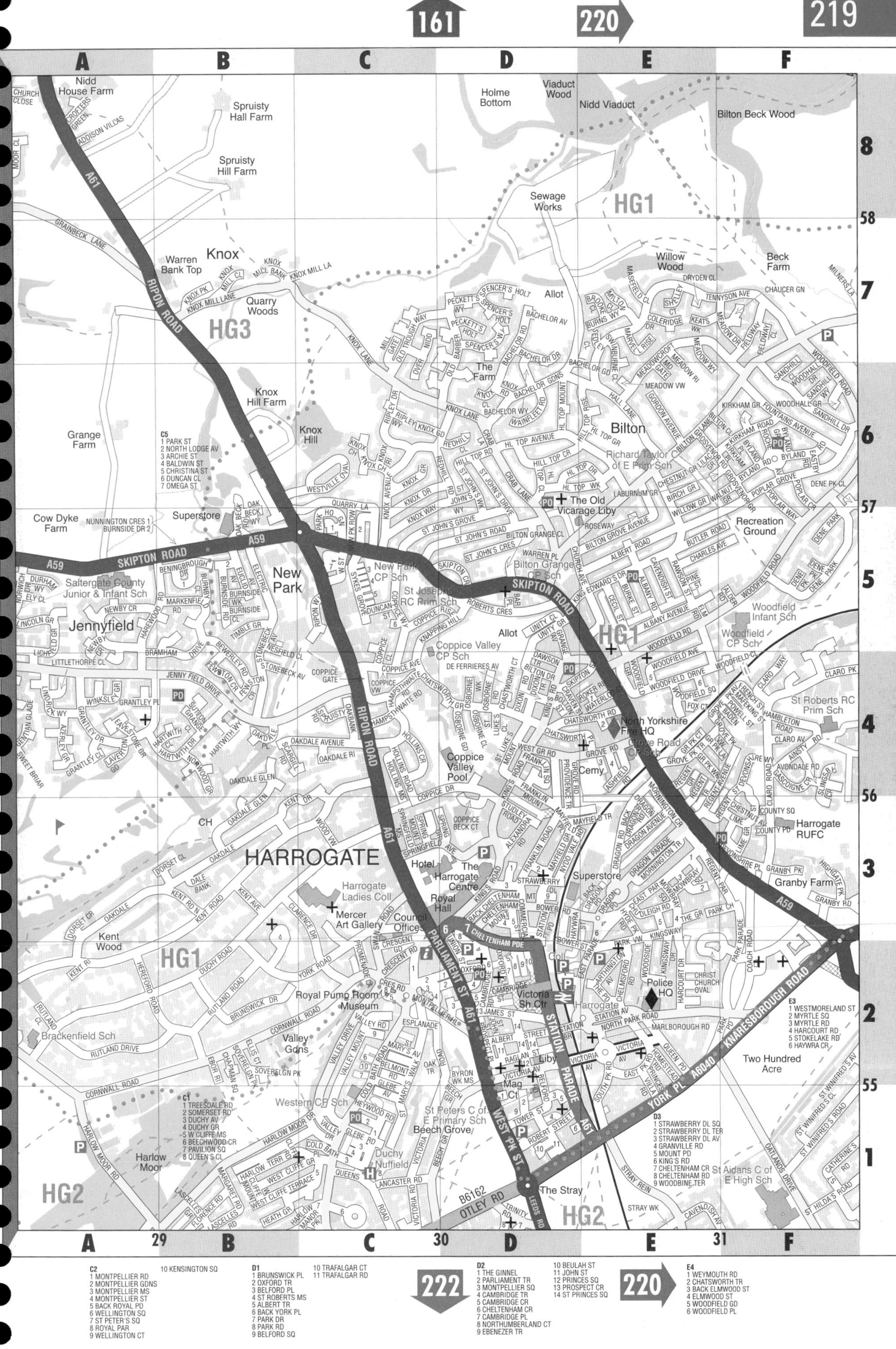
161
220
HARROGATE
Knox
New Park
Jennyfield
Bilton
HG1
HG2
HG3
Nidd House Farm
Spruisty Hall Farm
Spruisty Hill Farm
Holme Bottom
Viaduct Wood
Nidd Viaduct
Bilton Beck Wood
Sewage Works
Warren Bank Top
Quarry Woods
Willow Wood
Beck Farm
Allot
The Farm
Knox Hill Farm
Knox Hill
Grange Farm
Cow Dyke Farm
Superstore
Saltergate County Junior & Infant Sch
New Park CP Sch
St Josephs RC Prim Sch
Richard Taylor C of E Prim Sch
The Old Vicarage Liby
Recreation Ground
Bilton Grange CP Sch
Woodfield Infant Sch
Woodfield CP Sch
Coppice Valley CP Sch
St Roberts RC Prim Sch
North Yorkshire Fire HQ
Grove Road CP Sch
Cemy
Coppice Valley Pool
Harrogate RUFC
Granby Farm
Harrogate Ladies Coll
Mercer Art Gallery
Hotel
The Harrogate Centre
Royal Hall
Council Offices
Kent Wood
Royal Pump Room Museum
Victoria Sh Ctr
Harrogate
Police HQ
Christ Church Oval
Brackenfield Sch
Valley Gdns
Western CP Sch
St Peters C of E Primary Sch
Beech Grove
Duchy Nuffield
Harlow Moor
The Stray
Two Hundred Acre
St Aidans C of E High Sch
A61
A59
A6040
B6162
RIPON ROAD
SKIPTON ROAD
KNARESBOROUGH ROAD
PARLIAMENT ST
STATION PARADE
WEST PK ST
YORK PL
OTLEY RD
LEEDS RD
C5
1 PARK ST
2 NORTH LODGE AV
3 ARCHIE ST
4 BALDWIN ST
5 CHRISTINA ST
6 DUNCAN CL
7 OMEGA ST
C1
1 TREESDALE RD
2 SOMERSET RD
3 DUCHY AV
4 DUCHY GR
5 W CLIFFE MS
6 BEECHWOOD CR
7 PAVILION SQ
8 QUEEN'S CL
D3
1 STRAWBERRY DL SQ
2 STRAWBERRY DL TER
3 STRAWBERRY DL AV
4 GRANVILLE RD
5 MOUNT PD
6 KING'S RD
7 CHELTENHAM CR
8 CHELTENHAM RD
9 WOODBINE TER
E3
1 WESTMORELAND ST
2 MYRTLE SQ
3 MYRTLE RD
4 HARCOURT RD
5 STOKELAKE RD
6 HAYWRA CR
A
B
C
D
E
F
8
58
7
6
57
5
4
56
3
2
55
1
29
30
31
C2
1 MONTPELLIER RD
2 MONTPELLIER GDNS
3 MONTPELLIER MS
4 MONTPELLIER ST
5 BACK ROYAL PD
6 WELLINGTON SQ
7 ST PETER'S SQ
8 ROYAL PAR
9 WELLINGTON CT
10 KENSINGTON SQ
D1
1 BRUNSWICK PL
2 OXFORD TR
3 BELFORD PL
4 ST ROBERTS MS
5 ALBERT TR
6 BACK YORK PL
7 PARK DR
8 PARK RD
9 BELFORD SQ
10 TRAFALGAR CT
11 TRAFALGAR RD
222
D2
1 THE GINNEL
2 PARLIAMENT TR
3 MONTPELLIER SQ
4 CAMBRIDGE TR
5 CAMBRIDGE CR
6 CHELTENHAM CR
7 CAMBRIDGE PL
8 NORTHUMBERLAND CT
9 EBENEZER TR
10 BEULAH ST
11 JOHN ST
12 PRINCES SQ
13 PROSPECT CR
14 ST PRINCES SQ
220
E4
1 WEYMOUTH RD
2 CHATSWORTH TR
3 BACK ELMWOOD ST
4 ELMWOOD ST
5 WOODFIELD GD
6 WOODFIELD PL

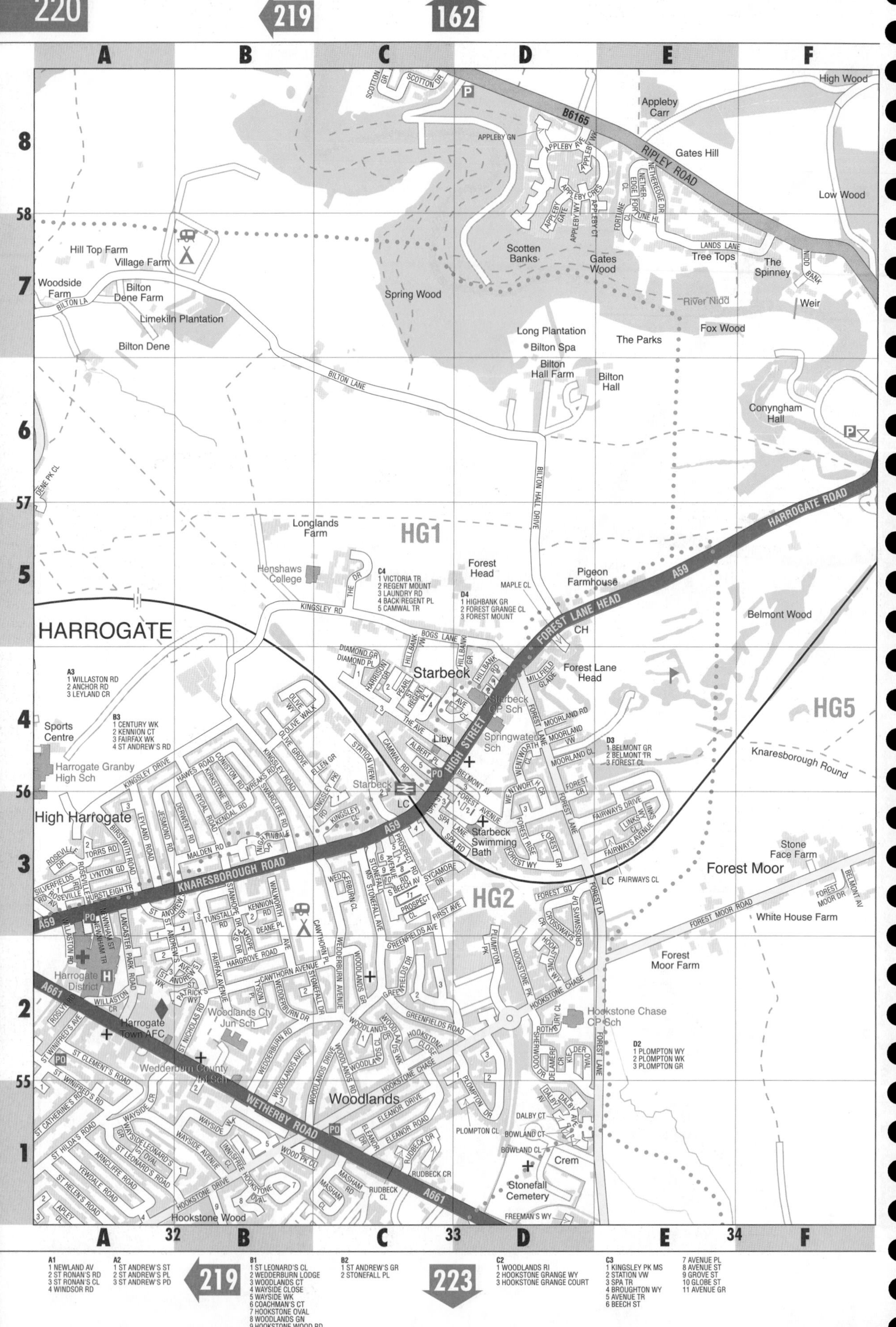

A1
1 NEWLAND AV
2 ST RONAN'S RD
3 ST RONAN'S CL
4 WINDSOR RD

A2
1 ST ANDREW'S ST
2 ST ANDREW'S PL
3 ST ANDREW'S PD

B1
1 ST LEONARD'S CL
2 WEDDERBURN LODGE
3 WOODLANDS CT
4 WAYSIDE CLOSE
5 WAYSIDE WK
6 COACHMAN'S CT
7 HOOKSTONE OVAL
8 WOODLANDS GN
9 HOOKSTONE WOOD RD

B2
1 ST ANDREW'S GR
2 STONEFALL PL

C2
1 WOODLANDS RI
2 HOOKSTONE GRANGE WY
3 HOOKSTONE GRANGE COURT

C3
1 KINGSLEY PK MS
2 STATION VW
3 SPA TR
4 BROUGHTON WY
5 AVENUE TR
6 BEECH ST
7 AVENUE PL
8 AVENUE ST
9 GROVE ST
10 GLOBE ST
11 AVENUE GR

219
223

162
163

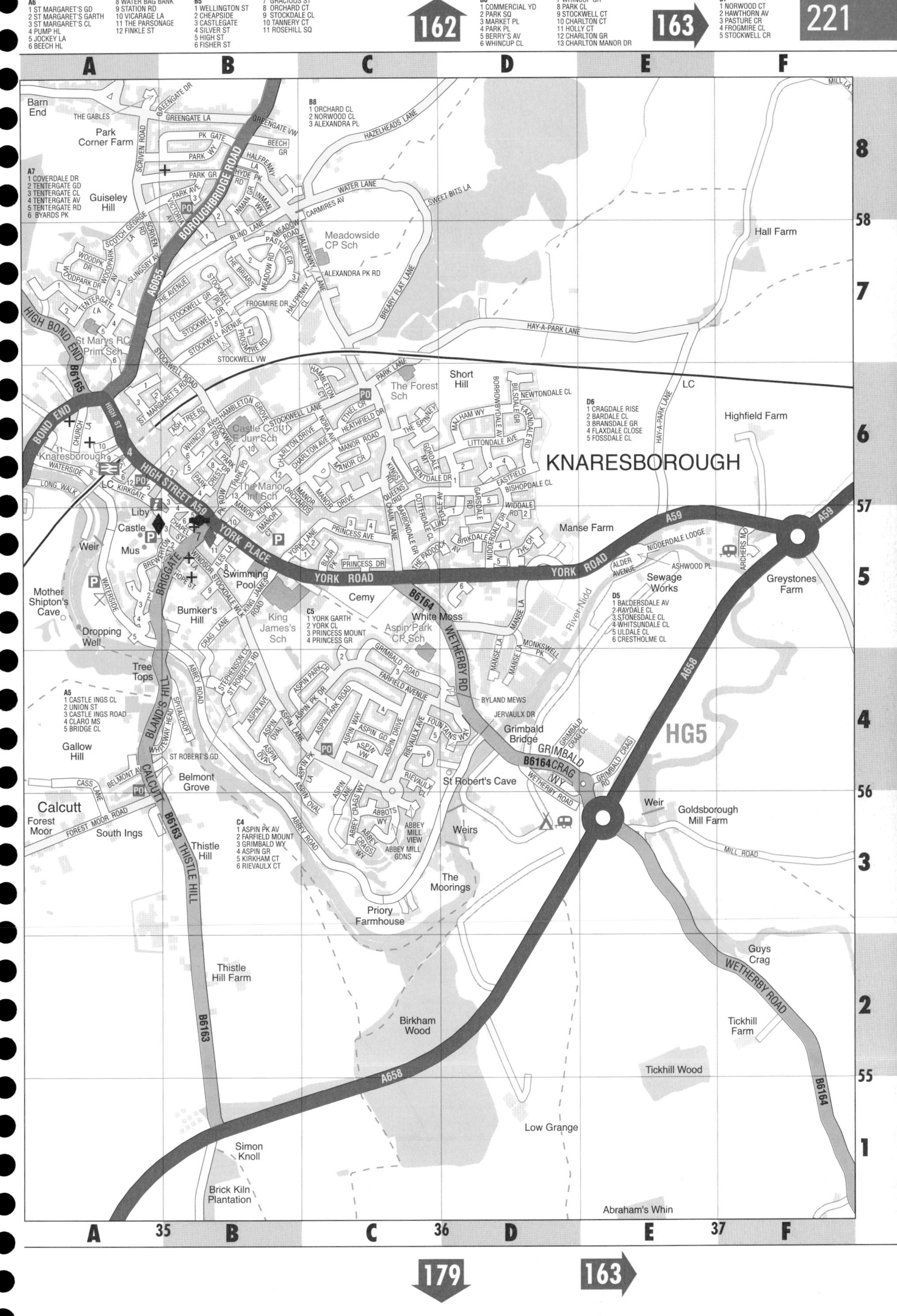

179
163

178
219

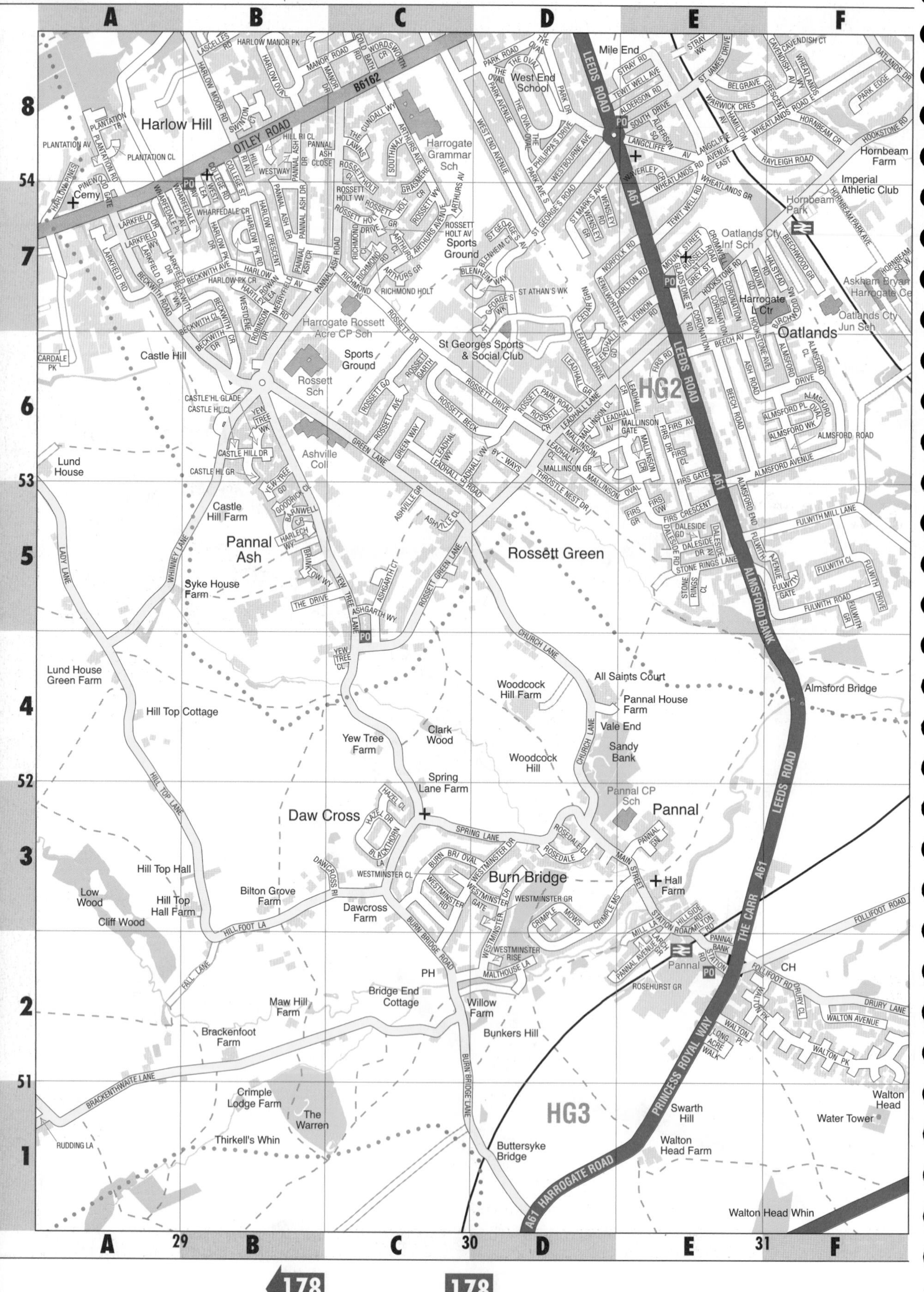

178
178

220 179

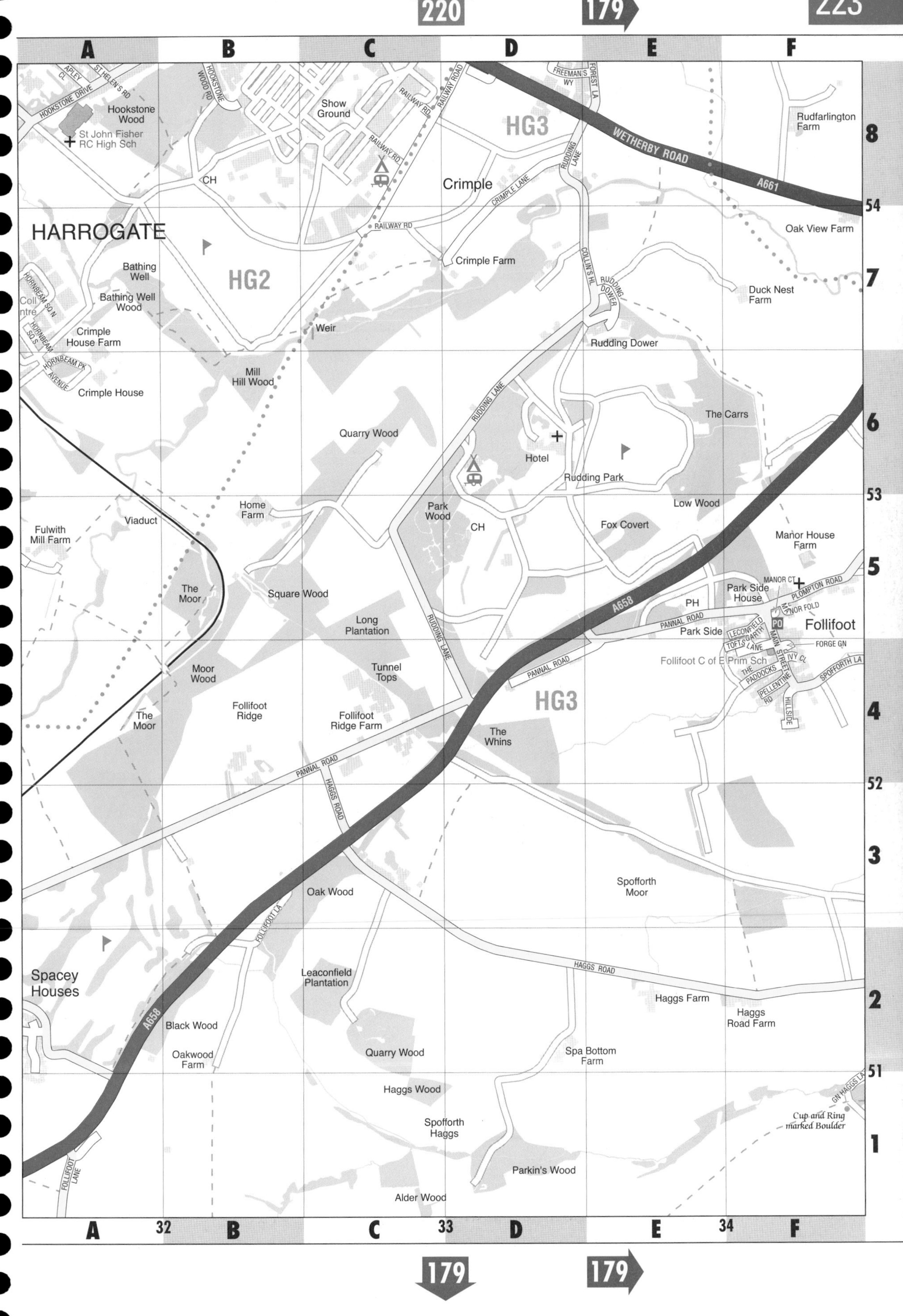

179 179

165 166

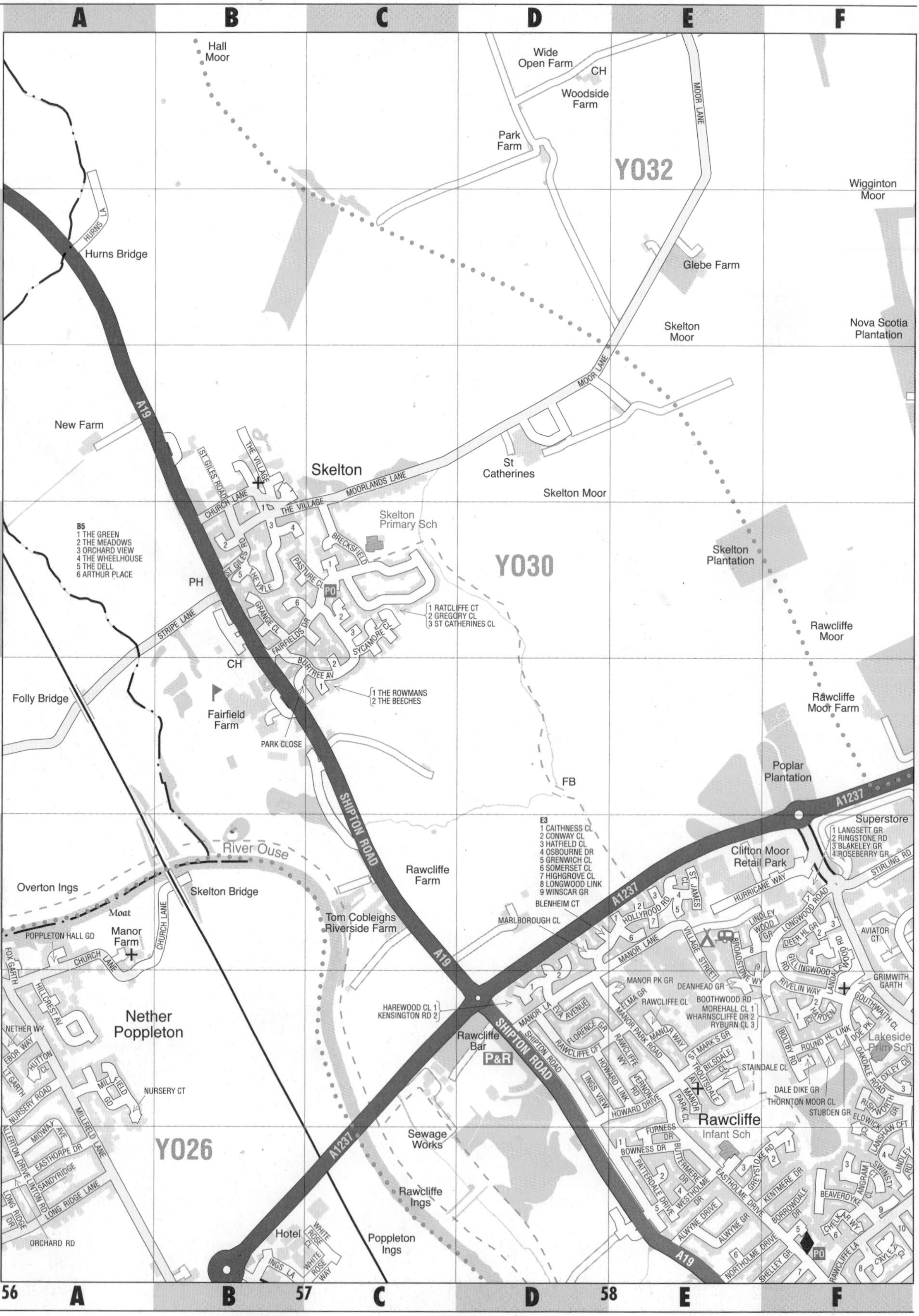

A B C D E F

8 7 57 6 5 56 4 3 55 2 1 54

Hall Moor
Wide Open Farm
CH
Woodside Farm
Park Farm
YO32
Wigginton Moor
Hurns Bridge
Glebe Farm
Skelton Moor
Nova Scotia Plantation
New Farm
St Catherines
Skelton
Skelton Moor
Skelton Primary Sch
YO30
Skelton Plantation

B5
1 THE GREEN
2 THE MEADOWS
3 ORCHARD VIEW
4 THE WHEELHOUSE
5 THE DELL
6 ARTHUR PLACE

PH
1 RATCLIFFE CT
2 GREGORY CL
3 ST CATHERINES CL

Rawcliffe Moor
CH
Folly Bridge
1 THE ROWMANS
2 THE BEECHES

Rawcliffe Moor Farm
Fairfield Farm
PARK CLOSE
Poplar Plantation
FB

E3
1 CAITHNESS CL
2 CONWAY CL
3 HATFIELD CL
4 OSBOURNE DR
5 GRENWICH CL
6 SOMERSET CL
7 HIGHGROVE CL
8 LONGWOOD LINK
9 WINSCAR GR

Superstore
1 LANGSETT GR
2 RINGSTONE RD
3 BLAKELEY GR
4 ROSEBERRY GR

River Ouse
Clifton Moor Retail Park
Rawcliffe Farm
Overton Ings
Skelton Bridge
Moat
Tom Cobleighs Riverside Farm
Manor Farm
POPPLETON HALL GD
BLENHEIM CT
MARLBOROUGH CL

Nether Poppleton
HAREWOOD CL 1
KENSINGTON RD 2
Rawcliffe Bar
P&R

MANOR PK GR
DEANHEAD GR
RAWCLIFFE CL
BOOTHWOOD RD
MOREHALL CL 1
WHARNSCLIFFE DR 2
RYBURN CL 3
STAINDALE CL
DALE DIKE GR
THORNTON MOOR CL
STUBDEN GR
Lakeside Prim Sch

NURSERY CT
Sewage Works
Rawcliffe
Rawcliffe Infant Sch
YO26
Rawcliffe Ings
Hotel
Poppleton Ings
ORCHARD RD

56 A B 57 C D 58 E F

165 227

E1
1 CONISTON CL
2 WASDALE CL
3 GARBURN GR
4 SCAFELL CL
5 LOWESWATER RD
6 FYLINGDALES AV

F1
1 EMBLETON DR
2 COLEDALE CL
3 LEIGHTON CFT
4 BARMBY CL
5 GRASMERE GR
6 BARDEN CT
7 SOUTHOLME DR
8 MILTON CARR
9 FEWSTON DR
10 REIGHTON DR

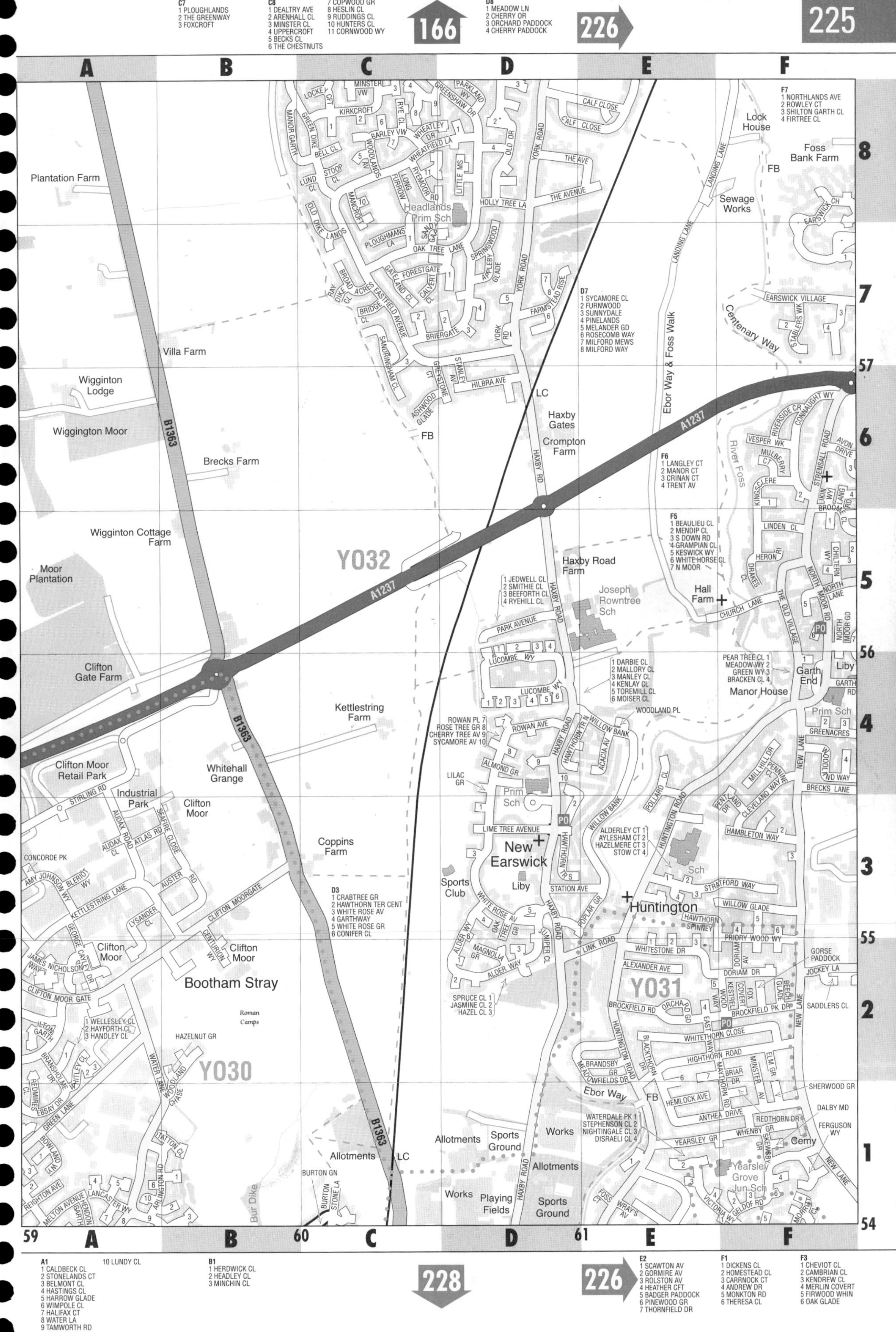
C7
1 PLOUGHLANDS
2 THE GREENWAY
3 FOXCROFT
C8
1 DEALTRY AVE
2 ARENHALL CL
3 MINSTER CL
4 UPPERCROFT
5 BECKS CL
6 THE CHESTNUTS
7 COPWOOD GR
8 HESLIN CL
9 RUDDINGS CL
10 HUNTERS CL
11 CORNWOOD WY
166
D8
1 MEADOW LN
2 CHERRY OR
3 ORCHARD PADDOCK
4 CHERRY PADDOCK
226
A
B
C
D
E
F
8
7
57
6
5
56
4
3
55
2
1
54
59
60
61
Plantation Farm
Villa Farm
Wigginton Lodge
Wiggington Moor
Brecks Farm
Wigginton Cottage Farm
Moor Plantation
Clifton Gate Farm
Clifton Moor Retail Park
Whitehall Grange
Industrial Park
Clifton Moor
Kettlestring Farm
Coppins Farm
Bootham Stray
Roman Camps
YO32
YO30
YO31
B1363
A1237
Headlands Prim Sch
Haxby Gates
Crompton Farm
Haxby Road Farm
Joseph Rowntree Sch
New Earswick
Sports Club
Liby
Huntington
Lock House
Foss Bank Farm
Sewage Works
Centenary Way
Ebor Way & Foss Walk
River Foss
Hall Farm
Garth End
Manor House
Prim Sch
Sch
Yearsley Grove Jun Sch
Cemy
Allotments
Sports Ground
Works
Playing Fields
Ebor Way
D7
1 SYCAMORE CL
2 FURNWOOD
3 SUNNYDALE
4 PINELANDS
5 MELANDER GD
6 ROSECOMB WAY
7 MILFORD MEWS
8 MILFORD WAY
F7
1 NORTHLANDS AVE
2 ROWLEY CT
3 SHILTON GARTH CL
4 FIRTREE CL
F6
1 LANGLEY CT
2 MANOR CT
3 CRINAN CT
4 TRENT AV
F5
1 BEAULIEU CL
2 MENDIP CL
3 S DOWN RD
4 GRAMPIAN CL
5 KESWICK WY
6 WHITE HORSE CL
7 N MOOR
1 JEDWELL CL
2 SMITHIE CL
3 BEEFORTH CL
4 RYEHILL CL
1 DARBIE CL
2 MALLORY CL
3 MANLEY CL
4 KENLAY CL
5 TOREMILL CL
6 MOISER CL
ROWAN PL 7
ROSE TREE GR 8
CHERRY TREE AV 9
SYCAMORE AV 10
D3
1 CRABTREE GR
2 HAWTHORN TER CENT
3 WHITE ROSE AV
4 GARTHWAY
5 WHITE ROSE GR
6 CONIFER CL
ALDERLEY CT 1
AYLESHAM CT 2
HAZELMERE CT 3
STOW CT 4
PEAR TREE CL 1
MEADOW WY 2
GREEN WY 3
BRACKEN CL 4
SPRUCE CL 1
JASMINE CL 2
HAZEL CL 3
WATERDALE PK 1
STEPHENSON CL 2
NIGHTINGALE CL 3
DISRAELI CL 4
1 WELLESLEY CL
2 HAYFORTH CL
3 HANDLEY CL
A1
1 CALDBECK CL
2 STONELANDS CT
3 BELMONT CL
4 HASTINGS CL
5 HARROW GLADE
6 WIMPOLE CL
7 HALIFAX CT
8 WATER LA
9 TAMWORTH RD
10 LUNDY CL
B1
1 HERDWICK CL
2 HEADLEY CL
3 MINCHIN CL
228
226
E2
1 SCAWTON AV
2 GORMIRE AV
3 ROLSTON AV
4 HEATHER CFT
5 BADGER PADDOCK
6 PINEWOOD GR
7 THORNFIELD DR
F1
1 DICKENS CL
2 HOMESTEAD CL
3 CARRNOCK CT
4 ANDREW DR
5 MONKTON RD
6 THERESA CL
F3
1 CHEVIOT CL
2 CAMBRIAN CL
3 KENDREW CL
4 MERLIN COVERT
5 FIRWOOD WHIN
6 OAK GLADE

225
167
167

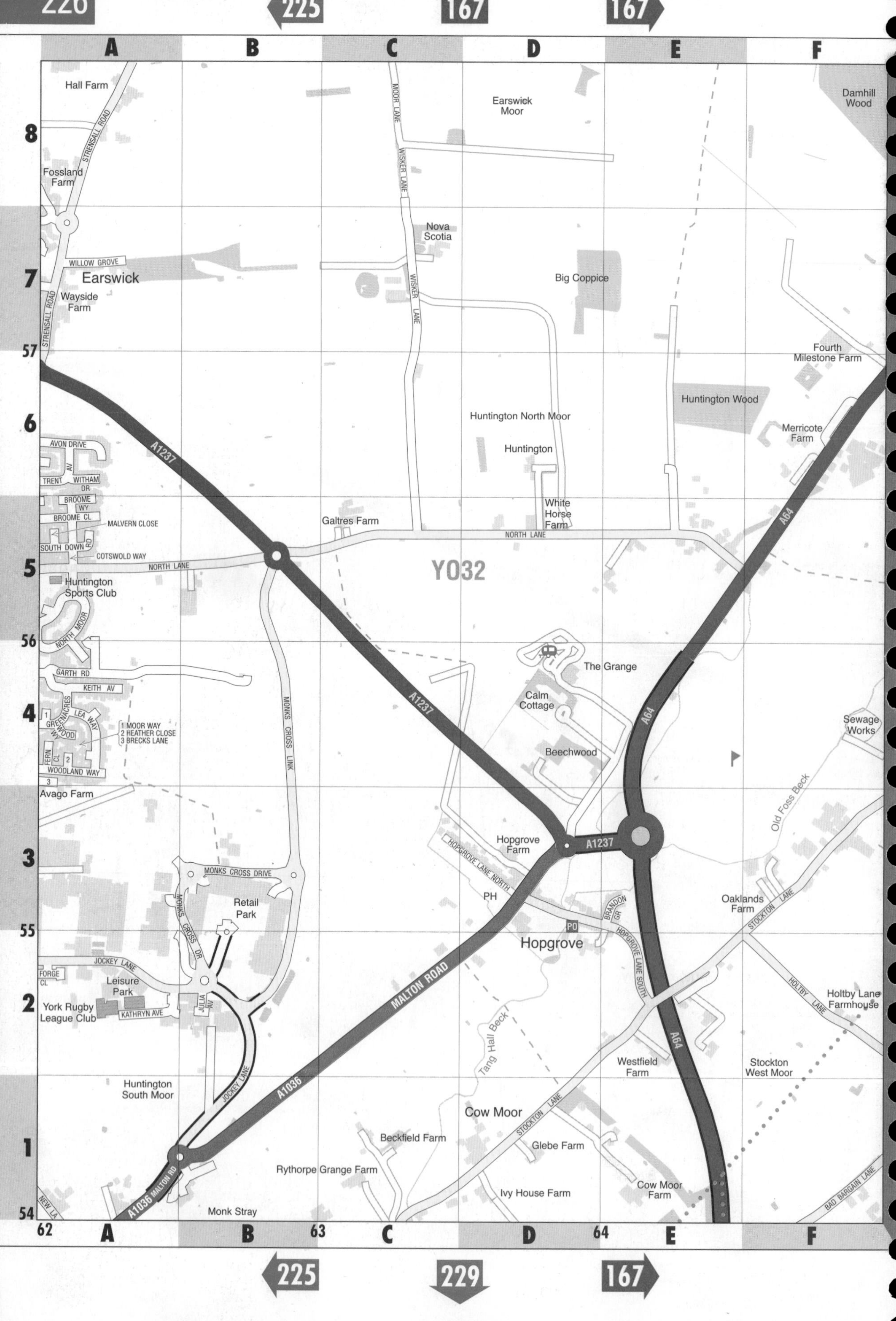

225
229
167

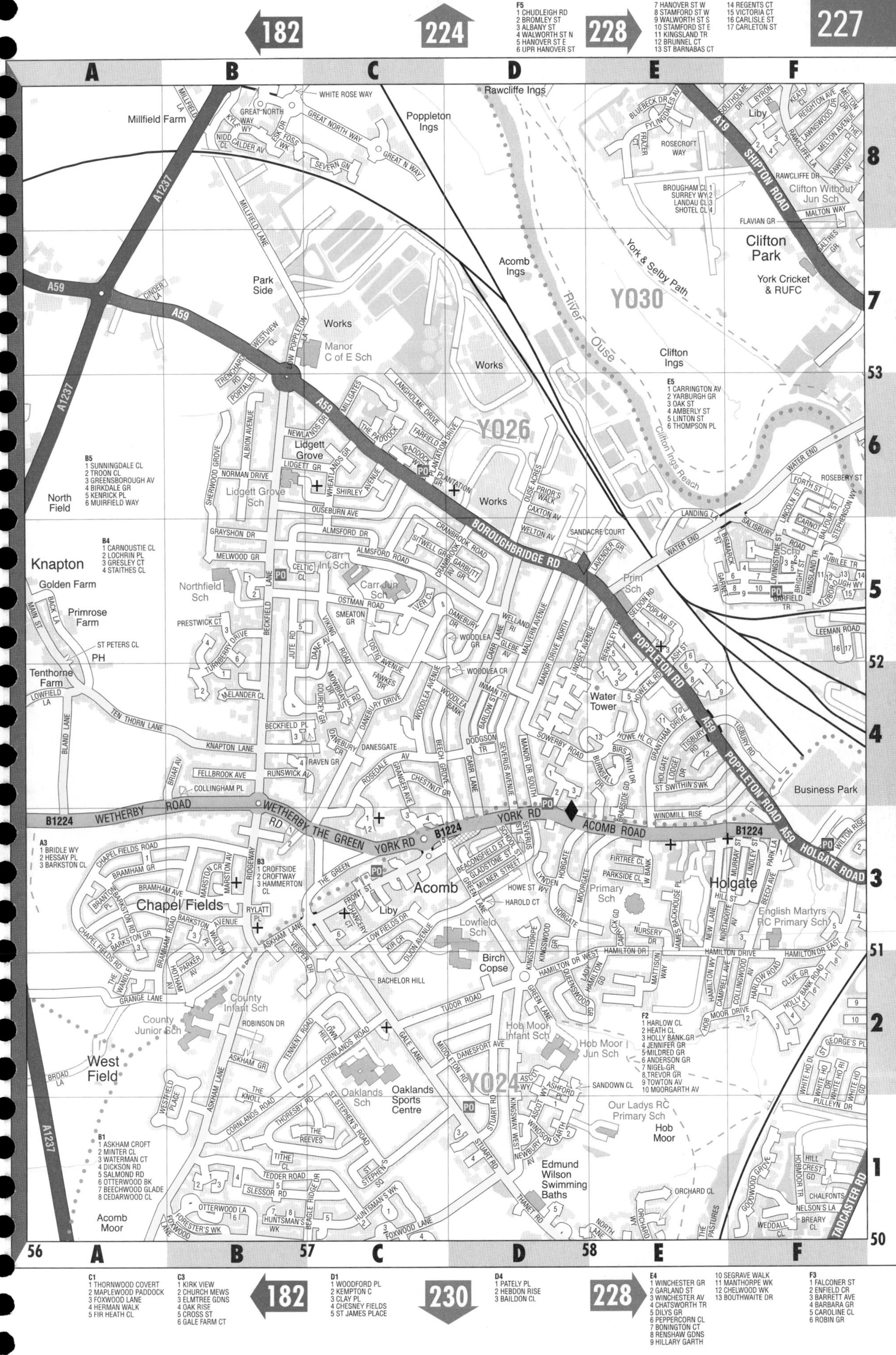
182
224
228
F5
1 CHUDLEIGH RD
2 BROMLEY ST
3 ALBANY ST
4 WALWORTH ST N
5 HANOVER ST E
6 UPR HANOVER ST
7 HANOVER ST W
8 STAMFORD ST W
9 WALWORTH ST S
10 STAMFORD ST E
11 KINGSLAND TR
12 BRUNNEL CT
13 ST BARNABAS CT
14 REGENTS CT
15 VICTORIA CT
16 CARLISLE ST
17 CARLETON ST
A
B
C
D
E
F
8
7
6
5
4
3
2
1
53
52
51
50
56
57
58
Millfield Farm
Rawcliffe Ings
Poppleton Ings
WHITE ROSE WAY
GREAT NORTH WAY
GREAT N WAY
SEVERN GN
CALDER AV
NIDD CL
KYLE WY
ESK DR
FOSS WK
MILLFIELD LANE
A1237
A59
CINDER LA
Park Side
Works
Manor C of E Sch
WESTVIEW CL
LOW POPPLETON LA
TRENCHARD RD
PORTAL RD
Acomb Ings
York & Selby Path
River Ouse
Y030
Clifton Ings
Clifton Park
York Cricket & RUFC
Clifton Without Jun Sch
Liby
A19
SHIPTON ROAD
RAWCLIFFE DR
MALTON WAY
FLAVIAN GR
BLUEBECK DR
FYLINGDALES AV
FRAZER CT
ROSECROFT WAY
BROUGHAM CL 1
SURREY WY 2
LANDAU CL 3
SHOTEL CL 4
E5
1 CARRINGTON AV
2 YARBURGH GR
3 OAK ST
4 AMBERLY ST
5 LINTON ST
6 THOMPSON PL
Clifton Ings Reach
Y026
Lidgett Grove
Lidgett Grove Sch
NEWLANDS DR
MILLGATES
THE PADDOCK
LANGHOLME DRIVE
FARFIELD
PLANTATION DRIVE
PLANTATION GR
WHEATLANDS GR
LIDGETT GR
SHIRLEY AVENUE
OUSEBURN AVE
ALMSFORD DR
ALMSFORD ROAD
NORMAN DRIVE
SHERWOOD GROVE
ALBION AVENUE
GRAYSHON DR
MELWOOD GR
B5
1 SUNNINGDALE CL
2 TROON CL
3 GREENSBOROUGH AV
4 BIRKDALE GR
5 KENRICK PL
6 MUIRFIELD WAY
North Field
B4
1 CARNOUSTIE CL
2 LOCHRIN PL
3 GRESLEY CT
4 STAITHES CL
Knapton
Golden Farm
Primrose Farm
Tenthorne Farm
PH
ST PETERS CL
MAIN ST
BACK LA
LOWFIELD LA
BLAND LANE
TEN THORN LANE
KNAPTON LANE
Northfield Sch
PRESTWICK CT
TURNBERRY DRIVE
MELANDER CL
BECKFIELD LANE
Carr Inf Sch
Carr Jun Sch
CELTIC CL
OSTMAN ROAD
SMEATON GR
JUTE RD
DANE AV
VIKING ROAD
TOSTIG AVENUE
FAWKES DR
MOWBRAY DR
COURCEY GR
DANEBURY DRIVE
BECKFIELD PL
RAVEN GR
DANEBURY CR
DANESGATE
RUNSWICK AV
FELLBROOK AVE
COLLINGHAM PL
BRIAR AV
CRANBROOK ROAD
SITWELL GR
GARBUTT GR
IVER CL
DANEBURY DR
WOODLEA GR
WOODLEA AVENUE
WOODLEA BANK
WOODLEA CR
WELLAND RI
GLEBE AV
CARR LANE
INMAN TR
BARLOW ST
DODGSON TR
BEECH GROVE
SEVERUS AVENUE
MALVERN AVENUE
MANOR DRIVE NORTH
MANOR DR SOUTH
OUSE ACRES
PRIOR'S WALK
CAXTON AV
WELTON AV
SANDACRE COURT
LAVENDER GR
BOROUGHBRIDGE RD
Works
Prim Sch
SELDON RD
POPLAR ST
ASH ST
BERKELEY TR
POPPLETON RD
HOWE HL RD
HOWE HL CL
Water Tower
LINDSEY AVENUE
SOWERBY ROAD
BURNSALL DR
BIRSTWITH DR
GRANTHAM DRIVE
HOLGATE LODGE DR
TISBURY RD
ST SWITHIN'S WK
BRAESIDE GD
WINDMILL RISE
WATER END
LANDING LA
ROSEBERY ST
FORTH ST
CARNOT ST
SALISBURY ROAD
BISMARCK ST
GARNET TR
LIVINGSTONE ST
BRIGHT ST
KINGSLAND TR
ALDBOROUGH WY
JUBILEE TR
LEEMAN ROAD
GARFIELD TR
STEPHENSON WY
BALFOUR ST
LINCOLN ST
Business Park
B1224
WETHERBY ROAD
WETHERBY RD
THE GREEN
YORK RD
ACOMB ROAD
A3
1 BRIDLE WY
2 HESSAY PL
3 BARKSTON CL
B3
1 CROFTSIDE
2 CROFTWAY
3 HAMMERTON CL
CHAPEL FIELDS ROAD
BRAMHAM GR
BRAMHAM AVE
BRANTON PL
BARKSTON ROAD
Chapel Fields
MARSTON AV
MARSTON CR
RIDGEWAY
RYLATT PL
BARKSTON AVENUE
BARKSTON GR
WALTON PL
BRAMHAM ROAD
HOTHAM AV
PARKER AV
THE WANDLE
GRANGE LANE
County Infant Sch
County Junior Sch
ROBINSON DR
ASKHAM GR
ASKHAM LANE
West Field
BROAD LA
Acomb
Liby
FRONT ST
CHANCERY CT
LOW FIELDS DR
KIR CR
DIJON AVENUE
VESPER DR
BACHELOR HILL
BEACONSFIELD ST
GLADSTONE ST
MILNER STREET
SCHOOL ST
SEVERUS ST
GREEN LANE
HOWE ST
HAROLD CT
Lowfield Sch
Birch Copse
LYNDEN WY
HOBGATE
MOORGATE
Primary Sch
FIRTREE CL
PARKSIDE CL
W BANK
NURSERY DR
JAMES BACKHOUSE PL
NEW LANE
NORTHCOTE AV
HILL ST
Holgate
MURRAY ST
LINDLEY ST
BEECH AVE
PARK LA
English Martyrs RC Primary Sch
HAMILTON DR WEST
HAMILTON DR
HAMILTON DRIVE
HAMILTON DR EAST
KINGSTHORPE
KINGSWOOD GR
QUEENSWOOD GR
LADY HAMILTON GD
MATTISON WAY
HAMILTON WY
CAMPBELL AVE
COLLINGWOOD AV
HARLOW ROAD
CLIVE GR
HOLLY BANK ROAD
HOB MOOR DRIVE
HOLGATE ROAD
WILTON RISE
TUDOR ROAD
TENNENT ROAD
LOWN HILL
CORNLANDS ROAD
GALE LANE
MIDDLETON RD
DANESFORT AVE
Hob Moor Infant Sch
Hob Moor Jun Sch
F2
1 HARLOW CL
2 HEATH CL
3 HOLLY BANK GR
4 JENNIFER GR
5 MILDRED GR
6 ANDERSON GR
7 NIGEL GR
8 TREVOR GR
9 TOWTON AV
10 MOORGARTH AV
ST GEORGE'S PL
WHITE HO DL
WHITE HO GD
WHITE HO RI
WHITE HO DR
PULLEYN DR
Oaklands Sch
Oaklands Sports Centre
Y024
ASCOT WY
ASHFORD PL
SANDOWN CL
Our Ladys RC Primary Sch
Hob Moor
WESTFIELD PLACE
THE KNOLL
CORNLANDS ROAD
THORESBY RD
THE REEVES
ST STEPHEN'S ROAD
ST STEPHEN'S SQ
STUART RD
KINGSWAY WEST
WINDSOR GARTH
NEWBURY AV
B1
1 ASKHAM CROFT
2 MINTER CL
3 WATERMAN CT
4 DICKSON RD
5 SALMOND RD
6 OTTERWOOD BK
7 BEECHWOOD GLADE
8 CEDARWOOD CL
TITHE CL
TEDDER ROAD
SLESSOR RD
HUNTSMAN'S WK
BEAGLE RIDGE DR
FOXWOOD LANE
OTTERWOOD LA
FORESTER'S WK
FOXWOOD LANE
Acomb Moor
Edmund Wilson Swimming Baths
THANET RD
NORTH LANE
ORCHARD WY
ORCHARD CL
THE PASTURES
GODWOOD GROVE
HORNOOR TR
HILL CREST GD
CHALFONTS
NELSON'S LA
WEDDALL CL
BREARY CL
TADCASTER RD
C1
1 THORNWOOD COVERT
2 MAPLEWOOD PADDOCK
3 FOXWOOD LANE
4 HERMAN WALK
5 FIR HEATH CL
C3
1 KIRK VIEW
2 CHURCH MEWS
3 ELMTREE GDNS
4 OAK RISE
5 CROSS ST
6 GALE FARM CT
182
D1
1 WOODFORD PL
2 KEMPTON C
3 CLAY PL
4 CHESNEY FIELDS
5 ST JAMES PLACE
230
D4
1 PATELY PL
2 HEBDON RISE
3 BAILDON CL
228
E4
1 WINCHESTER GR
2 GARLAND ST
3 WINCHESTER AV
4 CHATSWORTH TR
5 DILYS GR
6 PEPPERCORN CL
7 BONINGTON CT
8 RENSHAW GDNS
9 HILLARY GARTH
10 SEGRAVE WALK
11 MANTHORPE WK
12 CHELWOOD WK
13 BOUTHWAITE DR
F3
1 FALCONER ST
2 ENFIELD CR
3 BARRETT AVE
4 BARBARA GR
5 CAROLINE CL
6 ROBIN GR

A8
1 LINDEN GROVE
2 MARTEN CLOSE
3 RAINSBOROUGH WAY

A7
1 BELCOMBE WAY
2 HUDSON CRESCENT
3 CLIFTON PLACE
4 PINFOLD COURT

227

C7
1 UPR NEWBOROUGH ST
2 ALLAN ST
3 MURROUGH WILSON PL
4 FEVERSHAM CR
5 HILLSBOROUGH TR
6 HUDSON ST

225

E8
1 KIRKHAM AV
2 THE CROSSWAY
3 LILLING AV

E5
1 HAWTHORN ST
2 EMMERSON ST
3 FLEMING AV
4 SCROPE AV

F8
1 ALBERT CL
2 VICTORIA WY
3 MORRITT CL
4 FOSTON GR
5 THORNFIELD AV
6 LABURNUM GARTH

For full street detail of the highlighted area see page 233.

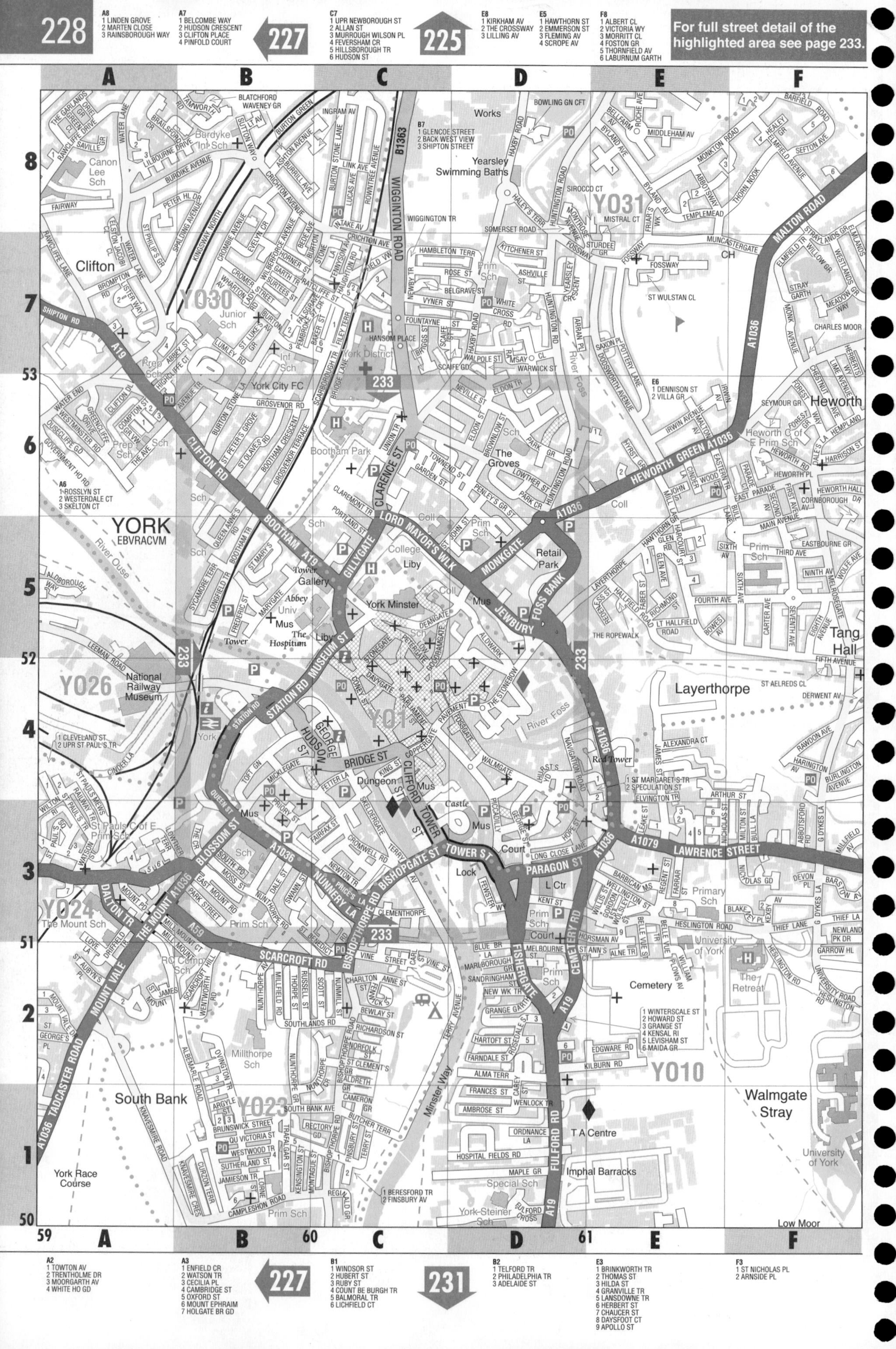

A2
1 TOWTON AV
2 TRENTHOLME DR
3 MOORGARTH AV
4 WHITE HO GD

A3
1 ENFIELD CR
2 WATSON TR
3 CECILIA PL
4 CAMBRIDGE ST
5 OXFORD ST
6 MOUNT EPHRAIM
7 HOLGATE BR GD

227

B1
1 WINDSOR ST
2 HUBERT ST
3 RUBY ST
4 COUNT BE BURGH TR
5 BALMORAL TR
6 LICHFIELD CT

231

B2
1 TELFORD TR
2 PHILADELPHIA TR
3 ADELAIDE ST

E3
1 BRINKWORTH TR
2 THOMAS ST
3 HILDA ST
4 GRANVILLE TR
5 LANSDOWNE TR
6 HERBERT ST
7 CHAUCER ST
8 DAYSFOOT CT
9 APOLLO ST

F3
1 ST NICHOLAS PL
2 ARNSIDE PL

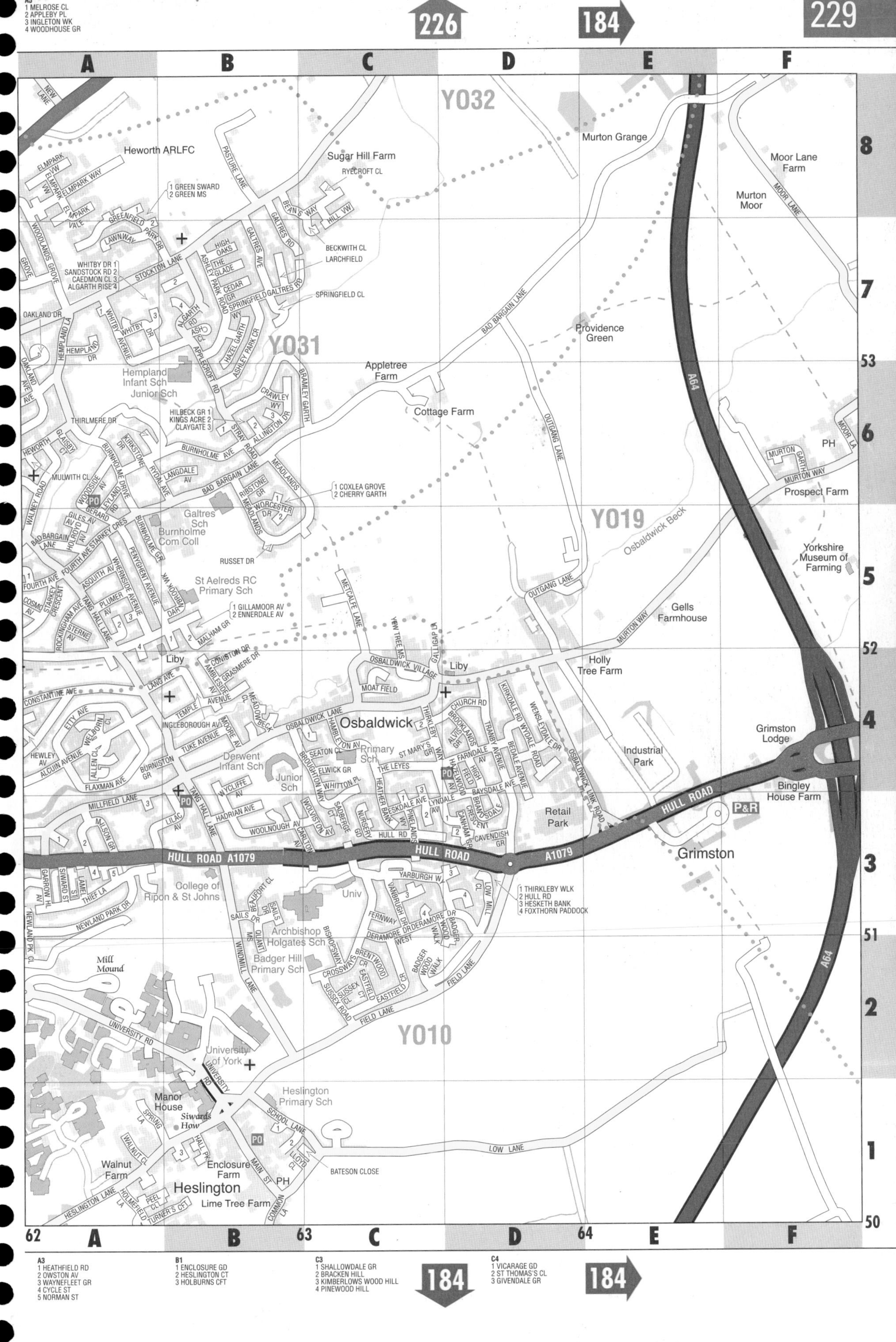
A5
1 MELROSE CL
2 APPLEBY PL
3 INGLETON WK
4 WOODHOUSE GR
226
184
A
B
C
D
E
F
8
7
53
6
5
52
4
3
51
2
1
50
62
63
64
YO32
YO31
YO19
YO10
Heworth ARLFC
Sugar Hill Farm
RYECROFT CL
Murton Grange
Moor Lane Farm
Murton Moor
MOOR LANE
1 GREEN SWARD
2 GREEN MS
PASTURE LANE
ELMPARK VW
ELMPARK WAY
ELMPARK VALE
GREENFIELD PARK DR
LAWNWAY
WOODLANDS GROVE
STOCKTON LANE
HIGH OAKS
THE GLADE
ASHLEY PARK ROAD
CEDAR GR
GALTRES AVE
GALTRES RD
BEAN'S WAY
HILL VW
BECKWITH CL
LARCHFIELD
SPRINGFIELD CL
SPRINGFIELD WY
WHITBY DR 1
SANDSTOCK RD 2
CAEDMON CL 3
ALGARTH RISE 4
OAKLAND DR
HEMPLAND LA
HEMPLAND DR
WHITBY AVENUE
WHITBY DR
ALGARTH RD
ASH CL
APPLECROFT RD
HAZEL GARTH
ASHLEY PARK CR
BRAMLEY GARTH
BAD BARGAIN LANE
Providence Green
Appletree Farm
Cottage Farm
Hempland Infant Sch
Junior Sch
CRAWLEY WY
ALLINGTON DR
HILBECK GR 1
KINGS ACRE 2
CLAYGATE 3
STRAY ROAD
THIRLMERE DR
HEWORTH
GLAISBY CT
BURNHOLME DR
KIRKSTONE DR
RYDAL AVE
BURNHOLME AVE
LANGDALE AV
RIBSTONE GR
MEADLANDS
WORCESTER DR
1 COXLEA GROVE
2 CHERRY GARTH
OUTGANG LANE
A64
MURTON GARTH
MURTON WAY
PH
MOOR LA
Prospect Farm
MULWITH CL
WALNEY ROAD
WOODSIDE AV
LEYLAND RD
BURNHOLME DRIVE
GERARD AV
GILES AV
HOLROYD AV
BAD BARGAIN LANE
FOURTH AVE
STARKEY CRES
Galtres Sch
Burnholme Com Coll
PENYGHENT AVENUE
RUSSET DR
Osbaldwick Beck
Yorkshire Museum of Farming
ASQUITH AV
WINDERMERE AVENUE
St Aelreds RC Primary Sch
1 GILLAMOOR AV
2 ENNERDALE AV
COSMO AV
STARKEY CRESCENT
ROCKINGHAM AVE
TANG HALL LANE
PLUMER AV
STERNE AV
MALHAM GR
METCALFE LANE
YEW TREE MS
GALLIGAP LA
MURTON WAY
Gells Farmhouse
Liby
CONISTON DR
GRASMERE DR
AMBLESIDE AV
LANG AVE
OSBALDWICK VILLAGE
Holly Tree Farm
MOAT FIELD
CONSTANTINE AVE
ETTY AVE
WELBORN CL
TEMPLE AVENUE
MEADOW BECK CL
CHURCH RD
KIRKDALE RD
WENSLEYDALE DR
INGLEBOROUGH AV
OSBALDWICK LANE
Osbaldwick
HAMILTON DR
THIRKLEBY WAY
BROOKLANDS
TRANBY AVENUE
WYDALE ROAD
HEWLEY AV
ALCUIN AVENUE
ALLEN CL
TUKE AVENUE
MOORE AV
Derwent Infant Sch
SEATON CL
Primary Sch
ST MARY'S GR
ALVIS GR
FARNDALE AV
BEDALE AVENUE
OSBALDWICK LINK ROAD
Industrial Park
Grimston Lodge
BURNISTON GR
FLAXMAN AVE
Junior Sch
ELWICK GR
BROUGHTON WAY
THE LEYES
HAZELWOOD AV
HIGH FIELD
BAYSDALE AVE
WHITTON PL
PO
LILAC AV
WYCLIFFE AV
HEATHER BANK
ESKDALE AVE
LYNDALE AV
BRANSDALE
Retail Park
HULL ROAD
Bingley House Farm
P&R
MILLFIELD LANE
HADRIAN AVE
WOLVISTON AV
SADBERGE CT
NURSERY GD
PINELANDS WY
CRESCENT
CANHAM GR
CAVENDISH GR
MILSON GR
WOOLNOUGH AV
CARLTON AV
HULL RD
HULL ROAD A1079
HULL ROAD
A1079
Grimston
GARROW HL AV
SIWARD ST
LAMEL ST
THIEF LA
College of Ripon & St Johns
BEAUFORT CL
Univ
YARBURGH WY
VANBRUGH DR
LOW MILL CL
1 THIRKLEBY WLK
2 HULL RD
3 HESKETH BANK
4 FOXTHORN PADDOCK
NEWLAND PARK DR
SAILS DR
QUANT MS
FERNWAY
DERAMORE DR WEST
DERAMORE DR
BADGER WOOD WALK
NEWLAND PK CL
Archbishop Holgates Sch
WINDMILL LANE
BISHOPSWAY
Badger Hill Primary Sch
BRENTWOOD CR
BADGER WOOD WALK
FIELD LANE
Mill Mound
CROSSWAYS
SUSSEX CL
SUSSEX CT
EASTFIELD CT
EASTFIELD CR
SUSSEX ROAD
FIELD LANE
UNIVERSITY RD
University of York
UNIVERSITY RD
Heslington Primary Sch
Manor House
Siwards How
SPRING LA
SCHOOL LANE
WALNUT CL
HALL PK
LLOYD CL
BATESON CLOSE
LOW LANE
Walnut Farm
Enclosure Farm
MAIN ST
PH
Heslington
HESLINGTON LANE
HOLMEFIELD LA
PEEL CL
TURNER'S CFT
Lime Tree Farm
COMMON LA
A3
1 HEATHFIELD RD
2 OWSTON AV
3 WAYNEFLEET GR
4 CYCLE ST
5 NORMAN ST
B1
1 ENCLOSURE GD
2 HESLINGTON CT
3 HOLBURNS CFT
C3
1 SHALLOWDALE GR
2 BRACKEN HILL
3 KIMBERLOWS WOOD HILL
4 PINEWOOD HILL
C4
1 VICARAGE GD
2 ST THOMAS'S CL
3 GIVENDALE GR
184
184

230
182
227
C8
1 HINTON AV
2 LYDHAM CT
3 MARTIN CHEESEMAN CT
4 CRANFIELD PL
ROGER COURT
D8
1 FARMLANDS RD
2 DRINGFIELD CL
3 HERDSMAN RD
4 SANDCROFT CL
5 DEEPDALE
E8
1 TURNMIRE RD
2 SOUTHFIELD CR
3 MEADOW CT
4 THE PASTURES
5 ST HELEN'S RD
F8
1 KENSINGTON CT
2 REGENCY MS
Great Knoll
B8
1 REDCOAT W
2 KITEMERE PL
3 HAWKSHEAD CL
4 OSPREY CL
5 PHEASANT DR
6 HOUNDSWAY
7 EATON CT
Acomb Moor
High Moor Close
B7
1 HALLADALE CL
2 TARBERT CR
3 WANSBECK
4 CAIRNBORROW
High Moor
Woodthorpe Prim Sch
Woodthorpe
ACOMB WOOD CLOSE
KINBRACE DR
SANDMARTIN CT
Hob Moor
Dringhouses
Prim Sch
Sports & Social Club
Liby
ST EDWARD'S CL
YO24
THE COVERT
THE SPINNEY
HUNTERS WAY
MIDDLETHORPE GROVE
1 CHALONER'S CR
2 WAIN'S GR
3 SILVERDALE CT
Hogg's Pond
WINDERMERE
BRAMBLE DENE
MOOR LA
OLD MOOR LA
ALDERSYDE
P&R
Askham Bar Park and Ride
York Coll of Further & Higher Education
WHIN GARTH
Eastfield Farm
DALMALLY CL
HELMSDALE
SPEY BANK
MOOR LANE
C7
1 QUAKER GN
2 LINDALE
3 CRUMMOCK
4 MITERDALE
5 STONETHWAITE
6 BANNISDALE
7 TROUTBECK
Marsh Farm
BOG LANE
Superstore
THE GROVE
CHESSINGHAM GD
York Sixth Form Coll
SIM BALK LANE
Sim Hills
TADCASTER ROAD DRINGHOUSES
A1036
A1237
ASKHAM BRYAN LANE
ASKHAM LANE
Askham Bogs
Middlethorpe Grange Farm
Bond Hill Ash Farm
A64
CH
PH
SARGENT AV 1
DEANS CL 2
COPMANTHORPE LANE
COPMANTHORPE LA
Cotton End
TOP LANE
PIKE HILLS MOUNT
ST NICHOLAS CR
ST NICHOLAS CL
WATTLERS CL
ROPERS CT
THATCHERS CFT
FLETCHER'S CFT
OSTLER'S CL
SAWYER'S CR
YO23
Glebe Farm
Prim Sch
Junior Sch
Copmanthorpe
Town Ings Drain
WHEELWRIGHT CL
Recreation Centre & Sports Club
Sewage
MOOR LANE
1 BEADLE GARTH
2 BELLMANS CFT
3 VAVASOUR CT
STATION RD
HOBSON CL
DROME ROAD
TEMPLE GARTH
TEMPLE LANE
Temple Hill Farm
HOMEFIELD CL 1
PADDOCK CL 2
BARNFIELD WY 3
NALTON CLOSE
Cemy
LEADLEY CFT
North Moor
A B C D E F
8 7 49 6 5 48 4 3 47 2 1 46
56 57 58
A3
1 LARKFIELD CL
2 HORSEMAN CL
3 LYNWOOD AV
4 LYNWOOD VW
B3
1 SADDLERS CL
2 FARRIERS CFT
3 WAGGONERS DR
4 POTTERS DR
5 WAINERS CL
6 MILLERS CFT
7 LORINERS DR
8 GARDENERS CL
182
191

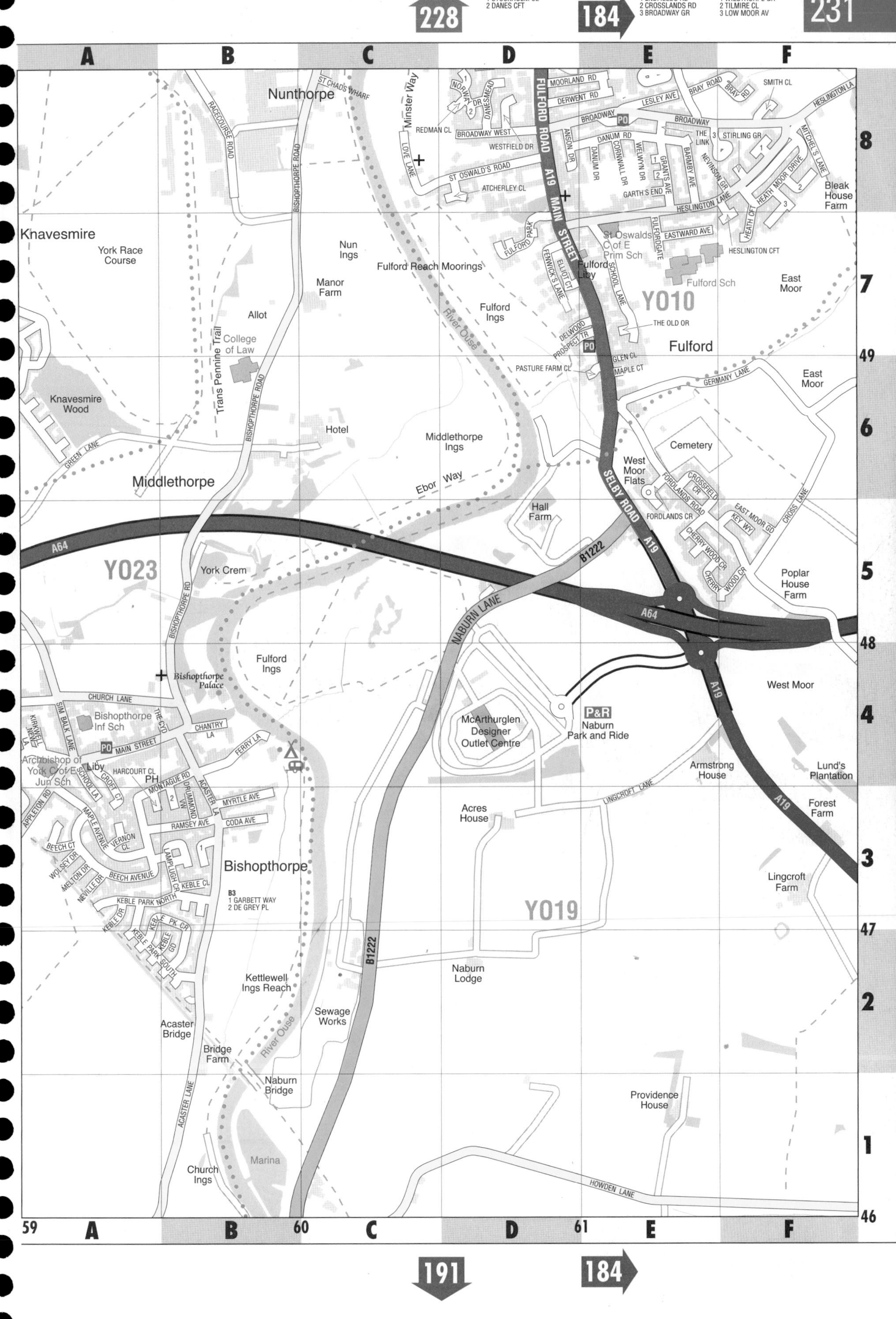
A
B
C
D
E
F
Nunthorpe
ST CHAD'S WHARF
Minster Way
NORWAY DR
DANESMEAD
REDMAN CL
BROADWAY WEST
WESTFIELD DR
LOVE LANE
ST OSWALD'S ROAD
ATCHERLEY CL
FULFORD ROAD
A19
MAIN STREET
MOORLAND RD
DERWENT RD
LESLEY AVE
BRAY ROAD
BRAY RD
SMITH CL
HESLINGTON LA
BROADWAY
PO
THE LINK
STIRLING GR
MITCHEL'S LANE
ANSON DR
DANUM RD
DANUM DR
CORNWALL DR
WELWYN DR
GRANTS AVE
BARMBY AVE
NEVINSON GR
HEATH MOOR DRIVE
GARTH'S END
HESLINGTON LANE
HEATH CFT
Bleak House Farm
8
RACECOURSE ROAD
BISHOPTHORPE ROAD
Knavesmire
York Race Course
Nun Ings
Manor Farm
Fulford Reach Moorings
FULFORD PARK
FENWICK'S LANE
ELLIOT CT
St Oswalds C of E Prim Sch
Fulford Liby
SCHOOL LANE
FULFORDGATE
EASTWARD AVE
HESLINGTON CFT
Fulford Sch
East Moor
7
Allot
College of Law
Trans Pennine Trail
River Ouse
Fulford Ings
YO10
THE OLD OR
DELWOOD
PROSPECT TR
PO
Fulford
GLEN CL
MAPLE CT
PASTURE FARM CL
GERMANY LANE
East Moor
49
Knavesmire Wood
GREEN LANE
Hotel
Middlethorpe Ings
Cemetery
West Moor Flats
6
Middlethorpe
Ebor Way
SELBY ROAD
FORDLANDS ROAD
CROSSFIELD CR
FORDLANDS CR
EAST MOOR GD
KEY WY
CROSS LANE
Hall Farm
CHERRY WOOD CR
A64
YO23
York Crem
B1222
A19
Poplar House Farm
5
BISHOPTHORPE RD
NABURN LANE
A64
48
Fulford Ings
Bishopthorpe Palace
CHURCH LANE
A19
West Moor
SIM BALK LANE
KIRKWELL
THE OLD
Bishopthorpe Inf Sch
CHANTRY LA
McArthurglen Designer Outlet Centre
P&R
Naburn Park and Ride
4
PO
MAIN STREET
FERRY LA
Archbishop of York C of E Jun Sch
Liby
PH
HARCOURT CL
MONTAGUE RD
DRUMMOND VW
ACASTER LA
SCHOOL LA
CROFT CT
MYRTLE AVE
Armstrong House
Lund's Plantation
APPLETON RD
MAPLE AVENUE
RAMSEY AVE
CODA AVE
LINGCROFT LANE
Acres House
Forest Farm
A19
BEECH CT
VERNON CL
WOLSEY DR
MELTON DR
BEECH AVENUE
LAMPLUGH CR
KEBLE CL
Bishopthorpe
3
NEVILLE DR
KEBLE PARK NORTH
KEBLE DR
KEBLE PK CR
KEBLE PARK SOUTH
KEBLE GD
B3
1 GARBETT WAY
2 DE GREY PL
Lingcroft Farm
YO19
47
B1222
Naburn Lodge
Kettlewell Ings Reach
2
Acaster Bridge
Sewage Works
Bridge Farm
River Ouse
Naburn Bridge
ACASTER LANE
Providence House
1
Marina
Church Ings
HOWDEN LANE
46
59
60
61

197
197
198
198

C5
1 YORK ST
2 HARPER ST
3 DOUGLAS ST
4 RAINCLIFFE ST
5 LONDESBOROUGH ST
6 HILDA ST
7 PORTHOLME CR
8 SOUTH PAR
9 TURNERS SQ
10 AUDUS ST
11 MARKET PL

D5
1 MICKLEGATE
2 WREN LA
3 CHURCH HL
4 CHURCH LA

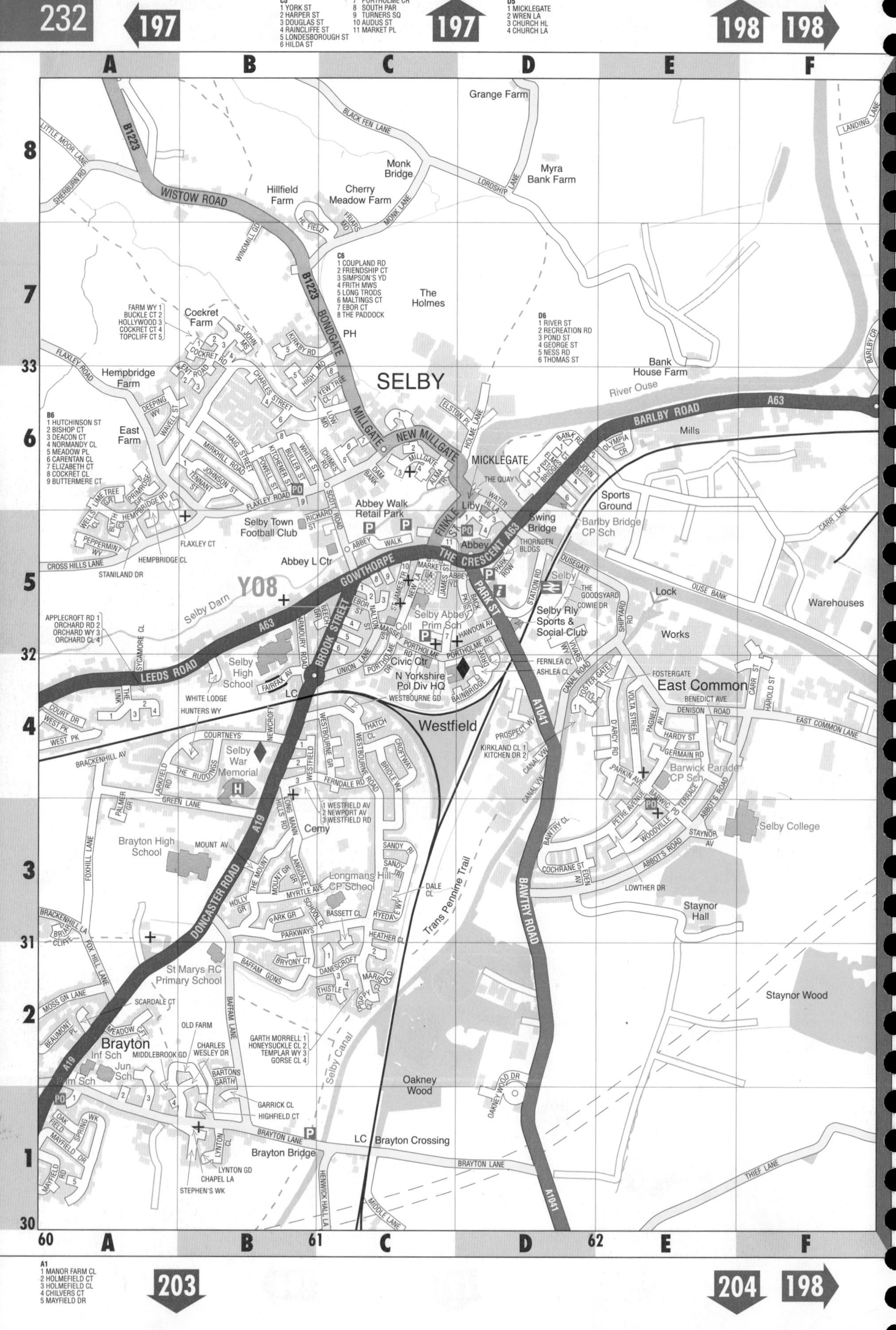

A1
1 MANOR FARM CL
2 HOLMEFIELD CT
3 HOLMEFIELD CL
4 CHILVERS CT
5 MAYFIELD DR

203
204
198

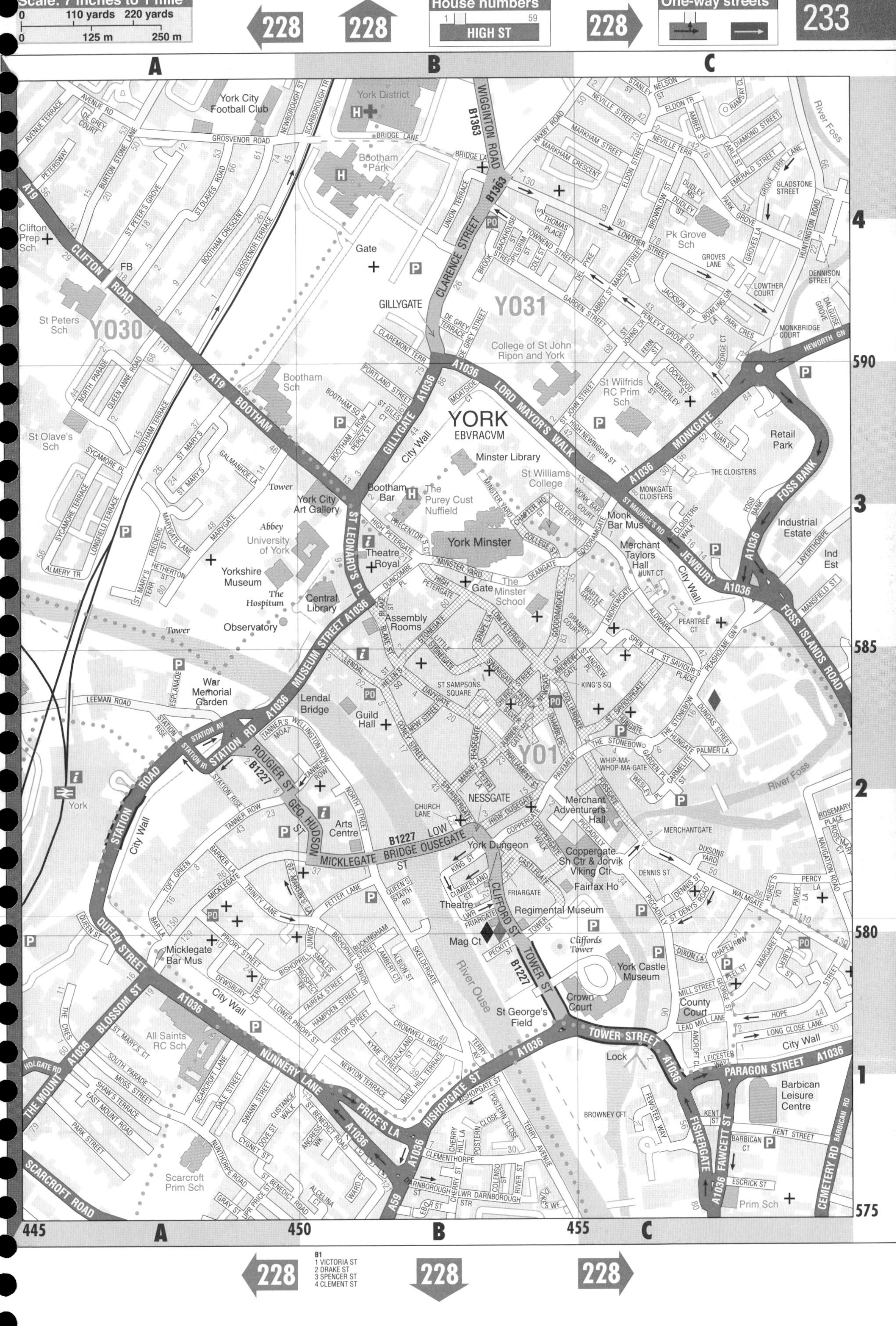

228 228 228 228 228 228

Index

Church Rd **6** Beckenham BR2..........**53** C6

Place name	**Location number**	**Locality, town or village**	**Postcode district**	**Page and grid square**
May be abbreviated on the map	Present when a number indicates the place's position in a crowded area of mapping	Shown when more than one place has the same name	District for the indexed place	Page number and grid reference for the standard mapping

Public and commercial buildings are highlighted in **magenta** **Places of interest** are highlighted in **blue** with a star★

Abbreviations used in the index

Acad	**Academy**	Comm	**Common**	Gd	**Ground**	L	**Leisure**	Prom	**Prom**
App	**Approach**	Cott	**Cottage**	Gdn	**Garden**	La	**Lane**	Rd	**Road**
Arc	**Arcade**	Cres	**Crescent**	Gn	**Green**	Liby	**Library**	Recn	**Recreation**
Ave	**Avenue**	Cswy	**Causeway**	Gr	**Grove**	Mdw	**Meadow**	Ret	**Retail**
Bglw	**Bungalow**	Ct	**Court**	H	**Hall**	Meml	**Memorial**	Sh	**Shopping**
Bldg	**Building**	Ctr	**Centre**	Ho	**House**	Mkt	**Market**	Sq	**Square**
Bsns, Bus	**Business**	Ctry	**Country**	Hospl	**Hospital**	Mus	**Museum**	St	**Street**
Bvd	**Boulevard**	Cty	**County**	HQ	**Headquarters**	Orch	**Orchard**	Sta	**Station**
Cath	**Cathedral**	Dr	**Drive**	Hts	**Heights**	Pal	**Palace**	Terr	**Terrace**
Cir	**Circus**	Dro	**Drove**	Ind	**Industrial**	Par	**Parade**	TH	**Town Hall**
Cl	**Close**	Ed	**Education**	Inst	**Institute**	Pas	**Passage**	Univ	**University**
Cnr	**Corner**	Emb	**Embankment**	Int	**International**	Pk	**Park**	Wk, Wlk	**Walk**
Coll	**College**	Est	**Estate**	Intc	**Interchange**	Pl	**Place**	Wr	**Water**
Com	**Community**	Ex	**Exhibition**	Junc	**Junction**	Prec	**Precinct**	Yd	**Yard**

Index of localities, towns and villages

A

Aberford 194 F7
Acaster Malbis 191 D8
Acaster Selby 191 B4
Acklam 169 E8
Acklam 6 E8
Acomb 227 C3
Addingham 174 F5
Agglethorpe 60 A1
Ainderby Quernhow 88 C4
Ainderby Steeple 64 B7
Ainthorpe 29 C6
Aire View 173 D1
Airedale 201 B4
Airmyn 205 E4
Airton 155 A6
Airy Hill 208 D4
Aiskew 63 A3
Aislaby 5 C3
Aislaby 31 F7
Aislaby 95 D8
Aldborough 141 C5
Aldbrough St John 2 A2
Aldfield 139 A8
Aldwark 142 C2
Allerston 97 C5
Allerton Bywater 200 D6
Allerton Mauleverer ...163 E4
Alne 142 F4
Alne Station 143 A5
Amotherby 121 B4
Ampleforth 92 C1
Angram 182 C3
Angram 35 E6
Appersett 56 C5
Appleton Roebuck 190 F5
Appleton Wiske 24 B3
Appleton-le-Moors 70 F2
Appleton-le-Street 120 F4
Appletreewick 157 D7
Archdeacon Newton 2 F7
Arkendale 163 B8
Arncliffe 107 D2
Arrathorne 62 A8
Asenby 115 B6
Askham Bryan 182 F3
Askham Richard 182 D3
Askrigg 57 F6
Askwith 176 D3
Asselby 205 D7
Aughton 193 C1
Austwick 130 E7
Aysgarth 58 E3
Azerley 113 A5

B

Bagby 90 C3
Bainbridge 57 D5
Baldersby 88 D1
Baldersby St James 114 E8
Balne 207 C5
Bank Newton 172 B8
Barden 61 A8
Barkston Ash 195 F7
Barlby 198 B5
Barlow 204 C7
Barmby on the Marsh ..205 B7
Barnoldswick 171 D1
Barnoldswick 103 A2
Barrowcliff 212 D7
Barton 21 D7
Barton Hill 146 D3
Barton-le-Street 120 E5
Barton-le-Willows 146 D1
Barwick in Elmet 194 B8
Battersby 27 D6
Beadlam 93 C7
Beal 202 D4
Beamsley 174 F7
Beckermonds 80 D3
Beckwithshaw 178 A7
Bedale 63 B2
Bedlam 161 A8
Bell Busk 155 A3
Bellerby 60 D7
Ben Rhydding 218 E3
Beningbrough 165 D4
Bent 187 D7
Bewerley 137 B3
Bickerton 181 A5
Biggin 196 E5
Bilbrough 182 D1
Bilton 219 E6
Bilton in Ainsty 181 E4
Binsoe 86 F2
Birdforth 116 E6
Birdsall 148 B4
Birkby 23 B1
Birkin 202 D6
Birstwith 160 E6
Bishop Monkton 140 A5
Bishop Thornton 138 F2
Bishop Wilton 169 F2
Bishopthorpe 231 B3
Bishopton 113 D2
Black Banks 3 D2
Blackwell 3 B4
Blades 37 B5
Blazefield 137 E4
Blubberhouses 159 D2
Boltby 66 F1
Bolton Abbey 174 E8
Bolton Bridge 174 F8
Bolton Percy 190 D4
Bolton-on-Swale 41 F6
Boosbeck 9 E8
Bootham Stray 225 B2
Boothferry 205 F5
Booze 17 F1
Bordley 133 D3
Boroughbridge 141 C5
Borrowby 11 D6
Borrowby 65 E4
Bossall 168 D7
Boston Spa 188 F8
Botton 29 B3
Bouthwaite 110 E2
Bracewell 171 C3
Brackenbottom 105 E3
Brafferton 116 A1
Braidley 83 B2
Bramham 188 F5
Brandsby 118 C3
Branksome 2 F6
Branton Green 142 A1
Brawby 94 F1
Brawith 26 A6
Braythorn 177 E4
Brayton 232 A2
Brearton 162 A7
Breighton 199 D5
Bridge Hewick 114 B1
Bridgehouse Gate 137 B4
Briggswath 32 B7
Briscoerigg 177 F5
Brockfield 167 E2
Brompton 43 F3
Brompton-by-Sawdon ..98 C5
Brompton-on-Swale 41 B7
Brookfield 6 E6
Brotherton 201 D5
Broughton 121 D4
Broughton 172 E6
Broxa 74 C6
Brunthwaite 174 D1
Bubwith 199 D7
Buckden 107 E8
Bugthorpe 169 D4
Bullamoor 44 B1
Bulmer 146 B6
Burley in Wharfedale ..176 B1
Burn 203 D7
Burn Bridge 222 D3
Burneston 87 E7
Burniston 75 C8
Burnsall 157 B8
Burnt Yates 160 F8
Burrill 62 E2
Burtersett 56 E4
Burton Fleming 126 E3
Burton in Lonsdale 102 F3
Burton Leonard 140 B2
Burton Salmon 201 F6
Burythorpe 147 F3
Buttercrambe 168 F5
Butterwick 120 E8
Butterwick 125 B2
Byland Abbey 91 E1
Byram 201 F4

C

- Calcutt 221 A3
- Caldbergh 84 B7
- Caldwell 1 B4
- Calton 155 B6
- Camblesforth 204 D5
- Camp Hill 87 F5
- Cantsfield 102 B4
- Carlbury 2 B7
- Carlesmoor 111 E4
- Carleton in Craven 173 A4
- Carlton 1 F3
- Carlton 204 D3
- Carlton 83 E7
- Carlton 68 E1
- Carlton Husthwaite 116 F7
- Carlton in Cleveland 26 A3
- Carlton Miniott 89 C4
- Carperby 58 E4
- Carthorpe 87 E6
- Castle Bolton 59 A6
- Castleford 200 E4
- Castleton 29 A6
- Castley 178 A1
- Cattal 164 A1
- Catterick 41 D5
- Catterick Bridge 41 D6
- Catterick Garrison 209 D2
- Catterton 190 B8
- Catton 88 F1
- Cawood 197 B8
- Cawthorne 71 D4
- Cawton 119 C7
- Cayton 100 C6
- Chantry 59 D2
- Chapel Fields 227 B3
- Chapel Haddlesey 203 C5
- Chapel-le-Dale 104 C8
- Charltons 9 C6
- Chop Gate 46 F6
- Church Fenton 196 B7
- Church Houses 48 F4
- Clapham 130 C8
- Clapham Green 160 E5
- Claxton 168 B7
- Cleasby 2 F4
- Cliffe 198 E2
- Cliffe 2 B6
- Clifford 188 E7
- Clifton 176 F3
- Clifton 228 A7
- Clifton Park 227 F7
- Clint 161 A6
- Clints 39 C8
- Clough 55 A7
- Cloughton 54 C1
- Cloughton Newlands 54 C2
- Coates 171 E2
- Cobby Syke 159 F2
- Cock Hill 165 B2
- Cockayne 48 A5
- Cockerton 3 B6
- Colburn 41 A5
- Cold Cotes 103 F2
- Cold Kirby 91 D7
- Collingham 188 A8
- Colsterdale 84 E4
- Colton 190 E7
- Commondale 9 D1
- Coneysthorpe 120 D2
- Coneythorpe 163 A5
- Coniston Cold 155 A1
- Conistone 134 C6
- Cononley 173 C2
- Cononley Woodside 173 C3
- Constable Burton 61 C5
- Coomboots 75 B6
- Copgrove 140 C2
- Copmanthorpe 230 B2
- Copt Hewick 114 C2
- Cotterdale 55 F8
- Cotton Tree 186 A2
- Coulby Newham 7 A5
- Coulton 119 B5
- Countersett 57 C2
- Coverham 60 C1
- Cowan Bridge 102 D7
- Cowesby 66 C4
- Cowling 62 D2
- Cowling 187 B6
- Cowthorpe 180 E7
- Coxwold 117 D8
- Crackpot 37 B3
- Cracoe 156 C7
- Crag 187 D6
- Crakehill 115 E4
- Crambe 146 F3
- Crambeck 146 F6
- Crathorne 25 A6
- Cray 81 E2
- Crayke 118 A1
- Cridling Stubbs 206 C8
- Crimple 223 D8
- Cringles 174 C3
- Crockey Hill 184 A1
- Croft-on-Tees 22 D8
- Cropton 71 B4
- Crosby Court 65 B6
- Cross Hills 187 E7
- Cross Lanes 143 D3
- Crossgates 99 E7
- Crowdon 54 A4
- Cubeck 57 F4
- Cundall 115 E3
- Cutsyke 200 E3

D

- Dacre 159 F7
- Dacre Banks 159 F8
- Dalby 119 B2
- Dalesbridge Centre 130 E6
- Dallow 111 F2
- Dalton 19 D7
- Dalton 115 F7
- Dalton Gates 22 D4
- Dalton-on-Tees 22 E6
- Danby 29 C7
- Danby Wiske 43 C5
- Darley 160 A6
- Darlington 3 E6
- Daw Cross 222 B3
- Deepdale 80 F2
- Deerstones 175 B8
- Deighton 44 A8
- Deighton 192 A7
- Denton 176 A3
- Dishforth 115 A4
- Downholme 39 D4
- Draughton 174 B7
- Drax 204 F5
- Drebley 157 D6
- Dringhouses 230 E8
- Duggleby 149 B6
- Dunkeswick 178 E2
- Dunnington 184 F7
- Dunsley 12 F2

E

- Eaglescliffe 5 E5
- Earby 172 B1
- Earswick 226 A7
- Easby 27 B7
- Easby 209 F5
- Easington 11 A8
- Easingwold 143 D8
- East Appleton 41 D2
- East Ayton 99 B8
- East Barnby 12 C3
- East Common 232 E4
- East Cottingwith 193 C5
- East Cowton 22 F2
- East Garforth 194 E4
- East Harlsey 44 E6
- East Hauxwell 61 D8
- East Heslerton 124 A7
- East Knapton 123 C6
- East Layton 20 C8
- East Lutton 150 C8
- East Marton 172 B6
- East Ness 94 B1
- East Newton 93 C2
- East Rounton 24 E2
- East Row 13 A3
- East Witton 61 A1
- Eastbourne 3 E4
- Eastburn 187 F7
- Eastby 156 F1
- Easterside 7 A7
- Eastfield 100 A7
- Eavestone 138 B7
- Ebberston 97 E5
- Eggborough 202 F2
- Egglescliffe 5 E4
- Egton 31 B5
- Egton Bridge 31 A4
- Eldroth 130 E4
- Ellerbeck 44 F3
- Ellerburn 96 E7
- Ellerton 193 C2
- Ellerton 41 F4
- Ellingstring 85 D6
- Elton 5 C8
- Elvington 185 B2
- Embsay 217 D8
- Enterpen 25 C4
- Eppleby 1 E4
- Eryholme 23 A7
- Escrick 192 B5
- Eshton 155 D3
- Everley 74 F4
- Exelby 63 D1

F

- Faceby 25 F2
- Fadmoor 69 F4
- Fairburn 201 D7
- Falsgrave 212 D3
- Fangdale Beck 47 A1
- Farlington 144 F6
- Farnham 162 D7
- Farnhill 173 E1
- Farnley 177 B2
- Faverdale 3 B8
- Fawdington 115 F3
- Fearby 85 F4
- Feetham 37 C5
- Feizor 131 B6
- Felixkirk 90 C7
- Fenwick 207 D3
- Ferrensby 162 F7
- Ferrybridge 201 D3
- Fewston 159 F1
- Fewston Bents 159 F1
- Filey 101 C3
- Finghall 61 D4
- Firby 63 A1
- Firby 147 A5
- Firth Moor 3 F4
- Fishpool 177 C2
- Flasby 155 E3
- Flawith 142 E4
- Flaxby 163 B4
- Flaxton 145 F1
- Fleets 156 A7
- Flixton 99 F2
- Folkton 100 B2
- Follifoot 223 F5
- Forcett 1 D3
- Fordon 126 A6
- Foredale 131 C8
- Forest 42 B7
- Forest Moor 220 F3
- Foston 146 B4
- Foul Green 9 E1
- Foulrice 118 F1
- Fowgill 129 B8
- Foxholes 125 D3
- Foxton 44 E3
- Foxup 106 C7
- Fremington 38 D6
- Fryton 120 A6
- Fulford 231 E7
- Full Sutton 169 A2
- Fylingthorpe 33 B3

G

- Gainford 1 D8
- Galphay 112 F3
- Gammersgill 83 C5
- Ganthorpe 120 A1
- Ganton 125 A8
- Garforth 194 C4
- Gargrave 155 D1
- Garriston 61 B7
- Gate Helmsley 168 B2
- Gateforth 203 A7
- Gatenby 64 A2
- Gauber 78 F1
- Gayle 56 D4
- Gayles 19 E6
- Gerrick 10 C3
- Giggleswick 131 C2
- Gill 187 A6
- Gillamoor 70 A5
- Gilling East 118 F8
- Gilling West 20 E4
- Girsby 23 D7
- Glaisdale 30 D4
- Glass Houghton 201 A3
- Glasshouses 137 C3
- Glusburn 187 D8
- Goathland 51 E8
- Goldsborough 163 A2
- Goldsborough 12 D5
- Gollinglith Foot 85 B3
- Goulton 25 E3
- Gowdall 204 A1
- Gowthorpe 169 C1
- Grafton 141 D2
- Grange 57 D5
- Grassington 134 E3
- Great Ayton 7 F2
- Great Barugh 95 A1
- Great Broughton 26 E5
- Great Burdon 3 F8
- Great Busby 26 C4
- Great Crakehall 62 E4
- Great Edstone 94 C7
- Great Fencote 63 C8
- Great Habton 121 B7
- Great Heck 207 D7
- Great Langton 42 D3
- Great Ouseburn 164 B8
- Great Preston 200 C8
- Great Smeaton 23 C3
- Great Thirkleby 90 D1
- Green Close 130 A8
- Green Hammerton 164 C3
- Green Hill 194 F8
- Greenhow 136 D3
- Grewelthorpe 112 D7
- Greygarth 111 F3
- Greystonegill 129 C8
- Grimston 229 E3
- Grindale 127 D2
- Grinton 38 C5
- Gristhorpe 100 E4
- Grosmont 31 D3
- Grunsagill 153 A1
- Guisborough 8 D7
- Gunby 199 D6
- Gunnerside 36 F4

H

- Hackforth 62 E8
- Hackness 74 F5
- Hall Garth 184 F6
- Halton East 174 C8
- Halton Gill 106 E7
- Halton West 154 A1
- Hambleton 174 D8
- Hambleton 196 F1
- Hampsthwaite 160 F5
- Hanlith 155 A8
- Hardgate 139 A1
- Hardraw 56 C6
- Harlow Hill 222 A8
- Harmby 60 E4
- Harome 93 C4
- Harrogate 219 D1
- Harrowgate Hill 3 C8
- Harrowgate Village 3 E8
- Hartforth 20 D5
- Hartley 14 A7
- Hartlington 157 C8
- Harton 168 C8
- Hartwith 160 B8
- Haughton Le Skerne 3 F6
- Hawes 56 D4
- Hawkswick 107 F1
- Hawnby 67 E4
- Hazlewood 175 A8
- Healaugh 182 A2
- Healaugh 37 F6
- Healey 85 E3
- Heathfield 136 F6
- Heathwaite 45 E8
- Hebden 135 A1
- Hellifield 154 B3
- Hellifield Green 154 B3
- Helm 57 D6
- Helmsley 92 F7
- Helperby 142 A8
- Helperthorpe 124 D1
- Helwith Bridge 131 D8
- Hemingbrough 198 F1
- Hemlington 6 F4
- Hensall 203 D2
- Heslington 229 B1
- Hessay 182 C8
- Hetton 155 F5
- Hew Green 160 D5
- Heworth 228 F6
- Heyshaw 159 D8
- High Bentham 129 B8
- High Birstwith 160 D5
- High Bradley 173 E4
- High Catton 185 D8
- High Coniscliffe 2 C6
- High Ellington 85 F6
- High Grantley 138 D8
- High Harrogate 220 A3
- High Hawsker 33 B6
- High Hutton 147 B7
- High Kilburn 91 B2
- High Leven 6 A3
- High Marishes 96 B1
- High Mowthorpe 149 D7
- High Shaw 56 D7
- High Stakesby 208 B5
- High Worsall 24 A8
- Highfield 199 E7
- Hillam 202 A7
- Hilton 6 C2
- Hinderwell 11 F7
- Hipswell 209 F1
- Hirst Courtney 203 F3
- Hole Bottom 135 A3
- Holgate 227 F3
- Hollinthorpe 194 A2
- Holly Hill 209 B5
- Holme 88 D5
- Holme Green 190 F4
- Holtby 167 F1
- Hopetown 200 C2
- Hopgrove 226 D2
- Hopperton 163 E3
- Hornby 23 E4
- Hornby 62 B8
- Horsehouse 83 C4
- Horton 171 B5
- Horton in Ribblesdale 105 C3
- Houlsyke 29 F6
- Hovingham 119 F6
- Howe 88 E3
- Howgill 157 E6
- Howsham 146 F1
- Hubberholme 81 C1
- Huby 144 A4
- Huby 178 B2
- Hudswell 40 A7
- Hummersknott 3 A5
- Hunmanby 126 F8
- Hunsingore 180 F8
- Huntington 225 E3
- Hunton 61 E7
- Hurgill 209 A7
- Hurworth Place 3 D1
- Hurworth-on-Tees 3 E1
- Hut Green 203 A2
- Hutton Bonville 43 C7
- Hutton Buscel 98 E7
- Hutton Conyers 114 A4
- Hutton Gate 8 D6
- Hutton Hang 61 D3
- Hutton Mulgrave 12 D1
- Hutton Rudby 25 C5
- Hutton Sessay 116 D7
- Hutton Village 8 E4
- Hutton Wandesley 182 A5
- Hutton-le-Hole 70 C5
- Huttons Ambo 147 B6

I

- Ickornshaw 187 A6
- Ilkley 218 B4
- Ilton 85 E1
- Ingerthorpe 139 C5
- Ingleby Arncliffe 45 B8
- Ingleby Barwick 6 B4
- Ingleby Cross 45 A7
- Ingleby Greenhow 27 C5
- Ingleton 103 D3
- Ingmanthorpe 180 E5
- Inholmes 189 C6
- Ireby 102 F6
- Irton 99 D6
- Ivelet 36 D5

J

- Jennyfield 219 A5
- Junction 187 F8

K

- Keasden 130 A5
- Kelbrook 186 A8
- Keld 35 E8
- Keld Houses 136 C2
- Keldholme 70 D1
- Kelfield 191 D1
- Kellingley 202 C2
- Kellington 202 F4
- Kennythorpe 147 F5
- Kepwick 66 C6
- Kettleness 12 D6
- Kettlesing 160 C3
- Kettlesing Bottom 160 D4
- Kettlewell 108 B3
- Kexby 185 C6
- Key Green 31 A3
- Kilburn 91 B2
- Kildale 27 E8
- Kildwick 187 F8
- Killerby 100 C5
- Killinghall 161 C5
- Kilnsey 134 B6
- Kilton Thorpe 10 B8
- Kiplin 42 B4
- Kippax 194 E1
- Kirby Grindalythe 149 E6
- Kirby Hill 20 A5
- Kirby Knowle 66 C2
- Kirby Misperton 95 D2
- Kirby Sigston 44 D1
- Kirby Underdale 170 A5
- Kirby Wiske 88 F8
- Kirk Deighton 180 B5
- Kirk Hammerton 164 C2
- Kirk Smeaton 206 B3
- Kirkbridge 62 F5
- Kirkby 26 D5
- Kirkby Fleetham 42 D1
- Kirkby Hill 141 B7
- Kirkby Malham 154 F8
- Kirkby Malzeard 112 D5
- Kirkby Mills 94 C8

Kirkby Overblow 179 A4
Kirkby Wharfe 190 A3
Kirkbymoorside 70 B1
Kirkham 147 A4
Kirklevington 24 F8
Kirklington 88 A4
Knapton 227 A5
Knaresborough 221 A6
Knavesmire 230 F7
Knayton 65 F2
Knedlington 205 F6
Knottingley 201 F3
Knottingley 202 B2
Knox 219 B7

L

Lane End 171 C2
Lane Ends 187 C6
Laneshaw Bridge 186 C4
Langbar 175 B6
Langbaurgh 7 F2
Langcliffe 131 E3
Langthorne 62 F6
Langthorpe 141 A6
Langthwaite 17 E1
Langtoft 151 D5
Langton 147 F6
Lastingham 70 F5
Laverton 112 D4
Lawkland 130 F5
Lawkland Green 131 A4
Layerthorpe 228 E4
Leake 65 F5
Lealholm 30 B6
Lealholm Side 30 D7
Leathley 177 D2
Leavening 147 E1
Lebberston 100 D5
Leck 102 E7
Ledsham 201 B8
Ledston 200 F7
Ledston Luck 194 F1
Leeming 63 D4
Leeming Bar 63 C5
Leighton 85 C2
Leppington 169 C8
Levisham 72 D5
Leyburn 60 D5
Leysthorpe 93 B1
Lindley 177 C4
Lingdale 9 F7
Lingerfield 162 B6
Lingfield 3 F5
Linton 180 A1
Linton 134 D1
Linton-on-Ouse 164 E7
Little Airmyn 205 E4
Little Ayton 8 B1
Little Barugh 95 C2
Little Crakehall 62 D5
Little Fencote 63 C8
Little Fenton 196 B6
Little Habton 121 A8
Little Heck 203 D1
Little Hutton 116 B7
Little Ouseburn 164 A7
Little Preston 194 B1
Little Ribston 180 A8
Little Sessay 116 C5
Little Skipwith 192 D1
Little Smeaton 23 C2
Little Smeaton 206 C3
Little Stainforth 131 D6
Little Studley 214 C7
Littlethorpe 214 F1
Litton 107 A5
Liverton 10 D6
Liverton Mines 10 C8
Lockton 72 D4
Lodge Green 36 F5
Lofthouse 110 C4
Londonderry 63 E2
Long Drax 205 A6
Long Lease 33 A7
Long Marston 182 A6
Long Preston 153 F5
Longnewton 5 A7
Longscales 160 C4
Loscoe 200 C1
Lothersdale 187 A8
Low Bentham 128 F8
Low Bradley 173 E3
Low Catton 185 C8
Low Coniscliffe 2 F4
Low Dalby 72 F2
Low Dinsdale 4 C1
Low Ellington 86 A6
Low Garth 29 F4
Low Gate 138 F6
Low Gatherley 21 D1
Low Green 160 A6
Low Grantley 112 E1
Low Hawsker 33 A6
Low Hutton 147 C6
Low Laithe 137 F2
Low Marishes 122 C8
Low Mill 48 E2
Low Row 37 C4
Low Snaygill 173 D4
Low Town 5 B1
Low Whita 37 D5
Low Worsall 24 A8
Lower Altofts 200 A3
Lower Dunsforth 142 A4
Lower Mickletown 200 D6
Lower Westhouse 103 B4
Lowgill 128 F3
Lowna 70 A6
Lumb 187 A4
Lumby 195 E1
Lund 198 D3
Lythe 12 E4

M

Malham 133 A1
Maltby 6 C4
Malton 215 C4
Manfield 2 B4
Manor Park 176 B2
Margrove Park 9 D6
Markington 139 D3
Marrick 38 F4
Marsett 57 A1
Marske 39 C7
Marton 94 F6
Marton 141 D1
Marton 7 B7
Marton-in-the-Forest 144 E7
Marton-le-Moor 114 F1
Masham 86 B3
Masongill 103 A6
Maunby 64 D1
Meagill 159 D3
Mearbeck 153 D7
Melmerby 83 F8
Melmerby 114 C7
Melsonby 21 A7
Menethorpe 147 D6
Menthorpe 199 C5
Merrybent 2 E5
Methley 200 B5
Methley Junction 200 A4
Mewith Head 129 E6
Mickleby 12 A4
Micklefield 194 F4
Mickletown 200 B5
Mickley 112 F7
Middlecave 215 A5
Middleham 60 E2
Middlesmoor 110 B5
Middlethorpe 231 B6
Middleton 187 A6
Middleton 218 C7
Middleton 95 E8
Middleton One Row 4 D3
Middleton Quernhow 88 B1
Middleton St George 4 B2
Middleton Tyas 21 D5
Middleton-on-Leven 25 D8
Milby 141 B6
Mill Dam 129 C6
Mill Hirst 159 F7
Minskip 141 A3
Monk Fryston 202 B8
Monkhill 201 B1
Monkroyd 186 D4
Moor End 188 D8
Moor Monkton 165 A3
Moorsholm 10 B5
Morton-on-Swale 64 A6
Moss 207 D1
Moulton 21 D3
The Mount 214 D3
Mount Pleasant 7 B5
Mowden 3 A6
Moxby 144 D5
Muker 36 A5
Murton 184 D7
Muscoates 94 A3
Muston 100 F2
Myton-on-Swale 141 F5

N

Naburn 191 D8
Nappa 171 B8
Nawton 93 E7
Neasham 4 A1
Nesfield 175 B4
Nether Burrow 102 B6
Nether Poppleton 224 A2
Nether Silton 66 B7
Netherby 179 B1
New Earswick 225 D3
New Fryston 201 B6
New Houses 105 C4
New Micklefield 195 A3
New Park 219 B5
New Road Side 187 B5
New Row 8 F1
New Thirsk 211 A3
New Town 201 B2
New York 137 F1
Newall 176 F1
Newbiggin 57 F6
Newbiggin 101 A5
Newbiggin 82 D8
Newbridge 96 A8
Newby 104 A1
Newby 7 A3
Newby 75 E5
Newby 140 D6
Newby Cote 104 B1
Newby Wiske 64 E2
Newholm 13 A1
Newland 205 B3
Newsham 19 D8
Newsham 89 A8
Newsholme 171 A6
Newsholme 205 E8
Newthorpe 195 D3
Newton Kyme 189 B7
Newton Morrell 21 E8
Newton Mulgrave 11 E6
Newton under Roseberry 8 B4
Newton upon Derwent 185 E4
Newton-le-Willows 62 B4
Newton-on-Ouse 165 B6
Newton-on-Rawcliffe 72 A5
Nidd 161 E6
Norby 211 A4
Normanby 94 F4
Normanton 200 C1
North Cowton 22 C3
North Deighton 180 B6
North Duffield 199 A8
North Featherstone 200 E1
North Grimston 148 E6
North Ings 119 D1
North Kilvington 89 E8
North Lees 113 E4
North Otterington 64 D4
North Rigton 178 B5
North Stainley 113 D7
Northallerton 210 D4
Norton 206 E2
Norton-le-Clay 115 C2
Norton-on-Derwent 215 D3
Nosterfield 87 B3
Nun Appleton 190 F3
Nun Monkton 165 A4
Nunnington 93 E2
Nunthorpe 7 D5
Nunthorpe 231 C8
Nunwick 114 A5

O

Oak Tree 4 E4
Oakdale 161 B2
Oatlands 222 F6
Octon 151 F8
Old Byland 91 F8
Old Malton 215 E7
Old Micklefield 194 F4
Old Thirsk 211 C4
Oldstead 91 C3
Ormesby 7 C8
Osbaldwick 229 C4
Osgodby 198 C4
Osgodby 100 B7
Osgodby Common 198 C6
Osmotherley 45 C4
Oswaldkirk 93 A1
Otterburn 154 E4
Oughtershaw 80 C4
Oulston 117 E5
Outhgill 34 A8
Over Burrow 102 B7
Over Silton 66 B8
Overton 165 F2
Overtown 102 C7
Oxton 190 A6

P

Padside 159 B6
Padside Green 159 C6
Painsthorpe 170 B5
Pannal 222 E3
Pannal Ash 222 B5
Park 186 F5
Park End 7 B8
Parlington 194 E6
Pateley Bridge 137 C5
Patrick Brompton 62 C5
Pickering 95 E6
Pickhill 88 C6
Picton 24 D6
Piercebridge 2 A6
Place Newton 123 C3
Pockley 69 B1
Pollington 207 F6
Poole 201 F5
Port Mulgrave 11 F8
Potterton 188 C1
Potto 25 D2
Preston-on-Tees 5 F7
Preston-under-Scar 59 E6
Primrose Valley 101 C1

R

Rainton 114 E6
Ramsgill 110 E1
Raskelf 116 E2
Rathmell 153 C6
Ravenseat 15 C2
Ravensworth 20 A7
Raw 33 B4
Rawcliffe 205 A1
Rawcliffe 224 E2
Raydale 57 A1
Raygill 186 E8
Red Hill 201 A4
Redmire 59 C6
Reeth 38 B6
Reighton 127 D6
Riccall 198 A8
Richmond 209 C7
Rievaulx 92 B8
Rillington 122 F5
Ripley 161 C7
Ripon 214 E5
Risplith 138 E7
Robin Hood's Bay 33 D4
Roecliffe 140 F4
Romanby 210 B3
Rookwith 62 A1
Rosedale Abbey 49 E3
Rossett Green 222 D5
Roundhill Village 5 F5
Rowden 160 F4
Roxby 11 C7
Rudby 25 D5
Rufforth 182 C6
Runswick Bay 12 A7
Rushton 98 D6
Ruswarp 208 B3
Rylstone 156 B5
Ryther 190 F1
Ryton 121 F6

S

Sadberge 4 B8
St John's 194 F8
Salton 94 D3
Sand Hutton 168 B5
Sandhutton 89 A4
Sandsend 13 A3
Satron 36 D4
Sawdon 98 C7
Sawley 138 F6
Saxton 195 D8
Scackleton 119 C4
Scagglethorpe 122 D3
Scalby 75 D6
Scaling 11 A4
Scaling Dam 11 A4
Scampston 123 A6
Scarborough 213 B5
Scarthingwell 195 F7
Scawton 91 E6
Scorton 41 F7
Scotton 40 F2
Scotton 162 A6
Scrayingham 168 F7
Scriven 162 D5
Scruton 63 D7
Seamer 6 F1
Seamer 99 E6
Seave Green 47 A7
Sedbusk 56 E6
Selby 232 C6
Selly Hill 32 A8
Selside 105 A6
Sessay 116 B6
Settle 131 E3
Settrington 122 D1
Sexhow 25 D4
Sharow 214 F6
Shaw Mills 138 F1
Sherburn 124 D8
Sherburn in Elmet 195 E5
Sheriff Hutton 145 C5
Shipton 165 F5
Sicklinghall 179 E3
Silpho 74 E7
Silsden 174 C2
Simonstone 56 D6
Sinderby 88 C4
Sinnington 95 A8
Skeeby 21 A1
Skelton 224 C6
Skelton on Ure 140 E7
Skerne Park 3 C3
Skewsby 119 A1
Skipton 216 F4
Skipton-on-Swale 88 E2
Skipwith 192 E1
Skirethorns 134 C2
Skirpenbeck 169 A4
Skyreholme 157 E7
Slapewath 9 C6
Sledmere 150 B3
Sleights 32 A6
Slingsby 120 C6
Small Banks 174 F3
Smelthouses 137 F3
Snainton 98 A5
Snaith 204 C1
Snape 87 A7
Sneaton 32 D6
Sneatonthorpe 32 F5
Sockburn 23 C5
Sourby 176 D8
South Bank 228 B1
South Duffield 199 A4
South Kilvington 211 B7
South Loftus 10 E8
South Milford 195 F1
South Otterington 64 F2
South Stainley 139 E2
Sowerby 211 C1
The Spa 213 B4
Spacey Houses 223 A2
Spaunton 70 E4
Speeton 127 F5
Spennithorne 60 F3
Spofforth 179 E5
Sproxton 92 F4
Stackhouse 131 D4
Stainburn 177 F3
Stainforth 131 E6
Stainsacre 32 F7
Stainton 39 C3
Stainton 6 D5
Staintondale 54 B5
Stalling Busk 81 B8
Stamford Bridge 168 D2
Stanwick-St-John 1 E2
Stape 71 F8
Stapleton 3 A2
Starbeck 220 C4
Starbotton 107 F5
Staupes 160 C4
Staveley 140 F1
Staxton 99 E2
Stead 176 A1
Stean 110 A4
Stearsby 118 F2
Stillingfleet 191 C3
Stillington 144 C6
Stirton 216 C6
Stock 171 C3
Stockton on the Forest 167 D3
Stokesley 26 D7
Stone House 78 F8
Stonegate 30 D8
Stonegrave 119 D8
Stranghow 9 F6
Street 29 F3
Street Houses 190 C8
Streetlam 42 F5
Strensall 167 A7
Strensall Camp 167 B6
Studfold 105 D1
Studley Roger 113 D1
Studley Royal 113 C1
Stutton 189 D4
Suffield 75 A5
Summerbridge 138 A1
Summerscales 158 C1
Sutton 201 F4
Sutton Howgrave 87 F1
Sutton upon Derwent 185 C1
Sutton-in-Craven 187 F6
Sutton-on-the-Forest 144 C3
Sutton-under-Whitestonecliffe 90 E5
Swainby 45 E8
Swaledale 37 C4
Swartha 174 D1
Swathgill 119 B4
Swetton 111 F4
Swillington 194 A1
Swillington Common 194 A3
Swincliffe 160 E4
Swinden 154 C1
Swinithwaite 59 C4
Swinton 121 C4
Swinton 86 B2

T

Tadcaster 189 D6

Tame Bridge 26 A7
Tang 160 D4
Tang Hall 228 F5
Tanton 7 C1
Temple Hirst 203 E4
Terrington 119 F1
Theakston 87 E8
Thimbleby 45 A2
Thirlby 90 E7
Thirn 86 B8
Thirsk 211 C2
Thixendale 170 E7
Tholthorpe 142 D5
Thoralby 58 E1
Thorganby 193 B4
Thorgill 49 C3
Thorlby 216 B6
Thormanby 116 F5
Thornaby-on-Tees 6 A7
Thornborough 87 C2
Thorns 35 E7
Thornthwaite 159 D6
Thornton 6 E4
Thornton in Lonsdale 103 C4
Thornton Rust 58 B4
Thornton Steward 61 D1
Thornton Watlass 86 D8
Thornton-in-Craven 172 A3
Thornton-le-Beans 65 B5
Thornton-le-Clay 146 A4
Thornton-le-Dale 96 D5
Thornton-le-Moor 65 B3
Thornton-le-Street 65 D1
Thorp Arch 188 F8
Thorpe 156 F8
Thorpe Bassett 123 A4
Thorpe Underwood 164 C6
Thorpe Willoughby 197 B2
Threshfield 134 D2
Thrintoft 64 A8
Throxenby 212 A7
Thruscross 159 A5
Thwaite 35 F5
Thwing 126 B1
Timble 176 D7
Tockwith 181 D7
Tollerton 143 A3
Tollesby 7 A6
Topcliffe 115 B7
Tosside 152 F3
Toulston 189 B7
Town Head 174 C1
Towthorpe 149 D1
Towthorpe 167 B5
Towton 189 E2
Trawden 186 B1
Tunstall 41 B2
Tunstall 102 B4

U

Uckerby 21 E1
Ugglebarnby 32 C6
Ugthorpe 11 F2
Ulleskelf 190 C2
Ulshaw 61 A2
Upper Dunsforth 142 A2
Upper Helmsley 168 B3
Upper Poppleton 165 F1
Upsall 66 B2
Ure Bank 214 D7
Urlay Nook 5 B5
Urra 47 A8

V

Vicar's Green 39 F7

W

Waithwith Banks 40 B5
Wake Hill 111 F1
Walden Stubbs 206 F3
Walkerville 41 A4
Walmgate Stray 228 F1
Walshford 180 D8
Walton 181 A2
Warlaby 64 D6
Warsill 138 C4
Warthermarske 86 A1
Warthill 167 F2
Washfold 18 D1
Wass 91 F2
Water Fryston 201 C5
Wath 137 A6
Wath 119 F6
Wath 114 A7
Weaverthorpe 124 E1
Weeton 178 C1
Welburn 94 A7
Welburn 146 D7
Welbury 24 B1
Well 87 A4
Wennington 102 B1
Wensley 60 A4
Wensleydale 57 A5
Wescoe Hill 178 B1
West Appleton 41 C1
West Ayton 99 A7
West Barnby 12 C3
West Burton 58 F1
West Cliff 208 B7
West Field 227 A2
West Garforth 194 B3
West Haddlesey 203 A5
West Harlsey 44 D5
West Heslerton 123 F7
West Knapton 123 B6
West Layton 20 A8
West Lilling 145 C4
West Lutton 150 B8
West Marton 171 F5
West Ness 94 B1
West Rounton 24 D2
West Scrafton 83 F6
West Stonesdale 15 E1
West Tanfield 87 A1
West Witton 59 E3
Westerdale 28 E4
Westfield 232 C4
Westhouse 103 C4
Weston 176 E2
Westow 147 B4
Wetherby 180 D4
Wharfe 131 A8
Wharram le Street 149 A4
Whashton 20 A5
Whashton Green 20 A5
Whaw 17 B3
Wheldale 201 B5
Wheldrake 192 F8
Whenby 145 B8
Whinfield 3 F8
Whitby 208 C6
Whitewall Corner 215 C1
Whitley 207 A7
Whitley Thorpe 206 F7
Whittington 102 A7
Whitwell 42 B6
Whitwell-on-the-Hill 146 E4
Whitwood 200 C3
Whixley 164 A5
Whorlton 25 E1
Wiganthorpe 119 E3
Wigginton 166 D5
Wigglesworth 153 C3
Wighill 181 D1
Wilberfoss 185 F5
Willerby 99 C2
Wilsill 137 E3
Wilton 97 A5
Winewall 186 B2
Winksley 112 F2
Winsley 160 D8
Winterburn 155 D5
Winton 44 C3
Wintringham 123 C4
Wistow 197 D6
Wold Newton 126 A3
Wombleton 93 F7
Womersley 206 C6
Wood Row 200 A6
Woodale 83 A2
Woodhall 58 B5
Woodhall 199 B2
Woodhouse 200 A1
Woodlands 220 C1
Woodthorpe 230 C7
Worton 57 F5
Wray 128 A6
Wrayton 102 B3
Wrelton 71 C1
Wressle 199 D2
Wycoller 186 C2
Wydra 160 A1
Wykeham 122 B6
Wykeham 98 E6

Y

Yafforth 43 C1
Yarm 5 D3
Yearsley 118 C5
Yedingham 97 D2
Yockenthwaite 81 A1
York 233 B3
Youlthorpe 169 C2
Youlton 142 E2

A

A W Nielson Rd DN14 . .205 F2
Abber La LS24 . . . . .182 A2
Abbeville Ave 1 YO21 . .208 B6
Abbey Cl 12 LS29 . . . . . .175 A4
Abbey Crags Way
HG5 . . . . .221 C3
Abbey Cty Inf Sch DL3 . . .3 B5
Abbey Gdns
Darlington DL3 . . . . .3 B5
Pontefract WF8 . . . . .201 B2
Abbey Hill BD23 . . . . . . .155 C5
Abbey Jun Sch DL3 . . . . . .3 B5
Abbey La YO22 . . . . .208 E7
Abbey Leisure Ctr
YO8 . . . . .232 C5
Abbey Mews WF8 . . . . .201 B2
Abbey Mill Gdns HG5 . .221 C3
Abbey Mill View HG5 . .221 C3
Abbey Rd Darlington DL3 . .3 B5
Knaresborough HG5 . . . . . .221 B3
Sadberge DL2 . . . . .4 C7
Abbey St YO30 . . . . .228 A7
Abbey Walk Ret Pk
YO8 . . . . .232 C6
Abbey Wlk
Pontefract WF8 . . . . .201 B2
Selby YO8 . . . . .232 C5
Abbey Yd YO8 . . . . .232 C5
Abbot St YO31 . . . . .233 C4
Abbot's Garth YO12 . . . .99 D6
Abbot's Rd Selby YO8 . .232 E3
Whitby YO22 . . . . .208 E5
Abbots Way HG5 . . . . . .221 C3
Abbot's Wlk YO22 . . . . .208 E5
Abbotsford Rd YO10 . . .228 F3
Abbotsway YO31 . . . . . .228 E8
Abbotts Cl LS25 . . . . . . .194 F8
Abbotts Ct YO17 . . . . . .215 E4
Abelton Gr 33 YO32 . . . .166 E5
Aberdeen La 19 YO11 . . .213 A6
Aberdeen Pl 20 YO11 . . .213 A6
Aberdeen Rd DL1 . . . . .3 E8
Aberdeen St 17 YO11 . . .213 A6
Aberdeen Terr 21 YO11 .213 A6
Aberdeen Wlk 16 YO11 .213 A6
Aberford C of E Prim Sch
LS25 . . . . .194 F8
Aberford Rd
Barwick in Elmet & Scholes
LS15 . . . . .194 C8
Bramham cum Oglethorpe
LS23 . . . . .188 E5
Garforth LS25 . . . . .194 D4
Abram's View YO11 . . . .213 B2
Acacia Ave YO32 . . . . . .225 E4
Acacia Dr WF10 . . . . . . .201 B3
Academy Gdns DL2 . . . . . .1 D8
Acaster Ave YO23 . . . . .191 A3
Acaster Dr LS25 . . . . . .194 D3
Acaster La
Acaster Malbis YO23 . . . . .231 B1
Acaster Selby YO23 . . . . .191 A4
Accommodation Rd
YO25 . . . . .151 D6
Acklam Grange Sec Sch
TS5 . . . . .6 D7
Acklam Rd TS17 . . . . .6 C8
Acklam Whin Prim Sch
TS5 . . . . .6 D6
Ackton La WF7 . . . . . . .200 D1
Ackton Pasture La
WF7 . . . . .200 D2
Ackton Pastures Jun & Inf
Sch WF10 . . . . .200 D3
Acomb Prim Sch
YO24 . . . . .227 E3
Acomb Rd YO24 . . . . . . .227 D3
Acomb Wood Cl YO24 .230 C7
Acomb Wood Dr YO24 .230 B7
Acorn Cl 6 YO8 . . . . . . .198 B4
Acorn Way
Gateforth YO8 . . . . .197 B1
York YO24 . . . . .230 D7
Acre Fold 21 LS29 . . . . . .174 F4
Acre Mdw 1 BD22 . . . . .187 B6
Acre Rd 2 BD22 . . . . . .187 B6
Acres Cl 24 YO62 . . . . . . .92 F6
Acres La Brompton YO13 .98 C4
Helmsley YO62 . . . . .93 A6
Scrayingham YO41 . . . . . .169 B8
Acres The
Addingham LS29 . . . . . . .175 A5
Glusburn BD20 . . . . .187 E6
Stokesley TS9 . . . . .26 C8
Acresfield 11 BB8 . . . . . .186 A3
Acworth St 3 YO12 . . . .212 E4
Adam's Field La YO61 .117 F4
Adcott Rd TS5 . . . . .6 E7
Addingham Mid Sch
LS29 . . . . .174 F5
Addingham Prim Sch
LS29 . . . . .174 F5
Addingham Wharfedale
LS29 . . . . .174 E4
Addison Ave 18 WF6 . . .200 B1
Addison Rd TS9 . . . . .8 A1
Addison Villas HG3 . . . .219 A8
Addlethorpe La LS22 . .179 C3
Adelaide Rd
Middlesbrough TS7 . . . . . . .7 B6
6 Norton DN6 . . . . .206 E2
Adelaide St 3 YO23 . . . .228 B2
Adlington Cl 8 YO32 . . .167 A7
Admirals Ct YO7 . . . . . .211 A2
Admirals' Ct YO7 . . . . . .211 A2
Agar St YO31 . . . . .233 C3
Agnes Ing La LA2 . . . . . .128 A7
Agnesgate HG4 . . . . . . .214 D5
Aikengill Rd LA2 . . . . . .129 A4
Ailcey Rd HG4 . . . . .214 D5
Ainderby Rd DL7 . . . . . .210 B2
Ainsford Way TS7 . . . . . . .7 D8
Ainstable Rd TS7 . . . . . . .7 D8
Ainsty Ave YO24 . . . . . .230 F8
Ainsty Dr 2 LS22 . . . . . .180 C4
Ainsty Gr YO24 . . . . . . .230 F8
Ainsty Rd
Harrogate HG1 . . . . .219 F4
Wetherby LS22 . . . . .180 C4
Ainsty View
Acklam YO17 . . . . .169 E8
Whixley YO26 . . . . .164 A4
Ainsworth Way TS7 . . . . . .7 D8
Ainthorpe La YO21 . . . . .29 C7
Aintree Ct
9 Darlington DL1 . . . . .3 F6
York YO24 . . . . .230 F8
Aire Cres BD20 . . . . . . .187 E7
Aire Rd LS22 . . . . .180 B4
Aire St Castleford WF10 .200 E4
Glusburn BD20 . . . . .187 F7
Knottingley WF11 . . . . . . .202 A3
Aire Valley Cl BD20 . . .173 D3
Aire Valley Dr BD20 . . .173 D3
Aire View Inf Sch
BD20 . . . . .174 C1
Airedale Ave
Gargrave BD23 . . . . .155 D1
Skipton BD23 . . . . .217 B4
Airedale Dr WF10 . . . . .201 B5
Airedale High Sch
WF10 . . . . .201 B4
Airedale Mews 1 BD23 .216 E3
Airedale Rd
Castleford WF10 . . . . .201 A4
Scotton DL9 . . . . .40 D4
Airedale Trading Pk
BD20 . . . . .187 F8
Airedale View 1 BD20 . .187 F8
Aireside Ave BD20 . . . .173 D1
Aireside Terr BD20 . . . .173 D2
Aireville Dr BD20 . . . . .174 C1
Aireville Sch BD23 . . . .216 D4
Aireville Swimming Baths
BD23 . . . . .216 D4
Aireyholme La TS9 . . . . . .8 B2
Airmyn Park Prim Sch
DN14 . . . . .205 E4
Airmyn Rd DN14 . . . . . .205 D3
Airy Hill CP Sch YO21 .208 D5
Airy Hill La TS12 . . . . . . .9 D8
Aiskew Leeming Bar C of E
Sch DL7 . . . . .63 C4
Aislabie Cl HG4 . . . . . . .214 A5
Aislabie Garth HG4 . . . .214 A5
Aislaby Carr La YO18 . . .95 C7
Aislaby La Aislaby YO21 . .32 A8
Aislaby YO18 . . . . .95 C6
Aislaby Rd TS16 . . . . .5 D4
Aismunderby Cl HG4 . .214 C3
Aismunderby Rd HG4 . .214 C4
Aisne Rd DL9 . . . . .209 C1
Aketon Rd WF10 . . . . . .200 D3
Alanbrooke Barracks Cty
Prim Sch YO7 . . . . .89 A1
Alanbrooke Ind Est
YO7 . . . . .115 B8
Alandale Cres LS25 . . . .194 B3
Alandale Rd LS25 . . . . .194 B4
Albany Ave HG1 . . . . . . .219 E5
Albany Rd
Harrogate HG1 . . . . .219 E5
Middlesbrough TS7 . . . . . . .7 B6
Albany St 3 YO26 . . . . . .227 F5
Albany Wlk LS29 . . . . . .218 A3
Albatross Way DL1 . . . . . .3 E5
Albemarle Back Rd 10
YO11 . . . . .212 F6
Albemarle Cres 18
YO11 . . . . .213 A6
Albemarle Rd YO23 . . . .228 B2
Albermarle Dr 3 DL9 . . . .40 F5
Albert Cl 1 YO32 . . . . . .228 F8
Albert Hill BD24 . . . . . . .131 E2
Albert Pl
Harrogate HG1 . . . . .220 C4
1 Whitby YO21 . . . . .208 D7
Albert Rd
Eaglescliffe TS16 . . . . .5 E5
12 Glusburn BD20 . . . . . .187 E7
Harrogate HG1 . . . . .219 E5
1 Scarborough YO12 . . . .213 A7
Albert St 33 Earby BB18 .172 A1
Glusburn BD20 . . . . .187 F7
Harrogate HG1 . . . . .219 D2
Normanton South WF6 . . .200 B2
8 Scarborough YO12 . . . .213 A7
York YO10 . . . . .233 C1
Albert Terr
5 Harrogate HG1 . . . . . .219 D1
Skipton BD23 . . . . .216 F4
Albion Ave YO26 . . . . . .227 B6
Albion Cres 3 YO11 . . . .213 A4
Albion Pl 14 YO21 . . . . .208 D6
Albion Rd 25 Earby BB18 172 A1
Scarborough YO11 . . . . . .213 A4
Albion St Boosbeck TS12 . . .9 E7
Boston Spa LS23 . . . . .188 E7
Castleford WF10 . . . . .200 E4
Albion St continued
28 Earby BB18 . . . . .172 A1
York YO1 . . . . .233 B1
Albion Terr 9 LS23 . . . . .188 E7
Alcelina Ct YO23 . . . . . .233 B1
Alcuin Ave YO10 . . . . . .229 A4
Aldborough Gate 13
YO51 . . . . .141 B4
Aldborough Way YO26 .227 F5
Aldbrough & Boroughbridge
CP Sch YO51 . . . . .141 C5
Aldenham Rd TS14 . . . . . .8 E5
Alder Ave HG5 . . . . .221 E5
Alder Carr La YO18 . . . . .49 E2
Alder Hill St 1 BB18 . . . .172 B1
Alder Rd HG1 . . . . .219 F5
Alder Way YO32 . . . . . . .225 D2
Alderley Ct YO32 . . . . . .225 E3
Alderman Leach Inf Sch
DL3 . . . . .3 B6
Alders Rd YO18 . . . . .49 C4
Aldersley Ave BD23 . . . .217 B3
Alderson Cres YO12 . . . .99 E7
Alderson Rd HG2 . . . . . .222 E8
Alderson Sq HG2 . . . . . .222 E8
Aldersyde YO24 . . . . . . .230 E7
Aldreth Gr YO23 . . . . . .228 C2
Aldridge Rd TS3 . . . . .7 B8
Aldwark YO1 . . . . .233 C3
Aldwych Cl TS6 . . . . .7 E8
Alexander Ave
6 East Ayton/West Ayton
YO13 . . . . .99 B8
York YO31 . . . . .225 E2
Alexander Cl YO7 . . . . .211 C4
Alexander Rd DL9 . . . . .209 C2
Alexandra Cres 10 LS29 218 A4
Alexandra Ct
Skipton BD23 . . . . .216 F2
York YO10 . . . . .228 E4
Alexandra Park Rd
HG5 . . . . .221 C7
Alexandra Pk YO12 . . . .212 D5
Alexandra Pl 3 HG5 . . .221 B8
Alexandra Rd
Harrogate HG1 . . . . .219 D3
Strensall YO32 . . . . .167 A6
Alexandra Way DL10 . . .209 C7
Alexandria Dr DL2 . . . . . .4 D4
Algarth Rd YO31 . . . . . .229 B7
Algarth Rise YO31 . . . . .229 B7
All Saints Jun & Inf Sch
WF7 . . . . .200 E1
All Saints Prim Sch
LS29 . . . . .218 B4
All Saints RC Comp Sch
YO24 . . . . .233 A1
All Saints RC Prim Sch
YO7 . . . . .211 B2
All Saints Rd 1 YO12 . . .212 F4
Allan St Darlington DL1 . . .3 D6
2 York YO30 . . . . .228 C7
Allen Cl YO10 . . . . .229 A4
Allen Gr TS9 . . . . .26 B7
Allenby Rd
20 Helmsley YO62 . . . . . . .92 F6
Hipswell DL9 . . . . .209 C1
Allendale YO24 . . . . . . .230 D8
Allendale Rd TS7 . . . . . . .7 D8
Allens West Sta TS16 . . . .5 D5
Allensway TS17 . . . . .6 C7
Allerdale Cl YO7 . . . . . .211 C4
Allerston La YO18 . . . . . .97 C4
Allerton Balk TS15 . . . . . .5 D2
Allerton Bywater Prim Sch
WF10 . . . . .200 D7
Allerton Dr
22 Poppleton YO26 . . . . . .165 F1
Poppleton YO26 . . . . .224 A1
Allerton La HG5 . . . . . . .163 D4
Allerton Wath Rd DL6 . . .65 D4
Allertonshire Sch DL6 .210 D6
Allhallowgate HG4 . . . .214 C5
Allington Dr YO31 . . . . .229 B6
Allington Way
Darlington DL1 . . . . .3 F5
Great Burdon DL1 . . . . .4 A5
Allison Ave TS17 . . . . . . .6 B4
Allison St TS14 . . . . .8 E6
Allotments La YO61 . . .143 F3
Alma Gdns HG4 . . . . . . .214 D4
Alma Par 2 YO11 . . . . . .212 F5
Alma Rd BB8 . . . . .186 B3
Alma Sq 3 YO11 . . . . . .212 F5
Alma Terr Selby YO8 . . .232 C6
3 Skipton BD23 . . . . . . .217 A4
York YO10 . . . . .228 D2
Alma Way 2 YO18 . . . . . .96 A6
Almery Terr YO30 . . . . .233 A3
Almond Cl 7 Filey YO14 .101 B4
Hambleton YO8 . . . . .197 B1
Almond Gr 11 Filey YO14 101 B4
Northallerton DL7 . . . . . . .210 D3
Scarborough YO12 . . . . . .212 D5
York YO32 . . . . .225 D4
Almond Tree Ave
Carlton DN14 . . . . .204 C3
Malton YO17 . . . . .215 D6
Almond Wlk 4 DL9 . . . .209 B1
Almscliffe Dr LS17 . . . .178 B2
Almscliffe Garth LS17 .178 B4
Almsford Ave HG2 . . . .222 E6
Almsford Bank HG2 . . .222 E5
Almsford Cl HG2 . . . . .222 F6
Almsford Dr
Harrogate HG2 . . . . .222 F6
York YO26 . . . . .227 C5
Almsford End HG2 . . . .222 E6
Almsford Oval HG2 . . . .222 F6
Almsford Pl HG2 . . . . . .222 E6
Almsford Rd
Harrogate HG2 . . . . .222 F6
York YO26 . . . . .227 C5
Almsford Wlk HG2 . . . .222 F6
Almshouse Hill 1 LS23 .188 E5
Alne CP Sch YO61 . . . . .142 F4
Alne Rd
Easingwold YO61 . . . . . . .143 B8
Tollerton YO61 . . . . .143 A3
Alne Terr YO10 . . . . . . .228 E2
Alness Dr YO24 . . . . . . .230 B7
Altofts La WF10 . . . . . . .200 B3
Altofts Rd WF6 . . . . . . .200 B1
Alum House La TS9 . . . . .26 B2
Alverton Cty Inf Sch
DL6 . . . . .210 F6
Alverton Dr DL3 . . . . .3 B8
Alverton La DL7 . . . . . .210 D4
Alvin Wlk 9 YO41 . . . . .185 B2
Alvis Gr YO10 . . . . .229 D4
Alwyn Rd DL3 . . . . .3 D8
Alwyne Dr YO30 . . . . . .224 E1
Alwyne Gr YO30 . . . . . .224 E1
Amber St YO31 . . . . . . .233 C4
Amberly St 4 YO26 . . . .227 E5
Amble Cl YO62 . . . . .70 B2
Ambler St WF10 . . . . . . .200 E4
Ambler's La YO30 . . . . .165 F7
Ambleside Ave
10 Barnoldswick BB18 . . .171 D2
York YO10 . . . . .229 B4
Ambleside Gr TS5 . . . . . . .6 E8
Ambrey Cl 16 YO14 . . . .126 F8
Ambrose Rd HG4 . . . . . .214 C4
Ambrose St YO10 . . . . .228 D1
America La BD20 . . . . . .187 F4
Amesbury Cres TS8 . . . . . .6 F5
Amiens Cres DL9 . . . . . .209 D1
Amotherby CP Sch
YO17 . . . . .121 A4
Amotherby La YO17 . . .121 A6
Amplecarr YO61 . . . . . . .117 B5
Ampleforth Abbey & Coll
YO62 . . . . .92 D1
Ampleforth Coll Jun Sch
YO62 . . . . .118 F7
Ampleforth St Benedicts RC
Prim Sch YO62 . . . . .92 C1
Amy Johnson Way
YO30 . . . . .225 A3
Anchor Rd 2 HG1 . . . . .220 A3
Anchorage La DL7 . . . .210 C5
Anchorage Way YO21 . .208 C5
Anchorite La 7 YO18 . . . .95 F7
Ancress Wlk YO23 . . . . .233 B1
Ancroft Cl YO1 . . . . . . .233 C1
Andersen Rd DN14 . . . .205 F2
Anderson Gr 6 YO24 . . .227 F2
Anderson St 6 WF8 . . . .201 B1
Anderton St 18 BD20 . . .187 E8
Andrew Dr 4 YO32 . . . .225 F1
Andrew La YO18 . . . . . . .71 B4
Anfield Ct 8 DL1 . . . . . . .3 F6
Angel Ct 8 TS9 . . . . .26 C7
Angel Yd 1 YO21 . . . . . .208 D6
Angelica Cl 12 HG3 . . . .161 B3
Angram Cl YO30 . . . . . .224 F1
Angram La
Barlby with Osgodby
YO19 . . . . .198 A6
Muker DL11 . . . . .35 E6
Tollerton YO61 . . . . .143 B3
Angram Rd YO26 . . . . . .182 A5
Angrove Cl TS9 . . . . .7 F1
Angrove Dr TS9 . . . . .7 F1
Annan Cl YO24 . . . . . . .230 C6
Annandale Gr 1 YO13 . . .75 D5
Annas Garth DL8 . . . . . . .60 F4
Anne St YO23 . . . . .228 C2
Annumhills Rd YO8 . . . .199 D7
Anserdale La YO62 . . . . .70 E5
Anson Croft 5 YO8 . . . . .196 E1
Anson Dr YO10 . . . . . . .231 D8
Anteforth View DL10 . . . .20 E3
Anthea Dr YO31 . . . . . .225 E1
Anthony La HG4 . . . . . .114 E1
Anvil Sq 3 DL11 . . . . .38 B6
Anzio Rd DL9 . . . . .209 C1
Apedale Rd
Castle Bolton with East &
West Bolton DL8 . . . . .37 F1
Redmire DL8 . . . . .59 C8
Apley Cl HG2 . . . . .220 A1
Apollo St 9 YO10 . . . . .228 E3
Apple Garth
10 Easingwold YO61 . . . . .117 D1
15 Poppleton YO26 . . . . .165 F1
Apple Tree Gdns 2
LS29 . . . . .175 C2
Appleby Ave HG5 . . . . .220 D8
Appleby Cres HG5 . . . . .220 D8
Appleby Ct HG5 . . . . . . .220 D8
Appleby Gate HG5 . . . .220 D7
Appleby Glade YO32 . . .225 D7
Appleby Gn HG5 . . . . . .220 D8
Appleby La
Aldbrough DL11 . . . . .1 F1
Kirkby Malzeard HG4 . . . .112 B4
Appleby Pl 2 YO31 . . . .229 A5
Appleby Way HG5 . . . . .220 D7
Appleby Wlk HG5 . . . . .220 D8
Applecroft Rd
Selby YO8 . . . . .232 A4
York YO31 . . . . .229 B7
Applegarth
Barnoldswick BB18 . . . . . .171 E2
Applegarth continued
Coulby Newham TS8 . . . . . . .7 A4
Applegarth Ct DL7 . . . .210 D5
Applegarth St 15 BB18 .172 A1
Applegartn CP Prim Sch
DL7 . . . . .210 D4
Appleton Ct YO23 . . . . .230 F3
Appleton La
Appleton-le-Street with
Easthorpe YO17 . . . . . . .120 F4
Coneysthorpe YO60 . . . . .120 E2
Appleton Rd YO23 . . . . .231 A3
Appleton Roebuck CP Sch
YO23 . . . . .190 F5
Appleton Wiske CP Sch
DL6 . . . . .24 B3
Appletree Dr YO8 . . . . .196 E1
Appletree Way
Malton YO17 . . . . .215 B4
10 Sherburn in Elmet LS25 195 F4
Appletreewick Stone Circle*
BD23 . . . . .135 E2
Appley Cl TS16 . . . . .5 E7
Apron La HG3 . . . . .140 B2
Arbour The
4 Glusburn BD20 . . . . . . .173 E1
Ilkley LS29 . . . . .218 A6
Arbour Way YO17 . . . . .215 E4
Archbishop Holgates Sch
YO10 . . . . .229 B3
Archbishop of York C of E
Jun Sch YO23 . . . . .231 A4
Archer La HG3 . . . . .140 B3
Archer Rd DL2 . . . . .4 D3
Archers Gn The DL10 . . .41 C7
Archers Mdw HG5 . . . . .221 F5
Archie St 3 HG1 . . . . . .219 C5
Arden La YO62 . . . . .92 B8
Arena View 12 DL10 . . . . .41 D5
Arenhall Cl 2 YO32 . . . .225 C8
Argam La YO25 . . . . . . .126 F1
Argill DL8 . . . . .60 F5
Argyle Rd YO21 . . . . . . .208 C7
Argyle St YO23 . . . . .228 B1
Arkendale La HG5 . . . . .141 A2
Arkendale Rd HG5 . . . . .162 F8
Arkengarthdale C of E Prim
Sch DL11 . . . . .17 D1
Arkengarthdale Rd
DL11 . . . . .38 B7
Arkle Cres DL1 . . . . .3 C3
Arlington Rd
Middlesbrough TS5 . . . . .6 F8
York YO30 . . . . .225 A1
Armoury Rd YO8 . . . . . .232 B5
Armstrong Cl 7 WF6 . . .200 A2
Army Foundation Coll
HG3 . . . . .161 A2
Arncliffe C of E Prim Sch
BD23 . . . . .107 D2
Arncliffe Dr WF11 . . . . .201 D2
Arncliffe Rd HG2 . . . . . .220 A1
Arndale Way 8 YO14 . . .101 B4
Arnold Rd DL1 . . . . .3 E6
Arnside Cres WF10 . . . .201 B4
Arnside Pl 2 YO10 . . . . .228 F3
Arran Ct LS25 . . . . .194 C3
Arran Dr LS25 . . . . .194 C3
Arran Pl YO31 . . . . .228 D7
Arrows Cres 10 YO51 . . .141 B5
Arrows Terr 9 YO51 . . . .141 B5
Arthington Ave HG1 . . . .219 E2
Arthur Pl 6 YO30 . . . . . .224 B5
Arthur St
6 Barnoldswick BB18 . . . .171 D2
Earby BB18 . . . . .186 A8
Great Ayton TS9 . . . . .8 A2
York YO10 . . . . .228 E4
Arthurs Ave HG2 . . . . . .222 C7
Arthurs Cl HG2 . . . . . . .222 C7
Arthurs Gr HG2 . . . . . . .222 C7
Arundel Gr YO24 . . . . . .230 C7
Arundel Pl
12 Scarborough YO11 . . . .212 F5
9 Whitby YO21 . . . . .208 C6
Arundel Rd 5 DN6 . . . . .206 E2
Ascot Rd TS5 . . . . .194 C1
Ascot Way YO24 . . . . . .227 D1
Ash Bank Ave 2 HG4 . .113 D2
Ash Bank Cl 1 HG4 . . . .113 D2
Ash Bank Rd HG4 . . . . .113 D2
Ash Cl 1 Ilkley LS29 . . . .175 C2
Newton on Derwent
YO41 . . . . .185 E4
York YO31 . . . . .229 B7
Ash Croft 7 DL10 . . . . . .41 D5
Ash Gn TS8 . . . . .7 A4
Ash Gr
13 Barnoldswick BB18 . . .171 D1
Danby YO21 . . . . .29 A6
12 Filey YO14 . . . . .101 B4
Glusburn BD20 . . . . .187 E7
Ilkley LS29 . . . . .218 C5
7 Kirkbymoorside YO62 . . .70 B1
1 Kirklevington TS15 . . . . .24 E8
Northallerton DL6 . . . . . . .210 F5
1 Riccall YO19 . . . . .197 F8
Ripon HG4 . . . . .214 A6
Scarborough YO12 . . . . . .212 C7
Whitby YO21 . . . . .208 B6
Ash Hill TS8 . . . . .7 B5
Ash La
Church Fenton LS24 . . . . .196 B6
Garforth LS25 . . . . .194 D4
8 Haxby YO32 . . . . .166 E5
Little Fenton LS25 . . . . . .196 C5
Ash Lea YO21 . . . . .29 A6
Ash Rd 13 Filey YO14 . . .101 B4

Ash Rd *continued*
Guisborough TS14 8 F7
Harrogate HG2 222 E6
Ash Ridge 5 DL6 210 E3
Ash St 11 Glusburn BD20 187 E7
Ilkley LS29 218 C5
Trawden BB8 186 B1
York YO26 227 E4
Ash Tree Cl DL8 62 F2
Ash Tree Garth LS24 195 E7
Ash Tree Rd
8 Bedale DL8 63 A2
Knaresborough HG5 221 B6
Ash Tree Wlk 22 LS29 176 C1
Ashbank La Firby DL8 62 F1
Sheriff Hutton YO60 145 F6
Ashbourne Cl 12 YO51 141 B4
Ashbourne Rd 10 YO51 141 B4
Ashbourne Way YO24 230 C8
Ashburn Pl LS29 218 A3
Ashburn Rd YO11 212 E4
Ashburn Rise 10 YO11 212 E4
Ashburn Way LS22 180 B4
Ashburnham Cl 4 DN6 206 F2
Ashburnham Wlk 5
DN6 206 F2
Ashdale Cl DL2 4 E4
Ashdale La LS22 180 B4
Ashdale Rd
19 Dunnington YO19 184 F7
Helmsley YO62 92 F6
Ashdene Gr WF8 201 D2
Ashdown Rise YO13 75 C8
Ashdowne Cl DL8 62 E5
Ashdowne Ct DL8 62 E5
Ashes The DL10 21 C7
Ashfield
2 Grassington BD23 134 E3
Wetherby LS22 180 C3
Ashfield Ave YO17 215 D5
Ashfield Cl
Constable Burton DL8 61 C5
Pateley Bridge HG3 137 B4
Ashfield Court Rd
HG3 137 B4
Ashfield Rd Danby YO21 29 B6
Harrogate HG1 219 E4
6 Pickering YO18 96 A6
Ashfield St WF6 200 A2
Ashford Ave TS5 6 D8
Ashford Pl YO24 227 D2
Ashgap La WF6 200 A2
Ashgarth Ct HG2 222 C5
Ashgarth Way HG2 222 C5
Ashgrove Cres LS25 194 D2
Ashlands Cl DL6 210 F4
Ashlands Ct DL6 210 F4
Ashlands Dr DL7 63 C5
Ashlands Prim Sch
LS29 218 C5
Ashlands Rd
Ilkley LS29 218 C5
Northallerton DL6 210 F4
Ashlea Cl YO8 232 D4
Ashlea Rd DL7 210 D4
Ashley Ct 2 YO14 101 B3
Ashley Park Cres
YO31 229 B6
Ashley Park Rd YO31 229 B7
Ashmead 4 LS23 188 E7
Ashmeade Cl YO24 230 B8
Ashton Ave YO30 228 B8
Ashton Rd WF10 200 E3
Ashtree Dr YO8 197 D1
Ashville Ave
Eaglescliffe TS16 5 E6
Scarborough YO12 212 F6
Ashville Cl HG2 222 C5
Ashville Coll HG2 222 B6
Ashville Dr 9 DL2 22 E8
Ashville Gr HG2 222 C5
Ashville St YO31 228 D7
Ashwood Cl 5 YO62 92 F7
Ashwood Dr TS9 26 C8
Ashwood Glade YO32 225 C6
Ashwood Pl HG5 221 E5
Ashworth Rd WF8 201 C2
Askam Ave WF8 201 C2
Askam Bryan Coll TS14 8 F7
Aske Ave DL10 209 E8
Aske Hall★ DL10 20 D2
Askern & Campsall Sports Ctr
DN6 206 F1
Askew Dale TS14 8 D6
Askew Rigg La YO18 71 A5
Askham Bryan Coll
Askham Bryan YO23 182 F2
Bedale DL8 63 A2
Pickering YO18 95 F8
Askham Bryan Coll Harrogate
Ctr HG2 223 A7
Askham Bryan La
YO23 230 A6
Askham Croft 1 YO24 227 B1
Askham Fields La
YO23 182 F2
Askham Gr YO24 227 B2
Askham La
Askham Bryan YO24 230 A8
York YO24 227 B1
Askrigg Prim Sch DL8 57 E5
Askwith CP Sch LS21 176 D3
Askwith La LS21 176 D3
Askwith Moor Rd
LS21 176 D5
Aspen Cl 3 YO19 184 F7
Aspen La BB18 172 A1
Aspen Way
Slingsby YO62 120 B5
Tadcaster LS24 189 D6
Aspin Ave HG5 221 B4
Aspin Dr HG5 221 C4
Aspin Gdns HG5 221 C4
Aspin Gr 4 HG5 221 C4
Aspin La HG5 221 C3
Aspin Oval HG5 221 B4
Aspin Park Ave 1 HG5 221 C4
Aspin Park CP Sch
HG5 221 C5
Aspin Park Cres HG5 221 B4
Aspin Park Dr HG5 221 B4
Aspin Park La HG5 221 C4
Aspin Park Rd HG5 221 C4
Aspin View HG5 221 C4
Aspin Way HG5 221 C4
Asquith Ave
Scarborough YO12 212 E3
York YO31 229 A5
Assembly St 7 WF6 200 A1
Astbury TS8 7 C4
Asterley Dr TS5 6 D8
Astley Ave LS26 194 A1
Astley La
Great & Little Preston
LS26 200 B8
Swillington LS26 194 A1
Astley Lane Ind Pk
LS26 200 B8
Astley Way LS26 200 A8
Atcherley Cl YO10 231 D8
Athelstan CP Sch
LS25 195 F3
Athelstan La 7 LS21 177 A1
Athelstans Ct LS25 195 F4
Atkinson Ave DL10 209 D8
Atkinson Ct WF6 200 A1
Atkinson La WF8 201 C1
Atlantis Water Pk★
YO12 212 F8
Atlas Rd YO30 225 A3
Atlas Wynd TS16 5 E3
Attermire Cave★
BD24 132 A3
Atterwith La YO26 182 A7
Auborough St 5 YO11 213 A6
Auckland Ave DL3 3 B6
Auckland Oval DL3 3 B7
Auckland St TS14 8 F7
Auckland Way 7 YO21 208 C6
Audax Cl YO30 225 A3
Audax Rd YO30 225 A3
Audby La LS22 180 C4
Audus St 10 YO8 232 C5
Augusta Cl DL1 3 F7
Aumit La YO62 92 E1
Aunums Cl 7 YO18 96 D5
Auster Bank Ave LS24 189 F7
Auster Bank Cres
LS24 189 F7
Auster Bank Rd LS24 189 F7
Auster Bank View
LS24 189 F7
Auster Rd YO30 225 B3
Austfield La LS25 202 B8
Austin Rd WF10 201 B4
Austwick C of E Prim Sch
LA2 130 E7
Austwick Rd BD24 131 C8
Ava Rd DL9 40 C4
Avens Way TS17 6 A5
Avenue A LS23 181 A2
Avenue B LS23 181 A1
Avenue Bank HG4 86 C4
Avenue C E LS23 181 B1
Avenue C W LS23 181 A1
Avenue Cl HG2 220 D4
Avenue D LS23 181 A1
Avenue E E LS23 181 B1
Avenue E W LS23 189 A8
Avenue F LS23 181 B1
Avenue G LS23 181 B1
Avenue Gr 11 HG2 220 C3
Avenue House Ct HG5 162 F3
Avenue Pl 7 HG2 220 C3
Avenue Prim Sch The
TS7 7 D6
Avenue Rd
Harrogate HG2 220 C3
Scarborough YO12 212 E4
York YO30 233 A4
Avenue St 8 HG2 220 C3
Avenue Terr
5 Harrogate HG2 220 C3
York YO30 233 A4
Avenue The
Campsall DN6 206 E1
Collingham LS22 180 A1
Dalby-cum-Skewsby
YO60 119 B2
Eaglescliffe TS16 5 E6
26 Filey YO14 101 B3
Gilling East YO62 118 E7
Great Ribston with Walshford
LS22 180 C8
Guisborough TS14 8 D6
Harrogate HG1 220 C4
5 Haxby YO32 166 E5
Haxby YO32 225 D8
Knaresborough HG5 221 A7
Masham HG4 86 C3
Middlesbrough TS5 6 F8
Middlesbrough TS7 7 D6
Norton YO17 215 C2
Nun Monkton YO26 165 A4
Nunnington YO62 93 E1
Avenue The *continued*
8 Pateley Bridge HG3 137 C4
Richmond DL10 209 D7
Rufforth YO23 182 C6
Skutterskelfe TS15 25 E6
1 Sleights YO22 32 A6
Snape with Thorp DL8 87 A7
South Milford LS25 195 F2
Stainton Dale YO13 54 A8
Stokesley TS9 26 C7
Thirkleby High & Low
with Osgodby YO7 116 D8
West Hauxwell DL8 61 C8
Whitby YO21 208 B6
Wighill LS24 181 D2
York YO30 228 A6
Avenue Victoria YO11 213 A3
Aviation Rd LS25 196 A4
Aviator Ct YO30 224 F3
Aviemore Ct 10 DL1 3 F6
Aviemore Rd TS8 6 F5
Avocet Cres 11 YO12 99 F6
Avon Dr
Barnoldswick BB18 171 E2
Guisborough TS14 8 E6
York YO32 225 F6
Avon Garth LS22 180 B3
Avon Rd 8 DL2 22 D8
Avondale Rd HG1 219 F4
Avondale St 7 BB8 186 A3
Avro Cl TS18 5 F7
Awnhams La YO42 169 D2
Axminster Rd TS8 6 F5
Axton Cl TS17 6 A6
Aylesham Ct YO32 225 E3
Aylton Dr TS5 6 E6
Aynham Cl 2 BD23 134 E2
Aynholme Cl 10 LS29 174 F4
Aynholme Dr 1 LS29 175 A4
Ayresome Way 1 DL1 3 F6
Aysgarth Gr DL7 210 B2
Aysgarth Rd DL1 3 D4
Aysgarth Sch DL8 62 A4
Ayton Castle★ YO13 99 A8
Ayton Rd YO12 99 C7
Azerley Gr HG3 219 A4
Azerley La HG4 112 F3

B

Babyhouse La BD20 173 A1
Bachelor Ave HG1 219 D7
Bachelor Dr HG1 219 D7
Bachelor Gdns HG1 219 D6
Bachelor Hill YO24 227 C2
Bachelor Rd HG1 219 D6
Bachelor Way HG1 219 D6
Back Ave Victoria 2
YO11 213 A3
Back Beck La LS29 174 F4
Back Bridge St BD23 216 F4
Back Cheltenham Mount
HG1 219 D3
Back Colne Rd 9 BD20 187 E7
Back Dragon Par HG1 219 E3
Back Dragon Rd HG1 219 E3
Back Elmwood St 3
HG1 219 E4
Back Gate LA6 103 D3
Back Gn BD23 153 F5
Back Grove Rd LS29 218 B4
Back La
Acaster Selby YO23 191 B3
Airton BD23 155 A6
Aiskew DL7 63 C5
Alne YO61 142 F4
Ampleforth YO62 92 C1
Appleton Roebuck YO23 191 A5
Appleton-le-Moors YO62 70 F2
Asselby DN14 205 D6
Bagby YO7 90 B3
Barkston Ash LS24 195 F6
Barlby with Osgodby
YO8 198 C4
Barton DL10 21 C7
Barton-le-Street YO17 120 E5
1 Bedale DL8 63 A3
Bilbrough YO23 182 D1
Birstwith HG3 160 D5
Bolton-on-Swale DL10 41 E5
7 Boroughbridge YO51 141 B5
Borrowby YO7 65 E4
Bradleys Both BD20 173 E4
10 Brafferton YO61 115 F1
Bramham LS23 188 E6
Burley in Warfedale
LS29 176 C1
Carlton Miniott YO7 89 B3
Carthorpe DL8 87 E7
Cawood YO8 197 A8
Cold Kirby YO7 91 C8
Copmanthorpe YO23 230 A2
Copt Hewick HG4 114 B2
Cottingwith YO42 193 C5
Crakehall DL8 62 E4
Crathorne TS15 24 F6
Dalton YO7 115 E7
Dishforth YO7 115 A4
Drax YO8 204 F5
Eaglescliffe TS16 5 E4
Easingwold YO61 117 D1
East Tanfield DL8 87 D2
Ebberston & Yedingham
YO13 97 D5
Ellerton YO42 193 C1
Fewston HG3 159 F1
Flaxton YO60 145 F1
Back La *continued*
Giggleswick BD24 130 F2
Great & Little Broughton
TS9 26 E5
Great Ouseburn YO26 164 A8
Great Preston WF10 200 D6
Gristlthorp YO14 100 E5
Guisborough TS9 8 A4
Hambleton YO8 196 F1
Harome YO62 93 C5
Hawsker-cum-Stainsacre
YO22 32 F5
11 Haxby YO32 166 D5
Hebden BD23 135 A2
Hellifield BD23 154 B3
Hemingbrough YO8 198 F1
Hetton BD23 155 F5
Hirst Courtney YO8 203 F3
Holtby YO19 184 E8
Hunsingore LS22 180 E8
Hutton-le-Hole YO62 70 C4
Huttons Ambo YO60 147 B7
Kirby Wiske YO7 88 E7
Kirkby Malham BD23 154 F8
Kirkby Malzeard HG4 112 C5
Lockton YO18 72 E4
Long Preston BD23 153 F5
Longnewton TS21 4 F8
Low Coniscliffe & Merrybent
DL2 2 E4
Low Worsall TS15 24 C7
Luttons YO17 150 B8
Malham BD23 132 F2
Markington with Wallerthwaite
HG3 139 C3
Marton YO62 94 F5
Marton cum Grafton
YO51 141 D1
Melmerby HG4 114 B7
8 Middleham DL8 60 E2
Morton-on-Swale DL7 64 A6
Moulton DL10 21 E3
Newby Wiske DL7 64 D3
Newholm-cum-Dunsley
YO21 13 A1
Newton-on-Ouse YO30 165 B6
North Cowton DL7 22 B3
North Duffield YO8 199 A7
Norton DN6 206 E2
Osmotherley DL6 45 B4
Raskelf YO61 116 F2
Rathmell BD24 153 C6
Reeth, Fremington & Healaugh
DL11 38 B6
2 Riccall YO19 198 A8
Rookwith HG4 86 A8
Scorton DL10 41 E6
Settrington YO17 148 D8
Sicklinghall LS22 179 E3
Sinnington YO62 95 A8
Skelton HG4 140 E7
Stillington YO61 144 C6
Sutton-under-Whitestonecliffe
YO7 90 E5
Thirkleby High & Low
with Osgodby YO7 116 D8
Thirsk YO7 211 B1
Tholthorpe YO61 142 D5
Thormanby YO61 116 F6
Thornton Steward DL8 61 C2
Topcliffe YO7 115 C7
Trawden BB8 186 A1
Tunstall DL10 41 B3
Tunstall LA6 102 A4
Weaverthorpe YO17 124 E1
Weeton LS17 178 C2
Wennington LA2 102 C2
West Tanfield HG4 87 A1
West Witton DL8 59 C4
Westerdale YO21 28 E5
Whixley YO26 164 A3
Whorlton DL6 45 D8
Wilberfoss YO41 185 F5
Wold Newton YO25 126 A4
Wombleton YO62 93 E7
Wray-with-Botton LA2 128 A6
York YO26 227 A5
Back La S
Middleton YO18 95 E8
Wheldrake YO19 192 F7
Back Middleton Rd 9
LS29 218 A4
Back Newton La
WF10 201 A7
Back Nook 1 DL8 58 F1
Back Northgate WF8 201 B1
Back O' Newton YO41 185 E3
Back of Parks Rd YO62 70 C2
Back of the Beck 6
BD23 216 F4
Back Parish Ghyll Rd 8
LS29 218 B4
Back Park St YO8 232 D5
Back Rd Birstwith HG3 160 B5
Thormanby YO61 116 F5
Back Regent Pl 4 HG1 220 C4
Back Royal Par 5 HG1 219 C2
Back Sea View YO14 101 C1
Back Side YO17 149 B5
Back St
Boroughbridge YO51 141 C5
Bramham LS23 188 E6
Burton Fleming YO25 126 E3
Langtoft YO25 151 D5
10 Middleham DL8 60 E2
Wold Newton YO25 126 A4
Back St Hilda's Terr
YO21 208 D7
Back Station Rd 17
BD20 187 E8
Back Syke DL8 57 D5
Back West View 2
YO30 228 B7
Back Weston Rd 5
LS29 218 B4
Back York Pl 6 HG1 219 D1
Backhouse St YO31 233 B4
Backside La YO62 93 E6
Backstone La LS29 218 C3
Backstone Way LS29 218 C4
Bacon Ave WF6 200 B2
Bad Bargain La YO31 229 A5
Baden St HG1 219 F4
Bader Ave TS17 6 B6
Bader Prim Sch TS17 6 B6
Badger Butt La BD23 155 B5
Badger Gate BD23 134 D3
Badger Hill Dr 14 DL8 63 B3
Badger Hill Prim Sch
YO10 229 B2
Badger La DN6 207 A3
Badger Paddock 5
YO31 225 E2
Badger Wood Glade
LS22 180 C4
Badger Wood Wlk
YO10 229 D3
Badgerbeck Rd 2 DL9 209 B1
Badgers Gate LS29 175 C6
Badminton Ct 18 DL1 3 F6
Baffam Gdns YO8 232 B2
Baffam La YO8 232 B2
Bagby La YO7 90 B2
Bagdale YO21 208 C6
Baghill La WF8 201 C1
Baildon Ave LS25 194 D2
Baildon Cl 3 YO26 227 D4
Baile Hill Terr YO1 233 B1
Bailey Ct DL7 210 C4
Bailey La BD23 152 E3
Bailey St BB18 172 B1
Bailey The BD23 217 A4
Bainbridge C of E Prim Sch
DL8 57 D5
Bainbridge Dr YO8 232 C4
Bairnswood Sch YO12 212 B6
Baker St
Appleton Wiske DL6 24 A3
York YO30 228 C7
Bakersfield Dr DN14 202 F3
Baldersby Garth YO7 88 D1
Baldersby St James C of E
Prim Sch YO7 114 E7
Baldersdale Ave 1
HG5 221 D5
Baldoon Sands TS5 6 D6
Baldwin St 4 HG1 219 C5
Balfour St YO26 227 F5
Balfour Terr TS5 6 D8
Balfour Way YO32 167 A6
Balk La DN14 207 F7
Balk The
Bishop Wilton YO41 169 C2
Marton-le-Moor HG4 114 E1
Slingsby YO62 120 B5
Balk Top YO7 115 B1
Balksyde YO62 120 B5
Ball Grove Dr BB8 186 A3
Ballhall La YO42 193 E6
Balmer Hill DL2 1 C8
Balmoral Ave TS17 6 C8
Balmoral Rd
Barmpton DL1 3 E8
Lingdale TS12 9 F6
Middlesbrough TS3 7 C8
Ripon HG4 214 C3
Balmoral Terr 5 YO23 228 B1
Balne Hall Rd DN14 207 F5
Balne Moor Rd DN14 207 B6
Balshaw Rd LA2 129 B3
Baltimore Way DL1 3 D7
Banbury Rd WF8 201 C2
Bancroft Fold 18 BB18 171 D1
Bancroft Steam Mus★
BB18 171 D1
Bands La DL8 56 C4
Bank Bottom LA6 103 D3
Bank Cl 2 YO22 32 A6
Bank Dike Hill HG3 159 A4
Bank Hall Cl LA6 103 D4
Bank House La LA6 103 B5
Bank La Egton YO21 30 E5
Faceby TS9 25 F1
Grassington BD23 134 E3
Great & Little Broughton
TS9 26 F3
Silsden BD20 174 C4
Bank Rd Glusburn BD20 187 E8
Selby YO8 232 D6
Bank Side
2 Eastfield YO11 100 A7
Rawcliffe DN14 205 A2
Bank St
Barnoldswick BB18 171 D1
Castleford WF10 200 E4
11 Wetherby LS22 180 C3
Bank The DL10 41 D4
Bank Top LA6 103 D3
Bank Top La 4 TS13 12 A7
Bank Wood Rd WF8 206 A6
Bankfield La DN14 205 A7
Bankfield St BB8 186 A2
Bankhead Cl DL6 210 F4

Bankhead Rd DL6 .....210 F4
Banklands Ave BD20 ...174 C1
Banklands La BD20 ....174 C1
Banks Bridge Cl BB18 .171 E2
Banks Hill 1 BB18 .....171 D2
Banks La DL10 ....41 E7
Banks Rd Brompton DL6 ..44 A2
Darlington DL1 ....3 E6
Bankside Cl 3 YO26 ...165 F1
Bankwell Rd BD24 ....131 D2
Bannisdale 6 YO24 ....230 C7
Bannister Cl BB8 ......186 B2
Bannister Wlk BD22 ...187 B6
Banqueting House*
LS21 ....176 D1
Bar La
Bramham cum Oglethorpe
LS23 ....188 F7
Garforth LS25 ....194 D4
Hambleton YO8 ....196 E1
Knaresborough HG5 .....162 D5
Roecliffe YO51 ....141 A5
York YO1 ....233 A2
Bar Pl HG1 ....219 D5
Bar St YO11 ....213 A6
Bar The 6 DL10 ....209 C6
Barbara Gr 4 YO24 ....227 F3
Barbeck YO7 ....211 C3
Barbeck Cl YO7 ....211 D3
Barberry TS8 ....7 B4
Barberry Cl Ingleby TS17 ..6 B5
20 Killinghall HG3 ....161 B3
Barbers Dr YO23 ......230 B4
Barbican Ct YO10 .....233 C1
Barbican Leisure Ctr
YO10 ....233 C1
Barbican Mews YO10 ..228 E3
Barbican Rd YO10 .....233 C1
Barbondale Gr HG5 ...221 C5
Barbondale Rd LA10 ....77 A7
Bardale Cl 2 HG5 .....221 D6
Barden Ct 6 YO30 .....224 F1
Barden Fell View 3
BD23 ....134 E2
Barden La DL8 ....40 B1
Barden Moor Rd DL1 ....3 E4
Barden Pl 9 YO14 .....101 A3
Barden Rd BD23 ......157 A1
Barden Twr* BD23 .....157 C4
Bardney Rd 14 YO14 ...126 F8
Bardsley Cl TS16 ....5 E7
Barefoot St HG4 ....214 C4
Barf Bank DL8 ....61 A2
Barf La YO41 ....169 D4
Barff Cl 10 YO8 ....197 D1
Barff Gr 6 YO8 ....197 B2
Barff La YO8 ....197 C1
Barff View YO8 ....203 D7
Barfield Rd YO31 ......228 F8
Bargate DL10 ....209 B6
Bark House La LA2 ....131 B8
Bark La
Addingham LS29 ....175 A5
Embsay with Eastby
BD23 ....157 A1
Barker La YO1 ....233 A2
Barker's La
Newholm-cum-Dunsley
YO21 ....13 A1
Snainton YO13 ....98 A4
Barkery The TS8 ....7 B3
Barkhouse Bank HG3 ..138 F4
Barkhouse Wood La
WF11 ....202 D6
Barknotts Terr YO17 ...215 C3
Barkston Ash RC Prim Sch
LS24 ....195 E7
Barkston Ave YO26 ....227 B3
Barkston Cl 3 YO26 ...227 A3
Barkston Gr YO26 .....227 A3
Barkston Rd YO26 .....227 A3
Barlby Bridge CP Sch
YO8 ....232 D5
Barlby By Pass 2 YO8 ..198 B4
Barlby CP Sch YO8 ....198 B4
Barlby Cres YO8 ....232 F7
Barlby High Sch YO8 ..198 B5
Barlby Rd YO8 ....232 E6
Barley Cl YO17 ....215 D2
Barley Horn Rd LS24 ..190 B2
Barley Rise YO32 ......167 A6
Barley View YO32 .....225 C8
Barleycroft YO11 ......213 C1
Barleyfields La 5 LS22 .180 C3
Barleyfields Rd
4 Wetherby LS22 ......180 C3
4 Wetherby LS22 ......180 C4
Barleyhill Rd LS25 ....194 B4
Barley's Yd YO7 ....211 B3
Barlow C of E Prim Sch
YO8 ....204 C7
Barlow Cl TS14 ....8 F6
Barlow Common Nature
Reserve* YO8 ....204 B7
Barlow Common Rd
YO8 ....204 B8
Barlow Rd YO8 ....204 B6
Barlow St YO26 ....227 D4
Barmby Ave YO10 ......231 E8
Barmby Cl 4 YO30 .....224 F1
Barmby Ferry Rd 1
YO8 ....198 F1
Barmby on the Marsh Cty
Prim Sch DN14 ....205 B7
Barmoor Cl YO13 ....75 D6
Barmoor Gn YO13 ......75 D6
Barmoor La YO13 ....75 C6
Barmpton La DL1 ....3 F7
Barn Field Cl BB8 .....186 A3
Barnaby Pl TS14 ....8 E7
Barnard La YO13 ....98 C4
Barnard's Rd YO21 .....31 A4
Barnbow La LS15 ......194 A6
Barnes Rd
Castleford WF10 ....200 E3
Darlington DL3 ....3 A6
Barney La YO60 ....146 A1
Barnfield Way YO23 ...230 A2
Barnhill La DN14 ......205 F7
Barningham Rd DL11 ...18 G7
Barnoldswick CE Sch
BB18 ....171 D1
Barnoldswick La LA6 ..103 A2
Barns Wray 2 YO61 ....117 D1
Barnsdale Est WF10 ...200 D3
Barnsdale Rd
Ledston WF10 ....200 E7
Mickletown LS26 ....200 B5
Barnsdale View DN6 ...206 E2
Barnwell Cres HG2 ....222 B5
Barnwood Cres BB18 ..172 B1
Barnwood Rd BB18 ....172 A1
Barnygate La YO60 ....147 A7
Barons Cres YO23 .....230 B2
Barr La YO32 ....167 D4
Barrack View DL10 ....209 C8
Barracks Bank DL10 ....21 A2
Barret St 13 BB18 ......172 A1
Barrett Ave 3 YO24 ....227 F3
Barrett Rd DL3 ....3 A5
Barrington Garth
DN14 ....202 F3
Barrowby La
Austhorpe LS15 ....194 A4
Kirkby Overblow HG3 ....179 A3
Barrowcliff Cty Jun Sch
YO12 ....212 C7
Barrowcliff Rd YO12 ...212 D7
Barry Bank YO21 ....11 F1
Barry's La YO12 ....212 E2
Barse Beck La HG3 ....160 D5
Barstow Ave YO10 .....228 F3
Barstow Fall 2 WF8 ...201 C2
Bartindale Rd YO14 ...127 A5
Bartle Garth YO1 ......233 C3
Barton C of E Sch DL10 .21 D7
Barton St DL1 ....3 E6
Bartons Garth YO8 ....232 B2
Barugh La
Barugh (Great & Little)
YO17 ....95 B2
Normanby YO62 ....94 F4
Barwic Par YO8 ....232 E4
Barwick Fields TS17 .....6 A5
Barwick Inf Sch LS15 ..194 C8
Barwick La Ingleby TS17 ..6 A4
Ingleby Barwick TS17 .....5 F5
Barwick Parade CP Sch
YO8 ....232 E4
Barwick Rd LS25 ......194 C5
Barwick St YO12 ......212 F5
Barwick Terr 1 YO12 ...212 F5
Barwick View TS17 ....6 A5
Barwick Way TS17 ....6 A4
Bassett Cl YO8 ....232 C3
Bassleton La TS17 ....6 A6
Baston La YO61 ....143 E4
Bates Ave DL3 ....3 B7
Bateson Cl YO10 ......229 C1
Bath St LS29 ....218 C5
Battersby Ave TS9 ....27 C7
Battersby Junc TS9 .....27 C6
Battersby Sta TS9 ......27 C6
Battle of Bramham Moor
(site of)* LS24 ....188 F4
Battle of Marston Moor (site
of)* YO26 ....181 E7
Battle of Standard Hill (site
of)* DL6 ....43 E4
Battle of Towton (site of)*
LS24 ....195 D8
Battleflats Way YO41 ..168 D2
Battling Hills La YO18 ..49 B5
Bawhead Rd 23 BB18 ...172 A1
Bawtry Cl YO8 ....232 D3
Bawtry Rd YO8 ....232 D3
Baxby Manor* YO61 ...117 B6
Baxby Terr 2 DL2 ....22 D8
Baxter Wood BD20 .....187 E8
Baxtergate YO21 ....208 D6
Baxton's Sprunt 1 YO62 .92 F7
Bay Bolton Ave DL8 .....59 D3
Bay Horse Yd 9 BD23 ..216 F4
Baydale Rd DL3 ....3 A4
Baysdale Ave YO10 ....229 D3
Baysdale Cl TS14 ....8 F6
Baysdale Rd TS17 ....6 B7
Bazeley's La YO17 .....215 E1
Beach Rd The YO14 ...101 B3
Beach The YO14 ....101 B3
Beacon Bank YO62 .....92 D1
Beacon Brow Rd YO13 ..75 A7
Beacon Grange Pk DL2 ..4 C7
Beacon Hill DL2 ....4 B7
Beacon Rd
Millington YO42 ....170 B1
Seamer YO12 ....99 D7
Beacon Rise 4 LS29 ...175 C2
Beacon St 5 LS29 .....175 A4
Beacon View 3 BD23 ..217 E8
Beacon Way YO22 ....32 D6
Beaconsfield St
Northallerton DL7 ....210 D4
Beaconsfield St *continued*
3 Scarborough YO12 ....212 E3
York YO24 ....227 D3
Beadlam Ave TS7 ....7 D6
Beadle Garth YO23 ....230 B2
Beagle Croft YO41 .....168 C1
Beagle Ridge Dr YO24 .227 C1
Beagle Spinney YO41 ..168 C1
Beal La Beal DN14 .....202 D4
Cridling Stubbs WF11 ....202 C1
Beale Cl TS17 ....6 B5
Beamsley Ct BD23 .....217 A2
Beamsley La BD23 .....174 F7
Beamsley View 13 LS29 .175 C2
Bean Sheaf La YO17 ....96 A3
Beancroft Rd WF10 ....200 E3
Beancroft St WF10 ....200 E3
Beanland La YO32 .....167 D2
Beanlands Dr 7 BD20 ..187 E7
Beanlands Par LS29 ...218 C5
Beanlands Pl
8 Glusburn BD20 ....187 E7
5 Glusburn BD20 ....187 E8
Bean's Way YO31 ......229 B8
Beatswell Lawn HG4 ...113 C8
Beaufighter Cl DL10 ....41 F6
Beaufort Cl YO10 ......229 B3
Beaulieu Cl 1 YO32 ...225 F5
Beaumont Hill Sch DL1 ..3 D8
Beaumont Pl YO8 ......232 A2
Beaverdyke YO30 ......224 F1
Becca La LS25 ....194 F8
Beck Cl 6 YO41 ....185 B2
Beck Closes Rd YO26 ..142 A3
Beck Hole 9 YO11 .....100 B6
Beck Hole Rd YO22 .....31 C1
Beck Isle Mus of Rural Life*
YO18 ....95 F7
Beck La Cloughton YO13 ..54 C1
Collingham LS22 ....180 A1
Farndale East YO62 ......48 F2
Lebberston YO11 ....100 D5
South Kilvington YO7 ....211 B6
Wheldrake YO19 ....193 A8
Beck Mdw LS15 ....194 C7
Beck Mill Cl YO17 .....215 D3
Beck Row YO41 ....169 D5
Beck Side BD23 ....173 B4
Beck Side Cl BD20 ....173 D1
Beckbridge La 2 WF6 ..200 B1
Beckbridge Rd WF6 ...200 B2
Beckbridge Way WF6 ..200 B1
Beckclose La DL8 ....87 F6
Beckdale Rd YO62 ......92 E7
Beckett Cl 8 YO62 .....93 D7
Beckfield La
Fairburn WF11 ....201 C7
York YO26 ....227 B5
Beckfield Pl YO26 .....227 B4
Beckfields Ave TS17 .....6 A4
Becklands Cl YO51 ....141 A5
Becklands La YO51 ....141 A4
Becks Brow BD23 .....153 C3
Becks Cl 5 YO32 ......225 C8
Beckside Catterick DL10 ..41 E4
7 Elvington YO41 ....185 B2
Northallerton DL7 ....210 B4
4 Staithes TS13 ....13 K2
Trawden Forest BB8 .....186 B2
Wilberfoss YO41 ....185 F6
Beckside Cl
13 Addingham LS29 .....174 F4
29 Burley in Warfedale
LS29 ....176 C1
Beckwith Ave HG2 ....222 B7
Beckwith Cl
Harrogate HG2 ....222 A6
Heworth YO31 ....229 C7
Beckwith Cres HG2 ...222 B7
Beckwith Dr HG2 .....222 B6
Beckwith Head Rd
HG3 ....178 C8
Beckwith Rd HG2 .....222 A7
Beckwith Wlk HG2 ....222 A7
Beckwithshaw CP Sch
HG3 ....178 A8
Bedale Ave
Scarborough YO12 ......212 E8
York YO10 ....229 D4
Bedale C of E Prim Sch
DL8 ....63 A2
Bedale High Sch DL8 ...63 A2
Bedale La HG4 ....114 A8
Bedale Mus* DL8 ......63 A3
Bedale Rd Aiskew DL7 ..63 C4
Scotton DL9 ....40 F2
Well DL8 ....87 A4
Bedburn Dr DL3 ....2 F5
Bede Ave YO30 ....228 B7
Bedern Bank 13 HG4 ...214 C5
Bedern Ct 16 HG4 .....214 C5
Bedford Rd TS7 ....7 D6
Bedford St 13 YO11 ...213 A6
Bedfords Fold 6 LS25 .202 A7
Bedlam Hill YO7 ....65 E4
Bedlam La
Fewston HG3 ....159 F2
Staveley HG5 ....140 E1
Beech Ave
3 Airmyn DN14 ....205 E4
Bishopthorpe YO23 ......231 A3
1 Earby BB18 ....172 A1
Harrogate HG2 ....222 E6
4 Topcliffe YO7 ....89 B1
York YO24 ....227 F3
Beech Cl Baldersby YO7 ..88 D1
6 Eastfield YO11 ....100 A7
2 Elvington YO41 ....185 B2
Beech Cl *continued*
Farnham HG5 ....162 D7
Great Ayton TS9 ....7 F1
Hunton DL9 ....40 E2
Scruton DL7 ....63 E7
7 Sherburn in Elmet LS25 195 F4
Snape with Thorp DL8 .....87 A7
3 South Milford LS25 ...195 F2
Tadcaster LS24 ....189 F6
Beech Cres
Castleford WF10 ....201 B3
Whitwell-on-the-Hill
YO60 ....146 E4
Beech Croft
Barlby with Osgodby
YO8 ....198 B6
Pontefract WF8 ....201 C2
Beech Ct YO23 ....231 A3
Beech Dr
6 Kirkbymoorside YO62 ...70 B1
12 Scalby YO13 ....75 D5
South Milford LS25 ......195 F2
Beech Glade YO31 .....225 F2
Beech Gr
1 Airmyn DN14 ....205 E4
Burton Salmon LS25 .....201 F6
Camblesforth YO8 ....204 C5
Harrogate HG2 ....219 C1
Knaresborough HG5 .....221 B8
Maltby TS8 ....6 C4
Northallerton DL6 ....210 E5
Selby YO8 ....232 C5
Sherburn in Elmet LS25 ..195 F4
Sowerby YO7 ....211 C1
Whitby YO21 ....208 B6
York YO26 ....227 C4
Beech Hill
Carleton BD23 ....173 A4
6 Knaresborough HG5 ...221 A6
5 Pontefract WF8 ....201 C1
Beech Hill Rd BD23 ...173 A4
Beech La
8 East Ayton/West Ayton
YO13 ....99 A7
3 Spofforth HG3 ....179 E6
Beech Pk YO19 ....198 A8
Beech Pl 5 YO32 ......167 A6
Beech Rd
Boston Spa LS23 ....188 E8
Campsall DN6 ....206 E1
Darlington DL1 ....3 F7
Harrogate HG2 ....222 E6
Ripon HG4 ....214 B3
Beech St
23 Barnoldswick BB18 ...171 D1
10 Glusburn BD20 ....187 E7
6 Harrogate HG2 ....220 C3
Beech Tree Ct 2 YO30 .164 F7
Beech Tree La YO8 ....204 C5
Beech View LS25 ......194 E8
Beech Wlk
5 Eastfield YO11 ....100 A7
Tadcaster LS24 ....189 D6
Beechcroft Cl TS12 .....9 F6
Beeches End LS23 .....188 F8
Beeches The
Skelton YO30 ....224 C4
11 Stokesley TS9 ....26 C7
Beechfield
Coulby Newham TS8 ....7 A5
Hawsker-cum-Stainsacre
YO22 ....33 A6
Newby Wiske DL7 ....64 F2
Newton-on-Ouse YO30 ...165 B6
Beechfield Cl YO8 .....197 B1
Beechfield Rd DL10 ...209 C8
Beechnut La WF8 .....201 B1
Beechtree Rd LS24 ....189 D5
Beechville Ave YO12 ..212 F6
Beechwood Ave 2 TS9 ..26 C8
Beechwood Cl
14 Bedale DL8 ....63 A2
Markington with Wallerthwaite
HG3 ....139 D4
Sherburn in Elmet LS25 ..195 F3
Beechwood Cres 6
HG2 ....219 C1
Beechwood Croft
LS25 ....195 F3
Beechwood Dr BD23 ..216 D5
Beechwood Glade
Sherburn in Elmet LS25 ..195 F3
7 York YO24 ....227 B1
Beechwood Gr
Harrogate HG2 ....222 F7
16 Ilkley LS29 ....175 C2
Beechwood Rd YO17 ..215 D2
Beechwood Rise 1
LS22 ....180 C4
Beeforth Cl YO32 .....225 D5
Beeston's La LS17 .....178 C4
Beggarmans Rd DL8 ....80 C8
Belbrough Cl 3 TS15 ...25 C4
Belbrough La TS15 .....25 C4
Belcombe Way 1 YO30 228 A7
Belford La HG4 ....112 A3
Belford Pl 3 HG1 ......219 D1
Belford Rd HG1 ....219 D2
Belford Sq 9 HG1 .....219 D1
Belgrave Cres
Harrogate HG2 ....222 E8
15 Scarborough YO12 ....212 F5
Belgrave St
3 Skipton BD23 ....216 E4
York YO31 ....228 C7
Belgrave Terr
3 Hurworth-on-Tees DL2 ..22 D8
14 Scarborough YO11 ....212 F5
Bell Cl Haxby YO32 ....225 C8
5 Seamer YO12 ....99 D6
Bell End Gn YO18 ......49 D3
Bell La Cawood YO8 ...197 A7
Huby YO61 ....144 A4
Husthwaite YO61 ....117 B5
Rawcliffe DN14 ....205 A2
Ulleskelf LS24 ....190 C2
Bellaby Pk 7 YO62 .....93 D7
Bellburn La DL3 ....3 B7
Belle Hill BD24 ....131 D3
Belle Vue LS29 ....218 C3
Belle Vue Cres 33 YO14 .101 B3
Belle Vue Par 9 YO11 ..212 F5
Belle Vue Pl 10 YO11 ..212 F5
Belle Vue St
34 Filey YO14 ....101 B3
Scarborough YO12 ......212 F5
York YO10 ....228 E3
Belle Vue Terr
Whitby YO21 ....208 D7
York YO10 ....228 E3
Bellerby Camp DL8 .....60 B7
Bellerby Rd DL8 ....60 D6
Bellerbyhurn Rd YO17 ..95 F2
Bellevue Terr
Ripon HG4 ....214 C5
2 Skipton BD23 ....216 E4
Bellfarm Ave YO31 ....228 E8
Bellground La YO30 ...165 D4
Bellhouse La YO21 .....29 C7
Bellhouse Way YO24 ..230 B8
Bellingham Cl YO7 ....211 C3
Bellman Wlk 3 HG4 ...113 D2
Bellmans Croft YO23 ..230 B2
Bell's Ct 15 YO62 ....92 F6
Bellwood Ave
Boston Spa LS23 ....188 E7
Lockwood TS12 ....9 E7
Bellwood Dr YO24 .....230 B8
Belmangate TS14 ....8 F6
Belmont WF11 ....201 D5
Belmont Ave
Harrogate HG2 ....220 D4
10 Otley LS21 ....176 F1
Belmont Cl 3 YO30 ....225 A1
Belmont Gr 1 HG2 .....220 D3
Belmont Prim Sch TS14 ..8 F6
Belmont Rd
Harrogate HG2 ....219 C2
Ilkley LS29 ....218 E4
Scarborough YO11 ......213 A4
Belmont St BD23 ......216 F4
Belmont Terr 2 HG2 ...220 D3
Belmont Wharf BD23 ..216 F4
Belthorpe La YO42 ....169 E1
Belton Park Dr 7 DL9 ..40 E4
Belvedere Pl YO11 ....213 A3
Belvedere Rd YO11 ....213 A3
Belvoir Ave 8 YO41 ....185 B2
Belvoir Dr WF11 ......201 F2
Ben La BB18 ....171 E2
Ben Rhydding Dr LS29 .218 F3
Ben Rhydding Prim Sch
LS29 ....218 E4
Ben Rhydding Rd
LS29 ....218 D3
Ben Rhydding Sta
LS29 ....218 F4
Bence The YO42 ......170 C3
Benedict Ave YO8 .....232 E4
Beningbrough Dr HG3 .219 B5
Beningbrough La
YO30 ....165 D5
Benjy La YO19 ....192 E7
Benkhill Dr 16 DL8 .....63 A2
Bennett St 11 BD23 ...216 F3
Bennions Way 5 DL10 ..41 E4
Bennison La YO21 ......13 A1
Bennymoor La YO8 ....198 C4
Bensham Rd DL1 ....3 D8
Benson La WF6 ....200 B2
Bent La Colne BB8 .....186 A3
Sutton BD20 ....187 E7
Bent Rigg La YO13 .....54 B7
Bentham Moor Rd
LA6 ....103 A2
Bentham Rd LA6 ......103 B3
Bentham Sta LA2 ......129 A7
Bentinck Ave TS5 ....6 F8
Bentley Wynd TS16 ......5 D3
Benton Cap La BD22 ..187 B7
Bents La YO18 ....71 A5
Beresford Cl 6 DL8 .....63 B2
Beresford Terr YO23 ..228 C1
Berghill La YO7 ....66 A7
Berkeley Terr YO26 ...227 E5
Berkley Dr TS14 ....8 F5
Bernard La YO26 ......164 B3
Bernica Gr TS17 ....6 A4
Berry Bank DL11 ....1 A6
Berry La LS26 ....200 C8
Berrygate La HG4 .....214 E7
Berry's Ave 5 HG5 ....221 B6
Berwick Rd
Archdeacon Newton DL3 ...3 A7
18 Scotton DL9 ....40 E4
Bestmire La DL6 ....65 A4
Betteras Hill Rd LS25 .202 A8
Betton Rise YO13 ....99 B8
Between Dikes Rd
YO8 ....204 F8
Beulah St 10 HG1 .....219 D2
Beverley Balk YO41 ...168 B2
Beverley Cl 12 YO11 ...100 B6
Beverley Gate YO12 ....99 D1
Beverley Rd
11 Eastfield YO11 ....100 B6

Beverley Rd *continued*
Middlesbrough TS7 . . . . .7 D6
Norton YO17 . . . . .215 E3
Beverley Rise LS29 . . . .175 C2
Beverley Sch TS4 . . . . .6 F8
Bewerley Rd HG1 . . . . .219 B5
Bewlay St YO23 . . . . . . .228 C2
Bewley Gr TS5 . . . . .6 E7
Bexhill Cl WF8 . . . . .201 C1
Bexley Dr TS6 . . . . .7 E8
Bickerton Way LS21 . . .176 F1
Bickley Gate YO13 . . . . . .73 F6
Bickley Howe YO12 . . . .212 B4
Bickley Way TS8 . . . . .7 A5
Bielby Cl 8 Bedale DL8 . . .63 B3
33 Scalby YO12 . . . . .75 D5
Big Meadow Dr 5 LS29 174 E4
Biggin La LS25 . . . . .196 C6
Bilsdale Cl
Northallerton DL7 . . . . . . .210 C2
York YO30 . . . . .224 E2
Bilsdale Gr HG5 . . . . . . .221 D6
Bilsdale Midcable Chop Gate C of E Prim Sch TS9 . . .46 F6
Bilton Cl HG1 . . . . .219 E6
Bilton Dr HG1 . . . . .219 D4
Bilton Grange Cl HG1 .219 D5
Bilton Grange CP Sch
HG1 . . . . .219 D5
Bilton Grove Ave HG1 .219 E5
Bilton Hall Dr HG1 . . . .220 D6
Bilton La HG1 . . . . .219 E6
Binks Cl DL6 . . . . .210 B7
Binnington Carr La
YO12 . . . . .99 B1
Binns La BD20 . . . . .187 D7
Binsley La YO61 . . . . . . .117 E2
Binsoe La HG4 . . . . .86 F3
Birch Ave Malton YO17 . .215 D6
Sleights YO22 . . . . .32 A6
Birch Cl 8 Filey YO14 . . .101 B3
9 Hunton DL9 . . . . .40 F2
2 Kirklevington TS15 . . . . .24 E8
4 Thorpe Willoughby YO8 197 B1
Birch Cres 10 YO22 . . . . . .32 A6
Birch Dr 2 Faceby TS9 . . . .25 F1
Kippax LS25 . . . . .194 D2
Birch Gr
Castleford WF10 . . . . .201 B3
Harrogate HG1 . . . . .219 E6
Kippax LS25 . . . . .194 D1
Birch Hall La BB18 . . . . .172 B1
Birch La 13 YO32 . . . . . . .166 E5
Birch Rd DL1 . . . . .3 D8
Birch View 8 YO18 . . . . . .96 A6
Birches The TS8 . . . . .7 A5
Birchfield Dr TS16 . . . . . . .5 D5
Birchwood Cl 16 BD24 . . .131 D2
Birchwood Ct 5 LS29 . . .218 A4
Birchwood Mews HG2 .222 F7
Birchwood Rd TS7 . . . . . . .7 C6
Bird Gdn★ LS25 . . . . . . .195 B7
Bird La Hensall DN14 . . .203 D2
Kellington DN14 . . . . . . .202 F4
Bird Ridding La DL8 . . . .60 B1
Birdale Field La LS22 . .188 B8
Birdforth Way 1 YO62 . . .92 C1
Birdwood Cl DL9 . . . . . .209 C2
Birk Brow Rd TS12 . . . . . .9 D5
Birk Field Bank YO21 . . .28 F6
Birk Head La YO62 . . . . .70 F4
Birk La YO42 . . . . .199 D8
Birkby La DL7 . . . . .23 B1
Birk-Crag Ct 2 HG3 . . .161 B2
Birkdale Ave HG5 . . . . .221 D5
Birkdale Gr 4 YO26 . . . .227 B5
Birker La
Newton on Derwent
YO41 . . . . .185 D4
Wilberfoss YO41 . . . . . . .185 F6
Birkett La CA17 . . . . .14 B7
Birkhills HG3 . . . . .140 A3
Birkin La WF11 . . . . . . .202 B4
Birkin Rd YO8 . . . . .202 F5
Birklands 1 YO62 . . . . . . .93 D7
Birkwith La LA2 . . . . . . .128 F7
Birstwith C of E Prim Sch
HG3 . . . . .160 E6
Birstwith Dr YO26 . . . . .227 E4
Birstwith Grange HG3 .160 E6
Birstwith Rd HG1 . . . . .220 A3
Birthwaite La HG3 . . . .161 C8
Birtley Ave TS5 . . . . .6 E7
Bishop Cl 1 HG3 . . . . . .137 C4
Bishop Ct 2 YO8 . . . . . .232 B6
Bishop Garth 2 HG3 . . .137 C4
Bishop Monkton C of E Prim Sch HG3 . . . . .140 B5
Bishop Thornton C of E Prim Sch HG3 . . . . .139 A2
Bishop Thornton RC Prim Sch HG3 . . . . .139 A2
Bishop Way 3 HG3 . . . . .137 C4
Bishop Witton Sch
YO42 . . . . .169 F2
Bishopdale Cl HG5 . . . .221 D6
Bishopdale Dr
7 Collingham LS22 . . . . .180 A1
1 Collingham LS22 . . . . .188 A8
Bishopdike Rd
Cawood YO8 . . . . .197 A6
Sherburn in Elmet LS25 . .196 A4
Bishopgate St YO23 . . .233 B1
Bishophill Jun YO1 . . . .233 A1
Bishophill Senior YO1 . .233 B1
Bishopsgarth DL7 . . . . .210 C4
Bishopsway YO10 . . . . .229 C3
Bishopthorpe Inf Sch
YO23 . . . . .231 A4
Bishopthorpe Pal★
YO23 . . . . .231 B4
Bishopthorpe Rd
YO23 . . . . .231 B5
Bishopton HG4 . . . . . . .214 A5
Bishopton La
Great Burdon DL1 . . . . .4 A7
Ripon HG4 . . . . .113 D2
Bisley Ct 13 DL1 . . . . .3 F6
Bismarck St YO26 . . . . .227 E5
Bitterdale La YO62 . . . . .70 A3
Black Abbey La 1 BD20 187 E8
Black Bank Rd LA2 . . . .130 E3
Black Dike La YO26 . . . .182 F8
Black Fen La YO8 . . . . . .232 C8
Black Gill La
Airton BD23 . . . . .154 B8
Settle BD23 . . . . .132 A1
Black Hill YO62 . . . . . . .118 E5
Black Hill Rd HG3 . . . . .157 F8
Black Horse La TS15 . . . .25 C3
Black Sike La YO13 . . . . .98 B4
Black Wlk WF8 . . . . .201 B1
Blackbird Way 8 YO12 . . .99 F6
Blackburn La WF11 . . . .202 B2
Blacklee Cl 4 YO32 . . . .167 B8
Blacksmith Bank DL8 . . .62 E5
Blacksmith Hill YO22 . . .53 A7
Blackthorn TS8 . . . . .7 B4
Blackthorn Dr YO31 . . .225 E2
Blackthorn La HG3 . . . .222 C3
Blackwell DL3 . . . . .3 B3
Blackwell La DL3 . . . . . . .3 B4
Blackwood La YO8 . . . .198 F7
Blackwood Rd YO8 . . . .198 E8
Blair Ave TS17 . . . . .5 F4
Blair Pk HG5 . . . . .221 C5
Blake Ct YO19 . . . . .193 A8
Blake Gate HG3 . . . . . .136 E1
Blake St YO1 . . . . .233 B3
Blakeley Cres 3 BB18 . .171 D2
Blakeley Gr YO30 . . . . .224 F3
Blakeney Pl YO10 . . . . .228 F3
Blakey Bank YO62 . . . . . .49 A5
Blakey Cl YO7 . . . . .211 C1
Blakey La YO7 . . . . .211 C1
Blakey Rd YO62 . . . . .70 B6
Bland La YO26 . . . . .227 A4
Blandford Rd DL9 . . . . . .40 E3
Blands Ave WF10 . . . . . .200 D7
Bland's Cliff 27 YO11 . . .213 A6
Blands Cres 3 WF10 . . .200 D7
Blands Gr 4 WF10 . . . . .200 D7
Bland's Hill HG5 . . . . . .221 A4
Blands Terr WF10 . . . . .200 D7
Blansby La YO17 . . . . . .121 C8
Blansby Park La YO18 . . .96 A8
Blatchford YO30 . . . . . .228 B8
Blawath Rd YO18 . . . . . . .51 A2
Blayshaw La HG3 . . . . . .110 B4
Blazefield Bank HG3 . . .137 D3
Blea Moor Rd LA6 . . . . . .78 E2
Blea Pit La HG4 . . . . . . .140 E8
Bleaberry La YO41 . . . . .169 B5
Blean La DL8 . . . . .57 D3
Bleara Rd BB18 . . . . . . .186 B8
Blenheim Ave 4 YO21 . . .208 B7
Blenheim Cl DL10 . . . . . .41 F6
Blenheim Ct
Harrogate HG2 . . . . .222 D7
Rawcliffe YO30 . . . . .224 D3
Blenheim St 12 YO12 . . . .213 A7
Blenheim Way HG2 . . . .222 C7
Bleriot Way YO30 . . . . . .225 A3
Blewhouse La DL8 . . . . . .61 E3
Blind La Aiskew DL8 . . . . .63 B3
Barton DL10 . . . . .21 D7
Burton in Lonsdale LA6 . . .102 F3
Guisborough TS14 . . . . .8 C6
Hurworth DL2 . . . . .22 E8
Knaresborough HG5 . . . . .221 B7
Scorton DL10 . . . . .42 B8
Tockwith YO26 . . . . .181 B8
Blind Piece La YO7 . . . . .116 A6
Bloe Beck La LA2 . . . . .129 E6
Bloody Beck Hill YO13 . . .54 A7
Blossom St YO24 . . . . . .233 A1
Blossomgate HG4 . . . . .214 B5
Blue Bank YO22 . . . . .32 A4
Blue Barn La TS15 . . . . . .25 C6
Blue Bell Gr TS5 . . . . .6 F6
Blue Bridge La YO10 . . .228 D2
Blue Nile Way 25 DL9 . . . .41 A5
Blue Slates Cl YO19 . . . .193 A8
Bluebeck Dr YO30 . . . . .227 E8
Bluebell Mdw 15 HG3 . . .161 B3
Bluebell Wlk 18 HG3 . . .161 B3
Blyth Cl YO8 . . . . .232 A5
Boar La TS17 . . . . .6 B5
Boat La Barforth DL11 . . . .1 C7
Great Ouseburn YO26 . . . .164 C8
Kirby Hall YO26 . . . . .142 C1
Mickletown LS26 . . . . . . .200 D5
Boatcliffe Rd YO14 . . . . .127 D7
Boathouse La DL2 . . . . . . .2 E4
Bob La YO7 . . . . .65 E3
Bodmin Dr WF6 . . . . . . .200 A2
Bodner Hill YO61 . . . . . .118 F1
Boeing Way TS18 . . . . .5 F7
Bog La
Askham Bryan YO24 . . . . .230 B6
Barwick in Elmet & Scholes
LS15 . . . . .194 A7
Stirton with Thorlby
BD23 . . . . .216 D7
Boggart La LS24 . . . . . . .190 C2
Boggy La DL10 . . . . .209 B5
Boghole Bank DL6 . . . . . .45 B3
Boghouse La TS13 . . . . . .10 F3
Bogs La
Bridge Hewick HG4 . . . . . .114 C1
Harrogate HG1 . . . . .220 C5
Bolckow St TS14 . . . . .8 F7
Bold Venture St BD23 . . .216 F2
Boldron Cl 8 TS18 . . . . . . .5 D8
Bolland St 16 BB18 . . . . .171 D2
Bolling Rd LS29 . . . . . . .218 D4
Boltby Rd YO30 . . . . . . .224 F2
Bolton Abbey Sta
BD23 . . . . .174 D8
Bolton Ave DL10 . . . . . .209 B7
Bolton Castle★ DL8 . . . .59 B6
Bolton Cross DL10 . . . . . .41 F5
Bolton Ct 14 DL8 . . . . . . .60 D5
Bolton Hall★ BD23 . . . .157 F1
Bolton La YO42 . . . . . . .169 E1
Bolton on Swale C of E Prim Sch DL10 . . . . .41 F6
Bolton Priory (rems of)★
BD23 . . . . .157 F1
Bolton Rd
Draughton BD23 . . . . .174 F7
Silsden BD20 . . . . .174 D3
Bolton St HG1 . . . . .219 D4
Bolton Way
13 Leyburn DL8 . . . . .60 D5
Richmond DL10 . . . . .209 C8
Bolton-on-Swale Nature Reserve★ DL10 . . . . .41 F5
Bonby La YO8 . . . . .192 E2
Bond End HG5 . . . . .221 A6
Bond La
Appleton Roebuck YO23 . .190 F5
Settle BD24 . . . . .131 D2
Bond St WF8 . . . . .201 C1
Bondgate Helmsley YO62 .92 F6
Pontefract WF8 . . . . .201 C1
Ripon HG4 . . . . .214 C4
Selby YO8 . . . . .232 B7
Bondgate Gn HG4 . . . . .214 D4
Bondgate Green Cl 6
HG4 . . . . .214 C4
Bondgate Green La
HG4 . . . . .214 C4
Bondings Rise 5 LS25 .196 A4
Bonington Ct 7 YO26 . .227 E4
Bonny Gr TS8 . . . . .7 C5
Bonnygate La YO61 . . . .118 F3
Bonnygrove Way TS8 . . . .7 B5
Boonhill Rd YO62 . . . . . . .69 F4
Boosbeck Rd TS12 . . . . . .9 D8
Boot St 26 BB18 . . . . . .172 A1
Booth Bridge La BD23 .172 A3
Booth Ferry Rd DN14 . . .205 F4
Booth St 27 LS29 . . . . . .176 C1
Bootham YO30 . . . . . . .233 A3
Bootham Bar★ YO31 . . .233 B3
Bootham Cres YO30 . . . .233 A4
Bootham Park Hospl
YO31 . . . . .233 B4
Bootham Row YO31 . . . .233 B3
Bootham Sch YO31 . . . .233 A3
Bootham Sq YO31 . . . . .233 B3
Bootham Terr YO30 . . . .233 A3
Boothferry Prim Sch
DN14 . . . . .205 F2
Boothferry Rd DN14 . . .205 F2
Boothwood Rd YO30 . . .224 E2
Bootiful La DN14 . . . . . .206 F7
Borage Rd 30 HG3 . . . . .161 B3
Bore Tree Baulk YO19 .184 D6
Borogate 9 YO62 . . . . . . .92 F6
Borough Mere La
YO17 . . . . .215 D8
Borough Rd
Darlington DL1 . . . . .3 D5
Richmond DL10 . . . . .209 B8
Boroughbridge High Sch
YO51 . . . . .141 B5
Boroughbridge Rd
Bishop Monkton HG3 . . . . .140 B5
Bridge Hewick HG4 . . . . . .114 B1
Dishforth YO7 . . . . .115 A2
Knaresborough HG5 . . . . .221 B7
North Otterington DL7 . . . . .64 E6
Northallerton DL7 . . . . . . .210 C1
Ripon HG4 . . . . .214 E3
Scriven HG5 . . . . .162 E6
Westwick YO51 . . . . .140 D4
Whixley YO26 . . . . .164 B4
York YO26 . . . . .227 D5
Borrage Green La
HG4 . . . . .214 B4
Borrage La HG4 . . . . . .214 B4
Borrowby Ave DL6 . . . .210 F3
Borrowby La
Borrowby TS13 . . . . .11 D7
Staithes TS13 . . . . .13 J1
Borrowbydale Ave
HG5 . . . . .221 D6
Borrowdale Dr
Castleford WF10 . . . . .201 B5
York YO30 . . . . .224 F1
Boss Moor La BD23 . . . .155 F8
Boston Dr TS7 . . . . .7 B5
Boston Rd Clifford LS23 .188 E7
Wetherby LS22 . . . . .180 C2
Boston Spa C of E Sch
LS23 . . . . .188 E8
Boston Spa Comp Sch
LS23 . . . . .188 D8
Boston Spa Primrose Lane Jun & Infants Sch
LS23 . . . . .188 E8
Botheby Wood BD23 . . .216 E5
Bottom House La YO22 .33 B5
Bottoms La YO22 . . . . . . .33 B6
Botton Rd LA2 . . . . .128 E2
Bouldershaw La DL11 . . .17 D1
Boulsworth Dr BB8 . . . .186 B1
Boulsworth Gr 9 BB8 . . .186 A3
Boundary Ave BD20 . . . .187 E7
Boundary Way DL10 . . .209 F8
Bourlon Rd DL9 . . . . . .209 A2
Bournemouth Rd TS3 . . . .7 C8
Bouthwaite Dr 13 YO26 .227 E4
Bow Bridge Dr BD23 . . .217 D7
Bow Bridge La YO21 . . . .29 A7
Bow Bridge View
LS24 . . . . .189 F7
Bow St TS14 . . . . .8 F7
Bowbridge La DL7 . . . . . .63 A8
Bowcarr La YO26 . . . . . .163 D8
Bowcliffe Rd LS23 . . . . .188 E5
Bowe Cres 8 DL8 . . . . . . .63 B2
Bowen Rd DL3 . . . . .3 B7
Bower Rd HG1 . . . . .219 D3
Bower St HG1 . . . . .219 D2
Bower Wlk YO17 . . . . . .215 E4
Bowes Ave YO31 . . . . . .228 E5
Bowes La YO14 . . . . . . .100 F5
Bowesfield Cres TS18 . . . .6 A8
Bowesfield Ind Est TS18 . .6 A8
Bowesfield La TS18 . . . . . .6 A7
Bowland Cl HG2 . . . . . .220 D1
Bowland Ct HG2 . . . . . .220 D1
Bowland La YO42 . . . . . .193 E2
Bowland View LA6 . . . . .103 E3
Bowland Way YO30 . . . .225 A1
Bowling Green Ct
YO31 . . . . .228 D8
Bowling Green La
9 Hunmanby YO14 . . . . . .126 F8
Manfield DL2 . . . . .2 B4
York YO31 . . . . .233 C4
Bowling La YO17 . . . . . .215 E4
Bowling View BD23 . . . .216 D3
Bowman St DL3 . . . . .3 D7
Bowness Dr YO30 . . . . . .224 E1
Bowthorpe La YO8 . . . . .199 B4
Bowyers Cl YO23 . . . . . .230 C4
Box Hill YO12 . . . . .212 C3
Box La WF8 . . . . .201 C1
Boyle & Petyts Sch
BD23 . . . . .174 F8
Boyle The LS15 . . . . . . .194 B8
Boynton La
Barton-le-Street YO17 . . . .120 F8
Rawcliffe DN14 . . . . .205 A1
Boynton Rd DL7 . . . . .22 E2
Bracewell La BD23 . . . . .171 B4
Bracewell St 15 BB18 . . .171 D2
Bracken Cl
Whitby YO22 . . . . .208 E4
York YO32 . . . . .225 F4
Bracken Cres TS14 . . . . . .8 D6
Bracken Field BD23 . . . .134 B3
Bracken Hill
Scarborough YO12 . . . . . .212 C7
2 York YO10 . . . . .229 C3
Bracken Rd YO24 . . . . . .230 F7
Brackenber Cl BD24 . . .131 C2
Brackenber La BD24 . . .131 C1
Brackenfield Sch HG1 . .219 A2
Brackenhill Ave YO8 . . .232 A4
Brackenhill La
Brayton YO8 . . . . .232 A3
Church Fenton LS24 . . . . .196 C8
Sleights YO22 . . . . .32 A5
Brackenhills YO26 . . . . .165 F1
Brackenhoe Sec Sch
TS4 . . . . .7 B8
Brackenley Ave 2
BD23 . . . . .217 C7
Brackenley Cl 3 BD23 .217 C7
Brackenley Cres BD23 .217 C7
Brackenley Dr BD23 . . .217 C7
Brackenley Gr 1 BD23 .217 C7
Brackenley La BD23 . . .217 A7
Brackenthwaite La
HG3 . . . . .222 A1
Brackenwell La LS17 . . .178 B4
Brackenwood Cl 2
LS29 . . . . .218 E4
Brackit La YO61 . . . . .91 B2
Bracknell Rd TS17 . . . . . .6 C8
Bradfords Cl 8 LS23 . . .188 E6
Bradley Ave
Castleford WF10 . . . . .200 E4
Northallerton DL6 . . . . . . .210 F2
Bradley Cres YO23 . . . .182 D6
Bradley Dr YO24 . . . . . .230 C8
Bradley Gr BD20 . . . . . .174 B1
Bradley La YO23 . . . . . .182 C5
Bradley Rd
Pickering YO18 . . . . .71 F4
Silsden BD20 . . . . .174 B2
Bradley Rise BD20 . . . . .174 B1
Bradleys Both CP Sch
BD20 . . . . .173 E3
Bradleys Terr 2 TS9 . . . . .8 A2
Bradworth Cl 3 YO11 . . .100 B7
Bradworth Dr 2 YO11 . .100 B7
Braeburn Cty Jun Sch
YO11 . . . . .100 A6
Braegate La LS24 . . . . .190 E7
Braemar Dr LS25 . . . . . .194 D4
Braeside 3 TS15 . . . . . . .24 E8
Braeside Gdns YO24 . . .227 E3
Brafferton C of E Prim Sch
YO61 . . . . .115 F1
Brafferton Hall Garde 3
YO61 . . . . .115 F1
Braham La HG5 . . . . . . .179 F7
Brailsford Cres YO30 . . .228 A8
Braimber La YO51 . . . . .141 C1
Braithegayte YO19 . . . .192 F8
Braithwaite Endowed C of E Prim Sch HG3 . . . . . . .159 B7
Braithwaite Hall★ DL8 .84 D8
Braithwaite La
Dacre HG3 . . . . .159 A7
East Witton Town DL8 . . . . .84 E8
Braker La YO26 . . . . . . .163 F4
Bramall La 6 DL1 . . . . . . .3 F6
Bramble Cl 11 HG3 . . . . .161 B3
Bramble Dene YO24 . . .230 D7
Bramble Wlk YO17 . . . .215 B4
Brambles 8 YO8 . . . . . .197 B1
Brambles The 6 LS29 . .175 C2
Bramcote Prep Sch for Boys
YO11 . . . . .213 A3
Brame La HG3 . . . . .177 A8
Bramham Ave YO26 . . .227 A3
Bramham CP Sch
LS23 . . . . .188 E6
Bramham Dr HG3 . . . . .219 A4
Bramham Gr YO26 . . . .227 A3
Bramham La LS23 . . . . .188 A6
Bramham Park Gdns★
LS23 . . . . .188 C4
Bramham Pk★ LS23 . . .188 C4
Bramham Rd
Boston Spa LS23 . . . . .188 E7
Thorner LS14 . . . . .188 A3
York YO26 . . . . .227 A2
Bramley Ave YO8 . . . . . .198 B5
Bramley Garth YO31 . . .229 B6
Bramper La DL7 . . . . .42 E1
Branch Rd BD23 . . . . . .216 F2
Brandon Gr YO32 . . . . .226 E3
Brandsby Bank YO61 . . .118 D3
Brandsby Gr YO31 . . . .225 E2
Brandsby Rd YO61 . . . .118 A1
Brandsby St YO61 . . . . .118 A1
Brandsdale Cres
YO10 . . . . .229 D3
Brankin Dr DL1 . . . . .3 E4
Brankin Rd DL1 . . . . .3 D3
Branklyn Gdns TS17 . . . . .6 A4
Branksome Comp Sch
DL3 . . . . .3 A6
Branksome Gr 1 TS18 . . . .5 E8
Bransdale TS14 . . . . .8 D6
Bransdale Ave
Northallerton DL7 . . . . . . .210 C2
11 Pontefract WF6 . . . . . .200 A2
Bransdale Cl 6 WF6 . . . .200 A2
Bransdale Gr 3 HG5 . . .221 D6
Bransdale Mews 10
WF6 . . . . .200 A2
Bransdale Rd YO62 . . . . .48 B1
Bransdale Wlk WF6 . . . .200 A2
Bransholme Dr YO30 . . .225 A2
Brant Bank La LS29 . . . .175 B3
Brant La LS24 . . . . .189 D4
Branton Cl YO26 . . . . . .142 A1
Branton Ct YO26 . . . . . .142 A1
Branton La YO26 . . . . . .142 A1
Branton Pl YO26 . . . . . .227 A3
Brass Castle La TS8 . . . . .7 C3
Brat La LS21 . . . . .177 A7
Bravener Ct YO30 . . . . .165 B6
Brawby La YO62 . . . . . . .94 E1
Bray Gate YO42 . . . . . . .169 E2
Bray Rd YO10 . . . . .231 F8
Braygate Balk YO18 . . . . .72 C5
Braygate La YO18 . . . . . .72 D5
Braygate St YO17 . . . . .121 A2
Braythorne La LS21 . . . .177 E4
Brayton C of E Prim Sch
YO8 . . . . .232 A2
Brayton Cty Inf Sch
YO8 . . . . .232 A2
Brayton Cty Jun Sch
YO8 . . . . .232 A2
Brayton High Sch
YO8 . . . . .232 A3
Brayton La YO8 . . . . . . .232 B1
Breakmoor Ave BD20 . . .174 C2
Brearlands BD23 . . . . . .172 A3
Brearton La HG3 . . . . . .161 E8
Breary Cl YO24 . . . . . . .227 F1
Breary Flat La HG5 . . . .221 C7
Brechin Dr TS17 . . . . .6 B6
Breckenbrough La
DL10 . . . . .41 A3
Breckenbrough Sch
YO7 . . . . .89 A6
Breckney La YO17 . . . . .122 D5
Brecks La Kippax LS25 . .194 C2
Pockley YO62 . . . . .93 B8
Strensall YO32 . . . . .167 B7
Swillington LS26 . . . . . . .194 B2
York YO32 . . . . .225 F4
Brecksfield YO30 . . . . . .224 C5
Brecon Cres TS17 . . . . . . .5 F4
Breedycroft La YO17 . . .121 C4
Breighton Rd
Bubwith YO8 . . . . .199 D6
Wressle YO8 . . . . .199 C3
Brendon Gr TS17 . . . . . . .6 A3
Brentwood DL8 . . . . .60 D5
Brentwood Cres YO10 . .229 C2
Brewers Ct YO7 . . . . . . .211 B3
Brewerton St HG5 . . . . .221 A5

Brewery La
5 Ripon HG4 214 C4
Skipton BD23 216 F4
Brewery Rd LS29 218 C4
Brewster Terr HG4 214 C6
Briar Ave YO26 227 B4
Briar Cliffe YO8 232 A3
Briar Dr YO31 225 F2
Briar Pk 5 YO62 93 D7
Briar Rd TS17 6 B7
Briar Wlk DL3 3 B3
Briardene Ave 9 YO12 75 E5
Briarfield Cl LS29 218 D3
Briars Ct YO23 190 E5
Briars Dr YO23 190 E5
Briars The HG5 221 B7
Briarwood Cl YO8 202 F7
Brick Kiln La YO8 203 D6
Brick Lands La YO8 203 F4
Brickfield La YO51 141 D4
Brickhill La YO8 204 F4
Brickkiln La
Aldbrough DL11 2 A3
Forcett & Carkin DL11 20 C8
Brickyard La YO7 89 C6
Brickyard Rd YO51 141 A4
Bridge Beck La YO7 66 C7
Bridge Cl
Burniston YO13 75 D7
3 Colburn DL9 41 A5
Haxby YO32 225 C7
5 Knaresborough HG5 221 A5
Bridge Cres DN14 205 C8
Bridge End DL6 65 B5
Bridge Foot LS23 188 F8
Bridge Garth
2 Boston Spa LS23 188 E7
South Milford LS25 195 F2
Bridge Gn YO21 29 C7
Bridge Hill LS21 176 C7
Bridge Holm La YO22 33 C2
Bridge La Ilkley LS29 218 A5
Pollington DN14 207 F6
York YO30 233 B4
Bridge Rd Airmyn DN14 205 E4
Bishopthorpe YO23 230 F3
Boston Spa LS23 188 F8
Brompton-on-Swale DL10 41 B6
Glusburn BD20 187 E7
Hurworth DL2 3 B3
Malton YO17 215 C5
Old Byland & Scawton
YO7 91 F7
10 Stokesley TS9 26 C7
Bridge St 5 Bedale DL8 63 A3
9 Brafferton YO61 115 F1
Castleford WF10 200 F4
Egglescliffe TS16 5 D4
12 Helmsley YO62 92 F6
8 Normanton South WF6 200 B2
16 Pickering YO18 95 F7
Richmond DL10 209 B6
Skipton BD23 216 F4
Tadcaster LS24 189 E6
Thirsk YO7 211 B3
Whitby YO22 208 D7
York YO1 233 B2
Bridge Terr DL10 209 B6
Bridge View Rd HG4 214 C7
Bridges Ct YO8 232 D6
Bridges La YO42 193 E4
Bridle Way 1 YO26 227 A3
Bridle Wlk YO8 232 C4
Bridlington Rd
Hunmanby YO14 127 A7
Sledmere YO25 150 C4
1 Stamford Bridge YO41 168 D2
Wold Newton YO25 126 A4
Bridlington St YO14 126 F8
Brier Hill YO21 29 C7
Brier La YO8 205 A4
Briercliffe YO12 212 C7
Briergate YO32 225 C7
Brierlands Cl LS25 194 D4
Brierlands La LS25 194 E4
Brierley Rd YO12 99 E7
Briery Cl 18 LS29 175 C2
Brigg La YO8 204 D5
Briggate HG5 221 B5
Brigg's Ave WF10 200 E3
Briggs St YO31 228 C7
Bright St 18 Colne BB8 186 A3
Darlington DL1 3 E5
1 Glusburn BD20 173 E1
Skipton BD23 216 E4
York YO26 227 F5
Bright Terr BB8 186 A1
Brighton Rd LS29 218 E3
Brigshaw Dr WF10 200 C8
Brigshaw High Sch
WF10 200 C8
Brigshaw La WF10 200 C8
Brind La DN14 199 F2
Brindle Park Dr WF10 201 A3
Brindleys La DN14 199 F3
Brinkburn Ave DL3 3 B7
Brinkburn Dr DL3 3 B6
Brinkburn Rd
Darlington DL3 3 B6
4 Scarborough YO12 212 E5
Brinklow Way HG2 222 B5
Brinkworth Terr 1
YO10 228 E3
Briscoe Ridge La HG3 177 F6
Briscoe Way TS8 6 E5
Britannia Rd DN14 205 F1
Britannia St 2 YO12 212 E5
Britannia Way DN14 205 F2
Broach La Heck DN14 203 D1
Kellington DN14 202 F3
Broach Rd Heck DN14 207 D8
Hensall DN14 203 C1
Broad Acres YO32 225 C7
Broad Balk YO17 149 A5
Broad Balk La YO7 115 B1
Broad Carr Rd HG3 110 D2
Broad Cl TS8 6 D5
Broad Dubb Rd HG3 177 C8
Broad Gate
Brompton YO13 98 B7
Hunsingore LS22 180 F8
Marton cum Grafton
YO26 141 F1
Broad Gate Rd YO21 28 E4
Broad Head La BD22 187 E2
Broad Highway YO19 192 F8
Broad La
Appleton Roebuck YO23 191 A6
6 Beal DN14 202 D4
Catton YO41 185 C7
Cawood YO8 197 A6
Church Fenton LS24 196 D6
Rufforth YO23 227 A2
Wistow YO8 197 A5
Broad Oak YO61 166 D8
Broad Oak La 18 YO32 166 E5
Broadacres DN14 204 D3
Broadacres Ave DN14 204 D3
Broadacres Garth
DN14 204 D3
Broadfield La HG4 138 B8
Broadfield Way 9 LS29 174 E4
Broadgate Rd TS5 6 E8
Broadlands YO19 193 A8
Broadlands Dr 5 YO13 99 B8
Broadmanor YO8 199 A7
Broadmires La YO18 96 C5
Broadrum La YO18 95 E6
Broadstone Way YO30 224 E3
Broadway
Scarborough YO12 212 D7
York YO10 231 E8
Broadway Gr 3 YO10 231 E8
Broadway The DL1 3 E5
Broadway W YO10 231 D8
Broadwell Rd TS4 7 A8
Brockfield Pk Dr YO31 225 F2
Brockfield Rd YO31 225 E2
Brockholme La DL6 65 A4
Brocklesby Rd TS14 8 F5
Brockley Cl LS24 196 B7
Broc-o-Bank 1 DN6 206 E2
Brogden La BB18 171 B1
Brokes La DL11 40 B6
Bromley La TS8 7 B3
Bromley St 2 YO26 227 F5
Brompton Carr La
YO13 98 B4
Brompton CP Sch DL6 43 F3
Brompton Hall Sch
YO13 98 C5
Brompton Ings Rd
YO13 98 D3
Brompton La DL6 43 E4
Brompton on Swale C of E
Prim Sch DL10 41 B7
Brompton Rd
Newton-le-Willows DL8 62 B4
Northallerton DL6 210 D5
York YO30 228 A7
Brompton-by-Sawdon CP
Sch YO13 98 C5
Bronte Cl YO12 212 D5
Bronte Ct WF8 201 B1
Bronte Dr DL9 41 A5
Brook House Croft
BD24 131 E6
Brook La Danby YO21 29 C6
Halton West BD23 153 F1
Thornton Dale YO18 96 D6
Weeton LS17 178 C2
Brook Pk YO21 32 A7
Brook St
Castleford WF10 201 B6
18 Earby BB18 172 A1
Hebden BD23 135 A2
Hellifield BD23 154 B3
Ilkley LS29 218 B4
12 Scarborough YO12 212 F6
Selby YO8 232 C4
Skipton BD23 216 F4
York YO31 233 B4
Brook View BD23 173 B4
Brookacre LA6 103 D3
Brooke Cl
Harrogate HG1 219 E7
12 Kirkbymoorside YO62 70 B1
Brookfield HG3 161 A5
Brookfield Cl HG3 161 A5
Brookfield Cres HG3 161 A5
Brookfield Ct 5 WF6 200 B1
Brookfield Garth HG3 161 A5
Brookfield Way
7 Earby BB18 172 A1
Hampsthwaite HG3 160 F5
Brookland 1 LA6 102 F2
Brooklands
43 Filey YO14 101 B3
York YO10 229 D4
Brooklands Cl 44 YO14 101 B3
Brooklands Cres DL6 210 E5
Brooklands Sch BD23 216 F2
Brooklands Terr BD23 216 F3
Brooksbank Rd TS7 7 D7
Brookside
Collingham LS22 188 A8
Hovingham YO62 119 E6
Skelton & Brotton TS12 9 D8
Sleights YO22 32 B6
Brookside Ave 1 DL8 63 B2
Brookside Cl 2 DL8 63 B2
Brookwood Way TS16 5 E4
Broom House La
Egton YO21 30 F4
Ugthorpe YO21 12 B2
Broom Rd LS24 189 D5
Broom Wlk YO12 212 E7
Broome Cl
14 Pontefract WF6 200 A2
York YO32 225 F5
Broome Way YO32 226 A5
Broomfield HG3 160 E6
Broomfield Ave DL7 210 D2
Broomfield CP Sch
DL7 210 D2
Broomhill WF10 201 A3
Broomhill Cl 23 WF11 202 A2
Broomhill Cres 25
WF11 202 A2
Broomhill Dr 26 WF11 202 A2
Broomhill Gr 19 WF11 202 A2
Broomhill Pl 22 WF11 202 A2
Broomhill Sq 24 WF11 202 A2
Broomhill Wlk 21 WF11 202 A2
Brootes La BD23 107 C2
Brotes La YO26 164 B5
Brotherton Cty Prim Sch
WF11 201 E4
Brough Ave 5 DL9 41 A5
Brough Hall★ DL10 41 B4
Brough Mdws 4 DL10 41 D5
Brough Rd 23 DL9 40 E4
Brougham Cl YO30 227 F8
Brougham St
Darlington DL3 3 C7
Skipton BD23 217 A3
Broughton Ave BD23 216 D3
Broughton Cres BD23 216 C3
Broughton Gr BD23 216 D3
Broughton Rd
Broughton YO17 121 C3
11 East Ayton/West Ayton
YO13 99 A7
Malton YO17 215 A5
Skipton BD23 216 C3
Broughton Way
4 Harrogate HG2 220 C3
York YO10 229 B4
Brow La LA2 129 D6
Browcliff BD20 174 C2
Brown Bank La BD20 174 D2
Brown Bank Rd
Kirkby Malzeard HG4 111 F5
Norwood HG3 177 B8
Brown Cow Rd YO8 204 C8
Brown Howe Rd YO18 51 A1
Brown La YO26 141 F1
Brown Moor 22 YO41 168 D2
Brown Rigg Rd YO13 53 F5
Browney Croft YO10 233 C1
Browning Cl 3 DL9 40 E4
Brownlow St YO31 233 C4
Brownmoor La
Huby YO61 144 A2
Sutton-on-the-Forest
YO61 166 B8
Brownroyd 14 BB18 172 B1
Browns Ct 4 BD20 173 E3
Browns Fold 3 BD23 134 E3
Brown's Terr 4 TS13 11 F7
Browsfield Rd 24 LS29 174 F4
Broxa Hill YO13 74 C6
Broxa La YO13 74 D5
Broxa Moor La YO13 74 C7
Bruce Way 5 YO18 95 F6
Brunel Ct 12 YO26 227 F5
Brunel Way DL1 3 D5
Brunsell La YO26 163 F7
Brunswick Cl 2 YO32 167 C8
Brunswick Dr HG1 219 B2
Brunswick Pl 1 HG1 219 D1
Brunswick Sh Ctr
YO11 213 A5
Brunswick St
Whitby YO21 208 D6
York YO23 228 B1
Brunt Acres Rd DL8 56 D4
Brunthwaite La BD20 174 E1
Brunton Bank DL8 59 A5
Brunton La HG5 163 B6
Brunton Rd LA2 131 A6
Bry Hills YO12 99 D6
Bryan Cl 13 DL2 3 E1
Bryden Cl DL6 210 E2
Bryony Ct YO8 232 B2
Bryony Rd 4 HG3 161 B3
Bryony Way 5 HG3 161 B3
Bubwith Cty Prim Sch
YO8 199 D7
Buck Haw Brow BD24 131 B4
Buck La YO60 147 B6
Buck Stone La BD22 187 C5
Buckden Cl 13 YO61 143 D8
Buckden Wood La
BD23 107 D8
Buckingham Sq
8 Helmsley YO62 92 F6
7 Helmsley YO62 92 F6
Buckingham St YO1 233 B1
Buckingham Way
WF11 201 F4
Buckle Ct YO8 232 B7
Buckle La WF6 200 A1
Bucks La 1 BD24 131 D2
Buess La DL1 4 A7
Buffet Hill La LA2 129 D7
Bugthorpe La YO41 169 D5
Bugthorpe La Town E
YO41 169 E5
Bull Alley La DN14 204 B3
Bull Balk YO41 185 E4
Bull Hill DL8 61 E8
Bull Ing La BD23 134 D3
Bull La Huby YO61 166 B7
York YO10 228 F3
Bull Moor La YO60 168 A8
Bull Piece La YO17 122 D3
Bullamoor Cl DL6 210 F5
Bullamoor Cty Jun Sch
DL6 210 F5
Bullamoor Rd DL6 210 E5
Buller St YO8 232 B6
Bullock La YO7 89 A5
Bullytree La LS25 195 E2
Bulmer Hill YO60 146 B6
Bungalow Rd BD20 187 D7
Bunkers Hill
Aberford LS25 194 F7
1 Skipton BD23 217 A4
BUPA Belvedere Hospl
YO11 213 A3
Burdale Cl YO17 215 F2
Burdike Ave YO30 228 A8
Burdock Cl 10 HG3 161 B3
Burdyke Inf Sch YO30 228 B8
Burgate YO18 95 F7
Burgoyne Cl HG4 113 D3
Burke Rd YO17 215 C5
Burke St HG1 219 E5
Burlands La YO26 182 F7
Burley Ave HG3 161 A2
Burley Bank Cl HG3 161 A3
Burley Bank Rd HG3 161 A3
Burley Cl LS25 195 F2
Burley in Wharfedale Sch
LS29 176 C1
Burley La HG3 161 A3
Burley Mid Sch LS29 176 C1
Burlington Ave YO10 228 F4
Burlyn Rd 3 YO14 127 A8
Burma Rd DL2 3 F2
Burn Bridge La HG3 222 C2
Burn Bridge Oval HG3 222 C3
Burn Bridge Rd HG3 222 C3
Burn Hall Cl YO8 203 D7
Burn La YO8 203 D6
Burn Wood Ct TS21 5 A7
Burnby Cl HG3 219 B5
Burneston C of E Prim Sch
DL8 87 E8
Burneston Hargill DL8 87 F8
Burnett Cl HG3 140 A2
Burnham Rd LS25 194 C3
Burnholme Ave YO31 229 B6
Burnholme Com Coll
YO31 229 A5
Burnholme Dr YO31 229 A6
Burnholme Gr YO31 229 A5
Burniston Gdns YO13 75 D7
Burniston Gr YO10 229 A4
Burniston Rd YO12 212 E8
Burnley Rd BB8 186 A1
Burnleys Ct LS26 200 B4
Burnleys Dr LS26 200 B4
Burnleys Mews LS26 200 B4
Burnleys View LS26 200 B5
Burnmoor Cres LA6 103 D3
Burnmoor Dr TS16 5 D5
Burnroyd Ave 17 BD20 187 E7
Burns Ct YO24 230 B7
Burns Hill 4 LS29 174 F4
Burns Way
Boston Spa LS23 188 E7
Harrogate HG1 219 E7
Burnsall Cl 6 YO14 101 A3
Burnsall Dr YO26 227 E4
Burnsall La BD23 135 A1
Burnsall Mews BD20 174 B2
Burnsall Prim Sch
BD23 157 B8
Burnside 4 YO11 100 A6
Burnside Ave BD23 216 F2
Burnside Cl HG1 219 B5
Burnside Cres BD23 216 F2
Burnside Dr HG1 219 B5
Burnside Rd
Darlington DL1 3 E4
Harrogate HG1 219 B5
Burnside Wlk HG1 219 B5
Burnt La HG4 87 A1
Burnt Yates C of E Endowed
Prim Sch HG3 160 F8
Burnthouse Bank DL6 45 B3
Burr Bank 15 YO11 213 B6
Burrard Ave DL10 209 B7
Burrill Ave YO30 228 B8
Burrill Dr 13 YO32 166 D5
Burrill Rd DL8 62 F2
Burrow Rd LA6 102 B7
Burstall Dr 2 DL9 209 C1
Burtersett Rd DL8 56 D4
Burton Ave YO30 228 B7
Burton Comm La
LS25 202 A6
Burton Fields Cl 12
YO41 168 D2
Burton Fields Rd 4
YO41 168 D2
Burton Fleming Rd
YO25 126 B3
Burton Gn YO30 228 B8
Burton Hill 3 LA6 102 F3
Burton La YO61 141 D8
Burton Leonard C of E Prim
Sch HG3 140 A2
Burton Rd LA2 128 E8
Burton Salmon CP Sch
LS25 201 F6
Burton Stone La YO30 233 A4
Burtondale Rd 1 YO12 99 F7
Burtree Ave YO30 224 B4
Burtree La YO21 29 B5
Burwains La BD23 155 F5
Burwen Castle (Roman
Fort)★ BD23 172 C4
Burwen Castle Rd
BD23 172 C4
Busby La TS9 26 C4
Busk La LS24 196 C8
Busky Dike La LS21 159 E2
Butcher La Potto DL6 25 C2
Whitley DN14 207 A6
Butcher Terr YO23 228 C1
Butcher's La YO25 126 E3
Butler Rd HG1 219 E5
Butt Fields La DN14 203 F1
Butt Hedge YO26 182 A5
Butt Hill 22 Haxby YO32 166 D5
Kippax LS25 194 D1
Butt La
Carlton Husthwaite YO7 116 F7
Guisborough TS14 9 A6
Wold Newton YO25 126 A3
Buttacre La YO23 182 D2
Butter Mkt 8 DN14 204 C1
Butterbur Way 34 HG3 161 B3
Buttercrambe Rd
YO41 168 C3
Buttercup Cl 6 HG3 161 B3
Butterfield Cl HG3 140 B5
Butterfield Dr TS16 5 D5
Butterfly World★ TS18 5 E6
Buttermere Ave
Middlesbrough TS5 6 E8
4 Wetherby LS22 180 B3
Buttermere Ct 9 YO8 232 B6
Buttermere Dr YO30 224 E1
Butters Cl 20 YO32 166 D5
Butterwick La YO17 120 F8
Butterwick Rd
Barton-le-Street YO17 120 E5
Foxholes YO17 125 B1
Langtoft YO25 151 C7
Butthouse Rigg DL11 35 F8
Buttle La 3 DN14 204 C1
Butts BB18 171 D1
Butts Cl 19 YO41 168 D2
Butts Hill YO14 127 C6
Butts La Bainbridge DL8 81 B8
Barton-le-Willows YO60 146 D2
Bentham LA2 129 A8
Eaglescliffe TS16 5 D4
Monk Fryston LS25 201 E8
South Milford LS25 195 E1
Butts The 12 WF8 201 B1
Buxton Ave TS7 7 B5
Byards Pk 6 HG5 221 A7
Byefield Gr YO13 99 B8
Byemoor Ave TS9 8 A1
Byemoor Cl TS9 8 A1
Byland Abbey (rems of)★
YO61 91 E1
Byland Ave
Northallerton DL6 210 E5
Thirsk YO7 211 C3
York YO31 228 E8
Byland Ct 5 YO21 208 B6
Byland Gr HG1 219 F6
Byland Mews HG5 221 D4
Byland Pl
Harrogate HG1 219 F6
Northallerton DL6 210 E5
Byland Rd
Harrogate HG1 219 F6
Whitby YO21 208 B6
Bylands Way DL3 3 A6
Byng Rd DL9 209 F1
Byram Cl 3 DL6 210 E3
Byram Ct 4 DL6 210 E3
Byram Park Ave WF11 201 F4
Byram Park Rd WF11 202 A4
Byron Ave 3 DN6 206 E1
Byron Ct DL2 22 D7
Byron Dr YO30 227 F8
Byron Rd 21 BB8 186 A3
Byron St 2 BD23 217 A3
Byron Wlk Mews HG2 219 D2
Byward Dr YO12 99 F7
Byway The DL1 3 E5
By-Ways HG2 222 D6

C

Cabin La 2 HG3 137 F1
Caburn Cl 2 YO12 212 B5
Caedmon Ave YO21 208 B8
Caedmon Cl YO31 229 A7
Caedmon Sch YO21 208 D5
Cairnborrow 4 YO24 230 B7
Caithness Cl 1 YO30 224 E3
Calcaria Cres LS24 189 D5
Calcaria Rd LS24 189 E5
Calcutt HG5 221 A4
Caldbeck Cl 1 YO30 225 A1
Calder Ave YO26 227 B8

Calder Cres DN14 207 F6
Caledonia St YO12 212 E5
Caledonian Way DL1 3 F8
Calf Cl YO32 225 D8
Calf Hall La BB18 171 D1
Calf Wood La BD20 172 E1
California Dr WF10 200 B3
California Gr 7 TS9 8 A2
California Rd YO22 208 E5
Calton La BD23 155 A6
Calvert Cl YO32 225 C7
Calvert Hos DL11 36 C4
Calverts Garth YO60 145 D5
Cam Gill Rd BD23 108 B4
Cam High Rd BD23 79 D5
Cam La BD23 172 A3
Camblesforth CP Sch YO8 204 C4
Cambrian Cl 2 YO32 225 F3
Cambridge Ave TS7 7 B5
Cambridge Cres 5 HG1 219 D2
Cambridge Pl
7 Harrogate HG1 219 D2
1 Scarborough YO12 212 E4
Cambridge Rd
Harrogate HG1 219 D2
Middlesbrough TS5 6 E8
Cambridge St
Harrogate HG1 219 D2
Normanton South WF6 200 A1
Scarborough YO12 212 F6
4 York YO24 228 A3
Cambridge Terr
4 Harrogate HG1 219 D2
1 Scarborough YO11 213 A4
Camden Rd WF10 201 B4
Camela La YO8 204 B6
Cameron Gr YO23 228 C1
Camm La DN14 204 C3
Cammock La BD24 131 D2
Camp Hill Cl HG4 214 D3
Campbell Ave
Ripon HG4 113 D3
York YO24 227 E2
Campbell St 11 BD20 187 E8
Campion Cl YO13 75 D5
Campion Dr TS14 8 D6
Campion Gr
Coulby Newham TS7 7 B6
6 Harrogate HG3 161 B3
Campion La TS15 25 B4
Campion Rd DL1 3 D7
Campleshon Rd YO23 228 B1
Campsall Balk DN6 206 E1
Campsall Hall Rd 12 DN6 206 E1
Campsall Park Rd 11 DN6 206 E1
Campsmount Sch DN6 206 D1
Camwal Rd HG1 220 C4
Camwal Terr 5 HG1 220 C4
Cana La HG4 114 E2
Canaan La DL8 60 E2
Canal Garth DN14 207 F6
Canal Rd
Cottingwith YO42 193 C5
Ripon HG4 214 D4
Selby YO8 232 D4
Canal St BD23 216 F4
Canal View YO8 232 D3
Canal Yd 8 BD23 216 F4
Canberra Rd TS7 7 B6
Canby La 4 HG3 179 E6
Candler Ave 12 YO13 99 A7
Candler St YO12 212 E5
Canham Gr YO10 229 D3
Cannon Hall La DN14 202 F1
Cannon St WF10 200 F3
Canon Gr TS15 5 E2
Canon Lee Sch YO30 228 A8
Canons Garth La 2 YO62 92 F6
Canterbury Cl
9 Haxby YO32 166 D5
Whitby YO21 208 C5
Canterbury Ct 5 WF8 201 C2
Canton Gdns TS5 6 E6
Caper Hill YO21 29 F1
Captain Cook & Staithes Heritage Ctr* TS13 13 K2
Captain Cook Birthplace Mus* TS7 7 B7
Captain Cook Cres YO22 208 E6
Captain Cook Meml Mus* YO22 208 E7
Captain Cook Prim Sch TS7 7 B6
Captain Cook's Cl
Hinderwell TS13 11 D8
Staithes TS13 13 K1
Captain Cook's Cres TS7 7 C6
Captain Cook's Mon* TS9 8 D1
Captain Cook's Schoolroom Mus* TS9 8 A1
Captain Cook's Way TS9 8 A1
Cardale Pk HG3 222 A6
Cardan Dr LS29 218 E4
Cardinal Cl 13 LS25 195 F4
Cardinals Cl 3 YO8 197 B8
Careless House La HG3 138 E4
Carentan Cl 6 YO8 232 B6
Carey St YO10 228 D1
Cargate Hill 32 YO14 101 B3
Cargo Fleet La TS3 7 C8
Carl St YO23 228 C2
Carla Beck La BD23 173 B4
Carlbury Ave TS5 6 D6
Carlbury Cres DL3 3 A5
Carless La YO14 100 F4
Carleton Ave BD23 216 E3
Carleton Dr DL3 3 A5
Carleton Endowed Prim Sch BD23 173 B4
Carleton La BD23 173 A4
Carleton New Rd BD23 216 E3
Carleton Rd BD23 216 E1
Carleton St
3 Skipton BD23 216 F3
17 York YO26 227 F5
Carlile Hill TS8 6 E5
Carline Mead 23 HG3 161 B3
Carlisle St 16 YO26 227 F5
Carlton & Faceby C of E Prim Sch TS9 26 A3
Carlton App 1 LS22 180 B3
Carlton Ave Thirsk YO7 211 B1
York YO10 229 B3
Carlton Cl
4 Carlton Miniott YO7 89 C4
Eggborough DN14 202 F1
19 Normanton South WF6 200 A1
Carlton Dr TS17 6 A6
Carlton Gdns 1 WF6 200 B1
Carlton La YO62 92 F7
Carlton Miniott CP Sch YO7 89 B4
Carlton Moor Cres DL1 3 E4
Carlton Rd
Carlton Miniott YO7 89 A3
Catterick Garrison DL9 40 F4
9 Filey YO14 101 B3
Harrogate HG2 222 D7
Helmsley YO62 92 F7
Sutton upon Derwent YO41 185 C1
Carlton St WF6 200 A2
Carlton Terr 6 YO11 213 A4
Carlton Twrs* DN14 204 D2
Carlton View WF10 200 C7
Carlton-in-Snaith CP Sch DN14 204 C3
Carlyle Cres WF10 201 A4
Carlyle Rd WF10 201 A4
Carmel Gr DL3 3 B4
Carmel RC Aided Comp Sch DL3 3 A5
Carmel Rd N DL3 3 B5
Carmel Rd S DL3 3 B4
Carmelite St YO1 233 C2
Carmires Ave
Haxby YO32 166 F5
Knaresborough HG5 221 C8
Carnagil Rd DL9 209 B1
Carnagill CP Sch DL9 40 D4
Carney St TS12 9 D7
Carnot St YO26 227 F5
Carnoustie Cl 1 YO26 227 B4
Carnoustie Dr TS16 5 E5
Carnoustie Gdns 20 WF6 200 B1
Carnoustie Way TS8 7 C5
Caroline Cl 5 YO24 227 F3
Carousel Wlk LS25 195 F4
Carpenters Yd YO17 215 C4
Carpley Green Rd DL8 57 D3
Carr Ave LS25 195 F4
Carr Bridge La DL6 24 D3
Carr Cl
13 Hemingbrough YO8 198 F1
Rainton with Newby YO7 114 F6
Ripon HG4 214 B3
Carr Field La YO26 141 F1
Carr Fields La YO12 99 B5
Carr Head La BD20 187 B7
Carr Hill YO60 145 D5
Carr Hill La YO21 32 B7
Carr Hill Ridge YO21 32 B7
Carr House La
Cayton YO11 100 A5
Heslerton YO17 98 A1
Carr Inf Sch YO26 227 C5
Carr Jun Sch YO26 227 C5
Carr La Ampleforth YO62 92 B1
Azerley HG4 113 A7
Barlby with Osgodby YO8 232 F5
Barlow YO8 204 C7
Castleford WF10 200 F3
Cawton YO62 119 C8
Cayton YO11 100 B4
East Ayton YO13 99 B7
Escrick YO19 192 B5
Glaisdale YO21 30 D4
Gristhorpe YO11 100 E4
Heslerton YO17 124 A8
Kilburn High & Low YO61 91 B3
Little Ouseburn YO26 164 A7
Long Drax YO8 204 F6
Muston YO14 100 F3
Newby & Scalby YO13 75 C5
Newton on Derwent YO41 185 F4
Rainton with Newby YO7 114 F6
Roecliffe YO51 140 E3
Sheriff Hutton YO60 145 E6
Stillington YO61 144 C6
Sutton-on-the-Forest YO61 144 D2
Thirlby YO7 90 F6
Thormanby YO61 116 E4
Wetherby LS22 180 D4
Carr La *continued*
Wistow YO8 197 A3
York YO26 227 D5
Carr Leys La YO7 66 A5
Carr Mill Mews BD22 187 B5
Carr Rd 7 BB18 171 D2
Carr Side Rd YO26 163 F8
Carr St YO8 232 F4
Carr The HG3 222 E2
Carr Wood Rd WF10 200 F3
Carrbank La YO32 167 E3
Carrfield YO24 230 C8
Carrfield Dr LS15 194 B8
Carrfield La LS15 194 B8
Carrfield Rd LS15 194 B8
Carrick Gdns YO24 227 E3
Carrier's Row BB8 186 B2
Carrington Ave 1 YO26 227 E5
Carrnock Ct 3 YO32 225 F1
Carrol Cl DL6 210 F2
Carroll Pl 2 DL2 22 C8
Carron Cres YO24 230 B7
Carrs Mdw YO19 192 B5
Carrs The YO21 208 A2
Carrside 2 YO11 99 F6
Carseylands Hill BD23 155 A4
Cart Riggin YO7 66 A8
Carter Ave YO31 228 F5
Carter La 22 YO62 70 B1
Carter's La Ilkley LS29 218 E6
Longnewton TS16 5 A4
Cartmell Terr DL3 3 C6
Cass House Rd TS8 6 E4
Cass La
Knaresborough HG5 221 A4
South Milford LS25 195 E1
Castelo Gr 1 YO18 96 A6
Castle Bank DL6 25 E1
Castle C of E Jun Sch HG5 221 B6
Castle Cl Cawood YO8 197 A8
1 Haxby YO32 166 D5
Killinghall HG3 161 C5
Middleton St George DL2 4 C3
Northallerton DL7 210 D5
2 Spofforth HG3 179 E6
1 Thornton Dale YO18 96 D5
Castle Dyke Wynd TS16 5 E3
Castle End DL8 59 B6
Castle Garth
Pontefract WF8 201 C1
4 Thornton Dale YO18 96 D5
Castle Gate 4 LS29 218 B4
Castle Gdns YO11 213 B6
Castle Hill
8 Hunmanby YO14 126 F8
2 Ilkley LS29 218 B4
Richmond DL10 209 C6
4 Settle BD24 131 E2
Castle Hill Cl HG2 222 B6
Castle Hill Dr HG2 222 B6
Castle Hill Glade HG2 222 B6
Castle Hill Gr HG2 222 B6
Castle Hill La YO8 204 F5
Castle Howard* YO60 120 D1
Castle Howard Dr YO17 215 A4
Castle Howard Rd YO17 215 A4
Castle Ings 1 HG3 179 E5
Castle Ings Cl 1 HG5 221 A5
Castle Ings Rd 3 HG5 221 A5
Castle La Danby YO21 29 D6
10 East Ayton/West Ayton YO13 99 B8
Castle Mdws DL8 87 A7
Castle Rd Colne BB8 186 A4
1 Ilkley LS29 218 B4
Killinghall HG3 161 C5
18 Pickering YO18 95 F7
Scarborough YO11 213 A6
Thornton Dale YO18 96 D5
Whitby YO21 208 A6
Castle Rise 1 YO13 99 A7
Castle Sch WF10 201 B4
Castle Side YO60 145 C5
Castle St Skipton BD23 217 A3
Spofforth HG3 179 E6
Castle Steads (Fort)* DL8 84 C8
Castle Steads* DL11 19 D6
Castle Terr
Richmond DL10 209 C6
16 Scarborough YO11 213 B6
Castle View
7 Newby & Scalby YO13 75 D5
Sheriff Hutton YO60 145 C5
Castle View Terr BD23 216 F4
Castle Yd 3 LS29 218 B4
Castleberg Hospl BD24 131 C2
Castleberg La 5 BD24 131 E2
Castleford High Sch WF10 200 F4
Castleford La
Featherstone WF7 200 D2
Knottingley WF11 201 D3
Castleford Mus Room* WF10 200 E4
Castleford Normanton & District Hospl WF10 200 D3
Castleford Park Sch WF10 200 F4
Castleford Rd WF6 200 B2
Castleford Redhill Mid Sch WF10 201 B4
Castleford RUFC WF10 200 C3
Castleford Sta WF10 200 E4
Castleford Three Land Ends Jun & Inf Sch WF10 200 D4
Castleford Tigers RLFC WF10 200 F5
Castlegate
East Ayton/West Ayton YO13 99 A7
6 Helmsley YO62 92 F6
Kirkbymoorside YO62 70 B1
3 Knaresborough HG5 221 B5
Malton YO17 215 C4
19 Pickering YO18 95 F7
Scarborough YO11 213 B7
Thirsk YO7 211 B2
York YO1 233 B2
Castlekeep Cl DL10 209 C8
Castlemount Ave YO13 75 D6
Castlereagh Cl TS21 5 A7
Castleton Ave
Middlesbrough TS5 6 D8
Northallerton DL7 210 C1
Castleton Moor Sta YO21 29 A7
Castleton Prim Sch YO21 29 A7
Castleton Rd DL9 40 F4
Castley La LS21 178 A1
Cat Bank DL11 39 C6
Cat La Balne DN14 207 E5
Bilbrough YO23 182 D1
Upper Poppleton YO26 182 D8
Cathcart Cl DN14 206 F7
Cathedral C of E Prim Sch HG4 214 D5
Cathedral Cl HG4 214 D5
Catherine Love Dr 15 YO61 143 C8
Catherine St 2 TS12 9 F7
Cattal Moor La YO26 181 B8
Cattal St YO26 164 A2
Cattal Sta YO26 164 A2
Catterick Bridge* DL10 41 C6
Catterick La DL10 41 D3
Catterick Race Course DL10 41 C5
Catterick Rd DL9 40 E4
Catterton La LS24 190 A8
Cattle La LS25 194 F8
Cattlelaith La WF11 201 E2
Catton La YO7 115 A7
Catton Moor La YO7 114 F8
Caudle Hill WF11 201 C6
Causeway BD23 81 E3
Causeway The DL1 3 E5
Cautley Dr HG3 161 C5
Cautley Gr HG3 161 C5
Cavalry Ct 9 YO12 75 F5
Cavendish Ave
Harrogate HG2 219 E1
8 Pontefract WF8 201 C2
Cavendish Ct HG2 222 F8
Cavendish Gr YO10 229 D3
Cavendish Rd TS4 7 A8
Cavendish St
Barnoldswick BB18 171 D1
Harrogate HG1 219 E5
Skipton BD23 216 F3
Cavendish Terr 8 HG4 214 C4
Caversham Rd TS4 7 A8
Cawcliff La YO18 97 A5
Cawdel Cl 4 LS25 195 F2
Cawdel Way LS25 195 F2
Cawder Ghyll BD23 217 A1
Cawder La BD23 217 A1
Cawder Rd BD23 217 A1
Cawood C of E Prim Sch YO8 197 B8
Cawood Cres LS24 190 C1
Cawood Dr TS5 6 F7
Cawood Rd
Stillingfleet YO19 191 D3
Wistow YO8 197 C7
Cawthorn Ave HG2 220 B2
Cawthorn Pl HG2 220 B3
Cawthorne Cres YO14 101 A3
Cawthorne La YO18 71 D3
Cawton Rd YO62 118 F8
Caxton Ave YO26 227 D6
Caxton Cl 1 DL10 41 C7
Caxton Gdns 4 WF8 201 B2
Caxton Way YO11 99 F6
Cayley Cl YO30 224 F1
Cayley La YO13 98 C5
Caymer Rd YO11 100 A7
Cayton Cty Prim Sch YO11 100 B6
Cayton Low Rd YO11 99 F6
Cayton Low Road Ind Est YO11 100 A6
Cecil Rd 7 YO14 127 A8
Cecil St HG1 219 E5
Cecilia Pl 3 YO24 228 A3
Cedar Cl
Hambleton YO8 197 B1
Ripon HG4 214 B3
Cedar Cres YO8 197 D2
Cedar Dr
Coulby Newham TS8 6 D4
Tadcaster LS24 189 D6
Cedar Glade YO19 184 E7
Cedar Gr Barton DL10 21 C7
3 Filey YO14 101 B4
Sutton BD20 187 E7
York YO31 229 B7
Cedar Grange HG2 222 D7
Cedar Mews 4 DL2 22 D8
Cedar Rd DL3 3 B6
Cedar Ridge LS25 194 E5
Cedar Vale 8 YO62 70 B1
Cedarhurst Dr TS12 9 F7
Cedarwood 3 DL2 4 C4
Cedarwood Ave 1 TS9 26 C8
Cedarwood Cl 8 YO24 227 B1
Cedarwood Glade TS8 6 E4
Celtic Cl YO26 227 B5
Cemetery La DL3 3 A5
Cemetery Rd
40 Earby BB18 172 A1
Normanton South WF6 200 B1
Thirsk YO7 211 A3
York YO10 233 C1
Centenary Rd DN14 205 F3
Central Av 6 YO61 143 D8
Central Dr
Castleford WF10 200 C4
Northallerton DL6 210 E4
Central St TS16 5 E3
Central Way 6 TS9 8 A2
Centre La LS24 189 E6
Centre Rd BD20 186 D7
Centurian Cl 7 DL10 41 E4
Centurion Way YO30 225 B3
Century Wlk 1 HG2 220 B3
Ceres Rd LS22 180 C3
Chacksfield Rd 17 DL10 41 E4
Chadderton Cl TS12 9 E8
Chadderton Dr TS17 6 C7
Chain Bar La HG3 161 A4
Chain La HG5 221 C6
Chair Wlk HG4 139 B8
Chaldon Cl 4 YO32 167 A6
Chaldron Way TS16 5 D6
Chalfield Cl TS17 6 B4
Chalfonts YO24 227 F1
Chalford Oaks TS5 6 D8
Challacombe Cres TS17 6 A3
Challoner Rd TS15 5 D2
Chaloner St TS14 8 F6
Chaloner's Cres YO24 230 D7
Chaloner's Rd YO24 230 D8
Chamber End Fold 5 BD23 134 E3
Chancery Ct YO24 227 C3
Chancery Rise TS18 6 A6
Chandler Cl DL10 209 F8
Chandlers Ct YO11 213 B2
Chandlers Ridge Prim Sch TS7 7 D5
Chandlers Wharf YO17 215 C3
Chanting Hill Cl YO60 146 E6
Chantry Ave 14 YO26 165 F1
Chantry Bank DL8 59 D3
Chantry Cl YO24 230 C8
Chantry Ct HG3 161 C7
Chantry Dr
East Ayton/West Ayton YO13 99 B8
2 Ilkley LS29 218 B3
Chantry Gap 11 YO26 165 F1
Chantry Garth DL8 59 D3
Chantry Gr 13 YO26 165 F1
Chantry La
Bishopthorpe YO23 231 B4
Scotton HG5 162 A6
Stutton with Hazlewood LS24 189 B3
Chantry Rd
9 East Ayton/West Ayton YO13 99 B8
Northallerton DL7 210 B3
Chapel Balk Rd YO8 198 F1
Chapel Bridge* DL11 1 C7
Chapel Cl
Bilton-in-Ainsty with Bickerton LS22 181 B5
21 Helmsley YO62 92 F6
Rawcliffe DN14 205 A1
Chapel Croft 7 BD23 134 E3
Chapel Ct
Gargrave BD23 155 D1
Huby YO61 144 A4
Chapel Fields Rd YO26 227 A3
Chapel Fold 6 BD23 134 E3
Chapel Garth
Dalton YO7 115 E7
Markington with Wallerthwaite HG3 139 C3
Thrintoft DL7 63 F7
Chapel Gate
Kirkby Malham BD23 154 F8
Malham BD23 132 F1
Sherburn YO17 124 D6
Chapel Haddlesey C of E Prim Sch YO8 203 B5
Chapel Hill
Boroughbridge YO51 141 C5
Kearby with Netherby LS22 179 B1
Skipton BD23 217 A5
Chapel Hill La LS21 178 A1
Chapel La
Askham Bryan YO23 182 F3
Barwick in Elmet LS15 194 C8
Boston Spa LS23 188 E7
Brayton YO8 232 B1
Brompton YO13 98 B7
5 Burton in Lonsdale LA6 102 F3

Chapel La *continued*
13 Easingwold YO61 ....143 C8
18 Eastfield YO11 ....100 B6
Finghall DL8 ....61 E4
Halton East BD23 ....174 C8
Harome YO62 ....93 C4
Hebden BD23 ....135 A2
Horton in Ribblesdale BD24 ....105 C3
Ilkley LS29 ....218 A4
Langtoft YO25 ....151 D5
Little Smeaton WF8 ....206 B3
Marton-le-Moor HG4 ....114 F1
Rawcliffe DN14 ....205 A2
Reighton YO14 ....127 E5
3 Riccall YO19 ....192 A1
2 Spofforth HG3 ....179 E5
3 Thornton Dale YO18 ....96 D5
Tollerton YO61 ....143 A3
Westow YO60 ....147 B4
Chapel of Our Lady* YO11 ....213 C7
Chapel Rd
23 Scarborough YO11 ....213 A6
Settrington YO17 ....122 D1
Chapel Riggs 4 DL10 ....41 E4
Chapel Row YO10 ....233 C1
Chapel Sq 7 BD24 ....131 E2
Chapel St
8 Addingham LS29 ....174 F4
6 Beadlam YO62 ....93 D7
Carleton BD23 ....173 B4
Cattal YO26 ....164 A1
22 Earby BB18 ....172 A1
27 Filey YO14 ....101 B3
Grassington BD23 ....134 E3
Hambleton YO8 ....196 F1
Hillam LS25 ....202 B7
Kirk Hammerton YO26 ....164 C2
Knaresborough HG5 ....221 B5
Middleton St George DL2 ....4 C4
Nunnington YO62 ....93 E2
12 Settle BD24 ....131 D2
Tadcaster LS24 ....189 E6
Thirsk YO7 ....211 B2
Chapel Wlk
Long Preston BD23 ....153 F5
4 Riccall YO19 ....192 A1
Chapman Cl 1 YO32 ....167 C8
Chapman La 8 HG4 ....86 C3
Chapman Sq HG1 ....219 B2
Chapmans Ct YO24 ....230 D6
Chapman's La YO30 ....165 E7
Chapter House St YO1 ....233 B3
Charles Ave HG1 ....219 E5
Charles Ct DL10 ....209 F7
Charles Moor YO31 ....228 F7
Charles St YO8 ....232 B6
Charles Wesley Dr YO8 ....232 B2
Charlock TS8 ....7 B4
Charlton Ave
Knaresborough HG5 ....221 B6
2 Whitby YO21 ....208 B7
Charlton Ct 10 HG5 ....221 B6
Charlton Dr HG5 ....221 B6
Charlton Gr 12 HG5 ....221 B6
Charlton Manor Dr 13 HG5 ....221 B6
Charlton St YO23 ....228 C2
Charnwood Dr TS7 ....7 D6
Charrington Ave TS17 ....6 A6
Charter Ave DN14 ....205 A1
Charters The YO8 ....198 B5
Chartwell Cl TS17 ....6 B4
Chase Garth Rd 16 YO61 ....143 C8
Chase Side Ct YO24 ....230 E8
Chase The
11 Boroughbridge YO51 ....141 B4
Garforth LS25 ....194 D4
Hurworth-on-Tees DL2 ....3 E1
Knaresborough HG5 ....221 D5
Norton YO17 ....215 E2
Chastworth Ct HG1 ....219 D4
Chatham Rd HG4 ....113 D2
Chatsworth Ave 7 WF8 201 C2
Chatsworth Dr
16 Haxby YO32 ....166 F5
2 Wetherby LS22 ....180 B3
Chatsworth Gdns YO12 ....212 E7
Chatsworth Gr
4 Boroughbridge YO51 ....141 B5
Harrogate HG1 ....219 C4
Chatsworth Pl HG1 ....219 D4
Chatsworth Rd HG1 ....219 D4
Chatsworth Terr
2 Harrogate HG1 ....219 E4
4 York YO26 ....227 E4
Chaucer Gn HG1 ....219 F7
Chaucer St 7 YO10 ....228 E3
Chaumont Way 1 YO32 167 D2
Chauvel Cl DL9 ....209 C2
Cheapside
2 Knaresborough HG5 ....221 B5
12 Normanton South WF6 ....200 A1
11 Settle BD24 ....131 D2
Cheapsides Rd YO17 ....215 B8
Checker La YO19 ....198 A7
Chelkar Way YO30 ....224 F1
Chelmsford Rd HG1 ....219 E2
Cheltenham Ave
Ilkley LS29 ....218 E4
Middlesbrough TS7 ....7 B5
Cheltenham Cres
6 Harrogate HG1 ....219 D2
7 Harrogate HG1 ....219 D3
Cheltenham Mount HG1 ....219 D3
Cheltenham Par HG1 ....219 D3
Cheltenham Rd 8 HG1 ....219 D3
Chelwood Wlk 12 YO26 ....227 E4
Chepstow Ct 14 DL1 ....3 F6
Cherry Ave
Malton YO17 ....215 D6
Swinton YO17 ....121 B4
Cherry Cl YO21 ....208 B6
Cherry Garth YO31 ....229 B5
Cherry Garth Rd DL7 ....210 C3
Cherry Gr 7 Bedale DL8 ....63 B3
2 Ilkley LS29 ....175 C2
16 Poppleton YO26 ....165 F1
Cherry Hill La YO23 ....233 B1
Cherry La YO24 ....230 F8
Cherry Orch 2 YO32 ....225 D8
Cherry Paddock
4 Haxby YO32 ....225 D8
Kexby YO41 ....168 C2
Cherry Rd 4 YO14 ....127 A8
Cherry St YO23 ....233 B1
Cherry Tree Ave
Newton-on-Ouse YO30 ....165 B6
1 Scarborough YO12 ....212 B5
York YO32 ....225 D4
Cherry Tree Cl 13 YO8 ....197 D1
Cherry Tree Dr YO14 ....101 A4
Cherry Tree Gdns 7 DL9 ....209 B1
Cherry Tree Way 14 DL9 ....41 A5
Cherry Tree Wlk
Amotherby YO17 ....121 A4
7 Barlby YO8 ....198 B4
Cherry Wood Cres YO19 ....231 E5
Cherrytree Cl HG4 ....140 E7
Cherrywood Ave 4 TS9 ....26 C8
Cherwell Croft YO8 ....196 F1
Cherwell Ct YO8 ....196 F1
Cheshire Ave YO32 ....167 A6
Cheshire Sq 5 YO7 ....89 B1
Chesler-Pit La YO61 ....117 F2
Chesney Fields 4 YO24 227 D1
Chessingham Gdns YO24 ....230 E6
Chessingham Pk YO19 ....184 F6
Chester Court Rd YO8 ....204 A6
Chester La DL6 ....65 D8
Chesterton Ave TS17 ....6 A6
Chestnut Ave
2 Airmyn DN14 ....205 E4
Harrogate HG1 ....219 F3
10 Hemingbrough YO8 ....198 F1
Malton YO17 ....215 D5
Thornton Dale YO18 ....96 D6
2 Topcliffe YO7 ....89 A1
1 Topcliffe YO7 ....89 B1
Welburn YO60 ....146 E6
York YO31 ....228 F6
Chestnut Bank YO12 ....212 D6
Chestnut Cl
3 Catterick DL10 ....41 D5
4 Ilkley LS29 ....218 E3
Richmond DL10 ....209 C8
Scarborough YO12 ....212 D6
Chestnut Cres
6 Catterick Garrison DL9 ....40 F5
1 Catton YO7 ....89 A1
Chestnut Croft 7 YO8 ....198 F1
Chestnut Ct 9 YO8 ....198 F1
Chestnut Dr
17 Barnoldswick BB18 ....171 D1
8 Hemingbrough YO8 ....198 F1
Middlesbrough TS7 ....7 C6
Chestnut Garth 4 YO8 ....198 F1
Chestnut Gr
Harrogate HG1 ....219 E6
Norton YO17 ....215 F2
York YO26 ....227 C4
Chestnut Mews YO8 ....197 A8
Chestnut Rd
Cawood YO8 ....197 A8
Eaglescliffe TS16 ....5 E6
Chestnut Rise 6 YO8 ....198 F1
Chestnuts The
6 Haxby YO32 ....225 C8
Hensall DN14 ....203 D2
Pontefract WF8 ....201 C2
Chevin Dr YO14 ....101 A3
Cheviot Cl 1 YO32 ....225 F3
Chew La
Gargrave BD23 ....155 D1
Seamer YO12 ....99 D6
Chichester Cl 13 YO13 ....75 D5
Chieftain Rd DL9 ....40 C4
Chiltern Ave WF10 ....200 C3
Chiltern Way YO32 ....225 F5
Chilvers Ct 4 YO8 ....232 A1
Chimes Rd YO8 ....232 C6
China St DL3 ....3 D7
Chippendale Jun Sch LS21 ....176 F1
Chippendale Rise 8 LS21 ....177 A1
Chippenham Rd TS4 ....7 A7
Cholmley Way YO22 ....208 F3
Christ Church C of E Sch BB8 ....186 A3
Christ Church Oval HG1 ....219 E2
Christchurch C of E Prim Sch BD23 ....216 F3
Christina St 5 HG1 ....219 C5
Christ's Hospl DL8 ....63 A1
Christy Gate Rd YO21 ....28 E4
Chubb Hill Rd YO21 ....208 C6
Chudleigh Rd
Harrogate HG1 ....219 E3
1 York YO26 ....227 F5
Church Ave
Clapham LA2 ....130 C8
4 Dacre HG3 ....137 F1
Harrogate HG1 ....219 D5
Swillington LS26 ....194 A1
Church Balk YO19 ....184 E7
Church Bank
Aysgarth DL8 ....58 F3
Hunton DL8 ....61 F7
Kirkby Malzeard HG4 ....112 D5
Church Cl
Askham Bryan YO23 ....182 F3
Bagby YO7 ....90 C3
4 Bubwith YO8 ....199 D7
Carleton BD23 ....173 B4
18 Filey YO14 ....101 B4
1 Hambleton YO8 ....196 F1
Killinghall HG3 ....219 A8
Kirby Hill YO51 ....141 B7
Middleton St George DL2 ....4 C3
Newby & Scalby YO13 ....75 C5
Sawley HG4 ....138 E6
Sharow HG4 ....214 F7
4 Swillington LS26 ....194 A1
5 Tollerton YO61 ....143 B3
Wheldrake YO19 ....193 A7
Church Cliff Dr 9 YO14 101 B4
Church Cres
Stutton with Hazlewood LS24 ....189 D4
Swillington LS26 ....194 A1
Church Croft
Barkston Ash LS24 ....195 F7
Gargrave BD23 ....172 C8
Church Cswy LS23 ....188 F8
Church Ct 18 WF6 ....200 A1
Church Dike La YO8 ....204 F5
Church Dr
Great Ayton TS9 ....7 F1
Lockwood TS12 ....9 E7
Church End
Cawood YO8 ....197 B8
Sheriff Hutton YO60 ....145 D5
Church Farm YO7 ....211 A6
Church Farm Cl YO23 ....182 C6
Church Farm View LS15 ....194 C8
Church Fenton La LS24 ....190 B3
Church Fenton Sta LS24 ....196 A8
Church Field La 2 YO26 ....164 A8
Church Field Rd DN6 ....206 E1
Church Fields 17 WF6 ....200 A1
Church Garth DL6 ....23 C3
Church Gdns LS25 ....194 C3
Church Gn 3 YO41 ....185 C2
Church Hill
4 Bramham LS23 ....188 E5
Crayke YO61 ....118 A1
Easingwold YO61 ....117 C1
10 Hunmanby YO14 ....126 F8
Hunsingore LS22 ....180 E8
Malton YO17 ....215 C4
Newby & Scalby YO13 ....75 C5
North Rigton LS17 ....178 B3
Reighton YO14 ....127 C6
3 Selby YO8 ....232 D5
Sherburn in Elmet LS25 ....195 E4
5 Spofforth HG3 ....179 E6
Stillingfleet YO19 ....191 D3
Thorner LS14 ....188 A3
Thornton Dale YO18 ....96 D6
8 Wistow YO8 ....197 D6
Church La
Allerston YO18 ....97 B5
Appleton Roebuck YO23 ....190 F4
Aysgarth DL8 ....58 F3
Bagby YO7 ....90 C3
Barton DL10 ....21 C8
Bishopthorpe YO23 ....231 A4
Bolton Percy YO23 ....190 D4
Boroughbridge YO51 ....141 B5
Brompton YO13 ....98 C5
Burnsall BD23 ....157 A8
Carlton DN14 ....204 C3
Catton YO41 ....185 D8
Cayton YO11 ....100 B6
Collingham LS22 ....180 A1
Cropton YO18 ....71 B4
Cundall with Leckby YO61 ....115 E3
Dunnington YO19 ....184 E7
Elslack BD23 ....172 D4
4 Elvington YO41 ....185 C2
Faceby TS9 ....25 F1
Fylingdales YO22 ....33 C4
Garforth LS25 ....194 C4
Gargrave BD23 ....172 D8
Gateforth YO8 ....202 F8
Gilling East YO62 ....118 F7
Guisborough TS7 ....7 E5
Guisborough TS9 ....8 A4
Guisborough TS14 ....8 F7
Hampsthwaite HG3 ....161 A6
17 Haxby YO32 ....166 E5
Hebden BD23 ....135 A1
Hensall DN14 ....203 C1
Hutton Buscel YO13 ....98 F7
Ingleby Greenhow TS9 ....27 B5
Kelbrook & Sough BB18 ....186 A8
Church La *continued*
Kellington DN14 ....202 E3
Kirby Hall YO26 ....164 B7
Kirby Hill YO51 ....141 B7
Knaresborough HG5 ....221 A6
Langtoft YO25 ....151 C5
Low Worsall TS15 ....24 A8
Marton cum Grafton YO51 ....141 D1
Martons Both BD23 ....172 A5
Micklefield LS25 ....194 F4
Mickletown LS26 ....200 B5
Middlesbrough TS5 ....6 E7
Middlesbrough TS7 ....7 D7
Middleton YO18 ....95 E8
Middleton St George DL2 ....4 C3
Milby YO51 ....141 B7
4 Monk Fryston LS25 ....202 A8
Moor Monkton YO26 ....165 B2
Nether Poppleton YO26 ....224 B3
New Earswick YO32 ....225 F5
11 Normanton South WF6 ....200 A1
North Featherstone WF7 ....200 E1
Pannal HG3 ....222 D4
Poppleton YO26 ....224 A3
Redmire DL8 ....59 C5
Ripon HG4 ....214 B5
Sadberge DL2 ....4 C7
Scarborough YO11 ....213 B7
4 Selby YO8 ....232 D5
Sessay YO7 ....116 C6
Settrington YO17 ....122 D1
Sinnington YO62 ....71 A1
Skelton YO30 ....224 B5
Slingsby YO62 ....120 B6
2 Snaith DN14 ....204 C1
South Stainley with Cayton HG3 ....139 E2
9 Spofforth HG3 ....179 E6
Stainburn LS21 ....177 E3
Stainforth BD24 ....131 E6
10 Stamford Bridge YO41 ....168 D2
Strensall YO32 ....167 A7
Stutton with Hazlewood LS24 ....189 E4
Swillington LS26 ....194 A1
Terrington YO60 ....119 F1
Thormanby YO61 ....116 F5
Thornton Dale YO18 ....96 D6
Thwing YO25 ....126 A1
Tunstall LA6 ....102 B4
Welburn YO60 ....146 E6
Weston LS21 ....176 D1
Westow YO60 ....147 B4
Wheldrake YO19 ....193 A7
Whitby YO22 ....208 E7
Whorlton DL6 ....25 D1
Wigglesworth BD23 ....153 D3
Wighill LS24 ....181 D1
Wintringham YO17 ....123 C4
York YO1 ....233 B2
Church Mdw DL10 ....21 D8
Church Mdws 9 LS23 ....188 E6
Church Mews
13 Boroughbridge YO51 ....141 B5
Sherburn in Elmet LS25 ....195 F4
2 York YO26 ....227 C3
Church Rd
26 Glusburn BD20 ....187 E7
Great Preston LS26 ....200 C8
Linton BD23 ....134 E2
Pontefract WF6 ....200 A3
Scotton DL9 ....40 E4
Stainton Dale YO13 ....54 A7
Stamford Bridge YO41 ....168 D2
Thornton in Craven BD23 ....171 F3
York YO10 ....229 D4
Church Rise YO19 ....167 F1
Church Row
Hurworth-on-Tees DL2 ....3 E1
Melsonby DL10 ....20 F7
Church Side LS26 ....200 B5
Church Sq YO21 ....208 C7
Church St
Addingham LS29 ....175 A4
Amotherby YO17 ....121 B4
Asenby YO7 ....115 B7
Barkston Ash LS24 ....195 F7
Bellerby DL8 ....60 D7
Bilton-in-Ainsty with Bickerton YO26 ....181 D5
Boston Spa LS23 ....188 E8
Broughton BD23 ....172 D7
Bubwith YO8 ....199 D7
Carleton BD23 ....173 B4
Church Fenton LS24 ....196 B7
Copmanthorpe YO23 ....230 B2
Danby YO21 ....29 B7
Dunnington YO19 ....184 E7
5 Easingwold YO61 ....143 C8
5 Filey YO14 ....101 B3
Gargrave BD23 ....155 D1
13 Glusburn BD20 ....187 E8
Goldsborough HG5 ....163 A3
Guisborough TS14 ....8 F7
5 Helmsley YO62 ....92 F6
Heslerton YO17 ....123 E7
Hovingham YO62 ....119 E6
Ilkley LS29 ....218 A4
Ingleton LA6 ....103 D4
Kirk Hammerton YO26 ....164 C2
Kirkby Malzeard HG4 ....112 D5
24 Kirkbymoorside YO62 ....70 B1
Knottingley WF11 ....201 E4
Long Preston BD23 ....153 F4
6 Masham HG4 ....86 C3
Church St *continued*
6 Middleham DL8 ....60 E2
Norton YO17 ....215 D3
Nunnington YO62 ....93 E2
2 Scarborough YO11 ....213 B6
Settle BD24 ....131 D3
4 Skipton BD23 ....216 F3
5 Staithes TS13 ....13 K2
Trawden BB8 ....186 B1
Ulleskelf LS24 ....190 C3
Well DL8 ....87 A4
West Tanfield HG4 ....87 A1
Whitby YO22 ....208 E6
Whixley YO26 ....164 A5
York YO1 ....233 B2
Church Stairs St 3 YO11 ....213 B6
Church View
12 Airmyn DN14 ....205 E4
3 Brompton DL6 ....43 F3
16 Hurworth DL2 ....3 E1
Kirby Hill YO51 ....141 B7
Ledston LS25 ....194 E1
Norton DN6 ....206 E1
Sherburn YO17 ....124 D8
Sherburn in Elmet LS25 ....195 F4
South Milford LS25 ....195 F2
Thirsk YO7 ....211 A3
Church View Mews 7 LS23 ....188 E7
Church Wind
Alne YO61 ....142 F4
Burneston DL8 ....87 E7
Church Wlk
Lindrick with Studley Royal & Fountains HG4 ....139 B7
1 Willerby YO12 ....99 D2
5 Wistow YO8 ....197 D6
Church Wynd DL10 ....209 C7
Churchfield Dr 23 YO32 ....166 E5
Churchfield La
Castleford WF10 ....200 F3
Little Smeaton DN6 ....206 C4
Churchill Cl 3 TS9 ....8 A2
Churchill Way 4 BD20 ....187 F8
Churchside Villas LS26 ....200 B5
Churchville LS25 ....195 A4
Churchville Ave LS25 ....194 F4
Churchville Dr LS25 ....195 A4
Churchville Terr LS25 ....195 A4
Churwell Cl WF10 ....200 E3
Cinder La
Castleford WF10 ....200 E4
Clifford LS23 ....188 F7
Lindley LS21 ....177 C3
Upper Poppleton YO26 ....165 F1
Upper Poppleton YO26 ....227 A7
York YO26 ....228 A4
York YO31 ....228 E6
Citadilla Cl 5 DL10 ....41 C7
Clack La DL6 ....45 A4
Clapdale Dr LA2 ....130 C8
Clapdale Way 2 LA2 ....130 C8
Clapgate Bank DL11 ....39 D8
Clapham C E Prim Sch LA2 ....130 C7
Clapham Sta LA2 ....130 A6
Clare Ave DL3 ....3 A5
Claremont 23 YO14 ....101 B3
Claremont Dr TS7 ....7 C5
Claremont La HG3 ....140 B5
Claremont St BB8 ....186 A3
Claremont Terr YO31 ....233 B4
Clarence Ave 47 YO14 ....101 B3
Clarence Dr Filey YO14 ....101 B3
Harrogate HG1 ....219 B3
Clarence Pl
7 Scarborough YO11 ....213 A6
2 Whitby YO21 ....208 D7
Clarence Rd
Middlesbrough TS7 ....7 D5
2 Scarborough YO12 ....213 A7
Scorton DL10 ....41 F7
Clarence St
2 Barnoldswick BB18 ....171 E1
6 Colne BB8 ....186 A3
1 Trawden Forest BB8 ....186 B1
York YO31 ....233 B4
Clarendon Rd
Boston Spa LS23 ....188 E8
Great Burdon DL1 ....3 F7
Thornaby TS17 ....6 B7
Clarendon St 15 BB8 ....186 A3
Clareton La HG5 ....163 B6
Clark Ct WF7 ....200 E1
Clark St 7 YO12 ....213 A7
Clarkson Ct 12 WF6 ....200 B1
Clarkson Dr LS25 ....201 F6
Clarkson St 7 YO21 ....208 D7
Claro Ave HG1 ....219 F4
Claro Mews 4 HG5 ....221 A5
Claro Pk HG1 ....219 F4
Claro Rd
Harrogate HG1 ....219 F3
Ripon HG4 ....214 C4
Claro Way HG1 ....219 F4
Claude Ave TS5 ....6 E8
Claver Cl DL6 ....45 D8
Clavery Ley La YO62 ....67 E1
Claxton Ave DL3 ....3 A6
Clay Bank TS9 ....27 A3
Clay Hill YO41 ....169 C3
Clay La Bubwith YO8 ....199 C5
Camblesforth YO8 ....204 C6
Cliffe YO8 ....198 D4
Clay Pit La YO51 ....141 A4
Clay Pl 3 YO24 ....227 D1

Claygate YO31 229 B6
Claypenny Hospl YO61 117 D1
Claypit La
Carlton DN14 204 C3
Ledston WF10 201 A8
Clayton Hall Rd BD20 187 F7
Clayton Mews 8 WF6 200 A2
Clayton Pl 9 WF6 200 A2
Clayton St 7 BB18 171 E1
Cleasby La DL2 2 F1
Cleasby Way TS16 5 D6
Clement St 4 YO23 233 B1
Clementhorpe YO23 233 B1
Clevedon House Sch LS29 176 A1
Clevegate TS7 7 C5
Cleveland Ave
Darlington DL3 3 C5
Knottingley WF11 201 F2
Scalby YO12 212 D8
Stokesley TS9 26 C8
Cleveland Coll of Art & Design TS5 6 E8
Cleveland Dr DL7 210 D2
Cleveland Rd Boltby YO7 91 B8
Catterick Garrison DL9 40 F4
Scarborough YO12 212 E6
Scorton DL10 41 F7
Cleveland Rein YO7 66 A3
Cleveland St
Darlington DL1 3 D6
Great Ayton TS9 8 A2
Guisborough TS14 8 E6
York YO24 228 A4
Cleveland Terr DL3 3 B5
Cleveland Trad Est DL1 3 D6
Cleveland View 1 TS9 25 F1
Cleveland Way
1 Carlton Miniott YO7 89 C4
York YO32 225 F3
Cliff Bridge Pl 6 YO11 213 A5
Cliff Bridge Terr 7 YO11 213 A5
Cliff Brow TS13 11 C7
Cliff Cres LS25 194 E1
Cliff Dr 24 DL8 60 D5
Cliff Gate Rd DL11 35 E4
Cliff Hill Rd DN6 206 D2
Cliff La
Newholm-cum-Dunsley YO21 13 B2
Snainton YO13 97 F5
Whitwell-on-the-Hill YO60 146 E4
Wilton YO18 97 A5
Wrelton YO18 95 B8
Cliff Rd
Stainton Dale YO13 54 A8
Staithes TS13 13 K2
Cliff St YO21 208 D7
Cliff The YO22 32 B6
Cliffe Prim Sch YO8 198 E2
Cliffe Rd HG2 219 B1
Clifford Ave LS29 218 A5
Clifford Moor Rd LS23 188 D8
Clifford Rd
Boston Spa LS23 188 F8
Ilkley LS29 218 A6
Clifford St
3 Barnoldswick BB18 171 E1
1 Skipton BD23 216 F3
York YO1 233 B2
Clifford's Terr 25 YO14 101 B3
Cliffords Twr* YO1 233 B1
Clifton Ave TS18 5 E6
Clifton Dale YO30 228 A6
Clifton La LS21 176 F3
Clifton Moor Gate YO30 225 A2
Clifton Moor Ret Pk YO30 224 E3
Clifton Moorgate YO30 225 B3
Clifton Pl 3 YO30 228 A7
Clifton Prep Sch YO30 233 A4
Clifton Rd Darlington DL1 3 D4
Ilkley LS29 218 D3
York YO30 233 A4
Clifton St Earby BB18 186 A8
5 Scarborough YO12 212 F6
Trawden Forest BB8 186 A1
Clifton Without Jun Sch YO30 227 F8
Clint Bank HG3 160 E6
Clint Bank La HG3 160 F6
Clint Garth HG3 160 F8
Clipt La YO7 65 D2
Clitheroe St 2 BD23 216 D3
Clive Gr YO24 227 F2
Clive Rd 1 HG3 179 E6
Clock Twr* HG4 214 C6
Clockhill Field La YO26 163 F3
Clockwood Gdns TS16 5 E3
Clogger La BD23 172 D3
Cloggerby Rigg DL11 35 E5
Cloisters The
15 Hemingbrough YO8 198 F1
Wilberfoss YO41 185 F6
York YO31 233 C3
Cloisters Wlk YO31 233 C3
Close La BD22 187 B5
Close Rd WF10 200 F4
Close The
Barwick in Elmet LS15 194 B7
Close The *continued*
Boroughbridge YO51 141 A3
Boston Spa LS23 188 E8
Cawood YO8 197 A7
6 Collingham LS22 188 A8
11 East Ayton/West Ayton YO13 99 B8
4 Fylingdales YO22 33 D4
Hunmanby Sands YO14 101 C1
Longnewton TS21 4 F7
Neasham DL2 4 A1
Northallerton DL7 210 B2
Norton DN6 206 E2
Riccall YO19 198 A8
Scalby YO12 212 B8
Skipton BD23 216 F3
Studley Roger HG4 113 D1
Thirsk YO7 211 C1
Thorner LS14 188 A3
Thornton Dale YO18 96 D5
Towton LS24 189 E2
York YO30 227 F8
Clotherholme Rd HG4 214 A5
Clough La DN6 207 B2
Clover Hill BD23 217 B5
Clover Way 9 HG3 161 B3
Cloverley Cl YO41 168 C2
Clowbeck Ct DL3 3 B8
Coach La
10 Hurworth-on-Tees DL2 3 E1
Lindley LS21 177 D3
Coach Rd
Harrogate HG1 219 F2
Sheriff Hutton YO60 145 D4
Sleights YO22 32 A6
Coach St BD23 216 F4
Coach Street Yd 13 BD23 216 F4
Coachman's Ct 6 HG2 220 B1
Coal Pit La
Kirk Smeaton WF8 206 A2
Rimington BB7 171 A1
Coalmire La DL6 45 D7
Coarse La HG3 159 A4
Coastal Rd YO13 75 D7
Coastguard Hill YO14 127 E5
Coates Ave BB18 171 E2
Coates Fields BB18 171 E2
Coates La
Barnoldswick BB18 171 E2
Kettlewell with Starbotton BD23 107 F5
Coate's La BD20 173 F2
Coates Lane Inf Sch BB18 171 E2
Coates Marsh La DN14 204 B2
Coatham Ave DL2 4 D3
Coatham La TS21 5 B7
Cob Castle* DL8 63 B1
Cob La BB18 186 A6
Cobble Carr TS14 8 E6
Cobblers La WF8 201 C1
Cobbler's La WF8 201 C1
Cobblers Lane Inf Sch WF8 201 D1
Cobby Syke Rd HG3 159 F1
Cobcroft La WF11 206 B8
Cobden St
Barnoldswick BB18 171 D1
Darlington DL1 3 E5
Thornaby TS17 6 B8
Coble La YO60 145 D5
Cobshaw La DL8 62 F6
Cochrane St YO8 232 D3
Cock Garth YO17 122 D1
Cock La Gainford DL2 1 E8
Piercebridge DL2 2 A7
Cock Lodge (site of)* YO7 115 C6
Cockburn St 5 TS12 9 F7
Cocked Hat HG4 139 C8
Cockerhill La YO62 93 E7
Cockerton C of E Prim Sch DL3 3 A6
Cockerton Gn DL3 3 B6
Cockhill La BB8 186 A4
Cocking La LS29 174 E3
Cocklakes La YO7 114 F1
Cockmoor Rd YO13 74 A1
Cockpit Cl HG4 113 C7
Cockrah Rd YO13 74 F2
Cockret Cl 8 YO8 232 B6
Cockret Ct YO8 232 B7
Cockret Rd YO8 232 B7
Cockshaw Bank La HG4 113 B4
Cockshott Pl 5 LS29 174 F4
Coda Ave YO23 231 B3
Codlin Rd 1 TS15 25 C5
Coeside YO24 230 B7
Coggan Way YO23 230 F4
Colber La HG3 138 F2
Colbert Ave LS29 218 E5
Colburn CP Sch DL9 41 A5
Colburn Dr DL9 40 F5
Colburn La DL9 40 F6
Colburn Sidings DL9 40 F4
Cold Bath Pl HG2 219 C1
Cold Bath Rd HG2 222 C8
Cold Cotes Rd HG3 160 B4
Cold Kirby Rd YO7 91 C8
Coldhill La LS25 195 C6
Coldie Hill 11 TS15 25 C5
Coldstone La YO7 88 B2
Coldyhill La YO12 212 B8
Cole St YO31 233 B4
Coledale Cl 2 YO30 224 F1
Colenso St YO23 233 B1
Coleridge Dr HG1 219 E7
Coleridge Gdns DL1 3 D3
Coleridge Way 1 WF8 201 B1
Colescliffe Cres YO12 212 C8
Colescliffe Rd YO12 212 C8
Colin St 14 BB18 171 D2
Coll of St John The YO31 233 B3
College Ave YO11 213 A2
College Ct
1 Low Bradley BD20 173 E3
4 Scarborough YO11 212 F4
College Farm Cl DN14 207 A8
College Farm La LS22 180 A2
College Gr WF10 200 D3
College La
Bradleys Both BD20 173 E3
5 Masham HG4 86 C3
Scarborough YO11 213 A1
College of Law YO23 231 B7
College of Ripon & York St Johns
York YO10 229 B3
York YO31 233 B3
College Rd
Bradleys Both BD20 173 E3
Copmanthorpe YO23 230 A3
Harrogate HG2 222 B8
Ripon HG4 214 B6
College St
Harrogate HG2 222 B8
York YO1 233 B3
Colley Broach Rd YO61 117 F7
Collier Hag La YO23 182 B3
Collier La
Lotherton cum Aberford LS25 195 A6
West Layton DL11 20 A8
Colliergate YO1 233 B2
Collin Ave TS4 6 F8
Collin Bank HG3 160 E6
Collinge Rd 9 BD22 187 B6
Collingham Way 12 YO14 101 A3
Collingwood Ave YO24 227 F2
Collingwood Gdns YO17 215 A3
Collingwood Rd WF6 200 A2
Collin's Hill HG3 223 D7
Collinsons La YO17 122 F5
Colliwath La DL8 60 F4
Colne & Broughton Rd BD23 172 C4
Colne Rd
Barnoldswick BB18 171 D1
Cowling BD22 187 A5
Earby BB18 172 A1
Kelbrook & Sough BB18 186 A8
Sutton BD20 187 C7
Trawden Forest BB8 186 A1
Colonel's Wlk 9 WF8 201 B1
Colorado Way WF10 200 F2
Colstan Rd DL6 210 E3
Colton Junc LS24 190 E7
Colton La YO23 190 E6
Coltsgate Hill HG4 214 B6
Columbine Gr 33 HG3 161 B3
Columbus Ravine YO12 212 F7
Colville Cres 8 DL9 41 A5
Colville Rd 12 DL9 41 A5
Comfort La DL10 20 C5
Comfrey Cl 32 HG3 161 B3
Comfrey Manor TS8 7 B4
Commercial St
9 Barnoldswick BB18 171 D1
Harrogate HG1 219 D3
Norton YO17 215 D3
Scarborough YO12 212 E5
10 Settle BD24 131 E2
Tadcaster LS24 189 E6
Commercial Yd 1 HG5 221 B6
Common Balk La HG3 140 A3
Common Croft La YO26 165 E1
Common Holme La LS29 175 C3
Common La Beal DN14 202 D3
Burn YO8 203 E7
Carlton Husthwaite YO7 116 F8
Catton YO41 185 E8
Coverham with Agglethorpe DL8 60 A2
Dunnington YO19 184 F5
Fangfoss YO41 169 B1
Glaisdale YO21 29 F1
Hambleton YO8 196 D2
Harome YO62 93 E5
Hartley CA17 14 A8
Knottingley WF11 202 B1
Norton DN6 206 E2
Scruton DL7 63 E7
South Milford LS25 195 F2
Sutton upon Derwent YO41 193 C8
Temple Hirst YO8 203 F4
Thorganby YO19 192 F5
Ulleskelf LS24 190 C2
Walden Stubbs DN6 206 F4
Warthill YO19 167 F2
West Witton DL8 59 F2
York YO10 229 B1
Common Rd
Barkston Ash LS24 195 F7
Church Fenton LS24 196 A7
Common Rd *continued*
Dunnington YO19 184 F7
Skipwith YO8 192 E1
Strensall YO60 145 D1
Commondale Sta YO21 9 E1
Compton La LS23 188 A7
Compton St YO30 228 A6
Conan Dr DL10 209 D8
Conan Gdns DL10 209 D8
Concorde Pk YO30 225 A3
Concorde Way TS18 5 F7
Coney Moor Gr LS26 200 C6
Coney St YO1 233 B2
Coneycroft 10 YO19 184 F7
Coneygarth La
Dunnington YO19 184 E5
Tunstall LA6 102 A4
Conference Cl YO17 215 B4
Conifer Cl 6 YO32 225 D3
Conifers Cl 2 YO8 197 D1
Coniscliffe Mews DL3 3 A4
Coniscliffe Rd DL3 3 A4
Coniston Ave BB18 171 D2
Coniston Cl 1 YO30 224 E1
Coniston Dr
Castleford WF10 201 C4
York YO10 229 B4
Coniston Gdns 6 YO12 99 F7
Coniston Gr
1 Colne BB8 186 A3
Middlesbrough TS5 6 E7
Coniston Rd HG1 220 B4
Coniston Way
3 Eastfield YO12 99 F7
Thirsk YO7 89 C4
Conistone La BD23 108 B3
Connaught Rd
Ilkley LS29 218 D3
Middlesbrough TS7 7 D6
Connaught Way YO32 225 F6
Cononley La BD20 173 D1
Cononley Prim Sch BD20 173 D2
Cononley Rd BD20 187 D8
Cononley Sta BD20 173 D1
Conowl Cl 23 YO62 92 F6
Conroy Cl 11 YO61 143 D8
Consort St BD23 217 B4
Constable Burton Hall* DL8 61 C6
Constable Rd
Hunmanby YO14 127 A8
Ilkley LS29 218 D3
Constable Ridge Rd HG3 160 B2
Constantine Ave
10 Colburn DL9 41 A5
York YO10 229 A4
Constantine Gr 11 DL9 41 A5
Constitution Hill 3 BD24 131 E2
Conway Cl 2 YO30 224 E3
Conway Cres BB18 171 E1
Conyers Ave DL3 3 A6
Conyers Cl DL10 209 D8
Conyers Ings YO13 99 A7
Conyers La DL8 61 D6
Conyers Rd DL7 22 E2
Conyers Sch TS15 5 E2
Cookgate TS7 7 C5
Cooks Cl 2 DL6 45 A7
Cooks Gdns 3 YO13 75 D5
Cook's Row 5 YO11 213 B6
Coolham La BB18 186 B8
Coombe Dr DL1 3 F6
Coombes Cl YO61 144 C3
Coomboots Brow YO13 75 A6
Cooper Cl DL6 25 D2
Cooper La
Blubberhouses LS21 159 C1
Potto DL6 25 D2
Cooper Lane Shepherd LS21 159 C2
Cooper Rd 49 YO14 101 B3
Coopers Dr YO23 230 B3
Copgrove La HG5 162 D8
Copgrove Rd HG3 140 A2
Cophill La YO7 66 A4
Copley La LS25 195 B7
Copmanroyd LS21 177 A2
Copmanthorpe Jun Sch YO23 230 B3
Copmanthorpe La YO23 230 E3
Copmanthorpe Prim Sch YO23 230 B3
Copmanthorpe Recn Ctr & Sports Club YO23 230 B2
Copper Beeches The 2 YO19 184 E7
Copperclay Wlk YO61 117 D1
Copperfield Cl YO17 215 C5
Coppergate
1 Riccall YO19 191 F1
York YO1 233 B2
Coppergate Wlk YO1 233 B2
Coppertop Mews 4 WF8 201 C2
Coppice Ave HG1 219 C4
Coppice Beck Ct HG1 219 D3
Coppice Cl
Harrogate HG1 219 C4
10 Haxby YO32 166 E5
Coppice Dr HG1 219 C3
Coppice Gate HG1 219 C4
Coppice La YO18 71 B1
Coppice Rise HG1 219 C5
Coppice The
Barwick in Elmet LS15 194 B7
Bishopthorpe YO23 230 F4
Brayton YO8 197 C1
Ilkley LS29 218 A6
Leeming DL7 63 F3
14 Sherburn in Elmet LS25 195 F4
19 Sutton BD20 187 E7
Coppice Valley CP Sch HG1 219 C5
Coppice Valley Pool HG1 219 D4
Coppice View HG1 219 C4
Coppice Way HG1 219 C5
Coppy La
Cononley BD20 173 C2
Sutton BD22 187 E4
Coppy Rd LS29 174 F4
Coppy Wood Dr LS29 218 B7
Copse Hill 1 YO14 101 A4
Copse The
3 North Featherstone WF7 200 E1
5 Scarborough YO12 212 B5
Copsewood Wlk 5 TS9 26 C8
Copwood Gr 7 YO32 225 C8
Corban La YO32 166 B6
Corban Way 21 YO32 166 D5
Corber Hill 7 DL6 43 F3
Corbie Way YO18 96 A7
Corby Ave TS5 6 D8
Cordike La
Birdsall YO17 148 D6
Langton YO17 147 F6
Cordilleras La DL11 39 C8
Corn Mill Gdns YO12 212 D7
Corn Mill La 39 LS29 176 D1
Cornbell Gate 4 HG4 113 D2
Cornborough Av YO31 228 F6
Cornborough Rd YO60 145 C5
Cornel Rise 26 HG3 161 B3
Cornelian Ave YO11 100 B8
Cornelian Cl
1 Scarborough YO11 100 B8
Scarborough YO11 213 C1
Cornelian Dr
2 Scarborough YO11 100 B8
Scarborough YO11 213 C1
Cornelius Cswy YO8 198 E8
Corner Cl 17 YO32 166 D5
Cornfield Rd TS17 6 A8
Cornflower Way 1 HG3 161 B3
Cornforth Hill DL10 209 B6
Cornlands YO17 215 D2
Cornlands Rd YO24 227 B1
Cornmill Cl YO8 197 B8
Cornwall Ave
Darlington DL1 3 E6
Silsden BD20 174 B1
Cornwall Dr YO10 231 E8
Cornwall Rd HG1 219 B2
Cornwood Way 11 YO32 225 C8
Coronation Ave
6 Colburn DL9 41 A5
Harrogate HG2 222 F7
1 Hinderwell TS13 11 F7
Coronation Gr HG2 222 E7
Coronation Hospl LS29 218 C3
Coronation Pl DL10 209 A7
Coronation Rd
Crakehall DL8 62 E5
Harrogate HG2 222 E7
Coronation St 8 BB18 171 E1
Corporation Rd DL3 3 C6
Corpse Rd
North Otterington DL7 64 E5
Thornton-le-Moor DL6 65 A4
Cosmo Ave YO31 229 A5
Costa La YO18 95 D6
Costa Way YO18 95 E7
Cotchers La LS24 195 D8
Cotcliffe Bank DL6 65 E5
Cote Hill Rd HG3 160 B4
Cote La Healey HG4 85 D5
Sproxton YO62 92 C4
Cotescue Bank DL8 60 C1
Cotswold Dr LS25 194 C3
Cotswold Way YO32 226 A5
Cottage Cl DL6 210 E5
Cottage La YO60 145 C4
Cottagers La DL2 2 C3
Cottam La YO25 151 C5
Cotterdale Cl HG5 221 C6
Cotterdale Holt 9 LS22 180 A1
Cottom La YO42 193 C2
Cotton Tree La BB8 186 A3
Coulby Farm Way TS8 7 A5
Coulby La YO18 97 A6
Coulby Manor Way TS8 6 F6
Coulby Newham Sec Sch TS8 7 A5
Coulson Cl 5 YO32 167 C8
Coulter Beck La LA6 102 D7
Coulthurst Craven Sports Ctr The BD23 216 F3
Coulton La YO62 119 A6
Count De Burgh Terr 4 YO23 228 B1
County Cricket Gd YO12 212 F7
County Par HG1 219 F3
County Sq HG1 219 F3

Coupland Rd
Garforth LS25 194 C4
1 Selby YO8 232 C6
Courby Hill HG4 86 F2
Courcey Gr YO26 227 C4
Court Dr YO8 232 A4
Court Green Cl YO13 54 D1
Court La BD23 217 A4
Court Moor La YO62 70 A4
Court The 6 DL8 63 A2
Courtneys Selby YO8 232 B4
Wheldrake YO19 193 A8
Courts Cl 7 DN14 205 E4
Courtyard The
Bishopthorpe YO23 231 B4
11 Pontefract WF8 201 C2
Coutances Way LS29 218 F5
Cove Rd BD23 132 F2
Cover La
Carlton Town DL8 83 E7
Marton-le-Moor HG4 114 E1
Coverdale Dr
1 Knaresborough HG5 221 A7
Scarborough YO12 212 B4
Coverdale Garth 2
LS22 188 A8
Coverdale La TS13 12 A4
Coverham Abbey (rems of)*
DL8 60 C1
Coverham Cl DL7 210 C2
Coverham La DL8 60 C1
Covert The
9 Topcliffe YO7 89 B1
York YO24 230 F7
Cow & Calf Rocks*
LS29 218 D2
Cow Close La
Kirkby Malham BD23 154 E8
Lockwood TS12 10 B4
Cow Gate La BD23 171 B7
Cow La Cowling BD22 187 B6
Knottingley WF11 202 A2
Lothersdale BD20 172 F1
Middleton Tyas DL10 21 E5
Womersley DN6 206 D6
Cow Pasture La YO42 193 C3
Cow Wath Bank YO22 51 E8
Cow Wath Cl 30 YO12 75 D5
Cowbar Bank 1 TS13 13 K2
Cowbar La TS13 13 J2
Cowcliff Hill YO17 148 F6
Cowgarth La 15 BB18 172 B1
Cowgill St 17 BB18 172 A1
Cowhouse Bank YO62 68 F3
Cowie Dr YO8 232 D5
Cowland La YO7 88 D3
Cowley Cl TS16 5 E7
Cowley Rd TS5 6 E7
Cowling Hill La BD22 186 F7
Cowling La DL8 62 D3
Cowling Prim Sch
BD22 187 A6
Cowling Rd DL8 62 D2
Cowlings Cl 16 YO14 127 A8
Cowpasture Rd LS29 218 C3
Cowper La YO23 191 C8
Cowper St 3 BD23 217 A3
Cowton Castle* DL7 22 D1
Cowton La YO14 127 C6
Cowton Way TS16 5 D6
Coxlea Gr YO31 229 B6
Coxwold Dr DL1 3 D4
Coxwold Hill 5 LS22 180 C4
Coxwold Pottery*
YO61 117 D7
Coxwold View 1 LS22 180 C3
Crab La Harrogate HG1 219 D6
Seamer YO12 99 E6
Crab Tree La WF8 206 A1
Crabmill La YO61 143 D8
Crabtree Gn LS22 188 A8
Crabtree Gr 1 YO32 225 D3
Crabtree Hill LS22 188 A8
Cracoe Prim Sch
BD23 156 B6
Cradley Dr TS5 6 E6
Crag Bank YO21 28 B8
Crag Cl 33 BD20 187 E7
Crag Gdns LS23 188 E5
Crag Hill La HG3 161 B6
Crag Hill Rd YO13 53 F8
Crag La
Bradleys Both BD20 173 E2
Felliscliffe HG3 160 D4
Huby LS17 178 B2
Killinghall HG3 161 B1
Killinghall HG3 161 C5
Knaresborough HG5 221 B5
North Rigton LS17 178 B3
Pannal HG3 178 C8
Sutton BD20 187 D6
Crag Side Rd DL8 57 B2
Crag The 3 LS23 188 E5
Crag View
Cononley BD20 173 D1
Threshfield BD23 134 B3
Weeton LS17 178 B2
Crag View Rd BD23 217 B3
Cragdale 13 BD24 131 D2
Cragdale Rise 1 HG5 221 D6
Cragg Bottom Rd
BD22 187 C1
Cragg Dr LS29 218 F3
Cragg Hill Rd BD24 105 C3
Cragg La LA2 130 C4
Craggs La
Arrathorne DL10 41 A1
Tatham LA2 129 A3
Craig St DL3 3 C6
Craiglands Pk LS29 218 C3
Craiglands Rd LS29 218 C3
Craigmore Dr LS29 218 E4
Craigs Way YO7 211 C4
Crake La HG3 159 F6
Crakehall C of E Prim Sch
DL8 62 E4
Cranberry TS8 7 B5
Cranbrook Ave YO26 227 C5
Cranbrook Rd YO26 227 C5
Cranbrooks The YO19 192 F8
Cranfield Pl 4 YO24 230 C8
Cranford Gdns TS5 6 D8
Crank La DL7 63 B7
Crankley La YO61 143 B7
Cranwell Gr TS17 6 B6
Craven Bank La BD24 131 B3
Craven Coll BD24 131 D2
Craven Cres 3 LS29 174 F4
Craven Ct
Cowling BD22 187 C6
Northallerton DL7 210 B3
Richmond DL10 209 B6
Silsden BD20 174 C1
Craven Dr BD20 174 C1
Craven Garth 5 DN14 202 D4
Craven Mus* BD23 217 A4
Craven Ridge La BD24 131 A2
Craven Ridge La Ends
BD24 131 B3
Craven St 8 Colne BB8 186 A3
Harrogate HG1 219 D4
Scarborough YO11 213 A4
Skipton BD23 216 F3
Craven Way
5 Boroughbridge YO51 141 B4
Dent LA10 78 B8
Cravendale Rd 4 DL9 40 F5
Cravengate DL10 209 B6
Craven's Hill YO13 54 C3
Crawford Cl YO26 181 C7
Crawley Way YO31 229 B6
Cray Thorns Cres YO7 115 A4
Crayke C of E Prim Sch
YO61 117 F1
Crayke Castle* YO61 117 F1
Crayke La YO61 117 F2
Crayke Manor* YO61 118 A2
Crescent Ave YO21 208 C7
Crescent Back Rd 8
YO11 213 A5
Crescent Ct LS29 218 B4
Crescent Gdns HG1 219 C2
Crescent Hill 53 YO14 101 B3
Crescent Par HG4 214 C6
Crescent Rd
Harrogate HG1 219 C2
Ripon HG4 214 B6
Crescent Terr 6 LS29 218 B4
Crescent The
13 Bedale DL8 63 B3
Burton Fleming YO25 126 E3
Carlton TS9 26 A2
Eaglescliffe TS16 5 D4
Filey YO14 101 B3
Garforth LS25 194 D4
2 Hartwith cum Winsley
HG3 138 A1
17 Helmsley YO62 92 F6
Ilkley LS29 218 E5
Kelfield YO19 191 D1
Kexby YO41 185 C5
Kippax LS25 194 D1
Micklefield LS25 195 A3
Middlesbrough TS7 7 D6
Middleton St George DL2 4 E4
North Rigton LS17 178 B3
Northallerton DL6 210 E4
Otley LS21 177 A1
6 Riccall YO19 197 F8
Richmond DL10 209 D7
Ripon HG4 214 B6
Scalby YO12 212 B7
Scarborough YO11 213 A5
Sicklinghall LS22 179 E3
Stainton Dale YO13 54 A8
Stamford Bridge YO41 168 D2
Thornaby TS17 6 B8
Thornton Dale YO18 96 D5
York YO24 233 A1
Crest Hill LS26 194 A1
Crest The LS26 194 A1
Crestbrooke DL7 210 D2
Crestholme Cl 6 HG5 221 D5
Crewe Rd WF10 201 B4
Creyke View DN14 205 A1
Crichton Ave YO30 228 B8
Cricket La TS6 7 E8
Cricketers Way 8 LS25 195 F4
Cridling Gdns DN6 206 F2
Crimple Ave LS22 180 A8
Crimple La HG3 223 D7
Crimple Mdws HG3 222 D3
Crinan Ct
Pontefract WF6 200 A2
3 York YO32 225 F6
Crindle Carr La DL7 65 B3
Cringle Moor Chase
TS9 26 F4
Cringles La BD20 174 C4
Cringley La DL8 57 E5
Crocus Ct 20 DL9 41 A5
Croft Ave
8 Knottingley WF11 202 A3
Croft Ave *continued*
Middlesbrough TS5 6 D8
4 Normanton South WF6 200 B2
Otley LS21 176 F1
Croft C of E Prim Sch
DL2 22 C8
Croft Cl
Carlton Husthwaite YO7 116 F7
14 Easingwold YO61 143 C8
Ingleton LA6 103 D3
Croft Ct YO23 231 A4
Croft Dr LS23 188 E6
Croft Farm Cl YO23 230 B3
Croft Gdns YO7 211 B1
Croft Head Terr 2
BD20 187 E7
Croft Heads YO7 211 B1
Croft Hill Carthorpe DL8 87 E6
32 Glusburn BD20 187 E7
Croft Hills TS9 26 A7
Croft House Dr 8 LS21 176 F1
Croft House Fold 10
LS29 175 A4
Croft House La BD23 135 A1
Croft La
Carlton Husthwaite YO7 116 F8
Newton Kyme cum Toulston
LS24 189 B7
Snainton YO13 97 F5
Walton LS23 181 A2
Croft Motor Racing Circuit*
DL2 22 C5
Croft Rd
Bramham cum Oglethorpe
LS23 188 E6
Camblesforth YO8 204 D4
Catterick Garrison DL9 209 E1
Eaglescliffe TS16 5 D4
Hurworth DL2 3 B2
Ingleton LA6 103 D3
Croft St 12 Earby BB18 172 B1
1 Glusburn BD20 187 E7
Croft The Beadlam YO62 93 D7
Burton in Lonsdale LA6 102 F3
Castleford WF10 200 F3
5 Collingham LS22 188 A8
Draughton BD23 174 B7
16 Filey YO14 101 B3
1 Filey YO14 101 B3
Knottingley WF11 202 A3
Langthorpe YO51 141 A7
Scalby YO12 212 B7
Sheriff Hutton YO60 145 D5
Stirton with Thorlby
BD23 216 C6
Thirsk YO7 211 B1
West Tanfield DL8 87 B3
Crofters Gn HG3 219 A8
Croftlands 7 WF11 202 A3
Crofts Ave
4 Pickering YO18 96 A6
Richmond DL10 209 B7
Crofts The
1 Glusburn BD20 173 F1
1 Sutton BD20 187 E6
Croftside 1 YO26 227 B3
Croftway
Barwick in Elmet LS15 194 C8
Camblesforth YO8 204 C5
Selby YO8 232 C4
Sherburn in Elmet LS25 195 F4
2 York YO26 227 B3
Crombie Ave YO30 228 B7
Cromer St YO30 228 B7
Cromwell Ave 22 YO14 101 B3
Cromwell Cl 5 WF11 201 E4
Cromwell Cres 6 WF8 201 C1
Cromwell Dr DL7 64 A6
Cromwell Gdns 6 YO11 212 F4
Cromwell Par 5 YO11 212 F4
Cromwell Rd
Harrogate HG2 222 E7
Scarborough YO11 212 F4
York YO1 233 B1
Cromwell Rise LS25 200 D8
Cromwell St 9 BD23 217 A3
Cromwell Terr 7 YO11 212 F4
Crook Bank La DL11 38 F6
Crook La HG4 85 E5
Crooked La YO26 164 C2
Crookland La YO32 166 F5
Croom Medieval Village*
YO25 150 B4
Croome Dale La YO17 150 C6
Croome Rd YO25 150 B4
Cropstones LS23 188 F5
Cropton La YO18 71 B2
Cropton Rise YO12 212 B4
Cropton Way TS8 7 B5
Crosby Rd DL6 210 E4
Crosby St DL3 3 C7
Crosland Cl 22 YO62 92 F6
Cross Bank BD23 217 B6
Cross End Fold 3 LS29 175 A4
Cross Gate YO13 97 D5
Cross Haw La 3 LA2 130 C8
Cross Head Bank DL8 60 D7
Cross Hill
Fairburn WF11 201 D6
Sutton-under-Whitestonecliffe
YO7 90 D5
Cross Hills La YO8 232 A5
Cross La Bentham LA2 128 E8
Brompton YO13 98 C5
Burneston DL8 87 E8
Burniston YO13 75 D7
Farndale East YO62 48 E4
Flaxton YO60 167 E8
Cross La *continued*
Fulford YO19 231 F5
Giggleswick BD24 130 F2
Great Ouseburn YO26 164 B8
Little Ayton TS9 27 A8
Pickhill with Roxby YO7 88 C6
Scalby YO12 212 C8
Sinnington YO62 95 A8
Snainton YO13 97 F3
Stonebeck Up HG3 110 B5
Cross Lane Hospl
YO12 212 D8
Cross Lanes DL10 209 E7
Cross Queen St 9 WF6 200 A1
Cross Rd LA2 128 E7
Cross Rein Bank DL7 23 A1
Cross Row Boosbeck TS12 9 E7
Swillington LS15 194 A3
Cross St 6 Cowling BD22 187 B6
14 Earby BB18 172 A1
Scarborough YO11 213 A6
Skipton BD23 216 F3
5 York YO24 227 C3
Cross The LS15 194 B8
Cross Top DL8 57 E7
Crossbeck Cl LS29 218 B3
Crossbeck Rd
Ilkley LS29 218 B3
Northallerton DL6 210 F5
Crossbeck Way TS7 7 D8
Crosscliff TS8 6 F5
Crossdale Rd YO18 72 E3
Crossfield Cl 2 DL2 3 E1
Crossfield Cres YO19 231 E6
Crossfields TS8 7 A4
Crossgate La
22 Pickering YO18 95 F6
10 Pickering YO18 96 A6
Crossgates HG3 138 B5
Crosshill La DN14 207 E6
Crosshills Rd BD20 173 D1
Crossings The 18 DN14 205 E4
Crosslands Rd 2 YO10 231 E8
Crossley Pl BD23 216 F4
Crossley St 8 LS22 180 C3
Crossman Dr 2 WF6 200 B2
Crossmoor La YO32 166 E6
Crossway The
Darlington DL1 3 E5
2 York YO31 228 E8
Crossways YO10 229 C2
Crossways Cres HG2 220 D3
Crossways Dr HG2 220 D2
Crossways The LS21 177 A1
Crow Hill La HG3 160 C4
Crow Nest Rd LA2 130 F6
Crowberry Dr HG3 161 B3
Crowdy Cl YO22 208 E4
Crowfoot La DL6 43 D5
Crowgarth HG4 140 D7
Crown Cres YO11 213 A4
Crown Gr YO17 215 E3
Crown Sq 26 YO62 70 B1
Crown St
34 Burley in Warfedale
LS29 176 C1
Darlington DL1 3 C5
Crown Terr YO11 213 A4
Crowood Ave TS9 26 C8
Crowtrees LA2 128 E8
Crummack La LA2 130 E8
Crummock 3 YO24 230 C7
Cuddy Brown Cl 7 YO18 96 A6
Cuddy La DL6 45 B4
Culvert La BD23 216 A4
Cumberland Cl 6 YO32 167 B6
Cumberland Gdns
DL10 21 C4
Cumberland Rd WF10 201 C5
Cumberland St
6 Skipton BD23 216 F3
York YO1 233 B2
Cumbernauld Rd TS17 6 C7
Cumbrian Ave 4 YO32 167 B6
Cundall Ave YO7 115 B6
Cundall Cl 6 YO32 167 C8
Cundall Manor Sch
YO61 115 E3
Cundall Way HG2 222 C8
Cunliffe Rd LS29 218 B4
Cunningham Ave TS17 6 B6
Cunningham Rd DL9 40 F4
Cupid's Alley YO17 149 B6
Curfew Rd HG4 214 C3
Curlew Cl 11 Ilkley LS29 175 C2
Leyburn DL8 60 E4
Curlew Cres 2 DL9 40 F2
Curlew Dr Eastfield YO12 99 E6
3 Filey YO14 101 A3
Curlew Glebe 8 YO19 184 E7
Curly Hill LS29 218 C7
Currer La LS29 175 B6
Currie Cl DL9 209 C2
Curson Terr YO8 198 E3
Curtain La DL11 1 D5
Curtain The DL11 1 D4
Curteis Dr DL10 41 B6
Curzon Terr YO23 228 B1
Custance Wlk YO23 233 A1
Cut Rd WF11 201 D6
Cut Throat La HG3 138 F1
Cutler La LS26 200 C6
Cutpurse La DL10 209 C8
Cutsyke Ave WF10 200 D3
Cutsyke Crest WF10 200 D3
Cutsyke Rd WF10 200 D2
Cycle St 4 YO10 229 A3
Cygnet Cl 7 YO14 101 A4
Cygnet St YO23 233 A1
Cypress Cl DL3 3 B4
Cypress Gdns HG4 214 B2
Cypress Rd TS7 7 C6

D

Dacre Ct LS24 195 D7
Dacre Hall Pk HG3 159 F7
Dacre La HG3 159 D7
Dacre Pasture La
HG3 159 D6
Daffy La YO61 117 E1
Dairy La HG3 159 E6
Daisy Cl 18 DL9 41 A5
Daisy Hill BD20 174 C1
Dakyn Cl DL7 22 F2
Dalacres Cres BD23 217 D8
Dalacres Dr BD23 217 D8
Dalby Ave HG2 220 D1
Dalby Bank YO60 119 C2
Dalby Cl YO12 212 B5
Dalby Ct HG2 220 D1
Dalby Forest Dr YO18 96 E8
Dalby Mead YO32 225 F1
Dalby Way TS8 7 A5
Dale Ave YO13 75 C8
Dale Bank HG1 219 B3
Dale Cl Burniston YO13 75 C8
Hampsthwaite HG3 161 A5
7 Hurworth-on-Tees DL2 3 E1
Selby YO8 232 C3
Thornton Watlass HG4 86 D8
Dale Cres BD23 173 A4
Dale Croft 20 LS29 175 C2
Dale Dike Gr YO30 224 F2
Dale Edge 11 YO11 99 F7
Dale End Danby YO21 29 C7
Kirkbymoorside YO62 70 B1
Dale End Rd YO62 70 A7
Dale Garth YO12 212 D4
Dale Gr DL8 60 D6
Dale Rd Carleton BD23 173 A4
Darlington DL3 3 B5
Sadberge DL2 4 C7
Dale Rise YO13 75 C8
Dale St Earby BB18 172 B1
York YO23 233 A1
Dale Stone Cl WF11 201 D5
Dale The LS25 188 F1
Dale View 6 Earby BB18 172 A1
Ilkley LS29 175 C2
Dale Way 2 DL8 60 D5
Dalefield Ave WF6 200 A1
Dalefield Rd WF6 200 A1
Dalehouse Bank TS13 13 J1
Dales Ave BD23 217 C7
Dales Countryside Mus*
DL8 56 D5
Dale's La YO31 228 F6
Dales Park Rd TS8 6 E5
Dales Sch DL7 64 A7
Dalesbridge Outdoor Ctr*
LA2 130 E6
Daleside Ave HG2 222 E5
Daleside Dr HG2 222 E5
Daleside Gdns HG2 222 E5
Daleside Pk HG3 160 A6
Daleside Rd
Farndale East YO62 48 C7
Farndale West YO62 48 B6
Harrogate HG2 222 E5
Rosedale East Side YO18 49 C5
Rosedale West Side YO18 49 C3
Dalewood Wlk 5 TS9 26 C8
Dalguise Gr YO31 233 C4
Dallamires Cl HG4 214 D3
Dallamires La HG4 214 E3
Dallamires Way N
HG4 214 D4
Dallamires Way S
HG4 214 D3
Dalmally Cl YO24 230 B6
Dalton Hill YO19 193 A8
Dalton La Dalton YO7 115 D7
Wothersome LS23 188 C5
Dalton Terr YO24 228 A3
Dam Bank YO8 232 C6
Dam Head Rd 14 BB18 171 D1
Dam Hill YO23 182 B4
Dam La
Appleton Roebuck YO23 190 F4
Leavening YO17 147 E1
Markington with Wallerthwaite
HG3 139 C3
Saxton with Scarthingwell
LS24 195 C7
Selby YO8 197 B3
Dame La DL8 58 F1
Danby C of E Prim Sch
YO21 29 B6
Danby Castle* YO21 29 D6
Danby La DL7 43 C5
Danby St DL9 40 F4
Danby Sta YO21 29 C7
Dandy Mill Ave WF8 201 C1
Dandy Mill Croft 8
WF8 201 C1
Dandy Mill View WF8 201 C1
Dane Ave
Thorpe Willoughby YO8 197 B1
York YO26 227 C5
Dane Rd DL9 209 E1
Danebury Cres YO26 227 C4
Danebury Dr YO26 227 C4
Danelaw Fields 1 DL6 43 F3
Danelaw Rd 2 DL6 43 F3

Danes Croft 2 YO10 231 D8
Danes Ct 5 YO19 198 A8
Danes Dyke 34 YO12 75 D5
Danescroft YO8 232 C2
Danesfort Ave YO24 227 D2
Danesgate YO26 227 C4
Danesmead YO10 231 D8
Danesmoor Cres DL3 3 B5
Daneswell Cl 3 YO41 168 D2
Dangerous Cnr HG3 160 A2
Dansk Way LS29 218 D5
Danum Ave YO7 211 A1
Danum Dr YO10 231 E8
Danum Rd YO10 231 E8
Darbie Cl YO32 225 D4
D'arcy Ct DL9 40 F4
D'arcy Rd YO8 232 E4
Dark La
Barwick in Elmet & Scholes LS15 194 B8
Brompton YO13 98 C5
Earby BB18 172 B1
Newsham DL11 19 C8
Sinnington YO62 71 A1
Spofforth with Stockeld HG5 179 F7
Stainburn LS21 177 E2
Sutton BD22 187 F1
Darkfield La WF8 201 C2
Darley Carr HG3 159 F6
Darley Cl 7 YO41 168 D2
Darley CP Sch HG3 160 A6
Darley Mill Ctr★ HG3 159 F6
Darley Rd HG3 160 D6
Darling La YO23 191 C8
Darlington (Bank Top) Sta DL1 3 D4
Darlington Arts Ctr★ DL3 3 C5
Darlington Back La DL2 4 E8
Darlington Coll of Tech DL3 3 B5
Darlington Meml Hospl DL3 3 C6
Darlington Rd
Easby DL10 20 F1
Longnewton TS21 5 A7
Northallerton DL6 210 C7
Richmond DL10 209 E8
Stockton-on-Tees TS18 5 E8
Darlington Rly Ctr & Mus★ DL3 3 C6
Darlington Rugby Football Club DL1 3 C3
Darnborough St YO23 233 B1
Darnbrook Rd 2 BB18 171 D1
Darnbrook Wlk YO31 229 B5
Darnholme La YO22 51 D8
Darnton Dr TS4 7 A7
Darrowby Cl YO7 211 C4
Darrowby Dr DL3 3 C6
Daskett Hill YO60 145 D5
Dauby La YO41 185 B3
Davenport Rd TS15 5 D2
David La YO18 72 F5
Davis Ave WF10 201 B3
Davison Rd DL1 3 D7
Davison St TS12 9 F7
Davygate YO1 233 B2
Daw La YO23 191 A5
Dawcross Rise HG3 222 B3
Dawes Ave WF10 201 A3
Dawnay Cl 5 YO12 99 F7
Dawnay Garth
Shipton YO30 165 E5
2 Snaith DN14 204 B1
Dawney La YO61 143 B6
Dawson St 16 BD23 217 A3
Dawson Terr HG1 219 D4
Dawson's La HG4 85 F4
Dawtrie St WF10 201 B4
Day La HG3 159 E4
Daysfoot Ct 8 YO10 228 E3
De Bruce Rd DL6 210 D8
De Brus Pk TS8 7 C4
De Brus Way TS14 8 F7
De Ferrers Rd DL6 210 D8
De Ferrieres Ave HG1 219 D4
De Gaunte Rd DL6 210 E8
De Grey Ct YO30 233 A4
De Grey Pl 2 YO23 231 B3
De Grey St YO31 233 B4
De Grey Terr YO31 233 B4
De Lacy Ave 1 WF7 200 E1
De Lisle Cres DL9 209 C2
De Mowbray Ct YO23 182 D3
Deacon Ct 3 YO8 232 B6
Deacons Ct YO23 230 B2
Dealtry Ave 1 YO32 225 C8
Dean Edge Rd BD22 187 C1
Dean Hall Brow YO22 32 C5
Dean La BD22 187 F3
Dean Rd Norton YO17 215 E3
Scarborough YO12 212 E6
Dean St Ilkley LS29 218 C5
Trawden Forest BB8 186 A1
Deane Pl HG2 220 B3
Deangate YO1 233 B3
Deanhead Gr YO30 224 E2
Deans Cl YO23 230 F4
Deans Sq YO7 115 C7
Debruse Ave TS15 5 D2
Dee Cl YO24 230 B7
Deep Dale LS23 180 E1
Deep Ghyll Croft HG4 214 C3
Deep Ghyll Wlk HG4 214 C3
Deepdale
Guisborough TS14 8 D6
Deepdale *continued*
7 Hutton Rudby TS15 25 C5
5 York YO24 230 D8
Deepdale Ave
Eastfield YO11 100 A8
Middlesbrough TS4 7 A8
Scarborough YO11 213 A1
Deepdale La
Boston Spa LS23 180 D1
Dent LA10 77 F8
Deepdale Way 7 DL1 3 F6
Deepfurrows La YO41 185 D3
Deeping Way YO8 232 A6
Deer Hill Gr YO30 224 F3
Deer Park Ct 1 LS25 202 A8
Deerstone Way 22 YO19 184 F7
Deighton Ave 18 LS25 195 F4
Deighton La
Brompton DL6 43 E5
Little Smeaton DL6 23 E1
Deighton Rd
Coulby Newham TS4 7 A7
Spofforth with Stockeld HG3 179 F6
Wetherby LS22 180 C4
Deigton Gate Jun & Inf Sch LS22 180 C4
Del Pyke YO31 233 C4
Delamere Cl 6 YO32 166 D5
Delamere Cres HG2 220 D1
Delamere Rd TS3 7 B8
Delaney Cl 19 BD24 131 D2
Delf La YO7 66 A4
Dell The 5 YO30 224 B5
Delves La YO22 30 F3
Delwood YO10 231 D7
Dene Cl DN14 203 C2
Dene Gr DL3 3 C6
Dene Mdw 1 YO13 99 B8
Dene Park Cl HG1 219 F6
Dene Pk HG1 219 F5
Dene Rd DL6 210 E5
Dene The YO12 212 E7
Deneside Rd DL3 3 B6
Denesway LS25 194 D3
Denevale TS15 5 E3
Denison Ave 8 YO12 99 D6
Denison Rd YO8 232 E4
Dennis La BD20 174 A2
Dennis St YO1 233 C2
Dennison St
1 York YO31 228 E6
York YO31 233 C4
Dentdale Dr HG5 221 C6
Denton Rd LS29 218 A5
Denton Terr WF10 200 F4
Denver Dr DL2 4 D4
Denver Rd 6 DN6 206 F2
Denwell Terr WF8 201 B1
Depot La 11 YO12 212 E4
Deramore Dr YO10 229 C3
Deramore Dr W YO10 229 C3
Derby Rd TS14 8 E6
Derby The TS7 7 B6
Dere Street Roman Rd★ DL11 2 B2
Derrings La YO61 142 D6
Derventio Roman Fort★ YO17 215 D4
Derwent Ave
Garforth LS25 194 C3
5 Scarborough YO12 212 E4
York YO31 228 F4
Derwent Cl 2 Colne BB8 186 A3
Elvington YO41 185 B3
2 Stamford Bridge YO41 168 D2
Derwent Ct YO41 185 C2
Derwent Dr
4 Barlby YO8 198 B5
Castleford WF10 201 C5
Wheldrake YO19 192 F7
Derwent Est YO19 184 E7
Derwent Inf Sch YO10 229 B4
Derwent Jun Sch YO10 229 B4
Derwent Pk YO19 193 A8
Derwent Rd
Harrogate HG1 220 B3
Huttons Ambo YO17 215 A2
Whitby YO21 208 A7
York YO10 231 D8
Derwent St 7 YO12 212 E4
Derwent Swimming Pool & Fitness Ctr YO17 215 D4
Desmond Rd DL2 4 C3
Deveron Way YO24 230 B7
Devil's Arrows Standing Stones★ YO51 141 B5
Devon Pl YO10 228 F3
Devonshire Dr YO12 212 E7
Devonshire Gn HG4 114 F1
Devonshire Pl
Harrogate HG1 219 E3
12 Skipton BD23 216 F4
Devonshire Rd DL1 3 E6
Devonshire St 13 BD23 217 A3
Devonshire Way HG1 219 F4
Dew La TS7 7 D7
Dewberry TS8 7 B4
Dewsbury Terr YO1 233 A1
Dexta Way DL7 210 C3
Diamond Gr HG1 220 C4
Diamond Pl HG1 220 C4
Diamond Rd TS17 6 B8
Diamond St YO31 233 C4
Dibble Bridge Bank YO21 28 F6
Dibdale Rd DL2 4 A1
Dick La BD22 187 B6
Dick Scot La DL11 19 D7
Dickens Cl 1 YO32 225 F1
Dickens Rd YO17 215 C6
Dickey La YO8 197 D5
Dickson Rd 4 YO24 227 B1
Dicky Grounds La YO17 121 D8
Dijon Ave YO24 227 C2
Dike La HG3 159 C8
Dikehollin La DL8 58 E2
Dikelands Cl 19 YO26 165 F1
Dikelands La YO26 165 F1
Dikes La TS9 8 C2
Dilys Gr 5 YO26 227 E4
Dimmingdale Rd TS12 10 A3
Dinsdale Ave TS5 6 E7
Dinsdale Cl 7 DL2 4 C4
Dinsdale Ct 6 DL2 4 C4
Dinsdale Dr TS16 5 E5
Dinsdale Sta DL2 4 C4
Diomed Ct TS7 7 B7
Dishforth Airfield YO7 115 A2
Dishforth Airfield CP Sch YO7 115 B2
Dishforth C of E Prim Sch YO7 114 F4
Dishforth Rd
Copt Hewick HG4 114 B2
Sharow HG4 214 F6
Disraeli Cl YO32 225 E1
Dixon La YO1 233 C1
Dixon Rd HG1 219 D4
Dixon St BD20 187 F7
Dixon Terr HG1 219 D4
Dixons Bank TS8 7 C5
Dixsons Yd YO1 233 C2
Dob Park Rd LS21 176 F4
Dobella Ave DN14 205 A1
Dobella La DN14 205 B1
Doctor Laithe 3 BD23 134 D2
Doctor's Hill LA2 128 E8
Doctors La WF10 200 D7
Doctor's La TS15 25 C5
Dodder Carr Rd TS13 10 F3
Dodford Rd TS8 6 F5
Dodgson La
Lothersdale BD20 186 D8
Thornton in Craven BB18 172 C1
Dodgson Terr YO26 227 D4
Dodmire Jun & Inf Sch DL1 3 E4
Dodsworth Ave YO31 228 E7
Doe Park La YO41 169 B4
Doe Pk YO30 224 F2
Dog Hill DL8 60 E3
Dog Hill Brow BD24 131 D6
Dog Kennel La YO18 96 E5
Dolegate YO41 168 F4
Dolly La DL7 64 C8
Dolphin Ctr The DL1 3 C5
Dolphin Way YO14 100 F5
Don Ave YO24 230 E8
Don Pedro Ave WF6 200 B1
Don Pedro Cl WF6 200 B1
Donald Smith Ct DL8 61 C5
Doncaster Rd
Brayton YO8 232 B3
Knottingley WF11 201 E2
North Elmsall WF8 206 A1
Doran Cl 45 YO14 101 B3
Dorchester Rd LS24 189 D5
Doriam Ave YO31 225 F2
Doriam Dr YO31 225 F2
Dorkings The TS9 26 E5
Dorset Cl HG1 219 A3
Dorset Cres HG1 219 A3
Dorset Rd TS14 8 E5
Dorset St BD23 217 A3
Dorts Cres LS24 190 C1
Dotcliffe Rd BB18 186 A7
Doublegates Ave 6 HG4 113 D2
Doublegates Cl 8 HG4 113 D2
Doublegates Ct 10 HG4 113 D2
Doublegates Gn 9 HG4 113 D2
Doublegates Wlk 7 HG4 113 D2
Doubting Castle★ YO21 10 D1
Douglas Cl TS18 5 F7
Douglas St 3 YO8 232 C5
Douky Bottom Cave★ BD23 133 F7
Dove Cl LS22 180 B4
Dove Cote Gdns DN14 203 D2
Dove St YO23 233 A1
Dove Way YO62 94 C8
Dovecot Cl YO14 100 E4
Dovecote Dr WF10 200 F7
Dovecote Garth 5 YO41 185 B2
Dovecote Mews YO7 115 C7
Dovedale Ave YO12 212 D8
Dovelands 14 BD20 187 E6
Dowber Way YO7 211 D4
Dower Chase YO19 192 A6
Dower Pk YO19 192 B6
Dowkell La LS23 180 F1
Downdale Rd YO13 54 B4
Downdinner Hill YO21 208 C6
Downholme Rd DL9 209 B1
Downland Cres WF11 202 A1
Downside Rd TS5 6 D8
Dragon Ave HG1 219 E3
Dragon Par HG1 219 E3
Dragon Rd HG1 219 E3
Dragon Terr HG1 219 E3
Drake Cl YO21 208 B5
Drake St 2 YO23 233 B1
Drakes Cl YO32 225 F4
Drapers Croft YO23 230 B4
Drax CP Sch YO8 204 F5
Dreaken Fold 4 YO13 99 A7
Drebley La BD23 157 D6
Dresser Cl DL10 209 C8
Driffield Rd YO25 151 C4
Driffield Terr YO24 228 A2
Drift La HG4 138 B8
Dringfield Cl 2 YO24 230 D8
Dringhouses Prim Sch YO24 230 F8
Dringthorpe Rd YO24 230 F7
Drive The
Harrogate HG1 220 C5
Harrogate HG2 222 B5
7 High & Low Bishopside HG3 137 C4
Kippax LS25 194 D1
12 Swillington LS26 194 A1
Threshfield BD23 134 B3
Drome Rd YO23 230 C2
Drovers Ct 8 YO61 143 C8
Drovers Way YO7 211 D4
Drovers Wlk BD23 154 B3
Druggist La 16 LS29 174 F4
Druggon Rd DL9 40 E3
Druids Mdw 8 YO51 141 B5
Drummond View YO23 231 B4
Drury Cl HG3 222 F2
Drury La HG3 222 F2
Drury St DL3 3 C6
Dryden Cl HG1 219 E7
Dryhurst Cl 9 DN6 206 F2
Dubbing Garth La DL11 37 B4
Dubb's La BD23 81 C1
Duchess of Kents Military Hospl DL9 40 F4
Duchy Ave
3 Harrogate HG2 219 C1
11 Scalby YO13 75 D5
Duchy Gr 4 HG2 219 C1
Duchy Nuffield Hospl HG2 219 C1
Duchy Rd HG1 219 B2
Duck Hill HG4 214 C5
Duck La YO12 125 A8
Duck St LA2 128 A6
Duck St La HG3 136 D2
Duckett Cl DL10 209 F8
Duckett St BD23 217 A3
Dudley Mews YO31 233 C4
Dudley Rd DL1 4 A5
Dudley St YO31 233 C4
Dudley Wlk HG4 214 B3
Duffield Cres 1 LS25 195 F4
Dugdale La BB7 152 C1
Duke St
6 Burton in Lonsdale LA6 102 F3
High Bentham LA2 129 A8
Settle BD24 131 D2
Skipton BD23 217 A4
20 Trawden Forest BB8 186 A3
Duke's La YO25 126 A1
Dukes Wharf YO23 233 B1
Dukesway TS17 6 B5
Dulverton Cl 13 WF8 201 C2
Dulverton Rise WF8 201 C2
Dulverton Way 14 WF8 201 C2
Dumb Tom's La LA6 103 B1
Dumfries Sq 8 DL9 40 E4
Duna Way 6 YO62 70 C1
Duncan Cl 6 HG1 219 C5
Duncan St HG1 219 C5
Dunce Mire Rd LS25 202 A8
Duncombe Cl
2 Eastfield YO12 99 F7
Malton YO17 215 A3
Duncombe La YO32 167 B8
Duncombe Pk★ YO62 92 E6
Duncombe Pl YO1 233 B3
Dundas Gdns YO21 208 B6
Dundas St
Richmond DL10 209 C7
York YO1 233 C2
Dunderdale Cres WF10 201 B5
Dunelm Wlk DL1 3 E7
Dunhill Rd DN14 205 F2
Dunkeswick La LS17 178 D4
Dunn Gr 3 YO11 100 A7
Dunnington C of E Prim Sch YO19 184 E7
Dunnington Dr YO8 196 E1
Dunroyal YO61 141 F8
Dunroyal Cl YO61 141 F8
Dunsley Cres YO21 208 A8
Dunsley La YO21 32 A8
Dunslow Ct YO11 99 F6
Dunslow Rd YO11 99 F6
Dunsmore Cl TS8 6 C4
Dunwell Ave 2 YO12 212 B7
Durham La TS16 5 D5
Durham Lane Ind Pk TS16 5 D6
Durham Lane Prim Sch TS16 5 D5
Durham Pl 5 YO12 213 A7
Durham St
6 Scarborough YO12 212 F7
6 Scarborough YO12 213 A7
Durham Way HG3 219 A5
Durlston Dr YO32 167 A7
Duxbury St 11 BB18 172 B1
Dyke Hall La LA10 78 A8
Dykelands Cl YO19 192 F7
Dykes La YO23 230 A1
Dyon La YO8 199 B3
Dyon Rd YO8 199 D7
Dyson la DL11 18 G7

E

Eagle Pk TS8 7 C5
Eaglescliffe Sta TS16 5 E6
Earby Springfield Prim Sch BB18 172 B1
Earfit La YO23 191 A8
Earl Edwin Dr DL10 209 D8
Earle St YO31 233 C4
Earlham St 10 BB18 172 B1
Earls Court Rd TS8 6 F5
Earls View 3 BD20 187 E6
Earlsdon Ave TS5 6 D7
Earlsway TS17 6 C5
Earswick Chase YO32 225 F7
Earswick Village YO32 225 F7
Easby Abbey (rems of)★ DL10 209 E5
Easby Ave TS5 6 F8
Easby Cl 4 Bedale DL8 63 B2
7 Ilkley LS29 175 C2
Easby Dr LS29 175 C2
Easby La Easby TS9 27 A8
Great Ayton TS9 7 F1
Easby Low Rd DL10 209 D7
Easingwold CP Sch YO61 117 C1
Easingwold Sch YO61 143 C8
Eason Rd YO24 230 E8
Eason View YO24 230 E8
Easson Rd DL3 3 C5
East Acres WF11 201 F4
East Ave
8 Easingwold YO61 143 D8
13 Glusburn BD20 187 E7
21 Scalby YO13 75 D5
East Ayton CP Sch YO13 99 A8
East Bank 2 LS25 195 F4
East Barnby La YO21 12 C3
East Beck Ct LS21 176 C3
East Brow Rd YO18 72 C4
East Carr 18 YO11 100 B6
East Castle St 6 BD23 217 A3
East Cl DL2 4 C7
East Comm La YO8 232 F4
East Cowton C of E Prim Sch DL7 22 E1
East Cres YO21 208 D7
East Down WF10 201 A4
East End YO60 145 D5
East Garforth Cty Prim Sch LS25 194 D4
East Garforth Sta LS25 194 D3
East Gate YO13 98 D6
East Heslerton La YO17 124 A8
East Ings La YO18 95 F4
East La Ampleforth YO62 92 D1
Castle Bolton with East & West Bolton DL8 59 B6
Embsay BD23 217 D7
Yafforth DL7 43 C1
East Lea View 21 YO11 100 B6
East Moor Gdns YO19 231 F5
East Mount YO17 215 C4
East Mount Rd
Darlington DL1 3 D6
York YO24 233 A1
East Neville St 14 BD23 217 A3
East Par Harrogate HG1 219 E2
Ilkley LS29 218 C4
York YO31 228 F6
East Park Rd
Harrogate HG1 219 E2
15 Scalby YO13 75 D5
5 Spofforth HG3 179 E5
East Rd Melsonby DL10 20 F7
Northallerton DL6 210 E4
Norton YO17 215 E3
East Sandgate 14 YO11 213 B6
East Side 5 TS15 25 D5
East St Gargrave BD23 155 D1
Gayles DL11 19 E6
Swinton YO17 121 B4
East Terr YO21 208 D7
East View Barton DL10 21 D8
7 Campsall DN6 206 E1
Kippax LS25 194 D1
10 Knottingley WF11 202 A2
Middleton St George DL2 4 D3
Sherburn in Elmet LS25 195 F3
3 Trawden BB8 186 B1
East View Ct HG5 162 F3
East Way Whitby YO21 208 B7
York YO31 225 E2
East Whitby CP Sch YO22 208 F4
East Witton Rd DL8 60 E2
Eastborough YO11 213 B6
Eastbourne Comp Sch DL1 3 E5
Eastbourne Gdns TS3 7 C8
Eastbourne Gr YO31 228 F5
Eastbourne Rd DL1 3 D5

Eastburn Jun & Inf Sch
BD20 187 F7
Eastbury Cl TS17 6 B4
Eastby Rd HG1 219 F6
Eastern Terr YO31 228 E6
Easterside La YO62 67 F4
Easterside Prim Sch
TS4 7 A7
Easterside Rd TS4 7 A7
Eastfield
Amotherby YO17 121 B4
Knaresborough HG5 221 D6
Eastfield Ave
Haxby YO32 225 C7
Norton YO17 215 E3
Richmond DL10 209 D8
Eastfield Cl LS24 189 F7
Eastfield Cres YO10 229 C2
Eastfield Ct YO10 229 C2
Eastfield Dr 14 WF8 201 C1
Eastfield Gr WF6 200 B2
Eastfield La
Dunnington YO19 184 F8
Kellington DN14 202 F4
Spennithorne DL8 61 A3
Thoralby DL8 58 E2
Eastfield Rd
Norton YO17 215 E3
Pickering YO18 96 A6
Eastfields TS9 26 C7
Eastgate 16 Helmsley YO62 92 F6
Pickering YO18 96 A6
3 Seamer YO12 99 D6
Eastholme Dr YO30 224 E1
Easthorpe Dr YO26 224 A1
Easton La YO21 29 D6
Eastward Ave YO10 231 E7
Eastway YO11 100 A7
Eastway Cl 2 YO62 70 C1
Eaton Ct 7 YO24 230 B8
Eaton Rd LS29 218 A3
Eavestone Gr HG3 219 A4
Ebenezer Terr 9 HG1 219 D2
Ebor Cl DL10 21 A1
Ebor Ct
Northallerton DL7 210 D3
7 Selby YO8 232 C6
Ebor Mount LS25 194 D1
Ebor Prep Sch YO30 228 A7
Ebor Rise HG1 219 B2
Ebor St Selby YO8 232 C5
York YO23 233 B1
Ebor Way
7 Poppleton YO26 165 F1
Poppleton YO26 224 A2
Ebsay Dr YO30 225 A1
Eden Ave YO8 232 D3
Eden Camp Modern History
Mus★ YO17 215 E8
Eden Cl
2 Hurworth-on-Tees DL2 3 D1
1 Hutton Rudby TS15 25 C4
York YO24 230 C7
Eden Cres DL1 3 C4
Eden Crest DL2 1 D7
Eden La DL2 1 D8
Eden Park Rd 2 TS15 25 C4
Eden Pk DL2 1 D7
Eden Rd DL7 210 B2
Edendale WF10 200 F4
Edenhouse Rd YO17 215 E8
Edens Way HG4 214 C2
Edge Dell YO12 99 E8
Edge La
Grassington BD23 134 F3
Long Preston BD23 153 E6
Edgecombe Dr DL3 3 A6
Edgehill Rd YO12 212 E2
Edgemoor Rd DL1 3 E3
Edgerton Cl LS24 189 D6
Edgerton Ct LS24 189 D6
Edgerton Dr LS24 189 D6
Edgerton Garth LS24 189 D6
Edgware Rd YO10 228 E2
Edinburgh Dr DL3 3 A4
Edmondson St 17 BB18 171 D2
Edmondson's La BD23 172 C5
Edmund Wilson Swimming
Baths YO24 227 D1
Edward St
27 Earby BB18 172 A1
Pontefract WF6 200 A3
Egglescliffe C of E Sch
TS16 5 E4
Egglescliffe Sch TS16 5 D4
Eggleston View DL3 3 A6
Eggshell La LA2 130 C8
Eglington Ave TS14 8 F6
Egremont Cl 11 YO41 168 D2
Egton Ave TS7 7 C5
Egton C of E Prim Sch
YO21 31 B5
Egton Cliff YO21 31 A4
Egton La YO21 30 F5
Egton Sta YO21 31 A4
Eight Acre La HG4 113 A5
Eighth Ave YO31 228 F5
El Alamein Rd 5 DL9 209 C1
Elbolton Cave★ BD23 156 E8
Elder Rd DL6 210 D4
Elder's St YO11 213 A6
Eldmire La YO7 115 D6
Eldon St YO31 233 C4
Eldon Terr YO31 233 C4
Eldroth Rd LA2 130 C5
Eldwick Cl YO30 224 F2
Eleanor Dr HG2 220 C1
Eleanor Rd HG2 220 C1
Electric Ave HG1 219 B5
Elgin Rd TS17 6 B6
Elgin St 16 YO21 208 D6
Elizabeth Ct
7 Selby YO8 232 B6
Sherburn in Elmet LS25 195 E4
Elizabeth Dr WF10 201 B4
Elizabethan Ct 4 WF8 201 C1
Elland Ct 12 DL1 3 F6
Ellarfield La LS25 195 F5
Ellen Gr HG1 220 C4
Ellenthorpe La YO51 141 D6
Eller Gates YO21 30 C6
Eller Gill La BD23 172 D4
Eller Mews 3 BD23 216 E3
Ellerbeck Ct TS9 26 D6
Ellerbeck Way
Great & Little Broughton
TS9 26 D6
Middlesbrough TS7 7 D8
Whitby YO22 208 E4
Ellerburn Rd YO18 96 F7
Ellerby Bank TS13 11 F4
Ellerby La TS13 11 F5
Ellerclose Rd 23 DL8 60 D5
Ellerholme La DL11 38 F5
Ellerington Cl LA6 103 D3
Ellerker La LS14 188 A3
Ellerker Rd LS14 188 A3
Ellers La DL8 59 A2
Ellers Rd BD20 187 E6
Ellerton Priory (rems of)★
DL11 39 A4
Ellerton Rd TS18 5 D8
Elliot Ct YO10 231 D7
Elliot St BD23 216 F4
Elliott St BD20 174 B1
Ellis Ct HG1 219 B2
Ellis La LS25 194 C5
Ellison Ave 32 YO12 75 D5
Ellwood Cotts BD24 131 D4
Elm Ave Kippax LS25 194 C2
Northallerton DL6 210 F5
Elm Cl
Barnoldswick BB18 171 D1
10 Filey YO14 101 B4
Hipswell DL9 209 F1
Northallerton DL6 210 F5
Elm Ct DL6 210 E5
Elm Dr TS7 7 B6
Elm End 9 YO32 166 E5
Elm Gn 7 YO62 92 F7
Elm Gr Sherburn YO17 124 D8
Thornaby TS17 6 B8
4 Whitby YO21 208 B6
York YO31 225 F2
Elm Pl WF11 201 F2
Elm Rd 34 Glusburn BD20 187 E7
Guisborough TS14 8 F7
Harrogate HG1 219 E5
Ripon HG4 214 B2
9 Scarborough YO12 212 E4
3 Topcliffe YO7 89 B1
Elm St YO8 232 D6
Elm Tree Ave 9 YO26 165 F1
Elm Tree Rise HG3 140 B5
Elm Tree Sq BD23 217 D8
Elm View YO18 96 A6
Elm Wlk 6 DL10 41 D5
Elma Gr YO30 224 E2
Elmet Dr LS15 194 C8
Elmet Rd LS15 194 C7
Elmete Ave LS25 195 F4
Elmete Rd WF10 201 B5
Elmfield Ave YO31 228 F8
Elmfield Rd
3 Glusburn BD20 187 F8
Hurworth DL2 3 D1
Hurworth-on-Tees DL2 22 D8
Elmfield Terr YO31 228 F7
Elmlands Gr YO31 228 F8
Elmpark Vale YO31 229 A8
Elmpark View YO31 229 A8
Elmpark Way YO31 229 A8
Elms Cl 2 YO19 191 F1
Elmslac Cl
9 Helmsley YO62 92 F6
1 Helmsley YO62 92 F6
Elmslac Rd 3 YO62 92 F7
Elmtree Gdns 3 YO26 227 C3
Elmville Ave YO12 212 E6
Elmwood Ave LS15 194 B8
Elmwood Chase LS15 194 B8
Elmwood Cl 6 TS9 26 C8
Elmwood La LS15 194 B8
Elmwood Rd TS16 5 E6
Elmwood St 4 HG1 219 E4
Elphin Bridge La
YO61 117 B6
Elslack La BD23 172 C4
Elston Cl YO30 228 A8
Elston Pl YO8 232 C6
Eltham Cres TS17 6 C6
Elton La HG3 160 E6
Elton Par DL3 3 B5
Elton Rd DL3 3 B5
Elvington C of E Prim Sch
YO41 185 B3
Elvington Ind Est
YO41 185 A3
Elvington La YO19 184 E5
Elvington Pk YO41 185 A3
Elvington Terr YO10 228 E4
Elwick Ave TS5 6 E7
Elwick Gr YO10 229 C4
Elwick La YO26 164 B7
Ely Cl HG3 219 A5
Embleton Dr 1 YO30 224 F1
Embleton Rd LS26 200 B4
Embsay C of E Prim Sch
BD23 217 D8
Embsay Junc BD23 217 C6
Embsay Sta BD23 217 D7
Embsay Steam Rly★
BD23 217 E7
Emerald St YO31 233 C4
Emerson Ave TS5 6 F8
Emerson Cl 2 DL6 25 D1
Emerson Rd DL2 3 E1
Emery Cl DL2 3 E1
Emgate 2 DL8 63 A3
Emley Moor Rd DL1 3 E4
Emmerson St 2 YO31 228 E5
Emmet La HG3 160 C5
Emmott Ct BB8 186 C3
Emmott La BB8 186 B4
Emsworth Dr TS16 5 D5
Enclosure Gdns 1
YO10 229 B1
Endcliff Cres YO12 212 D8
Endeavour Wharf 6
YO21 208 D6
Endfields Rd 1 YO10 231 E8
Endsleigh Dr TS5 6 D8
Enfield Chase TS14 8 F5
Enfield Cl 4 DL9 40 E4
Enfield Cres
2 York YO24 227 F3
1 York YO24 228 A3
Engine Shed La BD23 216 D3
England La WF11 201 F2
English Martyrs RC Prim Sch
YO24 227 F3
Ennerdale Ave YO31 229 B5
Enter La LA6 103 D3
Enterpen TS15 25 C4
Enterprise Way
Bradleys Both BD20 173 D4
Sherburn in Elmet LS25 196 B4
Whitby YO22 32 F8
Eppleby Forcett C of E Prim
Sch DL11 1 D4
Epsom Ct 11 DL1 3 F6
Eridge Rd TS14 8 F6
Ermysted St 4 BD23 217 A4
Ermysteds Gram Sch
BD23 216 F4
Eryholme La DL2 22 F7
Escrick C of E Prim Sch
YO19 192 A5
Escrick Ct YO19 192 B5
Escrick Park Gdns
YO19 192 B5
Escrick St YO10 233 C1
Esher Ave TS6 7 E8
Eshington La DL8 58 F2
Eshton Rd BD23 155 D2
Esk Dr YO26 227 B8
Esk Leisure Ctr YO21 208 C7
Esk Rd DL1 3 D3
Eskdale Ave
Normanton WF6 200 A2
York YO10 229 C3
Eskdale Cl
5 Pontefract WF6 200 A2
Sleights YO22 32 A5
Eskdale Croft WF6 200 A2
Eskdale Ct 12 WF6 200 A2
Eskdale Cty Modern Sch
YO22 208 E3
Eskdale Rd YO22 208 F3
Eskdaleside YO22 31 F5
Eskew La LA2 128 E7
Eskitt Hill YO12 212 D4
Esp La BB18 171 C1
Esplanade
Harrogate HG2 219 C2
Scarborough YO11 213 A4
Whitby YO21 208 D7
York YO26 233 A2
Esplanade Cres YO11 213 B2
Esplanade Gdns YO11 213 A4
Esplanade Rd YO11 213 A3
Estell La YO13 74 C5
Estill Cl 2 YO11 100 B6
Estoril Rd S DL1 3 F4
Ethel Cres HG5 221 C6
Ethel St 12 BB18 171 E1
Etive Pl YO24 230 B7
Eton Dr 7 YO32 166 D5
Eton Rd Goole DN14 205 F3
Middlesbrough TS5 6 E8
Ettersgill Dr DL3 3 A5
Ettington Ave TS3 7 B8
Etty Ave YO10 229 A4
Euclid Ave HG1 219 B5
Eva Ave YO30 224 D2
Evelyn Cres YO30 228 B7
Evelyn Ct 5 HG3 161 B2
Evelyn Dr YO12 212 D4
Evergreen Way 1 YO8 197 D1
Everingham Rd TS15 5 D2
Eversley Ave LS25 195 F3
Eversley Ct LS25 195 F4
Eversley Garth Cres
LS25 195 F4
Eversley Mount LS25 195 F3
Evesham Rd TS3 7 B8
Ewart St YO12 212 E3
Ewden Cl 16 YO14 101 A3
Ewe Leys La YO7 66 A5
Ewelands Hill YO7 90 C7
Exchange St 8 WF6 200 A1
Exelby Cl DL8 63 D1
Exelby La DL7 63 D3
Exeter Cres 10 HG3 161 B3
Exeter Dr DL1 3 F7
Express Way WF6 200 A3

F

Faber Cl YO23 230 B3
Faber St YO31 228 E5
Faceby Rd TS9 26 A2
Fadmoor Bank YO62 69 E6
Fadmoor La YO62 69 F4
Fair Head La YO22 31 D4
Fairburn Cty Prim Sch
WF11 201 D6
Fairburn Dr LS25 194 D3
Fairburn Sports & Recn Ctr
WF11 201 D6
Fairfax 15 YO41 168 D2
Fairfax Ave
Harrogate HG2 220 B2
North Featherstone
WF7 200 E1
Selby YO8 232 B4
Fairfax Cl
2 Ampleforth YO62 92 C1
Bolton Percy YO23 190 D4
Fairfax Cres YO26 181 C7
Fairfax Croft YO23 230 B2
Fairfax House★ YO1 233 C2
Fairfax Rd DL2 4 D4
Fairfax St
1 Scarborough YO12 212 E5
10 Skipton BD23 217 A3
York YO1 233 B1
Fairfax Wlk 3 HG2 220 B3
Fairfield
Fairburn WF11 201 D7
Thirsk YO7 211 C4
Fairfield Ave TS7 7 D7
Fairfield Cl 16 LS25 195 F4
Fairfield Cres YO12 212 B8
Fairfield La LS25 202 A6
Fairfield Link LS25 195 F4
Fairfield Rd
Staithes TS13 13 K2
Stokesley TS9 26 B7
Tadcaster LS24 189 E6
Fairfield St DL3 3 C6
Fairfield Way
9 Tadcaster LS24 189 E6
Whitby YO22 208 F3
Fairfields Dr YO30 224 B5
Fairheath Rd LA2 128 E5
Fairholme La DL7 64 A4
Fairmead Ct YO22 208 E4
Fairmead Way YO22 208 E4
Fairview TS21 5 A7
Fairview Gdns DL10 209 C8
Fairway
Normanton South WF6 200 B1
4 Scalby YO12 75 E5
York YO30 228 A8
Fairway App WF6 200 B1
Fairway Ave WF6 200 B1
Fairway Cl
8 Normanton South WF6 200 B1
15 Sherburn in Elmet LS25 195 F4
Fairway Dr
Normanton South WF6 200 B1
18 Poppleton YO26 165 F1
Fairway Gdns 4 WF6 200 B1
Fairway Mdws 9 WF6 200 B1
Fairway The
Darlington DL1 3 E5
Middlesbrough TS8 7 C5
8 North Featherstone
WF7 200 E1
Northallerton DL7 210 C3
Sherburn in Elmet LS25 195 F4
Tadcaster LS24 189 E5
Fairways Ave HG2 220 E3
Fairways Cl HG2 220 E3
Fairways Dr HG2 220 D3
Fairwood Pk TS8 7 C5
Fairy Hill La WF8 201 B3
Fairy La YO18 71 C3
Falcon Ave 7 YO12 99 E6
Falcon Cl 10 Haxby YO32 166 F5
1 Scotton DL9 40 F2
17 Settle BD24 131 D2
Falcon Dr WF10 200 E3
Falcon Gdns 20 BD24 131 D2
Falcon Terr 11 YO21 208 D6
Falcon Way TS14 8 D6
Falcon Wlk TS15 6 C2
Falconberg Way TS15 5 D2
Falconer St 1 YO24 227 F3
Falconers Rd YO11 213 A5
Falkland Rd 2 DL9 40 F5
Falkland St YO1 233 B1
Fall La Pannal HG3 222 B2
Thornthwaite with Padside
HG3 159 A6
Falling Foss (Waterfall)★
YO22 32 C2
Fallow Field 1 BD23 217 B5
Falmer Rd DL1 3 D4
Falmouth Ave WF6 200 A2
Falmouth Cres 20 WF6 200 A2
Falmouth Dr DL3 3 C8
Falmouth Rd WF6 200 A2
Falsgrave Cres YO30 228 B7
Falsgrave Mews 6
YO12 212 E5
Falsgrave Rd YO12 212 F5
Fanacurt Rd TS14 8 D6
Fancy Bank TS14 9 B6
Fanny La Knayton YO7 65 F2
Stutton with Hazlewood
LS24 189 D4
Far La
Hutton Buscel YO13 98 F8
Kettlewell with Starbotton
BD23 108 A3
Far Mead Croft 3 LS29 176 C1
Farfield YO26 227 C6
Farfield Ave HG5 221 C4
Farfield La YO19 184 E8
Farfield Mount 2 HG5 221 C4
Farfields Cl TS21 4 F6
Farm Cl YO21 208 A7
Farm Croft BD23 216 F1
Farm Garth TS9 8 A2
Farm La TS17 6 A5
Farm Way YO8 232 B7
Farmanby Cl 12 YO18 96 D5
Farmbank Rd TS7 7 E7
Farmers Way YO23 230 B3
Farmlands Rd 1 YO24 230 D8
Farmstead Rise YO32 225 D7
Farnborough Ct 10 DL2 4 C4
Farndale Ave
Northallerton DL7 210 C2
York YO10 229 D4
Farndale Cl 1 YO32 166 F5
Farndale Cres DL3 3 B6
Farndale Dr TS14 8 D6
Farndale Rd HG5 221 D6
Farndale St YO10 228 D2
Farnham La HG5 162 D7
Farnley C of E Prim Sch
LS21 177 B3
Farnley Hall★ LS21 177 B2
Farnley La LS21 177 B2
Farnley Pk LS21 177 C2
Farrar St YO10 228 E3
Farriers Croft 2 YO23 230 B3
Farside Garth YO13 75 D6
Farside Rd YO13 99 A7
Farthingale Way TS8 6 E4
Favell Ave WF6 200 A1
Faven Field Rd YO7 211 D4
Faverdale DL3 3 B7
Faverdale N DL3 3 B7
Faverdale Rd DL3 3 B7
Faverdale W DL3 3 B7
Favordale Rd BB8 186 A3
Fawcett Ave TS8 6 E4
Fawcett St YO10 233 C1
Fawdington Rd YO61 115 F2
Fawkes Dr YO26 227 C4
Fearby Rd Fearby HG4 85 F4
Masham HG4 86 A4
7 Stockton-on-Tees TS18 5 D8
Fearnhead TS8 7 C5
Feasegate YO1 233 B2
Featherbeck Cl LA6 103 D3
Featherbed La
Bilton-in-Ainsty with Bickerton
LS24 181 C3
Ellerbeck DL6 44 E4
Federation St 12 BB18 171 D1
Feeding Pasture La
YO60 147 B7
Feetham Ave DL1 3 F7
Feethams Sports Gd
DL1 3 C5
Felbrigg La TS17 6 A4
Feldom La DL11 19 E1
Felixstowe Dr 10 DL9 40 E4
Fell La Cracoe BD23 156 B7
Winton CA17 14 C8
Fell Rd LA6 77 A4
Fell View BD23 217 E8
Fell View Sq 4 BD23 134 E2
Fellbrook Ave YO26 227 B4
Felliscliffe Cty Prim Sch
HG3 160 C4
Fenby Ave DL1 3 E4
Fence Dike La DL7 63 C7
Fenton Ave BB18 171 E2
Fenton Cl 10 YO11 100 B7
Fenton La Malton YO17 215 C8
Sherburn in Elmet LS25 196 A5
Fenton St Boosbeck TS12 9 D7
38 Burley in Warfedale
LS29 176 C1
Fenwick Cl 1 YO11 100 B6
Fenwick Comm La
DN6 207 D2
Fenwick La DN6 207 B1
Fenwick St YO23 228 C2
Fenwick's La YO10 231 D7
Ferguson Cl DL7 210 C3
Ferguson Way YO32 225 F1
Fern Bank Ave BB18 171 D2
Fern Cl YO32 226 A4
Fern Gdns 1 LS29 218 A3
Fern St YO31 233 C4
Ferndale Rd YO8 232 C4
Fernie Rd TS14 8 F5
Fernlea Cl YO8 232 D4
Fernley Green Cl 6
WF11 202 A2
Fernway YO10 229 C3
Fernwood TS8 7 A4
Fernwood Cl 9 DL6 43 F3
Ferry Cl 11 YO8 198 F1
Ferry Farm Cl 2 YO19 191 D8
Ferry La Airmyn DN14 205 F4
Bishopthorpe YO23 231 B4
Bubwith YO8 199 C5
Snaith & Cowick DN14 204 C1

Ferry La *continued*
Thorganby YO19 193 B5
Ferrybridge By-Pass
WF11 201 E3
Ferrybridge Inf Sch
WF11 201 E3
Ferrybridge Rd
Castleford WF10 200 F4
Pontefract WF8 201 C1
Ferrybridge Service Area
WF11 201 E1
Fetter La YO1 233 B2
Feversham Cres 4
YO31 228 C7
Feversham Dr 16 YO62 70 B1
Feversham Rd YO62 92 F7
Fewster Way YO10 233 C1
Fewston Cl 11 YO14 101 A3
Fewston Cres HG1 219 B4
Fewston Dr 9 YO30 224 F1
Field Ave YO8 197 B1
Field Cl YO21 208 A7
Field Cl Rd 16 YO13 75 D5
Field Dr 1 Pickering YO18 95 F6
Tadcaster LS24 189 F7
Field Gr 7 DL9 40 E3
Field Head YO41 185 F6
Field House Rd 2 YO21 208 C7
Field La Aberford LS25 194 F8
Burniston YO13 75 D8
Gowdall DN14 207 F8
Hambleton YO8 196 F1
Hensall DN14 203 D2
Heslington YO10 229 C2
Newby & Scalby YO13 75 E5
Rawcliffe DN14 205 A1
Wistow YO8 197 C7
Field Lane Sports Ctr
YO8 197 B1
Field Rd YO8 203 A5
Field View
Norton YO17 215 E2
York YO31 228 C7
Fieldhead Cl 12 WF8 201 C1
Fieldhead Dr
Barwick in Elmet LS15 194 C8
15 Glusburn BD20 187 E7
Fieldhead Paddock
LS23 188 E8
Fielding's Yd DL10 209 A7
Fieldside YO12 212 D7
Fieldstead Cres YO12 212 B8
Fieldway
Harrogate HG1 219 F7
Ilkley LS29 218 E4
Fieldway Cl HG1 219 F7
Fifth Ave 24 Colburn DL9 41 A5
York YO31 228 F4
Filey Ave HG4 214 A6
Filey Brigg Nature Reserve★
YO14 101 D4
Filey C of E Inf Sch
YO14 101 B3
Filey Cl 12 DL9 40 E4
Filey CP Sch YO14 101 B3
Filey Folk Mus★ YO14 101 B3
Filey Rd Folkton YO11 100 A2
Hunmanby YO14 127 A8
Scarborough YO11 213 A2
Filey Sch YO14 101 A3
Filey Sta YO14 101 B3
Filey Terr YO30 228 C7
Finden Gdns HG3 160 F5
Fine Garth Cl LS23 188 E6
Finkills Way DL7 210 C6
Finkle Cl 4 HG4 214 C5
Finkle Hill LS25 195 F5
Finkle St Hensall DN14 203 D2
12 Knaresborough HG5 221 A6
Malham BD23 133 A1
3 Malton YO17 215 C4
Richmond DL10 209 C6
5 Ripon HG4 214 C5
Selby YO8 232 C5
Sheriff Hutton YO60 145 C5
Thirsk YO7 211 C3
Finsbury Ave YO23 228 C1
Finsbury St YO23 228 C1
Fir Gr TS17 6 B8
Fir Heath Cl 5 YO24 227 C1
Fir Tree Cl Hilton TS15 6 C2
Thorpe Willoughby YO8 197 B2
Fir Tree Dr Filey YO14 101 B4
11 Norton DN6 206 E2
Fir Tree La YO8 197 B2
Fir Tree View LS26 200 C6
Fir Tree Way YO8 197 B2
Fir Trees The YO8 197 B2
Firbank Cl 9 YO32 167 A7
Firbeck Rd LS23 188 E6
Firby La HG4 214 B5
Firby Rd Bedale DL8 63 A2
Richmond DL10 209 B8
Firs Ave Harrogate HG2 222 E6
Ripon HG4 214 D4
Firs Cl HG2 222 E6
Firs Cres HG2 222 E5
Firs Dr HG2 222 E6
Firs Gate HG2 222 E5
Firs Gr HG2 222 E5
Firs Rd HG2 222 E6
Firs View HG2 222 E5
First Ave 23 Colburn DL9 41 A5
Harrogate HG2 220 C3
Menwith with Darley
HG3 160 A4
10 Pickering YO18 95 F7
9 Wetherby LS22 180 C3
First Ave *continued*
York YO31 228 F6
First Comm La YO8 197 D4
Firth Moor Jun Sch DL1 3 F4
Firth St BD23 217 A2
Firthfields LS25 194 D4
Firthland Rd YO18 95 F7
Firthmoor Cres DL1 3 E4
Firtree Ave TS6 7 E8
Firtree Cl
4 Earswick YO32 225 F7
York YO24 227 E3
Firtree Cres LS24 189 D5
Firville Ave WF6 200 A1
Firwood Whin 5 YO32 225 F3
Fishbeck La BD20 174 D2
Fishburn Rd 4 YO21 208 D5
Fisher Green La HG4 214 F4
Fisher Row 14 HG4 86 C3
Fisher St 6 HG5 221 B5
Fishergate
3 Boroughbridge YO51 141 B5
Knottingley WF11 201 E3
17 Ripon HG4 214 C5
York YO10 233 C1
Fishergate Prim Sch
YO10 233 C1
Fishergreen HG4 214 D4
Fishers Garth 10 YO18 95 F6
Fitzalan Rd 18 DL8 63 A2
Fitzjohn Cl YO17 215 C6
Fitzwilliam Dr
Darlington DL1 3 D7
Malton YO17 215 A4
Five Hills La DL10 21 D5
Five Lane Ends HG4 86 D5
Flake La TS13 12 A3
Flamingo Land Zoo & Family
Funpark★ YO17 95 D2
Flashley Carr La DN6 207 F1
Flask La DL8 87 C3
Flass La WF10 200 E3
Flat Cliffs YO14 101 C1
Flat La
Bolton-on-Swale DL10 41 E6
Hellifield BD23 153 F3
Flats Bank DL11 19 F6
Flats La
Barwick in Elmet LS15 194 B7
Thirkleby High & Low
with Osgodby YO7 90 D1
West Witton DL8 59 D4
Flatts La
Eston & South Bank TS6 7 F7
Welburn YO62 94 A7
Wombleton YO62 93 F6
Flavian Gr YO30 227 F8
Flaxdale Cl 4 HG5 221 D6
Flaxley Ct YO8 232 B5
Flaxley Rd YO8 232 A7
Flaxman Ave YO10 229 A4
Flaxman Croft YO23 230 B3
Flaxmill Cl DL11 18 G7
Flaxton Rd YO32 167 B7
Fleck Way TS17 6 B5
Fleet Bank La YO61 143 C1
Fleet La
Barmby on the Marsh
DN14 205 A7
Mickletown LS26 200 A6
Tockwith YO26 181 C7
Fleetham La
Cundall with Leckby YO7 115 C4
Kirkby Fleetham with Fencote
DL7 63 C8
Fleets La BD23 156 A6
Fleming Ave 3 YO31 228 E5
Fletcher Ct 14 YO32 166 E5
Fletcher's Croft YO23 230 C3
Flintmill La LS23 180 E2
Flints Terr DL10 209 C7
Flixton Carr La YO11 99 F4
Flock Leys 24 YO13 75 D5
Flora Ave DL3 3 B5
Florence Ct 12 YO51 141 B5
Florence Gr YO30 224 D2
Florence Rd HG2 219 B1
Flotmanby La YO14 100 D2
Flow Edge DL8 57 F7
Flower Ct 19 YO11 100 B6
Flower Garth
40 Filey YO14 101 B3
Scarborough YO12 212 C6
Flowergate 12 YO21 208 D7
Fog La YO42 193 E4
Fold La BD22 187 B6
Fold The Filey YO14 101 B1
Thornton in Craven
BD23 172 A3
Foldshaw La HG3 159 C8
Folk Mus★ DL11 38 C6
Folks Cl 13 YO32 166 F5
Follifoot C of E Prim Sch
HG3 223 F4
Follifoot La HG3 223 B2
Follifoot Rd HG3 222 F3
Folliott Ward Cl YO17 215 B5
Folly La
Barnoldswick BB18 171 D1
Bramham cum Oglethorpe
LS23 188 E5
Folly View 2 LS23 188 E5
Fontenay Rd DL10 209 D8
Fonteyn Ct TS8 6 F5
Forcett Cl
East Layton DL11 20 C8
Middlesbrough TS5 6 E7
Forcett Gdns DL11 1 D3
Forcett La DL10 20 D5
Fordlands YO8 197 B2
Fordlands Cres YO19 231 E5
Fordlands Rd YO19 231 E6
Fordon La
Willerby YO12 125 E7
Wold Newton YO25 126 A6
Fordon Pl TS4 7 A8
Fordyce Rd TS8 6 E4
Fore La Cowesby YO7 66 B4
West Tanfield DL8 87 D3
Whorlton DL6 25 F1
Foreshore Rd YO11 213 A5
Forest Ave HG2 220 D3
Forest Cl
3 Harrogate HG2 220 D3
27 Haxby YO32 166 E5
Forest Cres HG2 220 D4
Forest Dr Colburn DL9 41 A5
Dishforth YO7 115 A4
Middlesbrough TS7 7 D7
Forest Gdns HG2 220 D3
Forest Gr
Harrogate HG2 220 D3
York YO31 228 F6
Forest Grange Cl 2
HG2 220 D4
Forest La Alne YO61 143 B5
Fulford YO19 184 A2
Harrogate HG2 220 D3
Kirklevington TS15 24 D8
Strensall YO32 167 A8
Forest Lane Head
HG2 220 D5
Forest Moor Dr HG5 220 F3
Forest Moor Rd HG5 220 E3
Forest Mount 3 HG2 220 D4
Forest of Galtres Prim Sch
YO30 165 F5
Forest Rd
Appletreewick HG3 157 F8
Northallerton DL6 210 E5
Pickering YO18 96 A6
Forest Rise HG2 220 D3
Forest Sch The HG5 221 C6
Forest Way
Harrogate HG2 220 D3
York YO31 228 F6
Foresters Ct 5 YO12 75 F5
Foresters Wlk YO41 168 C1
Forester's Wlk YO24 227 B1
Forestgate YO32 225 C7
Forge Cl YO32 226 A2
Forge Gn HG3 223 F4
Forge Hill La WF11 201 F3
Forge La
Deighton YO19 192 A7
Kirkby Fleetham with Fencote
DL7 42 C1
Tollerton YO61 143 A3
Forge Valley Wood Reserve★
YO13 75 A1
Forge Way DL1 3 D6
Forkers La YO17 122 D2
Forrester's Cl 3 DN6 206 E2
Forth St YO26 227 F6
Fortune Cl HG5 220 E7
Fortune Hill HG5 220 E8
Foss Ave LS22 180 B4
Foss Bank YO31 233 C3
Foss Ct YO31 225 E1
Foss Field La YO23 191 B8
Foss Garth YO41 185 F5
Foss Islands Rd YO31 233 C3
Foss La YO22 32 C2
Foss Wlk YO26 227 B8
Fossdale Cl 5 HG5 221 D6
Fosse Way LS25 194 D3
Fossgate YO1 233 C2
Fossland View 4 YO32 167 A7
Fossway
Stamford Bridge YO41 168 D1
York YO31 228 D7
Foster Ave
Normanton South WF6 200 A1
Silsden BD20 174 B1
Foster Cl 31 LS29 176 C1
Foster Gate YO8 232 D4
Foster Rd 4 BB18 171 D2
Foster Wlk LS25 195 F4
Fostergate YO8 197 A8
Foston C of E Prim Sch
YO60 146 A3
Foston Gr 4 YO31 228 F8
Foston La YO60 146 B2
Fother Ingay Dr DL1 3 F8
Fothergill Way 3 YO51 141 B4
Fothill La YO13 98 E6
Foulbridge La YO13 97 F3
Foulds Rd BB8 186 A1
Foulgate Nook La
HG4 112 B6
Foundry La 5 WF11 202 A2
Fountain St TS14 8 F6
Fountains Abbey★
HG4 139 B7
Fountains Ave
Boston Spa LS23 188 E8
Harrogate HG1 219 F6
Ingleby TS17 6 B5
Fountains C of E Prim Sch
HG4 138 D8
Fountains Cl
Guisborough TS14 8 F6
1 Whitby YO21 208 C6
Fountains Dr TS5 6 E8
Fountains Gate HG4 112 F1
Fountains La HG4 139 B7
Fountains Mill★ HG4 139 B7
Fountains Pl DL6 210 E6
Fountains Rd DL6 210 E6
Fountains View DL3 3 A6
Fountains Way
Knaresborough HG5 221 C4
Morton-on-Swale DL7 64 A7
Fountayne Rd
13 Hunmanby YO14 126 F8
13 Hunmanby YO14 126 F8
Fountayne St YO31 228 C7
Four La Ends
Burythorpe YO17 147 D4
Lawkland BD24 130 F3
Four Lanes Ends BB7 152 C1
Four Riggs DL3 3 C5
Fouracre Dr 11 YO22 32 A6
Fourth Ave
26 Colburn DL9 41 A5
York YO31 228 E5
Fox Cl 6 DL2 22 D8
Fox Covert YO31 225 F2
Fox Covert Cl 15 DL8 63 B3
Fox Covert Rd WF8 206 C1
Fox Ct HG1 219 E4
Fox Garth
5 Brafferton YO61 115 F1
Poppleton YO26 224 A3
Fox Glade YO41 168 C2
Fox Heads La LS22 179 D4
Fox Hill La YO8 232 A3
Fox La
Chapel Haddlesey YO8 203 C5
Hambleton LS25 196 D1
Thornton-le-Dale YO18 96 C3
Thorpe Willoughby YO8 197 B1
Fox Terr WF8 201 C1
Foxberry Ave TS5 6 D6
Foxbridge Way WF6 200 C2
Foxcliff WF11 201 E5
Foxcroft 3 YO32 225 C7
Foxdale Ave YO8 197 B1
Foxglove Cl
2 Killinghall HG3 161 B3
Northallerton DL7 210 C1
Foxglove Ct 19 DL9 41 A5
Foxhill La YO8 232 A3
Foxholme La HG4 86 B3
Foxthorn Paddock
YO10 229 D3
Foxton Cl YO24 230 C8
Foxton La DL6 44 E2
Foxwood La
3 York YO24 227 C1
York YO24 230 C8
Foxwood Sch BD24 105 C4
Frances Rd DL10 209 C7
Frances St YO10 228 D1
Francis Ct 7 YO8 197 B2
Frank La YO26 164 F4
Frank St
24 Barnoldswick BB18 171 D1
4 Barnoldswick BB18 171 E1
9 Barnoldswick BB18 171 E1
Franklin Mount HG1 219 D4
Franklin Rd HG1 219 D3
Franklin Sq HG1 219 D4
Franklin St 7 YO12 212 F6
Frank's La YO26 164 A5
Fraser Rd 8 TS18 5 E8
Frazer Ct YO30 227 E8
Frederic St YO30 233 A3
Freebrough Rd TS12 10 A4
Freehold La YO17 215 D8
Freely La LS23 188 E5
Freeman's Way HG3 223 D8
Freemans Way
Leeming DL7 63 C4
Wetherby LS22 180 D3
Freeston Ct 16 WF6 200 A2
Freeston Dr 18 WF6 200 A2
French Rd DL9 209 C2
French St HG1 219 F4
Frenchgate DL10 209 C6
Friarage CP Sch YO11 213 B6
Friarage Gdns DL6 210 D5
Friarage Hospl DL6 210 E5
Friarage Mount DL6 210 E5
Friarage St DL6 210 D5
Friargate
Scarborough YO11 213 A6
York YO1 233 B2
Friars Cl YO19 184 D7
Friar's Gdns 10 YO11 213 A6
Friars Hill YO62 95 A8
Friars Mdw YO8 232 C8
Friars Pardon DL2 3 E1
Friar's Way 11 YO11 213 A6
Friar's Wlk YO31 228 E8
Friary Com Hospl
DL10 209 B7
Friendship Ct 2 YO8 232 C6
Frith Mews 4 YO8 232 C6
Frobisher Dr 5 YO21 208 C5
Frogmire Cl 4 HG5 221 B7
Frogmire Dr HG5 221 B7
Frogmire Rd HG5 221 B7
Front Nook 2 DL8 58 F1
Front St
Appleton Wiske DL6 24 B3
6 Bramham LS23 188 E5
Burton Fleming YO25 126 E3
Burton Leonard HG3 140 A2
Castleford WF10 200 F3
Grosmont YO22 31 C4
Langtoft YO25 151 C5
Lastingham YO62 70 E5
Naburn YO19 191 D8
Front St *continued*
Thirsk YO7 211 C1
Topcliffe YO7 115 C7
Wold Newton YO25 126 A4
York YO24 227 C3
Front The DL2 4 D3
Fryer Cres DL1 3 F7
Fryston Comm La
LS25 202 A8
Fryston La WF11 201 C3
Fryston Rd WF10 201 B5
Fryton La YO62 120 A7
Fryup Cres TS14 8 E5
Fulbeck Rd TS3 7 D8
Fulford Cross YO10 228 D1
Fulford Cross Specl Sch
YO10 228 D1
Fulford Pk YO10 231 D7
Fulford Rd
Scarborough YO11 212 F3
York YO10 231 D8
Fulford Sch YO10 231 E7
Fulfordgate YO10 231 E7
Fulham La DN14 206 E7
Fuller-Good Rd 14 DL10 41 E4
Fullicar La DL6 43 F3
Fulmar Head TS14 8 D6
Fulthorpe Ave DL3 3 A5
Fulthorpe Gr DL3 3 A5
Fulwith Ave HG2 222 E5
Fulwith Cl HG2 222 F5
Fulwith Dr HG2 222 F5
Fulwith Gate HG2 222 F5
Fulwith Gr HG2 222 F5
Fulwith Mill La HG2 222 F5
Fulwith Rd HG2 222 F5
Fummerber La LA2 130 C5
Furlong Rd 23 YO41 168 D2
Furlongs Ave YO17 215 F3
Furnace La HG4 87 A1
Furness Dr
Bentham LA2 129 A8
York YO30 224 E1
Furnessford Rd LA2 128 D6
Furnwood 2 YO32 225 D7
Furrows The 16 YO11 100 B7
Fushetts La LA2 129 A8
Fyling Rd YO21 208 A6
Fylingdales Ave 6
YO30 224 E1
Fylingdales C of E Prim Sch
YO22 33 C4

G

Gable Ct YO7 115 A4
Gable Pk YO23 182 C6
Gables Cl 8 DN14 202 D4
Gables The
15 Hurworth-on-Tees DL2 3 E1
Knaresborough HG5 221 A8
Middlesbrough TS7 7 B6
Scriven HG5 162 C5
Gainford C of E Prim Sch
DL2 1 C7
Gainforth Wath Rd
YO13 53 F5
Gainsborough Ct
BD23 216 E4
Gaits DL8 56 C4
Gale Bank DL8 60 B3
Gale Farm Ct 6 YO24 227 C3
Gale Garth YO61 142 F4
Gale Gate YO26 142 A1
Gale La Beadlam YO62 93 D6
Stainburn LS21 177 E3
Thorganby YO19 192 F4
York YO24 227 C2
Gale Rd YO61 142 F4
Gale The YO19 191 D4
Gallabar La YO51 141 E1
Galley Hill Prim Sch
TS14 8 D6
Galligap La YO10 229 C4
Gallogate La LS17 178 C1
Gallops The
Norton YO17 215 E2
York YO24 230 B8
Gallowfields Rd DL10 209 B7
Gallowfields Trad Est The
DL10 209 B8
Gallowgate DL10 209 C7
Gallowheads La YO62 95 A6
Gallows Hill
Castleford WF10 201 B4
Ripon HG4 214 C2
Gallows Hill Dr HG4 214 C2
Gallows Hill La YO13 98 D5
Gallows Hill Pk HG4 214 D2
Galmanhoe La YO30 233 A3
Galphay La HG4 113 A3
Galtres Ave YO31 229 B7
Galtres Dr 7 YO61 143 D8
Galtres Gr YO30 227 F7
Galtres Rd
Northallerton DL6 210 E6
York YO31 229 B7
Galtres Sch YO31 229 B5
Ganton Cl 1 YO21 208 C5
Ganton Hill YO12 125 B7
Ganton Pl YO24 230 E7
Ganton Rd YO25 125 C4
Gaol The YO61 144 E7
Gap Rd YO14 127 D8

Garbett Way 1 YO23 ... 231 B3
Garburn Gr 3 YO30 ... 224 E1
Garbutt Gr YO26 ... 227 D5
Garbutt La
4 Whorlton DL6 ... 25 D1
1 Whorlton DL6 ... 25 D1
Garbutts La TS15 ... 25 B5
Garden Cl
3 Glusburn BD20 ... 187 D7
Sherburn in Elmet LS25 ... 195 E4
Garden Flats La YO19 ... 184 E7
Garden House Cl LS26 ... 200 B6
Garden La
11 Knottingley WF11 ... 202 A3
Sherburn in Elmet LS25 ... 195 E4
Garden Pl YO1 ... 233 C2
Garden St
Castleford WF10 ... 200 E3
13 Normanton South WF6 ... 200 A1
York YO31 ... 233 B4
Garden Village LS25 ... 195 A3
Garden Way 3 YO18 ... 95 F6
Gardeners Cl 8 YO23 ... 230 B3
Gardeners Row YO25 ... 150 B3
Gardens Rd BD23 ... 155 D2
Gardens The 15 YO14 ... 101 B4
Garfield Rd YO12 ... 212 E6
Garfield Terr YO26 ... 227 F5
Garforth Barleyhill Infants Sch LS25 ... 194 C3
Garforth Com Coll LS25 ... 194 C3
Garforth Green Lane Prim Sch LS25 ... 194 D3
Garforth Leisure Ctr LS25 ... 194 D3
Garforth St Benedicts RC Prim Sch LS25 ... 194 C4
Garforth Sta LS25 ... 194 C4
Gargrave C of E Prim Sch BD23 ... 155 C1
Gargrave House Gdn BD23 ... 155 C1
Gargrave Rd
Broughton BD23 ... 172 D6
Skipton BD23 ... 216 D4
Gargrave Sta BD23 ... 172 C8
Garibaldi St 1 YO11 ... 213 B6
Garland St 2 YO26 ... 227 E4
Garlands Hill 3 YO11 ... 212 F3
Garlands The
Scarborough YO11 ... 212 F3
York YO30 ... 228 A8
Garman Carr La YO8 ... 197 D6
Garnet Brow La LA2 ... 130 D2
Garnet La 1 LS24 ... 189 D5
Garnet Rd TS17 ... 6 B8
Garnet Terr YO26 ... 227 E5
Garrick Cl YO8 ... 232 B1
Garrow Hill YO10 ... 228 F2
Garrow Hill Ave YO10 ... 229 A3
Garroway Way YO10 ... 184 A4
Garrowby Hill YO41 ... 169 E3
Garrowby Rd YO42 ... 169 F2
Garrowby St YO41 ... 169 E3
Garrowby View 5 YO41 ... 168 D2
Garrs End La BD23 ... 134 E3
Garrs La 10 BD23 ... 134 E3
Gars The LA2 ... 128 A6
Garsbeck Way TS7 ... 7 D8
Garsdale Fold 8 LS22 ... 180 A1
Garsdale Rd HG5 ... 221 D6
Garsdale Sta LA10 ... 55 A6
Garth Ave
Collingham LS22 ... 188 A8
4 North Duffield YO8 ... 199 A7
Garth Cl 11 Catterick DL10 ... 41 D5
Hambleton YO8 ... 196 E1
6 Wistow YO8 ... 197 D6
Garth Dr YO8 ... 196 E1
Garth End
Collingham LS22 ... 188 A8
Kirk Deighton LS22 ... 180 B5
Garth End Rd YO13 ... 99 A7
Garth Glebe 5 YO8 ... 198 B5
Garth Grange 3 YO30 ... 164 F7
Garth La
Hambleton YO8 ... 196 E1
Snainton YO13 ... 98 A5
Garth Mdws 13 DL10 ... 41 D5
Garth Mill 1 DN14 ... 202 D4
Garth Morrell YO8 ... 232 C2
Garth Rd
4 Hambleton YO8 ... 196 E1
York YO32 ... 225 F4
Garth Terr YO30 ... 228 B7
Garth The
8 Collingham LS22 ... 188 A8
Sinnington YO62 ... 95 A8
4 Stokesley TS9 ... 26 C7
Tunstall DL10 ... 41 B2
Whitby YO21 ... 208 B7
Garth View YO8 ... 196 E1
Garthends La 3 YO8 ... 198 F1
Garthorne Ave DL3 ... 3 A5
Garths End 20 YO32 ... 166 F5
Garth's End YO10 ... 231 E8
Garthway 4 YO32 ... 225 D3
Gas House La LA2 ... 129 A8
Gas St BD23 ... 216 F3
Gas Works La LS23 ... 188 F8
Gascoigne Ave LS15 ... 194 B7
Gascoigne Cres HG1 ... 219 F4
Gascoigne Ct LS15 ... 194 B7
Gascoigne Rd LS15 ... 194 B7
Gascoigne View LS15 ... 194 B7
Gascoigne Wood Mine LS25 ... 196 C2
Gate Bridge Rd HG4 ... 112 D2
Gate La Borrowby YO7 ... 65 E4
Low Coniscliffe & Merrybent DL2 ... 2 E4
Gate Way YO21 ... 29 B4
Gatecliff Brow BD23 ... 155 F4
Gateforth Ct YO8 ... 196 F1
Gateforth La YO8 ... 196 F1
Gateforth New Rd YO8 ... 203 A8
Gatehead La YO42 ... 193 D7
Gatehowe Rd YO17 ... 170 A7
Gatela Rd YO13 ... 53 D2
Gateland Cl YO32 ... 225 C7
Gateland Field La DN14 ... 205 B6
Gatenby Garth YO61 ... 143 B8
Gatesgarth Cl YO12 ... 212 B8
Gatherley Rd DL10 ... 41 C7
Gauber Rd LA6 ... 78 F1
Gaudy La DL8 ... 56 C3
Gauk St WF11 ... 201 D6
Gaul Rd DL9 ... 209 E1
Gaw La BD23 ... 174 C8
Gawtersike La YO62 ... 94 B8
Gay La LS24 ... 196 C7
Gay Mdws YO32 ... 167 D2
Gaylands La BB18 ... 172 B1
Gayle La DL8 ... 56 C4
Gayton Sands TS5 ... 6 D6
Gazelle Way YO7 ... 115 B1
Geecroft La LS22 ... 179 D3
Geldof Rd YO32 ... 225 F1
General La YO42 ... 193 E6
Geneva Cres DL1 ... 3 D4
Geneva La DL1 ... 3 D4
Geneva Rd DL1 ... 3 E5
Gennell La YO60 ... 145 E1
Gentian Glade HG3 ... 219 A4
George Cayley Dr YO30 ... 225 A3
George Ct YO31 ... 233 C3
George Hudson St YO1 ... 233 B2
George St
15 Addingham LS29 ... 174 F4
Carleton BD23 ... 173 B4
19 Earby BB18 ... 172 A1
3 Scarborough YO12 ... 213 A6
4 Selby YO8 ... 232 D6
17 Skipton BD23 ... 217 A3
Snaith DN14 ... 204 C1
12 Whitby YO21 ... 208 D6
7 Wistow YO8 ... 197 D6
York YO1 ... 233 C1
George Terr 1 YO8 ... 198 B4
Gerard Ave YO31 ... 229 A5
Germain Rd YO8 ... 232 E4
Germany La YO19 ... 231 E6
Gerrick La TS12 ... 10 C3
Gerrie St TS12 ... 9 D7
Ghyll Brow YO21 ... 30 D4
Ghyll La BB18 ... 171 E2
Ghyll Mdws BB18 ... 171 E2
Ghyll Mews LS29 ... 218 A3
Ghyll The DL10 ... 209 D8
Ghyll Way BD23 ... 173 D4
Ghyll Wood 28 LS29 ... 175 C2
Gibb St BD22 ... 187 B6
Gibbet Hill YO61 ... 117 C5
Gibside La BD20 ... 173 C1
Gibson Cl 2 YO8 ... 196 F1
Gibson La LS25 ... 194 D1
Gibson Lane Jun Sch LS25 ... 194 D1
Giggleswick CP Sch BD24 ... 131 D3
Giggleswick Sch BD24 ... 131 C2
Giggleswick Sta BD24 ... 131 C1
Gilcar St WF6 ... 200 B2
Gilcar Way WF6 ... 200 B3
Gildercliffe YO12 ... 212 C7
Giles Ave YO31 ... 229 A5
Gill Bank Rd LS29 ... 218 A6
Gill Cl 6 LS29 ... 174 E4
Gill Croft YO61 ... 117 C1
Gill La Cowling BD22 ... 187 A6
Kearby with Netherby LS22 ... 179 C1
Nesfield with Langbar LS29 ... 175 B4
Rosedale West Side YO18 ... 49 E2
Gillamoor Ave YO31 ... 229 B5
Gillamoor Bank YO62 ... 70 A5
Gillamoor C of E Prim Sch YO62 ... 70 A4
Gillamoor Rd YO62 ... 70 A2
Gillann St 15 WF11 ... 202 A2
Gillgate Rd HG4 ... 112 B4
Gilling Castle* YO62 ... 118 E7
Gilling Cres DL1 ... 3 E4
Gilling Rd Aske DL10 ... 20 E1
Richmond DL10 ... 209 D7
Gilling Way YO17 ... 215 C5
Gillings Ct YO7 ... 211 B3
Gillingwood Cl DL10 ... 209 C8
Gillingwood Rd YO30 ... 224 F3
Gills Fold 8 BD23 ... 134 E2
Gills The LS21 ... 177 A1
Gillygate YO31 ... 233 B3
Gillylees YO12 ... 212 C5
Gilmonby Rd TS3 ... 7 B8
Gilsforth Hill YO26 ... 164 A3
Gilsforth La YO26 ... 164 A3
Gilstead Way LS29 ... 218 B5
Gilsthwaite La YO26 ... 164 A3
Gindhill La LS21 ... 178 A4
Ginnel The 1 HG1 ... 219 D2
Gipsey Cnr YO19 ... 184 E3
Girls High Sch BD23 ... 216 E4
Girton Wlk DL1 ... 3 D7
Girvan Cl YO24 ... 230 B7
Gisburn Rd
Barnoldswick BB18 ... 171 D2
Hellifield BD23 ... 154 B3
Gisburn Road CP Sch BB18 ... 171 D1
Gisburn St
Barnoldswick BB18 ... 171 D2
Skipton BD23 ... 216 D3
Givendale Gr 3 YO10 ... 229 C4
Givendale Rd YO12 ... 212 D8
Glade Rd YO19 ... 192 B2
Glade The
Escrick YO19 ... 192 A6
Scarborough YO11 ... 212 F3
York YO31 ... 229 B7
Gladstone La YO12 ... 212 E5
Gladstone Rd YO12 ... 212 E5
Gladstone Road Jun & Inf Sch YO12 ... 212 E5
Gladstone St
Darlington DL3 ... 3 C5
Harrogate HG2 ... 222 E7
Normanton South WF6 ... 200 B2
Scarborough YO12 ... 212 E6
14 Skipton BD23 ... 216 F4
York YO31 ... 233 C4
Glaisby Ct YO31 ... 229 A6
Glaisdale Ave TS5 ... 6 F8
Glaisdale CP Sch YO21 ... 30 D4
Glaisdale Hall La YO21 ... 30 C4
Glaisdale Rd TS15 ... 5 F3
Glaisdale Sta YO21 ... 30 E4
Glasgow Dr 3 DL9 ... 209 C1
Glasshoughton Fst Sch WF10 ... 200 F4
Glasshouses CP Sch HG3 ... 137 D3
Glaves Cl YO13 ... 99 B7
Glebe Ave
Full Sutton YO41 ... 169 A2
Harrogate HG2 ... 219 C2
York YO26 ... 227 D5
Glebe Cl Barton DL10 ... 21 C7
15 Bedale DL8 ... 63 A2
Bolton Percy YO23 ... 190 D4
Kirby Hill YO51 ... 141 B7
Manfield DL2 ... 2 C4
3 Strensall YO32 ... 167 B7
Glebe Ct DL10 ... 21 A7
Glebe Field Dr 11 LS22 ... 180 B3
Glebe Gdns TS13 ... 11 A8
Glebe La DL2 ... 2 C4
Glebe Mdw HG4 ... 214 F6
Glebe Rd Campsall DN6 ... 206 E1
Darlington DL1 ... 3 D8
Harrogate HG2 ... 219 C1
Stokesley TS9 ... 26 C7
Glebe Sq DL7 ... 63 C5
Glebe St WF10 ... 200 E4
Glebe Way 26 YO32 ... 166 E5
Gledstone Rd BD23 ... 171 E5
Gledstone View 8 BB18 ... 171 D2
Glen Ave YO31 ... 228 E5
Glen Cl
Newby & Scalby YO13 ... 75 C5
York YO10 ... 231 E6
Glen Esk Rd YO22 ... 208 C3
Glen Rd YO31 ... 228 E5
Glencoe Cl LS25 ... 200 C8
Glencoe Croft LS25 ... 200 C8
Glencoe Gdns LS25 ... 200 C8
Glencoe St 1 YO30 ... 228 B7
Glencoe Terr LS25 ... 200 C8
Glendale
Guisborough TS14 ... 8 D5
9 Hutton Rudby TS15 ... 25 C5
Glendale Rd TS5 ... 6 F8
Gleneagles Rd
Darlington DL1 ... 3 F8
Middlesbrough TS4 ... 7 A8
North Featherstone WF7 ... 200 E1
Glenfield Ave LS22 ... 180 C2
Glenmore Dr YO17 ... 215 E2
Glenn Cres TS7 ... 7 B5
Glenridding YO24 ... 230 D7
Glenside YO12 ... 212 E7
Globe St
10 Harrogate HG2 ... 220 C3
9 Scarborough YO11 ... 213 B6
Gloucester Ave BD20 ... 174 B1
Glusburn CP Sch BD20 ... 187 E7
Glynndale Dr YO12 ... 212 A8
Glynwed Ct 2 BD23 ... 216 E3
Goat La BD24 ... 131 F7
Goathland CP Sch YO22 ... 51 C8
Goathland Gr TS14 ... 8 E5
Goats Rd DL11 ... 18 D2
Godfrey Rd 12 DL10 ... 41 E4
Godley Cl DL9 ... 209 C2
Godwinsway 18 YO41 ... 168 D2
Goker La YO51 ... 141 E1
Gold Thread La 5 YO8 ... 197 B8
Golden Acres DL7 ... 22 E2
Golden Butts Rd LS29 ... 218 C4
Goldhill La YO7 ... 90 D6
Goldsborough C of E Prim Sch HG5 ... 162 F3
Goldsborough Ct HG5 ... 163 A3
Goldsborough La YO21 ... 12 C4
Golf Links Ave 5 LS24 ... 189 D5
Golf Links Cres 4 LS24 ... 189 D5
Golf Links Ct LS24 ... 189 E5
Good Hope Cl WF6 ... 200 B2
Goodall Cl 31 BB18 ... 172 A1
Goodenber Rd LA2 ... 129 A8
Goodramgate YO1 ... 233 B2
Goodrick Cl HG2 ... 222 B5
Goodsyard The YO8 ... 232 D5
Goodwood Ave LS25 ... 194 C1
Goodwood Cl YO12 ... 212 B6
Goodwood Gr YO24 ... 227 F1
Goodwood Rd 3 DL9 ... 40 E3
Goody Cross LS26 ... 194 B1
Goody Cross La LS26 ... 194 A1
Goole Coll DN14 ... 205 F2
Goole Gram Sch DN14 ... 205 F3
Goose Green Cl 2 DL9 ... 40 E3
Goose La YO61 ... 144 C1
Goose Mire La YO12 ... 99 C6
Goose Track La YO60 ... 145 C3
Goosecroft Gdns DL6 ... 210 D5
Goosecroft La
East Harlsey DL6 ... 44 D6
Northallerton DL6 ... 210 D5
Gooselands BD24 ... 153 C6
Gooselands Hill BD23 ... 107 D2
Goosepastures TS16 ... 5 E3
Gordale Cl 3 BB18 ... 171 D1
Gordale La BD23 ... 133 A2
Gordale Mount HG5 ... 221 C6
Gordon Ave HG1 ... 219 E6
Gordon Cres DL10 ... 209 D8
Gordon St
28 Glusburn BD20 ... 187 E7
Ilkley LS29 ... 218 C4
Scarborough YO12 ... 212 E5
York YO10 ... 228 E3
Gordon Terr BD20 ... 173 C1
Gore La DN14 ... 207 B5
Gore Sands TS5 ... 6 D6
Gormire Ave 2 YO31 ... 225 E2
Gormire Cl YO7 ... 211 D3
Gorse Cl YO8 ... 232 C2
Gorse Hill 1 YO19 ... 184 F7
Gorse La LS25 ... 195 D3
Gorse Paddock YO32 ... 225 F2
Goschen St 8 BD23 ... 217 A3
Goslipgate 9 YO18 ... 95 F6
Gough Rd DL9 ... 40 D4
Gouldings Cl YO11 ... 100 A7
Goulton La TS9 ... 25 E3
Gouthwaith Cl YO30 ... 224 F2
Government House Rd YO30 ... 228 A6
Gowans The YO61 ... 144 C3
Gowdall Broach DN14 ... 207 E8
Gowdall La
Pollington DN14 ... 207 F7
Snaith & Cowick DN14 ... 204 B1
Gowdall Rd DN14 ... 203 E2
Gower Rd Aske DL10 ... 20 D1
Richmond DL10 ... 209 C8
York YO24 ... 230 E8
Gowland La YO13 ... 54 B2
Gowthorpe YO8 ... 232 C5
Gracious St Huby YO61 ... 144 A4
7 Knaresborough HG5 ... 221 B5
Grafton Cl TS14 ... 8 F6
Grafton La YO51 ... 141 C3
Grafton St WF10 ... 200 F3
Graham Cl YO11 ... 213 B7
Graham Cres YO12 ... 212 C5
Graham Dr WF10 ... 201 A4
Graham Rd HG4 ... 113 D3
Graham Sch YO12 ... 212 B5
Grainbeck La HG3 ... 219 A7
Grainger Row HG4 ... 214 D5
Grainger St DL1 ... 3 D4
Grains La BD23 ... 154 E8
Grammar Sch La DL6 ... 210 D3
Grampian Cl 4 YO32 ... 225 F5
Granary Ct YO1 ... 233 B3
Granby Pk HG1 ... 219 F3
Granby Rd HG1 ... 219 F3
Grandage La BD22 ... 187 A7
Grange Ave Aiskew DL7 ... 63 C4
Filey YO14 ... 101 B3
Garforth LS25 ... 194 C3
Harrogate HG1 ... 219 D5
3 Hurworth-on-Tees DL2 ... 3 D1
5 Hurworth-on-Tees DL2 ... 22 D8
Ilkley LS29 ... 218 D4
Scarborough YO12 ... 212 E4
Spofforth HG3 ... 179 E6
Tadcaster LS24 ... 189 F6
Thorp Arch LS23 ... 181 A2
3 Willerby YO12 ... 99 D2
Grange Cl 10 Bedale DL8 ... 63 A2
Bishop Thornton HG3 ... 138 F1
Dishforth YO7 ... 114 F4
Full Sutton YO41 ... 169 A2
Ilkley LS29 ... 218 D4
Lebberston YO11 ... 100 D5
Northallerton DL7 ... 210 C3
Skelton YO30 ... 224 B5
Grange Cl E DL7 ... 63 E7
Grange Cres
Middlesbrough TS7 ... 7 B5
10 Tadcaster LS24 ... 189 E6
Grange Ct YO12 ... 99 D7
Grange Dr TS9 ... 26 C7
Grange Est LS29 ... 218 D4
Grange Garth YO10 ... 228 D2
Grange La 1 Dacre HG3 ... 137 F1
Rufforth YO26 ... 227 A2
Scackleton YO62 ... 119 C3
Stonebeck Down HG3 ... 137 A6
Sutton BD22 ... 187 F2
Grange Park Cl WF10 ... 200 D7
Grange Park Rd HG4 ... 214 B2
Grange Rd 19 Bedale DL8 ... 63 A2
Brompton-on-Swale DL10 ... 41 B6
Burley in Warfedale LS29 ... 176 C1
8 Campsall DN6 ... 206 E1
Castleford WF10 ... 201 B5
Colburn DL9 ... 40 F5
5 Dacre HG3 ... 137 F1
Darlington DL1 ... 3 C4
Farnhill BD20 ... 173 E1
Goole DN14 ... 205 F2
Tadcaster LS24 ... 189 E6
Thornaby TS17 ... 6 B8
Grange St YO10 ... 228 D2
Grange Terr HG4 ... 114 B8
Grange The
Kirby Hill YO51 ... 141 A7
Thirsk YO7 ... 211 B2
Grange View
11 Otley LS21 ... 176 F1
Towton LS24 ... 189 E2
Grangefield Ave 32 LS29 ... 176 C1
Granger Ave YO26 ... 227 C4
Grangeside DL3 ... 3 B4
Grant Cl DL6 ... 45 B4
Grantham Dr YO26 ... 227 E4
Grantley Cl HG3 ... 219 A4
Grantley Dr HG3 ... 219 A4
Grantley Hall Coll HG4 ... 138 E8
Grantley Pl HG3 ... 219 A4
Grants Ave YO10 ... 231 E8
Granville Rd
21 Filey YO14 ... 101 B3
4 Harrogate HG1 ... 219 D3
Scarborough YO11 ... 213 A6
Granville Sq 3 YO11 ... 213 A6
Granville St
20 Normanton South WF6 ... 200 A1
Skipton BD23 ... 216 E4
Granville Terr 4 YO10 ... 228 E3
Grape La Whitby YO22 ... 208 E7
York YO1 ... 233 B3
Grasmere Ave LS22 ... 180 A3
Grasmere Cl 4 BB8 ... 186 A3
Grasmere Cres HG2 ... 222 C7
Grasmere Dr YO10 ... 229 B4
Grasmere Gr 5 YO30 ... 224 F1
Grass Croft TS21 ... 5 A7
Grass Wood La BD23 ... 134 C3
Grassfield Cl HG3 ... 137 B4
Grassgill La DL8 ... 59 E3
Grassholme YO24 ... 230 C7
Grassington Ave DL7 ... 210 C2
Grassington C of E Prim Sch BD23 ... 134 E2
Grassington Rd
Middlesbrough TS4 ... 7 A8
Skipton BD23 ... 216 F5
Gravel Hole La
Sowerby YO7 ... 89 E3
Thirsk YO7 ... 211 C1
Gravelhill La DN14 ... 206 F7
Gravelly Hill La LS17 ... 178 A2
Gray La YO62 ... 70 D1
Gray St 13 Whitby YO21 ... 208 D6
York YO23 ... 233 A1
Grays Rd YO62 ... 69 F6
Grayshon Dr YO26 ... 227 B5
Grayston Plain La HG3 ... 160 F4
Graystonber La LA2 ... 130 E7
Great & Little Preston C of E Inf Sch LS26 ... 200 C8
Great & Little Preston Prim Sch LS26 ... 200 C8
Great Auk TS14 ... 8 D6
Great Ave DL10 ... 209 A7
Great Ayton Sta TS9 ... 8 B1
Great Cl YO8 ... 197 B8
Great Close La BD24 ... 153 A6
Great Croft Cl 9 BB18 ... 171 D2
Great Moor Rd YO13 ... 74 D2
Great North Rd
Ledsham LS25 ... 195 C1
Micklefield LS25 ... 194 F5
Great North Way YO26 ... 227 B8
Great Ouseburn Cty Prim Sch YO26 ... 164 B8
Great Pasture LS29 ... 176 C1
Great Sike Rd YO17 ... 215 D8
Great Smeaton Cty Prim Sch DL6 ... 23 C3
Greatwood Ave BD23 ... 217 A3
Greatwood Prim Sch BD23 ... 217 A2
Greavefield La WF8 ... 201 D1
Greaves Smithy LS29 ... 175 B4
Grebe Ave DL9 ... 40 E2
Green Ave LS25 ... 194 C2
Green Balk
Great & Little Broughton TS9 ... 26 F5
Millington YO42 ... 170 D1
Green Bank BB18 ... 171 E2
Green Bank La HG4 ... 139 A6
Green Cl
Bradleys Both BD20 ... 173 D3
2 Linton-on-Ouse YO30 ... 164 F8

Green Cl continued
Middlesbrough TS7 ....7 D5
Steeton with Eastburn BD20 ....187 F7
York YO30 ....228 A8
Green Cres The YO62 ..120 B5
Green Croft Gdns 24 YO11 ....100 B6
Green Dike YO32 ....225 C8
Green Dikes La YO25 ..151 F1
Green Dyke La YO62 ..120 C5
Green Dykes YO17 ....215 A3
Green Dykes La YO10 ..228 F3
Green End Ave 35 BB18 .172 A1
Green End Rd 34 BB18 .172 A1
Green Gate
Exelby, Leeming & Newton DL8 ....63 D2
Hawsker-cum-Stainsacre YO22 ....33 A6
Kirkby Malham BD23 ....154 F8
West Witton DL8 ....59 C3
Green Gate La
Crakehall DL8 ....62 E5
Kildale YO21 ....27 F8
Long Preston BD23 ....153 F5
Green Haggs La HG3 ..223 F1
Green Hammerton C of E Prim Sch YO26 ....164 B3
Green Head La BD24 ..131 E2
Green Hill YO62 ....118 E6
Green Hill La BD22 ....187 A5
Green Hills YO60 ....168 B7
Green Hills La DL7 ....64 B6
Green Howards & Regimental Mus★ DL10 ....209 C6
Green Howard's Dr 8 YO12 ....75 F5
Green Howards Rd
Pickering YO18 ....96 A6
Richmond DL10 ....209 B8
Green Island YO12 ....99 D7
Green La
Addingham LS29 ....174 F4
Appleton Roebuck YO23 ..191 B6
Barmby on the Marsh DN14 ....205 A6
Barton-le-Street YO17 ....120 E8
Bedale DL8 ....62 F3
Bishopthorpe YO24 ....231 A6
Boston Spa LS23 ....188 F7
Bradleys Both BD20 ....174 A3
Burton Leonard HG3 ....140 B2
Burton-on-Yore HG4 ....86 D6
Castleford WF10 ....200 E3
Castleford WF10 ....200 F5
Cawton YO62 ....119 B6
Collingham LS22 ....188 A8
Coneythorpe & Clareton HG5 ....163 B5
Constable Burton DL8 ....61 A6
Cottingwith YO42 ....193 C5
Cundall with Leckby YO61 ....115 D4
Darlington DL1 ....3 D8
Dishforth YO7 ....115 A2
East Rounton TS15 ....24 F4
Fadmoor YO62 ....69 E3
Farndale West YO62 ....48 E1
Folkton YO12 ....99 F1
Garforth LS25 ....194 D4
Glusburn BD20 ....187 D7
Great Ouseburn YO26 ....142 A1
Halton East BD23 ....157 C1
Harome YO62 ....93 C5
Harrogate HG2 ....222 C6
Heck DN14 ....207 D8
Horton BD23 ....171 B5
Hudswell DL11 ....39 F5
Hutton Rudby TS15 ....25 B4
Ilkley LS29 ....176 C2
Ingleton LA6 ....103 E2
Kippax LS25 ....194 C2
Kirby Wiske YO7 ....88 F7
Kirkby Overblow LS17 ....178 D2
Kirklevington TS15 ....5 E2
Langtoft YO25 ....151 D5
Lebberston YO11 ....100 D5
Ledston WF10 ....200 E7
Little Ayton TS9 ....27 A8
Littlethorpe HG4 ....140 A7
Marrick DL11 ....38 E7
Maunby YO7 ....64 D1
Menwith with Darley HG3 ....160 A6
Mickletown LS26 ....200 C5
Middlesbrough TS5 ....6 E8
Moor Monkton YO26 ....164 F1
Newby TS7 ....7 C3
North Cowton DL7 ....22 B2
North Duffield YO8 ....198 F8
Otley LS21 ....176 F1
Ripon HG4 ....113 C3
Sawley HG4 ....138 E7
Scalby YO12 ....212 C8
Selby YO8 ....232 A3
South Stainley with Cayton HG3 ....161 E8
Stutton with Hazlewood LS24 ....189 D4
Sutton BD22 ....187 F2
Sutton-on-the-Forest YO61 ....144 E4
Thirsk YO7 ....211 F3
Weaverthorpe YO17 ....124 F1
Welbury DL6 ....44 C8
Wensley DL8 ....60 A4
Whitby YO22 ....208 E5
Green La continued
Whorlton DL6 ....45 F7
Wigginton YO32 ....166 D5
Winksley HG4 ....112 F2
Wressle DN14 ....205 D8
York YO30 ....225 A1
York YO24 ....227 D2
Green La E YO7 ....211 B1
Green La W YO7 ....211 A1
Green Lane Prim Sch TS5 ....6 E8
Green Mdw BB8 ....186 A1
Green Mdws YO31 ....229 A7
Green Park Ave 15 YO11 ....100 B6
Green Park Rd 14 YO11 .100 B6
Green Pastures DL8 ....62 C5
Green Row LS26 ....200 B5
Green St
7 Cowling BD22 ....187 B6
Darlington DL1 ....3 D5
Green Sward YO31 ....229 A8
Green Sykes Rd BD20 ..187 F4
Green The Brompton DL6 ..43 F3
Castleford WF10 ....201 B4
1 Clapham LA2 ....130 C8
Cleasby DL2 ....2 F4
Conistone with Kilnsey BD23 ....134 B6
20 Dunnington YO19 ....184 F7
Garforth LS25 ....194 D3
Hellifield BD23 ....154 B3
High Coniscliffe DL2 ....2 C6
Kettlewell with Starbotton BD23 ....108 B3
Kirkby Malzeard HG4 ....112 D5
8 Kirklevington TS15 ....24 E8
Linton-on-Ouse YO30 ....164 F8
Longnewton TS21 ....5 A7
9 Otley LS21 ....176 F1
Rawcliffe DN14 ....205 A1
Scalby YO12 ....212 B7
Seamer TS9 ....6 F1
6 Seamer YO12 ....99 D6
1 Skelton YO30 ....224 B5
Slingsby YO62 ....120 B5
10 Thirsk YO7 ....211 C3
Tockwith YO26 ....181 C7
2 Tollerton YO61 ....143 B3
7 Topcliffe YO7 ....89 B1
Wistow YO8 ....197 D6
York YO26 ....227 C3
Green Village YO7 ....88 C5
Green Way
Glusburn BD20 ....187 E8
Harrogate HG2 ....222 C6
Middlesbrough TS7 ....7 D5
York YO32 ....225 F4
Green Ways 2 YO8 ....197 D6
Green Wlk 5 BB18 ....172 A1
Greenacre Cl TS9 ....7 F1
Greenacres Hunton DL8 ..61 E7
Morton-on-Swale DL7 ....64 A6
Skipton BD23 ....217 B5
Stainton & Thornton TS8 ....6 D5
York YO32 ....225 F4
Greenacres Cl 8 YO8 ..197 D1
Greenacres Cres 7 YO8 ....197 D1
Greenacres Dr 4 YO8 ..197 D1
Greenacres Gr 3 YO8 ..197 D1
Greenbank 5 DL6 ....210 E2
Greenbank Cl WF10 ....200 D3
Greenbank Rd DL3 ....3 C6
Greenberfield La BB18 ....171 E2
Greencliffe Dr YO30 ..228 A6
Greencroft Ct 14 YO19 ..184 F7
Greencroft La 17 YO19 ..184 F7
Greendown Cl LS29 ..218 D4
Greenfield Ave LS25 ..194 D1
Greenfield Cl DL2 ....3 E1
Greenfield Dr
6 Brayton YO8 ....197 D1
Eaglescliffe TS16 ....5 D5
Greenfield Gdns BD20 .187 F7
Greenfield Park Dr YO31 ....229 A7
Greenfield Rd 8 YO11 .213 A4
Greenfield St 5 BD23 ..216 D3
Greenfields DN14 ....207 F6
Greenfields Ave HG2 ..220 C2
Greenfields Dr HG2 ..220 C2
Greenfields Rd HG2 ..220 C2
Greenfinch Cl 1 YO12 ..99 E6
Greenfoot La LA2 ....128 E8
Greengales Ct YO19 ..193 A8
Greengales La YO19 ..193 A8
Greengate
Malton YO17 ....215 C4
Scarborough YO12 ....212 D4
Greengate Dr HG5 ..221 B8
Greengate La
Cliffe YO8 ....198 F6
Kirkby Fleetham with Fencote DL7 ....42 B1
Knaresborough HG5 ....221 B8
Thornton-le-Dale YO18 ....96 C6
Greengate Rd WF8 ....206 C1
Greengate View HG5 ..221 B8
Greengates La YO61 ..142 E3
Greenhill Cres DL6 ..210 E3
Greenhill La YO7 ....66 B4
Greenholme Cl
1 Boroughbridge YO51 ..141 B6
7 Burley in Warfedale LS29 ....176 C1
Greenhow Hill HG3 ....136 C2
Greenhow Hill Rd HG3 ....159 B6
Greenhow Pk LS29 ....176 B1
Greenhowsyke La DL6 .210 E4
Greenland La YO17 ....95 B3
Greenlands TS15 ....25 C6
Greenlands La YO8 ..197 C3
Greenlands Rd YO18 ....95 F6
Greenless La DL11 ....1 A2
Greenmires La LS21 ..177 E4
Greenroyd Gr 13 BD20 ..187 E6
Greens Yd YO22 ....208 E7
Greensborough Ave 3 YO26 ....227 B5
Greenshaw Dr YO32 ..225 C8
Greenside 18 YO19 ....184 F7
Greenside Cl 24 YO19 ..184 F7
Greenside Ct 9 DL2 ....3 E1
Greenside Wlk 23 YO19 .184 F7
Greenstead Rd YO12 ..212 B8
Greenway The
2 Haxby YO32 ....225 C7
2 Middleton St George DL2 .4 C4
Greenways Dr 1 YO8 ..197 D6
Greenways The DL7 ....63 C8
Greenwodd Rd HG3 ....137 B4
Greenwood Ave HG3 ..137 B4
Greenwood Gr YO24 ..230 C8
Greet's Hill YO17 ....169 E7
Gregory Cl YO30 ....224 C5
Grenadier Dr DL6 ....210 F3
Grendon Gdns 1 DL2 ....4 C4
Grenley St 8 WF11 ....202 A2
Grenville Rd TS17 ....6 B6
Grenwich Cl 5 YO30 ..224 E3
Gresham Cl DL1 ....3 D7
Gresley Ct 3 YO26 ..227 B4
Greta Heath 2 LA6 ....102 F2
Grewelthorpe C of E Prim Sch HG4 ....112 C7
Grey Cl YO61 ....144 C3
Grey St HG2 ....222 E7
Grey Thorn La HG5 ....163 D3
Grey Towers Dr TS7 ....7 D5
Greyfriars Cl DL3 ....2 F5
Greylands Park Ave YO12 ....212 C8
Greylands Park Dr YO12 ....212 C8
Greylands Park Gr 3 YO12 ....212 C8
Greylands Park Rd YO12 ....212 C8
Greystoke Rd YO30 ....224 E1
Greystone Cl 2 LS29 ..176 C1
Greystone Ct YO32 ..225 C7
Greystone Head HG4 ..112 A4
Greystone La
Aldbrough DL2 ....2 A4
Stanwick St John DL11 ....1 E4
Greystone Pk LS25 ....188 F1
Greystonegill La LA2 ..129 D7
Greystones Ave HG3 ..161 B4
Greystones Cl LS25 ..188 F1
Greystones La BD22 ..187 E4
Grimbald Crag Cl HG5 ....221 D4
Grimbald Crag Rd HG5 ....221 E4
Grimbald Crag Way HG5 ....221 D4
Grimbald Rd HG5 ....221 C5
Grimbald Way 3 HG5 ..221 C4
Grimston La YO17 ....148 D7
Grimston Rd 12 YO14 ..127 A8
Grimwith Garth YO30 ..224 F2
Grimwith Rd BD23 ....135 E2
Grindale Rd YO16 ....127 F2
Grinkle La TS13 ....10 F5
Grinton Rd TS18 ....5 D8
Grisedale Cres TS16 ....5 E4
Gristhwaite La YO7 ....89 D1
Grosmont Sta YO22 ....31 C4
Grosvenor Cres 2 YO11 ....213 A4
Grosvenor Gdns LS17 ..178 B2
Grosvenor Gr HG1 ....219 F6
Grosvenor House Sch HG3 ....160 D6
Grosvenor Pl TS14 ....8 E6
Grosvenor Rd
Harrogate HG1 ....219 E6
Scarborough YO11 ....212 F4
York YO30 ....233 A4
Grosvenor Sq 3 YO30 ..164 F8
Grosvenor Terr YO30 ..233 A4
Grove Ave 25 LS29 ....175 C2
Grove Bank 4 TS15 ....24 E8
Grove Cl HG4 ....214 C3
Grove Cres
Boston Spa LS23 ....188 F8
South Milford LS25 ....195 F2
Grove Gdns 12 YO26 ..165 F1
Grove Hill Rd 4 YO14 ..101 B4
Grove La
Knottingley WF11 ....201 F2
Ripon HG4 ....214 C3
Grove Park Ave HG1 ..219 E4
Grove Park Ct HG1 ..219 E4
Grove Park La HG1 ..219 E4
Grove Park Terr HG1 ..219 E4
Grove Park View HG1 ..219 E4
Grove Park Wlk HG1 ..219 E4
Grove Pk 7 YO8 ....198 B5
Grove Rd
Boston Spa LS23 ....188 F8
14 Filey YO14 ....101 B4
Harrogate HG1 ....219 D4
Grove Rd continued
Ilkley LS29 ....218 A3
Grove Road CP Sch HG1 ....219 E4
Grove St 33 Earby BB18 .172 A1
9 Harrogate HG2 ....220 C3
Norton YO17 ....215 E3
15 Whitby YO21 ....208 D6
Grove Terr 11 DL8 ....60 E2
Grove Terrace La YO31 ....233 C4
Grove The
Eaglescliffe TS15 ....5 E2
Guisborough TS14 ....8 D5
Harrogate HG1 ....219 E3
1 Hutton Rudby TS15 ....25 D5
Ilkley LS29 ....218 A4
Kellington DN14 ....203 A3
Kippax LS25 ....194 D1
Middlesbrough TS5 ....6 E6
Middlesbrough TS7 ....7 B7
Normanton South WF6 ..200 A1
Norton YO17 ....215 E2
1 Seamer YO12 ....99 D6
Skipton BD23 ....217 C3
Swillington LS26 ....194 A1
York YO24 ....230 E6
Grove View YO30 ....228 A6
Groves La YO31 ....233 C4
Grundy Way 11 DL10 ....41 E4
Grunton La DL2 ....2 C4
Grysedale La BD23 ....134 B2
Guadaloupe Rd DL9 ....40 C4
Guards Ct 10 YO12 ....75 F5
Guildford Rd TS6 ....7 E8
Guisborough Mus★ TS14 ....8 F7
Guisborough Rd
Aislaby YO21 ....31 F8
Great Ayton TS9 ....7 F1
Lockwood TS12 ....10 A5
Middlesbrough TS7 ....7 D5
Thornaby TS17 ....6 B8
Whitby YO21 ....208 A5
Guisborough RUFC TS14 .8 F6
Guisborough Swimming Pool TS14 ....8 E7
Gunby Rd YO8 ....199 D5
Gunbywood Rd YO8 ..199 D6
Guncroft La YO62 ....69 D1
Guning La DL11 ....36 B4
Gunnergate La TS8 ....7 B5
Gurney Pease Prim Sch DL1 ....3 D6
Gurney St DL1 ....3 D6
Guy La YO7 ....114 F2
Gyll Hall La DL10 ....41 E1
Gypsy La
Castleford WF10 ....201 B3
Middlesbrough TS7 ....7 C6
Gypsy Lane Sta TS7 ....7 D6

H

Habton La YO17 ....121 B7
Habton Rd YO17 ....95 D1
Hackforth & Hornby C of E Prim Sch DL8 ....62 E8
Hackforth Rd 2 TS18 ....5 D8
Hackness C of E Prim Sch YO13 ....74 E5
Hackness Dr YO12 ..212 A8
Hackness Rd YO12 ..212 A8
Haddlesey Rd WF11 ..202 D5
Haddocks La YO61 ..142 B4
Hadrian Ave YO10 ..229 B3
Hag La
Cottingwith YO42 ....193 C4
Raskelf YO61 ....142 E8
South Kilvington YO7 ....211 D6
Sproxton YO62 ....92 D4
Youlton YO61 ....142 F2
Hagg La Colton LS24 ..190 E8
Cottingwith YO42 ....193 E8
Cowesby YO7 ....66 C4
Dunnington YO19 ....184 F6
Hemingbrough YO8 ....198 F3
South Milford LS25 ....196 C2
Hagg Rd YO62 ....69 F2
Hagg Side La YO13 ....97 D6
Haggersgate 10 YO21 ..208 D7
Haggitt Hill La DL6 ....24 E3
Haggs La DN6 ....207 D2
Haggs Rd HG3 ....223 C4
Hague Ave 31 YO12 ....75 D5
Hagworm Hill★ YO12 ....75 C2
Haig Rd DL9 ....209 C2
Haig St YO8 ....232 B6
Haigh La DN14 ....207 A6
Hailsham Ave TS17 ....6 B5
Hailstone Dr DL6 ....210 F5
Hales La YO8 ....204 E5
Haley's Terr YO31 ....228 D8
Half Acres Jun & Inf Sch WF10 ....200 E4
Half Moon St 1 YO30 ..164 F7
Halfpenny Cl HG5 ....221 C7
Halfpenny La HG5 ....221 B7
Halifax Ct 7 YO30 ....225 A1
Halifax Way YO41 ....185 A3
Hall Arm La YO51 ....141 D5
Hall Ave 10 BD20 ....187 E6
Hall Brow BD23 ....155 A5
Hall Cl 5 Airmyn DN14 ..205 E4
Austwick LA2 ....130 E7
Burley in Warfedale LS29 ....176 B1
Hall Cl continued
Cawood YO8 ....191 D1
11 Glusburn BD20 ....187 E6
Hall Croft BD23 ....216 E4
Hall Ct WF11 ....201 E4
Hall Dr
Burley in Warfedale LS29 ....176 B1
Glusburn BD20 ....187 E6
Middlesbrough TS5 ....6 F7
Hall Farm Cl 4 YO19 ..197 F8
Hall Farm Pk LS25 ....194 F4
Hall Garth 25 YO18 ....95 F7
Hall Garth Cl LS24 ..190 C3
Hall Garth★ LS25 ....195 E4
Hall Gdns BD20 ....173 F1
Hall Green La LS17 ....178 C4
Hall Ings La YO62 ....70 E4
Hall La Askwith LS21 ..176 C4
Blubberhouses LS21 ....159 C2
Caldwell DL11 ....1 C4
Church Fenton LS24 ....196 C7
Harome YO62 ....93 C4
Harrogate HG1 ....219 E6
Hawnby DL6 ....46 B1
Huddleston with Newthorpe LS25 ....195 C3
Leathley LS21 ....177 D1
Ledston WF10 ....200 F7
Myton-on-Swale YO61 ....142 A6
Norton DN6 ....206 E2
Hall Mdws BB8 ....186 A2
Hall Moor Cl 7 TS15 ....24 E8
Hall Orchards Ave LS22 ....180 D3
Hall Park Cl 23 YO13 ....75 D5
Hall Park Croft LS25 ..200 D8
Hall Park Gr 25 YO13 ....75 D5
Hall Park Mdws LS25 ..200 D8
Hall Park Orch LS25 ..200 D8
Hall Park Rd
Hunmanby YO14 ....126 F8
Walton LS23 ....181 A2
Hall Pasture 9 YO22 ....32 A6
Hall Pk Wistow YO8 ....198 A5
York YO10 ....229 B1
Hall Rd
Swillington LS26 ....194 A1
Trawden Forest BB8 ....186 A2
Hall Rise
Burley in Warfedale LS29 ....176 B1
12 Haxby YO32 ....166 F5
Hall Sq 5 YO51 ....141 B5
Hall Tower Hill★ LS15 .194 B8
Hall View Gr DL3 ....3 A6
Hall Way 9 BD20 ....187 E6
Halladale Cl 1 YO24 ..230 B7
Hallam Cl 41 YO14 ....101 B3
Hallam La LS21 ....176 D3
Hallam's Yd 4 BD23 ..216 F4
Hallard Way 7 YO32 ..167 B7
Hallcroft Dr 13 LS29 ..175 A4
Hallcroft La YO23 ....230 A3
Hallfield Ave LS25 ....194 F4
Hallfield La
Nawton YO62 ....69 C3
Wetherby LS22 ....180 C3
Hallfield Rd YO31 ....228 E5
Hallfield Terr LS25 ....194 F4
Hallgarth Alne YO61 ..142 F4
Great & Little Broughton TS9 ....26 E5
Hallgarth Comp Sch TS5 .6 E7
Hallwith Rd DL8 ....61 A3
Halnaby Ave DL3 ....2 F5
Halstead Rd HG2 ....222 E7
Hambleton Ave
Northallerton DL7 ....210 C2
Thirsk YO7 ....211 D3
York YO10 ....229 C4
Hambleton C of E Prim Sch YO8 ....196 F1
Hambleton Cl
12 Easingwold YO61 ....143 D8
11 Thirsk YO7 ....211 C3
Hambleton Ct
Great Smeaton DL6 ....23 C3
Knaresborough HG5 ....221 C6
Hambleton Dr YO7 ....211 C3
Hambleton Garth 21 YO61 ....143 C8
Hambleton Gate TS9 ....26 C7
Hambleton Gr HG5 ....221 B6
Hambleton La YO61 ....91 F2
Hambleton Leisure Ctr DL6 ....210 D6
Hambleton Pl YO7 ....211 C3
Hambleton Rd
6 Catterick Garrison DL9 ..40 E3
Harrogate HG1 ....219 F4
Norton YO17 ....215 E2
Hambleton Terr YO31 ..228 C7
Hambleton View
10 Haxby YO32 ....166 D5
Thirsk YO7 ....211 D3
4 Tollerton YO61 ....143 B3
Hambleton Way
Easingwold YO61 ....143 D8
York YO32 ....225 F3
Hamer Bank YO18 ....49 F4
Hamerton Cl 14 YO14 ..127 A8
Hamerton Rd 10 YO14 ..127 A8
Hamhall La DL7 ....63 D6
Hamilton Ave HG2 ....222 E8

Hamilton Cl YO13 ...75 C5
Hamilton Ct WF6 ...200 A2
Hamilton Dr
Darlington DL1 ...3 D8
York YO24 ...227 E2
Hamilton Dr E YO24 ...227 F2
Hamilton Dr W YO24 ...227 D2
Hamilton Gn YO17 ...215 B3
Hamilton Way YO24 ...227 E2
Hamlet The 8 DN14 ...202 F2
Hamley La YO62 ...70 F3
Hammer Rd HG4 ...85 B7
Hammersike Rd
Cawood YO8 ...196 F5
Wistow YO8 ...197 A4
Hammerton Cl
Green Hammerton YO26 ...164 D3
3 York YO26 ...227 B3
Hammerton Dr
Garforth LS25 ...194 D3
Hellifield BD23 ...154 B3
Hammerton Sta YO26 ...164 D2
Hammond Dr DL1 ...3 C4
Hammond Rd YO13 ...54 A8
Hampden St YO1 ...233 B1
Hampden Way TS17 ...6 B6
Hampshire Cl
Ilkley LS29 ...218 D4
6 Pontefract WF8 ...201 C2
Hampsthwaite C of E Prim
Sch HG3 ...161 A5
Hampsthwaite Rd
HG1 ...219 C4
Hampton Rd YO12 ...212 E5
Hancow Rd
Hartoft YO18 ...50 A1
Rosedale East Side YO18 ...49 F3
Handale Cl TS14 ...9 A6
Handley Cl
Stockton-on-Tees TS18 ...5 F7
York YO30 ...225 A2
Hang Bank DL10 ...21 B8
Hanger La DN14 ...204 B3
Hanghow La DL8 ...84 C8
Hanging Stone La YO18 ...49 E4
Hangingstone Rd
LS29 ...218 D2
Hankins La YO42 ...193 D1
Hanover Pl WF11 ...201 D4
Hanover Rd 6 YO11 ...212 F5
Hanover St 2 BD20 ...173 E1
Hanover St E 5 YO26 ...227 F5
Hanover St W 7 YO26 ...227 F5
Hansom Pl YO31 ...228 C7
Hanson Ave WF6 ...200 A1
Harborough Cl 20 YO14 ...126 F8
Harbour Rise 5 DL8 ...63 A2
Harbour View 7 DL8 ...63 A3
Harcourt Ave YO12 ...212 E3
Harcourt Cl
Bishopthorpe YO23 ...231 A4
Wheldrake YO19 ...192 F7
Harcourt Dr
Addingham LS29 ...174 F5
Harrogate HG1 ...219 E2
Harcourt Pl 4 YO11 ...213 A5
Harcourt Rd 4 HG1 ...219 E3
Harcourt St YO31 ...228 E5
Hard Gate BD23 ...134 A3
Hard Stiles DL11 ...39 B7
Hardcastle Ave 8 WF8 ...201 B1
Harden Cl YO30 ...224 F2
Harden Rd BB18 ...186 A7
Hardenshaw La YO8 ...204 B4
Hardigate Rd YO18 ...72 B7
Hardings La
Glusburn BD20 ...187 F8
Middleton LS29 ...218 A8
Hardisty Hill HG3 ...159 C3
Hardrada Way 3 YO41 ...168 D1
Hardy Mdws 11 BD23 ...134 E2
Hardy St YO8 ...232 E4
Harebell Cl
17 Harrogate HG3 ...161 B3
Northallerton DL7 ...210 C1
Harecroft Rd 9 LS21 ...177 A1
Haregill Bank HG4 ...85 E6
Harehills La BD22 ...187 E1
Haresfield Way TS17 ...6 A5
Harewell Cl HG3 ...137 D3
Harewell La 3 HG3 ...137 F1
Harewood Ave
5 Normanton South WF6 ...200 B2
8 Scalby YO12 ...75 E5
1 Scalby YO12 ...212 D8
Harewood Chase DL7 ...210 B2
Harewood Cl
Morton-on-Swale DL7 ...64 A6
Rawcliffe YO30 ...224 D2
5 Wigginton YO32 ...166 D5
Harewood Dr 4 YO14 ...101 A3
Harewood La DL7 ...210 C3
Harewood Rd
Collingham LS22 ...188 A8
Harrogate HG3 ...219 A5
Ripon HG4 ...214 B3
Skipton BD23 ...216 E4
Harford Rd YO11 ...100 B6
Hargill
Gilling with Hartforth & Sedbury
DL10 ...20 E4
Harmby DL8 ...60 E4
West Witton DL8 ...59 C3
Hargill Cl DL8 ...60 E4
Hargill Dr DL8 ...59 C6
Hargill La Finghall DL8 ...61 E4
6 Leeming DL7 ...63 D4
Redmire DL8 ...59 C7
Hargill Rd DL8 ...61 A3
Hargrove Rd HG2 ...220 B2
Harington Ave YO10 ...228 F4
Harker Hill DL8 ...56 C4
Harker St 12 WF11 ...202 A2
Harkness Cl DL7 ...63 C4
Harkness Dr DL7 ...63 C4
Harland Cl YO61 ...144 C3
Harlech Way HG2 ...222 B5
Harley Cl YO12 ...212 E5
Harley Cres DL9 ...40 F4
Harley La DL9 ...40 F4
Harley St 5 YO12 ...212 E5
Harlow Ave HG2 ...222 B7
Harlow Cl 1 YO24 ...227 F2
Harlow Cres HG2 ...222 B7
Harlow Grange Pk
HG3 ...178 C8
Harlow Manor Pk
HG2 ...222 B8
Harlow Moor Dr HG2 ...219 B1
Harlow Moor Rd HG2 ...219 A1
Harlow Oval HG2 ...222 B8
Harlow Park Cres
HG2 ...222 B7
Harlow Park Dr HG2 ...222 B7
Harlow Park Rd HG2 ...222 B7
Harlow Pines HG2 ...222 A7
Harlow Rd YO24 ...227 F2
Harlow Terr HG2 ...219 B1
Harlsey Castle* DL6 ...44 D5
Harlsey Cres TS18 ...5 E8
Harlsey Rd TS18 ...5 E8
Harmby Rd 12 DL8 ...60 D5
Harness La 9 YO51 ...141 B4
Harold Ct YO24 ...227 D3
Harold St YO8 ...232 F4
Harolds Way 1 YO41 ...168 D1
Harome Heads La YO62 ...93 B6
Harome Heads Rd
YO62 ...93 C6
Harper Gr BD20 ...187 E6
Harper La HG3 ...159 C6
Harper St
Barnoldswick BB18 ...171 D1
2 Selby YO8 ...232 C5
Harper Terr 7 TS18 ...5 E8
Harpers Sq 7 BD20 ...187 E6
Harpers Terr DL2 ...4 B5
Harr Gill DL8 ...58 A6
Harris Dr 9 DL10 ...41 E4
Harris St DL1 ...3 E4
Harrison Gr HG1 ...220 C4
Harrison St
Barnoldswick BB18 ...171 E1
York YO31 ...228 F6
Harrogate Coll HG1 ...219 D2
Harrogate Ctr The*
HG1 ...219 D3
Harrogate District Hospl
HG2 ...220 A2
Harrogate Gram Sch
HG2 ...222 C8
Harrogate Granby High Sch
HG1 ...220 A4
Harrogate Hill Jun Sch
DL3 ...3 D7
Harrogate Ladies Coll
HG1 ...219 C3
Harrogate Leisure Ctr
HG2 ...222 E7
Harrogate Rd
Bishop Monkton HG3 ...139 E5
Boroughbridge HG5 ...141 A2
Ferrensby HG5 ...162 E7
Green Hammerton YO26 ...164 B3
Kirkby Overblow HG3 ...222 D1
Knaresborough HG5 ...220 F5
Littlethorpe HG4 ...214 C1
Spofforth with Stockeld
LS22 ...180 A4
Weeton LS17 ...178 B2
Harrogate Rossett Acre CP
Sch HG2 ...222 C7
Harrogate RUFC HG1 ...219 F3
Harrogate Sta HG1 ...219 D2
Harrogate Town AFC
HG2 ...220 A2
Harrow Cliff La YO18 ...96 E4
Harrow Glade 5 YO30 ...225 A1
Harrow Rd TS5 ...6 E8
Harrowing Dr 2 YO21 ...208 C6
Harry Moor La YO8 ...197 B2
Harryfield La YO61 ...144 C7
Hart Hill Cres YO41 ...169 A2
Hartburn Village TS18 ...5 E8
Hartforth La DL10 ...20 E4
Hartington St 19 BB8 ...186 A3
Hartley La CA17 ...14 A7
Hartley Pl BD22 ...187 B6
Hartley Rd HG2 ...222 B7
Hartley St 12 BB18 ...172 A1
Hartlington Raikes
BD23 ...157 B8
Hartoft St YO10 ...228 D2
Hartwith Ave 3 HG3 ...138 A1
Hartwith Bank HG3 ...138 A1
Hartwith Cl HG3 ...219 A4
Hartwith Dr HG3 ...219 B4
Hartwith Gn 4 HG3 ...138 A1
Hartwith Way HG1 ...219 B4
Harvard Ct YO12 ...212 A8
Harvest Cl 10 WF8 ...201 C2
Harvest Croft LS29 ...176 B1
Harvest Way YO11 ...100 B7
Harwood Dale Rd YO13 ...54 A1
Hassacarr La YO19 ...184 F6
Hastings Cl 4 YO30 ...225 A1
Hastings Cres WF10 ...201 A4
Hatcase La 23 YO18 ...95 F7
Hatfield Ave TS5 ...6 E8
Hatfield Cl 8 YO30 ...224 E3
Hatfield Rd DL7 ...210 D3
Hatkill La YO41 ...169 B1
Hatterboard Dr YO12 ...212 C6
Hatters Cl YO23 ...230 B3
Haugh La YO8 ...202 F8
Haughton Comp Sch
DL1 ...3 E7
Haughton Rd
Darlington DL1 ...3 D6
York YO30 ...228 C7
Hauling La YO23 ...191 C8
Hauxley Ct LS29 ...218 D5
Havelock St TS17 ...6 B8
Haven The 5 LS25 ...195 F2
Havercroft Rd 15 YO14 ...127 A8
Havernook La HG4 ...86 A3
Havers Hill YO11 ...100 A6
Haverthwaites Dr
LS25 ...188 F1
Havertop La WF6 ...200 C1
Havikil La HG5 ...162 A5
Havikil Pk HG5 ...162 A6
Havilland Rd TS17 ...6 B6
Havre Pk 11 BB18 ...171 E1
Haw Gr BD23 ...154 B3
Haw Hill View WF6 ...200 A2
Haw La BD23 ...154 B3
Haw Pk 1 BD23 ...217 E8
Hawber Cote Dr BD20 ...174 C1
Hawber La BD20 ...174 C1
Hawdon Ave YO8 ...232 D5
Hawes CP Sch DL8 ...56 D4
Hawes Rd HG1 ...220 B4
Hawes Visitor Ctr*
DL8 ...56 D4
Hawke Garth 5 YO14 ...127 A8
Hawkridge Cl TS17 ...6 A3
Hawkshead Cl 3 YO24 ...230 B8
Hawkstone TS8 ...7 C4
Hawkstone Cl TS14 ...8 E6
Hawkswell La DL8 ...40 E1
Hawkswood 1 DL2 ...3 D1
Hawley St BB8 ...186 B3
Hawse Rd YO8 ...204 E8
Hawshaw Rd BD22 ...186 E7
Hawsker C of E Prim Sch
YO22 ...33 A7
Hawsker Intake Rd
YO22 ...32 F5
Hawsker La
Hawsker-cum-Stainsacre
YO22 ...13 F1
Whitby YO22 ...208 F6
Hawson Cl 9 YO11 ...100 B7
Hawthorn Ave
2 Knaresborough HG5 ...221 B7
Knottingley WF11 ...201 E2
Malton YO17 ...215 D5
Tadcaster LS24 ...189 D5
Hawthorn Cl
11 Addingham LS29 ...174 E4
3 Pickering YO18 ...96 A6
Stutton with Hazlewood
LS24 ...189 E5
Hawthorn Cres TS7 ...7 C6
Hawthorn Croft 6 LS24 189 D5
Hawthorn Dr
2 Topcliffe YO7 ...89 B1
Wilberfoss YO41 ...185 E5
Wistow YO8 ...198 A5
Hawthorn Garth DN14 ...202 F4
Hawthorn Gr YO31 ...228 E5
Hawthorn La YO18 ...96 A6
Hawthorn Spinney
YO32 ...225 E3
Hawthorn St 1 YO31 ...228 E5
Hawthorn Terr Ctr 2
YO32 ...225 D3
Hawthorn Terr N
YO32 ...225 D4
Hawthorn Terr S
YO32 ...225 D3
Hawthorn Way YO14 ...101 C1
Hawthorn Wlk 1 YO11 ...100 A7
Hawthorne Ave
12 Haxby YO32 ...166 E5
10 Scotton DL9 ...40 F2
Hawthorne Cl YO13 ...75 D7
Hawthorne Dr
Barnoldswick BB18 ...171 E2
Guisborough TS14 ...8 E6
Hawthorns
3 Riccall YO19 ...197 F8
2 Riccall YO19 ...197 F8
Hawthorns La BD23 ...133 B2
Hawthorns The
20 Glusburn BD20 ...187 E7
10 Great Ayton TS9 ...8 A2
Haxby Moor Rd YO32 ...166 F7
Haxby Rd Clifton YO31 ...225 D1
Middleton St George DL2 ...4 C5
New Earswick YO32 ...225 D6
York YO31 ...233 B4
Haxby Road Prim Sch
YO31 ...228 D7
Hay Brow Cl YO13 ...75 C5
Hay Brow Cres YO13 ...75 C5
Hay La YO13 ...75 C5
Hay-a-Park La HG5 ...221 D7
Hayfield Ave LS23 ...188 E8
Hayforth Cl YO30 ...225 A2
Haygate La YO18 ...95 F5
Haygill Nook BD23 ...174 B5
Hayhills La BD20 ...174 B2
Hayton Wood View
LS25 ...194 F8
Haywain The LS29 ...218 D3
Haywra Cres 6 HG1 ...219 E3
Haywra St HG1 ...219 D3
Hazel Bank HG5 ...162 D6
Hazel Cl Pannal HG3 ...222 C3
York YO32 ...225 D2
Hazel Ct 11 DL8 ...63 B3
Hazel Dr HG3 ...222 C3
Hazel Garth YO31 ...229 B7
Hazel Gr
Middlesbrough TS7 ...7 C6
Pontefract WF8 ...201 C1
Sutton BD20 ...187 E7
Hazel Grove Rd BD20 ...187 E7
Hazel Hill YO12 ...75 A2
Hazel Old La DN14 ...203 C2
Hazel Rd
2 Boroughbridge YO51 ...141 B4
2 Filey YO14 ...101 A4
Knottingley WF11 ...201 F1
Hazel Rise LS26 ...200 B5
Hazelheads La HG5 ...221 C8
Hazelmere Ct YO32 ...225 E3
Hazelnut Gr YO30 ...225 B2
Hazelwood Ave
Garforth LS25 ...194 D3
York YO10 ...229 D4
Hazing La DN14 ...207 B6
Hazler La BD23 ...157 D7
Headingley Cres 3 DL1 ...3 F6
Headingley Rd 7 DN6 ...206 E2
Headland Cl 30 YO32 ...166 E5
Headland La YO18 ...72 B4
Headlands La
Howgrave DL8 ...87 F2
Knottingley WF11 ...201 F2
Pontefract WF8 ...201 B1
Headlands Prim Sch
YO32 ...225 D8
Headlands Rd YO62 ...70 E2
Headlands The DL3 ...3 A5
Headley Cl 2 YO30 ...225 B1
Headley La LS23 ...188 F5
Heads Bank DL8 ...58 F3
Heads La BB18 ...186 A7
Heads Rd Newton YO18 ...51 B1
Pickering YO18 ...71 F8
Headwell La LS24 ...195 E7
Healaugh La YO26 ...181 F4
Healaugh Priory*
LS24 ...181 E1
Heald Brow BB18 ...171 D2
Heald St WF10 ...200 F4
Healdfield Rd WF10 ...201 A4
Healdwood Rd WF10 ...201 A4
Healey Gr YO31 ...228 F8
Healthfield Prim Sch
DL1 ...3 E5
Heath Cl 2 YO24 ...227 F2
Heath Cres BD20 ...173 E3
Heath Croft YO10 ...231 F7
Heath Dr
Boston Spa LS23 ...188 D8
7 Low Bradley BD20 ...173 E3
Heath Gr HG2 ...219 B1
Heath Moor Dr YO10 ...231 F8
Heath Pk 27 LS29 ...175 C2
Heath Ride YO32 ...167 B8
Heathcliff Gdns 5
YO12 ...212 C8
Heather Bank
13 Stamford Bridge YO41 ...168 D2
York YO10 ...229 C4
Heather Brow 16 BB18 ...172 B1
Heather Cl Selby YO8 ...232 C3
3 Whorlton DL6 ...25 D1
York YO32 ...226 A4
Heather Croft 4 YO31 ...225 E2
Heather Dr YO22 ...208 E3
Heather View BD23 ...217 B3
Heather Way 16 HG3 ...161 B3
Heatherdene LS24 ...189 E6
Heatherdene Rd 1 DL9 ...40 E4
Heathfield Dr HG5 ...221 C6
Heathfield Pk DL2 ...4 C5
Heathfield Rd 1 YO10 ...229 A3
Heathness Rd LS29 ...174 E5
Heathrow TS17 ...6 C7
Heathrow Cl 18 DL2 ...4 C4
Hebden Bank HG3 ...138 F4
Hebden Rd BD23 ...134 E2
Hebdon Rise 2 YO26 ...227 D4
Heber Dr BD23 ...172 A5
Heber's Ghyll Dr 24
LS29 ...175 C2
Heber's Gr 21 LS29 ...175 C2
Hebron Rd TS9 ...26 B7
Heck & Pollington Lake
DN14 ...207 E7
Heck Gill La HG3 ...160 A5
Heck La DN14 ...207 C7
Heckler Cl 3 HG4 ...214 C4
Heckler La HG4 ...214 C4
Heddon Gr TS17 ...6 A3
Hedley St TS14 ...8 F7
Height La BD23 ...174 C6
Height Lands La YO23 ...182 D6
Heights La BD20 ...174 A2
Helena St LS25 ...200 C8
Helks Brow LA2 ...128 E2
Hell Wath Gr HG4 ...214 A2
Hell Wath La
Littlethorpe HG4 ...214 A2
Hell Wath La *continued*
Markingfield Hall HG4 ...139 E6
Hellifield CP Sch
BD23 ...154 B3
Hellifield Rd BD23 ...155 A6
Hellifield Sta BD23 ...154 B4
Helmsdale YO24 ...230 C6
Helmsley Castle*
YO62 ...92 E6
Helmsley Cty Prim Sch
YO62 ...92 F7
Helmsley Dr TS14 ...8 E7
Helmsley Gr 16 YO32 ...166 D5
Helmsley Rd TS9 ...26 C7
Helmsley Way DL7 ...210 C2
Helperby & Myton La
YO61 ...142 A7
Helperby La YO51 ...141 C7
Helredale Gdns YO22 ...208 E4
Helredale Rd YO22 ...208 E4
Helston Rd WF6 ...200 A2
Helwath Rd YO13 ...53 D5
Helwith Rd DL11 ...38 E7
Hemingbrough CP Sch
YO8 ...198 F1
Hemingford Gdns TS15 ...5 E2
Hemishor Dr LS26 ...200 C8
Hemlington Hall Rd TS8 ...6 E5
Hemlington Hall Sch
TS8 ...6 E5
Hemlington Lake & Recn Ctr
TS8 ...6 E5
Hemlington Rd TS8 ...6 E5
Hemlock Ave YO31 ...225 E1
Hempbridge Cl YO8 ...232 A5
Hempbridge Rd YO8 ...232 A5
Hempland Ave YO31 ...228 F6
Hempland Dr YO31 ...229 A7
Hempland Inf Sch
YO31 ...229 A6
Hempland Jun Sch
YO31 ...229 B6
Hempland La YO31 ...229 A7
Hemsby Rd WF10 ...200 E3
Henbusk La LA2 ...130 A8
Hendon Garth YO30 ...225 A1
Henlow La YO60 ...147 B4
Henrietta Cl DL10 ...209 F8
Henrietta St YO22 ...208 E7
Henry Moore Jun Sch
WF10 ...200 E3
Henry St BD23 ...216 F1
Hensall CP Sch DN14 ...203 C1
Hensall Sta DN14 ...203 C1
Henshaws Coll HG1 ...220 B5
Henside La BD24 ...132 A5
Henside Rd BD24 ...132 B6
Henson Gr WF10 ...201 A4
Henwick Hall La YO8 ...232 C1
Hepton Hill YO17 ...120 F2
Hepworth's La DN14 ...204 C2
Herbert St 6 YO10 ...228 E3
Herberts Way YO31 ...228 F7
Hercules St DL1 ...3 E7
Herdborough Rd
YO11 ...100 A7
Herdsman Dr YO23 ...230 C3
Herdsman Rd 3 YO24 ...230 D8
Herdwick Cl 1 YO30 ...225 B1
Hereford Rd HG1 ...219 A2
Hergill La Baldersby HG4 ...88 C1
Kirby Hill DL11 ...19 F5
Kirkby Fleetham with Fencote
DL7 ...63 C8
Herisson Cl 20 YO18 ...95 F7
Heritage Ctr The* TS12 ...9 D6
Herman Wlk YO24 ...230 C8
Hermitage The* HG4 ...86 C8
Hermitage Way YO22 ...32 A5
Heron Ave YO24 ...230 C8
Heron Cl 1 Bedale DL8 ...63 B3
11 Thornton Dale YO18 ...96 D5
Heron Ct 6 Filey YO14 ...101 A4
6 Hunton DL9 ...40 F2
Heron Dr DL1 ...3 E5
Heron Gate TS14 ...8 D6
Heron La YO12 ...99 E6
Heron Rise YO32 ...225 F5
Heron Tree Cl DL8 ...60 D7
Heron Way YO17 ...215 D2
Herriot Way YO7 ...211 C4
Hertford Cl 4 YO11 ...100 A7
Hertford Vale C of E Prim
Sch YO12 ...99 D2
Hesketh Ave TS4 ...7 A7
Hesketh Bank YO10 ...229 D3
Heslaker La BD23 ...216 C1
Hesleden Ave TS5 ...6 D6
Hesley La BD24 ...153 A6
Heslin Cl 8 YO32 ...225 C8
Heslington Croft YO10 ...231 F7
Heslington Ct 2 YO10 ...229 B1
Heslington La
Heslington YO10 ...229 A1
York YO10 ...231 E8
Heslington Prim Sch
YO10 ...229 C1
Heslington Rd YO10 ...228 E3
Hessay Pl 2 YO26 ...227 A3
Hetherton St YO30 ...233 A3
Hetton Garth 18 DL8 ...60 D5
Hewitson Rd DL1 ...3 E5
Hewitts La BD20 ...172 F2
Hewley Ave YO10 ...229 A4
Hewley Dr 9 YO13 ...99 A7
Heworth YO31 ...229 A6
Heworth ARLFC YO31 ...229 A8

Heworth C of E Prim Sch YO31 228 F6
Heworth Dr YO21 208 B6
Heworth Gn YO31 233 C4
Heworth Hall Dr YO31 228 F6
Heworth Pl YO31 228 F6
Heworth Rd YO31 228 F6
Heyford Rd YO7 115 B1
Heygate Bank YO18 49 F3
Heygate La LS23 188 F6
Heyshaw Rd HG3 159 C8
Heythrop Dr
Guisborough TS14 8 F6
Middlesbrough TS5 6 D7
Heywood Rd HG2 219 C1
Hibernia St YO12 212 E5
Hicks La LS26 200 B6
Hickstead Ct 16 DL1 3 F6
Hidcote Gdns TS17 6 A4
High Back Side YO18 95 E8
High Bank
Ampleforth YO62 92 B2
Bradleys Both BD20 173 E3
5 Threshfield BD23 134 D2
High Bank Cl 7 LS29 174 F4
High Barmer YO13 75 B7
High Bentham CP Sch LA2 129 B8
High Bond End HG5 221 A7
High Bradley La BD20 173 E4
High Catton Rd YO41 185 D8
High Church Wynd TS16 5 D3
High Cleugh HG4 214 A4
High Coniscliffe C of E Sch DL2 2 C6
High Cragwell YO21 31 F7
High Crest 6 HG3 137 C4
High Croft 7 YO14 126 F8
High Croft Way 5 BD20 173 E1
High Eggborough La DN14 203 A1
High Fell Cl BD24 131 D1
High Field YO10 229 D4
High Fold BB18 186 A7
High Garth
Eastfield YO11 100 A7
Richmond DL10 209 B8
High Gill Rd TS7 7 D6
High Gn Catterick DL10 41 D4
Hebden BD23 135 A2
High Green Dr BD20 174 B1
High Hill Gr St 14 BD24 131 D2
High Hill La BD24 131 E2
High La Beadlam YO62 93 C8
Birstwith HG3 160 C5
Cowling BD22 187 A4
Cropton YO18 71 C4
Dalby-cum-Skewsby YO60 119 A2
Dalton DL11 19 D7
Fylingdales YO22 33 C5
Gillamoor YO62 70 A6
Grassington BD23 134 E3
Grinton DL11 37 D4
Hawes DL8 56 F4
Howsham YO60 147 B1
Kirby Sigston DL6 44 E1
Leake DL6 65 E6
Maltby TS15 6 C4
Muston YO14 100 F1
Myton-on-Swale YO61 142 B6
Newsham DL11 18 G7
Reeth, Fremington & Healaugh DL11 37 F5
Spofforth with Stockeld HG3 179 C4
Sutton upon Derwent YO41 185 D3
Thirlby YO7 90 D6
Thornton Watlass DL8 62 C2
West Scrafton DL8 83 F6
West Witton DL8 59 D2
High Leir La YO7 67 D1
High Market Pl 27 YO62 70 B1
High Mdw
Gowdall DN14 204 A1
Selby YO8 232 B6
High Mill Dr 1 YO12 75 E5
High Mill La LS29 175 A5
High Moor Edge YO12 212 A7
High Moor La
Boroughbridge HG5 141 A2
Brearton HG3 161 F8
Newton-on-Ouse YO30 165 C8
Scotton HG5 162 A5
High Moor Rd
North Rigton HG3 178 A5
Skelton YO51 140 F7
High Moor Way 11 YO11 100 A6
High Newbiggin St YO31 233 B3
High Oaks YO31 229 B7
High Ousegate YO1 233 B2
High Peak TS14 8 F5
High Peter La HG3 140 A3
High Petergate YO1 233 B3
High Rd LA2 128 F5
High Riding Aske DL10 20 D1
Richmond DL10 209 C8
High Rifts TS8 6 E5
High Riggs La YO18 96 C3
High Row
Bugthorpe YO41 169 D4
Caldwell DL11 1 C4
Darlington DL1 3 C5
Melsonby DL10 20 F7
High Skellgate 7 HG4 214 C5
High St Airmyn DN14 205 E3
Ampleforth YO62 92 C3
Aske DL10 20 E2
Austwick LA2 130 E7
Barmby on the Marsh DN14 205 A7
Barnby YO21 12 C4
Barton-le-Street YO17 120 E5
Beadlam YO62 93 D7
Boosbeck TS12 9 D8
6 Boroughbridge YO51 141 B5
Boston Spa LS23 188 E8
Boston Spa LS23 188 F7
Bramham LS23 188 E5
Buckton/Bempton YO13 97 D6
Burniston YO13 75 C8
Burton in Lonsdale LA6 102 F3
Carlton DN14 204 C2
Castleford WF10 200 E4
Catterick DL10 41 D5
Cawood YO8 197 B8
Cottam YO25 150 E5
Cropton YO18 71 B4
Danby YO21 29 A6
Eaglescliffe TS15 5 D4
13 Eastfield YO11 100 A6
Gargrave BD23 155 D1
Glaisdale YO21 30 D4
Glusburn BD20 187 E6
Great Ayton TS9 7 F1
Great Broughton TS9 26 E4
Hampsthwaite HG3 160 F5
Harrogate HG2 220 C4
4 Helmsley YO62 92 F6
Heslerton YO17 123 F6
Hinderwell TS13 11 F7
Hovingham YO62 119 E6
Husthwaite YO61 117 B6
Ingleton LA6 103 D4
Kippax LS25 194 D1
Kirby Grindalythe YO17 149 D8
5 Knaresborough HG5 221 B5
Knottingley WF11 201 E5
Langtoft YO25 151 C8
Lastingham YO62 70 E5
9 Leyburn DL8 60 D5
Lingdale TS12 9 F7
Lockwood TS12 10 A5
Markington with Wallerthwaite HG3 139 C4
Mickleby TS13 12 A4
Middlesbrough TS7 7 C8
Newton Mulgrave TS13 11 E4
Normanton South WF6 200 A1
Northallerton DL7 210 D6
Norton DN6 206 E2
Old Byland & Scawton YO62 92 A4
Oldstead YO7 91 E5
Pateley Bridge HG3 137 B4
Rawcliffe DN14 205 A1
Rillington YO17 122 F5
Scalby YO13 75 D5
6 Settle BD24 131 E2
Settrington YO17 122 F1
Sherburn YO17 124 D7
Skipton BD23 217 A4
Slingsby YO62 120 B5
Snainton YO13 98 A5
Snaith DN14 204 B1
South Milford LS25 195 E2
Spofforth HG3 179 E5
3 Staithes TS13 13 K2
Stillington YO61 144 B6
Stokesley TS9 26 C7
Swinton YO17 121 B4
Tadcaster LS24 189 E6
Thornton Dale YO18 96 E6
Thornton-le-Clay YO60 146 A4
Wharram YO17 149 A6
Whitby YO21 208 B3
Whixley YO26 164 A4
Whorlton DL6 45 D8
Wombleton YO62 93 E7
Wrelton YO18 71 C1
High St Agnesgate HG4 214 C5
High Stakesby Rd YO21 208 A6
High Stell DL2 4 C4
High Town Bank Rd YO7 91 C5
High Trace DL6 210 E2
High Trees Ct LS25 195 F4
High Trees Sch LS23 188 F7
High View HG3 160 F8
High Wheatley LS29 218 E3
High Wlk YO12 212 E7
High Wood LS29 218 F3
Highbank Gr 1 HG2 220 D4
Highbury Ave TS5 6 F8
Highcliff Rd TS14 8 E4
Highcliffe Ct YO30 228 A6
Highcroft
Collingham LS22 188 A8
9 Grassington BD23 134 E3
Highdale Ave 5 YO12 212 D8
Highdale Rd YO12 212 E7
Higher Hartley St 2 BD20 187 D7
Higher Lodge St 1 BD20 187 D7
Higher Rd BD23 152 F4
Higherlands Cl BD23 155 D1
Highfield
Pollington DN14 207 F7
Scarborough YO12 212 E4
Highfield Ave WF8 201 D2
Highfield Cl YO25 126 A4
Highfield Cres YO8 198 B5
Highfield Ct YO8 232 B1
Highfield Dr
Allerton Bywater WF10 200 C7
Garforth LS25 194 C3
Highfield Gn
Allerton Bywater WF10 200 C7
Sherburn in Elmet LS25 195 F3
Highfield Gr WF10 200 C7
Highfield La
Barwick in Elmet & Scholes LS15 194 B7
Fangfoss YO41 169 B1
Gillamoor YO62 69 F5
Huddleston with Newthorpe LS25 195 B2
Nawton YO62 69 C2
Scagglethorpe YO17 122 E2
Womersley DN6 206 D5
Highfield Pl 1 WF10 200 D7
Highfield Rd
Aberford LS25 194 F8
29 Earby BB18 172 A1
Malton YO17 215 C5
Ripon HG4 214 B3
Whitby YO21 208 A7
Highfield View 3 YO8 198 B4
Highfield Villas LS25 195 F3
Highfields La YO7 115 A1
Highgate Balne DN14 207 D6
Glusburn BD20 187 D8
Highgate Pk HG1 219 F3
Highgrove Cl 7 YO30 224 E3
Highland Cl 9 WF8 201 C1
Highlands Ave 5 YO32 167 B7
Highlands Cl YO14 101 B1
Highmoor Cl YO24 230 D8
Highmoor Rd
Darlington DL1 3 F4
York YO24 230 D8
Highthorn Rd YO31 225 E2
Highthorne La YO61 117 B5
Highway BD24 131 E3
Hilbeck Gr YO31 229 B6
Hilbra Ave YO32 225 D6
Hilda St 6 Selby YO8 232 C5
3 York YO10 228 E3
Hildenley Cl 6 YO12 212 B5
Hilderthorpe TS7 7 C6
Hildewell 3 TS13 11 F7
Hildyard Cl TS9 26 C8
Hill Bank HG5 163 B7
Hill Cl DL11 38 B6
Hill Crest YO19 167 F1
Hill Crest Gdns YO24 227 F1
Hill End La BD22 186 F5
Hill Field YO8 232 B8
Hill Foot La HG3 222 B2
Hill House La DL2 4 C8
Hill La BB8 186 B4
Hill Rd WF10 200 F3
Hill Rise
Middleton St George DL2 4 D3
Skipton BD23 216 E5
Hill Rise Ave HG2 222 B8
Hill Rise Cl HG2 222 B8
Hill Side DL2 3 A3
Hill St
6 Barnoldswick BB18 171 E1
York YO24 227 E3
Hill The DL8 56 D4
Hill Top
24 Burley in Warfedale LS29 176 C1
Castleford WF10 200 C4
Ilkley LS29 218 A2
Knottingley WF11 201 F2
Hill Top Ave HG1 219 D6
Hill Top Cl
Embsay BD23 217 C8
Harrogate HG1 219 D6
Stutton with Hazlewood LS24 189 D4
Hill Top Cres HG1 219 D6
Hill Top Ct DL7 22 C3
Hill Top Dr HG1 219 D6
Hill Top Gr HG1 219 E6
Hill Top La Earby BB18 172 A1
Pannal HG3 222 A4
Hill Top Mount HG1 219 D6
Hill Top Rd
Harrogate HG1 219 D6
4 Wistow YO8 197 D6
Hill Top Rise HG1 219 E6
Hill Top View HG3 159 F8
Hill Top Wlk HG1 219 D6
Hill View
Langthorpe YO51 141 A6
Stillington YO61 144 C6
York YO31 229 C7
Hillam Comm La LS25 202 B7
Hillam Hall La 4 LS25 202 A7
Hillam Hall View 3 LS25 202 A7
Hillam La
Burton Salmon LS25 201 F7
Hillam LS25 202 A7
Hillam Rd YO8 202 F8
Hillary Garth 9 YO26 227 E4
Hillbank Gr HG1 220 D4
Hillbank Rd HG1 220 D4
Hillbank View HG1 220 C4
Hillcrest
8 Monk Fryston LS25 202 A8
Tadcaster LS24 189 D5
Hillcrest Ave
Newby & Scalby YO12 75 E5
Hillcrest Ave *continued*
Poppleton YO26 224 A2
Silsden BD20 174 C1
Hillcrest Cl WF10 201 B3
Hillcrest Ct 2 LS24 189 D5
Hillcrest Dr
Castleford WF10 201 B3
Loftus TS13 10 D8
Hillcrest Gdns YO51 141 A7
Hillcrest Gr 2 YO12 75 E5
Hillcrest Mount WF10 201 B3
Hillgarth WF11 201 F2
Hillgarth Ct 4 YO41 185 B2
Hillhouse DL2 4 C7
Hilliam Hall Cl 5 LS25 202 A7
Hillingdon Rd TS4 7 B8
Hillocks La TS12 10 A5
Hills La BD23 155 E5
Hillsborough Terr 5 YO30 228 C7
Hillshaw Parkway HG4 214 D5
Hillside Byram WF11 201 E4
Follifoot HG3 223 F4
3 Ingleby Arncliffe DL6 45 A7
Hillside Cl
18 Addingham LS29 174 F4
9 Monk Fryston LS25 202 A8
Threshfield BD23 134 B3
Hillside Cres BD23 217 C3
Hillside Dr BD23 134 B3
Hillside Gdns
Langtoft YO25 151 D5
Scarborough YO12 212 E1
Hillside Rd HG3 222 E3
Hillside Way YO17 150 B8
Hilltop Cres DL9 40 E4
Hilton Cl DL6 210 E8
Hilton Gn DL6 210 D8
Hilton Grange DL6 210 E8
Hilton La 7 HG5 221 A6
Hilton Rd TS9 6 F1
Hilton Sq DL6 210 E8
Hincks Hall La HG3 139 C3
Hinderwell CP Sch YO12 212 D2
Hinderwell La
Hinderwell TS13 11 E8
Staithes TS13 13 K1
Hinderwell Pl YO12 212 E2
Hinderwell Rd YO12 212 E1
Hindle Dr 39 YO14 101 B3
Hinsley La DN14 204 C2
Hinton Ave 1 YO24 230 C8
Hinton Cl 9 WF8 201 C2
Hinton La WF11 201 D3
Hipswell C of E Prim Sch DL9 209 F1
Hipswell Rd DL9 209 E1
Hipswell Rd W DL9 209 C1
Hird Ave 22 DL8 63 A2
Hird Rd TS15 5 D2
Hirds Yd 2 BD23 216 F3
Hirst Courtney & Temple Hirst CP Sch YO8 203 E3
Hirst La HG3 160 E5
Hirst Rd YO8 204 A3
Hirst St WF10 200 C8
Hirstead Gdns YO12 212 B8
Hirstead Rd YO12 212 B8
Hob Cote La BD22 187 F1
Hob Moor Dr YO24 227 E2
Hob Moor Inf Sch YO24 227 D2
Hob Moor Jun Sch YO24 227 E2
Hobart Rd WF10 201 B5
Hobb Nook La LS21 176 D4
Hobbs Cl DL9 209 C2
Hobgate YO24 227 D3
Hobmoor Terr YO24 227 F1
Hobson Cl YO23 230 B1
Hodge La WF8 206 B3
Hodgson Fold LS29 174 E5
Hodgson Hill YO13 54 B4
Hodgson La YO26 182 F8
Hodgson's La LS25 196 A5
Hogg La YO17 148 E6
Holbeck Ave
Middlesbrough TS5 6 E6
Scarborough YO11 213 B2
Holbeck Cl YO11 213 B2
Holbeck Hill YO11 213 B1
Holbeck Rd YO11 213 A2
Holbecks La YO51 141 F3
Holburns Croft 3 YO10 229 B1
Holden Gdns YO8 197 D2
Hole House La BB7 152 B2
Hole La BD20 174 A2
Holes La WF11 201 E2
Holgate DL6 45 E8
Holgate Bank HG5 163 A8
Holgate Bridge Gdn 7 YO24 228 A3
Holgate Cl YO17 215 C5
Holgate Lodge Dr YO26 227 E4
Holgate Rd YO24 233 A1
Holl Gate DL8 59 E3
Hollicarrs Cl YO19 192 A2
Hollies The YO8 198 C4
Hollin Gate LS21 176 E1
Hollin Hall Dr LS29 175 C2
Hollin La LA2 129 F6
Hollin Top La YO21 29 C7
Hollings The LS26 200 A6
Hollington St 14 BB8 186 A3
Hollingwood Gate 31 LS29 175 C2
Hollingwood Rise 32 LS29 175 C2
Hollinhurst Brow LA2 128 F2
Hollins DL8 60 B3
Hollins Beck Cl LS25 200 D8
Hollins Cl HG3 161 A5
Hollins Cres HG1 219 C4
Hollins Gr WF10 200 C7
Hollins Hall HG3 161 A4
Hollins La Firby DL8 63 B1
Hampsthwaite HG3 161 A4
Melmerby HG4 114 B8
Middleton Quernhow HG4 88 C1
Rosedale East Side YO18 49 D4
Hollins Mews HG1 219 C4
Hollins Rd
10 Barnoldswick BB18 171 D1
Harrogate HG1 219 C4
Hollis Cres YO32 167 B6
Hollow Gill Brow BD24 153 C5
Hollow Moor La DL8 62 E7
Holly Bank Gr 3 YO24 227 F2
Holly Bank Rd YO24 227 F2
Holly Cl
Acaster Malbis YO23 191 C8
Full Sutton YO41 169 A2
Thirsk YO7 211 B2
Wrelton YO18 71 C1
Holly Ct 11 HG5 221 B6
Holly Garth 1 YO61 115 F1
Holly Garth Cl TS9 7 F1
Holly Gr Selby YO8 232 B3
8 Thorpe Willoughby YO8 197 B2
Holly Pk LS17 178 B3
Holly Rd 10 Bedale DL8 63 B3
Boston Spa LS23 188 D8
Holly Tree Croft 2 YO19 184 F7
Holly Tree Ct 2 YO21 208 B6
Holly Tree Garth YO32 167 E3
Holly Tree La
Dunnington YO19 184 F7
Haxby YO32 225 D8
Holly Wlk YO12 212 D7
Hollybush Ave TS17 6 B5
Hollybush Gn LS22 188 B8
Hollygarth La DN14 202 D4
Hollyhurst Rd DL3 3 C6
Hollyrood Rd YO30 224 E3
Hollywalk Ave TS6 7 E8
Hollywood YO8 232 B7
Holm Hill YO13 54 C2
Holm La LA2 130 E6
Holme Cl Earby BB18 186 A8
23 Sutton BD20 187 E7
Holme Cres BB8 186 A2
Holme Croft 1 BD23 134 D2
Holme Farm La LS23 188 A5
Holme Green Rd YO23 190 F4
Holme Hill 2 YO11 100 A6
Holme Hill La YO10 184 C4
Holme Ings LS29 175 B4
Holme La
Glusburn BD20 187 E7
Halton East BD23 174 B8
Newbiggin DL8 58 E1
Rudby TS9 25 E7
Selby YO8 232 D6
Holme St 17 BB8 186 A3
Holme The TS9 26 E4
Holmebeck La HG4 88 B1
Holmefield Cl 3 YO8 232 A1
Holmefield Ct 2 YO8 232 A1
Holmefield La YO10 229 A1
Holmefield Rd
Glusburn BD20 187 E7
Ripon HG4 214 C3
Holmefields Rd TS6 7 E8
Holmes Dr 2 YO19 192 A1
Holmes House* YO8 199 B3
Holmfield HG4 112 D7
Holmfield Cl WF8 201 C2
Holmfield Cres HG4 214 C3
Holmfield La WF8 201 C2
Holmstead Ave YO21 208 A5
Holmtree La HG4 113 B8
Holmwood Ave TS5 6 F8
Holray Pk DN14 204 C2
Holroyd Ave YO31 229 A5
Holtby Gr YO12 212 D5
Holtby La Holtby YO19 167 D1
Stockton on the Forest YO32 226 F2
Holy Family RC High Sch DN14 204 C3
Holy Family RC Prim Sch DL3 3 B6
Holy Family RC Sch WF8 201 D1
Holy Rood La LS25 201 C8
Holy Trinity C of E Inf Sch HG4 214 B6
Holy Trinity Prim Sch HG4 214 B5
Holyrood Ave DL3 3 A5
Holystone Dr TS17 6 A4
Holywell Gn TS16 5 E5
Holywell La
Castleford WF10 201 A3
North Cowton DL7 22 C2
Home Farm Cl LA2 128 A6

Home Office Emergency Planning Coll YO61 . .143 D6
Homefield Cl YO23 . . . .230 A2
Homestead Cl
Eggborough DN14 . . . . . . .203 A2
2 York YO32 . . . . .225 F1
Homestead Rd HG1 . . .219 E2
Honey Pot 5 YO8 . . . . .199 D7
Honey Pot Rd 2 DL10 . . . .41 C6
Honeypot La DL3 . . . . .3 C7
Honeysuckle Cl
Romanby DL7 . . . . .210 C1
Selby YO8 . . . . .232 C2
Honister Gr TS5 . . . . .6 D7
Hood La YO13 . . . . .54 D2
Hoodstorth La HG3 . . . .158 F6
Hook La DN14 . . . . .205 F4
Hook Pasture La
DN14 . . . . .205 F1
Hookstone Ave HG2 . . .222 E7
Hookstone Chase
HG2 . . . . .220 D2
Hookstone Chase CP Sch
HG2 . . . . .220 D2
Hookstone Cl HG2 . . . .220 C2
Hookstone Dr HG2 . . . .223 A8
Hookstone Garth HG3 . .159 E5
Hookstone Grange Ct 3
HG2 . . . . .220 C2
Hookstone Grange Way 2
HG2 . . . . .220 C2
Hookstone Oval 7 HG2 220 B1
Hookstone Pk HG2 . . . .220 D2
Hookstone Rd HG2 . . . .222 E7
Hookstone Way HG2 . . .220 D2
Hookstone Wood Rd
9 Harrogate HG2 . . . . . .220 B1
Harrogate HG2 . . . . .223 B8
Hope St 30 Filey YO14 . . .101 B3
Knaresborough HG5 . . . . .221 B5
Scarborough YO12 . . . . . .213 A6
York YO10 . . . . .233 C1
Hopetown La DL3 . . . . . . .3 C6
Hopgrove La N YO32 . .226 C3
Hopgrove La S YO32 . .226 E3
Hopper Hill Rd YO11 . . . .99 F6
Hopper La LS21 . . . . . . .159 C2
Hopperton St HG5 . . . .163 E4
Hopps's Rd 6 BD20 . . . .187 E8
Horn La BD20 . . . . .174 B3
Hornbeam Cres HG2 . . .222 F8
Hornbeam Park Ave
HG2 . . . . .222 F7
Hornbeam Park Sta
HG2 . . . . .222 F7
Hornbeam Sq N HG2 . .223 A7
Hornbeam Sq S HG2 . .223 A7
Hornbeam Sq W HG2 . .222 F7
Hornblower Cl 5 HG4 . .113 D2
Hornby Castle★ DL8 . . . .62 C8
Hornby Cl 1 DL2 . . . . .3 E1
Hornby Rd
Appleton Wiske DL6 . . . . . .24 A3
Roeburndale LA2 . . . . . . .128 A2
Wray-with-Botton LA2 . . . .128 A6
Horndale Rd 5 YO14 . . .101 B4
Horne Rd DL9 . . . . .40 F4
Horner Ave YO61 . . . . . .144 A5
Horner Cl YO61 . . . . . . .144 A5
Horner St YO30 . . . . . . .228 B7
Hornsea Rd TS8 . . . . .6 E5
Hornsey Garth 25 YO32 .166 E5
Horse Bell Gate LA6 . . . .103 D4
Horse Course La YO17 .122 E1
Horse Mill La HG3 . . . .139 D5
Horsefair 2 YO51 . . . . . .141 B5
Horseman Ave YO23 . . .230 A3
Horseman Cl 2 YO23 . . .230 A3
Horseman Dr YO23 . . . .230 A3
Horseman La YO23 . . . .230 A3
Horsemarket Rd YO17 .215 B4
Horseshoe Cave★
BD24 . . . . .132 A3
Horseshoe The YO24 . .230 E7
Horseway Gn YO18 . . . . .49 D4
Horsfield Way YO19 . . .184 F7
Horsman Ave YO10 . . . .233 C1
Horton in Ribblesdale C of E Prim Sch BD24 . . . . .105 D3
Horton in Ribbleside Sta
BD24 . . . . .105 C3
Hospital Fields Rd
YO10 . . . . .228 D1
Hospital La YO8 . . . . . . .197 B4
Hospital Rd YO17 . . . . .215 B4
Hospitum The★ YO30 . .233 A3
Hostess La YO18 . . . . . . .72 E4
Hotham Ave YO26 . . . . .227 B2
Hothfield Street Jun Sch
BD20 . . . . .174 C1
Houghton Ave WF11 . . .201 D2
Houndgate DL1 . . . . .3 C5
Houndsway 6 YO24 . . . .230 B8
House of Correction Mus★
HG4 . . . . .214 D5
Hovingham C of E Prim Sch
YO62 . . . . .119 E6
Hovingham Dr YO12 . . .212 B4
Hovingham Hall★
YO62 . . . . .119 E6
How Hill Rd HG4 . . . . . .139 B6
How Stean Gorge★
HG3 . . . . .110 B4
Howard Dr YO30 . . . . . .224 E2
Howard Link YO30 . . . .224 D2
Howard Rd
Catterick Garrison DL9 . . .209 E1
Towthorpe YO32 . . . . .167 B6
Howard St
3 Scarborough YO12 . . . .213 A7
York YO10 . . . . .228 D2
Howden Dike TS15 . . . . . .5 E2
Howden La YO19 . . . . . .231 E1
Howden Rd
4 Barlby YO8 . . . . .198 B4
Romanby DL7 . . . . .210 B2
Silsden BD20 . . . . .174 C1
Howdenshire Way
DN14 . . . . .205 F6
Howdlands La HG4 . . . .140 E7
Howe Ave DL10 . . . . .41 E3
Howe Bank YO21 . . . . . . .29 B7
Howe End YO62 . . . . .70 B1
Howe Field Rd YO26 . . .142 A2
Howe Hill Bank TS8 . . . . .7 B2
Howe Hill Cl YO26 . . . . .227 E4
Howe Hill La DL10 . . . . . .41 C6
Howe Hill Rd YO26 . . . .227 E4
Howe La YO41 . . . . .170 A5
Howe Rd Malton YO17 . .122 A6
Norton YO17 . . . . .215 E3
Howe St YO24 . . . . .227 D3
Howes Rd 8 YO14 . . . . .127 A8
Howgate DL8 . . . . .57 F6
Howgill La
Barden BD23 . . . . .157 E6
Rimington BB7 . . . . .171 A1
Howhill Quarry Rd
HG3 . . . . .178 B7
Howhill Rd HG3 . . . . . . .178 B8
Howker La YO61 . . . . . .116 F2
Howl Gate YO41 . . . . . . .185 E8
Howlbeck Rd TS14 . . . . . .8 E7
Howldale La
Appleton-le-Moors YO62 . . .70 F4
3 Beadlam YO62 . . . . .93 D7
Howlgate La YO21 . . . . . .13 A1
Howsham Gates★
YO60 . . . . .146 F2
Howsham Hall Prep Sch
YO60 . . . . .146 F2
Howson La BD24 . . . . . .131 E4
Hoxton Rd YO12 . . . . . .212 F6
Hoylake Rd TS4 . . . . .6 F8
Hoylake Way TS16 . . . . . .5 E4
Hubert St 2 YO23 . . . . .228 B1
Huby Prim Sch YO61 . .144 A4
Huby Rd YO61 . . . . . . .144 B3
Hudgin La Lockton YO18 . .72 E4
Wykeham YO13 . . . . .98 D4
Hudson Cl
Malton YO17 . . . . .215 C6
Stamford Bridge YO41 . . .168 D2
2 Tadcaster LS24 . . . . . .189 E6
Hudson Cres 2 YO30 . . .228 A7
Hudson St
Whitby YO21 . . . . .208 D7
6 York YO30 . . . . .228 C7
Hudson View 1 LS24 . . .189 E6
Hudson Way LS24 . . . . .189 E6
Hugden Cl YO18 . . . . . . .96 A6
Hugden Way YO17 . . . .215 F4
Huggate Hill YO17 . . . .170 E7
Hugh Field La YO8 . . . .199 A8
Hugh Field North La
YO8 . . . . .193 A1
Hugh St WF10 . . . . .200 E4
Hull Rd Cliffe YO8 . . . . .198 E2
Hemingbrough YO8 . . . . .199 B1
Heslington YO19 . . . . . . .229 E3
Humber Dr 5 YO32 . . . .167 B6
Humber Rd TS17 . . . . .6 B7
Hummersknott Ave DL3 . .3 A5
Hummersknott Comp Sch
DL3 . . . . .3 A4
Humphrey Balk La
YO7 . . . . .114 D8
Humphrey Hill DL8 . . . . .58 D1
Hundale Rd 5 TS15 . . . . .25 C5
Hunday Field Rd YO51 .141 E2
Hundens Day Hospl DL1 . .3 E5
Hundens La DL1 . . . . .3 D6
Hungate
Bishop Monkton HG3 . . . .140 A5
Brompton YO13 . . . . .98 C5
Pickering YO18 . . . . .95 F6
York YO1 . . . . .233 C2
Hungate Cl LS24 . . . . . .195 D8
Hungate Ct 11 YO14 . . . .126 F8
Hungate Cty Prim Sch
LS25 . . . . .195 F4
Hungate La YO14 . . . . .126 F8
Hungate Rd LS25 . . . . .195 F4
Hunger Hill LS29 . . . . . .218 C7
Hungerhill La YO62 . . . . .93 F6
Hunmanby CP Sch
YO14 . . . . .126 F8
Hunmanby Rd
Burton Fleming YO25 . . . .126 E3
Reighton YO14 . . . . .127 C6
Hunmanby St YO14 . . . .100 F2
Hunmanby Sta YO14 . . .127 A7
Hunt Ct YO31 . . . . .233 C3
Hunt House Rd YO22 . . . .51 B6
Hunt St WF10 . . . . .200 D4
Hunter St 8 YO21 . . . . .208 D7
Hunters Cl
Dunnington YO19 . . . . . . .184 E7
19 Easingwold YO61 . . . . .143 C8
10 Haxby YO32 . . . . .225 C8
4 Hurworth-on-Tees DL2 . . . .3 D1
Hunters Croft BD23 . . . .156 F1
Hunters Gn DL2 . . . . .4 C3
Hunters Ride DL6 . . . . . .24 B3
Hunters Row 6 YO51 . . .141 B4
Hunters Way
Norton YO17 . . . . .215 D2
Selby YO8 . . . . .232 B4
York YO24 . . . . .230 F7
Hunters Wlk
Barlow YO8 . . . . .204 D7
Kirk Deighton LS22 . . . . . .180 C4
Hunters Wood Way 21
YO19 . . . . .184 F7
Huntington Prim Sch
YO32 . . . . .225 F4
Huntington Rd YO31 . . .233 C4
Huntington Sch YO32 . .225 E3
Hunton CP Sch DL8 . . . .61 F7
Hunton Rd DL8 . . . . .40 E1
Huntriss Row YO11 . . . .213 A6
Huntsmans La YO23 . . .168 C2
Huntsman's Wlk YO24 .227 B1
Hurdle Cl YO17 . . . . . . .215 E2
Hurgill Rd DL10 . . . . . .209 A7
Hurn Rd YO61 . . . . .144 A4
Hurns La YO30 . . . . . . .224 A7
Hurrell La YO18 . . . . .96 E5
Hurricane Way YO30 . . .224 E3
Hurrs Rd 3 BD23 . . . . . .217 B4
Hurst Hill HG3 . . . . .159 F7
Hurstleigh Terr HG1 . . .220 A3
Hurst's Yd YO1 . . . . . . .233 C2
Hurworth Comp Sch
DL2 . . . . .22 D8
Hurworth Cty Inf Sch
DL2 . . . . .3 E1
Hurworth House Sch
DL2 . . . . .3 E1
Hurworth Rd
Hurworth DL2 . . . . .3 F1
Hurworth-on-Tees DL2 . . . .22 D8
Neasham DL2 . . . . .4 A1
Hussars Ct 6 YO12 . . . . .75 F5
Husthwaite C of E Prim Sch
YO61 . . . . .117 B5
Husthwaite Rd
Coxwold YO61 . . . . .117 D7
Easingwold YO61 . . . . . . .117 B2
Hutchinson Dr DL6 . . . .210 E3
Hutchinson St 1 YO8 . .232 B6
Hutton Ave DL1 . . . . .3 E7
Hutton Bank
3 Hutton Rudby TS15 . . . .25 D5
Ripon HG4 . . . . .214 D7
Hutton Cl YO26 . . . . . . .224 A2
Hutton Cross Rd YO13 . .98 E8
Hutton La
Guisborough TS14 . . . . .8 E5
Hutton Conyers HG4 . . . . .114 A4
Sharow HG4 . . . . .214 E8
Hutton Rae La YO7 . . . .116 D7
Hutton Rudby CP Sch
TS15 . . . . .25 C5
Hutton St YO26 . . . . . . .182 A5
Hutton View Rd HG4 . . .214 C7
Hutton Village Rd TS14 . . .8 D5
Hutton's Mon★ DL11 . . .39 C6
Hutts La HG4 . . . . .112 C7
Hyde Park Rd
Harrogate HG1 . . . . .219 E3
Knaresborough HG5 . . . . .221 B8
Hydro Cl LS29 . . . . .218 F3
Hyrst Gr YO31 . . . . .228 E6

I

Ian St TS17 . . . . .6 B8
I'anson Cl DL8 . . . . .60 D6
I'anson Rd DL10 . . . . . .209 D7
Ibbetson Cl 16 HG4 . . . . . .86 C3
Iburndale La YO22 . . . . . .32 A6
Iddison Dr DL8 . . . . .63 A2
Ikin Way YO32 . . . . .225 F6
Iles La HG5 . . . . .221 B5
Ilkeston Ave DN14 . . . . .205 F3
Ilkley Gr TS14 . . . . .8 E5
Ilkley Gram Sch LS29 . .218 C3
Ilkley Hall Mews 5
LS29 . . . . .218 B3
Ilkley Hall Pk 4 LS29 . .218 B3
Ilkley Rd
Addingham LS29 . . . . . . .175 A4
Ilkley LS29 . . . . .176 C1
Ilkley Sch LS29 . . . . . . .218 E5
Ilkley Sta LS29 . . . . . . .218 B4
Ilkley Swimming Baths
LS29 . . . . .218 C5
Ilton Bank HG4 . . . . .85 E1
Ilton Garth YO30 . . . . . .225 A2
Imperial Athletic Club
HG2 . . . . .222 F8
Imperial Ave TS17 . . . . . . .6 B8
In Moor La HG3 . . . . . . .109 F6
Ingdale Howl YO62 . . . . .92 C7
Ingdale La YO7 . . . . .66 C3
Ingfield La BD24 . . . . . .131 D2
Ingham Cl YO22 . . . . .32 A6
Ingleborough Ave
YO10 . . . . .229 B4
Ingleborough Dr 4
BB18 . . . . .171 D1
Ingleborough Park Cl
LA6 . . . . .103 D3
Ingleborough Park Dr
LA6 . . . . .103 D3
Inglebrook Sch WF8 . . .201 B1
Ingleby Arncliffe C of E Prim Sch DL6 . . . . .45 A8
Ingleby Dr LS24 . . . . . . .189 E6
Ingleby Greenhow C of E Prim Sch TS9 . . . . .27 C5
Ingleby Manor★ TS9 . . .27 C4
Ingleby Mill Prim Sch
TS17 . . . . .6 A4
Ingleby Rd
Great & Little Broughton
TS9 . . . . .27 A5
Great Broughton TS9 . . . . . .26 E5
Ingleby Way TS17 . . . . . . .6 B5
Ingleton CP Sch LA6 . . .103 D3
Ingleton Dr 16 YO61 . . . .143 D8
Ingleton Ind Est LA6 . . .103 D3
Ingleton Mid Sch LA6 . .103 D3
Ingleton Wlk 3 YO31 . . .229 A5
Ingman Lodge Rd BD24 .78 F1
Ingram Ave YO30 . . . . . .228 C8
Ingramgate YO7 . . . . . .211 C3
Ingrish La YO23 . . . . . . .182 C1
Ings Cl 6 Pickering YO18 . .95 F6
5 Willerby YO12 . . . . .99 D2
Ings CP Sch BD23 . . . . .216 D3
Ings Ct DN14 . . . . .202 F4
Ings Dr
Low Bradley BD20 . . . . . . .173 E3
Mickletown LS26 . . . . .200 C6
Ings Field Rd YO26 . . . .142 A3
Ings La
Ainderby Quernhow YO7 . . .88 D4
Beal DN14 . . . . .202 D4
Bishop Monkton HG3 . . . .140 B5
Bishop Wilton YO42 . . . . .169 D2
Bradleys Both BD20 . . . . .173 E3
Brompton YO13 . . . . .98 C4
Carlton DN14 . . . . .204 E2
Cawood YO8 . . . . .197 D8
Cononley BD20 . . . . .173 D2
Cottingwith YO42 . . . . . . .193 C5
Crakehall DL8 . . . . .62 F5
Ebberston & Yedingham
YO13 . . . . .97 E4
Great Preston WF10 . . . . .200 E6
Harome YO62 . . . . .93 D4
Hensall DN14 . . . . .203 D2
Husthwaite YO61 . . . . . . .117 A6
Hutton Buscel YO13 . . . . . .99 A3
Kellington DN14 . . . . .202 F4
21 Kirkbymoorside YO62 . . .70 B1
Kirkbymoorside YO62 . . . . .94 B7
Lastingham YO62 . . . . .70 F5
Lillings Ambo YO60 . . . . . .145 C2
Nether Poppleton YO26 . . .224 B1
Pickering YO18 . . . . .95 E4
Riccall YO19 . . . . .197 E8
Skipton BD23 . . . . .216 D2
Snape with Thorp DL8 . . . . .87 B7
Stillington YO61 . . . . .144 A6
Thorganby YO19 . . . . .193 B5
Thorp Arch LS23 . . . . .189 A8
Tollerton YO61 . . . . .143 B2
Welburn YO62 . . . . .94 A5
Wheldrake YO19 . . . . .193 B7
Wighill LS24 . . . . .189 D8
4 Willerby YO12 . . . . .99 D2
Wistow YO8 . . . . .198 A6
Ings Mere Ct WF11 . . . .201 C6
Ings Rd Cliffe YO8 . . . . .198 D2
Dunsforths YO26 . . . . . . .142 A3
Snaith DN14 . . . . .204 C1
Thorganby YO19 . . . . .193 B4
Ulleskelf LS24 . . . . .190 C3
West Ayton YO13 . . . . .99 B6
Wilberfoss YO41 . . . . .185 E6
Ings Terr YO22 . . . . .31 C4
Ings View 2 Bedale DL8 . .63 B3
Castleford WF10 . . . . .201 A4
Mickletown LS26 . . . . .200 C6
York YO30 . . . . .224 D2
Ingsgarth YO18 . . . . .95 F6
Ingthorns La LS25 . . . . .195 F1
Ingthorpe La
Martons Both BD23 . . . . .171 E7
Monk Fryston LS25 . . . . . .196 A1
Inhams La YO26 . . . . . . .141 F2
Inholmes La
Tadcaster LS24 . . . . .189 D6
Walton LS23 . . . . .181 B2
Inman Gr HG5 . . . . .221 B8
Inman Terr YO26 . . . . . .227 D4
Inman Wlk HG5 . . . . . . .221 B8
Inn La 10 YO61 . . . . .143 C8
Innisfree Cl HG2 . . . . . .220 B1
Institute St 4 BD20 . . . .187 E7
Intake Ave YO30 . . . . . .228 C8
Intake La
Acaster Malbis YO23 . . . . .191 C7
Beal WF11 . . . . .202 D5
Carlton Miniott YO7 . . . . . . .89 C4
Dunnington YO19 . . . . . . .184 F7
Grassington BD23 . . . . . . .134 E3
Habton YO17 . . . . .121 E7
Heck DN14 . . . . .207 C8
Tollerton YO61 . . . . .143 B4
West Haddlesey YO8 . . . . .202 F6
Intakefield Rd YO8 . . . .199 D7
Invicta Ct YO24 . . . . . . .230 B8
Ireby Rd LA6 . . . . .102 F3
Ireton St 3 YO12 . . . . . .212 E5
Iron Row LS29 . . . . .176 C1
Irton Moor La YO12 . . . .212 A1
Irwin Ave YO31 . . . . . . .228 E6
Islebeck La YO7 . . . . . . .115 F8
Iver Cl YO26 . . . . .227 C5
Ivy Bank Ct 4 YO13 . . . . .75 D5
Ivy Cl HG3 . . . . .223 F4
Ivy Cres DL8 . . . . .62 B4
Ivy House Cl 6 YO11 . . .100 B6
Ivy House Gdns BD23 . .155 D1
Ivy La LS23 . . . . .188 E8

J

Jack Field La BD20 . . . .187 D6
Jack Hill La LS21 . . . . . .176 F6
Jack Hole YO61 . . . . . . .142 F4
Jack La Crayke YO61 . . .118 A1
Stillington YO61 . . . . .144 C7
Wigglesworth BD23 . . . . . .153 C4
Jackson Cl YO11 . . . . . .100 B6
Jackson Dr TS9 . . . . .26 C8
Jackson La YO41 . . . . . .185 E4
Jackson St
24 Glusburn BD20 . . . . . . .187 E7
York YO31 . . . . .233 C4
Jackson's La
Bradleys Both BD20 . . . . .173 F3
Eastfield YO11 . . . . .100 A8
Scarborough YO11 . . . . . .213 A1
Jackson's Wlk YO23 . . .182 D3
Jacobi Cl YO30 . . . . . . .228 A7
Jacques Gr BD20 . . . . . .174 C1
Jacques' La YO8 . . . . . .198 E4
Jaffa Rd DL9 . . . . .209 E2
Jagger La DL10 . . . . .20 E6
Jagoe Rd 8 BB18 . . . . . .172 A1
James Backhouse Pl
YO24 . . . . .227 E3
James Cl LS25 . . . . .194 D4
James Ct DL10 . . . . .209 F7
James La DL10 . . . . .41 A2
James Nicholson Way
YO30 . . . . .225 A2
James Pl 2 YO12 . . . . . .213 A6
James St 20 Earby BB18 . .172 A1
10 Glusburn BD20 . . . . . . .187 E8
Harrogate HG1 . . . . .219 D2
Scarborough YO12 . . . . . .213 A6
Selby YO8 . . . . .232 C5
York YO10 . . . . .228 E4
Jameson Cres YO12 . . . .212 D5
Jamesville Way YO7 . . .115 B6
Jamieson Terr YO23 . . .228 B1
Janesway LS25 . . . . . . .194 C1
Janet's Foss★ BD23 . . .133 B2
Jasmine Cl
10 Snaith DN14 . . . . .204 C1
York YO32 . . . . .225 D2
Jasper La HG3 . . . . .179 A3
Jay Ave TS17 . . . . .6 B4
Jaywick Cl 3 YO32 . . . .167 B8
Jedburgh Dr DL3 . . . . .2 F7
Jedwell Cl YO32 . . . . . . .225 D5
Jennifer Gr 4 YO24 . . . .227 F2
Jenny Field Dr HG3 . . .219 B4
Jenny Frisk Rd TS12 . . . . .9 E6
Jenny Gill Cres BD23 . .217 B3
Jenny La DN14 . . . . .207 B5
Jerry Carr Bank YO62 . . .92 B1
Jerry Croft 2 BD23 . . . .217 A4
Jerry La BD20 . . . . .174 F1
Jersey Ct YO12 . . . . .99 C7
Jervaulx Abbey★ HG4 . .85 D8
Jervaulx Dr HG5 . . . . . .221 D4
Jervaulx Rd DL7 . . . . . . .64 A6
Jervis Rd YO24 . . . . . . .230 E8
Jesmond Ct YO17 . . . . . .215 E3
Jesmond Gr 5 TS18 . . . . . .5 E8
Jesmond Rd
Darlington DL1 . . . . .3 F7
Harrogate HG1 . . . . .220 A3
Jew Leys La YO23 . . . . .190 F3
Jewbury YO31 . . . . .233 C3
Jewitt La LS22 . . . . .188 B8
Jin-Whin Hill WF10 . . . .200 C4
Jobbing Cross YO61 . . .116 C3
Jockey La
Huntington YO32 . . . . .225 F2
5 Knaresborough HG5 . . .221 A6
Joffre Ave WF10 . . . . . .200 F3
John Breckon Rd YO21 . .28 D5
John Dixon La DL1 . . . . . .3 D5
John of Gaunt's Castle★
HG3 . . . . .160 B1
John St Darlington DL1 . . . .3 D6
11 Earby BB18 . . . . .172 A1
35 Filey YO14 . . . . .101 B3
Great Ayton TS9 . . . . .8 A2
11 Harrogate HG1 . . . . . . .219 D2
Selby YO8 . . . . .232 D6
Whitby YO21 . . . . .208 D7
York YO31 . . . . .228 E6
Johnson Cl 1 YO7 . . . . .211 C3
Johnson St YO8 . . . . . . .232 B6
Johnson Way YO7 . . . . .211 D2
Jolby La Cleasby DL10 . . . .2 E1
Croft-on-Tees DL2 . . . . . . .22 B8
Newton Morrell DL10 . . . . .21 F8
Jonah's La HG3 . . . . . . .160 B1
Jonathan Garth 17 LS29 174 F4
Jorvik Viking Ctr★
YO1 . . . . .233 C2
Joseph Rowntree Sch
YO32 . . . . .225 E5
Jowett's La BD20 . . . . . .174 B4
Jowland Winn La YO8 .204 A4
Jubbergate YO1 . . . . . . .233 B2
Jubilee Bank TS7 . . . . . . .7 C8
Jubilee Cave★ BD24 . . .131 F4
Jubilee Rd
Norton YO17 . . . . .215 E3
Wistow YO8 . . . . .197 D6
Jubilee Terr YO26 . . . . .227 F5
Julia Ave YO32 . . . . . . .226 B2
Junction Farm Prim Sch
TS16 . . . . .5 D5

Juniper Cl YO32 ...225 D3
Juniper Gr TS21 ...5 C8
Juniper Way 28 HG3 ...161 B3
Jura Dr DL1 ...3 E8
Jute Rd YO26 ...227 B5
Jutland Rd DL9 ...209 C2

K

Kader Ave TS5 ...6 D7
Kader Prim Sch TS5 ...6 E7
Kail La BD23 ...156 F8
Kangel Cl HG4 ...214 E3
Kareen Ave 3 YO12 ...99 E6
Kathryn Ave YO32 ...226 A2
Kay House La TS15 ...24 D5
Kaye Dr YO8 ...198 B4
Kays Bank YO61 ...117 C5
Kearby Cliff LS22 ...179 B1
Kearsley Cl TS16 ...5 E7
Kearsley Rd HG4 ...214 B7
Kearton DL11 ...37 D6
Keasden Rd LA2 ...130 A3
Keats Cl
4 Pontefract WF8 ...201 B1
York YO30 ...227 F8
Keats Wlk HG1 ...219 E7
Keble Cl YO23 ...231 B3
Keble Dr YO23 ...231 A2
Keble Garth LS25 ...194 E1
Keble Gdns YO23 ...231 B2
Keble Park Cres YO23 .231 A2
Keble Pk N YO23 ...231 A3
Keble Pk S YO23 ...231 A2
Keeper's Cl YO61 ...118 A1
Keepers Gate 18 YO18 ...95 F6
Keeper's Hill YO25 ...150 A1
Keepers Way 11 YO19 ..184 F7
Keighley Rd
Bradleys Both BD20 ...173 D3
5 Colne BB8 ...186 A3
Cowling BD22 ...187 B6
2 Glusburn BD20 ...187 F7
Ilkley LS29 ...218 A2
Laneshaw Bridge BB8 ...186 D3
Skipton BD23 ...216 F2
Trawden Forest BB8 ...186 B3
Keilder Rise TS8 ...6 F5
Keith Ave YO32 ...226 A4
Keith Rd TS4 ...6 F8
Kelbrook Prim Sch BB18 ...186 A7
Kelbrook Rd BB18 ...171 D1
Kelcbar Cl LS24 ...189 D6
Kelcbar Hill LS24 ...189 D6
Kelcbar Way LS24 ...189 D6
Kelcow Caves★ BD24 .131 D3
Keld Bank HG4 ...85 E3
Keld Cl Pickering YO18 ...95 E7
Scalby YO12 ...212 B8
Keld Head Orch 1 YO62 .70 B1
Keld Head Rd YO62 ...70 A1
Keld La
Hutton-le-Hole YO62 ...70 C5
Newton YO18 ...72 A5
Thorpe Bassett YO17 ...123 A3
Keld Runnels Rd YO13 ...75 A4
Keldale 4 YO32 ...166 F5
Keldale Gdns HG4 ...214 F6
Keldgate Rd YO18 ...72 A3
Keldhead YO18 ...95 E8
Keldheads La DL8 ...59 F5
Kelfield Rd 9 YO19 ...197 F8
Kell Bank C of E Prim Sch HG4 ...85 E3
Kell Beck 1 LS21 ...176 F1
Kell Syke La BD23 ...155 A6
Kellington La DN14 ...202 F2
Kellington Prim Sch DN14 ...202 F3
Kemmel Cl DL9 ...40 E2
Kempton Cl 2 YO24 ...227 D1
Kempton Ct 15 DL1 ...3 F6
Kendal Cl
6 Dunnington YO19 ...184 F7
Hellifield BD23 ...154 B3
Kendal Dr WF10 ...201 B4
Kendal Gdns YO26 ...181 D7
Kendal La YO26 ...181 D7
Kendal Rd
Harrogate HG1 ...220 B3
Long Preston BD23 ...154 A3
Kendalmans 4 BD24 ...131 D2
Kendrew Cl 11 Bedale DL8 63 A2
3 York YO32 ...225 F3
Kenilworth Ave HG2 ...222 D7
Kenilworth Dr
3 Earby BB18 ...172 A1
Earby BB18 ...186 A8
Kenlay Cl YO32 ...225 D4
Kennedy Dr 32 YO32 ...166 E5
Kennels La LS14 ...188 A4
Kennet La LS25 ...194 D3
Kennion Ct 2 HG2 ...220 B3
Kennion Rd HG2 ...220 B3
Kenrick Pl 5 YO26 ...227 B5
Kensal Rise YO10 ...228 D2
Kensington Ave
Eston & South Bank TS6 ...7 E8
Thorner LS14 ...188 A3
Kensington Ct 1 YO24 .230 F8
Kensington Gdns DL1 ...3 E5
Kensington Rd YO30 ...224 D2
Kensington Sq 10 HG2 ..219 C2
Kensington St YO23 ...228 B1
Kent Ave HG1 ...219 B3
Kent Cl HG4 ...214 A2
Kent Dr HG1 ...219 B3
Kent Rd Goole DN14 ...205 F2
Guisborough TS14 ...8 E5
Harrogate HG1 ...219 B3
Selby YO8 ...232 A6
Kent Rd N HG1 ...219 B3
Kent Rise HG1 ...219 A2
Kent St YO10 ...233 C1
Kentmere Dr YO30 ...224 F1
Kenton Cl 4 TS18 ...5 E8
Kershaw Ave WF10 ...201 A4
Kerver La YO19 ...184 F7
Kesteven Rd TS4 ...7 A7
Kestrel Dr 7 DL9 ...40 F2
Kestrel View 2 YO12 ...99 E6
Kestrel Wood Way YO31 ...225 F2
Keswick Dr WF10 ...201 C5
Keswick Gr TS5 ...6 D7
Keswick Way 5 YO32 ..225 F5
Kettle Spring La HG3 ..139 B1
Kettlesbeck Brow LA2 .130 C5
Kettlestring La YO30 ..225 A3
Kettlewell CP Sch BD23 ...108 A3
Kettlewell La DL8 ...57 A5
Kex Gill Rd HG3 ...158 F2
Kexby Ave YO10 ...228 F3
Kexby Bridge★ YO41 ..185 C6
Kexby House★ YO41 ..185 C6
Kexby Stray YO41 ...185 A5
Key La YO61 ...118 A1
Key Way YO19 ...231 F5
Keys Beck Rd YO18 ...71 F8
Khyber Pass YO21 ...208 D7
Kiddal La LS15 ...188 C2
Kidstones Bank DL8 ...81 E3
Kielder Dr DL1 ...3 E7
Kielder Oval HG2 ...220 D2
Kilburn Rd YO10 ...228 D2
Kildale Sta YO21 ...27 E8
Kildare Garth 5 YO62 ...70 C1
Kildwick C of E Prim Sch BD20 ...187 F8
Kilgram La HG4 ...85 E8
Kilham Rd YO25 ...151 D5
Killerby Dr 2 DL10 ...41 E4
Killerby La YO11 ...100 C5
Killin Rd DL1 ...3 E7
Killinghall C of E Prim Sch HG3 ...161 C5
Kilmarnock Rd DL1 ...3 E8
Kiln Hill La
Lawkland LA2 ...131 A6
Silsden BD20 ...174 A3
Kiln La LA2 ...128 A6
Kilners Croft 11 LS29 ...174 F4
Kilnsey Fold BD20 ...174 B2
Kilnwick Ct DL7 ...210 D3
Kilton La TS12 ...9 F7
Kilton Thorpe La TS13 ..10 B8
Kimberlows Wood Hill 3 YO10 ...229 C3
Kinbrace Dr YO24 ...230 B7
King Edward Ave WF10 ...200 C7
King Edward Rd HG4 ..214 C3
King Edward St
27 Glusburn BD20 ...187 E7
Normanton South WF6 ...200 A1
King Edward's Dr HG1 ...219 D5
King George Rd 1 HG4 214 C3
King Hill YO14 ...101 A2
King James Rd HG5 ...221 B5
King James's Gram Sch HG5 ...221 B5
King Rudding Cl 6 YO19 ...198 A8
King Rudding La YO19 .198 B8
King St
Castleford WF10 ...200 F3
6 Cawood YO8 ...197 B8
Muston YO14 ...100 F2
Normanton South WF6 ...200 A1
Pateley Bridge HG3 ...137 B4
Richmond DL10 ...209 C6
Ripon HG4 ...214 C4
Scarborough YO11 ...213 A6
York YO1 ...233 B2
Kingfisher Cl 7 YO12 ...99 F6
Kingfisher Ct 3 DL9 ...40 F2
Kingfisher Dr
3 Bedale DL8 ...63 B3
Guisborough TS14 ...8 D6
14 Pickering YO18 ...95 F6
Whitby YO22 ...208 E3
Kingfisher Reach
17 Boroughbridge YO51 ..141 B5
5 Collingham LS22 ...180 A1
Kings Acre YO31 ...229 B6
Kings Ave 2 LS29 ...218 A4
Kings Cl 5 YO8 ...198 B5
King's Cl 9 DL10 ...41 D5
Kings Cl 19 LS29 ...175 C2
King's Gate LA2 ...130 D3
King's Gdns YO7 ...211 B1
Kings Keld Bank DL8 ...86 F8
Kings La YO13 ...97 D5
Kings Lea YO8 ...199 A8
Kings Manor Comp Sch TS5 ...6 E7
Kings Mdws YO7 ...89 E3
Kings Mead HG4 ...214 B7
Kings Mill La 8 BD24 ...131 D2
Kings Moor Rd YO32 ...167 D2
King's Rd 6 HG1 ...219 D3
Kings Rd Ilkley LS29 ...218 A4
Kings Rd *continued*
Knaresborough HG5 ...221 C6
King's Sq YO1 ...233 C2
King's St 7 BD23 ...217 B4
Kingsclere YO32 ...225 F6
Kingsland Terr 11 YO26 ...227 F5
Kingsley Ave WF11 ...201 D3
Kingsley Cl HG1 ...220 C3
Kingsley Dr
Harrogate HG1 ...220 A4
2 Middleham DL8 ...60 E2
Kingsley Park Mews 1 HG1 ...220 C3
Kingsley Park Rd HG1 .220 C3
Kingsley Rd
Harrogate HG1 ...220 B5
Trawden Forest BB8 ...186 B3
Kingsthorpe YO24 ...227 D2
Kingston Ave HG4 ...214 C3
Kingston Cres YO8 ...196 E2
Kingston Dr
Hambleton YO8 ...196 E1
16 Normanton WF6 ...200 B1
Norton YO17 ...215 E2
Kingston Garth 2 YO22 .33 C3
Kingston Gr 5 YO12 ...212 B7
Kingstonia Gdns 3 HG4 ...214 C3
Kingsway
Garforth LS25 ...194 B3
Harrogate HG1 ...219 E3
Pontefract WF8 ...201 B2
Scalby YO12 ...212 C8
Skipton BD23 ...217 B4
6 Stamford Bridge YO41 .168 D2
Weeton LS17 ...178 B2
Kingsway Dr
Harrogate HG1 ...219 E2
4 Ilkley LS29 ...218 A4
Kingsway Jun Sch YO30 ...228 B7
Kingsway N YO30 ...228 B7
Kingsway W YO24 ...227 D1
Kingswood Gr YO24 ...227 D3
Kinloss Cl TS17 ...6 C7
Kinsey Cave★ BD24 ...131 C4
Kintyre Dr TS17 ...6 B6
Kiplin Hall★ DL10 ...42 B4
Kipling Gr WF8 ...201 B2
Kippax Greenfield Prim Sch LS25 ...194 D1
Kippax Inf Sch LS25 ...194 D1
Kippax Leisure Ctr LS25 ...200 D8
Kippax North Jun & Inf Sch LS25 ...194 C2
Kir Cres YO24 ...227 C3
Kirby Hill C of E Prim Sch YO51 ...141 B7
Kirby La
Ebberston & Yedingham YO17 ...97 E1
Sledmere YO25 ...150 A4
Kirby Misperton La YO17 ...121 C7
Kirby Misperton Rd YO17 ...95 F2
Kirk Balk YO17 ...169 E8
Kirk Balk La YO60 ...168 B7
Kirk Bank
Conistone with Kilnsey BD23 ...134 B4
Kirkby Malzeard HG4 ...112 A5
Kirk Fenton C of E Prim Sch LS24 ...196 B8
Kirk Gate
Brompton YO13 ...98 C7
Silpho YO13 ...74 E6
Kirk Hammerton C of E Prim Sch YO26 ...164 C2
Kirk Hammerton La YO26 ...164 C3
Kirk Hills LS14 ...188 A3
Kirk Ings La YO7 ...66 B7
Kirk La
Embsay with Eastby BD23 ...217 E8
Tockwith YO26 ...181 C7
Kirk Rd Egglescliffe TS15 ...5 F2
Northallerton DL7 ...210 B3
Kirk Smeaton C of E Prim Sch WF8 ...206 B3
Kirk Syke La BD23 ...155 A5
Kirk View 1 YO26 ...227 C3
Kirkby & Great Broughton C of E Prim Sch TS9 ...26 E5
Kirkby Ave HG4 ...214 A6
Kirkby Cl HG4 ...214 A6
Kirkby Dr HG4 ...214 A6
Kirkby Fleetham C of E Prim Sch DL7 ...42 C1
Kirkby in Malhamdale Prim Sch BD23 ...154 F8
Kirkby La
Gillamoor YO62 ...70 A3
Kearby with Netherby HG3 ...179 B2
Kirkby TS9 ...26 D6
Kirkby Fleetham with Fencote DL7 ...42 C2
Sicklinghall LS22 ...179 D3
Kirkby Malzeard C of E Prim Sch HG4 ...112 D5
Kirkby Overblow C of E Prim Sch HG3 ...179 A4
Kirkby Rd
North Stainley with Sleningford HG4 ...113 C4
Kirkby Rd *continued*
Ripon HG4 ...214 A6
Selby YO8 ...232 B7
Kirkbymoorside Com Prim Sch YO62 ...70 B1
Kirkbymoorside CP Sch YO62 ...70 A1
Kirkcroft YO32 ...225 C8
Kirkdale La YO62 ...93 F8
Kirkdale Manor YO62 ...93 D8
Kirkdale Rd YO10 ...229 D4
Kirkfield Ave LS14 ...188 A3
Kirkfield Cres LS14 ...188 A3
Kirkfield La LS14 ...188 A3
Kirkfield Rd DL3 ...3 D8
Kirkgate
Knaresborough HG5 ...221 A6
7 Middleham DL8 ...60 E2
12 Ripon HG4 ...214 C5
Settle BD24 ...131 D2
Sherburn in Elmet LS25 ...195 E4
Silsden BD20 ...174 C1
Thirsk YO7 ...211 B3
Kirkgate La YO62 ...70 F4
Kirkham Augustinian Priory (rems of)★ YO60 ...146 F4
Kirkham Ave 1 YO31 ...228 E8
Kirkham Bridge★ YO60 ...146 F4
Kirkham Cl 6 YO21 ...208 C6
Kirkham Ct 5 HG5 ...221 C4
Kirkham Gr HG1 ...219 F6
Kirkham Pl HG1 ...219 F6
Kirkham Rd
Harrogate HG1 ...219 F6
Middlesbrough TS7 ...7 D6
Whitby YO21 ...208 C6
Kirkham View YO60 ...147 B4
Kirkhaw La WF11 ...201 D4
Kirkland Cl YO8 ...232 D4
Kirklands YO32 ...167 B6
Kirklands La YO41 ...169 C2
Kirklevington Cty Prim Sch TS15 ...24 F8
Kirkstall Dr BB18 ...171 E2
Kirkstone Dr YO31 ...229 A6
Kirkstone Rd HG1 ...220 B4
Kirkwell YO23 ...231 A4
Kit La BD20 ...174 B3
Kitchen Dr YO8 ...232 D4
Kitchener Rd
Ripon HG4 ...113 D3
Scotton DL9 ...40 E4
Kitchener St Selby YO8 .232 B6
York YO31 ...228 D7
Kitemere Pl 2 YO24 ...230 B8
Kitter La YO21 ...31 C8
Kitty Garth YO19 ...193 A7
Knapping Hill HG1 ...219 C5
Knapton Cl 1 YO32 ...167 B6
Knapton La YO26 ...227 B4
Knapton Wold Rd YO17 ...123 C5
Knaresborough Ave TS7 ..7 B5
Knaresborough Castle★ HG5 ...221 A5
Knaresborough Rd
Bishop Monkton HG3 ...140 B4
Harrogate HG2 ...219 F2
Little Ribston LS22 ...180 A8
Ripon HG4 ...214 C3
Knaresborough Sta HG5 ...221 A6
Knaresborough Swimming Pool HG5 ...221 B5
Knavesmire Cl YO62 ...93 C5
Knavesmire Cres YO23 ...228 B1
Knavesmire Prim Sch YO23 ...228 B1
Knavesmire Rd YO23 ...228 A1
Knayton C of E Prim Sch YO7 ...65 E3
Kneeton La DL10 ...21 C5
Knightsway LS25 ...194 B3
Knipe Point Dr 8 YO11 .100 B8
Knoll The
3 Bramham LS23 ...188 E6
York YO24 ...227 B2
Knolls Cl 11 YO11 ...100 B7
Knolls La YO62 ...67 F5
Knot La BB7 ...171 A5
Knott La
Easingwold YO61 ...143 C8
Steeton with Eastburn BD20 ...187 F7
Knott Rd YO18 ...49 D5
Knottingley England Lane Jun & Inf Sch WF11 ..202 A2
Knottingley High Sch WF11 ...202 A2
Knottingley Rd WF8 ...201 D1
Knottingley Rugby Union Club WF11 ...202 A3
Knottingley Sta WF11 ..201 F2
Knotto Bottom Cl DL6 ...210 F3
Knotto Bottom Way DL6 ...210 F3
Knotts La BD23 ...152 E1
Knowle La
Ilton-cum-Pott HG4 ...85 D1
Kirby Knowle YO7 ...66 C2
Knowles Cl 5 TS15 ...24 E8
Knox Ave HG1 ...219 C5
Knox Chase HG1 ...219 C6
Knox Cl HG1 ...219 D6
Knox Dr HG1 ...219 C6
Knox Gdns HG1 ...219 C6
Knox Gr HG1 ...219 C6
Knox La Harrogate HG1 .219 D6
Scarborough YO11 ...213 B1
Knox Mill Bank HG3 ...219 B7
Knox Mill Cl HG3 ...219 B7
Knox Mill La HG3 ...219 B7
Knox Pk HG3 ...219 B7
Knox Rd HG1 ...219 D6
Knox Rise HG1 ...219 C6
Knox Way HG1 ...219 C5
Kyle Cl 3 YO61 ...143 B3
Kyle Way YO26 ...227 B8
Kyme Castle★ LS24 ...189 C7
Kyme St YO1 ...233 B1

L

La Bassee Rd DL9 ...209 D1
Laburnum Ave
Fylingdales YO22 ...33 C4
Thornaby TS17 ...6 B7
Laburnum Cl
5 Catterick Garrison DL9 209 B1
Rufforth YO23 ...182 C6
7 Snaith DN14 ...204 C1
3 Thorpe Willoughby YO8 197 B1
Laburnum Dr HG3 ...140 A5
Laburnum Garth 6 YO31 ...228 F8
Laburnum Gr
Harrogate HG1 ...219 E6
Richmond DL10 ...209 D8
Stillingfleet YO19 ...191 D4
Whitby YO21 ...208 B6
Laburnum Rd TS7 ...7 D8
Lacey Ave YO12 ...99 D7
Lachman Rd BB8 ...186 A2
Lack La YO62 ...93 C2
Lackon Bank HG3 ...160 D6
Lacy Gr LS22 ...180 C2
Ladgate La TS5 ...6 F6
Lady Balk La WF8 ...201 B1
Lady Edith's Ave YO12 .212 B6
Lady Edith's Cres YO12 ...212 B6
Lady Edith's Dr YO12 ..212 A6
Lady Edith's Pk YO12 ..212 B7
Lady Elizabeth Hastings C of E Sch
Collingham LS22 ...180 A1
Thorp Arch LS23 ...180 F1
Lady Grace's Ride YO12 ...212 A3
Lady Hamilton Gdns YO24 ...227 E2
Lady Hullocks Ct 12 TS9 .26 C7
Lady La HG3 ...222 A5
Lady Lumleys Sch YO18 .95 F7
Lady Rd YO30 ...228 B7
Ladycarr La YO61 ...143 E8
Ladysmith Ave YO21 ...208 C7
Ladysmith Mews 13 YO32 ...167 A7
Ladysmith Rd DL9 ...40 C4
Ladywell La YO51 ...141 C5
Ladywell Rd YO51 ...141 B5
Lairs Cres YO13 ...98 A5
Lairs La YO13 ...98 A5
Lairum Rise LS23 ...188 E7
Laith Staid La LS25 ...195 D4
Laithbutts La LA2 ...130 B8
Lake View WF8 ...201 B2
Lakeber Ave LA2 ...129 A8
Lakeber Dr LA2 ...129 A8
Lakeside
Acaster Malbis YO23 ...191 C7
Darlington DL1 ...3 C4
Hunmanby Sands YO14 ...101 B1
Lakeside Cl LS29 ...218 A5
Lakeside Gr 1 YO32 ...167 B8
Lakeside Mdws 1 WF8 .201 B2
Lakeside Prim Sch YO30 ...224 F2
Lakeside Way YO17 ...215 D2
Laking La YO25 ...126 A3
Lamb Inn Rd 9 WF11 ...202 A2
Lamb La TS17 ...6 A4
Lambert Ct YO1 ...233 B1
Lambert Meml Hospl YO7 ...211 B2
Lambert St
11 Skipton BD23 ...217 A3
2 Trawden BB8 ...186 B1
Lambeth St 13 BB8 ...186 A3
Lambourne Dr TS7 ...7 C6
Lamb's La TS9 ...27 B4
Lambs La 12 YO18 ...95 F7
Lamel St YO10 ...229 A3
Lamplugh Cres YO23 ...231 B3
Lanacar La DL8 ...56 A4
Lancar Cl 18 YO32 ...166 D5
Lancaster Cl 9 YO13 ...75 D5
Lancaster Park Rd HG2 ...220 A3
Lancaster Rd
Harrogate HG2 ...219 C1
North Cowton DL7 ...22 C2
Lancaster St 6 YO11 ...213 A6
Lancaster Way
17 Scalby YO13 ...75 D5
York YO30 ...225 A1
Lancers Ct 4 YO12 ...75 F5
Landalewood Rd YO30 .224 F2
Landau Cl YO30 ...227 F8

Landing La
Asselby DN14 205 D6
Barlby with Osgodby YO8 232 F8
22 Haxby YO32 166 F5
Haxby YO32 225 E7
Hemingbrough YO8 204 F8
Riccall YO19 197 F8
York YO26 227 E6
Landing Rd YO8 203 A7
Landings The 21 YO32 166 F5
Lands La HG5 220 E7
Lane Ends La BD22 187 B7
Lane Foot Rd HG3 159 E8
Lane House La BB8 186 B1
Lane House Rd BD22 187 A6
Lane The
Gate Helmsley YO41 168 B2
Mickleby TS13 12 A4
Lanehead La DL11 18 H8
Lanehouse Rd TS17 6 B8
Laneshawbridge CP Sch BB8 186 B3
Lang Ave YO10 229 A4
Lang Gate YO13 74 E4
Lang Kirk Cl 2 BD20 173 F1
Lang Rd
Bishopthorpe YO23 230 F4
York YO32 225 F6
Langbar Rd LS29 218 A6
Langbaurgh Cl TS9 8 A2
Langbaurgh Rd TS15 25 C4
Langber End La LA6 103 D1
Langber La BD23 154 A6
Langbourne Rd YO21 208 D6
Langburn La YO21 29 A7
Langburn's Bank YO21 29 A7
Langcliffe Ave HG2 222 E8
Langcliffe Ave E HG2 222 E8
Langcliffe CP Sch BD24 131 E4
Langcliffe Garth BD23 108 B3
Langcliffe Rd BD24 131 D3
Langdale TS14 8 D6
Langdale Ave
3 Pontefract WF6 200 A2
York YO31 229 B6
Langdale Dr 2 WF6 200 A2
Langdale Gr YO8 232 B3
Langdale Mews 4 WF6 200 A2
Langdale Rd 3 YO12 212 F7
Langer Hill La HG3 160 B5
Langford Cl 21 LS29 176 C1
Langford Ct 17 LS29 176 C1
Langford La LS29 176 C1
Langford Mews 19 LS29 176 C1
Langford Rd LS29 176 C1
Langford Ride 30 LS29 176 C1
Langholm Cres DL3 3 C5
Langholme Dr YO26 227 C6
Langhorne Dr 2 DL11 38 B6
Langley Ct 1 YO32 225 F6
Langley Dr YO17 215 E1
Langleys Rd 6 DN6 206 E1
Langrickgate La YO42 193 C5
Langsett Ave 7 YO14 101 A3
Langsett Gr YO30 224 F3
Langstrothdale Rd BD24 105 D7
Langthwaite La DL8 59 C3
Langtoft CP Sch YO25 151 C5
Langton CP Sch YO17 147 F5
Langton Crossroads YO17 148 B6
Langton Ct 1 YO32 167 A6
Langton La YO17 148 C8
Langton Rd
Langton YO17 148 A7
Norton YO17 215 E2
Langwith Ave LS22 188 A8
Langwith Stray YO10 184 C2
Lansdown Rd DN14 205 F2
Lansdown Way 7 YO32 166 F5
Lansdowne Rd TS15 5 E3
Lansdowne Terr 5 YO10 228 E3
Lanshaw Bank BD23 175 A7
Lanshaw Croft YO30 224 F1
Lantsbury Dr TS13 10 D8
Larch Gr 1 Filey YO14 101 B4
Pannal HG3 222 E2
Larch Rd 6 YO7 89 A1
Larch Rise 4 YO61 117 D1
Larchfield YO31 229 C7
Larchfield Com TS8 6 F4
Larchfield Sports Ctr DL3 3 C5
Larchfield St DL3 3 C5
Lark Hill HG4 214 A7
Lark Hill Cres 13 HG4 113 D2
Lark Hill Dr HG4 214 A6
Lark La HG4 214 A6
Larkfield Cl
1 Copmanthorpe YO23 230 A3
Harrogate HG2 222 A7
Larkfield Dr HG2 222 A7
Larkfield Rd
Harrogate HG2 222 A7
Selby YO8 232 A4
Larkfield Way HG2 222 A7
Larkhill Cl HG4 214 A6
Larkspur Gr 14 HG3 161 B3
Larkspur Rd TS7 7 A6
Larpool Cres YO22 208 E4
Larpool Dr YO22 208 D3
Larpool La YO22 208 D4
Larsen Rd DN14 205 F2
Larun Beat The TS15 5 E2
Lascelles Ct DL6 210 E4
Lascelles Gr HG2 219 B1
Lascelles La
Malton YO17 215 E6
Northallerton DL6 210 E4
Lascelles Rd HG2 222 B8
Latimer La TS14 8 E6
Latimer Rd DL1 3 E7
Lauderdale Dr TS14 8 F6
Laughton Ave YO12 212 C5
Laundry La LA6 103 D3
Laundry Rd
4 Filey YO14 101 B3
3 Harrogate HG1 220 C4
Lauradale La BD23 134 D1
Laurel Ave TS4 7 A8
Laurel Cl Burniston YO13 75 D8
Gateforth YO8 197 B1
Laurel Croft BD23 217 D8
Laurels Garth YO60 145 C5
Laurels The 6 DL6 210 E2
Laurence Jackson Sch TS14 8 F7
Lavender Ct 21 DL9 41 A5
Lavender Gr YO26 227 E5
Laveracks Ind Est YO41 185 B3
Laverton Gdns HG3 219 A4
Law La HG3 138 F1
Lawn Ave LS29 176 C1
Lawn La DN6 207 E3
Lawn Rd 35 LS29 176 C1
Lawnfield Dr HG3 140 B5
Lawnfield Rd HG3 140 B5
Lawns Rd YO21 29 E6
Lawns The HG2 222 C8
Lawnswood Dr YO30 227 F8
Lawnway YO31 229 A7
Lawrence Cl YO12 212 A8
Lawrence Cres DL10 209 E8
Lawrence Gr YO12 212 A8
Lawrence St YO10 228 E3
Lawsings Brow LA2 130 B5
Lawson Ave 1 YO51 141 B4
Lawson Rd YO24 230 F7
Lawsons Cl YO14 126 F7
Layerthorpe YO31 233 C3
Layfield Prim Sch TS15 5 D2
Lazenby Dr 10 LS22 180 B3
Lazenby Moor La HG5 141 A2
Le Cateau CP Sch DL9 40 F4
Le Cateau Rd DL9 40 E4
Lea Croft LS23 188 E7
Lea La YO61 143 F4
Lea Way YO32 226 A4
Lead La Brompton DL6 43 F3
Nether Silton YO7 66 B7
Ripon HG4 214 B3
Westerdale YO21 28 E4
Lead Mill La YO1 233 C1
Leadhall Ave HG2 222 D6
Leadhall Cl HG2 222 D6
Leadhall Cres HG2 222 E6
Leadhall Dr HG2 222 D7
Leadhall Gdns HG2 222 D6
Leadhall Gr HG2 222 D6
Leadhall La HG2 222 D6
Leadhall Rd HG2 222 C6
Leadhall View HG2 222 C5
Leadhall Way HG2 222 C6
Leading Post St 8 YO11 213 B6
Leadley Croft YO23 230 A1
Leafield Rd DL1 3 D4
Leahope Ct TS17 6 C6
Leahurst Cl YO17 215 E2
Leake La YO7 65 F6
Leake St
Castleford WF10 200 F4
York YO10 228 E3
Lealholm C of E Sch YO21 30 C6
Lealholm Cres TS3 7 C8
Lealholm La YO21 30 B5
Lealholm Sta YO21 30 B6
Leamington Rd LS29 218 C5
Leamington Terr LS29 218 C5
Leas Head Rd YO22 32 B2
Leas La YO18 95 F5
Leas The
11 Brafferton YO61 115 F1
Darlington DL1 3 D8
8 Eastfield YO11 99 F7
Lease Rigg La YO22 31 A3
Leases La DL10 41 E2
Leases Rd DL7 63 C5
Leasmires Ave 10 YO61 143 D8
Leat Cl YO17 215 D2
Leather Bank LS29 176 C1
Leathley La LS21 177 D1
Leavening CP Sch YO17 147 E2
Leck C of E Sch LA6 102 E7
Leconfield Garth HG3 223 F5
Ledbury Way TS14 8 E6
Ledesway 1 BD23 134 E3
Ledgate La LS25 201 E6
Ledston Ave LS25 194 D3
Ledston Hall★ WF10 200 F8
Ledston Mill La WF10 200 F8
Leech La DL10 41 E4
Leeds Barnsdale Rd WF10 200 D3
Leeds La LS26 194 A3
Leeds Rd
Allerton Bywater WF10 200 D7
Barwick in Elmet & Scholes LS15 194 A7
Castleford WF10 200 E3
Collingham LS22 188 A8
Great Preston WF10 200 C7
Harrogate HG2 219 D1
Ilkley LS29 218 D5
Kippax LS25 194 C2
Mickletown LS26 200 A6
Pannal HG3 222 F3
Selby YO8 232 A4
Tadcaster LS24 189 D5
Leeman Rd YO26 233 A2
Leeming & Londonderry CP Sch DL7 63 D4
Leeming La
Brough with St Giles DL10 41 D5
Burneston DL8 87 F8
4 Burton in Lonsdale LA6 102 F3
Catterick DL10 41 E4
Kirklington-cum-Upsland YO7 88 A6
Langthorpe YO51 141 B6
Leeming DL7 63 C4
Melmerby HG4 114 D8
Theakston DL7 63 E1
Thornthwaite with Padside HG3 159 D5
Lees La DL7 210 B1
Leeside YO24 230 E8
Legion St LS25 195 F2
Legram La YO26 163 D8
Legram Rd YO26 163 D8
Leicester Way
Aislaby TS16 5 D4
York YO1 233 C1
Leighton Cl YO12 99 E6
Leighton Croft 3 YO30 224 F1
Leighton Rd 6 TS18 5 D8
Leith Rd DL3 3 A5
Lendal YO1 233 B2
Lendales La YO18 95 E3
Lennerton La LS25 196 C3
Lennox Ave DL10 209 D7
Lennox Cl 2 YO14 127 A8
Lennox Pl HG4 113 D3
Leonard St 15 BB18 171 D1
Leppington Dr YO12 212 C4
Leppington La YO17 147 D1
Lerecroft Rd YO24 230 D8
Lesley Ave YO10 231 E8
L'espec St DL7 210 D3
Leven Bank Rd TS15 5 F2
Leven Cl TS16 5 D4
Leven Ct TS9 8 A1
Leven Rd Eaglescliffe TS15 5 E3
Stokesley TS9 26 B7
York YO24 230 D7
Leven Wynd 9 TS9 26 C7
Levendale 6 TS15 25 C5
Levendale Prim Sch TS15 5 F3
Levens Cl HG3 161 B4
Levenside Great Ayton TS9 7 F1
4 Hutton Rudby TS15 25 D5
Stokesley TS9 26 C7
Levick Cres TS5 6 D8
Levisham St YO10 228 D2
Levisham Sta YO18 72 B5
Lewes Rd DL1 3 D4
Lewis Cl
1 Croft-on-Tees DL2 22 C8
Northallerton DL6 210 F5
Lewis Rd DL6 210 F5
Lexden Ave TS5 6 D8
Leyburn Com Prim Sch DL8 60 D5
Leyburn Gr 1 TS18 5 D8
Leyburn Pl 8 YO14 101 A3
Leyburn RC Prim Sch DL8 60 D5
Leyburn Rd Askrigg DL8 57 F6
Darlington DL1 3 D7
Masham HG4 86 B4
Middleham DL8 60 E3
Scotton DL9 40 C4
Leyes The YO10 229 C4
Leyfield Cl 1 YO32 167 A7
Leyland Cl BB8 186 A2
Leyland Cres 3 HG1 220 A3
Leyland Rd
Harrogate HG1 220 A3
York YO31 229 A5
Leys La
Boston Spa LS23 188 D8
Darrington WF11 206 A8
Glusburn BD20 187 B8
Knottingley WF11 201 F1
Little Smeaton WF8 206 B4
Leys Rd WF11 206 A7
Leysthorpe La YO62 93 B2
Liardet Rd DL10 41 E4
Lichfield Ct 6 YO23 228 B1
Lichfield Gr HG3 219 A4
Lickley St HG4 214 D5
Lidget La HG5 163 B5
Lidget Rd BD20 173 E3
Lidgett Gr YO26 227 B6
Lidgett Grove Sch YO26 227 B6
Lidgett La LS25 194 C3
Lidice Rd DN14 205 E2
Lidsty Hill YO62 70 E5
Lifeboat Mus★ YO21 208 D7
Light Bank La BD20 174 E2
Light La DL8 59 E5
Lightfoots Ave YO12 212 D3
Lightfoots Cl YO12 212 C3
Lightfoot's La YO12 212 D3
Lightfoots Rd YO12 212 D3
Lightmire La YO26 142 A1
Lightwater Valley Miniature Rly★ HG4 113 C6
Lightwater Valley Theme Pk★ HG4 113 C6
Lilac Ave
Appleton Roebuck YO23 190 F5
Thornaby TS17 6 B7
York YO10 229 B3
Lilac Cl 7 LS29 175 A4
Lilac Gr Harrogate HG1 219 E6
New Earswick YO32 225 D4
Lilac Rd TS7 7 D7
Lilac Wlk YO12 212 D7
Lilbourne Dr YO30 228 A8
Lile Cl DL10 209 C7
Lilla Cl YO21 208 A6
Lilling Ave 3 YO31 228 E8
Lilling La YO60 145 E3
Lilling Low La YO60 145 C2
Lilly Gate La HG3 162 A8
Limber Hill YO21 30 E4
Lime Ave YO31 228 F7
Lime Chase 10 YO62 70 B1
Lime Cl 10 LS29 174 E4
Lime Gr Harrogate HG1 219 F3
4 Whitby YO21 208 C6
Lime Kiln La LS22 180 B5
Lime La DL8 87 F2
Lime Rd Eaglescliffe TS16 5 E6
Guisborough TS14 8 E7
Sinnington YO62 94 D8
Lime St HG1 219 F3
Lime Tree Ave
8 Easingwold YO61 117 D1
Malton YO17 215 D6
York YO32 225 D3
Lime Tree Gr YO8 232 A6
Lime Tree Mews 15 YO19 184 F7
Limebar Bank Rd YO51 141 D1
Limebar La YO51 141 C2
Limegarth 10 YO26 165 F1
Limehouse La BD23 216 E1
Limekiln Bank HG4 113 C1
Limekiln Hill YO25 150 B3
Limekiln La
Burton Leonard HG3 140 A1
East Layton DL11 1 B1
8 Eastfield YO11 100 B6
Folkton YO11 100 A2
Halton West BD23 154 A1
North Stainley with Sleningford HG4 113 C5
Snape with Thorp HG4 86 D5
Limekiln Rd YO7 65 F5
Limes The
Burniston YO13 75 C8
Helmsley YO62 92 F6
Stockton on the Forest YO32 167 D2
Limestone Gr YO13 75 C8
Limestone La YO13 75 A5
Limestone Rd YO13 75 B7
Limestone Way YO13 75 C8
Limetree Cl 2 YO8 197 B1
Lime-Tree Cres LS25 194 E1
Limetrees WF8 201 D2
Limpsey Gate La YO18 72 D6
Limpton Gate TS15 5 E2
Linacre Way DL1 3 D7
Lincoln Gr HG3 219 A5
Lincoln Rd 30 BB18 172 A1
Lincoln St YO26 227 F5
Lindale 2 YO24 230 C7
Linden Ave Darlington DL3 3 B5
Great Ayton TS9 7 F1
Linden Cl Great Ayton TS9 7 F2
4 Hutton Rudby TS15 25 C4
Sleights YO21 32 B7
York YO32 225 F5
Linden Cres
Great Ayton TS9 7 F1
5 Hutton Rudby TS15 25 C4
Middlesbrough TS7 7 B6
Linden Dr Hurworth DL2 3 D1
1 Hurworth-on-Tees DL2 22 D8
Linden Gdns DL10 209 D7
Linden Gr Great Ayton TS9 7 F1
Thornaby TS17 6 B8
1 York YO30 228 A8
Linden Rd 9 Earby BB18 172 A1
Great Ayton TS9 7 F1
Northallerton DL6 210 E4
Scalby YO12 212 A8
Linden Way
9 Thorpe Willoughby YO8 197 B2
Wetherby LS22 180 B4
Lindhead CP Sch YO13 75 C8
Lindhead Rd YO13 75 B8
Lindisfarne Rd TS3 7 C8
Lindley Rd YO30 224 F1
Lindley St Skipton BD23 216 F2
York YO24 227 F3
Lindley Wood Gr YO30 224 E3
Lindon Rd DL10 20 F1
Lindrick Cl 3 HG4 214 B2
Lindrick Way HG3 219 A4
Lindsay Rd LS25 194 C3
Lindsey Ave YO26 227 D4
Ling Croft LS23 188 D8
Ling Hill YO12 212 B7
Ling La YO41 185 F6
Ling Trod YO17 123 D4
Lingcrag Gdns BD22 187 B6
Lingcroft Cl YO8 204 D4
Lingcroft La
Naburn YO19 231 E3
Tockwith LS22 181 A6
Lingdale Prim Sch TS12 9 F7
Lingdale Rd
Lockwood TS12 9 E7
Thornaby TS17 6 C7
Lingerfield Prim Sch HG5 162 B7
Lingfield Ash TS8 7 A5
Lingfield Cl DL1 4 A5
Lingfield Prim Sch TS7 7 B5
Lingfield Rd TS15 5 F3
Lingfield Way DL1 4 A5
Lingham La YO7 115 A3
Linghaw La LA2 129 C7
Lingholm Cres 9 YO11 99 F7
Lingholm La YO11 100 D4
Lingmoor La YO62 70 E3
Lingrow Cl 3 TS13 12 A7
Link Ave YO30 228 C8
Link Rd YO31 225 E2
Link The
Copmanthorpe YO23 230 A3
Middlesbrough TS3 7 C8
Northallerton DL7 210 B2
Northallerton DL6 210 E4
Selby YO8 232 A4
York YO10 231 E8
Link Wlk 5 YO11 100 A6
Linkfoot La YO62 93 A6
Links Cl HG2 220 E3
Links Dr LA2 129 A8
Links Prim Sch The TS16 5 E5
Links The
7 North Featherstone WF7 200 E1
Tadcaster LS24 189 E5
Links Way HG2 220 E3
Linkway DN6 206 E2
Linnburn Mews 1 LS29 218 B3
Linnet Way YO24 230 C8
Linton Ave 9 LS22 180 B3
Linton Cl
Cloughton YO13 54 D1
19 Filey YO14 101 B3
Linton Comm LS22 179 F1
Linton Ct 8 BD23 216 F3
Linton Falls 1 BD23 134 E2
Linton La LS22 180 B2
Linton Mdw 1 YO30 164 F7
Linton Mdws 7 LS22 180 B3
Linton Pl 4 YO30 164 F7
Linton Rd
Collingham LS22 180 A1
Poppleton YO26 224 A1
Wetherby LS22 180 B3
Linton Rise 17 DL9 40 E4
Linton St 5 YO26 227 E5
Linton Woods YO30 165 A7
Linton Woods La YO30 165 A8
Linton-on-Ouse Cty Prim Sch YO30 165 A7
Linwith La DN14 204 C3
Linwood Ave TS9 26 C8
Lisheen Ave WF10 200 F4
Lismore Pl YO12 212 E1
Lismore Rd YO12 212 E1
Lister Hill 5 BD20 187 E6
Lister St LS29 218 A4
Lister Way YO30 228 A7
Lisvane Ave YO12 212 D4
Litley Bank YO7 66 B5
Little Ave YO30 228 B8
Little Ayton La TS9 8 A1
Little Beck Bank YO22 32 C4
Little Beck La YO22 32 B3
Little Catterton La LS24 190 A7
Little Church La LS26 200 B5
Little Comm La DN14 207 C5
Little Croft HG3 139 C4
Little Crossing HG4 214 E2
Little Field La YO18 72 C5
Little Garth YO26 224 A2
Little Hallfield Rd YO31 228 E5
Little Harries La HG4 214 A7
Little Heck Comm La DN14 203 D1
Little Hutton La DL11 1 A4
Little Ings Cl LS24 196 C8
Little Ings La YO51 141 C5
Little King St HG3 137 B4
Little La Brompton DL6 44 A3
12 Easingwold YO61 143 C8
Ellerton YO42 193 C1
11 Haxby YO32 166 E5
Ilkley LS29 218 C4
Little Smeaton DN6 206 D4
North Stainley with Sleningford HG4 113 C4
Little Mdws YO32 225 D8
Little Moor Cl YO13 54 C1
Little Moor La YO8 232 A8
Little Stonegate YO1 233 B3
Little Studley Cl HG4 214 C7
Little Studley Rd HG4 214 C7
Little Westfield YO25 151 C3
Little Wood St YO17 215 E3
Littlebeck Dr DL1 3 E7

Littleboy Dr TS17 ... 6 C8
Littledale YO18 ... 95 F7
Littlefield Cl 5 YO26 ... 165 F1
Littleside DL8 ... 83 E7
Littlethorpe Cl HG3 ... 219 A4
Littlethorpe La HG4 ... 214 D2
Littlethorpe Pk HG4 ... 214 E3
Littlethorpe Rd HG4 ... 214 E3
Littondale Ave HG5 ... 221 D6
Liverton La TS13 ... 10 D6
Liverton Mill Bank TS12 ... 10 B6
Liverton Rd TS13 ... 10 D7
Livingstone Rd YO12 ... 212 E6
Livingstone St YO26 ... 227 F5
Lloyd Cl YO10 ... 229 B1
Lob La YO41 ... 168 D2
Lochrin Pl 2 YO26 ... 227 B4
Lock Cl DN14 ... 207 F6
Lock La
Castleford WF10 ... 200 E5
Normanton WF6 ... 200 A3
Lock Lane Sports Ctr WF10 ... 200 F5
Lock Wlk DL10 ... 41 E4
Locker La HG4 ... 214 C4
Lockey Croft YO32 ... 225 C8
Lockfield Dr BB18 ... 171 E2
Lockgate Rd DN14 ... 207 C4
Lockheed Cl TS18 ... 5 F7
Lockton Cres TS17 ... 6 A6
Lockton Ct LS24 ... 196 B7
Lockton La YO18 ... 72 E4
Lockton Rd YO21 ... 208 A6
Lockwood Chase YO13 ... 54 D1
Lockwood Prim Sch TS12 ... 9 D7
Lockwood St YO31 ... 233 C3
Loders Gn
5 Eastfield YO11 ... 99 F6
10 Eastfield YO11 ... 100 A6
Lodge Cl 7 YO11 ... 100 B6
Lodge Gdns
Gristlthorp YO14 ... 100 E4
5 Snaith DN14 ... 204 C1
Lodge La 5 Brompton DL6 ... 43 F3
Danby YO21 ... 29 D7
Gowdall DN14 ... 203 F1
Newby with Mulwith HG4 ... 140 E6
Wennington LA2 ... 102 B1
Lodge Rd
Hutton-le-Hole YO62 ... 70 C5
Lythe YO21 ... 12 E3
Settle BD24 ... 153 E8
Lodore Gr TS5 ... 6 D7
Lofthouse Endowed Prim Sch HG3 ... 110 B4
Lofthouse La YO41 ... 185 D7
Loftus Cl YO12 ... 212 B4
Lombards Wynd DL10 ... 209 C7
Londesborough Gr 5 YO8 ... 197 B2
Londesborough Pk 10 YO12 ... 99 D6
Londesborough Rd YO12 ... 212 E4
Londesborough St 5 YO8 ... 232 C5
London La DN6 ... 207 D1
Long Acre Wlk HG3 ... 222 E2
Long Ashes Leisure Ctr BD23 ... 134 B3
Long Band DL8 ... 58 A8
Long Bank DL11 ... 19 C6
Long Bank La BD23 ... 153 E1
Long Causeway Rd
Danby YO21 ... 29 E3
Hutton Buscel YO13 ... 99 A4
Long Close La YO10 ... 233 C1
Long Crag View 1 HG3 ... 161 B2
Long Cswy
Halton East BD23 ... 174 B8
Thirkleby High & Low with Osgodby YO7 ... 90 D1
Long Furrow YO32 ... 225 C8
Long Gate BD22 ... 187 D4
Long Gn 7 BB18 ... 172 B1
Long Heads La LS25 ... 195 F1
Long Hill End BD22 ... 187 B5
Long Ing La BB18 ... 171 E1
Long La
Barwick in Elmet LS15 ... 194 C7
Borrowby YO7 ... 65 E5
Brompton DL6 ... 44 A6
Catton YO41 ... 185 D6
Cawood YO8 ... 197 A6
Cowling BD22 ... 187 B7
East Ayton YO13 ... 99 B7
Ellerton YO42 ... 193 F1
Farndale East YO62 ... 48 F4
Felliscliffe HG3 ... 160 E3
Gayles DL11 ... 19 E6
Heck DN14 ... 207 D8
Heslington YO10 ... 184 C3
Kirk Smeaton WF8 ... 206 B1
Laneshaw Bridge BB8 ... 186 B4
Lockwood TS12 ... 10 B5
Normanby YO62 ... 95 A4
Picton TS15 ... 24 E6
Seamer YO12 ... 99 E6
Slingsby YO62 ... 120 D6
Tatham LA2 ... 128 E7
Well DL8 ... 87 C4
Long Level LA6 ... 102 C8
Long Mann Hills Rd YO8 ... 232 B4
Long Marston C of E Prim Sch YO26 ... 182 A6
Long Mdw 12 Colne BB8 ... 186 A3
Skipton BD23 ... 217 B5
Long Mdw Gate LS25 ... 194 C2
Long Mdws
Garforth LS25 ... 194 C3
6 Ilkley LS29 ... 176 C1
Rillington YO17 ... 122 F5
Long Newton La TS21 ... 5 A6
Long Preston Endowed Prim Sch BD23 ... 153 F5
Long Preston Sta BD23 ... 153 F4
Long Rampart YO42 ... 193 D3
Long Riddings LS29 ... 174 F5
Long Ridge Dr YO26 ... 224 A1
Long Ridge La YO26 ... 224 A1
Long Royd Rd BB18 ... 172 A1
Long St Asenby YO7 ... 115 B6
Easingwold YO61 ... 143 C8
Thirsk YO7 ... 211 C3
Topcliffe YO7 ... 115 C6
Long Stoop Standing Stone* HG3 ... 160 A2
Long Swales La HG4 ... 112 D5
Long Trods 5 YO8 ... 232 C6
Long Wlk
Knaresborough HG5 ... 221 A6
Scarborough YO12 ... 212 D7
Longacre WF10 ... 200 E3
Longbank Rd TS7 ... 7 D7
Longber La LA6 ... 102 D4
Longcroft 2 YO32 ... 166 E5
Longcroft Rd 1 LS29 ... 218 E3
Longdale Ave 18 BD24 ... 131 D2
Longdike La
Kippax LS25 ... 200 E8
Thornton Steward HG4 ... 61 E1
Longfield Comp Sch DL3 ... 3 C8
Longfield Ct 21 BB18 ... 171 D1
Longfield Rd DL3 ... 3 C7
Longfield Terr YO30 ... 233 A3
Longland La YO26 ... 164 A3
Longlands Field Rd YO26 ... 163 D8
Longlands La
Boroughbridge YO51 ... 141 A3
Danby YO21 ... 29 B6
Hetton BD23 ... 155 F5
Sicklinghall LS22 ... 179 E3
Thornton-le-Dale YO18 ... 96 E5
Longlands Rd YO17 ... 123 B3
Longmans Hill CP Sch YO8 ... 232 C3
Longtons La BD23 ... 152 F4
Longwestgate YO11 ... 213 B6
Longwood Bank DL10 ... 209 D5
Longwood Link 8 YO30 ... 224 E3
Longwood Rd YO30 ... 224 F3
Lonsdale Mdws LS23 ... 188 E8
Lonsdale Pl 12 YO13 ... 99 B8
Lonsdale Rd YO11 ... 213 A3
Loos Rd DL9 ... 40 F3
Loraine Cres DL1 ... 3 C4
Lord Ave TS17 ... 6 B5
Lord Mayor's Wlk YO31 ... 233 B3
Lord's Close Rd LA2 ... 129 B3
Lords La DL8 ... 41 F1
Lord's La DL8 ... 63 C2
Lords La DL8 ... 62 E8
Lords Moor La YO32 ... 167 C7
Lordship La YO8 ... 232 D8
Loriners Dr 7 YO23 ... 230 B3
Loring Rd YO13 ... 54 A7
Lorne St YO23 ... 228 B1
Lorraine Ave 3 YO41 ... 185 B2
Loscoe Cl WF6 ... 200 C2
Loscoe La WF7 ... 200 C1
Loshpot La LS22 ... 180 C5
Lothersdale CP Sch BD20 ... 186 F8
Lothersdale Rd BD20 ... 187 B8
Lotherton La LS25 ... 195 A7
Lotherton Way LS25 ... 194 C4
Louisa St DL1 ... 3 D5
Lousy Hill La YO22 ... 32 C3
Louvain St 5 BB18 ... 171 D2
Love La Brawby YO17 ... 94 F1
Castleford WF10 ... 200 E3
Easby DL10 ... 209 E4
8 Leyburn DL8 ... 60 D5
Whitby YO21 ... 208 A7
York YO24 ... 228 A2
Lovers' La DL7 ... 64 F2
Low Bank
4 Embsay BD23 ... 217 E8
Over Silton DL6 ... 66 A8
Low Bentham CP Sch LA2 ... 128 F8
Low Bentham Rd LA2 ... 128 F8
Low Catton Rd YO41 ... 185 C8
Low Cl LS29 ... 218 A5
Low Croft 6 YO32 ... 167 A7
Low Demesne LA6 ... 103 D3
Low Demesne Cl LA6 ... 103 D3
Low Farm LS26 ... 200 C8
Low Farm Cl YO23 ... 190 D4
Low Field La
Cold Kirby YO7 ... 91 D7
Goldsborough HG5 ... 163 A1
Marton cum Grafton YO51 ... 141 E2
Staveley HG5 ... 140 E1
Low Fields Dr YO24 ... 227 C3
Low Fold BB18 ... 186 A7
Low Garth YO22 ... 32 A6
Low Garth Link 17 LS25 ... 195 F4
Low Garth Rd LS25 ... 195 F4
Low Gate DL8 ... 57 F5
Low Gate La HG4 ... 138 F7
Low Gn Catterick DL10 ... 41 D4
Copmanthorpe YO23 ... 230 B2
18 Knottingley WF11 ... 202 A2
Menwith with Darley HG3 ... 160 A6
Low House La
Carlton Miniott YO7 ... 89 C2
Dishforth YO7 ... 115 B2
Low Hutton Pk YO60 ... 147 C6
Low La Askrigg DL8 ... 58 B4
Carperby-cum-Thoresby DL8 ... 58 F4
Cononley BD20 ... 173 C2
Cowling BD22 ... 187 A8
Cropton YO18 ... 71 B4
Dalby-cum-Skewsby YO60 ... 119 B2
Dalton DL11 ... 19 D7
Embsay with Eastby BD23 ... 217 E8
Grassington BD23 ... 134 E3
Grinton DL11 ... 37 E5
Grinton DL11 ... 38 C5
Heslington YO10 ... 229 D1
Howsham YO60 ... 147 A1
Hutton-Sessay YO7 ... 116 B7
Leck LA6 ... 102 D7
Leyburn DL8 ... 60 C4
Maltby TS17 ... 6 B3
Menwith with Darley HG3 ... 159 F6
Mickleby TS13 ... 12 A3
Middlesbrough TS5 ... 6 E6
Muker DL11 ... 36 C4
Newsham DL11 ... 18 H7
Reeth, Fremington & Healaugh DL11 ... 37 F5
Silsden BD20 ... 174 B3
Spofforth with Stockeld HG3 ... 179 C4
Stainburn LS21 ... 177 F3
Sutton-under-Whitestonecliffe YO7 ... 90 E6
Swinton YO17 ... 121 C4
Thirkleby High & Low with Osgodby YO7 ... 90 C1
West Rounton DL6 ... 24 D3
Westow YO60 ... 147 C4
Wigglesworth BD23 ... 153 D3
Low Mdw YO8 ... 232 C6
Low Mill Cl YO10 ... 229 D3
Low Mill La LS29 ... 175 A4
Low Mill Rd HG4 ... 214 D4
Low Moor Ave 3 YO10 ... 231 F8
Low Moor La
Askham Richard YO23 ... 182 D3
Brearton HG5 ... 162 B7
East Harlsey DL6 ... 44 C7
Fearby HG4 ... 85 F3
Hessay YO26 ... 182 C8
Rillington YO17 ... 122 E6
Low Moor Rd YO18 ... 71 F5
Low Moor S La YO17 ... 122 D6
Low Moorgate YO17 ... 122 F5
Low Ousegate YO1 ... 233 B2
Low Park Rd LS29 ... 176 A3
Low Peter La HG3 ... 140 A3
Low Petergate YO1 ... 233 B3
Low Poppleton La YO26 ... 227 B7
Low Rd Gainford DL2 ... 1 C7
Gowdall DN14 ... 204 A1
Irton YO12 ... 75 B3
Kellington DN14 ... 202 F4
Kirby Grindalythe YO17 ... 149 F7
Newby & Scalby YO12 ... 212 A6
Thirkleby High & Low with Osgodby YO7 ... 116 E8
Low Skellgate HG4 ... 214 C5
Low Sleights Rd LA6 ... 104 B7
Low St Aiskew DL7 ... 63 C6
Austwick LA2 ... 130 E7
Burton in Lonsdale LA6 ... 102 F3
Carlton DN14 ... 204 C2
Husthwaite YO61 ... 117 B6
Kirkby Fleetham with Fencote DL10 ... 41 F2
Knottingley WF11 ... 201 E4
Lastingham YO62 ... 70 E5
Nunnington YO62 ... 93 E2
Oswaldkirk YO62 ... 92 F3
Ripon HG4 ... 214 D5
22 Scalby YO13 ... 75 D5
Sherburn in Elmet LS25 ... 195 F4
Thornton-le-Clay YO60 ... 146 A4
Low Stanghow Rd TS12 ... 9 F6
Low Town Bank Rd YO61 ... 91 B4
Low Tun Way YO62 ... 69 A2
Low Wath Rd HG3 ... 137 B4
Low Way 5 LS23 ... 188 E5
Low Well Pk YO19 ... 192 F7
Low Westfield Rd YO23 ... 230 A1
Low Wood La
Glaisdale YO21 ... 30 C6
Leyburn DL8 ... 60 C4
Low Wood Rise LS29 ... 218 F3
Lowcroft 9 LS22 ... 188 A8
Lowcross Ave TS14 ... 8 E5
Lowcross Dr TS9 ... 26 E5
Lowdale Ave YO12 ... 212 E8
Lowdale Ct 4 YO22 ... 32 A6
Lower Clark St
2 Scarborough YO12 ... 212 F6
13 Scarborough YO12 ... 213 A7
Lower Constable Rd LS29 ... 218 D3
Lower Croft St 39 BB18 ... 172 A1
Lower Darnborough St YO23 ... 233 B1
Lower Derwent Valley Nature Reserve* YO42 ... 199 C8
Lower Flat Cliffs YO14 ... 101 C1
Lower Friargate YO1 ... 233 B2
Lower Greenfoot 15 BD24 ... 131 D2
Lower Mickletown LS26 ... 200 C6
Lower Oxford St WF10 ... 200 E4
Lower Park Marina* BB18 ... 171 E1
Lower Priory St YO1 ... 233 A1
Lower Station Rd 3 WF6 ... 200 A1
Lower Union St BD23 ... 216 F3
Lower Wellington Rd LS29 ... 218 B4
Lower William St 3 YO12 ... 212 F6
Loweswater Rd 5 YO30 ... 224 E1
Lowfield
3 Eastfield YO11 ... 100 A6
Hawes DL8 ... 56 C4
Lowfield Dr YO32 ... 166 E5
Lowfield La
Beamsley BD23 ... 174 F7
Kirkby Fleetham with Fencote DL7 ... 42 D2
Langthorpe YO51 ... 141 A6
Rufforth YO26 ... 227 A4
Scrayingham YO41 ... 169 A7
Sharow HG4 ... 214 F6
Snape with Thorp DL8 ... 87 A7
Lowfield Rd
Barlby with Osgodby YO8 ... 198 B5
Hillam LS25 ... 202 C8
Malton YO17 ... 215 C6
Lowfield Sch YO24 ... 227 D3
Lowfields 2 YO12 ... 99 D2
Lowfields Ave TS17 ... 6 A5
Lowfields La YO7 ... 88 C6
Lowgate DN14 ... 207 D5
Lowgill La LA2 ... 128 F4
Lowick YO24 ... 230 C7
Lowkber La LA6 ... 103 E2
Lowlands Dr DL7 ... 63 C5
Lowmoor Rd YO8 ... 198 E6
Lown Hill YO24 ... 227 C2
Lowna Rd YO62 ... 70 B5
Lownorth Rd YO13 ... 53 C2
Lowskellgate 15 HG4 ... 214 C5
Lowther Cres 3 LS26 ... 194 A1
Lowther Ct YO31 ... 233 C4
Lowther Dr
Garforth LS25 ... 194 C3
Selby YO8 ... 232 E3
2 Swillington LS26 ... 194 A1
Lowther St YO31 ... 233 C4
Lowther Terr YO24 ... 228 A3
Loxley Cl YO30 ... 224 F2
Loyne Pk LA6 ... 102 A7
Lucas Ave YO30 ... 228 C8
Lucas Gr N YO26 ... 181 C7
Lucas Gr S YO26 ... 181 C7
Lucas Rd YO26 ... 181 C7
Lucerne Dr TS14 ... 8 E6
Lucia La TS14 ... 8 E6
Lucky La YO7 ... 89 E8
Lucombe Way YO32 ... 225 D4
Luddith Rd YO17 ... 148 D5
Ludlow Ave LS25 ... 194 D4
Lulsgate TS17 ... 6 C7
Lumb Gill La LS29 ... 175 A3
Lumb La BD22 ... 187 A5
Lumb Mill Way BD23 ... 157 E7
Lumby Hill LS25 ... 202 A8
Lumby La
Monk Fryston LS25 ... 202 A8
South Milford LS25 ... 196 A1
Lumley Cl YO7 ... 211 D2
Lumley La Azerley HG4 ... 112 D2
Kirkby Fleetham with Fencote DL7 ... 42 B1
Lumley Rd YO30 ... 228 B7
Lumley St WF10 ... 200 D3
Lunar Pk* YO11 ... 213 C6
Luncarr La HG4 ... 114 B2
Lund Cl YO32 ... 225 C8
Lund Head La HG3 ... 179 B2
Lund La Bubwith YO8 ... 199 C4
Cliffe YO8 ... 198 D4
Hampsthwaite HG3 ... 161 A5
Lund Rd YO62 ... 70 B7
Lund Sand La
Easingwold YO61 ... 143 A8
Raskelf YO61 ... 117 A1
Lund Sike La LS25 ... 195 F2
Lundgreen La YO61 ... 144 A3
Lund's Twr* BD20 ... 187 C6
Lundy Cl 10 YO30 ... 225 A1
Lunebeck Wlk TS17 ... 6 C6
Lunedale Ave
Knaresborough HG5 ... 221 C5
Middlesbrough TS5 ... 6 E8
Lunedale Rd DL3 ... 3 A6
Lunn La DN14 ... 202 D3
Lunnfields La WF11 ... 201 E6
Lupton Bank HG3 ... 137 D3
Lupton Cl HG3 ... 137 D3
Lutton La YO17 ... 123 F4
Luttons CP Sch YO17 ... 150 B8
Lutyens The 22 LS29 ... 175 C2
Lycett Rd YO24 ... 230 F6
Lych Gate 14 DL2 ... 3 E1
Lydford Rd 18 DL10 ... 41 E4
Lydham Ct 2 YO24 ... 230 C8
Lyell St YO12 ... 212 E6
Lynbrook Cl YO7 ... 211 B4
Lyndale LS25 ... 200 D8
Lyndale Ave YO10 ... 229 C3
Lyndale Gr 14 WF6 ... 200 B1
Lynden Way YO24 ... 227 D3
Lyndhurst Cl
2 Norton DN6 ... 206 F2
9 Whitby YO21 ... 208 D6
Lyndhurst Dr 1 DN6 ... 206 F2
Lyndhurst Rise 3 DN6 ... 206 F2
Lyndon Ave
Bramham LS23 ... 188 E6
Garforth LS25 ... 194 C4
Lyndon Cl 1 LS23 ... 188 E6
Lyndon Cres 4 LS23 ... 188 E6
Lyndon Rd LS23 ... 188 E6
Lyndon Sq 2 LS23 ... 188 E6
Lyndon Way LS23 ... 188 E6
Lynmouth Cl TS8 ... 6 E5
Lynndale Ave 6 BD20 ... 187 F8
Lynton Ave LS23 ... 188 E8
Lynton Cl YO8 ... 232 B1
Lynton Gdns
Brayton YO8 ... 232 B1
Darlington DL1 ... 3 E5
Harrogate HG1 ... 220 A3
Lynton Way DL6 ... 210 D3
Lynwith Cl DN14 ... 204 C3
Lynwith Ct DN14 ... 204 C3
Lynwith Dr DN14 ... 204 C3
Lynwood Ave 3 YO23 ... 230 A3
Lynwood View 4 YO23 ... 230 A3
Lynx La YO7 ... 115 B1
Lyon Rd BD20 ... 187 F7
Lyonette Rd DL1 ... 3 E7
Lyons Rd DL10 ... 209 C8
Lys Cres DL9 ... 209 D1
Lysander Cl YO30 ... 225 A3
Lytham Cl BD23 ... 217 C3
Lytham Gdns BD23 ... 217 C3
Lytham Rd DL1 ... 3 D8
Lythe Bank Lythe YO21 ... 12 F4
Sutton with Howgrave DL8 ... 87 F2
Lythe C of E Prim Sch YO21 ... 12 E3
Lythe Fell Rd LA2 ... 129 B2
Lythe La LA2 ... 129 A2

M

M62 Trad Est DN14 ... 205 F2
Mac Arthur Cl YO7 ... 211 B2
Macdonell Cl 1 DL9 ... 209 C1
Mackeridge La YO62 ... 48 F4
Mackie Dr TS14 ... 8 F7
Mackinnon Ave 1 WF6 ... 200 B2
Maclagan Rd YO23 ... 230 F4
Mafeking St HG1 ... 219 F4
Magazine La YO8 ... 198 B3
Magazine Rd YO8 ... 198 B4
Magdalen's Cl HG4 ... 214 D6
Magdalen's Rd HG4 ... 214 D6
Magister Rd TS17 ... 6 B7
Magnolia Gr YO32 ... 225 D2
Maida Gr YO10 ... 228 D2
Maiden Bower (Motte & Bailey)* YO7 ... 115 D5
Maiden Castle* DL11 ... 38 A5
Maiden Greve YO17 ... 215 A4
Maidensgrave Henge* YO25 ... 126 F1
Maidstone Dr TS7 ... 7 C6
Main Ave YO31 ... 228 F5
Main Rd Drax YO8 ... 204 F5
Gainford DL2 ... 1 D7
Hambleton YO8 ... 196 E1
Hellifield BD23 ... 154 B3
Stainforth BD24 ... 131 E6
Steeton with Eastburn BD20 ... 187 F7
Weaverthorpe YO17 ... 124 E1
Main St Aberford LS25 ... 194 F8
Addingham LS29 ... 174 F4
Allerston YO18 ... 97 B5
Alne YO61 ... 142 F4
Amotherby YO17 ... 121 A4
Appleton Roebuck YO23 ... 190 F5
Askham Bryan YO23 ... 182 F3
Askrigg DL8 ... 57 E6
Asselby DN14 ... 205 D7
Austwick LA2 ... 130 E7
Aysgarth DL8 ... 58 E3
Barkston Ash LS24 ... 195 E7
Barwick in Elmet LS15 ... 194 B8
3 Beal DN14 ... 202 D4
Bentham LA2 ... 128 E8
Bilbrough YO23 ... 182 C1
Bilton-in-Ainsty with Bickerton LS22 ... 181 A5
Bishop Monkton HG3 ... 140 B5
Bishopthorpe YO23 ... 231 A4
Boroughbridge YO51 ... 141 A3
4 Brafferton YO61 ... 115 F1

Main St *continued*
Brafferton YO61 141 F8
Bubwith YO8 199 C7
Bugthorpe YO41 169 D4
Burley in Warfedale LS29 176 C1
Burton Salmon LS25 201 F6
Church Fenton LS24 196 B7
Cliffe YO8 198 E2
Cononley BD20 173 D1
Copmanthorpe YO23 230 A2
Cottingwith YO42 193 C5
Darley HG3 160 A6
Deighton YO19 192 A7
Earby BB18 186 A7
East Ayton/West Ayton YO13 99 A7
Eastfield YO11 100 B6
Ebberston & Yedingham YO13 97 D5
Ellerton YO42 193 C1
Elvington YO41 185 C2
Embsay BD23 217 E8
Escrick YO19 192 B5
Farnhill BD20 173 E1
Folkton YO11 100 A2
Follifoot HG3 223 F5
Ganton YO12 125 A8
Garforth LS25 194 C3
Gillamoor YO62 70 A4
Gilling East YO62 118 F7
Glusburn BD20 187 E7
Gowdall DN14 204 A1
13 Grassington BD23 134 E3
Great Ouseburn YO26 164 B8
Great Preston WF10 200 D6
Gristlthorp YO14 100 E4
Harome YO62 93 C5
Healaugh LS24 181 F2
Hebden BD23 135 A1
Heck DN14 207 C8
Helperby YO61 142 A8
Hemingbrough YO8 198 F1
Hensall DN14 203 D2
Hessay YO26 182 B8
High Bentham LA2 129 A8
Hovingham YO62 119 E6
Huby YO61 144 A4
Ingleton LA6 103 D3
Irton YO12 99 C6
Kelfield YO19 191 D1
Kellington DN14 202 F3
Kirk Deighton LS22 180 B5
Kirk Smeaton WF8 206 B3
Kirkby Malham BD23 154 F8
Kirkby Malzeard HG4 112 C5
Langcliffe BD24 131 E4
Ledston WF10 200 F7
Linton LS22 180 A1
Little Ouseburn YO26 164 A7
Long Preston BD23 153 F5
Low Bradley BD20 173 E3
Menwith with Darley HG3 160 A4
Mickletown LS26 200 B6
Middleton YO18 95 E8
Monk Fryston LS25 201 F8
1 Naburn YO19 191 D8
Newton Kyme cum Toulston LS24 189 C7
North Duffield YO8 199 A8
Pannal HG3 222 D3
Pollington DN14 207 F6
Poppleton YO26 165 F1
Rathmell BD24 153 C6
Reighton YO14 127 E5
Riccall YO19 198 A8
Ryther cum Ossendyke LS24 190 E2
Saxton with Scarthingwell LS24 195 D7
Scholes LS15 194 A7
Scotton HG5 162 A6
Seamer YO12 99 D6
Sheriff Hutton YO60 145 D5
Shipton YO30 165 F5
Sicklinghall LS22 179 D3
Sinnington YO62 95 A8
Stainforth BD24 131 E6
Stamford Bridge YO41 168 D2
Staveley HG5 140 E1
Stillington YO61 144 C6
Threshfield BD23 134 C2
Thwing YO25 126 B1
Tollerton YO61 143 A3
Ulleskelf LS24 190 C3
Walton LS23 181 A2
Wath HG4 114 A8
Weeton LS17 178 C1
West Tanfield HG4 87 A1
Westow YO60 147 B4
Wheldrake YO19 192 F7
Whittington LA6 102 A7
Wilberfoss YO41 185 E5
Wombleton YO62 93 E6
Womersley DN6 206 C6
Wray-with-Botton LA2 128 A6
York YO26 227 A5
York YO10 229 B1
York YO10 231 D8
Mains La YO60 146 D5
Mains The BD24 131 D3
Mainsfield Cl 1 BD24 131 D3
Mainsfield Rise 2 BD24 131 D3
Maison Dieu DL10 209 D7
Major St DL3 3 C6
Malais La BD20 187 D7
Malbys Gr YO23 230 B2
Malden Rd HG1 220 B3
Malham Gr YO31 229 B5
Malham Moor La BD23 133 F4
Malham Rakes BD23 133 A2
Malham Tarn Field Ctr★ BD24 132 F6
Malham Visitor Ctr★ BD23 133 A1
Malham Way HG5 221 D6
Malim Rd DL1 3 F5
Mallard Cl 8 Filey YO14 101 A4
12 Pickering YO18 95 F6
Mallard Rd 4 DL9 40 F2
Mallard View YO17 215 D2
Mallard Way
4 Eastfield YO12 99 F6
11 Haxby YO32 166 F5
Mallard Wlk 14 YO51 141 B5
Mallinson Cl HG2 222 D6
Mallinson Cres HG2 222 E6
Mallinson Gate HG2 222 E6
Mallinson Gr HG2 222 D6
Mallinson Oval HG2 222 D6
Mallinson Way HG2 222 D6
Mallinson Hill Dr 5 YO61 117 D1
Mallorie Cl HG4 214 A5
Mallorie Ct HG4 214 B5
Mallorie Park Dr HG4 214 A4
Mallory Cl YO32 225 D4
Mallory Ct 17 DL1 3 F6
Mallowdale TS7 7 C5
Malltraeth Sands TS17 6 D6
Malpas Dr DL7 210 D4
Malpas Rd
Brompton YO13 98 C4
Northallerton DL7 210 D3
Malsis Prep Sch BD20 187 C7
Malt Dubs Cl LA6 103 D3
Malt Kiln La YO23 190 F5
Malt Kiln Terr LS24 189 D4
Maltby Rd TS8 6 D4
Malthouse La HG3 222 D2
Maltings Ct Alne YO61 143 A5
6 Selby YO8 232 C6
Maltings The
8 Brafferton YO61 115 F1
13 Pontefract WF8 201 B1
Thirsk YO7 211 B2
Maltkiln La
Castleford WF10 200 F4
Killinghall HG3 161 C6
Malton Ave YO31 228 E6
Malton CP Sch YO17 215 D5
Malton Gate YO18 96 D5
Malton La
Allerston YO18 97 B4
Flaxton YO60 146 A1
Kirby Grindalythe YO17 150 A8
Malton Mus★ YO17 215 C4
Malton Norton & District Hospl YO17 215 B4
Malton Rd
Hunmanby YO14 126 F8
Huntington YO32 226 A1
Leavening YO17 147 E2
Pickering YO18 95 F6
Rillington YO17 122 E4
Scampston YO17 123 B7
Slingsby YO62 120 B5
Swinton YO17 121 C4
York YO31 228 F7
Malton Rugby Club YO17 215 E5
Malton St Marys RC Prim Sch YO17 215 D5
Malton Sch YO17 215 A5
Malton St YO61 117 D6
Malton Sta YO17 215 C3
Malton Way YO30 227 F8
Malvern Ave YO26 227 D5
Malvern Cl
Huntington YO32 226 A5
8 Hurworth-on-Tees DL2 3 E1
Stokesley TS9 26 C7
Malvern Cres
Darlington DL3 2 F7
Scarborough YO12 212 D5
Malvern Dr
Middlesbrough TS5 6 E6
Stokesley TS9 26 C7
Malvern Rd WF11 201 F2
Manchester Rd BB18 171 D1
Mancroft YO32 225 C8
Mandale Mill Prim Sch TS17 6 B8
Mandale Rd TS5 6 D8
Manfield C of E Prim Sch DL2 2 B4
Mangrill La LS14 188 C3
Manham Hill YO11 99 F7
Mankin La HG4 214 D1
Manley Cl YO32 225 D4
Manley Dr LS22 180 A3
Manley Gr LS29 218 D4
Manley Rd LS29 218 E4
Manley Rise LS29 218 D3
Manor Ave YO12 212 D6
Manor Beeches The 3 YO19 184 E7
Manor C of E Sch YO26 227 C7
Manor Chase YO26 181 F6
Manor Cl
Burton in Lonsdale LA6 102 F3
5 Hemingbrough YO8 198 F1
Ingleton LA6 103 D3
Kirk Smeaton WF8 206 B3
13 Kirkbymoorside YO62 70 B1
Low Worsall TS15 24 B8
6 North Duffield YO8 199 A7
12 Norton DN6 206 E2
5 Stokesley TS9 26 C7
Topcliffe YO7 115 C6
Wath HG4 114 B7
Whitby YO21 208 B6
Manor Cres HG5 221 C6
Manor Ct
6 Bubwith YO8 199 D7
Fairburn WF11 201 D7
Follifoot HG3 223 F5
Kirkby Malzeard HG4 112 D5
Knaresborough HG5 221 B5
2 York YO32 225 F6
Manor Dr
2 Brafferton YO61 115 F1
Camblesforth YO8 204 C4
4 Dunnington YO19 184 E7
Harrogate HG2 222 C8
Hilton TS15 6 C2
Kirby Hill YO51 141 A7
Knaresborough HG5 221 C6
5 North Duffield YO8 199 A7
North Featherstone WF7 200 E1
Pickering YO18 95 E7
Scotton HG5 162 A6
Manor Dr N YO26 227 D4
Manor Dr S YO26 227 D4
Manor Farm Cl
1 Brayton YO8 232 A1
Carlton DN14 204 C2
Copmanthorpe YO23 230 A2
Kellington DN14 202 F3
Manor Farm Ct YO8 203 C4
Manor Farm Way TS8 6 F5
Manor Fold HG3 223 F5
Manor Garth
Haxby YO32 225 B8
Kellington DN14 202 F3
12 Kirklevington TS15 24 E8
Ledsham LS25 201 B8
7 Norton DN6 206 F2
1 Riccall YO19 198 A8
7 Spofforth HG3 179 E6
Manor Garth Rd LS25 194 E1
Manor Gdns
6 Hunmanby YO14 127 A8
Killinghall HG3 161 C5
Scarborough YO12 212 E6
Thorner LS14 188 A3
Manor Gn DL8 62 C6
Manor Gr Colburn DL9 40 F5
Great Broughton TS9 26 E5
Manor Heath YO23 230 A3
Manor House Art Gall & Mus★ LS29 218 B4
Manor Inf Sch The HG5 221 B6
Manor La
Healaugh LS24 181 E1
Rawcliffe YO30 224 D2
Manor Orchards HG5 221 B6
Manor Park Ave
Great Preston WF10 200 D7
Pontefract WF8 201 C2
Manor Park Cl YO30 224 E2
Manor Park Gr YO30 224 E2
Manor Park Rd YO30 224 E2
Manor Pk
Arkendale HG5 163 A7
Cowling BD22 187 B6
Ledston WF10 200 F7
Swinton YO17 121 C4
Manor Rd Beal DN14 202 C4
Darlington DL3 3 C4
Easingwold YO61 117 C1
Fylingdales YO22 33 C4
Harrogate HG2 222 B8
Hurworth-on-Tees DL2 3 D1
Killinghall HG3 161 C5
Knaresborough HG5 221 B6
Scarborough YO12 212 E5
Stutton with Hazlewood LS24 189 D4
Manor Rise LS29 218 D4
Manor Vale La 28 YO62 70 B1
Manor View
Oswaldkirk YO62 93 A1
Rillington YO17 122 F5
Manor View Rd YO11 100 D5
Manor Way
Glusburn BD20 187 E6
York YO30 224 E2
Manor Wood TS8 6 F6
Manorcroft WF6 200 A1
Manorfields 11 DL2 3 E1
Manse Cres 23 LS29 176 C1
Manse La HG5 221 D4
Manse Rd LS29 176 C1
Manse Way BD20 187 E7
Mansfield Ave TS17 6 B8
Mansfield Rd LS29 176 B1
Mansfield St YO31 233 C3
Manston Ct 14 DL2 4 C4
Manston La LS15 194 A5
Manton Ave TS5 6 D8
Maple Ave
Bishopthorpe YO23 231 A3
Malton YO17 215 D6
Maple Cl 5 Colburn DL9 40 F5
Maple Cl *continued*
Hambleton YO8 197 B1
Knaresborough HG1 220 D5
2 South Milford LS25 195 F2
Maple Croft YO61 144 A5
Maple Ct YO10 231 E6
Maple Dr YO12 212 D7
Maple Gr 12 Brayton YO8 197 D1
7 Linton-on-Ouse YO30 164 F7
York YO10 228 D1
Maple La YO61 144 A5
Maple Rd DL10 209 A8
Maple Tree Ave YO8 198 B4
Maplewood Paddock 2 YO24 227 C1
Mar Head Balk HG5 163 A7
Marage Rd YO7 211 B3
Marazion Dr DL3 3 C8
Marbeck La HG5 140 F2
March St
Normanton South WF6 200 A1
York YO31 233 C4
Marchlyn Cres TS17 5 F4
Marcus St DN14 205 F2
Marderby La YO7 90 C7
Maresfield Rd DL9 40 E3
Margaret Rd HG2 219 B1
Margaret St YO10 233 C1
Margerison Cres LS29 218 E3
Margerison Rd LS29 218 E3
Maria St 15 LS29 176 C1
Marias Ct 9 YO11 213 A6
Marigold Cl YO8 232 C2
Marina Ave 3 DN14 204 B1
Marina Cres BD23 216 D3
Marina Rd DL3 3 D8
Marina Way HG4 214 A2
Marine Dr YO11 213 C7
Marine Espl YO13 54 A8
Marine Villa Rd WF11 201 F2
Mariner's Terr 16 YO14 101 B3
Marion Ave TS16 5 D4
Marishes La
Allerston YO17 97 A2
Thornton-le-Dale YO17 96 E1
Marishes Low Rd YO17 122 B8
Mark House La BD23 155 C1
Mark La
Fylingdales YO22 33 C3
Kirk Deighton LS22 180 B5
Markenfield Hall★ HG4 139 D6
Markenfield Rd HG3 219 B5
Market Flat La HG5 162 C6
Market Hill 5 YO51 141 B6
Market La YO8 232 C5
Market Pl 4 Bedale DL8 63 A3
2 Cawood YO8 197 B8
7 Easingwold YO61 143 C8
11 Helmsley YO62 92 F6
10 Helmsley YO62 92 F6
25 Kirkbymoorside YO62 70 B1
3 Knaresborough HG5 221 B6
Malton YO17 215 C4
9 Masham HG4 86 C3
9 Middleham DL8 60 E2
6 Normanton South WF6 200 A1
Pickering YO18 95 F7
Richmond DL10 209 C6
11 Selby YO8 232 C5
10 Settle BD24 131 D2
9 Snaith DN14 204 C1
Thirsk YO7 211 B3
12 Wetherby LS22 180 C3
11 Whitby YO22 208 D7
Market Pl E 20 HG4 214 C5
Market Pl N 19 HG4 214 C5
Market Pl S 21 HG4 214 C5
Market Pl W 22 HG4 214 C5
Market St Malton YO17 215 C4
Normanton South WF6 200 A1
24 Scarborough YO11 213 A6
York YO1 233 B2
Market Way 25 YO11 213 A6
Market Weighton Rd YO8 198 B6
Markham Cres YO31 233 B4
Markham St YO31 233 B4
Markington C of E Prim Sch HG3 139 C3
Marl Hill La BD20 186 D8
Marlborough Ave
3 Byram WF11 201 F4
Tadcaster LS24 189 D5
3 Whitby YO21 208 B7
Marlborough Cl YO30 224 D3
Marlborough Dr
Darlington DL1 3 C4
Tadcaster LS24 189 D5
Marlborough Gr
Ilkley LS29 218 D3
Ripon HG4 214 B6
York YO10 228 D2
Marlborough Rd HG1 219 E2
Marlborough Sq LS29 218 C3
Marlborough St 11 YO12 213 A7
Marmiam Dr 2 YO32 167 D2
Marmion Ct HG4 87 A1
Marmion Twr★ HG4 87 A1
Marne Cl 1 DL9 209 B1
Marne Rd DL9 209 D1
Marr The YO14 100 F5
Marrick Priory (rems of)★ DL11 38 E4
Marrick Rd TS18 5 D8
Marridales DL8 56 D4
Marriforth La HG4 61 F2
Mars La TS13 11 A4
Marsett La DL8 57 B2
Marsh Croft WF11 201 E4
Marsh End WF11 202 A3
Marsh La Asselby DN14 205 D7
Barlow YO8 204 B8
2 Beal DN14 202 D4
Bolton Percy YO23 190 D3
Byram cum Sutton WF11 201 F4
Cawood YO8 197 D8
Ingleby Greenhow TS9 27 B5
Knottingley WF11 202 A2
West Haddlesey YO8 202 F5
Marsh Lane Gdns DN14 202 F4
Marsh Rd WF10 200 D3
Marshall Dr YO18 96 A7
Marshfield Rd 7 BD24 131 D2
Marston Ave YO26 227 B3
Marston Bsns Pk YO26 181 B7
Marston Cres YO26 227 B3
Marston La YO26 182 A8
Marston Moor Rd DL1 3 F4
Marston Rd YO26 181 D7
Marston Way 3 LS22 180 B3
Marten Cl 2 YO30 228 A8
Martin Cheeseman Ct 3 YO24 230 C8
Martindale Rd DL1 3 D7
Martinet Rd TS17 6 B7
Marton Abbey (Priory)★ YO61 144 C8
Marton Ave TS4 7 B8
Marton Cum Grafton C of E Prim Sch YO51 141 D1
Marton La
Arkendale HG5 163 B8
Wrelton YO18 95 C7
Marton Manor Prim Sch TS7 7 B6
Marton Moor Rd TS7 7 D5
Marton Rd
Coulby Newham TS4 7 A7
Gargrave BD23 172 C8
Marton YO62 94 F6
Sinnington YO62 95 A7
Marton St BD23 216 D3
Marton Sta TS7 7 C7
Martonside Way TS4 7 A8
Marvell Rise HG1 219 E7
Marwood Dr TS9 7 F1
Marwoods C of E Inf Sch TS9 7 F1
Mary La YO26 141 F3
Mary St 3 BD20 173 F1
Marygate Barton DL10 21 D7
York YO30 233 A3
Marygate La YO30 233 A3
Marykirk Rd TS17 6 B6
Masefield Cl HG1 219 E7
Masham Bank HG4 85 D8
Masham C of E Prim Sch HG4 86 C3
Masham Cl HG2 220 C1
Masham La DL8 87 A4
Masham Rd Firby DL8 62 F1
Harrogate HG2 220 C1
Snape with Thorp DL8 86 E8
Mask La YO41 185 D4
Masongill Fell La LA6 103 A6
Masonic La YO7 211 B3
Maspin Moor Rd LS25 202 C7
Massa Flatts Wood BD23 216 E5
Massey St YO8 232 C5
Master Rd TS17 6 B7
Master's Gate YO18 49 D4
Mastil Cl DL8 62 D5
Mastiles La BD23 134 A6
Matfen Ave TS7 7 D6
Matthew La
Bradleys Both BD20 173 E3
Green Hammerton YO26 164 C4
Mattison Way YO24 227 E2
Maud La LS21 177 A6
Maude Rd DL9 209 A1
Maudon Ave YO18 96 A6
Maudon Gr YO17 215 F4
Maufe Way 3 LS29 218 B3
Maunby La YO7 64 D1
Mawson Gr DL6 65 B5
Mawson La HG4 214 C4
Maxim Cl 5 DL9 40 E4
Maxwell Rd LS29 218 D3
May Beck Farm Trail YO22 32 D1
Mayfair Ave TS6 7 E8
Mayfair Rd DL1 3 D8
Mayfield DL7 64 F2
Mayfield Ave
Ilkley LS29 218 D4
7 Scalby YO12 75 E5
Mayfield Cl
3 Glusburn BD20 187 E7
Ilkley LS29 218 D4
Mayfield Cres TS16 5 D5
Mayfield Dr
5 Brayton YO8 232 A1
4 Seamer YO12 99 D6
Mayfield Gdns LS29 218 D5
Mayfield Gr
Harrogate HG1 219 D3
York YO24 230 E8
Mayfield Pl
Harrogate HG1 219 D3
3 Whitby YO21 208 C5

Mayfield Rd
Brayton YO8 232 A1
Ilkley LS29 218 C4
Middlesbrough TS7 7 D6
Whitby YO21 208 B5
Mayfield Terr HG1 219 D3
Maypole Gdns YO8 197 B8
Maypole Gr 3 YO19 191 D8
Maypole Mews LS15 194 B8
Maythorn Rd YO31 225 E2
Maythorpe YO23 182 C6
Mayville Ave YO12 212 E6
Mcdonald Rd HG4 113 D3
Mcmullen Rd DL1 3 E6
Mead Cres TS17 6 C8
Meadlands YO31 229 B6
Meadow Ave 5 HG4 214 B2
Meadow Brook Chase 19 WF6 200 B1
Meadow Cl
Cononley BD20 173 D2
7 Eastfield YO11 100 A6
Hampsthwaite HG3 160 F5
Northallerton DL7 210 D2
Thorpe Willoughby YO8 197 C2
Meadow Croft
Brayton YO8 232 A2
Cononley BD20 173 C2
Meadow Ct
Rillington YO17 122 F5
Scruton DL7 63 E7
6 Willerby YO12 99 D2
3 York YO24 230 E8
Meadow Dale Ct TS12 9 F7
Meadow Dr
7 East Ayton/West Ayton YO13 99 B8
Harrogate HG1 219 E7
Scruton DL7 63 E7
Thorpe Willoughby YO8 197 B2
Meadow Garth
2 Tadcaster LS24 189 F6
Thorpe Willoughby YO8 197 C2
Meadow Gate HG1 219 E6
Meadow Gr 20 DL8 63 A2
Meadow La
Cononley BD20 173 C2
2 Darley HG3 160 A6
8 Eastfield YO11 100 A6
1 Haxby YO32 225 D8
Northallerton DL6 210 E6
Snape DL8 87 A7
Meadow Lea 21 BD20 187 E7
Meadow Pl 5 YO8 232 B6
Meadow Rd
Garforth LS25 194 D4
Knaresborough HG5 221 B7
2 Pickering YO18 95 F7
Meadow Rise
Harrogate HG1 219 E7
2 Skipton BD23 217 B5
Meadow Spring Bank HG4 214 C7
Meadow Springs Way 3 YO61 143 D8
Meadow Vale
Green Hammerton YO26 164 C3
2 Ripon HG4 214 B2
Meadow View
Barwick in Elmet & Scholes LS15 194 B8
Harrogate HG1 219 E6
Sherburn in Elmet LS25 195 F4
Meadow Way
Barnoldswick BB18 171 E2
Harrogate HG1 219 E7
3 Tadcaster LS24 189 F6
York YO32 225 F4
York YO31 228 F7
Meadowbank Rd TS7 7 D7
Meadowbeck Cl YO10 229 B4
Meadowcroft
Draughton BD23 174 B7
Harrogate HG1 219 E6
Meadowcroft Dr HG3 140 A5
Meadowfield
Amotherby YO17 121 A4
9 Bedale DL8 63 B3
1 Bubwith YO8 199 D7
Lythe YO21 13 A3
8 Stokesley TS9 26 C8
Meadowfield Dr TS16 5 D5
Meadowfield Rd
9 Colburn DL9 41 A5
Darlington DL3 3 A7
Meadowfields YO21 208 C6
Meadowfields Cl 9 YO61 143 D8
Meadowfields Ct 17 YO21 208 D6
Meadowfields Dr YO31 225 D2
Meadowings The TS15 5 D2
Meadowlands Cl 2 TS13 11 A8
Meadows The
Carlton DN14 204 C3
Coulby Newham TS8 7 B5
Hambleton YO8 196 F1
8 Middleton St George DL2 4 C4
7 Monk Fryston LS25 202 A8
Riccall YO19 197 F8
Richmond DL10 209 E7
Scalby YO12 212 B7
2 Skelton YO30 224 B5
South Milford LS25 195 F2
Meadowside CP Sch HG5 221 C7
Meads La YO12 99 E5
Meads The
3 Eastfield YO11 99 F6
9 Eastfield YO11 100 A6
Meadway YO8 197 D2
Meadway Dr YO8 197 D2
Meagill La LS21 159 E2
Meagill Rise LS21 176 E1
Meanee Rd 11 DL9 40 F2
Medbourne Gdns TS5 6 E6
Megson Pl YO7 211 C4
Melander Cl YO26 227 B4
Melander Gdns 5 YO32 225 D7
Melbourne Dr YO7 90 E5
Melbourne Pl YO7 211 B2
Melbourne St YO10 228 D2
Melcombe Ave 11 YO32 167 A7
Meldyke La TS8 6 D5
Mellersh Rd 16 DL10 41 E4
Melling with Wrayton C of E Sch LA6 102 A2
Melltown's Gn YO7 88 C6
Melmerby Green La HG4 114 C6
Melmerby Green Rd HG4 114 B6
Melmerby Ind Est HG4 114 B6
Melrose Cl 1 YO31 229 A5
Melrose Cres
Bishop Monkton HG3 140 A5
Guisborough TS14 9 A6
Melrose Dr 16 LS29 176 C1
Melrose Rd HG3 140 A5
Melrose St 4 YO12 212 F6
Melrosegate YO31 228 F5
Melsonby Methodist Prim Sch DL10 20 F7
Melton Ave YO30 227 F8
Melton Dr
Bishopthorpe YO23 231 A3
York YO30 227 F8
Melville Gr 1 LS29 218 E4
Melville Terr 52 YO14 101 B3
Melwood Gr YO26 227 B5
Mendip Cl 2 YO32 225 F5
Menethorpe La YO17 147 D7
Menin Rd DL9 209 B1
Menwith Hill Rd HG3 159 D4
Mercer Art Gall★ HG2 219 C3
Mercer Dr DL9 209 C1
Merchant Adventurers Hall★ YO1 233 C2
Merchant Taylors Hall★ YO31 233 C3
Merchant Way YO23 230 B3
Merchantgate YO1 233 C2
Merchant's Row 10 YO11 213 B6
Mercury Rd DL10 209 A8
Mere La YO11 212 F1
Mere View Gdns YO12 99 F8
Merewood Rd WF10 200 C4
Merlin Covert 4 YO31 225 F3
Merlinwood BD23 172 B4
Merrington Ave TS17 6 D6
Merry Dale YO11 100 A7
Merrybank La LS17 178 A3
Merrybent Dr DL2 2 F5
Merryfield HG2 222 B7
Mesnes La DL8 59 D3
Messines Rd DL9 40 E3
Metcalfe La YO19 229 C5
Metes La YO12 99 E5
Methley Cty Jun Sch LS26 200 B6
Methley La LS26 200 A6
Methley Park Hospl LS26 200 A6
Methley Rd WF10 200 D4
Methodist Prim Sch DL11 36 E5
Meuse Cl 4 DL9 209 C1
Mewburn Rd DL3 3 C8
Mewith La LA2 129 B6
Mews The WF6 200 A2
Meynell Rd DL3 3 C7
Michael Mount Rd YO11 213 C1
Michael Syddall C of E Prim Sch DL10 41 E5
Micklebury La HG4 86 A3
Mickleby Dr YO21 208 B6
Mickleby La TS13 11 F4
Mickledale La YO26 163 D8
Micklefield C of E Sch LS25 195 A4
Micklefield Sta LS25 195 A3
Micklegate
17 Pontefract WF8 201 B1
1 Selby YO8 232 D5
York YO1 233 A2
Micklegate Bar Mus★ YO24 233 A1
Micklethwaite View LS22 180 C2
Mickletown Rd LS26 200 B6
Middle Bank Rd TS7 7 D7
Middle Banks 24 YO32 166 E5
Middle Head Rd YO18 71 E8
Middle La Brayton YO8 232 C1
Brompton YO13 98 C7
Collingham LS22 180 B1
Hutton Buscel YO13 74 E1
Kettlewell with Starbotton BD23 108 A3
14 Knottingley WF11 202 A2
Snainton YO13 97 F4
Middle Moor La DL11 39 F5
Middle Oxford St WF10 200 E4
Middle Rd TS17 6 A5
Middle St Gayles DL11 19 E6
Swinton YO17 121 B4
Wilberfoss YO41 185 F5
Middle Wlk YO12 212 E7
Middlebrook Gdns YO8 232 A2
Middlecave Cl YO17 215 A4
Middlecave Dr YO17 215 A4
Middlecave Rd YO17 215 B4
Middlecroft Dr YO32 167 A7
Middlecroft Gr 2 YO32 167 B7
Middlefield Cl YO17 124 E1
Middlefield La
Kirk Smeaton WF8 206 A2
Melmerby DL8 84 A8
Middleham Ave YO31 228 E8
Middleham C of E Prim Sch DL8 60 E2
Middleham Castle★ DL8 60 E2
Middlesbrough Coll TS5 6 E8
Middlesbrough Rd TS7 7 E6
Middlesbrough Rugby & Cricket Clubs TS5 6 E8
Middlethorpe Dr YO24 230 E7
Middlethorpe Gr YO24 230 F7
Middleton Ave
Ilkley LS29 218 B6
Thornaby TS17 6 B6
Middleton Carr La YO18 95 D7
Middleton Cl YO17 122 D1
Middleton La
Middleton YO18 95 E8
Middleton St George DL2 4 C3
Middleton Rd
Hutton Rudby TS15 25 D6
Ilkley LS29 218 A4
Pickering YO18 95 E7
Sadberge DL2 4 C7
York YO24 227 C2
Middleton St George Cty Prim Sch DL2 4 C4
Middleton Tyas C of E Prim Sch DL10 21 C5
Middleton Tyas La DL10 21 B4
Middleway BD20 174 C1
Middlewood Cl
3 Fylingdales YO22 33 C3
Rufforth YO23 182 C6
Middlewood Cres 5 YO22 33 C3
Middlewood Garth 4 YO22 33 C3
Middlewood La YO22 33 C3
Middycar Bank HG4 138 F6
Midge Hall Cl 18 LS29 176 C1
Midgeley Gate HG5 162 F2
Midgley Cl
4 Embsay BD23 217 C7
21 Stamford Bridge YO41 168 D2
Midgley Rd LS29 176 C1
Midgley Rise 2 WF8 201 B2
Midhope Way 15 YO14 101 A3
Midland St BD23 216 E3
Midway Ave YO26 224 A1
Mightens' Bank DL8 60 D4
Milbank Rd DL3 3 B5
Milburn La YO7 89 D3
Mildred Gr 5 YO24 227 F2
Mildred Sylvester Way WF6 200 B1
Mile Hill Coldhill La LS25 195 E5
Mile Planting DL10 209 F8
Milestone Ave YO23 182 C6
Milford Mews 7 YO32 225 D7
Milford Rd LS25 195 F3
Milford Way 8 YO32 225 D7
Milking Hill YO61 118 B4
Mill Balk DN14 207 C8
Mill Bank
Bishop Thornton HG3 138 F1
Fylingdales YO22 33 D2
Lindrick with Studley Royal & Fountains HG4 113 A3
Norton YO17 215 E3
Mill Bank Rd YO18 72 D5
Mill Bridge BD23 216 F4
Mill Brow LA2 128 E2
Mill Brow Rd BB18 172 B1
Mill Cl
Monk Fryston LS25 202 A8
Ravensworth DL11 19 F6
Settle BD24 131 D2
6 Spofforth HG3 179 E6
Mill Croft
Cowling BD22 187 B6
Richmond DL10 209 A7
Mill Dam LS23 188 F7
Mill Dam La WF8 201 C1
Mill Dike La YO7 116 F8
Mill Field La YO61 91 B1
Mill Field Rd YO8 203 B5
Mill Flats La DL8 60 F3
Mill Garth 14 YO8 198 F1
Mill Gate
Gilling with Hartforth & Sedbury DL10 20 E3
Harrogate HG1 219 C7
Knayton with Brawith YO7 65 E2
Mill Green Way The YO22 51 D8
Mill Hill Escrick YO19 192 B5
16 Normanton South WF6 200 A1
Mill Hill Cl 8 DL6 43 F3
Mill Hill CP Sch DL6 210 E4
Mill Hill Cres DL6 210 E3
Mill Hill Dr YO32 225 F4
Mill Hill La
Giggleswick BD24 131 C3
Northallerton DL6 210 E3
Mill Hills La DL11 38 E4
Mill House YO7 65 D1
Mill La
Acaster Malbis YO23 191 C8
Ampleforth YO62 118 C8
Askham Richard YO23 182 D2
Askrigg DL8 57 E6
Aysgarth DL8 58 E3
Barlow YO8 204 B7
Bellerby DL8 60 E8
Bentham LA2 128 F7
Bewerley HG3 137 B4
Boroughbridge YO51 141 B5
Brayton YO8 203 C8
Buckton/Bempton YO13 97 D5
Burniston YO13 75 C8
Burton Leonard HG3 140 B2
Carlton DN14 204 D3
Castleford WF10 200 E5
Cayton YO11 100 C6
Constable Burton DL8 61 C5
Darlington DL1 3 F6
Earby BB18 172 B1
Easingwold YO61 117 D1
3 East Ayton/West Ayton YO13 99 A7
Eskdaleside cum Ugglebarnby YO22 32 B6
Exelby, Leeming & Newton DL7 63 D3
Faceby TS9 25 F2
Farndale East YO62 48 E4
Farndale West YO62 48 F1
Gargrave BD23 155 D1
Great Ouseburn YO26 164 C8
Hambleton YO8 196 F1
Haxby YO32 166 D5
Hebden BD23 135 A1
2 Hemingbrough YO8 198 F1
Hessay YO23 182 B7
High Coniscliffe DL2 2 C6
Kearby with Netherby LS22 179 C2
Kirk Hammerton YO26 164 C2
Knaresborough HG5 221 F8
Langtoft YO25 151 C7
Leyburn DL8 60 E4
6 Linton-on-Ouse YO30 164 F7
Long Preston BD23 153 F4
Longnewton DL2 4 F6
Low Bradley BD20 173 E3
Mickletown LS26 200 B6
Middleton St George DL2 4 D5
Muston YO14 101 A2
Nether Silton YO7 66 B6
Newland YO8 205 A3
Pannal HG3 222 E2
Pickering YO18 95 F6
Pontefract WF8 201 C2
Rawcliffe DN14 204 F1
Redmire DL8 59 C5
1 Riccall YO19 192 A1
Ryther cum Ossendyke LS24 190 E1
1 Scarborough YO12 212 E3
Scruton DL7 63 E5
Sherburn in Elmet LS25 195 F2
Skipton BD23 216 F3
Sledmere YO25 149 F3
Snape with Thorp DL8 87 B7
South Milford LS25 195 F2
Spofforth with Stockeld HG3 179 E6
Stillington YO61 144 C6
Stutton with Hazlewood LS24 189 E4
Swinden BD23 154 B1
Thirkleby High & Low with Osgodby YO7 90 D2
Thormanby YO61 116 E5
Thrintoft DL7 63 F8
Whitwood WF10 200 B2
Wilberfoss YO41 185 E6
York YO31 228 E6
Youlton YO61 142 F2
Mill Lane Ave YO60 145 C5
Mill Mount YO24 228 A3
Mill Mount Ct YO24 228 A3
Mill Race The 4 DL2 22 C8
Mill Rd
Burton Fleming YO25 126 D4
Gillamoor YO62 70 A5
Goldsborough HG5 221 F3
Mill Riggs TS9 26 D7
Mill Rise DL6 210 E2
Mill Row BD20 187 F7
Mill St
6 Barnoldswick BB18 171 D1
Glusburn BD20 187 F6
Guisborough TS14 8 F6
Harome YO62 93 C4
Norton YO17 215 E3
Scarborough YO12 212 F5
York YO1 233 C1
Mill View
5 Burley in Warfedale LS29 176 C1
Mill View *continued*
Knottingley WF11 201 D2
Mill Wynd TS16 5 E3
Millbank Ct YO7 89 D4
Millbank La TS17 6 B7
Millbeck Gn LS22 188 A8
Millenium Rd BD20 173 D4
Millers Cl YO17 215 D2
Millers Croft 6 YO23 230 B3
Millers La TS12 9 F6
Millers Rd 2 YO7 211 C3
Millfield YO51 141 D2
Millfield Ave
Northallerton DL6 210 E3
York YO10 228 F3
Millfield Cl
Eaglescliffe TS16 5 D4
1 Leeming DL7 63 D4
Pickering YO18 95 F6
Wilberfoss YO41 185 E5
Millfield Cres DL6 210 E3
Millfield Dr YO8 204 D4
Millfield Gdns YO26 224 A2
Millfield Glade HG2 220 D4
Millfield La
Easingwold YO61 117 C1
Nether Poppleton YO26 227 B8
Poppleton YO26 224 A2
York YO10 229 A3
Millfield Rd
17 Hemingbrough YO8 198 F1
Hemingbrough YO8 204 F8
York YO23 228 B2
Millfield Rise YO61 117 C1
Millfield St HG3 137 B4
Millfields BD20 174 B1
Millgarth Ct 7 LS22 188 A8
Millgate 10 Masham HG4 86 C3
Richmond DL10 209 C6
Selby YO8 232 C6
Thirsk YO7 211 B3
Millgates YO26 227 C6
Millholme Rise BD23 217 C8
Millings La YO51 141 B7
Millrace Cl YO17 215 D2
Millside YO17 215 D2
Millthorpe Sch YO23 228 B2
Millway YO62 92 C1
Milner La LS24 195 D8
Milner Rd DL1 3 D4
Milner St YO24 227 D3
Milners La HG1 219 F7
Milnthorpe Cl 6 LS23 188 E6
Milnthorpe Garth 7 LS23 188 E6
Milnthorpe Gdns 5 LS23 188 E6
Milnthorpe La LS23 188 E6
Milnthorpe Way LS23 188 D5
Milson Gr YO10 229 A3
Milton Ave
Malton YO17 215 D5
Scarborough YO12 212 E3
Milton Carr 8 YO30 224 F1
Milton Cl HG1 219 E7
Milton Gr 11 BB18 171 D2
Milton Rd Malton YO17 215 C5
Pannal HG3 222 E3
Milton St Darlington DL1 3 E5
4 Skipton BD23 217 A3
York YO10 228 F3
Minchin Cl 3 YO30 225 B1
Mine Mus★ BB18 172 A2
Minors Cres DL3 3 A7
Minskip Rd HG5 140 F2
Minster Ave YO31 225 F2
Minster Cl
3 Haxby YO32 225 C8
23 Ripon HG4 214 C5
Minster Rd HG4 214 C5
Minster Sch The YO1 233 B3
Minster View YO32 225 C8
Minster Wlk 12 DL2 3 E1
Minster Yd YO1 233 B3
Minsterley Dr TS5 6 D7
Minter Cl 2 YO24 227 B1
Mire Bank La DL8 56 F4
Mire Close La BD22 187 A8
Mire Ridge BB8 186 A2
Mire Syke La HG5 162 A5
Mires La Carthorpe DL8 87 D6
Ulleskelf LS24 190 B1
Mirkhill Rd YO8 232 B6
Miry La LS15 188 C1
Missies La HG4 112 C3
Mistral Ct YO31 228 E8
Mitchell Ave TS17 6 B7
Mitchell La Alne YO61 142 F4
Catton YO41 185 D8
Settle BD24 131 E1
Mitchel's La YO10 231 F8
Miterdale 4 YO24 230 C7
Mitford Cl 3 YO14 126 F8
Mitford Rd 2 YO14 126 F8
Mitford St 24 YO14 101 B3
Mitton La BD20 172 D1
Moat Field YO10 229 C4
Moat Way YO8 197 D1
Moatside Ct YO31 233 B3
Mock Beggar Hall★ BD23 157 D7
Moiser Cl YO32 225 D4
Mole End 15 YO18 95 F6
Monash Ave DL9 209 C1
Monckton Dr WF10 201 B3

Monk Ave YO31 .228 F7
Monk Bar Ct YO31 .233 B3
Monk Bar Mus★ YO31 .233 C3
Monk Fryston C of E Prim Sch LS25 .202 A8
Monk Fryston Prim Sch LS25 .202 A8
Monk Gardens La YO62 .93 A7
Monk Gn YO61 .142 F4
Monk Ing Rd HG3 .159 E8
Monk La YO8 .232 C7
Monkbridge Ct YO31 .233 C4
Monket House Bank YO62 .48 C4
Monkgate YO31 .233 C3
Monkgate Cloisters YO31 .233 C3
Monkhill Ave WF8 .201 B1
Monkhill Dr WF8 .201 B1
Monkhill La WF8 .201 B2
Monkhill Mount WF8 .201 B1
Monkholme La BD23 .134 C2
Monkroyd Ave BB18 .171 D1
Monks Cross Dr YO32 .226 A3
Monks Cross Link YO32 .226 B4
Monk's Rd BD23 .107 D2
Monkswell Pk HG5 .221 D5
Monkton Rd
5 York YO31 .225 F1
York YO31 .228 E8
Monmouth Dr TS16 .5 E5
Monmouth St 10 BB8 .186 A3
Mons Cl 3 DL9 .209 B1
Mons Rd
Catterick Garrison DL9 .209 D1
Colburn DL9 .40 F4
Montague Cres LS25 .194 D4
Montague Rd YO23 .231 A3
Montague St YO23 .228 C1
Montague Wlk 6 YO26 .165 F1
Montagu's Harrier TS14 .8 D6
Montgomery Rd DL9 .209 C2
Montgomery St BD23 .217 A3
Montpellier Gdns 2 HG1 .219 C2
Montpellier Hill HG2 .219 C2
Montpellier Mews 3 HG1 .219 C2
Montpellier Rd 1 HG1 .219 C2
Montpellier Sq 3 HG1 .219 D2
Montpellier St 4 HG1 .219 C2
Montrose Ave YO31 .228 D8
Moody Sty La 4 BD23 .134 E3
Mook St YO60 .169 B8
Moor Ave 1 LS23 .188 E7
Moor Carr La YO8 .198 B5
Moor Cl Killinghall HG3 .219 A8
10 Kirklevington TS15 .24 E8
Lockwood TS12 .10 A5
Wheldrake YO19 .192 F8
Moor Cres BD23 .217 B4
Moor Croft 8 BD23 .134 E3
Moor End La
Crakehall DL8 .62 C3
Sowerby YO7 .90 A2
Moor End Rd YO13 .53 F2
Moor Gn TS7 .7 D5
Moor Gr YO24 .230 E8
Moor Hill YO17 .147 E7
Moor House La YO61 .116 B1
Moor La
Addingham LS29 .174 D5
Aislaby YO21 .31 F7
Aldfield HG4 .138 F8
Arkendale HG5 .162 F7
Arrathorne DL10 .41 A2
Askwith LS21 .176 D4
Bagby YO7 .90 C4
6 Barlby YO8 .198 B5
Bilton-in-Ainsty with Bickerton YO26 .181 D5
Bishopthorpe YO23 .230 E2
Borrowby TS13 .11 C6
Brawby YO17 .94 F2
Brompton YO13 .74 B1
Broughton YO17 .121 C4
Burton Leonard HG3 .140 B4
Carthorpe DL8 .87 D4
Catterton LS24 .190 A8
Cleasby DL2 .2 F2
Cliffe YO8 .198 F4
Cloughton YO13 .54 C1
Collingham LS23 .188 C8
Coneythorpe & Clareton HG5 .163 B6
Copmanthorpe YO23 .230 A1
Cropton YO18 .71 B6
Crosby DL6 .65 C5
Dalton DL11 .19 C6
Dalton YO7 .116 B8
Dishforth YO7 .114 F3
Earswick YO32 .226 C8
East Ayton/West Ayton YO13 .99 B8
East Layton DL11 .20 B8
Eastfield YO11 .100 A6
Elslack BD23 .172 D3
Embsay with Eastby BD23 .156 F1
Full Sutton YO41 .168 F1
Grassington BD23 .134 E3
Great Ouseburn YO26 .163 D7
Great Ribston with Walshford LS22 .180 E8

Moor La *continued*
Halton East BD23 .157 B1
Haxby YO32 .166 D7
Hunton DL8 .61 E8
Hutton-le-Hole YO62 .70 C5
Kearby with Netherby HG3 .179 B2
Kelfield YO19 .191 E2
Kirby Hill HG4 .140 F8
Long Preston BD23 .153 F5
Milby YO51 .141 C7
Murton YO19 .229 F8
Myton-on-Swale YO61 .142 B5
Naburn YO19 .191 D8
Nether Silton DL6 .66 C8
Newsham DL11 .19 A7
Newsham with Breckenbrough YO7 .65 A1
Newton-on-Ouse YO30 .165 C7
Rufforth YO23 .182 E6
Ryther cum Ossendyke LS24 .196 E8
Scalby YO12 .212 A8
Settrington YO17 .122 C1
Sherburn in Elmet LS25 .195 F4
Skelton YO30 .224 D6
Snape with Thorp DL8 .86 E6
Steeton with Eastburn BD20 .187 F7
Stillington YO61 .143 F6
Strensall YO32 .167 B7
Stutton with Hazlewood LS24 .189 D4
Thirkleby High & Low with Osgodby YO7 .90 C1
Thirsk YO7 .89 D5
Tholthorpe YO61 .142 D6
Thormanby YO61 .116 E5
Thornton Steward HG4 .61 E2
Thornton-le-Clay YO60 .145 F2
Thorp Arch LS23 .180 E3
Threshfield BD23 .134 B2
Welburn YO62 .94 A5
West Tanfield HG4 .87 B2
Weston LS21 .176 E2
Wilstrop YO26 .181 D8
Yafforth DL7 .43 B2
York YO24 .230 C6
Moor Lane Trad Est LS25 .196 A3
Moor Lee La
Eggborough DN14 .207 B8
Heck DN14 .203 B1
Moor Park Cl
2 Addingham LS29 .174 E4
Pannal HG3 .178 A8
Moor Park Cres 3 LS29 174 E4
Moor Park Dr LS29 .174 E4
Moor Park Gr 2 LS29 .174 F4
Moor Park Way 1 LS29 174 F4
Moor Pk TS7 .7 D5
Moor Rd Askrigg DL8 .57 E6
Bishop Monkton HG3 .139 F5
Filey YO14 .101 B1
Hunmanby YO14 .127 B7
Ilkley LS29 .218 F1
Knayton with Brawith YO7 .65 F3
Leyburn DL8 .60 C5
Marton cum Grafton YO51 .141 C2
Melsonby DL10 .20 F6
Muston YO14 .101 A2
9 Sherburn in Elmet LS25 195 F4
Stamford Bridge YO41 .168 D2
Wykeham YO13 .74 B4
Moor Side LS23 .188 D8
Moor View 2 TS13 .11 F7
Moor Way YO32 .226 A4
Moorber La BD23 .171 F8
Moorberries TS15 .6 C2
Moorbridge Croft 6 LS25 .196 A4
Moorcock La HG3 .159 F5
Moorcroft Rd YO24 .230 D7
Moore Ave YO10 .229 B4
Moorfield Dr YO41 .185 E6
Moorfield Rd LS29 .218 F4
Moorfield Sch LS29 .218 C3
Moorfield Way YO41 .185 E6
Moorfields
Raskelf YO61 .116 F2
3 Wistow YO8 .197 D6
Moorfields La YO62 .93 E5
Moorfoot La BD20 .173 D2
Moorgarth Ave
10 York YO24 .227 F2
3 York YO24 .228 A2
Moorgate YO24 .227 D3
Moorgate Dr LS25 .194 D1
Moorgate Rd LS25 .194 D2
Moorhill La YO17 .147 E6
Moorhouse Cl 3 WF6 .200 B2
Moorhouse La YO7 .89 E8
Moorland Ave 6 BB18 .172 B1
Moorland Cl
5 Embsay BD23 .217 E8
Harrogate HG2 .220 D4
Moorland Garth 2 YO32 .167 A7
Moorland Rd
Harrogate HG2 .220 D4
Scarborough YO12 .212 F7
York YO10 .231 D8
Moorland Rise BD23 .217 E8
Moorland View HG2 .220 D4
Moorlands Ilkley LS29 .218 A2
Skelton YO32 .166 B5

Moorlands La
Skelton YO30 .224 C6
1 Tollerton YO61 .143 B3
Moorlands Pk YO21 .29 A6
Moors Ctr The★ YO21 .29 D7
Moorsholm La TS13 .10 C6
Moorside
Melling-with-Wrayton LA6 .102 A2
Scalby YO12 .212 A8
Moorside Ave HG4 .214 B2
Moorside Cl LA6 .102 A2
Moorside Cty Jun & Inf Sch HG4 .214 B3
Moorside Dale 6 HG4 .214 B2
Moorside La
Addingham LS29 .175 A2
Askwith LS21 .176 C4
Moorside Rd DL10 .209 E8
Moorside View HG4 .214 C2
Moorview Rd
Northallerton DL6 .210 F5
Skipton BD23 .217 B3
Moorview Way BD23 .217 B4
Morehall Cl YO30 .224 F2
Morgan Dr TS14 .8 E6
Morgan St 4 YO12 .212 F5
Morley Dr 10 YO13 .99 A7
Morley Gate DL11 .37 E5
Mornington Cres HG1 .219 E4
Mornington Rd LS29 .218 C4
Mornington Terr HG1 .219 E3
Morpeth Ave
Coulby Newham TS4 .7 A7
Darlington DL1 .3 E7
Morpeth Gate DL8 .58 F1
Morrets La YO8 .197 A1
Morrison Rd TS14 .8 F7
Morritt Cl 3 YO31 .228 F8
Morton Carr La TS7 .7 E6
Morton La YO8 .203 A8
Morton Rd DL1 .4 A5
Mosber La BD23 .172 C8
Moss Arc HG4 .214 C5
Moss End La BD22 .186 F5
Moss Green La
Brayton YO8 .232 A2
Hirst Courtney YO8 .203 F3
Moss Haven DN6 .207 D1
Moss Hill La YO26 .164 D5
Moss Rd DN6 .207 B1
Moss Side BB18 .171 E1
Moss St YO24 .233 A1
Moss Way TS18 .5 F7
Mossburn Dr YO62 .119 E6
Mossdale Gr TS14 .8 D6
Mossra La HG4 .85 F4
Mosswood Cres TS5 .6 D7
Mosswood La YO61 .118 A1
Mossy La DL8 .56 C4
Moulton Hall★ DL10 .21 D2
Moulton La DL7 .22 C3
Mounstrall La DL7 .43 C1
Mount Ave YO8 .232 B3
Mount Bank DL6 .45 A5
Mount Cres YO17 .215 B5
Mount Dr DL8 .60 D5
Mount Ephraim 6 YO24 .228 A3
Mount Farm Cl YO22 .208 E3
Mount Gdns HG2 .222 E7
Mount Gr YO8 .232 B3
Mount Grace Priory★ DL6 .45 B5
Mount Leven Rd TS15 .5 F3
Mount Par
5 Harrogate HG1 .219 D3
York YO24 .228 A3
Mount Park Ave YO12 .212 E5
Mount Park Rd 2 YO12 212 E4
Mount Pk YO19 .198 A8
Mount Pleasant
26 Addingham LS29 .174 F4
High Bentham LA2 .129 A8
Kippax LS25 .200 D8
Newby & Scalby YO13 .75 C5
Mount Pleasant Cl 9 DL2 .4 C4
Mount Pleasant E 2 YO22 .33 D4
Mount Pleasant Grange TS18 .6 A8
Mount Pleasant N 1 YO22 .33 D4
Mount Pleasant Prim Sch DL3 .3 A7
Mount Pleasant S 3 YO22 .33 D4
Mount Rd Malton YO17 .215 B4
Northallerton DL6 .210 F6
Mount Sch The YO24 .228 A3
Mount St HG2 .222 E7
Mount The
Barwick in Elmet & Scholes LS15 .194 B7
Castleford WF10 .201 B4
Malton YO17 .215 B4
Selby YO8 .232 B3
8 Thornton Dale YO18 .96 D5
York YO24 .233 A1
Mount Vale YO24 .228 A2
Mount Vale Dr YO24 .228 A2
Mount View YO14 .101 A2
Mount View Ave YO12 .212 E3
Mount View Cl 4 YO12 .212 E3
Mount View Rd 8 YO11 100 B6
Mountside YO11 .212 F3
Mouseman Visitor Ctr★ YO61 .91 B2

Mowbray Castle (site of)★ HG4 .112 D5
Mowbray Cres
17 Bedale DL8 .63 A2
Hovingham YO62 .119 E6
Kirkby Malzeard HG4 .112 D5
Mowbray Dr
4 Hurworth-on-Tees DL2 .3 E1
York YO26 .227 C4
Mowbray Pl YO7 .211 B2
Mowbray Rd
5 Catterick DL10 .41 D5
Northallerton DL6 .210 E6
Mowbray Sch DL8 .63 A2
Mowbray Sq HG1 .219 E3
Mowbray Terr HG4 .87 A2
Mowden Inf Sch DL3 .3 A6
Mowthorp Rd YO12 .75 A3
Mowthorpe La YO60 .145 F8
Mowthorpe Medieval Village★ YO17 .149 C6
Moxby La YO61 .144 D5
Moxby Priory★ YO61 .144 D5
Muddy La LS22 .180 A1
Muff La TS8 .7 A3
Muirfield TS7 .7 D5
Muirfield Ave WF7 .200 E1
Muirfield Rd TS16 .5 E5
Muirfield Way 6 YO26 .227 B5
Mulberry Ct YO32 .225 F6
Mulberry Dr 7 YO32 .166 E5
Mulberry Garth LS23 .188 F8
Mulgrave Castle★ YO21 .12 E2
Mulgrave Cres YO21 .208 B8
Mulgrave Dr 6 DL7 .210 D2
Mulgrave Pl YO11 .213 B7
Mulgrave Rd YO21 .208 A8
Mulgrave View YO22 .32 F7
Mullberry Gdns LS26 .200 A5
Mulwith Cl YO31 .229 A6
Mulwith La HG4 .140 E6
Muncaster Way YO22 .208 E3
Muncastergate YO31 .228 E7
Murchison Pl 8 YO12 .212 F6
Murchison St YO12 .212 E6
Murray St 31 Filey YO14 .101 B3
Scarborough YO12 .212 F5
York YO24 .227 F3
Murray Wlk DL3 .3 A5
Murrayfield Way 5 DL1 .3 F6
Murrough Wilson Pl 3 YO31 .228 C7
Murton Bank YO62 .67 E3
Murton Garth YO19 .229 F6
Murton La YO19 .184 D7
Murton Way YO19 .229 E5
Muscoates La YO62 .93 F3
Museum of Craven Life★ BD24 .131 E2
Museum St YO1 .233 B2
Musham Bank Rd YO11 .99 F7
Music in Miniature Ex★ YO22 .33 D3
Musterfield La HG4 .113 B7
Muston Rd Filey YO14 .101 A3
Hunmanby YO14 .126 F8
Mutton Scalp Rd TS12 .9 E7
My Love La HG3 .159 C5
Myer's Green La HG3 .161 B5
Myers La DL7 .64 A8
Myra Bank La YO61 .117 F3
Myrtle Ave
Bishopthorpe YO23 .231 B3
Selby YO8 .232 B3
Myrtle Gdns DL1 .3 D8
Myrtle Rd
Eaglescliffe TS16 .5 E6
3 Harrogate HG1 .219 E3
Myrtle Sq 2 HG1 .219 E3
Myson Ave WF8 .201 C2
Myton La YO61 .142 C5
Myton Rd TS17 .6 A4

N

Nab View BD20 .174 C2
Nabs View YO12 .212 A7
Naburn La
Deighton YO19 .192 A7
Fulford YO19 .231 D4
Naburn Park Mews YO19 .191 E8
Nairn Cl YO24 .230 C6
Nairnhead Cl TS8 .6 E5
Nalton Cl YO23 .230 A1
Nalton St YO8 .232 C5
Nanny Goat La
Barwick in Elmet & Scholes LS25 .194 B4
Hunton DL8 .61 F8
Nanny La LS24 .196 C7
Nansen St YO12 .212 E6
Nap Cote La HG4 .112 E4
Napier Cres YO12 .99 D7
Napier Rd HG4 .113 D3
Nares St YO12 .212 E6
Narrow La YO42 .193 D7
Narrowfield 8 YO22 .32 A6
Nasterfield Nature Reserve★ HG4 .87 B2
Nat La LS17 .178 A3
National Rly Mus★ YO26 .228 A4
Nattrass Wlk 7 DL8 .63 B2
Navigation Rd YO1 .233 C2
Nawton Cty Sch YO62 .93 D7

Nawton Rd YO62 .93 E7
Neasham Ct TS9 .26 C8
Neasham Hill DL2 .4 B1
Neasham Rd
Darlington DL1 .3 D4
Low Dinsdale DL2 .4 A3
Neile Cl DL7 .210 B4
Nell Bank Ctr★ LS29 .218 D6
Nelson Rd LS29 .218 B4
Nelson St
7 Normanton South WF6 .200 B2
Scarborough YO12 .212 F6
Skipton BD23 .217 A3
York YO31 .233 C4
Nelson's La YO24 .227 F1
Nesfield Cl
17 Eastfield YO11 .100 B6
Harrogate HG1 .219 B5
Nesfield Rd LS29 .218 A5
Nesfield View 12 LS29 .175 C2
Ness La
Pickhill with Roxby YO7 .88 B6
Tockwith YO26 .181 C8
Ness Rd 5 YO8 .232 D6
Nessgate YO1 .233 B2
Nestfield Cl WF8 .201 B2
Nether Way 20 YO26 .165 F1
Netherby Cl 6 YO22 .32 A6
Netherby La
Huttons Ambo YO60 .147 B6
Sinnington YO62 .71 A1
Netheredge Cl HG5 .220 E8
Netheredge Dr HG5 .220 E8
Netherfield Cl WF10 .200 C3
Nethergill La BD20 .173 B1
Netherside Hall Sch BD23 .134 C4
Netherwindings 18 YO32 .166 F5
Netherwoods 6 YO32 .167 B8
Nettledale Cl 1 TS13 .12 A7
Nettledale La YO13 .97 F6
Nevern Cres TS17 .5 F4
Neville Cres BD23 .155 D1
Neville Dr YO23 .231 A3
Neville Gr LS26 .194 A1
Neville Pits La DN14 .207 B4
Neville Rd Darlington DL3 .3 B5
Gargrave BD23 .155 D1
Neville St
Normanton South WF6 .200 A1
Skipton BD23 .217 A4
York YO31 .233 C4
Neville Terr YO31 .233 C4
Neville Wlk DL10 .209 D7
Nevinson Gr YO10 .231 E8
Nevis Way YO24 .230 B7
Nevison Ave WF8 .201 C2
New Brook St LS29 .218 B5
New Close La LA2 .130 C7
New Dales La BD20 .173 D4
New Earswick Prim Sch YO32 .225 D4
New Fen La YO8 .197 F6
New Forge Ct 15 YO32 .166 F5
New Hall Rd WF8 .201 C2
New House La BD23 .153 F5
New Ings La YO18 .96 E4
New Inn La DL8 .87 F6
New La Aislaby YO18 .95 D8
Beal DN14 .202 D3
Bishopthorpe YO23 .231 A4
Burton Salmon WF11 .201 E6
Green Hammerton YO26 .164 C3
Hawes DL8 .56 E4
Huntington YO32 .226 A1
Kildwick BD20 .173 F1
Lillings Ambo YO60 .145 C3
Little Ouseburn YO26 .164 A8
Long Marston YO23 .182 B3
Neasham DL2 .4 A1
Newland YO8 .205 A3
Ravensworth DL11 .20 A7
Selby YO8 .232 C5
Sherburn in Elmet LS25 .195 F3
Sheriff Hutton YO60 .145 D5
Stainburn LS21 .177 E4
Strensall YO32 .167 B8
West Tanfield DL8 .87 C2
York YO32 .225 F1
York YO24 .227 E3
New Laithe Cl 5 BD23 .217 B5
New Lennerton La LS25 .196 C3
New Mill La LS23 .188 F7
New Millgate YO8 .232 C6
New Park CP Sch HG1 .219 C5
New Park Rd 4 YO12 .212 E4
New Park Row HG1 .219 C5
New Parks Cres 8 YO12 .212 E4
New Potter Grange Rd DN14 .205 E2
New Quay Rd YO21 .208 D6
New Queen St 10 YO12 .213 A7
New Rd Allerston YO13 .73 D6
Allerton Mauleverer with Hopperton HG5 .163 E4
Appleton Roebuck YO23 .190 E5
Appletreewick BD23 .157 E8
Beningbrough YO30 .165 C6
Birstwith HG3 .160 D6
Bramham LS23 .188 E6
Earby BB18 .172 A1
Fylingdales YO22 .33 D4
Glaisdale YO21 .29 F3
Guisborough TS14 .8 F6

New Rd *continued*
Heck DN14 203 D1
Hessay YO26 182 C8
Hunmanby YO14 126 F7
Kirby Grindalythe YO17 149 B6
Kirby Hall YO26 164 B8
Kirkbymoorside YO62 70 B1
Knottingley WF11 201 D3
Ledsham LS25 201 B8
Lillings Ambo YO60 145 D3
Long Drax YO8 204 E6
Newsham DL11 18 J8
North Stainley with Sleningford HG4 113 B8
Norton DN6 206 F2
Rainton with Newby YO7 114 E6
Raskelf YO61 116 E3
Reighton YO14 127 E5
Richmond DL10 209 C6
Rosedale East Side YO18 49 E3
Scotton HG5 162 A5
Settrington YO17 122 D1
Spaunton YO62 70 E5
Stapleton WF8 206 B5
Terrington YO60 119 E2
Thornton in Lonsdale LA6 103 B4
Ulleskelf LS24 190 B3
Westerdale YO21 28 F6
Wheldrake YO19 192 C7
Whixley YO26 164 A4
New Row
15 Boroughbridge YO51 141 B5
Eppleby DL11 1 D4
Trawden Forest BB8 186 B2
New St Carleton BD23 173 B4
Kippax LS25 194 D1
Langcliffe BD24 131 E4
Tadcaster LS24 189 E6
York YO1 233 B2
New Sturton La LS25 194 D4
New Walk Terr YO10 228 D2
New Way YO21 29 C4
Newall Ave LS21 176 F1
Newall Carr Rd LS21 176 F3
Newall Hall Pk 10 LS21 177 A1
Newbiggin
Malton YO17 215 B5
Richmond DL10 209 B6
Newborough YO11 213 A6
Newborough St YO30 233 A4
Newbridge La BD23 174 B8
Newburgh Priory* YO61 117 E7
Newbury Ave YO24 227 D1
Newby Cl HG4 214 D4
Newby CP Sch YO12 212 B8
Newby Cres HG3 219 A4
Newby Farm Cl 35 YO12 75 D5
Newby Farm Cres 36 YO12 75 D5
Newby Farm Rd YO12 75 D5
Newby Hall* HG4 140 C6
Newby Hall C of E Prim Sch HG4 140 E7
Newby La DN14 207 F8
Newby Pk* HG4 140 D6
Newby St HG4 214 D4
Newby Terr YO31 228 C7
Newcastle Farm Ct 4 WF11 201 D6
Newchase Ct YO11 99 F6
Newcoln Rd YO12 212 E1
Newcroft YO8 232 B4
Newdale 3 YO32 166 F5
Newfield Ave 6 WF6 200 B1
Newfield Cl 7 WF6 200 B1
Newfield Cres
Middlesbrough TS17 6 D7
Normanton South WF6 200 B1
Newfield Ct 3 WF6 200 B1
Newfield La LS25 201 B8
Newgate 2 Malton YO17 215 C4
York YO1 233 B2
Newgate Bank YO62 68 A4
Newgate Ct YO1 233 B2
Newham Bridge Prim Sch TS5 6 F8
Newham Way TS8 7 B5
Newhay La YO8 198 E1
Newhold LS25 194 D4
Newington Rd TS4 7 A8
Newkin DL8 57 D5
Newlaithes Cres WF6 200 B1
Newland Ave 1 HG2 220 A1
Newland Park Cl YO10 229 A3
Newland Park Dr YO10 228 F3
Newlands DL6 210 F4
Newlands Ave
Scarborough YO12 212 E8
3 Whitby YO21 208 C7
Newlands Ct YO7 211 D3
Newlands Dr
2 Glusburn BD20 187 F8
Ripon HG4 214 B3
York YO26 227 B6
Newlands La
Burniston YO13 54 D1
Upper Poppleton YO26 182 E8
Wintringham YO17 123 F3
Newlands Park Ave YO12 212 D8
Newlands Park Cres YO12 212 D8
Newlands Park Dr YO12 212 D8
Newlands Park Gr 2 YO12 212 D8
Newlands Park Rd YO12 212 D8
Newlands Rd
Bishopthorpe YO23 230 F4
Darlington DL3 3 B6
Newlands Sch TS4 6 F7
Newlyn Dr DL3 3 C8
Newmarket St BD23 217 A4
Newnham St HG2 220 A3
Newnham Terr HG2 220 A3
Newport Ave YO8 232 B4
Newport St
Goole DN14 205 F2
5 Pontefract WF8 201 B1
Newsham Hill DL11 18 J8
Newsham La
Barugh (Great & Little) YO17 95 A1
Habton YO17 121 A8
Newsham Rd YO7 211 A3
Newsham Way DL7 210 B1
Newstead La HG4 85 C7
Newstead Prim Sch TS14 8 E5
Newsteads 12 DL8 63 B3
Newthorpe Rd 2 DN6 206 E2
Newton Cres 4 DL7 63 D4
Newton Dr TS17 6 B6
Newton House Ct YO61 144 C3
Newton La
Archdeacon Newton DL2 2 F8
Ledsham WF10 201 A6
Newton Mulgrave TS13 11 F6
Newton Pk YO30 165 B7
Newton Rd
Great Ayton TS9 8 A2
Tollerton YO61 143 B3
Newton St YO21 208 D6
Newton Terr YO1 233 B1
Newtondale Cl HG5 221 D6
Newtondale Forest Dr YO18 72 B6
Newtondale Halt YO18 51 D1
Nicholas Gdns YO10 228 F3
Nicholas St YO10 228 F3
Nichols Way LS22 180 A3
Nicholson Ave HG4 113 D3
Nickey Nackey La YO8 197 B8
Nicklaus Dr TS16 5 E5
Nickstream La DL3 3 A7
Nidd Bank HG5 220 F7
Nidd Cl YO26 227 B8
Nidd Dr HG3 160 E6
Nidd Gr YO24 230 E8
Nidd La Birstwith HG3 160 E7
Ripley HG3 161 D7
Nidd Orch 4 HG3 160 A6
Nidd Rise HG3 160 E6
Nidd Viaduct* HG3 219 E8
Nidd Wlk HG3 137 B4
Nidderdale Dr HG5 221 D5
Nidderdale Lodge HG5 221 E5
Nidderdale Mus* HG3 137 B4
Nidderdale Recn Ctr HG3 137 A5
Niddside HG3 160 A6
Niffany Gdns 7 BD23 216 D3
Nigel Gr 7 YO24 227 F2
Nightingale Cl YO32 225 E1
Nightingale Dr HG2 220 B3
Nightingale La 9 YO12 99 F6
Nile Rd LS29 218 B4
Ninelands La LS25 194 D3
Ninelands Lane CP Sch LS25 194 D4
Ninevah La WF10 200 C7
Ninth Ave YO31 228 F5
No Man's Moor La DL8 61 E3
Noel's Ct DL10 41 E5
Nook The LS25 195 F2
Nooking The YO61 117 B6
Nora Ave HG5 221 C6
Norby YO7 211 B3
Norby Front St YO7 211 B4
Norfolk Cl WF11 201 E4
Norfolk Cres TS3 7 C8
Norfolk Gdns YO26 181 C7
Norfolk Rd HG2 222 D7
Norfolk St YO23 228 C2
Norman Cl
22 Pickering YO18 95 F7
7 Thorpe Willoughby YO8 197 B1
Norman Cres 11 YO14 101 B3
Norman Dr YO26 227 B6
Norman Rd Aske DL10 20 D1
Catterick Garrison DL9 209 E1
Richmond DL10 209 C8
Norman Sq DL10 209 D8
Norman St 5 YO10 229 A3
Normanby Prim Sch TS6 7 F8
Normanby Rd
Middlesbrough TS7 7 D8
Northallerton DL7 210 D2
Normandy Cl 4 YO8 232 B6
Normanton Comm Sch WF6 200 B2
Normanton Freeston High Sch WF6 200 A1
Normanton Ind Est WF6 200 B1
Normanton Public Baths WF6 200 A1
Normanton Sta WF6 200 A2
Normanton Town Mid Sch WF6 200 A1
Norseman Cl 7 YO19 197 F8
Norseway 2 YO41 168 D1
North & South Cowton CP Sch DL7 22 C3
North App LS24 189 A2
North Ave
Castleford WF10 200 C4
12 Glusburn BD20 187 E6
North Back La YO60 119 E1
North Baileygate WF8 201 B1
North Bay Rly* YO12 212 E8
North Burton La YO14 127 B4
North Cl 5 WF7 200 E1
North Cliff Ave YO12 75 F5
North Cliff Ctry Pk* YO14 101 C4
North Cotes Rd
Hunmanby YO25 126 C5
Wold Newton YO25 125 E5
North Cres LS25 195 F5
North Croft Grove Rd 1 LS29 218 A4
North Dr Kippax LS25 194 D2
Sherburn in Elmet LS25 195 F5
North Duffield CP Sch YO8 199 A8
North End Bedale DL8 63 A3
2 Hutton Rudby TS15 25 C5
Osmotherley DL6 45 B4
North Field Ave YO23 190 F5
North Field Cl YO23 190 F5
North Field La
Askham Bryan YO23 182 F3
Upper Poppleton YO26 182 F7
North Field Way YO23 190 F5
North Garth La YO60 145 D5
North Gr 2 LS22 180 C3
North Grove Ave 6 LS22 180 C4
North Hill Rd YO7 115 B2
North La Eastfield YO11 100 B6
Gainford DL2 1 D8
Great Timble LS21 176 E8
Huntington YO32 226 D5
Hutton Hang DL8 61 C4
Wheldrake YO19 192 F7
York YO32 225 F5
York YO24 230 E8
North Leas Ave YO12 212 D8
North Lodge Ave 2 HG1 219 C5
North Marine Rd YO12 212 F7
North Moor 7 YO32 225 F5
North Moor Gdns YO32 225 F5
North Moor La YO61 118 C5
North Moor Rd
Easingwold YO61 117 B2
York YO32 225 F5
North Par
10 Burley in Warfedale LS29 176 C1
Ilkley LS29 218 C4
Skipton BD23 217 A2
York YO30 233 A3
North Park Rd HG1 219 E2
North Prom YO21 208 C7
North Rd Darlington DL1 3 D7
5 Fairburn WF11 201 D6
Glusburn BD20 187 E7
Grosmont YO22 31 C4
Hackforth DL8 62 E8
3 Middleham DL8 60 E2
Norton YO17 215 E3
Ripon HG4 214 D6
Stokesley TS9 26 C7
Whitby YO21 208 D6
North Road Prim Sch DL1 3 D7
North Road Sta DL1 3 D6
North Ribblesdale RUFC BD24 131 D2
North Riding Rise DL7 65 B3
North Rigton C of E Prim Sch LS17 178 C4
North Side TS15 25 C5
North St
Addingham LS29 175 A4
Barmby on the Marsh DN14 205 A7
Barnoldswick BB18 171 D1
Castleford WF10 201 B6
Folkton YO11 100 A2
Gargrave BD23 155 D1
31 Glusburn BD20 187 E7
14 Glusburn BD20 187 E8
Newby & Scalby YO13 75 C6
Ripon HG4 214 C6
Scarborough YO11 213 A6
Silsden BD20 174 C1
Wetherby LS22 180 C3
York YO1 233 B2
North Stainley C of E Prim Sch HG4 113 C8
North Street La 22 YO11 213 A6
North Terr Gainford DL2 1 D7
4 Scarborough YO11 213 A6
Whitby YO21 208 C7
North View
Knottingley WF11 201 F2
Little Ribston LS22 180 A8
North York Craven Inst of Further Ed BD23 217 A4
North Yorkshire Moors Rly* YO18 95 F7
Northallerton Coll DL6 210 E4
Northallerton Rd
Brompton DL6 210 E7
Dalton-on-Tees DL2 22 E6
Leeming DL7 63 C4
Thirsk YO7 211 A6
Thornaby TS17 6 B7
Northallerton Rigg DL6 43 D4
Northallerton Rugby Club DL6 210 D8
Northallerton Sta DL7 210 C3
Northcarrs La YO61 144 A4
Northcliffe Gr 3 TS15 25 C5
Northcote Ave YO24 227 E3
Northcote Fold 3 LS22 180 A1
Northcroft 5 YO32 166 F5
Northfield 3 YO8 198 B5
Northfield Cl
Stokesley TS9 26 C7
Womersley DN6 206 C6
Northfield Ct LS24 196 B8
Northfield Dr
Pontefract WF8 201 C1
Stokesley TS9 26 C8
Northfield La
Church Fenton LS24 196 B8
Pockley YO62 69 B2
3 Riccall YO19 191 F1
South Milford LS25 195 E2
Womersley DN6 206 C7
Northfield Pl LS22 180 C3
Northfield Rd YO8 199 E8
Northfield Sch YO26 227 B5
Northfield Way YO13 75 D6
Northfields
4 Hutton Rudby TS15 25 C5
5 Strensall YO32 167 B8
Northfields Ave 4 BD24 131 D3
Northfields Cres 5 BD24 131 D3
Northfields La YO61 142 C6
Northgate Darlington DL1 3 D5
Guisborough TS14 8 F7
Hunmanby YO14 126 F8
Muston YO14 100 F1
Pontefract WF8 201 B1
Northgate Cl 15 WF8 201 B1
Northgate Jun Sch TS14 8 F7
Northgate La
1 Linton LS22 180 A1
Warthill YO41 168 A3
Northgate Lodge 11 WF8 201 B1
Northgate Rise 2 LS22 180 A1
Northlands Ave 1 YO32 225 F7
Northleach Dr TS8 6 F5
Northminster Bsns Pk YO26 182 F7
Northolme Dr YO30 224 E1
Northstead Cty Prim Sch YO12 212 D8
Northstead Manor Dr YO12 212 E7
Northumberland Ct 8 HG1 219 D2
Northumberland Rd TS17 6 B8
Northway Pickering YO18 95 E7
11 Scarborough YO12 212 F6
6 Whitby YO21 208 B7
Northwell Gate LS21 176 F1
Northwold Rd YO11 100 A7
Norton & Kirk Smeat WF8 206 C3
Norton Back La DL2 4 D8
Norton Cl HG4 114 A8
Norton Comm La DN6 206 F2
Norton Comm Rd DN6 207 A1
Norton Comp Sch YO17 215 E2
Norton Conyers* HG4 113 F7
Norton CP Sch YO17 215 E3
Norton Cres DL2 4 C8
Norton Cty Jun & Inf Sch DN6 206 E2
Norton Grove Ind Est YO17 215 F3
Norton Mill La DN6 206 E2
Norton Priory DN6 206 E2
Norton Rd
Norton YO17 215 C3
Sadberge DL2 4 C7
Norton Twr* BD23 156 B4
Norway Dr YO10 231 D8
Norwich Cl YO13 75 D6
Norwich Dr HG3 219 A5
Norwood Ave LS29 176 C1
Norwood Bottom Rd LS21 177 A5
Norwood Cl
36 Burley in Warfedale LS29 176 C1
2 Knaresborough HG5 221 B8
Norwood Ct 1 HG5 221 B7
Norwood Gr HG3 219 B4
Norwood La
Glusburn BD20 187 B8
Pannal HG3 177 E7
Norwood Pl 8 YO12 212 F5
Norwood St
Normanton WF6 200 B2
Scarborough YO12 212 F5
Nossill La DL8 59 C3
Nosterfield Rd HG4 87 B2
Notagreen Rd DL11 39 F6
Nought Bank Rd HG3 137 B3
Nought Moor Rd HG3 137 B2
Nova Scotia Way 4 YO19 198 A8
Nun Monkton Prim Sch YO26 165 A5
Nuneaton Dr TS8 6 E5
Nunmill St YO23 228 C2
Nunnery La
Darlington DL3 3 A5
York YO23 233 B1
Nunnington Cres HG3 219 A5
Nunnington Hall* YO62 93 F2
Nuns Green La YO21 29 E3
Nunthorpe Ave YO23 228 B2
Nunthorpe Cres YO23 228 B1
Nunthorpe Gr YO23 228 B2
Nunthorpe Prim Sch TS7 7 E6
Nunthorpe Rd YO23 233 A1
Nunthorpe Sta TS7 7 E6
Nurseries The
3 Easingwold YO61 143 C8
East Ayton YO13 99 C8
10 Leyburn DL8 60 D5
3 Whitby YO21 208 B6
Nursery Ct YO26 224 A2
Nursery Dr YO24 227 E3
Nursery Gdns YO10 229 C3
Nursery La 4 LS29 175 A4
Nursery Rd YO26 224 A2
Nursery Way 8 LS23 188 E7
Nutgill La Bentham LA2 129 D8
Ingleton LA2 103 D1
Nutwith La HG4 112 B8
Nydd Vale Rd HG1 219 D3

O

Oak Ave
Appleton Roebuck YO23 190 E3
Garforth LS25 194 C4
Killinghall HG3 161 B2
Oak Beck Rd HG1 219 B5
Oak Beck Way HG1 219 B6
Oak Busk La YO60 145 F1
Oak Cl Filey YO14 101 B4
9 Kirkbymoorside YO62 70 B1
Oak Cres LS25 194 C4
Oak Dr Garforth LS25 194 C4
5 Thorpe Willoughby YO8 197 B1
3 Topcliffe YO7 89 A1
Oak Field YO8 232 A1
Oak Field Ave YO22 51 D8
Oak Glade 6 YO31 225 F3
Oak Gr DL6 210 E6
Oak Hill TS8 7 B5
Oak La HG3 159 F8
Oak Rd Eaglescliffe TS16 5 E6
Garforth LS25 194 C4
Guisborough TS14 8 F7
2 North Duffield YO8 199 A7
Ripon HG4 214 B2
Scarborough YO12 212 D4
Tockwith LS22 180 E7
Whitby YO21 208 B6
Oak Ridge 6 LS22 180 B3
Oak Rise 4 YO26 227 C3
Oak St 3 YO26 227 E5
Oak Terr HG2 219 C2
Oak Tree Cl
2 Bedale DL8 63 A2
Strensall YO32 167 B7
Tees-side Airport DL2 4 E4
Oak Tree Ct 7 YO8 199 D7
Oak Tree Dr DL8 62 F2
Oak Tree Gr YO32 225 D3
Oak Tree La YO32 225 C7
Oak Tree Rd 7 DL8 63 A2
Oak Tree Way 10 YO32 167 B7
Oak Wood Rd LS22 180 B4
Oakbank HG1 219 C4
Oakburn Rd LS29 218 A3
Oakbusks La YO61 142 F4
Oakdale HG1 219 A3
Oakdale Ave HG1 219 B4
Oakdale Glen HG1 219 B3
Oakdale Manor HG1 161 B2
Oakdale Pl HG1 219 B4
Oakdale Rd YO30 224 F2
Oakdale Rise HG1 219 C4
Oaken Grove Sch YO32 166 F5
Oakenshaw Dr TS5 6 E7
Oaker Bank HG3 161 B2
Oakfields DL10 21 D4
Oakhill Cres 3 YO32 167 A6
Oakland Ave YO31 229 A7
Oakland Comp Sch TS5 6 D8
Oakland Dr YO31 229 A7
Oaklands
Camblesforth YO8 204 C5
9 Great Ayton TS9 8 A2
5 Ilkley LS29 218 A3
5 Pickering YO18 96 A6
6 Strensall YO32 167 B7
Oaklands Cres YO8 204 C5
Oaklands Rd TS6 7 F8
Oaklands Sch YO24 227 C2

Oaklands Small Sch DN14 ... 205 E4
Oaklands Sports Ctr YO24 ... 227 C2
Oaklands The DL2 ... 4 D3
Oakley Bank YO22 ... 208 B2
Oakley Cl TS14 ... 8 F5
Oakley Rd TS12 ... 9 E7
Oakney Wood Dr YO8 . 232 D1
Oakridge Cty Prim Sch TS13 ... 11 F7
Oakridge View 3 HG3 .. 161 B3
Oaks La LS23 ... 188 E8
Oaks The
Coulby Newham TS8 ... 6 E5
Dalton YO7 ... 115 F7
7 Masham HG4 ... 86 C3
Oaksfield LS26 ... 200 B5
Oaktree Ave DL9 ... 40 E2
Oaktree Bank YO7 ... 65 F3
Oaktree Dr DL7 ... 210 C1
Oaktree Gr 5 TS18 ... 5 D8
Oaktree Hill DL6 ... 43 D6
Oaktree Junc DL2 ... 4 D4
Oakville Ave YO12 ... 212 E6
Oakwood Cl LS24 ... 196 B7
Oakwood Pk DN14 ... 207 F6
Oatlands Cty Inf Sch HG2 ... 222 E7
Oatlands Cty Jun Sch HG2 ... 222 F7
Oatlands Dr
Harrogate HG2 ... 222 F8
11 Otley LS21 ... 177 A1
Oatlands Gr 3 TS13 ... 11 A8
Occaney La HG3 ... 162 D8
Occupation La LS24 ... 188 E2
Occupation Rd TS6 ... 7 F8
Ocean Rd YO21 ... 208 C7
Ocean Terr YO14 ... 100 F6
Ochrepit Hill YO42 ... 170 A2
Oddie's La LA6 ... 103 D5
Offerton Dr TS8 ... 6 F5
Ogleforth YO31 ... 233 B3
Okehampton Dr TS7 ... 7 B6
Olav Rd DL10 ... 209 C7
Old Barber HG1 ... 219 D6
Old Boys Sch La 4 YO8 197 B8
Old Brewery Gdns 5 LS24 ... 189 F6
Old Bridge Rise 7 LS29 218 A4
Old Chapel Cl 7 HG3 .. 161 B2
Old Church Gn YO26 .. 164 C2
Old Church La 9 HG3 .. 137 C4
Old Church Sch DL8 ... 60 E2
Old Coach Rd HG3 ... 137 F2
Old Coppice 14 YO32 .. 166 F5
Old Courthouse Museum* HG5 ... 221 A5
Old Dike Lands YO32 .. 225 C8
Old Farm Cl 5 YO18 ... 95 F7
Old Farm Way YO8 ... 232 B2
Old Garth Croft 3 WF11 ... 201 D6
Old Gayle La DL8 ... 56 D4
Old Great North Rd WF11 ... 201 E4
Old Hall Cl BD20 ... 187 D7
Old Hall Croft BD23 .. 155 D1
Old Hall La
Gilling with Hartforth & Sedbury DL10 ... 20 D3
Kexby YO41 ... 185 C5
Old Hall Rd BD20 ... 187 D7
Old Hall Way BD20 ... 187 D7
Old La Addingham LS29 .. 175 B3
Broughton BD23 ... 172 D5
Cowling BD22 ... 187 B5
Earby BB18 ... 172 A2
Hambleton YO8 ... 196 E1
Hirst Courtney YO8 ... 203 F3
Horton in Ribblesdale BD24 ... 105 A7
Ilkley LS29 ... 218 D3
Kelbrook & Sough BB18 .. 186 A6
Long Marston YO26 ... 182 A6
Old Lane Ct LS24 ... 190 E7
Old London Rd LS24 .. 189 D3
Old Malton Rd
Malton YO17 ... 215 D5
7 Willerby YO12 ... 99 D2
Old Maltongate YO17 .. 215 C4
Old Market Pl 6 HG4 .. 214 C5
Old Mill Cl 8 LS29 ... 176 C1
Old Mill Row 3 YO7 ... 211 C3
Old Mill View YO60 ... 145 C5
Old Mill Wynd TS9 ... 8 A1
Old Moor La YO24 ... 230 E7
Old Moor Rd LA2 ... 128 B8
Old Oliver La BD24 ... 152 F6
Old Orch YO32 ... 225 D8
Old Orch The
1 Easingwold YO61 ... 143 C8
Fulford YO10 ... 231 E7
Shipton YO30 ... 165 F5
Old Park La YO21 ... 31 D6
Old Park Mews HG4 ... 214 B5
Old Quarry La LS25 ... 195 E1
Old Raike BD23 ... 152 F4
Old Rd
Appleton Roebuck YO23 .. 190 E5
Clapham LA2 ... 130 C8
Garsdale LA10 ... 55 A6
Ingleton LA6 ... 103 E3
Kirkby Overblow LS17 ... 178 E1
Old Rd *continued*
Kirkbymoorside YO62 ... 70 B1
Thornton in Craven BD23 ... 172 A3
Old Sawmill The BD24 . 153 B7
Old Sch The LS23 ... 188 E7
Old School Hall LS29 .. 174 F4
Old School La YO8 ... 198 B5
Old St The LS24 ... 190 C8
Old Station Rd 4 YO62 .. 92 C1
Old Station Way 20 LS29 ... 174 F4
Old Station Yd* YO62 .. 92 F6
Old Stone Trough La BB18 ... 186 A6
Old Stubble The 6 TS13 . 13 K2
Old Sutton Rd YO7 ... 211 E3
Old Trough Way HG1 .. 219 C6
Old Vicarage La 5 LS25 ... 202 A8
Old Village The YO32 .. 225 F5
Old Wife's Way YO18 .. 73 A8
Olde Mkt The TS16 ... 5 D3
Oldfield La
Collingham LS22 ... 180 C1
Spaunton YO62 ... 70 E4
Sutton BD22 ... 187 F1
Oldgate La LS25 ... 195 D6
Oldham Cl TS12 ... 9 E8
Oldham St TS12 ... 9 D7
Oldstead Rd YO61 ... 91 B3
Olicana Pk LS29 ... 218 B5
Olive Gr HG1 ... 220 B4
Olive Way HG1 ... 220 B4
Olive Wlk HG1 ... 220 B4
Oliver La YO17 ... 121 C8
Oliver St 4 YO11 ... 213 A4
Oliver's Cl 18 YO14 ... 126 F8
Oliver's Mount Rd YO11 ... 212 F2
Olliver La DL10 ... 20 F1
Olliver Rd DL10 ... 209 E8
Olympia Cres YO8 ... 232 E6
Omega St 7 HG1 ... 219 C5
Onams La YO62 ... 69 F4
One Acre Garth 2 YO8 . 196 E1
Onhams La YO60 ... 146 E4
Oran La DL10 ... 41 E4
Orcaber La LA2 ... 130 E6
Orchard Cl
Appleton Roebuck YO23 .. 190 F5
Barkston Ash LS24 ... 195 E7
Dalton-on-Tees DL2 ... 22 D7
1 Great Ayton TS9 ... 8 A2
6 Hartwith cum Winsley HG3 ... 137 F1
1 Knaresborough HG5 .. 221 B8
6 Monk Fryston LS25 .. 202 A8
9 Norton DN6 ... 206 E2
Selby YO8 ... 232 A4
Sharow HG4 ... 214 F6
6 South Milford LS25 .. 195 F2
York YO24 ... 227 E1
Orchard Cotts 4 YO19 .. 184 F7
Orchard Ct
Bramham cum Oglethorpe LS23 ... 188 F5
8 Knaresborough HG5 .. 221 B5
Orchard Dr
Fairburn WF11 ... 201 D7
Hambleton YO8 ... 196 F2
Linton LS22 ... 180 A2
Orchard Gdns YO31 .. 225 E2
Orchard Gr 4 DL6 ... 43 F3
Orchard Head Cres WF8 ... 201 C2
Orchard Head Dr WF8 . 201 C2
Orchard Head Jun & Inf Sch WF8 ... 201 C2
Orchard Head La WF8 . 201 B2
Orchard La
8 Addingham LS29 ... 175 A4
Barkston Ash LS24 ... 195 F6
Hebden BD23 ... 135 A2
Ripley HG3 ... 161 C7
Thirsk YO7 ... 211 B1
Orchard Paddock
34 Haxby YO32 ... 166 E5
3 Haxby YO32 ... 225 D8
Orchard Rd
Malton YO17 ... 215 B4
Selby YO8 ... 232 A4
3 Sleights YO22 ... 32 A6
Upper Poppleton YO26 .. 224 A1
Orchard The
5 Ampleforth YO62 ... 92 C1
Burniston YO13 ... 75 D8
6 North Featherstone WF7 ... 200 E1
Sadberge DL2 ... 4 C7
Scalby YO12 ... 212 C7
Snainton YO13 ... 98 A4
Thirsk YO7 ... 211 C4
Tholthorpe YO61 ... 142 D5
Orchard View
Markington with Wallerthwaite HG3 ... 139 E3
3 Skelton YO30 ... 224 B5
Orchard Way
Hensall DN14 ... 203 C2
Middlesbrough TS7 ... 7 D8
Selby YO8 ... 232 A4
1 Strensall YO32 ... 167 B7
Thorpe Willoughby YO8 .. 197 B2
York YO24 ... 227 E1
Orchards The
2 Beadlam YO62 ... 93 D7
6 Brafferton YO61 ... 115 F1
Orchards The *continued*
Leavening YO17 ... 147 E1
Mickletown LS26 ... 200 B5
Ripon HG4 ... 214 C6
Westow YO60 ... 147 B4
Orchid Ct 17 DL9 ... 41 A5
Orchid Way 8 HG3 ... 161 B3
Ordmerstones La YO18 . 96 C4
Ordnance La YO10 ... 228 D1
Oriel Bank YO11 ... 212 F3
Oriel Cl YO11 ... 212 F3
Oriel Cres YO11 ... 212 F3
Oriel Gr YO30 ... 228 A8
Ormesby Bank TS7 ... 7 D7
Ormesby Cres DL7 .. 210 D2
Ormesby Cty Modern Sch TS3 ... 7 D8
Ormesby Prim Sch TS7 .. 7 D8
Ormesby Rd TS3 ... 7 C8
Orms Gill Green La BD23 ... 154 D6
Orpington Rd TS3 ... 7 C8
Orrin Cl YO24 ... 230 C7
Osbaldwick La YO10 .. 229 B4
Osbaldwick Link Rd YO19 ... 229 D4
Osbaldwick Prim Sch YO10 ... 229 C4
Osbaldwick Village YO10 ... 229 C4
Osborne Cl HG1 ... 219 D4
Osborne Gdns HG1 ... 219 D4
Osborne Pk YO12 ... 212 D5
Osborne Rd HG1 ... 219 D4
Osborne Wlk HG1 ... 219 D4
Osbourne Dr 4 YO30 .. 224 E3
Osgodby Cl 9 YO11 ... 100 B8
Osgodby Cres YO11 .. 100 B7
Osgodby Gr 10 YO11 .. 100 B8
Osgodby Hall Rd YO11 . 100 B7
Osgodby Hill YO11 ... 100 B7
Osgodby La 12 YO11 ... 100 B8
Osgodby Way 11 YO11 .. 100 B8
Osgoodby Bank YO7 ... 90 F3
Osmington Gdns 10 YO32 ... 167 A7
Osmotherley CP Sch DL6 ... 45 B4
Osprey Cl
4 Collingham LS22 ... 180 A1
Guisborough TS14 ... 8 D6
5 Scotton DL9 ... 40 F2
4 York YO24 ... 230 B8
Osprey Garth 4 YO12 .. 99 E6
Ostler's Cl YO23 ... 230 C3
Ostman Rd YO26 ... 227 C5
Oswaldene DL6 ... 45 B4
Oswaldkirk Bank YO62 . 93 A1
Oswestry Gn TS4 ... 7 A7
Oswin Gr DL10 ... 20 E4
Oswy St 5 YO21 ... 208 D5
Otley Rd
Harrogate HG2 ... 222 B8
Killinghall HG3 ... 161 B4
Pannal HG3 ... 178 A7
Skipton BD23 ... 217 B4
Stainburn HG3 ... 177 F6
Otley St BD23 ... 217 A4
Otter Dr 18 YO18 ... 95 F6
Otter Way TS17 ... 6 A5
Otterbeck Way 16 DL8 .. 63 B3
Otterwood Bank 6 YO24 ... 227 B1
Otterwood La YO24 ... 227 B1
Otterwood Paddock YO41 ... 168 C2
Oucher La HG3 ... 140 B2
Oughtershaw Rd BD23 .. 80 B6
Oulston Rd YO61 ... 117 D1
Our Ladys RC Prim Sch YO24 ... 227 E1
Ouse Acres YO26 ... 227 D6
Ouse Bank YO8 ... 232 E5
Ouseburn Ave YO26 .. 227 C6
Ousecliffe Gdns YO30 . 228 A6
Ousegate YO8 ... 232 D5
Ouston Cl LS24 ... 189 F6
Ouston La LS24 ... 189 F6
Out Gang La BD23 ... 107 F1
Outgaits Cl 4 YO14 ... 126 F8
Outgaits La
Hunmanby YO14 ... 127 A8
Muston YO14 ... 100 F1
Outgang La
Osbaldwick YO19 ... 229 D6
21 Pickering YO18 ... 95 F6
Thornton-le-Dale YO18 ... 96 E6
Outgang Rd
Malton YO17 ... 215 B5
Pickering YO18 ... 96 A6
Scampston YO17 ... 122 F7
Outgang The YO17 ... 122 F4
Outgate Cnr DL6 ... 23 F4
Outwood La LS24 ... 190 C2
Oval The
Harrogate HG2 ... 222 D8
Hurworth DL2 ... 3 F1
Kellingley DN14 ... 202 C3
Middlesbrough TS5 ... 6 E6
Otley LS21 ... 176 F1
3 Scarborough YO11 ... 100 B8
Skipton BD23 ... 217 B3
Over Nidd HG1 ... 219 C6
Overburn Rd 8 BD20 .. 187 E6
Overdale YO11 ... 100 A7
Overdale Cl YO24 ... 230 D8
Overdale CP Sch YO11 ... 100 A7
Overdale Ct BD23 ... 217 A5
Overdale Grange 3 BD23 ... 217 B5
Overdale Rd TS3 ... 7 C8
Overgreen Cl YO13 ... 75 D8
Overgreen La YO13 ... 75 C8
Overgreen View YO13 .. 75 D8
Overscar La YO18 ... 72 E3
Overton Rd YO30 ... 165 F3
Ovington La DL11 ... 1 A6
Ovington Terr YO23 ... 228 B2
Owler Park Rd LS29 .. 175 C3
Owlwood Ct 7 YO19 .. 184 E7
Owlwood La 6 YO19 .. 184 E7
Owmen Field La YO62 .. 93 C5
Owston Ave 2 YO10 .. 229 A3
Owston Rd 1 YO14 ... 126 F8
Ox Calder Cl 16 YO19 .. 184 F7
Ox Carr La YO32 ... 167 B6
Ox Cl YO41 ... 168 D2
Ox Close La
Eldmire with Crakehill YO7 ... 115 E5
Myton-on-Swale YO61 ... 141 F5
North Deighton LS22 ... 180 B7
Whixley YO26 ... 163 F5
Ox Moor La
Cattal YO26 ... 164 A1
Hunsingore LS22 ... 180 E8
Oxcliff YO12 ... 212 C8
Oxclose La Huby YO61 .. 144 B4
Hutton-le-Hole YO62 ... 70 C4
Oxcroft 23 YO62 ... 70 B1
Oxen La YO8 ... 198 E3
Oxenby Pl 12 YO61 ... 117 D1
Oxford Dr LS25 ... 194 D1
Oxford Pl HG1 ... 219 D2
Oxford St
Harrogate HG1 ... 219 D2
6 Normanton South WF6 . 200 B2
Scarborough YO12 ... 212 F6
Skelton & Brotton TS12 ... 9 D7
5 York YO24 ... 228 A3
Oxford Terr 2 HG1 ... 219 D1
Oxmoor La LS24 ... 196 D7
Oxpasture Cl YO12 ... 212 C4
Oxton Dr LS24 ... 189 F6
Oxton La LS24 ... 189 F6
Oyster Park Inf Sch WF10 ... 201 B4
Oyster Park Mid Sch WF10 ... 201 B4

P

Packhorse Bridge*
Dacre HG3 ... 159 D6
Romanby DL7 ... 210 B4
Pad Cote La BD22 ... 187 A5
Padbury Ave 50 YO14 ... 101 B3
Padbury Cl 49 YO14 ... 101 B3
Paddock Cl
Copmanthorpe YO23 ... 230 A2
Norton YO17 ... 215 D3
2 Pickering YO18 ... 95 F6
Paddock Hill YO17 ... 215 A4
Paddock House La LS22 ... 179 E1
Paddock Rise 13 YO61 .. 117 D1
Paddock The
14 Airmyn DN14 ... 205 E4
Appleton Wiske DL6 ... 24 B3
Burton Salmon LS25 ... 201 F6
Knaresborough HG5 ... 221 C5
1 Linton-on-Ouse YO30 .. 164 F8
Melmerby HG4 ... 114 B7
Middleton St George DL2 ... 4 C3
Newby Wiske DL7 ... 64 E2
Normanton South WF6 ... 200 A1
8 Selby YO8 ... 232 C6
Stokesley TS9 ... 26 C8
9 Whitby YO21 ... 208 D7
Wilberfoss YO41 ... 185 E5
York YO26 ... 227 C6
Paddock Way YO26 ... 227 C6
Paddocks The HG3 ... 223 F4
Page La YO62 ... 93 E6
Pagnell Ave YO8 ... 232 E4
Painsthorpe La YO41 .. 170 B5
Painter La YO8 ... 196 E2
Palace Rd HG4 ... 214 B7
Pale La Carleton BD23 .. 216 E1
Gateforth YO8 ... 202 F7
Paley Green La BD24 .. 131 B2
Pallet Hill 10 DL10 ... 41 D5
Palmer Gr YO8 ... 232 A3
Palmer La YO1 ... 233 C2
Palmes Cl YO19 ... 191 E8
Panman La YO19 ... 184 F8
Pannal Ash Cl HG2 ... 222 C8
Pannal Ash Cres HG2 .. 222 B7
Pannal Ash Dr HG2 .. 222 B7
Pannal Ash Gr HG2 .. 222 B7
Pannal Ash Rd HG2 .. 222 B7
Pannal Ave HG3 ... 222 E2
Pannal Bank HG3 ... 222 E2
Pannal Cl 3 YO21 ... 208 B5
Pannal CP Sch HG3 .. 222 E3
Pannal Gn HG3 ... 222 E3
Pannal Rd HG3 ... 223 B4
Pannal Sta HG3 ... 222 E2
Pannett Way 8 YO21 .. 208 D6
Pannierman La TS9 ... 7 D1
Panorama Cl 10 HG3 .. 137 C4
Panorama Dr LS29 ... 175 C1
Panorama Wlk HG3 ... 137 C4
Pant La LA2 ... 130 E7
Parade Ct YO31 ... 228 F6
Parade The HG1 ... 219 E2
Paradise YO11 ... 213 B7
Paradise Cotts YO17 .. 170 F8
Paradise Field Est 2 YO61 ... 143 D8
Paradise La Dalton YO7 . 115 F8
Stutton with Hazlewood LS24 ... 189 A3
Paradise Rd YO7 ... 67 A2
Paragon St YO10 ... 233 C1
Parish Ghyll Dr LS29 .. 218 A3
Parish Ghyll La LS29 .. 218 A3
Parish Ghyll Rd LS29 .. 218 A3
Parish Ghyll Wlk LS29 . 218 A3
Park Ave Barlow YO8 .. 204 C7
Castleford WF10 ... 200 F4
Glusburn BD20 ... 187 E7
Great Preston WF10 ... 200 E6
Harrogate HG2 ... 219 C1
Hellifield BD23 ... 154 B3
Kippax LS25 ... 194 E1
Knaresborough HG5 ... 221 B8
New Earswick YO32 ... 225 D5
Normanton South WF6 .. 200 A1
Scarborough YO12 ... 212 D4
Sherburn in Elmet LS25 .. 195 E4
Skipton BD23 ... 216 F4
Swillington LS26 ... 194 A1
Thornaby TS17 ... 6 B8
Park Ave S HG2 ... 222 D8
Park Bank YO21 ... 29 E7
Park Chase
Harrogate HG1 ... 219 E3
Hornby DL8 ... 62 C8
Park Cl 6 Airmyn DN14 . 205 E4
1 Easingwold YO61 ... 143 D8
8 Knaresborough HG5 .. 221 B6
Skelton YO30 ... 224 B4
Park Cres
6 Addingham LS29 ... 175 A4
Castleford WF10 ... 201 B4
Darlington DL1 ... 3 D4
Embsay BD23 ... 217 C7
Hellifield BD23 ... 154 B3
York YO31 ... 233 C4
Park Crest HG5 ... 221 B6
Park Dale WF10 ... 201 B5
Park Dr Campsall DN6 .. 206 E1
Glusburn BD20 ... 187 E7
7 Harrogate HG2 ... 219 D1
Harrogate HG2 ... 222 D8
Knaresborough HG5 ... 221 B6
18 Masham HG4 ... 86 C3
Park Edge HG2 ... 222 F8
Park End Prim Sch TS3 .. 7 C8
Park Gate
Knaresborough HG5 ... 221 B8
Strensall YO32 ... 167 B8
Park Gr
Knaresborough HG5 ... 221 B8
Norton YO17 ... 215 C3
Selby YO8 ... 232 B3
Swillington LS26 ... 200 A8
York YO31 ... 233 C4
Park Grove Sch YO31 .. 233 C4
Park Hill BB18 ... 171 E1
Park House Gn
Harrogate HG1 ... 219 C5
7 Spofforth HG3 ... 179 E5
Park House La LA2 ... 128 D5
Park La Balne DN14 ... 207 C5
Barlow YO8 ... 204 C7
Bishop Wilton YO42 ... 169 F1
Borrowby YO7 ... 65 E4
Buckden BD23 ... 81 E2
Burn YO8 ... 203 D7
Carleton BD23 ... 173 A3
Cowling BD22 ... 186 F5
Darlington DL1 ... 3 D4
6 Easington TS13 ... 11 A8
Glusburn BD20 ... 187 E7
Great Preston WF10 ... 200 E7
Guisborough TS14 ... 8 E6
Kippax LS25 ... 200 E8
Kirkbymoorside YO62 ... 70 B1
Knaresborough HG5 ... 221 C6
Ledsham LS25 ... 201 B8
Luttons YO17 ... 150 C8
Mickletown LS26 ... 200 A5
5 Middleham DL8 ... 60 E2
North Featherstone WF8 .. 200 F1
North Stainley with Sleningford HG4 ... 113 E5
Spofforth with Stockeld HG3 ... 179 D5
Tatham LA2 ... 128 B8
West Tanfield HG4 ... 113 A8
Wilberfoss YO41 ... 185 E5
Womersley DN6 ... 206 D6
York YO24 ... 227 F3
Park Lands 4 HG3 ... 179 E5
Park Lane Cl YO42 ... 169 F1
Park Lane Inf Sch TS14 .. 8 E7
Park Mount 6 HG3 ... 179 E5
Park Nook Rd YO8 ... 196 F4
Park Par
Harrogate HG1 ... 219 F2
Knaresborough HG5 ... 221 B6
Park Pl Darlington DL1 ... 3 D5
Hellifield BD23 ... 154 B3
4 Knaresborough HG5 .. 221 B6
Park Rd Airmyn DN14 .. 205 E4
Asenby YO7 ... 115 B6
Barlow YO8 ... 204 C7
Castleford WF10 ... 201 A3
Cowling BD22 ... 187 B6
Glusburn BD20 ... 187 E8

Park Rd *continued*
8 Harrogate HG2 ......219 D1
Harrogate HG2 ....222 D8
Norton-on-Derwent YO17 ....215 C3
Pontefract WF8 ....201 A1
6 Scarborough YO12 ....212 E4
Spofforth HG3 ....179 E5
Park Rise 17 YO14 ......126 F8
Park Row
Knaresborough HG5 .....221 B5
Selby YO8 ....232 D5
Park Side BB18 ....186 A8
Park Sq
2 Knaresborough HG5 ..221 B6
9 Ripon HG4 ....214 C4
Park St 16 Glusburn BD20 187 E8
1 Harrogate HG1 ......219 C5
Hovingham YO62 ....119 E6
Masham HG4 ....86 C3
Pickering YO18 ....95 F7
Ripon HG4 ....214 B5
Scarborough YO12 ......212 D4
Selby YO8 ....232 D5
1 Skipton BD23 ....216 F4
York YO24 ....233 A1
Park Terr YO21 ....208 D6
Park The 14 YO13 ....75 D5
Park View
Castleford WF10 ....201 B3
Glaisdale YO21 ....30 D4
Harrogate HG1 ....219 E2
22 Leyburn DL8 ....60 D5
Middleton Tyas DL10 ......21 C4
Skipton BD23 ....216 D4
Swillington LS26 ....194 A1
Park View Dr BD23 ....134 B3
Park Way
Kirk Hammerton YO26 ....164 C2
Knaresborough HG5 .....221 B8
Park Wood BD23 ......216 D5
Park Wood Cl BD23 ...216 E5
Park Wood Cres BD23 .216 D5
Park Wood Way BD23 .216 D5
Park Wynd DL10 ......209 C6
Parker Ave YO26 ......227 B2
Parker Dr 21 DL8 ....63 A2
Parker La YO26 ....164 C3
Parker St 15 BD20 ......187 E8
Parkers Mount 20 YO62 ..70 B1
Parkfield Ave TS5 ....6 E8
Parkfield Cl YO12 .....212 D4
Parkfield Gdns YO12 ..212 D4
Parkfield La WF7 ......200 E1
Parkgate DL1 ....3 D5
Parkgate La DL10 ......41 B7
Parkin Ave YO8 ....232 E4
Parkinson App LS25 ..194 C4
Parkinson's La LS21 ...159 E2
Parkinson's Yd 5 DL10 .209 C6
Parkland Dr
Darlington DL3 ....3 A6
Tadcaster LS24 ....189 F6
Parkland Way YO32 ...225 D8
Parklands
Castleford WF10 ....200 F4
Ilkley LS29 ....218 D4
Parklands The
1 Ingleby Arncliffe DL6 ...45 A7
Scruton DL7 ....63 D7
Parkshill Ct DL10 ....20 F7
Parkside DL1 ....3 C4
Parkside Cl YO24 ......227 E3
Parkside Prim Sch DN14 ....205 F3
Parkway The YO12 ....212 B7
Parkways YO8 ....232 B3
Parkwood Dr 6 TS18 .....5 E8
Parliament Ave YO17 ..215 E4
Parliament St
Harrogate HG1 ....219 C3
Norton YO17 ....215 E3
York YO1 ....233 B2
Parliament Terr 2 HG1 .219 D2
Parlington Ct LS15 ....194 C8
Parlington Dr LS25 ....194 E8
Parlington La LS25 ....194 E7
Parlington Mdw LS15 ..194 C7
Parlington Villas LS25 .194 E8
Parrock St 7 BB18 .....171 D1
Parson Back La DL6 ....25 B2
Parsonage Rd LS26 ....200 C6
Parsonage The 11 HG5 .221 A6
Parsons Cl 10 DN14 ....205 E4
Parson's Cl YO21 .....208 A7
Parsons Close La BD24 ....131 A2
Parson's La
1 Addingham LS29 .....174 E4
Hutton Rudby DL6 ....25 A2
Parsons La YO26 ......165 E1
Parson's Wlk 11 DN14 ..205 E4
Pasley Rd HG4 ....113 D3
Pasture Ave LS25 .....196 A4
Pasture Cl
Barnoldswick BB18 ......171 E2
4 Sherburn in Elmet LS25 ....196 A4
Skelton YO30 ....224 B5
Skipton BD23 ....217 B5
2 Strensall YO32 ....167 B6
Wistow YO8 ....197 D6
Pasture Cres
Filey YO14 ....101 A4
3 Knaresborough HG5 ..221 B7
Pasture Ct LS25 ....195 F4
Pasture Dr Bedale DL8 ...63 A2
Castleford WF10 ....200 D3
Pasture Farm Cl YO10 .231 D6
Pasture Field La YO22 ..32 C5
Pasture Fold 4 LS29 ...176 C1
Pasture Hill YO17 .....169 E8
Pasture La
Ellerton YO42 ....193 C1
Helperby YO61 ....142 B8
Heworth YO31 ....229 B8
Hovingham YO62 ....119 E6
Kearby with Netherby LS22 ....179 C1
Malton YO17 ....215 C5
Marton-le-Moor HG4 ....140 D8
2 Seamer YO12 ....99 D6
Pasture Rd
Embsay with Eastby BD23 ....217 C8
Lockton YO18 ....73 A5
Pasture View LS25 .....195 F4
Pasture Way
Castleford WF10 ....200 D3
Sherburn in Elmet LS25 ...195 F4
Wistow YO8 ....197 D6
Pastures The
Carlton DN14 ....204 C3
Coulby Newham TS8 ....7 B5
16 Eastfield YO11 ....100 B6
Sherburn YO17 ....124 D7
4 York YO24 ....230 E8
Pateley Moor Cres DL2 ...3 E3
Pately Pl 1 YO26 ......227 D4
Paterson Cres DL6 ....210 E4
Patience La HG4 ......114 D3
Patrick Pool YO1 ......233 B2
Patterdale Dr YO30 ....224 E1
Patterham La DL8 ......59 D4
Paul's Row 5 YO17 ....215 C4
Pavement YO1 ....233 B2
Paver La YO1 ....233 C2
Pavilion Sq 7 HG2 .....219 C1
Peacock's Cl DL7 ....63 E7
Peacocks Cl TS9 ....26 C8
Peak Scar Rd YO62 .....67 C3
Pear Tree Acre LS23 ...180 F1
Pear Tree Ave
Long Drax YO8 ....204 F7
8 Poppleton YO26 ......165 F1
Pear Tree Cl
Skeeby DL10 ....20 F1
York YO32 ....225 F4
Pear Tree Wlk YO17 ...215 B4
Pearl Rd TS17 ....6 B8
Pearl St HG1 ....220 C4
Pearson Garth YO13 ....99 A7
Pearson St WF6 ....200 A3
Peart La BD23 ....154 C8
Peartree Ct YO1 ......233 C3
Pease Ct
Guisborough TS14 ....8 D5
4 Lingdale TS12 ....9 F7
Pease St Darlington DL1 ...3 E5
6 Lingdale TS12 ....9 F7
Peasey Hills Rd YO17 .215 C5
Peasholm Ave YO12 ...212 F7
Peasholm Cres YO12 ..212 F7
Peasholm Dr YO12 ....212 E7
Peasholm Gap YO12 ...212 F8
Peasholm Gdns YO12 ..212 F7
Peasholm Rd YO12 ....212 F8
Peasholme Bridge YO12 ....212 E7
Peasholme Gn YO1 ....233 C2
Peasland La YO7 ....66 B5
Peaslands La YO18 .....96 D5
Peat La HG3 ....137 B3
Peatmoor La DL8 ....58 E5
Peckett's Holt HG1 ....219 D7
Peckett's Way HG1 ....219 D7
Peckfield HG4 ....214 C2
Peckfield Cl HG3 ......160 F5
Peckitt St YO1 ....233 B1
Peel Cl YO10 ....229 A1
Peel Gn BD23 ....154 B2
Peel Pl 11 LS29 ....176 C1
Peel St Thornaby TS17 .....6 B8
York YO1 ....233 C1
Pefham La YO17 ......170 F4
Pegman Cl TS14 ....8 F7
Peirse Cl DL8 ....63 A2
Pelham Pl 15 YO32 ....167 A7
Pellentine Rd HG3 .....223 F4
Pemberton Cres TS4 .....7 A8
Pemberton Rd WF10 ..201 A4
Pembroke St
10 Skipton BD23 ....216 F3
York YO30 ....228 B7
Pembroke Way YO21 ..208 C5
Pembury Mews DL10 ....41 B6
Penders La TS15 ....5 E1
Penderyn Cres TS17 .....5 F4
Pendle St 4 BD23 .....216 D3
Pendleton Rd DL1 ....3 D7
Pendragon Castle★ CA17 ....14 A1
Penhill Ct DL7 ....210 C1
Penhowe La YO17 .....147 D4
Penistone Rd TS3 ....7 C8
Penley's Grove St YO31 ....233 C4
Penn La DL8 ....56 D4
Penn Rd DL10 ....209 B7
Pennine Way BD20 ...172 E2
Pennine Cl YO32 ......225 F4
Pennine View
Burneston DL8 ....87 E8
Northallerton DL7 ......210 B2
Pennine Way
11 Barnoldswick BB18 ...171 D1
Pennine Way *continued*
Ingleby TS17 ....6 A4
Penniston La YO13 .....97 C4
Penny Gn BD24 ....131 D1
Penny La
1 Easingwold YO61 .....117 D1
Ripon HG4 ....214 C7
Penny Pot Gdns 4 HG3 161 B2
Penny Pot La
Felliscliffe HG3 ....160 D2
Killinghall HG3 ....161 A2
Penny Royal Cl 7 HG3 .161 B3
Pennycarr La YO61 ....143 D7
Pennyman Prim Sch TS3 ....7 D8
Pennypot La TS18 ....5 E7
Pennywort Gr 15 HG3 ..161 B3
Penrith Cres WF10 ....201 B5
Penrith Rd TS3 ....7 B8
Pentland Dr YO32 .....225 E3
Penton Rd 20 YO11 ....100 B6
Penyghent Ave YO31 ..229 A5
Pen-y-Ghent Way 5 BB18 ....171 D1
Penyghent Way TS17 ....6 A3
Peppercorn Cl 6 YO26 .227 E4
Peppergarth The DL7 ..210 B3
Peppermint Dr 15 DL9 ...41 A5
Peppermint Way YO8 ..232 A5
Per Ardua Way 6 DL10 ..41 E4
Percy Cross Rigg YO21 ...9 A1
Percy Dr 4 DN14 ......205 E4
Percy Rd Darlington DL3 ...3 C7
14 Hunmanby YO14 .....127 A8
Percy St YO31 ....233 B3
Percy's La YO1 ....233 C2
Perie Ave HG4 ....113 D3
Perry Ave TS17 ....6 B5
Peter Hill Dr YO30 ....228 A8
Peter La
Burton Leonard HG3 .....140 A2
York YO1 ....233 B2
Petercroft Cl 5 YO19 ..184 F7
Petercroft La YO19 ....184 F7
Peterhouse Cl DL1 ......3 D7
Petersbottom La LA2 ..129 B4
Petersway YO30 ......233 A4
Petre Ave YO8 ....232 E3
Petty Whin Cl 25 HG3 ..161 B3
Petyt Gr BD23 ....217 A4
Pheasant Dr 5 YO24 ...230 B8
Philadelphia Terr 2 YO23 ....228 B2
Philip La YO8 ....196 E2
Philippa's Dr HG2 .....222 D8
Philpin La LA6 ....104 C8
Phlashetts La DL8 ......87 A4
Phoenix Pk TS8 ....6 F6
Piave Rd DL9 ....40 D4
Piccadilly YO1 ....233 C2
Pick Haven Garth DN14 ....202 F3
Pickard Cl BB18 ....171 E2
Pickard La BD20 ....174 C1
Pickering Castle★ YO18 ....95 F7
Pickering Cty Inf Sch YO18 ....96 A7
Pickering Cty Jun Sch YO18 ....95 F7
Pickering Rd
East Ayton/West Ayton YO13 ....99 A7
Thornaby TS17 ....6 B8
Thornton-le-Dale YO18 ....96 C6
Pickeringmoor La YO7 ..64 C2
Pickhill C of E Prim Sch YO7 ....88 C6
Picking Croft La HG3 ..161 B5
Pickrowfield La LS25 ..196 C6
Pickwick Cl YO17 .....215 C5
Piece Croft 2 BD23 ....134 D2
Piece Fields 4 BD23 ...134 D2
Pier Rd YO21 ....208 D7
Piercy End YO62 ....70 B1
Pierremont Rd DL3 ......3 B6
Piggy La DL2 ....1 C7
Pighill Nook Rd LS25 ..202 C7
Pike Hills Mount YO23 ....230 A3
Pike La BD24 ....131 E4
Pike Rd 8 YO18 ....95 F6
Pikepurse La DL10 ....209 D8
Pilgrim St YO31 ....233 B4
Pill White La LS21 ....177 C3
Pilmoor Cl DL10 ......209 E8
Pilmoor Dr DL10 ......209 E8
Pindar Leisure Ctr YO11 ....100 A6
Pindar Rd YO11 ....100 A6
Pindar Sch YO11 ......100 A6
Pinders Cres WF11 ....201 E3
Pinders Gn LS26 ......200 B4
Pinders Green Ct LS26 ....200 B5
Pinders Green Dr LS26 ....200 B5
Pinders Green Fold LS26 ....200 B5
Pine Cl
Castleford WF10 ....200 F3
Skipton BD23 ....216 E4
Pine Croft HG4 ....112 F2
Pine Gr 1 DL6 ....210 E3
Pine Hill TS8 ....7 B5
Pine Rd Guisborough TS14 .8 E7
Middlesbrough TS7 ....7 D8
Pine St HG1 ....219 E5
Pine Tree Ave YO17 ....122 F5
Pine Tree Cl YO8 ......197 B2
Pine Tree La 1 LS25 ...202 A7
Pinelands 4 YO32 .....225 D7
Pinelands Way YO10 ..229 C3
Pines Gdns 23 LS29 ....175 C2
Pines The LS17 ....178 B2
Pinetree Gr DL2 ....4 C4
Pinewood Ave YO14 ...101 B4
Pinewood Cl
5 Easington TS13 ....11 A8
2 Ilkley LS29 ....218 A3
5 Whitby YO21 ....208 C6
Pinewood Dr
Camblesforth YO8 ....204 D4
Scarborough YO12 ......212 D5
Pinewood Gate HG2 ...222 A7
Pinewood Gr
13 Bedale DL8 ....63 A2
6 York YO31 ....225 E2
Pinewood Hill 4 YO10 .229 C3
Pinewood Rd TS7 ....7 C6
Pinewood Wlk 7 TS9 ...26 C8
Pinfold Ave LS25 ......195 F4
Pinfold Cl
Bilton-in-Ainsty with Bickerton LS22 ....181 B5
5 Riccall YO19 ....192 A1
3 Sherburn in Elmet LS25 195 F4
Pinfold Ct
Kirkby Malzeard HG4 ....112 D5
4 Sherburn in Elmet LS25 195 F4
4 York YO30 ....228 A7
Pinfold Dr DL6 ....210 E5
Pinfold Garth
Malton YO17 ....215 A4
6 Sherburn in Elmet LS25 195 F4
1 Sherburn in Elmet LS25 ....196 A4
Pinfold Gn HG5 ....140 E1
Pinfold Hill YO8 ......197 D6
Pinfold La
Asselby DN14 ....205 F6
Kirk Smeaton WF8 ....206 B3
Mickletown LS26 ....200 C5
Moss DN6 ....207 D1
Norton DN6 ....206 E2
Norwood HG3 ....177 A8
Pollington DN14 ....207 F6
Pinfold Rise LS25 .....194 F8
Pinfold The 5 BD23 ....216 F4
Pinfold View DN14 ....207 F6
Pinfold Way
5 Sherburn in Elmet LS25 195 F4
2 Sherburn in Elmet LS25 ....196 A4
Pinhaw Rd BD23 ......217 A2
Pinnacle View BD22 ...187 A5
Pioneer Way WF10 ....200 C2
Piper Hill 1 WF11 .....201 D6
Piper La Cowling BD22 ..187 B5
Thirsk YO7 ....211 C3
Piper Rd DL6 ....45 F6
Pipers Acre 4 YO18 .....95 F7
Pipers La YO26 ....141 F1
Pippin Rd YO17 ....215 B4
Pippin's App 17 WF6 ...200 A2
Pit Ings La YO7 ....115 F6
Pit La Micklefield LS25 ..195 A4
Mickletown LS26 ....200 B6
Pitman Rd YO17 ......215 C5
Place Hill DL11 ....38 B6
Plane Tree Way YO14 ..101 A4
Planetree La
Kirkby Fleetham with Fencote DL7 ....42 A1
Thornville YO26 ....164 A1
Plantation Ave HG3 ...222 A8
Plantation Cl HG2 .....222 A8
Plantation Dr
Barlby with Osgodby YO8 ....198 B5
York YO26 ....227 C6
Plantation Gr YO26 ...227 C6
Plantation Rd HG2 ....222 A8
Plantation Terr HG2 ...222 B6
Plantation The BD23 ...152 E3
Plantation Way 23 YO32 166 E5
Pleasance The 6 LS26 .194 A1
Pleasant Mount YO22 ..208 F3
Pleasant View 5 BB18 ..172 B1
Plews Way DL7 ....63 C5
Plompton Cl HG2 ......220 D1
Plompton Dr HG2 .....220 D2
Plompton Gr 3 HG2 ...220 D2
Plompton Rd HG3 .....223 F5
Plompton Way 1 HG2 ..220 D2
Plompton Wlk 2 HG2 ..220 D2
Plough Garth The DN14 ....202 F3
Ploughlands 1 YO32 ..225 C7
Ploughman's Cl YO23 ..230 C3
Ploughmans Ct 14 YO11 100 B7
Ploughmans' La YO32 ..225 C7
Plover Gdns 1 YO12 ....99 F6
Plum St YO17 ....215 D3
Plumer Ave YO31 .....229 A5
Plumer Rd DL9 ....209 B1
Plumpton La HG4 .....139 D8
Plumpton Pk HG2 .....220 D3
Plumpton Rocks★ HG5 ....179 D8
Pluntrain Dale La YO18 .96 B7
Pocklington La YO42 ..169 F2
Pockthorpe La YO25 ...151 F2
Pocock Pl DL10 ....41 E4
Polam Hall Sch DL1 .....3 C4
Polam La DL1 ....3 C4
Pole Rd BD22 ....187 F4
Pollard Cl YO32 ......225 E3
Pollard Gdns YO12 ....212 C4
Pollington Balne C of E Sch DN14 ....207 F6
Polperro Cl 21 WF6 ....200 A2
Pond Farm Cl TS13 .....11 F7
Pond Field Cl DL3 ....3 A4
Pond St 3 YO8 ....232 D6
Pondfields Dr LS25 ....194 D1
Pontefract C of E Sch WF8 ....201 B1
Pontefract Castle★ WF8 ....201 C1
Pontefract Monkhill Sta WF8 ....201 B1
Pontefract Mus★ WF8 ....201 B1
Pontefract New Coll WF8 ....201 A1
Pontefract Park Race Course★ WF8 ....200 F2
Pontefract Rd
Castleford WF10 ....200 F4
Knottingley WF11 ....201 D2
Normanton South WF6 ...200 B2
Pool Ct 20 YO18 ....95 F6
Pool La YO26 ....164 E4
Poole La LS25 ....201 F6
Pope St WF6 ....200 B3
Poplar Ave
Castleford WF10 ....201 B4
6 Hutton Rudby TS15 ....25 D5
4 Kirkbymoorside YO62 ...70 B1
3 Wetherby LS22 ......180 C4
Poplar Cres
Harrogate HG1 ....219 F6
Northallerton DL7 ....210 C2
Poplar Dr WF6 ....200 A3
Poplar Gdns YO8 .....204 F5
Poplar Gn HG5 ....162 A6
Poplar Gr
Harrogate HG1 ....219 F6
York YO32 ....225 E3
Poplar Pl TS14 ....8 E7
Poplar Row 6 YO21 ...208 D7
Poplar St YO26 ....227 E5
Poplar Way HG1 ......219 F6
Poplars La YO17 ......123 A7
Poplars The
11 Brayton YO8 ....197 D1
2 Glusburn BD20 ....187 E6
Knottingley WF11 ....202 A1
Poppleton Hall Gdn YO26 ....224 A3
Poppleton Rd YO26 ...227 E4
Poppleton Road Prim Sch YO26 ....227 E5
Poppleton Sta YO26 ...182 F8
Poppy Cl YO8 ....232 C2
Poppy Ct 16 DL9 ....41 A5
Porch Farm Cl YO62 ..120 B5
Porch The DL10 ....21 D7
Pornic Ave YO13 ....75 D5
Porritt La YO12 ....99 D7
Portal Rd YO26 ....227 B6
Portholme Cres 7 YO8 .232 C5
Portholme Dr YO8 .....232 C4
Portholme Rd YO8 ....232 C5
Portisham Pl 12 YO32 ..167 A7
Portland St YO31 .....233 B4
Portland Way DL7 ......63 C5
Portman Rise TS14 ......8 F5
Post Office Row DN14 .205 A1
Postern Cl YO23 ......233 B1
Postern La YO42 ......193 D6
Pot Bank HG3 ....178 A8
Potlands DL7 ....63 C4
Pott Bank HG4 ....85 A1
Pott Moor High Rd HG4 ....110 F8
Potter Hill 11 YO18 ......95 F7
Potter La DL7 ....64 A5
Pottergate
Gilling East YO62 ....118 F7
14 Helmsley YO62 ....92 F6
Richmond DL10 ....209 C7
Potters Dr 4 YO23 .....230 B3
Potter's Side La YO21 ...9 D1
Potterton Cl LS15 .....194 C8
Potterton La
Barwick in Elmet LS15 ...194 C8
Barwick in Elmet & Scholes LS15 ....188 C1
Pottery La
Bishop Monkton HG4 ....140 A6
Knottingley WF11 ....201 E3
Littlethorpe HG4 ....214 E1
York YO31 ....228 E7
Pottery St WF10 ......200 D4
Potticar Bank YO62 ...119 D4
Pounteys Cl 4 DL2 ......4 C4
Powell St
Harrogate HG1 ....219 F4
Selby YO8 ....232 B6
Prail Cl 13 WF8 ....201 C1
Precentor's Ct YO31 ...233 B3
Preen Dr TS5 ....6 D8
Premier Rd TS7 ....7 D7
Premiere Pk 30 LS29 ...175 C2
Preston Field Cross Rd YO13 ....74 E1
Preston Hall Mus★ TS18 .5 F6
Preston La
Great Preston WF10 .....200 C7

Preston La *continued*
Preston-on-Tees TS18 .....5 E7
Preston Prim Sch TS16 ..5 E6
Preston View LS26 ....194 A1
Preston Way TS9 ....26 C8
Prestwick Ct
15 Middleton St George DL2 .4 C4
Rufforth YO26 ....227 B5
Pretoria St WF10 ......200 F4
Price's La YO23 ....233 B1
Priest Bank DL8 ....57 B4
Priest Bank Rd 4 BD20 .173 F1
Priest Cl YO14 ....126 F8
Priest Gill Bank DL11 ...19 F5
Priest La
Dunnington YO19 ....184 F5
Ripon HG4 ....214 D4
Priestcarr La YO26 ....163 D8
Primrose Ave
Hunmanby Sands YO14 ...101 B1
Swillington LS26 ....194 A1
Primrose Cl
Guisborough TS14 ....8 E6
13 Killinghall HG3 ....161 B3
Ripon HG4 ....214 C6
Primrose Ct 18 DL9 ....41 A5
Primrose Dene WF11 ..201 E4
Primrose Dr
Filey YO14 ....101 B1
Ripon HG4 ....214 C6
Primrose Gr YO8 ......232 A6
Primrose Hill
9 Knottingley WF11 ....202 A3
2 Skipton BD23 ....216 F4
Primrose Hill Cl LS26 ..194 A1
Primrose Hill Dr
Great & Little Preston
LS26 ....200 A8
15 Swillington LS26 .....194 A1
Primrose Hill Garth
LS26 ....200 A8
Primrose Hill Gdns
LS26 ....194 A1
Primrose Hill Gn LS26 .200 A8
Primrose Hill Gr 16
LS26 ....194 A1
Primrose La LS23 ......188 E8
Primrose Vale 1 WF11 .202 A2
Primrose Valley Rd
YO14 ....101 B1
Prince Henry Rd LS21 .177 A1
Prince Henrys Gram Sch
LS21 ....177 A1
Prince of Wales Terr
YO11 ....213 A4
Prince Rupert Dr
YO26 ....181 C7
Prince St WF10 ....200 C8
Princes Cres BD23 ....217 B4
Princes Dr BD23 ....217 A4
Princes Sq
12 Harrogate HG1 ......219 D2
Thornaby TS17 ....6 B6
Princes Villa Rd HG1 ..219 E2
Princess Ave HG5 .....221 C5
Princess Cl HG4 ....214 C6
Princess Ct 11 WF6 ....200 B1
Princess Dr HG5 ......221 C5
Princess Gr 4 HG5 ....221 C5
Princess La 12 YO11 ....213 B6
Princess Mead HG5 ....163 A3
Princess Mount 3 HG5 221 C5
Princess Pl 5 YO21 ....208 D6
Princess Rd
Darlington DL3 ....3 D8
Ilkley LS29 ....218 A3
Malton YO17 ....215 C4
Ripon HG4 ....214 C6
Strensall YO32 ....167 B7
Princess Royal La 4
YO11 ....212 F3
Princess Royal Pk 1
YO11 ....213 A3
Princess Royal Rd
HG4 ....214 C3
Princess Royal Terr
YO11 ....213 A3
Princess Royal Way
HG3 ....222 E1
Princess Sq 11 YO11 ...213 B6
Princess St
Castleford WF10 ....200 F5
Normanton South WF6 ...200 A1
Scarborough YO11 ......213 B6
Prior Ave DL10 ....209 B7
Prior Pursgrove Coll
TS6 ....7 E8
Prior Wath Rd YO13 ....54 A5
Priorpot Way YO17 ....215 F4
Prior's La BD23 ....174 C8
Prior's Wlk YO26 ......227 D6
Priorwood Gdns TS17 ....6 A4
Priory Cl
Guisborough TS14 ....8 F7
Northallerton DL6 ....210 E5
Wilberfoss YO41 ....185 F6
Priory La 1 DN14 ......204 C1
Priory Park Cl 3 LS25 .202 A8
Priory Park Gr 2 LS25 .202 B8
Priory Pk YO21 ....31 C4
Priory Pl YO11 ....100 B7
Priory Rd DN6 ....206 E2
Priory St YO1 ....233 A1
Priory View 2 BD23 ....217 E8
Priory Way
4 Ingleby Arncliffe DL6 ...45 A7
1 Snaith DN14 ....204 B1
Priory Wood Way
YO31 ....225 F2
Prissick Sports Ctr TS4 ..7 B8
Pritchett Rd TS3 ....7 C8
Promenade La HG1 ...219 C3
Prospect Ave
Normanton South WF6 ...200 A2
Sherburn in Elmet LS25 ...195 F4
Prospect Bank LS23 ...188 F6
Prospect Cl
Camblesforth YO8 ....204 D5
Harrogate HG2 ....220 C3
Pollington DN14 ....207 F6
Prospect Cres
13 Harrogate HG1 ......219 D2
Scarborough YO12 ......212 D6
Prospect Ct 3 LS24 ....189 E6
Prospect Dr LS24 .....189 E6
Prospect Field
5 Fylingdales YO22 ......33 D4
Hawsker-cum-Stainsacre
YO22 ....33 A6
Prospect Hill YO21 ....208 C5
Prospect Mount Rd
YO12 ....212 C6
Prospect Pk YO12 .....212 D6
Prospect Pl
Harrogate HG1 ....219 D2
Northallerton DL6 ....210 F4
28 Scarborough YO11 ....213 A6
Skipton BD23 ....216 F4
Thornton-le-Dale YO18 ....96 D6
Wistow YO8 ....197 D6
Prospect Rd
Harrogate HG2 ....220 C3
9 Scarborough YO12 ....212 F6
Prospect St 14 BD20 ...187 E7
Prospect Terr
Fulford YO10 ....231 D6
1 Lingdale TS12 ....9 F7
Micklefield LS25 ....195 A3
York YO1 ....233 B1
Prospect View DL6 ....210 E4
Prospect Way
5 Leeming DL7 ....63 D4
Selby YO8 ....232 D4
Providence Gn 16 WF8 .201 C2
Providence Pl
13 Filey YO14 ....101 B3
Mickletown LS26 ....200 D6
15 Scarborough YO11 ....213 A6
Skipton BD23 ....217 A4
Providence Terr HG1 ..219 D4
Pry Hills La
Hartoft YO18 ....71 A8
Rosedale East Side YO18 ...49 F2
Pudding Hill Rd DL11 ....1 B6
Pudding La YO13 ....97 F5
Pudding Pie Hill★
YO7 ....211 D1
Pulleyn Cl 3 YO32 .....167 C8
Pulleyn Dr YO24 ....227 F1
Pump Hill 4 HG5 ....221 A6
Pump La
Kirklevington TS15 ....24 F8
4 Malton YO17 ....215 C4
Purey Cust Nuffield Hospl
The YO31 ....233 B3
Pursglove Prior Coll
TS14 ....8 F7
Pye Busk Cl LA2 ......129 B8
Pye La HG3 ....160 F8

Q

Quaker Cl
1 Reeth, Fremington &
Healaugh DL11 ....38 B6
Scarborough YO12 ......212 C5
Quaker Gn 1 YO24 ....230 C7
Quaker La DL6 ....210 D5
Quaker's La DL6 ....44 D7
Quakers La DL10 ......209 B7
Quant Mews YO10 .....229 B3
Quarry Ave 20 WF11 ....202 A2
Quarry Banks YO7 .....116 E7
Quarry Dr TS8 ....6 E5
Quarry Gate YO13 ......74 C1
Quarry Hill YO17 ......120 F4
Quarry Hill La LS22 ....180 B3
Quarry La
Harrogate HG1 ....219 C6
Osmotherley DL6 ....45 C5
Pateley Bridge HG3 .....137 C4
Quarry Moor La HG4 ..214 C3
Quarry Mount YO12 ...212 E3
Quarry Rd Norton DN6 ..206 F2
Richmond DL10 ....209 B7
Ripon HG4 ....214 B2
Quay St YO11 ....213 B6
Quay The YO8 ....232 D6
Queen Anne's Ct 3 DL8 .63 A2
Queen Anne's Dr 4 DL8 .63 A2
Queen Anne's Rd
YO30 ....233 A3
Queen Elizabeth Dr 10
YO13 ....75 D5
Queen Elizabeth Sixth Form
Coll DL3 ....3 C5
Queen Ethelburgas Coll
YO26 ....164 C6
Queen Ethelburga's Dr 6
HG3 ....161 B2
Queen Ethelburga's Pa 8
HG3 ....161 B2
Queen Margarets Ave 4
WF11 ....201 E4
Queen Margarets Cl 3
WF11 ....201 E4
Queen Margaret's Dr
WF11 ....201 E4
Queen Margaret's Rd 6
YO11 ....212 F3
Queen Margarets Sch
YO19 ....192 A5
Queen Marys Sch YO7 .115 A7
Queen Par HG1 ....219 E2
Queen St
10 Cowling BD22 ....187 B6
Great Preston LS26 .....200 C7
Normanton South WF6 ...200 A1
18 Ripon HG4 ....214 C5
Scarborough YO11 ......213 A6
Skelton & Brotton TS12 .....9 D7
York YO24 ....233 A2
Queen Street Jun & Inf Sch
WF6 ....200 A1
Queen Victoria St
YO23 ....228 B1
Queens Ave DL9 ....40 E3
Queen's Cl 8 HG2 .....219 C1
Queen's Dr LS29 ......218 A3
Queens Dr
9 Stokesley TS9 ....26 C8
Whitby YO22 ....208 E3
Queen's Drive La LS29 .218 A3
Queens Garth BD23 ...172 A3
Queen's Gdns
4 Ilkley LS29 ....218 A3
Tadcaster LS24 ....189 E6
Queen's Par YO12 .....213 A7
Queen's Park Dr
WF10 ....201 A4
Queen's Rd
Harrogate HG2 ....219 C1
Ilkley LS29 ....218 A3
Queens Rd
Knaresborough HG5 .....221 C6
Richmond DL10 ....209 C7
Queen's St 6 BD23 ....217 B4
Queen's Staith Rd
YO1 ....233 B2
Queen's Terr
3 Filey YO14 ....101 B3
Scarborough YO12 ......213 A7
Queen's Way YO62 .....70 B1
Queensbury Ct 15 WF6 .200 B1
Queensway WF8 ......201 C2
Queenswood Gr YO24 .227 D2
Quentin Rd 19 DL9 ......40 E4
Quernmore Dr BB18 ...186 A7

R

Rabbit La YO17 ....215 F8
Raby La DL7 ....22 E3
Raby Pk LS22 ....180 B3
Raby Terr DL3 ....3 C5
Racca Ave 11 WF11 .....202 A2
Racca Gn WF11 ....202 A2
Race La Carlton YO8 ....204 B4
Sessay YO61 ....116 C4
Racecourse Ct DL10 ...209 A8
Racecourse La DL7 ....210 D3
Racecourse Mews
YO7 ....211 A2
Racecourse Rd
East Ayton/West Ayton
YO13 ....99 B8
Irton YO12 ....212 A1
Richmond DL10 ....209 B8
York YO23 ....231 B8
Rachel La DL11 ....20 B5
RAF Leeming CP Sch
DL7 ....63 F3
Rag Robin Turn YO7 ....66 D6
Raghill La YO61 ....142 A8
Raglan St HG1 ....219 D2
Raglan Terr 3 YO21 ....208 D5
Raikes Ave BD23 ......216 F5
Raikes La BD23 ....156 A6
Raikes' La YO22 ....32 E3
Raikes Rd BD23 ....216 F5
Raikes The HG3 ....137 E3
Raikeswood Cres
BD23 ....216 E5
Raikeswood Dr BD23 ..216 E5
Raikeswood Rd BD23 ..216 E5
Railer Bank HG4 ......112 E6
Railway Ave WF8 ......201 B1
Railway Rd
Follifoot HG3 ....223 C7
Ilkley LS29 ....218 B4
Railway St 16 Leyburn DL8 60 D5
Norton YO17 ....215 C3
Slingsby YO62 ....120 B5
Railway Terr
Hurworth-on-Tees DL2 ....22 D8
5 Normanton South WF6 .200 A1
Thirsk YO7 ....211 B2
York YO24 ....228 A4
Railway View DL7 .....210 D3
Raincliffe Ave
29 Filey YO14 ....101 B3
Scarborough YO12 ......212 C5
Raincliffe Cres YO12 ..212 C5
Raincliffe Gr YO12 ....212 C4
Raincliffe Sch YO12 ...212 B6
Raincliffe St 4 YO8 ....232 C5
Raindale Rd YO18 ......71 F6
Raines Dr 5 BD20 .....173 E3
Raines La BD23 ....134 D3
Raines Lea BD23 ......134 D3
Raines Mdws 6 BD23 ..134 D2
Raines Rd BD24 ....131 C1
Rainford Cl 7 YO12 .....99 D6
Rainhall Cres BB18 ....171 E1
Rainhall Rd BB18 .....171 D1
Rainham Cl TS17 ....6 B4
Rainhill Road Cty Prim Sch
BB18 ....171 D1
Rainsborough Way 3
YO30 ....228 A8
Rainsburgh La YO25 ...126 A3
Raisdale Rd TS9 ....26 D1
Rake La YO21 ....30 D6
Rake The LA6 ....103 D4
Rakehill Rd LS15 ......194 B8
Raker Cl YO19 ....192 F7
Rakes BD23 ....134 C1
Rakes La BD23 ....171 B5
Raleigh St YO12 ....212 E6
Ralph Butterfield Sch
YO32 ....166 F5
Ralph Garth YO26 .....181 D7
Rampart The YO23 ....190 D4
Ramsay Cl YO31 ......233 C4
Ramsden Cl WF11 .....201 D4
Ramsden St LS25 .....200 C8
Ramsey Ave YO23 .....231 B3
Ramsey St YO12 ....212 E6
Ramshaw Dr BD23 .....217 A1
Ramshill Rd YO11 .....213 A4
Randal La HG3 ....160 D4
Range Rd DL8 ....40 A2
Rankin's Well Rd 4
BD23 ....217 B4
Rantreefold Rd LA2 ....128 F4
Rape Close La YO62 ...118 E4
Rape La YO62 ....93 B7
Raper La YO61 ....117 B3
Raper View LS25 ......194 F8
Rarber Top La LA6 ....103 D2
Rarey Dr YO17 ....124 E1
Raskelf Rd
7 Brafferton YO61 ......115 F1
Easingwold YO61 ....117 B1
Ratcliffe Ct YO30 ......224 C5
Ratcliffe St YO30 ......228 B7
Rathmall La YO26 .....164 C2
Rathmell C of E Prim Sch
BD24 ....153 B7
Rattan Row YO25 .....151 C6
Ratten Row Hunton DL8 ..61 E7
Seamer YO12 ....99 C5
Raven Cl 10 Eastfield YO12 99 F6
Featherstone WF7 ....200 D1
Raven Gr YO26 ....227 C4
Raven Hall Rd YO13 ....53 F7
Ravens Close Brow
LA2 ....102 C1
Ravenscroft Way
BB18 ....171 E2
Ravensdale Rd DL3 ......3 B4
Ravensthorpe Prep Sch
DL3 ....3 B5
Ravensville 1 BD20 ....187 F7
Ravensworth C of E Prim Sch
DL11 ....20 A6
Ravensworth Castle★
DL11 ....20 A6
Ravine Hill 17 YO14 ....101 B4
Ravine Rd YO14 ....101 B4
Ravine Top 7 YO14 ....101 B3
Raw Bank DL11 ....37 E8
Raw La Fylingdales YO22 ..33 B4
Kirkby Wharfe with
North Milford LS24 .....190 A3
Towton LS24 ....189 F3
Raw Pasture Bank
YO22 ....33 B5
Raw Pasture La YO22 ...33 C5
Rawcliff Rd YO18 ....72 A5
Rawcliffe Ave YO30 ...227 F8
Rawcliffe Cl YO30 .....224 E2
Rawcliffe Croft YO30 ..224 D2
Rawcliffe Dr YO30 ....227 F8
Rawcliffe in Snaith Prim Sch
DN14 ....205 A2
Rawcliffe Inf Sch
YO30 ....224 E1
Rawcliffe La YO30 .....224 F1
Rawcliffe Rd DN14 ....205 D2
Rawcliffe Way YO30 ..224 E2
Rawdon Ave YO10 ....228 F4
Rawfield La WF11 ......201 D7
Rawlinson Rd DL9 .....209 D2
Rawson St HG1 ....219 E5
Ray Bridge La BD23 ...155 D1
Ray Dike Cl YO32 .....225 C7
Ray La HG4 ....114 B1
Raydale Cl 2 HG5 ....221 D5
Raygill La BD20 ....186 E8
Rayleigh Rd HG2 .....222 E8
Raylton Ave TS7 ....7 B5
Rayner St HG4 ....214 C5
Read Cl YO8 ....204 F5
Read Sch YO8 ....204 F5
Real Aeroplane Mus The★
YO8 ....199 D5
Reas La YO51 ....141 D1
Reasty Hill YO13 ....53 E1
Reasty Rd YO13 ....53 D2
Recreation Rd
17 Pickering YO18 ....95 F6
2 Selby YO8 ....232 D6
Rectory Cl
Bolton Percy YO23 ......190 D4
Rectory Cl *continued*
Heslerton YO17 ....123 F6
Rectory Gdns YO23 ...228 B1
Rectory La
Guisborough TS14 ....8 E6
3 Hurworth-on-Tees DL2 ..22 C8
Longnewton TS21 ....5 A7
Skipton BD23 ....217 A4
Thornton-le-Dale YO18 ....96 E5
Red Bank Cl HG4 .....214 A3
Red Bank Dr HG4 .....214 A3
Red Bank Rd HG4 .....214 A3
Red Barnes Way DL1 .....3 E6
Red Brae Bank HG3 ...137 A3
Red Brow YO13 ....74 C5
Red Gate DL8 ....57 C6
Red Hall La TS15 ....6 A1
Red Hall Prim Sch DL1 ...3 F6
Red Hill La LS25 ......195 E1
Red Hills La HG3 ......140 B3
Red Hills Rd HG4 .....214 B7
Red House Prep Sch
YO26 ....165 D3
Red La
Green Hammerton YO26 ..164 C3
4 Masham HG4 ....86 C3
Red Lion St BB18 .....172 B1
Red Scar Dr YO12 ....212 A7
Red Scar La
Newby & Scalby YO12 .....75 C4
Scalby YO12 ....212 A8
Red Twr★ YO1 ....228 E4
Red Way Brompton DL6 ...43 F6
Danby YO21 ....29 E6
Farndale East YO62 ......48 E4
Nether Silton DL6 ....45 D1
Redcap La YO42 ......193 C5
Redcar Rd
Guisborough TS14 ....8 F7
Thornaby TS17 ....6 B7
Redcliff Cl 12 YO11 .....100 B7
Redcliffe Ct YO12 .....212 D7
Redcliffe Gdns YO12 ..212 C6
Redcliffe La YO11 .....100 D6
Redcliffe Rd YO12 .....212 D6
Redcoat W 1 YO24 ....230 B8
Redeness St YO31 .....228 E5
Redhill Ave WF10 .....201 A3
Redhill Cl HG1 ....219 D6
Redhill Dr WF10 ......201 A3
Redhill Field La YO23 .182 D1
Redhill Inf Sch WF10 ..201 B4
Redhill Rd
Castleford WF10 ....201 A4
Harrogate HG1 ....219 C6
Redhouse La YO8 .....204 F6
Redlish Rd HG3 ....136 E1
Redman Cl YO10 ......231 C8
Redmayne Sq YO32 ....167 B8
Redmires Cl YO30 .....225 A2
Redruth Dr 22 WF6 ....200 A2
Redshaw Cl 1 HG4 ....214 C4
Redshaw Gr 2 HG4 ....214 C4
Redthorn Dr YO31 .....225 F1
Redwood Dr 6 YO32 ...166 E5
Reebys La LA2 ....129 F5
Reedshaw La BD22 ....186 F5
Reeth Rd
Middlesbrough TS5 ....6 E8
Richmond DL10 ....209 A7
2 Stockton-on-Tees TS18 ....5 E8
Reeval Cl 13 BB18 .....172 B1
Reeves The YO24 .....227 C1
Regency Ave TS6 ....7 E8
Regency Ct
3 Ilkley LS29 ....218 A3
Northallerton DL6 ....210 F3
Regency Mews 2 YO24 .230 F8
Regency Pk TS17 ....6 B4
Regent Ave
Harrogate HG1 ....219 E3
Skipton BD23 ....217 B5
Regent Cres BD23 ....217 B5
Regent Dr BD23 ......217 B5
Regent Gr HG1 ....219 E4
Regent Mount 2 HG1 ..220 C4
Regent Par HG1 ......219 E3
Regent Pl HG1 ....220 C4
Regent Rd Ilkley LS29 ..218 A4
Skipton BD23 ....217 B5
Regent St
Castleford WF10 ....200 E4
Harrogate HG1 ....219 F3
Normanton WF6 ....200 B2
1 Scarborough YO12 ....213 A6
York YO10 ....228 E3
Regent Terr HG1 ......219 E3
Regents Ct 14 YO26 ....227 F5
Reginald Gr YO23 .....228 C1
Reid Street Prim Sch
DL3 ....3 C6
Reid Terr TS14 ....8 F6
Reighton Ave YO30 ....227 F8
Reighton Dr 10 YO30 ...224 F1
Rein Ct LS25 ....194 F8
Reins HG5 ....163 A7
Reivaulx Dr TS5 ....6 F8
Renfield Gr WF6 ......200 B2
Renshaw Gdns 8 YO26 .227 E4
Renton Cl HG3 ....140 B5
Reservoir La 7 YO11 ...100 B8
Residence La HG4 ....214 D5
Resolution Way YO21 ..208 B5
Retreat Hospl The
YO10 ....228 F2
Reygate Gr YO23 .....230 B2
Reynard Crag La HG3 .160 C6
Reynolds St 15 YO14 ...101 B3

Rhode's Hill La LS23 ...188 F6
Rhodes La LS23 ...188 D7
Rhodes St WF10 ...200 D4
Rhyddings Gdns LS29 .218 D4
Rianbow La YO17 ...215 C6
Ribble Dr DL1 ...3 C3
Ribblehead Sta LA6 ...78 E1
Ribblehead Viaduct★ LA6 ...78 D2
Ribston Rd
Little Ribston LS22 ...180 A7
Spofforth with Stockeld HG3 ...179 F6
Ribstone Gr YO31 ...229 B6
Riccal Dr
25 Helmsley YO62 ...92 F6
Huttons Ambo YO17 ...121 C1
Riccal Moor La YO62 ...93 E4
Riccall CP Sch YO19 ...191 F1
Riccall La YO19 ...191 D1
Rice Gate YO13 ...74 D8
Rice La Aldwark YO61 ...142 C2
Flaxton YO60 ...145 F2
Richard St YO8 ...232 B5
Richard Taylor C of E Prim Sch HG1 ...219 E6
Richard Thorntons C of E Prim Sch LA6 ...102 E3
Richardson Ct YO8 ...196 F1
Richardson Rd TS17 ...6 A7
Richardson St YO23 ...228 C2
Richmond Ave
Harrogate HG2 ...222 C7
Knottingley WF11 ...201 D3
Richmond C of E Prim Sch DL10 ...209 D7
Richmond Castle★ DL10 ...209 C6
Richmond Cl HG2 ...222 C7
Richmond Garth HG4 ...112 C5
Richmond Holt HG2 ...222 C7
Richmond Methodist Prim Sch DL10 ...209 E7
Richmond Pl LS29 ...218 C3
Richmond Rd
12 Barnoldswick BB18 ...171 D2
Barton DL10 ...21 E6
Brompton-on-Swale DL10 ...41 A6
Croft-on-Tees DL10 ...21 F6
Harrogate HG2 ...222 C7
Hipswell DL9 ...209 D1
Leyburn DL8 ...60 D5
Skeeby DL10 ...20 F1
Richmond Sch
Richmond DL10 ...209 C6
Richmond DL10 ...209 D7
Richmond St YO31 ...228 E5
Richmond Swimming Pool & Gemini Fitness Ctr DL10 ...209 D6
Richmondfield Ave LS15 ...194 C7
Richmondfield Cl LS15 ...194 C7
Richmondfield Cres LS15 ...194 C7
Richmondfield Cross LS15 ...194 C7
Richmondfield Dr LS15 ...194 B7
Richmondfield Garth LS15 ...194 C8
Richmondfield Gr LS15 ...194 C7
Richmondfield La LS15 ...194 C7
Richmondfield Mount LS15 ...194 C7
Richmondfield Way LS15 ...194 C8
Richmondshire Mus★ DL10 ...209 C7
Richmondshire Sports Ctr DL10 ...209 C8
Ridding Cres DN14 ...205 A1
Ridding Gate 5 LS21 ...176 F1
Ridding La DN14 ...205 A1
Riddings Rd LS29 ...218 B3
Riders La YO60 ...146 F2
Ridge Gn YO13 ...75 D5
Ridge La Roxby TS13 ...11 A6
Silsden BD20 ...174 B4
Sleights YO21 ...32 B7
Staithes TS13 ...13 H1
Ridge Rd LS25 ...200 E8
Ridge The
Coulby Newham TS8 ...7 A4
Linton LS22 ...180 B2
Ridgedale Mount WF8 .201 B2
Ridgeway Darlington DL3 ..3 C8
10 Eastfield YO11 ...99 F7
Skipton BD23 ...216 E6
York YO26 ...227 B3
Ridgeway The WF11 ...201 F2
Riding Cl 4 BB18 ...171 E1
Ridings The
7 Boroughbridge YO51 ...141 B4
Norton YO17 ...215 D2
Ridley Ave TS5 ...6 E8
Ridleys Fold 14 LS29 ...174 F4
Ridsdale St DL1 ...3 D5
Rievaulx Abbey★ YO62 ..92 B8
Rievaulx Ave HG5 ...221 C4
Rievaulx Bank YO62 ...92 B8
Rievaulx Cl HG5 ...221 C4
Rievaulx Ct 6 HG5 ...221 C4
Rievaulx Dr DL7 ...64 A6
Rievaulx Rd YO21 ...208 C6
Rievaulx Terr★ YO62 ...92 B7
Rievaulx Way TS14 ...8 F6
Riffa La LS21 ...177 E2
Rigg Bank HG4 ...85 E3
Rigg The TS15 ...5 E2
Rigg View YO22 ...32 F7
Riggs Rd YO17 ...121 F5
Riggs Spring 8 HG3 ...137 F1
Rigton Hill LS17 ...178 B4
Riley St 41 BB18 ...172 A1
Rillington CP Sch YO17 ...122 F5
Rimington Ave DL10 ...209 D6
Rimington Way YO11 ...100 B7
Ringing Keld Hill YO13 .54 A3
Ringstone Rd YO30 ...224 F3
Ringstones La LA2 ...129 A4
Ringway LS25 ...194 B3
Ringway Gr 11 DL2 ...4 C4
Ringwood Rd DL9 ...40 F3
Ripley Bank HG3 ...137 C4
Ripley Castle★ HG3 ...161 C7
Ripley Cl
11 Kirkbymoorside YO62 ...70 B1
Normanton South WF6 ...200 B1
Ripley Dr
Harrogate HG1 ...219 C6
Normanton South WF6 ...200 B2
Ripley Endowed Prim Sch HG3 ...161 C7
Ripley Gr 3 YO32 ...166 E5
Ripley Rd
Knaresborough HG5 ...220 E8
Nidd HG3 ...161 E6
Scotton HG5 ...162 A5
Ripley Way HG1 ...219 C6
Ripley's Rd YO13 ...54 B1
Ripon & District Hospl HG4 ...214 B5
Ripon By-Pass HG4 ...214 C2
Ripon Cath HG4 ...214 C5
Ripon Cathedral Choir Sch HG4 ...214 A3
Ripon Coll HG4 ...214 A5
Ripon Dr DL1 ...3 D4
Ripon FC HG4 ...214 B5
Ripon Gram Sch HG4 ..214 A6
Ripon Greystone CP Sch HG4 ...214 C2
Ripon Horn The★ HG4 ...214 C5
Ripon Leisure Ctr HG4 ...214 D3
Ripon Race Course★ HG4 ...214 F2
Ripon Rd
Harrogate HG3 ...219 A7
Middlesbrough TS7 ...7 E6
Ripley HG3 ...161 D8
South Stainley with Cayton HG3 ...139 E2
Ripon Rugby Club HG4 ...214 B5
Ripon Swimming Baths HG4 ...214 B5
Ripon Way
Carlton Miniott YO7 ...89 C4
Harrogate HG1 ...219 C5
Rise Carr Prim Sch DL3 ..3 C7
Rise Richmond DL7 ...210 C3
Rise The
Huttons Ambo YO60 ...147 C6
Knottingley WF11 ...201 E4
Leavening YO17 ...147 E1
Thornton Dale YO18 ...96 D5
Riseber DL8 ...60 C5
Risedale Rd DL9 ...209 B1
Risedale Sch DL9 ...209 F1
Risewood YO41 ...168 B2
Rishworth Gr YO30 ...224 F2
Rivadale View LS29 ...218 B5
Rivelin Way
10 Filey YO14 ...101 A3
York YO30 ...224 F2
Rivendell BD23 ...134 B3
River Cl 2 YO8 ...198 B5
River La
Brompton-on-Swale DL10 ..41 B6
Kilburn High & Low YO61 ...91 B2
West Haddlesey YO8 ...203 A5
River Pl BD23 ...155 D1
River Rd YO61 ...91 C2
River St 1 Selby YO8 ...232 D6
Trawden BB8 ...186 B2
York YO23 ...233 B1
River View
1 Barlby YO8 ...198 B5
Boston Spa LS23 ...188 F8
River View Rd HG4 ...214 C7
Riverdale 4 DN14 ...202 D4
Rivergarth DL1 ...3 F7
Riversdale
17 Haxby YO32 ...166 F5
5 Settle BD24 ...131 D2
Riversdene TS9 ...26 B7
Riverside Clapham LA2 ..130 C8
Gargrave BD23 ...155 D1
Rawcliffe DN14 ...205 A2
28 Scalby YO12 ...75 D5
Riverside Ave LS21 ...177 A1
Riverside Cl
1 Elvington YO41 ...185 C2
Farnley LS21 ...177 A1
Riverside CP Sch LS24 ...189 E6
Riverside Cres
5 Otley LS21 ...177 A1
York YO32 ...225 F6
Riverside Ct DN14 ...205 A2
Riverside Dr 3 LS21 ...177 A1
Riverside Gdns
2 Boroughbridge YO51 ..141 B6
2 Elvington YO41 ...185 C2
2 Poppleton YO26 ...165 F1
Riverside Mews 6 YO7 .211 C3
Riverside Pk 4 LS21 ...177 A1
Riverside Rd DL10 ...209 C6
Riverside View YO17 ...215 B3
Riverside Way DL1 ...3 E7
Riverside Wlk
Airton BD23 ...155 A6
Ilkley LS29 ...218 A5
1 Poppleton YO26 ...165 F1
5 Strensall YO32 ...167 A7
Riverslea TS9 ...26 B7
Riversvale Dr 21 YO26 ...165 F1
Riversway BD23 ...155 C1
RNLI Mus★ YO21 ...208 D7
Roach Grange Ave LS25 ...194 D2
Roall La DN14 ...202 F4
Robert St HG1 ...219 D1
Robert Wilkinson Prim Sch YO32 ...167 A7
Roberts Cres HG1 ...219 D5
Robertson Rd
Colburn DL9 ...40 F4
Ripon HG4 ...113 D3
Robin Cl 6 WF8 ...201 B2
Robin Gr 6 YO24 ...227 F3
Robin Hood Cl YO21 ...29 A6
Robin Hood Rd YO13 ...53 F8
Robin Hood's Bay Rd YO22 ...33 A3
Robin La Bentham LA2 ..103 A1
High Bentham LA2 ...129 A8
Huby YO61 ...144 A4
Robinson Dr
Harrogate HG2 ...222 B6
York YO24 ...227 B2
Robinson Rd 13 DL10 ...41 E4
Robinson St WF10 ...200 D6
Robson Ave TS17 ...6 B5
Roche Ave
Harrogate HG1 ...219 F6
York YO31 ...228 E8
Rock Hill WF10 ...201 A3
Rockingham Ave YO31 ...229 A5
Rockingham Cl YO17 ..215 A3
Rockingham Ct LS24 ..189 E2
Rockingham Dr YO12 ..212 B7
Rockland Gdns YO12 ..212 D5
Rockley Grange Gdn LS25 ...194 B3
Rocks La YO13 ...75 D7
Rocks La Cl YO13 ...75 D7
Rockville Dr BD23 ...217 C8
Rockwell Ave DL1 ...3 E7
Rockwood Cl 1 BD23 ..216 E4
Rockwood Dr BD23 ...216 E5
Rodney Terr 15 HG4 ...86 C3
Roe La LS25 ...202 C7
Roebuck La LS21 ...176 F2
Roecliffe C of E Prim Sch YO51 ...140 F4
Roecliffe La YO51 ...141 B5
Roedean Dr TS16 ...5 E4
Roger La TS8 ...6 C4
Roker Rd HG1 ...219 E4
Rolston Ave 3 YO31 ...225 E2
Roman Ave N 17 YO41 ..168 D2
Roman Ave S YO41 ...168 D1
Roman Cl
Newby & Scalby YO12 ...212 A7
4 Tadcaster LS24 ...189 E6
Roman Cres DL9 ...209 C1
Roman Fort of Olicana★ LS29 ...218 B4
Roman Rd TS5 ...6 E8
Roman Signal Sta★ YO21 ...12 D6
Roman Town Mus★ YO51 ...141 C5
Roman Way YO12 ...212 A7
Romanby CP Sch DL7 .210 B2
Romanby Rd DL7 ...210 C3
Romans Cl YO19 ...197 F8
Romany Rd 11 TS9 ...8 A2
Rombalds Dr BD23 ...217 A2
Rombalds La LS29 ...218 E3
Rombald's View LS29 ..218 D5
Rombalds View LS21 ...176 E1
Romille St 15 BD23 ...217 A3
Ronaldshay Cl DL10 ...209 E8
Ronaldshay Dr DL10 ...209 E8
Ronway Ave HG4 ...214 B2
Rook St
25 Barnoldswick BB18 ..171 D1
Lothersdale BD20 ...186 F8
Rookery Rd BB18 ...171 E1
Rookwood Ave LS25 ...200 C8
Rookwood Rd TS7 ...7 D6
Roomer La HG4 ...86 B1
Rope Wlk BD23 ...217 A4
Roper Ct DL10 ...209 C7
Ropers Ct YO23 ...230 C3
Ropery La YO17 ...124 E1
Ropery The
15 Pickering YO18 ...95 F7
Whitby YO22 ...208 E6
Ropery Wlk YO17 ...215 C4
Ropewalk The YO31 ...228 E5
Rosamund Ave 21 YO18 ..95 F7
Roscoe St YO12 ...212 F5
Rose Ave
Sherburn in Elmet LS25 ..195 F3
Whitby YO21 ...208 B7
Rose Cres
Richmond DL10 ...209 B7
Sherburn in Elmet LS25 ...195 F3
Rose Ct LS25 ...194 D4
Rose Hill Dr 13 TS9 ...26 C7
Rose Hill Way TS9 ...26 C7
Rose La LS24 ...196 A7
Rose Lea Cl 2 LS25 ...202 A7
Rose St YO31 ...228 C7
Rose Tree Gr YO32 ...225 D4
Rose Wood Prim Sch TS8 ...7 A4
Roseberry Ave
Great Ayton TS9 ...8 A2
Stokesley TS9 ...26 D8
Roseberry CP Sch TS9 ...8 A2
Roseberry Cres TS9 ...8 A2
Roseberry Dr 8 TS9 ...8 A2
Roseberry Gn HG4 ...113 C7
Roseberry Gr YO30 ...224 F3
Roseberry La
Guisborough TS9 ...8 B3
Stillington YO61 ...144 B6
Roseberry Mount TS14 ...8 E6
Roseberry Rd TS9 ...8 A2
Roseberry Topping★ TS9 ...8 C3
Rosebery Ave YO12 ...212 E3
Rosebery St YO26 ...227 F6
Rosecomb Way 6 YO32 ...225 D7
Rosecroft Ave TS13 ...10 D8
Rosecroft La TS13 ...10 D7
Rosecroft Sch TS13 ...10 D8
Rosecroft Way YO30 ...227 E8
Rosedale HG3 ...222 D3
Rosedale Abbey CP Sch YO18 ...49 E2
Rosedale Ave YO26 ...227 C4
Rosedale Chy Bank YO18 ...49 E1
Rosedale Cl
Pannal HG3 ...222 D3
3 Whitby YO21 ...208 C6
Rosedale Cres
Darlington DL3 ...3 A6
Guisborough TS14 ...8 D6
Rosedale La
Hinderwell TS13 ...11 F8
Staithes TS13 ...13 L1
Rosedale St YO10 ...228 D2
Rosehill TS9 ...8 A1
Rosehill Sq 11 HG5 ...221 B5
Rosehurst Gr HG3 ...222 E2
Roseland Dr TS7 ...7 C7
Rosemary Ct
20 Easingwold YO61 ...143 C8
6 Tadcaster LS24 ...189 E6
York YO1 ...233 C2
Rosemary La 1 DL10 ..209 C6
Rosemary Pl YO1 ...233 C2
Rosemary Row 5 LS24 .189 E6
Rosemoor Cl
Coulby Newham TS8 ...7 B5
19 Hunmanby YO14 ...126 F8
Rosemount Rd 2 YO21 .208 C5
Rosendale Ave YO17 ..215 F2
Roseville Ave
Harrogate HG1 ...220 A3
Scarborough YO12 ...212 E6
Roseville Dr HG1 ...220 A3
Roseville Rd HG1 ...220 A3
Roseway HG1 ...219 E5
Roseworth TS9 ...26 E5
Rosley St BB8 ...186 B3
Roslyn Rd HG2 ...220 A2
Rossett Ave HG2 ...222 C6
Rossett Beck HG2 ...222 C6
Rossett Cres HG2 ...222 D6
Rossett Dr HG2 ...222 C6
Rossett Garth HG2 ...222 C6
Rossett Gdns HG2 ...222 C6
Rossett Green La HG2 .222 C5
Rossett Holt Ave HG2 ..222 C7
Rossett Holt Cl HG2 ..222 C8
Rossett Holt Dr HG2 ..222 C7
Rossett Holt Gr HG2 ..222 C7
Rossett Holt View HG2 ...222 C7
Rossett Park Rd HG2 ..222 D6
Rossett Sch HG2 ...222 B6
Rossett Way HG2 ...222 C7
Rossiter Dr WF11 ...201 E2
Rosslyn St 1 YO30 ...228 A6
Rossway DL1 ...3 F8
Rostle Top Rd 10 BB18 ..172 A1
Rotary Way HG4 ...214 D6
Roth Hill La YO19 ...192 E3
Rothbury Cl HG2 ...220 D2
Rothbury St YO12 ...212 E5
Rothesay Gr TS7 ...7 D6
Rothwell Methley CP Inf Sch LS26 ...200 B5
Rotunda Mus★ YO11 ..213 A5
Rough Rd HG3 ...161 A2
Roughaw Cl BD23 ...216 F2
Roughaw Rd BD23 ...217 A2
Roughley Bank DL7 ...63 C5
Rougier St YO1 ...233 A2
Round Hill Link YO30 ..224 F2
Roundell Rd BB18 ...171 E2
Roundhill Ave TS17 ...5 F4
Roundhill Cl 5 DL2 ...3 E1
Roundhill Jun Sch WF11 ...201 D3
Roundhill Rd DL2 ...3 E1
Routh Wlk 5 YO21 ...208 D7
Rowan Ave
3 Filey YO14 ...101 A4
Malton YO17 ...215 D6
York YO32 ...225 D4
Rowan Cl
Gateforth YO8 ...197 B1
Scarborough YO12 ...212 C6
Rowan Ct 8 DL10 ...41 D5
Rowan Dr 5 TS9 ...8 A2
Rowan Fields YO12 ...99 E7
Rowan Garth 22 BD20 ..187 E7
Rowan Lea HG2 ...222 B7
Rowan Pl YO32 ...225 D4
Rowan Sq 6 DL9 ...209 B1
Rowans The YO7 ...115 F7
Rowans Way DL7 ...210 B4
Rowden La HG3 ...160 F5
Rowedale Cl 15 YO14 ...126 F8
Rowen Ave 6 YO61 ...117 D1
Rowland Keld TS14 ...8 E5
Rowland St 18 BD23 ...217 A3
Rowlandhall La DN14 ..199 E1
Rowley Ct 2 YO32 ...225 F7
Rowley Dr LS29 ...218 F3
Rowmans The YO30 ...224 C4
Rowntree Ave YO30 ...228 C8
Roxburghe Dale WF7 ..200 C1
Roxby Ave TS14 ...8 E5
Roxby Gdns
4 Eastfield YO12 ...99 F7
5 Thornton Dale YO18 ...96 D5
Roxby La Roxby TS13 ...11 C7
Staithes TS13 ...13 J1
Roxby Rd YO18 ...96 D5
Roxby Terr 6 YO18 ...96 D5
Royal Albert Dr YO12 ..212 F8
Royal Ave YO11 ...212 F4
Royal Chase YO24 ...230 F8
Royal Cres YO21 ...208 C7
Royal Crescent La 8 YO11 ...212 F4
Royal Dragoon Guard Association Regimental Mus★ YO1 ...233 B2
Royal George Dr TS16 ...5 D5
Royal Hall★ HG1 ...219 D3
Royal Par 8 HG1 ...219 C2
Royal Pump House Mus★ HG2 ...219 C2
Royd Cl 18 BD20 ...187 E7
Royd The TS15 ...5 D2
Royds Ave WF10 ...201 B4
Royd's Rd YO8 ...202 F6
Ruby St 3 YO23 ...228 B1
Rudbeck Cl HG2 ...220 C1
Rudbeck Cres HG2 ...220 C1
Rudbeck Dr HG2 ...220 C1
Rudby Bank TS15 ...25 D5
Rudby Lea TS15 ...25 D6
Rudcarr La YO19 ...167 E1
Rudda Rd YO13 ...53 F6
Rudding Dower HG3 ..223 E7
Rudding La
Follifoot HG3 ...223 C5
North Rigton HG3 ...222 A1
Ruddings YO19 ...193 A8
Ruddings Cl 9 YO32 ..225 C8
Ruddings La
Cowesby YO7 ...66 C4
Crakehall DL8 ...62 D4
Ellerton YO42 ...193 E2
Ruddings Rd YO18 ...72 B3
Ruddings The YO8 ...232 A4
Rudgate
Bilton-in-Ainsty with Bickerton YO26 ...181 B6
Newton Kyme cum Toulston LS24 ...189 B6
Walton LS23 ...181 B1
Rudgate Gr YO26 ...164 A4
Rudgate Pk LS23 ...181 A2
Rudstone Gr LS25 ...195 F4
Ruebury La DL6 ...45 B4
Rues La LS21 ...176 C8
Ruff La YO61 ...142 B5
Ruffa La YO18 ...96 A6
Ruffhams Cl YO19 ...192 F8
Ruffin La YO17 ...147 D5
Rufford Cl TS14 ...8 F5
Rufforth Prim Sch YO23 ...182 C6
Rumford Way DL8 ...60 D6
Rumple Croft 4 LS21 ...176 F1
Runnymede TS7 ...7 D5
Runs Bank DL8 ...60 D8
Runswick Ave
Middlesbrough TS5 ...6 E6
Whitby YO21 ...208 B6
York YO26 ...227 B4
Runswick La TS13 ...11 F7
Rupert Rd LS29 ...218 A5
Rushmere TS8 ...7 B5
Rusholme La YO8 ...205 A5
Rushton Ave 21 BB18 ..172 A1
Rushwood Cl 6 YO32 ..166 F5
Ruskin Ave
Middlesbrough TS5 ...6 D7
6 Skipton BD23 ...216 D3
Ruskin Cl DL2 ...22 D7
Ruskin Dr WF10 ...201 A4
Russell St
Harrogate HG2 ...222 E7
Skipton BD23 ...217 A3

Russell St *continued*
York YO23 228 B2
Russet Dr YO31 229 B5
Russet Gr YO12 212 C8
Russett Rd YO17 215 B4
Ruston La YO13 98 D7
Ruswarp Bank YO21 208 B3
Ruswarp C of E Prim Sch
YO21 208 B3
Ruswarp La YO21 208 B4
Ruswarp Sta YO22 208 C3
Rutland Cl
Copmanthorpe YO23 230 A3
Harrogate HG1 219 A2
Rutland Dr HG1 219 A2
Rutland Pl 4 YO62 92 F7
Rutland Rd HG1 219 B2
Rutland St 38 YO14 101 B3
Rutmoor Rd YO18 71 E8
Rutson Hospl DL7 210 D5
Ryburn Cl YO30 224 F2
Rycroft Rd 3 YO12 75 E5
Rydal Ave
Middlesbrough TS5 6 E8
York YO31 229 A6
Rydal Cl 2 YO7 89 C4
Rydal Cres 7 YO12 99 F7
Rydal Pl 3 BB8 186 A3
Rydal Rd Darlington DL1 3 E4
Harrogate HG1 220 B3
Ryder Cres 3 YO62 70 B1
Ryder's Wynd 3 DL10 209 C6
Rye Cl Haxby YO32 225 C8
Huttons Ambo YO17 121 C1
Rye Hill Way TS8 7 B4
Ryecroft 7 YO32 167 A6
Ryecroft Ave
10 Norton DN6 206 E2
York YO24 230 C7
Ryecroft Cl YO31 229 C8
Ryecroft Gdns DN14 203 A2
Ryecroft Rd
Glusburn BD20 187 D8
Norton DN6 206 E1
Ryecroft Way 2 BD20 187 E8
Ryedale Cl
Helmsley YO62 92 F7
Norton YO17 215 F1
Pontefract WF6 200 A3
Ulleskelf LS24 190 B2
Ryedale Folk Mus★
YO62 70 C5
Ryedale Indoor Bowls Ctr
YO17 215 E4
Ryedale Leisure Ctr
YO18 95 F7
Ryedale Pk LS29 218 D3
Ryedale Pl WF6 200 A3
Ryedale Sch YO62 93 D7
Ryedale Swimming Pool
YO62 93 D4
Ryedale View 2 YO62 70 B1
Ryedale Way YO8 232 C3
Ryefield Cl 12 YO11 99 F7
Ryefield Rd 1 YO11 100 A6
Ryegate 13 YO62 92 F6
Ryehill Cl YO32 225 D5
Ryeland St 9 BD20 187 E8
Ryelands Pk 1 TS13 11 A8
Ryemoor Rd YO32 225 C8
Ryatt Pl YO26 227 B3
Rylstone Dr 1 BB18 171 D1
Rymer Way 4 YO7 211 C3
Ryndle Cres YO12 212 E8
Ryndle Wlk YO12 212 E8
Ryndleside YO12 212 E7
Ryngwoode Dr YO17 215 C6
Ryton Old La YO17 121 F5
Ryton Old Rd YO17 122 A5
Ryton Stile Rd YO17 215 C7

S

Sackville Rd BD20 174 C1
Sackville St
20 Barnoldswick BB18 171 D1
Skipton BD23 217 A3
Sacred Heart Cath Prim Sch
LS29 218 D4
Sacred Heart RC Prim Sch
DL7 210 D2
Sadberge C of E Sch
DL2 4 C8
Sadberge Ct YO10 229 C3
Sadberge Rd DL2 4 C5
Saddle Cl YO17 215 D2
Saddlers Cl
1 Copmanthorpe YO23 230 B3
Huntington YO32 225 F2
Saddlers Croft 8 LS29 218 A4
Saddlers La WF11 201 E5
Saddlers Way YO26 182 A6
Sadler Dr TS7 7 B6
Sadler Forster Way TS17 6 B5
Sadlers Ct YO61 143 A5
Saffron Dr 6 DN14 204 C1
Saffron Mdw 19 HG3 161 B3
Sails Dr YO10 229 B3
St Aelreds Cl YO31 228 F4
St Aelreds RC Prim Sch
YO31 229 B5
St Aidans C of E High Sch
HG2 219 F1
St Aidan's Rd DL9 209 D1
St Aidans Rd LS26 200 C8
St Alkelda's Rd 1 DL8 60 E2
St Andrew Pl YO1 233 C2
St Andrewgate YO1 233 B2
St Andrew's Ave HG2 220 A3
St Andrew's Cres HG2 220 A3
St Andrews Dr WF7 200 E1
St Andrews Gate HG4 112 D5
St Andrew's Gr 1 HG2 220 B2
St Andrews Gr 2 DL7 210 D2
St Andrew's Par 3 HG2 220 A2
St Andrew's Pl 2 HG2 220 A2
St Andrew's Rd
Castleford WF10 201 B5
4 Harrogate HG2 220 B3
St Andrews Rd YO21 208 B5
St Andrew's St 1 HG2 220 A2
St Andrew's Wlk HG2 220 A2
St Anne's Cres 3 DL10 41 E4
St Annes Gdns DL2 4 C3
St Ann's Ct YO10 228 D2
St Ann's Staith 13 YO21 208 D7
St Anthonys Ave 2 DL7 210 E2
St Athan's Wlk HG2 222 D7
St Aubyn's Pl YO24 228 A2
St Augustines RC Jun & Infants Sch DL3 3 C5
St Augustines RC Prim Sch
TS8 7 B5
St Augustines RC Sch
YO12 212 C4
St Barnabas Ct 13 YO26 227 F5
St Bedes Ave 4 DL7 210 D2
St Bedes RC Prim Sch
DL1 3 D8
St Benedict Rd YO23 233 A1
St Bernadettes RC Prim Sch
TS7 7 D6
St Boltophs Cl 4 WF11 202 A2
St Catherines YO30 224 D6
St Catherines Cl YO30 224 C5
St Catherine's Rd HG2 219 F1
St Chads Wharf YO23 231 C8
St Christopher Cl 3
DL7 210 D2
St Christophers Dr 27
LS29 174 F4
St Clares Abbey DL3 3 B5
St Clares RC Prim Sch
TS5 6 D6
St Clement's Gr YO23 228 C2
St Clement's Rd HG2 220 A2
St Cuthbert Dr DL7 210 B3
St Cuthbert's Ave 4 DL9 41 A5
St Cuthberts C of E Prim Sch
HG3 137 B4
St Cuthbert's Gn DL10 21 D8
St Davids Gr TS17 5 F4
St Davids Rd LS21 176 F1
St Davids Sec Sch TS5 6 E7
St David's View 9 DN14 205 E4
St Denys' Rd YO1 233 C2
St Edmunds Cl 1 DL10 41 C6
St Edwards Cl 2 WF11 201 F4
St Edward's Cl YO24 230 F8
St Edward's RC Prim Sch
LS23 188 E8
St Edwin's Cl DL2 2 C6
St Francis Xavier Sch
DL10 209 E8
St Gabriels RC Prim Sch
TS7 7 D8
St George's Ave HG2 222 D7
St George's Gr 3 DL7 210 E2
St George's Pl YO24 227 F2
St Georges RC Prim Sch
Eastfield YO11 100 A7
York YO10 228 D2
St George's Rd HG2 222 D7
St George's Wlk HG2 222 D6
St Giles' Cl 1 DL9 41 A5
St Giles Cl YO7 211 C3
St Giles Ct YO31 233 B3
St Giles Rd YO30 224 B5
St Giles Way YO23 230 A2
St Gregory's Cl DL8 62 E4
St Heddas RC Prim Sch
YO21 31 A4
St Helena 11 YO51 141 B5
St Helens Cl DL7 64 A7
St Helen's Dr LS25 194 F4
St Helens Dr DL7 64 A7
St Helen's La
Borrowby YO7 65 E4
Reighton YO14 127 C6
St Helen's Rd
Harrogate HG2 223 A8
5 York YO24 230 E8
St Helen's Rise YO19 193 A7
St Helen's Sq
26 Scarborough YO11 213 A6
York YO1 233 B2
St Helen's Way LS29 218 D4
St Hilary Cl DL10 209 B7
St Hilda's Bsns Ctr
YO22 208 E6
St Hildas C of E Sch
YO62 92 C1
St Hilda's Cres YO17 124 E8
St Hilda's Gdns 4 YO21 208 C7
St Hildas RC Prim Sch
YO21 208 D5
St Hilda's Rd HG2 219 F1
St Hildas Rd 5 DL7 210 D2
St Hilda's St YO17 124 D7
St Hilda's Terr YO21 208 D6
St Hilda's Wlk 6 YO62 92 C1
St Ians Croft 32 LS29 174 F4
St Ives Cl 3 WF8 201 B2
St Ives Cres WF10 201 B3
St James C of E Sch
LS22 180 C3
St James Cl
Melsonby DL10 20 F7
York YO30 224 E3
St James Ct DN14 205 A1
St James' Dr HG2 222 E8
St James Dr DL7 210 D2
St James Gn 9 YO7 211 C3
St James' Mdw 16 YO51 141 B5
St James Mount YO24 228 A2
St James Pl 5 YO24 227 D1
St James' Rd LS29 218 A3
St James Rd
Northallerton DL7 210 B2
Scarborough YO12 212 E4
St James Terr YO8 232 C5
St James's St 7 LS22 180 C3
St John Fisher RC High Sch
HG2 223 A8
St John Mews YO8 232 B7
St John of God Hospl
DL10 41 F7
St John St
Harrogate HG1 219 D2
York YO31 233 B3
St John the Baptist RC Aided Prim Sch WF6 200 B1
St Johns Ave 25 LS29 174 F4
St John's Ave
42 Filey YO14 101 B3
Milby YO51 141 B7
Scarborough YO12 212 E5
St Johns C of E Prim Sch
DL1 3 E4
St John's Cl
Aberford LS25 188 F1
Bishop Monkton HG3 140 B5
St Johns Cl
Northallerton DL6 210 E2
Sharow HG4 214 F7
St John's Cres
Bishop Monkton HG3 140 A5
Harrogate HG1 219 D5
3 Leeming DL7 63 D4
York YO31 233 C4
St Johns Ct LS24 190 C3
St John's Dr
Harrogate HG1 219 D6
North Rigton LS17 178 B4
St John's Garth LS25 194 F8
St John's Gr HG1 219 C5
St Johns Pk DL11 2 A1
St John's Rd
Bishop Monkton HG3 140 A5
Clifford LS23 188 E7
Harrogate HG1 219 D5
Ilkley LS29 218 E4
2 Leeming DL7 63 D4
Scarborough YO12 212 E5
Scotton HG5 162 A6
9 Stamford Bridge YO41 168 D2
St Johns Rd DL9 209 F1
St Johns Residential Sch for the Deaf LS23 188 E8
St John's St BD20 173 C1
St John's View LS23 188 E8
St John's Way
Bishop Monkton HG3 140 B5
Harrogate HG1 219 D6
St John's Wlk
Harrogate HG1 219 D6
Milby YO51 141 B7
St Joseph's Cl 2 YO12 212 C8
St Josephs RC Prim Sch
Harrogate HG1 219 C5
Loftus TS13 10 D8
Pickering YO18 95 F7
Tadcaster LS24 189 E6
Wetherby LS22 180 C3
St Josephs RC Sch
Barnoldswick BB18 171 D2
Castleford WF10 200 F4
St Joseph's St LS24 189 E6
St Lawrences C of E Prim Sch
YO10 228 E3
St Leonards Ave YO8 198 B4
St Leonards Cl 30 LS29 174 F4
St Leonard's Cl
1 Harrogate HG2 220 B1
8 Malton YO17 215 C4
St Leonard's Cres
YO12 212 D8
St Leonard's Oval
HG2 220 A1
St Leonard's Pl YO30 233 B3
St Leonards Rd TS14 8 E6
St Leonard's Rd HG2 220 A1
St Luke's Cl
6 Boston Spa LS23 188 E7
Harrogate HG1 219 D4
St Lukes Cl DL7 22 C2
St Luke's Cres YO12 212 C6
St Luke's Gr YO30 228 B7
St Lukes Hospl TS4 7 A8
St Luke's Mount HG1 219 D4
St Margaret's Ave
LS26 200 B6
St Margaret's Cl 3 HG5 221 A6
St Margarets Cl DL2 4 C3
St Margaret's Garth 2
HG5 221 A6
St Margaret's Gdns 1
HG5 221 A6
St Margaret's Rd
Knaresborough HG5 221 A6
St Margaret's Rd *continued*
Mickletown LS26 200 B6
St Margaret's Terr
6 Ilkley LS29 218 B3
York YO1 228 E4
St Mark's Ave HG2 222 D7
St Mark's Cl 1 YO12 212 C8
St Mark's Gr YO30 224 E2
St Martins Ave 2 LS21 176 F1
St Martin's Ave YO11 213 A4
St Martins C of E Prim Sch
YO11 213 C1
St Martins Cl 15 DL9 40 E4
St Martin's La YO1 233 A2
St Martin's Pl 10 YO11 213 A4
St Martin's Rd 9 YO11 213 A4
St Martin's Sq 5 YO11 213 A4
St Martins Way 11 TS15 24 E8
St Marygate HG4 214 D5
St Mary's YO30 233 A3
St Mary's App YO8 196 F1
St Mary's Ave
Barnoldswick BB18 171 E2
Harrogate HG2 219 C2
12 Hemingbrough YO8 198 F1
14 Swillington LS26 194 A1
Thirsk YO7 211 C4
St Marys C of E Prim Sch
Askham Richard YO23 182 D3
Longnewton TS21 5 A7
St Marys Cath TS8 7 B5
St Mary's Cl DL10 21 D7
St Marys Cl YO42 193 C5
St Mary's Cl
15 Haxby YO32 166 E5
Ilkley LS29 218 C4
South Cowton DL7 22 E2
Thirsk YO7 211 C4
St Mary's Cres YO22 208 E6
St Mary's Ct
Allerton Bywater LS26 200 D6
York YO24 233 A1
St Mary's Dr YO7 211 C4
St Mary's Gdns BD23 173 B4
St Mary's Gr YO10 229 C4
St Marys Hospl YO12 212 F6
St Marys RC Prim Sch
Knaresborough HG5 221 A7
Richmond DL10 209 E7
Selby YO8 232 B2
St Marys Sixth Form Coll
TS4 6 F7
St Mary's St 6 YO11 213 B6
St Mary's Terr YO30 233 A3
St Mary's Way YO7 211 C4
St Mary's Wlk
Harrogate HG2 219 C1
Micklefield LS25 194 F4
Middlesbrough TS5 6 E8
Scarborough YO11 213 A7
Thirsk YO7 211 C4
St Matthew's Cl
20 Leyburn DL8 60 D5
4 Naburn YO19 191 D8
St Maurice's Rd YO31 233 C3
St Michael St 6 YO17 215 C4
St Michaels Ct 1 DL7 210 D2
St Michaels Gn 15 WF6 200 A1
St Michael's La YO11 213 C1
St Michael's Mead
HG4 138 E6
St Michaels Way 29
LS29 174 F4
St Monica Hospl YO61 143 C8
St Monicas Ct 4 YO61 143 D8
St Nicholas Cl
Copmanthorpe YO23 230 A3
Richmond DL10 209 F8
St Nicholas Cliff 5
YO11 213 A5
St Nicholas Cres
YO23 230 A3
St Nicholas Croft
YO23 182 E3
St Nicholas Dr DL10 209 F7
St Nicholas Gdns TS15 5 F2
St Nicholas Pl 1 YO10 228 F3
St Nicholas Rd
Copmanthorpe YO23 230 A3
Harrogate HG2 220 B2
Ilkley LS29 218 A5
St Nicholas St
Norton YO17 215 D3
Scarborough YO11 213 A6
St Nicholas Way 22
YO32 166 E5
St Olave's Cl HG4 214 A3
St Olave's Rd YO30 233 A4
St Olave's Sch YO30 233 A3
St Oswalds C of E Prim Sch
YO10 231 E7
St Oswalds Cl 14 DL9 40 E4
St Oswald's Cl
Catton YO41 185 F6
Oswaldkirk YO62 93 A1
St Oswalds Cl YO7 89 F3
St Oswalds Ct 6 YO14 101 B3
St Oswalds Rd 13 DL9 40 E4
St Oswald's Rd YO10 231 D8
St Patricks RC Comp Sch
TS17 6 C7
St Patricks RC Prim Sch
TS17 6 B8
St Patrick's Way HG2 220 B2
St Paulinas RC Prim Sch
TS14 8 D6
St Paulinus Dr DL7 210 B3
St Pauls C of E Prim Sch
YO24 228 A3
St Paul's Cl DL10 41 B6
St Pauls Cl 4 DL7 210 E2
St Pauls Ct 3 WF8 201 C2
St Paul's Dr DL10 41 B6
St Paul's Gr LS29 218 D4
St Pauls Mews YO24 228 A3
St Paul's Rd TS17 6 B8
St Pauls Rise LS29 174 F4
St Paul's Sq YO24 228 A3
St Paul's Terr
Darlington DL3 3 C7
York YO24 228 A4
St Peter St YO17 215 D3
St Peters C of E Prim Sch
HG2 219 D1
St Peter's Cl 2 DL9 41 A5
St Peters Cl YO26 227 A5
St Peter's Cres YO17 215 D3
St Peters Ct 31 LS29 174 F4
St Peter's Ct YO22 208 F4
St Peter's Garth LS14 188 A3
St Peter's Gr YO30 233 A4
St Peters RC Prim Sch
YO12 212 D8
St Peter's Rd Drax YO8 204 F5
Whitby YO22 208 F4
St Peters Sch YO30 233 A4
St Peter's Sq 7 HG2 219 C2
St Philip's Gr YO30 228 A8
St Philip's Way 33 LS29 176 C1
St Princes Sq 14 HG1 219 D2
St Richards Rd 3 LS21 176 F1
St Robert's Gdns HG5 221 B4
St Roberts Mews 4
HG1 219 D1
St Roberts RC Prim Sch
HG1 219 F4
St Robert's Rd HG5 221 B4
St Ronan's Cl 3 HG2 220 A1
St Ronan's Rd 2 HG2 220 A1
St Sampsons Sq YO1 233 B2
St Saviourgate YO1 233 C2
St Saviour's Pl YO1 233 C2
St Sepulchre St 7
YO11 213 B6
St Simon's Chapel (rems of)★ DL8 84 A7
St Stephen's Cl BD23 216 F4
St Stephens Gdns 1
DL7 210 E2
St Stephens RC Prim Sch
BD23 216 F4
St Stephen's Rd YO24 227 C2
St Stephen's Sq YO24 227 C1
St Swithin's Wlk YO26 227 E4
St Teresa's RC Prim Sch
DL1 3 E4
St Thomas' Pl YO31 233 B4
St Thomas St YO11 213 A6
St Thomas's Cl 2 YO10 229 C4
St Thomas's Way
YO26 164 C3
St Trinians Cl DL10 209 F8
St Trinians Dr DL10 209 F8
St Wilfred Dr DL7 210 B3
St Wilfrids Cath High Sch
WF7 200 E1
St Wilfrid's Cl 7 YO32 167 B6
St Wilfrid's Cres 9 YO8 197 D1
St Wilfrid's Gdns HG4 214 C6
St Wilfrid's Pl 2 HG4 214 C5
St Wilfrids RC Prim Sch
Ripon HG4 214 B5
York YO31 233 C3
St Wilfrid's Rd
1 Ripon HG4 214 C5
8 Strensall YO32 167 B6
St Williams Coll YO31 233 B3
St Winifred's Ave HG2 219 F1
St Winifred's Cl HG2 219 F1
St Winifred's Rd HG2 219 F1
St Wulstan Cl YO31 228 E7
Salents La YO17 148 C4
Salerno Cl 6 DL9 209 C1
Salisbury Cl 15 WF6 200 A2
Salisbury Dr 9 HG3 161 B3
Salisbury Rd YO26 227 F5
Salisbury St
Scarborough YO12 212 E3
Skipton BD23 216 E5
Sallow Heath 16 HG3 161 B3
Salmon La DL8 87 B6
Salmond Rd 5 YO24 227 B1
Salt Pans Rd YO13 54 D2
Saltburn Rd TS17 6 B8
Salter Rd YO11 99 F6
Salterforth La BB18 171 E1
Salterforth Rd BB18 172 A1
Saltergate Bank YO18 72 F8
Saltergate Cty Jun & Inf Sch
HG3 219 A5
Saltergate Dr HG3 161 B3
Saltergill La TS15 24 C8
Saltergill Sch TS15 5 D1
Salters Ave DL1 3 E6
Salters La DL1 3 F4
Salters La N DL1 3 D8
Salters La S DL1 3 E7
Saltersgill Ave TS4 6 F8
Salton La
Nunnington YO62 94 B1
Salton YO62 94 E3
Salutation Rd DL3 3 A4
Sam La YO61 142 D8
San Carlos Cl 1 DL9 40 E3

Sand Hutton C of E Prim Sch YO41 168 B5
Sand Hutton Ct YO41 168 B5
Sand La
Barlby with Osgodby YO8 198 B4
Bubwith YO8 199 D5
Heslerton YO17 123 F7
Huby YO61 144 A5
Oldstead YO61 91 D3
Sherburn YO17 124 D7
South Milford LS25 195 F2
Stillington YO61 144 A6
Wistow YO8 197 E6
Sandacre Ct YO26 227 D5
Sandbeck DL10 209 C5
Sandbeck Ind Est LS22 180 C4
Sandbeck La LS22 180 D4
Sandbeck Way LS22 180 C4
Sandcroft Cl 4 YO24 230 D8
Sandcroft Rd YO24 230 D8
Sanders Way DL10 41 E4
Sanderson Ave WF6 200 A1
Sanderson Rd DL2 3 F1
Sandfield La YO7 88 D4
Sandfield Terr 4 LS24 189 F6
Sandgate 14 YO22 208 D7
Sandgate Dr LS25 194 D1
Sandgate La LS25 194 E2
Sandgate Rise LS25 194 E1
Sandgate Terr LS25 194 E1
Sandhill Bank YO21 9 E1
Sandhill Cl
Harrogate HG1 219 F6
Pontefract WF8 201 B2
Sandhill Dr HG1 219 F6
Sandhill La Bedale DL8 63 B3
Brayton YO8 197 D2
Sutton upon Derwent YO41 185 E2
Sandhill Rise WF8 201 B2
Sandhill Way HG1 219 F6
Sandholme 2 YO32 166 F5
Sandholme Cl
14 Easingwold YO61 143 D8
22 Settle BD24 131 D2
Sandholmes La YO7 89 E3
Sandhurst Gdns 4 YO12 212 B7
Sandhutton La YO7 89 B4
Sandiacres 5 YO8 197 D1
Sandmartin Ct YO24 230 D8
Sandmoor Cl 5 YO21 208 B5
Sandown Cl Bagby YO7 90 B3
York YO24 227 E2
Sandpiper Cl
6 Eastfield YO12 99 E6
1 Filey YO14 101 A3
Sandpit La YO62 69 B1
Sandriggs DL3 3 B7
Sandringham Cl YO32 225 C7
Sandringham Rd
Byram cum Sutton WF11 201 E4
Lockwood TS12 9 F6
Middlesbrough TS3 7 B8
2 Ripon HG4 214 C3
6 Wetherby LS22 180 C3
Sandringham St
4 Scarborough YO12 212 F7
York YO10 228 D2
Sandrock Rd 3 WF8 201 C1
Sands Cl YO14 127 D7
Sands La
Hunmanby YO14 127 A8
Rillington YO17 122 F5
Sands Rd YO14 127 B7
Sandsend Rd
Newholm-cum-Dunsley YO21 13 A3
Whitby YO21 208 A8
Sandside YO11 213 B6
Sandsprunt La YO13 97 E6
Sandstock Rd YO31 229 B7
Sandwath La LS24 196 A8
Sandway Ave 12 YO8 197 B1
Sandway Cl 11 YO8 197 B1
Sandway Dr
Camblesforth YO8 204 D4
1 Thorpe Willoughby YO8 197 B1
Sandwith La YO8 204 B4
Sandwood Pk TS14 8 D5
Sandy Bank
Northallerton DL6 210 F3
Romanby DL6 65 A7
Sandy Flatts La TS5 6 F6
Sandy Gap YO32 225 C7
Sandy Gate HG3 159 A6
Sandy La Alne YO61 143 A4
Dalton YO7 116 A8
5 Embsay BD23 217 C7
Harton YO60 168 B8
16 Haxby YO32 166 E5
High & Low Bishopside HG3 137 D3
Humberton YO61 141 D8
North Duffield YO8 198 F8
Ripon HG4 214 B2
Scampston YO17 123 B5
Stockton on the Forest YO32 167 E4
Sandy Leas La TS21 5 A8
Sandy Rise YO8 232 C3
Sandybed Cres YO12 212 C4
Sandybed La
Scarborough YO12 212 C4
Wykeham YO13 98 F6
Sandyforth La BD22 186 E5
Sandyland 29 YO32 166 E5
Sandyridge YO26 224 A1
Sarah's Croft BD23 155 A1
Sargent Ave YO23 230 F4
Saunters Way WF6 200 A2
Savile Rd
Castleford WF10 200 E4
Mickletown LS26 200 B6
Saville Gr YO30 228 A8
Saville St YO17 215 C4
Saw Wells La LS24 195 F6
Sawley Cl BD23 217 C7
Sawley Moor La HG4 138 D6
Sawley St 1 BD23 216 D3
Sawmill La YO62 92 F6
Sawyer's Cres YO23 230 C2
Sawyers Garth 9 LS29 175 A4
Sawyers Wlk 9 YO19 184 F7
Saxford Way 8 YO32 166 D5
Saxon Cl Shipton YO30 165 F5
6 Thorpe Willoughby YO8 197 B1
Saxon Dr YO17 122 F5
Saxon Pl YO31 228 E7
Saxon Rd
Catterick Garrison DL9 209 E1
Ripon HG4 214 D5
Stamford Bridge YO41 168 D2
Whitby YO21 208 B7
Saxon Vale YO30 165 F5
Saxonfield TS8 7 A6
Saxton C of E Prim Sch LS24 195 D7
Saxton Ct LS24 195 D8
Saxton La LS24 195 E8
Saxty Way YO7 211 A1
Scabbate Gate BD23 108 B3
Scackleton Bank YO62 119 C4
Scackleton La YO62 119 C3
Scafell Cl 4 YO30 224 E1
Scagglethorpe La YO17 122 C4
Scaife Gdns YO31 228 C7
Scaife Shay La YO7 116 A7
Scaife St YO31 228 C7
Scalby Ave YO12 212 C8
Scalby Beck Rd 27 YO13 75 D5
Scalby Cty Modern Sch YO12 212 B8
Scalby Mills Rd YO12 75 F5
Scalby Rd YO12 212 D5
Scaldhill La YO51 141 C7
Scale Hill LS21 177 D2
Scale The BD23 157 D3
Scallow Bank La DL8 59 B6
Scalm La
Hambleton YO8 196 F2
Selby YO8 197 A4
Scampton Cl TS17 6 A6
Scar Close Nature Reserve* LA6 104 D8
Scar Field 9 BD23 134 E2
Scar Hos DL11 35 F5
Scar Rd BD23 171 E6
Scar St BD23 134 E2
Scarah Bank HG3 161 B8
Scarah La HG3 140 A2
Scarbeck Bank DL11 19 D7
Scarborough Art Gall* YO11 213 A5
Scarborough Castle* YO11 213 C7
Scarborough Coll YO11 213 A2
Scarborough Football Club YO12 212 E2
Scarborough General Hospl YO12 212 B6
Scarborough Indoor Pool* YO12 212 E8
Scarborough Rd
Gristhorpe YO14 101 A4
Heslerton YO17 123 F6
Langtoft YO25 151 C7
Norton YO17 215 F4
Norton-on-Derwent YO17 122 A3
Seamer YO12 99 D6
Stainton Dale YO13 53 F8
Scarborough RUFC YO12 212 A8
Scarborough Sixth Form Coll YO12 212 C4
Scarborough Sports Ctr YO11 213 A2
Scarborough Sta YO11 212 F5
Scarborough Terr YO30 233 B4
Scarcroft Hill YO24 228 B2
Scarcroft La YO23 233 A1
Scarcroft Prim Sch YO23 233 A1
Scarcroft Rd YO24 233 A1
Scardale Cres YO12 212 E8
Scardale Ct YO8 232 A2
Scarer's La YO26 142 B2
Scargill Rd HG1 219 B4
Scarhouse La DL11 17 E2
Scarlet Balk La YO17 122 C1
Scarth Cl 3 TS12 9 F7
Scarth Nick
Preston-under-Scar DL8 59 E6
Whorlton DL6 45 D6
Scarthingwell Cres LS24 195 D8
Scarthingwell La LS24 195 E8
Scate Moor La YO26 163 F3
Scaudercroft 13 YO19 184 F7
Scawling End Rd YO61 91 C3
Scawthorpe Cl WF8 201 C1
Scawton Ave 1 YO31 225 E2
Scholes La BD22 187 F1
Scholes Park Ave 3 YO12 75 F5
Scholes Park Cliff 1 YO12 75 F5
Scholes Park Dr 2 YO12 75 F5
Scholes Park Rd YO12 75 E5
Scholes Rd WF10 201 B5
Scholla La DL6 210 F5
Scholla View DL6 210 F5
School Cl Huby YO61 144 A4
Selby YO8 232 B3
16 Stamford Bridge YO41 168 D2
School Croft WF11 201 E4
School Fields BB18 172 A2
School Garth YO7 89 E3
School Hill
Bainbridge DL8 57 D5
8 Settle BD24 131 E2
School House Dr YO12 99 D6
School La
Addingham LS29 174 F5
Askham Richard YO23 182 D3
Bellerby DL8 60 D7
Bishopthorpe YO23 231 A4
Burton Fleming YO25 126 E3
Collingham LS22 188 A8
Copmanthorpe YO23 230 A2
Dacre HG3 159 F8
Earby BB18 172 A1
Easington BB7 152 B3
Eppleby DL11 1 D4
Great Ayton TS9 8 A1
Laneshaw Bridge BB8 186 C3
Lawkland LA2 130 D3
Lotherton cum Aberford LS25 194 F8
Malton YO17 215 C4
4 Nawton YO62 93 D7
Newton-le-Willows DL8 62 B4
Osmotherley DL6 45 B4
23 Poppleton YO26 165 F1
South Milford LS25 195 F2
8 Spofforth HG3 179 E6
Thornton-le-Beans DL6 65 B5
Walton LS23 180 F2
Wray-with-Botton LA2 128 A6
York YO10 229 B1
York YO10 231 E7
School Rd
Hemingbrough YO8 198 F1
Wetherby LS22 180 C3
School St
Castleford WF10 200 F5
2 Earby BB18 186 A7
York YO24 227 D3
Schoolgate LS15 194 C8
Score Ray La YO26 164 A5
Scoreby La YO41 168 B1
Scoresby Terr 2 YO21 208 D5
Scosthrop La BD23 154 E6
Scotch Cnr
Middleton Tyas DL10 21 B4
Oldstead YO61 91 C4
Scotch George La HG5 221 A7
Scotchman La YO60 168 A8
Scotpit La DL6 43 E4
Scots Dike Terr DL10 209 D6
Scots Dyke Cl DL10 20 F7
Scott Cl
35 Glusburn BD20 187 E7
13 Swillington LS26 194 A1
Scott Moncrieff Rd YO32 167 B6
Scott Rd YO8 232 C6
Scott St YO23 228 C2
Scotton Bank DL8 40 D2
Scotton Ct HG5 162 A6
Scotton Dr HG5 220 C8
Scotton Gdns 8 DL9 40 E3
Scotton Gr
Knaresborough HG5 220 C8
Scotton HG5 162 A5
Scotton Pk DL9 40 E3
Scotton Rd DL9 40 E3
Scriftain La LS22 180 C5
Scriven Gr 8 YO32 166 F5
Scriven Rd HG5 221 A7
Scroggs La DL8 86 E7
Scrogs La DL8 59 B6
Scrope Ave 4 YO31 228 E5
Scugdale Rd DL6 45 E8
Scurragh House La DL10 21 C2
Scurragh La DL10 21 B2
Sea App YO14 100 F6
Sea Cliff Cres YO11 213 B2
Sea Cliff Rd YO11 213 B2
Sea Life Ctr* YO12 75 F5
Sea View YO14 101 C1
Sea View Cl 5 YO11 100 B8
Sea View Cres YO11 100 B8
Sea View Dr 13 YO11 100 B8
Sea View Gdns 6 YO11 100 B8
Sea View Gr 4 YO11 100 B8
Seafield Ave 1 YO11 100 B7
Seafire Cl YO30 225 A3
Seagram Cres DL10 209 C8
Seakel La YO23 182 C2
Seal Bank BD23 81 D1
Seamer & Irton CP Sch YO12 99 D6
Seamer Moor Hill YO12 212 B1
Seamer Moor La YO12 212 B1
Seamer Rd
East Ayton YO13 99 B7
Eastfield YO12 99 F8
Hilton TS15 6 C2
Maltby TS8 6 E3
Scarborough YO12 212 E3
Seamer St 2 YO12 212 E3
Seamer Sta YO11 99 F6
Seaton Cl YO10 229 C4
Seaton Cres TS13 13 K2
Seaton Cty Prim Sch TS13 13 K2
Seaton Garth TS13 13 K2
Seave Cl La YO26 164 D2
Seavegate 4 YO13 99 B8
Seavegate Cl 3 YO13 99 B8
Seaview Ave 5 YO12 75 E5
Seavy Rd DN14 205 F2
Second Ave
Menwith with Darley HG3 160 A4
9 Pickering YO18 95 F7
Wetherby LS22 180 C3
York YO31 228 F6
Second Common La YO8 197 C4
Sedber La 5 BD23 134 E2
Sedbergh Dr LS29 218 B3
Sedbergh Pk LS29 218 B3
Sedbusk La DL8 56 D6
Sedge Rise LS24 189 D5
Sedgefield Rd TS5 6 E6
Sedley Cl HG1 219 E7
Seed Hill LA6 103 D4
Sefton Ave YO31 228 F8
Sefton Dr LS29 218 B3
Sefton Way TS15 5 D2
Seg La YO8 204 F3
Seggans Rd YO26 142 A1
Segrave Rd DL9 40 E4
Segrave Wlk 10 YO26 227 E4
Selbourne 9 BB18 172 B1
Selby Abbey YO8 232 D5
Selby Abbey Prim Sch YO8 232 C5
Selby Coll YO8 232 F3
Selby Cres DL3 3 A7
Selby High Sch YO8 232 B4
Selby Rd
Eggborough DN14 202 F1
Fulford YO19 231 E6
Garforth LS25 194 B3
Ledston LS25 195 A2
Riccall YO19 198 A8
Snaith DN14 204 C1
Swillington LS15 194 A3
Wistow YO8 197 D6
Womersley DN14 207 A4
Selby Sta YO8 232 D5
Selby Town Football Club YO8 232 B5
Seldon Rd YO26 227 E5
Self Gdns YO62 70 F3
Selside Shaw BD24 105 A7
Selstone Cres 7 YO22 32 A6
Seph Way YO17 215 A2
Sergeant Bank HG4 86 B8
Sessay C of E Prim Sch YO7 116 C5
Sessions House Yd 10 WF8 201 B1
Settle C of E Prim Sch BD24 131 E2
Settle High Sch BD24 131 D2
Settle Junc BD24 153 D8
Settle Mid Sch BD24 131 D3
Settle Rd BD23 155 A6
Settle Sta BD24 131 D2
Settle Swimming Pool BD24 131 D3
Settrington C of E Prim Sch YO17 122 D1
Settrington Rd YO12 212 B5
Seven St YO17 121 C1
Seven Wells YO17 121 A4
Seventh Ave YO31 228 F5
Severfield Cl YO7 211 D2
Severn Dr
Garforth LS25 194 D3
Guisborough TS14 8 E6
Severn Gn YO26 227 C8
Severn Way DL1 3 D3
Severus Ave YO26 227 D4
Severus St YO24 227 D3
Sewell's Cave* LA2 131 A5
Sewerbridge La WF7 200 C1
Sexhow La TS9 25 F4
Seymour Cres TS16 5 D4
Seymour Gr
Eaglescliffe TS16 5 D4
York YO31 228 F6
Shackleton Cl YO21 208 C5
Shady La BD20 173 C2
Shaftesbury Ave
Goole DN14 205 F3
Kellingley DN14 202 C3
Shaker Stile Rd YO18 96 B7
Shakespeare Ave 2 DN6 206 E1
Shakespeare Cl 3 DL10 41 C7
Shakespeare Cres WF10 201 B3
Shallowdale Gr 1 YO10 229 C3
Shambles YO1 233 B2
Shambles La YO7 114 D5
Shambles The 2 YO17 215 B4
Shandon Pk TS8 7 B5
Shandy Hall* YO61 117 D8
Shannon Cl 26 LS29 175 C2
Shannon Lea DL2 4 D4
Sharow C of E Prim Sch HG4 214 F7
Sharow La HG4 214 E6
Sharp Hill La YO8 204 F6
Sharphaw Ave BD23 217 A2
Sharphaw View BD23 155 D1
Shaw Ave WF6 200 B1
Shaw Barn La LS22 180 B3
Shaw Cl WF6 200 B1
Shaw Cres YO61 144 A5
Shaw Dr YO62 70 B1
Shaw La Farnham HG5 162 C7
Fenwick DN6 207 D2
North Rigton HG3 178 B6
Spofforth with Stockeld HG3 179 D7
Shaw Rise WF6 200 B1
Shawclose La YO62 67 E4
Shawcroft Ct DL10 209 E8
Shawl Terr 11 DL8 60 D5
Shaws La
Barwick in Elmet & Scholes LS15 194 B7
Hawes DL8 56 E4
Shaw's Terr YO24 233 A1
Sheep Rake La YO25 151 F4
Sheep St 11 BD23 216 F4
Sheepcote La HG3 159 F5
Sheepdyke La YO14 127 A8
Sheepfoot Hill YO17 215 D4
Sheepwalk La
Castleford WF10 201 B3
Kirby Grindalythe YO17 150 B7
Sheepwash Bank YO7 66 D5
Sheepwash La DN14 207 A7
Sheldrake Cl 9 YO14 101 A4
Sheldrake Rd WF10 200 E3
Shelley Cl YO11 100 B6
Shelley Ct HG1 219 E7
Shelley Dr WF11 201 D2
Shelley Gr YO30 224 F1
Shelley Rd TS4 6 F8
Shelton Ave 2 YO13 99 B8
Shepherd Ct TS12 9 E7
Shepherd Gate LA2 130 F5
Shepherd Hill DL6 45 D8
Shepherdfields La YO60 146 E5
Shepherdies The HG4 113 C8
Shepherds Dr 13 YO11 100 B7
Shepherd's Rd YO62 70 B4
Sherbrooke Cl 18 YO62 70 B1
Sherburn C of E Prim Sch YO17 124 D7
Sherburn High Sch LS25 195 F3
Sherburn Rd YO8 232 A8
Sherburn St 1 YO8 197 B8
Sherburn in Elmet Sta LS25 196 A4
Sheridan Rd BB8 186 B3
Sheriff Hutton Castle (rems of)* YO60 145 D5
Sheriff Hutton CP Sch YO60 145 C5
Sherriff Hutton House* YO60 145 D4
Sherringham Dr YO24 230 D8
Sherwood Brow BD24 131 D7
Sherwood Cl
Hunton DL8 61 E7
13 Norton DN6 206 E1
Sherwood Dr HG2 220 D2
Sherwood Gr
Huntington YO32 225 F1
York YO26 227 B6
Sherwood St 5 YO12 212 F5
Shetland Cl TS5 6 E6
Shilton Garth Cl 3 YO32 225 F7
Shipton Low Rd YO30 165 E5
Shipton Rd
Clifton YO30 227 F8
Rawcliffe YO30 224 D2
York YO30 228 A7
Shipton St 3 YO30 228 B7
Shipton Street Inf Sch YO30 228 B7
Shipyard Rd YO8 232 E5
Shirbutt La YO26 182 C8
Shire Cl 18 YO11 100 B7
Shire Croft 17 YO11 100 B7
Shire Fold YO11 100 B6
Shire Garth DL6 24 B1
Shire Gr YO17 95 D2
Shire Rd YO7 211 B4
Shirehorse Ctr* YO13 54 C5
Shires Croft BD23 217 E8
Shires La BD23 217 D8
Shirley Ave Ripon HG4 214 B4
York YO26 227 C6
Shoebridge Ave BD20 187 F7
Shop Hill YO22 33 B4
Shop La Cowling BD22 187 A6
Danby YO21 29 B3
Middleton YO18 95 D8
Short La
Farndale East YO62 48 F4
West Haddlesey YO8 202 F6
Short Lee La BD23 216 F6

Short Rd YO7 ....115 B2
Shortacre La YO42 ....193 E2
Shortbank Cl BD23 ....217 B3
Shortbank Rd BD23 ...217 B3
Shortsill La HG5 ......163 B5
Shotel Cl YO30 ....227 F8
Showfield Cl LS25 .....195 F4
Showfield Dr 17 YO61 ..143 C8
Showfield La YO17 ....215 C6
Shrubberies The YO8 ..198 E2
Shute Rd DL9 ....209 E1
Shutt La DL8 ....56 E6
Shuttleworth St 36
BB18 ....172 A1
Shuttocks Fold LS25 ..194 D2
Sicklinghall CP Sch
LS22 ....179 D3
Sicklinghall Rd LS22 ...179 F3
Side Gate YO12 ....99 D1
Sidegate La BD20 .....186 F8
Sidgwick Ct 7 BD23 ...217 A3
Siding La YO8 ....198 B5
Sidings La YO61 ......143 B4
Sidings The
Settle BD24 ....131 D2
Skipton BD23 ....216 E3
Sidmouth Sq 9 DL9 .....40 E4
Signals Ct 7 YO12 ......75 F5
Sigston Castle★ DL6 ...44 D2
Sike La YO7 ....115 B6
Sikelands La DL11 ......38 F4
Silicar La HG4 ....88 B1
Sills La YO30 ....165 B6
Silly La LA2 ....129 A2
Silsden Rd
Addingham LS29 ....174 D4
Low Bradley BD20 ......173 E3
Silver Garth DL10 ......21 C7
Silver Hill DL7 ....22 C2
Silver Mdws DL10 ....21 D7
Silver St Askrigg DL8 ....57 E5
Barton DL10 ....21 C7
Fairburn WF11 ....201 D6
Hackforth DL8 ....62 E8
4 Knaresborough HG5 ..221 B5
Masham HG4 ....86 C3
Reeth, Fremington & Healaugh
DL11 ....38 B6
3 Riccall YO19 ....198 A8
8 Scarborough YO11 ....213 A6
Thirsk YO7 ....211 C1
Whitby YO21 ....208 D7
Whitley DN14 ....207 A7
York YO1 ....233 B2
Silverdale Cl 5 HG3 ...160 A6
Silverdale Ct YO24 ....230 D7
Silverdale Rd BD24 ....131 F8
Silverfields Rd HG1 ...220 A3
Silverton Rd TS14 ....8 F5
Silverwood Ave 5
YO14 ....101 A3
Sim Balk La YO24 .....230 E5
Simbach Cl BD23 ......217 B3
Simon Howe YO12 .....124 F6
Simpson Ave 6 YO14 ...126 F8
Simpson Cl BB18 ......171 E2
Simpson Lane Jun & Inf Sch
WF11 ....201 E2
Simpsons La WF11 .....201 E2
Simpson's Yd 3 YO8 ...232 C6
Sinderby La YO7 ....88 B4
Sinks La DL8 ....62 C4
Sinnington Cl TS14 ......8 F6
Sinnington Cliff Rd
YO62 ....95 A8
Sinnington CP Sch
YO62 ....94 F8
Sinnington Rd TS17 .....6 B6
Sir John's La LS25 ....195 E4
Sirocco Ct YO31 ....228 D8
Sissy Bank DL8 ....59 D6
Sitwell Gr YO26 ....227 C5
Sitwell St YO12 ....212 E5
Siward St YO10 ....229 A3
Sixth Ave YO31 ....228 E5
Skates La YO61 ....144 B3
Sked Dale YO17 ....124 E6
Skeeby Cl 3 TS18 ....5 D8
Skegmer La YO60 ......145 F4
Skelda Rise LS29 .....218 B3
Skelder Rd YO21 ....31 E8
Skeldergate YO1 ......233 B2
Skelf St LS24 ....190 C1
Skelgate La DL11 ....38 B6
Skellbank HG4 ....214 B4
Skellbank Cl HG4 .....214 B4
Skelldale Cl HG4 .....214 E4
Skelldale View HG4 ...214 E4
Skellfield Terr HG4 ...214 D4
Skellgill La DL8 ....57 C6
Skelton Ct 3 YO30 ....228 A6
Skelton Ellers TS14 .....9 A8
Skelton La
Givendale HG4 ....140 C8
Marske DL11 ....39 B7
Skelton Prim Sch
YO30 ....224 C5
Skelton Rd
Skelton YO51 ....140 E6
Thornaby TS17 ....6 B8
Skelton Windmill★
YO51 ....140 F8
Skerne Park Cty Inf Sch
DL1 ....3 D4
Skerne Park Cty Jun Sch
DL1 ....3 C4
Skeugh Head La DL11 ...35 E6
Skeugh La YO61 ....144 D6
Skewsby Gr YO31 ......225 F1
Skibeden BD23 ....217 E6
Skibeden Ct 4 BD23 ...217 B5
Skiddaw YO24 ....230 C7
Skiddaw Ct TS7 ....7 C6
Skinner La 14 WF8 .....201 B1
Skinner St YO21 ......208 D7
Skiplam Cl 4 YO12 ....212 B5
Skiplam Rd YO62 ....69 D2
Skipper La YO25 ......125 E3
Skipton Castle★
BD23 ....217 A5
Skipton Cres HG1 .....219 D5
Skipton General Hospl
BD23 ....216 F3
Skipton High Sch
BD23 ....216 E5
Skipton Hospl BD23 ...216 E3
Skipton Old Rd BB8 ...186 A3
Skipton Parish Church Sch
BD23 ....217 A3
Skipton Rd
Addingham LS29 ....174 E5
Barnoldswick BB18 ....171 E2
Bradleys Both BD20 ....173 D4
Colne BB8 ....186 A2
Cononley BD20 ....173 C2
Earby BB18 ....172 A2
Embsay with Eastby
BD23 ....217 C7
Farnhill BD20 ....187 E8
Felliscliffe HG3 ......160 E3
Fewston LS21 ....159 D2
Gargrave BD23 ....155 D1
Glusburn BD20 ....187 F8
Harrogate HG3 ....219 A5
Hellifield BD23 ......154 B3
Ilkley LS29 ....218 A4
Silsden BD20 ....174 B1
Skipton BD23 ....217 B6
Skipton RUFC BD23 ....216 D3
Skipton St HG1 ....219 D4
Skipton Sta BD23 .....216 E3
Skipwith Comm Nature
Reserve★ YO8 ....198 E8
Skipwith Rd YO19 .....192 B6
Skirt Bank YO7 ....66 C7
Skottowe Cres TS9 ....7 F2
Skottowe Dr TS9 ....7 F2
Skuff Rd BD23 ....157 B8
Skurkhill La YO62 ......92 E7
Skyreholme Bank
BD23 ....157 F7
Skyreholme La BD23 ...157 E7
Slack La HG3 ....160 B4
Slackgap La CA17 ....14 A8
Sladeburn Dr 2 DL6 ...210 E3
Slaidburn Rd LA2 .....129 B4
Slate Hill YO21 ....29 D4
Slates La LS29 ....218 B7
Slayde The TS15 ....5 E2
Sled Gates YO22 ....33 B3
Sled La DL10 ....41 F4
Sledgate YO17 ....122 F5
Sledgate Garth YO17 ..122 F5
Sledmere Rd YO25 .....151 B6
Sledmere Sch YO25 ....150 B3
Sleigh La YO60 ....120 A1
Sleightholme Dale Rd
YO62 ....69 D5
Sleightholme Moor Rd
DL11 ....16 D7
Sleights C of E Prim Sch
YO22 ....32 A6
Sleights La
Acklam YO17 ....169 E7
Amotherby YO17 ....121 A6
Birstwith HG3 ....160 C4
Rainton with Newby YO7 ..114 E5
Sleights Rd YO62 ....69 D6
Sleights Sta YO22 ......32 A7
Sleights The LS17 .....178 A2
Slessor Rd
8 Catterick DL10 ....41 E4
York YO24 ....227 B1
Slice La LS24 ....190 A6
Slim Rd DL9 ....209 C2
Slingsby Ave HG5 .....221 A7
Slingsby Bank YO62 ...120 C4
Slingsby Castle (rems of)★
YO62 ....120 B5
Slingsby Cres HG1 ....219 F4
Slingsby Cty Prim Sch
YO62 ....120 B5
Slingsby Garth 19 YO62 ...70 B1
Slingsby Gdns DL7 ....210 B3
Slingsby Gr YO24 .....230 E8
Slip Inn Bank DL11 .....19 E6
Slippery Ford La
BD22 ....187 E3
Smales' St YO1 ....233 B1
Smary La YO19 ....184 D7
Smawthorne Ave
WF10 ....200 E4
Smawthorne Gr WF10 ..200 E4
Smawthorne La WF10 ..200 E4
Smay La YO22 ....33 D5
Smearbottoms La
BD23 ....133 C3
Smeathorns Rd TS12 ......9 F4
Smeatley's La DN6 ....206 C4
Smeaton Gr
5 Swillington LS26 ....194 A1
York YO26 ....227 C5
Smeaton Rd YO41 .....185 D7
Smiddy Hill
19 Pickering YO18 ......95 F6
Walton LS23 ....181 A2
Smiddyfields 5 YO22 ...32 A6
Smirthwaite View 14
WF6 ....200 A1
Smith Cl YO10 ....231 F8
Smith La HG4 ....114 A4
Smith St 19 BB18 .....171 D1
Smithfield Cl 7 HG4 ...214 B2
Smithfield Rd DL1 ....3 D4
Smithgutter La DL10 ....21 C4
Smithie Cl YO32 ......225 D5
Smith's La Egton YO22 ...30 E3
Flaxton YO60 ....145 D1
Smithson Ave WF10 ...201 B3
Smithson Cl DL10 ....21 D2
Smithson Ct YO17 .....215 B5
Smithson Gr 4 YO51 ...141 B4
Smithson's La HG3 ....177 A8
Smithy Croft Rd BD23 .155 D1
Smithy La Denton LS29 .176 A4
Scotton HG5 ....162 A6
Thornton in Lonsdale
LA6 ....103 A4
Ulleskelf LS24 ....190 C2
Smuts Rd DL9 ....209 D1
Smythy La YO25 ......125 D4
Snainton C of E Prim Sch
YO13 ....98 A5
Snainton La YO13 ......97 F7
Snaith Rd
Pollington DN14 ......207 F7
Rawcliffe DN14 ....205 B2
Snaith Sta DN14 ......204 C1
Snaizeholme Rd DL8 ....55 E1
Snape Castle★ DL8 ....87 A7
Snape CP Sch DL8 ......87 A7
Snape Hill YO62 ....93 E7
Snargate Hill YO61 ...118 E3
Sneaton La YO22 .....208 B1
Sneaton Thorpe La
YO22 ....32 E5
Sneck Gate La TS8 ......7 B2
Sneck Yate Bank YO7 ...67 A2
Snipe Cl 5 YO14 ......101 A4
Snipe La Hurworth DL2 ....3 C3
Loftus TS13 ....11 A6
Snowden Carr Rd
LS21 ....176 E5
Snowden Cl 4 HG4 ....214 B2
Snowdon Cl YO23 .....182 D3
Snowfield La YO61 ....142 F5
Snydale Ave WF6 ......200 B1
Snydale Cl WF6 ....200 B1
Snydale Ct 10 WF6 ....200 B1
Snydale Gr WF6 ....200 B1
Snydale Rd WF6 ....200 A1
Sober Hall Ave TS17 .....6 A4
Socarrs La YO62 ......119 F7
Sockburn La DL2 ....23 B8
Somerset Cl 6 YO30 ...224 E3
Somerset Rd
2 Harrogate HG2 ......219 C1
York YO31 ....228 D8
Somerset Terr YO11 ...213 A5
Somme Barracks DL9 ....40 F3
Sommerset Pastures
YO61 ....116 F2
Sorrel Gr 29 HG3 .....161 B3
Sorrell Gr TS14 ....8 D6
Sough La BB18 ....186 A8
Sour La BD23 ....216 B6
Sourby La LS21 ....176 D7
Soursikes Field Rd
YO51 ....141 D5
South App
Aberford LS25 ....188 F1
Bramham cum Oglethorpe
LS23 ....188 C5
Stutton with Hazlewood
LS24 ....189 A2
South Ave
Castleford WF10 ......200 C4
20 Scalby YO13 ....75 D5
South Back La
Stillington YO61 .....144 C6
Terrington YO60 ......119 E1
Tollerton YO61 ....143 B2
South Baileygate WF8 .201 C1
South Bank Ave YO23 .228 B1
South Beech Ave HG2 .220 C3
South Cleveland Hospl
TS4 ....7 B8
South Cliff Dr YO14 ...101 B1
South Craven Sch
BD20 ....187 E7
South Cres HG4 ....214 C4
South Crescent Ave 54
YO14 ....101 B3
South Crescent Cl 51
YO14 ....101 B3
South Crescent Rd
YO14 ....101 B3
South Dowber La YO7 .211 D4
South Down Rd 3 YO32 225 F5
South Dr HG2 ....222 E8
South Duffield Rd
YO8 ....198 C4
South End Bedale DL8 ...63 A3
Burniston YO13 ....75 D7
Osmotherley DL6 ....45 B3
South End Ave 6 DL8 ...63 A3
South End Cl YO13 .....75 D7
South End La DN14 ....207 B4
South Field La YO26 ...181 B6
South Gate 18 YO62 .....92 F6
South Grange Rd HG4 .214 B2
South Hawksworth St 7
LS29 ....218 B4
South Ings La YO62 .....70 F3
South Kilvington C of E Prim
Sch YO7 ....211 B4
South La
Bishop Wilton YO42 ...169 F1
Cawood YO8 ....197 B7
Thornton Dale YO18 ....96 D6
South Milford CP Sch
LS25 ....195 F2
South Milford Sta
LS25 ....195 F2
South Moor La
Garriston DL8 ....61 A7
Sowerby YO7 ....89 F3
South Otterington C of E
Prim Sch DL7 ....64 F2
South Par
Hurworth-on-Tees DL2 ....22 C8
Ilkley LS29 ....218 A4
Northallerton DL7 ....210 D3
Norton YO17 ....215 E3
8 Selby YO8 ....232 C5
York YO24 ....233 A1
South Park Ave TS6 .....7 E8
South Park La LS22 ...180 A8
South Park Rd HG1 ...219 E1
South Ridge LS25 .....194 D1
South Ruddings La
YO19 ....192 F7
South Side TS15 ....25 C5
South St
Barmby on the Marsh
DN14 ....205 A7
Burton Fleming YO25 ..126 E2
Scalby YO13 ....75 D5
7 Scarborough YO11 ...213 A4
South Town La TS13 .....10 E8
South Vale DL6 ....210 E2
South View
Burniston YO13 ....75 D7
Castleford WF10 ......201 B5
3 Glusburn BD20 .....173 E1
Healaugh LS24 ....182 A2
Hunton DL8 ....61 E7
19 Leyburn DL8 ....60 D5
Northallerton DL6 ....210 F6
2 Rudby TS15 ....25 D5
South View Terr BD20 ..174 B1
South Wood La 11 BD23 134 E3
Southdean Dr TS8 ....6 F6
Southdene 48 YO14 ....101 B3
Southend Ave DL3 ....3 C4
Southend Gdns 8 YO21 208 C6
Southey St 1 BD23 ....217 A3
Southfield YO17 ......122 D3
Southfield Ave HG4 ...214 B2
Southfield Cl
6 Hurworth-on-Tees DL2 ...3 E1
Rufforth YO23 ....182 D6
Southfield Cres 2
YO24 ....230 E8
Southfield La
23 Addingham LS29 ....174 F4
Kellington DN14 ......202 E2
Southfield Rd
28 Addingham LS29 ....174 F4
Burley in Warfedale
LS29 ....176 C1
Littlethorpe HG4 .....214 B2
Southfield Terr
22 Addingham LS29 ....174 F4
7 Skipton BD23 ....216 F3
Southfields Rd YO32 ..167 B7
Southgate
Eastfield YO12 ....99 E6
Pickering YO18 ....95 F7
Ripon HG4 ....214 C4
Southgate Ave HG4 ...214 C4
Southgate Cl 7 HG4 ..214 C4
Southlands
4 Haxby YO32 ....166 E5
19 Helmsley YO62 ....92 F6
16 Hemingbrough YO8 ...198 F1
High & Low Bishopside
HG3 ....137 B4
Southlands Cl
Escrick YO19 ....192 B6
8 South Milford LS25 ...195 F2
Southlands Gr YO12 ..212 B7
Southlands Rd YO23 ..228 B2
Southlea YO17 ....122 F5
Southmoor La WF11 ...202 B1
Southmoor Rd YO19 ...192 F5
Southolme Cl 22 YO51 ..141 B5
Southolme Dr 7 YO30 .224 F1
Southolme Wlk 23 YO51 141 B5
Southway
Harrogate HG2 ....222 C8
Ilkley LS29 ....218 D3
Southwold 7 YO11 ....100 B7
Southwold Cl 5 YO11 ..100 B7
Southwold Rise 6
YO11 ....100 B7
Southwood TS8 ....7 B4
Southwood Rd YO41 ...193 C8
Sovereign Gdns 2 WF6 200 A1
Sovereign Pk HG1 ....219 B2
Sowarth Field 21 BD24 .131 D2
Sowerby Cres TS9 ......26 B7
Sowerby Cty Prim Sch
YO7 ....211 B1
Sowerby Rd Thirsk YO7 .211 B2
York YO26 ....227 D4
Sowerby Terr YO7 .....211 B2
Sowerby Way TS16 ....5 D5
Sowgate La WF8 ......201 D2
Spa Complex The★
YO11 ....213 B4
Spa La Harrogate HG2 ..220 C3
Middleton YO18 ....95 B6
Spa Rd Gainford DL2 .....1 C7
Harrogate HG2 ....220 C3
Spa St HG2 ....220 C3
Spa Terr 3 HG2 ....220 C3
Spalding Ave YO30 ...228 B7
Sparrington La YO61 ..144 B5
Sparrow Hall Dr DL1 .....3 E8
Sparrow La TS14 ....8 F5
Spartal La LS25 ......200 F8
Spaunton Bank YO62 ....70 E5
Spaunton La YO62 ......70 E4
Spawd Bone La WF11 ..201 F2
Speculation St YO1 ...228 E4
Speedwell Rd WF10 ...200 C3
Speeton Ave TS5 ....6 F7
Spellow Cres HG5 .....140 E1
Spellow Gr HG5 ....140 E1
Spen Brow LA2 ....128 E6
Spen Common La
LS24 ....188 F3
Spen La YO1 ....233 C3
Spence Ct 4 TS9 ....8 A2
Spenceley Pl DL11 ....2 A2
Spencer Cl 5 BD20 ....187 F8
Spencer St
29 Glusburn BD20 .....187 E7
3 York YO23 ....233 B1
Spencer Wlk BD23 ....217 C3
Spencer's Holt HG1 ...219 D7
Spencer's Way HG1 ...219 D7
Speng La YO26 ....182 B4
Spennithorne C of E Prim
Sch DL8 ....60 F4
Spey Bank YO24 ......230 C6
Spiker's Hill La YO13 ...74 F2
Spindle Cl YO24 ......230 C8
Spink La WF8 ....201 B1
Spinksburn La HG3 ...159 F1
Spinner La HG3 ......161 A8
Spinney The
Darlington DL3 ....3 B4
Draughton BD23 ......174 B7
6 Easingwold YO61 ....143 C8
Knaresborough HG5 ....221 C6
3 Scarborough YO12 ...212 B5
Tees-side Airport DL2 ....4 D4
York YO24 ....230 F7
Spinniker Dr 4 YO21 ..208 C5
Spital Bridge YO22 ...208 E5
Spital Field Ct 1 YO17 .215 C4
Spital Rd YO12 ....99 E3
Spital St YO17 ....215 B4
Spital The TS15 ....5 D3
Spitalcroft HG5 ......221 B4
Spitalfields TS15 ....5 D2
Spitfire Ct DL10 ....41 F6
Spitfire Way LS25 ....196 B4
Spitlands La HG5 .....163 B7
Spittal Hardwick La
WF10 ....201 B3
Spittlerush La DN6 ...206 D2
Spofforth Castle★
HG3 ....179 D6
Spofforth Hill LS22 ...180 B3
Spofforth La
Follifoot HG3 ....223 F4
North Deighton LS22 ...180 A6
Spofforth Prim Sch
HG3 ....179 E5
Spofforth La LS22 ....180 A7
Spout La LA2 ....102 B2
Spring Bank YO12 ....212 E3
Spring Bank Cl HG4 ...214 C7
Spring Bank Rd HG4 ..214 C7
Spring Cl
Garforth LS25 ....194 D4
12 Sleights YO22 ....32 A6
Spring Ct HG3 ....160 E6
Spring Field Garth
YO17 ....215 D3
Spring Gdns 10 YO11 ..100 B6
Spring Gr
Harrogate HG1 ....219 C3
Laneshaw Bridge BB8 ....186 B3
Spring Hall Garth
YO17 ....215 A3
Spring Hill
Stonegrave YO62 ....93 C1
Welbury DL6 ....24 B1
Whitby YO21 ....208 D6
Spring Hill Sch HG4 ..113 E4
Spring Hill Terr 10
YO21 ....208 D6
Spring La Birdforth YO7 .116 F8
Kirkby Overblow HG3 ...179 A2
Long Marston YO26 ....182 A5
Pannal HG3 ....222 C3
Wetherby LS22 ....180 E3
York YO10 ....229 A1
Spring Mount HG1 ....219 C3
Spring Rise BD23 .....174 B7
Spring St
11 Easingwold YO61 ....117 D1
2 Easingwold YO61 ....143 C8
Spring Vale YO21 ....208 C6
Spring Way TS18 ....5 F8
Spring Wlk YO8 ....232 A1
Springbank
Marton cum Grafton
YO51 ....141 E2
Swillington LS25 ......194 B3
Springbank Ave YO19 ..184 E7

Springfield
Bentham LA2 ....129 B8
Clifford LS23 ....188 E7
4 Scarborough YO11 ....213 B6
Skeeby DL10 ....21 A1
Stokesley TS9 ....26 C7
Springfield Ave
4 Earby BB18 ....172 B1
Harrogate HG1 ....219 C3
Ilkley LS29 ....218 C4
11 Pontefract WF8 ......201 C1
Springfield Cl
Barlby with Osgodby
YO8 ....198 B5
20 Boroughbridge YO51 ..141 B5
Heworth YO31 ....229 C7
1 Leyburn DL8 ....60 D5
5 Pateley Bridge HG3 ...137 C4
Ripon HG4 ....214 B7
Thirsk YO7 ....211 B4
Springfield Cres
Bentham LA2 ....129 B8
3 Kirk Smeaton WF8 ....206 C3
Springfield Ct
7 Grassington BD23 ....134 E2
Sherburn in Elmet LS25 ...195 F5
Springfield Cty Prim Sch
DL1 ....3 E7
Springfield Dr
9 Barlby YO8 ....198 B5
19 Boroughbridge YO51 ..141 B5
Springfield Gdns 1 TS9 .26 C7
Springfield Gr
21 Boroughbridge YO51 ..141 B5
Kirklevington TS15 ....5 F1
Springfield La
3 Kirkbymoorside YO62 ...70 C1
Tockwith YO26 ....181 C7
Springfield Mews
HG1 ....219 C3
Springfield Mount
LS29 ....174 F5
Springfield Rd
18 Boroughbridge YO51 ..141 B5
Darlington DL1 ....3 E7
6 Grassington BD23 ....134 E2
4 Poppleton YO26 ......165 F1
Sherburn in Elmet LS25 ...195 F5
Springfield Rise 1
YO26 ....164 A8
Springfield Terr YO17 ..124 D7
Springfield Way
4 Pateley Bridge HG3 ...137 C4
York YO31 ....229 B7
Springfields
18 Knottingley WF11 ....202 A2
5 Skipton BD23 ....217 B4
Springfields Ave 17
WF11 ....202 A2
Springhead Specl Sch
YO12 ....212 E2
Springhill Cl YO12 .....212 E4
Springhill Ct 7 LS24 ....189 E6
Springhill La YO12 ....212 D3
Springhill Rd YO12 ....212 E4
Springmead Dr LS25 ..194 C3
Springmount 3 BB18 ..172 B1
Springs La
Ellerton-on-Swale DL10 ....41 F4
Ilkley LS29 ....218 C4
Walton LS23 ....180 F3
Whashton DL11 ....20 B4
Springs Leisure Ctr TS17 .6 B8
Springs The 4 DL8 ......60 E2
Springwater Sch HG2 .220 D4
Springwell Ave 11 LS26 .194 A1
Springwell Cl 8 BD22 ..187 B6
Springwell Gdns 3
DL7 ....210 D4
Springwell La DL7 .....210 B4
Springwell Rd 10 LS26 .194 A1
Springwell Terr E 1
DL7 ....210 D4
Springwell Terr W 2
DL7 ....210 D4
Springwood YO32 .....225 D7
Spruce Cl YO32 ....225 D2
Spruce Gill Ave 4 DL8 ..63 B3
Spruce Gill Dr 5 DL8 ...63 B3
Spruisty Rd HG1 ......219 C4
Spurn Lightship*
YO23 ....233 B1
Spurriergate YO1 .....233 B2
Square The
Boston Spa LS23 ....188 F8
Castleford WF10 ....201 B4
Ingleton LA6 ....103 D4
Kippax LS25 ....194 D1
Knottingley WF11 ....201 E3
Leeming DL7 ....63 F3
1 Tadcaster LS24 ......189 F6
Stable Rd YO8 ....204 D7
Stabler Cl 15 YO32 ....166 D5
Stablers Wlk
Earswick YO32 ....225 F7
13 Pontefract WF6 ......200 A2
Stables La LS23 ....188 F8
Stackhouse La
Giggleswick BD24 ....131 D4
Lawkland BD24 ....130 F2
Stainburn Ave WF10 ...201 A3
Stainburn La LS21 .....177 E2
Staindale TS14 ....8 D6
Staindale Cl YO30 .....224 E2
Staindrop Dr TS5 ....6 E7
Staindrop Rd DL3 ....3 A6
Stained Glass Ctr*
YO11 ....100 C5
Stainforth Gdns TS17 ....6 B5
Stainforth La BD24 ....131 D5
Stainforth Rd BD24 ....131 E4
Stainsacre La
Hawsker-cum-Stainsacre
YO22 ....32 F6
Whitby YO22 ....208 F3
Stainsby Rd TS5 ....6 D8
Stainton Rd TS9 ....6 F1
Stainton Way
Coulby Newham TS8 ....7 A5
Stainton & Thornton TS8 ....6 E5
Staithe St 3 YO8 ......199 D7
Staithes Cl 4 YO26 ....227 B4
Staithes La TS13 ....13 K2
Stake Rd DL8 ....57 C1
Stakesby Com Prim Sch
YO21 ....208 B6
Stakesby Rd YO21 .....208 B6
Stakesby Vale YO21 ....208 C6
Stamford Bridge Prim & Inf
Sch YO41 ....168 D2
Stamford Bridge Rd
YO19 ....184 E7
Stamford Bridge W
YO41 ....168 C2
Stamford St E 10 YO26 .227 F5
Stamford St W 8 YO26 .227 F5
Stammergate YO7 .....211 C3
Stammergate La LS22 .180 A1
Stamp Hill Cl 7 LS29 ..174 E4
Stan Valley 2 WF8 .....206 C3
Standard Way DL6 ....210 B6
Standard Way Ind Est
DL6 ....210 C6
Standridge Clough Lan
BB18 ....172 B1
Standroyd Dr BB8 .....186 A3
Standroyd Rd BB8 .....186 A3
Stang La
Arkengarthdale DL11 .....17 E3
Farnham HG5 ....162 C7
Hope DL11 ....18 A8
Stang Top
Arkengarthdale DL11 ......17 F5
Hope DL11 ....18 A6
Stanghow Rd TS12 ....9 F8
Stangs La BD23 ....157 D6
Stanhope Dr HG2 .....220 B2
Stanhope Gr TS5 ....6 E8
Stanhope Rd N DL3 ......3 C5
Staniland Dr YO8 .....232 A5
Stanley Ave YO32 .....225 D7
Stanley Cl
4 Catterick Garrison DL9 ..40 E3
22 Eastfield YO11 ....100 B6
Stanley Gr Aske DL10 ...20 D1
Richmond DL10 ....209 D8
Stanley St
Castleford WF10 ....200 F4
4 Scarborough YO12 ....213 A7
York YO31 ....233 C4
Stansfield Brow BD20 .187 A8
Stansfield Dr WF10 ...201 B4
Stansfield Rd WF10 ...201 A4
Stanstead Way TS17 .....6 C7
Stansted Gr DL2 ....4 D4
Stanyforth Cres YO26 ..164 C2
Stape Rd YO18 ....71 F7
Stape Sch YO18 ....71 F7
Stapleton Bank DL2 .....3 A2
Stapleton Cl
3 Bedale DL8 ....63 B2
11 Seamer YO12 ....99 D6
Stapley La DL8 ....87 F4
Star Carr La YO12 ......99 E4
Starbeck Cl 4 YO21 ....208 B5
Starbeck CP Sch HG2 .220 D4
Starbeck Sta HG2 .....220 C4
Starbeck Swimming Baths
HG2 ....220 D3
Starfits La
Fadmoor YO62 ....69 F3
Welburn YO62 ....94 A8
Stark Bank Rd HG4 .....85 C7
Starkey Cres YO31 ....229 A5
Starkey La 5 BD20 ....173 F1
Starmire BD22 ....187 A6
Starra Field La YO26 ..163 F5
Station Ave
20 Filey YO14 ....101 B3
20 Filey YO14 ....101 B3
Harrogate HG1 ....219 E2
Whitby YO21 ....208 B7
York YO32 ....225 D3
York YO1 ....233 A2
Station Bridge HG1 ...219 D2
Station Cl Dacre HG3 ...159 F8
6 East Ayton/West Ayton
YO13 ....99 A7
Hambleton YO8 ....196 F2
Sharow HG4 ....214 D7
Station Dr HG4 ....214 D7
Station Fields LS25 ....194 C4
Station La
Barmby on the Marsh
DN14 ....205 B7
Burton Leonard HG3 .....139 F3
Cliffe YO8 ....198 E3
Cloughton YO13 ....54 D1
Gristhorpe YO14 ....100 E4
Morton-on-Swale DL7 .....64 A7
Shipton YO30 ....165 E5
Station Par HG1 ....219 D2
Station Rd
Ampleforth YO62 ....92 C1
Beadlam YO62 ....93 D7
Brompton DL6 ....43 F4
Station Rd *continued*
Brompton-on-Swale DL10 ..41 B6
Burley in Warfedale
LS29 ....176 C1
Carlton DN14 ....204 C3
Castleford WF10 ....200 E4
Cayton YO11 ....100 B5
Church Fenton LS24 .....196 B7
Clapham LA2 ....130 C7
Copmanthorpe YO23 .....230 B2
Danby YO21 ....29 A7
Fylingdales YO22 ....33 C4
Gainford DL2 ....1 C8
Gilling East YO62 ....118 F8
Glusburn BD20 ....187 E8
Goldsborough HG5 ....163 A3
Great Ayton TS9 ....8 A1
Great Preston WF10 .....200 E6
Hambleton YO8 ....196 F1
Haxby YO32 ....166 F5
Hellifield BD23 ....154 B4
Helmsley YO62 ....92 F6
Hensall DN14 ....203 C1
Heslerton YO17 ....97 D1
High Bentham LA2 ....129 A8
Hinderwell TS13 ....11 F7
Horton in Ribblesdale
BD24 ....105 C3
Ilkley LS29 ....218 B4
Kildale YO21 ....27 E8
Kippax LS25 ....200 C8
Kirk Hammerton YO26 ...164 D2
9 Knaresborough HG5 ....221 A6
Long Preston BD23 ......153 F4
Menwith with Darley
HG3 ....160 A6
Mickletown LS26 ....200 A6
Middleton St George DL2 ....4 C5
Normanton WF6 ....200 A2
Norton DN6 ....206 F2
Nunnington YO62 ....93 E2
Pannal HG3 ....222 E2
24 Poppleton YO26 ......165 F1
Poppleton YO26 ....182 F8
Rawcliffe DN14 ....205 A1
Riccall YO19 ....198 A8
Richmond DL10 ....209 C7
Scalby YO13 ....75 D5
Scruton DL7 ....63 E6
Selby YO8 ....232 D5
Settle BD24 ....131 C2
Sleights YO22 ....32 A6
Snainton YO13 ....97 F4
South Otterington DL7 .....64 F4
Sowerby YO7 ....211 A2
Stainton Dale YO13 ....54 A8
Stokesley TS9 ....26 C7
Tadcaster LS24 ....189 D6
Thirsk YO7 ....89 D4
Threshfield BD23 ....134 D2
Tollerton YO61 ....143 B3
Wharram YO17 ....148 F4
Whixley YO26 ....164 A3
Wistow YO8 ....197 C6
Womersley DN6 ....206 D5
York YO1 ....233 A2
Station Rise YO1 ......233 A2
Station Sq
4 Strensall YO32 ....167 B7
4 Whitby YO21 ....208 D6
Station Terr
4 Boroughbridge YO51 ...141 B6
Great Preston WF10 .....200 E6
Station View
Cliffe YO8 ....198 D3
2 Harrogate HG1 ....220 C3
Seamer YO12 ....99 E7
8 Skipton BD23 ....216 D3
Station Way YO17 .....215 C3
Staupes Rd HG3 ....160 B4
Staveley CP Sch HG5 .140 E1
Staxton Carr La YO12 ...99 D3
Staxton Hill YO12 .....125 C8
Staynor Ave YO8 ......232 E3
Stead La LS14 ....188 A3
Stean La HG3 ....110 A4
Steelmoor La YO60 ....146 C2
Steeple Cl 4 YO32 ....166 D5
Steeton La LS24 ......190 D7
Steeton Way LS25 .....195 E2
Steincroft Rd 7 LS25 ..195 F2
Stella Gdns 10 WF8 ....201 C1
Stelling Rd DL11 ....38 E7
Stephen Bank DL11 .....18 H8
Stephen's Wlk YO8 ....232 B1
Stephenson Cl
Knaresborough HG5 ......221 B4
York YO31 ....225 E1
Stephenson Rd 2 DL10 ..41 C7
Stephenson Way
YO26 ....227 F5
Stephenson's La YO26 .164 A2
Stephensons Way
LS29 ....218 C4
Stephenwath La YO41 .169 C5
Stepin Turn YO62 ....49 B1
Stepney Ave YO12 .....212 D4
Stepney Cl YO12 ......212 C5
Stepney Dr YO12 ......212 C5
Stepney Gr YO12 ......212 C5
Stepney Hill YO12 .....212 B3
Stepney Rd YO12 .....212 D4
Stepney Rise YO12 ....212 D5
Sterne Ave YO31 ......229 A5
Sterne Way YO61 .....144 C3
Stewart La YO19 ......191 C4
Stillington Cty Prim Sch
YO61 ....144 C7
Stillington Rd
Easingwold YO61 ....143 D8
Huby YO61 ....144 A4
Stinton La
Boroughbridge YO51 .....141 C4
Helperby YO61 ....142 A8
Stirling Gr YO10 ......231 F8
Stirling Rd
Burley in Warfedale
LS29 ....176 B1
York YO30 ....224 F3
Stirling Way TS17 ....6 B6
Stirrup Cl Norton YO17 .215 E2
York YO24 ....230 B8
Stirton La BD23 ....216 C5
Stirtonber BD23 ....216 E5
Stittenham Hill YO60 ..146 A6
Stobarts La TS15 ....5 E6
Stock Stile La HG3 ....160 D5
Stockdale Cl 9 HG5 ...221 B5
Stockdale Ct DL6 ......210 F3
Stockdale La BD24 ....131 F2
Stockdale Wlk HG5 ....221 B5
Stockeld La LS22 ......179 E3
Stockeld Rd LS29 .....218 A4
Stockeld Way LS29 ....218 A5
Stockfield La YO51 ....141 D2
Stockfield Park House*
LS22 ....179 F4
Stockhill Cl 1 YO19 ...184 E7
Stockholm Cl 1 YO10 ..231 D8
Stocking Hill TS9 ....25 E2
Stocking La
Hambleton YO8 ....196 E1
Hillam LS25 ....202 B7
Knottingley WF11 ....202 B2
Lotherton cum Aberford
LS25 ....195 A7
Stockinger La LS29 ....174 F4
Stockings La YO62 ......92 F2
Stocks La 1 HG3 ......160 A6
Stockshill YO12 ....99 D6
Stockshott La BD20 ...173 C2
Stockton Football Club
TS17 ....6 C8
Stockton La
Heworth YO32 ....226 D1
York YO31 ....229 A7
Stockton on the Forest Cty
Prim Sch YO32 ......167 D3
Stockton Rd
Darlington DL1 ....3 F7
Sadberge DL2 ....4 C7
South Kilvington YO7 .....211 B6
Stockwell Ave
Ingleby TS17 ....6 B5
Knaresborough HG5 ......221 B7
Stockwell Cres 5 HG5 .221 B7
Stockwell Ct 9 HG5 ...221 B6
Stockwell Dr HG5 .....221 B7
Stockwell Gr HG5 .....221 B7
Stockwell La HG5 .....221 B6
Stockwell Pl HG5 .....221 B7
Stockwell Rd HG5 .....221 B6
Stockwell View HG5 ...221 B7
Stockwith La YO8 .....204 A4
Stokelake Rd 5 HG1 ...219 E3
Stokesley CP Sch TS9 ..26 C7
Stokesley Leisure Ctr
TS9 ....26 D7
Stokesley Rd
Brompton DL6 ....44 A3
Coulby Newham TS7 ....7 B7
Guisborough TS14 ....8 C6
Middlesbrough TS7 ....7 B6
Northallerton DL6 ....210 E7
Stokesley Sch TS9 ......26 D7
Stone Bramble 22 HG3 .161 B3
Stone Bridge Dr YO41 .185 F5
Stone Ct 6 YO13 ....75 D5
Stone Dale YO42 ......170 D3
Stone Garth 3 YO62 .....92 F6
Stone Gate YO26 ......164 A4
Stone Head La BD22 ..186 E6
Stone Man La DL11 .....19 C5
Stone Quarry Rd YO13 ..75 C8
Stone Riggs YO32 .....167 D2
Stone Rings Cl HG2 ...222 E5
Stone Rings La HG2 ...222 E5
Stone Stoup Hill TS9 ...27 C5
Stonebeck Ave HG1 ...219 B4
Stonebeck Gate La
YO21 ....29 D4
Stonebow The
Thornton-le-Beans DL6 ....65 B5
York YO1 ....233 C2
Stonebridgegate HG4 .214 D5
Stonecrop Ave 5 HG3 ..161 B3
Stonecrop Dr 1 HG3 ...161 B3
Stonecross Rd YO21 ...208 A6
Stoned Horse La
YO26 ....164 C4
Stonefall Ave HG2 .....220 C3
Stonefall Dr HG2 .....220 B2
Stonefall Mews HG2 ..220 C3
Stonefall Pl 2 HG2 ....220 B2
Stonefield Ave YO61 ..143 C8
Stonefield Garth 9
YO61 ....143 C8
Stonefield La 4 YO61 ..143 C8
Stonegate
Hunmanby YO14 ....126 F8
York YO1 ....233 B2
Stonehaven Way DL1 ....3 F8
Stonelands Ct 2 YO30 .225 A1
Stoneleigh Gate YO26 .164 B3
Stonepit Balk YO17 ....149 C5
Stonepit Hill YO17 ....149 C4
Stonepit La
Birdsall YO17 ....148 D6
Gristhorpe YO14 ....100 E5
Stonesdale Cl 3 HG5 ..221 D5
Stonesdale La DL11 ....35 E8
Stonethwaite 5 YO24 ..230 C7
Stoney Bank Rd BB18 ..172 B1
Stoney Haggs Rd YO12 ..99 E7
Stoneyborough Cl
YO7 ....211 C4
Stoneybrough La YO7 .211 C4
Stony Cross YO62 ......93 E7
Stony La
East Harlsey DL6 ....44 F5
8 Scalby YO13 ....75 D5
Stonygate Bank DL11 ...20 A5
Stoop Cl YO32 ....225 C8
Stooperdale Ave DL3 ....3 B7
Stoopes Hill 8 BB18 ...172 B1
Storey Cl 26 YO62 ......92 F6
Storiths La BD23 ......175 A8
Storking La YO41 ......185 F6
Storr La YO13 ....74 E5
Storth Gill La BD24 ....131 A1
Stourton Rd LS29 .....175 C3
Stow Ct YO32 ....225 E3
Strafford Rd 15 DL10 ....41 E4
Straight La
Addingham LS29 ....174 E3
Aldwark YO61 ....142 C3
Burton Leonard HG3 .....140 A3
Holtby YO19 ....184 F8
Middleham DL8 ....60 F2
Straights The DL8 ......58 C4
Strait La
Copt Hewick HG4 ....114 B2
Danby YO21 ....29 C6
Hurworth DL2 ....3 F1
Stainton & Thornton TS8 ....6 D5
Weeton LS17 ....178 B2
Well DL8 ....87 A3
Straits La YO13 ....99 A3
Stranglands La WF11 ..201 C3
Stratford Way YO32 ...225 E3
Strathmore Dr 9 TS15 ..24 E8
Strathmore Rd LS29 ...218 E4
Straw Gate DL2 ....3 A2
Strawberry Ct YO12 ...212 D4
Strawberry Dale HG1 ..219 D3
Strawberry Dale Ave 3
HG1 ....219 D3
Strawberry Dale Sq 1
HG1 ....219 D3
Strawberry Dale Terr 2
HG1 ....219 D3
Strawgate Gr DL2 ....3 A3
Stray Garth YO31 ......228 F7
Stray Rd
Harrogate HG2 ....222 D8
York YO31 ....229 B6
Stray Rein HG2 ....219 E1
Stray The Darlington DL1 ...3 E5
Henderskelfe YO60 ......146 D8
Longnewton TS21 ....5 A7
Stray Wlk HG2 ....222 E8
Straylands Gr YO31 ...228 F8
Street 1 LS23 ....189 A8
Street 2
Thorp Arch LS23 ....181 A1
Walton LS23 ....189 A8
Street 3 LS23 ....181 A1
Street 5 LS23 ....181 A1
Street 6 LS23 ....181 A2
Street 7 LS23 ....181 B1
Street 8 LS23 ....181 B1
Street Head La BD22 ..187 F1
Street La Bewerley HG3 .137 B4
Bubwith YO8 ....199 F5
Colton LS24 ....190 D7
Glaisdale YO21 ....29 E3
Middleton YO18 ....95 E7
Pickhill with Roxby YO7 ....88 B6
Street The 8 LS29 .....174 E4
Strensall Dr 11 YO12 ....75 F5
Strensall Pk YO32 .....167 A5
Strensall Rd
Earswick YO32 ....226 A7
York YO32 ....225 F6
Stretton Cl WF7 ....200 D1
Strickland Rd 18 YO14 .127 A8
Strikes La BD20 ....187 F6
Stripe La
Hartwith cum Winsley
HG3 ....160 B8
Skelton YO30 ....224 B5
Stripe The 6 TS9 ....26 C7
Stuart Ave DL10 ......209 C8
Stuart Cl
4 Scarborough YO11 ....100 B7
4 Strensall YO32 ....167 C8
Stuart Gr
Eggborough DN14 ....203 A2
1 Pontefract WF6 ......200 A2
9 Thorpe Willoughby YO8 197 B1
Stuart Rd
Pontefract WF8 ....201 B1
York YO24 ....227 D1
Stuart St
10 Barnoldswick BB18 ...171 E1
Pontefract WF8 ....201 B1
Stubbing La BD23 ......81 B1
Stubbing Nook La DL8 ..62 B2
Stubbs La
Cridling Stubbs WF11 ....206 A8
Norton DN6 ....206 E2

Stubbs La *continued*
Stainton Dale YO13 ....53 F5
Stubbs Rd DN6 ....206 D3
Stubden Gr YO30 ....224 F2
Stubham Rise LS29 ....218 A5
Stud Fold Bank HG3 ....110 B3
Studford Ring★ YO62 ....92 C2
Studley Cl DL7 ....210 B2
Studley La DL10 ....113 C1
Studley Rd
Harrogate HG1 ....219 D3
Ripon HG4 ....214 A4
Studley Roger HG4 ....113 D1
Stumpcross Ct 14 WF8 ....201 C2
Stumpcross La WF8 ....201 C2
Stumpcross Way 15 WF8 ....201 C2
Stumps La HG3 ....160 A5
Stunstead Rd BB8 ....186 B2
Sturdee Gr YO31 ....228 D7
Sturdy House La
Marske DL11 ....19 E2
Whashton DL11 ....20 A4
Sturton Grange La LS25 ....194 D4
Sturton La LS25 ....194 D4
Stuteville Cl 4 YO62 ....70 C1
Stutton Rd LS24 ....189 D4
Stygate La DN6 ....206 E1
Sudforth La DN14 ....202 C3
Suffield Hill YO13 ....75 A5
Sugar Hill 9 LS29 ....174 F4
Summer Hill Rd LS26 ....200 B6
Summerbridge CP Sch HG3 ....138 A1
Summerfield Cl 1 WF11 ....201 F4
Summerfield Dr WF11 ....201 F4
Summerfield La YO22 ....33 A7
Summerfield Rd YO24 ....230 C7
Sun La LS29 ....176 C1
Sun Lounge Theatre YO14 ....101 B3
Sun St Cononley BD20 ....173 C1
4 Cowling BD22 ....187 B6
Thornaby TS17 ....6 A8
Sunderland Rd BD20 ....173 E3
Sundew Heath 24 HG3 ....161 B3
Sunmoor Dr BD23 ....217 A4
Sunningdale LS25 ....194 F4
Sunningdale Cl 1 YO26 ....227 B5
Sunningdale Dr TS16 ....5 E5
Sunningdale Gr 1 YO21 ....208 B5
Sunningdales WF6 ....200 B1
Sunny Bank 3 WF11 ....202 A2
Sunny Bank Rd 6 BD20 ....187 E7
Sunnybank Rd LS25 ....195 A3
Sunnycrest Ave DL10 ....209 D8
Sunnydale 3 YO32 ....225 D7
Sunnyside Prim Sch TS8 ....7 A6
Sunset Dr LS29 ....218 D5
Sunstar Gr TS7 ....7 B6
Sur Gate
Harwood Dale YO13 ....53 F1
Suffield-cum-Everley YO13 ....74 F8
Surrey Way YO30 ....227 F8
Surtees St Darlington DL3 ....3 C6
York YO30 ....228 B7
Sussex Cl Bedale DL8 ....63 A2
York YO10 ....229 C2
Sussex Rd YO10 ....229 C2
Sussex St Bedale DL8 ....63 A2
14 Scarborough YO11 ....213 A6
Sussex Way 14 YO32 ....167 A7
Sutcliffe Ct 6 YO21 ....208 B6
Sutherland Rd YO18 ....71 C6
Sutherland St YO23 ....228 B1
Sutor Cl YO23 ....230 B3
Sutton Ave 7 DL9 ....41 A5
Sutton Bank YO7 ....91 A5
Sutton Bridge★ YO41 ....185 C2
Sutton C of E Prim Sch YO7 ....90 E5
Sutton CP Sch BD20 ....187 E7
Sutton Ct 5 YO7 ....211 C3
Sutton Dr DL7 ....210 C2
Sutton Grange Cl HG3 ....219 B4
Sutton in Craven C of E Prim Sch BD20 ....187 E7
Sutton La Byram WF11 ....201 E4
Byram cum Sutton WF11 ....202 A4
Ellington High & Low HG4 ....86 A5
Fearby HG4 ....85 F4
Steeton with Eastburn BD20 ....187 F7
Sutton on Derwent C of E Prim Sch YO41 ....185 C2
Sutton Rd YO7 ....211 E3
Sutton St YO17 ....215 D3
Sutton Way
Middlesbrough TS4 ....6 F8
York YO30 ....228 B8
Sutton-on-the-Forest C of E Prim Sch YO61 ....144 C3
Swadford St BD23 ....216 F4
Swain Ct DL6 ....210 D5
Swainby Abbey★ DL8 ....88 B8
Swainby Ellers DL6 ....25 D1
Swainby La DL8 ....87 F7
Swainsea Dr 3 YO18 ....95 F7
Swainsea La YO18 ....95 F8
Swainstead Raike BD24 ....153 B8
Swainston Cl TS5 ....6 E7
Swale Ave YO24 ....230 E8
Swale Hall La DL11 ....38 B5
Swale La Catterick DL10 ....41 E5
Pickhill with Roxby YO7 ....88 C7
Swale Pasture La DL10 ....41 E5
Swale View YO7 ....115 B6
Swaledale Ave DL3 ....3 B6
Swaledale Rd 22 DL9 ....40 E4
Swalegate DL10 ....209 C8
Swallow Cl TS14 ....8 D6
Swan Cl YO19 ....192 A7
Swan Farm Ct YO19 ....192 A7
Swan Hill Rd YO11 ....213 A6
Swan La YO7 ....65 F2
Swan Rd HG1 ....219 C2
Swan St BD23 ....173 B4
Swan Syke Dr 8 DN6 ....206 F2
Swang Rd YO13 ....75 A6
Swanhills La YO13 ....98 F3
Swanland Rd YO62 ....92 F7
Swann St YO23 ....233 A1
Swarcliffe Rd HG1 ....220 B4
Swartha La BD20 ....174 D2
Swarthlands La YO13 ....75 D7
Sweeming La LS25 ....196 C5
Sweet Bits La HG5 ....221 C8
Sweet Briar
18 Harrogate HG3 ....161 B3
Harrogate HG3 ....219 A4
Sweetbecks Cl 12 YO11 ....100 A6
Swillington La LS26 ....194 A2
Swillington Prim Sch LS26 ....194 A1
Swinburn Ct 12 HG4 ....86 C3
Swinburn Rd 11 HG4 ....86 C3
Swinburne Cl HG1 ....219 E7
Swinburne Rd TS16 ....5 E6
Swindale La TS12 ....9 F5
Swindon La HG3 ....178 E4
Swinegate YO1 ....233 B2
Swineherd La YO62 ....70 C1
Swinneybeck Bank HG4 ....85 E5
Swinsty Ct YO30 ....224 F1
Swinton Ct HG2 ....222 B8
Swinton La YO17 ....121 B3
Swire Way DL10 ....20 F7
Swires La BD20 ....173 C3
Swordfish Way LS25 ....196 B4
Sycamore Ave
4 Catton YO7 ....89 A1
Filey YO14 ....101 A4
Kippax LS25 ....194 C1
Knottingley WF11 ....201 E1
Malton YO17 ....215 D5
Richmond DL10 ....209 A8
York YO32 ....225 D4
Sycamore Cl
Bishop Monkton HG3 ....140 A5
Clint HG3 ....160 F8
1 Haxby YO32 ....225 D7
3 Hurworth-on-Tees DL2 ....3 E1
Selby YO8 ....232 A4
Skelton YO30 ....224 C5
Slingsby YO62 ....120 B5
Spennithorne DL8 ....60 F4
Sycamore Ct
2 Catterick DL10 ....41 D5
2 Pontefract WF8 ....201 C1
Sycamore Dr
11 Addingham LS29 ....175 A4
9 Bedale DL8 ....63 A2
Harrogate HG2 ....220 C3
Norton-le-Clay YO7 ....115 B1
Sycamore Gr BD20 ....187 F7
Sycamore La DL7 ....63 D4
Sycamore Pl YO30 ....233 A3
Sycamore Rd
Barlby with Osgodby YO8 ....198 B5
Ripon HG4 ....214 B2
Sycamore Terr YO30 ....233 A3
Sycamore View 17 YO26 ....165 F1
Sycamore Way 16 BB18 ....171 D1
Sydall's Way 1 DL10 ....41 E4
Sydney St 5 YO12 ....212 F7
Sykehead La YO62 ....93 D6
Sykes Barrel 3 BD24 ....131 D3
Sykes Gr HG1 ....219 C5
Sykes La YO61 ....143 B3

T

Tabard Hamlet 5 DN14 ....202 F2
Tabard Rd 6 DN14 ....202 F2
Tabards The 7 DN14 ....202 F2
Tadcaster Albion FC LS24 ....189 E6
Tadcaster East CP Sch LS24 ....189 F6
Tadcaster Gram Sch LS24 ....189 B5
Tadcaster Leisure Ctr LS24 ....189 E6
Tadcaster Rd YO24 ....230 F8
Tadcaster Road Dringhouses YO23 ....230 E5
Tadcaster Sports & Leisure Ctr LS24 ....189 E6
Talbot St WF6 ....200 A1
Tameside TS9 ....26 C8
Tamworth Rd 9 YO30 ....225 A1
Tanfield Dr 1 LS29 ....176 C1
Tanfield La HG4 ....114 A8
Tang Hall La YO31 ....229 A5
Tang Hall Prim Sch YO31 ....228 F5
Tang Rd HG3 ....160 D4
Tanner Row YO1 ....233 A2
Tanner's Moat YO1 ....233 A2
Tannery Ct 10 HG5 ....221 B5
Tannery La DL7 ....210 D5
Tanpit La
Easingwold YO61 ....143 C8
Walden Stubbs DN6 ....206 E3
Tanshelf Sta WF8 ....201 A1
Tansy Cl 2 HG3 ....161 B3
Tansy Rd 3 HG3 ....161 B3
Tanton Rd TS9 ....7 B1
Tarbard Ave 14 HG4 ....113 D2
Tarbert Cres 2 YO24 ....230 B7
Tarn Moor Cres BD23 ....216 E6
Tarr Steps TS17 ....6 A3
Tasmania Sq TS7 ....7 C6
Tate Cl YO8 ....197 D6
Tate Rd DL10 ....209 C8
Tatham Fells Sch LA2 ....128 F3
Tatton Cl YO30 ....225 A1
Taylor Gr LS26 ....200 C6
Taylor Hill YO18 ....71 F7
Taylor La LS15 ....194 A7
Taylor St 8 BB18 ....171 D1
Teal Cl Castleford WF10 ....200 E3
2 Filey YO14 ....101 A3
Teal Dr YO24 ....230 C8
Teal La 6 YO18 ....95 F7
Teal Rd DL1 ....3 E5
Teasel Gr 31 HG3 ....161 B3
Tebay Cl TS7 ....7 D8
Tedder Ave TS17 ....6 B6
Tedder Prim Sch TS17 ....6 C6
Tedder Rd YO24 ....227 B1
Tedworth Cl TS14 ....8 F5
Tees Bank Ave TS18 ....5 E6
Tees Grange Ave DL3 ....3 A5
Tees View Hurworth DL2 ....3 C1
Hurworth-on-Tees DL2 ....22 C8
Teesdale Ave DL3 ....3 A4
Teesdale Rd DL9 ....40 E4
Teesgate TS17 ....6 C8
Teeside Tertiary Coll TS4 ....7 B8
Teesside High Sch TS16 ....5 E5
Teesside Ind Est TS17 ....6 C5
Teesside International Airport DL2 ....4 F4
Teesway DL2 ....4 A1
Telford Cl WF10 ....200 D4
Telford Terr 1 YO24 ....228 B2
Templar Cl DN14 ....202 F1
Templar Gdns LS22 ....180 C4
Templar Way YO8 ....232 C2
Temple Ave YO10 ....229 B4
Temple Bank DL8 ....59 A3
Temple Garth YO23 ....230 C1
Temple La
Burton cum Walden DL8 ....82 D3
Copmanthorpe YO23 ....230 C1
Temple Manor★ YO8 ....203 D4
Temple Rd YO23 ....230 F4
Temple St WF10 ....200 E4
Templemead YO31 ....228 E8
Tems Side 3 BD24 ....131 D2
Tems St 2 BD24 ....131 D2
Ten Thorn La YO26 ....227 A4
Tennant Cl DL7 ....210 B6
Tennant St YO8 ....232 B6
Tennent Rd YO24 ....227 B2
Tennis Court La YO61 ....143 A3
Tennyson Ave
1 Campsall DN6 ....206 E1
Harrogate HG1 ....219 E7
Scarborough YO12 ....212 F7
York YO30 ....228 C7
Tennyson Way 3 WF8 ....201 B1
Tenter Hill LS23 ....188 D5
Tentergate Ave 4 HG5 ....221 A7
Tentergate Cl 3 HG5 ....221 A7
Tentergate Gdns 2 HG5 ....221 A7
Tentergate La HG5 ....221 A7
Tentergate Rd 5 HG5 ....221 A7
Tenters Cl WF11 ....201 E3
Tern Pk 6 LS22 ....180 A1
Terrington Bank YO60 ....119 C2
Terrington C of E Prim Sch YO60 ....119 E1
Terrington Hall Sch YO60 ....119 F1
Terrington South Bank YO60 ....119 D1
Terrington View YO60 ....145 C5
Terry Ave YO1 ....233 B1
Terry St YO23 ....228 C1
Tetherings La YO13 ....98 F5
Tewit Well Ave HG2 ....222 D8
Tewit Well Rd HG2 ....222 E7
Thackadale La YO17 ....121 A1
Thackeray Gr TS5 ....6 E8
Thacking La LA6 ....103 D4
Thames Ave
Guisborough TS14 ....8 E6
Thornaby TS17 ....6 B7
Thanet Rd YO24 ....227 D1
Thanets Ct 9 BD23 ....216 F3
Thatch Cl YO8 ....232 C4
Thatchers Croft YO23 ....230 C3
Theakston Brewery Visitor Ctr★ HG4 ....86 C4
Theakston Hargill DL8 ....87 E8
Theakston La DL10 ....209 C5
Theresa Cl 6 YO31 ....225 F1
Thickrash Brow LA2 ....129 A7
Thief La Barlow YO8 ....232 F1
York YO10 ....228 F3
Thiefgate La HG4 ....86 E3
Thiefhole La DL7 ....65 B3
Third Ave
10 Wetherby LS22 ....180 C3
York YO31 ....228 F5
Thirkleby Way YO10 ....229 C4
Thirlmere Cl 3 YO7 ....89 C4
Thirlmere Dr YO31 ....229 A6
Thirsk Athletic Club YO7 ....211 A3
Thirsk Bank
Angram Grange YO61 ....117 B8
Thornton-le-Moor DL7 ....65 B3
Thirsk Bsns Pk YO7 ....211 B2
Thirsk CP Sch YO7 ....211 C4
Thirsk Ind Pk YO7 ....211 D2
Thirsk Mus★ YO7 ....211 B3
Thirsk Race Course★ YO7 ....211 A3
Thirsk Rd
Eaglescliffe TS15 ....5 E2
Easingwold YO61 ....117 B1
Kirkby TS9 ....26 C6
Romanby DL6 ....210 F1
Thirsk Sch YO7 ....211 B1
Thirsk Sta YO7 ....89 D4
Thirsk Swimming Pool YO7 ....211 C2
Thirty Acre La HG5 ....163 A6
Thirwall Dr TS17 ....6 A4
Thistle Cl
Northallerton DL7 ....210 D1
Selby YO8 ....232 C2
Thistle Hill HG5 ....221 B3
Thistle Rise TS8 ....6 F6
Thistlebar Rd YO51 ....141 D2
Thomas Gill Rd 7 HG3 ....137 F1
Thomas St 6 Selby YO8 ....232 D6
2 York YO10 ....228 E3
Thomason Foss (Waterfall)★ YO22 ....31 C1
Thompson Cl
9 Barlby YO8 ....198 B4
29 Scalby YO12 ....75 D5
Thompson Dr 2 YO32 ....167 B8
Thompson Pl 6 YO26 ....227 E5
Thompson St E DL1 ....3 D7
Thompson St W DL3 ....3 C7
Thoresby La DL8 ....59 B5
Thoresby Rd YO24 ....227 B1
Thorington Gdns TS17 ....6 B4
Thorn Nook YO31 ....228 F8
Thorn Tree Ave 6 YO14 ....101 B4
Thorn Wath La YO62 ....48 E4
Thornaby Com Sch TS17 ....6 B7
Thornaby Rd TS17 ....6 B7
Thornaby Swimming Baths TS17 ....6 A8
Thornaby Village Prim Sch TS17 ....6 B7
Thornborough Cres 4 DL8 ....60 D5
Thornbrough Rd DL6 ....210 E3
Thornburgh Rd 6 YO11 ....99 F6
Thorncroft 8 YO19 ....184 F7
Thorndale St BD23 ....154 B3
Thornden Bldgs YO8 ....232 D5
Thorndikes La HG5 ....141 A2
Thorne Cl 13 WF6 ....200 B1
Thorner C of E Prim Sch LS14 ....188 A3
Thorner Gr BD20 ....174 C2
Thorner La LS23 ....188 B5
Thorner Rd LS23 ....188 B4
Thornfield Ave
Dishforth YO7 ....115 A4
5 York YO31 ....228 F8
Thornfield Bsns Pk DL7 ....210 B6
Thornfield Dr 7 YO31 ....225 E2
Thornfield Gr TS5 ....6 E8
Thornfield Rd DL8 ....87 C3
Thornhill
6 Eastfield YO11 ....100 A6
Northallerton DL6 ....210 E3
Thornhill Rd WF10 ....200 F3
Thornhills 19 YO32 ....166 F5
Thornlands 6 YO61 ....117 D1
Thornley Ave DL7 ....210 D3
Thorns La YO51 ....140 F4
Thornthwaite Brow HG3 ....159 E5
Thornton Cl
15 Easingwold YO61 ....143 D8
Stainton & Thornton TS8 ....6 D4
Thornton in Craven CP Sch BD23 ....172 A3
Thornton La Dent LA10 ....78 A4
Marishes YO17 ....96 B1
Thornton in Lonsdale LA6 ....103 C4
Thornton-on-the-Hill YO61 ....117 D4
Thornton le Dale C of E Prim Sch YO18 ....96 C5
Thornton Moor Cl YO30 ....224 F2
Thornton Rd
Coulby Newham TS8 ....6 D4
Pickering YO18 ....96 A6
Thornton St
14 Burley in Warfedale LS29 ....176 C1
Darlington DL3 ....3 C5
3 Skipton BD23 ....216 D3
Thornton Vale TS8 ....6 E4
Thornton Watlass C of E Prim Sch HG4 ....86 D8
Thorntree Gdns DL2 ....4 C4
Thorntree La DN14 ....207 C6
Thorntree Rd
Northallerton DL6 ....210 F6
Thornaby TS17 ....6 B7
Thornview Rd BD23 ....154 B3
Thornwood Ave TS17 ....6 A5
Thornwood Covert 1 YO24 ....227 C1
Thorny Hill La YO51 ....141 E2
Thorny La YO42 ....169 F2
Thorp Arch Pk LS23 ....180 F1
Thorp Arch Trad Est LS23 ....189 A8
Thorpe Bassett La YO17 ....122 E1
Thorpe Chase HG4 ....214 E3
Thorpe Green Bank 1 YO22 ....33 C3
Thorpe Green La YO26 ....164 B7
Thorpe La
Ampleforth YO62 ....118 B8
Cawood YO8 ....197 B8
Cracoe BD23 ....156 C7
Fylingdales YO22 ....33 C4
Thorpe BD23 ....156 D8
Thorpe Rd HG4 ....86 C2
Thorpe St YO23 ....228 B2
Thorpe Willoughby Cty Prim Sch YO8 ....197 B1
Threapland BD23 ....156 C7
Three Tuns Wynd 7 TS9 ....26 C7
Threshfield Prim Sch BD23 ....134 D2
Thrintoft La DL7 ....64 A7
Thrintoft Moor La DL7 ....64 A8
Thrope La HG3 ....110 C4
Throstle Farm Sch WF11 ....201 F1
Throstle Nest Cl LS21 ....176 E1
Throstle Nest Dr HG2 ....222 D6
Throxenby Gr 3 YO12 ....212 B7
Throxenby La YO12 ....212 B7
Thruscross La HG3 ....159 B5
Thrussendale Rd YO17 ....169 E8
Thurland Castle★ LA6 ....102 B3
Thwaite Holme La DL8 ....57 F5
Thwaite La LA2 ....128 E5
Thwaites Ave LS29 ....218 C4
Thwaites La
Markington with Wallerthwaite HG3 ....139 D5
Nether Silton YO7 ....66 C7
Thirkleby High & Low with Osgodby YO7 ....90 E1
Thweng Way TS14 ....8 E5
Thwing Rd YO25 ....126 E2
Tib Garth LS22 ....180 A2
Tibby Butts 26 YO13 ....75 D5
Tickergate La DL7 ....63 A8
Tidkin La TS14 ....8 E6
Tile Cl BD23 ....217 B3
Tillman Cl 6 BD24 ....131 D2
Tilmire Cl 2 YO10 ....231 F8
Timble Gr HG1 ....219 B5
Timmys La DL2 ....3 F1
Tindall St YO12 ....212 F5
Tinker La YO23 ....182 D6
Tinkers' La HG3 ....139 A1
Tinkingfield La LS22 ....181 A5
Tinkler La YO51 ....141 C6
Tinkler's La WF11 ....202 D6
Tinley Garth YO62 ....70 B1
Tinley Gdns 14 YO62 ....70 B1
Tintagel Ct WF6 ....200 A2
Tiplady Cl 18 YO61 ....143 C8
Tippaty La WF11 ....202 A4
Tirril Way TS7 ....7 C5
Tisbury Rd YO26 ....227 E4
Tithe Barn Fold LS15 ....194 B8
Tithe Barn Rd 2 WF11 ....202 A2
Tithe Barn Way DN14 ....202 F3
Tithe Cl YO24 ....227 B1
Tithe Way HG4 ....114 F1
Tivoli Pl LS29 ....218 C3
Toadham La DN14 ....207 C5
Toby Ct YO32 ....167 A7
Toc La YO18 ....97 C5
Tockwith C of E Prim Sch YO26 ....181 C7
Tockwith La YO26 ....181 D6
Tockwith Rd
Long Marston YO26 ....181 F6
Tockwith LS22 ....180 F7
Tod Holes La BD23 ....153 B4
Todd La DL7 ....63 B8
Todds Ct 8 YO7 ....211 C3
Todley Hall Rd BD22 ....187 F3
Todmanhaw La BD23 ....153 E3
Toft Gn YO1 ....233 A2
Toft Ings La YO61 ....143 B8
Tofta Rd YO13 ....54 A5
Tofting La YO17 ....148 B5
Tofts Cl TS15 ....24 B8
Tofts Fort The★ DL11 ....1 E2
Tofts La Danby YO21 ....29 B5
Follifoot HG3 ....223 F4
Humberton YO61 ....141 F8
Pickering YO18 ....95 F3
Tholthorpe YO61 ....142 D6
Welbury DL6 ....24 B1
Tofts Rd YO18 ....95 F3
Toll Bar Cl 3 YO8 ....196 E1

Toll Bar Rd WF10 200 C4
Toll Bar Way LS24 189 F7
Tollergate YO11 213 A7
Tollerton Rd YO30 165 B7
Tollesby La TS7 7 B6
Tollesby Rd TS5 6 F8
Tom Cat La
Bilton-in-Ainsty with Bickerton LS22 181 A5
Birdsall YO17 148 B4
Tom Dando Cl WF6 200 C1
Tom Hall Ct 12 DL8 63 A2
Tom La Cowling BD22 186 E7
Dunsforths YO26 141 F3
Tom Smith's Cross YO62 92 B4
Tomahawk Trail WF10 200 F3
Tomgill Bank DL8 58 E2
Tomlinson Way LS25 195 E4
Top Fold WF11 201 D6
Top House Farm Mews 2 WF11 201 D6
Top La Colne BB8 186 B2
Copmanthorpe YO23 230 B3
Norwood LS21 177 A6
Top Stone Cl LS25 201 F6
Topcliff Ct YO8 232 B7
Topcliffe C of E Prim Sch YO7 115 C7
Topcliffe Rd
Sowerby YO7 89 E3
Thirsk YO7 211 B1
Thornaby TS17 6 C7
Toremill Cl YO32 225 D4
Torrance Dr DL1 3 F8
Torridon Pl YO24 230 B7
Torrs Rd HG1 220 A3
Tostig Ave YO26 227 C5
Tostig Cl 14 YO41 168 D2
Toulston La LS23 188 F5
Tout Hill YO60 146 E5
Tow Scar Rd LA6 103 C5
Tow Top La BD20 173 A1
Tower Cres LS24 189 D6
Tower Croft 7 YO61 117 D1
Tower Rd Darlington DL3 3 B6
Ripon HG4 214 C6
Tower St
Harrogate HG1 219 D1
York YO1 233 B1
Tower Street Castle W 4 DL10 209 C6
Tower The★ HG4 139 B6
Tower View DN14 204 C2
Towers Paddock WF10 201 A4
Town End Ave DN14 204 C3
Town End Cl
16 Glusburn BD20 187 E7
9 Pickering YO18 96 A6
Town End Gdns 3 YO32 166 D5
Town Farm Cl 15 YO62 70 B1
Town Green Dr TS9 26 E5
Town Head Ave 1 BD24 131 E2
Town Head Way 14 BD24 131 D2
Town Hill LS23 188 E5
Town St
Bishop Thornton HG3 138 F1
Brandsby-cum-Stearsby YO61 118 D3
Malton YO17 215 E6
Nidd HG3 161 E7
Scampston YO17 123 A6
Settrington YO17 122 C1
Townend Ct 3 YO26 164 A8
Townend Pl 5 BD20 187 E7
Townend Rd YO42 193 D1
Townend St YO31 233 B4
Townhead 2 BD24 131 E2
Townhead Fold 12 LS29 174 F4
Townhead La LA2 130 E8
Towthorpe Moor La YO32 167 C5
Towthorpe Rd YO32 166 F5
Towton Ave
9 York YO24 227 F2
1 York YO24 228 A2
Toy Mus★ YO12 212 F5
Trafalgar Ct 10 HG1 219 D1
Trafalgar Rd
11 Harrogate HG1 219 D1
Ilkley LS29 218 B4
Trafalgar Sq YO12 212 F7
Trafalgar St YO23 228 B1
Trafalgar St W YO12 212 F6
Trafalgar Terr YO12 212 F7
Trafford Ct 19 DL1 3 F6
Trafford Rd 4 DN6 206 E2
Train La 14 YO18 95 F7
Tranby Ave YO10 229 D4
Tranmire Cl YO7 211 D4
Tranmore La DN14 203 B3
Trans Wlk LS24 190 B1
Tranter Rd TS4 6 F8
Trapping Hill HG3 110 C4
Trattles Hill YO13 54 D2
Travellers Garth YO17 121 C1
Trawden CP Sch BB8 186 A1
Trawden Rd BB8 186 A3
Treesdale Rd 1 HG2 219 C1
Trefoil Cl TS14 8 D6
Trefoil Dr 4 HG3 161 B3
Trefoil Wood TS7 7 B7
Trencar La YO61 91 A2
Trenchard Ave TS17 6 B6
Trenchard Rd YO26 227 B6
Trenchard St 8 YO7 89 B1
Trenholme La TS15 25 B3
Trent Ave
Garforth LS25 194 D3
Pontefract WF6 200 A2
4 York YO32 225 F6
Trent Way YO24 230 D7
Trentholme Dr 2 YO24 228 A2
Trevine Gdns TS17 5 F4
Trevor Gr 8 YO24 227 F2
Trimdon Ave TS5 6 D6
Trinity Cl 1 YO11 212 F3
Trinity Gdns 2 YO11 212 F3
Trinity La Ripon HG4 214 B5
York YO1 233 A2
Trinity Pk HG4 214 B6
Trinity Rd Darlington DL3 3 C5
Harrogate HG2 219 D1
Scarborough YO11 212 F3
Trinket La LA2 128 B6
Trip Garth LS22 180 A1
Trip La Collingham LS22 180 A1
Sicklinghall LS22 179 F1
Triplins La HG4 113 B6
Troon Cl 2 YO26 227 B5
Trousdale Hill YO60 147 A7
Troutbeck 7 YO24 230 C7
Troutbeck Cl 11 YO18 95 F6
Troutsdale Ave YO30 224 E2
Trumfleet La DN6 207 D1
Trundles La 7 WF11 202 A2
Truro Cres 8 HG3 161 B3
Truro Dr 19 WF6 200 A2
Truro Rd 7 HG3 161 B3
Truro Wlk 23 WF6 200 A2
Trust Fold LS25 201 E6
Tudor Cl 10 YO8 197 B1
Tudor Rd
Richmond DL10 209 D7
York YO24 227 C2
Tudor Way YO32 167 C8
Tuke Ave YO10 229 B4
Tumbledown Cl 5 DL9 40 E3
Tune St YO8 198 B4
Tunstall Rd
Catterick DL10 41 D4
Harrogate HG2 220 B3
Turbary Rd LA6 103 B7
Turfy Hill DL8 56 C4
Turker Cl DL6 210 E5
Turker La DL6 210 F6
Turkey La YO7 114 F8
Turnberry Ave TS16 5 E4
Turnberry Dr YO26 227 B4
Turnberry Way TS8 7 C5
Turner Cl DL9 209 C2
Turner Cres 6 LS21 177 A1
Turner La 4 LS29 174 E4
Turner's Croft YO10 229 A1
Turners Sq 9 YO8 232 C5
Turnham La YO8 198 C2
Turnhead Cres YO8 198 B5
Turnhead Ct YO8 198 B6
Turnmire Rd 1 YO24 230 E8
Turnpike La LS22 181 B5
Turnpike Rd LS24 189 F7
Turnshaw Rd BD22 187 F1
Turpin La LS25 196 A2
Turton Rd TS15 5 D2
Turver's La WF11 202 C2
Tuscany Way WF6 200 A3
Tuthill 13 YO11 213 B6
Tutin Rd DL7 63 C5
Tweed Ave TS17 6 B7
Twelve Acre Bank DL8 40 E1
Twin Pike Way 14 YO32 166 D5
Twine Wlk 7 LA6 102 F3
Twizzie Gill View 7 TS13 11 A8
Two Laws Rd BB8 187 B1
Tyler Cl WF6 200 C1
Tyn Garth YO19 191 D8
Tyne Cres DL1 3 D3
Typhoon Cl DL10 41 F6
Tyseley Gr 4 BB18 172 A1
Tyson Pl HG2 220 B2

U

Uldale Cl 5 HG5 221 D5
Uldale Dr TS16 5 E4
Ulla Gn LS24 190 B1
Ulleskelf Sta LS24 190 B2
Ullswater YO24 230 D7
Ullswater Ave TS5 6 E8
Ullswater Dr LS22 180 B3
Ullswater Rise 5 LS22 180 B3
Ulnaby La DL2 2 C7
Under Cliffe 17 YO18 95 F7
Undercliffe Rise LS29 218 E2
Undercroft 7 YO19 184 F7
Underlands La HG4 114 C7
Underwit Rd YO8 204 C4
Union La YO8 232 C4
Union St 28 Filey YO14 101 B3
Harrogate HG1 219 D3
2 Knaresborough HG5 221 A5
12 Scarborough YO11 213 A6
Union Terr
5 Skipton BD23 216 F3
York YO31 233 B4
Unity Cl HG1 219 D5
Unity Gr HG1 219 D5
Unity St 1 BB18 186 A7
University Coll of Ripon & York St John HG4 214 B6
University College of Scarborough YO12 213 B1
University of York
Heslington YO10 228 F1
York YO10 228 E3
York YO10 229 B2
York YO30 233 A3
University Rd YO10 228 F2
Upgang La YO21 208 B7
Upgarth Cl 2 TS13 12 A7
Uplands BD23 217 B5
Uplands Ave 8 YO13 99 B8
Uplands Rd DL3 3 B5
Uplands The YO12 212 A7
Upper Carr La YO18 96 A4
Upper Green La TS18 6 A7
Upper Hanover St 6 YO26 227 F5
Upper Newborough St 1 YO30 228 C7
Upper Nidderdale High Sch HG3 137 B4
Upper Poppleton Jun Sch YO26 165 F1
Upper Price St YO23 233 A1
Upper Sackville St 5 BD23 217 A3
Upper St Paul's Terr YO24 228 A4
Upper Union St BD23 216 F3
Upper Wharfdale Mus★ BD23 134 E2
Upper Wharfedale Sch BD23 134 D2
Uppercommon La DN14 202 F3
Uppercroft 4 YO32 225 C8
Uppergate LA6 103 D4
Upsall Dr DL3 3 C4
Upsall La
South Kilvington YO7 211 C7
Thornbrough YO7 90 A8
Upsall YO7 66 B1
Upwell Rd DL7 210 D4
Ure Bank HG4 214 D7
Ure Bank Terr HG4 214 C7
Ure Bank Top HG4 214 D7
Urlay Nook Rd TS16 5 C5
Usher La YO32 166 F6

V

Vale Ave WF11 201 E2
Vale Cres
Bishop Wilton YO42 169 F2
Knottingley WF11 201 E2
Vale Crest WF11 201 E2
Vale Sch WF11 201 E2
Vale The
10 Collingham LS22 188 A8
Middlesbrough TS5 6 F8
Skelton YO30 224 B5
Vale View HG4 114 B2
Valley Bridge Par YO11 213 A5
Valley Dr
Barnoldswick BB18 171 E2
Eaglescliffe TS15 5 E3
Great Preston LS26 200 C8
Harrogate HG2 219 C1
Ilkley LS29 218 D4
Valley Gdns TS16 5 D4
Valley Gdns★ HG2 219 C2
Valley Mount HG2 219 C2
Valley Rd
Barnoldswick BB18 171 E1
3 Darley HG3 160 A6
32 Earby BB18 172 A1
Harrogate HG2 219 C2
Ilkley LS29 218 D5
Kippax LS25 194 C2
Northallerton DL6 210 F3
Scarborough YO12 212 E4
Whitby YO21 208 A8
Valley Ridge LS25 194 C2
Valley St N DL1 3 D5
Valley View
3 Ampleforth YO62 92 C1
Clint HG3 160 F8
Danby YO21 29 C6
3 Glusburn BD20 187 E8
Wheldrake YO19 192 F7
Valuation La 1 YO51 141 B5
Vanbrugh Dr YO10 229 C3
Vane Ct TS21 4 F7
Vane Terr DL3 3 C5
Vasey Cl 5 DL8 63 B2
Vaughan Rd 10 DN6 206 E1
Vavasour Ct YO23 230 B2
Venables Rd TS14 8 E7
Vernon Cl YO23 231 A3
Vernon Gr 4 YO12 212 D8
Vernon Pl 3 YO11 213 A5
Vernon Rd
Harrogate HG2 222 E7
2 Scarborough YO11 213 A5
Trawden Forest BB8 186 B3
York YO30 224 E2
Vesper Dr YO24 227 B3
Vesper Wlk YO32 225 F6
Vicar Hill La YO7 116 D8
Vicarage Cl
2 Bubwith YO8 199 D7
12 Hunmanby YO14 126 F8
Seamer YO12 99 D6
Vicarage Gdns 1 YO10 229 C4
Vicarage La
Bishop Wilton YO42 169 F2
Bramham LS23 188 E5
10 Knaresborough HG5 221 A6
Naburn YO19 191 E8
Sherburn YO17 124 D8
Vicarage Rd
Barnoldswick BB18 171 E2
16 Catterick Garrison DL9 40 E4
3 Kelbrook & Sough BB18 186 A7
Vicars Ct YO23 230 B2
Vicars Croft DL6 210 E5
Vicar's La YO61 144 C6
Vicars Terr WF10 200 D6
Vickers Rd 2 DL9 40 E4
Victor St YO1 233 B1
Victoria Ave
10 Filey YO14 101 B3
Harrogate HG1 219 D2
Ilkley LS29 175 C2
Knaresborough HG5 221 B8
Ripon HG4 214 D5
Thirsk YO7 211 B2
Victoria Cave★ BD24 131 F4
Victoria Cl
Great Preston WF10 200 E6
Ilkley LS29 218 A4
Victoria Ct 15 YO26 227 F5
Victoria Dr 9 LS29 175 C2
Victoria Emb DL1 3 C4
Victoria Farm Cl YO23 182 C6
Victoria Gdns 17 LS29 175 C2
Victoria Gr
5 Ilkley LS29 175 C2
Ripon HG4 214 C5
Victoria Par 13 YO11 212 F5
Victoria Park Ave 2 YO12 212 F7
Victoria Park Mount YO12 212 E7
Victoria Pk 1 YO12 212 F7
Victoria Pl 3 YO21 208 D6
Victoria Rd
1 Barnoldswick BB18 171 E1
28 Burley in Warfedale LS29 176 C1
Cowling BD22 187 B6
Darlington DL1 3 C5
Earby BB18 172 A1
Glusburn BD20 187 E7
Harrogate HG2 219 C1
10 Ilkley LS29 175 C2
1 Malton YO17 215 B4
Richmond DL10 209 B7
Scarborough YO11 212 F5
Thornaby TS17 6 B8
Victoria St
24 Earby BB18 172 A1
Glusburn BD20 187 E7
Great Preston WF10 200 D6
Pontefract WF8 201 B2
Scarborough YO12 212 F6
Settle BD24 131 E2
10 Skipton BD23 216 F4
1 York YO23 233 B1
Victoria Terr
1 Harrogate HG1 220 C4
1 Skipton BD23 216 F4
Victoria Way 2 YO32 228 F8
Victoria Works Ind Est BD20 187 F8
Victory Rd LS29 218 B4
Viewley Hill Ave TS8 6 F5
Viewley Hill Sch TS8 6 F5
Viking Cl 20 YO41 168 D2
Viking Dr 5 YO19 197 F8
Viking Rd
Stamford Bridge YO41 168 D2
York YO26 227 C5
Vikings Ct 6 DL6 43 F3
Villa Cl YO8 198 F1
Villa Fields 4 DN14 204 C1
Villa Gr 2 YO31 228 E6
Village Farm Ct 7 DN14 202 D4
Village Fold DL7 42 B1
Village Garth 1 YO32 166 E5
Village Paddock TS18 5 E8
Village Rd TS15 24 B8
Village St YO30 224 E3
Village The
Boston Spa LS23 180 F1
Haxby YO32 166 E5
Skelton YO30 224 B5
Stockton on the Forest YO32 167 D3
Strensall YO32 167 B7
Village Wy DL7 42 B1
Villiers Ct 8 YO62 92 F6
Vimy Rd DL9 40 E3
Vincent St 9 YO12 213 A7
Vincent Way YO24 230 C8
Vine Cl TS14 8 F6
Vine Farm Cl YO26 164 A4
Vine St Darlington DL3 3 B6
Norton YO17 215 E4
6 Scarborough YO12 212 F6
York YO23 228 C2
Vinstra Cl DL10 209 D8
Virginia Gdns TS5 6 E6
Vivars Way YO8 232 D5
Vivers Pl 1 YO62 70 C1
Vivis La YO18 95 F6
Volta St YO8 232 E4
Vulcan Way TS17 6 B6
Vyner St Ripon HG4 214 D4
York YO31 228 C7

W

Waddington St 37 BB18 172 A1
Wade House La YO8 204 F4
Waggoners Dr 3 YO23 230 B3
Wain Cl
15 Eastfield YO11 100 B7
South Milford LS25 195 E2
Wain Gap LS25 195 F2
Waincroft 8 YO32 167 A6
Waindyke Way WF6 200 B1
Wainers Cl 5 YO23 230 B3
Wainfleet Rd HG1 219 D6
Waingates La YO51 140 F4
Wainman's Cl BD22 187 B6
Wain's Gr YO24 230 D7
Wain's La YO12 99 D2
Wain's Rd YO24 230 D8
Wainstones Cl TS9 7 F1
Wainstones Dr TS9 7 F1
Waite La YO13 53 F2
Waithwith Rd DL9 209 B1
Waitlands La DL11 20 A7
Wakefield Coll WF10 200 D3
Wakefield Rd
Garforth LS25 194 B3
10 Normanton South WF6 200 A1
Swillington LS26 194 A2
Wakeman Rd HG4 214 C3
Walburn Head DL11 39 D3
Walden Stubbs Rd DN6 206 E2
Wales St DL3 3 C7
Walker Cl BD20 187 D7
Walker Dr YO24 230 C8
Walker La
Menwith with Darley HG3 160 A6
Wheldrake YO19 192 F7
Walker St YO21 208 D6
Walker's La BD20 174 B4
Walkers Row TS14 8 F7
Walkerville Ave 22 DL9 41 A5
Walkington La YO30 165 B8
Wallgates La YO17 215 D4
Walmgate YO1 233 C2
Walmsley Gdns YO12 212 C5
Walney Rd YO31 229 A5
Walnut Cl
Saxton with Scarthingwell LS24 195 D8
York YO10 229 A1
Walnut Gr HG1 219 E6
Walpole St YO31 228 D7
Walton Ave
Gargrave BD23 155 C1
Middlesbrough TS5 6 E8
Pannal HG3 222 F2
Walton Chase LS23 180 F2
Walton Cl
Gargrave BD23 172 C8
Huby YO61 144 A4
Walton Head La HG3 178 F4
Walton Pk HG3 222 E2
Walton Pl Pannal HG3 222 E2
York YO26 227 B3
Walton Rd
Walton LS23 181 A2
Wetherby LS22 180 E2
Walton St
5 Cowling BD22 187 B6
Skipton BD23 216 F1
Walworth Ave HG2 220 B3
Walworth St N 4 YO26 227 F5
Walworth St S 9 YO26 227 F5
Wand Hill TS12 9 E8
Wand La DN14 203 C3
Wandale La YO17 95 A2
Wandales Cl YO17 215 F3
Wandales Ct YO13 75 D8
Wandales Dr YO13 75 D8
Wandales La YO60 146 B6
Wandales Rd YO13 75 D8
Wandell Balk YO61 144 B6
Wandels La YO21 29 B6
Wandesford Gr DL9 209 F1
Wandhill 31 YO32 166 E5
Wandhill Gdns TS12 9 E8
Wandhill La YO7 66 D1
Wandle The YO26 227 A2
Wansbeck 3 YO24 230 B7
Wapping La YO62 94 C7
War Dike La YO13 54 B6
War Field La LS22 180 F6
Warbler Cl TS17 6 A5
Ward Ct YO23 233 B1
Ward St BD23 217 A4
Wardale Ave TS5 6 E6
Wardrop Rd DL9 209 C1
Wareham Rd YO11 99 F6
Warehill La YO61 143 C2
Warlbeck 23 LS29 175 C2
Warley Wise La BB8 186 D6
Warren Ave WF11 201 E2
Warren La
Bramham cum Oglethorpe LS24 189 A5
Brearton HG3 162 A8
Kirkby Malzeard HG4 112 D4
Warren Pl HG1 219 D5
Warrener La DL10 20 C6
Warth La LA6 103 C3

Warthill C of E Prim Sch YO19 ... 167 F2
Warwick Cl YO60 ... 145 D5
Warwick Cres HG2 ... 222 E8
Warwick Dr 2 BB18 ... 172 A1
Warwick Pl 2 YO62 ... 92 F7
Warwick St YO31 ... 228 D7
Wasdale Cl 2 YO30 ... 224 E1
Wash Beck La YO62 ... 93 F6
Washbeck Cl YO12 ... 212 E4
Washbrook Dr DL3 ... 3 C8
Washburn Cl 13 YO14 ... 101 A3
Washburn Dr 4 BD20 ... 187 E8
Washfold La DL8 ... 60 B6
Washford Cl TS17 ... 6 A3
Washington Ave DL2 ... 4 D4
Washington Cl HG4 ... 214 E2
Wass Bank Rd YO61 ... 91 F2
Wass Way TS16 ... 5 D5
Waste La YO62 ... 48 F2
Watchet Rd 11 DL9 ... 40 E4
Water Bag Bank 8 HG5 221 A6
Water End YO26 ... 227 E5
Water Gap YO18 ... 97 B5
Water Garth DN14 ... 202 F4
Water Hill La YO8 ... 232 D6
Water Houses BD24 ... 132 E6
Water La
Camblesforth YO8 ... 204 D5
8 Clifton YO30 ... 225 A1
Dalton YO7 ... 115 E7
Dunnington YO19 ... 184 F7
Eggborough DN14 ... 203 A2
Exelby, Leeming & Newton DL7 ... 63 D4
Hemingbrough YO8 ... 198 F1
Huttons Ambo YO60 ... 147 C6
Kirby Grindalythe YO17 ... 149 B6
Kirby Underdale YO41 ... 170 A5
Kirk Smeaton WF8 ... 206 C3
Knaresborough HG5 ... 221 C8
Loftus TS13 ... 10 E8
North Stainley with Sleningford HG4 ... 113 C6
7 Pontefract WF8 ... 201 C1
South Stainley with Cayton HG3 ... 139 D2
Thorpe Bassett YO17 ... 123 A3
Welburn YO60 ... 146 E7
Whitby YO21 ... 208 B3
York YO30 ... 228 A7
Water Skellgate HG4 ... 214 C5
Water Slack La YO26 ... 164 C4
Water St Earby BB18 ... 172 A1
Gargrave BD23 ... 155 D1
Malton YO17 ... 215 C4
Skipton BD23 ... 216 F4
Water Street CP Sch BD23 ... 216 F4
Water Way Garth DN14 ... 207 F6
Water World York* YO32 ... 226 A2
Waterdale Pk YO31 ... 225 E1
Waterfall Fold 1 WF8 ... 201 C2
Waterfalls Wlk LA6 ... 103 D6
Watergate
Mickletown LS26 ... 200 A5
7 Pontefract WF8 ... 201 B1
Watergate Rd HG3 ... 139 A4
Waterhouse La 29 YO11 213 A6
Waterings 19 YO32 ... 166 D5
Waterloo YO22 ... 31 C4
Waterloo Cl WF10 ... 200 C3
Waterloo Rd BB18 ... 186 A7
Waterloo St
Harrogate HG1 ... 219 E4
2 Richmond DL10 ... 209 C6
Waterman Ct 3 YO24 ... 227 B1
Watermill Croft HG4 ... 113 C7
Watermill La HG4 ... 113 C7
Waters End DL2 ... 1 D7
Waters La DL10 ... 20 E3
Watershed Mill Bsns Ctr BD24 ... 131 D3
Waterside
3 Boroughbridge YO51 ... 141 B6
Knaresborough HG5 ... 221 A5
4 Ripon HG4 ... 214 C4
7 Thirsk YO7 ... 211 C3
Watersole La LS22 ... 180 D2
Waterstead Cres 1 YO21 ... 208 D5
Waterstead La YO21 ... 208 C5
Waterways Mus & Adventure Ctr The* DN14 ... 205 F1
Watery La Airton BD23 ... 155 A5
Giggleswick BD24 ... 131 C1
Snape with Thorp DL8 ... 86 F7
Wath La Catton YO41 ... 185 C8
Copgrove HG3 ... 140 D1
High & Low Bishopside HG3 ... 137 B6
Humberton YO61 ... 141 E8
Ulleskelf LS24 ... 190 B2
Wath Rd HG3 ... 137 B5
Wathcote Cl DL10 ... 209 F8
Wathcote Pl DL10 ... 209 F8
Wathgill Camp DL11 ... 39 C3
Watlass La DL8 ... 86 E8
Watlass Moor La HG4 ... 86 D7
Watling Cl DL11 ... 19 E6
Watling Rd WF10 ... 201 C5
Watson Cl 9 YO14 ... 127 A8
Watson St
4 Normanton South WF6 . 200 A1
York YO24 ... 228 A3
Watson Terr 2 YO24 ... 228 A3
Watson's Houses 7 BD23 ... 216 F4
Watson's La
Newton Kyme cum Toulston LS24 ... 189 B7
Norwood HG3 ... 177 B8
Reighton YO14 ... 127 D6
Wattle Syke LS22 ... 180 B1
Wattlers Cl YO23 ... 230 C3
Wattlesyke LS22 ... 188 C8
Wavell Cty Jun Sch DL9 ... 209 D1
Wavell Rd DL9 ... 209 D1
Wavell St YO8 ... 232 A6
Waveney Gr YO30 ... 228 B8
Waver La DL6 ... 43 F8
Waverley Cl DN14 ... 204 C2
Waverley Cres HG2 ... 222 E8
Waverley St YO31 ... 233 C3
Waydale Cl YO62 ... 70 A2
Wayne Tarbard Cl 12 HG4 ... 113 D2
Waynefleet Gr 3 YO10 ... 229 A3
Wayside Ave HG2 ... 220 B1
Wayside Cl 4 HG2 ... 220 B1
Wayside Cres HG2 ... 220 A1
Wayside Gr HG2 ... 220 A1
Wayside Terr LS17 ... 178 B2
Wayside The DL2 ... 3 E1
Wayside Wlk 5 HG2 ... 220 B1
Weaponness Dr YO11 ... 213 A2
Weaponness La
Eastfield YO11 ... 99 F8
Scarborough YO11 ... 212 F1
Weaponness Pk YO11 ... 213 A2
Weaponness Valley Cl 5 YO11 ... 212 F3
Weaponness Valley Rd YO11 ... 212 E3
Weardale TS14 ... 8 D5
Weardale Rd 20 DL9 ... 40 E4
Weary Bank TS15 ... 25 B8
Weavers Cl YO23 ... 230 B3
Weavers Ct 3 TS9 ... 26 C7
Weavers Gn DL7 ... 210 C3
Weaverthorpe C of E Prim Sch YO17 ... 124 E2
Webster Pl 1 WF6 ... 200 A1
Weddall Cl YO24 ... 227 F1
Wedderburn Ave HG2 ... 220 C2
Wedderburn Cl HG2 ... 220 C3
Wedderburn Cty Inf Sch HG2 ... 220 B2
Wedderburn Dr HG2 ... 220 B2
Wedderburn Lodge 2 HG2 ... 220 B1
Wedderburn Rd HG2 ... 220 B2
Weedling Gate LS24 ... 189 D4
Weeland Ct 16 WF11 ... 202 A2
Weeland Rd Beal DN14 ... 202 E3
Hensall DN14 ... 203 E2
Weeton La LS17 ... 178 D1
Weeton Sta LS17 ... 178 B2
Weets View BB18 ... 171 E2
Welbeck Ave DL1 ... 3 E7
Welborn Cl YO10 ... 229 A4
Welborn Ct YO11 ... 99 F2
Welbourn Dr 12 YO12 ... 99 D6
Welburn Cty Prim Sch YO60 ... 146 D6
Welburn Gr TS7 ... 7 D7
Welburn Hall Sch YO62 . 94 A7
Welburn La YO60 ... 147 A8
Welbury Cl 2 BB18 ... 172 B1
Welfare Ave LS15 ... 194 C8
Welford Rd 36 YO14 ... 101 B3
Welham Hill YO17 ... 147 E7
Welham Rd YO17 ... 215 D3
Well Bank DL8 ... 87 A4
Well Cl
Great & Little Preston LS25 ... 200 C8
3 Whitby YO21 ... 208 D7
Well Close Terr 4 YO21 ... 208 D7
Well La Kippax LS25 ... 194 D1
Redmire DL8 ... 59 C5
Seamer TS9 ... 6 F2
Snape with Thorp DL8 ... 87 A6
South Milford LS25 ... 195 F2
Yearsley YO61 ... 118 C5
Welland Dr LS25 ... 194 D3
Welland Rise YO26 ... 227 D5
Wellbrook Cl TS17 ... 6 B4
Wellesley Cl YO30 ... 225 A2
Wellfield La 13 LS29 ... 176 C1
Wellhouse St 5 BB18 ... 171 E1
Wellington Ct 19 HG2 ... 219 C2
Wellington Mews 9 HG4 ... 214 C5
Wellington Rd
Ilkley LS29 ... 218 B4
Richmond DL10 ... 209 B7
2 Whitby YO21 ... 208 D6
Wellington Row YO1 ... 233 A2
Wellington Sq 6 HG2 ... 219 C2
Wellington St
1 Knaresborough HG5 ... 221 B5
10 Ripon HG4 ... 214 C5
12 Skipton BD23 ... 217 A3
York YO10 ... 228 E3
Wellington Terr YO21 ... 208 D7
Wellington Way 4 DL10 . 41 C7
Wellingtonia Dr 5 DN6 . 206 E1
Wells Cl YO8 ... 232 A5
Wells La Barton DL10 ... 21 D7
Kellington DN14 ... 202 E3
Malton YO17 ... 215 C4
Wells Prom LS29 ... 218 B4
Wells Rd LS29 ... 218 B3
Wells Wlk Ilkley LS29 ... 218 B4
13 Pickering YO18 ... 95 F7
Wellspring Cl TS17 ... 6 D7
Welton Ave YO26 ... 227 D5
Welwyn Dr YO10 ... 231 E8
Wemyss Rd 11 HG4 ... 113 D2
Wendel Ave LS15 ... 194 B8
Wendy Ave HG4 ... 214 B3
Wenham Rd YO24 ... 230 C8
Wenlock Dr YO19 ... 192 B6
Wenlock Terr YO10 ... 228 D1
Wenning Ave LA2 ... 129 A7
Wenning Bank LA2 ... 130 A6
Wennington Hall Sch LA2 ... 102 B1
Wennington Rd LA2 ... 128 A6
Wennington Sta LA2 ... 128 B8
Wensley Gr HG2 ... 222 D7
Wensley Rd
Harrogate HG2 ... 222 D7
15 Leyburn DL8 ... 60 D5
Northallerton DL7 ... 210 B2
Wensleydale Ave 2 BD23 ... 217 B4
Wensleydale Dr YO10 ... 229 D4
Wensleydale Rd 21 DL9 ... 40 E4
Wensleydale Rugby Club DL8 ... 60 C5
Wensleydale Sch DL8 ... 60 D5
Wentcliffe Dr BB18 ... 172 A1
Wentdale 1 WF8 ... 206 C3
Wentworth Ave YO61 ... 116 F5
Wentworth Cl
Camblesforth YO8 ... 204 D4
Harrogate HG2 ... 220 D4
Kellington DN14 ... 203 A2
Wentworth Cres
Harrogate HG2 ... 220 D3
2 Whitby YO21 ... 208 B5
Wentworth Gate LS22 ... 180 A3
Wentworth Rd YO24 ... 228 B2
Wentworth St YO17 ... 215 B5
Wentworth Way
Eaglescliffe TS16 ... 5 E4
5 Hunmanby YO14 ... 126 F8
Wescoe Hill La LS17 ... 178 B1
Wesley Pl YO1 ... 233 C2
Wesley Rd YO22 ... 33 C4
Wesley Sq 2 TS13 ... 13 K2
Wesson Cl 6 DL9 ... 40 E4
West Acres 2 WF11 ... 201 E4
West Acres Cl 7 YO13 ... 99 A7
West Auckland Rd DL3 ... 3 A7
West Ave
Boston Spa LS23 ... 180 E1
Burton Fleming YO25 ... 126 E3
5 Easingwold YO61 ... 143 D8
Filey YO14 ... 101 B3
19 Scalby YO13 ... 75 D5
West Bank
Scarborough YO12 ... 212 E4
York YO24 ... 227 E3
West Bank Rd BD23 ... 216 E4
West Barnby La YO21 ... 12 B3
West Beck Way TS8 ... 7 B6
West Burton C of E Prim Sch DL8 ... 58 F1
West Cam Rd BD23 ... 79 E6
West Cl Carthorpe DL8 ... 87 E6
Normanton WF6 ... 200 A1
Swinton YO17 ... 121 B4
West Cliff Ave 5 YO21 ... 208 B7
West Cliffe Gr HG2 ... 219 B1
West Cliffe Mews 5 HG2 ... 219 C1
West Cliffe Mount HG2 ... 219 B1
West Cliffe Terr HG2 ... 219 B1
West Close Rd 13 BB18 ... 171 D2
West Craven High Sch BB18 ... 171 E1
West Craven Swimming Pool BB18 ... 171 E1
West Croft
19 Addingham LS29 ... 174 F4
6 Glusburn BD20 ... 187 E6
West Ct 8 YO19 ... 197 F8
West Dale LS23 ... 180 E1
West Dike Rd YO18 ... 71 F5
West Edge Rd WF8 ... 206 A3
West End
Boston Spa LS23 ... 180 E1
Guisborough TS14 ... 8 E6
Hurworth-on-Tees DL2 ... 3 E1
Hutton Rudby TS15 ... 25 C5
Kirkbymoorside YO62 ... 70 B1
Muston YO14 ... 100 F2
Osmotherley DL6 ... 45 B4
Pollington DN14 ... 207 F6
Rawcliffe DN14 ... 205 A2
Sheriff Hutton YO60 ... 145 C5
Stokesley TS9 ... 26 C7
Strensall YO32 ... 167 A7
West End App LS24 ... 190 B3
West End Ave
Appleton Roebuck YO23 ... 190 F5
Harrogate HG2 ... 222 D8
Richmond DL10 ... 209 A7
West End Cl
North Duffield YO8 ... 199 A8
9 Strensall YO32 ... 167 B7
West End Ct 5 YO11 ... 100 B6
West End Gdns
Egglescliffe TS16 ... 5 D4
Pollington DN14 ... 207 F6
West End Rd DN6 ... 206 E2
West End View 4 YO11 ... 100 B6
West End Way TS18 ... 5 F8
West Field La
Arkendale HG5 ... 163 A8
East Witton Town DL8 ... 60 F1
Upper Poppleton YO26 ... 165 E1
West Field Rd 2 BB18 ... 171 D2
West Fields YO62 ... 70 B1
West Garforth Jun Sch LS25 ... 194 C3
West Garth
Cayton YO11 ... 100 B6
Sherburn YO17 ... 124 D8
Ulleskelf LS24 ... 190 B3
West Garth Gdns 23 YO11 ... 100 B6
West Gate
Thornton-le-Dale YO18 ... 96 C5
Wetherby LS22 ... 180 B3
Wykeham YO13 ... 98 D6
West Gr
Bishop Thornton HG3 ... 139 A2
Swinton YO17 ... 121 B4
West Grove Rd HG1 ... 219 D4
West Hall La LS29 ... 175 A5
West Heslerton C of E Prim Sch YO17 ... 123 F6
West Ing La BD23 ... 171 A5
West Ings Cl 4 WF11 ... 202 A3
West Ings Cres 5 WF11 ... 202 A3
West Ings Ct 1 WF11 ... 202 A3
West Ings La 2 WF11 ... 202 A3
West Ings Mews 6 WF11 ... 202 A3
West Ings Way 3 WF11 202 A3
West La
Appleton Wiske DL6 ... 24 A3
Askwith LS21 ... 176 C3
Azerley HG4 ... 112 F3
Bewerley HG3 ... 136 E4
Boston Spa LS23 ... 180 E1
Burn YO8 ... 203 C6
Burniston YO13 ... 54 C1
Burton Fleming YO25 ... 126 E3
Caldwell DL11 ... 1 B4
Caldwell DL11 ... 1 D5
Cononley BD20 ... 173 C2
Dalton-on-Tees DL2 ... 22 D6
Danby YO21 ... 29 C8
East Layton DL11 ... 20 A8
Embsay BD23 ... 217 D8
Hampsthwaite HG3 ... 161 A4
Hornby DL6 ... 23 F4
Littlethorpe HG4 ... 214 A2
2 Low Bradley BD20 ... 173 E3
Melsonby DL10 ... 20 E7
Mickleby TS13 ... 12 A4
Nether Silton YO7 ... 66 B7
North Deighton LS22 ... 179 F6
Snainton YO13 ... 97 F5
Stillington YO61 ... 143 F7
Sutton BD20 ... 187 E6
Sykehouse DN14 ... 207 F2
Whixley YO26 ... 163 F5
West Lea Ave HG2 ... 222 B7
West Lodge Gdns YO17 ... 215 A4
West Lund 17 YO62 ... 70 B1
West Lund La YO62 ... 94 B8
West Mead WF10 ... 201 A4
West Moor La DL8 ... 61 E4
West Moor Rd
Darlington DL2 ... 3 E3
Raskelf YO61 ... 116 E2
West Mount LS24 ... 189 E5
West Oaks Sch LS23 ... 188 E8
West Par LS29 ... 218 C4
West Parade Rd 11 YO12 ... 212 F5
West Park Ave YO12 ... 212 C8
West Park Cres YO12 ... 212 C7
West Park Rd 13 YO13 ... 75 D5
West Park St HG2 ... 219 D1
West Pasture
Kirkbymoorside YO62 ... 70 B1
7 Pickering YO18 ... 95 F6
West Pk YO8 ... 232 A4
West Rd Carleton BD23 ... 173 A4
12 Filey YO14 ... 101 B3
Melsonby DL10 ... 20 F7
West Row DL2 ... 4 C7
West Side Rd YO13 ... 53 A1
West Sq 7 YO11 ... 212 F5
West St
Castleford WF10 ... 200 E4
Eaglescliffe TS15 ... 5 D4
Gargrave BD23 ... 155 D1
Gayles DL11 ... 19 E6
Harrogate HG1 ... 219 C5
Ilkley LS29 ... 218 B4
Muston YO14 ... 100 F2
Normanton South WF6 ... 200 A1
Scarborough YO11 ... 213 A4
Swinton YO17 ... 121 B4
West Tanfield C of E Prim Sch HG4 ... 87 A1
West Thorpe YO24 ... 230 D8
West Vale 37 YO14 ... 101 B3
West View
Carleton BD23 ... 173 B4
Darlington DL3 ... 3 A5
Draughton BD23 ... 174 B7
Kippax LS25 ... 194 D1
West View *continued*
Micklefield LS25 ... 195 A3
North Deighton LS22 ... 180 A6
Sherburn in Elmet LS25 ... 195 E3
West View Ave 25 LS29 ... 176 C1
West View Rd 26 LS29 ... 176 C1
West View Terr TS16 ... 5 D4
West Villa YO61 ... 144 A4
West Way YO61 ... 118 A1
West Wood La YO23 ... 182 E4
Westacres 5 DL2 ... 4 C4
Westbeck Gdns TS5 ... 6 F8
Westborough 1 YO11 ... 213 A5
Westbourne Ave
Harrogate HG2 ... 222 D8
Whitby YO21 ... 208 A6
Westbourne Cl YO21 ... 208 A6
Westbourne Cres LS25 ... 194 B3
Westbourne Gdns YO8 ... 232 C4
Westbourne Gr
8 Pickering YO18 ... 95 F7
3 Ripon HG4 ... 214 C5
11 Scarborough YO11 ... 213 A4
Selby YO8 ... 232 C4
Whitby YO21 ... 208 A6
Westbourne Pk YO12 ... 212 E4
Westbourne Rd
Scarborough YO11 ... 212 F3
Selby YO8 ... 232 C4
Whitby YO21 ... 208 A6
Westbourne Terr YO7 ... 211 A2
Westbury Cty Jun Sch TS17 ... 6 B8
Westbury St TS17 ... 6 B8
Westcliff Prim Sch YO21 ... 208 C7
Westcroft La YO8 ... 196 E1
Westdene HG2 ... 222 B7
Westend La DN14 ... 207 B6
Westerdale 4 YO18 ... 95 F6
Westerdale Ct 2 YO30 ... 228 A6
Western Ave WF8 ... 201 C1
Western CP Sch HG2 ... 219 C1
Western Ct 15 WF8 ... 201 C1
Western Gales Way WF6 ... 200 B1
Western Rd
Goole DN14 ... 205 F3
Skipton BD23 ... 217 B3
Western Way 1 YO18 ... 95 E7
Westerns La HG3 ... 139 C4
Westfield YO8 ... 232 B4
Westfield Ave
Castleford WF10 ... 200 E2
3 Eggborough DN14 ... 202 F2
Rawcliffe DN14 ... 205 A1
6 Scalby YO12 ... 75 E5
Selby YO8 ... 232 B4
Westfield Cl
2 Eggborough DN14 ... 202 F2
21 Haxby YO32 ... 166 E5
South Milford LS25 ... 195 E2
Westfield Cres LS24 ... 189 E6
Westfield Ct 1 LS25 ... 195 F2
Westfield Cty Inf Sch YO24 ... 227 B2
Westfield Cty Jun Sch YO26 ... 227 A2
Westfield Dr
Hurworth-on-Tees DL2 ... 3 E1
York YO10 ... 231 D8
Westfield Gn YO26 ... 181 C7
Westfield Gr
Allerton Bywater WF10 ... 200 D7
4 Eggborough DN14 ... 202 F2
12 Haxby YO32 ... 166 D5
Westfield La
Exelby, Leeming & Newton DL8 ... 63 C2
Kippax LS25 ... 194 C1
Ledsham LS25 ... 195 C1
Lockton YO18 ... 72 E4
Normanby YO62 ... 94 F4
Norton WF8 ... 206 C2
South Milford LS25 ... 195 F2
Thirsk YO7 ... 211 A3
Thoralby DL8 ... 58 D1
Thorganby YO19 ... 193 A5
Thornton-le-Dale YO18 ... 96 C5
Westfield Pl
19 Haxby YO32 ... 166 E5
York YO24 ... 227 A1
Westfield Rd
1 Eggborough DN14 ... 202 F2
20 Haxby YO32 ... 166 E5
3 North Duffield YO8 ... 199 A7
Rawcliffe DN14 ... 205 A1
Selby YO8 ... 232 B4
2 Stokesley TS9 ... 26 C7
Tockwith YO26 ... 181 C7
Westfield Sq 8 LS24 ... 189 E6
Westfield Terr
2 Great Preston WF10 ... 200 D7
Tadcaster LS24 ... 189 E6
9 Thornton Dale YO18 ... 96 D5
Westfield Way YO17 ... 215 F4
Westfields
Castleford WF10 ... 200 E3
Richmond DL10 ... 209 A7
Scorton DL10 ... 41 E7
Westfields Ct DL10 ... 209 B7
Westfold YO17 ... 215 E6
Westgarth LS22 ... 180 A2
Westgate
22 Barnoldswick BB18 ... 171 D1
Guisborough TS14 ... 8 F6

Westgate *continued*
Malton YO17 ....215 E6
Pickering YO18 ....95 E7
Rillington YO17 ....122 F5
Ripon HG4 ....214 C5
Tadcaster LS24 ....189 E6
Thirsk YO7 ....211 B2
Westgate Carr Rd YO18 ....95 D5
Westgate La
Malton YO17 ....215 D6
Thornton in Lonsdale LA6 ....103 C5
Westgate Rd DL3 ....3 B7
Westholme 10 TS15 ....25 C5
Westholme Bank DL8 ....58 F2
Westholme Cres 2 HG4 ....86 C3
Westholme Ct 3 HG4 ....86 C3
Westholme Dr YO30 ....224 E1
Westholme Rd 1 HG4 ....86 C3
Westland Cl 3 BD20 ....187 F7
Westlands
Bilton-in-Ainsty with Bickerton YO26 ....181 D5
6 Kirklevington TS15 ....24 E8
Pickering YO18 ....96 A7
Stokesley TS9 ....26 B7
Westlands Ave 1 YO21 ....208 C7
Westlands Gr YO31 ....228 F7
Westlands La YO7 ....211 A4
Westlands Rd DL3 ....3 B6
Westminster Cl HG3 ....222 C3
Westminster Cres HG3 ....222 D2
Westminster Dr HG3 ....222 D3
Westminster Gate HG3 ....222 C3
Westminster Gr HG3 ....222 D3
Westminster Rd
Pannal HG3 ....222 C3
York YO30 ....228 A6
Westminster Rise HG3 ....222 D2
Westmoreland St
Darlington DL3 ....3 C7
1 Harrogate HG1 ....219 E3
19 Skipton BD23 ....217 A3
Westmount Cl HG4 ....214 B6
Weston Cres 7 LS21 ....176 F1
Weston Dr LS21 ....176 E1
Weston La LS21 ....176 F1
Weston Moor Rd LS21 ....176 E4
Weston Park View LS21 ....176 E1
Weston Rd LS29 ....218 B4
Weston Ridge LS21 ....176 F1
Westover Rd YO12 ....212 F4
Westpit La YO32 ....167 A7
Westridge Cres 1 DL9 ....40 F5
Westside Cl YO17 ....215 B4
Westside Rd
Bransdale YO62 ....48 B5
Fadmoor YO62 ....69 E7
Westview Cl
3 Low Bradley BD20 ....173 E3
York YO26 ....227 B7
Westville Ave LS29 ....218 A4
Westville Cl 6 LS29 ....218 A4
Westville House Prep Sch LS29 ....218 D7
Westville Oval HG1 ....219 C6
Westville Rd LS29 ....218 A4
Westway Eastfield YO11 ....99 F7
Harrogate HG2 ....222 B8
Westwood
Carleton BD23 ....173 B4
Scarborough YO11 ....212 F5
Westwood Cl 2 YO11 ....212 F4
Westwood Dr LS29 ....218 A2
Westwood Gdns 3 YO11 ....212 F4
Westwood La
Ampleforth YO62 ....92 A2
West Tanfield HG4 ....86 E1
Westwood Mews
Carleton BD23 ....173 B4
12 Dunnington YO19 ....184 F7
Westwood Rd
Ripon HG4 ....214 A2
Scarborough YO11 ....212 F4
Westwood Terr YO23 ....228 B1
Westwood Way LS23 ....188 E8
Wetherby Bsns Pk LS22 ....180 C3
Wetherby High Sch LS22 ....180 C3
Wetherby Jun Sch LS22 ....180 C3
Wetherby La LS22 ....180 D7
Wetherby Leisure Ctr LS22 ....180 C2
Wetherby Race Course* LS22 ....180 E3
Wetherby Rd
8 Boroughbridge YO51 ....141 B4
Bramham cum Oglethorpe LS23 ....188 E6
Harrogate HG2 ....220 B1
Kirk Deighton LS22 ....180 B5
Knaresborough HG5 ....221 D4
Sicklinghall LS22 ....179 E3
Tadcaster LS24 ....189 D6
Walton LS23 ....180 F2
Wetherby LS22 ....180 B2
York YO26 ....227 B3
Wethercote La YO7 ....67 C1
Wetlands La DL11 ....18 G7
Weydale Ave YO12 ....212 E8
Weymouth Ave TS8 ....7 A7
Weymouth Rd 1 HG1 ....219 E4
Whaddon Chase TS14 ....8 F6
Whaites La YO7 ....115 C5
Whales La DN14 ....202 E3
Wham La BD24 ....130 F1
Wharfe Dr YO24 ....230 D8
Wharfe Gr 8 LS22 ....180 B3
Wharfe La
Grassington BD23 ....134 D3
Kearby with Netherby LS22 ....179 B1
Wharfe Pk 2 LS29 ....175 A4
Wharfe View
Grassington BD23 ....134 D3
Kirkby Overblow HG3 ....179 A4
Wharfe View Rd LS29 ....218 B4
Wharfedale YO14 ....101 A3
Wharfedale Ave HG2 ....222 A7
Wharfedale Cl 1 BD23 ....217 B4
Wharfedale Cres
Harrogate HG2 ....222 B7
Tadcaster LS24 ....189 E6
Wharfedale Dr
Ilkley LS29 ....218 C4
Normanton WF6 ....200 A3
Wharfedale General Hospl LS21 ....176 F1
Wharfedale Pl HG2 ....222 A7
Wharfedale RUFC BD23 ....134 D3
Wharfedale View 6 LS29 ....174 F4
Wharfeside Ave BD23 ....134 D3
Wharfeside La LS29 ....218 C5
Wharncliffe Pl 14 YO14 ....101 A3
Wharnscliffe Dr YO30 ....224 F2
Wharton Ave YO30 ....228 B7
Wharton Rd 8 YO41 ....168 D2
Whartons Prim Sch The LS21 ....177 A2
Whartons The LS21 ....177 A1
Whashton Rd Aske DL10 ....20 C1
Richmond DL10 ....209 C8
Wheatcroft 6 YO32 ....167 A6
Wheatcroft Ave YO11 ....213 B1
Wheatcroft Cty Prim Sch YO11 ....213 B1
Wheatdale Rd LS24 ....190 B2
Wheatear La TS17 ....6 A5
Wheatfield La YO32 ....225 C8
Wheatlands
Great Ayton TS9 ....8 A2
Ilkley LS29 ....218 C4
Wheatlands Ave 8 BD20 ....187 E8
Wheatlands Dr 4 TS13 ....11 A8
Wheatlands Gr
Harrogate HG2 ....222 E8
York YO26 ....227 C6
Wheatlands La
7 Glusburn BD20 ....187 E8
Roecliffe YO51 ....140 E4
Wheatlands Rd HG2 ....222 E7
Wheatlands Rd E HG2 ....222 E8
Wheatlands Way HG2 ....222 F8
Wheatley Ave
Ilkley LS29 ....218 E3
Normanton South WF6 ....200 A1
Wheatley Dr YO32 ....225 C8
Wheatley Gdns 2 LS29 ....218 E3
Wheatley Gr LS29 ....218 E3
Wheatley La 3 LS29 ....218 E3
Wheatley Rd LS29 ....218 C3
Wheatley Rise LS29 ....218 E3
Wheeldale Cres TS17 ....6 B7
Wheeldale Rd YO18 ....51 A4
Wheelgate YO17 ....215 C4
Wheelgate Sq 7 YO17 ....215 C4
Wheelhouse The 4 YO30 ....224 B5
Wheels La YO8 ....204 F3
Wheelwright Cl
Copmanthorpe YO23 ....230 B2
Sutton upon Derwent YO41 ....185 C1
Wheldale La WF10 ....201 B5
Wheldon Rd WF10 ....201 A5
Wheldrake C of E Prim Sch YO19 ....193 A8
Wheldrake Ings Nature Reserve* YO19 ....193 C7
Wheldrake La
Deighton YO19 ....184 B1
Escrick YO19 ....192 B5
Whenby Gr YO31 ....225 F1
Whenby La YO60 ....145 C6
Whernside TS7 ....7 C5
Whernside Ave YO31 ....229 A5
Whessoe Rd DL3 ....3 C8
Whin Bank YO12 ....212 D5
Whin Cl
3 Strensall YO32 ....167 B6
York YO24 ....230 F7
Whin Garth YO24 ....230 F6
Whin Gn YO22 ....32 A6
Whin Hill YO17 ....147 E1
Whin La
South Milford LS25 ....195 D2
Warlaby DL7 ....64 C5
Whin Rd YO24 ....230 F6
Whinbeck Ave WF6 ....200 B1
Whinbush Way DL1 ....3 F8
Whinchat Tail TS14 ....8 D6
Whincup Ave HG5 ....221 B6
Whincup Cl 6 HG5 ....221 B6
Whincup Gr 7 HG5 ....221 B6
Whinfield Rd DL1 ....3 E7
Whinfield Road Jun & Inf Sch DL1 ....3 F7
Whinfields The 1 HG3 ....138 A1
Whingroves TS17 ....6 C8
Whinmoor Hill YO7 ....66 C2
Whinney La HG3 ....222 A5
Whinney Mire La LA2 ....103 E1
Whinny Bank YO61 ....117 C8
Whinny Gill Rd BD23 ....217 B3
Whinny Hagg La YO8 ....197 A2
Whinny Hill DL9 ....40 E3
Whinny La YO60 ....168 A7
Whinnythwaite La YO26 ....181 C8
Whins La
Spofforth with Stockeld HG3 ....179 E4
Thorp Arch LS23 ....180 F1
Whins The YO12 ....212 A7
Whinstone Prim Sch TS17 ....6 A5
Whinstone View 13 TS9 ....8 A2
Whinwath La DL8 ....87 F4
Whipley Bank HG3 ....161 A8
Whipley La HG3 ....161 A7
Whip-ma-whop-ma-gate YO1 ....233 C2
Whipperdale Bank DL8 ....60 A8
Whiston Dr 18 YO14 ....101 B3
Whit Moor Rd HG3 ....158 F5
Whitby Archives & Heritage Ctr* YO22 ....208 E7
Whitby Ave
Guisborough TS14 ....8 F6
York YO31 ....229 A7
Whitby Benedictine Abbey (rems of)* YO22 ....208 E7
Whitby Com Coll YO21 ....208 C5
Whitby Dr YO31 ....229 A7
Whitby Gate YO18 ....96 D6
Whitby Hospl YO21 ....208 D6
Whitby Mus & Art Gall* YO21 ....208 C6
Whitby Pavilion & Theatre YO21 ....208 C8
Whitby Rd
Guisborough TS14 ....9 A7
Pickering YO18 ....96 B8
Staithes TS13 ....13 K2
Whitby Sta YO21 ....208 D6
Whitby Town Football Club YO21 ....208 B7
Whitby Way DL3 ....3 A7
Whitcliffe Ave HG4 ....214 B4
Whitcliffe Cres HG4 ....214 B3
Whitcliffe Dr HG4 ....214 B3
Whitcliffe Gr HG4 ....214 B3
Whitcliffe La
Littlethorpe HG4 ....139 D8
Ripon HG4 ....214 A2
Whitcliffe Pl DL10 ....209 A7
White Bridge Rd YO21 ....208 B8
White Canons Ct 4 DL10 ....209 E8
White Canons Wlk 3 DL10 ....209 E8
White Cross Rd YO31 ....228 D7
White Cross Way YO41 ....169 A2
White Friars Cl DL10 ....209 F8
White Friars Gdns 6 DL10 ....209 E8
White Friars Wlk 5 DL10 ....209 E8
White Gate
Heslerton YO17 ....123 E6
Sherburn YO17 ....124 C6
White Gate Hill YO11 ....100 B2
White Hart Cres 4 DL1 ....3 F6
White Hill La BD20 ....172 E1
White Hills Croft BD23 ....216 E6
White Hills La BD23 ....216 E6
White Horse Cl 6 YO32 ....225 F5
White Horse Fold WF10 ....200 F7
White Horse La 9 YO12 ....99 D6
White Horse Mews 3 HG3 ....179 E5
White Horse of Kilburn* YO61 ....91 B4
White House Croft TS21 ....5 A7
White House Dale YO24 ....227 F1
White House Dr YO24 ....227 F1
White House Gdns 4 YO24 ....228 A2
White House Gr 1 YO41 ....185 B2
White House Rise YO24 ....227 F1
White La BD22 ....187 F1
White Lands DL10 ....209 E7
White Lee Ave BB8 ....186 B1
White Ley Rd DN6 ....206 C1
White Leys Rd YO21 ....208 A7
White Lilac Cl DL10 ....209 E7
White Lodge YO8 ....232 B4
White Pastures DL10 ....209 E7
White Point Ave 1 YO21 ....208 B7
White Point Rd YO21 ....208 B8
White Rose Ave 3 YO32 ....225 D3
White Rose Cl
Huby YO61 ....144 A5
8 Linton-on-Ouse YO30 ....164 F7
White Rose Cl *continued*
Nether Poppleton YO26 ....224 C1
White Rose Cres DL10 ....209 E7
White Rose Gr 5 YO32 ....225 D3
White Rose Way
Nether Poppleton YO26 ....227 C8
Thirsk YO7 ....211 D4
White Sprunt Hill YO17 ....125 A1
White St YO8 ....232 B6
White Wall La HG3 ....160 D4
White Way YO13 ....54 C1
White Way Heads YO18 ....51 F4
Whitebridge Dr DL1 ....3 D8
Whitecarr La YO62 ....95 A5
Whitecliffe Cres LS26 ....194 A1
Whitecliffe Dr 1 LS26 ....194 A1
Whitecliffe Rise LS26 ....194 A1
Whitecote La LS25 ....195 D2
Whitecross Hill DL8 ....87 F3
Whitefield Bglws DN14 ....206 F8
Whitefield La DN14 ....202 E1
Whitefields Dr DL10 ....209 E7
Whitefields Gate 1 DL10 ....209 E8
Whitefields Wlk 2 DL10 ....209 E8
Whitefriars Ct 9 BD24 ....131 D2
Whitegate Cl 7 TS13 ....13 K2
Whitegate La HG4 ....114 F1
Whitehill Rd BD22 ....187 E3
Whitehouse Ave LS26 ....200 B8
Whitehouse Cres LS26 ....200 B8
Whitehouse Dr LS26 ....200 B8
Whitehouse La
Great & Little Preston LS26 ....200 B8
Swillington LS26 ....194 B2
Whitelass La YO7 ....211 B4
Whitemoor La YO8 ....198 C6
Whiteoak Ave YO61 ....143 C8
Whitepits La LA2 ....129 A5
Whiterose Dr YO41 ....168 D2
Whiterow Rd DL8 ....82 F7
Whitestone Dr YO31 ....225 E2
Whitethorn Cl YO31 ....225 E2
Whitewall YO17 ....215 D1
Whitewall Corner Hill YO17 ....147 E8
Whiteway Head HG5 ....221 A4
Whitfield Ave YO18 ....96 A6
Whitkirk Pl 17 YO14 ....101 B3
Whitley & Eggborough Cty Prim Sch DN14 ....202 F1
Whitley Bridge Sta DN14 ....202 F1
Whitley Cl YO30 ....225 A1
Whitley Pl WF10 ....200 E6
Whitley Rd
Elvington YO41 ....185 A3
Norton-le-Clay YO7 ....115 B1
Thornaby TS17 ....6 B6
Whitley Thorpe La DN14 ....206 F7
Whitsundale Cl 4 HG5 ....221 D5
Whittle St 6 YO7 ....89 B1
Whitton Croft Rd 9 LS29 ....218 B4
Whitton Pl YO10 ....229 C4
Whitwell Rd YO60 ....146 E5
Whitwood Common La WF10 ....200 C3
Whitwood La WF10 ....200 C3
Whitworth Way BB18 ....171 E2
Whixley Field La YO26 ....164 B4
Whixley La YO26 ....163 E2
Whorlton Castle (rems of)* DL6 ....25 D1
Whorlton La DL6 ....45 E8
Whorlton Parochial Sch DL6 ....45 D8
Whyett Bank YO21 ....28 F6
Wickets The 8 TS15 ....25 C5
Widdale Rd HG5 ....221 D5
Widdale Sch DL8 ....55 E2
Widdowfield St DL3 ....3 C6
Wide Howe La YO7 ....114 E8
Wide La YO14 ....127 E5
Widgeon Cl 4 YO14 ....101 A4
Wigby Cl HG3 ....140 A2
Wigginton Prim Sch YO32 ....166 D5
Wigginton Rd YO31 ....233 B4
Wigginton Terr YO31 ....228 C8
Wigglesworth Sch BD23 ....153 C3
Wighill Garth LS24 ....189 E6
Wighill La
Healaugh LS24 ....181 F3
Healaugh LS24 ....189 E7
Wighill St 25 BD20 ....187 E7
Wilberforce Ave YO30 ....228 B7
Wilberfoss Sch YO41 ....185 E6
Wilcock La BD20 ....173 F2
Wild Rd DL1 ....4 A4
Wilfreds Gr 8 YO8 ....198 B4
Wilfreds Rd 5 YO8 ....198 B4
Wilken Cres TS14 ....8 F7
Wilkinson St TS12 ....9 E7
Wilkinson Way
6 Otley LS21 ....176 F1
3 Strensall YO32 ....167 A7
Willance Gr DL10 ....209 A7
Willaston Cres HG2 ....220 A2
Willaston Rd 1 HG1 ....220 A3
Willerby Carr La YO12 ....99 C3
Willgutter La BD22 ....187 F1
William Crossthwaite TS17 ....6 B4
William Jacques Dr YO8 ....198 E2
William Plows Ave YO10 ....228 E2
William Rd YO8 ....198 B4
William St 16 BB18 ....172 A1
William's Hill Ring & Bailey* DL8 ....60 E2
Williamson Cl 14 HG4 ....214 C5
Williamson Dr 8 HG4 ....214 C5
Willins Cl 13 TS15 ....25 C5
Willis St YO10 ....228 E3
Willitoft Rd YO8 ....199 F6
Willoughby Way YO24 ....230 B8
Willow Ave
Catterick Garrison DL9 ....209 B1
Clifford LS23 ....188 E7
Willow Bank YO32 ....225 E4
Willow Bank Dr 1 WF8 ....201 C1
Willow Beck Rd DL6 ....210 D6
Willow Bridge La YO7 ....115 F8
Willow Chase The TS21 ....4 F7
Willow Cl
20 Burley in Warfedale LS29 ....176 C1
2 Filey YO14 ....101 B4
Willow Cres
Clifford LS23 ....188 E7
Richmond DL10 ....209 D8
Willow Ct Kexby YO41 ....168 C2
2 North Featherstone WF7 ....200 E1
16 Pickering YO18 ....95 F6
Willow Dr 6 Bedale DL8 ....63 B3
Eston & South Bank TS6 ....7 E8
1 North Duffield YO8 ....199 A7
Willow Garth
Ferrensby HG5 ....162 F7
Scalby YO12 ....212 A7
10 Thornton Dale YO18 ....96 D5
Willow Garth Ave BD20 ....187 E8
Willow Garth La DN6 ....207 A1
Willow Glade
5 Boston Spa LS23 ....188 E7
York YO32 ....225 F3
Willow Gr
3 Boston Spa LS23 ....188 E7
Earswick YO32 ....226 A7
Harrogate HG1 ....219 E5
York YO31 ....228 F7
Willow La
Boston Spa LS23 ....188 E7
North Featherstone WF7 ....200 E1
Willow La E 4 WF7 ....200 E1
Willow Park Rd YO41 ....185 F5
Willow Rd
9 Campsall DN6 ....206 E1
Darlington DL3 ....3 B6
10 Knottingley WF11 ....202 A3
Northallerton DL7 ....210 D2
Willow Rise
5 Kirkbymoorside YO62 ....70 B1
Tadcaster LS24 ....189 D5
Thorpe Willoughby YO8 ....197 B1
Willow Tree Gdns 9 LS29 ....176 C1
Willow View 1 DL10 ....41 D5
Willow Way 4 BD20 ....187 E6
Willow Wlk 1 HG4 ....214 B2
Willowbank TS8 ....7 A5
Willowbridge Rd WF8 ....206 C2
Willowbridge Way WF10 ....200 C3
Willowdene La WF8 ....201 B2
Willowgate 24 YO18 ....95 F7
Willows Ave TS8 ....6 C4
Willows The
1 Hambleton YO8 ....196 E1
Middlesbrough TS7 ....7 C6
8 Strensall YO32 ....167 B7
Willymath Cl YO13 ....75 D7
Wilmot Rd LS29 ....218 C4
Wilson St
Castleford WF10 ....200 E4
Guisborough TS14 ....8 F6
Lockwood TS12 ....9 F7
16 Pontefract WF8 ....201 B1
Sutton BD20 ....187 F7
Wilson's La 5 YO13 ....99 A7
Wilsthorpe Gr 1 YO10 ....231 F8
Wilstrop Farm Rd YO23 ....230 A2
Wilton Carr La YO18 ....97 A3
Wilton Ings La YO18 ....97 A4
Wilton La TS14 ....8 F7
Wilton Rd LS29 ....218 A3
Wilton Rise YO24 ....227 F3
Wimbledon Cl 2 DL1 ....3 F6
Wimpole Cl 6 YO30 ....225 A1
Winchester Ave 3 YO26 ....227 E4
Winchester Gr 1 YO26 ....227 E4
Winchester Way DL1 ....3 F6
Windermere YO24 ....230 D7
Windermere Ave BB8 ....186 A3
Windermere Dr WF11 ....201 F1
Windgate Hill La YO8 ....197 B6
Windle La BD20 ....173 D1
Windleston Dr TS3 ....7 B8
Windmill Gdns YO8 ....232 B7

Windmill Gr LS24 189 D5
Windmill La
Norton DN6 206 D1
York YO10 229 B2
Windmill Mdws YO41 185 E6
Windmill Rd LS23 188 F6
Windmill Rise
Aberford LS25 194 F7
Tadcaster LS24 189 D5
York YO26 227 E3
Windrose Cl WF6 200 A2
Windross Sq 11 YO61 143 C8
Windsor Ave
Richmond DL10 209 D8
Skipton BD23 217 A4
Windsor Cl 17 WF6 200 B1
Windsor Cres
Middlesbrough TS7 7 D6
7 Whitby YO21 208 D6
Windsor Dr
2 Haxby YO32 166 D5
Lockwood TS12 9 F7
Windsor Garth YO24 227 D1
Windsor La HG5 221 B5
Windsor Pl BB18 171 E2
Windsor Rd
24 Catterick Garrison DL9 40 E4
4 Harrogate HG2 220 A1
Ripon HG4 214 C3
Thornaby TS17 6 B7
Windsor St 1 YO23 228 B1
Windsor Terr YO21 208 D6
Windy Hill LA2 129 B8
Winewall La BB8 186 B2
Winewall Rd 16 BB8 186 A3
Winksley Banks Rd
HG4 112 E2
Winksley Gr HG3 219 A4
Winn La YO7 115 C6
Winnow La LS23 188 D8
Winscar Gr 9 YO30 224 E3
Winston Ave BD20 187 F8
Winston Ct
Northallerton DL6 210 E6
Norton YO17 215 E3
Winter Gap La BD20 186 D8
Winter Gn 21 HG3 161 B3
Winterburn La BD23 155 D5
Winterscale St YO10 228 D2
Winthropp Cl YO17 215 C5
Winton Rd DL6 210 E6
Wise House La YO17 215 F7
Wisker La YO32 226 C7
Wisp Hill 12 BD23 134 E3
Wistow Parochial C of E Prim
Sch YO8 197 D6
Wistow Rd YO8 232 A8
Wistowgate YO8 197 B8
Witch La YO25 127 B2
Witham Dr YO32 226 A6
Withington Rd 6 YO62 92 F7
Witton Cres DL3 3 A7
Witton Steeps DL8 59 E2
Wobeck La HG4 114 B7
Wold La Willerby YO12 99 D1
Willerby YO12 125 E8
Wold Newton GM Sch
YO25 126 A4
Wold Newton Rd
YO25 126 E3
Wold Rd YO17 149 E8
Wold St YO17 215 D3
Wold View YO14 100 F2
Wold View Gr 5 YO12 99 E6
Woldcroft YO41 185 C2
Wolfe Ave YO31 228 F5
Wolsey Ave YO8 197 B8
Wolsey Cl 11 LS25 195 F4
Wolsey Croft LS25 195 F4
Wolsey Dr YO23 231 A3
Wolsey Gdns 12 LS25 195 F4
Wolsingham Dr TS5 6 E7
Wolsley St YO10 228 E3
Wolviston Ave YO10 229 C3
Womersley C of E Prim Sch
DN6 206 C6
Womersley Rd WF11 202 A2
Wood Acre Cl BD23 134 C3
Wood Aven Cl 35 HG3 161 B3
Wood Cl
Bradleys Both BD20 173 D3
Skipton BD23 216 E5
7 Strensall YO32 167 A7
14 Thorpe Willoughby
YO8 197 B1
Wood End La DL8 59 D5
Wood End Mus★
YO11 213 A5
Wood Gate YO13 74 A1
Wood Gn WF10 200 C3
Wood Hill Cl YO51 141 D1
Wood La
Acaster Selby YO23 191 B2
Austwick LA2 131 A8
Birkin WF11 202 D6
Gainford DL2 1 D8
10 Grassington BD23 134 E2
Great Preston LS26 200 C7
Low Coniscliffe & Merrybent
DL2 2 E4
Spennithorne DL8 61 A3
Thorp Arch LS23 180 F2
13 Thorpe Willoughby
YO8 197 B1
Threshfield BD23 134 B3
Wood La *continued*
Whitwood WF10 200 C3
Wood Lea 1 WF11 201 E4
Wood Park Cl HG2 220 B1
Wood Row LS26 200 A6
Wood St
Castleford WF10 200 E4
Norton YO17 215 D3
York YO31 228 E6
Wood View
Airmyn DN14 205 E3
Embsay BD23 217 C7
Harrogate HG1 219 C3
Wood View Ave WF10 200 D4
Wood Way YO32 226 A4
Woodall Ave YO12 212 F7
Woodall Ct 9 YO8 197 D6
Woodbine Cl 12 TS9 8 A2
Woodbine Terr 9 HG1 219 D3
Woodburn Dr 3 DL8 60 D5
Woodcock Cl
Eston & South Bank TS6 7 F8
9 Haxby YO32 166 F5
Woodcock Dr 8 DL9 40 F2
Woodcrest Rd DL3 3 B4
Wooden Hill La DL7 210 B2
Woodend WF10 200 C7
Woodend Cres WF10 200 C7
Woodfield Ave HG1 219 E4
Woodfield Cl HG1 219 E4
Woodfield CP Sch
HG1 219 F5
Woodfield Dr
Harrogate HG1 219 E4
6 Low Bradley BD20 173 E3
Woodfield Gdns 5 HG1 219 E4
Woodfield Gr HG1 219 E4
Woodfield Inf Sch
HG1 219 F5
Woodfield Pl 6 HG1 219 E4
Woodfield Rd
Goole DN14 205 F3
Harrogate HG1 219 F7
Woodfield Sq HG1 219 E4
Woodford Pl 1 YO24 227 D1
Woodgate YO12 212 D5
Woodgate La LS17 178 B2
Woodhall Dr HG1 219 F6
Woodhall Gr
Harrogate HG1 219 F6
Mickletown LS26 200 B6
4 Stockton-on-Tees TS18 5 D8
Woodhall La
Hemingbrough YO8 199 B3
Womersley DN6 206 D6
Woodhead Field La
YO62 70 A4
Woodhill View 3 LS22 180 C3
Woodhouse Gr 4 YO31 229 A5
Woodhouse La BD23 157 B7
Woodhouse Rd
Guisborough TS14 8 E6
Thorganby YO19 193 A3
Woodland Ave
Scarborough YO12 212 D6
9 Swillington LS26 194 A1
Woodland Chase
YO30 225 B1
Woodland Cl YO12 212 D6
Woodland Cres 8 LS26 194 A1
Woodland Dr DL7 63 F3
Woodland Gr
Scarborough YO12 212 C6
7 Swillington LS26 194 A1
Woodland Pl
New Earswick YO32 225 E4
Scarborough YO12 212 C6
Woodland Ravine
YO12 212 D6
Woodland Rd DL3 3 B6
Woodland Rise YO12 212 D6
Woodland St 3 BD22 187 B6
Woodland Terr DL3 3 B5
Woodland View 5 YO7 89 A1
Woodland Way
8 Airmyn DN14 205 E4
Longnewton TS21 4 F7
York YO32 225 F4
Woodlands
Escrick YO19 192 B5
Ilkley LS29 218 D4
Woodlands Ave
Harrogate HG2 220 B1
Haxby YO32 225 C8
Norton YO17 215 E2
Rillington YO17 122 F5
Tadcaster LS24 189 D5
Woodlands Cl
Goldsborough HG5 163 A3
Harrogate HG2 220 C2
15 Ilkley LS29 175 C2
Sherburn in Elmet LS25 195 F2
Woodlands Cres HG2 220 C2
Woodlands Croft
LS25 200 D8
Woodlands Ct 3 HG2 220 B1
Woodlands Cty Jun Sch
HG2 220 B2
Woodlands Dr
Egglescliffe TS15 5 E3
Garforth LS25 194 D3
Harrogate HG2 220 C1
Scarborough YO12 212 B5
Skipton BD23 216 E5
Woodlands Gn 8 HG2 220 B1
Woodlands Gr
Harrogate HG2 220 C2
8 Ilkley LS29 175 C2
Woodlands Gr *continued*
Kippax LS25 200 E8
Rillington YO17 122 F5
York YO31 229 A7
Woodlands La LS25 202 B7
Woodlands Rd
Harrogate HG2 220 C2
Rillington YO17 122 F5
Woodlands Rise
1 Harrogate HG2 220 C2
14 Ilkley LS29 175 C2
Norton DN6 206 E1
Woodlands Sch The
YO12 212 B5
Woodlands The TS7 7 D5
Woodlands View
Barlby with Osgodby
YO8 198 B4
Kippax LS25 200 E8
3 Tadcaster LS24 189 D5
2 Thornton Dale YO18 96 D5
Woodlands Way
Hurworth DL2 3 D1
7 Hurworth-on-Tees DL2 22 D8
Woodlands Wlk
Harrogate HG2 220 C2
Skipton BD23 216 E5
Stokesley TS9 26 C8
Woodlea Ave YO26 227 C4
Woodlea Bank YO26 227 D4
Woodlea Cres YO26 227 D4
Woodlea Gr YO26 227 D5
Woodleigh Cl 2 YO32 167 A6
Woodleigh Sch YO17 148 A6
Woodley Gr TS7 7 D7
Woodman La LA6 102 B6
Woodman Terr BD23 216 F4
Woodmanwray La
HG3 159 C8
Woodpark Ave HG5 221 A7
Woodpark Dr HG5 221 A7
Woodpecker Rd 12
LS29 176 C1
Woodrow Ave TS7 7 B6
Woodrow Cres LS26 200 A6
Woodroyd Gdns LS29 218 F3
Woodruff Cl 27 HG3 161 B3
Woodrush TS8 7 B4
Wood's Cl YO13 75 C8
Wood's Gr YO13 75 C8
Woods La YO26 142 B2
Woods Pl LS29 218 C4
Woodside
Castleford WF10 201 B4
Harrogate HG1 219 E2
Hutton Rudby TS15 25 C6
5 Leyburn DL8 60 D5
Woodside Ave YO31 229 A6
Woodside Cl 3 YO61 117 D1
Woodside Gr
Allerton Bywater WF10 200 C7
3 Stockton-on-Tees TS18 5 E8
Woodside La BD20 173 C2
Woodside Rd
Ganton YO12 125 A8
Silsden BD20 174 B1
Woodside St WF10 200 C7
Woodthorpe Prim Sch
YO24 230 C7
Woodvale TS8 7 B5
Woodvale Rd DL3 3 B4
Woodville Ave
Middlesbrough TS4 6 F8
3 Scalby YO12 212 D8
Woodville Terr YO8 232 E3
Wooldale Dr YO14 101 B4
Wooler St YO12 212 E5
Woolmoor Cl YO7 211 D4
Woolnough Ave YO10 229 B3
Woolpots La YO61 117 B4
Woolsington Dr DL2 4 C4
Worcester Dr YO31 229 B5
Wordsworth App 2
WF8 201 B1
Wordsworth Ave 4
DN6 206 E1
Wordsworth Cl YO13 75 C5
Wordsworth Cres
Harrogate HG2 222 C8
York YO24 230 D7
Wordsworth Dr WF11 201 D3
Workhouse Museum★
HG4 214 C6
Worsall Rd TS15 5 D2
Worsall Toll Bar TS15 24 B7
Worsendale Rd YO42 169 F2
Worsley Cl TS16 5 E7
Worsley Cres TS7 7 B5
Worsley Ct YO17 215 A3
Woundales La
Knayton with Brawith YO7 65 F4
Upsall YO7 66 A2
Wrangham Dr 1 YO14 127 A8
Wray with Botton Endowed
Sch LA2 128 A6
Wray's Ave YO31 225 E1
Wrea Head Cl 2 YO13 75 D5
Wrea La 1 YO12 212 F6
Wreaks La HG4 111 E6
Wreaks Rd
Birstwith HG3 160 E6
Harrogate HG1 220 B3
Wrelton Cliff Rd YO18 95 B8
Wrelton Hall Gdns
YO18 71 C1
Wren Croft 5 WF8 201 B2
Wren Hall La YO8 204 E6
Wren La 2 YO8 232 D5
Wrenbeck Ave 1 LS21 177 A1
Wrenbeck Cl 2 LS21 177 A1
Wrenbeck Dr LS21 177 A1
Wressle Sta YO8 199 D2
Wrexham Rd LS29 176 B1
Wreyfield Dr YO12 212 C7
Wright St 30 BD20 187 E7
Wrights La WF11 206 B8
Wycar 1 DL8 63 A2
Wycliffe Ave
Northallerton DL7 210 C2
York YO10 229 B3
Wycliffe Rd DL7 22 E1
Wycoller Ctry Pk★
BB8 186 D2
Wydale La YO13 98 B6
Wydale Rd YO10 229 D4
Wydale Rise YO13 98 A5
Wydra La HG3 159 F1
Wykeham Abbey★
YO13 98 E5
Wykeham Ave TS14 8 E5
Wykeham C of E Prim Sch
YO13 98 E6
Wykeham Carr Rd
YO13 98 E3
Wykeham Dale YO62 93 B8
Wykeham La YO13 98 E7
Wykeham Rd YO17 122 A5
Wykeham St YO12 212 E5
Wykeham Way TS8 7 A6
Wylam Ave DL1 3 D7
Wynbrook Ct YO13 75 C5
Wynd Cl 12 TS15 25 C5
Wynd The 3 Bedale DL8 63 A3
Hawes DL8 56 D4
Hutton Rudby TS15 25 D5
Skeeby DL10 20 F1
Wyvil Cres LS29 218 E4
Wyvil Rd LS29 218 E5
Wyville Gr DL8 61 E7

Y

Yafforth Rd DL7 210 B6
Yall Flat La YO21 29 B6
Yan Brow YO62 70 C3
Yarborough Cl DL10 41 B2
Yarburgh Cl 4 DN14 204 B1
Yarburgh Gr 2 YO26 227 E5
Yarburgh Way YO10 229 C3
Yarde Ave DL10 41 E4
Yarker Bank La DL8 60 C6
Yarlside La BD23 171 B4
Yarm Back La TS18 5 D8
Yarm Cty Jun Sch TS15 5 E2
Yarm La TS9 7 D1
Yarm Rd Darlington DL1 3 E5
Egglescliffe TS16 5 E5
Hilton TS15 6 C2
Middleton St George DL2 4 C4
Yarm Road Ind Est DL1 3 F5
Yarm Sch TS15 5 E3
Yarm Sta TS15 5 E2
Yarrow Dr HG3 161 B3
Yatts Rd YO18 96 A8
Yaud Sike La YO18 95 E5
Yeadon Wlk 12 DL2 4 C4
Yealand Ave BD24 131 D3
Yearby Cl TS5 6 D7
Yearsley Cres YO31 228 D7
Yearsley Gr YO31 225 E1
Yearsley Grove Jun Sch
YO32 225 F1
Yearsley Moor Bank
YO62 118 B7
Yearsley Swimming Baths
YO31 228 D8
Yederick Rd YO13 98 B8
Yedingham Priory (site of)★
YO17 97 D2
Yedmandale Rd
2 East Ayton/West Ayton
YO13 99 A7
Hutton Buscel YO13 98 F7
Yeomans Mount HG3 137 B4
Yew Tree Cl
Acaster Malbis YO23 191 C8
Harrogate HG2 222 C4
8 Low Bradley BD20 173 E3
Rufforth YO23 182 C6
Selby YO8 232 C6
18 Sleights YO22 32 A6
Yew Tree Gdns HG2 222 B5
Yew Tree La HG2 222 C5
Yew Tree Mews YO19 229 C5
Yew Tree Pk DN14 207 A7
Yew Tree Wlk HG2 222 B6
Yew Wlk The TS21 4 F7
Yewbank Cl 3 LS29 218 A4
Yewbank Terr LS29 218 A4
Yewdale Rd HG2 220 A1
Yiewsley Dr DL3 3 A5
YMCA Leisure Ctr
YO11 213 A6
Yoadwath Bank YO62 70 C3
Yoredale Ave
Darlington DL3 3 B6
17 Leyburn DL8 60 D5
York Abbey★ YO30 233 A3
York Barbican Leisure Ctr
YO10 233 C1
York Bridge Rd YO61 143 B2
York Castle Mus★
YO1 233 C1
York City Art Gall★
YO30 233 B3
York City Football Club
YO30 233 A4
York Cl 2 HG5 221 C5
York Coll of Further & Higher
Ed YO24 230 E6
York Cricket & RUFC
YO30 227 F7
York District Hospl
YO30 233 B4
York Dungeon★ YO1 233 B2
York Garth 1 HG5 221 C5
York Ind Pk YO17 121 C1
York La Flaxton YO60 167 E8
Knaresborough HG5 221 B5
York Minster★ YO1 233 B3
York Pl Harrogate HG2 219 E1
Knaresborough HG5 221 B5
Scarborough YO11 213 A5
York Race Course (The
Knavesmire)★ YO24 228 A1
York Rd Bagby YO7 211 D2
Barlby YO8 198 B5
Bilbrough YO23 182 B2
Bilton-in-Ainsty with Bickerton
LS22 181 A4
Boroughbridge YO51 141 B5
37 Burley in Warfedale
LS29 176 C1
Cliffe YO8 198 E3
Cottam YO25 151 B2
Dunnington YO19 184 D6
Easingwold YO61 143 C7
Flaxby HG5 163 B5
Green Hammerton YO26 164 B3
Harrogate HG1 219 C2
Haxby YO32 225 D7
Kilham YO25 151 F3
Kirk Hammerton YO26 164 C3
Knaresborough HG5 221 D5
Leavening YO17 147 E2
Long Marston YO26 182 A6
Malton YO17 215 A3
Middlesbrough TS7 7 D6
Naburn YO19 191 D8
North Duffield YO8 199 A8
Riccall YO19 192 A1
Sledmere YO25 150 E1
Sowerby YO7 211 E1
Stillingfleet YO19 191 D4
Strensall YO32 167 A6
Sutton-on-the-Forest
YO61 144 C2
Sutton-on-the-Forest
YO61 166 C8
Tadcaster LS24 189 F6
Wetherby LS22 180 C3
York YO26 227 C3
York Rugby League Club
YO32 226 A2
York Sixth Form Coll
YO24 230 E6
York St
Barnoldswick BB18 171 D1
Castleford WF10 200 E4
Crathorne TS15 24 E6
5 Dunnington YO19 184 E7
12 Glusburn BD20 187 E8
1 Selby YO8 232 C5
York Sta YO24 233 A2
York Steiner Sch
YO10 228 D1
York View DL10 209 E8
York Villas WF6 200 A1
Yorkdale Ct 4 YO8 196 F1
Yorkdale Dr 3 YO8 196 F1
Yorkersgate YO17 215 B4
Yorkshire Air Mus★
YO41 184 F3
Yorkshire Carriage Mus★
DL8 58 F3
Yorkshire Coast Coll
YO12 212 B6
Yorkshire Dales National
Park Ctr★ BD24 131 D3
Yorkshire Mus★ YO30 233 A3
Yorkshire Mus of Farming★
YO19 229 F5
Young Bank La YO62 70 C2
Young's Ct LS25 194 F7
Young's Dr 3 HG3 161 B2
Youngs Way 10 DL10 41 E4
Ypres Rd DL9 209 D1
Yule La YO26 164 C3

Z

Zetland Dr DL10 209 F8
Zetland St DL6 210 D4

Using the Ordnance Survey National Grid

Any feature in this atlas can be given a unique reference to help you find the same feature on other Ordnance Survey maps of the area, or to help someone else locate you if they do not have a Street Atlas.

The grid squares in this atlas match the Ordnance Survey National Grid and are at 500 metre intervals. The small figures at the bottom and sides of every other grid line are the National Grid kilometre values (**00** to **99** km) and are repeated across the country every 100 km (see left).

To give a unique National Grid reference you need to locate where in the country you are. The country is divided into 100 km squares with each square given a unique two-letter reference. Use the administrative map to determine in which 100 km square a particular page of this atlas falls.

The bold letters and numbers between each grid line (**A** to **F**, **1** to **8**) are for use within a specific Street Atlas only, and when used with the page number, are a convenient way of referencing these grid squares.

Example *The railway bridge over DARLEY GREEN RD in grid square B1*

Step 1: Identify the two-letter reference, in this example the page is in **SP**

Step 2: Identify the 1 km square in which the railway bridge falls. Use the figures in the southwest corner of this square: Eastings **17**, Northings **74**. This gives a unique reference: **SP 17 74**, accurate to 1 km.

Step 3: To give a more precise reference accurate to 100 m you need to estimate how many tenths along and how many tenths up this 1 km square the feature is (to help with this the 1 km square is divided into four 500 m squares). This makes the bridge about **8** tenths along and about **1** tenth up from the southwest corner.

This gives a unique reference: **SP 178 741**, accurate to 100 m.

Eastings (read from left to right along the bottom) come before Northings (read from bottom to top). If you have trouble remembering say to yourself "Along the hall, THEN up the stairs"!

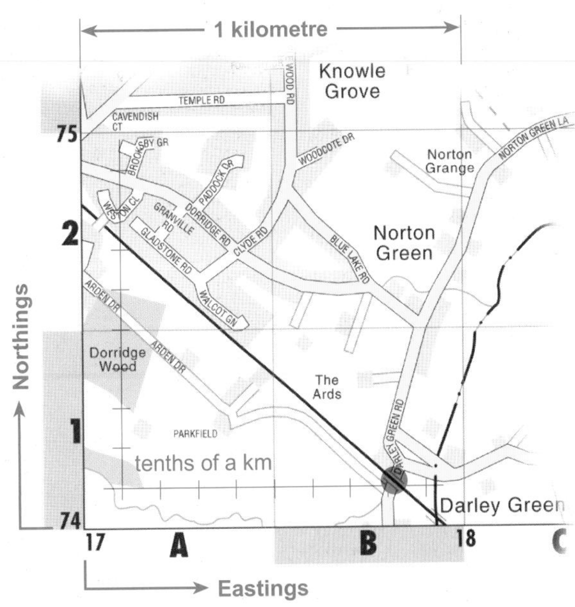

Notes

Name and Address	Telephone	Page	Grid reference

Street Atlases from Philip's

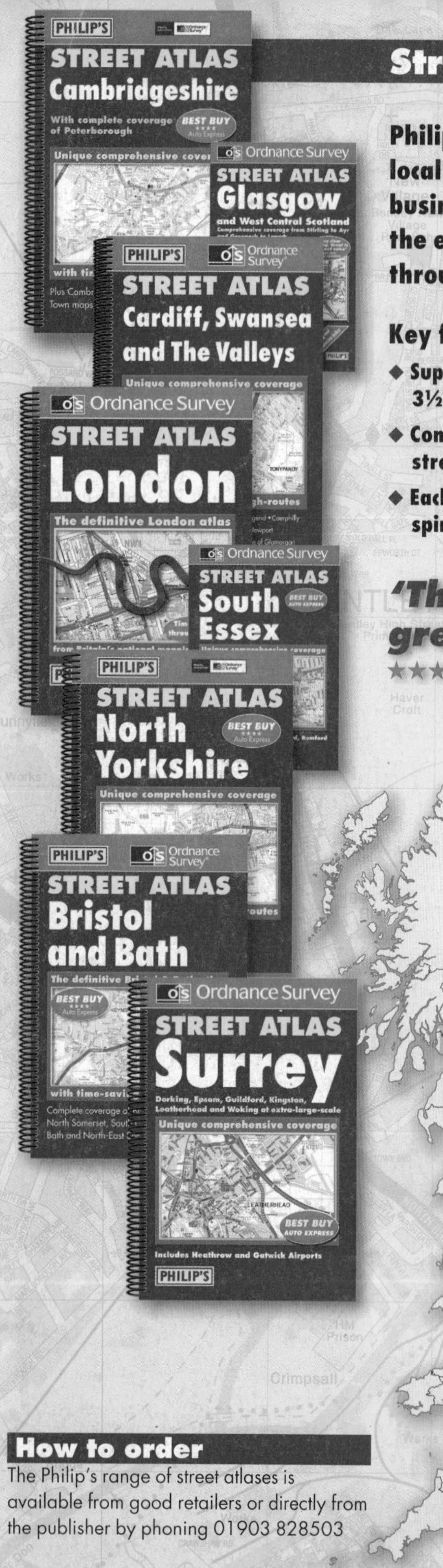

Philip's publish an extensive range of regional and local street atlases which are ideal for motoring, business and leisure use. They are widely used by the emergency services and local authorities throughout Britain.

Key features include:

- **Superb county-wide mapping at an extra-large scale of 3½ inches to 1 mile, or 2½ inches to 1 mile in pocket editions**
- **Complete urban and rural coverage, detailing every named street in town and country**
- **Each atlas available in three handy formats – hardback, spiral, pocket paperback**

'The mapping is very clear... great in scope and value'

★★★★ BEST BUY AUTO EXPRESS

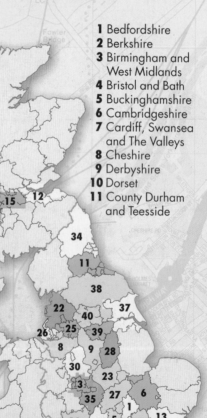

1 Bedfordshire
2 Berkshire
3 Birmingham and West Midlands
4 Bristol and Bath
5 Buckinghamshire
6 Cambridgeshire
7 Cardiff, Swansea and The Valleys
8 Cheshire
9 Derbyshire
10 Dorset
11 County Durham and Teesside
12 Edinburgh and East Central Scotland
13 North Essex
14 South Essex
15 Glasgow and West Central Scotland
16 Gloucestershire
17 North Hampshire
18 South Hampshire
19 Hertfordshire
20 East Kent
21 West Kent
22 Lancashire
23 Leicestershire and Rutland
24 London
25 Greater Manchester
26 Merseyside
27 Northamptonshire
28 Nottinghamshire
29 Oxfordshire
30 Staffordshire
31 Surrey
32 East Sussex
33 West Sussex
34 Tyne and Wear and Northumberland
35 Warwickshire
36 Wiltshire and Swindon
37 East Yorkshire and Northern Lincolnshire
38 North Yorkshire
39 South Yorkshire
40 West Yorkshire

How to order

The Philip's range of street atlases is available from good retailers or directly from the publisher by phoning 01903 828503